SEX IN ANTIQUITY

Looking at sex and sexuality from a variety of historical, sociological and theoretical perspectives, as represented in a variety of media, *Sex in Antiquity* represents a vibrant picture of the discipline of ancient gender and sexuality studies, showcasing the work of leading international scholars as well as that of emerging talents and new voices.

Sexuality and gender in the ancient world is an area of research that has grown quickly with often sudden shifts in focus and theoretical standpoints. This volume contextualises these shifts while putting in place new ideas and avenues of exploration that further develop this lively field or set of disciplines. This broad study also includes studies of gender and sexuality in the Ancient Near East which not only provide rich consideration of those areas but also provide a comparative perspective not often found in such collections. *Sex in Antiquity* is a major contribution to the field of ancient gender and sexuality studies.

Mark Masterson is Senior Lecturer of Classics at Victoria University of Wellington, New Zealand. He is author of *Man to Man: Desire, Homosociality, and Authority in Late-Roman Manhood* (2014). He has published articles and book chapters on Statius, Vitruvius, the *Historia Monachorum*, Eugene O'Neill, Emperor Julian, St. Augustine and Current New Zealand health policy, and the state of masculinity studies in Classics. He is currently completing a monograph on same-sex desire between Byzantine men, entitled *Between Byzantine Men: Desire, Brotherhood, and Male Culture in the Medieval Empire*.

Nancy Sorkin Rabinowitz is Professor of Comparative Literature at Hamilton College, USA. Author of *Anxiety Veiled: Euripides and the Traffic in Women* (1993) and *Greek Tragedy* (2008), she has co-edited *Vision and Viewing in Ancient Greece*, with Sue Blundell and Douglas Cairns (2013), *Feminist Theory and the Classics*, with Amy Richlin (1993), *Among Women: From the Homosocial to the Homoerotic in the Ancient World*, with Lisa Auanger (2002), as well as *From Abortion to Pederasty: Addressing Difficult Topics in the Classics Classroom,* with Fiona McHardy (2014), which won the Teaching Literature Book Award 2015. She is one of the co-editors and translators of *Women on the Edge: Four Plays by Euripides* (1999).

James Robson is Senior Lecturer in Classical Studies at the Open University, UK. His previous publications include *Humour, Obscenity and Aristophanes* (2006); *Aristophanes: An Introduction* (shortlisted for the Anglo-Hellenic League's Runciman Award; 2009); *Ctesias'* History of Persia: *Tales of the Orient* (with Lloyd Llewellyn-Jones; 2010) and *Sex and Sexuality in Classical Athens* (2013).

Rewriting Antiquity

Rewriting Antiquity provides a platform to examine major themes of the ancient world in a broad, holistic and inclusive fashion. Coverage is broad both in time and space, allowing a full appreciation of the selected topic rather than an exclusive view bound by a relatively short timescale and place. Each volume examines a key theme from the Ancient Near East to Late Antiquity, and often beyond, to break down the boundaries habitually created by focusing on one region or time period.

Volumes within the series highlight the latest research, current developments and innovative approaches, situating this with existing scholarship. Individual case studies and analysis held within sections build to form a comprehensive and comparative overview of the subject enabling readers to view matters in the round and establish interconnections and resonance across a wide spectrum. In this way the volumes allow new directions of study to be defined and provide differing perspectives to stimulate fresh approaches to the theme examined.

Available:

Sex in Antiquity – Mark Masterson, Nancy Sorkin Rabinowitz, James Robson
Women in Antiquity – Stephanie Lynn Budin and Jean Macintosh Turfa
Disability in Antiquity – Christian Laes

Forthcoming:

Childhood in Antiquity – Lesley Beaumont, Matthew Dillon, Nicola Harrington
Globalisation in Antiquity – Konstantin Vlassopoulos

SEX IN ANTIQUITY

Exploring Gender and Sexuality in the Ancient World

Edited by Mark Masterson, Nancy Sorkin Rabinowitz, and James Robson

Routledge
Taylor & Francis Group

LONDON AND NEW YORK

First published in paperback 2018

First published 2014
by Routledge
2 Park Square, Milton Park, Abingdon, Oxon OX14 4RN

and by Routledge
711 Third Avenue, New York, NY 10017

Routledge is an imprint of the Taylor & Francis Group, an informa business

British Library Cataloguing-in-Publication Data
A catalogue record for this book is available from the British Library

Library of Congress Cataloging-in-Publication Data
Sex in antiquity : exploring gender and sexuality in the ancient world / edited by Mark Masterson, Nancy Sorkin Rabinowitz and James Robson.
pages cm
Includes bibliographical references and index.
ISBN 978-0-415-51941-0 (hardback : alk. paper) -- ISBN 978-1-315-74791-0 (e-book : alk. paper) 1. Sex role--History--To 1500. 2. Sex--History--To 1500. I. Masterson, Mark. II. Rabinowitz, Nancy Sorkin. III.Robson, James.
HQ1075.S474 2014
306.7093--dc22
2014029289

ISBN: 978-0-415-51941-0 (hbk)
ISBN: 978-1-138-48041-4 (pbk)
ISBN: 978-1-315-74791-0 (ebk)

Typeset in Bembo
by Servis Filmsetting Ltd, Stockport, Cheshire

This book is dedicated:

To the memory of T. R. Heartt

To Ella and Sophie Gold, granddaughters extraordinaire

To Owain Thomas, *cariad* and *ffrind mawr*

CONTENTS

PART II
Archaic, classical and Hellenistic Greece 97

ILLUSTRATIONS

Figures

Tables

ACKNOWLEDGEMENTS

The editors would like to extend their thanks to Matt Gibbons and Amy Davis-Poynter at Routledge for their vision, assistance and patience while this volume was in process. We thank Luc Arnault for his work on the translation of two of the essays from French.

Thanks are also due to Caroline Grunewald and Courtney Kaplar, both students at Hamilton College, New York, for research assistance, and to Hamilton College and the Faculty of Humanities and Social Sciences at Victoria University of Wellington, New Zealand, for financial assistance. Finally, we are grateful to Lloyd Llewellyn-Jones for his help with this book, and particularly for his contribution to the Introduction.

LIST OF ABBREVIATIONS

ABV	Beazley, J. (1956) *Attic Black-Figure Vase*-Painters, Oxford: Clarendon.
Adam.	Adamantius, *Physiognomonica*
ADB	*Allgemeine Deutsche Biographie*
Add²	Carpenter, T. (1989) *Beazley Addenda*, 2nd edn, Oxford: Oxford University Press.
AE	*L'Année épigraphique*
APA	American Philological Association
Anon. Lat.	Anonymous, *De Physiognomonia Liber*
ARV²	Beazley, J. (1963) *Attic Red-Figure Vase-Painters,* 2nd edn, Oxford: Clarendon.
b-f	black–figure
CAT	Dietrich, M., Loretz, O. and Sanmartín, J. (eds) (1995) *The Cuneiform Alphabetic Texts from Ugarit, Ras Ibn Hani and Other Places*, 2nd edn, Münster: Ugarit-Verlag.
CGL	*Corpus Grammaticorum Latinorum*
CIL	*Corpus Inscriptionum Latinarum*
CTh.	*Codex Theodosianus*
HTR	*Harvard Theological Review*
ETCSL	Electronic Text Corpus of Sumerian Literature
ICTR	International Criminal Tribunal for Rwanda
ILAlg	*Inscriptions latines d'Algérie*
in de An.	*In de Anima*
Jul.	Emperor Julian
Lampe	Lampe, G. (ed.) (1961) *A Patristic Greek Lexicon*, Oxford: Oxford University Press.
LSJ	Liddell, H. Scott, R. and Jones, H. (eds) (1940) *Greek-English Lexicon*, Oxford:Oxford University Press.
LSO	*Lateres signati Ostienses*, Appendix
MT	Masoretic Text (the text of the Hebrew Bible)
Myst.	Iamblichus, *De Mysteriis*
NRSV	*New Revised Standard Version* of the Bible
ODNB	*Oxford Dictionary of National Biography*

OLD	Clare, P.G.W. (ed.) (2012) *Oxford Latin Dictionary*, 2nd edn, 2 vols, Oxford: Oxford University Press.
P. Oxy.	Grenfell, P., Hunt, A. S. *et al.* (eds) (1898-) *The Oxyrhynchus Papyri,* London: Egypt Exploration Fund.
Para	Beazley, J. (1971) *Paralipomena,* Oxford: Clarendon.
PPF	*Passion of Perpetua and Felicitas*
RE	Pauly, A., Walz, C. and Teuffel, W. S. (eds) (1894–1978) *Realencyclopädie der classischen Altertumswissenschaft*, Stuttgart: J. B. Metzler.
r-f	red-figure
RIB	*The Roman Inscriptions of Britain*
RPF	Rwandan Patriotic Front
Suppl. Ital.	*Corporis inscriptionum Latinarum supplementa Italica*
TLG	*Thesaurus Linguae Graecae*
TLL	*Thesaurus Linguae Latinae*
Victric.	Victricius, *De Laude Sanctorum*
VP	Iamblichus, *De Vita Pythagorica*

The names of Greek and Latin authors and works are generally abbreviated according to the conventions used in reference works such as *LSJ* and *OLD*. Where authors have departed from this practice, the abbreviations used are self-explanatory.

NOTES ON CONTRIBUTORS

Susan Ackerman is the Preston H. Kelsey Professor of Religion at Dartmouth College, USA. She is the author of *Under Every Green Tree: Popular Religion in Sixth-Century Judah* (1992); *Warrior, Dancer, Seductress, Queen: Women in Judges and Biblical Israel* (1998); and *When Heroes Love: The Ambiguity of Eros in the Stories of Gilgamesh and David* (2005). She has recently completed a draft of a new book on women and the religion of ancient Israel.

Alastair Blanshard is the Paul Eliadis Chair of Classics and Ancient History at the University of Queensland, Australia. He is the author of *Sex: Vice and Love from Antiquity to Modernity* (2010).

Sandra Boehringer is Maîtresse de Conférences in Classics at the University of Strasbourg, France. She is author of *L'homosexualité féminine dans l'Antiquité grecque et romaine* (2007). She has co-edited *Homosexualité. Aimer en Grèce et à Rome* (with L.-G. Tin, 2010) and *Hommes et femmes dans l'Antiquité* (with V. Sebillotte Cuchet, 2011). Along with Nadine Picard she has translated into French John J. Winkler's *The Constraints of Desire* (2005) and Maud Gleason's *Making Men: Sophists and Self-Presentation in Ancient Rome* (2013).

Roland Boer is the Xin Ao Professor of Literature at Renmin University of China, Beijing, and a researcher at the University of Newcastle, Australia. When not undertaking voyages by ship and long train journeys, he researches in the area of Marxism and religion, as well as biblical criticism. Among numerous publications, his most recent are *In the Vale of Tears* (2013); *Lenin, Religion, and Theology* (2013), and *The Sacred Economy* (2015).

Daniel Boyarin is Taubman Professor of Talmudic Culture and Rhetoric at UC Berkeley, USA, and has been a Fellow of the American Academy of Arts and Sciences since 2006. His publications include *Border Lines: The Partition of Judaeo-Christianity* (2004; winner of the AAR award for best book on religion in the area of historical studies in 2006); *Socrates and the Fat Rabbis* (2009), and *The Jewish Gospel: The Story of the Jewish Christ* (2012).

Stephanie Lynn Budin is an ancient historian who focuses on ancient Greece and the Near East. Her published works include *Images of Woman and Child from the Bronze Age* (2011), *The Ancient Greeks: An Introduction* (2009), *The Myth of Sacred Prostitution in Antiquity* (2008), *The*

Origin of Aphrodite (2003), and *Women in Antiquity* (2016), as well as numerous articles on ancient religion and iconography. She has delivered papers in England, Ireland, Germany, Sweden, Cyprus, Israel, Japan, and Canada, as well as throughout the United States.

Claude Calame is the Directeur d'études of the Ecole des Hautes Etudes en Sciences Sociales, Centre AnHiMA (Anthropologie et Histoire des Mondes Anciens), France, and has written widely on gender and sexuality in ancient Greece. His major works include: *Choruses of Young Women in Ancient Greece: Their Morphology, Religous Role, and Social Functions* (2nd ed., 2001), *The Craft of Poetic Speech in Ancient Greece* (1995), *The Poetics of Eros in Ancient Greece* (1999), *Masks of Authority. Fiction and Pragmatics in Ancient Greek Poetics* (2005) and *Poetic and Performative Memory in Ancient Greece: Heroic Reference and Ritual Gestures in Time and Space* (2009). He has also written numerous articles and book chapters.

Monica S. Cyrino is Professor of Classics at the University of New Mexico, USA. Her academic research centres on the erotic in ancient Greek poetry, and the reception of the ancient world on screen. She is the author of *Aphrodite* (2010), *Big Screen Rome* (2005), *In Pandora's Jar: Lovesickness in Early Greek Poetry* (1995), and the editor of *Screening Love and Sex in the Ancient World* (2013) and *Rome, Season One: History Makes Television* (2008).

Dorota Dutsch is Associate Professor of Classics at the University of California, Santa Barbara, USA. Her research centres on various forms of social performance, ancient and modern. She has published articles and book chapters on Plautine jokes, Roman lament, pharmacology of seduction, the language of gesture, and political appropriations of Greek drama. She is the author of *Feminine Discourse in Roman Comedy: On Echoes and Voices* (2008), co-editor with Ann Suter of *Ancient Obscenities* (2015) and co-editor with Sharon L. James and David Konstan of *Women in the Drama of the Roman Republic* (2014).

Matthew Fox grew up in London, the child of a pathologist and a psychoanalyst. After study in Oxford and Berlin, he taught at the University of Birmingham. In 2007 he became Professor of Classics at the University of Glasgow. His work centres on the intersection between literature, and history, and myth, and he has a strong interest in hermeneutics and classical reception. His *Roman Historical Myths* appeared in 1996 and *Cicero's Philosophy of History* in 2007. He is currently working on Roman ideas of materialism.

Kathy L. Gaca is Associate Professor of Classics at Vanderbilt University, USA. Her research focuses on exploring how sexual norms rooted in antiquity inform current concerns of social injustice and violence. She is the author of *The Making of Fornication: Eros, Ethics, and Political Reform in Greek Philosophy and Early Christianity* (2003; winner of the CAMWS 2006 Outstanding Publication Award) and of numerous articles. She is currently at work on her second book, *Rape as Sexual Warfare against Girls and Women: Ancient History, Modern Witness, Overpowering Injustice*.

Hunter H. Gardner is an Associate Professor of Classics and an affiliate of the Women's and Gender Studies Program at the University of South Carolina, USA. She is also the author of *Gendering Time in Augustan Love Elegy* (2013) and numerous articles on Latin poetry. Current projects include a study of the reception of the Pygmalion myth in horror films and a monograph on the traditions of plague narratives in Latin.

Allison Glazebrook is Associate Professor of Classics at Brock University, USA. Her research focuses on women, gender and sexuality in ancient Greece. She is co-editor with Madeleine M. Henry of *Greek Prostitutes in the Ancient Mediterranean, 800 BCE-200 CE* (2011).

Barbara K. Gold is Edward North Professor of Classics at Hamilton College, USA. She is the editor of *Literary and Artistic Patronage in Ancient Rome* (1982), author of *Literary Patronage in Greece and Rome* (1987), and co-editor of *Sex and Gender in Medieval and Renaissance Texts: The Latin Tradition* (1997) and *Roman Dining* (2005). She has published widely on satire, lyric and elegy, feminist theory and late antiquity. Her *Blackwell Companion to Roman Love Elegy* was published in 2012, and *Roman Literature, Gender and Reception: Domina Illustris* (co-edited) was published in 2013. Forthcoming is *Perpetua: A Martyr's Tale*.

Simon Goldhill is Professor of Greek at the University of Cambridge, UK, where he is also director of CRASSH, the Cambridge Centre for Research in Arts, Social Sciences and the Humanities. He has published widely on many aspects of Greek literature. His most recent book, *Sophocles and the Language of Tragedy*, won the 2013 Runciman Prize for the best book on a Greek subject, ancient or modern, and his book, *Victorian Culture and Classical Antiquity: Art, Opera and the Proclamation of Modernity*, won the Robert Lowry Patten award for the best book on Victorian Literature for 2011-2.

Judith P. Hallett is Professor of Classics and Distinguished Scholar-Teacher at the University of Maryland, USA. She has published widely in the areas of Latin language and literature; women, sexuality and the family in ancient Greece and Rome; and the reception and study of classics in nineteenth and twentieth century North America and Europe. Among these publications is *Roman Sexualities* (1997), which she co-edited with Marilyn B. Skinner. In 2013 Routledge published *Roman Literature, Gender and Reception: Domina Illustris*, edited by Donald Lateiner, Barbara K. Gold and Judith Perkins, nineteen essays in her honor.

Edward M. Harris received a BA in Classics from Stanford University, USA, a BA in Literae Humaniores from Oxford University, UK, and an MA and PhD in Classical Philology from Harvard University, USA. He taught at Brooklyn College/CUNY from 1983 to 2005 and at the Graduate School/CUNY from 1986 to 2005. He was Professor of Ancient History from 2005-2009 and Research Professor from 2009-2013 at Durham University, UK. He has been a member of the Institute for Advanced Study (Princeton), NEH Fellow at the American School of Classical Studies at Athens, Professeur invité at the Sorbonne, and Directeur d'études invité at the École pratique des hautes études, Paris.

Deborah Kamen is an Associate Professor of Classics at the University of Washington, USA. She has written a number of articles on ancient slavery, gender, and sexuality. Her book *Status in Classical Athens* was published in 2013.

Andrew Lear has taught at Harvard, Columbia, Pomona, and NYU. His first book was *Images of Ancient Greek Pederasty: Boys Were Their Gods* (2008, co-author Eva Cantarella); his second, *Ancient Greek Pederasty: History of a Custom and its Idealization*, is forthcoming.

Gwendolyn Leick studied Assyriology at Karl-Franzens University, Graz, Austria. She is Senior Lecturer at Chelsea College of Art (London). Her publications include *Dictionary of Ancient Near*

Eastern Mythology (1998), *Sex and Eroticism in Mesopotamian Literature* (1994), *Mesopotamia: The Invention of the City* (2001). She also edited *The Babylonian World* (2007).

Sarah Levin-Richardson is an Assistant Professor of Classics at the University of Washington, USA. She has published articles on Pompeian graffiti and modern receptions of Pompeii, and is working on a monograph exploring the physical, social, and emotional environment within Pompeii's "purpose-built" brothel. She has excavated at Pompeii, in the Roman Forum, and on Crete.

Mark Masterson is Senior Lecturer of Classics at Victoria University of Wellington, New Zealand. He is author of *Man to Man: Desire, Homosociality, and Authority in Late-Roman Manhood* (2014). He has published articles and book chapters on Statius, Vitruvius, the *Historia Monachorum*, Eugene O'Neill, Emperor Julian, St. Augustine and Current New Zealand health policy, and the state of masculinity studies in Classics. He is currently completing a monograph on same-sex desire between Byzantine men, entitled *Between Byzantine Men: Desire, Brotherhood, and Male Culture in the Medieval Empire*.

Shiela Murnaghan is the Alfred Reginald Allen Memorial Professor of Greek at the University of Pennsylvania, USA. She works in the areas of ancient Greek literature, especially Homer and tragedy, gender in classical culture, and classical reception. She is the author of *Disguise and Recognition in the Odyssey* (2nd ed, 2011) and the co-editor of *Women and Slaves in Greco-Roman Culture: Differential Equations* (1998) and *Odyssean Identities in Modern Cultures: The Journey Home* (2014). Her current projects include a co-authored book on classics and childhood in the 19th and 20th centuries and an edition with commentary of Sophocles' *Ajax*.

Kelly Olson is an Associate Professor in the Department of Classical Studies at the University of Western Ontario, USA. Her research focuses on Roman society, sexuality, and appearance. She is the author of several articles and book chapters on female clothing in Roman antiquity, published in *Mouseion, The American Journal of Ancient History, Fashion Theory,* and *Classical World.* Her books *Dress and the Roman Woman: Self-Presentation and Society* and *Masculinity and Dress in Roman Antiquity* were published in 2008 and 2017 respectively.

Walter Duvall Penrose, **Jr.** received his PhD from the City University of New York Graduate Center, USA, in 2006. Walter is currently an Assistant Professor in the History Department at San Diego State University, USA, specializing in the history of gender and sexuality. His book *Postcolonial Amazons: Female Masculinity and Courage in Ancient Greek and Sanskrit Literature* was published in 2016. Walter has published several essays on homoeroticism and masculinity in South Asian history, and has forthcoming publications on teaching homoeroticism in the Classics classroom and on the reception of Sappho from antiquity to the early Renaissance.

Nancy Sorkin Rabinowitz is Professor of Comparative Literature at Hamilton College, USA. Author of *Anxiety Veiled: Euripides and the Traffic in Women* (1993) and *Greek Tragedy* (2008), she has co-edited *Vision and Viewing in Ancient Greece*, with Sue Blundell and Douglas Cairns (2013), *Feminist Theory and the Classics*, with Amy Richlin (1993), *Among Women: From the Homosocial to the Homoerotic in the Ancient World*, with Lisa Auanger (2002), as well as *From Abortion to Pederasty: Addressing Difficult Topics in the Classics Classroom,* with Fiona McHardy (2014), which won the Teaching Literature Book Award 2015. She is one of the co-editors and translators of *Women on the Edge: Four Plays by Euripides* (1999).

Amy Richlin is Professor of Classics at the University of California, Los Angeles, USA. She has been publishing on Roman sexuality since 1981. Current projects include *How Fronto's Letters Got Lost: Reading Roman Pederasty in Modern Europe*, and a book on Roman comedy as slave theater.

James Robson is Senior Lecturer in Classical Studies at the Open University, UK. His previous publications include *Humour, Obscenity and Aristophanes* (2006); *Aristophanes: An Introduction* (shortlisted for the Anglo-Hellenic League's Runciman Award; 2009); *Ctesias'* History of Persia: *Tales of the Orient* (with Lloyd Llewellyn-Jones; 2010) and *Sex and Sexuality in Classical Athens* (2013).

Steven D. Smith is Associate Professor of Classics and Comparative Literature at Hofstra University, USA. He is the author of *Greek Identity and the Athenian Past in Chariton: The Romance of Empire* (2007) and *Man and Animal in Severan Rome: The Literary Imagination of Claudius Aelianus* (2014).

Elna K. Solvang is Associate Professor in the Religion Department at Concordia College, USA. She is the author of *A Woman's Place is in the House: Royal Women of Judah and their Involvement in the House of David* (2003) and essays examining women's agency in ancient royal households and in the Hebrew Bible.

Craig Williams is Professor of Classics at the University of Illinois at Urbana-Champaign, USA. He is author of *Roman Homosexuality* (2nd ed., 2010), *Reading Roman Friendship* (2012), and two commentaries on the epigrammatist Martial.

INTRODUCTION

Mark Masterson, Nancy Sorkin Rabinowitz, and James Robson,
with assistance from Lloyd Llewellyn-Jones

When we were asked by Routledge to edit a volume on gender and sexuality, we knew that we wanted a set of new and forward-looking essays, not a summation of where we had been. We wanted to present what people were currently working on. Throughout the editing process, however, we struggled about what to call it – "Sex in Antiquity" was our attempt at a catchy title, but what should the subtitle be? We were concerned for a while that the eventual choice, "gender and sexuality in the ancient world," might lead to a redundancy between the two halves – before and after the colon. Antiquity and the ancient world might seem to be synonyms, even though they are not really identical: one refers to time and the other designates a space as well. In a similar fashion, sex is not the same as gender and sexuality but is refined and expanded on in those terms. Looked at in this way, the subtitle explains and complicates the word sex. The apparent redundancy is even less significant because each term – sex, gender, sexuality – might be said to contain multitudes; they are not only internally complex but lie in complex relationships with one another, and are sometimes even in conflict with one another. The essays in this collection take gender and sexuality, in all the richness that these terms possess, as their starting point; thus the book is about sex, as refracted through these lenses.

The terms themselves are difficult to define because they are ideologically laden, historically fluid, and, of course, dependent on the English language for their articulation here. Indeed it is a live question as to how well the words sex, gender, and sexuality apply to antiquity. Clearly we, as editors of this volume, believe that it is worthwhile to look at the ancient world through these modern terms. Thus, we agree with those who would say it is not an anachronistic effort. In a recent book on gender, Lin Foxhall goes so far as to assert that the ancients were what we would call essentialist (2013: 3–4). Moreover, as Brooke Holmes points out in *Gender: Antiquity and Its Legacy*, not only did the ancient Greeks and Romans have ideas of sex, gender, and sexuality, but those ideas have had an impact on the ways in which we moderns conceptualize them (Holmes 2012: 6–11).

We must nonetheless be aware of changing meanings. Consider, for example, understandings of "sex" in recent decades. Sex is a complicated term, in English at least, because it is something an individual might "be" or "have" or "do." In Foucauldian terms it is both an identity and an act. Traditionally, sex has been taken to be physical. In the introduction to the important volume *Before Sexuality*, the editors (Halperin *et al.* 1990) state that "sex lies outside history," that it refers to the "erogenous capacities and genital functions of the human body" (3).[1] In antiquity and until comparatively recently, gender seemed to flow seamlessly from the binary of biological sex, with two sexes leading to two genders.

The "being" of sex referred to above has been typically limited to male and female, but the expansion of contemporary studies of the body (e.g. Laqueur 1990; Bordo 1993; Grosz 1994) emphasizes that that binary opposition is an oversimplification.[2] Recent developments around transgendered and transsexual individuals increasingly question the idea that there are only two sexes. In any case, although bodies and pleasures may not change that much, their enactment and reactions to them do shift in different historical periods and in different places. In short, what counts as sex (and how it counts) varies over time.

Theories of gender have tended to emphasize first the constructedness of gender, as opposed to the seemingly essential physiology of the body, pointing out that the dichotomy of gender is not intrinsic but is imposed on the body. It has further been pointed out that the dichotomy of sexed bodies is itself an imposition owing to binary thinking, which is in a mutually reinforcing relationship with gender (Wohl 2014).[3] The idea (in the quotation above, p. 1, from *Before Sexuality*) that the body is a residue and outside of history has been implicitly challenged by, for instance, Judith Butler's work, which argues that there is no secure anchor point for gender in the body (*Gender Trouble* [1990], *Bodies that Matter* [1993]). But Butler's move has hardly settled matters. There is still extensive debate, with some arguing against the extreme constructivist position.

Sexuality is a slippery term that obviously has a close relation to sex. It might be used to speak of the sex one has, or to refer to an individual's sexual object choice. In the wake of Michel Foucault's influential *The History of Sexuality* (1978, 1985, 1986) the word has been more cautiously deployed and now is taken most often to signify the set of discourses and practices that are in effect around sexual behavior (with a suite of identity effects, if persons in the modern West are meant). Foucault was crucial in making sexuality an object of study with a history (more about Foucault below, pp. 3–4). From that point on, there has been much work done emphasizing the delineation of sexuality as an area of inquiry. Influential in this regard were the works of Judith Butler and Eve Kosofsky Sedgwick, both of whom, as founding figures of queer theory, were building on and reacting to the work of Foucault, French feminists (such as Luce Irigaray), and Gayle Rubin, among others.

How does this volume fit into this terrain of "sex," "gender," and "sexuality," a terrain in which there is much that is not settled and lively debate is the rule? To answer this question, we will address historical moments, geographical locations, and disciplinary contexts.

First of all, the historical moments. We are talking about the ancient periods in (here comes geography) the Near East, Greece, and Rome. This portion of the introduction will for the most part focus on Greece and Rome, with a later section on the Ancient Near East (ANE). There are further details about the specific ancient locations in time and space in the table of contents and in the summary of the book that follows this part of the introduction. But we are also using the theoretical framework provided primarily by post-World War II Euro-American scholarship, so that is a second relevant time frame as well.

The bulk of modern and postmodern work on sex, gender, and sexuality must be put in the context of the liberation movements of the 1960s and 1970s, in particular the women's and gay liberation movements. Like Africana Studies, for instance, these academic disciplines were spawned by student pressure for a more inclusive curriculum. The Australasian, British, French, and North American settings of our authors differ from one another in their histories but are still interconnected, and all were affected by this activism in the academy.

As a sign of the interrelationships in the academic community, it is striking that one of the earliest figures cited in the American scene was a French woman. Simone de Beauvoir made the initial rupture between sex and gender, saying "one is not born, but rather becomes, a woman" (1953: 267). The phrase initiated a long period (in which we still are) of parsing those distinctions and others that follow from this first de-coupling. De Beauvoir's underlying point was that womanliness is not a biological condition but rather something imposed on the female child. She continues: "It is civilization as a whole that produces this creature, intermediate between male and eunuch, which is described as feminine. Only the intervention of someone else can establish an individual as an *Other*" (de Beauvoir 1953: 267).

Studying women was at first almost synonymous with studying gender, and vice versa. But gradually there came to be a concentrated emphasis on gender itself as a category of analysis. Rubin was one of the early voices theorizing the relationship between biological sex and gender with her influential essay "The traffic in women: Notes on the 'political economy' of sex." In that essay, she first of all pointed out that there *is* a sex/gender system constructing what is posited as an inert fact of human existence by, for instance, Claude Lévi-Strauss in his description of the exchange of women in kinship systems. She further defined the sex/gender system as the set of practices whereby "biological sexuality is transformed into products of human activity" (Rubin 1975: 159).

We might make the following list of distinctions based to some extent on de Beauvoir's formulation and Rubin's posited sex/gender system: biological sex, that with which one is born, the gender (man/woman) into which one is socialized with more or less pain and effort, and the traits associated with that gender (cultural masculinity and femininity). Overlaid on that set of binaries was taken, by the dominant culture, to be that of sexual orientation (when it was discussed at all) based on the sex (or is it the gender?) of the desired person. In the regime of heteronormativity, that meant desire for the "opposite sex." All of this has been disrupted and problematized in the years following. For instance, is there one object of desire? Why does the object have to have one sex or gender?

Within the immediately relevant setting of Classics in the United States we could conveniently center on three moments: 1978–84, marked by two volumes from *Arethusa* on women in antiquity;[4] 1990–93, when several volumes on gender and sexuality appeared;[5] and the present moment, which does not have such a clear stamp – but is marked by a certain retrospective quality. It might best be regarded as the moment of the survey or companion, which, if so, is a moment we are querying with the focus of this volume on new work. To be clear, however, these are not stages (or waves) with clear beginnings and endings; rather they need to be understood as interwoven with one another.

What we are calling the first moment (1978–84) was part of a general feminist body of work in the humanities and social sciences, for the most part focusing on women in antiquity as a field. It involved recovering historical women and engaging in feminist critique of male authors; that is, reading the literary material differently and for difference. The Women's Classical Caucus of the APA was founded in 1972 and has since then offered panels at the annual meetings of the association. There have been a number of important publications showing the continuing interest in the topic of women in antiquity, such as *Images of Women in Antiquity* (1983); *Women in Ancient Societies* (1994); and *Women in Antiquity: New Assessments* (1995). The wider project, of giving voice and reading differently, also led to feminist classicists becoming to some extent "resisting readers," in the words of Judith Fetterley (1978).

In Classics, the practice of looking for women in history and texts gradually changed into a concern with the organization of gendered relations in society, perhaps because of an early influence of structuralism on Classics. Froma Zeitlin is a good example; her early essay on Aeschylus' *Oresteia* published in the *Arethusa* volume (1978) undertook to analyze the misogyny of the myth (Zeitlin 1978); she was also one of the first to look for the feminine, as opposed to actual females. Writing in 1996, in the introduction to a collection of her essays from the previous decades, she counseled

> prob[ing] the cognitive, symbolic, and psychological functions of the feminine in a highly coded system of androcentric authority, a system whose own quest for universal categories and success in making culture pass for nature has left its imprint on us even today.
>
> *(Zeitlin 1996: 1)*

Zeitlin and others recognized the importance of "the category of gender and the dynamics of its manifold and varying uses as an integral structuring element of Greek literature and, more generally, of the social imagination" (Zeitlin 1996: 1). A fear that is often expressed, however, is that we might find ourselves forgetting women when attention turns to gender. It is worthwhile keeping both in play as we move forward.

Rubin was also in the vanguard of what might be taken to be the divergence, if not the outright war, between gender studies and sexuality studies, the next stage in this trajectory we are sketching in here. Ten years after her first groundbreaking essay, Rubin suggested that gender might not actually be the best hermeneutic tool for the discussion of sexuality. In "Thinking Sex" from 1984, she called for a radical politics of sexuality, and she explicitly separated the methodology for studying sexuality from that useful for gender studies, countering in this move, to some extent, her earlier essay.

One could say that the force of these questions and similar ones burst into Classics to form the second moment, a moment in which sexuality increasingly came to the fore, joining gender and sex as topics of discourse and providing further complications. In the study of sexuality in antiquity, an important or even dominant voice has been that of Michel Foucault. The scholarship we have associated above with the second moment was responsive to these trends and scholarship and indeed helped to shape them (for example Foucault knew and learned from Jack Winkler and Kenneth Dover; David Halperin's work has proven to be influential within and outside of Classics). The groundbreaking collection from 1990, *Before Sexuality*, has already been mentioned (p. 1). It, and both other works from around the same time and subsequent scholarship, foregrounded sexuality in a way that had not been done before.[6] Corollary to the appearance of the Women's Classical Caucus in 1972 and responsive to the increased interest in sexuality in Classics, the Lesbian and Gay Classical Caucus (now called the Lambda Classical Caucus) was founded in 1989 with an expressed interest in politically and intellectually supporting lesbian, gay, and now, queer classicists and their allies. The caucus has sponsored a panel at the APA annual meeting every year since then. Also at around this time, the study of ancient masculinity and men, as men, emerged and continued throughout the 1990s and into the next century.[7]

There has been vigorous debate accompanying this elaboration of Classics into considerations of gender and sexuality. While we agree with Foucault that sexuality is usefully regarded as having a history and as being responsive to its discursive situation, his influence on the shape of many research agendas in Classics has produced contention. The masculinist emphasis that underlies the second and third volumes of *The History of Sexuality* was problematic from the start and has only come to seem more so. The contours of these volumes seemed to justify the fear that women would be forgotten when attention turned to gender and sexuality: all subjectivities but that of the elite free man were erased from consideration,[8] and, making the erasure more profound, this man was even disembedded from his place in his world, specifically the *oikos/domus* and *polis/respublica*, and made into the solipsistic competitor with his urges and desires. Indeed, it is possible that the masculinist tendencies of work on sexuality that has come out since the very late 1980s stem from Foucault's influence.

Accompanying the debate about the influence of Foucault has also been considerable discussion about how to understand sexuality *itself* in antiquity, indeed if we can even use this term. Foucault's insight that there is a "history of sexuality" to be written was generally accepted and sexuality studies became a field. While this was a positive development, one consequence of it was the excessive emphasis on male same-sex relations because of this debt to Foucault and his generally masculinist orientation. It was in speaking of male desire that Foucault articulated his by-now canonical phrase: "the sodomite had been a temporary aberration; the homosexual was now a species" (1978: 43). As a result of this distinction and the attendant historicism, some modern scholars eschew the terms homosexual, homosexuality, sexuality, and related ones altogether when discussing pre-modern periods, arguing that the idea that there was a kind of person based on their choice of sexual object was not thinkable before modernity. Others maintain, however, that there was a category in antiquity at least for the man with desires to be penetrated, the *kinaidos* or *cinaedus*.[9]

But sexuality, despite often seeming a code for male same-sex sexual activity in Classics and elsewhere too, also refers to women's relations to men – and to women (though it has taken some effort to bring lesbianism into view). Sex between men and women (*mutatis mutandis*, heterosexuality), since it was and is the majority practice, was the norm that long tacitly dominated work in Classics: ubiquitous, heterosexual sex generally stood for all sexual activity prior to the development of the study of sex, gender, and sexuality. Work on gender in Classics initially continued with this default heterosexual matrix. It was easy enough to give in to: the ancient male speaking voice was sexually interested in women most of the time, though at other times in younger males (and occasionally ostentatiously refusing interest in other men). Women's desire for men and, especially, for other women does not figure prominently in this dynamic. Furthermore, male dominance in the sources, even those addressing women's desire, such as tragedy, leads to a healthy skepticism as to whose desire we are really seeing. Given that these desires and the erotic practices related to them surely existed in some form in the ancient world, scholars have been working in the interstices of the sources and been looking for gaps through which a woman's desire might be glimpsed, and this has come to include women's desires for other women.[10] This area of inquiry has been the one to arrive last in Classics, though of course Sappho was a name to conjure with in the earliest days of Women's Studies, with the iconic volume on lesbianism by Sidney Abbott and Barbara Love, *Sappho Was a Right-on Woman* (1972).

Studies of gender, sex, and sexuality in the ANE have moved in similar directions, but with differences based to some extent on the kind of evidence available and the nature of the field(s) involved. And, notably, they have a shorter history, beginning in earnest only a quarter of a century ago. Before this time the notion of ANE sexuality was dominated by anthropologically oriented Victorian notions of cultic Oriental "institutions" such as sacred prostitution, royal fertility, and orgiastic worship. By and large these ideas were popularized by Sir James Frazer (1854–1941), whose work, especially *The Golden Bough*, dominated the discipline for some fifty years, with later scholars adding to his anthropological investigations ideas such as "sacred marriage" and ritual castration. None of these notions can be found in the Near Eastern and Egyptian sources, and many of the nineteenth-century "truisms" about the role of sex in Mesopotamia and Egypt have now been overturned (Robins 1988; Assante 2003, 2006; Graves-Brown 2008). But these notions do persist, as Simo Parpola (2002: xiii) points out.

Increasingly scholars are turning their attention to the "daily" sexual habits of the people of the Near East, and diverting their interest from the mythic-sexual interests of earlier studies.

After all, unlike the Greeks, the Mesopotamians and Egyptians did not think of their literature as "mythic"; there was no demarcation between sacred and secular so that sexual metaphor, even of a cosmic level, is to be found in practically every genre of literary text from omen-list to love song (Leick 2002). It should be borne in mind that, as Zainab Bahrani (2001: 6) stresses, "the Near Eastern [sexual] tradition is quite unlike those of Greece and Rome, [the ones] with which the practitioners of women's history and ancient history are most familiar." Sex was woven into every fiber of life in Egypt and the rest of the Near East. Sexual language entered into prayers, hymns, dedications, magic spells, medical treatises, royal records, school texts, and humor. Sexual images decorated tomb walls, temple architecture, and household structures. Sexual potency was the key to all life – and to a healthy afterlife also (Biggs 1967, 2002; Manniche 1987; Sefati 1998).

More recently, studies of (male) same-sex relationships in Near Eastern cultures have begun to emerge. There is clear evidence for such relationships, but assessing their role and impact on the various cultures of the ancient orient is problematic. Male same-sex relations generally receive bad press – mainly because sex between men could not be centered on the life-giving bounty of fertility. There is some evidence that sexual passivity in particular was disliked and disrespected. An Egyptian Middle Kingdom story, for instance, tells how the pharaoh Neferkare (Pepi I or II) carried on a sexual liaison with one of his army officers – but the sexual act only occurred at night and in secret (Parkinson 1995). Myths such as *The Contendings of Horus and Seth* clearly regard male–male coupling as abnormal. Mesopotamian literature is more accepting to some extent in its attitudes towards male–male sex: some of the Middle Assyrian Laws (A §19–20) state that sex between men was to be punished only if anal penetration occurred (suggesting that other forms of sexual play were less egregiously offensive). Nonetheless if a man was charged with buggery – that is, taking the penetrative role – then he was condemned to be castrated and sodomized by a group of men (Asher-Greve 1997). In spite of this evidence, we find that same-sex unions of emotional intensity were lauded in literary masterpieces such the *Gilgamesh Epic*, and enter too into the Hebrew Bible in the story of David and Jonathan (2 Sam. 1). While it no doubt occurred, evidence for female same-sex practices is almost entirely lacking.

The essays in this volume represent the authors' latest thoughts on the subject of sex, gender, and sexuality in the ancient world at a time when across the academic disciplines, companions and surveys abound.[11] While in some sense this moment, our third one, looks increasingly like the effect of publishers wanting to get in on the act, the need to compile, summarize, and reflect upon the accomplishments of previous scholarship has generated similar effects before. The impulse to create Pauly-Wissowa (the *Realencyclopädie der classischen Altertumswissenschaft*) is surely an example. And the existence of the *Aufstieg und Niedergang der römischen Welt* series attests to a moment similar to this one. Taking stock is always a good idea, but there is also a need for new work. In terms of the topics of sex, gender, and sexuality, the work of previous decades poses particular challenges. As we said above (p. 3), the present moment, possessor of an inheritance fractured by previous battles over definition, is and must be hybrid since bodies of research with radically different assumptions remain in the mix. Progress forward can feel like disavowal of important elements from the past and functionally may be so since not every topic can remain at the top of the agenda.

Even so the effort to move forward must be made. As we change, and we have been doing so in the matters of sex, gender, and sexuality as the decades pass, we must reassess our relationship with the ancient world. For even as it was a time and place different from now – remember that the Greeks' strangeness has been part of the argument for social construction, post-Foucault – nonetheless the ANE, Greece, and Rome remain important to western culture. Once used to authorize the superiority of western culture (though less so in our multicultural present), assertions of similarity and even of origin are part of what makes the study of the ancient world and Classics important today, as Holmes argues (2012: 6–7). Last, we said above that in the title sex is to some extent explained as the amalgam of gender and sexuality. But we cannot just string together these terms; the relationships between them are not simply additive. We must ask how gender inflects sex and sexuality. The separation of sex and gender was accomplished by the hard work of denaturalization or de-essentialization. Gender norms are produced; they are not the inevitable consequences of physical bodies. And they importantly have ideals of sexual behavior and norms inscribed in and on them. In sum, then, it is not really possible, or productive, to separate out the terms of the title too sharply since they affect one another, and even determine one another. And all are interwoven with the questions of time and space. While we cannot rely on our contemporary point of view – especially since there is no single one in the present moment and historical difference is real – we also cannot escape this contemporaneity. We must always revisit and renegotiate our relationship with the past and this volume is part of that process.

The chapters

The thirty essays which make up this volume seek to intervene in existing debates, open up new areas for study, and articulate the authors' latest thinking on the subjects of sex, gender, and sexuality in antiquity. As you will see from the table of contents, the pieces have been divided into three (overlapping) sections along geographical-cum-chronological lines: Part I, the *Ancient Near East*; Part II, *Archaic, classical and Hellenistic Greece*; and Part III, *Republican, imperial and late-ancient Rome*.

Taken as a whole, the chapters in Part I of this volume, on the *Ancient Near East*, examine issues of gendered roles and the limits of normalized sexual behavior in a variety of Near Eastern cultures. The issue of gender surfaces in Susan Ackerman's contribution on women's reproductive magic in ancient Israel, for example (Chapter 1), where she examines both the nature of the magical rituals themselves and their harsh assessment by the male writers of the Hebrew Bible. Gender is also key to Budin's study (Chapter 2) which looks at the complementary roles of males and females in fertility and reproduction in ancient Mesopotamia, Egypt, Anatolia, and the Levant. Budin argues that in these ANE societies fertility – the ability to generate new life – was seen as a masculine rather than a feminine attribute. In Chapter 3, Solvang examines the use of rape as a strategy in ancient and modern conflicts, drawing out instructive parallels between the role played by rape in the 1994 Rwandan genocide and Absalom's decision to sexually violate the concubines of his father, King David, in 2 Sam. 16.

The limits of normalized sexual behavior form the subject of chapters by Boer and Leick. Boer (Chapter 4) undertakes a study of paraphilias – sex beyond that with living human beings – examining the assumptions and practices that written laws and rituals reveal. In his discussion, he uncovers not only prohibitions on bestiality and necrophilia in ANE cultures but also instances of more relaxed attitudes towards such acts. Leick (Chapter 5), on the other hand, looks at the issues of age and sex in Sumerian and Akkadian sources, demonstrating how neither extreme youth nor old age seem to have provided barriers to sex in ancient Mesopotamia.

The essays in Part II of this volume, on *Archaic, classical and Hellenistic Greece*, engage with a number of key areas in the study of ancient gender and sexuality, including pederasty and same-sex relationships, the construction of gender, prostitution, sexual ethics and rape.

Part II begins with Blanshard (Chapter 6) who re-examines the evidence for male same-sex orgies in ancient Athens. Blanshard argues that orgies were seen as far from desirable – indeed, the specter of such encounters was used to regulate normative sexual experiences. Lear (Chapter 7) also tackles same-sex relationships when he scrutinizes the idea (originating with Foucault) that the custom of pederasty was "problematized" in ancient Greek culture. Lear's view is that what scholars have observed is an essentially classical Athenian phenomenon, and that in other eras and locales, pederasty is idealized in a relatively unquestioning way. Penrose's piece (Chapter 8) on the iconography of the Tomb of the Diver complements Lear's study in that it suggests that the homoerotic scenes depicted, rather than being countercultural, points to a homonormativity to pederastic male relationships in ancient Poseidonia. Exploring the Orphic symbolism of these paintings, Penrose goes on to suggest that Orphic rites included pederastic or other homoerotic behavior.

Pederastic relationships also feature in the contribution by Glazebrook (Chapter 9), which examines the eroticized figures of the *pais* (boy) and *hetaira* (prostitute) in the context of the symposium. As Glazebrook's study demonstrates, these two figures are not infrequently juxtaposed and compared in poetry and art, with the female prostitute often differentiated from (and used as a negative role model for) the *pais* in terms of her erotic and ethical behavior. In a different vein, Goldhill also explores the world of, and attitudes towards, prostitutes (Chapter 10). He asks whether there is such a thing as a history of prostitution, exploring the diverse ways in which different societies are organized, structurally and socially, and questioning the extent to which a single term – "prostitution" – can usefully capture the range of phenomena we find in different eras and locations.

Calame's essay on the figure of Helen in Greek melic poetry (Chapter 11) speaks to a number of the theoretical strands outlined in this introduction in the way it engages with questions of sex and gender. In particular, he explores how different forms of lyric poetry construct gender identities and erotic relationships which in turn impact on the formation of social and gender relations. Rabinowitz's study of the figure of Electra in tragedy (Chapter 12) also breaks new ground in the way in which she uses theory – this time queer theory and, in particular, the concept of melancholy – to highlight various tensions in the way this figure is portrayed. As Rabinowitz demonstrates, Electra is variously portrayed by the tragedians as a marginal figure, ambiguous in gender and resistant to those in power – but also as a site where heterosexual norms are reimposed.

Other case studies based on ancient texts include Cyrino's essay on Euripides' *Hippolytus* (Chapter 13); she explores the violent way Eros is depicted in the play and how the lover's body is represented as vulnerable to violation. Boundaries and boundedness thus become key themes, with metaphors expressing loosening and fastening for grounding the destructive power of a deity denied. Dutsch's essay (Chapter 14) centers around Diogenes Laertius' *Lives of the Philosophers* and the concept of *kynogamia*, "dog marriage," a playful term associated with the marriage of Crates to a fellow Cynic, Hipparchia, in the late fourth century BCE. Dutsch uses this word, which denotes a partnership between individuals entitled to make free choices, as a springboard to examine the sexual ethics of the early Cynics. Murnaghan's essay (Chapter 15) concerns narratives in Greek literature which feature the exposure of a sexual secret. In a discussion which takes in a broad range of sources, she teases out key aspects of the power dynamics of heterosexual relationships and the gender dynamics that such stories expose.

The last group of essays in Part II engage with the subject of rape in ancient Greece. In Chapter 16, for example, Gaca looks at the use of rape in war, in a piece which self-conciously intersects with other studies of women, sex, and gender in antiquity. Building on her earlier work in this field, her study foregrounds, and explores the consequences of the extreme sexual and physical violence perpetrated against women by ancient armies. Harris's essay (Chapter 17) is also highly relevant to discussions of rape, since it critiques notions that women's consent was unimportant to men in ancient Greece. As Harris demonstrates, evidence from Athenian literature reveals that men did in fact pay attention to when women said "yes" and "no." Finally in this section, Robson (Chapter 18) examines the representation of rape in Old Comedy. He argues that the Aristophanic passages in question display a complex mixture of, on the one hand, male fantasies of rape as uncomplicated sexual acts, and on the other, recognition of rape's ability both to degrade and harm the female victim.

The essays in Part III of the volume, *Republican, imperial and late-ancient Rome*, engage with same-sex relationships, Roman manliness and unmanliness, and the gendered reception of female figures and sexual ethics in late antiquity.

Homoeroticism features heavily in the essay by Fox (Chapter 19), who uses psychoanalytic theory to read the myth of Orpheus as told in Ovid's *Metamorphoses*. Fox takes as his starting point the "bisexuality" of Orpheus, who transfers his affections to boys after the death of Eurydice, in a piece that tackles head on the problems inherent in reading poetic texts for historical data on ancient sexuality. And same-sex desire takes center stage in Richlin's essay (Chapter 20) which comprises a reassessment of the evidence for pederasty in Rome. Her conclusion is that pre-pubescent slave boys were used for sex and that pre-pubescent free boys were also the object of sexual desire at Rome. A key part of her discussion is an examination of how nineteenth- and twentieth-century scholars have previously read the evidence.

One chapter that spans the Greek and Roman divide is that of Boehringer (Chapter 21) whose subject matter is an erotic manual, *Peri Aphrodision*, attributed to the female author Philaenis. As Boehringer demonstrates, the issue of the author's sex raises broad and complex questions about authorship and sexual knowledge in antiquity – as well as attitudes towards prostitution and female homoeroticism. The presentation of female sexuality is also the subject of the essay by Gardner (Chapter 22) on Apuleius' *Metamorphoses*. Gardner uses Barbara Creed's notion of the "monstrous-feminine" to explore the thematic use of threatening aspects of feminine sexuality in the work.

Notions of manliness in Rome are scrutinized in a number of chapters. Hallett, for example (Chapter 23), examines the portrayal by Suetonius of the emperor Tiberius' "erectile dysfunction." Here she makes links with similar sexual scenarios described by the poets Catullus and Horace and also explores the way in which Tiberius' predecessors, Julius and Augustus Caesar, presented their sexual inadequacies publicly. A very different study of Roman manliness is undertaken by Olson (Chapter 24), who looks at the bearing that the occasional adoption of Greek costume by Roman men had not only on the formation of cultural identity but also on the construction of gender and sexual personality.

The sexual manliness and unmanliness of Roman men feature prominently in two further chapters. First, Kamen and Levin-Richardson (Chapter 25) revisit the topic of penetrated males through a study of literature and graffiti. Their findings are that Romans made a hitherto unnoticed distinction between penetrated men who exhibited agency and those who did not. Williams (Chapter 26) also turns to the Latin vocabulary of unmanly men for his essay, in a discussion which employs conceptual and terminological tools developed by linguists to add further nuance to interpretations of ancient Greek and Roman sex-gender systems.

A number of chapters in Part III focus on later antiquity. In Chapter 27, for example, Gold looks at the third-century CE Christian martyr Perpetua, and the way in which later male editors in antiquity sought to reframe the narrative that Perpetua wrote before her execution. In Smith's essay (Chapter 28), female personae feature in a very different way. His subject matter is the sixth-century CE epigrams of Agathias of Myrina and Paul the Silentiary. As Smith demonstrates, these poets, writing at a time when same-sex sexual activity had been criminalized by Emperor Justinian, sublimate these desires in two key ways: both by the adoption of female personae in their poetry and by the representation of an erotic triangle, wherein the relationship of two men is intensified through their mutual relationship with a woman. In a related vein, Boyarin (Chapter 29) considers relations between male Talmudic scholars, one married to the sister of the other. Revising to some extent his earlier thoughts on the "carnality" of Israel, Boyarin perceives an underlying Platonism in Talmudic homosociality that privileges non-carnal relations between men over the carnal ones of man and wife. This scene of talmudic scholarship therefore not only looks back to Plato, it also prefigures the friendships of men and women among Christian ascetics in late antiquity. Also considering late antiquity, Masterson (Chapter 30) places the anonymous fourth-century CE Latin physiognomy, the *De Physiognomonia Liber*, firmly in the temporal context of its writing. Resonances of late-Platonic philosophy in this work suggest perceptible connections to late-ancient notions of elite manhood.

It is nearly impossible to sum up a volume of essays as wide-ranging as this one. In the end there will be many versions of this book, as readers pick and choose what interests them. We close with the hope that you will find here ideas that stimulate further thought.

Notes

1 Brooke Holmes (2010) takes on the question of the body as the site not of sex, but of the symptom. Her "central argument … is that this body, designated in Greek by the word *soma*, emerges through changes in the interpretation of symptoms in the Greek world of the fifth and fourth centuries BCE" (2010: 2). On work on the body in antiquity in general, see Porter 1999, for example. In her second book, which is on gender, Holmes (2012) does interrelate body and sex.
2 The existence of intersex individuals challenges this neat duality, even on the level of the physiological, as Anne Fausto-Sterling (2000) pointed out. Although this work is not represented in this volume, it has been taken up elsewhere in Classics (e.g., Montserrat 1998; Brisson 2002).
3 Response to Brooke Holmes, *Gender: Antiquity and Its Legacy*, talk delivered at the APA Panel, Authors Meet Critics: Gender and Race in Antiquity and its Reception; APA annual meeting, January 3–5, 2014, Chicago.
4 Issues of *Arethusa* were published in 1973 (6.1), 1978 (11.1, 2), edited by John J. Peradotto, and, revised, issued as a book, *Women in the Ancient World: The Arethusa Papers* in 1984, edited by John J. Peradotto and J. P. Sullivan.
5 Halperin 1990; Halperin et al. 1990; Winkler 1990.
6 For consideration of Greece, see, e.g., Halperin 1990; Winkler 1990; Cohen 1991; Thornton 1997; for the situation at Rome, there are, e.g., Richlin 1992, 1993; Hallett and Skinner 1997; Williams 1999 [2010]; for both Greece and Rome, see Skinner 2005.
7 See, e.g., Gleason 1995; Bassi 1998; Foxhall 1998; Foxhall and Salmon 1998a, 1998b; Gunderson 2000, 2003; Rosen and Sluiter 2003; McDonnell 2006. Also see Masterson 2013 for an overview of the development of masculinity studies in Classics.
8 See, e.g., Richlin 1991; Foxhall 1998.
9 For the materiality of the *cinaedus*, see Richlin 1993. For insistence on the ultimate difference of antiquity in such matters, see, e.g., Halperin 2002.
10 See, e.g., Brooten 1996; Rabinowitz and Auanger 2002; Boehringer 2007.
11 There are, e.g., "Blackwell Companions," "Cambridge Companions," and "Oxford Readings" for any number of topics.

Bibliography

Abbott, S. and Love, B. (eds) (1972) *Sappho Was a Right-on Woman: A Liberated View of Lesbianism*. New York: Stein and Day.
Asher-Greve, J. (1997) "The essential body: Mesopotamian conceptions of the gendered body", *Gender and History* 9(3): 432–61.
Assante, J. (2003) "From whores to hierodules: The historiographic invention of Mesopotamian female sex professionals", in A.A. Donohue and M.D. Fullerton (eds) *Ancient Art and its Historiography*. Cambridge: Cambridge University Press, pp. 13–47.

——(2006) "Undressing the nude: Problems in analyzing nudity in ancient art, with an Old Babylonian case study", in S. Schroer (ed.) *Images and Gender: Contributions to the Hermeneutics of Reading Ancient Art.* Fribourg: Academic Press, pp. 177–207.

Bahrani, Z. (2001) *Women of Babylon: Gender and Representation in Mesopotamia.* London: Routledge.

Bassi, K. (1998) *Acting Like Men: Gender, Drama, and Nostalgia in Ancient Greece.* Ann Arbor, MI: Michigan University Press.

Biggs, R.D. (1967) *ŠÁ.ZI.GA: Ancient Mesopotamian Potency Incantations.* Locust Valley, NY: JJ Augustin.

——(2002) "The Babylonian sexual potency texts", in S. Parpola and R.M.Whiting (eds) *Sex and Gender in the Ancient Near East: Proceedings of the 47th Rencontre Assyriologique Internationale, Helsinki, July 2–6, 2001.* Helsinki: Neo-Assyrian Text Corpus Project, pp. 71–8.

Boehringer, S. (2007) *L'Homosexualité Féminine dans l'Antiquité Grecque et Romaine.* Paris: Belles Lettres.

Bordo, S. (1993) *Unbearable Weight: Feminism, Western Culture, and the Body.* Berkeley, CA: University of California Press.

Brisson, L. (2002) *Sexual Ambivalence: Androgyny and Hermaphroditism in Graeco-Roman Antiquity*, trans. J. Lloyd. Berkeley, CA: University of California Press.

Brooten, B.J. (1996) *Love Between Women: Early Christian Responses to Female Homoeroticism.* Chicago, IL: University of Chicago Press.

Butler, J. (1990) *Gender Trouble.* New York: Routledge.

——(1993) *Bodies that Matter: On the Discursive Limits of "Sex".* New York: Routledge.

Cohen, D. (1991) *Law, Sexuality, and Society: The Enforcement of Morals in Classical Athens.* Cambridge: Cambridge University Press.

de Beauvoir, S. (1953) *The Second Sex*, trans. H.M. Parsley. New York: Knopf.

Dover, K.J. (1989) *Greek Homosexuality*, updated and with a new postscript. Cambridge, MA: Harvard University Press.

Fausto-Sterling, A. (2000) *Sexing the Body: Gender Politics and the Construction of Sexuality.* New York: Basic Books.

Fetterley, J. (1978) *The Resisting Reader: A Feminist Approach to American Fiction.* Bloomington, IN: Indiana University Press.

Foucault, M. (1978) *The History of Sexuality, Vol. 1: Introduction.* New York: Pantheon Books.

——(1985) *The History of Sexuality, Vol. 2: The Use of Pleasure.* New York: Vintage Books.

——(1986) *The History of Sexuality, Vol. 3: The Care of the Self.* New York: Vintage Books.

Foxhall, L. (1998) "Pandora unbound: A feminist critique of Foucault's History of sexuality", in D.H.J. Larmour, P.A Miller and C. Platter (eds) *Rethinking Sexuality: Foucault and Classical Antiquity.* Princeton, NJ: Princeton University Press, pp. 122–37.

——(2013) *Studying Gender in Classical Antiquity.* Cambridge: Cambridge University Press.

Foxhall, L. and Salmon, J.B. (eds) (1998a) *Thinking Men: Masculinity and its Self-Representation in the Classical Tradition.* London: Routledge.

——(1998b) *When Men Were Men: Masculinity, Power, and Identity in Classical Antiquity.* London: Routledge.

Gleason, M.W. (1995) *Making Men: Sophists and Self-Presentation in Ancient Rome.* Princeton, NJ: Princeton University Press.

Graves-Brown, C. (ed.) (2008) *Sex and Gender in Ancient Egypt: "Don your Wig for a Joyful Hour".* Swansea: Classical Press of Wales.

Grosz, E.A. (1994) *Volatile Bodies: Toward a Corporeal Feminism.* Bloomington, IN: Indiana University Press.

Gunderson, E. (2000) *Staging Masculinity: The Rhetoric of Performance in the Roman World.* Ann Arbor, MI: University of Michigan Press.

——(2003) *Declamation, Paternity, and Roman Identity: Authority and the Rhetorical Self.* Cambridge: Cambridge University Press.

Hallett, J.P. and M.B. Skinner (eds) (1997) *Roman Sexualities.* Princeton, NJ: Princeton University Press.

Halperin, D.M. (1990) *One Hundred Years of Homosexuality: And Other Essays on Greek Love.* New York: Routledge.

——(2002) *How to Do the History of Homosexuality.* Chicago, IL: University of Chicago Press.

Halperin, D.M., Winkler, J.J. and Zeitlin, F.I. (1990) *Before Sexuality: The Construction of Erotic Experience in the Ancient Greek World.* Princeton, NJ: Princeton University Press.

Holmes, B. (2010) *The Symptom and the Subject: The Emergence of the Physical Body in Ancient Greece.* Princeton, NJ and Oxford: Princeton University Press.

——(2012) *Gender: Antiquity and its Legacy.* Oxford and New York: Oxford University Press.

Laqueur, T.W. (1990) *Making Sex: Body and Gender from the Greeks to Freud*. Cambridge, MA: Harvard University Press.

Leick, G. (1994) *Sex and Eroticism in Mesopotamian Literature*. London: Routledge.

——(2002) *The Babylonians: An Introduction*. Abingdon and New York: Routledge.

McDonnell, M.A. (2006) *Roman Manliness: Virtus and the Roman Republic*. Cambridge: Cambridge University Press.

Manniche, L. (1987) *Sexual Life in Ancient Egypt*. New York: Kegan Paul.

Masterson, M. (2013) "Studies of ancient masculinity", in T.K. Hubbard (ed.) *A Companion to Greek and Roman Sexualities*. Malden, MA: Wiley-Blackwell, pp. 17–30.

Montserrat, D. (1998) *Changing Bodies, Changing Meanings: Studies on the Human Body in Antiquity*. London: Routledge.

Parker, H.N. (1997) "The teratogenic grid", in J.P. Hallett and M.B. Skinner (eds) *Roman Sexualities*. Princeton, NJ: Princeton University Press, pp. 47–65.

Parkinson, R.B. (1995) "'Homosexual' desire and middle kingdom literature", *Journal of Egyptian Archaeology* 81: 57–76.

Parpola, S. (2002) "Introduction", in S. Parpola and R.M. Whiting (eds) *Sex and Gender in the Ancient Near East, Proceedings of the 47th Rencontre Assyriologique Internationale, Helsinki, July 2–6, 2001*. Helsinki: Neo-Assyrian Text Corpus Project, pp. xiii–xv.

Peradotto, J. and Sullivan, J.P. (eds) (1984) *Women in the Ancient World: The Arethusa Papers*. Albany, NY: State University of New York Press.

Porter, J. (ed.) (1999) *Constructions of the Classical Body*. Ann Arbor, MI: University of Michigan Press.

Rabinowitz, N.S. and Auanger, L. (eds) (2002) *Among Women: From the Homosocial to the Homoerotic in the Ancient World*. Austin, TX: University of Texas Press.

Richlin, A. (1991) "Zeus and Metis: Foucault, feminism, classics", *Helios* 18(2): 160–80.

——(1992) *The Garden of Priapus: Sexuality and Aggression in Roman Humor*. New York: Oxford University Press.

——(1993) "Not before homosexuality: The materiality of the *cinaedus* and the Roman law against love between men", *Journal of the History of Sexuality* 3(4): 523–73.

Robins, G. (1988) "Ancient Egyptian sexuality", *Discussions in Egyptology* 11:61–72.

Rosen, R.M. and Sluiter, I. (eds) (2003) *Andreia: Studies in Manliness and Courage in Classical Antiquity*. Leiden: Brill.

Rubin, G. (1975) "The traffic in women: Notes toward a political economy of sex", in R. Reiter (ed.) *Toward an Anthropology of Women*. New York: Monthly Review Press, pp. 157–210.

——(1984) "Thinking sex: Notes for a radical theory of the politics of sexuality", in C. Vance (ed.) *Pleasure and Danger*. London: Routledge & Kegan Paul, pp. 267–309.

Sedgwick, E.K. (1985) *Between Men: English Literature and Male Homosocial Desire*. New York: Columbia University Press.

——(1990) *Epistemology of the Closet*. Berkeley, CA: University of California Press.

Sefati, Y. (1998) *Love Songs in Sumerian Literature: Critical Edition of the Dumuzi-Inanna Songs*. Ramat Gan: Bar Ilan University Press.

Skinner, M. (2005) *Sexuality in Greek and Roman Culture*. Malden, MA and Oxford: Blackwell.

Thornton, B.S. (1997) *Eros: The Myth of Ancient Greek Sexuality*. Boulder, CO: Westview Press.

Williams, C.A. (1999 [2010]) *Roman Homosexuality*. New York: Oxford University Press.

Winkler, J.J. (1990) *The Constraints of Desire: The Anthropology of Sex and Gender in Ancient Greece*. New York: Routledge.

Zeitlin, F. (1978) "The dynamics of misogyny: Myth and mythmaking in the *Oresteia* of Aeschylus", *Arethusa* 11: 149–84.

——(1996) *Playing the Other: Gender and Society in Classical Greek Literature*. Chicago: University of Chicago Press.

PART I

Ancient Near East

1

"I HAVE HIRED YOU WITH MY SON'S MANDRAKES"

Women's reproductive magic in ancient Israel

Susan Ackerman

Genesis 30:14–16; 38:28; and Ezekiel 13:17–23

There are three texts in the Hebrew Bible that arguably depict women engaged in acts of reproductive magic. In Genesis 30:14–16, Rachel, who is barren (Genesis 29:31), and her sister Leah, who has ceased to bear children (Genesis 30:9), vie to use the "love plants" (*dûdā'îm*, a term kindred to the noun *dôd*, meaning "love, beloved")[1] that Leah's son Reuben has found in a field, in the hope that one of these sisters might benefit from the love plants' powers as an aphrodisiac and their ability to bestow fertility. In Genesis 38:28, the midwife who attends Judah's daughter-in-law Tamar as she gives birth ties a red thread around the hand of her son Zerah as his arm emerges from the womb, most probably an act of apotropaic magic meant to protect the baby from malevolent agents. And in Ezekiel 13:17–23, an anonymous cadre of "daughters who prophesy" are said to sew bands of cloth onto wrists,[2] to put head bands[3] on heads (v. 18), and to be associated as well with "handfuls of barley" and "pieces of bread" (v. 19) – all magical rites, according to an interpretation put forward by Nancy R. Bowen (1999), that can be enacted on behalf of expectant women during the course of their pregnancies and at the time of delivery.

To be sure, the classifying of each of these texts as an instance of reproductive magic can be debated. For example, Hector Avalos uses the language of medicine, not magic, to describe Leah's and Rachel's efforts to use the "love plants" that Reuben has found; more specifically, Avalos compares moderns' "medicinal" use of tea, or lemon juice, or chicken soup to treat various ailments to Rachel's and Leah's vying to perform an act of "self-medication" or "self-help," in which the "love plants" serve as a "natural remedy" that "cure[s] infertility" (Avalos 1995: 254–5; see similarly Avalos 1997: 454).[4] Yet as has been long and often pointed out, the boundary between "medicine" and "magic" in the ancient world was largely unmarked,[5] and thus Marten Stol (2000a: 56), who follows the standard interpretation that Leah's and Rachel's "love plants" were mandrake roots, can describe the mandrake of Genesis 30:14–16 as "a *magical* plant" (emphasis added). Likewise, Carol Meyers (2005: 38; see similarly Meyers 2002: 289) writes of Rachel and Leah engaging in a "*magical* act performed to promote fertility" (emphasis added).

Somewhat similarly Meyers, while noting that the purpose that is intimated in Genesis 38:28 for the red thread that is tied around Zerah's wrist is not magical, but pragmatic (it marks him as the first of Tamar's twin sons to have breached the womb), nevertheless proposes that the thread has a significance that transcends the rather idiosyncratic function that is described for it on the occasion of Zerah's birth. In her words, "its [the red thread's] use may reflect a set of practices involving the apotropaic character of strands of dyed yarn, with both their red color and the fact that they are bound on the infant's hand having magical protective powers" (Meyers 2002: 290, 2005: 38–9).[6] Meyers goes on to remark that in Mesopotamian and Hittite birth rituals, binding with red thread is used in exactly this sort of apotropaic fashion (although in the Mesopotamian example, which is from the Old Babylonian period [1894–1595 BCE], and in one Hittite text, red wool threads are bound not to the baby, but to the *mother* during delivery to protect her).[7]

As for Ezekiel 13:17–23, Katheryn Pfisterer Darr (2000: 336) proposes that there are allusions in this text to "séance-like practices," which indicates to her that the "daughters who prophesy" are women engaged not in rituals of reproductive magic but in necromancy. This interpretation has also been urged by several other scholars, based on the description of these daughters' "hunting for souls" in Ezekiel 13:18.[8] This phrase is taken, under the terms of these scholars' interpretation, to refer to spirits of the dead, given that, according to at least some among these commentators, "the dead can manifest themselves in the shape of birds" (van der Toorn 1994: 123, quoting Spronk 1986: 100, n. 3, 167, 255).[9] Ann Jeffers (1996: 94) somewhat similarly finds allusions in Ezekiel 13:17–23 to death-related, as opposed to reproductive, magic but she posits that a far more sinister practice than necromancy is being enacted: according to her analysis, the "daughters who prophesy" "mak[e] images of people tied up … [and] search for personal objects belonging to them," which is followed by "their burying" (whether Jeffers means the burying of the images, or of the personal objects, or of both, is unclear to me). Jeffers then goes on to say that in this way, "through the system of correspondences, the person represented by the image should die." In support of this argument, Jeffers cites Babylonian accounts of witchcraft that describe witches as making images of their victims and binding these images' knees and arms, which she sees as analogous to the binding practices depicted in Ezekiel 13:18.

That Ezekiel 13:18 refers to images, rather than the wrists and heads of actual individuals, is, however, an interpretation that Jeffers must impose upon the text, as this is nowhere explicitly indicated; moreover, Jeffers has no compelling explanation to offer for Ezekiel 13:19 and its association of the daughters' actions with barley and bread (she can suggest only that "the grain or the barley may have been used to block the mouth of an image" [1996: 94]). Conversely, those who interpret the daughters' acts as necromantic rituals that summon bird-like spirits of the dead can explain the allusions to barley and bread (this food is "meant to allure the bird-like souls," according to Marjo C. A. Korpel [1996: 103–4]). But these scholars are less able to explain the binding practices. Korpel, for example, can only suggest that the daughters "sew bird-nets which they spread out over their arms," in order to snare the bird-like dead spirits (1996: 103). But this defies the (admittedly difficult) syntax of the passage, which is best understood as distinguishing between those who sew the wrist and head bands and those upon whom these fabrics are bound. Moreover, the proposition that the dead can take on the shape of birds according to West Semitic religious thought has been challenged by such noted experts as Marvin H. Pope (1987: 452, 463) and Mark S. Smith and Elizabeth Bloch-Smith (1988: 277–84).[10]

Bowen turns, therefore, to consider some of the same sorts of Mesopotamian and Hittite data that I cited above to suggest that the binding acts performed by the Ezekiel 13 "daughters who prophesy" may be magical rites executed on behalf of women of childbearing age during their pregnancies and at the time of parturition.[11] For example, Bowen points out that in addition to the Hittite and Mesopotamian texts that speak of apotropaic red threads that can be bound to a delivering mother and/or her newborn infant, Mesopotamian sources describe how threads of various colors could be twined together, knotted, and then bound on a woman's hand or other body parts to stop excessive vaginal bleeding during pregnancy (Bowen 1999: 424, citing Scurlock 1991: 136–8). This act reminds her of the binding on of wrist bands performed by the "daughters who prophesy"; indeed, the specific term for the "wrist bands" that the "daughters who prophesy" in Ezekiel 13 apply, *kĕsātôt*, is arguably related to the Akkadian verb *kasû*, "to bind" (Bowen 1999: 424, n. 31; also Davies 1994: 121). A cloth band could also be tied on a Mesopotamian mother-to-be to prevent miscarriage (Bowen 1999: 424, citing Scurlock 1991: 138–9), and special amulet stones could likewise be tied to a mother-to-be's body if she was experiencing difficulties. One Neo-Assyrian text, for example, refers to nine stones that were tied around the waist of a pregnant woman who was experiencing profuse vaginal bleeding during the course of her pregnancy (Scurlock 1991: 136; Stol 2000a: 203). Mesopotamian sources describe as well a set of twelve amulet stones that can be tied to the hands, feet, and hips of a woman who struggles during labor and "does not give birth easily" (Stol 2000a: 132–3; see also ibid: 49–52, 116, 203; Stol 2000b: 491; Gursky 2001: 98–9).

Note, moreover, that it is not the amulet stones alone that protect the mother-to-be according to these texts: the knot-magic that is deployed when securing the amulets to the woman's body also has significant apotropaic powers according to Mesopotamian lore. Mesopotamian ritual texts (as well as Egyptian tradition) moreover speak of the removal of bands or the untying of knots at the time of the actual birth (Bowen 1999: 424, citing Scurlock 1991: 139, 141; Foster 1996: 1.138), given that "knots [otherwise] … constrain birth" (so much so that, in Egypt, a delivering woman's hair was intentionally unbraided and left to hang unbound [Ritner 2008: 174]).

Additionally, in Mesopotamian tradition, a midwife might sprinkle a circle of flour on the floor during a pregnant woman's delivery, and offerings of bread could be made (Bowen 1999: 424, citing Scurlock 1991: 140, 151, 182). This latter ritual, Jo Ann Scurlock hypothesizes, was meant to sate the hunger of demons that might otherwise snatch newborn infants (Bowen 1999: 424, citing Scurlock 1991: 157; Foster 1996: 2.545). Bowen suggests that the association of the "daughters who prophesy" in Ezekiel 13:17–23 with barley and bread indicates that they used these foodstuffs in a similar way. All in all, she concludes (Bowen 1999: 424),

> the activities that Ezekiel ascribes to the female prophets … share some of the same imagery as these various incantations associated with childbirth. In particular they share the imagery of the binding and removal of knots or bands of cloth (13:18, 20, 21) and the use of grain and bread for ritual use (13:19).

The biblical tradition's assessment of reproductive magic: Ezekiel 13:17–23

After putting forth her interpretation that identifies motifs that come from the arena of ancient Near Eastern reproductive magic in Ezekiel 13:17–23, Bowen turns to ask why the "daughters who prophesy" are excoriated in this oracle, as in v. 17, for example, where Ezekiel is commanded by God to prophesy against them, or in v. 19, where Ezekiel, speaking for God, accuses the "daughters who prophesy" of having "profaned" the deity. The question is a good one, especially given that Ezekiel's scathing denunciation of the daughters' acts of reproductive magic is unparalleled in either Genesis 30:14–16 or Genesis 38:28. Rather, in Genesis 30:14–16, Leah's and Rachel's vying to use the mandrake roots that Leah's son Reuben has found in a field, in the hope that one of them might benefit from the mandrake's aphrodisiac and fertility properties, is presented by the biblical writers in a manner that is wholly matter of fact, without any reservations being expressed about this use of "plant magic" (although it is important to note that the sisters' endeavors are not necessarily judged positively, by being treated as, say, praiseworthy; more on this below in the section entitled Women reproductive magicians). Likewise, in Genesis 38:28, although one could argue that the biblical writers move to obscure the magical significance of Tamar's midwife's endeavors by suggesting that her motivation was only pragmatic (to make clear which of Tamar's twin sons first breached the womb), the magical act performed by the midwife – the tying of a red band around the newborn's wrist as an apotropaic rite – is not judged negatively.

Why this difference between Ezekiel 13:17–23, on the one hand, and Genesis 30:14–16 and 38:28, on the other? The case of Ezekiel is easier to explain, as the prophet represents a point of view whereby (to quote Bowen [1999: 431]) "any religious practice that lies outside Ezekiel's priestly worldview is considered to be illegitimate and dangerous, and therefore must be condemned and destroyed." These illegitimate religious practices include anything Ezekiel's priestly cohort classifies as magic – although one must quickly admit that distinguishing between legitimate "religion" and illegitimate "magic" according to the worldview of Ezekiel's priestly cohort, and according to the worldview of biblical tradition more generally, is a tricky matter. After all, how different is magic – which we might define as "a form of communication involving the supernatural world in which an attempt is made to affect the course of present and/or future events by means of ritual actions ... and/or ... formulaic recitations" (Scurlock 1992: 464b) – from religion, which is also "a form of communication involving the supernatural world" that employs "ritual actions ... and/or ... formulaic recitations," often with the goal of affecting present and/or future events? Or, to phrase this question in somewhat more concrete terms: why is it praiseworthy, in 2 Kings 2:19–22, for the prophet Elisha to throw a bowl of salt into a spring near Jericho, a seemingly magical rite that purifies the spring, whereas the seemingly magical rite of binding on wrist and head bands in Ezekiel 13:17–23 is condemned? Both acts arguably defend against miscarriages: in Elisha's case, the "miscarriages (měšakkālet) of the land" (that is, its lack of fertility) and perhaps, by implication, the actual miscarriages being suffered by the city's pregnant women.[12] So too are actual miscarriages one of the things that the Ezekiel 13 binding rituals, according to Mesopotamian parallels, might serve to prevent.

The answer is that what distinguishes the "religious" from the "magical" in the minds of the biblical writers – or more specifically here, in the minds of Ezekiel and the author(s) and/or redactor(s) of 2 Kings 2:19–22 – is not the performance of a particular ritual by any given individual, but the value judgment that is made about that ritual's performer and whether he or she is regarded as properly authorized to execute said deed. "It is not the nature of the action itself," Stephen D. Ricks writes of the Hebrew Bible (2001: 131–2), "but the conformity of the ... actor to, or deviation from, the values of Israelite society – as these values are reflected in the canonical text of the Bible – that determines whether it [the action] is characterized as magic." Bowen (1999: 420) tellingly cites in this regard Jacob Neusner (1989: 4), "one group's holy man is another's magician," and Robert K. Ritner (2001: 44) is almost as pithy: "magic," he writes, "is simply the religious practices of one group viewed with disdain by another." Sarah Iles Johnston makes the same point more fully (2004: 140): "In antiquity, *magic* ... almost always referred to someone else's religious practices; it was a term that distanced those practices from the norm – that is, from one's own practices, which constituted religion." The Bible's magicians are, in short, its "others." We can again quote Ricks (2001: 132): "magic ... is quintessentially the activity of the 'outsider' in the Bible."[13]

Yet who, more specifically, are the Bible's "others" or "outsiders"? Most obviously, they are foreigners, those who are treated by the biblical writers as ethnically "other" to the Israelites and who, in terms of their political and religious affiliations, stand "outside" the Israelite commonwealth. Deuteronomy 18:9–12 particularly illustrates this understanding. The text envisions Moses as speaking to the Israelites at the end of their Exodus sojourn and immediately prior to their entry into the "promised land." As he speaks, Moses warns that, "When you come into the land that Yahweh your God is giving you, you shall not learn to act according to the abominable practices" of the nations already within it. He then enumerates what some of these "abominable practices" are by listing at least five different magical specialties (for example, divination, augury, sorcery, the casting of spells, and necromancy).[14] He concludes by reiterating the notion that such practices are "abominable" and also stresses that it is on account of the nations' engaging in these magical acts that Yahweh is driving them out of the land that Israel will inhabit. Again, what is indicated is that magicianship is to be characterized as "foreign" and, as such, unacceptably "other."

But the "other" can also come from within; paradoxically, that is, the "insider" can simultaneously occupy the position of unacceptable "outsider." This is particularly the case for ancient Israelite women. In her 1993 book *Fragmented Women: Feminist (Sub)versions of Biblical Narrative*, for example, J. Cheryl Exum includes a chapter whose title, "The (M)other's Place," and especially the parentheses within it, tries to capture the "othered" position that the otherwise "insider" matriarchs Sarah, Rebekah, Rachel, and Leah occupy in the book of Genesis. On the one hand, as Exum sees it, these matriarchs are central to the movement forward of the Genesis narrative, since the generational progression on which Genesis relies cannot be accomplished without the patriarchs Abraham, Isaac, and Jacob begetting a son or sons with a "right" or proper wife. What makes a wife "right," moreover, is her *insider* status: she is not of the Canaanites nor, like the Egyptian Hagar, of some other people. Rather, the "right" wife is of the patriarchs' ethnos and, indeed, of their own family (as Sarah is Abraham's half-sister, for example, according to Genesis 20:12). On the other hand, however, the matriarchs stand as outsiders: Rebekah, Leah, and Rachel, for example, are residents of faraway lands that they must leave to dwell with their husbands in Canaan, and once there, as Exum writes (1993: 110), "they are 'other.'" More important, as Joseph Blenkinsopp points out, *all* ancient Israelite women are construed by the patrilocal conventions of Israelite marriage as, at least to some degree, "other." In his words (1997: 59): "the woman introduced into her husband's household always remained, in a certain sense, an outsider."

To construe ancient Israelite women, at least in part, as "outsider" and "other" is, though, to affiliate them with those things "foreign" and "alien" about which the biblical writers can express so much suspicion and concern. For women magicians, the effect can be, colloquially speaking, a double whammy, as magic, the art of the "other," and women, the "other sex," come together in an ideological synthesis that renders women magicians the subject of particularly harsh censure. This is why no biblical text speaks positively about women as magical practitioners, not even Genesis 30:14–16 and 38:28, which we can only describe as refraining from negativity (again, more on this below in the section entitled Women reproductive magicians), and certainly not Ezekiel 13:17–23. Indeed, we see in Ezekiel 13:17–23 how determinative gender is as an "othering" principle for women magicians, so much so that although Ezekiel 13's "daughters" arguably lay some claim to the title of prophet that otherwise can mark one as a ritual actor who is legitimately allowed, like the prophet Elisha, to perform magical rites, the text's "daughters who prophesy" are nevertheless censured for the exercise of miscarriage-prevention magic. Conversely Elisha, as we have seen, is presented as worthy of praise when he performs an analogous ritual.

Again, then, we note the degree to which it is not the perform*ance* of (in this case) miscarriage-prevention magic, but the position of the magic's perform*er* (in this case, the gender position) that determines the propriety of the act. This also explains why the claim that the "othered" *daughters* of Ezekiel 13:17–23 "practice divination" (*tiqsamnâ*) is evoked in a condemnatory way (v. 23), even as the occasional biblical text can extend to *male* diviners, as well as to other *men* engaged in divinatory practice, a modicum of respect. In Isaiah 3:2–3, for example, the "(male) diviner" (*qōsēm*) is included in a seemingly matter-of-fact way (certainly, without opprobrium) in a list of community leaders: the *gibbôr*, or "warrior"; the *šōpēṭ*, or "judge"; the *nābî'*, or "prophet"; the *zāqēn*, or "elder"; and the *yô'ēṣ*, or "counselor." Somewhat similarly, in 1 Kings 20:33, it passes unremarked that the unnamed king of Israel (presumably King Ahab; see Cogan 2001: 471–4) is perceived by the defeated soldiers of the Syrian king Ben-Hadad as engaging in an act of cledonomancy, or the giving of an omen that they are able to divine (*yĕnaḥăšû*) through the interpreting of the king's "chance utterances," which are "overheard and considered endowed with ominous meanings" (Cogan 2001: 468, quoting Oppenheim 1954–6: 55). Proverbs 16:10, moreover, speaks approvingly of a just and praiseworthy king who gives voice to divinatory oracles (*qesem*).[15]

There are other texts we might adduce to demonstrate just how negatively the Bible judges women magical practitioners in comparison to their male counterparts, but to conclude this part of my discussion, I will evoke just one: the treatment of the female "sorcerer" (*mĕkaššēpâ*). She, according to Exodus 22:17 (in most of the Bible's English versions, 22:18), is to be put to death (literally, "not let live"; *lō' tĕḥayyeh*),[16] and indeed, in 2 Kings 9:33, the usurper King Jehu orders Jezebel, whom he has earlier condemned for her "sorceries" (2 Kings 9:22), to be thrown out of a window and killed. To be sure, 2 Kings 9:22 is best interpreted figuratively: that is, not as a literal denunciation of Jezebel as a sorcerer but rather as an attack upon Jezebel that uses the charge of sorcery as a pejorative slur.[17] Note in this regard that in the same breath that Jehu speaks of Jezebel's sorceries, he denounces as well her "harlotries," even though sexual improprieties are not among the otherwise manifold wrongdoings of which Jezebel, in the opinion of the biblical writers, is guilty. Instead, in the same way that, elsewhere in the Bible, the term "harlot" can be used metaphorically to accuse its subjects of "going after" gods other than the Israelite god Yahweh, regardless of these accuseds' sexual proclivities,[18] so too does Jehu use the accusation of harlotry to describe metaphorically what he takes Jezebel to represent: a devotee of the Canaanite storm god Baal (1 Kings 16:31–2; 18:19; 21:5). The accusation of "sorcery" likewise describes metaphorically the position of illegitimate "outsider" or "other" that Jehu takes Jezebel to represent,[19] not who she is literally.

Still, the identification of Jezebel as a "sorcerer," even a figurative one, is enough to justify, according to the rhetoric of 2 Kings 9, Jehu's sentencing of Jezebel to death, just as Exodus 22:17 (English 22:18) requires. However, in none of the texts in which sorcery is denounced elsewhere in the Bible (for example, in Deuteronomy 18:10, as one of the abhorrent magical practices of the alien "other") is it said the sorcerer – a term rendered, in each case, in forms that are grammatically male – should be killed. Rather, according to Malachi 3:5, the judgment to which sorcerers (*mĕkaššĕpîm*) are subject is left ambiguous, determined by the will of God. Granted, it could be that these sorcerers include women, given that Hebrew uses grammatically masculine forms when referring to collectives that include both men and women; it could thus also be that women are included in the collective "sorcerer" in Deuteronomy 18:10. Still, in 2 Chronicles 33, God – although angered enough by King Manasseh's practice of sorcery (*kiššēp*) to have him made prisoner of the king of Assyria (2 Chronicles 33:11–12) – ultimately forgives him and restores him to his throne (2 Chronicles 33:13). Thus, it seems clear that the negative judgments the biblical writers render concerning sorcery accrue disproportionately to women, since women accused of sorcery (as in Exodus 22:17 [English 22:18] and 2 Kings 9:33) remain subject to execution, even as their male counterparts (as in 2 Chronicles 33:13) can be absolved. Ezekiel 13:17–23, the text that has been our particular focus in this discussion, is but part and parcel of this tendency, as it also excoriates women magical practitioners to a degree beyond that experienced by male magicians.

The biblical tradition's assessment of reproductive magic: Genesis 30:14–16 and 38:28

Yet what of Genesis 30:14–16 and Genesis 38:28? As I have previously remarked, it is the case that in these texts, even if there is some obfuscation in Genesis 38:28 regarding the red thread, neither Leah's and Rachel's engagement in acts of "plant magic" nor the apotropaic magic performed by Tamar's midwife is judged negatively.

To explain, we can begin by again noting that in both Genesis 30:14–16 and Genesis 38:28, the magical acts in question are deployed in the interests of facilitating reproduction, either by enhancing women's reproductive abilities (Genesis 30:14–16) or by safeguarding the well-being of a newly delivered child (Genesis 38:28). This has led Ann Fritschel, who is one of the few scholars who has commented specifically on women's magicianship in ancient Israel, to suggest that women's magical practice is sanctioned by the biblical authors, or at least tolerated, as long as it is performed in the service of the constitutive social unit of Israelite society, the patriarchal family.[20] Conversely, women who perform magically outside the family sphere or in ways that act against family interests are, Fritschel argues, condemned.[21] Fritschel, I should perhaps make clear, does not unequivocally follow Bowen in suggesting that the women prophets of Ezekiel 13:17–23 perform magical acts associated with pregnancy and childbirth (Fritschel 2003: 126–42), and thus she need not see Ezekiel's denunciation of these women as contradicting her thesis regarding sanctioned magical practices. Yet even if Bowen's reading of Ezekiel 13:17–23 is accepted, Fritschel's overarching understanding of women's magicianship remains compelling. Indeed, it reminds me again of an aspect of J. Cheryl Exum's work: in this case, Exum's compelling studies (1983: 63–82, 1994: 75–87) of the women of Moses' birth story as recounted in Exodus 1:8–2:10. In this text, no fewer than six women are portrayed as laudatory characters (the two midwives, Shiphrah and Puah; Moses' mother; Moses' sister; the Pharaoh's daughter; and the daughter's maidservant). However, these women are portrayed as praiseworthy, Exum argues, because all act in service of a patriarchal agenda: saving the lives of Hebrew male babies in general and the life of the baby boy Moses in particular. Likewise, Fritschel suggests, women who deploy magical practices in the service of the patriarchal family are, if not commended, at least treated as acting acceptably by the biblical writers.

We might in addition posit that Fritschel's "sanctioned" magic – women's performance of magical acts in service of the reproductive needs of the patriarchal family – was quite prevalent in ancient Israel. Fritschel has proposed regarding Ezekiel's "daughters who prophesy," for example, that the "double *kl* [meaning 'all'] in verse eighteen [of Ezekiel 13:17–23] suggests that the women had many clients" (Fritschel 2003: 153; see similarly ibid: 148–9). The ubiquity of women practitioners of reproductive magic is also suggested by some of the realities of ancient Israelite demographics, for while, as just noted, the reproductive success of the patriarchal family unit was considered to be a social good, the challenges in ensuring that success were considerable. As many as one out of two children may have died before reaching adulthood, for instance, or even before reaching the age of five (Meyers 1988: 112, 1997a: 19, 44, n. 47, 2002: 283, n. 27, 2005: 16). Yet children were an extremely important source of labor on the self-sufficient family farms that were the means of livelihood for most ancient Israelites (Ebeling 2010: 97; Meyers 1989: 273, 1997a: 27, 29, 1997b: 282, 2005: 16). Indeed, modern population studies show that even in locales that might seem to non-agriculturalists to be vastly overpeopled, farm families seek to bear and raise as many children as possible, to the extent that they will eschew an increased standard of living in favor of an increased family size (Hopkins 1987: 189). This may have particularly been the case in ancient Israel, as its agrarian economy required that the essentials of each family's subsistence be painstakingly procured from the marginally fertile Levantine highlands that were the heartland of Israel's territorial holdings. To create an adequate labor supply to survive in such a difficult environment, "successful reproduction was essential" (Meyers 2005: 59). Tikva Frymer-Kensky similarly states (1992: 97): "The terrain and climactic conditions of Israel demanded a large labor force," and therefore "the encouragement of childbirth was vital to Israel's survival needs." Any and all acts that helped facilitate reproduction and a newborn's well-being must therefore have been quite common, including, as I posited above, practices of reproductive magic.

That reproductive magic was widely practiced in Israel is further suggested by the many rituals of reproductive magic that, as I catalogued earlier in this essay, were enacted within the larger ancient Near Eastern and eastern Mediterranean worlds of which Israel was a part. Indeed, certain objects that have been excavated at Israelite archaeological sites are well paralleled by magical reproductive aids known from other ancient Near Eastern and eastern Mediterranean cultures. For example, the many small statues and other representations (those carved on seals and scarabs, for example) of the demigod Bes that have been found in the remains of Israelite domestic sites (Keel and Uehlinger 1998: 217–23, especially 219–22; Meyers 2002: 287–8; Meyers 2005: 31–3; Zevit 2001: 387–8) can be readily compared to Bes amulets that come from ancient Egypt. We know, moreover, that in Egyptian tradition Bes was the deity preeminently associated with safe pregnancies and deliveries, and, indeed, the use of Bes amulets by pregnant and delivering Egyptian women is well attested (Robins 1994–5: 29; Willett 1999: 309–10). In Israel too, it follows, Bes images could have been used to safeguard a woman during pregnancy and labor.

Exemplars of the sorts of "pregnancy vases" used in Egypt, which are designed to resemble a childbearing figure (Ritner 2008: 182; Romano 1996: 63), have also been found in Syria-Palestine, dating from both the Late Bronze Age period as well as the Iron Age era that is the focus of our study (Keel and Uehlinger 1998: 106).[22] These vases held anointing oil that was used by parturient women as part of the delivery process, not only in Egypt and in Israel, but also in Mesopotamia and Hatti (Glassner 2004: 440; Hammons 2008: 64; Janssen and Janssen 1990: 3–4; Pringle 1983 [1993]: 131; Stol 2000a: 124). On the basis, moreover, of kindred rituals regarding the anointing of newborns, we can reasonably presume that the anointing oil of parturition was used for magical purposes. Consider, for example, a Hittite birth ritual in which a lamb stands in for a newborn child.[23] As part of the ritual, this lamb had a red thread tied to it, as well as being rubbed with oil. The tying of the red thread, as we have seen in our discussion of Genesis 38:28, is a magical means of ensuring the newborn's well-being, and, likewise, the act of anointing the proxy lamb can only have had a magical, not a pragmatic, purpose. An Assyrian text that describes a newborn's chest being massaged with oil during the course of an incantation (Stol 2000a: 177) similarly implies the oil's function is magical. So too, then, should we take the use of anointing oil during parturition in ancient Israel to be magical in nature. Other archaeological finds from Israelite sites that have been associated with reproductive magic include small model couches such as those found in the remains from Buildings (or Houses) 25 and 430 of eighth-century BCE Beersheba (Schmitt 2012: 82; Willett 1999: 142, 150; Zevit 2001: 175–6). These may represent full-size birth stools or birthing beds (a standard apparatus used during labor in the ancient Near East and eastern Mediterranean worlds)[24] and thus were meant magically to promote a woman's "ability to give birth" (Zevit 2001: 175–6).

As I have hypothesized, this archaeological evidence, when coupled with other data, suggests that reproductive magic would have been commonly practiced in ancient Israel, and it thereby follows that practitioners of reproductive magic were likewise common. To be sure, not all of these practitioners should be classified as professionals in the vein of Ezekiel's "daughters who prophesy" and Tamar's midwife, as Rachel and Leah, along with their benefactor Reuben, seem better regarded (for lack of a better term) as amateurs – or what we might think of in today's parlance as DIY-ers, who aim to help themselves, not others.

The story of Rachel, Leah, and Reuben also shows us that practitioners of reproductive magic, at least among the amateur community, could include both men and women. Still, the Genesis 38:28 story of Tamar's midwife and the Ezekiel 13:17–23 account of the "daughters who prophesy" intimate that specialists who render "medico-magical" reproductive services on behalf of others were more likely to be female. In particular, any specific rites that a medico-magical reproductive specialist enacted at the time of a woman's actual delivery – for example, the tying and untying of knotted threads and bands; the application of magical anointing oil; bread offerings to baby-snatching demons – would more likely than not have been the responsibility of women functionaries, given what seems to be the Israelite tendency to separate men from a woman who is giving birth. Certainly, it seems clear that Israelite women were separated from their *husbands* during childbirth, given that word must be brought after delivery to the fathers of Jeremiah (Jeremiah 20:15) and Job (Job 3:3) that a son has been born to them (van der Toorn 1994: 85). According to Leviticus 12:1–8, moreover, pregnant women are rendered impure at the time of their delivery and for one to two weeks afterwards, and this impurity is contagious (the nature of this impurity is said to have been identical to the impurity associated with menstruation, meaning, presumably, that anyone who touched the new mother or touched anything on which she had sat or lain was rendered impure for one day). We can thereby surmise that, in addition to their husbands, members of a recently delivered woman's community would have kept their distance from the polluted parturient – with the exception, of course, of those such as a woman's midwife and possibly other women attendants (1 Samuel 4:20; Ruth 4:14), whose presence at childbirth was required.

In turn we can presume, as I suggested above, that any magical rites that were enacted at the time of a woman's delivery would have been performed by her midwife (as in Tamar's case) and/or by her other women attendants. This leads to the conclusion that I have already proposed: that because reproductive magic must have been a widespread phenomenon in Israel and because practitioners of this reproductive magic, at least during the crucial periods of delivery and its aftermath, most logically would have been women, women reproductive magicians – both magically skilled midwives and other types of magical functionaries specializing in reproduction – must have been common within Israelite society. Yet this conclusion leads only to further questions, most notably: if the community of women reproductive magicians was as numerous in ancient Israel as I have argued, why are they not more richly represented in our primary witness to ancient Israelite culture and traditions, the Bible?

Women reproductive magicians: The Bible's ambivalence

Where, I have just asked, are the women reproductive magicians of ancient Israel, given that beyond our three focal texts (and three fairly oblique texts at that!), Genesis 30:14–16; 38:38; and Ezekiel 13:17–23, this numerous community is unrepresented in the Bible?

The simplest answer is to observe that women generally are underrepresented in the Bible, as the Bible tends to focus its attention instead on the lives of men (Meyers 1988: 4–5, 11–13) – and perhaps understandably so, given that men are arguably the authors of all of our biblical texts.[25] Moreover, these male authors, who were typically members of ancient Israel's elite classes (for example, royal scribes and priests), were primarily concerned with the public arenas of Israelite society with which they, as elites, were most commonly associated – political forums such as the king's palace and religious forums such as Israel's great state temples, located in Jerusalem, Samaria, Bethel, and Dan. The setting in which reproductive magic was most obviously practiced, however, is the home. As a result, it could be suggested that the reason women's reproductive magic is so rarely mentioned in the Bible is that both its agents – women – and the location of its agency – domestic venues – are in large part ignored by the biblical authors because these authors' interests and spheres of experience lay elsewhere.

But I would suggest that something more intentional is at play here, which has to do with domestic spaces more generally and women's role as ritual agents within them. In Israel, it turns out, domestic venues are not only the site where women reproductive magicians would most naturally be found, but where all women agents of the supernatural – both women reproductive magicians and other religious functionaries – are most easily able to exercise ritual power.[26] According to Judges 17:1–5, for example, a woman (Micah's mother) could take responsibility for producing or commissioning a precious icon that signified the god Yahweh who was venerated in her household and could further expect to see that image placed in her household's associated shrine room, where it was arguably revered as the shrine's most sacred object. Such a woman should be readily understood as the primary patron of her household's shrine. Likewise, the women who are described as making bread cakes for a goddess known in Jeremiah 7:16–20 only as the Queen of Heaven should be understood as their household cult's primary patrons.[27] After all, the role of the woman in Jeremiah 7:18 in kneading the dough for the Queen of Heaven's offering cakes, and presumably baking them, was surely more important to the ritual than responsibilities assigned to others in their households (the children's gathering of wood and the fathers' kindling of fire). Women are also specifically identified in Jeremiah 44:19 and 25 as having burned incense and poured out libations to the Queen of Heaven in the past and as intending to do so in the future.[28] The making of such food, drink, and incense offerings – what the great historian of Mesopotamian civilization A. Leo Oppenheim has famously described as "the care and feeding of the gods" (1977: 183) – was, moreover, the ritual central to ancient Israelite religion generally (and, indeed, to all ancient Near Eastern worship). Thus, if women are as crucially involved as Jeremiah 7:18 and 44:19 and 25 suggest in preparing and apportioning to their households' god or gods the food and drink offerings that are the essence of ancient Israelite worship, then women must be seen as utterly critical actors within Israelite household cult.

Yet it is often the case in the Bible that biblical writers, even when they hint at a powerful role for women within ancient Israelite tradition, do not affirm this absolutely. In Judges 17:1–5, for example, the text fails to assign its woman protagonist a name, instead referring to her only as *immô*, "his [Micah's] mother," six times in the space of three verses (17:2–4).[29] This is significant, for the giving of names in the Bible – especially the giving of names to women – is often an important marker of those women's autonomy and authority. Conversely, to deny a woman a name is often to mark her as powerless and someone easily victimized by patriarchal culture (Meyers 1996: 120–2 [= Meyers 1994: 96–9]).[30] In this way, the autonomy and authority the woman might otherwise claim as a religious actor are undermined.

In the case under consideration here, the female ritual agents whose autonomy and authority are being undermined are reproductive magicians. One way of achieving this goal, of course, is outright denunciation, as in Ezekiel 13:17–23. Still, the magic for which women reproductive magicians are responsible is essential, as we have seen, for families', and thus the society's, survival. Hence, whatever the biblical writers' desire to undercut these women reproductive magicians' ritual power, they generally seem to opt for a means of subjugation other than explicit condemnation. Instead, the importance of reproductive magic and its women practitioners can be subverted by their being largely ignored. Or, as in Genesis 30:14–16 and 38:28, I have suggested, the significance of women's reproductive magic can be suppressed by avoiding any language praising the magical practices and/or its practitioners, even as the necessity of women's reproductive magic means the language of negativity is avoided as well. Also in Genesis 38:28, as I have proposed, women's engagement in reproductive magic is marginalized by obscuring the magical aspects of the midwife's work. Another means by which the power of women reproductive magicians is held in check is through the condemnation of the larger community of women magicians throughout the Bible, a condemnation that can be expressed, as we have seen, in the harshest possible terms.

Karel van der Toorn has argued that women in ancient Israel and in the ancient Near East turned to magic because positions of power were otherwise so unavailable to them (van der Toorn 1994: 113, 116). My argument is in many respects the converse: that women as practitioners of reproductive magic would have been accorded so much power in Israelite tradition that, however much the society needed them, biblical writers acted to downplay their significance, through ignoring these women and their work; through failing to acknowledge the work's importance and/or its true nature (Genesis 30:14–16 and 38:28); through denunciation (Ezekiel 13:17–23); and through specially stigmatizing the larger class of women magicians as paradigmatic of all kinds of wrongdoing. Despite the power that women reproductive magicians should have been able to claim, biblical writers moved resolutely to enforce their position as "others" and so to place them at the margins of ancient Israelite tradition and culture.

Notes

1 I take the translation "love plants" from Avalos 1995: 255.
2 Reading here *yādayīm*, "hands, wrists," for the Masoretic Text *yāday*, "my hands."
3 This is the translation of the Hebrew *mispāḥôt* proposed by Bowen 1999: 424, n. 31, for the more usual "veils."
4 This latter reference brought to my attention by Meyers 2005: 38, 81, n. 4.
5 The bibliography is extensive. For a recent survey and discussion, see Chrysovergi 2011: 24–6.
6 See also in this regard Bowen 1999: 426.
7 Meyers 2002: 290 and 2005: 39, citing Gursky 2001: 66, n. 6 (see also ibid: 75), who gives as her source for the Old Babylonian ritual in which a red thread is tied to the mother during a difficult birth Finkel 1980: 37–52, especially 47. Gursky's Hittite source is "The Ritual of Papanikri," in which a red thread is tied to a lamb that substitutes for the newborn, as discussed in Beckman 1978: Text 6 (p. 18) and Beckman 1983: "The Ritual of Papanikri" (pp. 116–23): IV, lines 6–7 (pp. 118–19). Comments on the use of a red thread in "The Ritual of Papanikri" can also be found in Pringle 1983 [1993]: 140. For a Hittite ritual in which a red thread is tied to the delivering mother, see Beckman 1978: Text 5 (pp. 12–13) and Beckman 1983: Text H (pp. 86–115): II, lines 26–7 (pp. 90–1), a text that is also cited in Gursky 2001: 69 and Pringle 1983 [1993]: 140.
8 For example, Dumermuth 1963: 228–9; Korpel 1996: 102–9; Mowinckel 1961: 65; and van der Toorn 1994: 123 (the Mowinckel and Dumermuth references brought to my attention by Fritschel 2003: 133–4 and nn. 28 and 29 on those pages).
9 See similarly, with far more extensive discussion, Korpel 1996: 99–102.
10 These references brought to my attention by Fritschel 2003: 136, n. 38 and Korpel 1996: 99.
11 Ezekiel 13:21–2, where the bands are said to be tied to "your [masculine plural] arms" and where the head bands are likewise described using a second-person masculine plural suffix, might seem to disallow any suggestion that the wrist and head bands are bound onto *women*, whether parturient or not. But as Walther Zimmerli points out (1979: 289), these and other masculine forms used in vv. 21 and 22 are extremely problematic (note preeminently the wholly illogical use of a *masculine* plural pronoun, *'attem*, to denounce the "*daughters* who prophecy" at the end of v. 21). The masculine forms of vv. 21–2, Zimmerli therefore concludes, may be the result of textual corruption or come from textual material that was secondarily added to Ezekiel's original oracle. In either case, they need not contradict Bowen's analysis.
12 This is, for example, how Meyers (2002: 290 and 2005: 40) interprets.
13 See similarly Fritschel 2003: 40, n. 1, who speaks of the importance of the "social location of the practitioner" within Israelite society in determining his or her legitimacy.

14 For discussion of how to understand the precise meanings of the terms that are used of magical practitioners in Deuteronomy 18:10–11 (and elsewhere), see Fritschel 2003: 40–80 (ch. 2, "Biblical Terminology for Magic Users and Diviners"); Jeffers 1996: 25–124; Kuemmerlin-McLean 1992: 468b–69b; Schmitt 2004: 107–22 (ch. 3, "Zur Terminologie"); also Lewis 1989: 102 and Schmidt 1996: 179–90.

15 The examples of 1 Kings 20:33 and Proverbs 16:10 were brought to my attention by Fritschel 2003: 4.

16 On the legal implications of this phrase, see, most recently, Westbrook 1997: 61–70.

17 See the very similar analysis of Fritschel 2003: 234–45, concerning the rhetoric of the Jezebel story.

18 I have recently discussed this metaphor in Ackerman 2009: 651–2.

19 Fritschel 2003: 253 describes Jehu's metaphorical language as referring to Jezebel's "real political, economic, and social power," a claim which, although it might seem contrary to my comments here, is in fact quite consonant with the thesis I eventually wish to argue: see pp. 23–5 below.

20 Fritschel hints at this in her Ph.D. thesis (2003: 39); the idea was much more fully developed in Fritschel 2006.

21 Note also in this regard Meyers (2002: 300, n. 110 and 2005: 65), who suggests (following Brenner 1997: 84–6) that the reason the female sorcerer is condemned in Exodus 22:17 (English 22:18) is that she may have been "expert at preventing conception or inducing abortion, both procedures abhorrent to clan ideology encouraging procreation."

22 See also Janssen and Janssen 1990: 4, although the Janssens unfortunately do not indicate any specifics about the find spots or dates of such vessels.

23 Beckman 1978: Text 6 (p. 14); Beckman 1983: "The Ritual of Papanikri" (pp. 116–23): IV, line 6 (pp. 118–19); Gursky 2001: 74, 88; Pringle 1983 [1993]: 140, commenting on "The Ritual of Papanikri" from Beckman 1983, all as cited above in n. 7.

24 Birthing stools are mentioned in a Late Bronze Age text from the city-state of Ugarit, on the north Levantine coast (*CAT* 1995: 1.12.1.17–18) and are also well attested among Ugarit's Hittite neighbors, with various Hittite texts describing several combinations of special stools and cushions that can be used at birth: two stools and three cushions according to one text; two footstools according to another; a single birthstool – some sort of seat on which the woman sits, holding on to pegs for support during delivery – according to other sources (see Beckman 1978: 5; Beckman 1983: 250; and [less fully] Imparati 2000: 575). The birthstool also seems to be the norm in Greek and Roman culture (Stol 2000a: 121–2; also see, for Rome, McGeough 2006: 306).

25 The occasional scholarship that posits a female author or authors at certain points in the Bible is so highly speculative that it has convinced few. Phyllis Bird's comments in 1989: 285–6, n. 8, are particularly salient; Bird observes that while the Hebrew Bible does attribute some literary pieces to women, "these few works have all been transmitted to us in the compositions of scribal guilds, which I would view as male associations. Hence I believe that we have no *direct* or *unmediated* access to the words or lives of women in the Hebrew scriptures." See similarly Bird 1994: 32.

26 For what follows, see Ackerman 2008: 136–45.

27 The consonantal Hebrew text in Jeremiah 7:18 reads *lmlkt*, "for the Queen of." But the Masoretic tradition in 7:18, and also in Jeremiah 44:17–19 and 25, vocalizes *limleket*, as if the word were *lml'kt*, "for the work of [heaven]," i. e., "for the heavenly host." Many Hebrew manuscripts in fact read *lml'kt* (with an *'ālep* between the *lāmed* and the *kap*) in 7:18 and in 44:17–19 and 25. The Targumic text and the Peshitta support *lml'kt* in all five instances, as, apparently, does the ancient Greek translation of the Hebrew Bible (the LXX) in 7:18, which reads *tē stratia*, "to the [heavenly] host." But as is commonly recognized, the Masoretic pointing is an apologetic attempt to remove any hint that the people of Judah worshiped the Queen of Heaven: see Gordon 1978–9: 112. The correct reading, *lĕmalkat*, "for the Queen of," is supported by the translations of Aquila, Symmachus, and Theodotian, by the Latin Vulgate, and by the Greek translation of 44:17–19 and 25.

28 Reading Jeremiah as addressing "you women" in 44:25, as in the ancient Greek translation of the Hebrew Bible (the LXX), for the Masoretic Text's *'attem ûnĕšêkem*, "you and your wives," since the verbs that follow are second-person feminine forms. Still, the text remains confused, since the objects of these second-person feminine verbs are rendered using forms that are in the second-person masculine plural.

29 In addition to my discussion here, see Mueller 2001: 54 and 88, n. 18, who correctly notes that, in contrast to other female protagonists in Judges, Micah's mother's anonymity has generally been unnoticed by scholars.

30 But cf. the important cautions offered by Reinhartz 1998: *passim*.

Bibliography

Ackerman, S. (2008) "Household religion, family religion, and women's religion in ancient Israel", in J. Bodel and S.M. Olyan (eds) *Household and Family Religion in Antiquity*. Oxford: Blackwell Publishing, pp. 127–58.

——(2009) "Prostitution", in K.D. Sakenfeld (ed.) *The New Interpreter's Dictionary of the Bible*, vol. 4. Nashville, TN: Abingdon.

Avalos, H. (1995) *Illness and Health Care in the Ancient Near East: The Role of the Temple in Greece, Mesopotamia, and Israel*. Atlanta, GA: Scholars Press.

——(1997) "Medicine", in E.M. Meyers (ed.) *The Oxford Encyclopedia of Archaeology in the Near East*, 3. New York and Oxford: Oxford University Press, pp. 450–9.

Beckman, G.M. (1978) *Hittite Birth Rituals: An Introduction*. Malibu, CA: Undena Publications.

——(1983) *Hittite Birth Rituals*, 2nd rev. edn. Wiesbaden: Harrassowitz.

Bird, P. (1989) "Women's religion in ancient Israel", in B.S. Lesko (ed.) *Women's Earliest Records, from Ancient Egypt and Western Asia*, Proceedings of the Conference on Women in the Ancient Near East, Brown University, Providence, Rhode Island, November 5–7, 1987, Brown Judaic Studies 166. Atlanta, GA: Scholars Press.

——(1994) "Women in the ancient Mediterranean world: Ancient Israel", *Biblical Research* 39: 31–45.

Blenkinsopp, J. (1997) "The family in First Temple Israel", in L.G. Perdue, J. Blenkinsopp, J.J. Collins, and C. Meyers, *Families in Ancient Israel*. Louisville, KY: Westminster/John Knox, pp. 48–103.

Bowen, N.R. (1999) "The daughters of your people: Female prophets in Ezekiel 13:17–23", *Journal of Biblical Literature* 118: 417–33.

Brenner, A. (1997) *The Intercourse of Knowledge: On Gendering Desire and "Sexuality" in the Bible*. Leiden: Brill.

Chrysovergi, M. (2011) "Attitudes towards the use of medicine in Jewish literature from the third and second centuries BCE", unpublished PhD thesis, Durham University.

Cogan, M. (2001) *I Kings: A New Translation with Introduction and Commentary*. New York: Doubleday.

Darr, K.P. (2000) "Daughters who prophesy (Ezek 13:17–23)", in C. Meyers (ed.) with T. Craven and R.S. Kraemer, *Women in Scripture: A Dictionary of Named and Unnamed Women in the Hebrew Bible, the Apocryphal/Deuterocanonical Books, and the New Testament*. Boston, MA: Houghton Mifflin.

Davies, G.I. (1994) "An archaeological commentary on Ezekiel 13", in M.D. Coogan, J.C. Exum, and L.E. Stager (eds) *Scripture and Other Artifacts: Essays on the Bible and Archaeology in Honor of Philip J. King*. Louisville, KY: Westminster/John Knox, pp. 108–25.

Dumermuth, F. (1963) "Zu Ez. XIII 18–21", *Vetus Testamentum* 13: 228–9.

Ebeling, J.R. (2010) *Women's Lives in Biblical Times*. London and New York: T&T Clark.

Exum, J.C. (1983) "'You shall let every daughter live': A study of Exodus 1:8–2:10", in M.A. Tolbert (ed.) *The Bible and Feminist Hermeneutics* (= *Semeia* 28), pp. 63–82.

——(1993) "The (m)other's place", in *Fragmented Women: Feminist (Sub)versions of Biblical Narratives*, ch. 4. Valley Forge, PA: Trinity Press International.

——(1994) "Second thoughts about secondary characters: Women in Exodus 1.8–2.10", in A. Brenner (ed.) *A Feminist Companion to Exodus to Deuteronomy*. Sheffield: Sheffield Academic Press, pp. 75–87.

Finkel, I. (1980) "The crescent fertile", *Archiv für Orientforschung* 27: 37–52.

Foster, B.R. (1996) *Before the Muses: An Anthology of Akkadian Literature*, 2 vols. Bethesda, MD: CDL Press.

Fritschel, A. (2003) "Women and magic in the Hebrew Bible", unpublished PhD thesis, Emory University.

——(2006) "Gender and magic in the Hebrew Bible: Sex, lies, and amorphous shapes", paper presented at the annual meeting of the European Association of Biblical Studies, Pázmány Péter Catholic University, Piliscaba, and Károly Gáspar Reformed University, Budapest, August.

Frymer-Kensky, T. (1992) *In the Wake of the Goddesses: Women, Culture, and the Biblical Transformation of Pagan Myth*. New York: Free Press.

Glassner, J.-J. (2004) "Rites of passage: Mesopotamia", in S.I. Johnston (ed.) *Religions of the Ancient World: A Guide*. Cambridge, MA: Harvard University Press, pp. 440b–1b.

Gordon, R.P. (1978–9) "Aleph Apologeticum", *Jewish Quarterly Review* 69: 112–16.

Gursky, M.D. (2001) "Reproductive rituals in biblical Israel", unpublished PhD thesis, New York University.

Hammons, M.B. (2008) "Before Joan of Arc: Gender identity and heroism in ancient Mesopotamian birth rituals", unpublished PhD thesis, Vanderbilt University.

Hopkins, D.C. (1987) "Life on the land: The subsistence struggles of early Israel", *Biblical Archaeologist* 50: 178–91.

Imparati, F. (2000) "Private life among the Hittites", in J.M. Sasson (ed.) *Civilizations of the Ancient Near East*, vol. 1–2. Peabody, MA: Hendrickson, pp. 571–86.

Janssen, R.M. and Janssen, J.J. (1990) *Growing Up in Ancient Egypt*. London: Rubicon.

Jeffers, A. (1996) *Magic and Divination in Ancient Palestine and Syria*, Leiden, New York and Köln: Brill.

Johnston, S.I. (2004) "Magic", in S.I. Johnston (ed.) *Religions of the Ancient World: A Guide*. Cambridge, MA: Harvard University Press, pp. 139–52.

Keel, O. and Uehlinger, C. (1998) *Gods, Goddesses, and Images of God in Ancient Israel*. Minneapolis, MN: Fortress.

Korpel, M.C.A. (1996) "Avian spirits in Ugarit and Ezekiel 13", in N. Wyatt, W.G.E. Watson, and J.B. Lloyd (eds) *Ugarit, Religion, and Culture*. Proceedings of the International Colloquium on Ugarit, Religion and Culture, Edinburgh, July 1994: Essays Presented in Honour of Professor John C.L. Gibson. Münster: Ugarit-Verlag.

Kuemmerlin-McLean, J.K. (1992) "Magic (OT)", in D.N. Freedman (ed.) *Anchor Bible Dictionary*, vol. 4. New York: Doubleday, pp. 468a–71a.

Lewis, T.J. (1989) *Cults of the Dead in Ancient Israel and Ugarit*. Atlanta, GA: Scholars Press.

McGeough, K. (2006) "Birth bricks, potter's wheels, and Exodus 1, 16", *Biblica* 87: 305–18.

Meyers, C. (1988) *Discovering Eve: Ancient Israelite Women in Context*. New York and Oxford: Oxford University Press.

——(1989) "Women and the domestic economy of early Israel", in B.S. Lesko (ed.) *Women's Earliest Records, from Ancient Egypt and Western Asia*, Proceedings of the Conference on Women in the Ancient Near East, Brown University, Providence, Rhode Island, November 5–7, 1987, Brown Judaic Studies 166. Atlanta, GA: Scholars Press.

——(1994) "Hannah and her sacrifice: Reclaiming female agency", in A. Brenner (ed.) *A Feminist Companion to Samuel and Kings*. Sheffield: Sheffield Academic Press, pp. 93–104.

——(1996) "The Hannah narrative in feminist perspective", in J.E. Coleson and V.H. Matthews (eds) *Go to the Land I Will Show You: Studies in Honor of Dwight W. Young*. Winona Lake, IN: Eisenbrauns.

——(1997a) "The family in early Israel", in L.G. Perdue, J. Blenkinsopp, J.J. Collins, and C. Meyers, *Families in Ancient Israel*, Louisville, KY: Westminster/John Knox. 1–47.

——(1997b) "Recovering objects, re-visioning subjects: Archaeology and feminist biblical study", in A. Brenner and C. Fontaine (eds) *A Feminist Companion to Reading the Bible: Approaches, Methods and Strategies*. Sheffield: Sheffield Academic Press, pp. 270–84.

——(2002) "From household to house of Yahweh: Women's religious culture in ancient Israel", in A. Lemaire (ed.) *Congress Volume: Basel 2001*. Leiden and Boston: Brill, pp. 277–303.

——(2005) *Households and Holiness: The Religious Culture of Israelite Women*. Minneapolis, MN: Fortress.

Mowinckel, S. (1961) *Psalmenstudien*, vol. 1, reprinted edition of the 1921 publication. Amsterdam: P. Schippers.

Mueller, E.A. (2001) *The Micah Story: A Morality Tale in the Book of Judges*. New York: Peter Lang.

Neusner, J. (1989) "Introduction", in J. Neusner, E.S. Frerichs, and P.V. McCracken Flesher (eds) *Religion, Science and Magic: In Concert and in Conflict*. New York: Oxford University Press, pp. 3–7.

Oppenheim, A.L. (1954–6) "Sumerian: *inim.gar*; Akk: *egirrû* = Greek: *kledon*", *Archiv für Orientforschung* 17: 49–55.

——(1977) *Ancient Mesopotamia: Portrait of a Dead Civilization*, rev. edn. Chicago, IL and London: University of Chicago Press.

Pope, M.H. (1987) "Review of Klaas Spronk, *Beatific Afterlife in Ancient Israel and in the Ancient Near East* (Kevelaer: Butzon & Bercker; Neukirchen-Vluyn: Neukirchener Verlag, 1986)", *Ugarit Forschungen* 19: 452–63.

Pringle, J. (1983 [1993]) "Hittite birth rituals", in A. Cameron and A. Kuhrt (eds) *Images of Women in Antiquity*. London: Routledge, pp. 128–41.

Reinhartz, A. (1998) *"Why Ask My Name?" Anonymity and Identity in Biblical Narrative*. New York and Oxford: Oxford University Press.

Ricks, S.D. (2001) "The magician as outsider in the Hebrew Bible and the New Testament", in M. Meyer and P. Mirecki (eds) *Ancient Magic and Ritual Power*. Boston, MA and Leiden: Brill, pp. 131–43.

Ritner, R.K. (2001) "The religious, social, and legal parameters of traditional Egyptian magic", in M. Meyer and P. Mirecki (eds) *Ancient Magic and Ritual Power*. Boston, MA and Leiden: Brill, pp. 43–60.

——(2008) "Household religion in ancient Egypt", in J. Bodel and S.M. Olyan (eds) *Household and Family Religion in Antiquity*. Oxford: Blackwell Publishing, pp. 171–96.

Robins, G. (1994–5) "Women and children in peril: Pregnancy, birth and infant mortality in ancient Egypt", *KMT* 5(4): 24–35.

Romano, J.F. (1996) "Jar in the form of a woman", in A.K. Capel and G.E. Markoe (eds) *Mistress of the House, Mistress of Heaven: Women in Ancient Egypt*. New York: Hudson Hills, in conjunction with the Cincinnati Art Museum, p. 63.

Schmidt, B.B. (1996) *Israel's Beneficent Dead: Ancestor Cult and Necromancy in Ancient Israelite Religion and Tradition*. Winona Lake, IN: Eisenbrauns.

Schmitt, R. (2004) *Magie im Alten Testament*. Münster: Ugarit-Verlag.

——(2012) "Elements of domestic cult in ancient Israel", in R. Albertz and R. Schmitt, *Family and Household Religion in Ancient Israel and the Levant*. Winona Lake, IN: Eisenbrauns, pp. 57–219.

Scurlock, J.A. (1991) "Baby-snatching demons, restless souls and the dangers of childbirth: Medico-magical means of dealing with some of the perils of motherhood in ancient Mesopotamia", *Incognita* 2: 135–83.

——(1992) "Magic (ANE)", in D.N. Freedman (ed.) *Anchor Bible Dictionary*, vol. 4. New York: Doubleday.

Smith, M.S. and Bloch-Smith, E. (1988) "Death and afterlife in Ugarit and Israel", *Journal of the American Oriental Society* 108: 277–84.

Spronk, K. (1986) *Beatific Afterlife in Ancient Israel and in the Ancient Near East*. Kevelaer: Butzon & Bercker; Neukirchen-Vluyn: Neukirchener Verlag.

Stol, M. (2000a) *Birth in Babylonia and the Bible: Its Mediterranean Setting*. Groningen: Styx.

——(2000b) "Private life in ancient Mesopotamia", in J.M. Sasson (ed.) *Civilizations of the Ancient Near East*, vols 1–2. Peabody, MA: Hendrickson, pp. 485–99.

van der Toorn, K. (1994) *From Her Cradle to Her Grave: The Role of Religion in the Life of the Israelite and the Babylonian Woman*. Sheffield: JSOT Press.

Westbrook, R. (1997) "A matter of life and death", *Journal of the Ancient Near Eastern Society* 25: 61–70.

Willett, E. (1999) "Women and household shrines in ancient Israel", unpublished PhD thesis, University of Arizona.

Zevit, Z. (2001) *The Religions of Ancient Israel: A Synthesis of Parallactic Approaches*. London and New York: Continuum.

Zimmerli, W. (1979) *Ezekiel: A Commentary on the Book of the Prophet Ezekiel*, vol. 1. Philadelphia, PA: Fortress.

2

FERTILITY AND GENDER IN THE ANCIENT NEAR EAST

Stephanie Lynn Budin

Human females and males make very different contributions to the process of reproduction. Females conceive and incubate the embryo/fetus within their bodies for nine months, with concomitant inconveniences and health risks such as pica, high blood pressure, hemorrhoids, and potential death during pregnancy (especially in cases of incompatible, positive/negative blood types) or parturition. Should the infant be born healthy, the female might make an additional multi-year physical investment in breast-feeding. Males ejaculate. Anecdotal evidence suggests that this is a wholly positive experience.[1]

In modern times, this imbalance in contributions combined with the discovery of the ovum in 1827 has led to the belief that fertility and reproduction are essentially *feminine* attributes, that the sex responsible for life is the female.[2] This ideology then has been cast back onto the past to the great detriment of gender studies in ancient history: While it might seem that our view of the process stems from older paradigms, I would argue instead that we have imposed our own perspective onto the past. The "female = fertility" paradigm obscures studies of both ancient women and goddesses, with the result that all images of the female throughout antiquity have been interpreted as symbols of fecundity and maternity.[3] For example, James Mellaart interpreted his finds from Çatal Höyük as evidence of a Bachofen-style early matriarchy, complete with Mother Goddess.[4] Jacqueline Karageorghis's analysis of Cypriot cruciform figurines concluded that, "It is difficult to say whether this is the representation of a goddess of fertility or simply a magic image of the forces of fertility, but the main point is that the image of fertility is identified as a woman."[5] In her discussion of the Minoan "mother goddess" Nanno Marinatos affirms (2010: 151):

> [T]he mother goddess is still very much alive in both popular and specialized scholarship, although she has taken various guises. She has been linked to Babylonian Ishtar or Syro-Palestinian Astarte by scholars who rightly acknowledge Near Eastern influence on Crete. But even so, she remains the great mother of vegetation and fertility.

The pendulum is now swinging the other way concerning the "female = fertility" equation. The innately sexist implications of the theory that somehow females are nothing but wombs was questioned by JoAnn Hackett in her 1989 article "Can a Sexist Model Liberate Us? Ancient Near

Eastern 'Fertility' Goddesses." In her critique of androcentric tendencies in biblical studies Peggy Day noted,

> Generally speaking, traditional Hebrew Bible scholarship characterized the major Canaanite goddesses almost exclusively in terms of their alleged sexual and/or reproductive functions, labelled them as fertility goddesses and characterized worship of them as fertility cult worship … As this … characterization was so firmly embedded and widely accepted prior to the advent of feminist engagement, it is simply impossible to cite all of its proponents.[6]

In an earlier essay concerning the apparently abundant maternal iconography from the Bronze Age Aegean, I have noted that (Budin 2014: 93):

> An insufficiently recognized problem in the study of ancient iconographies is the tendency to assume that any female in the proximity of a child or infant is a mother, and the icon itself is a symbol of maternity and fertility. Not only do such blanket assessments fail to recognize culturally specific semantics, they also discourage careful analysis of the female in question.

Critics are now interested in exploring associations for women other than the merely reproductive, and at the same time there has been an incipient interest in male fertility. Scholars such as John Baines and Jerry Cooper have published on the masculine role in fertility in Egyptian iconography and Sumerian literature respectively.[7] However, much of this recent scholarship focuses on non-reproductive fertility—the fertility of field or stream—rather than on sexual reproduction *per se*. Furthermore, and perhaps oddly, there is a general tendency in scholarship to divide notions of fertility along gendered lines: One studies female fertility (or not), or masculine fertility, but not the combined contributions of both.

As a result, our study of ancient reproduction has been incomplete so far, for in ideology as well as biology both male and female were necessary to reproduce. In the Ancient Near East (ANE), it was men who were believed to be the founts of initial fertility: Men created new life (Asher-Greve 2002: 16):

> Attributing the sole source of procreation to semen, man was seen as "creator" and became *first* gender. This Mesopotamian idea may have influenced Aristotle's statement "sperma makes the man," which spread over the Western world where it remained medical wisdom until the contributive role of the ovaries was recognized in the late 18th century.

By contrast, it was women's role to receive that new life, to form it, and to nourish it.[8] The division of the sexes in terms of sexual reproduction could basically be summarized as: Males created seed—progeny, children—whereas females incubated, nourished, and nurtured the seed given to them by the male. As a late second-millennium Babylonian incantation well expressed it, "My father begot me, my mother bore me" (Foster 1993: 554).

This essay is an examination of how the societies of the ANE—Bronze and Iron Age Mesopotamia, the Levant, Anatolia, and Egypt—engendered their notions of fertility and reproduction. The data show that most references to baseline fertility—the ability to create new life—involve male agents, whereas examples of human reproduction (the creation of human offspring) involve both sexes[9]—male and female. Birth itself fell mainly within the female domain. Infertility was understood as impotence on the part of men, "barrenness" on the part of women, with concomitant cures for both. This division of reproductive "responsibilities" entailed different attitudes and appreciations for reproduction between the two sexes. It was men who, having established their primary role in the creation of progeny, more emphatically valued offspring in the documentary evidence. By contrast, outside of the Hebrew Bible, women were less likely to emphasize their maternal status, preferring to highlight other roles, such as occupation. In the end, it becomes clear that fertility and reproduction—both male and female aspects—are more highly valued and emphasized when presented from a male perspective. By contrast, when the female voice is explicit, issues of progeny and maternity pale. Although this in part might be explained by the patrilinear societies exclusive to the ANE, it might also be understood in light of the masculine emphasis placed on fertility in the process of creation as seen throughout all of the regions and periods covered in this survey.

Male fertility and "parthenogenesis" in Near Eastern mythology

Male sexuality is the dominant force for fertility in ANE mythology—it is associated with baseline creation, either of reality itself or of the natural phenomena constituting the world. In Egypt, the male instigation of cosmogony is expressed in the Old Egyptian Pyramid Text Spell 527, wherein creation commences with the god Atum (Allen 2003: 7): "Atum evolved growing ithyphallic, in Heliopolis. He put his penis in his grasp that he might make orgasm with it, and the two siblings were born—Shu (air) and Tefnut (moisture)."

In Mesopotamia, although cosmogony *per se* is consistently heterosexual (e.g. *Atrahasis*, *Enuma Eliš*, *Theogony of Dunnu*), the masculine nature of fertility is nevertheless expressed in the exploits of some particularly creative deities, most notably the god of fresh water, Enki. Enki was remarkable for his phallic fertility, giving rise to fertilizing waters, vegetal, animal, and human/divine abundance. This is most explicitly presented in the Sumerian hymn *Enki and the World Order*. Focusing on the passages which reference the god's phallic fecundity (ll. 250–65), we read (Black *et al.* 2004: 220–1):

> After he had turned his gaze from there, after father Enki had lifted his eyes across the Euphrates, he stood up full of lust like a rampant bull, lifted his penis, ejaculated and filled the Euphrates with flowing water … The Tigris … at his side like a rampant bull. By lifting his penis, he brought a bridal gift. The Tigris rejoiced in its heart like a great wild bull, when it was born … It brought water, flowing water indeed: its wine will be sweet. It brought barley, mottled barley indeed: the people will eat it. It filled the E-kur, the house of Enlil, with all sorts of things.

Additional passages in the hymn refer to Enki's control over fertility, although with less phallic language. Lines 18–30 note Enki's control over vegetal fertility; lines 32–7 note that Enki makes young men and women sexually appealing and amorous; lines 52–60 and 326–34 establish the god's ability to spark fertility in herd animals and the produce of the fields; and lines 193–205 even attribute to the god the birth of mortal kings. This is a deity with consummate control of fertility, often associated with the fertilizing "waters" of his penis.[10]

Perhaps the greatest font of masculine creation and fertility in the ANE corpus is the god of Genesis, who, in two separate accounts, creates all life on earth through the force of his word. In Genesis 1 we read how a transcendent male deity brought forth the earth from the *tohu wabohu*—the waste and void—while in Genesis 2 he brought rain, fertility, vegetal, and animal life to his "garden."

Some ANE gods express their fertility functions through absence: The motif of the vanishing god includes descriptions of the earth's lack of fertility while the god is absent. When the Anatolian Rain/Storm god Telipinu disappeared (Hoffner 1998: 15):

> Telipinu too went away and removed grain, animal fecundity, luxuriance, growth, and abundance to the steppe, to the meadow … Therefore barley and wheat no longer ripen. Cattle, sheep, and humans no longer become pregnant. And those (already pregnant) cannot give birth. The mountains and trees dried up, so that the shoots do not come (forth). The pastures and springs dried up, so that famine broke out in the land. Humans and gods are dying of hunger.

A similar situation emerges when Baal, the Ugaritic storm god, was vanquished by Mot ("Death"). While the god is dead, "Parched are the furrows of the fields," but when he returns, "The heavens rain oil, the wadis run with honey" (Smith in Parker 1997: 158–9).[11]

At the most extreme, in myths from Egypt, Mesopotamia, and Anatolia male deities can and do get pregnant. The New Kingdom Egyptian tale *The Contendings of Horus and Seth* relates how Seth's attempts to bugger Horus were reversed by Isis, leading to Seth's impregnation (Simpson 1972: 120 (= 11,4–10)):

> Now afterward, at evening time, bed was prepared for them, and they both lay down. But during the night Seth caused his phallus to become stiff and inserted it between Horus's thighs. Then Horus placed his hands between his thighs and received Seth's semen. Horus / went to tell his mother Isis: "Help me, Isis, my mother, come and see what Seth has done to me." And he opened his hand and let her see Seth's semen. She let out a loud shriek, seized her copper knife, and cut off his hands … Then she fetched some fragrant ointment and applied it to Horus's phallus. She caused it to become stiff and inserted it into a pot, and he caused his semen to flow down into it.
>
> Isis at morning time went carrying the semen of Horus to the garden of Seth and said to Seth's gardener: "What sort of vegetable / is it that Seth eats here in your company?" So, the gardener told her: "He doesn't eat any vegetable here in my company except lettuce." And Isis added the semen of Horus onto it. Seth returned according to his daily habit and ate the lettuce, which he regularly ate. Thereupon he became pregnant with the semen of Horus.

In the Sumerian tale *Enki and Ninhursag*, Enki eats a large quantity of his own semen that the mother goddess Ninhursag had placed in a variety of plants. Although the text is damaged, it appears that Enki gets quite sick from this, as he becomes impregnated with plant deities which he cannot remove from his body. The deities call for Ninhursag, who functions as a surrogate birth canal for Enki (Jacobsen 1987: 202–3):

> Ninhursaĝa laid Enki in her vulva,
> [placed cool hands. …
> "My brother, what part of you hurts you?"
> "My brainpan hurts me!"
> She gave birth to Abu out of it.
> "My brother, what part of you hurts you?"
> "The top of my hair hurts me!"
> She gave birth to Ninsikila out of it. … [12]

In the Hurrian *Song of Kumarbi*, the god Kumarbi becomes pregnant after biting off the loins of the sky-deity Anu, whom he is attempting to overthrow.

> Kumarbi bit Anu's loins, and his "manhood" united with Kumarbi's insides like bronze. When Kumarbi had swallowed the "manhood" of Anu, he rejoiced and laughed out loud. Anu turned around and spoke to Kumarbi: "Are you rejoicing within yourself because you have swallowed my manhood?

> "Stop rejoicing within yourself! I have placed inside you a burden. First, I have impregnated you with the noble Storm God. Second, I have impregnated you with the irresistible Aranzah River. Third, I have impregnated you with the noble Tasmisu. And two additional terrible gods I have placed inside you as burdens. In the future you will end up striking the boulders of Mount Tassa with your head!
>
> *(Hoffner 1998: 42–3 (= A I 25–36)).*[13]

Heterosexual reproduction

Males, then, are the source of new life in ANE ideologies, be that vegetal life or (divine) reproduction. Nevertheless, the basic understanding was that *both* sexes were required for human creation or reproduction. Male seed/semen gave the "spark" of new life, but the female body was needed to mold that seed into a human being. This notion comes across strongly in two Mesopotamian myths featuring, once again, the god Enki—*Atrahasis* and *Enki and Ninmah*. In the former, dating to the Old Babylonian period (*c.*1800 BCE), the deities decide to create humans to labor for them. Enki summons Nintu the womb goddess to create humanity, but the goddess counters that Enki must first provide her with purified clay. In this act, Enki infuses his "water," the Mesopotamian equivalent of semen, into the matter of creation. Furthermore, the god Geštu-e is slaughtered, and his blood is mixed with the clay, also infusing it with life. Thus, male liquids cause the inert clay to live. However, once the clay is properly invigorated, Nintu, either by herself or with the help of birth goddesses, forms the clay into human females and males who henceforth will reproduce themselves sexually (Dalley 1989: 16–17):[14]

> She pinched off fourteen pieces (of clay)
> (And set) seven pieces on the right, seven on the left,
> Between them she put down a mud brick.[15]
> She made use of a reed, opened it to cut the umbilical cord,
> Called up the wise and knowledgeable
> Womb-goddesses, seven and seven
> Seven created males,
> Seven created females,
> For the womb-goddess is creator of fate.

The importance of the female's molding of the seed into a human comes across even more emphatically in the Sumerian tale of *Enki and Ninmah* ("Great Lady," a Mesopotamian mother goddess). Here, after having created humankind, these two deities get a bit tipsy while celebrating and devise a bet that no matter how bad a human the one can make, the other will find a place for it in society. Ninmah begins, creating humans who are blind, incontinent, paralyzed, or stupid. In every instance, wise Enki can find an employment for the disabled individual, even if it is merely "standing by the king." But when Enki must form a human himself, he creates:

Umul (= "My day is far off"): its head was afflicted, its place of.... was afflicted, its eyes were afflicted, its neck was afflicted. It could hardly breathe, its ribs were shaky, its lungs were afflicted, its heart was afflicted, its bowels were afflicted. With its hand and its lolling head it could not put bread into its mouth; its spine and head were dislocated. The weak hips and the shaky feet could not carry (?) it on the field.[16]

Put simply, Enki created not the standard, adult human, but an infant, possibly a fetus, for which no independent occupation might be found. Ninmah lost the bet, but the point was that a male alone could not form a human. He could, and did, provide the seed for the being, but a human could only be fully formed with the participation of a female.

Our limited Canaanite/Ugaritic repertoire offers a similar understanding of this paradigm. In the *Birth of the Gracious Gods* (*CAT* 1.23), the focus is on the father god El whose phallic activities give rise to a pair of voracious deities who suckle at the breasts of Athirat, the Canaanite mother goddess. Once again, we have the division of male as engenderer and female as bearer and nourisher (T.J. Lewis in Parker 1997: 210–13):

El's "hand" grows long as the sea,[17]
El's "hand" is the ocean.
…
El charms the pair of maids.
If the maiden pair cries out:
"O husband! husband!
Lowered is your scepter,
Generous the 'staff' in your hand."
…
He bows down to kiss their lips,
Ah! their lips are sweet,
Sweet as succulent fruit.
In kissing, conception,
In embracing, pregnant heat.
The two travail and give birth
to the gods Dawn and Dusk.
…
Both travail and give birth,
Birth to the gracious gods.
Paired devourers of the day that bore them,
Who suck the teats of the Lady's breasts.[18]

Counter examples come from both Israel and Egypt. In Israel, where our primary source is the Hebrew Bible, masculine monotheism worked against any gender complementarity in the divine realm. Unlike the creation myths from the rest of the ANE, neither version of the creation of humanity in Genesis has a female creatrix complementing the creator. Nevertheless, there are some data which suggest a feminine *aspect* to the god of the Jews. Genesis 1:27 may indicate a dual-sexed nature to the creator deity:

So God created humankind in his image,
In the image of God he created them;
Male and female he created them.[19]

This notion reflects what we saw in the creation of humanity in *Atrahasis*, where the birth goddesses made seven males and seven females, reflecting the genders of the deities themselves and allowing for future sexual reproduction. Another passage cited for suggesting a feminine element in the Hebrew god is Genesis 49:25, wherein, among other blessings, Jacob blesses his sons:

> "By the God your father, who will help you,
> By the Almighty who will bless you
> With blessings of heaven above,
> Blessings of the deep that lies beneath,
> Blessings of the breasts and of the womb."[20]

The idea of God's assumption of female characteristics also plays out in the realm of reproduction, where God is credited with forming the fetus in the womb. Thus in Psalm 139 (ll. 13–14):

> For it was you who formed my inward parts;
> You knit me together in my mother's womb.
> I praise you, for I am fearfully and wonderfully made.
> Wonderful are your works.

Likewise, the lord claims to the prophet Jeremiah (l. 5):

> "Before I formed you in the womb I knew you,
> And before you were born I consecrated you … "

The archaeological evidence combined with the close cognates between the ancient Israelite and Canaanite religions suggest that the ancient Israelites were originally polytheistic, with female goddesses such as Asherah (Ugaritic Athirat) complementing male gods such as El and Baal. Although these goddesses and "extraneous" gods were removed in the process of creating Israel's monotheism, the texts seem to indicate an original feminine presence, especially those involving reproduction.[21]

In Egypt, humans were understood to be modeled by the god Khnum, the potter deity. He moistened his clay with waters from the Nile, which was understood to be the male deity Hapy. As such, we see a continuation of the ANE motif that water is a masculine attribute that provides fertility. What is odd is that Khnum alone makes humans, without a female complement. For example, the Middle Kingdom *Admonitions of Ipuwer* laments (Lichtheim 2006, Vol. I: 151) that:

> "Lo, women are barren, none conceive,
> Khnum does not fashion because of the state of the land."

Likewise, in the New Kingdom *Tale of Two Brothers* (Lichtheim 2006, Vol. II: 207):

> Pre-Harakhti said to Khnum: "Fashion a wife for Bata, that he not live alone!" Then Khnum made a companion for him who was more beautiful in body than any woman in the whole land, for (the fluid of) every god was in her.

Nevertheless, when the deities themselves reproduced, it was done in standard heterosexual fashion. The paradigmatic union is that between Osiris and his sister/spouse Isis, as recounted in Pyramid Text §§632–3 (Faulkner 2007: 120–1):

Your sister Isis comes to you rejoicing for love of you. You have placed her on your phallus and your seed issues into her, she being ready as Sothis, and Ḥar-Sopd has come forth from you as Horus who is in Sothis. It is well with you through him in his name of "Spirit who is in the *Dndrw*-bark"; and he protects you in his name of Horus, the son who protects his father.

In general, then, reproductive fertility required both sexes, excluding, for the most part, those tales of male impregnation mentioned above. The roles were fixed: Males provided the fluid seed of life; females incubated, molded, and ultimately nourished that new life. But the masculine element was considered dominant in this process of creation: It was the male who created new life which he then "gave" to the female. Thus as Ann Macy Roth comments on Egypt (Roth 2000: 189):

> If we define fertility specifically as the act of creation itself, it can be argued that in ancient Egypt, women were not credited with creating new life. Instead, the creative role is attached exclusively to the male sex. This association can be seen clearly in the language, where the verb that we translate as "to conceive a child" is the same as the Egyptian verb used for "to receive" or "to take." In the Egyptian view, the woman "receives" the child, already fully created, from the man. This view is stated explicitly in Akhenaton's Hymn to the Aton: praising the god as creator of human life, the hymn says that he has "placed seed in a woman and made the sperm into a person."

Similar understandings for Iron Age Israel are expressed by Baruch Levine (Levine 2002: 341–2):

> The womb provides the same nutrients to the embryo as the mother earth does to vegetation that grows in it. There is, however, no indication in the Hebrew Bible, as far as we can ascertain, that the female contributes a life essence, an egg, to the embryo; the role of the female is entirely that of nurturer. The seed is provided by the male, and it grows inside the womb.

Birth goddesses

When the infant is ready to be born, the feminine role becomes dominant. With the obvious exception of the Bible, ANE pantheons had named mother goddesses in charge of childbirth, as well as groups of semi-anonymous goddesses known by various collective names and understood in modern scholarship as birth goddesses. These latter goddesses helped the dominant mother goddess to create humankind (as above: *Atrahasis*), or assisted mortal women during parturition.

In Mesopotamia, the mother goddesses are known by several names: Ninhursag, Nintu, Aruru, Belet-ili, Ninmah, Dingir-maḫ, Mami. As noted above, they are responsible not so much for divine reproduction (which the deities do themselves, heterosexually for the most part), but for the creation of humans. In this aspect they are often shown making or sculpting human beings out of clay, and their epithets reflect this role in reproduction. Three epithets of the Sumerian Mother Goddess are "Lady Potter" (dNIN-BAHAR), "Sculptor of the Land" (dTIBIRA-KALAM.MA), and "Sculptor of the Gods" (dTIBIRA-DINGIR.RE.E.NE) (Stol 2000: 74 and no. 158). In Akkadian-language texts Dingir-maḫ is "the great mother who molds creatures" (Stol 2000: 76). An Old Babylonian hymn to Belet-ili calls her the "one who molds the creature" (Stol 2000: 77–8). These goddesses may also serve as midwives, and the reference above to Nintu making "use of a reed, opened it to cut the umbilical cord" shows how they cared for the neonate as would a mortal *femme sage*.

More typically, the role of midwife went to the anonymous collective of birth goddesses, those goddesses who assisted Nintu in the creation of humanity in the Assyrian version of *Atrahasis*. They specifically appear during scenes of mortal parturition. An incantation from the first half of the second millennium has Sîn (the Mesopotamian lunar deity) sending assistance to the parturient woman, calling on, "the daughters of Anu, seven [and seven],/ [May] they [ ] their pots of [ ]. May they bring this baby straight forth!" (Foster 1993: 135) The first-millennium tale of "Sîn and the Cow" refers to the birth of the moon god's bovine offspring. At the critical time (ll.18–27; Foster 1993: 891–2):

> He sent down the daughters of Anu from heaven.
> One brought a jar of oil,
> The other brought water of labor.
> She rubbed oil from the jar on her brow,
> She sprinkled her whole body with water of labor.
> A second time she rubbed oil from the jar on her brow,
> She sprinkled her whole body with water of labor.
> A third time she rubbed oil from the jar on her brow,
> As she sprinkled the front of her body.
> The calf fell like a (running) gazelle to the ground.

In spite of the obvious importance of females in the birthing process, both in terms of the mother herself and the consistently female midwives present to assist her, there is evidence that the role of the birth goddesses diminished in the official literature of late second-millennium Babylon. As noted by Tikva Frymer-Kenski and Marten Stol, by the time of the composition of the later Mesopotamian account of creation—*Enuma Eliš*—females no longer had any role in the creation of humanity.[22] Marduk, god of Babylon and head of the pantheon, commands the creation of humankind, and it is Ea/Enki[23] alone who creates them, once again with the blood of a slaughtered god—Qingu (Dalley 1989: 261–2):

> He (Ea) created mankind from his blood,
> Imposed the toil of the gods (on man) and released the gods from it.
> When Ea the wise had created mankind,
> Had imposed the toil of the gods on them—
> That deed is impossible to describe,
> For Nudimmud[24] performed it with the miracles of Marduk.

In this myth, the primary mother goddess is Tiamat, who turns against her children and engages them in war with an army of demons and monsters. It is by slaughtering her that Marduk is made king. As such, there is a very different take on maternity in the *Enuma Eliš*, and the feminine is wholly removed from the process of human creation.

Such a patriarchal takeover in this myth notwithstanding, the role of mother and birth goddesses remains significant in the other ANE societies. In Anatolia, the wisest deity is the mother goddess Ḫannaḫanna, who, among other things, was the one to find and return Telipinu when he disappeared and wrought havoc on the fertility of the land. Her name in the Hittite repertoire can be written syllabically, or with the Sumerogram DINGIR.MAH, sometimes in alternation with the signs for ^dNIN.TU (Beckman 1983: 239). In the syncretistic tendencies of the Late Bronze Age, Ḫannaḫanna was deemed the equivalent of Akkadian Nintu, and in later Anatolian religion she is seen as one of the forerunners (or at least a contributor) to the Phrygian goddess Kybele (Beckman 1983: 240).

Ḫannaḫanna was understood to be present at births and to have all of humanity as her domain. Thus a Hittite birth spell reveals (*KUB* XXX 29; Beckman 1983: 23, Text A):

> [When] a woman is giving birth, then the midwife prepa[re]s the following:
> [two sto]ols (and) three cushions. On each
> Stool is placed one cushion.
> And one spreads out [on]e cushion between the stools
> On the ground. When the child begins to fall,
> [then] the woman seats herself on the stools. And the midwife
> Holds the receiving blanket with (her) [ha]nd.
> [And] you shall repeatedly conjure as follows:
> To the [go]ds allotments are given. The Sun-goddess in Arinna
> Has [se]ated herself, and Halmašuitt in Harpiša likewise,
> And Hatepi < nu > in Maliluha likewise, ^dLAMA in Krarhna likewise,
> The [awe]some Telepinu in Taw(i)niya likewise,
> And Huzziya in Hakmiš likewise.
> But for Ḫannaḫanna there did not remain a place; so for her, man < kind >
> Remained (as) a [pl]ace.

Likewise, when a child was born (*KUB* XXX 30; Beckman 1983: 201, Text M):

> When a male child [… is born.]
> Then let her (Ḫannaḫanna) make (him) str[ong …]
> When a female child [… is born,]
> Then let her (Ḫannaḫanna) [. …].

All the data suggest that Ḫannaḫanna was responsible for mother and child after the birth of the infant. Once again, the female was responsible for the new life after it had been provided by the male; the female's role was that of molder and nurturer.

Often mentioned alongside this DINGIR.MAH were the DINGIR.MAH^{meš}—the plural birth goddesses. Like Ḫannaḫanna, these goddesses were present at the birth of a child, and along with the Gilšeš—fate goddesses—were responsible for decreeing a fate for the neonate. Thus at the birth of the god Kumarbi's son in the *Song of Ullikummi* (A iii 10–15):

> [The …] women made her give birth. The Fate Goddesses and the Mother Goddesses [lifted the child] and cradled [him] on Kumarbi's knees. Kumarbi began [to amuse] that boy, and he began to clean him, and he gave [to the child] a fitting name. Kumarbi began to say to himself: "What name [shall I put on] the child whom the Fate Goddesses and Mother Goddesses have given to me?"
>
> *(Hoffner 1998: 57–8)*

These two sets of goddesses were also worshipped together in birth rituals. According to a Hittite ritual prescription (*KBo* XXX 4, 3'–11'; Beckman 1983: 243):

And a woman who is pregnant breaks three [thin loaves] for the Mother-goddesses. Thereupon she places a liver (and) a heart, cooked. And on top she scatters mutton-fat cake (and) meal. And she places (it all) before the Mother-goddesses.

But three thin loaves she breaks for the Fate-deities. Thereupon she places a li[ver (and) a heart, cooked]. And on top she scat[ters mutton-fat cake (and) meal. And she places (it all) before the Fate-deities].

In Ugarit, the mother goddess of the pantheon was Athirat. Her role as mother goddess is confirmed by an epithet of the gods themselves, who are known as "Athirat's sons" (*bn.atrt*). In the literature she is notable for her nursing abilities, suckling the "Gracious Gods" born to her husband El. She resumes this role in the *Kirta Epic*, nursing Yassib, the late-born son of King Kirta.

The collective birth goddesses in Ugarit are the Katharat (or Kotharat), daughters of the moon god. They play their most prominent role in the extant literature in the *Tale of Aqhat*, which in many ways exemplifies the engendered roles of fertility (and infertility) in the ANE. In the beginning of the tale, the wise man Danel is without an heir. He makes offerings to the deities and performs a seven-day incubation ritual, ultimately drawing the attention of Baal. Baal intercedes on Danel's behalf with El, and they both agree that they will provide Danel with a son. Thus, the initial problem of (in)fertility is a masculine matter. The gods tell Danel to go home (*CAT* 1.17, col. i, 38–40; Parker 1997: 53–4):

Let him mount his couch […]
In kissing his wife, [conception]!
In embracing her, pregnancy!

Thus, heterosexual intercourse leads to birth. However, before he engages in these *rites du plaisir* with his wife, the Katharat come to his home to be feasted for seven days, after which come "[…] the joys of the bed […]/ The delights of the bed of childbirth" (Parker 1997: 57). Their role in the story at this point is atypical, as birth goddesses normally attend to the mother upon parturition, not before conception. In this instance, these "moon's radiant daughters" might be understood as erotic stimulators—goddesses who arouse and intensify Danel's passions so that his lovemaking with his wife proves fruitful.[25] Unfortunately, the text is badly abraded, so the portion containing the birth of Danel's son Aqhat is not preserved; we cannot know if the birth goddesses or Athirat were present.

This arrival of birth deities before the conception of a desired, late-born son is reflected in the Biblical narratives of Isaac (Genesis 18:1–15) and Samson (Judges 13:2–24). In the former, three strangers approach Abraham as he sits beneath the oaks of Mamre. Abraham, the perfect host, takes them in and slaughters a calf for them to eat, while bidding Sarah to make them bread. After their meal the three strangers:

said to him [Abraham], "Where is your wife Sarah?" And he said, "There, in the tent." Then one said, "I will surely return to you in due season, and your wife Sarah shall have a son." And Sarah was listening at the tent entrance behind him. Now Abraham and Sarah were old, advanced in age; it had ceased to be with Sarah after the manner of women. So Sarah laughed to herself saying, "After I have grown old and my husband has grown old, shall I have pleasure?"

In Judges 13:

> There was a certain man of Zorah, of the tribe of Danaites, whose name was Manoah. His wife was barren, having born no children. And the angel of the LORD appeared to the woman and said to her, "Although you are barren, having born no children, you shall conceive and bear a son … " Then the woman came and told her husband, "A man of God came to me, and his appearance was like that of an angel of God, most awe-inspiring … "

Manoah tracks down this "man of God" and offers him a feast. The man, being an angel, declines, but bids Manoah and his wife to offer the feast as a burnt sacrifice to God.

In both instances we have either God and his "assistants" or merely one of those assistants visiting an old, barren couple, receiving a feast from them, and prophesying that the old woman would bear a son. As James Kugel notes, such scenes of "Unrecognized Angels" reflect back on the more polytheistic times of Israel's past, before the roles and responsibilities of all the deities were absorbed by the single god YHWH (Kugel 2007: Ch. 7). With these specific scenes we get an echo of the tales of Kirta and especially Aqhat, where the father god El promises a child to an heirless old man, and where unnamed birth divinities (the Katherat in Ugaritic, the unnamed angels in the Bible) are feasted before the desired conception. Thus, even in monotheistic Israel there are echoes of birth goddesses in the preserved narratives.

Egypt, too, had its birth divinities. The god Bes and the goddess Taweret are those best known for protecting new mothers and infants, and Bes imagery is especially prominent on paraphernalia belonging to women. However, even the more prominent deities, including the creator god Khnum, could take part in the rites of childbirth. The Westcar Papyrus (= P. Berlin 3033) tells the story of the birth of the first three kings of the Fifth Dynasty (presented here as triplets):

> On one of those days Ruddedet felt the pangs and her labor was difficult. Then the majesty of Re, lord of Sakhbu, (said) to Isis, Nephtys, Meskhenet, and Khnum: "Please go, deliver Ruddedet of the three children who are in her womb, who will assume this beneficent office in this whole land. … "
>
> These gods set out, having changed their appearance to dancing girls, with Khnum as their porter. When they reached the house of Rawoser, they found him standing with his loincloth upside down. They held out to him their necklaces and sistra. He said to them: "My ladies, look, it is the woman who is in pain; her labor is difficult." They said "Let us see her. We understand childbirth." He said to them, "Come in!" They went in to Ruddedet. They locked the room behind themselves and her.
>
> *(Lichtheim 2006, Vol. I: 220).*

In all cases, the standard paradigm manifests itself. The actual creation of offspring is in the hands of a male deity, be he Enki/Ea, El or Baal, Khnum or YHWH. For the birth of mortals, a goddess is invoked to shape, nourish, and most importantly deliver the infant, as with Nintu or Ninmah, Hannahanna, Athirat, or the various collectives of birth goddesses, including angels.

Infertility

Most of the texts presented above are mythological. They pertain to the actions of the deities, both among each other and in dealing with the affairs of humankind. These are the texts that produce the majority of our evidence concerning ANE understandings of fertility. By contrast, when dealing with infertility, workaday mortals suddenly come into sharp relief. This is because the process of reproduction is never so important as when it is not functioning. That is the point at which mortals seek out the experts, invoking deities and performing rituals to allow their organs to function and their offspring to emerge. We have already seen numerous tales of infertile couples—Abraham and Sarah, Manoah and his wife, Danel, and Kirta. The problem of infertility, especially at the royal level, was critical in the ANE.

Considering the gendered divide in the understandings of ancient fertility, it is not surprising that two separate avenues of approach existed regarding the diagnosis of infertility. For men, the problem was impotence, either because of magic or insufficient manliness. Either way, he is incapable of getting his seed, the new life, into the female body. For women, the problem was barrenness, the inability to hold the seed given them by a man. Magical, medical, and psychological treatments existed for both.

Concerning male impotence, the ŠÀ.ZI.GA, or "rising of the 'heart'" texts were extensive.[26] They date to the Middle Babylonian period and have come to light in both Mesopotamia and the Hittite capital at Boğazköy. From a medical perspective, therapy might include rubbing the penis and lower body with an ointment made of plant oil and iron. Other concoctions were made with animal parts, preferably those engaged in mating or of known sexual potency. Thus the saliva of aroused animals; dried, copulating lizards; or stag penis.[27] More psychological aspects involved women "talking dirty" to their men, sometimes with props. To quote Robert Biggs (Biggs 2002: 72–3, excerpted):

> A striking feature of these incantations is that they are mostly ostensibly recited by women to increase the sexual ability of men … Some incantations are quite explicit, as, for example, the one that says, "My vagina is the vagina of a female dog. His penis is the penis of a dog. Just as the vagina of a female dog holds fast the penis of a dog, (so may my vagina hold fast his penis)!"
>
> …
>
> "Get an erection like a wild bull!" and "At the head of my bed is tied a buck. At the foot of my bed is tied a ram. The one at the head of my bed, get an erection, make love to me! The one at the foot of my bed, get an erection, caress me!" In a similar text we have "Buck, caress me! [Ram], copulate with me!" and "[At the head] of my bed a ram is tied. [At the foot of my bed] a weaned sheep is tied. Around my waist their wool is tied. [Like a ram eleven times], like a weaned sheep twelve times, like a bat thirteen times [make love to me, and like a pig] fourteen times, like a wild bull fifty times, like a s[ta]g fifty times!" And in another text we have "Make love to me with the love-making of a wolf!"

While such prescriptions were used in Anatolia, the Hittites also had their own means of dealing with erectile dysfunction. The most detailed ritual we have is Paškuwatti's ritual to the goddess Uliliyassi against impotence. The ultimate purpose of this ritual is to take away a man's femininity and replace it with masculinity. As such, there is some debate as to whether this is a rite to cure impotence, or a rite to cure male effeminacy/passivity.[28] In either event, the stated aims are for the man to impregnate his wife. In this ritual the female functionary Paškuwatti explicitly uses sympathetic magic to "cure" the man of femininity (l. 4); it results in the production of children (Hoffner 1987: 277):

> I place a spindle and distaff in the patient's [hand], and he comes under the gates. When he steps forward through the gates, I take the spindle and distaff away from him. I give him a bow (and) [arro]w(s), and say (to him) all the while: "I have just taken femininity away from you and given you masculinity in return. You have cast off the (sexual) behavior expected [of women]; [you have taken] to yourself the behavior expected of men!"

The man performs a three-day long ritual involving incubation, invoking the goddess' presence by his side (l.8; Hoffner 1987: 278):

> "Come to this man! You are his 'wife of children' for him! So look after him! Turn to him (in favor) and speak to him! Turn your maidservant (his wife) over to him, and he will become a yoke. Let him take his wife and produce for himself sons and daughters!"

The Egyptians used both medicine and magic in curing erectile dysfunction. One recipe from the end of the Middle Kingdom recommends (*P. Ram.* V no. XII): "Leaves of Christ thorn, 1; leaves of acacia, 1; honey, 1. Grind (the leaves) in this honey, and apply as a bandage" (Manniche 1997: 103). On the more magical side we have a spell from circa 1000 BCE (*P. Chester Beatty* X; Manniche 1997: 103):

> "Hail to you great god, who created the upper class, you, Khnum, who established the lower class. May you test the mouth of every vulva ... be erect, be not soft; be strong, be not weak ... You strengthen your testicles with Seth, son of Nut." To be recited over ... the member to be anointed with it.

Even our comparably limited corpus from Ugarit has a ritual for curing impotence. Text RIH 78/20 cites sorcery for the "pain of your rod" (Pardee 2002: 160–1, excerpted):

> This recitation casts out the tormentors of a young man:
> The pain of your rod it has banished,
> The producers of the pain of your rod.
> It goes forth at the voice of the ta'iyu priest
> Like smoke from a window,
> Like a serpent from a pillar,
> Like mountain goats to a summit,
> Like lions to a lair.
> The rod has recovered.
> …
> Then, as for the sorcerers, the tormentors,
> Ḥôranu will drive them out,
> Even the companions and the "lads of wisdom" he will drive out for you.
> With respect to heat, do not sag,

May your tongue not stutter,
May your canal not be decanalized.[29]

...

For the man, descend from the rod to the earth, O flow;
For the son of man, from illness he is delivered.

Matters could be more difficult for barren women. The easiest way to deal with barrenness, from a male perspective, was simply to get another woman. The ancient documents are full of such attestations. The *Codex Hammurabi* (§§144–7) regulates the process by
which non-reproducing *naditu*-priestesses provide a *šugitu* to their husbands for the bearing
of children. According to the final statute, "If she does not bear children, her mistress may
sell her" (Roth 2003: 344–5). Two legal texts from the Late Bronze Age Syrian city of
Alalakh (Level IV) document the replacement of female bodies for producing children.
Document AT 92 (3.101B) is a marriage contract between Naidu (wife) and Iri-halpa
(husband). According to lines 15'–16' of the contract, "If Naidu does not give birth to an
heir, then the daughter of her brother, Iwaššura, will be given (to Iri-halpa)" (Hess 2003:
252). Document AT 93 (3.101C) is a similar contract between Zunzuri and Idatti (ll.2–9;
Hess 2003: 252):

> From this day, before [Niqmepa the king:]
> The daughter of Ilimili,
> Zunzuri, Idat[ti
> Has taken for a wife.
> Two hundred shekels of silver and thirty shekels of gold
> He has given as a bride price.
> [I]f she has not given birth after seven years,
> He may take a second wife.

A papyrus from New Kingdom Egypt relates how Rennefer allowed her younger brother
Padiu to marry Taiemniut, the eldest of three children born to a slave girl bought by her
husband Nebnefer. Gay Robins suggests that, since the couple had no recorded children of
their own, Nebnefer may have bought the slave girl specifically for reproduction, and that the
three children were, in fact, his own.[30]

Perhaps the most famous story of a woman providing her husband with a surrogate is the
narrative of Abram, Sarai,[31] and Hagar (Genesis 16: 1–4):

> Abram's wife Sarai had borne him no children. Now she had an Egyptian slave-girl
> whose name was Hagar, and she said to Abram, "You see that the LORD has not
> allowed me to bear a child. Take my slave-girl; perhaps I shall found a family through
> her." Abram agreed to what his wife said; so Sarai, Abram's wife, brought her slave-
> girl, Hagar the Egyptian, and gave her to her husband Abram as a wife/concubine ...
> He lay with Hagar and she conceived.

Women were at pains to avoid such replacement. "Fixing" her body consisted of practices such as
using magical incantations and/or objects and/or the use of specific plants to promote fertility.
One Babylonian text prescribes "Silver, gold, iron, copper, in total 21 (amulet) stones, in order
that a woman who is not pregnant become pregnant: you string it on a linen yarn, you put it on
her neck" (Stol 2000: 35). Another (really horrible) prescription was:

> To make a not child-bearing woman pregnant: You flay an edible mouse, open it up, and fill it with myrrh; you dry it in the shade, crush and grind it up, and mix it with fat; you place it in her vagina, and she will become pregnant.
>
> *(Stol 2000: 53).*

In the Bible, barrenness is seen as having been sent by God so that he might later intervene and bless the woman with a late-born son. One such example was Sarai/Sarah, discussed above. The quintessential example of a woman coping with barrenness is Jacob's wife Rachel. In Genesis 30 we read:

> When Rachel saw that she bore Jacob no children, she envied her sister; and she said to Jacob, "Give me children or I shall die!" Jacob became very angry with Rachel and said, "Am I in the place of God, who has withheld from you the fruit of your womb?" Then she said, "Here is my maid Bilhah; go in to her that she may bear upon my knees and that I too may have children through her." ... In the days of wheat harvest Reuben went and found mandrakes[32] in the field, and brought them to his mother Leah. Then Rachel said to Leah, "Please give me some of your son's mandrakes." ... Then God remembered Rachel, and God heeded her and opened her womb. She conceived and bore a son.

Here we see the use of a replacement female body, use of medicinal herbs, and finally divine intervention from a father deity.

In cases where the male is convinced that it is he who is "barren," the adoption of heirs emerges as a solution. A Twentieth-Dynasty personal letter from Deir el-Medina to the scribe Nekhemmut reads (Robins 1993: 77–8):

> You are not a man since you are unable to make your wives pregnant like your fellow men. A further matter: You abound in being exceedingly stingy. You give no one anything. As for him who has no children, he adopts an orphan instead [to] bring him up. It is his responsibility to pour water onto your hands as one's own eldest son.

Adoption did occur for reasons other than infertility, including the adoption of one's own children born to slaves (as with Nebnefer above), or the adoption of a new spouse's children from a previous marriage, or to settle a debt (the bride price acquired by adopted daughters could be quite high in some areas, such as Mesopotamian Nuzi), or simply through pity for an orphaned child. A late-second-millennium legal training exercise from Mesopotamia—*ana ittišu* (VII iii, 9–10)—records, "This *qadištu* (a cultic midwife) took in a child from the street; at the breast with human milk [she nursed him]" (Westenholz 1989: 251). However, adoption as a remedy for infertility specifically appears as a solution only once the infertility can be ascribed to the male; no female body would "work" for him.

Sex, gender, and voice

These data reveal important aspects of the gender dynamic in the ANE. They show that gender is indeed relative and socially constructed, varying over time and place. In contrast to modern conceptions, in the ANE fertility was seen to be a masculine quality: The source of life was male. The role of the female was not creatrix of new life, be that human, divine, or even vegetal, but as the molder and nourisher of the life created by the male. As a consequence, men were anxious to advertise their paternal status: To have children was an ideal in all the societies here considered (*Bilgames and the Netherworld*, ll. 255–69; George 1999: 187–8):

> "Did you see the man with one son?" "I saw him." "How does he fare?"
> "For the peg built into his wall bitterly he laments."
> "Did you see the man with two sons?" "I saw him." "How does he fare?"
> "Seated on two bricks he eats a bread-loaf."
> "Did you see the man with three sons?" "I saw him." "How does he fare?"
> "He drinks water from the waterskin slung on the saddle."
> "Did you see the man with four sons?" "I saw him." "How does he fare?"
> "Like a man with a team of four donkeys his heart rejoices."
> "Did you see the man with five sons?" "I saw him." "How does he fare?"
> "Like a fine scribe with a nimble hand he enters the palace with ease."
> "Did you see the man with six sons?" "I saw him." "How does he fare?"
> "Like a man with ploughs in harness his heart rejoices."
> "Did you see the man with seven sons?" "I saw him." "How does he fare?"
> "Among the junior deities he sits on a throne and listens to the proceedings."
> "Did you see the man with no heir?" "I saw him." "How does he fare?"
> "He eats a bread-loaf like a kiln-fired brick."

Women were also concerned about having children, of course, especially as, unlike the males, they could be replaced if thought to be barren. The emotional strain must have been considerable, especially evident in the Biblical texts, where no man is ever presented as sterile.

Nevertheless, women in the ANE seem rarely to have *vaunted* their maternal status. For them, there was a greater sense of the difficulties involved, rather than an apparently effortless flow of offspring. The same Sumerian society that composed the above quotation from *Bilgames* also had a proverb, "A mother who has given birth to eight youths lies down in weakness" (Alster 1997: 72). Such a statement expresses perfectly the dichotomy presented at the start of this essay. For males, reproduction is simple, almost effortless. There is no downside to a plethora of offspring, merely the pride of being of proven fertility and potency.

For females, reproduction was dangerous, stressful, and exhausting. Not credited with the creation of new life, women bore the full drudgery of childbirth and rearing. Perhaps then it is not surprising that in much of the ANE their prestige came not from (their husbands') offspring, but from lineage and occupation.[33] The women who appeared in early art portrayed themselves in positions of status that derived either from lineage or profession. Queens, princesses, and nobility derived and portrayed status vis-à-vis their fathers and husbands. Priestesses did the same with their cultic positions. Servants who had any status acquired it through their more noble connections, and these connections were emphasized in the inscriptions and iconography. As Julia Asher-Greve has noted (Asher-Greve 2006: 74):[34]

> … independent women worked for queens or other court women, some were priestesses, or daughters of priestesses. Apart from marriage, court and temple offered positions that apparently gave women at least some independence as well as the means to donate votive gifts or acquire high quality seals of expensive materials. Imagery rarely shows women with husband or children but primarily in religious, ceremonial and/or public contexts.

The exceptions to this pattern come only when a woman's status is directly linked to her role as mother. A prime example is Queen Uqnitum of Urkeš, modern Tell Mozan.[35] The queen's personal seal that uses her longest title—Wife of (King) Tupkiš—shows the queen in the midst of the royal family, with one child on her lap, another standing before the king. Here Uqnitum emphasizes her role as Queen Mother and with that title, that of Chief Royal Consort. By contrast, the queen and royal consort of the next generation—Tar'am-Agade—was the daughter of Naram-Sîn of Akkad, a lineage of sufficient importance that the queen felt no need to portray herself as a mother in her iconography, but instead took status from her father. Her seals show combat scenes, and her inscription reads: "(Of) Naram-Sîn, the king of Akkad, Tar'am-Agade, his daughter."[36]

The emphasis on maternity comes across most strongly in the Hebrew Bible. Here, the Biblical matriarchs, denied any access to the religious or political hierarchy available to women in other ANE societies, wielded power and status *exclusively* through their male offspring, offspring pointedly given by a male deity and recorded in a text voiced and penned exclusively by males.

Ultimately it is a matter of voice. As the male voice dominates the ancient texts, male concerns come to the fore, such as children and the masculine credit for them. In wholly male-voice texts such as the Bible, women are valued almost exclusively for their ability to give men sons. When the woman's voice slips through, especially in societies that had greater opportunities for women, women *may* self-identify as mothers, but they are more likely to highlight their less reproductive accomplishments. Perhaps that gender construct is not so different from our own, after all.

Notes

1 This is not to discount the extensive non-biological contributions males make to the rearing of off-spring, such as bathing and feeding.
2 Roth 2000: 188.
3 Budin 2011: 12; Keel and Schroer 2004: 17–19.
4 Keel and Schroer 2004: 17.
5 Karageorghis 1992: 19.
6 Day 2012: 299.
7 Baines 1985; Cooper 1989.
8 A similar sentiment is expressed in the Greek repertoire in Aeschylus' *Eumenides*, ll. 657–62.
9 It is clear that male and female were deemed the standard sexes and genders in all the regions under discussion, and that those two sexes were understood as necessary for reproduction, especially human reproduction. This fact remains valid even if some members of the various communities felt themselves to be, or were perceived as, of a different gender-orientation than the one normally associated with their sex, thus effeminate men, masculine women, transvestites, eunuchs, or otherwise. On such categories, especially what might be dubbed "effeminate males" in ancient Mesopotamia, see Nissinen 1998: 28–36. On alternate genders (if not sexes) in the ANE, see McCaffrey 2002: *passim*. On normative and non-normative sex and gender in Mesopotamia, see Asher-Greve 2002: *passim*.
10 On the translation of the Sumerian A as "water," "urine," or "sperm" see Leick 1994: 25.
11 Similar dynamics occur when the Hittite birth goddess Ḫannaḫanna disappears, and one might compare this to the flight and return of Demeter in the *Homeric Hymn to Demeter*.
12 With several more lines of similar aches, pains, and births.
13 In the later Greek tradition, the sky god Zeus becomes "pregnant" twice. In Hesiod's *Theogony* (l. 924), upon swallowing his pregnant first wife Metis, Zeus incubates his future daughter Athena in his head. According to Euripides' *Bakkhai* (ll. 95–6), Zeus seized the immortal fetus Dionysos from the burning remains of his mother Semele and sewed him into his thigh until he was ready for birth. Both deities—Athena and Dionysos—were recognized as inverting the normal gender paradigms of ancient Greece, and this inversion began with their birth from a male.
14 Stol emphasizes that this passage is only preserved in two later, Assyrian versions of the text discovered in Assurbanipal's library. Thus, they may be later additions to an earlier text, and not part of the original conception of the origins of humanity (Stol 2000: 113–14).
15 A reference to the mud bricks upon which women in labor in Mesopotamia and Egypt kneeled or crouched during parturition.

16 ETCSL translation t.1.1.2, available online at http://etcsl.orinst.ox.ac.uk/cgi-bin/etcsl.cgi?text=t.1.1.2# (accessed 27 June 2014). It is interesting to note here the contrast with Greek mythology, where it is the *females*, notably Gaia and Hera, who parthenogenically produce monstrous offspring, such as the Cyclopes, Typhaon, and the lame god Hephaistos. My thanks to Aislinn Melchior for this insight.
17 On the euphemism "hand" for penis, see Paul 2002.
18 The "Lady" is identified as Athirat in an earlier stanza.
19 All translations are *NRSV*.
20 On this "breast and womb" passage see Smith 2002: 48–52.
21 On the archaeological evidence for "pre-Biblical" polytheism, see especially Keel and Uehlinger 1998. On the deities of ancient Israel, see Smith 2002.
22 Frymer-Kensky 1992: 70–80; Stol 2000: 71–2, 78.
23 Enki is the Sumerian form of the god's name, Ea is the Akkadian.
24 An epithet of Ea.
25 On the role of female as erotic stimulator, see Budin 2011: 20–5.
26 "Heart" is a euphemism here.
27 Biggs 2002: 76.
28 On this interpretation of the ritual, see J.L. Miller 2010: *passim*. According to Miller, the ritual was intended to "cure its patient of his proclivity for passive sexual acquiescence and to replace it with an inclination toward normative male, i.e. penetrative behavior."
29 May liquid continue to flow through.
30 Robins 1993: 58.
31 Abraham and Sarah before their names were changed.
32 Believed to be a cure for barrenness.
33 On maternity and status in the ancient world, see Budin 2011: ch. 7.
34 See also Asher-Greve 2002: 16–17.
35 Kelly-Buccellati 2010: 191–3.
36 Buccellati and Kelly-Buccellati 2002: 13.

Bibliography

Allen, J.P. (2003) "From pyramid texts spell 527 (1.3)", in W.M. Hallo and K.L. Younger Jr (eds) *The Context of Scripture*, Vols 1, 2, and 3. Leiden: Brill, p. 7.

Alster, B. (1997) *Proverbs of Ancient Sumer: The World's Earliest Proverb Collection*. Bethesda: CDL Press.

Asher-Greve, J. (2002) "Decisive sex, essential gender", in S. Parpola and R.M. Whiting (eds) *Sex and Gender in the Ancient Near East*. Helsinki: Neo-Assyrian Text Corpus Project, pp. 11–26.

——(2006) "'Golden Age' of women? Status and gender in third millennium Sumerian and Akkadian art", in S. Schroer (ed.) *Images and Gender: Contributions to the Hermeneutics of Reading Ancient Art*. Fribourg: Academic Press/Göttingen: Vandenhoeck & Ruprecht, pp. 41–81.

Baines, J. (1985) *Fecundity Figures: Egyptian Personification and the Iconology of a Genre*. Chicago, IL: Bolchazy-Carducci Publishers.

Beckman, G.M. (1983) *Hittite Birth Rituals*, 2nd rev. edn. Wiesbaden: Otto Harrassowitz.

Biggs, R. (2002) "The Babylonian sexual potency texts", in S. Parpola and R.M. Whiting (eds) *Sex and Gender in the Ancient Near East*. Helsinki: Neo-Assyrian Text Corpus Project, pp. 71–8.

Black, J., Cunningham, G., Robeson, E., and Zólyomi, G. (2004) *The Literature of Ancient Sumer*. Oxford: Oxford University Press.

Buccellati, G. and Kelly-Buccellati, M. (2002) "Tar'am-Agade, daughter of Naram-Sin, at Urkesh", in L. al-Gailani Werr (ed.) *Of Pots and Plans: Papers Presented to David Oates*. London: Nabu Publications, pp. 11–31.

Budin, S.L. (2011) *Images of Woman and Child from the Bronze Age: Reconsidering Fertility, Maternity, and Gender in the Ancient World*. Cambridge: Cambridge University Press.

——(2014) "Mother or sister? Finding adolescent girls in Minoan figural art", in A. Kieburg and S. Morrow (eds) *Mädchen im Altertum* [Girls in Antiquity]. Münster: Waxmann Verlag, pp. 93–104.

Cooper, J.S. (1989) "Enki's member: Eros and irrigation in Sumerian literature", in *DUMU E₂ DUB-BA-A: Festschrift in Honor of Å. Sjöberg*. Philadelphia, PA: University Museum Publications, pp. 87–9.

Dalley, S. (1989) *Myths from Mesopotamia*. Oxford: Oxford University Press.

Day, P. (2012) "Hebrew Bible goddesses and modern feminist scholarship", *Religion Compass* 6/6: 298–308.

Faulkner, R.O. (2007) *The Ancient Egyptian Pyramid Texts*. Stilwell, KS: Digireads.com Publishing.

Foster, B.R. (1993) *Before the Muses: An Anthology of Akkadian Literature.* Bethesda, MD: CDL Press.

Frymer-Kensky, T. (1992) *In the Wake of the Goddesses: Women, Culture and the Biblical Transformation of Pagan Myth.* New York: Fawcett Columbine.

George, A. (1999). *The Epic of Gilgamesh: A New Translation.* London: Penguin Classics.

Hackett, J.A. (1989) "Can a sexist model liberate us? Ancient near eastern 'fertility' goddesses", *Journal of Feminist Studies in Religion* 5: 65–76.

Hallo, W.M. and Younger, K.L. Jr (eds) (2003) *The Context of Scripture*, Vols 1, 2, and 3. Leiden: Brill.

Hess, R.S. (2003) "Contracts: Alalakh", in W.M. Hallo and K.L. Younger Jr (eds) *The Context of Scripture*, Vols 1, 2, and 3. Leiden: Brill, pp. 249–54.

Hoffner, H.A. Jr (1987) "Paškuwatti's ritual against sexual impotence (CTH 406)", *Aula Orientalis* 5: 271–87.

——(1998) *Hittite Myths*, 2nd edn. Atlanta, GA: Scholars Press.

Jacobsen, T. (1987) *The Harps that Once … : Sumerian Poetry in Translation.* New Haven, CT: Yale University Press.

Karageorghis, J. (1992) "On some aspects of Chalcolithic religion in Cyprus", *Report of the Department of Antiquities, Cyprus*, pp. 17–27.

Keel, O. and Schroer, S. (2004) *Eva: Mutter alles Lebendigen.* Fribourg: Academic Press.

Keel, O. and Uehlinger, C. (1998) *Gods, Goddesses, and Images of God in Ancient Israel.* Minneapolis, MN: Fortress Press.

Kelly-Buccellati, M. (2010) "Uqnitum and Tar'um-Agade: Patronage and portraiture at Urkesh", in J.C. Finke (ed.) *Festschrift für Gernot Wilhelm anläßlich seines 65. Geburtstages am 28. Januar 2010.* Dresden: ISLET, pp. 185–202.

Kugel, J.L. (2007) *How to Read the Bible: A Guide to Scripture Then and Now.* New York: Free Press.

Leick, G. (1994) *Sex and Eroticism in Mesopotamian Literature.* London: Routledge.

Levine, B. (2002) "'Seed' versus 'womb': Expressions of male dominance in biblical Israel", in S. Parpola and R.M. Whiting (eds) *Sex and Gender in the Ancient Near East.* Helsinki: Neo-Assyrian Text Corpus Project, pp. 337–44.

Lichtheim, M. (2006) *Ancient Egyptian Literature.* Berkeley, CA: University of California Press.

McCaffrey, K. (2002) "Reconsidering gender ambiguity in Mesopotamia: Is a beard just a beard?", in S. Parpola and R.M. Whiting (eds) *Sex and Gender in the Ancient Near East.* Helsinki: Neo-Assyrian Text Corpus Project, pp. 379–91.

Manniche, L. (1997) *Sexual Life in Ancient Egypt*, London: Kegan Paul International.

Marinatos, N. (2010) *Minoan Kingship and the Solar Goddess: A Near Eastern Koine.* Urbana and Chicago, IL: University of Illinois Press.

Miller, J.L. (2010) "Paškuwatti's ritual: Remedy for impotence or antidote to homosexuality?", *Journal of Ancient Near Eastern Religions* 10(1): 83–9.

Nissinen, M. (1998) *Homoeroticism in the Biblical World: A Historical Perspective.* Minneapolis, MN: Fortress Press.

Pardee, D. (2002) *Ritual and Cult at Ugarit.* Atlanta, GA: Society of Biblical Literature.

Parker, S.B. (1997) *Ugaritic Narrative Poetry.* Atlanta, GA: Scholars Press.

Parpola, S. and Whiting, R.M. (eds) (2002) *Sex and Gender in the Ancient Near East.* Helsinki: Neo-Assyrian Text Corpus Project.

Paul, S.M. (2002) "The shared legacy of sexual metaphors and euphemisms in Mesopotamian and biblical literature", in S. Parpola and R.M. Whiting (eds) *Sex and Gender in the Ancient Near East.* Helsinki: Neo-Assyrian Text Corpus Project, pp. 489–98.

Robins, G. (1993) *Women in Ancient Egypt.* Cambridge, MA: Harvard University Press.

Roth, A.M. (2000) "Father earth, mother sky: Ancient Egyptian beliefs about conception and fertility", in A.E. Rautman (ed.) *Reading the Body: Representations and Remains in the Archaeological Record.* Philadelphia, PA: University of Pennsylvania Press, pp. 187–201.

Roth, M.T. (2003) "The laws of Hammurabi", in W.M. Hallo and K.L. Younger Jr (eds) *The Context of Scripture*, Vols 1, 2, and 3. Leiden: Brill, pp. 335–53.

Simpson, W.K. (1972) *The Literature of Ancient Egypt.* New Haven, CT: Yale University Press.

Smith, M.S. (2002) *The Early History of God: Yahweh and the Other Deities in Ancient Israel*, 2nd edn. Grand Rapids, MI: William B. Eerdmans.

Stol, M. (2000) *Birth in Babylonia and the Bible: Its Mediterranean Setting.* Groningen: Styx Publications.

Westenholz, J.G. (1989) "Tamar, Qedeša, Qadištu, and sacred prostitution in Mesopotamia", *Harvard Theological Review* 82(3): 245–65.

3

GUARDING THE HOUSE

Conflict, rape, and David's concubines

Elna K. Solvang

Almost immediately after Rwandan president Juvenal Habyiramana's plane was shot down as it approached Kigali Airport the night of 6 April 1994, soldiers of the Rwandan armed forces surrounded the house of the prime minister Agathe Uwilingiyimana to keep her from assuming her responsibilities as temporary head of state and from going on national radio to plead for calm and promise an investigation into the fatal attack. In the early morning hours of 7 April, Rwandan military officials ordered soldiers to storm the residence and kill the prime minister and others with her. The assassination of Prime Minister Uwilingiyimana was a critical element of the opening salvo in the 100-day Hutu-Power genocidal assault on the Tutsi population of Rwanda that resulted in the killing of over 800,000 Tutsis and moderate Hutus. Prime Minister Uwilingiyimana had nothing to do with the shooting down of the president's plane. She was a member of the Hutu ethnic majority. Uwilingiyimana was targeted because she was not opposed to power-sharing with the Tutsi ethnic minority and because she was now in a position for those changes to go forward.

When Uwilingiyimana's body was recovered, it was clear that in addition to having been shot, she had been sexually violated. Her body "was riddled with bullets." She lay naked on the ground and "an empty Fanta bottle had been thrust into her genitals" (*Prosecutor v Augustin Ndindiliyiman, Augustin Bizimungu, François-Xavier Nzuwonemeye, Innocent Sagahutu* [17 May 2011] ICTR-00-56-T 363 ¶1629).[1] Over the next 100 days, as the targeted killings of Tutsis spread across Rwanda, rape and other forms of sexual violence and mutilation were directed and systematically employed as part of the genocide. The primary focus was Tutsi women. They were hunted and trapped and subjected to a range of abuses including gang rapes, battering, and the insertion of guns, sharp sticks, hot water, and acid into their vaginas in order to destroy their reproductive organs, transmit the HIV-AIDS virus, or conceive a "Hutu" child. The sexual violence was also intended to maim women's economic productivity, and cause them to be rejected by their families and the wider community because of extramarital sexual contact. The sexual violence was deliberately orchestrated, promoted, and rewarded by political and military leaders at all levels (Nowrojee 1996: 48).

That female non-combatants are targets of sexual violence during civil conflict is, sadly, no news. Elisabeth Meier Tetlow notes that in their royal accounts of war the ancient Assyrian kings "made frequent reference to captive women and girls put to death, tortured, or sent to Assyria as booty or slaves" (Tetlow 2004: 168). The violent subjugation of the enemy was immortalized in palace reliefs, among those one that "portrayed Assyrian soldiers raping a woman[2] and beating captives while forcing them to grind up the bones of their fathers"[3] (Tetlow 2004: 170). Similar sadistic and sexual horrors have been documented as widespread in modern conflicts in Bosnia-Herzegovina, Sudan, Democratic Republic of Congo, and Rwanda.

Though the use of sexual violence is not new, investigations into the sexual violence directed toward civilian women in these contemporary conflicts is leading to a clearer recognition that there are varying perpetrators of and objectives for the attacks, as well as varying ways in which these sexual assaults are regarded as "morally defendable, ethically palatable and socially acceptable (and therefore, arguably not *really* rapes …)" (Baaz and Stern 2009: 497). It is the hope of this paper that careful consideration of contemporary uses of sexual assault in civil conflict might lead to richer understandings of the ancient accounts, more wisdom in interpreting such texts with contemporary audiences, and more insight in responding to such violence.

This paper begins by examining uses of sexual violence in civil conflicts, drawing examples primarily from the 1994 Rwandan genocide. The focus then turns to biblical texts in 2 Samuel related to King David's son Absalom's decision to go "in to his father's concubines in the sight of all Israel" (2 Sam 16:22)[4] as part of his plan to seize the kingdom from David. Absalom's actions are considered in light of his stated purpose and the practices of other ancient Near Eastern conquering kings. The paper concludes with some observations about how the story of David's concubines might serve as a basis for contemporary conversation and reflection on sexual violence.

Uses of sexual violence in civil conflicts

It is important to note at the outset of this discussion that the victims of sexual violence in civil conflict may be female or male, including children. They may be combatants or just citizens living in the conflict area. Sexual violence is used in connection with other forms of violence to destroy and to control.

Contemporary forms of violence have gruesome ancient parallels. The Middle and Late Assyrian kings boasted in royal annals and inscriptions of "their cruelty to conquered peoples. … War captives, including women and girls, were regularly decapitated, impaled, flayed alive, burned alive, mutilated, and sold into slavery" (Tetlow 2004: 169). Typical of this propaganda is King Ashurnasirpal II's claim (Grayson 1991: 201):[5]

> I felled 3,000 of their fighting men with the sword. I carried off prisoners, possessions, oxen [and] cattle from them. I burnt many captives from them. I captured many troops alive: from some I cut off their arms [and] hands; from others I cut off their noses, ears, [and] *extremities*. I gouged out the eyes of many troops. I made one pile of the living [and] one of heads. I hung their heads on trees around the city. I burnt their adolescent boys [and] girls. I razed, destroyed, burnt, [and] consumed the city.

The Assyrian royal annals may have exaggerated the number of victims but not the terrifying forms of violence through which royal strength was demonstrated and royal control exercised. The violence against citizens and officials alike received further royal sanction in the carved wall reliefs in the court and private chambers of Assyrian palaces. A relief series in the Southwest Palace in Nineveh depicting Ashurbanipal's victory at Til-Tuba includes the beheading of the Elamite king Teumman.[6] In a subsequent scene Teumman's head is shown being carried for delivery to Ashurbanipal by a soldier riding in a chariot.[7] The head's final destination is depicted in a relief in one of Ashurbanipal's private apartments in the North Palace at Nineveh. As the king and queen enjoy a garden banquet tended by servants and musicians Teumman's head dangles from a tree.[8] The reliefs likely served as a reminder to senior Assyrian officials and a warning to visiting dignitaries of the power of the king's army and the fate of those who attempt to rebel (Reade 1979; Russell 1991).

The actual number of victims of the 1994 genocide in Rwanda will never be known. In 2000 an international panel assembled by the Organization of African Unity (OAU) reported: "Soon after the genocide ended, more than 250,000 widowed victims registered with the Ministry of Family and Women in Development. … By 1996, the government was faced with about 400,000 widows who needed help to become self-supporting" (OAU 2000: 147). Estimates are that up to 75 percent of the Tutsi population was exterminated. Tutsi males were initial targets for extermination (Des Forges 1999: 11):

> Authorities first incited attacks on the most obvious targets—men who had acknowl-edged or could be easily supposed to have ties with the RPF[9]—and only later insisted on the slaughter of women, children, the elderly and others generally regarded as apolitical.

While Tutsi males were typically rounded up and slaughtered en masse, Tutsi women were particularly subject to sexual violence, and "[t]hroughout the genocide … were often raped, tortured and mutilated before they were murdered" (Des Forges 1999: 10).

Sexual violence can take different forms in civil conflict. One form of sexual violence is the trafficking and appropriation of women by governments, militias, gangs, entrepreneurs, and family members to service the "sexual needs" of soldiers (Baaz and Stern 2009: 505). The Japanese Imperial Army's conscription of women and girls from Korea and other Asian nations to serve as "comfort women" to Japanese soldiers in the 1940s is just one example of the assumption that utilizing certain populations of women to satisfy the "natural" sexual desires of soldiers is in the interest of military readiness and civic order.[10] The soldier is regarded as "acting as a 'normal' heterosexual man, who *needs* to have sex" (Baaz and Stern 2009: 510). Linking military strength with sexual gratification, however, depersonalizes the women designated for this service and justifies utilizing them for personal and military gain. The idea that men have sexual needs that require servicing is regarded as socially acceptable, while the women providing the services become socially repugnant.

In civil conflict there are also opportunistic incidences of sexual violence as militia on patrol or conquering a city or village randomly seize and violate women and girls to demonstrate their ability to overpower and destroy (Baaz and Stern 2009: 510–11). Resentment and frustration over "hunger, poverty, neglect and the craziness of warring" might fuel the sexual violence that is intended to confirm their masculinity (Baaz and Stern 2009: 513) and their dominance. Additionally, as Meredeth Turshen notes, "[t]he unpredictability of rape serves to terrorize the community and warn all people of the futility of resistance—those targeted as victims as well as those who might wish to protect the intended targets" (2000: 810). Permission and encour-agement to take advantage of opportunities for sexual violence can be part of an army or militia's cultivation of a willingness to fight, a bonding among the combatants, and a perk for those men or young boy soldiers who can be trained to see sexual assault—even torture and mutilation—as natural expressions of manhood and military strength.

When examined closely, in both the trafficking and the opportunistic demonstrations of destructive power the violation of women is not about a surplus of sexual desire but is part of those systems in which sexual dominance is regarded as indicative of normative manhood and military prowess. Such systems are pervasive across cultures but they are clearly not inevitable, since they must operate within social frameworks in which such sexual violence is not normative. As Baaz and Stern discerned in their interviews with soldiers in the Congo, rape was viewed as "bad and forbidden, both in military and civilian life" (2009: 512). Nevertheless, a collective logic evolved which made such violence "understandable" (497), "'exceptional' and the result of the extraordinary circumstances of the deprived warscape which they inhabited" (512).

In discussing sexual violence in civil conflict, the temptation, as Cynthia Enloe cautions, is "reducing the cause of wartime rape to raw primal misogyny" and ignoring "the war-waging objectives to which rape is put" (2000: 134). Rape is not an inevitable by-product of civil conflict; it is a tool employed in the conflict for particular strategic purposes. Among the purposes, Enloe observes, might be the destruction of cultural identity, reproductive capacity, economic viability, and family honor (2000: 134).

In the Rwandan genocide, ethnic Tutsis were the population targeted for destruction. Through a system of checkpoints and house-to-house searches, Tutsi men and boys were rounded up, then shot or hacked to death and thrown into mass graves, rivers, latrines, or left to be eaten by dogs and wild animals drawn to the smell of flesh and blood. The decimation of Tutsi women was equally systematic and involved sexual violence, captivity, mutilation, and destruction. Such violence often took place after the women were forced to witness the killing of their husbands and children. Many of the women were killed by their tormenters and disposed of like the men (Nowrojee 1996: 39–40). Others died later of their injuries. Other women were "spared" by their attackers in order to die from having been intentionally infected with HIV-AIDS or left to raise the fatherless children born from the rapes. Other survivors were so severely injured that they were rendered unable to care for themselves physically and economically. Additionally, the attackers often sliced or disfigured their victims to permanently mark the women as having been raped. Given the deep cultural assumption that the women have been made "dirty" by the rapes and that such dirtiness brings dishonor to their families, the disfigurement is a perpetual reminder of their shame and a signal to others to have nothing to do with these women.

Like the "sexual need" and opportunistic systems of rape, the "war-waging" use of rape saddles the victims with shame while casting the deeds of their tormenters as matters of civic duty. In Rwanda the genocide killings and rapes were referred to as "the work" and the workers organized by the same system of local units used for civic projects such as road building and clearing brush. "Clear the remaining brush" was an instruction to search out and annihilate any Tutsis who remained in hiding (Des Forges 1999: 409–13).

The selection of the targets in "war-waging" rape is intentional, as is the rhetorical process by which they are transformed from neighbors, citizens, co-workers, friends, spouses, and extended family members into foreign and dangerous forces requiring control and removal. The intentionality is necessary to make the sexual violence ethically acceptable. The question of whether Tutsi wives of Hutu men could be raped and killed was debated at varying levels of the Rwandan government. Since the women were viewed as belonging to their husbands, in the initial weeks of the genocide some commune burgomasters (mayors) instructed that those women be left alone. According to the burgomaster of Huye commune, "anyone who attacks these women does it as a deliberate provocation because the husband will certainly take vengeance" (Des Forges 1999: 535). Tutsi women who were not officially married to their Hutu male partners were not protected and neither were Tutsi women forced by Hutu men into sexual servitude. "Referring presumably to sexual servitude involving Tutsi women with family ties in the Hutu community or Hutu widows of Tutsi husbands, the councilor of Cyarwa sector, Ngoma commune" described such "unions of couples" as "a form of kidnapping" and "rape" that "could cause much enmity … that could lead far" (Des Forges 1999: 564–5). The enmity would be intra-Hutu. It could be reasoned, since these women were not "wives," the Hutu men would have no legitimate basis for exempting the Tutsi women from the commands to rape and kill. When the effort to achieve total annihilation of Tutsis took hold in Nyakizu in late May (Des Forges 1999: 412–13):

> There were single women who had been forced to cohabit with Hutu men and they were still alive. So there was a meeting in the marketplace ... After that, there were eight children who had been hidden by their grandmother—all eight little grand-children were killed. And the girls married by force, who had accepted in order to have a hiding place, they were killed that night.

Overcoming the normal social and ethical prohibitions and punishments for rape involves both active and tacit sanctioning by governing authorities, educational institutions, religious leaders, and others in authority. In April 1994 Laurent Semanza, burgomaster of Bicumbi commune and a ranking leader of the National Republican Movement for Democracy and Development (MRND), traveled with Paul Bisengimana, burgomaster of Gikoro commune, and three members of the Presidential Guard to Musha to encourage the genocide. Speaking to a local crowd he asked "how far have you gotten with the work?" and urged "You have to kill Tutsi women. You should also rape them to see what they are like" (*Prosecutor v Paul Bisengimana* [1 July 2000] ICTR-2000-60-I ¶3.22).[11] The Rwandan minister of family and women's affairs, Pauline Nyiramasuhuko, not only supervised the slaughter and burning of Tutsis in the town of Butare but gave the instruction "Before you kill the women, you need to rape them" (Landesman 2002). Father Wenceslas Munyeshyaka, the priest in charge of Sainte-Famille parish in Kigali, aided military officials and *Interahamwe* militia in selecting and removing for extermination Tutsi civilians who sought refuge in the church. He aided, abetted, and himself raped Tutsi women and girls in the church, and shot a Tutsi woman and her children. After the genocide ended, Father Munyeshyaka, along with 28 other Hutu Rwandan Catholic priests, wrote to Pope John Paul II explaining the killing of Tutsis as "provoked by the RPF's actions" (*Prosecutor v Wenceslas Munyeshyaka* [20 July 2005] ICTR-2005-87-I ¶11).

In her 1995 discussion of the legal status of war rape in international courts, Rhonda Copelon notes (1995: 200–1):

> Traditionally, rape has been condemned as a violation of a man's honour and exclusive right to sexual possession of his woman/property, rather than an assault on a woman. Today the mass rape in Bosnia is often referred to as the rape of "the enemies' women"—the enemy in this formulation being the male combatant and the seemingly all-male nation or religious or ethnic group. The victim is male, humiliated and emasculated by having failed as both warrior and protector. While this describes a significant patriarchal dimension of rape, it ignores the fact that women, too, are the enemy, and are raped as such.

In the Rwandan genocide Tutsi women were specifically targeted as the enemy. Those who incited and directed the genocide were not focused only on male "honor." They "viewed sexual violence against Tutsi women as an effective method to shame and conquer the Tutsi popula-tion" (Eftekhari 2004: 8). Females were raped as wives, mothers, and potential mothers in a deliberate attempt to block the future for the Tutsi population. Genocide propaganda portrayed Tutsi women (Nowrojee 1996: 18):

as calculated seductress-spies bent on dominating and undermining the Hutu … [and] as beautiful and desirable, but inaccessible to Hutu men whom they allegedly looked down upon and were "too good" for. Rape served to shatter these images by humiliating, degrading, and ultimately destroying the Tutsi woman. … Most of the women interviewed described how their rapists mentioned their ethnicity before or during the rape.

The first of the "Hutu Ten Commandments" published in the December 1990 issue of the Hutu-Power *Kangura* ("Wake Up") warned: "Every Hutu should know that a Tutsi woman, wherever she is, works for the interest of her Tutsi ethnic group." A January 1992 issue blamed Tutsi women for "contributing to the unemployment rate of the Hutu, particularly Hutu women" by "monopolizing positions of employment in both the public and private sectors, hiring their Tutsi sisters … " (Nowrojee 1996: 13). The targeting of Tutsi women for rape and destruction was part of a deliberate strategy to secure Hutu political power, cultural dominance, and economic advantage.

Rhonda Copelon (above) points to the problem of overlooking the women victims of mass rape. Jill Trenholm, Pia Olsson, and Beth Maina Ahlberg point to the necessity of examining "the extent of traumatisation entire communities suffered" (Trenholm et al. 2011: 139). Based on their research on war rape in eastern Democratic Republic of Congo, they note that mass raping "is designed to destroy the very fabric of society through public humiliation, moral destruction and erosion of both mental and physical health and security" (2011: 142–3). The effect upon victims and their communities is "a paralysing sense of powerlessness" (2011: 144).

This brings us back to the murder and sexual assault of Prime Minister Agathe Uwilingiyimana on the morning of 7 April 1994. The prime minister was killed because she had previously resisted the military training and distribution of arms to Hutu militias, supported the power-sharing Arusha Accords, and now stood in the way of the planned extermination of Tutsis that was about to unfold. She was Hutu but for her willingness to work with Tutsis, Hutu-Power propaganda had labeled her "one of the puppets of the Tutsi" (Des Forges 1999: 138) and depicted her in sexual poses with other moderate Hutu politicians (Nowrojee 1996: 172). The sexual assault of Prime Minister Uwilingiyimana revealed a primary strategy in the unfolding campaign to wipe out Tutsis and moderate Hutus. The public humiliation in the exhibiting of the prime minister's body was intended to assert the unquestionable domination of the new regime and quash any thoughts of resistance.

Absalom and David's ten concubines

Utilizing self-promotion, a network of collaborators, and political cunning as brazen as the planners of the genocide in Rwanda, King David's son Absalom "stole the hearts of the people of Israel" (2 Sam 15:6), invited 200 men from Jerusalem to worship with him in Hebron, and before his unsuspecting guests had himself declared king. Absalom enlisted David's own counselor Ahithophel the Gilonite and "the conspiracy grew in strength, and the people with Absalom kept increasing" (2 Sam 15:12). When the news of Absalom's actions reached King David in Jerusalem, David commanded his officials to flee with him. If they remain in the city, he warned, "there will be no escape for us from Absalom" and Absalom will "attack the city with the edge of the sword" (2 Sam 15:14). David did not seem to expect the city to be harmed if he and his officials left. In fact, when the Levitical priests Abiathar and Zadok tried to join the departing entourage and bring the ark of the covenant with them, David told them to return to the city and to take the ark back to Jerusalem (2 Sam 15:25). God's favor and presence, represented by the ark, would remain in the city. David was confident enough that Zadok and Abiathar—though clearly associated with David's reign (e.g., 2 Sam 8:17)—would be able to continue their work under Absalom that he enlisted them and their two sons (Ahimaaz and Jonathan) to act as spies on his behalf.

When David departed Jerusalem "all of his house" (וְכָל־בֵּיתוֹ) went with him (2 Sam 15:16). No specifics are provided in this passage but earlier references to David's "house" mention his wives and concubines, and his sons and daughters (e.g., 2 Sam 3:1–5, 14; 5:13–16). It is logical that they would flee with David as he seeks refuge and establishes residence beyond Absalom's reach. It is critical that David takes them with him since his royal legitimacy, political efficacy, and dynastic future are dependent on the familial alliances, political wisdom, finances, fecundity, and mentoring skills of his wives and concubines, as well as his sons and daughters.

Strangely—and strategically—when David flees Jerusalem, he leaves behind ten concubines "to guard/watch over (שָׁמַר) the house" (2 Sam 15:16). Guarding associated with the verb שָׁמַר involves attentiveness, authority, the fending off of danger, and preserving what is being guarded. In Genesis 2:15, God puts the man in the Garden of Eden to keep/guard/watch over it. In 1 Samuel 7:1, Eleazar is consecrated to keep/guard/watch over the ark of the LORD. In 1 Samuel 26:15 and 16, David taunts Saul's army commander Abner and his troops saying they "deserve to die, because [they] have not kept watch over" Saul.

In each of the three passages where David's ten concubines are specifically mentioned they are described as the ones he left "to guard/watch over the house" (2 Sam 15:16, 16:21, 20:3). The "house" these women are to guard could be the house/palace where David and his household reside (2 Sam 7:1), but the "house" of which they are members and which is now in dispute is the royal house of David, i.e., the Davidic dynasty. Repetition of the descriptor draws attention to the intended role of these women in the battle over royal power launched by Absalom's coup. Like Prime Minister Agathe Uwilingiyimana of Rwanda, these ten women are in positions of political responsibility at the start of a civil war.

The ten women left to guard the house are the first of several persons David assigns to look after matters that could facilitate his return. The priests Abiathar and Zadok are sent back to function as spies (2 Sam 15:24–9). Hushai the Archite is directed to offer a false pledge of loyalty to Absalom in order to defeat the advice David's former counselor Ahithophel might offer to Absalom and to work with Zadok and Abiathar in keeping David informed on matters in Absalom's court (2 Sam 15:32–6). David prays that the LORD will "turn the counsel of Ahithophel into foolishness" (2 Sam 15:31). David indicates that his restoration to kingship in Jerusalem will take place if he finds "favor in the eyes of the LORD" (2 Sam 15:25), but David also takes care to deputize individuals to protect his dynasty and anticipate his return. While the details of how the priests and Hushai are to provide political assistance to David are spelled out in the text, no instructions are given to the ten women assigned to guard the house. Royal houses are always in danger of being toppled by rebellion. Guarding the "house" is the life work of everyone born, married, or brought into the royal household.

That a royal wife might be deputized to look after the royal house in the king's absence is not without historical analogue. The royal archives from Mari, an ancient (*c.*1800 BCE) capital city in the Euphrates Valley region in present-day Syria, provide a window into the personnel, politics, duties, and challenges of maintaining a monarchy and administering a kingdom in the ancient world. The archives contain extensive documentation of correspondence between Queen Šibtu and King Zimrî-Lîm about how to handle matters while the king was away on military campaigns. Two daughters of Zimrî-Lîm were married to Haya-Sumu of Ilan-Ṣura. Unlike the relationship of Zimrî-Lîm and Šibtu, the relationship between one of the daughters, Kirum, and Haya-Sumu became so hostile that Kirum begged her father to arrange her return to Mari. Through one of her father's envoys she reported that previously "Haya-Samu did nothing without me, placing his affairs, all of them before me" (Heimpel 2003: 291), but now "Haya-Samu never cares about me" and because of that "either a woman is killed, or else she falls from a roof" (Heimpel 2003: 292).[12] As bad as the situation was, Haya-Samu may, nevertheless, have planned to use Kirum's connection to Zimrî-Lîm as collateral to ensure his own safety and that of Ilan-Sura from any reprisal from Zimrî-Lîm for insufficient loyalty. According to Kirum, when Haya-Samu was summoned to Mari he told her: "To whom will we leave the city? Stay over here until I return from Mari!" (Heimpel 2003: 492).[13]

Inbatum, another daughter of Zimrî-Lîm, was the principal wife of Atamrum king of Andarig. While Atamrum was at Babylon, Inbatum carried out administrative matters on his behalf involving correspondence with her father. Zimrî-Lîm expected Inbatum's assistance in alerting him to vassals who might be pursuing other alliances. They corresponded concerning the rebellion of the city of Amaz and the unauthorized military intervention of Himdiya (Heimpel 2003: 147).[14] Inbatum detained a group of 30 Assyrian merchants and 60 donkeys who had crossed over into Andarig without authorization and wrote to Zimrî-Lîm for instructions on whether or not to release them (Heimpel 2003: 365).[15] Regarding the detention, Aškur-Addu, king of Karana, accused Inbatum of "set[ting] confusion in the land" (Heimpel 2003: 368).[16] Over the objections of Yasim-El, Zimrî-Lîm's designee to Andarig, Inbatum released the detainees (Heimpel 2003: 368).[17]

Monarchies are complex, dynamic, and highly structured institutions. The Mari archives also illustrate how royal succession and conquest might affect rank and privilege within royal households. When Himdiya succeeded Atamrum as king of Andarig, Atamrum's widow, Inbatum, wrote to Zimrî-Lîm complaining of her loss of royal position: Himdiya "brought in his wife and his earlier (born) sons against (the interest) of my household and your little boys" (Heimpel 2003: 490).[18] Himdiya incorporated Atamrum's household into his own, moved the women "from the capital to a village and deprived her [Inbatum] of all personal attendants" (Heimpel 2003: 160). Not all royal women experienced such a reduction in status at the change of political ruler. Women of Yahdun-Lîm's household were incorporated into the household of his successor Yasmah-Addu. Nele Ziegler reports that one wife of Yahdun-Lîm was appointed as a priestess and some of his daughters "married high officials of Yasmah-Addu or [his successor] Zimrî-Lîm" (1999: 56). Yasmah-Addu arranged to marry one of the daughters of Yahdun-Lîm to the son of Warad-Sîn, a high-ranking noble in the land (Ziegler 1999: 57).

In 2 Samuel 15:16, the ten women remaining in Jerusalem are concubine wives (נָשִׁים פִּלַגְשִׁים) of David. As concubine wives they are not the highest ranked wives in terms of seniority and dynastic succession of sons, but they count alongside David's "wives" in the royal household (2 Sam 19:5) and as mothers of David's sons and daughters (2 Sam 5:13–14). They all have a stake in the continued existence of the Davidic dynasty. In the political economy of the royal house, these women are assets. David's leaving behind ten women signals a significant investment in guarding the "house."

The biblical text suggests that many of David's marriages, as in other ancient Near Eastern dynasties, were made to secure some form of political treaty, strategic family alliance, or regional connection. When Aškur-Addu became king of Karana, he sought support for his rule through an alliance with Zimrî-Lîm secured through marriage. In a message to Zimrî-Lîm, Aškur-Addu reported that the citizens of Karana had urged him to "Seize the coattail of [Zimrî-Lîm]! Do what he says! And let Zimrî-Lîm dispatch his daughter, and let her exercise kingship in Karana!" (Heimpel 2003: 484).[19] David's wives Abigail and Ahinoam were both from southern Judah (1 Sam 25:42–3). Absalom's mother Maacah was the daughter of King Talmai of Geshur (2 Sam 3:3). A daughter's marriage to a foreign king would connect two lands. King Išhi-Addu of Qatna described his daughter Bēltum's marriage to King Yasmah-Addu of Mari as creating a very close connection (Sasson 2010: 246, n.10):[20] "I am placing in your lap my flesh and future, for this throne ('House') has now become yours and Mari's has now become mine."

The biblical text notes that after moving from Hebron to Jerusalem, "David took more concubines and wives" (2 Sam 5:13). It is quite probable that some of those wives and concubines were daughters of leading families of Jerusalem. Andrew Hill suggests that the ten concubines left behind in 2 Samuel 15:16 were "Jebusite ... tokens of an alliance or treaty between David and the residue of the local regime in Jerusalem after its capture by David's mercenaries" (Hill 2006: 135). Hill speculates that David left them behind because "their travels were restricted to the confines of Jerusalem, if not the palace complex" (136). Evidence for travel restrictions is lacking, however, and it does not explain why David leaves them "to guard/watch over the house."

In fleeing Jerusalem David would be wise to take with him wives and concubines with connections to places where he might seek refuge or kingdoms upon whom he might call for military assistance. He could reasonably consider leaving resident lower ranking wives whose familial, political, economic, and religious connections were integral to the acceptance and functioning of the royal house, particularly in Jerusalem.

The ten concubine wives are non-combatants in the civil war. As part of David's house they can be instrumental in preserving that house. They can also become an asset to the usurper, Absalom. In 1 Kings 20:3, King Ben-hadad of Syria leads an international army against King Ahab of Israel, laying siege to the capital Samaria and announcing: "Your silver and gold are mine; your fairest wives and children are also mine." Like silver and gold, wives and children are assets that can be given, sold, invested, or held onto.

In dynastic succession the new king inherits the household of his predecessor. As God says to David, through Nathan, "I anointed you king over Israel, and I rescued you from the hand of Saul; I gave you your master's house, and your master's wives into your bosom" (2 Sam 12:7b-8a). These would include Saul's concubine Rizpah (2 Sam 3:7) and her two sons (2 Sam 21:8). That Rizpah is referred to as "Saul's concubine" long into David's reign suggests not only that she and David are not to be perceived as sexual intimates but that within David's "house" she continues to represent Saul's "house." Many—perhaps most—of the women in the royal house are sexually off-limits to the king. The "house" Solomon inherits at the time of David's death includes his own mother, Bathsheba, any of David's surviving wives and concubines, and perhaps his half-sister Tamar who may have needed a new home after her brother Absalom was killed (2 Sam 13:20b; 18:15).

The combining of houses necessitates a new social ordering of women and children in the blended house and can create some interesting household dynamics. When Zimrî-Lîm took the throne in Mari, it may have been necessary to decide what to do with Bēltum, daughter of Išḫi-Addu of Qatna and wife of Yasmaḫ-Addu, the deposed ruler of Mari. Jack Sasson observes that the relationship between Mari and Qatna would be jeopardized if Bēltum did not receive sufficient honor in Zimrî-Lîm's household but "taking her as a prize wife would have compromised his plans to marry the daughter of Yarim-Addu of Aleppo, a staunch opponent of Qatna" (Sasson 2010: 246).

Sarah Melville notes (2004: 40) that:

> Concubines in Assyrian palaces represented a variety of individual circumstances and relationships, including aging women who had lived with the previous king, women related to the king but without another male protector (aunts or widowed sisters-in-law, for example), women from the household of a defeated king, women who belonged to the entourage of some foreign princess sent to Assyria for diplomatic

marriage, foreign hostages and their companions, and women who were sent to live at the palace by their families in hopes of achieving advancement.

The Hebrew word פִּלֶגֶשׁ that is commonly translated "concubine" is used in a more limited way than the MÍ.ERIM.É.GAL of the Assyrian texts, but the biblical texts assume the reader's familiarity with the kind of diversity and social complexity of royal houses highlighted by Sasson and Melville. Moreover, Absalom can be understood in 2 Samuel to have grown up in this type of royal household and to be familiar with and known to many of the women in it. He might know well some of the concubines David left in Jerusalem "to guard the house."

In the ancient (and contemporary) world royal wives and children can be punished for the actions of royal husbands/fathers. In a Hittite treaty between Muršili II of Ḫattuša and Niqmepà of Ugarit the wives and children of Niqmepà "were held co-responsible in case the Ugaritic king should violate the treaty" (Marsman 2003: 660). Tetlow notes "when the king of Elam ran away from the Assyrians, his mother, wife, and sons surrendered to the Assyrian king" (Tetlow 2004: 171). Some sons of defeated kings might be raised within the Assyrian royal family, learn to be loyal to it, and then be set upon the throne in their homeland as vassal kings (Parpola and Watanabe: 1988: xxi). In the biblical text, King David attempts a redirection of association and loyalty when he insists that Mephibosheth, grandson of King Saul and son of Jonathan, Saul's presumed heir, be incorporated into David's household and seated at his table (2 Sam 9:7), though there is never any indication that Mephibosheth will be given territory to rule. Previously David had reincorporated Michal, Saul's daughter and David's (former) wife, into his household (2 Sam 3: 13–15). As with Mephibosheth, the return of Michal allows David a measure of access to and control over the political and economic authority and networks of the prior king. The continuation of those networks provides some stability and a measure of legitimacy particularly when the successor is a usurper.

Absalom is a usurper. It is an anticipated military confrontation that prompts King David to flee Jerusalem (2 Sam 15:14), yet David leaves in Jerusalem priests to gather information to guard him (2 Sam 15:27–8) and concubine wives to "guard the house" (2 Sam 15:16). When Absalom enters Jerusalem, he is accompanied by David's counselor Ahithophel (2 Sam 16:15) and met by David's "friend" (2 Sam 15:37) Hushai the Archite, whom David had deputized to "defeat … the counsel of Ahithophel" (2 Sam 15:34). There is no mention of any armed resistance to Absalom. It appears to be up to Absalom to determine how to establish his authority and incorporate David's "house" into his.

Strangely, Absalom chooses to violate—not incorporate—the women of David's "house" as he enters Jerusalem. A tent is pitched on the roof for Absalom, and he "went in to his father's concubines in the sight of all Israel" (2 Sam 16:22). A.A. Anderson suggests (1989: 214) that: "the tent was, most likely, the bridal tent (cf. Ps 19:5[4]; Joel 2:16), and the whole proceedings were, more or less, equivalent to a royal wedding (so Stolz 1981: 262) but with wider implications."

The matrimonial association is problematic for a number of reasons. First, it depends on interpreting the tent (אֹהֶל) in 2 Sam 16:22 on the basis of an association made in Psalm 19:4–5 [MT 5–6]:

> [4] In the heavens he has set a tent (אֹהֶל) for the sun,
> [5] which comes out like a bridegroom from his wedding canopy (חֻפָּה)

Joel 2:16 uses the noun חֻפָּה to refer to a bridal chamber but the word "tent" does not appear there. The only other use of חֻפָּה in the biblical text is Isaiah 4:5 where God will create a canopy that "will serve as a pavilion, a shade … a refuge … and a shelter" (Isa 4:6). There is no marital imagery and the word "tent" does not appear.

A biblical passage that does depict the "marriage" of a king and a princess is Psalm 45 in which (vv.13b–15):

> The princess is decked in her chamber with gold-woven robes;
> in many-colored robes she is led to the king;
> behind her the virgins, her companions, follow.
> With joy and gladness they are led along as they enter the palace of the king.

It is a strikingly tender portrait of royal marriage, even in its hint at the sadness the new queen might feel having left "[her] people and [her] father's house" (v. 10). There is nothing in this psalm that is compatible with the description in 2 Sam 16:22 of Absalom having sexual intercourse with ten of his father's wives "upon the roof" and "in the sight of all Israel."

There is nothing normative or customary—in the ancient world, the biblical narrative world, or the modern world—about the public spectacle that Absalom stages. Absalom's behavior here can only be described as rape.

There are elements of comparison between Absalom's spectacle and the sexual violation of Prime Minister Agathe Uwilingiyimana. In the immediate aftermath of the rocket attack that brought down President Habyiramana's plane, the prime minister, though legitimately in charge of watching over the government and broadly connected to different constituencies in the land, was blocked from assuming those responsibilities. She was sexually assaulted, shot, and left uncovered on the ground. The usurpers chose to use sexual violence to underscore their power, command allegiance, and eliminate a targeted portion of the population. They made certain there would be no room for compromise, either on that day or in the weeks to come.

Absalom does not kill his father's concubines, but he, too, chooses to build support for his rebellion—"and the hands of all who are with you will be strengthened" (2 Sam 16:21)—through multiple rapes. The concubines are not elected leaders but they are functionaries in and symbols of the legitimate royal house that Absalom has determined not only to usurp but now signaled his intention to destroy. Absalom's intended audience for his actions is "all Israel." This would include the networks, families, friends, and beneficiaries of the ten concubines in their roles as part of the royal house, and all treaties and alliances connected to them. Walter Brueggemann observes that Ahithophel's advice to Absalom "is ruthless and daring but also realistic. He understands that the seizure of the symbols of power is a blatant, risky gesture, but likely to gain support from the people" (Brueggemann 1990: 310).

In the Rwandan conflict, the orders to rape came from the Hutu-Power leaders and flowed through the political chain of command. "Reasoned" excuses and brute force overcame ethical hesitance to participation. In 2 Samuel, authority for Absalom's treatment of David's concubines would appear to come directly from God: "Now in those days the counsel that Ahithophel gave was as if one consulted the oracle of God; so all the counsel of Ahithophel was esteemed, by both David and by Absalom" (2 Sam 16:23). Earlier in the narrative, when David learned that Ahithophel was conspiring with Absalom, David prayed: "O LORD … turn the counsel of Ahithophel into foolishness" (2 Sam 15:31). Regarding Absalom's treatment of the concubines, one must ask whether it is "as if one consulted the oracle of God" or if it is foolishness regarded as esteemed counsel.

On the matter of David's concubines, Absalom does not question Ahithophel's advice. Absalom's high regard for Ahithophel's counsel, however, does not stop him from summoning Hushai for a second opinion regarding a strategy for pursuing David (2 Sam 17:5). Ahithophel's counsel to pursue David that night was right/pleasing (יָשָׁר) in the eyes of Absalom and all the elders of Israel (2 Sam 17:4), but Absalom and the men of Israel decided Hushai's advice was better (2 Sam 17:14a). The narrator reveals to the reader that Ahithophel's advice was "the good counsel" but through Hushai "the LORD had ordained to defeat the good counsel of Ahithophel, so that the LORD might bring ruin on Absalom" (2 Sam 17:14b).

In the Rwandan genocide, the rape of Tutsi women was often justified as retribution for harms categorically suffered by Hutus, including "that Tutsi women were 'working for the interest of their Tutsi ethnic group' and threatened to steal the jobs and husbands of Hutu women" (Hogg 2010: 87). A retributive lens is also frequently applied to Absalom's treatment of his father's concubines. Absalom becomes the instrument of divine retribution, punishing David for despising God and taking "the wife of Uriah the Hittite to be [his] wife" (2 Sam 12:10b).

> Thus says the LORD: "I will raise up trouble against you from within your own house; and I will take your wives before your eyes, and give them to your neighbor, and he shall lie with your wives in the sight of this very sun. For you did it secretly; but I will do this thing before all Israel, and before the sun." (2 Sam 12:11–12)

Yahweh's announcement to David is similar in form to the divine retribution the Assyrian king Esarhaddon summons upon treaty violators: "May Venus, the brightest of the stars, before your eyes make your wives lie in the lap of your enemy … " (Parpola and Watanabe 1988: 46 §42). Absalom's actions in 2 Samuel 16:22 can be seen as David's punishment. Ken Stone suggests (2006: 217–18):

> Absalom's sexual activity with the concubines of his father constitutes a sort of message to other male Israelites, in whose eyes Absalom hopes to shame David by demonstrating publicly David's inability to control sexual access to the women of David's household. Within the games and power struggles of manhood, as "manhood" is understood in the ancient Mediterranean and Near Eastern world, such a demonstration amounts to a kind of symbolic castration.

This shaming perspective fits into the retributive lens of 2 Samuel 12:10–14, in which God declares that David will be powerless to protect his house, his wives, and his child.

When read apart from the lens of 2 Samuel 12, 2 Samuel 16:20–3 offers another perspective on shame and powerlessness. In the passage Absalom's stated intention is to "make [himself] odious to [his] father" (2 Sam 16:21). Absalom lies with ten of his father's wives, not "before [David's] eyes" (2 Sam 12:11) but "in the sight of all Israel" (2 Sam 16:22). All eyes in 2 Samuel 16 are directed to Absalom's violation of the ten concubine wives responsible for guarding the house. It is the women who are powerless. In the conventions of ancient Near Eastern royal protocols, the politics of David's marriages, and contemporary civil order, Absalom's behavior is truly odious.

Absalom's public attack on the ten concubines was intended not just to strengthen the hands of "all who are with [him]" but to signal victory over all who were not. As Claudia Card has noted (1996: 7):

> The activity of martial rape, often relatively public, can serve as a bonding agent among perpetrators and at the same time work in a variety of ways to alienate family members, friends, and former neighbors from each other, as in cases where the perpetrators had been friends or neighbors of those they later raped.

The names of the concubine wives Absalom rapes are not listed in the text but their familial connection to Absalom is stressed through the repeated mention of their relationship to David and their responsibility for guarding his house (2 Sam 15:16; 16:21, 22). Absalom and the women have been members of the same house.

In the narratives of the Hebrew Bible, the rape of women can become a summons to war, e.g., the rape of Dinah in Genesis 34 and the rape of the Levite's concubine in Judges 19 (see Keefe 1993). Absalom had previously used the rape of his sister Tamar by their half-brother Amnon as reason to enlist his servants to kill Amnon (2 Sam 13:28–9). Now by his own acts of rape Absalom seeks support for his attack on his father's house. If Absalom's political use of rape is to be effective, "all Israel" must no longer see what Absalom holds in common with his father's concubines, and no foe can be allowed to use Absalom's rapes as cause to advance his/her own political agenda, as Absalom had done in claiming to avenge the rape of Tamar.

Absalom's coup eventually fails and Absalom's body, speared three times in the heart by Joab and beaten to death by ten armor-bearers, is hastily thrown into a forest pit and covered with a pile of rocks (2 Sam 18:9–17). As David makes his way back to Jerusalem he rewards with forgiveness and favor those who had cursed him (2 Sam 19:16–23), likely conspired against him (2 Sam 19:24–30), and openly backed Absalom (2 Sam 19:9–10); but when he arrives at "his house at Jerusalem," he takes the ten concubines whom he had left to guard the house (לִשְׁמֹר הַבָּיִת) and puts them in a guarded house (בֵּית־מִשְׁמֶרֶת). David "provided for them, but did not go in to them" (2 Sam 20:3a). David, who had insisted on reclaiming Michal from her husband Paltiel (2 Sam 3:14–16) for his house, without incarcerating her (2 Sam 6:20), leaves the ten concubines "shut up until the day of their death, living as if in widowhood" (2 Sam 20:3b).

David's concubines and the survivors of rape

No reason is given in the biblical text for David's confinement of the concubine wives he left to guard the house. Their isolation from their family and rejection by their husband—after having been attacked while guarding his house—is shocking, though, tragically, not unlike the experience of women who survived rapes in the Rwandan civil conflict. Many Rwandan rape survivors have been rejected by their families and ostracized by their communities. Women who have not revealed their experience of sexual assault fear doing so because of the rejection, the assumption that they carry the HIV-AIDS virus, the unwillingness of men to marry them, and the poverty and isolation that accompany such rejection. David's concubines have two things most survivors of conflict rape do not: secure shelter and economic security. Their widowhood, as described in the biblical text, however, echoes that of the Rwandan widows: "We are not understood by society … Widows are without families … We are the living dead" (Nowrojee 1996: 73).

The pernicious genius of the political use of rape is its ability to simultaneously disempower and obscure its multiple victims (Nowrojee 1996: 2):

> The humiliation, pain and terror inflicted by the rapist is meant to degrade not just the individual woman but also to strip the humanity from the larger group of which she is a part. The rape of one person is translated into an assault upon the community …

It is not clear in the biblical text whether Joab is including the ten concubines who remained in Jerusalem when he recounts the sons and daughters, wives and concubines whose lives were delivered by David's officers, but it is clear that Joab berates David, as he mourns the death of Absalom, for David's failure to acknowledge what the larger community has suffered and sacrificed in the civil war (2 Sam 19:5–6 [MT 6–7]). Joab instructs David to "go out at once and speak kindly to your servants" (2 Sam 19:7 [MT 8]). David takes his seat in the gate. He never does acknowledge the suffering and sacrifice of his ten concubine wives. Ahithophel had suggested that Absalom's rape of his father's concubines would make Absalom odious to his father, but David displays no such reaction.

In both the biblical narrative and the Rwandan context, the women who are sexually victimized in the struggle over the house/the nation find themselves put out of the house. Their abandonment and rejection have recognizable roots in cultural, political, and religious assumptions about masculinity, purity, sexuality, shame, and power. In the Rwandan context the abandonment and rejection are exacerbated by limited resources for addressing the disease, dislocation, poverty, and trauma resulting from the victimization.

What is striking in the accounts of the Rwandan genocide and the biblical account of Absalom's treatment of his father's concubine wives is that, in both, the leaders and perpetrators speak openly about what they are doing: Hutu men and women gave orders to rape; Ahithophel advised Absalom to "go in to [his] father's concubines." In contrast, the community and the victims are silent. The reason for the silence in the biblical passage is unknown. There is a pervasive, cross-cultural reluctance on the part of victims and on the part of their communities to speak of rape, the circumstances that surround it, and its consequences. In Rwanda and other places where rape has been and continues to be used as a strategy in conflict, victims are silent not only because of the shame that is directed to them, but out of fear of reprisal from perpetrators and their family members who continue to live in the community, guilt for having survived when so many were killed, despair over being infected with HIV-AIDS, and determination not to let the rapes cut off their chance for marriage and family.

The biblical text makes no comment when Absalom rapes David's concubines and when David puts the concubines in a guarded house, but it does supply evidence for two judgments:

1   The narrative identifies Absalom and David as the ones who bring dishonor.

    Absalom makes himself odious (2 Sam 16:21) and David brings shame on those who rescued his life (2 Sam 19:5 [MT 6]). In neither their rape nor their rejection are the ten concubines described as shamed or as having brought dishonor upon anyone.

2   David's kingship has returned to Jerusalem but it is not as kingship should be.

    Regarding the "widowhood" of David's concubines, Suzanne Scholz poses the question "Why would the women want to be with any man, including David, who had abandoned them earlier?" She suggests to readers that "Perhaps they should rather be viewed as being relieved; they are finally left alone" (Scholz 2010: 79). The freedom to live in safety that Scholz envisions for the women in the narrative is something to be desired for all women who have been victims of rape. In Rwanda, there are groups of women victims of rape who live together and care for one another. For many, however, this arrangement is a result of the unwillingness and/or the inability of their own households to embrace and care for them. David's enclosure of the ten concubines is akin to this unwillingness.

    The text makes it clear that David does not resume sexual relations with any of the ten concubines ("[he] did not go in to them"). The text goes further. It describes the women "living as if in widowhood." If they are widows, then it is David as husband who must be declared dead. Moreover, in the ancient Near East and in the Bible, widows symbolized and are counted among those persons who are socially, economically, and judicially vulnerable. Widows were among those persons kings bore special responsibility for defending. The Babylonian king Hammurabi declares in the epilogue of his law code that he has set out these laws so "that the strong might not injure the weak, in order to protect the widows and orphans." In the biblical psalms the model for such protection is God, who is described in Psalm 68:5 as "Father of orphans and protector of widows." Kings were to use their power for the protection of those in need. In 2 Samuel 14 David is prepared to give orders for the protection of a woman who has come to him as a widow to ask for his help in preserving the life of her last living son. By describing David's concubines in 2 Samuel 20:3 as "living as if in widowhood," the text invites readers to judge how well these ten women have been defended by the newly returned king.

These judgments do not change the outcome for the concubines in the biblical narrative, but they press readers to consider who are the authors of dishonor, and who are the intended beneficiaries of the duty to defend.

In closing

In the biblical text Absalom chooses to advance his political ambitions through rape, a strategy also adopted by Hutu-Power leaders in Rwanda. The seemingly unstoppable horror of "war-waging" rape in so many places across the globe today compels this paper's consideration of ancient texts that narrate, boast of, or justify rape, as well as those that pass it by in silence. There are striking similarities between the ancient and modern worlds in how conflict rape is utilized and how it terrorizes. It is also abundantly clear that rape is a chosen—not inevitable—strategy in civil conflict.

The testimonies of individuals and communities victimized by conflict rape continue to reveal the processes and rhetoric by which such a strategy becomes "natural," "necessary," and organized. They also point to the need to lift the silence and the burden of shame off victims, hold perpetrators accountable for their deeds, and put defense of the vulnerable at the center of civic life.

This paper's examination of the narrative of David's ten concubine wives in 2 Samuel discerns ancient biblical resonances with the identified contemporary needs. It recognizes the concubines' role as guardians of the "house" and their rape as an attack on the nation, akin to the targeting and sexual violation of Prime Minister Agathe Uwilingiyimana and Tutsi women in the Rwandan genocide. In the absence of voices of protest in the 2 Samuel narrative, it identifies textual resistance to the dishonorable way the concubines were treated by Absalom and the widowhood imposed by David. In these ways this paper attempts to encourage readers of the 2 Samuel narrative to resist the "logic" of the use of rape in contemporary conflicts, and to honor and care for those who are its victims.

Notes

1 The testimony gathered by Human Rights Watch indicates "Witnesses who came to the house soon after [she had been shot] found her nearly naked body on the terrace and carried it into the house. Another witness who passed an hour or so later found that her dressing gown had been thrown up over her upper body and that a beer bottle had been shoved into her vagina" (Des Forges 1999: 190).
2 BM 124927. See Parpola and Watanabe 1988: 47, fig. 13.

3 BM 124801a.
4 Biblical citations are from the *NRSV*. Translations of some phrases are the author's.
5 AO 101.1.
6 WA 124801.
7 WA 124801.
8 ME 124920.
9 Rwandan Patriotic Front, the Uganda-based movement formed by diaspora Tutsis and some Hutus, politically and militarily challenging the government of President Habyarimana.
10 For an extensive review of militarized prostitution see Cynthia Enloe's chapter on "The Prostitute, the Colonel, and the Nationalist" (2000: 49–107).
11 The context and details are in *Prosecutor v Laurent Semanza* [15 May 2003] ICTR-97-20-T ¶252, ¶253.
12 Text 26 304.
13 Text 10 34+.
14 Text 10 84 (Heimpel 2003: 492).
15 Texts 26 432 and 26 433.
16 Text 26 436.
17 Text 26 436.
18 Text 10 29+.
19 Text 6 26.
20 A.3518.

Bibliography

Anderson, A.A. (1989) *2 Samuel*, Word Biblical Commentary, vol. 11. Dallas, TX: Word Books.
Baaz, M.E. and Stern, M. (2009) "Why do soldiers rape? Masculinity, violence, and sexuality in the armed forces in the Congo (DRC)", *International Studies Quarterly* 53: 495–518.
Brueggemann, W. (1990) *First and Second Samuel*, Interpretation. Louisville, KY: John Knox Press.
Card, C. (1996) "Rape as a weapon of war", *Hypatia* 11(4): 5–18.
Copelon, R. (1995) "Gendered war crimes: Reconceptualizing rape in time of war", in J. Peters and A. Wolper (eds) *Women's Rights, Human Rights: International Feminist Perspectives*. New York: Routledge, pp. 197–214.
Des Forges, A. (1999) *"Leave None to Tell the Story": Genocide in Rwanda*, 2nd edn. New York: Human Rights Watch.
Eftekhari, S. (2004) *Struggling to Survive: Barriers to Justice for Rape Victims in Rwanda*. New York: Human Rights Watch.
Enloe, C. (2000) *Maneuvers: The International Politics of Militarizing Women's Lives*. Berkeley, CA: University of California Press.
Grayson, A.K. (1991) *Assyrian Rulers of the Early First Millennium BC, I (1114–859 BC)*, Royal Inscriptions of Mesopotamia, Assyrian Periods 2. Toronto, ON: Toronto University Press.
Hammurabi, Law Code of, trans. 1915 L.W. King. Available online at <http://www.fordham.edu/halsall/ancient/hamcode.asp> (accessed 22 July 2013).
Heimpel, W. (2003) *Letters to the King of Mari: A New Translation with Historical Introduction, Notes, and Commentary*, Mesopotamian Civilizations, vol. 12. Winona Lake, IN: Eisenbrauns.
Hill, A.E. (2006) "On David's 'taking' and 'leaving' concubines (2 Samuel 5:13; 15:16)", *Journal of Biblical Literature* 125(1): 129–50.
Hogg, N. (2010, March) "Women's participation in the Rwandan genocide: Mothers or monsters?", *International Review of the Red Cross* 92(877): 69–102.
Keefe, A.A. (1993) "Rapes of women/wars of men", *Semeia* 61: 79–97.
Landesman, P. (2002) "A woman's work", *New York Times Magazine*. Available online at <http:www.nytimes.com/2002/09/15/magazine/a-woman-s-work.html> (accessed 15 May 2012).
Marsman, H.J. (2003) *Women in Ugarit and Israel: Their Social and Religious Position in the Context of the Ancient Near East*, Oudtestamentische Studiën, vol. 49. Atlanta, GA: Society of Biblical Literature.
Melville, S.C. (2004) "Neo-Assyrian royal women and male identity: Status as a social tool", *Journal of the American Oriental Society* 124(1): 37–57.
Nowrojee, B. (1996) *Shattered Lives: Sexual Violence during the Rwandan Genocide and Its Aftermath*. New York: Human Rights Watch.

Organization of African Unity (OAU) (2000) *Rwanda: The Preventable Genocide*. Available online at <http://www.africa-union.org/official_documents/reports/Report_Rowanda_Genocide.pdf> (accessed 20 July 2013).

Parpola, S. and Watanabe, K. (1988) *Neo-Assyrian Treaties and Loyalty Oaths*, State Archives of Assyria, vol. 2. Helsinki: Helsinki University Press.

Prosecutor v Augustin Ndindiliyimana, Augustin Bizimungu, François-Xavier Nzuwonemeye, Innocent Sagahutu [2011, 17 May] ICTR-00-56-T.

Prosecutor v Laurent Semanza [2003, 15 May] ICTR-97-20-T.

Prosecutor v Paul Bisengimana [2000, 1 July] ICTR-2000-60-I.

Prosecutor v Wenceslas Munyeshyaka [2005, 20 July] ICTR-2005-87-I.

Reade, J.E. (1979) "Ideology and propaganda in Assyrian art", in M.T. Larsen (ed.) *Power and Propaganda: A Symposium on Ancient Empires*. Copenhagen: Akademisk Forlag, pp. 329–43.

Russell, J.M. (1991) *Sennacherib's Palace without Rival at Nineveh*. Chicago, IL: University of Chicago Press.

Sasson, J.M. (2010) "On the 'Ishi-Addu' seal from Qatna with comments on Qatna personnel in the OB period", in S. Dönmez (ed.) *Veysel Donbaz'a Sunulan Yazilar, DUB.SAR.ÉDUB.BA.A: Studies Presented in Honour of Veysel Donbaz*. Istanbul: Ege Publications, pp. 243–50.

Scholz, S. (2010) *Sacred Witness: Rape in the Hebrew Bible*. Minneapolis, MN: Fortress Press.

Stolz, F. (1981) *Das erste und zweite Buch Samuel*, ZBKAT, vol. 9. Zürich: Theologischer Verlag.

Stone, K. (2006) "1 and 2 Samuel", in D. Guest, R.E. Goss, M. West, and T. Bohache (eds) *The Queer Bible Commentary*. London: SCM Press, pp. 195–221.

Tetlow, E.M. (2004) *Women, Crime, and Punishment in Ancient Law and Society, Volume 1: The Ancient Near East*. New York: Continuum.

Trenholm, J.E., Olsson, P., and Ahlberg, B.M. (2011) "Battles on women's bodies: War, rape and traumatisation in eastern Democratic Republic of Congo", *Global Public Health: An International Journal for Research, Policy and Practice* 6(2): 139–52.

Turshen, M. (2000) "The political economy of violence against women during armed conflict in Uganda", *Social Research* 67(3): 803–24.

Ziegler, N. (1999) "A questionable daughter-in-law", *Journal of Cuneiform Studies* 51: 55–9.

4

FROM HORSE KISSING TO BEASTLY EMISSIONS

Paraphilias in the Ancient Near East

Roland Boer

On the sexual deviancy hierarchy, it's widely held that bestiality is worse than humping your relatives.[1]

Sex with sheep, horses, and donkeys – surely the ban on bestiality is universal, much like the incest taboo. Fortunately, in the Ancient Near East (ANE), this is not quite the case. I propose to explore some of the manifestations of bestiality in this context, with a particular focus on the ancient Mesopotamians, Hittites, and then the Hebrews. To that examination I propose to add necrophilia, so that my study properly concerns paraphilias.[2] Or rather, I deal with texts containing rituals and laws, which have their own well-known limitations concerning the troubled and complex connections between textual representation and real life. Always to be kept in mind is that these texts are literary creations first, the work of scribes with their imaginations. In what follows, I seek to exploit their imaginations as I deal with a couple of ancient Mesopotamian texts, then more extensively with the Hittite laws, and then the Hebrew Bible.[3]

Before proceeding, let me define bestiality, which in today's usage refers primarily to sexual acts between human beings and animals. However, older meanings of bestiality include "the instinct of beasts" and the "beast signs" in astrology. If one was, in the Middle Ages, showing signs of bestiality it meant not that all furry beasts in the area need watch their rear ends, but that one was behaving like a beast. For terminological specificity, the terms *zoosexuality* or *zooerasty* have been used to refer to sex between human beings and other animals. *Zoophilia* may refer to affections for and relations with animals that are not sexual.[4] Nonetheless, since bestiality has become the term in common usage since the seventeenth century, I use it here.

Babylonians

The first moment in this survey stops briefly with the Babylonians of the second millennium. Given that sheep and goats formed the basis (as far as fauna are concerned) of the sacred economy in the ANE, one would expect creative uses of such animals. That is, every conceivable part of the animal was used, and the animals performed all manner of functions. Some would be expected – fiber, milk, meat, bones – but others less so. For instance, if a woman quarreled with her man, she could seek to overcome his anger by knifing a sheep, touching its death wound, holding a magnet in her right hand and an iron boat in the left – along with the necessary prayer to the goddess Ishtar. Why? Her man's anger would be as dead as the sheep and he would, like the iron boat, find her magnetism simply irresistible.[5]

More intriguing is the ritual for the man who, in a moment of introspection, suddenly suffers a twinge of regret for intercourse with a goat. Yes, there is a ritual for this too:

> You take hair from the she-goat. On the roof, before Shamash [the sun-god], you tie up a virgin she-goat and you take hair from a she-goat whose hair and body are red. You lay them out before the virgin she-goat and pour a libation of beer over them.

Of course one wonders why, but it may well be that the opposition between one's recent dalliance and the goat with whom one has not copulated, along with the opposition between the colors red and white (hair from the respective goats), all point to the wish for putting the recent affair behind one.

The instructions continue:

> You tie that hair up in a linen cloth. You put it on the ground before Shamash. You kneel on it and say as follows … You say this three times and report your doings and then prostrate yourself. You throw that linen cloth into the gate of a beer distributor and after fifteen days you remove it. The gain of the beer distributor will be diminished but the omen will stand to one side and its evil will not approach the man and his household.[6]

Why a beer distributor? Not only was beer a crucial product of agriculture, perhaps one of the reasons why human beings gathered together in the first place, but it may also be due to the fact that the goddess Ishtar was the patron of beer, goats, and sex.

A question that arises from such a text is whether it was an exercise in theoretical jurisprudence or an actual law. Scholars have been divided over such an issue concerning ANE law in general,[7] although in this case there is further incentive for those who take the position that such "laws" are theoretical exercises, since the proposed law may be seen as the product of a slightly depraved, albeit morally upright, legal scribe. At least the law fits in with the assumed moral codes of the few scholars who deal with such matters, namely, that the people of ANE shared the modern abhorrence of bestiality. Not so the omen of the horse-kisser.

In the list of omens in the Cuneiform Texts in the Kuyunjik Collection at the British Museum, one stumbles across the following: if a man ejaculates into a horse and then kisses it afterwards, it is a *good omen*. Apart from imagining the intricacies of horse-kissing while the plumbing is still connected, and speculating on whether the benefit of the omen lies in the timing of the kiss (is it a bad omen if he kisses the horse beforehand?), it is worth noting that this is very much a man-made omen. Unlike most omens, one may create this omen for oneself … unless of course you happen to stumble across another hippophiliac at work.

What are we to do with this omen? It clearly does not fit into accepted modern codes of sexual behavior, so much so that its ethical assumptions are enough to make an upright scholar squirm. A case in point is JoAnn Scurlock, who appears to be slightly unsettled by the relaxed approach of some of our civilizational forebears to matters sexual and bestial. Having reported on our horse-loving Babylonian, she offers this twisted assessment:

This would appear to be an endorsement; however, behavioral omens inhabit an amoral universe where the only calculation is of whether anything about the behavior could be interpreted as being of benefit or harm to the solicitor of the omen. It does not follow that good-omened behavior is necessarily desirable or even legal.[8]

I must admit to being mightily puzzled by the sheer absence of logic here. How is a collection of omens amoral, especially when the purpose of such omens is to ensure benefit or harm? And how can good-omened behavior not be desirable? The presence of bestiality does seem to unsettle the normal processes of logic.

Hittites

Nonetheless, the question remains as to whether such behavior was legal. In order to find out, let us now turn to the Hittites, from the second millennium. Given the strong sense of felt continuity in the ANE, manifested – among many examples – in copying law codes over millennia, and in at least the sense that one was restoring what had declined earlier, the Hittites may be able to answer the question I raised earlier concerning the Babylonians. In the Hittite laws we find the following:

> 187 If a man has sexual relations with a cow, it is an unpermitted sexual pairing;[9] he will be put to death …
> 188 If a man has sexual relations with a sheep, it is an unpermitted sexual pairing; he will be put to death …
> 199 If anyone has sexual relations with a pig or a dog, he shall die … If an ox leaps on a man (in sexual excitement), the ox shall die; the man shall not die. They shall substitute one sheep for the man and put it to death. If a *pig leaps on a man (in sexual excitement), it is not an offense.*
> 190 If they [have sexual relations] *with the dead* – man, woman – it is not an offense …
> 200 If a man has sexual relations with *either a horse or a mule, it is not an offense* … [10]

The obvious and initial point is that horses and mules, aroused oxen and pigs, and the dead are more liberated sexually among the Hittites. I would like to explore what the Hittites permitted and what they did not, but before I do so, a few general details concerning these laws: they date from the Old Hittite Period (*c.*1650–1500 BCE) and were then copied through to the thirteenth century. Some of the laws have undergone revision over time, but generally not in the case of sexual matters. Unlike laws elsewhere in the ANE (including the Hebrew Bible), there is no principle of *lex talionis* in these Hittite laws, nor do they claim to have a divine origin (rather astonishing, given the way religion permeated nearly every aspect of Hittite life). In other respects, these laws are similar to other ANE collections: many of them are case laws, and they do not pretend to be comprehensive (there are 200). Further, scholars remain nonplussed by the apparent lack of organization among the laws, seeking to identify some pattern, while admitting that whatever pattern one might find, it is not perfect.[11] I leave those debates aside as so much avoidance by scholars of the far more enticing issue of sexual practices.

What were the unacceptable sexual practices relating to non-human animals among the Hittites? From the laws it is obvious that becoming intimate with one's sheep, cow,[12] dog, or pig was out of the question – although if the ox or pig took the initiative since it found you were quite hot, then the law lets you off the hook. Indeed, the issue of the pig immediately raises what may appear to be a contradiction: one may not initiate sex with a pig, but it is fine if the pig should mount you. Penetration is clearly in question: penetrating a pig (given that a "man" is addressed) is unacceptable, but being penetrated by a pig causes less concern.[13]

The ox raises a slightly more delicate issue, for even though it is an offense for an ox to mount a man, the man in question is not to be killed (unlike the deviant ox). Instead, with a hint of the Christian theological doctrine of substitutionary atonement, a lamb is led to the slaughter to take the punishment for him. On a more general level, one gains the clear impression of a thoroughly agricultural society, in which there is an everyday possibility that an ox or a pig – two of the key animals domesticated in the ANE by human beings – might take a fancy to you as you bend over to perform some menial chore on the land. In a situation where labor was chronically short, it would be a waste of human beings to do away with yet another one every time such a connection of the plumbing occurred. However, the laws are less keen on the image of a randy farmer going about penetrating at will any and all of his domesticated animals – except of course horses, mules, and the dead.

These are precisely the exceptions that are so fascinating. Why were these sexual acts sanctioned, as not an offense against the gods? The few who have noted these laws are puzzled, since one would expect that the assumed codes of pollution applied here as they are supposed to have done with the sheep, pigs, and cows. Yet, a tortured sentence by Collins points to at least two possible reasons for the exception that applies to horses and their cousins: "The indemnification of the equids probably has less to do with a perverse fondness on the part of the Hittites for their horses than with the distinct status of the equids among the domesticates."[14] Obviously not comfortable with the topic – her prose is usually lucid and engaging – Collins disavows one reason and postulates another. I would suggest both apply: Hittites, particularly the men in question, *were* perversely fond of their horses, just as they were perversely fond of their wives and the dead. Given that Hittite men undertook campaigns when there were threats to the empire – that is, just about every year – and that they spent long periods of time away from home, the horse would have become like a wife on the road (as long as one avoided fellatio).[15]

But Collins's other reason is also important: the "equids" (horses, mules, donkeys) did have a different status from the other domesticated animals. They had, to put it in terms I will explore more fully later, a distinct role within the extended Hittite family. Not only were the Hittites among the first to make extensive use of the horse for burden and warfare, but the care for and training of a horse became a comprehensive, detailed, and much-loved pastime – as indicated by the training manual for a chariot horse written by one Kikkuli from *c.*1345 BCE.[16] The massed and disciplined Hittite chariotry was widely feared, although perhaps for more reasons – fear for their own horses and mules perhaps – than are usually adumbrated. For example, the Egyptians depicted this central feature of the Hittite military with great care, noting especially three men in the chariot, one a driver, one an archer, and one to protect both of them.[17] In short, not only did horses have an elevated status, especially for males who had the time and opportunity to devote themselves to a horse, but Hittite and horse became terms of automatic association (see 1 Kings 10:20 and 2 Chronicles 1:17).

If the horse was the beast of glory, the mount, companion, and soul mate of the charioteer on campaign, the mule or donkey was the beast of everyday labor. Plainer, smaller, and less glamorous than its stately and graceful cousin, the mule was sturdier and more reliable, less given to fits of temper, jealousy, and petulance and much more patient in the face of quotidian drudgery. The Hittite sentiment may be expressed in a saying that should have been: a horse for the road and a mule and a wife at home, what more can a man want? Admittedly, there is the curious qualification in regard to the horse and mule: the man who happened to insert his member into an equid must not approach the king or become a priest.[18] The suggestion that this was to avoid pollution of the king or priesthood seems rather lame; why say such an act was not an offense if it was polluting? Instead, I would suggest that since it was not an offense, the man need not approach the king for judgment. Further, since humping one's horse was the sign of total commitment to a vocation, it would be unconscionable to have such a man give up his vocation in order to become a priest.

What about the dead? Note the gender inclusiveness of this law: it matters not whether one takes a fancy to a male or female corpse. It may be possible that the text refers to a man or a woman having sex with a corpse: in that case, given the physical arrangements of body parts on male and female mammals, one may assume that a woman might avail herself of that brief period of rigor mortis, of penis, fingers, toes, and so on – unless we allow the very real possibilities of penetrative necrophilia by women as well.[19] In this case, both male and female corpses have orifices into which all manner of items might be worked with a little lubrication.

The opportunity for such acts was obviously briefer with cremations – the preferred option for the ruling class – than burials, either in a grave or in a large jar. From what can be ascertained from the archaeological and written materials, Hittite funerary and especially mortuary practices were elaborate and detailed.[20] For a king or queen, the funeral ran over fourteen days, with the body cremated at the end of the second day. Sacrifices and feasting followed, with the construction of an image of the diseased made of figs, olives, and raisins. Obviously, the opportunity for a last moment of passion was brief. Perhaps it was less appropriate on the first day, when an ox was slaughtered and placed at the feet of the dead royal, and when a goat was swung over the body to purify it. The second day was another matter, for now food offerings and libations were made to the gods who would receive the king's spirit. In that party atmosphere, the moment would be right for a comprehensive romp with the royal body, a last send-off to ensure that the seeds of new life may accompany him or her to the next world.[21]

By contrast, the common people had more fun, for they preferred burial. In this situation, any time was a good time, especially after a few beers and much feasting, to show one's love one last time … or two or even three last times. If the border between life and death was a fluid one, then one might from time to time pass some fluids across that border. It is worth noting that the dead were often buried with an ox, pig, sheep, goat, dog, horse, or mule.[22] This of course raises the question as to exactly which of these dead animals might be blessed with the good graces of their master. I would suggest that what applied in life applied to the dead: no pigs, cows, or dogs, but certainly one's wife, horse, or mule.

To conclude, most of the laws concern the Hittite male, at least a Hittite male of reasonable means. His wife, horse, donkey, and the dead were all within the range of acceptable sexual partners. Some laws mention both women and men, explicitly with the dead and implicitly concerning a pig or a dog. From the perspective of the one initiating sex, the active agent seems to have held a higher status within the network of Hittite life; from the perspective of the one on the receiving end, to be selected by the man (and less often the woman) of the house was thereby a sign of one's elevated status. For a man it may have been a wife and mule at home, a horse on campaign, and then the dead when one was thinking about one's own mortality. A woman seems to have had less range, restricted to pondering her own short life and thereby engaging with the dead in more ways than one.

I have, however, slipped into a common approach when dealing with laws – selecting a few that fit a category familiar to us and analyzing them as though they were also part of a category coherent to the framers and users of those ancient laws. In my case, I have – thus far – isolated the laws concerning bestiality and necrophilia and treated them as distinct. Yet, when we consider these laws in their context, they are part of a larger collection of Hittite laws concerning what one does with one's genitals, although the laws mostly assume a male as the subject: one must not have sex with one's mother, daughter, son, with two sisters and their mother,[23] a living brother's wife, a wife's daughter by another man, or a wife's mother or sister (Laws nos. 189, 191, 195). Even here we face a challenge, since the first three – mother, daughter, son – are what we would usually call consanguineous incest, but not the remainder. Add to this the prohibition of sex with a cow, sheep, dog, or pig (where one should happen to penetrate one of our porcine cousins rather than be penetrated by one) and we have a very different sexual economy. In other words, mother, cow, daughter, sheep, son, dog, two sisters and their mother, pig, a living brother's wife, and so on, all belong to the same group: one (a man) should not penetrate them with his penis. If we wish to continue to use the term "incest," we will need to stretch it considerably to fit quite a number of unexpected items, well beyond Lévi-Strauss's great and already accommodating text on the universality of the incest taboo.[24]

It should be obvious where my argument is headed (that family, gens, or clan in the Hittite world extended well beyond its human limitations); but what of the other group of permitted sexual activities? One may have sex with a horse, a donkey, or the dead. But one may also have sex with one's stepmother if your father is dead, two sisters who do not live in the same country,[25] the sister of your deceased wife, sisters or mother or daughter who are slaves; or father and son may have sex with the same slave or prostitute, or indeed two brothers with a free woman (Laws nos. 191–4). Once again, an extraordinary list in which – in the perpetual tension between identity and difference in relation to ancient societies – the Hittites become even more different from our own context.[26]

The few who have analyzed the rather different approach to sex in these laws have usually opted to see them in terms of pollution and purity,[27] but I am interested in another issue entirely, namely, the tendency for these laws to deal with what can only be called group sex. In the number of condoned sexual acts, note how many concern sexual multiples – threesomes, foursomes, and on and on. So we find what are known in the business as FFM (two sisters are fine, as long as one travels from country to country to do so); FMM (father and son with slave or prostitute; two brothers with a free woman); and FFFFM (mother, daughter, and sisters who are slaves). And if we go back and consider the prohibited acts, then here too we find a concern with group sex: two sisters, a living brother's wife, and a wife's mother or sister – threesomes and even a possible foursome. To be sure, there is a concern with one-on-one sex, but it is by no means foregrounded. As for the animals in this wide family, here too multiples appear: both horse and mule offer their services in the same law, as do dog and pig in another, and then ox and pig in subsequent elaboration of the same law. It may not be the case that one should be so fortunate as to be penetrated by an ox and pig in the same session, or indeed to have the pleasure of both a horse and a mule at one time, but the literary pairing is the crucial issue here.

The Hittite sexual laws lead to three conclusions: first, let me pick up the preceding comment on literary pairing. As mentioned in my opening comments, these texts are literary creations, recording not merely laws but also enabling scribes to give voice, through their imaginations, to wider cultural norms and expectations. I mean that texts often function in a way to provide metaphors and tropes of social, economic, and cultural life, at times in unexpected and indirect ways. In this case, the tendency toward collective acts, or group sex, may be seen as a metaphor for the fundamental collective social assumptions in the ANE. Second, the notion of what constitutes a family or clan or gens is far wider than human beings, for it includes domesticated animals as well; third, within this sexual economy the line of what may at a stretch be called the incest taboo runs according to a very different logic. More than the Hittite woman, the Hittite male had a range of sexual options, such as the dead, horses (and their cousins), wife, but also stepmothers and sisters of wives as long as one's father or wife is dead, and then slaves, prostitutes, and free women (even sisters if they lived in different countries). But not everything was permitted, for one must draw the line somewhere. Now the incest taboo swings into action with mothers, cows, daughters, sheep, sons, dogs, two sisters, pigs, living brothers' wives, and so on.

Hebrews

The third group to be considered in this survey is the people on the margins of the ANE, the Hebrews. How do they compare to their neighbors? I suggest the answer may be found in two areas: the first in relation to the law; the second concerning a sexual culture assumed across the ANE. I take each in turn. At first sight, do the laws of the Hebrew Bible suggest that they are an uptight exception to the liberal laws of the ANE? Those prohibitions read as follows:

> Whoever has sex with [*shokhev*][28] a beast shall be put to death.
>
> *(Exod. 22:18)*

> And you shall not ejaculate [*titten shekhovtekha*][29] into any beast and defile yourself with it, neither shall any woman bend over before [*ta'amodh lifne*][30] a beast to copulate [*rv'*] with it: it is a perversion.
>
> *(Lev. 18:23)*

> If a man ejaculates [*yitten shekhovto*] into a beast, he shall be put to death; and you shall kill the beast. If a woman approaches any beast to copulate [*rv'*] with it, you shall kill the woman and the beast; they shall be put to death, their blood is upon them.
>
> *(Lev. 20:15–16)*

> "Cursed be he who has sex [*shokhev*] with any beast." And all the people shall say, "Amen".[31]
>
> *(Deut. 27:21)*

It is worth noting, first, that these texts ban sex with any animal[32] and, second, that the command explicitly (and graphically in the case of Lev. 18:23) addresses on two occasions women as well as men. On the first count these prohibitions differ from the Hittite laws, while on the second they overlap with those laws, where women are mentioned in relation to the dead, to dogs, and to pigs. But do they share more with the Hittite laws? In order to gain a deeper (no pun intended) sense of these laws, I take a similar tack to my reading of the Hittite laws, avoiding the tendency among those who comment on these laws to separate those on "bestiality" from their wider textual context. So also with these laws from the Hebrew Bible: three of the four occurrences of the ban on bestiality occur in a context very similar to the Hittite laws.[33] In Leviticus 18:23, bestiality comes at the conclusion of a long passage on the incest taboo (Lev. 18:6–18), where we find bans on the following: sex with one's (assuming a man's) mother, father's wife (who is obviously different from one's mother), sister or even stepsisters (daughters of one's mother or father), granddaughters, half-sisters, paternal and maternal aunts, a paternal uncle's wife, daughter-in-law, brother's wife, sisters, and a mother, her daughter, and her granddaughter. At the close of this collection of incest taboos, we also find laws against sex with a menstruating woman, sex with a man's neighbor's wife, devoting one's children in the fire to the god Molech (a reference either to exposure of infants or to Canaanite religious practice), a ban on sex between human males,[34] and finally on sex with animals. Rather similar lists of incest taboos, albeit with fewer examples, appear in Leviticus 20:10–21 (in which vv. 15–16 are found) and in Deuteronomy 27:20–3 (the context for v. 21).[35] In other words, the ban on bestiality is one instance of a much more flexible and extended incest taboo, a taboo that includes not merely relations by blood, but also wider clan relations, menstrual sex, male-on-male sex, and bestiality.[36]

In light of these connections, the apparently straightforward laws of the Hebrew Bible reveal a much more complex picture, leading to the following conclusions. First, they operate with an approach to sex markedly different from modern and postmodern ones.[37] There is no sliding scale of sexually forbidden acts; bestiality is no worse than having sex with one's aunt by marriage or a menstruating woman. Sex with animals, the same sex, and extended relatives are all on par. Second, the Hebrew laws are much closer to the Hittite laws in terms of the assumed scale and range of sexual acts. Minor variations apart, both collections share the fundamental assumption that animals were contiguous with, sexually, the extended family or clan. The clan did not stop with blood relatives or living human beings, for it also included domesticated animals. Hence the laws on bestiality are located within a much expanded range of incest taboos.[38]

All of which brings me to my second point concerning the pervasiveness of such sexual conventions. Here I can provide only a glimpse of that pervasiveness, which would have to include the prominent roles of the patriarch's and matriarch's genitals;[39] the persistent theme in Genesis 2:18–20[40] of Adam's sex with the animals in the Garden; Eve and the serpent in Genesis 3:1–7, 14–16; and the account of Balaam and his ass in Numbers 22. Instead, I sadly restrict myself to some observations concerning our friends the Hittites. In the context of the prophet Ezekiel's lurid condemnations of Israel and Judah (called Ololah and Oholibah in the texts), he speaks of the latter's lust. She is worse than her sister, lusting not merely after "horsemen riding on horses" (Ezek. 23:12), but after donkey-sized and horse-like cocks: "She was horny [ta'gevah] for her toyboys [pilgeshehem], whose cocks [besaram] were the size of donkey schlongs [besar-hamorim] and whose ejaculations [zirmatam] were like horse cum [zirmat-susim]" (Ezek. 23:20).[41]

Of course, as the prophets know well, horses have large cocks and balls: in Jeremiah 5:8 we find the observation that the Jerusalemites are "horny [meyuzanim] stallions with massive balls [mashkim]."[42] Perhaps we can go further: the text from Ezekiel, with its donkey schlongs and horse cum, offers us a spattered word play. Zirmah – ejaculation – comes from zrm: to pour or overwhelm, with the noun, zerem, meaning a downpour or a rainstorm. So what Ezekiel 23:20 is really saying is that Jerusalem longs for an equine cum-storm, a zoological zirmah, if I may coin a phrase, or bestial bukkake,[43] as it is known in the business. Does this not take us back to the Hittites and their appetites for horses and donkeys? Even more, it is a good bet that by saying that Oholibah was attracted to cocks of donkey-like proportions and horse-like ejaculatory capacity, Ezekiel was making a sly allusion to her maternal Hittite ancestry: "Like mother, like daughter" (Ezek. 16:44).[44]

Conclusion

I have attempted to offer a glimpse of the range of perceptions and practices concerning paraphilias in the ANE. Inevitably, we are subject to the vagaries of time and the serendipitous preservation of materials that provide such a glimpse. It is quite feasible that the picture was much richer and fuller, robustly including far more than the scarce texts indicate. Another qualification is that we are condemned to rely on certain types of written sources, mostly laws. But that raises the inevitable question concerning the nature of the law, with which I close this discussion.

Earlier, I noted the intermittent debate concerning the traditions of law in the ANE, with some suggesting they were speculative exercises while others hold that they were actual law codes enacted by rulers and their judges. A full engagement with that debate is beyond my remit here, except to raise the question concerning the stern prohibition of bestiality in the laws of Exodus, Leviticus, and Deuteronomy and the curious pervasiveness of bestial themes in the Hebrew Bible. I have already argued that variations in the laws between the Hittites and the Hebrew Bible are superficial, for at a deeper level they partake of the same assumptions concerning the gens or clan and the (lack of) difference between human beings and other animals. Perhaps we can go further, and pick up Doniger's argument in relation to mythology, namely that the hypocrisy of the prohibition on bestiality is that it marks the covert pervasiveness of bestial themes in our social and cultural imagination.[45] As a couple of examples among many, think of the colloquial term for sex, "doggy-style," or "beaver" for a vagina, or that teenagers copulate "like rabbits," or the Australianism, that one is like a wombat: one "eats, roots [has sex], and leaves."

I would go further still and argue that the prohibition is itself the very means of that pervasiveness. This entails going beyond the common position in legal theory that a prohibition is in response to an existing transgression, that the law is based on its transgression.[46] Rather, I think of the dialectical point that law itself produces the transgression in the first place.[47] That is, a certain act becomes illegal only when the law designates it so. Rather than giving expression to cultural norms, to codifying those norms in a way that fixes them, the law functions to transform the act in question into something forbidden. It thereby seeks to reshape cultural expectations, usually in terms of the ideological agenda of a certain group that seeks influence and power. A codified law also makes a certain ban universal, and thereby seeks to make the transgression universal too. However, I would also suggest that the law's imagination may also bring certain acts into existence. I think here in particular of the Hittites or the good omen of horse-kissing among the Babylonians. Here it is entirely possible that a legal scribe's fantasy simultaneously creates and recognizes an act that may not have been previously contemplated.

Notes

1 Rinella 2006: 1.
2 Paraphilia designates an "abnormal" sexual practice, a "love that is to the side." The immediate question is then what constitutes normal and abnormal and, more importantly, who determines the boundaries of such categories. Overlapping legal, cultural, and religious codes desperately spend an inordinate amount of time policing and censoring what counts as acceptable and "normal."
3 Illuminating scholarly works on bestiality are few and far between, making one suspect that most scholars invoke the biblical taboo: a scholarly lying with an animal may well lead to a scholarly death. To be sure, there are the "scientific" studies of sexual "deviancy." See Dubois-Desaulle 1933; Ellis 1940; Kinsey et al. 1948, 1953; Krafft-Ebing 1965; Beetz and Podberscek 2005; Earls and Lalumiere 2007. Among these is Kinsey's (in)famous finding: in 1950s USA about 8 percent of males (mostly of rural background) had sexual contact with animals and 3.6 percent of females, the former preferring penetration of and fellatio by farm animals and the latter masturbation of aforesaid beasts. I would also note the occasional ethical reflection, political advocacy and animal liberation, and nervous avoidance of the topic by nearly all scholars of the ANE and the Hebrew Bible. See Ullendorf 1979; Borowski 1987; Brenner 1994; Magonet 1995; Stępień 1996; Rashkow 2000; Singer 2001; Ellens 2006, 144; Rinella 2006. Three works that do address such matters in full frontal are noticeably unhelpful, reducing a fascinating topic to a dreary catalogue or attempting to impose a prissy ethical code on material that simply does not sustain such an effort. See Aggrawal 2009; Hoffner 1973; Scurlock 2011. Even in the calculated edginess of porn studies, bestiality is notable for its absence from mainstream analyses. See, for example, Arcand 1993; Goulemot 1994 [1991]; Kaite 1995; Williams 2004. A beacon of scholarship, which leaves these other studies in a veritable dark age, is *Lief Dier* by the former zoo-keeper Midas Dekkers. First published in Dutch, it has now appeared in English (1992, 2000).
4 To this collection should be added *mixoscopic zoophilia*: sexual pleasure gained from watching copulating animals. Adding to the confusion, sodomy and buggery have also been used to denote bestiality, especially in legal texts. These are rather unhelpful, since they include male-on-male sex (not female-on-female sex), sex with Jews and Muslims, and even sex with Africans (Dekkers 2000: 118–19).

5 Scurlock 2002: 372.
6 Scurlock 2002: 379.
7 See Kozyreva 1991: 114–21.
8 Scurlock 2011: 937.
9 The term here is *hurkel*, which means an offense against the gods.
10 Hoffner 1997: 236–7, emphasis added.
11 Roth 1997: 215; Collins 2007: 118. For some strange reason, Roth bypasses the organizing category of the Hittite scribes: the first hundred were known as "If a man" and the second hundred as "If a vine" – simply because these are the first words of each section. Any serious consideration of the economic nature of Hittite society would pay much closer attention to such terms, since they indicate the primary role of agriculture in that socioeconomic system.
12 Unless one is the Sun-God, since then sex with a cow leads to the production of a human being. Collins 2007: 149.
13 Unless of course the law actually means not so much porcophilia but "pig-sex" as a generic term, that is, a sexual act that is considered outrageous or outside the norms of societal sexual behaviors, such as water sports, defecation, bondage, group-sex, and bestiality. But perhaps that is taking a little too much interpretive license, although the terminology in the Hittite texts is actually quite vague, so it leaves some room for interpretive exploration, let alone the possibilities of smooching, fellatio, cunnilingus, and so on.
14 Collins 2007: 121.
15 Curiously, the Hittite laws do not mention sex between men while on campaign. Either it was not an issue, or the relevant law had been lost.
16 This method has been revived by Anne Nyland. See her translation (2008) of this early work on equine training.
17 Garstang 2009 [1910]: 344, 364.
18 Hoffner 1997: 237.
19 It is worth noting here an awareness, at least among the Romans (who were fascinated by the ancient cultures further east), of the occasional projecting clitoris, which Martial's *Philaenis* sports (7.67). Many thanks to Mark Masterson for this point.
20 Bryce 2002; Collins 2007: 169–72, 192–5.
21 Of course, it is possible that the carefully cleaned bones, washed in olive oil, might also provide certain opportunities for enterprising necrophiliacs.
22 Collins 2007: 195.
23 The text does not stipulate whether this is a simultaneous matter of four-way sex, a sequential arrangement, or perhaps discrete coupling over the same period.
24 Lévi-Strauss 1969: 12–25, 1978 [1973]: 211–21. That stretching will need to go beyond Freud, Lacan, Žižek, and others in the psychoanalytic tradition; despite the great attention to incest via the Oedipus complex, it is difficult to find any references to bestiality or zoophilia in their work.
25 No clarification is given as to how this law relates to the one concerning two sisters and their mother. Are two sisters fine if the mother is dead, or if one does not have sex with the mother and the sisters live in different places? Or was no contradiction seen by the scribes who pressed these laws into clay?
26 I allude here to the various permutations of an ongoing debate concerning the ANE, and indeed ancient Greece and Rome, a debate in which opponents are characterized in terms of primitivism and modernism, substantivism and formalism, and so on. All are variations of identity and difference: either they were much like us, or a vast gulf separates us from them, or somewhere in between.
27 Cohen 2002: 93–4; Collins 2007: 121.
28 The basic sense of *shkhv* is to lie (down), but it includes within its semantic cluster sex and dying. For transliteration I follow the conventions of the "general purpose" style, according to *The SBL Handbook of Style* (Atlanta: Society of Biblical Literature, 2011).
29 Very euphemistically translated as "lie with" in RSV and other translations, *titten shekhovtekha* means literally to give a load of semen; hence "ejaculate."
30 As is so often the case, the translations try to "civilize" the explicit earthiness of the Hebrew text. The RSV has "give herself to," while the Hebrew literally reads "stand" or "take a position before"; and what position does a woman take before an animal? She turns her bum towards it and bends over.
31 Imagine for a moment the liturgical scene in this text: the Levites say with a loud voice on Mt Gerizim (after the people have crossed the Jordan) that anyone who has sex with an animal shall be put to death. The congregation reverently intones "Amen." Strange that it has not entered into any Christian books of common prayer. Of course, these laws were pervasive in the late Middle Ages and early

capitalism, in which the animal in question was put to death along with the human being, especially during waves of mass hysteria. In earlier centuries, animals were put on trial, judged, sentenced, and (sometimes) acquitted for biting, goring, trampling, for plagues and swarms, and even for sins of omission (preventing a rape in the house, for instance). With the separation of church and state, first with the Code Napoléon, it was no longer the role of the state to appease God and enforce his law. See Dekkers 1992: 130–40, 2000: 116–25; Evans 1998 [1906].

32 It seems that relatively large, domestic animals are in mind here, and that practices such as formicophilia are simply off the radar. Formicophilia is, strictly speaking, sex with ants, but includes any small creatures, such as snails, slugs, and frogs. It is said that to have them crawling – enticed perhaps by some honey or other tidbit – over one's genitals produces the most exquisite orgasm.

33 In the fourth, Exodus 22:19, the prohibition of bestiality is preceded by the commandment to kill sorceresses, and it is followed by a ban on sacrificing to other gods. The immediate context concerns religious practice, which touches on the central role of animal and theriomorphic images and sculptures in all areas of the ANE. On this material, see the extensive collection by Collins 2002.

34 The Hebrew Bible does not mention sex between human females.

35 The text in Leviticus 20:15–26, the liturgical recitation on Mt Gerizim, becomes even more intriguing, since the four incest laws appear in the midst of 12 laws that can justifiably be regarded as a variation on the ten commandments.

36 It may be possible to suggest that they constitute more of a ban on exogamy, but even then the place of animals in these lists does not work with conventional senses of exogamy. At this point the studies of incest by Brenner, Rashkow, and Carmichael simply fail to see that incest applies beyond human beings (Brenner 1994; Rashkow 2000; Carmichael 2010: 125–36). Schloen suggests that those mentioned in the collection would have cohabited in one dwelling. If so, then for some strange reason he leaves out bestiality and male-on-male sex (Schloen 2001: 148–9).

37 So different, in fact, that Frymer-Kensky's careful study concludes that she cannot discern any coherent system for dealing with sex in the Bible (Frymer-Kensky 1995).

38 What about the dead? No law appears in the Hebrew Bible concerning sex with the dead, but some mention at least of veneration of the dead. The dead often dwelt in a chamber beneath the floor or were represented by anthropomorphic statues. Here we find the daily pattern of invoking their names (a task for the eldest son), breaking some bread for them as part of the meal of the living, and in the presence at meals and gatherings of the "chair for the ghost." They were not so much tools of the living, but were part of a "living" household, which was also "the household of the dead, because deceased ancestors continued to participate in the social life of their descendants" (Schloen 2001: 346). On ancestor cults and veneration for the dead, see van der Toorn 1996; 2008; Schloen 2001: 342–6; Bloch-Smith 2009; Steinberg 2009.

39 Boer 2011.

40 Lawee 2007.

41 *RSV* has, lamely, "and doted upon her paramours there, whose members were like those of asses, and whose issue was like that of horses." Van Dijk-Hemmes offers a slightly better but still very tame translation: "She lusted after the paramours there, whose organs are like the organs of asses and whose ejaculation is like the ejaculation of stallions." Van Dijk-Hemmes 1995: 252. Runions and Halperin also note the fascination with mega-cocks (Halperin 1993: 117, 146; Runions 2001: 166, n. 27).

42 One soon becomes accustomed to an image of polite translators squirming over such passages and thereby producing limp offerings such as "well-fed lusty stallions." Carroll has some fun with the difficulties of commentators, suggesting "well hung" for *mashkim* (1986: 178).

43 Bukkake is a far more appropriate translation of *zirmah* than it at first seems to be. Bukkake is the noun form of the Japanese verb *bukkakeru* (ぶっ掛ける, to dash or splash water), and means a "dash," "splash," or "heavy splash." The word *bukkake* is often used in Japanese to describe pouring out water with sufficient momentum to cause splashing or spilling. Indeed, bukkake is used in Japan to describe a type of dish where the broth is poured on top of noodles, as in bukkake-udon and bukkake-soba. In pornography it describes a scene where a number of men ejaculate on a woman, or indeed men on men or women on women. It is a form of hygrophilia, sexual arousal from contact with bodily secretions. So I would suggest a formula: zoological *zirmah*: bestial bukkake.

44 Following the impetus of Halperin, many are keen to see these and other texts as signs of Ezekiel's – even if he is understood to be a literary construct – psychological problems (Halperin 1993; Garber 2004; Schmitt 2004). I am not so sure, since Ezekiel seems spot on to me, but see Jobling's excellent essay (2004).

45 Doniger 1995.
46 Knight 2011.
47 It is worth noting that this dialectical poststructural approach to the law is actually found in the Apostle Paul's reflections in Romans 7.

Bibliography

Aggrawal, A. (2009) "References to the paraphilias and sexual crimes in the Bible", *Journal of Forensic and Legal Medicine* 16(3): 109–14.

Arcand, B. (1993) *The Jaguar and the Anteater: Pornography Degree Zero*, trans. W. Grady. London: Verso.

Beetz, A.M. and Podberscek, A.L. (2005) *Bestiality and Zoophilia: Sexual Relations with Animals*. West Lafayette, IN: Purdue University Press.

Bloch-Smith, E. (2009) "From womb to tomb: The Israelite family in death as in life", in P. Dutcher-Walls (ed.) *The Family in Life and Death: The Family in Ancient Israel: Social and Anthropological Perspectives*. London: T & T Clark, pp. 122–31.

Boer, R. (2011) "The patriarch's nuts: Concerning the testicular logic of Biblical Hebrew", *Journal of Men, Masculinities and Spirituality* 5(2): 41–52.

Borowski, O. (1987) *Agriculture in Iron Age Israel*. Winona Lake, IN: Eisenbrauns.

Brenner, A. (1994) "On incest", in A. Brenner (ed.) *A Feminist Companion to Exodus to Deuteronomy*. Sheffield: Sheffield Academic Press, pp. 113–38.

Bryce, T. (2002) *Life and Society in the Hittite World*. Oxford: Oxford University Press.

Carmichael, C. (2010) *Sex and Religion in the Bible*. New Haven, CT: Yale University Press.

Carroll, R. (1986) *Jeremiah*. London: SCM.

Cohen, Y. (2002) *Taboos and Prohibitions in Hittite Society: A Study of the Hittite Expression natta āra ("Not Permitted")*. Heidelberg: Universitätsverlag.

Collins, B.J. (2002) *A History of the Animal World in the Ancient Near East*. Leiden: Brill.

——(2007) *The Hittites and Their World*. Atlanta, GA: Society of Biblical Literature.

Dekkers, M. (1992) *Lief Dier: Over Bestialiteit*. Amsterdam: Uitgeverij Contact.

——(2000) *Dearest Pet: On Bestiality*, trans. P. Vincent. London: Verso.

Doniger, W. (1995) "The mythology of masquerading animals, or bestiality", *Social Research* 62(3): 751–72.

Dubois-Desaulle, G. (1933) *Bestiality: An Historical, Medical, Legal and Literary Study*. New York: Panurge.

Earls, C.M. and Lalumiere, M.L. (2007) "A case study of preferential bestiality (Zoophilia)", *Sexual Abuse: A Journal of Research and Treatment* 14(1): 83–8.

Ellens, J.H. (2006) *Sex in the Bible: A New Consideration*. Westport, CT: Praeger.

Ellis, H. (1940) *Studies in the Psychology of Sex*, Volume 5. New York: Random House.

Evans, E.P. (1998 [1906]) *The Criminal Prosecution and Capital Punishment of Animals*. Clark, NJ: Lawbook Exchange.

Frymer-Kensky, T. (1995) "Law and philosophy: The case of sex in the Bible", in J. Magonet (ed.) *Jewish Explorations of Sexuality*. Providence, RI: Berghahn Books, pp. 3–14.

Garber, D.J. (2004) "Traumatizing Ezekiel, the exilic prophet", in J.H. Ellens and W.G. Rollins (eds) *Psychology and the Bible: A New Way to Read the Scriptures*. Westport, CT: Praeger, pp. 215–36.

Garstang, J. (2009 [1910]) *The Land of the Hittites: An Account of Recent Explorations and Discoveries in Asia Minor, with Descriptions of the Hittite Monuments*. Piscataway, NJ: Gorgias.

Goulemot, J.M. (1994 [1991]) *Forbidden Texts: Erotic Literature and Its Readers in Eighteenth-century France*. London: Polity.

Halperin, D.J. (1993) *Seeking Ezekiel: Text and Psychology*. University Park, PA: Pennsylvania State University Press.

Hoffner, H. (1973) "Incest, sodomy and bestiality in the ancient Near East", in H. Hoffner (ed.) *Orient and Occident: Essays Presented to Cyrus H. Gordon*. Neukirchen-Vluyn: Neukirchener Verlag, pp. 81–90.

——(1997) "Hittite laws", in M.T. Roth (ed.) *Law Collections from Mesopotamia and the Asia Minor*. Atlanta, GA: Scholar's Press, pp. 213–40.

Jobling, D. (2004) "An adequate psychological approach to the Book of Ezekiel", in J.H. Ellens and W.G. Rollins (eds) *Psychology and the Bible: A New Way to Read the Scriptures*. Westport, CT: Praeger, pp. 203–14.

Kaite, B. (1995) *Pornography and Difference*. Bloomington, IN: Indiana University Press.

Kinsey, A.C., Pomeroy, W.B., and Martin, C.E. (1948) *Sexual Behavior in the Human Male*. Philadelphia, PA: W.B. Saunders.

Kinsey, A.C., Pomeroy, W.B., Martin, C.E., and Gebhard, P.H. (1953) *Sexual Behavior in the Human Female*. Philadelphia, PA: W.B. Saunders.

Knight, D. (2011) *Law, Power, and Justice in Ancient Israel*. Louisville, KY: Westminster John Knox.

Kozyreva, N.V. (1991) "The old Babylonian period of Mesopotamian history", in I.M. Diakonoff and P.L. Kohl (eds) *Early Antiquity*. Chicago, IL: University of Chicago Press, pp. 98–123.

Krafft-Ebing, R. von. (1965) *Psychopathia Sexualis*. New York: Scarborough Books.

Lawee, E. (2007) "The reception of Rashi's commentary on the Torah in Spain: The case of Adam's mating with the animals", *The Jewish Quarterly Review* 97(1): 33–66.

Lévi-Strauss, C. (1969) *The Elementary Structures of Kinship*, trans. J.H. Bell, J.R. von Sturmer, and R. Needham. London: Eyre & Spottiswoode.

——(1978 [1973]) *Structural Anthropology 2*, trans. M. Layton. London: Penguin.

Magonet, J. (1995) *Jewish Explorations of Sexuality*. Providence, RI: Berghahn Books.

Nyland, A. (2008) *The Kikkuli Method of Horse Training*. Sydney, NSW: Smith and Stirling.

Rashkow, I. (2000) *Taboo or Not Taboo: Sexuality and Family in the Hebrew Bible*. Minneapolis, MN: Fortress.

Rinella, S. (2006) "Depraved indifference", *Nerve*. Available online at <http://www.nerve.com/personalessays/rinella/depravedindifference> (accessed 22 February 2013).

Roth, M.T. (1997) *Law Collections from Mesopotamia and Asia Minor*. Atlanta, GA: Scholar's Press.

Runions, E. (2001) "Violence and the economy of desire in Ezekiel 16:1–45", in A. Brenner (ed.) *Prophets and Daniel*. Sheffield: Sheffield Academic Press, pp. 156–69.

Schloen, J.D. (2001) *The House of the Father as Fact and Symbol: Patrimonialism in Ugarit and the Ancient Near East*. Winona Lake, IN: Eisenbrauns.

Schmitt, J.J. (2004) "Psychoanalyzing Ezekiel", in J.H. Ellens and W.G. Rollins (eds) *Psychology and the Bible: A New Way to Read the Scriptures*. Westport, CT: Praeger, pp. 185–202.

Scurlock, J. (2002) "Animals in ancient Mesopotamian religion", in B.J. Collins (ed.) *A History of the Animal World in the Ancient Near East*. Leiden: Brill, pp. 361–88.

——(2011) "Bestiality I: Ancient Near East", in *Encyclopedia of the Bible and Its Reception, Volume III: Athena – Birkat ha-Minim*. Berlin: Walter De Gruyter, pp. 935–8.

Singer, P. (2001) "Heavy petting", *Nerve*. Available online at <http://www.nerve.com/personalessays/rinella/depravedindifference> (accessed 22 February 2013).

Steinberg, N. (2009) "Exodus 12 in light of ancestral cult practices", in P. Dutcher-Walls (ed.) *The Family in Life and Death: The Family in Ancient Israel: Social and Anthropological Perspectives*. London: T & T Clark, pp. 89–105.

Stępień, M. (1996) *Animal Husbandry in the Ancient Near East: A Prosopographic Study of Third-Millennium Umma*. Bethesda: CDL Press.

Ullendorf, E. (1979) "The bawdy Bible", *Bulletin of the School of Oriental and African Studies University of London* 42(3): 425–56.

Van der Toorn, K. (1996) *Family Religion in Babylonia, Syria and Israel: Continuity and Change in the Forms of Religious Life*. Leiden: Brill.

——(2008) "Family religion in second millennium West Asia (Mesopotamia, Emar, Nuzi)", in J. Bodel and S.M. Olyan (eds) *Household and Family Religion in Antiquity: Contextual and Comparative Perspectives*. Malden, MA: Blackwell, pp. 20–36.

Van Dijk-Hemmes, F. (1995) "The metaphorization of woman in prophetic speech: An analysis of Ezekiel 23", in A. Brenner (ed.) *A Feminist Companion to the Latter Prophets*. Sheffield: Sheffield Academic Press, pp. 244–55.

Williams, L. (2004) *Porn Studies*. Durham, NC: Duke University Press.

5

TOO YOUNG – TOO OLD?

Sex and age in Mesopotamian literature

Gwendolyn Leick

In use for some 4,000 years (from the end of the fifth millennium until the last hundred years BCE), cuneiform, the "wedge"-writing on clay tablets, served primarily the needs of complex productive and distributive administrations. Originating in southern Mesopotamia, the writing system was adopted eventually by other societies in the Ancient Near East desirous to benefit from the advantages of keeping permanent records of important transactions. During the latter part of the second millennium, scribes able to write Akkadian (a Semitic language) were employed by all self-respecting royal courts aspiring to form part of the international political elite, from Hattusa on the Anatolian plateau to Ugarit on the Levant and Akhetaten on the Nile Valley. A corpus of sign lists, lexical lists, as well as literary material (from proverbs to lengthy narratives), was transmitted from generation to generation of scribes to facilitate the mastery of writing Akkadian. Such scholarly collections from palaces, temples and private residences, in Babylonia, Assyria, as well as the areas peripheral to Mesopotamia, provided the majority of texts that could be described as "literary". One of the best stocked of such "libraries", the one belonging to the Assyrian king Ashurbanipal (668–*c.*627 BCE), happened to be discovered as early as 1848 by Henry Austen Layard at the site of Nineveh and was subsequently shipped to London. Access to the ancient lexical lists greatly contributed to the understanding of the texts themselves and this triggered scholarly and popular interest in this "oldest known" literature. Sumerian tablet collections from southern Iraqi sites, especially Nippur (excavated by the University of Pennsylvania since 1851), provided even earlier material, dating to the late third millennium BCE. Editions of these literary tablets, with transliterations of the Akkadian texts, began to be published in the early nineteenth century; the Sumerian sources rather later, after the Second World War.

Since the first publication of Stephen Langdon's 1931 summaries of mythological narratives, entitled "Semitic myths" (Vol. V of *Mythologies of all the Races*), several generations of Assyriologists have worked with this material, and the erotic contents of some of these compositions gave rise to comments on ancient Mesopotamian sexuality. Inevitably such interpretations reflected contemporary attitudes to sexuality. Latin would replace English or German for passages that were deemed rather risqué (*Enki super me procubuit, procubuit*, as Langdon had put it). Babylon, long before it was excavated in the nineteenth century, had a reputation as "the great whore" of the Apocalypse and the city where all women had to sell themselves at least once (Herodotus 1.25). Quite a few Assyriologists were too keen to stress how wrong Herodotus was and how respectable (i.e., patriarchal) the Babylonians had really been and these scholars also reflected an andocentric and, more often than not given the institutional tradition of linking Assyriology to Biblical Studies, the Judeo-Christian bias of their own upbringing.[1] French scholars, most notably Jean Bottéro, would look at the subject of ancient sexuality from the perspective of liberal Parisian notions of *amour libre*, claiming that Mesopotamian men and women were able to make love without too much moral censure and the fear of divine punishment for sin:[2]

> (ils) n'avaient pas du tout, de la sexualité et de son exercice, les mêmes appréhensions et censures que nous, héritiers du discrédit et du soupçon dans lesquels le christianisme pastoral traditionnel nous a durablement appris à les tenir.[3]

My own generation, who came of age in the 1960s, experienced the invention of reliable methods of birth control, the decriminalization of homosexuality and were more or less enthusiastic practitioners of Free Love. We could read Sumerian poems celebrating the joys of sex as documents untainted by a long, repressive Judeo-Christian morality. We also witnessed the inexorable spread of consumerism and sexualized marketing strategies and learnt to "deconstruct" texts, becoming aware of our own cultural baggage. Even so, as had happened in classical scholarship rather earlier, the exegesis of our ancient texts was more or less consciously influenced by feminism(s), psychoanalysis, critical theory and queer studies. Hence our desire to deal with particular subjects can also be seen as a response to issues that trouble a contemporary audience.

Turning once more to the subject of sex in antiquity, some twenty years after I published *Sex and Eroticism in Mesopotamian Literature* (Leick 1994), I am now interested in examining a hitherto rather overlooked aspect of Ancient Near East culture, to see how the correlation between age and sexuality was addressed in cuneiform sources. This is motivated not just by my own ageing but by the almost obsessive preoccupation of western media with the sexuality of legal minors on the one hand and the efforts by the postwar generations to maintain their libido well into retirement age on the other. In recent months, at least in Britain, transgressions against "under-age" youths by people who had wielded some form of power, either through access to fame or money or institutional structures, has led to the arrest of octogenarian professionals, while websites catering for older women looking for "toy-boys" more than keep pace with those for older men looking for much younger sexual partners.

In what follows I discuss some Sumerian and Akkadian narratives in which the age of at least one of the partners plays a significant part. We cannot infer too much from these compositions, which after all describe the actions of divine beings and had some, usually obscure, connection to cult and ritual. Still, the tenor of the narrative gives some clues as to when a girl might be seen as too young, just right or too old for sexual relations. As for males, there is even less material, privileging the old over the precocious.

From child to adult

Unlike most other mammals, human beings give birth to immature infants who have a long period of maturation and need considerable social investment. A Sumerian myth describes how the creation of mankind and of various "faulty" specimens common among human beings, such as blind, lame and otherwise crippled beings, was the result of a competition between the goddess Ninmah and Enki, god of wisdom and magic. Enki is able to assign some station in life to even the most unviable creation of Ninmah's but Ninmah cannot find any use for a being called Umul (literally "My Days are Long"). Anne Draffkorn-Kilmer (1976) was the first to suggest that Umul is a good match for the extraordinarily helpless condition of the newly born child. In the translation provided by the online Electronic Text Corpus of Sumerian Literature (ETCSL 1. trl 12) the relevant passage reads as follows:

> [The goddess] Ninmah stood by for the newborn (…) and the woman brought forth (…) in the midst (…) In return (?), this was Umul: its head was afflicted, its place of (…) was afflicted, its eyes were afflicted, its neck was afflicted. It could hardly breathe, its ribs were shaky, its lungs were afflicted, its heart was afflicted, its bowels were afflicted. With its hand and its lolling head it could not put bread into its mouth; its spine and head were dislocated. The weak hips and the shaky feet could not carry (?) it on the field – [The god] Enki fashioned it in this way.
>
> Enki said to Ninmah: "For your creatures I have decreed a fate, I have given them their daily bread. Now, you should decree a fate for my creature, give him his daily bread too." Ninmah looked at Umul and turned to him. She went nearer to Umul and asked him questions but he could not speak. She offered him bread to eat but he could not reach out for it. He could not lie on (…), he could not (…) Standing up he could not sit down, could not lie down, he could not (…) a house, he could not eat bread. Ninmah answered Enki: "The man you have fashioned is neither alive nor dead. He cannot support himself (?)."

There is no resolution as to what is to be done offered in this text; Ninmah simply concedes defeat and Enki decrees that "his penis be praised". The myth seems to suggest that the many imperfections and afflictions of human beings, as well as the terrible vulnerability of infants, could be ascribed to the whim or the folly of competitiveness among the gods.

It has been argued that the evolutionary advantages of the long period of dependence of children, apart from being able to give birth to large-brained but helpless infants, lay in the potential for social imprinting (e.g. Bjorklund 2007). All aspects of childcare, from the age of weaning to the way puberty is handled, are subject to sociocultural context. There are many degrees of autonomy or restrictions, of incorporating children in subsistence activities, and of gender-based distinctions. In stratified societies elite children are often exempt from physical labour in order to be educated for the skills appropriate to their social status. The transition to adulthood with the conferment of full and gender-specific adult rights and responsibilities may be subject to specialized training and initiation that instil the norms, values and knowledge of the society in often painful rites.

The medievalist Philippe Ariès (1966) was one of the first scholars to show that the prevalent western idea of childhood was a relatively recent construction, dating back to the seventeenth century. The "age of consent" (to sexual activity) in Elizabethan Britain was ten, raised to thirteen in the eighteenth century and finally to sixteen in 1885 (Lee 2009: 26). The idea of the innate innocence of children was also promulgated in the nineteenth century while at the same time compulsory elementary schooling was instituted to discipline body and mind, a measure directed, according to Foucault's (1991) analysis, to produce a less volatile working class. State intervention, in terms of the imposition of expert guidance and welfare provisions, greatly increased in the twentieth century in the United States and central Europe (Schumann 2010) when industrialization all but eliminated child labour.

While Freud's theories of sexual development acknowledged the "polymorphous perversity" of children, it also insisted on the primary importance of the successful resolution of Oedipal desire for the well-adjusted adult. The Margaret Mead books (1928, 1930) on children and teenagers in Samoa, based on fieldwork in the 1920s, reached a much wider audience than most ethnographic accounts because the account of sexual freedom experienced by the native children and adolescents drew attention to the social construction of sexuality by comparing restrictive "western" norms and attitudes with the lack of inhibition experienced by the native children of Samoa. This chimed with the liberalization experienced by the generation who read her most avidly, while the backlash against 1960s "permissiveness" (especially among young people) could also be said to have made Freeman's refutation of her work in terms of field methods to have such a huge echo.[4]

Greater tolerance of teenage sexuality and indeed the lowering of the age of homosexual consent in the UK and other European countries were followed at the end of the twentieth century by revelations that children had been and continued to be subject to various forms of abuse, from domestic violence to "satanic" and finally sexual. In 2000 the UK Department of Health defined child sexual abuse as an action that:

> involves forcing or enticing a child or young person to take part in sexual activities, whether or not the child is aware of what is happening. The activities may involve physical contact, including penetrative (e.g. rape or buggery) or non-penetrative acts. They may include non-contact activities, such as involving children in looking at, or in the production of, pornographic material or watching sexual activities, or encouraging children to behave in sexually inappropriate ways.[5]

Some social scientists warned that the widespread reporting of child sexual abuse revelations should be seen in the context of capitalism and that such allegations and reports served also "to unmask the masking that takes place through the ideology of consumption" and that "more importantly, child sexual abuse epitomizes the culture of consumption, where no boundaries are known" (Lee 2009: 57). While the condition of the "post-modern child" in the wealthy countries of the twenty-first century is highly circumscribed by laws meant to protect its sexual innocence and secure it from other forms of "abuse", children in other parts of the world are portrayed as victims of famine and warfare, forcibly enlisted to commit acts of violence, manning the factories in the Far East and serving the demands of sex tourists. These are some of the current tropes about the contradictions and ambiguities of what childhood means in the "post-modern", globalized world. What evidence do we find in the cuneiform material as to the discourse about the decidedly pre-modern "Mesopotamian" childhood?

Age classification

There is no indication in the cuneiform sources that either age grades or formal initiations into male or female adulthood age existed in Mesopotamia. There was no equivalent of a boy from a well-to-do family donning the *toga virilis*. The terminology for different age categories derives from various cuneiform sources: lexical lists (especially the list of professions known as Lú = ša, which gives the main sign (logogram) its Sumerian pronunciation and in the later versions from the Old Babylonian period onwards, the translation into Akkadian); economic texts (such as ration lists); literary compositions (myths, proverbs, literary dialogues, etc); omens, incantations against evil spirits and witches, as well as documents (law collections) (see Figure 5.1).

The sign[6] "tur" was the most common way of denoting something being "small". Applied to human beings it stood for "child" (Sumerian "dumu", Akkadian *šerru*) in most periods of cuneiform writing. Determinatives[7] for male and female would be used to indicate whether the "child" was to be read as "boy" or "girl". The same sign also had the meaning of "son" or "daughter" (Sumerian uses the same word as for child, "dumu", Akkadian has another word,

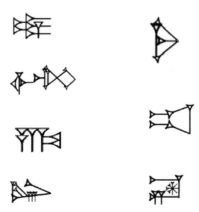

Figure 5.1 The signs for (top to bottom in first column) "tur", "henzer", "KAL", "lú" (male), (top to bottom in second column) "lú" (female), "abba", "ama".

maru). The same word as for "calf" ("amar") is often used to mean a small child, rather like the English use of "kid".

In the Old Babylonian period the sign "henzer" which denotes "weak" and "a low social class" can also stand for "infant, suckling" (Sumerian "bunga", Akkadian *lakû*). For older youths we find gender-specific terminology; in contrast to the "weak" and "small" child, the sign KAL (rendered in Akkadian as *dananu*) means "strong". It can also stand for an adolescent or young male: Sumerian "guruš", Akkadian *eṭlu*; "guruš" can also mean "hero" in literary works, whereas in economic contexts it also refers to an able-bodied male worker. The same sign, preceded by a female determinative and the suffix "tur" ("small", "young"), can be written for Akkadian *batultu* "young, adolescent girl". A more common form of writing this, especially in literary texts, as an epithet for goddesses, is "ki.sikil", a compound of "place" and "pure". The Akkadian *ardatu*, however, is the female form of *ardu* "slave". There are several Sumerian terms for "young man" (such as "mu", "mes", "šul" and "šuba"), all rendered as *eṭlu* in Akkadian. The generic term for "person" is "lú" (Akkadian *amēlu* or *ša*) as in the title of the lexical list already mentioned. This is one of the very early lists, originating in the late Uruk period (later fourth millennium BCE). It deals with terminology pertaining to people, and importantly for the purposes of scribal training, the various official titles, offices and professions. The female equivalent depicts the pudenda as a *pars pro toto* – denoting "female" in general, as well as Sumerian "munus", "woman", Akkadian *sinništu*. The adjective "male" derives from the sign "geš₃", "penis", which the archaic form depicted very clearly. The words for "father", Sumerian "abba", and Akkadian *abu,* are clearly babbling words, written "ama" (GÁxAN); Akkadian *ummu* means "mother". The word and sign for "father" can also stand for "old man" (Akkadian *šibu*) and as a sign of respect when a younger man addresses a senior, and "namabba" means "old age". The word "buršuma" (Akkadian *puršumu*) is usually rendered as "dowager, matriarch, matron" and found mainly in third-millennium and Old Babylonian records, while at the same period "šugi" is used for "senior, elder, old person; old", rendered in Akkadian as *šibu*. This brief survey shows that Sumerian seems to have had greater vocabulary for age grades than Akkadian but we also notice that they are fluid categories – from childhood to young adulthood to old age via parenthood.

According to economic tablets dealing with rations of barley and oil dispensed to workers or slaves, allowances were made for any dependants in the household, children and old people no longer able to work. Much of the Sumerian economy involved organized labour, for infrastructure projects (such as canal maintenance), construction and manufacturing, while female labour dominated in the textile sector. Rations were calibrated according to gender and age; old people received rations in significantly lower quantities than adults. A Sumerian literary composition known as the "Marriage of Martu" (ETCSL 1.7) describes how Martu, a young man from the country, probably a nomad, gets in the mood for marriage when he receives, though single, the double ration usually reserved for married men. Vanstiphout (1999: 468) suggested that such double rationing may have possibly been a strategy adopted by the city to pacify or integrate nomads living beyond the urban region. When Martu asks his mother for advice she tells him to follow his heart's desire. At a festival, Martu impresses the daughter of god Numushda with his wrestling skills and so, despite her family's disapproval of Martu's uncouth and uncivilized ways, the daughter chooses to have no other. Martu becomes the husband of a Sumerian city girl and thus achieves the married status he had anticipated through the double rations he had been allocated, presumably by mistake.

The age terminology in legal texts differentiates also between married and unmarried persons and between those who have not been married before, especially pertinent to females, and those who are widowed or divorced (see Wilcke 1985, 1998). In the first-millennium BCE Babylonian and Assyrian texts, a young girl about to be married and still living in her father's house is a *batultu* ("ki.sikil.tur"). Given that girls married when they were teenagers, the description tallies with the age category. The word "e_2-nu-gi_4-a" specified a girl who had not been deflowered (Akkadian *la naqbat*), as well as "nu-mu-un-zu-a" "her not having known (a man)". Once a suitable groom was found, she became an "e_2-gi4-a", Akkadian *kallatu*, "bride" – a word that also signified her status as "daughter-in-law". Martha Roth (1987) found from her work on the first-millennium BCE texts that the age of marriage for girls was between fourteen and twenty and for men from twenty-six to thirty-two. According to Cooper (2002: 93) a *batultu* was expected not to have had sexual intercourse before marriage although virginity as such was not a *sine qua non* condition. Families who would draw up written contracts belonged to a social class in which patriarchal values and the safeguarding of inheritance were important and where respectable young girls would live under close supervision. Cooper (2002: 100) points out that:

> Mesopotamian law and legal records leave no doubt that a girl's virginity was considered an asset to her father or her owner, and defloration was the implicit prerogative of a husband secured through the marriage agreement. Violation of a betrothed girl's chastity was very serious, punishable as adultery in most cases.

A clause in the "Code of Urnammu"[8] (twenty-first century BCE) states that "if a man violates the right of another and deflowers the virgin wife of a young man, they shall kill that male".

It also stipulates that a fine was payable to the owner of a deflowered slave girl. In either case a girl's value in terms of realizing a suitable bride prize was diminished if somebody had sexual intercourse with her. This was a serious issue and to make a false accusation against a young girl's reputation was punished by the hefty fine of ten shekels of silver, according to the "Code of Lipit Ishtar" (Isin-Larsa period, *c.*1930 BCE) (Roth et al. 1997: 23–35). Negotiations for future marriages, especially between wealthy families, could begin while the future partners were still children. The groom's parents would wish to ascertain that the bride would perpetuate their patriline and hence she would be subject to supervision and seclusion before marriage. The various legal texts reflect the patriarchal setting of Mesopotamian marriages and the point of view of the contractual partners' parents rather than the couple betrothed.

Very different in tone and purpose are the Sumerian "love songs", which take as their subject the union between the goddess Inanna and her lover Dumuzi. These compositions (collected by Sefati 1998) had a ritual context and arise from the idea that Sumerian kings could be ritually married to the goddess and receive from her blessings, and especially fertility of fields and flocks. While some of these texts describe the ritual contexts to some extent, most consist simply of dialogues or monologues, giving voice to the young lovers, and especially Inanna in her persona as in poems a nubile "ki.sikil.tur". Tivka Frymer-Kensky (2000) in an article entitled "Lolita-Inanna" drew attention to the fact that Inanna is here acting and speaking like a "child of privilege and leisure", even a "child of luxury", who eagerly awaits her wedding gifts, such as lapis lazuli, gold and jewels, as well as milk and butter, from the "shepherd Dumuzi". One of the poems (Dumuzi-Inanna C) (ETCSL 4.08.3) reads:

"My sister, what have you been doing in the house? Little one, what have you been doing in the house?"

"I was bathing, I was rubbing myself with soap. I was washing myself with water from the holy kettle, I was rubbing myself with the soap from the white stone bowl. I was anointing myself with good oil from the stone bowl, and dressing myself in the formal dress proper to Inanna. That is how I was busying myself in the house."

"I have put lots of kohl on my eyes, I have arranged ... the nape of my neck. I have washed my dangling hair, I have tested my weapons that make his reign propitious. I have straightened my tousled head of hair, I have tightened my loosened hairgrips, and let my hair fall down the back of my neck. I have put a golden bracelet on my wrist. I have put little lapis-lazuli beads round my neck, and arranged their buttons over my neck muscles."

"Sister! I will bring you whatever you desire. I will bring the loving heart of your heart. Your goddess has given you good looks. Sister, shining bright, you are the honey of your own mother. My sister, to whom I shall bring five things, my sister, to whom I shall bring 10 things, she has perfected your appearance for you; sister, shining bright, she has really made it a delight."

"When my brother enters from the palace, the singers shall ... and I shall pour wine into his mouth. That should gladden his heart, should please his heart."

"Let him bring, let him bring, now let him bring pats of butter and cream!" "My sister, I will bring them with me to the house." "Let him bring, let him bring me lambs like ewes." "My sister, I will bring them with me to the house." "Let him bring, let him bring me kids like goats." "My sister, I will bring them with me to the house!" "Let the lambs be as comely as ewes!" "My sister, I will bring them with me to the house!" "Let the kids be as fine as goats!" "My sister, I will bring them with me to the house!"

"See now, our (1 ms. has instead:) my breasts stand out; see now, hair has grown on our (1 ms. has instead:) my genitals, signifying (?) my progress to the embrace of a man. Let us be very glad! Dance, dance! O Bau, let us be very glad about my genitals! Dance, dance! Later on it will delight him, it will delight him!"

Here the anticipation of gifts ("pats of butter and cream", "lambs like ewes") is part of the general preparation of Inanna's body by bathing, anointing with oil, putting on eye make-up and jewellery, brushing her hair – though nothing is said of putting on clothes. In fact it is her naked body that she herself rejoices over, a body that is showing the signs of sexual maturation, "signifying my progress to the embrace of a man", as this translation puts it. Frymer-Kensky (2000: 93) wrote that the:

> image of Inanna that emerges from these texts is of a beautiful young girl in first bloom, self-absorbed and materialistic, preening and primping and prone to day-dreaming and infatuated love. She is, in short, the archetypical pre-teen and in our culture, this quintessential object of love would be in sixth or seventh grade.

Mentioning Dante's nine-year-old Beatrice, Petrarch's twelve-year-old Laura and Nabokov's fictional Lolita, she goes on to surmise that:

> this love for the very young girl is the heterosexual equivalent of the boy-love of Greek society. It is love for the eternal almost, the one who already holds the promise of sexual delight, and yet is still "on the verge" of limitless potential, still untouched by the experiences and sorrows into the person she will someday be.

There is no hint in this girl-child of the complex Inanna that she will later become.

I feel that this interpretation places too much weight on Inanna as a "beloved", the recipient of an older man's passion. In the Sumerian texts it is Inanna herself who initiates amorous encounters and anticipates her own as well as her lover's "delight". She may not come across as wild and dangerous or angry but her exultant celebration of sensual delight is in keeping with her persona imbued with what the Sumerian termed "hi.li" – voluptuousness and sex appeal. Her lover, Dumuzi "the Shepherd", is the lover of her choice, the "man of my heart", as she says. Such freedom of choice and such unconditional celebration of burgeoning sexuality of such a very self-conscious "Lolita" appear to me to be rather more characteristic of Inanna and her well-known impetuosity and sex drive than of an "archetypical Sumerian pre-teen". Importantly for our subject matter, it is Inanna who declares herself ready to go to the bridal bed, it is she who decides that she is young but old enough. We cannot know to what extent these literary configurations about Inanna or her Akkadian equivalent, Ishtar, reflect the reality of Mesopotamian women. However, it appears to me that the generally positive attitude to female sexuality to which many cuneiform sources attest would make it less likely for an Assyriologist to assert, as did Carson (1990: 144), in respect of women in classical Greece, that "a woman's life has no prime, but rather a season of unripe virginity, followed by a season of overripe maturity, with the single occasion of defloration as the dividing line".

In a longer Sumerian narrative, known as "Enlil and Ninlil" (Behrens 1978; also available on ETCSL), which is set in the city of Nippur, the protagonists are introduced at the beginning as two youngsters, ("ĝuruš tur") Enlil and ("ki-sikil tur") Ninlil, whose mother is identified as Nunbaršegunu, an old(er) woman ("um-ma"). She warns her daughter not to bathe in the river since Enlil seeing her there, presumably naked, will look at her and "[s]traight away he will want to have intercourse, he will want to kiss! He will be happy to pour lusty semen into the womb, and then he will leave you to it!"

Ninlil, however, does not heed this advice. Rivers and canals are the proverbial site for erotic encounters in Sumerian literature, much as beaches were in some Greek epics. Reeds provided cover from prying eyes and boats could convey lovers to secluded thickets. The scenario predicted by Ninlil's mother duly unfolds; Enlil makes his advances, which the young girl verbally, at least, rejects, citing her inexperience:

"I want to have sex with you!", but he could not make her let him. Enlil said to her, "I want to kiss you!", but he could not make her let him.

"My vagina is small, it does not know pregnancy. My lips are young, they do not know kissing. If my mother learns of it, she will slap my hand! If my father learns of it, he will lay hands on me! But right now, no one will stop me from telling this to my girl friend!"

Here Ninlil draws attention to her physical immaturity, as well as to her fear of punishment. Enlil is not easily deterred. Since he appears to be on the other side of the river when they have this dialogue he commands his minister to provide a boat for the crossing.

He grasped hold of her whom he was seeking – he was actually to have intercourse with her, he was actually to kiss her! – so as to lie with her on a small bank [break in the text]. He actually had intercourse with her, he actually kissed her. At this one intercourse, at this one kissing he poured the seed of Suen-Ašimbabbar into her womb.

When Enlil is declared "ritually impure" and has to leave the city – whether as a result of his intercourse with Ninlil is not expressively stated – Ninlil follows him and contrives to be impregnated three more times by Enlil in various disguises. Each time a different male deity is engendered. The composition ends with the praise of "father" Enlil and "mother" Ninlil. Various commentators, beginning with Jerrold Cooper (1980: 180), saw Enlil's banishment from the city as punishment for being a "sex offender". This is not explicitly stated in the Sumerian text and rape of a young girl was not generally punished in such a manner. Behrens and Jacobsen stressed the mythical character of the composition and that the main theme is fertility; for Jacobsen (1987: 169), Enlil and Ninlil "form a mythopoeically divine couple" as a couple embodying the "fertility and productivity of the spring winds". In a similar composition Enlil meets a more resolute maiden (called Sud, actually another manifestation of the goddess Ninlil) who compels her suitor to follow the correct procedures of engagement before she becomes his wife.

The point about "Enlil and Ninlil" that merits attention in our context is that her immediate conception proves that she was "old enough" despite her own doubts about her physical readiness for love-making and its consequences. In fact, her and Enlil's fertility befits their divine status as she successfully "receives the seed" for four simultaneous pregnancies. Generally in Mesopotamian texts, youth was correlated to sexual potency, for males as much as females. As the Sumerian proverb expresses: "Your exuberance is something that creates a household; the young people get married" (Alster 1997: 331).

In contrast to the hymns and myths that celebrate fertile young gods are the Babylonian witchcraft incantations evoking human life as perpetually threatened by disease and an early death. Evil witches and warlocks, as well as malevolent supernatural agents, demons and spirits, were said to single out infants and the young for their work of destruction. In hymns and incantations malevolent agents are said (Dalley 1989: 158):

to go round and enter every house; (...) to take away the young man in his prime, to remove the young girl from her bedroom;
to drag the young man from the marriage chamber, make the young woman leave the bedroom.
The witch,
who goes on the roads,

Who invades the houses,
Who walks in the alleys,
Who hunts over the square;
She turns around, front and back,
She stays standing in the street, and turns her feet,
In the square she blocks the way.
She took away the strength of the beautiful man,
She took away the fruit of the beautiful girl.[9]

This passage conveys the view, perpetuated by the professional exorcists, that life was precarious even for healthy and vigorous young people.

The disappearance of the goddess Ishtar, temporarily held captive in the Underworld, was also said to affect the sexual desire of animals and humans. Without her even the young lose their libido, according to the well-known passage in the Babylonian myth "Ishtar's Descent to the Netherworld":

No bull mounted a cow, no donkey impregnated a jenny,
No young man impregnated a girl in the street,
The young man slept in his private room,
The girl slept in the company of her friends.

Old age

Average life expectancy in antiquity was, as already mentioned, rather low.[10] Far fewer people than in today's affluent parts of world survived long enough to experience a ripe old age (see Harris 2000). In the standard Mesopotamian blessings (which can follow curses in official documents) the most commonly expressed wish is to be able to "perpetuate one name" and to have numerous offspring, rather than simply to live for a long time. In the poem "Bilgames and the Netherworld" (George 1999: 175–99; ETCSL) the conditions of departed souls are described as particularly sad for the woman who dies before having given birth:

like a *defective* pot she is cast aside, no man takes pleasure in her.

Equally sad for the fate of her who had never consummated her marriage:[11]

you have her finish a hand-worked reed mat, she weeps over it,
while a husband who died before having "bared the lap of his wife" is also "weeping while finishing an old rope".

Multiple childbirth, however welcome and necessary the support of surviving children were to women, takes quite a toll on women's bodies and few would live long beyond menopause, even among the elite who had not been subjected to hard menial work. The best-known group of powerful old women were those from wealthy and influential families (often daughters of kings) who joined a "cloister" and had to remain childless. This was a practice that arose in Old Babylonia to keep landed property from dispersal and allowed daughters to invest their share of paternal property during their lifetimes. Some accrued considerable wealth and, spared from bearing children, often outlived their male siblings. Some passages in a collection of omens related to sexual practices mention cloistered women resorting to anal intercourse to avoid pregnancy; but there is no reference to an old *naditum* having sex.

Omen 104 of the collection *Shumma alu* reads:

> If a man has sexual relations with an old woman (*shibtum*), he will quarrel daily.

Rivkah Harris (2000: 93) quotes a personal comment by Ann Guinan, who had published the sex omens (1997), as saying that the negative prognostication pertains primarily to the male partner engaged in such a relationship, but it may be due to strained power relations rather than any aversion to "old women" having sex.

A saying in the Sumerian–Assyrian proverb collection has been translated by Lambert (1960: 248) as:

> My vagina is fine; (yet) according to my people (its use) for me is ended.

His suggestion that this is an utterance made by an ageing prostitute has since been generally accepted.[12] Such a reading is of course related to the conventional and somewhat prudish view that only a prostitute would be interested in the condition of her vagina. It is to my knowledge the only reference in Mesopotamian sources that expresses the tension between a subjective female viewpoint and what may count as public opinion. Generally, old women feature in Mesopotamian literature as mothers; an exceptional text is the so-called "Autobiography of Adad-Guppi", the mother of King Nabunaid (Longman 1991: 102):

> He (Sîn) raised my head; he gave me a fine reputation in the land and years of well-being he added to me. From the period of Assurbanipal, king of Assur, until the ninth years of Nabunaid, king of Babylon, my offspring, they established for me 104 years in the worship of the gods. He kept me alive and well. My eyesight is clear and my mind is excellent. My hands and my feet are healthy. Well-chosen are my words; food and drink still agree with me. My flesh is vital; my heart is joyful. My little ones living four generations from me I have seen. I have reached a ripe old age.

Although this composition had a didactic and political purpose, to affirm the religious policies of Nabunaid, the claims about his mother's longevity and state of health were probably based on fact. The life of Adad-Guppi could indeed be taken as having been exceptionally blessed by the god she worshipped: she bore children, exercised high office as priestess of the Moon-god, and saw her offspring into the fourth generation while retaining lucidity of mind and excellent health. In the Bible (Genesis 18), Sarah, the barren and ninety-year-old wife of the centenarian Abraham, "for whom it had ceased to be after the manner of women", can only laugh when she hears that she is to bear a son, saying:

> After I am waxed old shall I have pleasure, my lord being old also?

The Lord resents her laughter as it shows doubts in His ability to do anything. Not only can the Lord restore a centenarian's powers to procreate, he can allow, even more miraculously, the fertility of an already unusually aged female, allowing her the pleasure of conception and of motherhood.

These positive experiences of old age in women contrast with the more common complaints about infirmities and pain (see Curchin 1980; Harris 2000). In the myth "Enki and Ninhursaja"

(ETCSL t.1.1.1) the pristine world of Dilmun is described as a virginal place, "where the lion did not slay, the wolf not carrying off lambs", where the birds did not eat the malt spread out to dry on the roof, and where:

> No eye-diseases said there: "I am the eye disease." No headache said there: "I am the headache." No old woman belonging to it said there: "I am an old woman." No old man belonging to it said there: "I am an old man."

Old age, with its common ailments such a weak eyes and headaches, does not yet exist. According to another myth, "Inanna and Enki" (ETCSL t 1.3.1), "nam.ab.ba", "old age", constitutes part of the divine prerogatives (Sumerian "me"), where it is listed just after "loud musical instruments and the art of song", and which include also "strife, triumph, counselling, comforting, judging, decision-making", crafts and other requisites of human civilization that Inanna takes from an inebriated Enki.

There are several words for old age, with the most general being nam.ab.ba (Akkadian *abbūtu*). This derives from the word for "father" ("ab.ba"), signifying that fatherhood leads to maturity, while "sumun" (Akkadian *sumkīnu*) denotes a state of decay and rot, and the term "šugi" (Akkadian *šību*) denotes the social status of "senior, elder" and has a more positive connotation of respect. Groups of such "seniors" appear in various literary texts in opposition to a collective of young men, as for example in "Bilgames and Akka" (George 1999: 143–8).

In western culture, the term *geriatrics* was coined in 1909 by the Austro-American physician Ignatz Leo Nascher, who drew attention to the fact that in old age the distinction between normal and pathological is lost and that the old people's afflictions need to be seen in their own epistemological context (Cohen 1994: 142). Cohen's survey of anthropological interpretations of ageing also draws attention to the correlations between social inequalities based on age.

There is one Sumerian text, which seems to have enjoyed such popularity that it was included in a teaching compendium of proverbial sayings. It is entitled "The Old Man and the Young Girl" and was published by Bendt Alster (1975, 1996).[13]

> ... the old man addressed the king [for help]:
> "My blood was good, my growth(?) (was like a) shining horn, my 'yield'
> was brilliant, (but now) my 'grain roasting' (= digestion?) has no success."
> The king did not give an answer.
> He turned to the (wise) *zikrum*[14]
> and repeated the words to the (wise) *zikrum*:
> "My blood was good, my growth(?) (was like a) shining horn, my 'yield'
> was brilliant, (but now) my 'grain roasting' (= digestion?) has no success.
> Thus he spoke to me."
> The (wise) *zikrum* answered the king:
> "My king, supposed that the old man took a young girl as a wife,
> [(in the rest of) his days] – as long as they last, as long as they are the old man will regain
>   his youthful vigour,
> [and the young girl] will become a mature woman."
> The king fetches the old man and asks him,
> "Why are you sorry?"
> The old man answered the king:
> "(I used to be) a warrior, but now my luck, my strength, my personal god and my youthful
>   vigour have left my loins like a runaway donkey.

My black mountain has produced white gypsum.
My mother turned a man from the forest toward me(?), he is giving me 'caught hands' [i.e. they are paralyzed?]
My mongoose that used to eat strong smelling things can no longer stretch its neck towards the jar(?) of good butter
My teeth that used to chew strong things can no more chew strong things
My urine that used to break a hole like a strong torrent, you have to extract it from myself.
My son, whom I used to feed on cream and milk, I can no longer give him anything.
And my slave-girl, whom I bought, has become a demon that […]"
The king paid attention to the words of the old man.
The king spoke to the girl:
"After I have given him to you, he will lie in your lap like a young man.
Come! Let your slave announce it, let him enter your house!"
After the girl had left the palace, (she cried) "Dance, dance, all young girls, rejoice!"

Many of the metaphors used here form part of the literary repertoire of proverbial sayings. The Old Man's allusive descriptions of his symptoms string together several of these familiar tropes; the "black mountain" now only producing "white gypsum" refers to the whitening of his previous dark hair,[15] the "mongoose that can no longer stretch its neck to the fragrant butter jar" denotes a lack of appetite. Less clear is what the "man from the forest" could mean; perhaps it's a walking stick or crutches. The other complaints, the general loss of vigour, of teeth unable to bite, of a weakened flow of urine, are more straightforward symptoms of ageing. Apart from these physical disabilities, he seems to experience a fall in income, since he can no longer spoil his son with cream and milk, as well as a lessening of his authority over his slave girl. The solution to all these problems is his marriage to a "ki.sikil", a young girl, which would allow him to recover his strength in "her lap".

This popular Sumerian tale differs markedly from the response given by Diogenes the Cynic, who when asked when was the right time to marry, quipped "For young men, not yet; for old men, never!" (Aristotle, *Politics* 7.14.6). Aristotle also thought that emitting seed, while being "helpful to young men hurt the old" (McLaren 2007: 12).

Closer to the Mesopotamian story is another Biblical account of a very aged man who finds, if not rejuvenation, then solace and warmth in the arms of a young girl (1 Kgs. 1:1–5). King David "stricken in years" was given Abishag, "a young virgin", to lie at his bosom, but this time there was no miraculous restoration of his sexual prowess, since it is said that "he knew her not".

In summary, we can conclude that Mesopotamian attitudes towards the correlation between sex and age were defined by the prevailing patriarchal society and by the relatively low life expectancy. The goddess Inanna rejoicing in the outward signs of coming of age stands for the idealized nubile girl who joyfully anticipates marriage to "the man of her heart". The myth of Ninlil hinges around the warning not to risk exposure to excitable young gods, keen to "pour their semen" into young wombs. The dangers of childbed and the fragility of good health are conjured in incantations and magic rituals. Not only would women and children become prey to malevolent spirits, young men too could be cut down in their prime. As in the words said to Gilgamesh by Siduri, the wise tavern-keeper at the edge of sea, given that the gods had dispensed death for mankind, keeping (eternal) life for themselves, all he could do was to (George 1999: 124):

Make merry each day, dance and play day and night!
Let your clothes be clean, let your head be washed, may your body bathe in water!
Gaze on the child that holds your hand, let your wife enjoy your repeated embrace!

This advice of *carpe diem* reflects the Mesopotamian view that death was both inevitable and could strike at any time, and that conditions in the Netherworld were dismal, alleviated only slightly for those with offspring able to procure them regular libations. The Old Man's hopes of being rejuvenated by marrying a young girl were as illusive as Gilgamesh's attempt to secure the plant that would make the old grow young again. Teenage sex and nubile bedfellows for ageing men showed that, at least for Mesopotamian males, there was never a too young or too old as soon or as long they were able to enjoy an embrace.

Notes

1 For the issue of a gender perspective in Assyriology, see Asher-Greve 2000.
2 "They did not have any of the fear and censure when it comes to sexuality and its practice that we have, heirs to the discredit and suspicion which traditional Christian teaching has so lastingly instilled in us." (My translation).
3 See Bottéro 1980 and the remarks by Cooper 2009.
4 Freeman 1983.
5 *Working Together to Safeguard Children*, Home Office, Dept. of Health and Dept. of Education and Employment, 1999.
6 See the Pennsylvania Sumerian Dictionary. Available online at http://psd.museum.upenn.edu/epsd/nepsd-frame.html (accessed 4 January 2010).
7 These are signs which signalled to the reader that the following or the preceding sign(s) referred to a category, such as human being, divine being, country, city, astral body, etc.
8 For an edition of the text and notes on the various arguments for and against ascribing the collection of laws to the king of the Third Dynasty of Ur, called Ur-Nammu, or to his son and successor Shulgi, see Frayne 1997: 43–9 and Roth 1987.
9 Maqlu Tablet III. Available online at http://enenuru.net/html/cuneiform_magic/maqlu_3.htm (accessed 4 January 2010).
10 Cf. for Roman soldiers of the principate period "between twenty and thirty years": Scheidel 2005; Morris 2005: 25 states that the average life expectancy for women rose to 36.8 in classical times.
11 Lines 274–8; George 1999: 188.
12 See Harris 2000: 93.
13 For the version presented here I used Alster's original translation from 1975 as well as his amended one from 1996.
14 The meaning of this term in this context is not clear; Alster 1996 renders it as "cloistered woman", since the word appears together with other similar terms, such as *naditu*, in lexical lists.
15 In a rather "ageist" terminology, all inhabitants of Sumer were known collectively as "the black-headed people".

Bibliography

Alster, B. (1975) *Studies in Sumerian Proverbs*. Copenhagen: Mesopotamia Copenhagen Studies in Assyriology, 3: 90–9.
——(1996) "Literary aspects of Sumerian and Akkadian proverbs", in M.E. Vogelzang and H.L.J. Vanstiphout (eds) *Mesopotamian Poetic Language: Sumerian and Akkadian*. Groningen: Styx, pp. 1–21.
——(1997) *Proverbs of Ancient Sumer: The World's Earliest Proverb Collections*. Bethesda, MD: CDL Press.
Ariès, P. (1966) *Centuries of Childhood: A Social History of Family Life*, trans. Robert Baldick. London: Pimlico.
Asher-Greve, J. (2000) "Stepping into the maelstrom: Women, gender and Near Eastern scholarship", *NiN, Journal of Gender Studies in Antiquity* 1: 1–22.
Behrens, H. (1978) *Enlil und Ninlil: Ein sumerischer Mythos aus Nippur* (Studia Pohl Series Maior, 8). Rome: Biblical Institute Press.
Bjorklund, D.F. (2007) *Why Youth is Not Wasted on the Young: Immaturity in Human Development*. Oxford: Blackwell.
Bottéro, J. (1980) "'L'amour libre' à Babylone et ses 'servitudes'", in L. Poliakov (ed.) *Le couple interdit: Entretiens sur le racism*. Paris and The Hague: De Gruyter, pp. 27–42.

Carson, A. (1990) "Putting her in her place: Woman, dirt and desire", in D.M. Halperin, J.J. Winkler and F.I. Zeitlin (eds) *Before Sexuality: The Construction of Erotic Experience in the Ancient Greek World*. Princeton, NJ: Princeton University Press, pp. 135–69.

Cohen, L. (1994) "Old age: Cultural and critical perspectives", *Annual Review of Anthropology* 23: 135–58.

Cooper, J.S. (1980) "Critical review of Hermann Behrens, 'Enlil und Ninlil'", *Journal of Cuneiform Studies* 32: 175–88.

——(2002) "Virginity in ancient Mesopotamia", in S. Parpola and R. Whiting (eds) *Sex and Gender in the Ancient Near East*, Proceedings of the 47th Rencontre Assyriologique Internationale, Helsinki, 2–6 July 2001. Helsinki: Helsinki University Press, pp. 91–112.

——(2009) "Free love in Bablyonia", in X. Faivre, B. Lion and C. Michel (eds) *Et il y eut un esprit dans l'homme: Jean Bottéro et la Mésopotamie*. Paris: Maison René Ginouvès, pp. 257–60.

Curchin, L. (1980) "Old age in Sumer: Life expectancy and social status of the elderly", *Florilegium* 2: 61–70.

Dalley, S. (1989) *Myths from Mesopotamia: Creation, the Flood, Gilgamesh and Others*. Oxford/New York: Oxford University Press.

Draffkorn-Kilmer, A. (1976) "Speculations on Umul, the first baby", in B.L Eichler (ed.) *Sumerological Studies in Honour of Samuel Noah Kramer*, Alter Orientund Altes Testament 25. Kevelaer/Neukirchen-Vluyn: Butzon and Bercker, pp. 265–70.

Foucault, M. (1991) *Discipline and Punish: The Birth of the Prison*, trans. A. Sheridan. Harmondsworth: Penguin.

Frayne, D.R. (1997) *The Royal Inscriptions of Mesopotamia, Early Period, Vol. 3/2: Ur III Period (2112–2004 BC)*. Toronto, ON: University of Toronto Press.

Freeman, D. (1983) *Margaret Mead and Samoa: The Making and Unmaking of an Anthropological Myth*. Cambridge, MA: Harvard University Press.

Frymer-Kensky, T. (2000) "Lolita-Inanna", *NIN: Journal for Gender Studies in Antiquity* 1: 91–4.

George, A. (1999) *The Epic of Gilgamesh*. London: Penguin.

Guinan, A.K. (1997) "Auguries of hegemony: The sex omens of Mesopotamia", *Gender & History* 9 (3 November): 462–79.

Harris, R. (2000) *Gender and Aging in Mesopotamia: The Gilgamesh Epic and Other Ancient Literature*. Norman, OK: University of Oklahoma Press.

Jacobsen, T. (1987) *Harps That Once … : Sumerian Poetry in Translation*. New Haven, CT and London: Yale University Press.

Lambert, W.G. (1960) *Babylonian Wisdom Literature*. Oxford: Oxford University Press.

Lee, J. (2009) *Celebrity, Pedophilia, and Ideology in American Culture*. Amhurst, NY: Cambria Press.

Leick, G. (1994) *Sex and Eroticism in Mesopotamian Literature*. London and New York: Routledge.

Longman, T. (1991) *Fictional Akkadian Autobiography: A Generic and Comparative Study*. Winona Lake, IN: Eisenbrauns.

McLaren, A. (2007) *Impotence: A Cultural History*. Chicago, IL: University of Chicago Press.

Mead, M. (1928) *Coming of Age in Samoa*. Harmondsworth: Penguin.

——(1930) *Growing up in New Guinea*. Harmondsworth: Penguin.

Morris, I. (2005) "The Athenian Empire (478–404 BC)", Princeton/Stanford Working Papers in Classics, Version 1.0 December 2005. Available online at <http://www.princeton.edu/~pswpc/pdfs/morris/120508.pdf> (accessed 19 June 2013).

Müller, E.W. (ed.) (1985) *Geschlechtsreife und Legitimation zur Zeugung*, Veroffentlichungen des "Instituts fur Historische Antrhopologie e.V.". Freiburg: Alber.

Parpola, S. and Whiting, R. (eds) (2002) *Sex and Gender in the Ancient Near East*, Proceedings of the 47th Rencontre Assyriologique Internationale, Helsinki, 2–6 July 2001. Helsinki: Helsinki University Press, vol. 1.

Poliakov, L. (ed.) (1980) *Le couple interdit: Entretiens sur le racism*. Paris and The Hague: De Gruyter.

Roth, M.T. (1987) "Age at marriage and the household: A study of Neo-Babylonian and Neo-Assyrian forms", *Comparative Studies in Society and History* 29: 715–47.

Roth, M.T., Hoffner, H. and Michalowksi, P. (1997) *Law Collections from Mesopotamia and Asia Minor*. Atlanta, GA: Scholars Press.

Scheidel, W. (2005) "Marriage, families, and survival in the Roman imperial army: Demographic aspects", Princeton/Stanford Working Papers in Classics, Version 1.0 November 2005. Available online at <http://www.princeton.edu/~pswpc/pdfs/scheidel/110509.pdf> (accessed 19 June 2013).

Schumann, D. (ed.) (2010) *Raising Citizens in the "Century of the Child": The United States and German Central Europe in a Comparative Perspective*. Chicago, IL: Berghahn.

Sefati, Y. (1998) *Love Songs in Sumerian Literature: Critical Edition of the Dumuzi-Inanna Songs*. Ramat Gan: Bar Ilan University Press.

Stol, M. and Vleeming, S.P. (eds) (1998) *The Care of the Elderly in the Ancient Near East*. Leiden: Brill.

van Lerberghe, K. and Voet, G. (1999) *Languages and Cultures in Contact: At the Crossroads of Civilizations in the Syro-Mesopotamian Realm*. Leuven: Peeters Publishers.

Vanstiphout, H.L.J. (1999) "A meeting of cultures? Re-thinking the 'Marriage of Martu'", in K. van Lerberghe and G. Voet (eds) *Languages and Cultures in Contact: At the Crossroads of Civilizations in the Syro-Mesopotamian Realm*. Leuven: Peeters Publishers, pp. 461–74.

Vogelzang, M.E and Vanstiphout, H.L.J. (1996) (eds) *Mesopotamian Poetic Language: Sumerian and Akkadian*. Groningen: Styx.

Wilcke, C. (1985) "Familiengründung im alten Babylon", in E.W. Müller (ed.) *Geschlechtsreife und Legitimation zur Zeugung*. Freiburg: Alber, pp. 229–40.

——(1998) "The care of the elderly in Mesopotamia in the third millennium", in M. Stol and S.P. Vleeming (eds) *The Care of the Elderly in the Ancient Near East*. Leiden: Peeters, pp. 23–58.

PART II

Archaic, classical and Hellenistic Greece

6

FANTASY AND THE HOMOSEXUAL ORGY

Unearthing the sexual scripts of ancient Athens

Alastair Blanshard

Intercourse is often much more of an intellectual activity than a physical one. Desire mixes with the imagination to produce a narrative. At its base level, intercourse just requires two bodies, but the nature of those bodies – who they are, how and where they meet, the positions (both physical and intellectual) they adopt in relation to each other, and the manner in which they negotiate both the beginning and ending of their coupling – are determined by scripts that exist long before (and persist long after) any sexual encounter.[1] The study of sex is really the study of storytelling.

In the field of the sociology of sexuality, it is the work of John Gagnon and Bill Simon that has done most to promote the idea that sex conforms to narrative conventions, and is essentially "scripted".[2] Coming in the wake of Alfred Kinsey's pioneering studies of human sexual behaviour, they offered a break with Kinsey's essentialist transhistorical model of sex as an act driven by biologically determined libidinous urges. Individually and together, most notably through their co-authored monograph *Sexual Conduct: The Social Sources of Human Sexuality* (1973), they ushered into the social sciences the social–constructionist model for sexuality that would take root elsewhere in post-structuralist critical theory. As such the work of Gagnon and Simon represents a paradigm of social constructionism that exists independently of the Foucauldian tradition. Their ideas were formed a decade or so prior to Foucault's writing; and *Sexual Conduct* (1973), their path-breaking work, was published three years before the publication of *La volonté de savoir* (1976), the first volume of Foucault's *Histoire de la sexualité*. Yet, while their work has been extraordinarily influential among social scientists, they have been comparatively neglected in the field of classical studies, which has tended to look towards Foucault and the Continental tradition for its theoretical underpinnings.[3] So while debates have raged about the validity of Foucault's analysis of the ancient world, there has been little work done utilizing sociological models that permit similar conclusions and forms of analysis.[4]

Gagnon arrived at his ideas through his interest in criminology. In particular, he was heavily influenced by the Chicago school of urban sociology and criminology in which crime was treated like any other career, without the imposition of any moral judgment or ethical concern.[5] One became a mugger in much the same way as one became a banker, namely through "learning how to do a job, acquiring skills and insider knowledge, learning how to deal with all of the other social actors in a particular social milieu".[6] This approach, which treated all behaviour (occupational, deviant, etc.) as learned and acculturated, had profound implications for the study of sex. It meant that (Gagnon 1977: 2):

> in any given society, at any given moment, people become sexual in the same way as they became everything else. Without much reflection, they pick up directions from their social environment. They acquire and assemble meanings, skills, and values from the people around them. Their critical choices are often made by going along and drifting.

In the process of "drifting", subjects learned to put together "scripts" for their sexual behaviour; scripts that were in turn developed and reinforced through interpersonal interaction. These personal and interpersonal scripts were derived in turn from larger societal narratives. Scripting for Gagnon and Simon exists on three levels – the societal, the interpersonal, and the "intrapsychic" (the internal mental life of the individual). For historians of the ancient world, these last two forms of scripting are largely unrecoverable. The authorial "I" is such a slippery construct that searching for genuine internal monologues would seem a fruitless task.[7] Similarly, reasons of genre and preservation conspire against reliable accounts of interpersonal interactions. Instead, we are left with material that is best seen as reflecting the societal scripts of normative behaviour – the raw material out of which interpersonal and interpsychic scripts were derived.

One advantage of Gagnon and Simon's approach is that it focuses our attention away from questions of sexual identity and back onto narratives of behaviour, and in particular the place that raw ideological material plays in a narrative. It makes us analyse and appreciate events prior to and consequent upon sex, and makes us organize material within a more synthetic whole. Just as Foucault brought to our attention the way in which the discourse of sexuality was implicit in architecture, systems of social organization, regimes of medicine and education, so too does the work of Gagnon pressure us to consider how elements such as the movement of people through space, the organization of age-classes, the reading habits of youths, the stories that people hear, and the images to which men and women are exposed contribute to the formation of narratives about how sex should be.[8]

In this chapter, I want to examine the scripting of male-to-male group sexual behaviour in the classical period. Two types of sources feature in this account; the first is Greek vase painting and the second is Attic oratory. Both are the types of evidence that lend themselves readily to incorporation within normative sexual scripts. Attic vase painting may have exhibited a preference for elite motifs in its iconography, but the use of those vases spread beyond elite circles.[9] Moreover, their role in the symposium locates them at precisely the occasion where, as we shall see, sexual scripts have a habit of unfolding. In contrast, forensic rhetoric often best captures the gossip-driven discourse of the type most likely to form popular opinions.[10] It is the type of literature that comes closest to the background noise that influences those "critical choices" made by our hypothetical drifting sexual subject.[11]

My decision to focus on male-to-male sex reflects the contested, volatile, and problematic nature of these sexual encounters. This was an area in which expectations about age, status, and gender intersected. Sex between men was different because masculinity (both in its actuality and latent potentiality) occupies a privileged position. As numerous studies of Athenian homosexuality have shown, every element in the transaction – who was involved in sexual acts, their roles, and their courtship – was subject to complex negotiation. Male-to-male sexual encounters in ancient Greece involved an elaborate dance in a minefield of expectations and preconceptions. One misstep could prove disastrous. These liaisons were ripe for scripting. Indeed, without a firm script, sex could never have taken place.

Focusing on sex acts involving groups allows us to engage with one of the most pervasive constructs in the historical construction of sexuality, namely the "orgy". One of the persistent modern myths about antiquity is the existence of orgiastic sex. Strangely the meaning of what the term "orgy" signifies has shifted, but the belief that the ancients indulged in it (whatever the term means) has remained resolute.[12] Initially, driven by Christian religious anxiety, the term "orgy" was used in post-antique discourse to signify degenerate pagan cults and rites. Seventeenth-century sermons that rail against the "orgie" were not warning against the dangers of profligate sex, but blasphemy. Group sexual activity in the seventeenth-century imagination of the orgy, if it was even present, played only a small and inconsequential part in the conception of the orgy. At the start of the eighteenth century, writers on sexual activity, such as Fredrich Karl Forberg, struggled to find a term to denote group sexual activity. In *De figuris Veneris*, he eventually settled on the term *spintria*, which he derived from the pliable prostitutes mentioned in Suetonius' *Tiberius* (43.1). At no stage does he seem to have contemplated using the term "orgy" for group sexual activity. It took until the nineteenth century for the term to lose its strong religious connotations and end up signifying group sexual activity. From that point onwards, the notion of the "orgy" and group sex have become synonymous in the English language.

A fascination with group sex is understandable. It breaks so many taboos. It obliterates notions of monogamy and exclusivity; it collapses distinctions of private and public, and wraps up sexual activity in a charged environment of voyeuristic possibilities.[13] One can forgive outraged moralists or wistful sensualists for wanting such an institution to exist in the "bad/good old days". Yet, it is the contention of this chapter that our projections with regards to group-sex activity have blinded us to quite complex issues of representation. "Orgy scenes" in Greek vase painting are rarely unproblematic depictions of desirable fantasies designed to titillate their viewers. Instead, they are deeply coded and didactic. When more than one figure is involved, the scene is marked. We are not on familiar territory, but one pregnant with unusual, possibly dangerous, possibilities. The term "orgy" tends to normalize and becomes reductive; it makes us think that we understand the game at play. Instead, we need to recognize that as bodies proliferate, so do meanings.

Courtship scenes

The most common scene of men collectively involved in homosexual activity involves the courting of adolescents by older men.[14] We have a number of scenes in which groups of men approach younger men offering them traditional lovers' gifts. The challenge becomes to locate the "truth value" of these images. Is this a depiction of a social practice in action or an artfully constructed metaphor for the politics of engaging with a lover?

In practice, Greek art seems rarely bound by the demands of real life in its depictions. For example, Greek warfare was fought in phalanxes of dozens of men working tightly together. Yet the phalanx is largely absent from our artistic record. Instead, scenes of personal valour proliferate on classical red-figure vases.[15] Here we tend to see individuals fighting alone or in small groups. To find the phalanx, we need to look elsewhere. The most famous depiction of the phalanx is the seventh-century Proto-Corinthian Chigi oinochoe. However, the representation is practically unique. As Lissarrague remarked: "This first representation of the phalanx clearly also seems to be its last!"[16] Hoplite battle, the most distinctive and important male group activity for the Athenian citizen, deliberately seems to avoid any notion of the collective in its representation. The absence of the phalanx in Athenian art highlights the political and ideological dimension to Greek vase painting. In choosing to depict only individual hoplites in battle,

Greek art chooses the heroic and the aristocratic over the realistic. So if vase painting prefers to see individuals whereas the reality of the battlefield saw groups, what should we expect in games of love? Is this a case of the reverse applying? That art sees groups, where life saw more individual action?

Confirmatory evidence for the reality of group courting scenes is slight. Literary discussions of seduction rarely represent courting as an activity simultaneously involving numerous individuals pursuing numerous boys. Homosexual love poetry often laments the presence of rivals, but there is no sense that these rivals constituted a pack that moved together.

Indeed, there is an odd disjunction between the literary discourse surrounding seduction and its artistic representation. Greek art seems much less agonistic than Greek literature. In poetry, there are always numerous implicit rivals for the beloved's attention, and this is never a friendly rivalry. Theognis worries about losing his beloved to others who mischievously spread lies about the poet (Theognis 1238a–1242). Similarly, other literary sources give an impression of high-stakes, cut-throat competition for beautiful boys. All friendship seems to go out the window when Charmides enters the gymnasium as colleagues jostle to sit next to the beautiful young man.[17] The stories about the scores of lovers pursuing Alcibiades collected in Plutarch are no doubt gossipy exaggerations, but they attest to a view in which the beloved was always outnumbered by would-be seducers who gave each other no quarter.[18] The figure of the "wing-man", the confidant and associate in seduction, who has been a feature of western erotics since the eighteenth century, seems largely absent from Greek discourse. While friends may aid in the abduction of youths or applaud success in seduction, they do not seem to assist in the process of courting either by praising the attributes of the seducer or ingratiating themselves with the beloved's friends to facilitate access to the beloved; standard features of a "wingman".[19] Instead, in the literary depiction of Greek courtship, every lover seems to find himself alone fighting a battle against innumerable rivals.

Greek art gives no sense of such rivalry or such insurmountable odds. In scenes of group courtship, the beloved is rarely significantly outnumbered by needy lovers.[20] For every man, there seems to be a boy, and there is no sense of one boy being preferred over others. No man seems to have settled for a second choice. Theognis may have worried about ending up with an uncomely youth (1344), but in Greek vase painting this never seems to be a problem.

The pleasure world of Greek pottery is a place of superabundance.[21] Its vision is utopian. Wine is always flowing, vines are heavy with grapes, the effects of starvation and poverty are absent. It should not surprise us that its lovers should find themselves freed from the burdens of competition as well as every other care.

On one level, this is the very particular pleasure that these group seduction scenes identify. The point is not the joy of seducing boys in groups, but the joy of being able to stand alongside another man, and not have to worry about a rival. The pairings of man and youth are pointedly lost in each other's eyes. Limbs do not cross from one couple to the other. There is no hint of voyeurism. Each couple is very much alone in the throng of seduction. Occasionally, we find an "odd man out" in such scenes who stands off to the side, but the pathos of his position only increases our perception of the desirability of the scene unfolding (Figure 6.1).[22] He provides the frame, often both literally and figuratively.

Yet these group seduction scenes often serve another purpose. They are didactic as well as fantastic. The range of bodies allows for the representation of a range of courting behaviour. Through the group it is possible to sketch out the limits of the normative. These images become exercises in expressing the acceptable.

The imagery is often precisely targeted towards those issues that we know were most problematic. So, for example, we know that lovers' gifts were a topic of anxiety. The line between

Figure 6.1 Detail of red-figure kylix; the Peithinos cup. Berlin, Antikensammlung, inv. no. F2279.

courtship and prostitution was thin. Gifts needed to be precisely calibrated to the *arête* ("virtue") of the beloved. They could not be so little as to be insulting nor so great that they implied a mercenary nature to the encounter.[23] In such circumstances, vases that choose to rehearse the variety of suitable lovers' gifts provide a useful and timely reminder of what constitutes appropriate behaviour. Like the endless repetition of the gifts of "chocolates and flowers" in depictions of mid-twentieth-century courting, these images also normalize such gifts, draining them of the potential to misfire. At the same time, they can also serve to remind the viewers of the complexities of courtship.

A kylix from the first half of the fifth century attributed to Macron (but potted by Heiron) provides a good example of such an interest in the intricacies of homosexual gift exchange.[24] The vase features a καλός-inscription to Hippodamas on its interior. At the same time as declaring its love for the boy, the vase also indulges in instruction about how such boys should be approached. The vase provides the viewer with an intriguing repertoire of lovers' gifts. One side of the vase shows a standard courtship scene of boys paired with youths. However, on the other side of the vase, we see the lovers offering a range of gifts to the beloved (Figure 6.2). These include a sprig of flowers, a rabbit, and a fighting cock. All of these gifts as standard lovers' gifts can be paralleled in vase painting.[25] What makes this scene distinctive is the attitude that the boys adopt in relation to the gifts.[26] Read from right to left, we see the boys increasingly unwrapping themselves from their cloaks and exposing their bodies as each gift is offered in turn. The boy receiving the garland remains tightly bound in his cloak, the boy receiving the rabbit bares a shoulder to his suitor and reaches out for it with an open hand while the boy receiving the cockerel has undressed himself almost completely. In this game of seduction, the power of the cockerel seems to trump all.

Yet, while the image seems a ringing endorsement of the cockerel as a lover's gift (and on one level functions as such), it also prompts the viewer to interrogate the attitudes of the beloved. Should one admire or think less of the boy who has undressed for the cockerel? The vase refuses to endorse any one position over the other. The ardour of the man offering the garland seems in no way diminished by the refusal of the boy to undress. Is the flirtatious undressing of the middle youth a sensible compromise between the exhibitionism and frigidity of his companions?

Certainly over-eagerness is problematized in vase painting. Again, it is a moral best illustrated in a group courting scene where a range of actions can be stylized and eagerness contexualized.

Figure 6.2 Detail of red-figure kylix, *c.*500–450 BC. Munich, Antikensammlungen, inv. no. 2655.

Over-eager youths are a figure of fun from some of our earliest black-figure examples.[27] One motif used to illustrate an unseemly interest in the lover's gift is the "snatched gift" motif where the lover is shown, seemingly in censure, to take back the gift from the outstretched arms of the youth.[28]

A kylix by Douris plays with this motif particularly effectively. The vase is dated to the first half of the fifth century BC and represents one of the most engaged depictions of the politics of courtship in the Athenian repertoire. The politics of pederasty dominates the vase. In the tondo, beneath a καλός-inscription, we see a bearded man approaching a seated youth. In his left hand he holds out a bag. The contents of such bags have intrigued scholars. They regularly feature in scenes of erotic courtship of both men and women. They have been read as money-bags and as containers for knucklebones.[29] One's view of the contents often depends on how mercenary you see the unfolding transactions. Those who favour exploitative readings prefer to see the object as a money-bag; those who prefer more romantic associations see the bags as containing gifts. The image plays with the ambiguity that lies at the heart of all gift exchange.[30] One sees what one wants to see. No real clue is given by the surrounding context in this kylix. We see the scene at precisely the moment where courtship is poised between success and failure. The eyes of the lover and the beloved are locked, but what each party is thinking remains a mystery. The beloved's hand is raised, but it is uncertain whether it is to accept or reject the gift.

The indeterminacy of the central image is given increased potency by the images that decorate the sides of the cup. A series of courting men and youths are depicted. On one side, the courtship seems to be going badly. Two youths are approached by three men. Two older men offer a youth a fillet and a wreath respectively. Standing between them, the youth shows pleasure at neither. He stares downcast at the ground, making eye-contact with neither suitor. The other youth is even more emphatic in his rejection of the suitor's gift of a tendril. Such scenes of rejection are unusual. In the fantasy world of pederastic courtship, gifts are almost always successful. This bleak scene adds a dark note to an otherwise joyful repertoire.

The scenes of rejection demonstrate the importance of understanding images in terms of a vase's overall decorative schema. In this case, the scenes of rejection need to be seen as operating alongside (and balanced by) the other side of the kylix, which shows a scene of resoundingly successful courtship (Figure 6.3). The scenes are constructed as polar opposites. This time the men are outnumbered by the youths. Three youths delight in their lovers' gifts. On this side of the vase, the offer of a fillet has had the desired effect with a youth standing off to the right holding it out in admiration. On the far left, a youth plays with the chest of a man who holds a sprig very similar to the one rejected previously. However, the most successful suitor occupies the centre position of the scene. Here we see a naked youth grasping for a long tendril held just out of reach by his lover. In his eagerness he leans forward, reaching to grasp it, not realizing that as he does so, he offers his genitals to the caress of his pursuer. It is a jokey image that plays with the dangers of seeming too eager to accept a lover's gift. The boy with his lack of modesty and restraint ends up looking foolish, easy prey.

Looking for the orgy

While the corpus of pederastic imagery is generous with advice about the opening stages of a sexual script, it provides less guidance about negotiating the problems of consummation of desire. Scenes depicting homosexual intercourse are rare. They are "inherently exceptional".[31] The same stricture applies even more so where consummation occurs as part of a group.

In his study of Athenian erotic vase painting, Kilmer (1993) lists only one example of male homosexual group copulation. It is not a straightforward example. The scene is found on a red-figure kylix in Turin (inv. 4117) dated to 500–475 BC (Figure 6.4). The piece was found in the 1830s near Vulci and originally formed part of the collection of Lucien Bonaparte, Prince of Canino and Musiagno (inv. 3032).

The tondo of the cup features an unbearded helmeted warrior holding a shield decorated with a bull's head device and a lance. He is depicted in a running pose and so is tentatively identified as performing in the hoplitodromos. The head of the figure is bracketed on each side

Figure 6.3 Detail of red-figure kylix, attributed to Douris, *c*.480–470 BC. New York: Metropolitan Museum of Art, inv. no. 52.11.4.

Figure 6.4 Detail of red-figure kylix, *c.*500–475 BC. Turin, Museo di Antichità, inv. no. 4117.

by the word παῖς written so that it was possible to read the formula ὁ παῖς καλός ("the boy is beautiful") both forward and retrograde round the rim. The inscription of this sentiment as both description and exclamation of desire seems appropriate given the paradigmatic example of youthful masculinity that it frames.

If the tondo represents the acceptable face of young male behaviour, the sides of the cup present its riotous inverse. On one side we have four youths clustered around a wineskin.[32] Inebriation rather than sex is the pleasure that they seek. One youth ladles out unmixed wine into the cups of his compatriots. One youth is receiving his share. The two youths behind him holding skyphoi turn their heads, seemingly distracted by the scene on the other side of the vase.

That the sight of the activity occurring on this side of the vase should prove distracting seems understandable. The attitudes of the figures are unparalleled in Greek art. The vase features two youths bent over with their buttocks pressed against each other; between them stands a youth facing the viewer front-on. The details are indistinct here. However, there is (perhaps) the suggestion that the figure in the centre has placed his penis between their buttocks and is enjoying an act of frottage in a manner that mimics intercrural intercourse. He balances, resting his hands on the hips of the two bent over youths. This central grouping is surrounded by four youths, two on either side. To the far left, one youth looks back at the central scene over his shoulder. He is possibly masturbating. However, damage to the vase prevents confirmation of this, and the gesture he adopts would equally be acceptable as a dancing gesture. To his right a youth stands with his arms raised with an erect phallus. On the other side of the central grouping we see one youth largely naked with his cloak over his extended arm. On the far right, a naked youth mimics the gesture of the youth on the far left.

As a depiction of an "orgy", this vase raises more questions than it answers. First, many of the key details remain sketchy. The identification of masturbation is tentative. The precise mechanics of the central group are unclear. Kilmer suggests "we are meant to imagine that the middle youth has his penis caught between the buttocks of his young friends, his hands on their sides controlling the pressure on it" (Kilmer 1993: 26). However, it is equally plausible that the central youth is merely resting his hands as he guides the buttocks of his companions together. That something sexual is happening here would seem to be indicated by the erection of one of the figures. But this remains the only certain signifier of strong erotic content and that this scene is not some convoluted form of drunken gymnastics.[33] At the very least, it seems to be an inefficient orgy where eleven figures gather, but only potentially one participant gets any sexual release.

Even if we could determine the mechanics of the scene, its register would remain elusive. It is hard to see this scene as unquestionably aspirational. Sympotic vases were equally keen to stress the dangers of the symposium as much as its delights. The drinking of the wine straight from the skin, at the very least, raises questions about its legitimacy.[34] The frontal face of the key participant is striking. Frontal faces are comparatively rare, usually reserved for figures in a high emotional state, drunk, or dead.[35] They are never normative. Whatever pleasure he is taking from his colleagues, it is marked out as extraordinary.

One can compare the Turin vase with another kylix from the Canino collection with a homoerotic sensibility, now in the British Museum.[36] This celebrated cup by Douris reverses the iconographic arrangement we have previously seen. Here normative behaviour, this time a very restrained symposium, with bearded men and naked slave boys, dominates the outside, while the scene of trangressive abandon is limited to a drunken komast staggering with kylix and staff in the tondo. There is clearly eroticism at play in the scene of the symposium as the reclined drinkers admire the naked serving boys. In particular, the gaze of the figure on the far right on both panels seems acutely intense. However, looking is where the action ends. Pleasure lies in restraint. The viewer is warned about what happens if this lesson is not heeded by the figure in the tondo.

The unusualness of the Turin orgy (if this is what it is) is strengthened when we look at it alongside other scenes of group sex involving female prostitutes.[37] Not only is the sexual intercourse much more graphic in these vases, but the scenes feature many more participants involved in the act. Furthermore, as a number of commentators have observed, these orgies are not scenes of "good sex".[38] The female figures are depicted as old and flabby. The sex is brutal and degrading. These sex acts are arguably a sign that matters have gone terribly wrong rather than terribly right for the participants.

The idea that the orgy is the result of affairs getting out of hand is confirmed by one of our most graphic depictions of group homosexual sex. This occurs on the side of a kylix attributed to the Nikosthenes painter (see Figure 7.5).[39] This involves an orgy of five satyrs. On the left, one stands with his arms outstretched as he is fellated by another satyr bent over. At this satyr's feet lies a satyr staring face up as his legs are hoisted onto the shoulders of yet another satyr who is about to penetrate him anally with his large erection. To his right the final member of the group is seen sneaking off clutching his phallus. His intent is obvious. He is off to molest a sphinx that stands guard as a decorative border element for the scene.

The scene is designed as a shocking counterpoint to the rest of the vase, which adopts fairly conventional and respectable imagery. On the other side we have Heracles and Apollo in contest over the Delphic tripod. The interior features a seated warrior. As always with satyrs, the scene is supposed to disgust and amuse.[40] We are not supposed to take this scene as a serious invitation to join in the frolic. We are supposed to recoil. That is the joke. The orgy repels. It puts the drinker in a difficult position. How does he hold the vase? Which side does he show? Which does he keep for himself? As the drinker twirls the vase, the image just becomes more obscene.

Dionysian excess and transgression informs another influential early example of homosexual group sex in Attic vase painting. This is found on a Tyrrhenian amphora dated to the mid- to late sixth century that was found during the excavations of the Orvieto necropolis in the 1870s–80s (Figure 6.5).[41] Although the export nature of the vase already compromises the imagery for a discussion of the raw material for sexual scripting in Athens, there are further reasons to doubt the realia of the imagery.

This image has featured in a number of discussions of erotic art. However, it has rarely been acknowledged that this scene is not an independent panel, but actually half of a frieze that runs around the shoulder of the vase. In order to fully understand this scene, we need to examine the other side of the vase.[42] It is this other side that provides the context for this riotous outbreak of sex. Here we see that the catalyst for all this commotion is the god Dionysus. He occupies a central position in this panel seated on a stool. Behind him stands a masturbating satyr. Behind the satyr, we see others in procession: a man with a huge flaccid phallus and a dancing maenad. The man looks over his shoulder at the scene behind him, linking the two panels. Further links between the panels are established by the presence of dancing maenads and the male figure who is not patting "his rump invitingly as he turns back to face a man approaching with his phallus at the ready" (Sutton 2000: 185), but who has in fact adopted a standard dancing pose and so is choreographed like a number of other figures in the two scenes.[43]

The scene of sexual congress occurs in the train of a Dionysiac ensemble. It is part of a thiasos. Sex is what that this god of carnivalesque disorder leaves in his wake. This scene represents the inverted, dangerous, and destabilizing power of Dionysus' presence. The anti-nomian nature of this "orgy" is underlined by the age discrepancy of the two principal figures. Only Dionysus can create a world where young men penetrate their elders.

It is worth stressing that at no stage in our discussion of scenes of group sex has the depiction ever been about the pleasure of sex in a group. Where multiple bodies have piled up, there have always been other considerations to the fore. Groups have served technical iconographic functions allowing a range of attitudes and consequences to be properly and simultaneously displayed. Where group sex has occurred the sex has always been marginal, suspicious, or fantastic. Reading these images as evidence of an orgy culture is highly problematic. The scripts that these images engender are not scripts about the pleasure of collective copulation. If anything, they push in the opposite direction and normalize sex as an encounter between individuals.

It is important to stress the abnormality of these scenes because the alternative, namely reading these images as straightforwardly aspirational, has important consequences. Significant interest, for example, has been shown in the Turin kylix because, as Dover pointed out, the scene belongs to a small group of images which depict sexual activity between coevals and so challenges notions of a strict hierarchy of age and status between the *erastes* and the *eromenos*.[44] While Dover was quick to dismiss these scenes as "peripheral, special or ambiguous" (1978: 86), others have been keen to incorporate the Turin vase into a more mainstream depiction of homosexuality.[45] Claiming the Turin kylix as a portrayal of standard practice between youths makes a large difference to how we conceive of Greek male-to-male sexual activity. It throws out a number of important coordinates and demands that, at the very least, we rethink the criteria for how roles are determined in sexual congress (what makes the boy in the middle so special?). However, we only tie ourselves up in such knots if we treat this image as standard rather than freakish.

Epilogue: A threesome at the Dionysia

I want to conclude this examination of homosexual group couplings by suggesting a reading of a literary text that plays with the potential of such an act. It occurs in the course of Aeschines' prosecution speech against his political rival Timarchus.

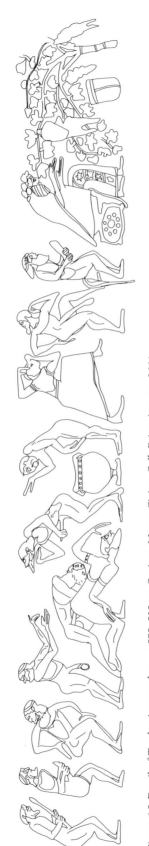

Figure 6.5 Detail of Tyrrhenian amphora, *c*.575–525 BC. Orvieto, Museo Civico, Coll. Faina, inv. no. 2664.

Ever since Dover, the speech has occupied a central place in discussions of Greek homosexuality.[46] Aeschines' central allegation in the speech was that Timarchus had acted as a male prostitute.[47] Over the course of the speech, Aeschines rehearsed a litany of tropes about acceptable and unacceptable homosexual activity. He argued that Timarchus should be punished not only because he accepted money for sex, but also because he took an unacceptable number of lovers and those lovers were often of particularly low status, including public slaves.[48]

According to Aeschines' narrative, early on in Timarchus' career he had been taken up by an Athenian citizen named Misgolas. Aeschines is frank about the undesirability and unacceptability of this relationship (1.42):

> This abomination, while still in the bloom of youth, felt no shame in leaving his father's house and taking up with Misgolas, a man who was not a friend of his father nor a contemporary, but an older stranger, who could not slake his desires.

His affair with Misgolas represents the start of Timarchus' decline into depravity. After Misgolas, his lovers become more frequent and base.

One of the first signs of Timarchus' corrupt nature is an incident that Aeschines reports as occurring at the City Dionysia (*Against Timarchus* 43–4). Misgolas and Timarchus had arranged to process together as part of the festivities. However, Timarchus never made his scheduled rendezvous. Misgolas and his associate Phaedrus go looking for the youth, and they encounter him lunching with a group of foreigners in a boarding-house (ἐν συνοκίᾳ).

In anger, Misgolas and Phaedrus accuse the foreigners of corrupting a free youth and threaten them with imprisonment. Alarmed, the foreigners run away, leaving Timarchus to his outraged lover. It is worthwhile speculating precisely what the jury imagined either had happened in that room or was about to happen when Misgolas and Phaedrus burst in. Aeschines deliberately avoids setting up a picture of a symposium. The verb to describe the dining (συναριστάω) is not used of sympotic banquets.[49] The only figures mentioned as present are the foreigners, and Timarchus was clearly outnumbered. Aeschines is vague about the number of foreigners (μετὰ ξένων τινῶν), but the stress on the plural is clear. Moreover, all of the foreigners are accused of the crime of corruption. It is tempting to read into this scene an implication of a group-sex act in which Timarchus services a number of clients. The fact that this occurred during the festival of the City Dionysia, a time of inversion and licence, adds extra supporting colour.

If this was Aeschines' implication, then, given the preceding discussion, this episode, described by Aeschines as "known to everyone" (44), takes on a particularly damning character. Assuming that group-sex activities were regarded as particularly base and abnormal, the charge against Timarchus demonstrates just how depraved Timarchus' character was. Central to Aeschines' allegations were the charges that Timarchus lacked a moral compass and was unable to exercise any restraint. What better sign of this than an inability to limit himself to just one lover. It deepens his betrayal of Misgolas and prepares the jury for the subsequent claims of Timarchus' debasement with the public slave Pittalacus.

The Timarchus case demonstrates that group sex was never an unproblematic issue for the Athenians. The politics of sexual couplings was difficult enough without adding extra bodies into the mix. Athenian sexual protocols were based on a strongly hierarchical schema. The mutuality and the desire to share that underlies group sexual activity was largely absent from the culture. The problem with an orgy is that you never could be certain that you were getting the better deal. There was always the suspicion that your compatriot is enjoying greater pleasures. Some resolution of these issues could be achieved if the sexually penetrated was debased enough so that the penetrators' status was heavily reinforced, but the sex that resulted was never pretty. This was a script that the intelligent actor avoided.

Notes

1 Cf. Gagnon (2004: 61): "scripts name the actors, describe their qualities, indicate the motives for behavior of participants, and set the sequence of appropriate activities, both verbal and non-verbal, that should take place to conclude behavior successfully and allow transitions into new activities".

2 For a retrospective view of the contribution of Gagnon and Simon, see Kimmel 2007. Gagnon 2004: 59–87 (reprint of his 1974 essay "Scripts and the co-ordination of sexual conduct") provides a useful introduction to the concept of scripting and its applicability to the study of human sexual behaviour.

3 Cf. Halperin 1990: 6–8, 62–71, 1995: 3–6, 2002: 7–10, 25–6; Halperin et al. 1990; Larmour et al. 1998; Winkler 1990: 3–4.

4 For criticism of the influence of Foucault in classics from a variety of perspectives, see Cohen and Saller 1994; Davidson 2001; Goldhill 1995; Paglia 1991; Richlin 1991, 1993; Sissa 1999.

5 For discussion of the Chicago School and its contribution, see Abbott 1998; Bulmer 1986; Rubin 2002: 21–35; Williams and McShane 1998: 53–112.

6 Gagnon quoted in "Revisiting the text: An interview with John Gagnon" in Kimmel 2007: 276.

7 The problems of the authorial "I" in the discourses of love have long been recognized, most notably in the study of Roman elegy and satire, see Allen 1950; Anderson 1982; Nappa 2001; Veyne 1988.

8 For example, see Foucault 1978: 27–8 on the manner in which sexual discourse permeates the regimes of the eighteenth-century secondary school.

9 A useful summary of the issues relating to social status and the consumption of Greek vase imagery is provided in Pritchard 1999. Admittedly, most of the vases discussed were found outside of Athens. However, they were not, except in the case of the Tyrrhenian amphorae, specifically produced for export and so may fairly represent the types of imagery in circulation within Athens. Cf. Osborne 2004.

10 On the importance of gossip and its preservation in Attic oratory, see Hunter 1990.

11 For Attic oratory as the best type of evidence for popular morality, see Dover 1975: 5–14, 1978: 13–14.

12 Blanshard 2010: 48–56 discusses the shifting nature of the term "orgy" and the history of popular fascination with it as an ancient institution.

13 For studies on the history of the orgy and its appeal, see Arno 1988; Barker and Langdridge 2010: esp. chs by McDonald and Phillips; Bartell 1971; Partridge 1964.

14 The term "courtship scene" was coined by John Beazley in *Some Attic Vases in the Cyprus Museum* (Oxford, 1948). For discussion of this and the scene type, see Shapiro 1981.

15 Lorimer 1947 collects the evidence for depictions of the phalanx.

16 Lissarrague (1990a: 14): "[L]a première représentation de la phalange semble bien être aussi la dernière!"

17 Cf. Plato, *Charmides* 155b–c.

18 Plutarch, *Alcibiades* 3.1, 4.1.

19 For assistance in the abduction of youths, see Lysias 3.12; Ephorus of Cyme fr. 149 *FGrH* (practices on Crete). Ion of Chios fr. 8 (Athen. 13.603f–604d) for friends applauding skill in seduction at a symposium. For the modern sociological phenomenon of friends as enablers in seduction, see Ackerman and Kenrick 2009.

20 Hubbard 2003: 11. There are a few examples where there is the odd spare lover. For discussion of these examples, see below.

21 Lissarrague 1990b: esp. 3–16.

22 The Peithinios cup (Berlin, Antikensammlung F2279) provides a good example of the motif; cf. Shapiro 1981: 143 n.76 with pl. 26 and Davidson 2007: 425–39 ("here the gymnasium looks more like an occasion for a teen orgy": 426).

23 On the problematics of gift-giving, see Kurke 1999: 178–82 and Von Reden 1995: esp. 195–206.

24 ARV^2 471.196 (Munich, Antikensammlungen 2655).

25 See, for example, rabbits: ARV^2 471.193 (Kunsthistoriches Museum, Vienna, IV, 3698); 375.68 (Vatican H550); fighting cocks: ABV 134.30 (Vatican Museum 352); flowers: ARV^2 437.114 (Metropolitan Museum, NY 52.11.4).

26 Contrast ARV^2 471.193, another vase by Macron, where we see a similar exercise in providing a repertoire of gifts (money-bag? knucklebones? and rabbit); but there is no attempt to differentiate between attitudes of the courted.

27 Cf. Black-figure kantharos (Boston, Museum of Fine Arts: 08.292), Dover 1978: B 598.

28 *ARV²* 375.68 (Vatican H550, attrib. Brygos) illustrates the motif with a hare snatched from a youth. Surrounding youths enjoy dogs as gifts.

29 For discussion, see Keuls 1993: 260–5; Pinney 1986; Rabinowitz 2011: 129–36; Von Reden 1995: 195–203.

30 Lear and Cantarella 2008: 85–6 who stress the incongruity between a potentially mercenary gift and the fact that "the *eromenos* is portrayed canonically as a praiseworthy *eromenos*".

31 Lear and Cantarella 2008: 106.

32 For the symbolism of the wine-skin, see Lissarrague 1990b: 68–76.

33 In a number of features, the scene is reminiscent of a kylix (London, British Museum, inv. 1866,0805.4) attributed to the Brygos painter in which drunken youths cavort, including one who bends over to expose his anus. Cf. *ARV²* 113.4 (Warsaw, National Museum, inv. no. 198514) for another example of drunken japes with a sexual colouring.

34 On drinking unmixed wine, see Lissarrague 1990b: 7–9.

35 The classic study of the connotations of frontality in Greek art is Frontisi-Ducroux 1995: esp. 77–132.

36 *ARV²* 432.52 (London, British Museum, inv. 1843,1103.15).

37 The two most infamous examples are the cups by the Pedieus painter (Louvre G 13) and the Brygos painter (Florence 3912). For illustrations, see Keuls 1993: 184–6.

38 Cf. the observations of Sutton 2000: 195–7 and Lear and Cantarella 2008: 126–7.

39 *ARV²* 1700 (Berlin, Antikensammlung: 1964.4).

40 For the world of satyrs as "a counter-model produced by proximity and distance", see Lissarrague 1990c.

41 *ABV* 102.100 (Orvieto, Museo Civico, Coll. Faina, inv. 2664).

42 For a similar highly eroticized band on a Tyrrhenian amphora that draws the viewer's eye around the vase, see the band of satyrs and maenads on Florence, Museo Archeologico Etrusco, inv. no. 3773 (560–550 BC).

43 For similar poses, see the collection in Smith 2007.

44 For the scene as emblematic of homosexual sex between those of the same age, see Dover 1978: 86–7 with discussion.

45 See, for example, Hubbard who describes the Turin kylix as an example of "graphic scenes of sexual experimentation between youths" (Hubbard 2003: 5).

46 Cf. Dover 1978: 9, 13–14 (on the importance of Aeschines, *Against Timarchus*).

47 Fisher 2001: 1–67 provides an excellent introduction to the speech and its historical and social background.

48 Aeschines, *Against Timarchus* 51–2 (frequency of lovers), 54–5 (Pittalacus, public slave as Timarchus' lover). On the issue of Pittalacus' real status, see Fisher 2004: 66–7.

49 See, for example, Aristophanes *Birds* 1486–7.

Bibliography

Abbott, A. (1998) "Of time and space: The contemporary relevance of the Chicago School", *Social Forces* 75: 1149–82.

Ackerman, J.M. and Kenrick, D.T. (2009) "Cooperative courtship: Helping friends raise and raze relationship barriers", *Personality and Social Psychology Bulletin* 35: 1285–300.

Allen, A.W. (1950) "'Sincerity' and the Roman elegists", *Classical Philology* 45: 145–60.

Anderson, W.S. (1982) *Essays on Roman Satire*. Princeton, NJ: Princeton University Press.

Arno, K. (1988) *Threesomes: Studies in Sex, Power, and Intimacy*. New York: Beech Tree Books.

Barker, M. and Langdridge, D. (eds) (2010) *Understanding Non-monogamies*. New York: Routledge.

Bartell, G.D. (1971) *Group Sex. An Eyewitness Report on the American Way of Swinging*. New York: Signet.

Blanshard, A.J.L. (2010) *Sex: Vice and Love from Antiquity to Modernity*. Malden, MA: Wiley Blackwell.

Bulmer, M. (1986) *The Chicago School of Sociology: Institutionalization, Diversity, and the Rise of Sociological Research*. Chicago, IL: University of Chicago Press.

Cohen, D. and Saller, R. (1994) "Foucault on sexuality in Greco-Roman antiquity", in J. Goldstein (ed.) *Foucault and the Writing of History*. Oxford: Blackwell, pp. 35–62.

Davidson, J. (2001) "Dover, Foucault and Greek homosexuality: Penetration and the truth of sex", *Past and Present* 170: 3–51.

——(2007) *The Greeks and Greek Love: A Radical Reappraisal of Homosexuality in Ancient Greece*. London: Weidenfeld and Nicolson.

Dover, K.J. (1975) *Greek Popular Morality in the Time of Plato and Aristotle*. Oxford: Oxford University Press.

——(1978) *Greek Homosexuality*. London: Gerald Duckworth.

Fisher, N. (2001) *Aeschines, Against Timarchos: Introduction, Translation, and Commentary*. Oxford: Oxford University Press.

——(2004) "The perils of Pittalakos: Settings of cock fighting and dicing in classical Athens", in S. Bell and G. Davies (eds) *Games and Festivals in Classical Antiquity*. Oxford: Archaeopress, pp. 65–78.

Foucault, M. (1976) *Histoire de la sexualité*. Paris: Gallimard.

——(1978) *The History of Sexuality: Volume 1, An Introduction*, trans. R. Hurley. Harmondsworth: Penguin.

Frontisi-Ducroux, F. (1995) *Du masque au visage: Aspects de l'identité en Grèce ancienne*. Paris: Flammarion.

Gagnon, J.H. (1977) *Human Sexualities*. Glenview, IL: Scott Foresman.

——(2004) *An Interpretation of Desire: Essays in the Study of Sexuality*. Chicago, IL: University of Chicago Press.

Gagnon, J.H. and Simon, W. (1973) *Sexual Conduct: The Social Sources of Human Sexuality*. Chicago, IL: Aldine.

Goldhill, S. (1995) *Foucault's Virginity: Ancient Erotic Fiction and the History of Sexuality*. Cambridge: Cambridge University Press.

Halperin, D.M. (1990) *One Hundred Years of Homosexuality and Other Essays on Greek Love*. New York: Routledge.

——(1995) *Saint Foucault: Towards a Gay Hagiography*. Oxford: Oxford University Press.

——(2002) *How to Do the History of Homosexuality*. Chicago, IL: University of Chicago Press.

Halperin, D.M., Winkler, J.J. and Zeitlin, F.I. (eds) (1990) *Before Sexuality: The Construction of Erotic Experience in the Ancient Greek World*. Princeton, NJ: Princeton University Press.

Hubbard, T.K. (2003) *Homosexuality in Greece and Rome: A Sourcebook of Basic Documents*. Berkeley and Los Angeles, CA: University of California Press.

Hunter, V. (1990) "Gossip and the politics of reputation in Classical Athens", *Phoenix* 44: 299–325.

Keuls, E.C. (1993) *The Reign of the Phallus: Sexual Politics in Ancient Athens*. Berkeley and Los Angeles, CA: University of California Press.

Kilmer, M.F. (1993) *Greek Erotica on Attic Red-Figure Vases*. London: Duckworth.

Kimmel, M. (ed.) (2007) *The Sexual Self: The Construction of Sexual Scripts*. Nashville, TN: Vanderbuilt University Press.

Kurke, L. (1999) *Coins, Bodies, Games, and Gold: The Politics of Meaning in Archaic Greece*. Princeton, NJ: Princeton University Press.

Larmour, D.H.J., Miller, P.A. and Platter, C. (eds) (1998) *Rethinking Sexuality: Foucault and Classical Antiquity*. Princeton, NJ: Princeton University Press.

Lear, A. and Cantarella, E. (2008) *Images of Greek Pederasty: Boys Were Their Gods*. London: Routledge.

Lissarrague, F. (1990a) *L'autre guerrier: Archers, peltastes, cavaliers dans l'imagerie attique*. Paris and Rome: La Découverte/École française de Rome.

——(1990b) *The Aesthetics of the Greek Banquet: Images of Wine and Ritual*, trans. A. Szegedy-Maszak. Princeton, NJ: Princeton University Press.

——(1990c) "The sexual life of satyrs", in D.M. Halperin, J.J. Winkler and F.I. Zeitlin (eds) *Before Sexuality: The Construction of Erotic Experience in the Ancient Greek World*. Princeton, NJ: Princeton University Press, pp. 53–82.

Lorimer, H.L. (1947) "The hoplite phalanx with special reference to the poems of Archilochus and Tyrtaeus", *Annual of the British School at Athens* 42: 76–138.

Nappa, C. (2001) *Aspects of Catullus' Social Fiction*. Frankfurt am Main: P. Lang.

Osborne, R. (2004) "Images of a warrior: On a group of Athenian vases and their public", in C. Marconi (ed.) *Greek Vases: Images, Contexts and Controversies*. Leiden: Brill, pp. 41–54.

Paglia, C. (1991) "Junk bonds and corporate raiders: Academe in the hour of the wolf", *Arion* 1(2): 139–212.

Partridge, B. (1964) *A History of Orgies*. London: Spring Books.

Pinney, G.F. (1986) "Money-bags?", *American Journal of Archaeology* 90: 218.

Pritchard, D.M. (1999) "Fool's gold and silver: Reflections on the evidentiary status of finely painted Attic pottery", *Antichthon* 33: 1–27.

Rabinowitz, N.S. (2011) "Sex for sale? Interpreting erotica in the Havana collection", in A. Glazebrook and M.M. Henry (eds) *Greek Prostitutes in the Ancient Mediterranean, 800 BCE–200 CE*. Madison, WI: University of Wisconsin Press, pp. 122–46.

Richlin, A. (1991) "Zeus and Metis: Foucault, feminism, Classics", *Helios* 18: 160–80.

——(1993) "Not before homosexuality: The materiality of the *cinaedus* and the Roman law against love between men", *Journal of the History of Sexuality* 3: 523–73.

Rubin, G. (2002) "Studying sexual subcultures: Excavating the ethnography of gay communities in North America", in E. Lewin and W. Leap (eds) *Out in Theory: The Emergence of Gay and Lesbian Anthropology*. Urbana, IL: University of Illinois Press, pp. 17–68.

Shapiro, H.A. (1981) "Courtship scenes in Attic vase-painting", *American Journal of Archaeology* 85: 133–43.

Sissa, G. (1999) "Sexual bodybuilding: Aeschines against Timarchus", in J.I. Porter (ed.) *Constructions of the Classical Body*. Ann Arbor, MI: University of Michigan Press, pp. 147–68.

Smith, T.J. (2007) "The corpus of komast vases: From identity to exegesis", in E. Csapo and M.C. Miller (eds) *The Origins of Theater in Ancient Greece and Beyond*. Cambridge: Cambridge University Press, pp. 48–76.

Sutton, R.F. (2000) "The good, the base, and the ugly: The drunken orgy in Attic vase-painting and the Athenian self", in B. Cohen (ed.) *Not the Classical Ideal: Athens and the Construction of the Other in Greek Art*. Leiden: Brill, pp. 180–202.

Veyne, P. (1988) *Roman Erotic Elegy: Love, Poetry, and the West*. Chicago, IL: University of Chicago Press.

Von Reden, S. (1995) *Exchange in Ancient Greece*. London: Duckworth.

Williams, F.P. and McShane, M.D. (1998) *Criminological Theory: Selected Classic Readings*. Cincinnati, OH: Anderson Publishing.

Winkler, J.J. (1990) *The Constraints of Desire: The Anthropology of Sex and Gender in Ancient Greece*. London: Routledge.

7

WAS PEDERASTY PROBLEMATIZED?

A diachronic view

Andrew Lear

In his influential 1985 study *The Use of Pleasure*, Foucault declared that pederasty was "problematized" in Greek culture: it was (1985: 192) "the object of a special—and especially intense—moral preoccupation" and consequently (1985: 191) "subjected to an interplay of positive and negative appraisals so complex as to make the ethics that governed it difficult to decipher." This concept has been generally accepted as part of the scholarly consensus. In fact, rather than being criticized for portraying pederasty as problematized, Foucault, along with Kenneth Dover, has been attacked for the opposite—for claiming, wrongly in their critics' view (Cohen 1991: 171–3; Hubbard 1998: 48–9), that the Greeks took a generally positive or neutral view of pederasty. In this article, I will open Foucault's—and the scholarly consensus'—view on this point to question. I will argue that problematization—at least as I have defined it above—was not an inherent characteristic of the practice of pederasty; instead, it is something that happened to pederasty at some point in the fifth century BC, initially (at least on the extant evidence) in Athens.

Thus the overemphasis in current scholarship on classical Athenian doubts about this practice masks the history of the practice and of those doubts. It occludes the relatively unquestioning idealization that is typical of our sources from the archaic period and from conservative cities such as Sparta and Thebes in the classical period, and it thereby banalizes the problematization in authors such as Aristophanes and Plato by denying the novelty of their views.[1]

Before proceeding, I should make clear that I am aware that my critique of Foucault is Foucaultian.[2] It is Foucault who first posited that sexuality is not an invariable fact of nature but rather (at least in part) a fact of culture that has a history (Foucault 1978, esp. 42–3).[3] He showed this, in part, by demonstrating that the mental categories through which the ancient Greeks experienced sexual desire were different from those through which modern Westerners experience it. Foucault discussed the fact that categories of sexuality have shifted within the modern period (and others, such as Chauncey 1994, have done so in greater detail): I am in effect merely extending his argument by suggesting that concepts of sexuality also had a history *within* ancient Greek culture. It is also the case that Foucault, in interviews given at the end of his life, seems occasionally to anticipate my point, as for instance when he says (Foucault 1994: 126) that for a ... behavior to enter the domain of thought, it is necessary for a certain number of factors to have made it uncertain, to have made it lose its familiarity, or to have provoked a certain number of difficulties around it. ... They [the factors] can exist and perform their action for a very long time, before there is effective problematization by thought.[4]

Thus one could also claim that I am merely correcting Foucault's use of his own concept, by applying his later thoughts to his earlier ones.

Far more importantly, one could object that I rely (or have relied up to this point) on a partial account of the concept of problematization: I defined being problematized as being the subject of ethical concern and debate. This is, in fact, only one aspect of the term's meaning in Foucault's work: it also means, more broadly, being a complex custom with an elaborated ethics of its own and a focus of cultural attention and production (Foucault 1985: 214). Given pederasty's apparent complexity as a custom and its overwhelming presence in Greek literature and art, one could hardly deny that it was in this sense always problematized. Indeed, under this broader definition, the idealization of which I speak could easily be seen as a genus of problematization. Foucault's account of pederasty (1985: 187–225), however, focuses on the narrower meaning of the term. It is also possible that the term itself creates some confusion: even if idealization and criticism are both evidence of concern, it does not clarify matters to refer to them with the same word. As a result, I argue that it would be better, for the purposes of history, to divide this concept into two quite different sub-concepts. I very tentatively propose (and use in this article) the terms "proto-problematization" for the broader sense of the term (cultural focus/idealization) and "hyper-problematization" for the narrower (criticism/debate).

I want, however, to emphasize that this article is only partly about Foucault; again, it is in a bigger sense about the current scholarly consensus (and of course Greek pederasty itself). I have discussed Foucault mainly because he invented the term that is commonly used to refer to the classical Athenian ethical debate on which today's scholarship centers; but Foucault is in fact no more focused on it than most other recent scholars.[5] Indeed, in my view, the roots of this consensus go back farther than Foucault, to the book that almost single-handedly energized modern studies of Greek sexuality and set the paradigm for them: Dover's (1989) *Greek Homosexuality*.

Dover's relationship to previous scholarship is hard to discuss, as he magisterially ignored the scholarly tradition,[6] and one is forced to construct one's own view of his methodology, as he explicitly discussed little aside from his (often criticized; e.g. Davidson 2001: 9–11) view of "homosexuality" as quasi-sexual or pseudo-sexual (Dover 1989: vii–viii). On the whole, however, Dover seems to have intentionally rejected the diachronic approach typical of earlier scholarship (and to which, *mutatis mutandis*, I am recommending a return).[7] He dedicated a short chapter at the end of his book (Dover 1989: 185–203) to the questions of variation over place and time, but on the whole he used a synchronic approach centered on classical Athenian evidence (though he used archaic vase painting extensively, but only to confirm and extend his theory, without ever acknowledging that it might represent the views of an earlier period). In fact, there are excellent reasons in favor of Dover's approach. The great majority of our textual evidence is from classical Athens. While our sources for other places/times are all fragmentary or otherwise obscure (depending on the case, in terms of authorship, context, meaning, etc.), a number of our classical Athenian texts are well preserved, and we are relatively well informed about their intellectual and historical context. Finally, a number of these texts (e.g. Aristophanes' *Clouds*, Plato's *Symposium* and *Phaedrus*, Xenophon's *Symposium* and *Memorabilia*, Aeschines' *Against Timarchus*) contain explicit praise or blame of pederasty, or statements that distinguish between praiseworthy and blameworthy versions of it, making it far easier to understand the ethics of this custom, at least for classical Athens. As a result, Dover centered his investigation on these ethically explicit texts, and this has remained the focus of most scholarship since.

Reasonable as this approach might seem, however, it does have drawbacks. First of all, we have evidence for pederasty from a wide variety of places and times in Greek history: from around the eighth century BC—the period of the Homeric bard(s)—to at least the third century AD, from Southern Italy to Syria, Macedonia to Alexandria. Our ancient sources furthermore often refer to variations in custom over place (e.g. Plato *Symposium* 182a–d) or time (e.g. Aristophanes *Clouds* 961–1073). However plausible we consider the specific claims made in these texts, Greek culture was in fact profoundly marked by local variation in law and custom, and Athens, although powerful, had little or no influence over local custom elsewhere. Thus it seems unwise to assume that classical Athenian customs or views were in any way definitional.

I would furthermore argue that the ethical explicitness that seems to be the greatest strength of our classical Athenian evidence is actually, potentially, a weakness. The relative ease of interpreting the ethics of a custom through ethically explicit texts can lead to the assumption that the ethical concerns expressed in them are latent in the discourse of other periods in which they are not expressed. In fact, however, there are many different latent conflicts in any social practice; at most, only some of these will ever become widespread concerns, and this may not happen to the obvious candidates. There is, furthermore, a difference between the experience of a participant in a practice with latent conflicts inherent in it and that of a participant in one that is the subject of explicit ethical concern and debate. Thus, whatever one's assumptions, the shift in attitudes toward a practice constitutes a history.

The best account of Greek pederasty must therefore take into account the issue of variation over time and place in a more than parenthetical way. Indeed, it must grapple with the complex and obscure evidentiary record to attempt to wrest a history from it—one that uses the evidence for earlier and non-Athenian times/places to set our classical Athenian sources in their historical context as much as it uses classical Athenian sources to provide a vocabulary for the interpretation of the other sources. In this chapter, I will attempt to give a brief sketch of such a view, or at least how such a history would use the main bodies of evidence up to the classical Athenian texts on which most modern scholarship focuses.[8]

Up to this point, I have proceeded as if there were no scholarship since Dover that treated Greek pederasty diachronically. This is not true, although synchronic theories dominate the scholarly consensus. In a rare direct protest, for instance, Martin Kilmer says (1993a: 192):[9]

> Evidence from Plato, and from forensic speeches … of late fifth and early fourth centuries reflect Athens of an age after Ephialtes' reforms, after the age of Perikles, during and after the Peloponnesian war … Transfer of evidence from this time onto any time within the Archaic period ought never to be carried out without making allowances for changes over time.

There are two key groups that have worked on pederasty in a diachronic way. The first is a group of continental scholars, including Patzer, Sergent, and Bremmer, that have expanded on a theory first proposed by Bethe in 1907. Using anthropological and mythological comparanda, they argue that pederasty derived from (or in some places constituted) adolescent initiation rituals, analogous to rites practiced in some Micronesian societies that involve pederastic sex. In their view, the customs of Sparta, Crete, and Thebes represent an earlier phase in pederasty's development than do those of Athens, and a general discussion of pederasty must start with these non-Athenian customs.[10]

The second is a loosely defined group of scholars working on archaic Greek culture, particularly vase painting and/or lyric/elegiac poetry, who take note of the differences between the views/versions of pederasty in these sources and our classical Athenian evidence. These differences are, for instance, central to the argument, first proposed by Frel (1963) and later developed by Shapiro (1981, 2000) and Hubbard (1998, 2000), for a decline in the degree of public approval accorded pederasty in fifth-century BC Athens—a theory on which I will comment in the section on classical Athens. A key influence on my own work is Edmunds' (1988) demonstration that the problematization of pederasty as Foucault defines it is not found in the *Theognidea*'s pederastic verses.[11] This article attempts to build on the work of these scholars in presenting a general argument in favor of diachronicity.

Origins?

There are, as the last paragraph has already made clear, several theories about the origin of Greek pederasty. Indeed, most of the scholarship that acknowledges diachronic change in pederasty focuses on this question. According to some, pederasty developed out of relations between soldiers in the Greek Dark Ages. Some believe that it developed as a means of population control.[12] The most popular—and most contested—theory is the one already mentioned, which I will call the "initiation theory." A subset of scholars subscribing to the initiation theory believe that these rites were widespread among the Indo-European peoples from whom the Greeks descended (and of whom they were one).[13] The evidence for this last view is very weak. It relies heavily on evidence from myths with pederastic elements, but the versions we have of these myths are literary, and the pederastic elements could have been added to them in historic times (as we know such elements were added in some cases).[14] The evidence presented from non-Greek Indo-European peoples is inadequate to establish an Indo-European heritage; the lack of substantial evidence from broad swathes of the Indo-European world is more striking. The other theories are all logically plausible, though none is provable in the current state of evidence.

While all three of these theories are plausible, the initiation theory is the only one for which there is any evidence worth noting. Two of the oldest pieces of evidence suggest that pederastic sex had a role in cultic rites of some kind, at least in the places from which this evidence comes. One of these is a group of sculptures excavated at a sanctuary of Hermes and Aphrodite at Kato Syme in Crete, which seems to represent initiator/initiand couples (Lebessi 1976; Koehl 1986: 107–8; Marinatos 2003: 134–5). Figure 7.1 in particular makes the sexual aspect of this relationship explicit: it is a double statuette, probably from the mid–late eighth century BC, representing two largely nude ithyphallic figures, an adult male and a boy, holding hands. The other is a group of inscriptions, probably dating to the late eighth or early seventh centuries BC, found on the island of Thera, a Spartan settlement, behind the remains of the temple of Apollo Carneius, of which several refer to penetrative sex between males.[15] There has been much debate over whether these record sacral relations or obscene boasts, and the evidence is ambiguous.[16] One point is conclusive to my mind, however: one of the inscriptions (*IG* 12.3 537a) reads, "By Apollo Delphinios, Krimon here penetrated the son of Bathykles and the brother of (illegible name)." There are no Greek parallels for the invocation of a deity in an obscene boast; thus this seems to be the record of a cultic ritual (and it also makes clear the pederastic nature of the sex act in question).

The initiation theory's advocates also adduce accounts of customs from classical Crete, Sparta, and Thebes. They rely particularly on a passage from the historian Ephorus (Strabo 10.4.21 70F, 149 *FGrH*) describing a ritual involving a mock abduction by an erastes (adult male lover) of his eromenos (his beloved boy/youth);[17] a period in which man and boy hunt together in the

Figure 7.1 Double statuette in bronze, mid–late eighth century BC. An adult male and a youth, both with erections, hold hands, probably in an initiation rite. Heraklion Archeological Museum. Photo: Deutsches Archäologisches Institut, Athens, neg. no. 2000/18.

countryside; and a ritual of return leading to a change in the boy's status. Even the most skeptical admit that there are some parallels to tribal initiation rituals here, though there are, as many have pointed out, also marked differences: the Cretan ritual involves only specially selected boys, for instance, while a tribal initiation ritual involves all of the boys in a certain age class.[18] The initiation theory's advocates also rely on Sparta's highly regulated education system for boys, which many see as constituting (or deriving from) a multi-year initiation system—and in which pederasty seems to have played an official or quasi-official role (Xenophon *Constitution of the Lacedaimonians* 2.12–14; Plutarch *Lycurgus* 17–18; Aelian 3.10; see Cartledge 1981: 19–23). They also frequently mention Plutarch's report (*Erotic Dialogue* 761b) that Theban lovers gave their beloveds a suit of armor when they came of age.

The initiation theory posits a connection between the rituals of eighth/seventh-century Thera and (at least in such recent versions of the theory as Koehl 1986 [particularly 107–8]) Kato Syme and the rituals and education systems of classical Crete, Sparta, and Thebes. They do this partly on the view that such conservative places as Crete and Sparta may have retained customs over long periods of time. Yet the evidence tends instead to suggest that Spartan customs changed considerably over time and that those Spartan customs that seemed archaic in later periods often represented self-conscious archaisms (Kennell 1995: 109–48). Indeed, aside from other problems with the evidence, it is hard to see what the early evidence for cultic rituals involving intercourse and taking place in, near, or in relation to temples has to do with the later evidence, which does not seem to involve any pairing rituals in temples or intercourse (which, if practiced, is mentioned in none of our accounts).[19]

We seem, in fact, to have two rather different groups of evidence here—with little if any evidence of a connection between them. Whether or not they help us to reconstruct the origin of pederasty, however, they do give us evidence about both the distant past of pederasty and non-Athenian Greek pederasty in the classical period—and in both cases, they indicate that pederasty had a formal role in various kinds of initiation and/or education.[20] This of course also tells us something about classical Athenian pederasty, by setting it in context. For instance, while modern scholarship, following Aristophanes (see for instance *Wealth* 149–59), is skeptical about the pedagogical rhetoric we find in many classical Athenian texts (e.g. Halperin 1990: 91–2), the existence of a traditional and institutional link between pederasty and pedagogy in parts of the speakers' cultural world suggests that this rhetoric represents some kind of belief, rather than just a set of excuses for lusting after teenagers.[21]

Archaic poetry

There is more substantial evidence from the later archaic period than from the Dark Ages. This consists largely of lyric and elegiac poetry, on the one hand, and of vase paintings on the other.[22] Pederasty was apparently an important theme in the poetry of this period: despite the decimation that time has wrought on Greek lyric and elegiac, there remain poems or fragments on pederastic themes by Solon, Mimnermus, Alcaeus, Ibycus, Theognis (and/or the tradition that comes to us under his name, today generally called the *Theognidea*), Anacreon, Simonides, Pindar, and Bacchylides (as well as poetry by Alcman and Sappho referring to female–female relations that may have been structured in a similar way). Of these, the most abundant sources are the *Theognidea*, Anacreon, and Pindar.[23]

Given the initiation theory and the evidence presented for it, one might expect a pedagogical/initiatory model to predominate in archaic poetry. In fact, however, the *Theognidea* and Anacreon present two contrasting styles of pederasty.[24] Indeed, the poets/traditions may provide an interesting example of proto-problematization. Both connect pederasty with their ideals, but though there is no conflict over its ethical value, there is a conflict over style. In each case, the ideals of the poet/tradition are embodied by the poetic persona. The *Theognidea*'s ideals can more easily be connected to a culture that links pederasty and initiation/education: indeed the "I"'s love for his beloved is inseparable from a process of inculcating wisdom in him and inducting him into the lover's elite political faction.

Anacreon by contrast eschews politics and pedagogy; he is bisexual and promiscuous, and his love poems center on desire, seduction, and rejection. Yet Anacreon's persona does not represent a bad or comic lover; instead, he clearly conforms to a different set of ideals, involving withdrawal from the political world and a focus on protecting the self from the overwhelming experience of passion. This is clear both from his "self"-praise (elegy 2) and from the contrast between his "self" and the figures he mocks for their failure to adhere to ideals of male gender and sexuality (Anacreon 388, 424, 458; see Brown 1983; Lear 2008: 53 n. 21).

Pindar is from a subsequent generation; he expresses nostalgia for the gentlemanly pederasty of the earlier lyrics (*Isthmian* 2.1–5). Nonetheless the slight fragments of his sympotic poetry include pederastic verses (frs. 123, 128), and his choral poems in praise of athletic victors confirm pederasty's high status in late archaic society: they show that addressing a youth as the object of pederastic desire and/or comparing him to famous pederastic love objects such as Ganymede (*Olympian* 10.99–106) could function as a mode of public flattery.

Vase painting and archaic Athens

Given the central position of Athens in the history that this chapter proposes, it is a problem that so little of the material mentioned so far is Athenian. The three pederastic poems attributed to Solon do, however, conform to the attitudes of other archaic poetry, though, perhaps surprisingly, given our image of Solon as a lawgiver, they are Anacreontic rather than Theognidean in their vision of pederasty (Lear 2011: 390–1). It should further be noted that Anacreon also lived in Athens for many years and seems to have been popular there.[25] There is also one other possible piece of textual evidence for archaic Athens. Aeschines, in *Against Timarchus* (e.g. 1.9–15), attributes to Solon a number of laws relating to (or which he relates to) pederasty. While there is almost universal agreement among scholars that most of these laws are of later date, it seems likely that the law forbidding slaves from having erotic relations with free boys is Solonian (Aeschines 1.139, Fisher 2001: 37). As Aeschines notes, this implies that free men can court boys; thus it too conforms to the general archaic approval of pederasty.

Most of our evidence for archaic Athens, however, comes from the artistic genre of vase painting. Pederastic scenes are among the commonest subgenres among the (so-called) scenes of everyday life, and kalos inscriptions (inscriptions praising the beauty of boys) appear so commonly on vases that they have never been counted.[26] Pederastic scenes, like lyric/elegiac, unanimously present a highly idealistic/idealized vision/version of pederasty. They do so by setting pederastic relations at the heart of a nexus of ideal elite activities—athletics, the hunt, and the symposium—either by blending the iconographies of pederastic courtship with those of these other activities/scene types or by juxtaposing images on different sides of vases.[27] They portray both lovers as handsome/beautiful and their erotic relations as exciting. Paradoxically the lovers—and in particular eromenoi—are portrayed as sexually self-controlled. Finally, vase painting creates a sharp contrast between the ideal figures and activities found in pederastic scenes and the comic or blameworthy figures and activities found in such other erotic scene types as satyr scenes and heterosexual (or, if I may coin a term, "hetaera-sexual") komos and orgy scenes. Indeed, although I see little evidence that different vase painters had different sexual ideologies, vase painting too might be seen as representing the proto-problematization of pederasty. Its idealized portrayal of pederasty is carefully constructed in opposition to various cultural "opposites"; but unlike our classical Athenian sources, vase painting generally does not juxtapose the ideal with the non-ideal or otherwise imply that the distinction is open to question.

I will demonstrate this by discussing five vase paintings. The first three will represent the three main pederastic scene types, as identified by Beazley: the "up and down" courtship scene, the courting-gift scene, and the scene of intercrural intercourse.[28] Then I will discuss two contrasting scenes, a satyr scene and a scene of Zeus and Ganymede, which is a common pederastic scene type of the mid-fifth century BC but contrasts sharply with scenes of mortal courtship.[29]

Figure 7.2 (Würzburg 241, black-figure amphora, Phrynos Painter, *ABV* 169.5 top, 688, *Para* 70, *Add²* 48) is a courtship scene: an erastes (left) courts his eromenos (right) by making the gestures that Beazley called "up and down" and that are typical of black-figure courtship scenes. The lover reaches for his beloved's chin with his left "up" hand and his genitals with his right "down" hand. I have argued elsewhere that this is not a single gesture drawn from real life but, as is typical of vase painting, a combination of two unrelated gestures portrayed as simultaneous in order to define the activity portrayed in symbolic terms (Lear and Cantarella 2008: 27, 54, 114–15). The down gesture symbolizes lust; parallels in both literature and art suggest that the up gesture is one of supplication.[30] By portraying the erastes as begging the eromenos to yield, the scene type elevates the eromenos to the position of victor or patron. Nothing in vase painting ever implies the opposite (see below on the hunter theory), but it is hard not to see this vision as,

Figure 7.2 Black-figure amphora by the Phrynos Painter, mid-sixth century BC. 'Up and down scene': a bearded man courts a beardless youth with the 'up and down' gesture(s). Martin-von-Wagner Museum der Universität Würzburg 241 (*ABV* 169.5 top, 688, *Para* 70, *Add²* 48). Photo: Martin-von-Wagner Museum der Universität Würzburg.

if not defensive, at least carefully constructed: an adult could seduce an adolescent in various ways, but this common scene type chooses to portray him as begging.³¹

The pair in Figure 7.2 is in any case idealized in other ways as well. Their sexual moderation is clearly symbolized by their unrealistically non-erect genitalia. They are also clearly portrayed as athletes, both by their muscular thighs and chests and by the wreaths they wear, which in combination with their muscle structure probably identifies them as athletic victors; this is particularly likely for the wreath hanging on the erastes' arm, which probably indicates a victory won with the arm, as in boxing.

Figure 7.3 (Würzburg 482, red-figure kylix, Douris, *ARV²* 444.239, *Add²* 238) is a courting-gift scene, the commonest type of pederastic scene. Here too the lovers are portrayed as athletes, this time by the inclusion of a rub-down kit (sponge and oil flask) on the "wall" behind the eromenos. Their clothing and props also connect them to certain ideals. The eromenos is wrapped to his chin and over his head in his cloak. This "opposite" of nudity at least temporarily protects his genitals from the erastes' fondling and precludes his own immediate acceptance of the courting gift; along with his lowered eyes, it symbolizes modesty.³² The erastes leans, as most erastai in such scenes in red-figure do, on his cane, symbolizing the leisureliness of courtship and hence also the leisure of a gentleman.³³ The gift in this scene is a hare.³⁴ Most interpretation of these scenes has focused on gifts of hares, which are one of the two commonest gifts in them. One of the prevalent theories, which I will call the "pedagogy theory," sees these hares as symbolizing

Figure 7.3 Red-figure cup by Douris, early fifth century BC. Courting-gift scene: bearded man courts a hooded youth by offering him a live hare. Martin-von-Wagner Museum der Universität Würzburg 482 (*ARV2* 444.239, *Add*² 238). Photo: Martin-von-Wagner Museum der Universität Würzburg.

the pedagogical nature of pederasty: the erastes, a hunter, gives the eromenos a game animal so that he will learn to hunt too (Koch-Harnack 1983: 35–128). The other, which I will call the "hunter theory," sees the hare as symbolizing the status of the eromenos: the erastes gives the eromenos a gift which symbolically indicates his status as the victim of erotic pursuit.[35] There are a few (though very few) vases that might support the first theory,[36] and it fits well with the archaic textual sources. The second reflects a critical "hyper-problematizing" view found not in archaic but in classical Athenian texts.[37] It also, at a basic level, relies upon a misreading of the act of gift giving. Gifts can symbolize many things, including the relationship that the giver offers (as a wedding ring symbolizes unity). No one, however, is likely to offer a gift that presents the relationship he offers and the recipient in an unflattering light. Nor is it clear to me why vase painters would so radically misrepresent the act of gift giving. The theory furthermore relies on a misunderstanding of the exchange involved in pederastic courtship, as will be made clear in the discussion of Figures 7.3 and 7.4.

Both theories, however, are weakened by their focus on gifts of game animals and the association between pederasty and hunting. Vase painting does connect pederasty with hunting, and this association is more frequent in earlier, black-figure scenes. However, the association with athletics is a constant from the earliest to the latest pederastic scenes.[38] A cogent interpretation of pederasty's associations in vase painting must cover both (if not also the association with the symposium).

123

Figure 7.4 Red-figure pelike by the Triptolemos Painter, early fifth century BC. Intercrural scene: a
bearded man engages in intercrural intercourse with a youth holding a live hare and a leashed
dog. Mykonos Museum 966 (*ARV²* 362.21, 280.18, *Add²* 222). Photo: Hellenic Republic,
Ministry of Culture, Mykonos Museum. © Hellenic Ministry of Education and Religious
Affairs, Culture and Sports/21st Ephorate of Antiquities.

Furthermore, a number of different gifts appear in courting-gift scenes, and by no means all of
them are game animals. Indeed, on extant vases, fighting cocks are as or more common than hares.
There are even scenes in which analogous erastai give analogous eromenoi different gifts, indicating that the gifts are all equivalent as such. In one such scene, Munich 2655 (red-figure kylix,
Makron, *ARV²* 471.196, 482, *Add²* 246), Side A, the three gifts are a hare, a fighting cock, and a
flower (see Figure 6.2). The fighting cock might be considered pedagogical, in that it might serve
as a role model for fighting spirit.[39] It does not, however, work with the hunter theory. Indeed, if
gifts were intended as symbolic of the boy's status, the erastes—or plural erastai—in a scene such as
Boston 08.291 (black-figure lekythos, Painter of Boston 08.291, *ABV* 92 top, *Para* 34, *Add²* 25),
upper register, who offer the eromenos both a hare and a fighting cock, among other gifts, would
be sending rather mixed messages: is he a victim or a fighter? The flower in any case fits with
neither theory: it has none of the implications hares are thought to have.

   Another much-discussed gift is a kind of small, closed sack that appears relatively frequently
in red-figure courting-gift scenes. Some evidence seems to indicate that these are intended as
money sacks (Sutton 1981: 290–7; Meyer 1988: 112–16), and on this basis some have argued
that the eromenoi in these scenes must be prostitutes (Koch-Harnack 1983: 167–72; Reinsberg
1989: 210–11) and somehow distinct from the eromenoi in other scenes. If this were the case,
vase painting would again reflect a concern central to classical Athenian hyper-problematization:

the potentially questionable distinction between respectable eromenoi and prostitutes (or between gifts and payment). An iconographical reading does not support this idea, however: the eromenoi in these scenes generally bear all the signs of idealized elite status that other eromenoi do (see Figure 6.3; New York 52.11.4, red-figure kylix, Douris, *ARV²* 437.114, 1653, *Add²* 239, on which Lear and Cantarella 2008: 85). It is, furthermore, not clear whether these sacks are actually money sacks: there is some evidence suggesting that they may be intended instead as containing astragaloi (pigs' knucklebones, with which the Greeks played a game resembling jacks) (Ferrari 1986: 218, 2002: 13–17). In fact, what is striking here is how rarely vase painting identifies the contents of these sacks. Yet again, the symbolism of the specific gift is downplayed because, no matter what it is, it plays the same role in the scene: that of a gift.

Indeed I would argue that both of these theories fail because they concentrate on the nature of the gifts in these scenes, rather than on the overall meaning of the scenes, or of the scene type. The question one must ask is: how does this scene type, using all of its various elements, portray pederastic courtship? And the answer is that it portrays it as an exchange. This is clearest in scenes, such as Oxford G 279 (red-figure kylix, Euaichme Painter, *ARV²* 785.8, *Para* 418, *Add²* 289), that merge the up and down and courting-gift scenes: the erastes here offers a gift with one hand and reaches for the boy's genitals with the other. In modern times, we are squeamish about the elements of exchange in erotic relations, and classical Athenians were also suspicious of them: thus in Aristophanes' *Wealth* 149–59, a character (though a slave, and not the author's *portavoce*) says that gifts to an eromenos are equivalent to the payment of a prostitute. In archaic Greece, however (as anyone who has read the Homeric epics will recall), exchange was highly valorized, between mortals and gods, or mortals and mortals. Indeed, I would argue that this scene type represents another form of idealization or proto-problematization: of all the different aspects of courtship, it focuses on exchange, because that is the most valorized possible social relationship.[40]

Figure 7.4 (Mykonos 966, red-figure pelike, Triptolemos Painter, *ARV²* 362.21, 280.18, *Add²* 222) will make the high status of exchange clearer. This is a scene of intercrural intercourse: the erastes bends down with his head on the eromenos' shoulder while inserting his penis (visible despite the vase's fragmentary state) between his thighs to engage in frottage. The eromenos gazes straight over the erastes' head, as is typical in this scene type. I have argued elsewhere that this is the effect that this scene type strives to achieve: while our literary sources suggest that pederastic couples had sex lying down (Plato *Symposium* 219b–c, Athenaeus 604d–e), vase painting always portrays the couple engaged in intercourse standing up, and I suggest that it does so in order to position the eromenos, as in the up and down scene, in the position of a victor, standing upright before his bending victim, the erastes (Lear and Cantarella 2008: 114). In this scene, the painter has emphasized the aspect of exchange: the eromenos is not staring into mid-air, but rather at his courting gift, a hare. Thus each member of the couple focuses on what he receives in the erotic exchange, which is as it were the organizing fiction of the scene. The vase painter has associated the scene with several valorized activities. It is connected to the hunt—both by the hare and by the hunting dog that the eromenos holds on a leash—and also to the gymnasium: indeed both the indoor and outdoor of the gymnasium are present, at least symbolically, in the form respectively of a terma (the end-post of a race course) and flute cases hanging from the "wall." The emphasis on exchange, furthermore, makes clear that the eromenos is not (viewed by his culture as) a victim; nor is he in any sense the equivalent of a hare. He is instead an active participant in an exchange, who gives not himself but access to his genitals and thighs in return for a gift.

The contrast to other, non-pederastic erotic scene types also underlines the idealization of the intercrural scene. Several different groups of vases could be discussed here,[41] but I will confine myself to an example that contrasts particularly clearly with Figure 7.4. Figure 7.5 (Berlin

Figure 7.5 Red-figure cup by the Pamphaios potter, late sixth century BC. Satyrs engage in orgiastic sex among grape-vines. Antikensammlung, Staatliche Museen, Berlin 1964.4 (*ARV*2 1700, *Para* 334, *Add²* 177). Photo: BPK Berlin/Antikensammlung/Jutta Tietz-Glagox/Art Resource, NY.

1964.4, red-figure kylix, Pamphaios potter, *ARV²* 1700, *Para* 334, *Add²* 177) is a satyr scene. One satyr attempts rear entry with a sphinx; one satyr–satyr couple engages in fellatio; another engages in anal intercourse. Recent scholarship has tended to follow Dover in emphasizing the issue of penetration in its view of Greek sexual ethics: in this view, anal sex is a defining element of the crude relations with which idealized pederasty contrasts. The prevalence of intercrural scenes in vase painting has been used as evidence for this proposition, but in fact there are a few scenes in vase painting that indicate acceptance of anal sex—or at least the erastes' desire for it—in respectable pederastic relations.[42] Thus, along with the satyrs' ugliness (marked among other things by their large lips and noses) and their oversized genitalia, it is fellatio that separates this scene from pederastic iconography most clearly. Whatever the status of anal sex, however, the satyr who is being anally penetrated serves as an "opposite" for the eromenos in Figure 7.4 (or indeed for all eromenoi): he is upended, rather than upright; he has an erection, as opposed to the eromenos' demurely small and (unrealistically) non-erect penis;[43] and above all he and his lover have open mouths, so they are talking or communicating in some vocal way, as opposed to the eromenos in Figure 7.4, who ignores his erastes and the sex act taking place between his thighs. It should also be noted that there are no gifts in this scene. This is invariably true in orgiastic scenes in vase painting: in this imaginary world, courtship by gifts does not precede unrestrained sex (on the orgy, see also Chapter 6, Blanshard, this volume).

Another scene type that helps by contrast to define the representation of pederasty in the three Beazley scene types is a pederastic one from the mid-fifth century BC (by which time up and down and intercrural scenes had largely disappeared). In these scenes, Zeus chases or seizes his eromenos Ganymede.[44] The contrast with mortal courtship scenes is rendered particularly clear by Figure 7.6 (Naples 3152, red-figure column krater, Harrow Painter, *ARV²* 275.60, *Add²* 207), in which

Figure 7.6 Red-figure column-krater by the Harrow Painter, early fifth century BC. Zeus seizes Ganymede, who drops his courting-gift in shock. Museo Nazionale Archeologico di Napoli 3152 (*ARV*2 275.60, *Add²* 207). Photo: Ministero per i Beni e le Attività Culturali, Soprintendenza Speciale per i Beni Archeologici di Napoli e Pompei.

Ganymede loses his grip on his courting gift of a fighting cock as Zeus stretches out his scepter to seize him. As so often, the vase painter renders two temporal phases of the action: clearly Zeus pretended to engage in courtship like a mortal, by making an exchange with Ganymede; now that he has dispensed with the fiction, the boy drops his courting gift in shock. The painter thus uses the element of the gift to show the difference between mortal courtship and divine rape: the exchange of gifts for sex does not function when the erastes is a hunter and the eromenos his prey. That exchange instead is one of the elements in a seamlessly idealizing (or proto-problematizing) portrayal of pederasty, in which handsome couples of athlete/hunter/symposiasts engage in decorous and limited though exciting erotic relations as part of the exchange of favors that archaic Greek culture valorized, leaving the eromenos, who is unconcerned with the sexual aspect of the relationship, in the superior position of a victor or patron—far apart from the contrasting worlds of ugly satyrs and orgiasts who engage in diverse and unrestrained sexual activities with no element of exchange and no concern for the dignity of their sex objects.

Classical Athens

But then, to put it simply, something happened. By the late fifth/early fourth centuries BC, pederasty seems to have passed from the proto-problematization of the archaic period to a full-blown period of hyper-problematization. Characters such as the Stronger Argument in

Aristophanes' *Clouds* (961–1023) or Phaedrus in Plato's *Symposium* (178c–179a) speak of pederasty in a highly idealistic/idealizing way: both associate pederasty with education, and specifically with education that leads to military courage. The Stronger Argument's interest in young boys is, however, portrayed as hypocritical: his rhetoric of pedagogical pederasty masks, or fails to mask, an obsessive interest in their bodies. And the speakers who follow Phaedrus in the *Symposium* problematize his views. The next speaker, Pausanias, presents in particular a highly idealized/idealistic view of pederasty as pedagogical, but also sets up an "opposite" consisting of crude sexuality, which includes a baser kind of pederasty and is therefore not automatically and obviously distinct from idealized pederasty (181a–b); moreover he specifically argues that Athenian views of pederasty are complex (182d–185b). Indeed one could view Pausanias' speech as both expressing and embodying hyper-problematization; the entire dialogue, with its multi-sided debate—formally about eros, but mostly about pederastic eros—might also seem to embody the concept, as might Plato's *Phaedrus* and Xenophon's *Symposium*, both of which also present multi-sided debates about this practice. It is, furthermore, the case that despite much effort, scholars have never convincingly connected the sharply differing perspectives on pederasty in Plato's various works, and Xenophon's perspective is also difficult to pin down (Hindley 1994, 1999, 2004). Finally, Aeschines' *Against Timarchus* would seem to show that this hyper-problematization also obtained outside the world of elite intellectuals, in that his argument, based on a division between decent pederasty and venal grossness very like that made by Plato's Pausanias,[45] convinced an Athenian jury to convict the accused of having been, in his youth, not an eromenos but a prostitute.

It would be, however, otiose to discuss the fact of hyper-problematization at length, as most current scholarship focuses on it exclusively. Instead, I will turn my attention to a set of questions opened up by acknowledging that hyper-problematization was a characteristic not of pederasty in general but of pederasty in classical Athens: when and why this change took place. Unfortunately, there is little evidence from the mid-fifth century BC, so it is impossible to be certain, but I consider it likely that hyper-problematization was new in the Athens of Socrates and Aristophanes, as this was a period of intellectual revolution, in which many archaic values and practices were subjected to questioning. Plato and Xenophon both seem, furthermore, to suggest this in their *Symposia*, dramatic dialogues that they set in late fifth-century BC Athens, in a milieu in which pederasty and its high value are taken for granted by most participants but questioned (though in different ways in each author) by Socrates, and in Plato's dialogue to a lesser degree by Pausanias and Aristophanes.

The view I am proposing runs counter to a now commonly accepted theory, which claims that pederasty disappears from vase painting after the 470s, and that this should be seen as evidence for a shift in attitudes toward the practice (Frel 1963; Shapiro 1981: 141–2, 2000: 21). I believe that the vase evidence should be seen differently. It is true that explicit portrayals of sex, including foreplay, are rare in vase painting after this time; this is, however, as true in heterosexual scenes as in pederastic (Shapiro 1981: 142; Hubbard 2000: 7). Pederastic courting-gift scenes, on the other hand, remain common until the fourth century. Most of these in later periods are so schematic and reduced that they are often considered merely scenes of "conversation in the palaestra," but on careful study, it is clear that the basic markers of the courting-gift scene type—often including gifts—remain (Lear and Cantarella 2008: 175–81). Kalos inscriptions also remain relatively common until the 440s.[46] One should finally not misinterpret the implications of the Ganymede scene (which, again, is a scene type of the early–mid-fifth century BC). While to a modern eye, this might seem to place pederasty in a negative light by connecting it to rape, in ancient Greek eyes it was generally honorific to connect anything/anyone to Zeus. Thus while vase painting may indicate that fifth-century Athenians were less open to sexual display, it does not seem to demonstrate a change in attitudes toward pederasty.

The idea of pederasty's disappearance is central to the main (or indeed only) current theory about why Athenian attitudes toward pederasty changed in the fifth century BC. This theory, which I will call the "elite theory," has been argued most extensively by T. K. Hubbard (1998, 2000), following a long tradition of considering pederasty an exclusively elite practice.[47] Hubbard argues that as the democracy grew more inclusive in the fifth century, the lower classes' dislike of this elite custom came to dominate discourse about it. The relationship between the view that I am proposing and this theory is complex. It is my closest predecessor; yet it proposes a view of pederasty as always (perhaps even *a priori*) a subject of class conflict and consequently, in a sense, hyper-problematized.

The evidence for pederasty's connection to the elite class is however less certain than is commonly believed. Certainly many portrayals of pederastic relations place them in the world of the elite, but a few sources show non-elite Greeks engaging in them as well.[48] Indeed Thucydides (6.54) tells us that Aristogeiton was a *mesos polites* (middling citizen), and one of Timarchus' *erastai* was a public slave (Aeschines 1.54–64). Xenophon, furthermore, mentions regular soldiers falling in love with boys (*An.* 4.1.14) and refers (*Oec.* 12.14–15) to the possibility that a farm bailiff— clearly not a member of the elite—might be an erastes. Finally, it seems (Shapiro 2000; Neer 2002: 123–8; Lear and Cantarella 2008: 168–70) that in the late archaic period, certain vase painters—paradigmatically lower-class men (Plato *Republic* 420d–421a)—participated, if perhaps in part jokingly, in the cult of the youths whose kalos inscriptions they painted.

In any case, more than vase painting, the elite theory depends on Aristophanes, whom it treats as a *vox populi* whose obloquy expresses popular contempt. Yet as has often been pointed out, Aristophanes' politics (if his comedies express a political point of view) are not populist in a simple sense.[49] He often criticizes the people (*demos*) quite bitterly, and the politicians he attacks most bitterly were popular and populist. He also does not on the whole attack "old money"— the class with which pederasty is most strongly associated.[50] Instead, his most intense mockery is reserved for innovators in politics, thinking, and the arts, such as Cleon, Socrates, and Agathon. Hubbard (1998: 53) suggests that Aristophanes views pederasty as a kind of formative training for these adult degenerates. Yet the evidence cited for this idea derives on the whole from contextless fragments capable of quite different interpretations.[51] In the eleven complete extant comedies, this connection is never made.

Certainly, Aristophanes portrays pederasty in a coarser, less idealistic way than our archaic sources. At *Peace* 724, it is clear that Zeus' sexual relations with Ganymede are anal (and that anal intercourse involves excrement); eromenoi are called venal at *Wealth* 149–59, and the erastai portrayed at *Wasps* 1025–8 are unconcerned with the reputations/futures of their eromenoi. Yet Aristophanes' comic every-Athenian heroes often express desire for boys, as for instance the old democrat Philocleon in the *Wasps* (578), Peisetaerus in the *Birds* (137–42), and the Demos itself in the *Knights* (1384–7). And although in the *Clouds* the Stronger Argument's pederastic desires are the subject of mockery, his opponent's new education is the ultimate subject of the play's attack: the old pederastic education, whatever its failings, was nonetheless better.

Indeed, on the whole, a subtler reading of Aristophanes' portrayal of pederasty is probably called for: rather than attacking pederasty, he seems to gently deflate the traditional idealizing view. On the whole, I suspect that a subtler view of history is called for as well. Chauncey (1994) has shown how complex the shifts in concepts of sex and sexuality were that took place in New York in the mid-twentieth century. Our evidence for the ancient world is inevitably thinner. That does not, however, mean that the historical processes at work were less complex. I suspect that more could be done by comparing the issues central to the proto-problematization in the archaic period and those central to the hyper-problematization in classical Athens. There is overlap: the honor of the eromenos seems to be an issue of concern both in vase painting—where, though never questioned, it is carefully constructed—and in classical Athenian texts, where, as Foucault famously argued (1985: 204–25), it is a central worry. There are also issues on which there is clear difference. A boy in the *Theognidea* (e.g. 1299–1304) can be criticized for promiscuity, but this is clearly sometimes not a serious concern, as the boy is still an object of desire, both sexual and political; in classical Athens, as *Against Timarchus* among other texts makes clear, promiscuity (whether real or only rumored) put a boy's status at risk. Most interesting are issues which are of concern in both periods, but in different ways. One of these is gift exchange. Vase painting marks the association between pederasty and gift exchange because this underscores the valorization of pederasty. In classical Athens, on the other hand, exchange between erastes and eromenos is open to question.

The relationship between pederasty and pedagogy is another such issue, and more complex. The archaic poets present alternate pedagogical and non-pedagogical models of pederasty, both apparently valorized. In classical Athens, only pedagogical pederasty is valorized, and (simultaneously) the pedagogical nature of pederasty is open to question. Is it possible that shifts in attitudes toward gift exchange and pedagogy, rather than attitudes directly about sex, undermined the status of pederasty? Both of these possibilities seem plausible to me. In the more monetized culture of classical Athens, relations based on an exchange of gifts or favors would not make the kind of cultural sense that they did in archaic Greece—leading to worries about corruption, prostitution, and so on. The changes in pedagogy taking place in the Athenian elite at the end of the fifth century BC could also be a key issue here. With the new professional model of pedagogy brought to Athens by the Sophists, the old ideal of education by *synousia* (being together, sc. with an appropriate older man or men)[52] will have lost some of its cultural prestige and thus perhaps stranded pederasty, in cultural terms, since it derived much of its prestige from its central role in the old education, again opening it to question.[53]

Finally, one should always remember that there is a great difference between problematization, even hyper-problematization, and condemnation. Even the sharpest criticism of pederasty in classical Athens falls far short of a proposal to ban it. Probably the most severe critic is the Athenian Stranger of Plato's *Laws* (836b–842a), and even he only desires to repress non-reproductive intercourse, rather than pederastic love *per se* (see in particular 837c–d). And he refers to his own ideas, given the context of Greek culture, as *euchai* (prayers, perhaps here visions) in a story (*mythos*) (841c). Plato's Athenian Stranger did not influence practice in classical Athens, much less in other Greek cities. Indeed, one must also remember that the Sacred Band was still in the future at this point,[54] and that as far as we can tell from the spotty (though abundant)[55] evidence for the Hellenistic and Imperial periods, pederasty continued not only to be practiced but also idealized—even if its idealization was often questioned—for another seven centuries after Plato's *Laws*, until the Roman or Byzantine Imperial state enforced Christian strictures on sex and sexuality as a matter of law and religion.[56] Thus, just as there is no point in looking for the signs of the Roman Empire's decline in the (purported) shenanigans of the Julio-Claudian emperors, we must not overemphasize the negative aspect of classical Athenian problematization, because there is no reason to think that Greek pederasty was in any sense in decline in classical Athens. It is, instead, merely in classical Athens that it first (as far as we know) passed from being proto-problematized (i.e. idealized) to being hyper-problematized.

Notes

1 Note that Hubbard implicitly recognizes this at 1998: 49, when he says "It was never, *at least in Classical Athens*, unproblematic" (emphasis added). In a forthcoming publication, Hubbard comes closer to the perspective of this article, or at least that of Lear 2004 (especially 3–12, 252–307), in which I make a similar argument but with a less complex stance toward Foucault.

2 I thank James Panero (*Arma Virumque*, the weblog of the *New Criterion*, 3/21/2005) for calling my dissertation—until then regarded both by myself and my colleagues in Classics as critical of Foucault—"more-Foucault-than-Foucault" and thereby prompting me to rethink my relationship to Foucault's work. For a similar point as regards James Davidson, see Wohl 2002: 15 n. 30.

3 See Halperin 1990: 6–7 for a deserved paean to this breakthrough.

4 I thank Meryl Altman and Richard Lynch for helping me find this reference.

5 Both Halperin and Cohen focus exclusively on classical Athens. See Halperin (1990: 29), who claims that "the surviving evidence for the classical period effectively restricts our powers to generalize" to Athens (though he uses evidence from other times/places several times, see e.g. Halperin 1990: 21–4, 37) and Cohen 1991: 8 n. 22.

6 Note for instance that Pogey-Castries 1930, "(still) the most useful introductory work on the subject" according to one of Dover's reviewers (Demand 1980: 123–4), is not even listed in his bibliography. Eighteenth- and nineteenth-century scholarship on Greek pederasty has recently come into vogue as a topic: see Blanshard 2010: 143–63 and Orrells 2011.

7 Dover and Foucault are undoubtedly responsible for other shifts in perspective on ancient sexuality as well. Until Dover, scholars generally considered it necessary to judge ancient customs in modern moral terms; see for example Pogey-Castries 1930: 3–4 (translating Meier 1837), where, after dismissing contemporary moralizing (or apologetic) views, he nonetheless refers to pederasty as a "tâche" (blemish), and Pogey-Castries 1930: 109, where he refers to consummated pederastic relations as an "impurity" which he finds impossible to attribute to Socrates. Dover, who famously denied that any sex act ("providing that it is welcome and agreeable to all the participants") can be judged moral or immoral (Dover 1989: viii), helped to sweep this away, and Foucault finished it off by extending the historical consciousness to the topic of sexuality. As a result, scholarship today is free to consider ancient sexual ethics on their own terms; I encourage a return to nineteenth-century practice only in terms of diachronicity.

8 For a more extensive version of this argument, see Lear 2004, 2014.

9 See also Kilmer 1993b: 1–4, 1997: 47.

10 So also Cantarella 1992: 5–8. Two other scholars (Percy 1996, 2005; Scanlon 2005) have also recently argued for a Cretan or Spartan origin for pederasty, although they do not connect it with initiation.

11 For the term *Theognidea*, see below at n. 24.

12 See Percy 1996: 62, following Aristotle (*Politics* 2.1272a).

13 For the initiation theory, see Bethe 1907; Jeanmaire 1939; Brelich 1969; and Patzer 1982; for the Indo-European version, see Bremmer 1980 and Sergent 1986a, 1986b.

14 See Sergent 1986a in particular for the overuse of myth. For an example of the addition of pederastic elements into myth, see Aeschylus frs. 135 and 136 Radt, on which Dover 1989: 128–9.

15 See *IG* 12.3 536, 537a, 538, 539. On dating, see Jeffery 1990: 318–19.

16 See for instance, on one side Patzer 1982: 85–7 and Cantarella 1992: 7; on the other Dover 1988: 126, 1989: 123.

17 These are the most common ancient terms and are used in this article as in most contemporary scholarship.

18 For a recent summation of differences, see Dodd 2000; for a defense of the comparison's aptness, see Graf 2003: 14–15.

19 Indeed, in the classical period, it seems to have been traditional to deny that Spartan pederastic relations were consummated (Xenophon *Const. Lac.* 2.13; Plutarch *Inst. Lac.* 7; Aelian 3.12). See Cartledge's (1981: 19–20) well-expressed doubts on our sources' veracity on this point.

20 Note that initiation and education are not as clearly separated in these sources as standard anthropological theory would predict. This is clearest in Sparta, where the education system was mixed with a series of initiatory events (and/or structured like a multi-year initiation) (Brelich 1969: 29, 113). Ephorus reports on the Cretan ritual as a variant on courtship and does not connect it to the educational system, but if men take boys into the countryside to hunt, there is presumably a large element of hunting/war training involved.

21 For another idea that sits ill with our information about Greek traditions, see Cohen's (1991: 187–90) argument in favor of a (1991: 190) "traditional one (sc. order) with its implicit valuation of heterosexuality"—an argument Cohen makes on the basis exclusively of classical Athenian texts (indeed of Socratic philosophy, à la Foucault)—and comparative evidence from modern Mediterranean societies of dubious relevance (see Hubbard 2011: 189–90 on the implicit racism behind such comparisons).

22 See below on the supposed laws of Solon. There are relevant artworks in other genres from the end of the archaic period, such as the symposium scene from the Tomb of the Diver at Paestum (see

particularly the North wall) and the terracotta akroterion of Zeus and Ganymede from Olympia (Olympia T 2/T 2A/Tc 1049), but the vast bulk of the evidence is from vase painting.

23 For Anacreon and Theognis, respectively, see Lear 2008, 2011. For Pindar, see Steiner 1998. For the poets of whose pederastic work less remains, see Solon (23, 24, 25); Mimnermus (1.9); Alcaeus (306A fr. 77, 366, 388); Ibycus (282.41–6, 282A frs. 8.7 and 16.10, 282C fr. 27, and 288); Simonides (22W); and Bacchylides (10.42–3). As I am writing this article and a companion chapter on pederasty (Lear 2014) simultaneously, some small passages such as this note and the two sentences to which it refers will appear verbatim or almost verbatim in the two articles.

24 See Selle 2008: 373–89 for a judicious recent view of the authorship of the *Theognidea* and the status of the largely pederastic elegies of Book 2 (though note the question about the ideological profile of the collection posed by Lear 2011).

25 See especially Shapiro 2012, esp. 16–21.

26 For an extensive list of pederastic scenes, see Lear and Cantarella 2008: 194–233. See Lissarrague 1999 for a good recent discussion of kalos inscriptions. There were also kalos inscriptions (or graffiti) on walls, trees, etc. For literary and archaeological evidence, see Lear and Cantarella 2008: 246 n. 1. Lynch 2011: 175 concludes, on the basis of a study of a well from the Athenian agora, that erotic scenes were made for export (to Etruria, where the best-preserved vases have been found, presumably because of Etruscan burial practices), rather than the Athenian market. Erotic scenes on ceramics from the Acropolis would tend to contradict this (see Lear and Cantarella 2008: 185–8 and figs 7.4–7); there is also little evidence for Etruscan influence on vase iconography (Johnston 1991; Spivey 1991). Kalos inscriptions are in fact a case in point: it would make little sense for vases designed for the export market to be decorated with inscriptions in Greek praising the beauty of clearly Greek (and sometimes clearly Athenian) boys. Note further the presence of kalos inscriptions on ceramics at Lynch 2011: 229–33.

27 For decorative program, see Lear and Cantarella 2008: 27, figs. 2.15 A–C (discussed on 90–1) providing a particularly good example; a good example of the blending of scene types is fig. 2.17 (discussed on 95–6). I cite my own book a great deal in this section, as it contains the most recent work on many of these topics; in every case of course I direct the reader to the excellent work referred to in the notes and bibliography.

28 See Beazley 1947: 198–223. For a quick introduction to the scene types and to iconographical interpretation in general (with reference to pederastic scenes), see Lear and Cantarella 2008: 25–37.

29 For Ganymede scenes, see Lear and Cantarella 2008: 141–51, with figs. 4.3–11, and relevant bibliography (in particular Kaempf-Dimitriadou 1979).

30 Berlin 1685 (amphora by Lydos, *ABV* 109.24, *Add*² 30), where Priam uses it to plead for his life; also Aeschines 1.61 and *Iliad* 10.454–5.

31 Note that in poetry too, the poet/lover often begs his beloved: see for instance Theognis 1235, 1237, 1286, 1344. The youth makes a gesture in return in this scene, as in many up and down scenes: he holds the erastes' left wrist. This has often been seen as a gesture of resistance, but as DeVries has shown (1997: 14–24), it is more likely to be the opposite. Among other things, if he were resisting, he would presumably hold the down hand, not the up.

32 Ferrari 1990, 2002: 54–6, 72–81.

33 See Kaeser 1990: 154, who invents the name "Ausruhestock" (resting stick) for these canes, which rarely if ever function as walking sticks. Also Kunisch 1997: 120.

34 See Schnapp 1997: 342–7 on the question of whether these are hares or rabbits; I follow scholarly convention in calling them hares.

35 See Schnapp 1989, in particular 79–80; Schnapp 1997, in particular 255; Barringer 2001: 70–124.

36 See Lear and Cantarella 2008: 72–3 (with fig. 2.4); Mykonos 966 (fig. 5 in this article) is another possible case.

37 See for instance Plato *Sophist* (222d–e), where the Elean says that the "lovers' hunt" takes place when lovers "give gifts to the hunted ones." This makes an interesting contrast to an archaic poem (Kydias 714P), paraphrased at Plato *Charmides* 155D as recommending, "when he spoke about a beautiful boy … 'to beware of coming before a lion like a fawn and being taken as a portion of meat.'" In the archaic quote, the eromenos, not the erastes, is the hunter; the lovers are, furthermore, compared to animals more heroic than dogs and hares.

38 See Scanlon 2002: 236–49; Lear and Cantarella 2008: 91–7 (with figs. 2.16–18).

39 See Hoffmann 1974; for arguments against this idea, see Lear and Cantarella 2008: 73–5.

40 See MacLachlan 1993: 3–12 and 56–72 on the exchange of charis (favor[s]) for charis (gratitude), both in non-erotic and erotic contexts (where charis also denotes grace/beauty).

41 There are two other principal scene types involving crude sexuality. For orgy scenes, see Lear and Cantarella 2008: 119–20 (with fig. 3.10) and 244 n. 8. Another group is the sex scenes on the so-called Tyrrhenian amphorae; see Lear and Cantarella 2008: 124–6 (with figs. 3.14–15). These scenes have been misinterpreted by Hupperts 1988 and Kilmer 1997, who view them as merely representing an aspect of Athenian reality ignored by other vase painters. Neither scene type, however, represents reality: pederastic scenes represent an idealized reality, while the Tyrrhenian amphorae, like satyr scenes, represent a comic and/or shameful "opposite" reality. Note in particular the satyrs on Orvieto 2664, side B (Lear and Cantarella 2008, fig. 3.14), which make clear that this scene type is analogous to the satyr scene, not courtship scenes.

42 See Shapiro 2000: 18–19 and Lear and Cantarella 2008: 115–18 (with figs. 3.6–9).

43 For exceptions, see Lear and Cantarella 2008: 65 (with fig. 2.1) and 240 n. 2.

44 The god Eros also sometimes chases and/or seizes boys; see Lear and Cantarella 2008: 162–3 (with figs. 4.22–3). Certain scenes in the work of the Affecter are often seen as representing erastai pursuing eromenoi. It is however unclear whether these scenes in fact represent pursuit or dancing. Indeed, the meaning of the Affecter's scenes, if any, is generally obscure (so Boardman 1974: 65; Mommsen 1975: 56).

45 Hubbard (1998: 67–8, 2007: 192–3) argues that the sections of the speech affirming the existence of ideal pederasty were added for publication, to appeal to an audience of readers wealthier than the actual jurors. This argument "underestimates the coherence of the speech" (Fisher 2001: 59): the distinction between legitimate eros and prostitution is a focal theme not only of these passages but the entire speech (see J. Shapiro 2010: 141–90).

46 See Shapiro 1987: 117 (with n. 37 for later exceptions) and Lissarrague 1999: 362.

47 See for instance Ehrenberg 1951: 100–2; Flacelière 1962: 62–3, 216; Dover 1989: 149–51.

48 See Fisher 1998, 2000 for the idea that non-elite Athenians may have participated in the paradigmatically elite activities of athletics, the symposium, and pederasty.

49 On the difficulty of pinning down Aristophanes' political perspective (or even that of his plays), see Robson 2009: 162–87; also Carey 1994; Olson 2010.

50 See Sommerstein 1996: 334–5; Robson 2009: 179–80.

51 For instance, Hubbard (1998: 53) cites an unattributed comic fragment (Adesp. 12 K), which he translates "there is no long-hair who is not pollinated with the gall-fly." Hubbard argues that "the reference is to the horticultural practice of placing branches of a wild fig next to a blooming cultivated fig, so that the gall fly native to the wild species may pollinate the other. Erastes and eromenos are the wild and cultivated fig respectively. The active partner infects the other, as in the process of pollination." This line comes down to us, however, not only in the version cited by Hubbard (Synesius 104.244a) but also in two others (Macarius 6.74; Photius and the Suidas) which replace the main verb and mean simply "there is no long-hair who is not buggered," a statement with many parallels in Old Comedy (e.g. *Knights* 877–80 and *Assemblywomen* 112–13) and without the implications that Hubbard finds in the Synesius version.

52 See Plato *Meno* 91c–92e for *synousia*. Also Robb 1994: 197–207, and in particular 1994: 204: "the final institutionalization of the paideia of young men in their *meirakion* years, a development of the advancing literacy of fourth century and of the Athenian philosophical schools, was greatly to diminish the importance of *sunousia, including the erotic* [emphasis added], as part of the Greek educational process," and "it was the older sophists and Socrates who" began the process of "undermining familial and tribal *sunousia*."

53 I am delighted that Hubbard has come to agree with me on this point: see Hubbard 2014, in particular p.138, which was published after this article was completed.

54 See in particular Plutarch *Pelopidas* 18.5. Leitao 2002 questions the existence of the Sacred Band, by showing that the sources for this regiment's existence all derive from the utopian philosophical tradition. He also (152–6) raises doubts about the evidentiary value of Xenophon *Symposium* 8.34 for a more general Theban custom in this regard. Xenophon's knowledge of and interest in military matters was too keen, however, for him to let a false rumor of this kind pass; if he did not believe in it, furthermore, he could easily have had Socrates deny its existence, as this would have suited his/Socrates' argument.

55 Pederasty is an important theme in Theocritus, Callimachus, and the Palatine Anthology; it appears in Plutarch (particularly the *Erotic Dialogue*), Achilles Tatius, Lucian, Maximus of Tyre, Philostratus, and so on. Yet little or no work has been published on the changing visions/versions of this practice in the Hellenistic and Imperial periods—which is to say that this is a particularly rich area for future research.

56 See Cantarella 1992: 173–86 for the increasingly restrictive Imperial edicts of the fourth to sixth centuries AD. See Gaca 2003, in particular 1–11, for the sharp discontinuities between ancient Greek philosophical ideas of sexual restraint and Christian sexual morality.
57 I list this interview as by Foucault, because the interviewer/editor is unnamed (though Richard Lynch claims that it was Thomas Zummer). Note that this interview is reprinted in Lotringer, Sylvère, ed. 1996 *Foucault Live: Interviews, 1961–1984*. New York: Semiotext, pp. 416–22.

Bibliography

Barringer, J. (2001) *The Hunt in Ancient Greece*. Baltimore, MD: Johns Hopkins University Press.
Beazley, J. (1947) "Some Attic vases in the Cyprus Museum", *Proceedings of the British Academy*, 195–247.
Bethe, E. (1907) "Die Dorische Knabenliebe", *Rheinisches Museum für Philologie* 62: 438–75.
Blanshard, A. (2010) *Sex: Vice and Love from Antiquity to Modernity*. Chichester: John Wiley & Sons.
Boardman, J. (1974) *Athenian Black Figure Vases*. London: Thames & Hudson.
Brelich, A. (1969) *Paides e parthenoi, Incunabula Graeca* 36. Rome: Edizioni dell'Ateneo.
Bremmer, J. (1980) "An enigmatic Indo-European rite: Paederasty", *Arethusa* 13: 279–98.
Brown, C. (1983) "From rags to riches: Anacreon's Artemon", *Phoenix* 37(1): 1–15.
Cantarella, E. (1992) *Bisexuality in the Ancient World*. New Haven, CT: Yale University.
Carey, C. (1994) "Comic ridicule and democracy", in S. Hornblower and R. Osborne (eds) *Ritual, Finance, Politics: Athenian Democratic Accounts Presented to David Lewis*. Oxford: Oxford University Press, pp. 69–83.
Cartledge, P. (1981) "The politics of Spartan pederasty", *Proceedings of the Cambridge Philological Society* 201: 17–36.
Chauncey, G. (1994) *Gay New York: Gender, Urban Culture, and the Makings of the Gay Male World, 1890–1940*. New York: BasicBooks.
Cohen, D. (1991) *Law, Sexuality and Society: The Enforcement of Morals in Classical Athens*. Cambridge: Cambridge University Press.
Davidson, J. (2001) "Dover, Foucault and Greek homosexuality: Penetration and the truth of sex", *Past & Present* 170: 3–51.
Demand, N. (1980) "Review of Kenneth Dover, *Greek Homosexuality*", *American Journal of Philology* 101: 121–4.
DeVries, K. (1997) "The 'frigid eromenoi' and their wooers revisited", in M. Duberman (ed.) *Queer Representations: Reading Lives, Reading Cultures*. New York: NYU Press, pp. 14–24.
Dodd, D. (2000) "Athenian ideas about Cretan pederasty", in T. Hubbard (ed.) *Greek Love Reconsidered*. New York: W. Hamilton Press, pp. 33–41.
Dover, K.J. (1988) "Greek homosexuality and initiation", in K.J. Dover, *The Greeks and their Legacy (Greek and the Greeks: Collected Papers*, vol. 2). Oxford: Blackwell, pp. 115–34.
——(1989) *Greek Homosexuality*, 2nd edn. Cambridge, MA: Harvard University Press.
Edmunds, L. (1988) "Foucault and Theognis", *Classical and Medieval Literature* 8(2): 79–91.
Ehrenberg, V. (1951) *The People of Aristophanes: A Sociology of Old Attic Comedy*. Oxford: Basil Blackwell.
Ferrari, G. (1986) "Money-Bags?", *American Journal of Archaeology* 90: 218.
——(1990) "Figures of speech: The picture of *aidos*", *Métis* 5: 185–200.
——(2002) *Figures of Speech: Men and Maidens in Ancient Greece*. Chicago, IL: University of Chicago Press.
Fisher, N. (1998) "Gymnasia and the democratic values of leisure", in P. Cartledge, P. Millett and S. von Reden (eds) *Kosmos: Essays in Order, Conflict and Community in Classical Greece*. Cambridge: Cambridge University Press, pp. 84–104.
——(2000) "Symposiasts, fish-eaters and flatterers: Social mobility and moral concern in Old Comedy", in F.D. Harvey and J. Wilkins (eds) *The Rivals of Aristophanes*. London: Duckworth and the Classical Press of Wales, pp. 355–96.
——(2001) *Aeschines, Against Timarchos*. New York: Oxford University Press.
Flacelière, R. (1962) *Love in Ancient Greece*. New York: Crown Publishers.
Foucault, M. (1978) *The History of Sexuality, Volume 1: An Introduction*. New York: Random House.
——(1985) *The History of Sexuality, Volume 2: The Use of Pleasure*. New York: Random House.
——(1994) "Problematics: Excerpts from conversation", in R. Reynolds and T. Zummer (eds) *Crash: Nostalgia for the Absence of Cyberspace*. New York: Random House, pp. 121–7.[56]
Frel, J. (1963) "Griechischer Eros", *Listy filologické* 86: 60–4.
Gaca, K. (2003) *The Making of Fornication: Eros, Ethics, and Political Reform in Greek Philosophy and Early Christianity*. Berkeley, CA: University of California Press.

Graf, F. (2003) "Initiation: A concept with a troubled history", in D. Dodd and C. Faraone (eds) (2003) *Initiation in Ancient Greek Rituals and Narratives: New Critical Perspectives*. London: Routledge, pp. 3–24.

Halperin, D.M. (1990) *One Hundred Years of Homosexuality and Other Essays on Greek Love*. New York: Routledge.

Hindley, C. (1994) "Eros and military command in Xenophon", *Classical Quarterly* 44: 347–66.

——(1999) "Xenophon on male love", *Classical Quarterly* 49: 74–99.

——(2004) "*Sophron Eros*: Xenophon's ethical erotics", in C. Tuplin (ed.) *Xenophon and his World: Papers from a Conference Held in Liverpool in July 1999*. Stuttgart: Franz Steiner Verlag, pp. 125–46.

Hoffmann, H. (1974) "Hahnenkampf in Athen", *Revue Archéologique* 195–220.

Hubbard, T. (1998) "Popular perceptions of elite homosexuality in Classical Athens", *Arion* 3, 6(1): 48–78.

——(2000) "Pederasty and democracy: The marginalization of a social practice", in T. Hubbard (ed.) *Greek Love Reconsidered*. New York: W. Hamilton Press, pp. 1–11.

——(2007) "Getting the last word: Publication of political oratory as an instrument of historical revision-ism", in E. Anne Mackay (ed.) *Orality, Literacy, Memory in the Ancient Greek and Roman World* (*Mnemosyne*, Suppl. 298). Leiden: Brill, pp. 185–202.

——(2011) "Athenian pederasty and the construction of masculinity", in J. Arnold and S. Brady (eds) *What is Masculinity? Historical Dynamics from Antiquity to the Contemporary World*. New York: Palgrave Macmillan, pp. 189–224.

——(2014) "Peer Homosexuality", in T. Hubbard (ed) *A Companion to Greek and Roman Sexualities* (Oxford: Blackwell, pp. 128–49).

Hupperts, C. (1988) "Greek love: Homosexuality or pederasty?", in J. Christiansen and T. Melander (eds) *Proceedings of the 3rd Symposium on Ancient Greek and Related Pottery*. Copenhagen, pp. 255–68.

Jeanmaire, H. (1939) *Couroi et Courètes: Essai sur l'éducation spartiate et sur les rites d'adolescence dans l'antiquité hellénique*. Lille: Bibliothèque universitaire.

Jeffery, L. (1990) *The Local Scripts of Archaic Greece*, rev. edn. Oxford: Clarendon Press.

Johnston, A. (1991) "Greek vases in the marketplace", in T. Rasmussen and N. Spivey (eds) *Looking at Greek Vases*. Cambridge: Cambridge University Press, pp. 203–32.

Kaempf-Dimitriadou, S. (1979) *Die Liebe der Götter in der attischen Kunst des 5. Jahrhunderts v. Chr*. Bern: Antike Kunst Beiheft 11.

Kaeser, B. (1990) "Zuschauerfiguren", in B. Kaeser and K. Vierneisel (eds) *Kunst der Schale/Kultur des Trinkens*. München: Staatliche Antikensammlung und Glyptothek, pp. 151–6.

Kennell, N. (1995) *The Gymnasium of Virtue: Education and Culture in Ancient Sparta*. Chapel Hill, NC: University of North Carolina Press.

Kilmer, M. (1993a) *Greek Erotica on Attic Red-figure Vases*. London: Duckworth.

——(1993b) "In search of the wild *kalos*-name", *Echos du Monde Classique/Classical Views* 12: 173–99.

——(1997) "Painters and pederasts", in M. Golden and P. Toomey (eds) *Inventing Ancient Culture: Historicism, Periodization, and the Ancient World*. London: Routledge, pp. 36–49.

Koch-Harnack, G. (1983) *Knabenliebe und Tiergeschenke: Ihre Bedeutung im päderastischen Erziehungssystem Athens*. Berlin: Gebrüder Mann Verlag.

Koehl, R. (1986) "The chieftain cup and a Minoan rite of passage", *Journal of Hellenic Studies* 106: 99–110.

Kunisch, N. (1997) *Makron*. Mainz: Philipp von Zabern.

Lear, A. (2004) "Noble Eros: The idealization of pederasty from the age of Homer to the Athens of Socrates", unpublished PhD thesis, University of California, Los Angeles.

——(2008) "Anacreon's 'Self': An alternative role model for the Archaic elite male?", *American Journal of Philology* 129: 47–76.

——(2011) "The pederastic elegies and the authorship of the Theognidea", *Classical Quarterly* 61: 378–93.

——(2014) "Ancient Greek pederasty: An introduction", in T.K. Hubbard (ed.) *A Companion to Greek and Roman Sexualities*. Chichester: Wiley Blackwell, pp. 102–27.

Lear, A. and Cantarella, E. (2008) *Images of Ancient Greek Pederasty: Boys Were Their Gods*. London: Routledge.

Lebessi, A. (1976) "A sanctuary of Hermes and Aphrodite in Crete", *Expedition* 18: 2–13.

Leitao, D. (2002) "The legend of the sacred band", in M. Nussbaum and J. Sihvola (eds) *The Sleep of Reason: Erotic Experience and Sexual Ethics in Ancient Greece and Rome*. Chicago, IL: University of Chicago Press, pp. 143–69.

Lissarrague, F. (1999) "Publicity and performance: *Kalos* inscriptions in Attic vase-painting", in S. Goldhill and R. Osborne (eds) *Performance, Culture and Athenian Democracy*. Cambridge: Cambridge University Press, pp. 359–73.

Lynch, K. (2011) *The Symposium in Context: Pottery from a Late Archaic House near the Athenian Agora.* Princeton, NJ: American School of Classical Studies at Athens.

MacLachlan, B. (1993) *The Age of Grace: Charis in Early Greek Poetry.* Princeton, NJ: Princeton University Press.

Marinatos, N. (2003) "Striding across boundaries: Hermes and Aphrodite as gods of initiation", in D. Dodd and C. Faraone (eds) (2003) *Initiation in Ancient Greek Rituals and Narratives: New Critical Perspectives.* London: Routledge, pp. 130–50.

Meier, M. (1837) "Päderastie", *Allgemeine Enzyklopädie der Wissenschaften und Künste* 9(3): 147–89.

Meyer, M. (1988) "Männer mit Geld", *Jahrbuch des Deutschen Archäologischen Instituts* 103: 87–125.

Mommsen, H. (1975) *Der Affecter.* Mainz: Philipp von Zabern.

Neer, R. (2002) *Style and Politics in Athenian Vase-painting.* Cambridge: Cambridge University Press.

Olson, S.D. (2010) "Comedy, politics, and society", in G. Dobrov (ed) *Brill's Companion to the Study of Greek Comedy.* Leiden: Brill, pp. 35–69.

Orrells, D. (2011) *Classical Culture and Modern Masculinity.* Oxford: Oxford University Press.

Patzer, H. (1982) *Die griechische Knabenliebe.* Wiesbaden: Franz Steiner Verlag.

Percy, W. (1996) *Pederasty and Pedagogy in Archaic Greece.* Urbana, IL: Board of Trustees of the University of Illinois.

——(2005) "Reconsiderations about Greek homosexualities", in B. Verstraete and V. Provencal (eds) "Same-sex Desire and Love in Greco-Roman Antiquity and in the Classical Tradition of the West", *Journal of Homosexuality* 49(3/4): 13–61.

Pogey-Castries, L.-R. (aka Georges Hérelle) (1930). *Histoire de l'amour grec.* Paris: Stendhal et compagnie.

Reinsberg, C. (1989) *Ehe, Hetärentum und Knabenliebe im antiken Griechenland.* München: C.H. Beck Verlag.

Robb, K. (1994) *Literacy and Paideia in Ancient Greece.* Oxford: Oxford University Press.

Robson, J. (2009) *Aristophanes: An Introduction.* London: Duckworth.

Scanlon, T. (2002) *Eros and Greek Athletics.* Oxford: Oxford University Press.

——(2005) "The dispersion of pederasty and the athletic revolution in sixth-century BC Greece", in B. Verstraete and V. Provencal (eds) "Same-sex Desire and Love in Greco-Roman Antiquity and in the Classical Tradition of the West", *Journal of Homosexuality* 49(3/4): 63–85.

Schnapp, A. (1989) "Eros en chasse", in C. Bérard (ed) *A City of Images.* Princeton, NJ: Princeton University Press, pp. 67–83.

——(1997) *Le chasseur et la cité.* Paris: Editions Albin Michel.

Selle, H. (2008) *Theognis und die Theognidea.* Berlin: Walter de Gruyter.

Sergent, B. (1986a) *Homosexuality in Greek Myth.* Boston, MA: Beacon Press.

——(1986b) *L'homosexualité initiatique dans l'Europe ancienne.* Paris: Payot.

Shapiro, H. (Harold) A. (1981) "Courtship scenes in Attic vase painting", *American Journal of Archaeology* 85: 133–43.

Shapiro, H. (1987) "Kalos-inscriptions with patronymic", *Zeitschrift für Papyrologie und Epigraphik* 68: 107–18.

——(2000) "Leagros and Euphronios", in T. Hubbard (ed.) *Greek Love Reconsidered.* New York: W. Hamilton Press, pp. 12–32.

——(2012) *Re-fashioning Anakreon in Classical Athens.* Munich: Wilhelm Fink Verlag.

Shapiro, J. (2010) "Speaking Bodies: Physiognomic consciousness and oratorical strategy in 4th-century Athens", unpublished PhD thesis, University of Michigan, Ann Arbor.

Sommerstein, A. (1996) "How to avoid becoming a *komodoumenos*", *Classical Quarterly* 46: 327–56.

Spivey, N. (1991) "Greek vases in Etruria", in T. Rasmussen and N. Spivey (eds) *Looking at Greek Vases.* Cambridge: Cambridge University Press, pp. 131–50.

Steiner, D. (1998) "Moving images: Fifth-century victory monuments and the athlete's allure", *Classical Antiquity* 17: 123–49.

Sutton, R. (1981) "The interaction between men and women portrayed on Attic red-figure pottery", unpublished PhD thesis, University of North Carolina, Chapel Hill.

Wohl, V. (2002) *Love among the Ruins: The Erotics of Democracy in Classical Athens.* Princeton, NJ: Princeton University Press.

8

BEFORE QUEERNESS?

Visions of a homoerotic heaven in ancient Greco-Italic tomb paintings

Walter Duvall Penrose Jr

The paintings decorating the walls and ceiling of the early fifth-century BCE Tomb of the Diver in the ancient Greek colony of Poseidonia (modern-day Paestum, Italy) have achieved much acclaim since their 1968 discovery. One of the five paintings portrays an expression of homo-erotic desire which has gained widespread notoriety, becoming an icon of male "homosexuality" (Figure 8.1). Not only did the painting appear as evidence in the landmark work *Greek Homo-sexuality* by K. J. Dover (1978 [1989]), it went on to grace the cover of *Bisexuality in the Ancient World* by Eva Cantarella and more recently the covers of both the *Columbia Anthology of Gay Literature: Readings from Western Antiquity to the Present Day* and James Saslow's *Pictures and Passions: A History of Homosexuality in Visual Arts.*[1] Yet, based on our understanding of the ancient Greek past, this depiction is neither a representation of homosexuality nor of gayness unless we are to speak in an anachronistic, essentialist way.

Should we then perhaps use the broader, more flexible category of queer, which after all denotes a site of marginalization from and resistance to dominant culture, to try to link the male–male eroticism of the past to the homosexuality of the present? On the one hand, *every-thing* about the Tomb of the Diver paintings would fit into the context of "queer" if the paintings were modern, from the *erōmenos* who in Figure 8.1 seems to be wearing lipstick to the *erastēs* who seems to be ready to kiss him, particularly as their ultimate setting is in a homo-erotic, homosocial afterlife, which defies a modern heteronormative ideology. Indeed what could be a more transgressive space in a modern, Christian context than a male–male erotic vision of heaven? Taken in the context of their own time, however, the paintings rather invite us to view a space that was neither queer nor marginalized, but was rather a privileged location of the Greek patriarchy—the symposium. In this sense, the Tomb of the Diver paintings are like the pederastic symposium scenes found on Attic pottery and described in philosophical and other Greek treatises. Ancient Greek societies did not operate under the heteronormativity of Western modernity, but, I will argue, were *homonormative* in that they privileged males and prioritized relationships between men through the institution of pederasty. It is this homo-normativity that we are viewing in the Tomb of the Diver paintings.

Furthermore, the symposium scene of the tomb seems to offer a reward to the deceased in the afterlife of both homoeroticism and hedonism, and what could be more normative than eschatology? In terms of eschatology, the paintings show local Italic influences, especially

Figure 8.1 Gli Amanti: "The Lovers"; detail of a fresco from the Tomb of the Diver, *c.*480–470 BCE. Found in località Tempa del Prete, near Paestum. Museo Archeologico Nazionale, Paestum, Italy. Photo: Gianni Dagli Orti/ Art Resource, NY.

associations of death, sexuality, and banqueting that seem to have been borrowed from the Etruscans. At the same time, they show a pederastic Greek homosocial environment that is different from Etruscan funerary painting. In the Etruscan depictions, the male–female or married couple is privileged, but in the Tomb of the Diver it is the male–male couple that stands out. The cultural blending present suggests that the Greeks of Poseidonia borrowed heavily from Etruscan conceptions of the afterlife, but adapted these ideas to suit their own social milieu. The result was a homoerotic, homosocial, and homonormative conception of the afterlife, an idea that is clearly displayed in the tomb paintings.

Both the eroticism and the eschatology of the iconography of the Tomb of the Diver paintings suggest that the deceased buried there was an initiate of the Orphic cult. The most convincing analysis of the iconography to date has identified Orphic themes in the Tomb of the Diver paintings, particularly labeling four of the five paintings as depicting a symposium of the dead similar to the Orphic conception of the afterlife described by Plato in the *Republic* (363c; Somville 1979; see also Otto 1990; cf. Holloway 2006). That said, Orphic and other analyses of the iconography of the tomb have focused on eschatological readings that have either avoided the eroticism presented by the paintings or subordinated it to other concerns. The main exception to this is the analysis of Cerchiai (1987), who instead subordinates the eschatological themes to the erotic.[2] A more balanced approach is needed—one that interprets the iconography in terms of *both* eschatology and eroticism. In this essay, I propose to bring these motifs together in one reading, in which I will demonstrate that the Orphic rites were, in much more of a Greek than an Etruscan fashion, both homosocial and homoerotic.[3] In Orphic thought, the symposium served both as a means to worship Dionysus and other gods in this life, and as an image of the eternal hereafter in the next life. Crucially, on the tomb paintings, that world is male and homoerotic.

I will begin this essay in earnest by describing each of the five paintings found in the tomb. Next, I will briefly survey the secondary scholarship on the paintings to date, paying careful attention to the blending of Greek and Etruscan elements present as well as the debates that have developed regarding the eschatological program outlined in the iconography, specifically asking whether the iconography is Pythagorean, Hesiodic, Etruscan, or Orphic. Then, expanding on current Etruscan and Orphic interpretations, I will present my own explication of the tomb's iconographic program, in which I will demonstrate that the Orphic cult in Italy was heavily influenced by Etruscan eschatological ideas. I will incorporate the erotic, ritual, and eschatological elements of the paintings into a new and revised Orphic reading. Finally, I will return to the questions of the use of the images to mark homosexuality or gay identity, or even queerness as raised above. I will argue that the scene we are viewing is neither gay nor queer, but rather offers a "homonormative" paradigm. To be useful for analysis of ancient Greek evidence, queer theory must be adapted and refined, as concepts like "heteronormative" do not really apply.

The paintings

The interior decorations of the Tomb of the Diver consist of five painted slabs—four on the walls or sides of the chamber and one on the top or lid. The tomb itself is relatively small, only slightly larger than a modern coffin. Based on pottery found in the tomb, the paintings have been dated to approximately 480–470 BCE (Napoli 1970: 68–9; Pontrandolfo 1996: 458). The two long-sided slabs depict partygoers lounging on couches at what has been identified as a symposium (Figures 8.2 and 8.3). Most of the male guests appear in couples, and the celebrated pair mentioned earlier (Figure 8.1; Figure 8.2, far right) have been labeled *gli amanti* "the lovers" by Mario Napoli, the archeologist who discovered the tomb. On the opposite wall, one of the symposiasts is playing music while his couchmate holds his hand to his forehead (Figure 8.3), a gesture which has been interpreted to indicate a state of ecstasy (Pontrandolfo 1996: 458). The symposiast on the left in Figure 8.3 is holding an egg, an item which has been identified as a symbol of the Greek Orphic religious movement (Somville 1979),[4] but also appears in a similar fashion in the Etruscan Tomb of the Lionesses at Tarquinia (Figure 8.7) (Napoli 1970: 141; Steingräber 1986: 316–17, no. 77; Holloway 2006: 379).[5]

On the middle *klinē* (couch) of Figure 8.2, the symposiast has raised his kylix at an angle, indicating that he is playing *kottabos*. The game of *kottabos* was played like modern-day darts—the object was to hit a target with lees of wine. Whereas the initial libation at a symposium was poured to the god Dionysus, the dregs offered in *kottabos* were done so in the name of an *erōmenos* (Athenaeus 10.427d). While throwing the wine, the participant would shout out the name of a youth that he was courting or wished to court (Lissarague 1989: 85–6; Lynch 2012: 537).

On the shorter side slabs, the theme of the symposium is continued. A youth is pictured walking away from a garlanded krater which appears to contain wine (Figure 8.4). He is most likely the designated wine pourer for the guests (Pontrandolfo 1996: 458). A procession of symposiasts appears on the opposing short slab, led by a female flautist followed by a naked youth with a blue scarf draped over his arms and a clothed, bearded man (Figure 8.5).[6] Finally, on the lid of the tomb a naked young man is pictured diving into a body of water (Figure 8.6).

Figure 8.2 Fresco on the north wall of the Tomb of the Diver. Museo Archeologico Nazionale, Paestum, Italy. Photo: © Vanni Archive/ Art Resource, NY.

Figure 8.3 Fresco on the south wall of the Tomb of the Diver. Museo Archeologico Nazionale, Paestum, Italy. Photo: © Vanni Archive/ Art Resource, NY.

Figure 8.4 Fresco on the east wall of the Tomb of the Diver. Museo Archeologico Nazionale, Paestum, Italy. Photo: © Vanni Archive/ Art Resource, NY.

As the oldest known examples of Greek wall paintings, the Tomb of the Diver frescoes occupy a unique position in the canon of Classical art. The Poseidonian paintings, despite similarities in the symposium scenes, otherwise fall outside of the norms of Attic art.[7] In particular, the association of the symposium with the afterlife, and of eschatology with eroticism, are reflective of Etruscan influence, as Pontrandolfo (1996: 458) has argued:[8]

> The way the figures have been represented, and the composition of the scenes, especially that of the symposiasts lounging on their *klinai*, are perfectly "Greek" and just like the widespread pictures on the coeval red figure Attic pottery. While full of Greek conceptual models, the paintings in the Diver's Tomb are in fact an exception, even as far as their contents are concerned, because they do not mirror the typical mental attitude of Greeks who would normally never decorate the interior of tombs with paintings, nor place the world of death together with that of the *symposium*, for the two worlds contradict each other. The homosociality of the symposium participants, nevertheless, is very Greek.

The Tomb of the Diver is like Attic symposium scenes in that the only female is a young flute girl, possibly a slave due to her diminished stature, in the *kōmos* or procession scene (Figure 8.5).[9] In contrast, Etruscan paintings show women, probably wives, at symposia (see Figure 8.7).

Figure 8.5 Fresco on the west wall of the Tomb of the Diver. Museo Archeologico Nazionale, Paestum, Italy. Photo: © Vanni Archive/ Art Resource, NY.

The Tomb of the Diver is also a one-of-a-kind artifact—no other comparable funerary paintings from the fifth century have been discovered in the vicinity of Poseidonia. Other painted tombs from the fourth century BCE have been found, but they date to the period after the Lucanian invasion/conquest of Poseidonia (when the name of the city was changed to Paestum), thus after the period of Greek rule of the *polis* of Poseidonia. Nevertheless, some continuities can be noted. For example, fourth-century male burials are usually accompanied by kraters (Pontrandolfo et al. 2004: 35) and other wine vessels which suggest that, for men, the afterlife might include a symposium.

Eschatology of the tomb's iconography

Scholars have disputed the eschatological symbolism of the iconography of the tomb's paintings. When he discovered the tomb, Napoli interpreted the dive scene as Pythagorean, representing the purifying passage of the soul through water (Napoli 1970: 165).[10] While this is an interesting proposition, it fails to account for the relationship of the diver to the symposium scene.[11]

Bianchi-Bandinelli (1970–1: 142) has asserted that the symposium scenes represent the heroic afterlife in the Isles of the Blessed beyond the western limits of the Mediterranean described by Hesiod (*Works and Days* 156–79), that the structure from which the diver leaps represents the Pillar of Heracles, and that the body of water he plunges into is the Atlantic

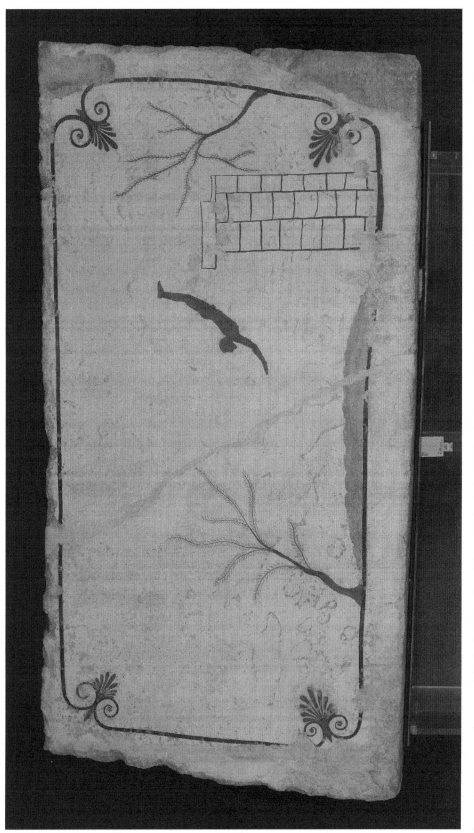

Figure 8.6 Fresco on the cover slab, Tomb of the Diver. Museo Archeologico Nazionale, Paestum, Italy. Photo: © Vanni Archive/ Art Resource, NY.

Figure 8.7 Fresco from the Tomb of the Leopards, Tarquinia. © 2014. Photo Scala, Florence. Courtesy of the Soprintendza per i Beni Archeologici dell'Etruria Meridionale, Ministero dei Beni e delle Attività Culturali e del Turismo.

Ocean, which represented the limits of the known world to the Greeks. Several centuries separate the time of Hesiod and the tomb, however, and the body of water into which the diver plunges looks much more like a small lake or spring than an ocean (Moreno 1996: 105; Pontrandolfo 1996: 458).

The most convincing explanations of the Tomb of the Diver iconography have noted either Etruscan or Orphic influence. These readings need not be mutually exclusive, however. Greek Orphic eschatology found in texts shows Etruscan influence, as do the paintings. I will first explain the Etruscan influence in the iconography, and then I will turn to the Orphic understanding, at which point I will draw connections between the two. I will then suggest that, like the iconography of the paintings, Orphic eschatology is also "hybrid," meaning that it shows both Etruscan and Greek cultural influences.[12]

The diver, the association of the symposium with the afterlife, and the procession of the deceased are all themes that surface in Etruscan funerary art. The influx of Etruscan eschatology into Magna Graecia (the Greek settlements of Southern Italy) is not surprising when one looks at a map of ancient Italy. The Greek colony of Poseidonia lay just to the south of Naples, and the *polis* shared a border, along the River Sele, with ancient Campania. Campania was already "deeply Etruscanized" by the end of the seventh century BCE, when Poseidonia was founded (Pontrandolfo et al. 2004: 5; Holloway 2006: 365–6). The inhabitants of Poseidonia mingled and possibly intermarried with Etruscans and other native inhabitants of the region. The

Etruscans had spread their influence into Campania long before the fifth century BCE, and had built an important trading colony at Capua. Hence, Greeks, Etruscans, native Campanians, traders from abroad, and others probably mingled in the *polis* of Poseidonia. Inscriptions on an *olpē* manufactured at Poseidonia and found at Fratte di Salerno (just up the coast from Poseidonia) contains short erotic verses involving persons with Greek, Etruscan, and other Italic names. Inscriptions suggest that the intermingling of persons of different cultures living at or near Poseidonia was perhaps not uncommon (Pontrandolfo 1987; Pontrandolfo et al. 2004: 20), although it is hard to be entirely sure due to a paucity of other written sources.[13]

At first glance, the association of the *symposium* with the afterlife is a feature which appears to be more of an Italic/Etruscan than a Greek phenomenon, as Pontrandolfo (1996: 459) has argued.[14] But the paintings *do* represent the attitude of at least *some* Greeks—those Greeks called "Orphics" who followed the teachings of Musaeus (Plato *Republic* 363c). As mentioned above (p. 138), the most convincing reading of the iconography thus far has been presented by Somville (1979: 44), who equates the symposium scene with a passage from Plato (*Republic* 363c), in which the Orphic conception of the afterlife is described as a banquet where the reward is eternal drunkenness.[15] Orpheus was a prophet of Dionysus, and hence the "Orphic" cult was associated with and perhaps even synonymous with the Dionysiac/Bacchic mysteries in ancient Southern Italy. Archeological finds attest to the fact that beginning perhaps as early as the sixth century BCE, the "Orphic" movement became particularly notable in Southern Italy.[16]

Furthermore, although previous scholars have tended to separate Etruscan and Orphic readings of the tomb's iconography,[17] Orphic beliefs demonstrate a number of commonalities with Etruscan eschatology, including: (1) a procession of the dead to a blessed afterlife;[18] (2) a need to either pass through or drink water to reach that afterlife;[19] and, most striking of all, (3) the representation of that afterlife as a banquet or symposium.[20] In fact, one might argue that Orphism as it appeared in the fifth-century Greek cities of Southern Italy had been heavily influenced by Etruscan ideology. Whereas Etruscan artwork in ancient Italy shows an afterlife of sympotic pleasure in the early sixth century BCE, the Tomb of the Diver shows such an afterlife in the fifth century (with a Greek pederastic twist); and by the fourth century BCE Plato refers to the "Orphic" idea of the afterlife as a symposium being a reward for the just, whereas the unjust went to the house of Hades as punishment for their wrongdoings. This chronology suggests that the Etruscan idea of the afterlife was borrowed by Greeks, who adapted it for their own needs in the Orphic cult.[21]

The eschatology of Orphism appears to be a radical departure from archaic Greek religion, in which humans were thought to be forever separated from the immortal gods. Instead, they went to the gloomy "land of the shadows" described by Homer in the *Odyssey* (11.57), save for a select few of the heroic race who transcended mortality to dwell in the paradise of the Elysian fields at the end of the earth described by Hesiod (*Works and Days* 157–69).[22] In Orphic belief, however, the afterlife was a reunion with the gods, in the form of a symposium. According to Plato (*Gorgias* 493a), Orpheus' followers subscribed to a doctrine that considered the human body a "tomb" of an immortal soul. Because of wicked deeds committed in the distant past, humans had been separated from the gods, but through initiation into special mystery rites that purified the soul, they could eventually be rejoined to the gods (Sassi 1996: 515).

Burials identified as Orphic in other, nearby Greek colonies provide further insight into the iconography of the Tomb of the Diver paintings.[23] Some Orphic initiates were buried with a tablet, considered by archeologists to be a type of passport which would give the Orphic initiate access to the afterlife. A fifth-century tablet found in Hipponium in Southern Italy contained a small text inscribed on soft gold which was rolled up and attached to a necklace worn around the deceased's neck. The text reads as follows:[24]

This (dictate) is sacred to Memory (for the *mystes* [initiate]) on the point of death.
You will go to the well-built house of Hades,
where, on the right, there lies a spring,
and next to that a white cypress tree stands.
There the souls of the dead seek refreshment.
Do not even approach this spring.
Beyond it you will find the cold water that runs
from the lake of Memory, with its keeper to the fore,
and they will ask you, with clear penetration,
what you seek in the shades of murky Hades.
Reply: "I am the son of the Earth and of starry Heaven;
I burn with thirst and I am fainting; quick, give me
to drink the cold water that comes from the lake of Memory.
They are merciful, as the king of the underworld wills,
and will give you to drink from the lake of Memory;
and when you have drunk you will travel the sacred path where
the other *mystai* and *bakkhoi* proceed in glory."

This text is the oldest of a group of gold tablets describing the landscape of the underworld, including a cypress tree, cold water from a pool of Memory, and a special road reserved for initiates of the Bacchic mysteries (Cole 1993: 276). In this context, the procession depicted on the west wall of the tomb (Figure 8.5) may be none other than a sacred procession of *bakkhoi* as mentioned in the Hipponium tablet above. Furthermore, Bacchic worshippers in Lerna believed that Dionysus had descended to Hades through a bottomless marsh to rescue his mother from death (Pausanias 2.37.5).

Some skepticism over the "Orphic" associations in this text has been expressed because the deceased buried with it was a woman (Edmonds 2004: 65–9; Avramidou 2009: 83, n. 38; see also Parker 1995: 498). From this perspective, the term "Bacchic" or "Dionysiac" might be better, given that Greek women worshipped Dionysus in maenadic rites that excluded men. What we can loosely term "Orphic/Dionysiac" cults were marked by sex-segregated rites. Although Orpheus allegedly excluded women from his rites, the eschatology of "Orphic" and "Dionysiac" cults seem to be similar—whether for men or women.[25] In typically Greek fashion, the "Orphic" or "Dionysiac" afterlife was also gender-segregated.

The elements of water and earth are also invoked in what Clement of Alexandria (*Stromata* 6.2.17.1–2) alleges is the writing of Orpheus himself:

Water is death for souls,
But from water comes earth, from earth again water,
and thence soul, rushing to all the ether.

The Orphic association between water and death expressed in these verses is reminiscent of the leap of the diver into the water and also into the afterlife in the tomb painting.

On Southern Italian Greek vases both Orpheus and Dionysus are shown in the presence of Hades (Schmidt 1975: 112). Orpheus was thought to have been a prophet of the god Dionysus, as well as someone who could potentially lead the way to the afterlife. Both Orpheus and Dionysus journey to the underworld and return from it in Greek myth, and it stands to reason that both of these mythical characters, the god and his prophet, were believed to have the power to intercede on behalf of the dead with the rulers of the underworld.[26] Initiation into Orphic/Dionysiac rites served to ensure salvation.

The symposium and Orphic rites: Higher forms of knowledge, homosociality, and homoeroticism

Orphic/Dionysiac mystery rites ultimately sought to provide the initiate with a better afterlife through the purification provided by traveling Orphic priests, or *orpheotelestai* (Graf and Johnston 2007: 59–60). Bone tablets found in the Black Sea colony of Olbia dating to the fifth century BCE explicate the relationship between Orpheus and Dionysus.[27] One of these bone tablets is more revealing than the Hipponium text, as it reads: "Dion[usos] life death life truth" with either the word *Orphikoi* or *Orphikon* inscribed in the lower left corner (Graf and Johnston 2007: 64). With the phrase "life death life truth," this inscription seems to argue for reincarnation at least once before reaching the Orphic afterlife of "truth." "Liberation from the wheel of life" in Orphism could be achieved, it was thought, through religious rites (Guthrie 1988: 31).

According to Pausanias (9.30.3), at the first Orphic rites Orpheus charmed the Thracians with his music, and led the men into ecstatic, homoerotic, male-only mystery rites.[28] Beginning in the 480s BCE, and hence contemporary to the Tomb of the Diver paintings, Attic vases show Orpheus surrounded by males only (Bremmer 1991: 22). Extant texts (Conon *FGrH* 26 F 1.45; Pausanias 9.30) tell us that women were excluded from Orpheus' rites, and Phanocles further explains that Orpheus introduced "male love" (*erōtas arrenas*) to the Thracians. Eventually, the Thracian women killed Orpheus out of jealousy for taking their husbands away from them. This scene is depicted on Greek vases from *c*.490 BCE onward (see *LIMC* vol. 7, pt. 1: 85–8). The action of the women expresses resentment at the homosocial and homoerotic activities of their husbands, by whom they felt abandoned. Hyginus (*Astronomica* 2.7) indicates that this love was pederastic: "Some say that because Orpheus was the first to introduce the love of boys [*puerilem amorem*], he had made the women angry, and for this reason they killed him."[29] In terms of the pederasty and homosociality, the "Orphic rite" has much in common with the Greek concept of the symposium.

According to Cerchiai (1987: 115–16), the reveler would obtain access to higher forms of knowledge through the symposium. This knowledge is similar to the "truth" obtained from the Orphic rite. Truth and wine were associated in the idea of the symposium, and the symposium of the here and now served as the model for the ideal Orphic afterlife. In the symposium, "the phrase 'wine and truth' was proverbial for those who talked frankly while inebriated" (Scholiast on Plato *Symp.* 217e; Alcaeus, fr. 366, ed. Lobel and Page; Skinner 2005: 46). Sympotic discussions strove both to enlighten one's contemporaries with regard to politics but even more to educate the *erōmenoi* present, just as the Orphic rite strove to educate the initiate as to how to find an eternity of sympotic pleasure.[30]

Therefore, we get to the main point here: the sexuality displayed is consistent with an eschatological Orphic reading. The male-only party displayed in the Tomb of the Diver may be Orphic, as both homosociality and same-sex eroticism are present. Cerchiai (1987: 117–23) suggests that the procession on the west wall of the tomb is an erotic hunt, in which the older bearded man is chasing the younger, nude man (Figure 8.5). By the same token, if the afterlife *includes* eroticism, the nudity could have multiple meanings. Indeed, associations of the komast's nudity with heroic death, divinity, revelry, and erotic lure may all have been intended by the artist.

Ancient paintings, modern queerness

Despite their modern deployment as symbols of gay identity (as noted above), the sympotic scenes denote what is, for all intents and purposes, a specifically ancient context; it is a paradigmatic scene in an ancient aristocratic Greek milieu where male pederasty was enjoyed without blame.[31] The Tomb of the Diver paintings occupy the intersection between religion (or at least eschatology) and eroticism in antiquity that one would never find in a Judeo-Christian paradigm or in a modern, Western, secular context. The symposium scene was more than a drinking party; it was a ritual, wherein a libation was poured to the god Dionysus, paeans were sung, and divination was sought through the game of *kottabos*. By calling out the name of a prospective beloved, a suitor might also hope to find romantic success if he made a successful throw.[32] Hence, even in daily life, homoeroticism and religious ritual were intertwined in the Greek symposium. Furthermore, the Tomb of the Diver symposium seems to represent *both* the best of this life and the hereafter, given Plato's description of the Orphic afterlife as sympotic.

The Tomb of the Diver paintings are derived from a Greek cultural setting that is not as well understood as that of Athens, or even Sparta, Thebes, or Macedon. Nonetheless, the Greek homosocial symposium at least allows us to begin to understand and contextualize the ideology displayed. First of all, the roles of the Greek lover, or *erastēs*, and the beloved or *erōmenos*, are generally considered to have been "two stages in the social development of a Greek citizen rather than … life-long identities" (Golden and Toohey 2003: 6–7, based upon Dover 1964: 31–42). The youth was meant to begin his sexual and social development as an *erōmenos*, then, when his beard came in, to become the *erastēs*, and finally, around the age of 30, to give up youthful same-sex *erōs* and marry. This was normative, and the homoeroticism engaged in by youths did not raise eyebrows.

The numerous scenes of Greek male–male eroticism on vases and other objects, most of which were exported to and later found in Italy, make it difficult to argue that, from an ancient Greco-Italic perspective, there is anything "queer" going on here, at least where queerness is identified with marginalization or transgression. I would argue that we instead should call these paintings *homonormative*. I do not mean homonormative in the sense of "upper-middle class gay male homosexual-centered," as one might conceive the term when thinking of the gay community and its standards of fashion and beauty in modern West Hollywood, California. Nor do I mean the "new homonormativity" that Lisa Duggan (2002) identified with "the sexual politics of neoliberalism" among Log Cabin gay Republicans in the United States. Rather, in an ancient Greek context, homonormativity would define the centrality of social and/or erotic relationships among men to the institutions, such as the symposium, that reify and promote exclusive male privilege in the power structures of society.[33]

The Tomb of the Diver paintings may, however, manipulate the norms of pederasty while still enforcing them, or, at least, displaying them.[34] Of course, the pederastic paradigm was central to Athenian social mores, although it was not always followed, and exact ages of an *erōmenos* and his *erastēs* are difficult, if not impossible, to pinpoint given the evidence available for the ancient Greeks.[35] On *some* Attic vases, particularly in courtship scenes, *erōmenoi* look barely pubescent, though they tend to look a bit older on symposia scenes from Athens. The *erōmenoi* shown in the Poseidonian tomb paintings look to be in their late teens or even early twenties. They are depicted as beardless, but otherwise they generally appear to be fully-grown males, most with very muscular bodies and well-defined abdominal muscles. They are of the same size and stature as their lovers. One *erōmenos* even has sideburns (Figure 8.8). Some might decipher this as peach fuzz, but otherwise he looks to be of the same physical stature as his *erastēs* and almost of a similar age. One might even ask, "could he be trimming the rest of his beard to fit into the role of *erōmenos* for which a beard might seem inappropriate"? According to Cohen (1991: 16):

> … when an Athenian man courts a boy he does so according to the normative
> expectations of the boy, his family, and the community of which he is a part
> (all social interaction is normatively structured by such expectations, though these

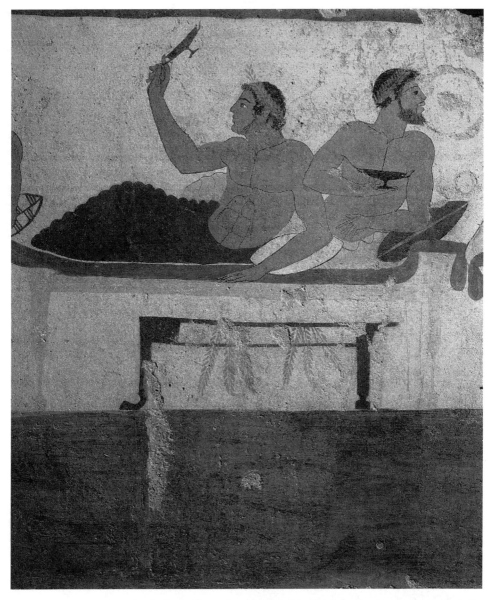

Figure 8.8 Banquet scene; fresco from the north wall of the Tomb of the Diver. Museo Archeologico Nazionale, Paestum, Italy. Photo: Gianni Dagli Orti / The Art Archive at Art Resource, NY.

expectations may conflict or reflect moral ambivalences about the conduct). Yet the norms reflected in such expectations do not simply *determine* his behavior. He possesses the knowledgeability that almost all individuals have about the norms, values, beliefs, and practical expectations of the society in which they live. This knowledgeability enables individuals to influence evaluations of their behavior by interpreting and manipulating their words and deeds and the normative categories by which they are judged.

The youth might also modify his actions, in this case trimming his facial hair, to continue being an *erōmenos* into young adulthood. Perhaps there is some transgression against Greek norms in the paintings after all, despite my earlier reluctance to think so. On the other hand, what we are viewing in the Tomb of the Diver may be the result of a more hedonistic environment than that of Athens.

Despite its proximity with Etruria, Poseidonia was a Greek *polis* as the symposium scene from the tomb reminds us. But that still allows for wide variety in social customs, as Dover (1978 [1989]: 3) suggests. Xenophon discusses the marked distinctions between homoerotic customs in the various Greek city-states. For instance, he notes (*Symposium* 8.34) that the Thebans and Eleans share common beds with their beloveds and are stationed beside them in battle formation, whereas at Athens such customs would be "banned by the severest reprobation." Could the restraints placed upon Poseidonia have been different than those at Athens or Thebes? While little is known of the customs and social history of ancient Poseidonia, its mother city has left a few more details behind. Poseidonia was founded *c.*600 BCE as a colony of Sybaris (Cerchiai et al. 2004: 62), itself an Achaean colony that was known for its wealth and luxurious way of life in antiquity (Athenaeus 12.501; Diodorus Siculus 12.1.1–2).

Sybaris was the most agriculturally rich Greek city of Magna Graecia, and its inhabitants the most indulgent of the Western Greeks. Athenaeus goes into great detail on the luxurious banquets, carriages, and other extravagances of the Sybarites, though he does not provide much detail about their sexual habits. He does, however, tell us that the Sybarites liked and befriended the Etruscans to the north and the Ionians to the east because both peoples lived luxuriously (Athenaeus 12.518a). Moreover, he says that the fourth-century BCE historian Theopompus wrote that the Etruscans "consort very eagerly with women, much more, however, do they enjoy consorting with boys [*paisi*] and striplings [*meirakiois*]. For in their country these are very good-looking, because they live in luxury and keep their bodies smooth."

Could this indicate Etruscan influence on Poseidonian sexuality? The Poseidonians lived between the Sybarites and the Etruscans, and, as we have noted in the section entitled "Eschatology of the tomb's iconography", seemed to have absorbed some of the Etruscan ideology of the afterlife into their own eschatology. Were their sexual *mores* influenced by Etruscan or other local Italic customs as well? This certainly is a possibility. Inscriptions on an *olpē* made in Poseidonia and found in a tomb at nearby Fratte di Salerno suggests that same-sex activity was enjoyed between Greeks and Etruscans (Pontrandolfo 1987). The inscriptions read:

> Apollodoros Scyllas eratai
> Wolchas apugei Apollodoron
> Onatas Niksous eratai
> Hubrichos Parmunios ēratai.

> Apollodorus loves Kscylla
> Wolchas buggers Apollodorus.
> Onatas loves Nikso
> Hybrichus has loved Parmynio.

Five males (Apollodorus, Wolchas, Onatas, Hubrichus, and Parmynio) and two females (Ksylla and Nikso) are named in the inscriptions. Pontrandolfo (1987) labels lines two and four here as pederastic and indicative of the mixed community which existed at Poseidonia and the nearby Etruscan towns of Fratte and Pontecagnano (where a similar inscription has been found). Athenaeus points out that the Etruscan men enjoyed sex with both boys (*paides*) and young men (*meirakia*), a term that refers to approximately twenty-year-old males (*LSJ* s.v. *meirakion*). The Etruscan Folkas (Latin: Vulca) is doing the Greek Apollodorus, who in turn is in love with a woman. Apollodorus seems more likely to be a *meirakion* than a *pais*, given his involvement with a woman. Nor does his literal role of passive partner to another male seem to be interfering with his seeking to be the penetrator of a woman. The inscription problematizes the scholarly idea of distinct "life-stages" of both the *erastēs* and the *erōmenos*. In other words, we as modern scholars have wanted to neatly define these categories, but the inscriptions suggest that these life-stages could have overlapped—a young male who was the *erōmenos* of an older male might in a place like Poseidonia or Fratte be simultaneously the lover of a woman.

Conclusion

The paintings analyzed suggest that the idea of a drunken, sexy hereafter derived from an Etruscan context was imported into Greek thought and altered to fit Greek norms of homosociality and pederasty in the "Orphic" religious movement. The Tomb of Diver paintings also display both Greek and Etruscan influences, as well as Orphic symbolism, all of which suggest that the deceased buried in the tomb was an initiate of the Orphic cult. Furthermore, the tomb can be called "Orphic" in terms of not only eschatology but also of sexuality. The Tomb of the Diver paintings display a relationship between male–male eroticism and the afterlife that is Orphic. While the tomb has been called Orphic for a number of other reasons, the pederastic, homosocial aspect of its Orphism has been overlooked.

The Tomb of the Diver paintings show a pederastic ideal, even if it is not as stringent as the Athenian model. The close proximity of Poseidonia to Etruscan and other Italic communities may offer a rationale for this phenomenon—the construction of pederastic norms at Poseidonia was perhaps more fluid than in other Greek cities. Hence, the paintings of the Tomb of the Diver would seem to position Poseidonia somewhere between Athens and Etruria on the map of homoerotic (and religious) subjectivity.

Notes

I would like to thank Larissa Bonfante for her generous assistance with many drafts of this article; Sarah B. Pomeroy for comments on an early draft; and the editors of this book, Nancy Rabinowitz, Mark Masterson, and James Robson, for their insightful suggestions. Any inaccuracies in this essay are my own.

1 Dover (1978 [1989]); Fone, ed. (1998); Saslow (1999); Cantarella (2002).

2 See p. 148 below. In 1977, Holloway pointed to the importance of the eroticism in the tomb's iconographic program, but in 2006 (365), Holloway wrote that "Although the diver may make reference to the moment of death, the symposium may have been intended to create a welcoming scene to surround the dead man in the tomb."

3 I have here chosen to use the more general term "homoerotic" as opposed to the more specific label "pederastic" because some depictions of Orphic rites do not seem to be showing pederasty (see e.g. *LIMC* s.v. "Orpheus", no. 9). Literary sources, on the other hand, indicate that Orpheus initiated the "love of boys," but these are late. Leitao (1996); see further p. 148.

4 The egg symbolizes the Orphic belief in eventual reunification with a divine source. According to Aristophanes (*Birds* 695–7), in Orphic cosmogony, Phanes, also called Eros, the creator of all things, was an androgynous being who was originally thought to have hatched from a shell. A simple set of grave goods found in a fifth-century tomb near ancient Metapontum included a small egg from which an androgynous figure identified as Phanes is emerging (Maddoli 1996: 498).

5 The egg has also been identified, like flowers, as a "gift of love" in vase paintings. See further Rabinowitz (2002: 113, fig. 5.2a,b). As the man holding the egg in the Tomb of the Diver is not involved in an exchange, however, the egg is more likely to be an Orphic symbol, probably pointing to the idea that the symposium represents an Orphic rite and/or the Orphic hereafter.

6 On the flautist, see Holloway (2006: 371), who argues that "she is not a child; she has fully developed breasts". Her small stature may indicate that she is a slave rather than a child.

7 As much of extant Greek art was made in Attica but exported to the rest of the Mediterranean, our understandings of artistic convention and iconography are heavily reliant on an understanding of the Attic pottery industry.

8 Cf. my assessment, p. 146.

9 See further Chapter 9, Glazebrook, this volume.

10 Cf. Holloway 2006: 379–80.

11 Other objections to the Pythagorean interpretation have been raised by scholars elsewhere. See further Rouveret 1976; Holloway 2006: 380; Avramidou 2009: 81 n. 24; cf. Warland 1998.

12 On cultural hybridity, see further Bhabha (1994 [2004]); Young (1995).

13 See further p. 151–52.

14 Pontrandolfo's assessment of the composition of the paintings is quoted above, p. 142.

15 Plato specifically attributes the idea to Musaeus, who in turn was either a son or disciple of Orpheus (Diod. 4.25; Serv. *ad Virg. Aen.* 6.667).

16 This movement also appears to have occurred in other areas which were colonized by the Greeks, as archeological evidence from Olbia on the Black Sea indicates. While Edmonds (2004: 29) has questioned whether the "so-called Orphic texts" found in Greek graves are actually Orphic, the label "Orphic" has otherwise held up to the scrutiny of other scholars, e.g., Bernabé and Jiménez San Cristóbal (2011); Graf (2011). Some tablets which are found in Orphic burials call to Persephone or Kore, the queen of the Underworld, while others invoke the goddess Mnemosyne, or Memory in English. Also see Graf and Johnston 2007.

17 Holloway (2006: 379) has rejected the possibility of Orphic influence in the paintings, and Torelli (1997: 138) is so swayed by the Etruscan influence that he has argued an Etruscan alien was buried in the tomb at Poseidonia.

18 On Etruscan procession scenes to the afterlife, see further Roncalli (1996: 47–8).

19 Cf. the diver in the Etruscan Tomb of Hunting and Fishing (Steingräber 2006: 104–5; Holloway 2006: 375, fig. 10). On Orphics equating water with death, see p. 147 of this essay.

20 On Etruscan banqueting in the afterlife, see further Bonfante (1986): 233–5.

21 Likewise, Etruscan specialists (Steiner 2003: 281; Avramidou 2009: 78, n. 10) have noted the influence of Dionysiac and "Orphic Pythagorean" myths in Etruscan painting of the last two decades of the sixth century BCE. Cultural exchange between Greeks and Etruscans was clearly two-way.

22 See further Sourvinou-Inwood 1995: 19–20; Sassi 1996: 515.

23 This idea has also been explored to some extent by Otto (1990: 270–1); cf. Holloway 2006: 379.

24 Based upon the translation of Gigante (1996: 503).

25 On misogyny in Orphic cultic practice, see Böhme (1970: 197); Avramidou (2009: 74, 80, n. 13).

26 Dionysus was equated with the vegetation god Flufluns, who was also a god of the underworld in Etruscan mythology (Bonfante 1993).

27 For a more thorough understanding of the "Orphic" cult and texts associated with it, see Bernabé and Jiménez San Cristobal (2008); Edmonds (2011).

28 I have here used the term "homoerotic" instead of "pederastic" because we are told that the men who participated in these rites were married. Leitao (1996: 58–60) argues that "many different forms of same-sex fellowship and eroticism, particularly in the domain of myth, were slowly assimilated to the pederasty model, a process which was more or less complete by the Hellenistic period … Orpheus sometimes appears to be a figure who crosses gender and sex boundaries." Leitao (1996: 57–8) further asserts that Phanocles' use of the phrase *arrenes erōtes*, "love of males," is not necessarily pederastic but rather "reflects an entirely different ethos," wherein Orpheus rejected the love of women in a role perhaps like that of the North American berdache, a "third sex" or effeminate male whose "sexual and spiritual functions" were intertwined. The fact that Orpheus was Thracian, Leitao (1996: 58) suggests, may also explain why Phanocles does not use pederastic terminology to describe Orpheus' relations with other men.

29 Ovid (*Metamorphoses* 10.79–85) and Philargyrius (*Comment. Ad. Verg. Georg.* 4.520) assert that Orpheus was the first to introduce pederasty. Bremmer (1991: 21) asserts that "Orpheus' homosexuality … does not belong to the original myth." The problem in general is that the sources calling Orpheus' homoeroticism pederastic are late.

30 Pederasty was ultimately the terrain of aristocrats, and the symposium was an elite, oligarchic activity (Skinner 2005: 47; Lear and Cantarella 2008: xvi).

31 For a critical analysis of the identification of modern gay men with the ancient Greeks, see Halperin 2002: 13–17.

32 See above, p.139.

33 Are new words and more precise terminology necessary to refine queer theory for analysis of the remote past? As Halberstam (1998: 46) argues, "the challenge for new queer history has been, and remains, to produce methodologies sensitive to historical change but influenced by current theoretical preoccupations". Neither of the dominant current methodologies at our disposal to study pederasty/homoeroticism in ancient sources and art—philology and queer theory—have achieved this goal. The former is trapped in the past forever, while the latter has been developed in a modern setting and, at least as currently configured, has a vocabulary that cannot adequately describe ancient Greek history. When available, Greek categories such as *erastēs* and *erōmenos* offer the preferable word choice for terminology (Halperin 2002: 14; Calame (Chapter 11, this volume)). That said, these categories in some ways limit us from finding that delicate balance between our own interests and taxonomies and those of the remote past. The term *erastēs*, for example, can refer to a male "lover" of women as well as youths. Redefining, or perhaps better stated, historicizing concepts such as homonormativity provides a means to extend our "current theoretical preoccupations" to the study of ancient texts and artwork. As mentioned above, that which is normative is typically *not* defined, at least not until those power structures which create it are analyzed by those on the margins.

34 Stewart (1997: 8) writes that "though Greek art may look broadly naturalistic and therefore lifelike, it actually offers more insights into ideology rather than reality." Neer (2002: 2), discussing Attic vase images, argues that "these objects convey meaning in a social field … it is about *form* (or, how an image shows what it shows)", and "*ideology* (or, how people interact with each other and the world in ways mediated by the representations)." As McNiven (2012) notes, however, "the conflict between our visual and textual evidence forces us to question the reality behind both. It is important to realize that ideals and taboos are at work here. Some things were not depicted; they violated the ideology."

35 The youngest *erōmenoi* tend to show up in these courtship scenes as opposed to *symposia* on Attic ware, however (see further Lear and Cantarella 2008). And, even at Athens, some relationships apparently continued on past youth and broke the rules, such as the relationship of Euripides and his *erōmenos* Agathon (Plut. *Amat.* 770c). We hear that when he noticed that Agathon's beard had grown in, Euripides kissed him anyway and mused "even the autumn of the fair is fair."

Bibliography

Avramidou, A. (2009) "The Phersu game revisited," *Etruscan Studies* 12: 73–87.

Bernabé, A. and Jiménez San Cristóbal, A.I. (2008) *Instructions for the Netherworld: The Orphic Gold Tablets*. Leiden: Brill.

——(2011) "Are the 'Orphic' gold leaves Orphic?," in R. Edmonds (ed.) *The "Orphic" Gold Tablets and Greek Religion: Further Along the Path*. Cambridge: Cambridge University Press, pp. 68–101.

Bhabha, H. (1994 [2004]) *The Location of Culture*. London: Routledge.

Bianchi-Bandinelli, R. (1970–1) "Review of Mario Napoli *La Tomba del Tuffatore*," *Dialoghi di Archeologia* 4–5: 135–42.

Böhme, R. (1970) *Orpheus: Der Sänger und Seiner Zeit*. Bern/Munich: Francke.

Bonfante, L. (1986) "Life and afterlife," in L. Bonfante (ed.) *Etruscan Life and Afterlife: A Handbook of Etruscan Studies*. Detroit: Wayne State University Press, pp. 232–78.

——(1993) "Fufluns Pacha: The Etruscan Dionysus mystery cult," in T.H. Carpenter and C.A. Faraone (eds) *Masks of Dionysus*. Ithaca, NY: Cornell University Press, pp. 221–38.

Bremmer, J. (1991) "Orpheus: From guru to gay," in P. Borgeaud (ed.) *Orphisme et Orphee: En l'honneur de Jean Rudhart*. Geneva: Droz, pp. 13–30.

Cantarella, E. (2002) *Bisexuality in the Ancient World*, trans. C.Ó. Cuillanáin. New Haven, CT: Yale University Press.

Cerchiai, L. (1987) "Sulle Tombe del Tuffatore e della Caccia e Pesca: Proposta di lettura iconologica," *Dialghi di Archeologica* 2:113–23.

Cerchiai, L., Jannelli, L. and Longo, F. (2004) *The Greek Cities of Magna Graecia and Sicily*. Los Angeles, CA: J. Paul Getty Museum.

Cohen, D. (1991) *Law, Sexuality, and Society: The Enforcement of Morals in Classical Athens*. Cambridge: Cambridge University Press.

Cole, S. (1993) "Voices from beyond the grave: Dionysus and the dead," in T.H. Carpenter and C.A. Faraone (eds) *Masks of Dionysus*. Ithaca, NY: Cornell University Press, pp. 276–95.

Dover, K.J. (1964) "Eros and nomos (Plato, *Symposium*182A–185C)," *Bulletin of Classical Studies* 27: 31–42.

——(1978 [1989]) (updated with a new postscript 1989) *Greek Homosexuality*. Cambridge, MA: Harvard University Press.

Duggan, L. (2002) "The new homonormativity: The sexual politics of Neoliberalism," in R. Castronovo and D.D. Nelson (eds) *Law, Sexuality, and Society: The Enforcement of Morals in Classical Athens*. Durham, NC: Duke University Press, pp. 175–94.

Edmonds, R.G. (2004) *Myths of the Underworld Journey: Plato, Aristophanes and the "Orphic" Gold Tablets*. Cambridge: Cambridge University Press.

——(2011) *The "Orphic" Gold Tablets and Greek Religion: Further along the Path*. Cambridge: Cambridge University Press.

Fone, B.S. (ed.) (1998) *The Columbia Anthology of Gay Literature: Readings from Western Antiquity to the Present Day*. New York: Columbia University Press.

Gigante, M. (1996) "Literary culture in Magna Graecia and Sicily," in G. Pugliese Caratelli (ed.) *The Western Greeks*. Venice: Bompiani, pp. 499–500.

Golden, M. and Toohey, P. (2003) "Introduction," in M. Golden and P. Toohey (eds) *Sex and Difference in Greece and Rome*. Edinburgh: Edinburgh University Press, pp. 1–20.

Graf, F. (2011) "Text and ritual: The corpus eschatologicum of the Orphics," in R. Edmonds (ed.) *The "Orphic" Gold Tablets and Greek Religion: Further along the Path*. Cambridge: Cambridge University Press, pp. 53–67.

Graf, F. and Johnston, S.I. (2007) *Ritual Texts for the Afterlife: Orpheus and the Bacchic Gold Tablets*. London: Routledge.

Guthrie, K.S. (1988) *The Pythagorean Sourcebook and Library*, ed. D.R. Fideler. Grand Rapids, MI: Phanes Press.

Halberstam, J. (1998) *Female Masculinity*. Durham, NC: Duke University Press.

Halperin, D. (2002) *How to Do the History of Homosexuality*. Chicago, IL: University of Chicago Press.

Holloway, R.R. (1977) "High flying at Paestum: A reply," *American Journal of Archaeology* 81: 554–5.

——(2006) "The Tomb of the Diver", *American Journal of Archaeology* 110: 365–88.

Lear, A. and Cantarella, E. (2008) *Images of Ancient Greek Pederasty: Boys Were Their Gods*. London: Routledge.

Leitao, D. (1996) "Orpheus and the third sex: Some thoughts on sexual diversity in Ancient Greece" (published only in the campus – printed San Francisco State University), *Humanities Magazine* 14(2): 47–68.

Lissarague, F. (1989) *The Aesthetics of the Greek Banquet*. Princeton, NJ: Princeton University Press.

Lynch, K.M. (2012) "Drinking and dining," in T.J. Smith and D. Plantzos (eds) *A Companion to Greek Art*. Malden, MA: Wiley-Blackwell, pp. 525–42.

McNiven, T. (2012) "Sex, gender, and sexuality," in T.J. Smith and D. Plantzos (ed.) *A Companion to Greek Art*. Malden, MA: Wiley-Blackwell, pp. 510–24.

Maddoli, G. (1996) "Cults and religious doctrines of the western Greeks," in G. Pugliese Caratelli (ed.) *The Western Greeks*. Venice: Bompiani, pp. 481–98.

Moreno, P. (1996) "Il cielo in una tomba: Come decifrare il significato di una famosa pittura funeraria del V secolo A.C.," *Archeo* 11/12(142): 102–5.

Napoli, M. (1970) *La tomba del tuffatore*. Bari: De Donato.

Neer, R. (2002) *Style and Politics in Athenian Vase Painting: The Craft of Democracy 530–460 BCE.* New York: Cambridge University Press.

Otto, B. (1990) "Die Fresken der 'Tomba del Tuffatore' in Paestum," *Innsbrucker Beiträge zur Kulturwissenschaft* 27: 263–78.

Parker, R. (1995) "Early Orphism," in Anton Powell (ed.) *The Greek World*. London: Routledge, pp. 483–510.

Pontrandolfo, A. (1987) "Un'iscrizione posidoniate in una tomba di Fratte di Salerno," *Atti di Istituto Universitario Orientale di Napoli* 9: 55–63.

——(1996) "Wall painting in Magna Graecia," in G. Pugliese Caratelli (ed.) *The Western Greeks*. Venice: Bompiani, pp. 457–70.

Pontrandolfo, A., Rouveret, A. and Cipriani, M. (2004) *The Painted Tombs of Paestum*, trans. F. Poole. Paestum, Italy: Pandemos.

Rabinowitz, N.S. (2002) "Excavating women's homoeroticism in ancient Greece: The evidence from Attic vase painting," in N.S. Rabinowitz and L. Auanger (eds) *Among Women: From the Homosocial to the Homoerotic in the Ancient World*. Austin, TX: University of Texas Press, pp. 106–66.

Roncalli, F. (1996) "Laris Pulenas and Sisyphus: Mortals, heroes, and demons in the Etruscan underworld," *Etruscan Studies* 3: 45–64.

Rouveret, A. (1976) "La peinture dans l'art funéraire: La Tombe du Plongeur a Paestum," in R. Bloch (ed.) *Recherches sur les religions de l'Italie antique*. Geneva: Droz, pp. 99–129.

Saslow, J. (1999) *Pictures and Passions: A History of Homosexuality in the Visual Arts*. New York: Viking Press.

Sassi, M.M. (1996) "Philosophy in the western Greek world," in G. Pugliese Caratelli (ed.) *The Western Greeks*, Venice: Bompiani, pp. 515–22.

Schmidt, Margot (1975) "Orfeo e orfismo nella pittura vasculare italiota," in P. Romanelli (ed.) *Orfismo in Magna Grecia, Atti del XIV convegno di studi sulla Magna Graecia. Taranto 6–10 ottobre 1974*, Naples: Arte tip. editrice.

Skinner, M. (2005) *Sexuality in Greek and Roman Culture*. Malden, MA: Blackwell.

Somville, P. (1979) "La tombe du plongeur," *Revue de l'Histoire des Religions* 196: 41–51.

Sourvinou-Inwood, C. (1995) *Reading Greek Death*. Oxford: Clarendon Press.

Steiner, D. (2003) *Jenseitsreise und Unterwelt bei den Etrusken, Untersuchung zur Ikonographie und Bedeutung*. Munich: Herbert Utz.

Steingräber, S. (1986) *Etruscan Painting: Catalogue Raisonné of Etruscan Wall Paintings*, trans. M. Blair. New York: Harcourt, Brace, Jovanovich.

——(2006) *Abundance of Life: Etruscan Wall Painting*, trans. R. Stockmann. Los Angeles, CA: J. Paul Getty Museum.

Stewart, A. (1997) *Art, Desire, and the Body in Ancient Greece*. Cambridge: Cambridge University Press.

Torelli, M. (1997) *Il rango, il rito, e l'imagine: Alle origini della rappresentazione storica romana*. Milan: Electa.

Warland, D. (1998) "Tentative d'exégèse des fresques de la tombe 'du Plongeur' de Poseidonia," *Latomus* 57(2): 261–91.

Young, R.J.C. (1995) *Colonial Desire: Hybridity in Theory, Culture, and Race*. London: Routledge.

9

"SEX ED" AT THE ARCHAIC SYMPOSIUM

Prostitutes, boys and *paideia*[1]

Allison Glazebrook

Both the *pais*[2] and *hetaira*-figure[3] were eroticized in sympotic poetry, drinking games and dedications. Their common identity as objects of desire resulted in similarities that might have produced anxiety among symposiasts. Aeschines' attack on the character of Timarchus in *Aeschines* 1, although a fourth-century example, demonstrates how easily the pederastic relationship could slip into the realm of prostitution. It is this slippage between boy-youths and prostitutes that might have made archaic symposiasts apprehensive.[4] In fact, the increasing popularity of boy courtship as a sympotic theme in the mid- to late sixth century BCE (in poetry and on pots) suggests a desire to explore and define the pederastic relationship and even a need to distinguish the boy-youth (free and future active citizen) from the *hetaira*-prostitute (slave/freed and foreign).[5] The female body, in its guise as a prostitute at the drinking party, was an essential element in this discourse. While her presence at symposia was multi-faceted and attitudes toward her body were complex and varied, I focus here on the use of the *hetaira*-figure as a pedagogical tool and negative paradigm for boy-youths and adult males at symposia. I investigate attitudes toward the boy beloved and the prostitute discernible in sympotic poetry and in images on sympotic ware and suggest that the relationship of the *hetaira*-prostitute and her client versus that of the boy beloved and his *erastēs* was an important focus of *paideia* (education) at symposia; the symposium was not simply an erotic space, but a forum for a kind of sexual ethics.

The Greek symposium

The Greek word *symposion* is literally "a drinking together," and wine consumption among friends is the defining feature.[6] The Greeks participated in symposia in both public and private contexts. While free women of the citizen class likely celebrated with symposia in sanctuaries, like that of Demeter at Brauron, they were excluded from private symposia hosted by a male citizen in his own home. By the classical period, the private drinking party occurred after the *deipnon*, the evening meal.[7] It was not necessarily an extension of the *deipnon*, but was often its own event. An Athenian might dine at home or with a friend, and then head to the home of another friend for the symposium. Once there, he might find entertainers, acrobats and musicians.[8] Prostitutes were often present, but entertainers, like *aulos*-players, could also perform this role. Their function as

Figure 9.1 Terracotta kylix (drinking cup), exterior, tilted, side A, c.510 BCE. Attributed to the Class of Palmette Eye-cups. Fletcher Fund, 1956 (56.171.61). Image copyright © The Metropolitan Museum of Art. Image Source: Art Resource, NY.

Figure 9.2 Terracotta kylix (drinking cup), exterior, tilted, side B, c.510 BCE. Attributed to the Class of Palmette Eye-cups. Fletcher Fund, 1956 (56.171.61). Image copyright © The Metropolitan Museum of Art. Image Source: Art Resource, NY.

Figure 9.3 Terracotta kylix (drinking cup), interior, c.510 BCE. Attributed to the Class of Palmette Eye-cups. Fletcher Fund, 1956 (56.171.61). Image copyright © The Metropolitan Museum of Art. Image Source: Art Resource, NY.

performers and sexual partners likened them to wine, something to be consumed. While females are thus present, their common status as slave, freed and foreign kept such women distinct from the male symposiasts and made the symposium a masculine space.[9]

The private symposium is traditionally thought to be a gathering of elite males of varying ages, but recently its elite status has been brought into question, making it a more widespread phenomenon even in the late archaic period.[10] In the classical period, it took place in the *andrōn*, a room typically recognizable in the archaeological record by its offset door.[11] The size of room dictated the number of *klinai* (couches) lining the walls, typically seven or eleven. One couch could fit two people, making intimate parties of 14 to 22 participants. The couches could be placed either head to toe or head to head, keeping all symposiasts in full view of one another and creating an intimate communal atmosphere. Visual representations of the symposium on archaic Attic vases (even when set on the ground without *klinai*) suggest a similar arrangement in this earlier period. Based on images of the symposium and literary accounts, such as the works of Theognis, Plato and Xenophon, the purpose of the symposium was an intimate gathering of companions, who drank, watched performances, played drinking games, drank some more, recited verses and discussed important topics of the day. Both boys and youths were present at symposia. In Xenophon's *Symposium*, Lycon accompanies his son Autylochus to a symposium in the boy's honor. Also present is the youth Critobolus. The sympotic verses of Theognis indicate the presence of boys at the archaic symposium as well (19–20, 1319). Boy-youths add to the erotic nature of a gathering, since prepubescent boys and beardless youths were courted as objects of desire (*erōmenoi*). Critobolus is described by Xenophon as *kalos* and, despite having soft down beside his ears, is clearly admired and desired by the other symposiasts (*Symp.* 4.23–8).[12]

The symposium itself is an important context for instilling values into these future citizens by providing them with models of acceptable conduct and exposing them to an intellectual culture grounded in discussion and poetry.[13] Theognis points to the banquet as the principal venue for learning (32–3, 563–6) (Levine 1985: 179–80). This tradition continues into the classical period. In Xenophon's *Symposium*, Socrates quotes a verse of Theognis about the importance of associating with good men (*esthloi*) who teach (*didaskein*) good values and of avoiding morally lax men (*kakoi*) who corrupt the mind. Lycon makes sure to check that his son has heard Socrates and has paid attention to the verse's meaning (2.4). In a comic reversal in Aristophanes' *Wasps*, the son (Bdelykleon) teaches his father (Philokleon) about proper behavior at the symposium and expects his father to reuse stories he learns (*manthanein*) there (1256–61).[14] Just as they witnessed particular values in action and what it was to be a citizen at the gymnasium, in school and in a pederastic relationship, boys and youths also learned at symposia through watching the behavior of their elders and listening to them as they recited poetry and discussed various topics.

Prostitutes and boys in the *Theognidea*

The *Theognidea* (a collection of poems by Theognis and others dating from 640 to 479 BCE) was well known in archaic and classical times for its focus on important social values including how to live the good moral life (Cobb-Stevens et al. 1985: 1–3). These teachings, moreover, were not specific to Megara, but became the foundation of an education delivered at symposia throughout Greece (Donlan 1985: 228; Ford 1985: 89).[15] Many of the verses in the *Theognidea* address a *pais* by the name of Cyrnus. Their thematic focus is *paideia*: Theognis comments that with his verses he is passing on to Cyrnus advice that he gleaned from worthy men: "the very things, Cyrnus, I myself learned (*manthanein*) from good men (*agathoi*) while still a boy (*pais*)" (28–9). He advises him first and foremost to drink and dine only with men of noble character (*agathoi*) (33–4) "for you will learn (*manthanein*) worthy things (*esthla*) from worthy men (*esthloi*), but if you associate with base men (*kakoi*), you will even destroy your current common sense (*ton eonta noon*)" (35–6). This same sentiment is passed on again later in the verses when an unknown speaker tells the addressee to sit by a man of worth and use his time at the banquet to learn from him, confirming once again the symposium as an important place for *paideia* (education): "whenever he speaks (*legein*) some bit of wisdom, you should learn it (*didaskesthai*) and with this golden nugget (*kerdos*) go home" (563–6). While *agathos* and *esthlos* are broad in their meaning (good, noble, worthy), the terms relate specifically to behavior toward others and conduct in one's actions. *Didaskesthai* commonly refers to the knowledge acquired through a teacher and mentor, knowledge acquired through guidance, while *manthanein* refers to knowledge based on study and observation, frequently under the guidance of another, but not always. Food and drink are thus the context for *paideia*, and the symposium of *agathoi* an important place of pedagogy for boys and youths.[16]

Theognis addresses Cyrnus on many topics, focusing on friendship, wine drinking, love and politics and encouraging a moderate lifestyle. Another topic of the verses to Cyrnus is the appropriate behavior of the *pais* and *philos* in the pederastic relationship. Verses 237–54 relate the benefits Cyrnus has received from Theognis: *kleos* (fame) throughout Greece on account of verses in his honor. Yet Theognis complains that he does not get the proper respect (*aidōs*) from Cyrnus, his beloved. In fact, he states further that Cyrnus is deceiving him:[17]

αὐτὰρ ἐγὼν ὀλίγης παρὰ σεῦ οὐ τυγχάνω αἰδοῦς,
ἀλλ' ὥσπερ μικρὸν παῖδα λόγοις μ' ἀπατᾶις.

I, however, don't win a little respect from you, but you deceive me just like a small child with words.

The verb *apataō* (deceive) indicates that Cyrnus is not the loyal beloved. The phrase *ōsper micron paida* (just like a small child) suggests naivety on the part of Theognis who put his trust in Cyrnus. Cyrnus, however, turns out to be untrustworthy and an unworthy companion. Other verses addressed simply to *pais* (*ō pai*) relate additional complaints. A lover tells a boy to stop fleeing and show some *charis* (gratitude) to his pursuer: ἐμοὶ δὲ δίδου χάριν (1303). The verse makes clear that *charis* is expected from a boy.

Charis is a hard term to pin down in a single definition. While the context of these verses suggests sexual favors, the term is much more complex. It defines the bond between two individuals (either divine or human) as a worthy relationship built on reciprocity in which one favor is repaid with another favor at some indefinite point in the future.[18] In the context of courtship, *charis* represents a particular type of behavior expected of the *pais* toward his lover and admirer, the *philos*.[19] Boys who accept the favors of a lover but do not reciprocate with *charis* meet with complaint. Lines 1263–6 emphasize reciprocity as being essential to the relationship:

ὦ παῖ, ὃς εὖ ἔρδοντι κακὴν ἀπέδωκας ἀμοιβήν,
οὐδέ τις ἀντ' ἀγαθῶν ἐστὶ χάρις παρὰ σοί·
οὐδέν πώ μ' ὤνησας· ἐγὼ δέ σε πολλάκις ἤδη
εὖ ἔρδων αἰδοῦς οὐδεμιῆς ἔτυχον.

Boy, you repay badly the one granting you favors. You offer no gratitude in exchange for kindnesses. You never benefit me. But I who have by now often done you a favor win no special regard.

The open criticism for being unfaithful in other verses similarly suggests a *philos* imagined the *pais* would repay him by being loyal (*pistos*) and constant.[20] But the actions of the boy were not to come from a feeling of compulsion. At line 1238 the speaker comments:

ὦ παῖ, ἄκουσον ἐμεῦ δαμάσας φρένας· οὔ τοι ἀπειθῆ
μῦθον ἐρῶ τῆι σῆι καρδίηι οὐδ' ἄχαριν.
ἀλλὰ τλῆθι νόωι συνιδεῖν ἔπος· οὔ τοι ἀνάγκη
τοῦθ' ἔρδειν, ὅ τι σοὶ μὴ καταθύμιον ἦι.

Boy, subduing your mind, listen to me: I will relate a tale neither unpersuasive nor without gratification for your heart. But venture to understand my pledge prudently. You are not compelled to do whatever is not heartfelt.[21]

Noteworthy, I think, is that *anankē* alludes to a reciprocity that is forced and undertaken by compulsion and can thus be usefully seen as the opposite of *charis* which depends on a willingness to reciprocate.[22]

Through these verses, the boys and youths attending symposia were presented with advice as to how best to conduct themselves in public and with a *lover*. Boys are directly critiqued for being flighty and too easy (1263–6, 1267–70, 1271–4). Model behavior is also emphasized: fathers are told that they can leave their sons no better treasure than knowledge of *aidōs* (409–10, 1161–2), thus emphasizing the importance of modest behavior for boy-youths, including, as MacLachlan argues, "respectful attention" toward a *philos*. It is in this specific aspect that *aidōs* is related to *charis*.[23]

In a particularly interesting verse (1367–8), boys and women are directly contrasted as companions:

παιδός τοι χάρις ἐστί· γυναικὶ δὲ πιστὸς ἑταῖρος
οὐδείς, ἀλλ' αἰεὶ τὸν παρεόντα φιλεῖ.

You get gratitude from a boy. No one has a faithful companion in a woman, but she always loves the one close at hand.

The verse notes that no one expects a woman to be a loyal companion (*pistos hetairos*), to exhibit *charis*. She, instead, enjoys the nearest available lover (*ton pareonta*). The *gunē* here, as Leslie Kurke and others have interpreted in the case of Arguris in 1211–16 (see Kurke 1997: 143–5), makes most sense as a *hetaira*-prostitute, given the sympotic themes and sympotic context of the poetry. The *Theognidea* in general, and especially Book II (from which this verse comes), contains verses about and composed for the symposium, a setting in which prostitutes appear but not wives or daughters.[24] The mention of *hetairos* (companion) in this verse directly evokes such a location for this woman. The use of *ton pareonta* in line 1368 to refer to the one she loves further suggests prostitution. The term hints at the woman's open availability and highlights her fickleness and promiscuity. It contrasts her with wives and associates her instead with prostitutes who are indiscriminately available to everyone (see Chapter 10, Goldhill, this volume). The pairing of *pais* and *gunē* here further suggests the woman referred to is a prostitute, since both are present together at the symposium.[25]

The comparison of *gunē* to *hetairos*, the term for a male sympotic companion, has further significance because it implicates all symposiasts in a comparison with her. The woman here does not live up to the expectations of a *pistos hetairos*, a loyal companion and a worthy drinking partner. Instead, she falls short of expectations. Given that the *hetaira* is *not* a *pistos hetairos*, she must represent the *kakos* and *deilos hetairos*, and thus embody all the negative characteristics outlined in the *Theognidea*. Like the *deiloi* (base and vile companions) who are referenced at length in the first book of the corpus, she is deceitful and lacking in control in addition to *charis* (the reciprocity expected of loyal companions). The couplet not only presents a negative stereotype for female banqueters at the male symposium, but also associates the negative behavior of male symposiasts with the behavior common to the *hetaira*-prostitute.

The main purpose of the couplet, however, is her comparison with a *pais*. It constructs the *pais* and *hetaira*-prostitute as opposites. It begins by stating that boys offer *charis* and suggests that a lover should expect no less. Other verses, as we have seen, support the view that the behavior of the prostitute is contrary to what the lover should expect of a male beloved. Unlike verse 1238, discussed above, the *hetaira*-prostitute is under compulsion to please regardless of her personal feelings because she makes a living and maintains her standard of living by attracting lovers/clients (see [Dem.] 59.26). Yet the verses that criticize boys associate them with traits that we could easily associate with prostitution. In lines 1267–70, a *pais* is blamed for the very same offence as the *hetaira*-prostitute in 1367–8: for loving the one close at hand (*ton pareonta philei*). In this verse the boy is compared directly to a horse who cares not who his rider is as long as he continues to have his fill of barley. The comparison highlights the potential fickleness and inconstancy of a boy beloved. It also makes the bad behavior of a *pais* like the behavior of the prostitute, since both love *ton pareonta*.

In another example (lines 1271–4), the boy possesses *margosune* (immodesty) as opposed to the ideal quality of *aidōs*. While *aidōs* highlights modest behavior and habits, *margosune* emphasizes the excessive conduct of the boy, including flirting, and hints at a hyper-sexuality, which a free and noble person needs to control. In another verse, lines 1351–2, the *pais* is advised *not* to exhibit wild merry making (*komazein*).[26] Such excessive appetites and behavior, in contrast, are commonly associated with women and female prostitutes from as early as Archilochos in the seventh century BCE. In learning to be good beloveds (and by extension *agathoi* [meaning good and noble companions in the context of the verses]), these boy-youths are also learning *not* to be women.

While the verses address the *pais*, they also indirectly teach about the proper conduct of a *philos* toward a beloved. The verses make clear the mentoring aspect of this relationship: the lover is expected to transmit important social values to the boy (Lewis 1985: 214–21). As John Lewis points out, the faithfulness of the admirer and lover is also valued. Self-control is another important trait of the *agathoi* (Levine 1985: 180–5). Such control is also essential to the pederastic relationship and should define conduct with the *pais*.

> νεβρὸν ὑπὲξ ἐλάφοιο λέων ὣς ἀλκὶ πεποιθώς
> ποσσὶ καταμάρψας αἵματος οὐκ ἔπιον·
> τειχέων δ᾽ ὑψηλῶν ἐπιβὰς πόλιν οὐκ ἀλάπαξα·
> ζευξάμενος δ᾽ ἵππους ἅρματος οὐκ ἐπέβην·
> πρήξας δ᾽ οὐκ ἔπρηξα, καὶ οὐκ ἐτέλεσσα τελέσσας·
> δρήσας δ᾽ οὐκ ἔδρησ᾽, ἤνυσα δ᾽ οὐκ ἀνύσας.

> Just as a lion relying on his might and with his speed overtaking a fawn separated from a deer, I do not drink its blood; I do not sack the city, after mounting its lofty walls; nor yoking horses, do I mount the chariot. Although doing, I do not do; though finishing, I do not finish; while I can accomplish, I do not accomplish; even though I can obtain [my desire], I do not.

In Lewis's interpretation, these verses (949–54) comment on the appropriate treatment of the *pais* by the lover and associate the behavior outlined with the *agathoi* – in contrast to how *deiloi* react to attractive boys.[27] The verses compare the lover to one who overcomes prey, an enemy city or wild horses, but does not claim the prize. The unclaimed prize is not a result of a lack of ability, but a choice and decision on the part of the victor. Despite the vulnerable position of the victim, the speaker holds back and does not taste the final victory. The verses emphasize the ability of the *agathos* lover to control his erotic feelings. His relationship with the *pais* is not simply about conquering and sexual gratification.

Prostitutes and boy-youths on pots

The erotic themes of sympotic poetry find parallels in the images painted on wine vessels, a central component of the Athenian symposium.[28] Such wares have been found in Athenian excavations in sympotic contexts (Steiner 2007: 232–3, 237–9) and also appear in the sympotic scenes painted on these very vases.[29] The different shapes fulfill a specific function associated with storing, serving and consuming wine.[30] While these pots were functional, they also engaged the participants with their painted images, entertaining with their narratives and humor.[31] Most importantly for our purposes here, the images may be assumed to reflect (and construct) the sociocultural values of the symposiasts.[32] As a representation of the actual symposium itself,[33] the scenes force the viewer to reflect on the practice and its participants, including him/herself. Just like sympotic poetry, the vessels have the potential to engage the attention of its viewers just as poetry recited engrosses its listeners, and to teach as well as entertain.[34] Although sharing a common iconography, the composition of each image is to some extent unique.

Erōmenoi (the preferred scholarly term for boy beloveds depicted in vase painting) and prostitute-figures are commonly represented on Attic vases.[35] But there are important observable differences between the two depictions.[36] While relations with female prostitutes are common in depictions of the symposium and *kōmos*, scenes of *erōmenoi* and *erastai* (lovers) are more frequent in courting scenes that seem to take place in more generic spaces not easily identified with a sympotic context. Different attitudes toward the treatment of each are also observable. A few images depict clients abusing female prostitutes, but there is no scene showing a lover abusing his male beloved.[37] As Alan Shapiro argues, the status of the male beloved as free most likely explains this discrepancy (1992: 56–8, 1981: 136). While Robert Sutton has observed that vase painters rarely, if at all, depicted the meretricious and pederastic relationship together on the same pot,[38] an interesting class of image appears to contrast prostitutes and *erōmenoi* directly: the image of the female banqueter.[39] These vases are typically discussed for the scenes of women banqueting alone, but when we examine the full decorative programme of these vessels, interesting patterns emerge – in particular, allusions to pederasty might also occur on these same vases.

A red-figure cup (526–475 BCE) depicts two female banqueters on the exterior and a seated youth in its tondo (Figures 9.1, 9.2 and 9.3).[40] Both female figures are fully naked, except for head coverings and earrings. The figure on side A wears a turban and has earrings. She holds a large kylix in outstretched arms and sits on a pillow, suggestive of the symposium. The stem of the kylix is fashioned in the shape of a penis. The position of the kylix makes it unclear whether or not she is going to drink from the kylix or take another sort of pleasure from it, but the association of the female banqueter with wine and sex is clear. The ambiguous nature of her intention suggests an overeagerness for both. The figure on side B wears a headband, earrings and has an *aulos* bag hanging over her mid-calf, suggesting her role as flute-player, an entertainer at symposia. She reclines on a pillow like a symposiast. She holds a wine amphora with both hands and appears to lift it toward her face, likely intending to drink from it. The amphora, however, is for storing and transporting wine. Drinking directly from it demonstrated a lack of decorum, since the Athenians drank their wine mixed with water.[41] Drinking unmixed wine was thought to be uncivilized and non-Greek.[42] Such would be the view of the behavior of this female banqueter, who drinks her wine straight and ignores the symposium as a context for sharing wine. She represents excessive behavior that is not appropriate for the symposium.[43] While a clear example of female excess, the sympotic context of the two scenes along with the *aulos* bag on side B suggests their identity as *hetaira*-prostitutes.[44] The fact that citizen wives and daughters did not attend such gatherings further reinforces the view that symposiasts would link the figures with the sexually available prostitutes frequently present among them.

The interior of the cup, however, adds another dimension. It depicts a boy-youth seated on a stool wearing a wreath and wrapped in a cloak on the lower half of his body in the manner of a symposiast. In his left hand he holds what appears to be fruit, a gift of courtship and so likely the gift of a lover and admirer.[45] The boy-youth has most probably accepted this gift as an *erōmenos*, making the scene in the tondo a reference to the pederastic relationship. Unlike the fully nude *hetaira*-prostitutes on the exterior of the vase, the boy-youth is more restrained. He rests his right arm on a walking stick, while his left hand holding the gift rests on his thigh. His modesty accentuates the insatiability of the prostitute figures on the exterior of the vase. The connection of all three images with the symposium invites further comparison. While both the prostitute-figure and *erōmenos* are regularly eroticized on pots and an object of fantasy, the *hetaira*-prostitutes are openly on display and available, ready for sex, as suggested by the position of the kylix on side A and the presence of the *aulos* bag on side B. In contrast, the availability of the youth is more ambiguous.[46] He holds an erotic gift, suggesting he is being courted and has accepted a lover. He is available to admire, but not openly available for sex. In fact, the images suggest an effort to distinguish, to shore up the virtue of the boy. This contrast in the deportment of the figures suggests that *erōmenoi* and female prostitutes are not to be confused as erotic objects and require different methods of approach by their admirers. The vase also teaches boys and youths about appropriate behavior as love objects. *Aidōs* (modesty), as we have previously seen, is a trait admired in the boy-youth, but is not required or desired of a female prostitute.

The tondo of another red-figure drinking cup (510–490 BCE) displays a woman reclining on a couch, made more comfortable by a pillow (Figure 9.4).[47] The head of the figure is missing, but the rest of the body is intact.[48] Her nudity is openly displayed, despite a himation draped over her left shoulder and right thigh. She leans on her left elbow and looks about to fling the wine from her cup in a game of *kottabos*.[49] A wine jug is visible below the couch. It is not decorative, but appears to be part of the scene and suggests a ready flow of wine for the figure. An inscription above her right arm reads TOI TEN[DE], "this one's for you," a dedication for her wine toss. Once again the sympotic context of the scene, along with the viewing context for the vase, suggests her identity as a *hetaira*-prostitute to any symposiast.

The exterior of the cup depicts four male symposiasts wearing himations reclining on pillows: a pair of youths on side B and a bearded male with a fragmentary figure on side A (Figures 9.5 and 9.6). The youths wear wreaths. One youth holds what might be a musical instrument, but only the top part remains extant, making identification difficult. The second youth holds a myrtle branch in his upraised right arm. An inscription, emanating from the mouth of this second youth, declares, K[ALO]S EI, "you are handsome," making a direct reference to pederasty and the desirability of *erōmenoi* (see Lear and Cantarella 2008: 170–3). The bearded figure wears a headband and holds out a kylix in his right hand, perhaps offering it to the symposiast near him. At the same time he exclaims, EGEI[RE], "arouse or awaken," an inscription appearing above his right arm.

Anne Steiner notes that the repetition of pillows, cups, himations and poses "connect three different types of symposiasts – adult men, youths and a hetaira-figure – in one location" (Steiner 2007: 244). The similarity of poses, the draping of the himation, the upraised arms and utterances confirm the female figure's status as a symposiast, but also connect her in particular

Figure 9.4 Red-figure kylix, interior, *c.*510–490 BCE, by Onesimos. Staatliche Antikensammlungen und
Glyptothek 2636, München. Photography by: Renate Kühling. Photograph © Staatliche Antikensammlungen und Glyptothek München.

with the youth holding the myrtle branch and the bearded figure with the kylix. All three
recline with their right knee bent and upright and their left knee bent, resting on the couch. All
three drape the himation over the right thigh and left shoulder. All three have their right arm
raised holding an object, and inscriptions associate all three with sympotic utterance. In the case
of the two male figures, there is a more frontal view of the legs, showing the shin and foot. In
the case of the youth and prostitute-figure, the genitalia are fully exposed despite the himation.

The similarities predominate over the differences and invite comparison between the three figures. The exposure of genitals connects the youth and the female figure in particular and suggests a
lack of modesty on the part of both. Such an assimilation, however, does not elevate the status of

Figure 9.5 Red-figure kylix, exterior, side B, c.510–490 BCE, by Onesimos. Staatliche Antikensammlungen und Glyptothek 2636, München. Photography by: Renate Kühling. Photograph © Staatliche Antikensammlungen und Glyptothek München.

Figure 9.6 Red-figure kylix, exterior, side A, *c.*510–490 BCE, by Onesimos. Staatliche Antikensammlungen und Glyptothek 2636, München. Photography by: Renate Kühling. Photograph © Staatliche Antikensammlungen und Glyptothek München.

the prostitute, but denigrates the youth and his behavior. He lacks *aidōs*, a trait highly valued in boys and youths as *erōmenoi*, and he instead represents the exact opposite of the *kalos* youth he invokes: the *katapugōn*, whom Theognis describes as *margosunē*.[50] His large penis confirms this interpretation, since genitalia in Greek art are conventionally small (and even infantile to our eyes) as a way to indicate modesty and self-restraint (see Lear and Cantarella 2008: 24–5, 64–5).

The inscriptions add a level of humor. The youth points to the beauty of another, when typically the boy-youth is the one praised as *kalos* by men instead. Likewise, the prostitute-figure plays a drinking game, when she is more commonly the object of such a game. Anne Steiner calls the two "parodies of 'correct' behavior" (2007: 244). As reversals the images are comic.[51] But as parodies, they also imply the behavior of the youth and prostitute is inappropriate. The affinity between the youth and prostitute would act as a warning to boy-youths at the symposium by presenting a model that is not to be emulated. The bearded figure, on the other hand, acts as a positive model for all symposiasts. He is modestly draped with his himation. While the inscription associated with this figure is only brief, it indicates a sympotic performance. Scholars connect EGEI[RE] ("Awaken" or "Be stirred up with passion") with sympotic poetry.[52] He thus offers a recitation, demonstrating his *paideia*, and passes the cup on to the next symposiast to continue the poem. This figure contrasts with the *hetaira*-prostitute in the tondo, whose image confronts the symposiast each time he drains his cup. The bearded figure acts as a reminder not to become too much like the female banqueter. The cup hints that boy-youths (and *erōmenoi*) should emulate the behavior of their betters, as also advised in the *Theognidea*, not female drinking companions who are prostitutes.

A comparison of *erōmenoi* with female prostitutes is also a theme of the decorative programme on a red-figure cup by Oltos (525–475 BCE).[53] Palmettes decorate the interior of the cup. Side B depicts two female banqueters (Figure 9.7). The figures are fully nude, but wear bracelets, necklaces and earrings. One wears a *sakkos* (hairnet) and the other has her hair loose. Both women wear wreaths and recline on cushions, like male symposiasts. The context of the symposium once again calls to mind working women available for pleasure.[54] Their legs are awkwardly rendered – but this appears to be purposeful rather than a technical shortcoming.[55] The figure on the left plays the *aulos*, further hinting at her role as a sexual companion, and perhaps kicks her legs to the music. Her companion cradles a skyphos and stretches out her arm, holding a kylix in her hand. She appears to be passing the cup to the *aulētris* (*aulos* player) and the inscription confirms this: PINE KAI SU, "You drink too." While the inscription might suggest commensality typical of the symposium, the figure offering wine does so at the expense of interrupting the *aulos* playing. The wreathed boy-youth on side A contrasts dramatically with these female figures. He carries a rolled up cattle rope in his right hand and chases a bull (Figure 9.8). An inscription, DIO SIPIS KALOS, reconstructed as *dios pais kalos*,[56] "the child of Zeus is beautiful," once again associates the image with pederasty.

Nudity, wreaths and outstretched limbs connect the images on both sides of the vase and invite comparison between them. While the outstretched limbs of the female figures, particularly their lower limbs, are disorderly and awkward, the youth's limbs indicate he is running. His nakedness shows off his buttocks and infantile genitalia, and the well-defined musculature of his chest, thighs and upper arms highlights his athleticism. These physical features associate the youth with the ideal body of the beloved. Undersized genitalia, as mentioned above, indicate self-restraint and modesty, qualities important in free citizens and typical in the depiction of *erōmenoi*.[57] Like the two other cups discussed previously, the decorative programme of this cup provides both a positive and negative paradigm for a boy-youth at a symposium: an ideal beloved versus the excess associated with the female prostitute. The vase is thus another medium for instilling values in youths and boys and motivating them toward a particular type of behavior.[58]

Figure 9.7 Red-figure kylix, c.525–475 BCE, by Oltos. Museo Arqueológico Nacional L151/11267, Madrid, Spain. Photo: Albers Foundation/Art Resource NY.

Figure 9.8 Red-figure kylix, c.525–475 BCE, by Oltos. Museo Arqueológico Nacional L151/11267, Madrid, Spain. Drawing by Tina Ross.

Conclusion

Pederasty is a common theme in the *Theognidea* and clearly alluded to in these images depicted on Attic vases. While the male figures in the examples discussed are not shown in an actual scene of courtship, their physical bodies and accompanying inscriptions evoke the pederastic relationship. The similarities between figures of female banqueters, boy-youths and adult males on the pots discussed invite comparisons between *hetaira*-prostitutes, *erōmenoi* and *erastai*. These images are erotic and also humorous for the male viewers on account of their role reversals and use of negative stereotypes, particularly in the case of the female, but they also perform another function: they provide both negative and positive paradigms for the boy-youth and thus teach behavior appropriate for an *erōmenos*.[59] In addition, they remind *erastai* of appropriate conduct and thus act as a guide for them at symposia as well. In both cases, the female banqueter represents the opposite of appropriate behavior and teaches and guides the viewer by negative example. For the boy-youth in particular, she represents a lack of *charis* and *aidōs*, exhibiting instead excessive behavior to be avoided and thus feminizing such behavior. In addition, for the adult male viewer, the *erastēs*, she is a reminder of the differences between *erōmenoi* and prostitutes as objects of desire.[60] These same themes feature in the verses in the *Theognidea*. Addressed to boys, they outline appropriate behavior and advisable company to spend time with and learn from. They critique the bad behavior of *deiloi* and prostitutes and praise the behavior of the *agathoi*. The actual presence of the *hetaira*-prostitute (commonly foreign and slave or freed) at symposia likely bolstered these differences and reinforced these lessons.

The distinctions observed here between female prostitutes and boy-youths in particular become further developed as a stereotype in Athens in the classical period. While *hetairai* are described in Greek oratory as "sexually available to anyone who can pay," *erōmenoi* must be discreet about their availability and not appear "too easy" to win over and seduce. The fourth-century BCE trial of Timarchus (see p. 157) makes clear the fine line that boys and youths had to walk as objects of desire. Aeschines accuses Timarchus of having prostituted himself as a youth. The defense maintains that any such relationships were legitimate and respectable relations between an *erōmenos* and an *erastēs*. Which account is the correct one? Although Aeschines accuses Timarchus of abusing his parents, squandering his patrimony and stealing from the treasury, he likely focused on the charge of prostitution because it was easy to construe pederastic courtship as prostitution – hence the anxiety surrounding boy courtship.

Emphasis is on the *aidōs* and *sōphrosynē* of the beloved and the appropriate behavior of the lover in Xenophon's *Symposium*. The boy Autylochus is described as possessing both *aidōs* and *sōphrosynē* (1.9). Socrates refers to Callias' love for the boy as grounded in the soul (*psychē*), friendship (*philia*) and virtuous conduct (*kala erga*), rather than the body and carnal desire. Socrates concludes this from the excellence (*kalokagathia*) of the youth and because Callias always includes the father in his meetings with Autylochus. His discussion leads Hermogenes to comment that Socrates is in fact teaching (*paideuein*) Callias how to behave toward Autylochus (8.12). But, I would add, he is also teaching about the appropriate behavior of a beloved toward his lover through the example of Autylochus.

This last example illustrates well that while the symposium is an erotically charged space, it is also a forum for a theory of erotics, a kind of sex-education class for ancient Athenians. The archaic vases and verses discussed here reflect the start of this discourse, which instructs boys, youths and adults in the parameters of their social roles and acceptable ways to manifest their desires. One focus for this discussion is the prostitute body, constructed as the opposite of the *erōmenos*. Despite the variety in kinds of prostitutes available in ancient Greece, in these ideological comparisons with the *erōmenos*, the prostitute body is depicted undifferentiated and female. The construction serves a purpose: it allays an anxiety about the similarity between the *pais/erōmenos* and the *hetaira*-prostitute that might remain despite any protocols designed to distinguish them. At the same time, the comparison between the *pais/erōmenos* and the *hetaira*-prostitute reveals a concern with how to distinguish between prostitutes and citizen boys as erotic objects in archaic society, especially in the context of the symposium.

Notes

1 Versions of this chapter were presented to audiences at the Annual Meeting of the Classical Association of Canada, the University of Cincinnati and the University of Florida. I would like to thank these audiences for their comments. I would also like to thank the editors for their many helpful suggestions.

2 The term *pais* frequently has an erotic connotation in the context of the symposium implying a beloved. See Book II of the *Theognidea*, for example. By the classical period the *pais* is more commonly known as the *erōmenos*. The courting lover is known as the *philos* and then later as the *erastēs*. Conventionally, modern scholars (particularly in the context of vase painting) prefer these later terms when indicating the pederastic relationship. Even though discussing archaic Greece, I employ these later terms in addition to *pais* and *philos*.

3 The *hetaira* (female companion) first made her appearance in sympotic poetry and on painted pots in the sixth century BCE, when, according to Leslie Kurke, elite symposiasts were concerned to distinguish their female sexual companions from *pornai* (women for sale) (1997: 112–13). See also Reinsberg 1989: 161. Note that the actual term, *hetaira*, is absent from archaic elegy and lyric, but used by Kurke to encapsulate the different attitudes present in such poetry (1997: 145). Henceforth, I use *hetaira*-figure (and *hetaira*-prostitute) to highlight the complexity of prostitution and the fact that *hetaira* and *pornē* are sometimes interchangeable.

4 I use the term boy-youth because the age limit of the male beloved is unclear. Rather than age defining the beloved, it is more accurately the lack of facial hair that distinguishes him from the one courting. As soon as facial hair begins to appear, the boy-youth ceased his role as beloved and might even take on the role of lover to another boy. See Dover 1978; Ferrari 2002: 139–40. In vase painting, the age distinction is clear in black-figure, but by the fifth century and in red-figure the courting lover is frequently shown as another youth. See Lear and Cantarella 2008: 3–6, 67. See Shapiro 1992: figs. 3.1–2 for courting scenes depicting mature men with beardless youths and young men with just the beginnings of beards courting boys and beardless youths.

5 See Cantarella 1992: 12–16 on references in lyric poetry. Also see Fisher 2001: 30–3; Skinner 2005: 42–4, 46. On representation of pederasty in vase painting see Sutton 1992: 12–14. Sutton comments that scenes of pederasty become popular in the mid-sixth century and are very different from heterosexual scenes set in the symposium or during the *komos*. Shapiro comments that the same artist might depict a scene of pederasty and then a scene of a prostitute and her client (1992: 55).

6 For an excellent and accessible discussion of *symposia*, see Lissarrague 1990.

7 The term *symposium* appears in 298 and 498 of the *Theognidea*. The terms *eilapinē* (238) and *dais* (563) also appear (238), and references to wine, wine drinking and drinking companions are frequent (e.g. 33, 497–8, 500, 503–4, 509–10). These references also include eating together and so the archaic drinking party may not always have been separate from the *deipnon* as in classical times; see Levine 1985: 176.

8 See Xen. *Symp.* Note also that at the start of Plato's *Symposium* the guests dismiss the aulos player.

9 While Kurke argues, using archaic poetry, that symposiasts might assimilate themselves with the *hetairai* (1997), I maintain that distinctions between male and female, free and slave, and Athenian and foreign were paramount (even more so than elite and non-elite) for the symposiasts of the late archaic and early classical periods. The *hetaira*-prostitute was a visible other at the symposium; see further Glazebrook 2012.

10 See Lynch 2007: 246–8; Pütz 2007: xii, 119; Topper 2009: 4–5, 22–3; Corner 2010: 352–80.

11 The offset door enabled the arrangement of *klinai* (couches) lining the walls. On the material remains of the *andrōn* see Bergquist 1990 and Nevett 1995, 2010: 45–62. For depictions of the *andrōn* on Greek vases see Lissarrague (1990: 20–2) and Steiner (2007: 239–40). Note Lynch who argues that neither an *andrōn* nor *klinai* were a necessity for the symposium and that in some cases it might even have taken place in the open courtyard of the Greek house or out of doors in a vineyard (Lynch 2007: 243–6).

12 Ferrari agues that soft down beneath the ears and on cheeks indicates a youth at his peak of desirability (2002: 134–7, 140–1). Lear and Cantarella disagree and counter that in red-figure it distinguishes the *erastēs* from the *erōmenos* (2008: 239, n. 7).

13 See Levine 1985: 178–80; Bremmer 1990: 136, 137; Robb 1994: 35; Percy 1996: 17; Skinner 2005: 47.

14 On the symposium in Aristophanes, see Pütz 2007.

15 Most iambs and lyric were composed for or adapted for the symposium. See Percy 1996: 117 and Rossi 1983: 44. On the *Theognidea* as composed for the symposium, see Gerber 1997: 120, also n. 7. See also Vetta 1980: xi; Collins 2004: 114–23.

16 See further Lewis 1985 on the *paideia* of Book II in particular. Also Donlan 1985: 237; Levine 1985: 177–80, 194.

17 I follow Gerber 1999: 209, n. 4, in connecting the negative (*ou*) with the verb.

18 See MacLachlan 1993: 5–8. Also Hewitt 1927, esp. 149–51; Mitchell 1997: 18–21. On reciprocity more generally see Hands 1968: 28–48.

19 See MacLachlan 1993: 56–72, esp. 67–71 on the *Theognidea*.

20 On the connection between erotic *charis* and constancy see Vetta 1980: 67. For complaints on inconstancy and disloyalty see 1243–4, 1249–62, 1267–70.

21 On the ambiguity of the first line of this verse see Vetta 1980: 44–5 and Lewis 1985: 213. I follow Lewis here. See also 1091–4 where the *erastēs* expresses frustration at the feelings of the *erōmenos*, but acknowledges that an *erōmenos* cannot love against his will.

22 See Padilla's comments on *anankē* versus *charis* in Euripides' *Alcestis* (2000: 200).

23 MacLachlan 1993: 69. See the verses 237–54 and 1263–6 above under subheading *Prostitutes and boys at the* Theognidea. *Aidōs* is also an important quality of girls and women of free citizen status. Prostitutes, by the nature of their profession, lack this quality. A comprehensive study of *aidōs* is Cairns 1996; see further on *aidōs* throughout the main text.

24 On Book II as sympotic see Gerber 1997: 120, also n. 7; and Vetta 1980: XXVII–XXXVII.

25 See Kurke who makes this argument for such a pairing in an Attic *skolia* (1997: 117–18).

26 See Lewis 1985: 219. Levine points out that verse 242 uses *eukomos* to describe appropriate behavior at the symposium and argues the term is for the benefit of youths in particular (Lewis 1985: 186).

27 Lewis 1985: 218–19. See verses 1363–4 and 1029–36. On the expected conduct of the lover toward the beloved see further Dover 1978; Foucault 1985.

28 See Lissarrague 1990; Neer 2002; Steiner 2007: 246–7.

29 Lissarrague 1990: 22. Steiner notes, however, that the hydria and amphora rarely appear (2007: 237–9).

30 For a detailed discussion of vase shapes and their function, see Kanowski 1984.

31 Lissarrague 1990: 87–106; Neer 2002: 11–23; Steiner 2007: 194–211. On humor in particular see Mitchell 2009.

32 Lissarrague 1990: 11–14; Steiner 2007: 245–6.

33 Steiner argues that artists were "well aware of the space in which the vessels were used" (2007: 240).

34 On the context of viewing see Stansbury-O'Donnell 2006: 70–9.

35 For an overview of the difficulty of identifying prostitutes on pots see Lewis 2002: 101–12. On the slippage between images of "being courted" and "being purchased" and the contemporary practice of classifying male figures as lovers and female figures as prostitutes see Rabinowitz 2011.

36 On the differences, see Sutton 1992: 12–14. Also see Lear and Cantarella 2008: 119–20, 131–5.

37 One exception might be a pelike by Euphronios (Villa Giulia 12109) depicting a seated youth raising a sandal to a boy with a semi-erection. Shapiro 2000: 29 interprets the scene as shared sado-masochism. Other scholars, however, interpret the boy as a slave and do not consider it a pederastic scene. See Lear and Cantarella 2008: 121–3.

38 Sutton 1992: 14. But note the exceptions discussed in Lear and Cantarella 2008: 111, 131–5.

39 For discussion of female banqueters see Peschel 1987: 70–4, 110–12; Reinsberg 1989: 112–14; Kurke 1997: 136; Venit 1998: 127; Lewis 2002: 113–15; Neer 2002: 131–2; Steiner 2007: 244; Lyons 2008: 78; Topper 2009: 21; Glazebrook 2012. Scholars have identified a total of ten vases, dating between 520 and 450/425 BCE, with female banqueters banqueting alone. See Lewis (2002: 233, nn. 77–8 with images 3.18–19). The scenes model sympotic scenes on Attic vases with male figures. For example, see the red-figure neck amphora by Euphronios (*c*.520–505 BCE), Paris, Louvre G 30 (Steiner 2007: figs. 8.16–17); the red-figure kylix by the Colmar Painter (*c*.500 BCE), New York, Metropolitan Museum 16.174.41 (Lissarrague 1990: fig. 1).

40 Red-figure kylix, 525–475 BCE. New York, Metropolitan Museum of Art 56.171.61. *ARV²* 50.192, 1622. Para 325. Ingeborg Peschel grouped this scene with other scenes of female banqueters, referring to them as "reine Hetärensymposia" (*hetaira*-only drinking parties) (Peschel 1987: 70–4, 110–12).

41 On the practice of wine drinking see Lissarrague 1990: 6–10.

42 Lissarrague 1990: 7. See Hdt. 6.84 and Ath. 10.427a–b.

43 On the *hetaira*-figure in Attic vase painting as representative of the excessive female nature see Venit 1998. On the parallels of this scene with scenes of satyrs see Glazebrook 2012: 513–14.

44 As I have argued elsewhere, images of female banqueters represent female excess more generally, but also make specific reference to the prostitute body when viewed in the context of the symposium (Glazebrook 2012). On the aulos player as prostitute see Starr (1978: 401–10); Davidson (1998: 80–2). Also see Ath. 13.607 d and Theophr. *Char.* 20.10.

45 See Lear and Cantarella on gifts as synecdoche for pederastic courtship (2008: 34–5), with a list of common gifts on p. 39.

46 On the slippage between *erōmenos* and male prostitute in Attic vase painting see Rabinowitz 2011.

47 Red-figure kylix. 510–490 BCE. Onesimos. Munich, Staatliche Antikensammlungen und Glyptothek 2636. *ARV²* 317.16. 214. AttScr 502. CVA Munich, Antikensammlungen 16, 14–16, Beilage 2.1, Pls. (4667, 4668, 4728) 2.1–4, 3.1–5, 63.1.

48 An image with the head still intact appears in Peschel 1987: Pl. 47. Her hair is short with a headband.

49 See Lissarrague 1990: 80–6; Sparkes 1960. For further details of this game see Ath. 11.487d–e and 15.665c–668f.

50 See discussion under subhead Prostitutes and boys at the *Theognidea*. On *katapugon* as the opposite of *kalos* see Lear and Cantarella 2008: 170–1.

51 The inscriptions add to the competition of the symposium by ridiculing any adult male reader of the inscription. On inscriptions being read aloud see Slater 1999: 161; Steiner 2007: 240.

52 See Immerwahr 1990: 84 for its identification as "perhaps the beginning of a poem." See Steiner for its association with Pindar O. 9.47 (2007: 244).

53 Red-figure kylix. 525–475 BCE. Oltos. Madrid, Museo Arqueologico Nacional L151/11267. *ARV²* 38.46. *ARV²* 58.53, 1622, 1574. Add 80. CVA Madrid 2, III-IC.3, Pls. (58, 59, 61, 62) 1.3A–B, 2.2, 4.1, 5.1. Note that there is no image in the tondo of the cup.

54 See note 44 above.

55 Rabinowitz comments that the intertwined legs suggest intimacy and an erotic connection between the women (2002: 135).

56 CVA Madrid 2, III-IC.3c. It possibly identifies the figure as Theseus on his labor to free Attica from the bull of Marathon or Herakles after the Cretan bull. On the myths of Herakles and Theseus and their representation in art see Carpenter 1991; see also Steiner 2007: 157.

57 The genitalia of the youth contrast with the enlarged genitalia frequently associated with satyrs and non-Greeks and as depicted in group-sex scenes; see Lear and Cantarella 2008: 24–5, 64–5.

58 These images of prostitutes also enforce negative stereotypes about women more generally; see further Glazebrook 2012.

59 Lear argues that scenes of anal intercourse and group sex contrast with pederastic scenes and highlight the pederastic relationship as the ideal (Lear and Cantarella 2008: 106–7, 119–20, 126–7, 192).

60 Note that Apollodoros refers to Neaira's clients as *erastai* ([Dem.] 59.26, 29, 30, 31, 32).

Bibliography

Bergquist, B. (1990) "Sympotic space: A functional aspect of Greek dining rooms", in O. Murray (ed.) *Sympotica: A Symposium on the Symposion*. Oxford: Clarendon Press, pp. 37–65.

Bremmer, J. (1990) "Adolescents, symposion, and pederasty", in O. Murray (ed.) *Sympotica: A Symposium on the Symposion*. Oxford: Clarendon Press, pp. 135–48.

Cairns, D. (1996) *Aidos: The Psychology and Ethics of Honour and Shame in Ancient Greek Literature*. Oxford: Clarendon Press.

Cantarella, E. (1992) *Bisexuality in the Ancient World*, trans. C.Ó. Cuilleanáin. New Haven, CT: Yale University Press.

Carpenter, T.H. (1991) *Art and Myth in Ancient Greece: A Handbook*. London: Thames and Hudson.

Cobb-Stevens, V., Figueira, T.J. and Nagy, G. (1985) "Introduction", in T.J. Figueira and G. Nagy (eds) *Theognis of Megara: Poetry and the Polis*. Baltimore, MD: Johns Hopkins University Press, pp. 1–8.

Collins, D. (2004) *Master of the Game: Competition and Performance in Greek Poetry*. Washington, DC: Center for Hellenic Studies.

Corner, S. (2010) "Transcendent drinking: The symposium at sea reconsidered", *Classical Quarterly* 60(2): 352–80.

Davidson, J. (1998) *Courtesans and Fishcakes: The Consuming Passions of Classical Athens.* London: Harper-Collins.

Donlan, W. (1985) "Pistos Philos Hetairos", in T.J. Figueira and G. Nagy (eds) *Theognis of Megara: Poetry and the Polis.* Baltimore, MD: Johns Hopkins University Press, pp. 223–43.

Dover, K.J. (1978) *Greek Homosexuality.* Cambridge, MA: Harvard University Press.

Ferrari, G. (2002) *Figures of Speech: Men and Maidens in Ancient Greece.* Chicago, IL: University of Chicago Press.

Fisher, N.R.E. (2001) *Aeschines: Against Timarchos.* Oxford: Oxford University Press.

Ford, A.L. (1985) "The politics of authorship in archaic Greece", in T.J. Figueira and G. Nagy (eds) *Theognis of Megara: Poetry and the Polis.* Baltimore, MD: Johns Hopkins University Press, pp. 82–95.

Foucault, M. (1985) *The Use of Pleasure, The History of Sexuality*, vol. 2, trans. R. Hurley. New York: Random House.

Gerber, D.E. (trans. and ed.) (1997) "Elegy", in D.E. Gerber (ed.) *A Companion to the Greek Lyric Poets.* Leiden: E.J. Brill, pp. 89–132.

——(1999) *Greek Elegiac Poetry.* Cambridge, MA: Harvard University Press.

Glazebrook, A. (2012) "Prostitutes, plonk and play: Female banqueters on a red-figure psykter from the Hermitage", *Classical World* 105(4): 497–524.

Hands, A.R. (1968) *Charities and Social Aid in Greece and Rome.* London: Camelot Press.

Hewitt, J.W. (1927) "The terminology of 'gratitude' in Greek", *Classical Philology* 22(2): 142–61.

Immerwahr, H.R. (1990) *Attic Script: A Survey.* Oxford: Clarendon Press.

Kanowski, M.G. (1984) *Containers of Classical Greece: A Handbook of Shapes.* St. Lucia: University of Queensland Press.

Kurke, L. (1997) "Inventing the *hetaira*: Sex, politics, and discursive conflict in archaic Greece", *Classical Antiquity* 16(1): 106–50.

Lear, A. and Cantarella, E. (2008) *Images of Ancient Greek Pederasty: Boys Were Their Gods.* New York: Routledge.

Levine, D.B. (1985) "Symposium and the polis", in T.J. Figueira and G. Nagy (eds) *Theognis of Megara: Poetry and the Polis.* Baltimore, MD: Johns Hopkins University Press, pp. 176–96.

Lewis, J.M. (1985) "Eros and the polis in Theognis Book II", in T.J. Figueira and G. Nagy (eds) *Theognis of Megara: Poetry and the Polis.* Baltimore, MD: Johns Hopkins University Press, pp. 197–222.

Lewis, S. (2002) *The Athenian Woman: An Iconographic Handbook.* London: Routledge.

Lissarrague, F. (1990) *The Aesthetics of the Greek Banquet: Images of Wine and Ritual*, trans. A. Szegedy-Maszak. Princeton, NJ: Princeton University Press.

Lynch, K. (2007) "More thoughts on the space of the symposium", in R. Westgate, N. Fisher and J. Whitley (eds) *Building Communities: House, Settlement, and Society in the Aegean and Beyond.* London: British School at Athens, pp. 243–9.

Lyons, C.L. (2008) "Objects of affection: Genre and gender on some Athenian vases", in K. Lapatin (ed.) *Papers on Special Techniques in Athenian Vases: Proceedings of a Symposium Held in Connection with the Exhibition The Colors of Clay: Special Techniques in Athenian Vases, at the Getty Villa, June 15–17, 2006.* Los Angeles, CA: Getty Publications, pp. 73–84.

MacLachlan, B. (1993) *The Age of Grace: Charis in Early Greek Poetry.* Princeton, NJ: Princeton University Press.

Mitchell, A. (2009) *Greek Vase Painting and the Origins of Humour.* Cambridge: Cambridge University Press.

Mitchell, L.G. (1997) *Greeks Bearing Gifts: The Public Use of Private Relationships in the Greek World, 435–323 BC.* Cambridge: Cambridge University Press.

Neer, R.T. (2002) *Style and Politics in Athenian Vase Painting: The Craft of Democracy, ca. 530–460 B.C.E.* Cambridge: Cambridge University Press.

Nevett, L.C. (1995) "Gender relations in the Classical Greek household: The archaeological evidence", *Annual of the British School at Athens* 91: 89–108.

——(2010) *Domestic Space in Classical Antiquity.* Cambridge: Cambridge University Press.

Padilla, M. (2000) "Gifts of humiliation: *Charis* and tragic experience in *Alcestis*", *American Journal of Philology* 121(2): 179–211.

Percy, W.A. (1996) *Pederasty and Pedagogy in Archaic Greece.* Campagne/Urbana, IL: University of Illinois Press.

Peschel, I. (1987) *Die Hetäre bei Symposion und Komos in der attisch-rotfigurigen Vasenmalerei des 6.-4. Jahrhunderts v. Christus.* Frankfurt am Main: P. Lang.

Pütz, B. (2007) *The Symposium and Komos in Aristophanes.* Oxford: Aris and Philips.

Rabinowitz, N.S. (2002) "Excavating women's homoeroticism in ancient Greece: The evidence from Attic vase painting", in N.S. Rabinowitz and L. Auanger (eds) *Among Women: From the Homosocial to the Homoerotic in the Ancient World*. Austin, TX: University of Texas Press, pp. 106–66.

——(2011) "Sex for sale? Interpreting erotica in the Havana Collection", in A. Glazebrook and M.M. Henry (eds) *Greek Prostitutes in the Ancient Mediterranean 800 BCE–200 CE*. Madison, WI: University of Wisconsin Press, pp. 122–46.

Reinsberg, C. (1989) *Ehe, Hetärentum und Knabenliebe im antiken Griechenland*, Beck's Archäologische Bibliothek. München: C.H. Beck.

Robb, K. (1994) *Literacy and Paideia in Ancient Greece*. Oxford: Oxford University Press.

Rossi, L.E. (1983) "Il simposio Greco arcaico e classico come spettacolo a se stesso", *Spettacoli conviviali dall' antichità classica alle corti italiane del 400*. Atti del VII convegno di studio, 27–30 Maggio 1982. Viterbo: Agnesotti, pp. 41–50.

Shapiro, H.A. (1981) "Courtship scenes in Attic vase-painting", *American Journal of Archaeology* 85: 133–44.

——(1992) "Eros in love: Pederasty and pornography in Greece", in A. Richlin (ed.) *Pornography and Representation in Greece and Rome*. Oxford: Oxford University Press, pp. 53–72.

——(2000) "Leagros and Euphronios: Painting pederasty in Athens", in T.K. Hubbard (ed.) *Greek Love Reconsidered*. New York: W. Hamilton Press, pp. 12–32.

Skinner, M.B. (2005) *Sexuality in Greek and Roman Culture*. Oxford: Blackwell.

Slater, N. (1999) "The vase as ventriloquist: *Kalos*-inscriptions and the culture of fame", in E.A. Mackay (ed.) *Signs of Orality: The Oral Tradition and its Influences in the Greek and Roman World*. Leiden: Brill, pp. 143–61.

Sparkes, B. (1960) "Kottabos: An Athenian after dinner game", *Archaeology* 13: 202–7.

Stansbury-O'Donnell, M.D. (2006) *Vase Painting, Gender, and Social Identity in Archaic Athens*. Cambridge: Cambridge University Press.

Starr, C. (1978) "An evening with the flute-girls", *La Parola del Passato* 33: 401–10.

Steiner, A. (2007) *Reading Greek Vases*. Cambridge: Cambridge University Press.

Sutton, R.F. (1992) "Pornography and persuasion on Attic pottery", in A. Richlin (ed.) *Pornography and Representation in Greece and Rome*. Oxford: Oxford University Press, pp. 3–35.

Topper, K. (2009) "Primitive life and the construction of the sympotic past in Athenian vase painting", *American Journal of Archaeology* 113: 3–26.

Venit, M.S. (1998) "Women in their cups", *Classical World* 92: 117–30.

Vetta, M. (1980) *Teognide libro secondo: Introduzione, testo critico, traduzione e commento*. Rome: Edizioni dell'Ateneo.

10

IS THERE A HISTORY OF PROSTITUTION?

Simon Goldhill

Between the politics of recognition and the politics of compulsion, there is no bright line.

Appiah 1994: 163

There is a strong case to be made that there is no history of prostitution. That is, there is an unbroken and unchanging story throughout recorded experience in the West of the sexual exploitation and violent mistreatment of especially the female body by men with the social, financial or political power to use and abuse women. The female body is instrumentalized and objectified – a relationship encapsulated in the purchase of sexual use – within the structures of patriarchal social norms. Of course, numbers can be gathered, some exceptional stories garnered, and visual representations change in different communities, but such superficial differences do not alter the deep and continuing structure of violent abuse. It remains the same old story.[1]

This is a strong argument, which stands as a shadow throughout what follows – and explains the question of my title. For both Greek and Roman society, from the fifth century BCE to the fourth century CE – the period I will be looking at in this chapter – the vast majority of sex workers were females (we will also look at some male cases); they were mainly slaves, compelled to have sex within a degrading and violent power structure, and had lives that were nasty, brutish and short. These lives also largely stand outside the historical record, at least in the sense that they do not produce narratives. These women appear occasionally in the stories of others as objects; they turn up in the graffiti or fantasies of others; they may be represented by others; they may be pursued by archaeologists and cultural historians through their loom-weights or cubicles – but the celebrated stories of the *hetairai*, *pornai*, *meretrices* and *scorta* that fill ancient comedies, satire, historiography and erotic fantasy are best seen not simply as exceptions to the grim normality of forced bodily exploitation, but as discursive alibis that keep such normality in place and veiled – much as the rags to riches stories of the American dream play an active role in keeping the normality of economic exploitation and inequality in place.

This is a strong and necessary political argument, but it also needs development for two reasons: first, because it does not allow us to interrogate our contemporary complicity with the language of exploitation; and second, because it can obscure structural social differences that go to the heart of how power and gendered relations are organized differently within ancient and modern cultures.[2] In this chapter, I will test this argument first by looking at some of the ways in which the current discussion of prostitution – which has become a staple of political, economic and cultural

179

history, a commodity in itself – requires a set of self-implicating complicities. The first section will start to outline from a single passage of Victorian writing what could be called a tool-box of categories for exploring ancient prostitution, with the aim of developing a wider perspective than is sometimes formulated in contemporary critical discussion. I start with this Victorian material partly because it allows me to articulate concisely the broad categories of analysis with which I will be working, and partly, and more importantly, because modern writing on sexuality has so often defined itself through a genealogical contrast with Victorian culture – both in the popular imagination which still sets Victorian repression or corruption against modern liberation or openness, and in the headier theoretical world of the history of sexuality, where Foucault's trajectory from the Victorian era in volume 1 to the ancient world in volumes 2 and 3 of his history have set the agenda for many subsequent accounts.

This exemplary Victorian material, consequently, is a particularly good place from which to view what I called above the self-implicating complicities of our contemporary discourse on prostitution; this past is an integral part of how modern views are constructed, to the degree that it is difficult to discuss modern attitudes *without* this particular and continuing inheritance, just as modern legal discourse in this area is hard to disentangle from its Victorian precedents. It is a crucial defining other against and with which the narrative of the modern sexual self is formulated. The second section, The prostitute and the citizen, and third section, The palace and the prostitute, of the chapter – based on this tool-box – will contrast the cases of the fourth-century Athenian *polis* with the Hellenistic court of Alexandria, a contrast which will be suggestive, I hope, for the possibilities of writing a history of prostitution. In particular, they will argue that the different political systems of democracy and monarchic, courtly hierarchy offer differently nuanced patterns of agency, exploitation and positionality, especially for the category of *hetaira* across time. This will provide one model for seeing how the history of prostitution may not be simply the same old story.

The pornography of the street

I shall begin, then, in the Victorian era and with the broad categories through which we can understand the category of prostitution, and with the self-implicating strategies the language of prostitution involves. I have chosen a brief and nasty passage from an extraordinarily unpleasant Victorian pornographic book, *My Secret Life* by "Walter", which has achieved a certain notoriety in studies of the history of sexuality, but which, with detailed analysis, will help reveal the deep confusions that persist in the discourse around the idea of prostitution, for all the advances of modern scholarship.[3] *My Secret Life* was privately and anonymously published in the late 1880s, possibly written by the bibliophile of erotica Henry Spencer Ashbee.[4] In this passage, the narrator, walking in the country, has met and, with the usual pornographic fantasy, instantly seduced a girl. He wants, as ever, more:

> Two minutes after she was back over the gate, and after having closed the shed door I followed her. – "Don't let us go to **** together," said she. – "Dad's there." – "All right, here are two sovereigns." She looked at them wistfully, then angrily, – "I know what yer thinks me but I ain't." – "I know that but take it." – "Thank you." – taking it she spat on it. "How old are you?" – "Just turned seventeen," she'd said it before. – "How long has Jack fucked you?" – She coloured up. – "Just a year ago on my birthday." "He won't marry you." – "Yes he will at Christmas, and I hope you ain't filled me up." After our first coupling she let me say anything baudy, and I revelled in it but she wasn't a bit baudy herself. – I would feel her cunt again. – "Don't my thighs are wet". – Then she started off alone.

This is a fascinating passage for thinking about the exchange of money for sex, and the enactment of a dominating power relation. After having sex in the shed, they are back on the street: from the space of private concealment to the open thoroughfare. "Two minutes after" defines the act within a specific temporality of gratification – swift, time-bound, daytime, non-lasting, and, above all, non-romantic, in inherent and normative contrast here to the ideal love of a marital relation, a whole night, a life together, non-time-bound. Sexuality always has an ideologically laden rhetoric of temporality: "Had we but world enough and time … ", "Who, this time, Sappho … ?", "love, all alike, no season knows nor clime, Nor hours, days, months which are the rags of time". With the discourse of prostitution, this is inevitably tied in with notions of accessibility and repetition and thus the instrumentalizing of time. "Have you got the time?" is a standard euphemism of modern British soliciting. Time, for prostitution of all professions, is money.

That the conversation takes place "over the gate" and in the street is also marked. The leap over the fence embodies a physical looseness and energy that is contrary to the standard expectations of proper Victorian upper-class femininity, a small sign of the far wilder sexual transgression already enacted in the shed (matched by her directness, "my thighs are wet"). Whether a prostitute or even a sexually desiring woman had a different physical nature from a "proper woman" was a commonplace debate of Victorian medicine and its social and class-bound expectations: there is no understanding of prostitution outside a construction of the body in society.[5] So, ancient and modern connections of prostitution with "unusual requests", "sexual positions", are beholden to a socially constructed norm of bodily use (and thus the ancient comic fascination with *keletizein*, "straddling", "riding", as a sexual position associated with prostitution should be seen in relation to the familiar social anxiety about "women on top").[6] Paradigmatically, the vast array of Aristophanic metaphors for sex with a prostitute multiplies the materiality and instrumentalization of the prostitute's body: almost any activity, within the comic and pornographic world, can become an expression of sex; any activity can make a (prostitute's) body a sexualized object, an increasingly depersonalized thing.

The return to the street itself encapsulates one of the distinctive difficulties in the definition of prostitution, especially for the law. The public nature of soliciting – the street – is integral to modern and ancient definitions of prostitution (street walking/curb crawling), and much legal wrangling depends on the *place* of any sexual transaction, to the extent that the same request – money for sex – may be illegal on the street but legal within a house, provided the house is not further defined as a brothel. The growth of the industrial city – and the culture of regulation that followed it – alters the perception and practice of prostitution, but "openness" is a crucial category in its shifting understanding.[7] This was already true in antiquity. So, Ulpian, with regard to the Lex Papia and Lex Julia, declares (*Dig* 23.2.43):

> Because she has intercourse with one or two, having taken money, it is not under-stood that she has openly made a living by her body. And, as Octavenus says, most correctly, that even a woman who makes herself openly available [*palam se prostituerit*] without making a living [*sine quaestu*] ought to be counted in this category.

That is, a woman who has sex with a couple of people for money is not to be regarded as a prostitute if the transaction is private, but a woman who is *openly available* to many, even if no money or gifts are exchanged, should be regarded legally as a prostitute. For this jurist, open availability rather than monetary exchange defines prostitution. The threat of prostitution in Victorian society (and often elsewhere) is that it might be seen, and seen to take place, to have a place, to be open. How prostitution is conceived in ancient and modern societies depends on the constructed boundaries of the public and private spheres, and on the ideological, topographic work in making such boundaries, and in keeping sex and women within them. Hence the overheated legal and social wrangling about the place (in all senses) of the brothel, which stretches from Aeschines to Cato to modern Western democracies: how the brothel fits into the civic space of a community remains a problem for the discourse of sexuality, especially with regard to the idea of personal value, autonomy and desire, even when legalized and fully institutionalized.[8]

The girl here is unnamed, as so many prostitutes are in such narratives, a depersonalizing classification (the professional name, "Goldie", "Sweetie", commonly used by ancient sex workers, has the same depersonalizing function). But she refuses to walk with Walter to the village because her father is there. A woman without a *kurios* (a male authority figure) is an anomaly within patriarchy. Here, the mention of her father sets her in a family network – which forms a poignant frame to the exchange that follows – no pimp for her. Walter offers her the large sum of two pounds – the equivalent of the expected weekly expenditure of a middle-class woman. She recognizes that he seems to want to categorize her as a whore although any such word itself is unexpressed. She refuses the categorization ("I ain't"). He assents, but the money is accepted, and she spits on it. This is a deeply troubling moment in this deeply uncomfortable scene. Does this exchange make her a prostitute (and in whose eyes?)? She has taken money after sex: is it money for sex? She refuses his further touching. As so often in *My Secret Life*, the narrator sees such an exchange as payment, but here the recipient wishes to see it or herself as something else. She indicates the ambivalence – or deep disgust – by spitting on the money, as she also looks "wistfully" at it. The power relation is enacted, for sure – he is a higher class than her, economically and socially and linguistically – but the reversal of offering money after the act, luring her into a financial relation where none was proposed or anticipated before, confuses the expected boundaries of exchange. "Gift exchange" is not (to be) a mercenary, financial, commodity exchange.

It is essential to the discourse of prostitution that different forms of exchange are kept separate. So, Holly Golightly in *Breakfast at Tiffany's* will accept gifts and money from wealthy men – it is her only income – but Truman Capote, the author, in an interview referred to her precisely as not a prostitute but an "American Geisha".[9] Theodote, the *hetaira* memorably portrayed in Xenophon's *Memorabilia*, paradigmatically tells Socrates, "If anyone who has become my friend [*philos*] wishes to be generous [*eu poiein*], that is how I make my living" (3.11.4).[10] A mistress, in modern Western culture, may accept money, gifts, property, and have sex with the giver – it may be her only source of income – but the relationship is not to be construed as prostitution, nor as formally or even informally contractual.[11]

At work in such divisions – and other examples could easily be developed, as these could be treated at greater length – are at least three sets of anxieties. First, the opposition of financial and personal values: both in ancient society and in Victorian culture, financial relations are denigrated as signs of an impersonal contract, and expressive of an instrumental or mechanical and thus hierarchical social interaction, to be set against the personal values of (aristocratic) status, trust, friendship, affection and so forth. Prostitution is criticized – and there is little vocabulary of prostitution that is not denigrating – because it replaces personal value by financial exchange in an area where personal value is most valued.

Second, and this follows immediately from the first, the autonomy of the individual is threatened by a monetary exchange, in a way which prostitution doubly exacerbates. Theodote, the *hetaira*, can make or refuse an appointment with a man. A *pornê* in a brothel has no such freedom. In the politics of contemporary British law, there is a long-running and heated debate whether it is right to base the criminalization of prostitution on the assumption that prostitution must be exploitative – that is, on the assumption that a woman *cannot* freely agree to offer herself for money. Similarly, it is debated whether strict liability can be placed on a man, a liability which makes it a criminal offence to pay for sex, even if the buyer is unaware of any exploitation, or even if no exploitation can be shown to exist, even if both parties appear willing. Those who wish to criminalize any act of prostitution in this way argue on the grounds that, as Archbishop Sentamu put it, "Prostitution is an inherently abusive and exploitative system."[12] What political costs are there in defending women from exploitation by denying women autonomy? How *could* the values of autonomy be preserved or expressed in a power-based relationship such as prostitution? From Helen of Troy onwards, the question of female autonomy – did she want to? Was she forced? – is integral to sexual discourse, and brought into sharp focus by attempts to comprehend or regulate prostitution.

Third – and this in turn follows from the first two anxieties – to break the veils that are in place to keep such oppositions safe is likely to produce contestation and anger. For a man to ask "If I take you out for dinner and pay for it and give you a gift, will you have sex with me?" would be socially offensive, however much it might be part of an unwritten and unexpressed negotiation, because on the one hand it replaces personal value with financial instrumentaliza-tion, and, on the other, because it replaces autonomy ("choice", "interest", "desire") with a contractual relationship. The distaste – anger, upset – caused by such a question is also because it refuses to recognize and uphold the necessary veils of social interaction. Giving money after the act of sex nastily makes explicit the inequalities otherwise inherent in their interaction. It works to turn the girl – the exchange – into something she wishes to refuse.

One consequence of these three sets of anxieties is that it is extremely hard to produce a coherent and objective definition of prostitution that covers the range of (self)-interested accu-sations and defences encoded within its rhetoric – and the language of prostitution, from the playground to the law court, has little claim to neutrality. The slippage between shop-girl, actress, seamstress, fallen woman, mistress, prostitute, courtesan (and so forth) shows the power of persuasive definition and the manipulation of social interactions within Victorian discourse.[13] A mistress may be accused by a wife of being a whore, even if the wife also has no means of income beyond the man with whom she has sex. Having one's body exploited for money is a decent Marxian definition of all manual labour. A prostitute who is paid just to talk to a client about sex is still considered a prostitute, although a psychoanalyst is not. What is more, although there is plenty of evidence of women engaging in prostitution irregularly, or for short periods under particular pressures,[14] the use of the term "prostitute" still veers between determining a state and an activity. Would selling one's body for sex once make one a prostitute? For ever – or just for the period of the exchange? Is it really a *profession*? It is a central claim of Aeschines' successful prosecution of Timarchus that because he could be shown – by the conviction of gossip – to have been a prostitute when young, this means that all his future behaviour, espe-cially his political loyalties, may be anticipated as corrupt. Prostitution may be considered, as with Bernard Shaw's Mrs Warren, to be a profession – but it is also an act whose significance depends on a series of partial moral, political and social narratives (often grimly enforced in society). One could read the history of one strand of early Christianity – with its privileging of virginity at all costs and yet its promotion of prostitute saints such as Mary of Egypt or Pelagia – as struggling with the idea of the (ir)reversibility of a sexual fall.[15] Moralists and orators and censors of all sorts have so often been rather too quick to assert that the consequences of an act of prostitution are self-evident and inevitable and lasting.

The definition of prostitution – not its dictionary entry but its social conceptualization, which is always persuasive rather than denotative – is thus articulated not just as a question of "sex for money", but within overlapping frameworks of ideals of exchange and reciprocity, social value and financial value, temporality and autonomy, the body and labour, private and public spheres. To use the inherently normative discourse of prostitution is to place oneself within this self-defining network of social categories, where one's own values are on display. Consequently, the rhetoric of prostitution is necessarily self-implicating, self-positioning.

Walter, however, continues to press the girl. He asks her about her boyfriend/fiancé (whom she had mentioned earlier). Walter, as part of the power-play of pornography, is keen to take another man's woman, as he is quick to offer a woman's sexual history as part of his own. The age of consent is perhaps an issue here (the law raising it to 16 had just been passed in a storm of public debate),[16] but more important is the taunt about marriage – rebutted with the marriage date of Christmas – and the fear of pregnancy. This sets their act of sex and payment against the standard social proprieties of marriage and the stigma of illegitimacy. The social understanding of prostitution depends on the social understanding of marriage.

Compare, for example, Cato's famous suggestion that it is good for young men to visit prostitutes rather than pay attention to other men's wives, with Charles Kingsley's anxious terror that a single experience with a prostitute made him unfit for the purities of marriage;[17] or an upper-class Greek man's expectation to invite *hetairai* into his home for symposia with the twentieth-century English prosecution of prostitutes and confinement of single mothers to lunatic asylums … The ideals of marriage as the framework for sexual experience in society, and thus for conceptualizing prostitution, lead us inevitably to law and to religion, the regulatory systems which help define both marriage and prostitution. Law has regularly struggled to comprehend prostitution, and to find adequate regulation to reflect or direct society's values. Who is to be criminalized, if anyone, in such a transaction? What is the wrongdoing? How is it to be policed? The transgression of prostitution in Western culture is inevitably linked to the normativities of religion, either implicitly or explicitly. It is only with Christianity that prostitution *per se* becomes an institution to be crushed, and only with the industrial city of the nineteenth century that full-scale legal and regulatory systems attempt such control. If we are to construct a history of prostitution, it will necessarily engage with the regulatory systems with which it is as a practice in constant dynamic interaction.[18]

Walter, again adopting a position of power over the girl, finally insists on his licence to be "baudy" – adding linguistic transgression to the sexual – and performs it for us, his readers, by his blunt and knowingly obscene expression of desire: "I would feel her cunt again." The violence of the aggressive sexualized vocabulary is for his (male) readers to share – that is the logic of pornography.[19] (It is a bitter little irony that the name of the village is decorously asterisked out while the obscenity is paraded. So too the girl's worried sense of propriety is cancelled by the pornographer's leer.) Yet prostitution produces social anxiety precisely because of how the practice becomes a site for the expression of desire: prostitution constantly raises the question of the degree to which desire *can* be separated from personal values into a mechanical, instrumental, financial relationship.

As another Walter, Walter Benjamin, suggestively remarked, with prostitution "an always fictive pleasure arises".[20] This emphasis on the fictive is insightful (though his unwillingness to consider the location of the pleasure also telling). Narratives about prostitution love to explore just how far reciprocal physical, social or psychological response can be denied, imitated, controlled. Are you faking when you say you love me? So, at one extreme a character in Plutarch shockingly dismisses any concerns of a *hetaira*'s care for him with "Wine and fish do not love me, but I use both with pleasure,"[21] as if desire could be expressed wholly as use value; at the other end of the spectrum are the multiple tales of the "whore with the heart of gold" from Menander to Hollywood (a bad faith act which proclaims "see, no faking!"). "The heart of gold" precisely replaces the gold of the financial transaction with a felt personal value. The prostitute saved for decency reasserts the triumph of (good) social value over (bad) commercial exploitation: money trumped by feelings. Narratives about prostitution flourish in part because prostitution vividly poses the question: was will das Mensch? How do sexual desire, social process and personal value interrelate? What does matter in the exchanges of sex? Desire is always caught up with fiction and in pursuit of its truth, and prostitution above all sets at risk how we understand, recognize, hope for "the real thing".

I started with this squalid paragraph of *My Secret Life* partly because it allows in a small compass an exploration of the rich complexity of how prostitution as a social act is conceived and articulated: temporality, financial and social value, agency and autonomy, legal and religious regulation, the ideals of marriage, constructions of boundaries between the public and private, cultural constructions of the body, the social expression of desire, all play their role. These broad categories will structure my argument about ancient prostitution in the second half of this chapter, and it is part of the contention of this chapter that this very broadness and complexity of the discourse of prostitution has all too often been insufficiently recognized in current histories. But this pornographic prose, both in its wilfully coarse vocabulary and in its portrayal of a dominating, manipulative relationship of power, is also implicating in its obscenity.

Walter offers money to construct or make aggressively explicit a humiliating relationship of financial objectification; the girl resists but is lured angrily and wistfully from her poverty into his pornographic world, in which any female is potentially a *pornê*, every woman open to his financed lust. Pornography wants to lure its readers into its own world, where even resistance is framed by its own logic of desire. Pornography sets out to make its readers complicit, so that even citing a passage like this for critical analysis is an uncomfortable gesture. This paragraph of *My Secret Life* was chosen in short not despite its nastiness, but because its nastiness also suggests how self-implicating is the discourse of prostitution – how definitions of prostitution are persuasive rather than simply denotational, how the rhetoric of prostitution involves a self-positioning within the normative narratives of marriage, social propriety, personal value. This chapter is located, that is, between the bitter and necessary recognition of the continuing abuse and violence involved in prostitution, on the one hand, and, on the other, the difficult recognition that the very term prostitution conceals a confusion of normative rhetoric and social expectation, compulsions which render its definition a quagmire of complicity, misplaced certainty and self-projection, especially around the category of agency (autonomy, choice, compulsion, responsibility, criminality). This tension is everywhere at work in the modern historiography of prostitution.

The prostitute and the citizen

The difficulty of the catch-all term prostitution is immediately evident when we turn to the classical city of Athens. It is a commonplace of the scholarly discussion that there are at least three basic categories at play: *pornê*, *hetaira* and *pallakê*. *Aulêtris*, often translated "flute-girl", is a further common term for a woman hired for a party as a performer and potential sexual partner.[22] There is also a full panoply of insulting vocabulary, innuendo and pun. (For male prostitution, as in English, the language is more restricted in range and occurrence.) The conceptualization of these categories has been well articulated in a string of fine analyses by recent scholarship.[23]

So, a *pornê*, as its etymology from *pernêmi* suggests, is located within the business of commodity exchange. She – or he (*pornos*) – is a slave, owned by a pimp (*pornoboskos*), and is available for purchase for a price in a brothel. The *pornê* is bought for a short period of time, offers gratification, has no choice in the matter of her sale and at the lowest level is associated with dirt, poverty, drink and a humiliating and desperate life. As Aristotle says, the slave is an instrument, and the body of the *pornê* is fully instrumentalized. The *aulêtris* is also hired, specifically in a sympotic context, but comes into the home of the man, has specific musical performance skills and may or may not provide sexual gratification, although her body is on display and for the entertainment of men.[24]

A *pallakê* by contrast is established in a long-term relationship with a single man, either in place of or, far more rarely, alongside a wife. According to pseudo-Demosthenes [59.122] – in a quotation cited by every scholar in the field – a *pallakê* is "for the everyday care of our bodies" – that is, is inscribed in a temporality of normality ("the everyday"), is not solely for pleasure, but also for "care", and although the relationship is physical and affective, it is separated from marriage in the legal and social restrictions which prevent the production of legitimate children from it.[25] Although a *pallakê* is kept by a man and may have been purchased by him, there is no direct financial exchange involved in "everyday care". Thus, the *pallakê*, as a category, is marked out against the *hetaira* and *pornê* in terms of the dynamics of exchange, temporality, pleasure, domestic space, autonomy.

A *hetaira*, often translated "courtesan", exchanges her sexual favours in return for material benefits, but may have considerable autonomy in her choice of partner. Indeed, as with Aspasia, Pericles' consort, she may have a single partner over a long period (and thus be categorized as a *pallakê*). The pleasures of a *hetaira* are conceived to embrace more than a sexual physicality, but to include conversation, wit, musical skill, intelligence; and, as with the modern term "courtesan", fantasies of exoticism, fascination, heightened desire and manipulation are built into the discourse of pleasure surrounding the *hetaira*.[26] A *hetaira* could be imagined as very rich, and could be a citizen,[27] but the encounter is often idealized as a gift exchange (as we saw with Theodote in Xenophon's description), and as requiring a man's persuasion and potential rejection. Phryne became so rich, we are told, that she could offer to rebuild the walls of Thebes destroyed by Alexander – an offer refused by the citizens, ashamed to take money publicly for civic space from a *hetaira*.[28]

Now the slippage between these categories has also been discussed in a sophisticated manner by historians of sexuality, especially with regard to the rhetorical *glissement* between *pornê* and *hetaira*. It should be no surprise that "the two terms are frequently applied to the same woman", and not simply because "porne is what a speaker resorts to when he wants to insult a woman, or her male relatives, while hetaira is a more euphemistic term".[29] As James Davidson argues, we should "view such representations not as reflections of discrete realities, but as discursive strategies, attempting to create distinctions in precisely those areas where difference is most awkward and problematic".[30] Indeed, Davidson goes on to analyse the definitional space of the *hetaira* within the discourse of gift exchange and seduction as "a never-ending cycle of *involvement, founded on dissimulation and avoidance of definition*".[31] That is, for Davidson, the *hetaira* functions by a self-aware manipulation and shiftiness of categories and positions, precisely to escape clear and objective definition – in contrast to the depersonalized, reified, objectified *pornê*.

Leslie Kurke follows Davidson's insistence on "discursive strategies" to approach the rhetoric of the sexual traffic of women, but adds two provisos. First, she argues that even if Davidson's characterization is an effective representation of fourth-century Athens, from where most of his evidence is drawn, it is also possible to see this discursive conflict "as an *active* process in the archaic period", when aristocratic and democratic values were still in dynamic tension with one another.[32] Second, she insists that the interplay of gift and financial exchange which Davidson takes as central to the opposition of *pornê* and *hetaira* must also be seen as political, a term which she characteristically unpacks as a conflict between elite and non-elite status. I wish here to extend this style of analysis through the categories outlined in the opening section of my chapter, first to reconsider the "discursive system" of definition of the traffic of women, and second to contrast the case of the fourth century with the later period of the Hellenistic court.

It should be immediately clear that the system of thinking which links *pornê*, *hetaira*, *pallakê*, *aulêtris* and other related terms is a system (rather than discrete fields of definition), and, as a system, is constructed in opposition to marriage, as a legal and social institution. This matrix of ideas sets pleasure and reproduction in opposition to each other, and this opposition provides the ideological staging for Menander's plots of pregnant *hetairai* (imagined or real), legitimate daughters who appear to have been sexually louche, and intrigues of mistaken sexual status. It also provides the "ideological fault lines", as Kurke would put it, that motivate the rhetoric of a speech such as *De Neaira*.[33] The question of female autonomy is structured within this frame-work. I have discussed in detail elsewhere how Xenophon dramatizes Socrates' encounter with the *hetaira* Theodote as a male anxiety about control, not just the gendered control of man over woman, but the sexual self-control of a man over his desires – a set of ideas integrally linked to the ideological values of *sôphrosunê* and *enkrateia* (as Foucault and others have debated).[34] Davidson has made such a dynamic central to his understanding of the threat and thus the narratability of the *hetaira*.

It is worth stressing how this dynamic of seduction and control needs to be seen in relation to the position of a wife. What autonomy does a wife have? As Greek tragedy dramatically exposes, when a wife does attempt to take action or control within the *oikos*, even in protection of the *oikos*, violent troubles arise.[35] The control over a wife is – with whatever irony – central to dialogues such as Xenophon's *Oikonomikos* (with its inheritance in works such as Plutarch's *Conjugalia Praecepta*). Lysias 1 portrays a wife who is passive in the face of seduction, but active in dissimulation, and thus a profound danger to the patriarchal household.[36] Yet a wife is not to be like a *pornê* in her lack of autonomy, nor like a *hetaira* in seductiveness and dissimulation, nor as removed from the prime value of the continuation of the *oikos* as a *pallakê*, without, that is, responsibility for her and the family's sexual chastity and continuation. This could be expressed in temporal terms also, where the wife alone has a commitment to the long-term maintenance of the *oikos*, with its corresponding issues of legitimacy, property and inheritance – in contrast to the brief encounter with the *pornê* and the fragility of engagement with *hetaira* or *pallakê* (with a corresponding need to find a language to deal with a *hetaira* or *pallakê* if the relationship is genuinely long-term and exclusive, as is made evident by the profound ambivalence about the proper social status of Aspasia in ancient and modern representations of her, especially when Pericles sought to flout his own citizenship law for the children of this relationship).

In this light it is fascinating that in our extant plays and fragments of Menander, no legitimate young girl (*parthenos*) ever speaks, nor indeed does even a wife speak unless she has been deserted on a charge of sexual misconduct – though *hetairai* are central speakers and plotters. The authority – the activity – of speech, forever gendered in Greek thinking, is distributed by the proprieties of sexual roles. A good girl, unlike a *hetaira,* can be expected to have nothing to say. When and how a wife can take action, be responsible, without transgression, is a question at the heart of gender relations in the classical family, which is constantly expressed through the opposition of dowried wife to trafficked woman – and the complexity of the narratives which explore such an opposition. Medea's recognition that a wife "purchases" a husband with her dowry and thus buys a "master of her body" [Eur. *Med* 230–3] is rhetorically so potent and flamboyant because it bitterly uncovers the normatively concealed similarities between the exchanged wife and trafficked whore.

The preceding two paragraphs were written, as are most texts of the classical period, as if the default subject were the citizen – the adult, enfranchised male. It is through the citizen that the law is focalized. So, prostitution at any level is not criminalized in Athenian law, for either the client or the pimp or the prostitute. There was a *pornikon telos*, a prostitute tax, which institutionalizes the practice under state authorities. There is an obvious social stigma attached to a *pornê* as a slave and as someone whose body is degraded by its use (though, as David Halperin has influentially suggested, the citizen body is established in its hard, masculine impenetrability in contrast to multiple forms of feminine negativity).[37]

For a wife to behave as a *hetaira*, or a *hetaira* as a wife, however, is not merely shameful, but also criminalized. So, for a man not to divorce a wife who has committed adultery, let alone behaved as a prostitute, is punishable by his loss of citizen rights, and equally a man to pass off a prostitute as a wife demands drastic legal response (as in ps-Demosthenes' *De Neaira*). Sexual activity becomes not merely transgressive but criminalized when it comes up against the secure status of the citizen and his values. Prostitution becomes a legal issue only when it comes into direct conflict with the secure structures of patriarchal, civic inheritance – and political competition between men.

A woman caught in the sexual transgression of adultery, what is more, cannot take part in the city's religious rites and must not appear in public in jewellery or other finery: that is, not merely is her exclusion from religion as a sign of communal life enforced, but also her public status as attractive or valued figure must be curtailed: A ritualized humbling. So too if a citizen enters another man's house without his permission or enters the woman's quarters under almost any circumstances, he is likely to end up in a court case, whereas the admission of *hetairai*, *aulêtrides* and male guests to the *andrôn* for a symposium, concluding perhaps in a *kômos* to the streets, dramatizes not just a topography of gendered, public and private space, but also a licensed crossing of the boundaries of inside and outside, pleasure and propriety: the prostitute's work is expressed as a dimension of the citizen's domestic space and public role.[38]

Equally telling is the law that proscribes action by the *astunomoi,* the state's legal regulators, if two men wish to hire the same *aulêtris* for a symposium. The issue is not to become a matter of supply and demand – no price rises are allowed beyond the state's agreed rate. Nor, however, is the choice left to the girl. Rather, the decision must be made by the men drawing lots. In other words, competition for a desirable woman is not to lead to social division or the triumphant assertion of one man's superior status but is to be solved by a democratic process, that is by a process which enforces the performance of democratic civic values, enshrined in law as an expression of those values. The organization of prostitution in fourth-century Athens is not merely constructed in relation to marriage in terms of autonomy and self-control, temporality, the boundaries of public and private space, the social ordering of desire and the conceptualization of the body, but also in each case is mediated through the specifics of the ideals of the democratic citizen.

Thus too, as several scholars have pointed out, male prostitution, as most fully represented in Aeschines' *In Timarchum*, is denigrated as a failure of proper citizen behaviour, which deserves disenfranchisement as a condign punishment.[39] The discursive regime of prostitution in the classical city is organized through the categories of citizenship.

This argument is not to refute Kurke's claim that the *hetaira* was "invented" at the same time as money to (re-)introduce a classed evaluation of privileged pleasure over and against incipient democratization; but rather to note that the proclamation of such entitled pleasures is also reframed by the dominant democratic language. The self-positioning of the rhetoric of prostitution is the self-positioning of citizenship.

Two contrasting passages will help illustrate this claim. Both examples are from Athenian comedy, that is, from public performances in front of the body of citizens, and thus are telling test cases for the public representation of this citizen politics of prostitution. The first is from Aristophanes' *Wasps*. The old man, Philocleon, has behaved appallingly at a symposium of rather too high a class for him, and has bolted with an *aulêtris* in tow. The first joke is that the old man is behaving exactly like the archetypal youth on the rampage of a post-party *kômos*, fighting, carousing and getting into sexual scrapes in public. He gets the girl to grab his (stage) phallus to pull her up the steps. "Watch out," he says, "the 'rope' is rotten, but it doesn't mind a good rub" (*Vesp.* 1343–4). The old man's grotesque and sexualized body is flaunted just as is the party girl's. Philocleon's extreme comic language goes on to expose the logic of exchange involved in prostitution in a set of increasingly outrageous deals: "Do you see how cleverly I stole you away when you were about to suck off the party goers? So do this prick of mine a favour in return" [*apodos charin*] (1345–7). In a shameless parody of the required politesse with a *hetaira* like Theodote, Philocleon claims that as he has acted as a friend to her by saving her from her tasks, so she should "pay him back" – a failing attempt at compulsion dressed up as repayment. When it becomes clear this is not going to happen, Philocleon ups the price: "If you act like a good girl [*gunê*], when my son dies, I will buy you out and make you my *pallakê*, pussy" [1351–3]. On the one hand, the joke here is simply if outrageously the image of the old man taking on the full rhetorical desperation of the familiar young man of comedy – "wait till I inherit!" – to the point of blithely anticipating his own son's death. On the other, the joke is in the display of the arrant self-interest of the lover's promise, which manipulates the familiar sexual categories. Philocleon, trying to persuade the slave he cannot order to comply, offers to buy her from her current master and to make her a *pallakê*, a mistress – the *De Neaira* offers the full and serious version of such a narrative of social climbing – but by calling her *choirion*, a slang term for female genitals, his actual interests remain all too clear. Philocleon's comic performance is a bravura parody of Athenian negotiations of sexual exchange.

Throughout the scene the girl says nothing. Her body is there to prompt Philocleon's performance. His monologue is precisely shameless: it ignores and thus reveals the usual normative veils of exchange. He becomes a parody of citizen propriety. It is a display for the citizen audience to revel in. The audience response itself becomes a performance of shared pleasure in the image of transgression, an act of social bonding by laughing together that enacts a shared set of values. The girl – whose status in Philocleon's language veers between sexual worker, party girl, promised mistress, mere genitals – becomes a way for the masculine propriety of citizenship to represent itself to itself.

My second example is also an old man's monologue, struggling with desire – though from a social framework with quite different horizons of propriety. In Menander's *Samia*, Demea believes his *pallakê* to have had a child with his own adopted son. With an easy denigration, he immediately blames the woman (*autê gar estin aitia* [338]), and assumes, with the same stereotypes as we saw in Aristophanes, that the recklessness of youth coupled with wine let him be led astray. For he knows his son's character: he is *kosmios* and *sôphrôn* [344] (exactly the traits missing in Philocleon), "well-behaved", "self-controlled", the two privileged qualities of the proper citizen. But his own feelings for the Samian girl are not so easily controlled: "She's a common whore [*chamaitupê*], damn her. But what of it? She won't win. Demeas, now you must be a man. Forget your longing, stop desiring!" [348–50]. His *pallakê* is insulted as a "street-walker"; he sees his position as a battle that she must not win. He has to display his masculinity. To do so he must control his desire – and kick her out of the house [352–4]. Like a tragic hero, Demea's monologue is a struggle in practical reasoning, where what is at stake is his status as a man, and what imperils this status is his desire. In *Samia*, too, then, sexual intrigues with a prostitute stage and embroil the citizen as masculine, desiring subject.

Both of these passages are from comedy, a normative discourse which Foucault largely avoids discussing.[40] Both offer telling visions of the citizen performing his citizenship specifically through an engagement with a *hetaira*. The representation of the prostitute is formulated within and through the concerns of the citizen.

The palace and the prostitute

This "politics of prostitution" is central to the contrast I wish to explore between the classical *polis* and the world of the Hellenistic kingdoms and with the court at Alexandria in particular.

It is a striking fact that many texts of later Greek, especially those of the so-called Second Sophistic, demonstrate an extraordinary nostalgia for the prostitute world of the classical *polis*. The *Letters of Prostitutes* of Alciphron, for example, not only are set in this earlier period – as if the world were (still) the world of a Menandrian comedy – but also fictionalize the relationship of the playwright Menander and his *hetaira* as an epistolary love story, written from one side. The thirteenth book of Athenaeus' *Deipnosophistae* collects a vast anthology of quotations about prostitutes – the majority of which are taken from classical sources, and many of which feature the "sayings" of *hetairai*: "The desire to recover an authentic Attic past is displaced onto the figure of the courtesan who is in turn fragmented and fetishized into a series of names, jokes and monuments."[41] Lucian's *Letters of Prostitutes* is also written in the elegant Attic Greek of this earlier period; refers only to classical Athenian literary, political, artistic landmarks; is full of names from Menander's plays; and seems to be set in a similar fictional world of a city imagined through New Comedy and the rhetoric of the classical Athenian law court. For all of this Empire literature, monologues and dialogues, the *hetaira* is a speaking subject, as male writers imagine the verbal world and imaginative life of the *hetaira* in a quite different way from Aristophanes. Where in the democratic *polis* men are paradigmatically imagined competing over *hetairai*, many of these texts imagine *hetairai* vying for men's attention, and even (Lucian *Dial.* 7) finding themselves paying men. So too, paradigmatically, in this later period, the practical reasoning, parodies and anxieties are now those of the *hetaira* (too). From an earlier era, Herodas' *Mimiamb* 2, "The *Pornoboskos*" ("Pimp", "Brothel Keeper"), and *Mimiamb* 1, "The Go-Between or the Temptress", stage a "composite type" "representative of … Middle and New Comedy" in a similar way.[42]

This nostalgia has the effect of apparently closing the gap between the classical *polis* and the Hellenistic court or the regimes of Greek culture in the Roman Empire, and consequently many scholars have used this later material to gloss the representation of courtesans in the earlier period. This has had two worrying consequences. First, there has been insufficient attention paid to the nostalgia itself (and its new genres of representation). Turning back to a fictionalized world of the past creates an imagined rule-book through which the games of *erós* are to be played out. The *kalos kagathos*, the "gentleman" of New Comedy, becomes part of the projected self of the *pepaideumenos* of the Empire; the plots and behaviour of the heroes of comedy and the villains of rhetoric inform the armoury of personality, the imagination of the desiring subject. Much as Walter Scott's fictionalized world of chivalry became for his huge nineteenth-century readership a horizon of expectation, an idealism, a fuel of desire, that took shape in lovers' exchanges, architecture, social institutions, so the fictionalized image of Menander's courtesans structures the imaginary of later Greek erotics.

Second, and, for the purposes of my argument, more importantly, this nostalgia has allowed a radically different politics of prostitution to remain obscured. Here, I wish to focus closely on the Hellenistic kingdoms, where the role of the courtesan has been expertly catalogued by Daniel Ogden, and to look at the general structuring of political life as a framework for the conceptualization of the *hetaira*.[43] Two parameters of the discussion can be outlined swiftly. First, in this case in particular the debate concentrates on women of the highest status, especially so-called "royal courtesans". Although by definition these women are exceptional – and no doubt the lower levels of prostitution scarcely changed – they also form the fascination of a good deal of ancient anecdote – that is, they significantly enter and redefine public discourse about prostitution, and thus redefine horizons of expectation. Such "imaginative embroidery and indeed fiction" is a vexing "problem",[44] only if one is committed to a form of empirical historiography that eschews public discourse and social imagination as a culturally significant historical force. Second, the Hellenistic kingdoms represent a radical realignment of the political subject. Citizenship is no longer the defining category of the self, nor is there a recognized dominant place for the proclamations of equality that define citizenship especially in a democracy: the king's court is aggressively hierarchical; the ruler would be characterized as a tyrant by the standards and expectations of classical rhetoric; power is located and contested within the authority of an individual, and the status of his courtiers defined by closeness to that apex of power.

Ogden has demonstrated that the Hellenistic kingdoms were distinctively drawn into repeated internal violence of dynastic succession because the kings were polygamous – had sexual relations with more than one woman concurrently – and produced children from these various partners, who, along with their mothers, competed to succeed in murderous rivalry with each other. Marriage was also a central part of international diplomacy for these royal figures. Accusations of illegitimacy and the characterization of a woman as a courtesan are endemic refractions of malicious propaganda between competing factions, but, even so, Ogden argues not merely that "courtesans could shade into other types of courtier" but also that "a number of courtesans are said to have been married by their kings".[45] Indeed, "Laodice progressed from the status of wife, to that of courtesan, and back again to that of wife."[46]

Children of women declared to be courtesans and yet married to kings could progress to become major actors on the political stage. Their children could become high officials or rulers in their own right: Leontiscus, the admiral of the Alexandrian fleet, was the son of Ptolemy 1st Soter and Thais, a celebrated *hetaira*. Their daughter Eirene was married to a king of Cyprus.[47] The status of such royal courtesans is marked not merely by wealth and power in a way which might be recognizable for a very few very famous *hetairai* of the earlier era, but also by marks of honour and position inconceivable in the classical *polis*. Bilistiche, the courtesan partner of Ptolemy Philadelphus, entered a winning chariot team in 268 at Olympia. Glycera, Harpalus' consort, was a dominant figure in grain supply. Lamia funded a stoa in Sicyon.[48] By contrast, Phryne's offer to rebuild the walls of Thebes was a taunt declined. Monumental memorials to *hetairai* were built, for example, by Harpalus.[49] Most strikingly, while the rhetoric of insult looks back to a continuing privilege of the legal and social institution of marriage, Hellenistic practice reveals an extraordinarily porous boundary between the *hetaira* and the wife.

Again, comedy provides a fascinating illustration of this shift in representation. Herodas' first *Mimiamb* dramatizes a visit of an old woman, Gryllis, to the house of Metriche in an attempt to get her to take on Gryllus as a lover. The conversation is ribald and direct, but Gryllis' plan is rejected. The females may appear as familiar stereotypes, but it is noticeable that Mandris, Metriche's current man, "went to Egypt ten months ago, and hasn't even sent a letter and has been drinking out of a new cup" (24–5). The man is absent. We have no idea of his status, though the suggestion that "he is drinking from a new cup" may imply that Metriche is a *pallakê*, open to the fickleness of her man; any such identification, however, remains inexplicit. We have no idea where the poem is set (apart from "not Egypt").[50] Like Penelope or Deianeira, Metriche is languishing at home, and part of the poem's pleasure is eavesdropping on a scabrous version of Penelope's choice. But the questions of citizenship familiar from the classical city are nowhere in evidence. Status, legitimacy, the boundary between wife and *hetaira*, are not part of the practical reasoning. Metriche is assumed to have a good measure of sexual autonomy, and the rejection of Gryllis' offer is followed by a cup of wine rather than outrage.

The settings of the *Mimiambs* are far removed from the Hellenistic royal palaces, of course, but their discourse is also markedly different from either Menander or Aristophanes, for all that the *Mimiambs* share some stereotypes with their comic genealogy. The different articulations of the masculine subject within the new socio-political environment of the Hellenistic city go hand in hand with redrafting how the *hetaira* is *bon à penser*, good to think with. Citizenship no longer frames the representation of the *hetaira*.

The contrast with the classical *polis* is vivid. The politics of citizenship in the classical era focuses on marriage, inheritance and patriarchal authority; legal and social regulation follow and enforce such a politics; the conceptualization of the autonomy and thus the threat of the *hetaira* is articulated against a model of marriage and of *porneia*; the status of the *hetaira* is linked to the laws of legitimacy through which citizenship is maintained; consequently the division between wife and *hetaira* is fiercely policed. The Hellenistic kingdoms, however, offer different, hierarchical power structures, with a quite different conceptualization of political affiliation, where citizenship and its claims of equality have far less purchase. The logic of autonomy, authority and exchange alters. The *hetaira*, now as a political actor, can move nearer to and further from the centre of power by virtue of her own financial and social status gained through her sexuality and skills of seduction, and, perhaps more importantly, by virtue of her reproductive success. The success of her children with a royal ruler retrospectively (and prospectively) changes social status. Competition for power now includes competition between collaborations of women and their sons. The *hetaira* can take on the roles not just of wives but also of high status men through the financial and social prestige of spectacular donations and display. The monarchies of the Hellenistic kingdoms, with their different power structures, create the conditions of possibility for a different politics of prostitution. As in the classical city, comedy – written by men – reflects this shifting discourse in its own sphere, where the *hetaira* is shaped by the contours of a different socio-political masculinity.

In short, sexual autonomy is framed by the system of political autonomy.

Is there a history of prostitution?

The question posed by the chapter title is: is there a history of prostitution? I have offered three answers. The first, which I have suggested is powerful and necessary, but in need of nuancing, is that there is no history of prostitution, in that there is an unbroken and, despite superficial variations, unchanging tradition of abuse and exploitation of largely women largely by men, who remain dominant in economic, social and financial terms in Western cultures. Important though the institutions of prostitution may be for economic, or cultural, history, and should be for the politics of gender, such everyday violence and humiliation over the *longue durée* repeatedly produces the same story, and shows a similar brutal structure across different times and societies. On this account, the narratives of the glamorous, successful courtesan – from Phryne to Harriet Wilson to Belle de Jour – are myths, which do little more than keep the deep structure in place – even and especially when the narratives are demonstrably true (as the best myths are).[51]

A second answer suggests rather that prostitution is itself a very difficult term to define, not least because it marks site of shifting and dissimulated relationships where the social construction of desire is set at stake. We need a rich cultural understanding of the rhetoric and practice of specific regimes of prostitution, which would include the formation of citizenship, in terms of agency and autonomy; the institution of marriage; cultural notions of the body, desire, temporality; the competing claims of financial and personal value, gift exchange and commodity exchange; the topography of public and private, domestic and civic space; the intricate matrix of pleasure and reproduction within and without the family. The historiography of prostitution has often resisted developing such a thick description, and, all too often, has resisted in particular the dynamics of complicity and self-positioning in the rhetoric of prostitution. The question remains: to what degree does such a rich, conceptual and rhetorical analysis of the concept of prostitution across time challenge, develop or stand in tension with the perception of the *longue durée* of unchanging exploitation?

Third, building on recent sophisticated critical approaches to ancient prostitution that have emphasized "discursive strategies" as a key interpretative method for approaching the field, it has been suggested that the contrast between the rhetoric and practice of the *hetaira* in the cultural imagination of the classical *polis* and the Hellenistic kingdoms demonstrates how the issue of sexual autonomy is reframed by the structures of political autonomy – that is, how political change enables and requires a different politics of prostitution. The politics of *citizenship* in the classical *polis* frames and defines the concept of the *hetaira* – its rhetoric, narratives, tension points, institutions. The different political structure of the hierarchical, polygamous, Hellenistic court, where citizenship plays so little a role at least in contrast with the classical city, *reframes* and *redefines* the concept of the *hetaira* – its rhetoric, narratives, tension points, institutions. Aspasia is an anomaly, made possible by Pericles' unique position in the state, and is a source of anxiety as such. Thais, Eurydice, Artacama and even Berenice, all wives of Ptolemy 1st Soter, are paradigmatic of the Hellenistic court; Thais fully part of the dynastic genealogies of the Hellenistic kingdoms and its power brokers, not only through her military sons but also through her daughter, married into another royal hierarchy. In this light, Kurke's influential critical focus on elite and non-elite males as a political framework proves an inadequate matrix to comprehend the shifting politics of prostitution. This third answer attempts also to provide a test case for exploring the central category of agency within a political framework as a way of opening the *longue durée* to historical analysis.

This chapter has made no attempt, of course, at providing a full account of prostitution of any period or even at outlining how such a narrative could be written. Rather, it has tried to bring together a necessary recognition of the political complicities of writing about prostitution with a recognition of how nuanced and broad the categories of analysis need to be in order to explore so complex a social and political institution across time. This double recognition, I would suggest, is integral to writing a history of prostitution.[52]

Notes

1 This is the argument, of course, of much important feminist thinking of the 1980s and 1990s in particular: see, for examples, Barry 1979; Dworkin 1979; Bristow 1982; MacKinnon 1987; Pateman 1988; and Kappeler 1986, influential on e.g. Richlin 1992; Bland 1995. It continues still: Jeffreys 1997 (republished in 2008), 2009.

2 There are particularly strong, local histories for prostitution in the nineteenth century, which are central to the debate: see Finnegan 1979; Walkowitz 1980; Harsin 1985; Gibson 1986; Corbin 1990; Best 1998; Luddy 2008; Harris 2010. In general, see the fine studies of Levine 2003 and most recently Laite 2012, which go beyond Hyam 1990 and Bristow 1977, 1982. There are many broad histories of varying use, see e.g. Simons 1975; Roberts 1993. The classical material has been most influentially discussed in recent years by Davidson 1997; McGinn 1998; Flemming 1999; Kurke 1999; Ogden 1999; McClure 2003; Faraone and McClure 2006; Budin 2008; Glazebrook and Henry 2011a – all with further bibliography.

3 Marcus 1966 has been particularly influential.

4 The identification was first made by Gershon Legman in the introduction to the 1966 Grove Press edition of *My Secret Life*, and, although doubted by Marcus 1966, has been defended at length by Gibson 2001.

5 Texts collected in Helsinger *et al.* 1983; good discussion in Michie 1987; Mort 1987; Bland and Doan 1998; Levine 2003. For classical material, see in particular Lloyd 1983; Dean-Jones 1994; King 1998; Flemming 2000, all with further bibliography.

6 And not just about unwilling male effort in the heat, as is suggested by Sommerstein 1983: 188 *ad* 501. See Henderson 1991: 164–5. For "Women on Top" as an expression for the anxieties of female dominance see e.g. Zeitlin 1996.

7 Decker 1979; Walkowitz 1980; Harsin 1985. Corner 2011 is a stimulating discussion of the classical material.

8 Aeschines, *In Tim.* 122–31 (the rhetoric of this passage is under-appreciated by Glazebrook and Henry 2011b: 48; Hor. *Sat.* 1.2, with ps-Acro 1.2 for the continuation of the anecdote (cf. Cicero, *Pro Caelio* 20), discussed in context by Harper 2011: 281–325); for the modern problem, see now the insightful discussion from Laite 2012, especially 54–69.

9 The interview, it should be noted, was in *Playboy* in 1968; this context is significant in evaluating how Capote is also responding knowingly to a particular need to deny any simple exchange of money for sex – an idea that *Playboy*'s fantasy, especially in its early years, is set against.

10 Discussed in detail in Goldhill 1998; on the background of exchange see also von Reden 1995.

11 Ovid *Amores* 1.10 is a brilliant treatment of this issue.

12 *Sunday Times* 2009: Oct 11.

13 See Pullen 2005. "The difference between wife and harlot ... resides in man's ability to define and maintain the borders between the two" (Henry 1986: 127).

14 See e.g. Walkowitz 1980; Harris 2010.

15 See Brown 1988; Rouselle 1988; Jansen 1999; Burrus 2004.

16 To 16, in 1885, thanks to Stead's celebrated "The Maiden Tribute of Modern Babylon": see Goldhill 2011: 42–4; Walkowitz 1992; with Levine 2003.

17 See in particular Chitty 1974; Klaver 2006 and n. 8 above.

18 See Cohen 1991, 2000, 2006; McGinn 1998 for classical materials; and Harsin 1985; Levine 2003; Harris 2010 from the works cited in n. 2.

19 See e.g. Butler 1997.

20 Benjamin 1999: 361.

21 *Amatorius* 750d–e.

22 See Henderson 1975: 1–107; Davidson 1997: 73–136; Kurke 1999: 175–219; McClure 2003: 9–26; Glazebrook and Henry 2011a: 4–8; Kapparis 2011. The artistic representation is equally slippery: see Beard 1991; Kilmer 1993: 159–69; Rabinowitz 2011; also Keuls 1985: 153–273, and the less satisfactory Reisenberg 1989.

23 See for examples Davidson 1997; McGinn 1998; Kurke 1999; Ogden 1999; McClure 2003; Miner 2003; Faraone and McClure 2006; Budin 2008; Glazebrook and Henry 2011a – all with further bibliography.

24 The *aulos* itself has a great range of connotations, and, especially in male lips, does not imply prostitution: see Wilson 1999.

25 Useful comments on *pallakê* in Miner 2003.

26 This discursive construction has resulted also in much modern fantasy about the ancient courtesan. Images of Aspasia in particular play to this: see Henry 1995.

27 Most forcibly expressed by Cohen 2000. Antiphanes (*Ath.* 572a), who glowingly describes the moral virtue of an *aste hetaira*, appears to be setting up a comic plot – and I do not understand why Cohen 2000: 127 calls it a parody.

28 *Ath.* 13.591d.

29 McClure 2003: 11.

30 Cited by Kurke 1999: 179.

31 Davidson 1994: 141, cited by Kurke 1999: 179.

32 Kurke 1999: 180.

33 Kurke 1999: 199. On Neaira, see Hamel 2003; Glazebrook 2005.

34 Goldhill 1998. On Xenophon's other hired women see Wohl 2004; Gilhuly 2009.

35 Zeitlin 1996 is seminal here.

36 See in particular Omitowoju 2004.

37 Halperin 1989: 88–112.

38 See Corner 2011.

39 See Dover 1978; Halperin 1989; Winkler 1989, 1990; Fisher 2001.

40 See Goldhill 1995.

41 McClure 2003: 28. See also Henry 1992.

42 Zanker 2009: 66.

43 Ogden 1999.

44 Ogden 1999: 218.

45 Ogden 1999: 217, 231.

46 Ogden 1999: 215.
47 *Ath.* 576e.
48 Fine discussion in van Bremen 1996.
49 *Ath.* 595e–f. Its scale is the subject of shocked rhetoric – but Stratonice's memorial (576f) is mentioned without comment.
50 Scholars have debated inconclusively whether there is a hint that Cos is the setting: see Zanker 2009: 21.
51 On Phryne, see Morales 2011. Harriet Wilson's autobiography awaits rehabilitation as one of the most engrossing narratives of the Regency period.
52 Thanks especially to Helen Morales, and to Carrie Vout, who have helped form my thinking on these issues, and to Daniel Orrells for discussions of Herodas over the years.

Bibliography

Appiah, A. (1994) "Identity, authenticity, survival: Multicultural societies and social reproduction", in A. Gutmann (ed.) *Multiculturalism: Examining the Politics of Recognition*. Princeton, NJ: Princeton University Press, pp. 149–64.

Barry, K. (1979) *Female Sexual Slavery*. New York: New York University Press.

Beard, W.M. (1991) "Adopting an approach II", in T. Rasmussen and N. Spivey (eds) *Looking at Greek Vases*. Cambridge: Cambridge University Press, pp. 12–35.

Benjamin, W. (1999) *The Arcades Project*, trans. H. Eiland and K. McLaughlin. Cambridge, MA: Harvard University Press.

Best, J. (1998) *Controlling Vice: Regulating Brothel Prostitution in St. Paul 1865–1883*. Columbus, OH: Ohio State University Press.

Bland, L. (1995) *Banishing the Beast: Feminism, Sex and Morality*. London: Penguin.

Bland, L. and Doan, L. (eds) (1998) *Sexology in Culture: Labelling Bodies and Desires*. Cambridge: Polity.

Bristow, E. (1977) *Vice and Vigilance: Purity Movements in Britain since 1700*. Dublin: Gill and McMillan.

——(1982) *Prostitution and Prejudice*. Oxford: Oxford University Press.

Brown, P. (1988) *The Body and Society*. New York: Columbia University Press.

Budin, S. (2008) *The Myth of Sacred Prostitution in Antiquity*. Cambridge: Cambridge University Press.

Burrus, V. (2004) *The Sex Lives of Saints: An Erotics of Ancient Hagiography*. Philadelphia, PA: University of Pennsylvania Press.

Butler, J. (1997) *Excitable Speech: A Politics of the Performative*. New York and London: Routledge.

Chitty, S. (1974) *The Beast and the Monk: A Life of Charles Kingsley*. London: Hodder and Stoughton.

Cohen, D. (1991) *Law, Sexuality and Society: The Enforcement of Morals in Classical Athens*. Cambridge: Cambridge University Press.

Cohen, E. (2000) "Whoring under contract? The legal context of prostitution in fourth-century Athens", in V. Hunter and J. Edmondson (eds) *Law and Social Status in Classical Athens*. Oxford: Oxford University Press, pp. 113–48.

——(2006) "Free and unfree sexual work: An economic analysis of Athenian prostitution", in L. McLure and C. Faraone (eds) *Courtesans and Prostitutes in the Ancient World*. Madison, WI: University of Wisconsin Press, pp. 95–124.

Corbin, A. (1990) *Women for Hire: Prostitution and Sexuality in France after 1850*, trans. A. Sheridan. Cambridge, MA: Harvard University Press.

Corner, S. (2011) "Bringing the outside in: The *andrôn* as brothel and the symposium's civic sexuality", in A. Glazebrook and M. Henry (eds) *Greek Prostitutes in the Ancient Mediterranean: 800 BCE–200 CE*. Madison, WI: University of Wisconsin Press, pp. 60–85.

Davidson, J. (1994) "Consuming passions: Appetite, addiction and spending in classical Athens", DPhil thesis, Oxford: University of Oxford.

——(1997) *Courtesans and Fishcakes: The Consuming Passions of Classical Athens*. London: Fontana.

Dean-Jones, L. (1994) *Women's Bodies in Classical Greek Science*. Oxford: Oxford University Press.

Decker, J. (1979) *Prostitution: Regulation and Control*. Littleton, CO: F.B. Rothman.

Dover, K. (1978) *Greek Homosexuality*. London: Duckworth.

Dworkin, A. (1979) *Pornography: Men Possessing Women*. New York: Penguin.

Faraone, C. and McClure, L. (eds) (2006) *Prostitutes and Courtesans in the Ancient World*. Madison, WI: University of Wisconsin Press.

Finnegan, F. (1979) *Poverty and Prostitution: A Study of Victorian Prostitution in York*. Cambridge: Cambridge University Press.

Fisher, N. (2001) *Aeschines: Against Timarchus*. Oxford: Oxford University Press.

Flemming, R. (1999) "*Quae corpore quaestum facit*: The sexual economy of female prostitution in the Roman Empire", *Journal of Roman Studies* 89: 38–61.

——(2000) *Medicine and the Making of Roman Women: Gender, Nature, and Authority from Celsus to Galen*. Oxford: Oxford University Press.

Gibson, I. (2001) *The Erotomaniac: Secret Life of Henry Spencer Ashbee*. London: Faber.

Gibson, M. (1986) *Prostitution and the State in Italy, 1860–1915*. New Brunswick, NJ: Rutgers University Press.

Gilhuly, K. (2009) *The Feminine Matrix of Sex and Gender in Classical Athens*. Cambridge: Cambridge University Press.

Glazebrook, A. (2005) "The making of a prostitute: Apollodorus' portrait of Neaira", *Arethusa* 38: 161–87.

Glazebrook, A. and Henry, M. (eds) (2011a) *Greek Prostitutes in the Ancient Mediterranean 800 BCE–200 CE*. Madison, WI: Wisconsin University Press.

Glazebrook, A. and Henry, M. (2011b) "Introduction: Why prostitutes? Why Greek? Why now?", in A. Glazebrook and M. Henry (eds) *Greek Prostitutes in the Ancient Mediterranean, 800 BCE–200 CE*. Madison, WI: University of Wisconsin Press, pp. 3–13.

Goldhill, S. (1995) *Foucault's Virginity: Erotic Fiction and the History of Sexuality*. Cambridge: Cambridge University Press.

——(1998) "The seductions of the gaze: Socrates and his girlfriends", in P. Cartledge, P. Millet and S. von Reden (eds) *KOSMOS: Essays in Order, Conflict and Community in Classical Athens*. Cambridge: Cambridge University Press, pp. 105–24.

——(2011) *Victorian Culture and Classical Antiquity: Art, Opera, Fiction and the Proclamation of Modernity*. Princeton, NJ: Princeton University Press.

Halperin, D. (1989) *One Hundred Years of Homosexuality and Other Essays on Greek Love*. New York: Routledge.

Hamel, D. (2003) *Trying Neaira: The True Story of a Courtesan's Scandalous Life in Ancient Greece*. New Haven, CT: Yale University Press.

Harper, K. (2011) *Slavery in the Late Roman World AD 275–425*. Cambridge: Cambridge University Press.

Harris, V. (2010) *Selling Sex in the Reich: Prostitutes and German Society, 1915–1945*. Oxford: Oxford University Press.

Harsin, J. (1985) *Policing Prostitution in Nineteenth-Century Paris*. Princeton, NJ: Princeton University Press.

Helsinger, E., Sheets, R. and Veeder, W. (1983) *The Woman Question*. Chicago, IL: Chicago University Press.

Henderson, J. (1975) *The Maculate Muse: Obscene Language in Attic Comedy*. Oxford: Oxford University Press.

Henry, M. (1986) "*Êthos, mythos, praxis*: Women in Menander's comedy", *Helios* 13: 141–50.

——(1992) "The edible woman: Athenaeus' concept of the pornographic", in A. Richlin (ed.) *Pornography and Representation in Greece and Rome*. Oxford: Oxford University Press, pp. 250–68.

——(1995) *Prisoner of History: Aspasia of Miletus and her Biographical Tradition*. New York: Oxford University Press.

Hyam, R. (1990) *Empire and Sexuality*. Manchester: Manchester University Press.

Jansen, K. (1999) *The Making of the Magdalene*. Princeton, NJ: Princeton University Press.

Jeffreys, S. (1997) *The Idea of Prostitution*. North Melbourne, VIC: Spinifex.

——(2009) *The Industrial Vagina: The Political Economy of the Sex Trade*. London: Routledge.

Kapparis, C. (2011) "The terminology of prostitution in the Ancient Greek world", in A. Glazebrook and M. Henry (eds) *Greek Prostitutes in the Ancient Mediterranean, 800 BCE–200 CE*. Madison, WI: University of Wisconsin Press, pp. 222–55.

Kappeler, S. (1986) *The Pornography of Representation*. Cambridge: Polity.

Keuls, E. (1985) *The Reign of the Phallus: Sexual Politics in Ancient Athens*. Berkeley, CA: University of California Press.

Kilmer, M. (1993) *Greek Erotica on Attic Red-figure Vases*. London: Duckworth.

King, H. (1998) *Hippocrates' Woman: Reading the Female Body in Ancient Greece*. London: Routledge.

Klaver, J. (2006) *Apostle of the Flesh: A Critical Life of Charles Kingsley*. Leiden: Brill.

Kurke, L. (1999) *Coins, Bodies, Games and Gold: The Politics of Meaning in Archaic Greece*. Princeton, NJ: Princeton University Press.

Laite, J. (2012) *Common Prostitutes and Ordinary Citizens: Commercial Sex in London 1885–1960*. Basingstoke and New York: Ashgate.

Legman, G. (ed.) (1966) *My Secret Life*. New York: Grove Books.

Levine, P. (2003) *Prostitution, Race and Politics: Policing Venereal Disease in the British Empire*. London: Routledge.

Lloyd, G.E.R. (1983) *Science, Folklore, Ideology: Studies in the Life Sciences in Ancient Greece*. Cambridge: Cambridge University Press.

Luddy, M. (2008) *Prostitution and Irish Society, 1800–1940*. Cambridge: Cambridge University Press.

McClure, L. (2003) *Courtesans at Table: Gender and Greek Literary Culture in Athenaeus*. New York and London: Routledge.

McGinn, T. (1998) *Prostitution, Sexuality and the Law in Ancient Rome*. New York: Oxford University Press.

MacKinnon, C. (1987) *Feminism Unmodified: Discourses on Life and Law*. Cambridge, MA: Harvard University Press.

Marcus, S. (1966) *The Other Victorians: A Study of Sexuality and Pornography in Mid-Victorian Britain*. New York: Bantam Books.

Michie, H. (1987) *The Flesh Made Word: Female Figures and Female Bodies*. Oxford: Oxford University Press.

Miner, J. (2003) "Courtesan, concubine, whore: Apollodorus' deliberate use of terms for prostitute", *American Journal of Philology* 124: 19–37.

Morales, H. (2011) "Fantasizing Phryne: The psychology and ethics of *ekphrasis*", *Cambridge Classical Journal* 57: 71–104.

Mort, F. (1987) *Dangerous Sexualities: Medico-Moral Politics in England since 1830*. London: Routledge.

Ogden, D. (1999) *Polygamy, Prostitutes and Death*. London: Duckworth.

Omitowoju, R. (2004) *Rape and Politics of Consent*. Cambridge: Cambridge University Press.

Pateman, C. (1988) *The Sexual Contract*. Cambridge: Polity.

Pullen, K. (2005) *Actresses and Whores: On Stage and in Society*. Cambridge: Cambridge University Press.

Rabinowitz, N.S. (2011) "Sex for sale? Interpreting erotica in the Havana Collection", in A. Glazebrook and M. Henry (eds) *Greek Prostitutes in the Ancient Mediterranean, 800 BCE–200 CE*. Madison, WI: University of Wisconsin Press, pp. 122–46.

Reisenberg, C. (1989) *Ehe, Hetärentum und Kanbenliebe in antiken Griechenland*. Munich: Beck.

Richlin, A. (ed.) (1992) *Pornography and Representation in Ancient Greece and Rome*. New York: Oxford University Press.

Roberts, N. (1993) *Whores in History: Prostitution in Western Society*. London: Harper Collins.

Rouselle, A. (1988) *Porneia: On Desire and the Body in Antiquity*, trans. F. Pheasant. Oxford: Oxford University Press.

Simons, G.L. (1975) *A Place for Pleasure: The History of the Brothel*. Lewes, UK: Harwood-Smart.

Sommerstein, A. (1983) *Wasps*. Warminster, UK: Aris & Phillips.

van Bremen, R. (1996) *The Limits of Participation: Women and Civic Life in the Greek East in the Hellenistic and Roman Periods*. Amsterdam: J.C. Gieben.

von Reden, S. (1995) *Exchange in Ancient Greece*. Cambridge: Cambridge University Press.

Walkowitz, J. (1980) *Prostitution and Victorian Society: Women, Class and the State*. Cambridge: Cambridge University Press.

——(1992) *City of Dreadful Delight: Narratives of Sexual Danger in Late-Victorian London*. Chicago, IL: Chicago University Press.

Wilson, P. (1999) "The *aulos* in Athens", in S. Goldhill and R. Osborne (eds) *Performance Culture and Athenian Democracy*. Cambridge: Cambridge University Press, pp. 58–95.

Winkler, J. (1989) *Constraints of Desire: The Anthropology of Sex and Gender in Ancient Greece*. New York: Routledge.

——(1990) "Laying down the law: The oversight of men's sexual behavior in Classical Athens", in D.M. Halperin, J.J. Winkler and F.I. Zeitlin (eds) *Before Sexuality: The Construction of Erotic Experience in the Ancient Greek World*. Princeton, NJ: Princeton University Press, pp. 171–209.

Wohl, V. (2004) "Dirty dancing: Xenophon's *Symposium*", in P. Murray and P. Wilson (eds) *Music and the Muses: The Culture of Mousikê in the Classical Athenian City*. Oxford: Oxford University Press, pp. 337–63.

Zanker, G. (2009) *Herodas: Mimiambi*. Warminster, UK: Aris & Phillips.

Zeitlin, F. (1996) *Playing the Other: Gender and Society in Classical Greek Literature*. Chicago, IL: Chicago University Press.

11

RELATIONS OF SEX AND GENDER IN GREEK MELIC POETRY

Helen, object and subject of desire[1]

Claude Calame

If there is one body of evidence that seems to me to be relevant when trying to appreciate the sexuality of Greek men and women in the so-called archaic period according to the criteria of "gender," it is indeed lyric poetry. Yet it appears that neither our modern concept of sexuality, nor that of "lyric," nor even the concept of "gender"—if it is based only on a simple structural opposition between male and female—is relevant for a poetry of love, which is, in reality, a poetry of ritual action. The concept of "the archaic" with all its negative connotations is likewise unhelpful. Let us return then to the indigenous categories with our modern issues in mind—from a perspective of historical and cultural anthropology, and especially of ethnopoetics—with full awareness of the interpretive and relative nature of such an approach. Therefore not "lyric" but *melos*, not "sex" but *eros*, not "gender" but, in the case of ritual erotic poetry during the pre-classical period, the traditional language used by both male and female poets, a language that tends to juxtapose and blend social relations of sex and sexual identities which, for us moderns, are highly marked by a male/female opposition.

Forms of erotic melic poetry

Let us start with some examples. First a few lines from erotic poetry attributed to Alcman:[2]

> Eros again, by Cypris' will
> warms me, softly flooding my heart.

Then a distich by Sappho:

> Eros again agitates me, he who breaks limbs,
> the soft sting, the impossible animal,

And to finish, a fragment by Anacreon:

> Again, Eros has hit me with his long axe,
> like a bronze-smelter, and he pushed me into a freezing stream.

According to their syntax and the way they are cited, these three fragments correspond to the beginnings of poems. The three poems open with a traditional poetical language formula, with expected variations owing to different metrical structures: *Erōs me deute*. These three distiches name differing physical effects created by the strength of amorous desire. An integral part of modern sexuality, this impulse is incarnated, in pre-classical Greece, in the figure of the young Eros as well as the goddess Aphrodite of whom the adolescent with wings is the assistant.

Greek sexuality depends then on an anthropology, that is to say, on a conception both physical and moral of man and woman; on a conception (in some manner medical) of the human being, in which the physiology of emotions plays an essential role. It is the case, in particular, with erotic desire, the physiology of which is represented and described in poetry or in iconography more often than the sexual acts themselves. Considered etymologically by Plato as deriving from *rhein* (to run, to stream), *erōs* is perceived as a flow emanating from the body of a young person inspiring desire, conveyed by the look in the eyes and hitting the organs of sense and thought of adult individuals; this is independent from "biological sex" or sex statuses, and the relationship being either "hetero-" or "homo-sexual"—again, two modern concepts not relevant to classical Greek culture. We will come back to that later on, but let us note right away that, in the eyes of the Greeks, poetry can provoke the same effects of charm and bewitchment as the erotic desire it stages.[3]

In a poetry of musical and oral performance, the formal similarities observable in the first examples would not be very surprising if the lines under consideration did not originate from poets active in cities with very diverse political regimes; and especially if these distiches did not bear the marks of very different conditions of enunciation: a poem probably sung by a chorus of young girls, with the poet, Alcman, presented as their educator; a poem that also may be sung by a chorus in the case of Sappho's lines, in which the "I" is never explicitly identified as the poetess herself; a poem, no doubt a "monody," as far as Anacreon's beginning is concerned, who often delegated the poetic "I" in his pieces to the guests of the symposium, the ones to whom his songs were generally devoted. Three "texts" then that refer to differentiated singing performances.

The three also differ in their "enunciatory" scenarios (to be distinguished from the real situations of performance) from the point of view of actors personifying the poetical "I" and from the point of view of sexual identity conveyed by the *persona poetica*. First, a young girls' chorus states the erotic sentiments that the beauty of a female choregus inspires and also sings, from the perspective of adolescents, lines composed by an adult poet who takes an educational role in the service of the city (Alcman). Second, we have a choral group in which a young woman sings about the effects of a feminine Eros in songs composed by the adult leader of a group whose members are young aristocratic girls; they become complete women in the practice of song rituals (Sappho). Finally, a grown up individual, or the poet himself, sings for his gathered peers at a symposium about the *eros* inspired alternatively by a young and untamed mare in Thrace or by a young man who looks like a young girl (Anacreon).[4] In these three cases, a double distinction operates: on the one hand, between those—males and females— who, in the poem, personify the enunciation and use "I" (the *persona loquens* or *poetica*, the speaker) and those—males or females—who perform the poem in a ritual singing performance. On the other hand, a distinction between the one or several performers and the author-poet, more present here in his or her "author function" than in a sexed individual and biographical identity to be associated with a proper name with all its psychosocial implications.[5]

An approach to *melos:* Processes of enunciation and deictic gestures

The different forms of Greek poetry belonging to the expansive genre of *melos* should not be confused with other pieces that we understand as "lyric" because we think they are the direct poetical expression of the poet's feelings. It is certainly true that Greek melic pieces are distinguished, although with varying linguistic forms, by a strong presence of a singing "I"; but before claiming to have been hit by feelings such as Eros creates, this "I" describes itself in the process of singing. That is to say with forms such as "I sing" or "I am getting ready to dance," this poetical "I" engages in speech acts that transform the poem, in a performative way, into a (ritual) singing act. This self-referential "I," bearing values of enunciation and performativity, is regularly located in time and space. Through different movements of *deixis*, through different processes of verbal designation, this locating in space and time refers to the *hic et nunc* of enunciation; that is, this enunciatory marking refers to the "here" and "now" of the ritual and musical performance, whether it be individual or collective, "monodic" or choral.[6]

Yet melic poetry is not only characterized by a strong presence of the first person's self-referential and performative forms; its various forms also include narrative allusions to the community's heroic past in their argumentation: stories that we traditionally label as "myths." In these heroic stories, "mythical" for us, scenes of seduction and erotic union play a major part. In this regard, there is an essential distinction—borrowed from the French linguist Emile Benveniste—operative between two levels of verbal and discursive expression which, in fact, often coincide: on the one hand, the level of "story" (*histoire* or *récit*), grammatically marked by forms of *they*, or *there* and the aorist; and, on the other hand, the level of "discourse" characterized by *I/you (us/you)* and *here* and *now*. In the poetical genre of *melos*, the forms of discourse refer to the poem's musical and ritual performance, whereas the forms of story refer to the action, to the space and to the time of myth. But equally important for melic poetry there is another distinction (established by German linguist Karl Bühler) operating between *Deixis am Phantasma* and *demonstratio ad oculos*. This distinction signifies the dual ability of any form of discourse to refer internally to what is being said while appealing to the reader/spectator's imagination on the one hand, and on the other hand, to designate verbally what is exterior to the speech, what the hearer has before his or her eyes; these gestures of verbal *deixis* rely on the *Hier-Jetzt-Ich System*; focused on the "position of enunciation," it corresponds in Benveniste's "formal apparatus of enunciation" with the mentioned forms of the *I/you*, of the "now" and of the "here."[7]

This ability to make external reference, in particular the ability of poetic discourse through the "I" via the parameters of enunciation, does not refer only to the pragmatic dimension of any verbal (discursive) utterance and, in this particular case, the forms of melic poetry. It also allows us to justify, from the linguistic point of view, an essential distinction already mentioned above concerning gendered poetical expression: on the one hand, through the grammatical forms of *I/we* and the qualifications attributed to them, the figure of the *persona poetica*; on the other hand, the figure of the *performer* who takes the collective role and ethos of the "speaker" in the actual poetical performance. In an intermediate situation the figure of the poet who recognizes him or herself in his or her "author function" can, through different enunciatory strategies of "choral delegation," integrate his or her voice into the choral "we" who sings the poem.

Thus, the amorous *melos* as self-referential, ritual, and pragmatic poetry implies a collective and ritualized expression of desire inspired by Eros and his mistress Aphrodite; amorous passion is expressed through poetry in musical performance, in a relation of gender that complicates the enunciatory games between male or female poet and male or female singers.

Identities of the *persona loquens* and "gender"

Significant from this perspective are verse fragments from Sappho, whether they came to us through the indirect tradition or through papyrological discoveries. As far as the traditional classification of these lines under the label of "lyric poetry" goes, the focus of scholars has essentially been concerned since the beginning with the issue of the sexual identity of the *persona loquens*, in connection with the nature of sentiments expressed by this poetical "I" within these verse fragments. Two issues in contemporary Western civilization have contributed to regenerating or renewing our readings of Greek erotic poetry: the salutary debate around the moral and legal acknowledgement of homosexuality, in the modern sense of the term, and the critical issue of the natural or cultural characteristics of identities, roles, and social relations of sex (together with representations based on them). As for antiquity, this dual issue regarding the nature of homosexuality and of sexual differences has essentially been focused on poetry attributed by the ancients to the poet Sappho.

We have thus been led to question, from these two contemporary points of view, the love relationships between women poetically expressed in the—alas—fragments which have come to us under the name of "Sappho." From an Anglo-Saxon point of view, representatives of "lesbian studies" and "gay studies"—as well as "gender studies"—have vied with each other to find within the lines attributed to Sappho the traits of a specifically feminine "intimacy." To that extent, some readings inspired by different trends in gender studies have given back to Sappho the romantic role of a lyric poet who confides her passionate emotions to poetic writing. Essentially textual, put in the field of literature in the modern sense of the term, Sappho's poetry would create a subjectivity which would be specifically feminine; it would likely be conveyed to other women, offering the possibility of its being assumed by these women in an intersubjective way. Limited to the private domain in contrast with public melic poetry written by the male poets, her poetry would avoid "the tyranny of the performance culture."[8]

From the side of a gay engagement and in the frame of a "feminist anthropology," it would mean that, for example in the *Hymn to Aphrodite* (fr. 1 Voigt), Sappho borrowed from the masculine *Iliad* the conflicting relationship which opposes Diomedes to Aphrodite. In an intertextual game implicitly referring to written poems, she would reorient this male/female relationship in order to make, on the contrary, the goddess her ally. Consequently, the reformulation by a woman of the Homeric relationship between a hero and the divinity would transform the poetical relationship of "Sappho" with the goddess of erotic desire into an intimate connection, from person to person, mediated by writing. In this textual and literary sphere of a personal dialogue with Aphrodite tending to become a monologue with oneself, this would be the inner expression of a woman based on a reading (sic!) of Homer; therefore, on the one hand, the androcentric world of a public culture, and on the other, the intimate sphere of feminine privacy; on the one hand, the public ceremonies of men, marked by sacrifices and rituals, and on the other, the "poetical meetings" of women, of a private and intimate character.[9]

No doubt driven by a well-intentioned feminism, such interpretive positions are a sign of the need for the previously mentioned enunciatory distinction between the one who says "I" in the poem (the *persona loquens* or *cantans*), the one who composes the poem, and the one who sings it (and finally the one who reads it …). With its positions of enunciation, and with its mask of authority, the textual figure of the poetical "I" first refers to the one who sings the poem, then, indirectly, to the poet defined not as a biographical and psychosocial identity, but in his or her "author function."[10] Before being a woman unveiling the intimacy of her amorous passions in the form of written poetry, Sappho is a master in the arts of the Muses. Across various ancient testimonies, the poetess of Lesbos appears as some sort of choregus for a group of young girls who follow a musical and ritual collective education under her poetic direction; this musical training aims at nurturing feminine beauty as well as affective and sexual maturity. We will come back to this in our conclusion.

Yet one must highlight differences; the correct anthropological and ethnopoetical method demands a comparative process, proceeding by contrast. The possible feminine specificities of

Sappho's erotic poetry can only be confirmed through confrontation with masculine erotic poetry coming from the same melic tradition, staging feminine and masculine homoerotic relationships, as well as heteroerotic relations.

Pragmatics of melic poetry and gendered "anthropopoiesis"

Though a personal dimension without doubt plays an important part in Sappho's poetry, let us not forget that it does so through local poetic language, for a melic poem taken on collectively and designed for a particular ritual performance. This local elocution relies on a language of traditional erotic poetry, apparently pan-Hellenic, whose lexical and metaphorical turns of phrase are equally used by male poets. Metric and strophic rhythms belong to this tradition of love poetry that crosses masculine and feminine; it refers to poetical performances, musical and cadenced, that are also ritualized bodily practices. This is far from modern conceptions of melic poetry which are assimilated to romantic conceptions of lyric poetry and to the literary notion of written poetry in an intertextual connection with other poetic genres.

In the debate on Sappho's poetry's femininity and on the gendered specificity of emotions she seems to express, one has essentially focused on the "position of enunciation," i.e., on the *origo* of the *Hier-Jetzt-Ich-System* mentioned in the earlier section, *An approach to* melos. With this focus on the "lyric I," one has almost put into brackets the parameters which define the spatial and temporal anchoring of the moment of enunciation. In the field of space and time, these marks are however constitutive of the "formal apparatus of enunciation"; by their deictic reference (*demonstratio ad oculos*) to the singing performance's frame of space and time, they play a major part in particular in the poetical forms of the *melos* and are characterized by their very strong pragmatic dimension.

Moreover, through procedures of *Deixis am Phantasma* with their demonstrative appeals to imagination, the same poetical compositions regularly refer to a past situation (historical or heroic) in a different space than *hic et nunc* (level of the *performance*). Attention given to marks of space and time can therefore equally shed light on the subtle relations which any melic poem weaves between past and present: between a past and heroic space which appears to us as a "myth" and a poetic present which refers to the *hic et nunc* during the poem's performance. Understood according to the indigenous terms of *ta arkhaia, ta palaia*, or *ta patrōia* (the times of the beginning, the times of the past, or the times of the fathers' actions and therefore of the ancestors), the feats of heroic times have nothing fictitious about them; their fiction (to be understood in the etymological sense as fabrication) finds itself in an effective and dialectical relation with the situation of performance indicated as enunciation in the poem.[11]

Thus through the intermediary of creative imagination based in a long tradition of poetic language and poetic genres, by way of scanned and rhythmic verbal expression, in the medium of various enunciatory procedures, Greek storytelling, which appears to us as "mythical," is fully integrated in the enunciatory system that makes the execution of melic poetry a poetical and musical action. Through cadenced poetical forms and modes of ritualized "performance," heroic stories relative to the past of civic communities foster "anthropopoietic" constructions and identifications, marked by representations of sex, around a culturally and socially shared memory.[12] In reality, "myth" contributes to the making of the social being, in its cultural and religious identity as well as in its sexual identity; through this role as collective intermediary, it contributes to the social and cultural making of individuals implied in the anthropopoietic process of rhythmic and poetic performance. This last constitutes the central point of the choral education which is at the base of Greek culture, defined as a "chorus and song culture."

The participants in the choir's poetical celebration are the protagonists in a process of musical education, in which asymmetrical erotic relationships between members of the choir group and the directing person play an essential part: and not homosexual relations but homophile ones. Indeed, such homophile and homoerotic relationships between adult male or female and male or female adolescents are temporary, but no less real. Propaedeutic, they provide a role of initiation through a constant shift in mature love, in the sense that they provide a transition role toward what we see as adult "heterosexual" relationships. These homophile relationships, strongly marked by the presence of Eros and particularly fulfilled in melic poetry performances, are, to our eyes, paradoxical: they contribute to the (hetero)sexual and affective maturity of individuals, male and female, through relationships which appear to us as "homosexual" and through a collective and ritualized poetical expression. Even if it is not really attested in the iconography as far as feminine erotic homophilia is concerned, the numerous images of the late archaic period showing (ritualized) sex between an adolescent and an adult man show that the pederastic and homophile relationship was not a Platonic one: homoerotic education continued to completed love through poetry and through practice![13]

From a poetical language to common forms of rhythm and music, this musical and erotic education and initiation prepared young people for social and cultural roles clearly marked from the point of view of sexed identities: marriage, motherhood, and cultural roles for young girls; soldiering and civic duties of political power for young males. Yet the reality of Greek poetry in performance eludes what reassurance such binary logic could bring. Gender ambiguities in pre-classical erotic poetry are illustrated in particular, in differential comparison, in the poetical use made of the figure of Helen. It legitimizes love relationships which are very different from those typical of the modern point of view of sexual orientation; as expressed in melic poems by Alcman, Sappho, Alcaeus, Stesichorus, between "epichoric" and "pan-Hellenic" poetical traditions, these relations blur the distinction we are used to make between "heterosexual" and "homosexual."

Alcman and Spartan cults of Helen

Dawn goddess or morning goddess, as Orthia or Aotis, Helen is no doubt the recipient of rituals described in the first *Partheneion* by Alcman; as a singing act or as a musical offering, the poem's performance is itself part of the cult sequence into which it comes. Yet as a heroic figure attached to the city's founding history with her brothers the Dioscuri, through the double paternity of Zeus and Tyndareus, Helen was, in Sparta, the object of a double cult.

On the one hand, near the Platanistasa, on the plane trees' island—also the theatre for ritual battles between ephebes—not far from Alcman's grave and the sanctuary devoted to Herakles, the young Helen was the recipient of heroic honors. According to the epithalamion that Theocritus dedicated to the future spouse of Menelaus, the heroine was worshiped in particular by races of girls who could find an echo in Alcman's poem; be that as it may, the aetiological myth represents the future Helen at the Plane Tree singing on the lyre for the virgin goddesses Artemis and Athena and distinguishing herself in those adolescent races.[14] On the other hand, in Therapne, on a hill situated on the other bank of the Eurotas River, beautiful Helen was no longer heroicized, but divinized in a shrine shared with her spouse Menelaus. An anecdote reported by Herodotus attributes to Helen, worshiped as a goddess in Therapne, the metamorphosis of the future spouse of Ariston, king of Sparta: first a child of no account, the young girl soon became the most beautiful woman of Sparta. Thus, history associates the heroine, who became a goddess, with the adolescent's maturation and transformation into a young spouse, endowed with Aphrodite's grace and arousing *eros*.

Again, according to the classical Athenian perspective, Isocrates was not mistaken when he showed evidence of the excellence of Helen's great beauty as worshiped in Sparta; according to the orator, in Therapne even in his time, the Spartans, following the tradition of the fathers, offered sacrifices to both spouses Helen and Menelaus, not considered as heroes but as divinities.[15]

The link between the cults given to Helen as a young girl not only with the choral practice, but also with her role as choregus receives striking confirmation in classical times by the Athenian poets' perspective on Spartan musical culture. On the one hand, at the end of Euripides' *Helen*, the chorus evokes the association of Helen as a young girl with the young Leucippidai, the future spouses of her brothers the Dioscuri; then the members of the chorus sing about the participation of the beautiful heroine in choral dances executed in front of Athena's temple and offered to Apollo, for the occasion of the great civic festival called the Hyacinthia, in order to commemorate the god's love for the young athlete Hyacinthus. On the other hand, in *Lysistrata,* Aristophanes portrays Helen as the "divine and splendid choregus" (*hagna choragos euprepēs*) in a chorus of young girls compared to mares dancing along the Eurotas for the city's tutelary gods; matching the Lacedaemonian evocation of Euripides, the song in choral style and in Laconian diction imagined by Aristophanes, precisely gives the names of those divinities: Athena Chalcioicos, Amyclaean Apollo, and the Tyndaridai themselves![16] Everything happens as if Helen had, in this legendary scene revisited by Aristophanes, the leading role in a young Spartans' choral group, a role which is attributed to Hagesichora in the ritual whose musical performance, as a central facet, is the "first" *Partheneion* of Alcman.

These striking correspondences in the choral songs staged respectively by Euripides and Aristophanes invite us to imagine that the poem of Alcman was intended for one of the ceremonies in honor of the beautiful Helen, maybe on the occasion of the heroic cult which had been given to her. Yet, most probably, it was performed on the occasion of the Hyacinthia: celebrations introducing young adults, males and females, to the civic community at the end of their initiatiory cursus. For Sparta's young girls, Helen, worshiped near the Platanistas and in Therapne, is without doubt a protective figure in their initiation process—this course, musical and educational, that led adolescents belonging to Sparta's aristocratic families to the maturity of adult women.[17] What about sex in these practices of worship?

An attentive study of the vocabulary and metaphors used by the chorus in the *Partheneion* of Alcman, when singing about the beauty of Hagesichora and her consort Agido, shows that the praise is filled with erotic desire aroused by the grace of the choregus among the chorus of young girls. The presence of *eros* is fully confirmed by fragments of a second *Partheneion* by Alcman, in which the female chorus explicitly sings: "by the desire that tears limbs, she threw me a glance that liquefies even more than sleep or death." Although it is contrary to the distinction we make in contemporary Western culture between "homosexuality" and "heterosexuality," one has to acknowledge that for the woman of archaic Greece, as for the man, there is a strong homoerotic link between an adolescent and a more mature woman; it leads to the heteroerotic relationship with the future husband; both are placed under the power of Eros. Erotic desire aroused by perfected feminine beauty is as essential for the homoerotic education through music and poetry to completed womanhood as it is for successful marriage and breeding beautiful children. Contrary to previous assertions, Aphrodite and her assistant Eros (in his theogonic role) play also an essential part in marriage and the birth of a first child, who makes the young bride (*numphē*) an adult woman.[18] Archaic Greek poetry offers the example of a real culture of erotic desire, between women as well as between women and men.

Helen, subject and object of desire in Sappho's poetry

By contrast, if we focus on the remaining tatters of Sappho's poetry, we find the figure of Helen again, not for ritual purposes, as in the perspective of melic songs, but in a "mythical" storytelling often integrated as a narrative argument. Helen thus appears at the centre of a poem focused on a definition, a game frequent in banquet poetry and which Plato reuses in some Socratic dialogues. Tackling the issue of knowing what the most beautiful things are (*to kalliston*), Sappho offers an answer, much discussed later on: "as for me, I assert that it is whatever one loves (*ottō tis eratai*)." Contrasting with a cavalry or infantry troop, or a fleet, examples offered by others as *kalliston*, the figure of Helen is chosen as an illustration, until this point without the slightest allusion to the sexual orientation ("heterosexual" or "homosexual") of the implied love relationship.[19]

The heroine is considered both as a heroic figure representing human beauty, in an epic manner, and as a woman led astray by the power of love; she simultaneously represents a paradigmatic figure asserting a general affirmation accepted by the poetical "I" about the loved thing and a woman who abandons spouse, daughter, and parents, and joins a young man for love (in this particular case: Paris of Troy). The heroine is at the same time the object and subject of the erotic desire she rouses and experiences. Helen is therefore in the same situation as Anactoria, the young girl sung of as following the heroine in Sappho's verses: her walk full of grace and her brilliant look arouse erotic desire, as it is with Hagesichora in Alcman's poem. But this woman is herself absent probably because she has left Sappho's group, in order to meet a young man, her future spouse. Now an adult, she is also taken by the power of Aphrodite.

Is the gracious Anactoria another paradigmatic figure adding to Helen's example? In fact, the young girl is not a figure belonging to the time of heroes. In addition, from the point of view of erotic orientation, she does not arouse the desire of a man like Menelaus or Paris, but that of a woman. The relationship between Anactoria and the woman singing (or composing) the poem extends itself into the *hic et nunc* of the poem, thus bearing a pragmatic connection with an actual situation. Assuming in some way the position of Menelaus abandoned by Helen, the feminine "I" of the poetic persona can only evoke the young girl through memory. Physically absent in the poem's place of enunciation (*lieu d'énonciation du poème*) and performance, Anactoria is now without doubt already married, in some other place; maybe in Lydia, as is probably true in the case of a young girl sung of in one of the poems called "of memory," or as is also without doubt the case in the famous triangular relationship from the poem "he is like a god to me."[20] Implicitly, Anactoria has gone from a transitional homoerotic relation (as an adolescent who sings) to a heteroerotic one (as a grown woman) with a young man; and the heroic example of Helen, a victim of Aphrodite in love with Paris, illustrates just as well the homoerotic relationship of the young woman with "Sappho" as the heteroerotic relationship with her future spouse.

In a circular echo with the priamel at the beginning of the poem and following the double exemplification created by this formulation, the feminine "I" of the *persona cantans* can firmly distinguish the masculine field of war from the feminine-oriented field of love, and reject one in favor of the other. The epic episode of Helen's betrayal and departure to Troy by Aphrodite's will is therefore reoriented onto the beauty of feminine figure at the dawn of adult eroticism. The heroine's actions are therefore cut off from their heavy consequences in the war to be of service in the erotic situation in which Sappho and the young girls of her group are involved, here and now, in particular regarding this present Helen: Anactoria. In Sappho's poem, beautiful Helen finds, through a narrative argumentation of how beauty awakens *eros*, a role somehow similar to the one she has in the ritual, to which the enunciation and pragmatics in Alcman's *Partheneion* refer; and this as in the Spartan poem refering to the heroic wedding of the Dioscouri with the Leucippidai, that means through a transition from a "heterosexual" relationship between two adults, in heroic times, to a homoerotic and asymmetrical relationship between a young girl and a more mature woman, *hic et nunc*.

Helen between love and war in Alcaeus

But that is not all. In two successive compositions, Alcaeus, a contemporary co-citizen of Sappho, offers a representation of Helen that seems to be the complete opposite of the one in the poem aiming at a definition of the *kalliston*. Written at about the same time on the island of Lesbos, these two short strophic compositions offer poetry of the same diction and dialect as Sappho's verses; written in Sapphic strophes, these two poems were also sung in the same metric rhythm.

Via the overlapping of three ring structures, Alcaeus's first fragmentary poem opposes the successful marriage of Thetis and Peleus to the ruin of the Trojans and their city: it is Helen's fault, though she was without doubt manipulated by Aphrodite. From a perspective which, in contrast with Sappho's poem, privileges the field of war, Achilles is introduced as "happy among the semi-gods"; born from a harmonious union, the hero is in opposition to Helen, the female cause and guilty of great evils.[21] The main protagonists of the Trojan War are thus opposed according to a crossed criterion of "gender": the masculine hero is valorized by the love from which he was born; the beautiful heroine is condemned for the destruction she has caused in war. Paradoxically, this means that Achilles is not praised for his deeds of war. If, in contrast with the feminine point of view in Sappho's poem, the perspective of Alcaeus's poem is certainly masculine, war is nevertheless condemned as in fragment 16. But here the woman, not the man, is the cause of wars; as far as he is concerned, the man is referred to as belonging to the domain of a productive love union. Moreover, perhaps invoked in the second person at the beginning of the poem, Helen the destroyer is opposed to Thetis, "the best of the Nereids," a young girl of erotic charm. Her marriage—placed under the sign of *philotēs*—leads to the birth of an excellent son; her union with Peleus makes a mature woman of this young heroine, according to the expected sex role in classical Greece.

In a more linear movement, another fragment of melic poetry, also by Alcaeus, describes love as experienced by Helen in a perspective both masculine and Trojan. Under the influence of passion presented in the Greek tradition as a fit of madness (*mania*), the Spartan heroine abandons her daughter and leaves the marital bed for a man (Paris) "who cheats on his host." Consequences of this heteroerotic and adulterous relationship are again destructive: "because of them," the land of Troy can only host Paris' brothers tamed by death, chariots thrown into the dust, and corpses of numerous warriors.[22] The fragment of a melic poem by Ibycus, the context of which is unfortunately lost, presents the Trojan War as a struggle often celebrated in song, but destructive about the beauty (*eidos*) of Helen, under the influence of Cypris.[23] Conforming to the double nature of Eros, the "bittersweet," the effects of love can either lead to the breeding of beautiful children or to the worst destruction in war.

Therefore, in these two melic poems by Alcaeus, it is the speaker and narrator "I" who takes all responsibility which, in the *Iliad*, is successively the work of Hera, of Athena, of old Trojan men, then of Achilles himself, when it is not Helen accusing herself for the war she has provoked.[24] On the enunciatory level, the perspective here is not only Trojan, but masculine above all: violence and destruction which are caused by military activity lead back to a woman and to the negative aspect of erotic passion. Nevertheless, in contrast with Helen, the epic male figure Achilles is connected to an exemplary love union. As for the heroic feminine figure representing the influence of Eros' and Aphrodite's action, she is on the contrary emphasized positively in Sappho's strophes; the poet eludes the phase of punishment in a heroic story reduced to a mere episode of the plot: the ruins of Troy and its inhabitants are not mentioned in the poem about the *kalliston*.

If there is any opposition between "the bed and the war," to quote Nicole Loraux's structural expression, it does not coincide, from the perspective of representations of sex, with an analogous opposition between feminine and masculine.[25] Eros' ways are more complex.

Erotic poetry, sex relations, and enunciatory circumstances

The argumentative and pragmatic use of Helen's figure in Spartan poetry on the one side and Lesbos' poetry on the other leads to the issue of plasticity in Greek heroic traditions entitled "myth." Let us remember that this fictional (and not fictitious) narrative act, in which protagonists are gods or heroes, and which is endowed with cultural values, exists only in various poetical forms, and later on in discursive forms; they confer on it its pragmatic meaning and discursive efficacy, in a particular performance context and in a particular historical and cultural context.[26]

In Alcman's *Partheneion*, Helen is just a name taking the form of a double *epiklēsis* (Orthia and Aotis) and merely appears in the third person. But this name refers to a complex of worship in which Helen, as a young girl and as a young bride, plays a major part. No doubt the heroine owes her accession to the Lacaedemonian pantheon to her double descent from Zeus and from Tyndareus, the king who re-founded Sparta: she assumes there the functions and scope of action which, between love and war, partly overlap those of Aphrodite. The performance of this erotic praise and choral poem indirectly consecrated to Helen may therefore have coincided with one of the many musical events marking the great festival of the Hyacinthia. On that ritual opportunity, young girls of the prominent Spartan families would be carried to the sanctuary of Apollo in Amyclae on special chariots.

Yet it is precisely in this celebration where newly initiated persons were being introduced to the Spartan community that a fragment of Hellenistic commentary sees Alcman as a "master for the homeland's choirs"; in this allusion to the Lydian poet's "author function" as a *(khoro-) didaskalos*, the commentator carefully specifies that these choral groups were formed from the city's girls and ephebes.[27] Another poetic fragment mentions chorus members "noble and full of charm," beardless young men of the same age, who maintain a certain relationship with the choral "we" and therefore with the members of the chorus; they may be able to be related to the *Dymainai*, a choral group which is mentioned in the same context according to the naming of one of the three tribes in Sparta.[28] Beyond the cultural ceremony to which they were devoted, the songs composed and "taught" by Alcman are in line with the city's familial and political structures from the point of view both of their enunciation and of their ritual performance: adolescent members and adolescents of families belonging to one of the city's tribes and one of its neighborhoods, when they were not direct representatives of one of the two ruling families, as a third fragment of Hellenistic commentary attests.[29]

In regard to Sappho, if one ignores the epithalamia (that is to say the wedding songs) devoted to choral performances during key moments of wedding ceremonies, the other poems, such as the *kalliston* and poems "of memory," recount the beauty of a young girl who has left what one could carefully call "Sappho's group." Pieces of information which the editor of Sappho's biographical notice in the *Suda* undoubtedly extracted from the poems themselves also state special homoerotic relationships with three "dear companions" (*hetairae*): Atthis, Telesippa, and Megara. Over time, the homophile relationships the poetic "I" weaves with these young girls, whose names refer like Anactoria to figures of beauty and to exemplary love relationships, have become *aiskhrai philiai,* "shameful friendships." But the Byzantine also includes the names of three other young girls in the list of Sappho's three companions; three students (*mathētriai*) respectively coming from Miletus, Colophon, and Salamine (Cyprus).[30]

A papyrus fragment from another Hellenistic commentary has brought striking confirmation to the hypothesis drawn from these few pieces of information regarding the composition of Sappho's choral group and the erotic relationships weaving its social and affective web. In an excerpt commenting on lines in which both Aphrodite and the Muses were mentioned, Sappho is introduced as one who "educates for serenity not only the best young girls from local families but also from Ionia."[31] Poems such as *Hymn to Aphrodite* or the *ostrakon* fragment show that strophes composed by Sappho were meant to be sung in sanctuaries during religious ceremonies devoted in particular to Aphrodite, the goddess of erotic desire. The poetic and religious group led by Sappho was composed of young girls belonging to aristocratic families of Lesbos and neighbouring Lydia sojourning on the island in order to receive the poetess' education in singing, music and dance, erotic charms of beauty, and cultural and social maturity leading a woman of good descent to marriage.[32] Homoerotic relationships staged in these poems are therefore real, though transitory, as well as largely ritualized under the aegis of Aphrodite and Eros. The second (marital) relationship will certainly recall the first (homoerotic) one.

In contrast, Alcaeus' compositions allude to various political struggles between aristocratic families for power in a Mytilene otherwise dominated by tyrannical figures such as the highly criticized Pittacus. With Sappho on the one hand we have then poetry devoted to cult in the service of the production of feminine beauty through musical education and the culture of erotic desire; with Alcaeus on the other hand, we have poetry devoted to political struggle generally directed to groups of *hetairoi* gathered in the *symposion* in exchanges based on poetic exercises and diction.[33] Yet some rare testimonies and poetical fragments attribute songs to Alcaeus which show homophile relationships between adolescents and adults of a kind such as are attested in the many groups of elegiacs attributed to Theognis and where they are deployed in the ritual context of the *symposion*.[34] In melic poetry, lines in which Ibycus compares the young Troilos' tremendous erotic beauty to the beauty of the poem's recipient, the tyrant Polycrates, while he refuses to narrate the lofty feats of the heroes in the Trojan War, offer this testimony too. We have said elsewhere that these poetic performances at the banquet perform a pedagogical and initiatory role of bringing the young lad to the adult status of soldier-citizen.[35]

For the adolescent, who generally belongs to an aristocratic family, the pederastic courtship by an adult by means of ritualized poetry serves as a poetical example of physical, political, and moral values that the future *kalos kagathos* must adopt. But beyond the perspective of social relations of sex which, as much from the perspective of content as from the perspective of the enunciation and pragmatics, separate Sappho's poems from Alcaeus' in spite of formal commonalities (meter, dialect, lexicon), the two contemporary poets' verses depend on the same social and political context for their pragmatic function. In both bodies of work, indeed, one finds allusions to the same aristocratic families and the same political struggles. There is the case, for example, of the clan of Cleanax's descendants to which the tyrant Myrsilus belongs: allusion to their exile in a poem "of memory" by Sappho, perhaps dedicated to her "daughter" Cleis; for Alcaeus, poetry of blame directed at Myrsilus, Melanchrus, and the Cleanactidai.[36]

To conclude: Helen's simulacrum and Eros' power

Thus, from the point of view of gender, if the initiatory role played by masculine homophile relations ritualized at the symposium is formally analogical to the homoerotic relation sung in the feminine choral group; if traditional vocabulary, formal expressions, and erotic metaphors are practically identical when used in masculine and feminine poetical performances that play an initiatory role (at least in the case of educational praise poetry), the narrative content is often marked from the point of view of sexual identities: Helen always, or Atalanta, or, again, Hermione, young heroines are subjugated in various ways by erotic desire inspired by Aphrodite.[37] These beautiful desirable ones are protagonists in a narrative action which is generally heteroerotic: The partners of those "mythical" relationships are differentiated in comparison to the actual partners' sex in a relationship which is on the contrary homoerotic and asymmetrical; this actual homophile relationship is expressed and played out musically and ritually in and by the poetic performance, whether the poet is man or woman. Can we say that this homophile relationship, which is performed in a poetical manner, is not realized sexually? If the melic poetry that has come down to us is very discreet on the topic, the iconography leaves no doubt of the very sexual character of homophile relationships, at least regarding ritualized erotic relationships of citizen *erastai* with their young *eromenoi*.[38] From a comparative anthropological perspective, one should also evoke the reality of highly ritualized asymmetrical homosexual practices attested for adolescents in several communities of Papua New Guinea. Relying on the young man's absorption of the semen of his adult "godfather" through fellatio and sodomy, these initiatory ("homo"-) sexual acts are integrated into a physiological specifics respectively attributed, as in ancient Greece, to the man and to the woman: the absorbed male adult semen will reinforce the bones and the male strength of the young man, in contrast with the girl where, as I argue elsewhere, it is related to menstrual blood and milk.[39]

Relations of sex and representations founding sexed identities depend on an anthropopoietic molding proper to each culture; that it takes its start from a genetic (and psychic?) given is largely confirmed by the modern life sciences, but it happens in a much more complex way than through a mere masculine/feminine opposition. Pre-classical Greece provides evidence for very sophisticated processes of the making and realization of men and women in their sexual and symbolic identities through poetic tradition and performances. The anthropological perspective brings out a surprising anthropopoietic use of a particular form of homosexuality, through the practice of ritual poetry, for male and female adolescents.

> This tale is not the real story (*logos*)
> You did not go aboard the ships of strong armature
> You did not penetrate the citadel of Troy.

According to Socrates, those lines by the poet Stesichorus were inspired by the Muses, and may have been composed in a palinode to exculpate Helen: only the heroine's *eidōlon* would have been present at Troy.[40] Whatever this poetical game of truth and appearances may be, Socrates in Plato's *Phaedrus* invokes these lines, probably citharoedic, in the speech, also a palinode, in which he tries to give justice to the excellence of Eros: for a woman in the myth, for men in the philosophical reality!

Notes

1 This chapter was translated from the French by Luc Arnault and Mark Masterson.
2 Alcman fr. 59 (*a*) Page-Davies = 148 Calame; Sappho fr. 130, 1–2 Voigt; Anacreon fr. 413 Page. Uses of a formula that has come to be known in other metrical variations in erotic poetry are mentioned in my (Calame 1997) study; see also Nagy 1996: 94–100. Apologies for numerous self-references to previous sttudies on which this chapter relies heavily.
3 Concerning this physiology of Eros, consult my bibliography, in Calame 2009a: 23–60, 209–22 (= 1999: 13–38, 153–64). Cf. Plato, *Cratylus* 420ab.
4 I return to these multiple conditions of communication of pre-classical Greek erotic poetry infra, pp. 207–8.

5 These various enunciatory situations implying different poetical scenarios (from the point of view of the enunciation) have been the object of several of my studies, particularly in Calame 2000a: 17–48 (= 1995: 3–26), 2004: 415–23, where highly useful references will be found on the work of scholars on whom I have depended in completing these essays.

6 Concerning this essential return to the indigenous category of *melos* (μέλος), see my contribution (Calame 2006), with a comparison between a melic poem by Sappho (fr. 2 Voigt) and a poem entitled "Lyrisches" by J.W Goethe; see also Calame 1998 [2008].

7 Classical reference on the one hand to Benveniste 1966: 237–50, 258–66; 1974: 79–88, and on the other to Bühler 1934: 102–48 (= 1990: 137–57). For Greek poetry in particular, see Calame 2004; Edmunds 2008.

8 Stehle 1997: 287–311, 322–5 (p. 323 for the quote; cf. also 288: "a seductive atmosphere apart from family life must have fused women's individual ties into a common intimacy"); also see, in the same sense, suggestions from duBois 1995: 107–11 (on the emergence of the individual) or Greene 1996a: 236–43 ("gender specificity" in poetical intimacy in reaction against patriarchal order and phallic representations of desire). Read the response from Gentili and Catenacci 2007, two male philologists … ; for a francophone feminine perspective, see Bruit Zaidman and Schmitt Pantel 2007: 27–38.

9 Winkler 1981 [1990]: 162–6, 174–5, as well as 186, 187 (for the quotes), notably in regard to Sappho, fr. 1 Voigt. Resuscitated by readings of Sappho's poetry inspired by various streams of feminism, the debate regarding the (homo)sexual character of erotic sentiments expressed in these poems is considered in the comprehensive study by Boehringer 2007: 43–66.

10 On notions of the mask of authority and "author-function" (coined by Michel Foucault), see Calame 2005: 14–36 (= 2005: 13–40).

11 "Fiction" is according to the definition given by Borutti 2003: 75–8; for Greek poetry see my study, Calame 2009b.

12 On the concept of "anthropopoiesis" as the cultural realization of men and women, see the contribution by Remotti 2003: 36–69.

13 On the meaning of "homophilia," as well as the places and processes of Greek musical and gymnastic education in the respective qualities of masculine and feminine, see Calame 2009a: 119–75 (= 1999: 91–129); regarding the "anthropopoietical" construction of adults via initiation rituals in particular in ancient Greece, refer to Calame 2003: 149–66. For the iconography of male homoerotic relationships, see the corpus commented on by Lear and Cantarella 2008: 106–38 (consummation); for representation of female homoeroticism, see Rabinowitz 2002. This past is not erased since the young man as an adult may in turn have homoerotic experiences with young men.

14 Alcman fr. 1 Page-Davies = 3 Calame; cf. Pausanias 3.14.8, 15.2–3, Theocritus 18.28–48; cf. Calame 1977: 333–50 (= 2001: 191–202).

15 Pausanias 3.19.9, also Isocrates, *Helenae Encomium* 63; the sanctuary of Therapne was built on Mycenaean foundations, cf. Musti and Torelli 1991: 249–50. The anecdote is told by Herodotus 6.61.1–62 and summed up by Pausanias 3.7.7.

16 Euripides, *Helen* 1465–78 and Aristophanes, *Lysistrata* 1296–1315; cf. Calame 1977: 305–13, 323–33 (= 2001: 174–9, 185–91); on the Hyacinthia, see now Richer 2012: 343–82.

17 This is said in order to further develop the study followed in Calame (1977: 385–419; 439–49 [= 2001: 221–44; 258–63]), as well as one of the points elaborated in Calame 1983: 333, 343, to see in this partheneion a poem devoted to a ritual celebrating Helen. For the initiation role of the Hyacinthia, cf. Calame 1977: 443–4 (= 2001: 260–1).

18 Alcman fr. 3.61–2 Page-Davies = 26.61–2 Calame; see commentary, Calame 1983: 403–4; on the status of the *numphē* (νύμφη) and the role of Aphrodite, see Calame 2009a: 170–5 (= 1999: 125–9).

19 Sappho fr. 16 Voigt; see the interpretation of the poem I proposed in Calame 2005: 107–30 (= 2005: 55–69), as well as readings by Bierl 2003: 101–23 and Blondell 2010: 377–86; see also Greene 2002: 99–100, on Helen's "erotic agency."

20 Sappho fr. 96.1–9, 31.1–6 Voigt; in this regard read interpretations made by Burnett 1983: 300–13, 230–43.

21 Alcaeus fr. 42 Voigt; it is difficult to determine to whom the pronominal expression *ek sethen* (ἐκ σέθεν) refers, cf. Burnett 1983: 190–8, and, thus, Blondell 2010: 351–9 in particular on the figure of Thetis. The interventions of Aphrodite in the field of war are now the object of an excellent study by Pironti 2007: 209–30.

22 Alcaeus fr. 283 Voigt, a fragmentary poem that one can read with the help of Burnett's commentary, 1983: 185–90; see also Pironti 2007: 94–100, regarding violence caused by erotic desire (driven by Aphrodite).

23 Ibycus fr. S 151 Page-Davies; cf. Blondell 2010: 362–4.

24 Homer *Iliad*, 2.160–1 (Hera), 176–8 (Athena), 3.159–60 (the old Trojans), 9.338–41 (Achilles); Helen herself: 3.172–4; see for instance Bettini and Brillante 2002: 86–96; on the figure of Helen in the *Odyssey*, see Austin 1994: 71–89.
25 See Loraux 1989: 29–53 for Heracles' femininity.
26 Hypothesis developed notably in Calame 2000b: 11–69 (= 2009: 1–66).
27 Alcman fr. 10 (*b*) Page-Davies = fr. 82 Calame; for the connection between the Hyacinthia and for the "author-function" of Alcman, see Calame 1977: 322–3, as well as 393–4, 399 (= 2001: 184–5, 226–8, 230–1). For the Hyacinthia in general, see note 16 above.
28 The complex issue on the *Dymainai* chorus is raised in my work, Calame 1997: 115–17, 274–6, 382–5 (= 2001: 58–60, 154–6, 219–21); for comprehension of the details of these fragments, see Calame 1983: 454–61.
29 Cf. again Alcman fr. 11 Page-Davies = 24 Calame: this other fragment of *hupómnēma* discusses some missing lines dealing with *parthenoi* (παρθένοι) and it seems to associate a *Dymainai* chorus with a group of Pitanatides (from Spartan township/*oba* of Pitané); cf. Calame 1983: 387–92.
30 *Suda s.v. Sappho* (*S* 107 Adler) = Sappho test. 2 Campbell.
31 Sappho fr. 214 B Campbell (= fr. S 261 A Page).
32 Concerning the composition of Sappho's group, the erotic relations present in it and its educational role for feminine beauty by the ritual practice of the arts of Muses, again I must refer to a personal study (Calame 1996) based on points made by other colleagues. See also Lardinois 1996 and now, in a thorough study, Caciagli 2011: 41–56.
33 On the forms and roles of various *hetairiai* (ἑταιρίαι) of Alcaeus, see Caciagli 2011: 49–52, 88–96.
34 Refer to the critical work by Vetta, 1982.
35 Ibycus fr. 282 (a) Page-Davies, cf. Blondell 2010: 364–72; on the propaedeutic role of homophile relationships at the symposium, see the numerous references I have given in Calame 2009a: 119–33 (= 1999: 91–102).
36 Sappho fr. 98 (b) Voigt (see also fr. 99 and 155 Voigt) is to be compared with Alcaeus test. 1 Campbell (= Strabon 13.2.3) and fr. 112, 23 Voigt; for details see Caciagli 2011: 207–16.
37 Hermione is compared for her beauty to her mother Helen by Sappho fr. 23 Voigt; for Atalante, cf. Theognis 1283–94, in a context of masculine homophile intercourse!
38 See the group of images revisited by Lear and Cantarella 2008: 106–38 showing that pederastic sex scenes, masturbation, group sex, oral sex, and acts of violence were excluded.
39 For that comparative material, see Calame 2013: 27–31.
40 Stesichorus fr. 192 Page-Davies, quoted by Plato, *Phaedrus* 243a; see my commentary on this and other melic and erotic use of the figure of Helen (Calame 2000b: 153–6 [= 2009c: 166–70]) with numerous bibliographical references; see also, in the detail, Austin 1994: 90–117.

Bibliography

Austin, N. (1994) *Helen of Troy and Her Shameless Phantom*. Ithaca, NY: Cornell University Press.
Benveniste, E. (1966) *Problèmes de linguistique générale*. Paris: Gallimard.
——(1974) *Problèmes de linguistique générale* II. Paris: Gallimard.
Bettini, M. and Brillante, C. (2002) *Il mito di Elena: Immagini e racconti dalla Grecia a oggi*. Turin: Einaudi.
Bierl, A. (2003) "'Ich aber (sage), das Schönste, ist, was einer liebt': Eine pragmatische Deutung von Sappho Fr. 16 LP/V", *Quaderni Urbinati di Cultura Classica* 103: 91–124.
Blondell, R. (2010) "Refractions of Homer's Helen in archaic lyric", *American Journal of Philology* 131: 349–91.
Boehringer, S. (2007) *L'homosexualité féminine dans l'antiquité grecque et romaine*. Paris: Les Belles Lettres.
Borutti, S. (2003) "Fiction et construction de l'objet en anthropologie", in F. Affergan, S. Borutti, C. Calame, U. Fabietti, M. Kilani, and F. Remotti (eds) *Figures de l'humain: Les représentations de l'anthropologie*. Paris: Éditions de l'EHESS, pp. 75–99.
Bühler, K. (1934) *Sprachtheorie: Die Darstellungsfunktion der Sprache,* Jena: G. Ficher; [trans. D.F. Goodwin (1990) *Theory of Language: The Representational Function of Language*. Amsterdam: John Benjamins.]
Burnett, A.P. (1983) *Three Archaic Poets: Archilochus, Alcaeus, Sappho*. London: Duckworth.
Caciagli, S. (2011) *Poeti e società: Comunicazione poetica e formazioni sociali nella Lesbo del VII/VI secolo a.C.* Amsterdam: Hakkert.
Calame, C. (1977) "Diction formulaire et fonction pratique dans la poésie mélique archaïque", in F. Létoublon (ed.) *Hommage à Milman Parry: Le style formulaire de l'épopée homérique et la théorie de l'oralité poétique*. Amsterdam: Gieben, pp. 215–22.

——(1983) *Alcman: Introduction, texte critique, témoignages, traduction et commentaire.* Rome: Ateneo.

——(1996) "Sappho's group: An initiation into womanhood", in E. Greene (ed.) *Reading Sappho: Contemporary Approaches.* Berkeley and Los Angeles, CA, and London: University of California Press, pp. 113–24.

——(1997) *Les chœurs de jeunes filles en Grèce archaïque I. Morphologie, fonction religieuse et sociale.* Rome: Ateneo. [English edn: (2001) *Choruses of Young Women in Ancient Greece: Their Morphology, Religious Role, and Social Functions,* 2nd edn, trans. D. Collins and J. Orion. Lanham, MD: Rowman & Littlefield.]

——(1998) "La poésie lyrique grecque, un genre inexistant?", *Littérature* 111: 87–110; reprinted in (2008) *Sentiers transversaux: Entre poétiques grecques et politiques contemporaines.* Grenoble: Jérôme Million, pp. 85–106.

——(2000a) *Le récit en Grèce ancienne: Énonciations et représentations de poètes.* Paris: Belin [English edn: (1995) *The Craft of Poetic Speech in Ancient Greece,* trans. J. Orion. Ithaca, NY and London: Cornell University Press.]

——(2000b) *Poétique des mythes dans la Grèce antique.* Paris: Hachette. [English edn: (2009c) *Greek Mythology: Poetics, Pragmatics and Fiction,* trans. J. Lloyd. Cambridge: Cambridge University Press.]

——(2003) "Modes rituels de la fabrication de l'homme: L'initiation tribale", in F. Affergan, S. Borutti, C. Calame, U. Fabietti, M. Kilani, and F. Remotti (eds) *Figures de l'humain: Les représentations de l'anthropologie.* Paris: Éditions de l'EHESS, pp. 129–73.

——(2004) "Deictic ambiguity and auto-referentiality: Some examples from Greek poetics", *Arethusa* 37: 415–43.

——(2005) *Masques d'autorité: Fiction et pragmatique dans la poétique grecque antique.* Paris: Les Belles Lettres. [English edn: (2005) *Masks of Authority: Fiction and Pragmatics in Ancient Greek Poetics,* trans. P.M. Burk. Ithaca, NY and London: Cornell University Press.

——(2006) "Identifications génériques entre marques discursives et pratiques énonciatives: Pragmatique des genres 'lyriques' (Goethe et Sappho)", in R. Baroni and M. Macé (eds) *Le savoir des genres.* Rennes: La Licorne, pp. 35–55.

——(2009a) *L'Éros dans la Grèce antique,* 3rd edn, Paris: Belin. [English edn: (1999) *The Poetics of Eros in Ancient Greece,* trans. J. Lloyd. Princeton, NJ: Princeton University Press.]

——(2009b) "Referential fiction and poetic ritual: Towards a pragmatics of myth (Sappho 17 and Bacchylides 13)", *Trends in Classics* 1: 1–17.

——(2013) "Itinéraires initiatiques et poésie rituelle en Grèce ancienne: Rites de passage pour adolescentes à Sparte", *Tumultes* 41: 13–33.

duBois, P. (1995) *Sappho is Burning.* Chicago, IL: University of Chicago Press.

Edmunds, L. (2008) "Deixis in ancient Greek and Latin literature: Historical introduction and state of the question", *Philologia Antiqua* 1: 67–98.

Gentili, B. and Catenacci, C. (2007) "Saffo 'politicamente corretta'", *Quaderni Urbinati di Cultura Classica* 115: 77–87.

Greene, E. (1996) "Apostrophe and women's erotics in the poetry of Sappho", in E. Greene (ed.) *Reading Sappho: Contemporary Approaches.* Berkeley and Los Angeles, CA, and London: University of California Press, pp. 233–47.

——(2002) "Subjects, objects, and erotic symmetry in Sappho's fragments", in L. Auanger and N.S. Rabinowitz (eds) *Among Women: From the Homosocial to the Homoerotic in the Ancient World.* Austin, TX: University of Texas Press, pp. 82–105.

Lardinois, A. (1996) "Who sang Sappho's songs?", in E. Greene (ed.) (1996) *Reading Sappho: Contemporary Approaches.* Berkeley and Los Angeles, CA, and London: University of California Press, pp. 150–72.

Lear, A. and Cantarella, E. (2008) *Images of Ancient Greek Pederasty: Boys Were Their Gods.* London and New York: Routledge.

Loraux, N. (1989) *Les expériences de Tirésias: Le féminin et l'homme grec.* Paris: Gallimard.

Musti, D. and Torelli, M. (1991) *Pausania. Guida della Grecia. Libro III: La Laconia.* Milan: Mondadori.

Nagy, G. (1996) *Poetry as Performance. Homer and Beyond.* Cambridge: Cambridge University Press.

Pironti, G. (2007) *Entre ciel et guerre: Figures d'Aphrodite en Grèce ancienne* (Kernos Suppl. 18). Liège: CIERGA.

Rabinowitz, N.S. (2002) "Excavating female homoeroticism: The evidence from Greek vase painting", in N.S. Rabinowitz and L. Auanger (eds) *Among Women: From the Homosocial to the Homoerotic in the Ancient World.* Austin, TX: University of Texas Press, pp. 106–66.

Remotti, F. (2003) "De l'incomplétude", in F. Affergan, S. Borutti, C. Calame, U. Fabietti, M. Kilani, and F. Remotti (eds) *Figures de l'humain: Les représentations de l'anthropologie.* Paris: Éditions de l'EHESS, pp. 19–74.

Richer, N. (2012) *La religion des Spartiates: Croyances et cultes dans l'antiquité*. Paris: Les Belles Lettres.

Stehle, E. (1997) *Performance and Gender in Ancient Greece: Nondramatic Poetry in its Setting*. Princeton, NJ: Princeton University Press.

Vetta, M. (1982) "Il P. Oxy 2506 fr. 77 e la poesia pederotica di Alceo", *Quaderni Urbinati di Cultura Classica* N. S. 10: 7–20.

Winkler, J.J. (1981) "Gardens of nymphs: Public and private in Sappho's lyrics", in H.P. Foley (ed.) *Reflections of Women in Antiquity*. New York and London: Gordon & Breach, pp. 63–89. [reprinted in Winkler, J.J. (1990) *The Constraints of Desire: The Anthropology of Sex and Gender in Ancient Greece*. New York and London: Routledge, pp. 162–187.]

Zaidman, L.B. and Schmitt Pantel, P. (2007) "L'historiographie du genre: État des lieux", in V. Sebillotte Cuchet and N. Ernoult (eds) *Problèmes du genre en Grèce ancienne*. Paris: Publications de la Sorbonne, pp. 27–48.

12

MELANCHOLY BECOMES ELECTRA

Nancy Sorkin Rabinowitz

My title is an obvious play on Eugene O'Neill's version of the *Oresteia*, "Mourning Becomes Electra,"[1] with a twist which is a nod to the emphasis on melancholy and loss in recent work in queer theory. In the past, I have worked extensively on tragedy's strategies of containment of women, arguing that one of those was keeping women away from other women; I turned to vase painting for any evidence of women's intimate relationships to women (Rabinowitz 2002a). I will admit that, for this essay in a volume on "sex in antiquity," I was hoping to find resistance to that strategy in the figure of Electra. I asked myself "What about Electra and her sisters and mother?", inspired perhaps by watching the Strauss-Hofmannsthal *Elektra*, based on the Sophocles version, where Elektra practically seduces her sister, Chrysothemis.

Eventually, I shifted to a queer perspective, because the term queer seems more appropriate, indicating resistance to dominant norms.[2] It takes in gender performance and sexuality per se, both at issue in this volume. Moreover, one prominent strand of queer theory has been work on loss and melancholy, which seems relevant to this heroine known for her mourning.[3] Since each of the tragedians (and Euripides twice) turns to the story of revenge in the house of Atreus, we are provided with a wide range of representations of the figure.[4] We will see that Electra does seem (in some plays) to resist gender norms, while in other ways (and other plays) she is a model for the imposition of heterosexuality through marriage.

Significantly, the epic version of the story is a male heroic myth in which Orestes is held up to Telemachus as a model of filial behavior: be like Orestes who killed Aigisthos (Clytemnestra is hardly mentioned) and take the throne (*Od.* 1. 40, 1.298–300, 3.195–200, 3.308). In tragedy, however, gender and mourning play central roles (on tragedy and revenge, see Burnett 1998: esp. 99–104). Once Clytemnestra becomes the killer, the heroic vengeance becomes matricide. His sister, Electra, is introduced, but left to grieve; her mourning is circumscribed, however, by her mother and Aigisthos.[5] I will argue that mourning and gender are intimately related: Electra mourns because she is a woman, and she becomes a woman through her mourning, which at times appears to be what Freud calls melancholy (Freud 1957).

Judith Butler has addressed Freud's attempt to distinguish mourning from melancholy, which she argues is not wholly convincing (Butler 1997b: 132–4). According to Freud, mourning is completed by "de-cathexis," but the melancholic does not accomplish that resolution, instead showing a profoundly painful dejection, cessation of interest in the outside world, loss of the capacity to love, inhibition of all activity, and a lowering of the self-regarding feelings to a degree that finds utterance in self-reproaches and self-revilings, and culminates in a delusional expectation of punishment.[6]

Butler contests that simplistic distinction, and points out that Freud himself acknowledged a slippage between the terms. She further argues that gender itself is "melancholy" or "one of melancholy's effects" (Butler 1997b: 132); that is, normative gender is only constituted by giving up the previous same sex object of desire, or by introjecting elements of it: "The resolution of the Oedipal complex affects gender identification through not only the incest taboo, but, prior to that, the taboo against homosexuality" (Butler 1990: 63).[7] Luce Irigaray, however, calls Freud's version of female homosexuality "hom(m)osexuality" to underline the fact that it is all about masculinity (Irigaray 1985: 98). Jill Scott (2005: 10) points out that Electra is still useful to modern audiences because she offers these possibilities for their consideration.

There are several elements within the figure of "Electra" that make her a potentially anti-normative or queer figure (if not quite a heroine).[8] Two plays present her as unmarried and waiting for her brother: *Libation Bearers* and Sophocles' *Electra*. As I said above, her female gender typically prohibits her from taking violent action; it thus defines her as a mourner, waiting for her brother to arrive.[9] In these plays, her mourning turns into melancholy (both because it seems endless and because it is to some extent forbidden); it can also have political repercussions, as queer activism around death would point out (e.g. Butler 1997b; Crimp 2002).

In Aeschylus and Sophocles, that act of mourning is intertwined with her liminality. Electra is emphatically a girl but one unable to marry,[10] to grow into an adult, and thus to become the normative woman of her society (cf. Sorum 1982: 209; Ormand 1999, 2009). She is at odds with traditional femininity and heterosexuality; she pathologically hates the females of the family (her mother and sister). At the same time she appears masculinized and is overly attached to the masculine, almost to the point of expressing incestuous desire for the father and brother. In these ways, the unmarried Electra is resistant to normative gender categorization and seems a female warrior.

Euripides' *Electra* and *Orestes* present slightly different versions of the story, but they participate in some of these same structures: here Electra is also marginal, and she hates her mother; she is masculine and is overly attached to her father/brother. In these plays, however, she is eventually to be married off to Orestes' best friend from boyhood, Pylades.[11] Thus, her gender and sexuality are stabilized in those versions.

Electra the unmarried: Aeschylus' *Oresteia*—the urtext

Gender ideology: Electra's liminality

In the *Oresteia*, Aeschylus sets out some of the themes that will be taken up and varied by Sophocles and Euripides.[12] The matricide is the second act of a trilogy that depicts Clytemnestra as both a sexual monster and a tyrant.[13] Thus, Aeschylus' treatment of Electra must be seen in the context of the trilogy's overarching ideology of gender. As has often been asserted, gender confusion is pronounced in the *Oresteia*: Clytemnestra is a woman who acts like a stereotypical man in her assumption of rule and her lust for power; Aigisthos is a man who acts like a woman.[14] The watchman introduces this note by calling Clytemnestra a woman with an *androboulon kear* (Aesch. *Ag.* 11); her debate with the chorus is set in gendered terms, and her triumph over Agamemnon in the tapestry scene is also highly gendered: her insistence is unbecoming to a woman, he says (940). Cassandra continues the theme, horrified that the woman is killing the man (1231). In the end, the chorus is especially appalled at the murder because Agamemnon was both her husband and their king. Her action has brought down the legitimate authority and left a tyranny in its place (1355).

This then is the backdrop for *Choephoroi* (*Libation Bearers*). It is left to the children to put things "right." The revenge action is presented in terms that make it a coming of age ritual for Orestes—he has been away on the borders like a typical ephebe; he returns and must act with stealth (Vidal-Naquet 1986; Dodds 2003; Wheeler 2003: 388). Identifying with Apollo and his father, as well as with his companion Pylades, he is placed in a male hierarchy, even though or especially because he has been displaced from his patriarchal home and denied access to its wealth (Aesch. *Cho.* 275, 301 [277 Hartung]).

Electra, on the other hand, is in limbo. She too is young; she is labeled inexperienced (*apeiron*, Aesch. *Cho.* 118) and seeks advice from the slave women who surround her. She stresses that she is unmarried and living at home (486–8). Since in ancient Greece girls were imagined as like little wild animals,[15] marriage constituted a taming or yoking, the imposition of culture (*damazein, zeugnunai*).[16] Electra is unmarried, thus untamed, and potentially dangerous. While Orestes is allowed to grow up (he has the rest of this play and the sequel to work out his guilt), there is no future whatsoever for Electra. At line 712 her mother sends her inside, and she is never heard from again. This curt dismissal of her after her early prominence suggests that for Electra there can be no progress, and certainly no resolution.

Mourning and melancholy

At the play's opening, Electra has been mourning her father and waiting for her brother for many years. She and the chorus have been sent on a mission by Clytemnestra, to put offerings at Agamemnon's tomb, which would have dominated the stage. Thus, the ritual offerings are prominent. The chorus advises her to reverse the desired discourse and deploy the requested prayer against Aigisthos and Clytemnestra, and for herself and Orestes (111–15). From the first, Electra shows telltale signs of melancholia, and these are clearly related to her gender. While Orestes is in physical exile, Electra is the abjected other within the house. She laments, complaining that she is thrust aside and dishonored, like a dog, worth nothing (444–6); indeed her mourning makes her the object of laughter, she says, and she has to hide her tears (449). Because as a woman she cannot act without her brother, she is fated to mourn; because she lives under the rule of her mother and her lover, her mourning is curtailed. Thus, she seems what Freud would term melancholic.

Suppressed desire for the mother and identification with the masculine

Electra's relationship to her mother is responsible for this melancholy/mourning. Since her mother murdered her father, she violently rejects her mother (her first object of desire in psychoanalytic theory). As a result, her gender identity is conflicted, as well. Her dominant wish is to be more modest and restrained (*sôphronesteran*) than her mother (140). At a slightly later time, she claims to be wolfish (421) and will not let her mother fawn on her, implying that she is in the dog family as well. But her anger will not be softened (*asantos … thumos* 421, 422). It seems clear then that Electra is concerned about her identity as a female, and about how she will turn out. What will genetics mean for her? Or socialization? With Helen and Clytemnestra as examples, how can she grow up into a sexual woman *and* a proper woman, a *gynê*?

In this situation, Electra not only turns from her mother, but she identifies with the male. Her mourning and her tie to her brother are all she has: Orestes is everything to her (235–42); he plays all the family parts. In their famous recognition scene, they are identified with one another: his hair and foot an exact match for hers; any plot against her would be one against him too (172). On the one hand, her dedication to her father and waiting for the brother align her with masculinity. On the other hand, in this version of the story, she gives up all claims to action and exits the scene; in this way, she may be seen to conform to her role as a proper woman.

Electra the unmarried: Sophocles' *Electra*—almost an avenger

Sophocles takes the revenge plot, makes it stand alone, and, most important for my purposes, places emphasis on Electra and the construction of her gender by delaying her recognition of Orestes and by adding scenes with her sister, Chrysothemis, and her mother. Two traditional critical problems—the play's ending and its characterization of Electra—have a tight connection to the representation of gender.[17] Electra is more emphatically liminal in this version, more markedly melancholic, and while her hatred for her mother and heterosexual femininity is stressed, she is more markedly attached to her male relations as well.

Liminal gender

Like the *Choephoroi*, the play opens with the return of Orestes, but instead of staging an immediate reunion between the two, Sophocles defers it.[18] The prologue, then, establishes the division between the siblings (Woodard 1964) and further marks it as gendered: the three men (Orestes, Paidagogos, Pylades), appropriately for men, have come from afar, and they exit without addressing Electra. Their mobility is contrasted with her immobility. Even when Orestes thinks he hears her (Soph. *El.* 80, 86–90), he does not stay to talk to her, departing instead on the explicit advice of the Paidagogos (83–5; cf. Aesch. *Cho.* 20–1) that he put the (male) god's orders first. This discussion draws attention to Electra's plight and to the existence of two worlds: that of men and that of women.[19] Electra is left to lament, while the men plan the action.

While the male avenger delays his return and disguises his presence, Electra is or at any rate feels abandoned. Although in the male–female binary, Electra is strongly marked as female, waiting and wailing, she is prevented from marrying and bearing children, so she has not moved from being a girl to being a full *gunē*. Her lament for herself underlines her anomalous and liminal status. Waiting for Orestes has put her in limbo; she is unmarried and without children (*ateknos, anumpheutos*, Soph. *El.* 164, 165); she repeats this complaint at 185–92 with added details. She emphasizes her virginal status and the fact that she cannot marry (see Ormand 1999). Worn out with her mourning and waiting, without children or man to take her part, she is like an outsider: "as if I were a stranger or settler (*epoikos*) in the bed chambers (*thalamous*) of [her] father" (187–90). Further on, she says she is like a servant in the house (*oikonomô* 190). Thus, her status is definitely marginal—her clothing is shameful (cf. Euripides), and she only gets crumbs from the family table (264–5, 354, 379–82, 597–600, 626–7, 814–15, 911–12, 1181, 1192–6).

Mourning and melancholy

Electra does not merely lament her own condition, of course; she endlessly and appropriately, as she argues, mourns for her father and the shameful way he was murdered.

But never shall I cease my dirges and painful laments, as long as I look on the glittering radiance of the stars and on this light of day; no, like a nightingale who has lost her young, I will cry aloud, for all to hear, sorrows without end before my father's doors. … come, help me, avenge my father's murder and send my brother home to me. For I no longer have the strength to hold up alone against the load of grief that weighs me down.

(March 2001: 103–20)

She claims to conform to the role of the well-born woman (*gunē*), asserting that she is not mad (257); that no one thinking rightly would dissuade her because it is an obligation to mourn one's parents (145–6, 237, especially the father 341–2; see Jebb 1894 on lines 338ff.).[20]

The play offers a conflicting interpretation, however, one that makes her mourning into melancholy. Those around her specifically view her as going too far.[21] The chorus is made up of noble women (*genethla gennaiôn* 129), citizens of the city (*polities* 1227); while they are sympathetic to the plight of the Atreidai (134), they express doubts about Electra's behavior.[22] They ask, "Why do you eternally waste away in this unceasing lament" (*tin' aei takeis hôd' akoreston oimôgan* 122–3); they blame her then for what she offers as reason to pity her (187, cf. 834).[23] The language represents her as insatiable; she cannot get enough of mourning, and she depletes herself in the process. It seems that her grief feeds on her flesh. As her friends and her mother surrogate (234), the chorus seek to restrain her. They urge her to be reasonable;[24] they counsel moderation in mourning (140), and plead with her not to go over into *cholos*, the word for anger that is at the root of melancholy (176). In this view, Electra's behavior is excessive; she brings more suffering on herself (*polu gar ti kakon huperektêsô* 217) than is necessary. Those around her recommend silence (213) and furthermore counsel avoiding fights with the powerful (219–20).

While Electra is positioned by her allies as mourning insatiably, she does so in resistance to the state, which attempts to prohibit her free expression of lament. Electra is not a proper woman, according to Athenian norms. She is outside the doors, speaking to all who come by (109).[25] We are told that Aigisthos keeps her under control; her wandering outside depends on his absence (310–13, 517). Clearly she is under constraints from the authorities (221, 256). Not only is her mourning forbidden, but the sacrilegious celebrations that Clytemnestra conducts on Agamemnon's death day make it impossible to observe it properly (278–81; cf. Aesch. *Cho.* 434–43). Electra has to cry to herself (282–6). In Butler's terms, then, Electra would be a melancholic, denied the opportunity to grieve publicly. In mourning anyway, Electra seems to be an outlaw and in resistance to gender norms.

Femininity rejected

In this play, Electra actively rejects women and veers toward a masculine gender identity. Sophocles emphasizes gender here by introducing a sister, Chrysothemis, who is a law-abiding woman (cf. *Antigone*). The two have a heated debate about Electra's behavior, with Chrysothemis announcing that the powers that be intend to punish her with the fate of a living death (379–82, cf. the fate of Antigone). Chrysothemis claims that she gains freedom because she gives in to power (339), but that seems to mean freedom to be a "normal" Greek woman of her status, to eat well and dress luxuriously (*chlidê* 365), not the freedom to speak out, for she agrees that Electra is morally right (338–9). Here appropriately obedient femininity is aligned with wealth: Chrysothemis has luxurious hair, unlike Electra, whose hair is unattractive since it is "not oiled" (*liparê* 451) and whose *zomê* is unadorned (*ou chlidais* 452, in contrast to Chrysothemis at 365).

She is the feminine to Electra's masculinity or gender indeterminacy, the desirable object as opposed to the abjected other.

In Sophocles, we get to see the daughter's rejection of her mother, as well as her sister; he adds an encounter between mother and daughter which also amplifies Electra's role as a gender non-conformist. The scene opens with Clytemnestra's assertion of the gender norms and male power; yet Electra is not a proper woman; she shames her (debatably) "dear ones" (*philous*) by being outdoors (516–18).[26] From Clytemnestra's point of view, the problem is one of male identification. Electra cares about nothing but her father (cf. Electra's accusation that Chrysothemis favors her mother [341–5]). Electra chooses the heroic path of the male over attachment to her sister and mother. She would like to replace her "dead" brother and overthrow the despots (she calls her mother *despotin* [597]), but she is aware that she lacks the strength (604–5); as a girl/woman, and without her sister's help, she cannot be an active partner in the overthrow of the tyrannical regime. Yet Electra comes very close to taking on the man's role and acting without a man's help. And even though she defers to Orestes' leadership when he does finally disclose himself to her, she participates in the killing by calling on Orestes to strike their mother a second time (1415).

The queer threads of melancholy and gender non-conformity come together in Electra's painful relationship to her mother. She argues that she has experienced hubristic behavior and returned it; she has been reviled, so she reviles. Electra's situation is an exaggeration of what psychoanalysis would call the requisite denial of the original desire for the mother (see above, pp. 214–15). She has vigorous contempt for her sister and her mother and in both cases her hatred has to do with their sexuality (on Clytemnestra, 255–80). In Aeschylus, Electra prays to be more modest than her mother; in Sophocles, living with Clytemnestra has taught her shamelessness (*anaideias* 607, 607–9). But she is capable of feeling shame, *pace* Clytemnestra (612–15, 622–3, 625), at the thought of turning out like her mother. Electra says "I am ashamed, (*aischunên*); I do feel it [shame], even if I do not seem to; I know that I act unseasonably (*exôra prassô*) and not like myself" (*emoi proseikota* 616–18). Thus she poses the question of what is her real identity. Electra's trauma has worn her down and made her who she is in the present. Her disavowal of her mother's behavior, then, reveals the conflict she is placed in as a mourning Greek daughter. She cannot simply blithely accept her role as rebel, nor can she assume the identity of a traditional married woman.

Thus far we have seen that Electra has been put in a liminal space, condemned to melancholy (in Freud's sense of incomplete mourning and in the sense that she is prevented from mourning as she would like). She has pushed the boundary of femaleness as far as she can—wandering outside the house, complaining to all who pass by, contesting her sister's and mother's choices.

Electra's revenge and masculinization

She has some limited success in her resistance. Her continuing lamentation is represented as a revenge action (*pace* Burnett 1998: 121–3). It pains the rulers (*lupô toutous*) and thus gives honor to the dead (355–7; see Kitzinger 1991: 309 on speech act). Furthermore, she persuades the chorus that she is right (251–3). More importantly, she dissuades Chrysothemis from making offerings for Clytemnestra. At the end of their first debate she gets Chrysothemis to turn Clytemnestra's apotropaic prayer into a prayer for the children. Her steadiness of purpose is contagious: Chrysothemis leaves the stage with the exhortation "be bold" (*tolmêsein*) ringing in the audience's ears (471). Electra has won an ally for the time being.

Other effects are implicit. As a result of her complaints, the queen must speak in code when she makes her offerings (637–8), and she fears Electra's tongue, lest it run throughout the city

(642). Thus, her mourning has political ramifications—it extends to the polis.[27] It seems that, as in *Antigone*, there might be a political movement around this dissident girl since she must be sent out of the land before being entombed (Jebb 1894 on lines 380ff.).

Sophocles, as is often noted, has deferred the recognition between brother and sister, further isolating Electra. When she believes that Orestes is dead, she then goes further toward revenge action, and an avowed masculinity. Sophocles again underlines the factor of gender by adding another scene with Chrysothemis. This time the two women exchange insults and finally break off along the lines of masculine and feminine gender performance (cf. Antigone and Ismene, Soph. *Ant.* 917). Electra wants Chrysothemis to be her ally in active revenge. She argues that they are similarly deprived of the wealth of the house (960), fated to remain unmarried and without marriage bed (*alektra, anumenaia* 962, cf. 164–5 of Electra), and as a result, they will not have children as long as Aigisthos lives (965–6).

Moreover, she claims that by taking revenge they will win praise for their piety (*eusebeia*) from their dead father and their brother (968–9); a good name, worthy of their status as free women (970); and noble marriages (971–2). The implicit glory is made explicit at 973: they will win great reputation (*eukleian*) if Chrysothemis is persuaded by Electra to kill Aigisthos. All the citizens and the strangers too will welcome them with praise (976), recognizing that they have saved their father's house (977). They will say that, without thought for their own lives, the two women dealt blood to their enemies (979–80).

Of course, this is contradictory behavior for women in fifth-century BCE Athens. Winning glory and good reputation through killing one's mother is not feminine behavior and surely not calculated to win great marriages. Completing the revenge themselves would clearly identify the girls as manly; thus, Electra uses the word "*andreias*" (983) when "quoting" what will be said of them. The description of the glory they will achieve goes beyond the norms for women, as Chrysothemis makes clear when she says that "you are a woman, not a man" (997); she first promises to help as far as she has the strength to do so (946), but she becomes afraid when she sees Electra arming herself, behaving like a hoplite (996); she reminds her that they do not have the strength of those opposing them (998). Chrysothemis sees her sister as foolish and once again advises controlling her temper (*orgê*) and giving in to those in power. But Electra will not live by such norms (1043), which are gender norms—she sends Chrysothemis inside, explicitly rejecting her feminine sister (cf. Ismene and Antigone, see Honig 2011).[28] In her desire for heroism, then, Electra seems masculine.[29]

Recognition of the self in the brother

The delay also heightens the emotion and underlines the incestuousness of the baroque recognition scene (which is doubly queer given Electra's performance of masculinity). When Orestes gives Electra the urn containing "his" ashes, her previous death wish is transformed into a suggestively incestuous desire for the brother: he is all to her, and when she sees the urn, she says she would like to lie with him in it (1164 ff.).[30] She will not give up the urn because of what it holds; it is her most precious possession (1208). He is the offspring of the "best beloved of bodies" (or corpses, *sômatôn* 1232–3).

The scene between the two of them when he makes himself known to her recapitulates the gendered dynamic of the rest of the play. She is not a "real" woman: her body is wasted (dishonorably and godlessly); he mourns her unmarried and ill-fated life. Then, she is both feminine and masculine. She heroically rescued and sent Orestes away (masculine) (321); but the act was also life-giving and defined as maternal (feminine) (1130–42). Her unfeminine body is later associated with very feminine emotion. Orestes and the Paidagogos both try to restrain her free expression of emotion.[31] When Orestes tries to silence her with a warning about Aigisthos and Clytemnestra, she says she will not fear the "women" inside (1242); he reminds her that she should know well that women can be warlike within (1243–4). Thus, gender performance is pointed out and rendered highly ambiguous.[32]

How does the ending fit with this non-normative play? In order to lure Aigisthos into the house and to his death, Electra says sardonically that "my part is complete" (*teleitai tap' emou* 1464) and that she has learned her lesson, presumably to obey the powerful (1465).[33] The word translated here as "complete" implies ritual accomplishment, as does the last line of the play (1510).[34] My reading argues strongly that there is no end or no conclusion for this Electra. She must remain outside while the men go within. She cannot participate in the *oikos*, which would be the woman's place, but she also cannot escape it. In Sophocles, Electra still has no place. She is between genders and without recognized sexuality. In Strauss' *Elektra*, with a libretto by Hofmannsthal, she dances herself to death. Perhaps they have it right.[35]

Euripides' *Electra*: The married virgin

Liminal gender

Euripides' *Electra* retains some of the queer elements I have been working with thus far. In this version, Aigisthos has chosen to marry Electra off to a safely non-aristocratic husband, having originally kept her in his house and away from any bridegroom (*hêrmoze numphiôi*, Eur. *El.* 23–4). This change does not, however, mitigate her liminal status; it rather exacerbates it. She is clearly labeled a wife (*damarta* 35), and Orestes has heard that she is married and so no longer a *parthenos* (99). But in contradiction, her "husband" stresses that that she is still a *parthenos* and that he has never shamed her in bed (*eunêi* 44); she is untouched (51, 254–7, 270–1, 945–6, 1284 cf. 99). Her marriage is like death (247) because it is chaste (255).[36]

Her status is contradictory, married but a maiden still. As is typical of this heroine, she is associated with a chorus of women, but they serve to underline her liminal status. They invite her to celebrate the *partheneia* for Hera with other women, "the brides (*numphais*) of Argos" (179).[37] She rejects their invitation because she does not have the appropriate attire (175–85); Euripides thus emphasizes her isolation (Zeitlin 1970: esp. 647). Her anomalous role is explicitly at stake in her shame since she notes her discomfort at being a virgin among married women at the festival (311). She continues to refuse the community they extend to her even when they take a pragmatic approach and offer to lend her the appropriate attire and adornment (*aglaia* 192; on her clothing, see also 304–13).

Like the other Electras, Euripides' heroine is de-feminized by her mourning: her body is *xeron*, wasting away with suffering (239), and her hair, cut in mourning (241), would be masculine in appearance. These markers refer not only to her dedication to the dead, but also to her lack of sexual activity. Her contradictory gender construction is also very much at issue. Moreover, she receives explicit instructions in gender norms. Electra is exhorted to be a proper woman when her "husband" says it is shameful for her to be standing among young men (*aischron* 344) and tells her to "Go inside, there is much that a woman can find to fix a meal" (421–3). In contrast, she explicitly notes the masculinity required of Orestes: he must live up to his father's warlike behavior (cf. the ending of the choral song [432–86], where Clytemnestra's adultery is mentioned in contrast with the warrior status of the prince it killed [480–1]). After the children's reunion, when Orestes departs to find Aigisthos, Electra admonishes him to be a man (*andra* 693).

Mourning and melancholy

Electra's problematic gender construction is related to her mourning. We could say that she is a melancholy heterosexual. Euripides takes her away from the daily insults that Sophocles' Electra received from Clytemnestra, and he thus makes her continued suffering more a matter of her own choice. For instance, she complains that she performs physical labor, such as carrying the water herself from the stream (55–6, 309); she later says that she weaves her own clothing (307–8). Her husband points out that the water-carrying in particular is not necessary (64–5), and in this way it is like her self-exclusion from ritual. Thus, she seems almost to relish her suffering.

Her mourning is implicitly melancholic because needlessly long.[38] As in Sophocles, her mourning is extended by the absence of Orestes (330), and it is similarly circumscribed (320–2). It is intensified by the desecration of Agamemnon's grave by Aigisthos' dance and insults (326–9). She correlates her suffering with her father's (300–1), and then sends this weird message to Orestes: "Many send this message, I, its interpreter (hermêneus), these hands, this tongue, and this wretched mind, my shorn head, and he who begot him" (332–5). Electra's self-indulgent suffering, her fractured body, and identitification with Agamemnon all imply that her mourning verges into melancholy.

Electra's revenge and masculinization

The revenge action as a whole underlines both the norms of gender and their subversion (Michelini 1987: 228–30). First, Electra identifies with her brother in his attack on Aigisthos. If he dies, being outwrestled, then she too is dead (686–7). Second, she is divided from the other more womanly women—they will stand guard and cry out, but she will actually hold a sword. And she asserts, like a hero, that if she is not victorious, she will not allow her body to be desecrated (sôm'emon kathubrisai 698).

Electra displays improper femininity and even masculinity when Orestes gives her the corpse of Aigisthos and encourages her to insult it. Gender makes up an important part of her attack on the dead king; he arranged her deathly marriage (911). He somehow avoided fighting in the war (917), and he is effeminate (948), as is typical of Aigisthos (see Cropp 1988 on these lines). Furthermore, the gender structure of his marriage to Clytemnestra is the subject of gossip among the Argives, who say that the man is the woman's, not vice versa ("O tês gunaikos—ouchi tandros hê gunê" 931). They find it shameful for the woman to run things, for the children to take their name from the mother, and for him to take her fortune (932–7).[39] As a maiden (945) Electra says that she cannot speak of Aigisthos' exploits with women, but she does so cryptically nonetheless: he committed hubris (947), and the implication is that he was able to do so because he had a royal house and good looks (947–8), which Electra disdains as "maidenly" and not "manly" (949; see Mossman 2001).[40]

In the preamble to the murder of Clytemnestra, this Orestes articulates his dilemma; he considers his mother the one who bore and nurtured him and doubts that it can be right to kill her (964–71; cf. Ag. Cho. 899, 908–9). Electra, not Pylades, urges him on with the threat of cowardice and "unmanliness" (982). Crucially, Clytemnestra will be called to her death with the pretense that Electra has had a male child (656–7); that is, the virginal wife performs the role of mother in this deceitful plot. Euripides emphasizes the femaleness of her situation by having her attract her mother with this ruse of childbirth.

But Electra is simultaneously more violent. In the killing, she takes on the most active and masculine role of all three versions, for she actually participates. She furthermore takes responsibility for the act: "I am to blame; I was the one who burned against this mother who bore me as a daughter" (1182–4). Euripides has the chorus say that she did terrible things to her brother who was not willing (1204–5, see above, on 964–7). Electra later repeats that she did terrible things (1224–6). Tellingly in this gender confusion, Orestes becomes feminine, veils himself from the sight of his mother's body (1221),[41] while Electra becomes more masculine and seizes the sword (1225). But their responses are also somewhat appropriately gendered in another way: he asks what city or what house will have him; he cannot stay,[42] whereas she wonders about marriage and what chorus, what dance, she will participate in (1198–1200) (also noted by Ormand 2009: 251). Thus at the end she is back to where she was at the beginning when she could not participate in the ritual with the other women.

The heterosexual imperative

Whatever disruption to gender roles has been implied, the return to non-incestuous hetero-normativity is explicit in the conclusion to this play. The Dioskouroi arrive (Castor was mentioned earlier as a potential groom for Electra) and provide closure. They tell Orestes to give Electra to Pylades (1249); thus the exchange of the woman avoids the incestuous attachment of the pair and gets her out of the household, where her Sophoclean avatar is stuck. Pylades agrees to take Electra, who is both maiden and wife (*korê te kai damart'* 1284).

This restoration of order is tenuous at best, however. The marriage to Pylades arranged at the end is completely perfunctory; the sister and brother experience deep suffering at their separation. Orestes grieves leaving her, and the sentence structure emphasizes their identity: *kai s'apoleipso sou leipomenos* (1310). The gods point out that her fate is not so bad—she at least has a husband and a home. But Electra is not satisfied with that fate: the loss of her real home is grievous (1314–15). Her attachment to Orestes is reiterated in language of identity: "breast to breast" (*sterna … sterna* 1321); he bids her wrap herself around his body and sing a dirge for him as on a tomb (1326). Thus, for these two, parting is equivalent to death. His final farewell to Pylades includes another reference to the body of Electra with a word that can also mean corpse ("Marry the *demas Elektras*" 1340–1).

Euripides' *Orestes*: An imaginary (queer?) interlude

Euripides' *Orestes* (408) is arguably the strangest of the plays. It introduces events following the matricide and includes a trial by the Argives, hostage taking, and the threat of more murder and mayhem. The action gets wilder and wilder, madder and madder, adding more and more characters and elements, before once more returning to the path set out by tradition. As editor and translator M. L. West says, "*Orestes* almost goes 'over the top,' with touches of self-commentary and self-parody" (1987: 27). The play shows the effect of the matricide on Orestes, not externalized in the Furies but internalized and embodied as illness. Whereas we have a potentially deranged Electra in the *Electra* plays, here we have an Orestes with a disordered mind. While *Libation Bearers* resolves into the *Eumenides* and an elaborate ritual and trial, leading to the establishment of a court at Athens, *Orestes* shows the failure of the civic order and spins off into increasingly irrational violence. The traditional mythic solution (marriage) seems more unnatural, more forced, than ever. Orestes goes from holding a knife to Hermione's throat to agreeing to marry her.

Gender norms

Electra is once again unmarried and childless (Eur. *Or.* 206). While this complaint might seem irrelevant in the play's context, where they are facing a death sentence from the Argives, the passage makes clear that she is still concerned with the sexual consequences of her mourning and revenge. She emphasizes her birth from an abhorrent mother, and points out that her maidenhood prevents her from speaking (*parthenôi* 26, cf. 108, 282) of her mother's (sexual) motives. Her appropriate behavior is discussed: she claims that her participation in the vengeance was according to what was suitable for a woman (*gunê* 32); later, Orestes instructs her not to be like the evil daughters of Tyndareus (251–2).

Electra shows some of her earlier masculinity in this play; her manliness (1204–6, cf. Soph. *El.* 1242) is indicated, but it is specifically correlated to an embodied form of femininity. When Orestes thinks they will all die, he says: "Oh you who possess a manly heart/mind (*phrenas arsenas* 1204), a body outstanding in womanliness among women (*en gunaixi thêleiais*), how worthy you are to live not to die. Pylades, such a woman will you be deprived of, or if she is living, her bed will make you blessed" (1205–8). Her manly spirit in her woman's body makes her a suitable wife for a hero like Pylades; their marriage is further emphasized in 1210: "May that happen, and may she come into the city of the Phocians deemed worthy of fair wedding songs."

Incest

Because Euripides stages Electra and Orestes after they have killed their mother, their almost incestuous love is placed in high relief. The situation underlines their intimacy: they are alone together for much of the first episode (Electra tries to dismiss the chorus because they disturb Orestes' rest at 170; 305–6), and his illness is a catalyst for much physical closeness since she is nursing him. Their desire for one another, implicit in the other versions, seems more overt here. Their reciprocity is revealed through the use of repeated terms—brother/sister (222), side to side (223)—and their parallel actions (marked by the repetition of *hotan* (296, 298)) fit their relationship of *philia* (298–300; see Willink 1986: 134–5, on lines 299–300). In facing death, Electra underlines her dependence on him: as a woman there is no life for her without him (309–10).

In the penultimate scene, after the death sentence has been pronounced, the siblings' relationship is a bit more testy, but it is still intimate and erotic. Orestes is afraid that her tears will rub off on him and unman him, make him melt away: *anandrian* 1031, *m'etêxas* 1047. Electra wants Orestes to kill her; when he refuses, she chooses the sword and wants the same sword to kill them both and wants to be buried with him (1052–3). She clings to him passionately and wants to put her arms around his neck. Although he calls such an embrace an empty pleasure, he gives in, and asks why he should be ashamed to hug her (1048). He compares their loving death to a marriage bed (1050).

Pylades, who has one line in Aeschylus and is not present at all in Sophocles, here takes on an expanded role; he claims a part in the murder, while Electra's role in the murder is also deepened (1236, 1237—she puts her hand to the sword, while Pylades urges Orestes on). His presence adds a note of homoeroticism. He replaces Electra to some extent as the support for the invalid (e.g. 1015–17) and does many of the things that she had done as caregiver; their friendship is, at least in the second century, construed as homoerotic, as specified by Lucian in the *Erotes*.[43] That intense closeness also troubles the brother–sister bond. Orestes and Pylades do not tell Electra they are going to the citizens lest she shed ill-omened tears (787–8). It also reinscribes her femininity; Orestes silences her with impatience, calling her wailing "womanish" (1022). When the men get together, then, the woman is excluded. Thus, the norms of gender are reinforced through the dynamics of male friendship.

The imposition of heterosexuality

In this context, it is significant that Pylades' place as Electra's husband is emphasized. Given the intense tie to Orestes, perhaps we can see here an example of the kind of exchange of women that Eve Sedgwick first theorized in *Between Men* (1985). Electra would then function as a way for the men to remain connected. At the same time, Pylades might be seen as a way for her to marry her brother, since he is little more than Orestes' alter ego.[44] The reimposition of hetero-normativity is even more tendentious in this play than it was in Euripides' *Electra*, for it includes the marriage of Hermione to Orestes; the plot has involved taking her hostage, since Helen has disappeared, and threatening Menelaus with her death. Apollo intervenes: he will set right Orestes' relationship to the city (*thêso kalôs*), since he ordained that he kill his mother (1664). At the same time, he arranges his marriage to Hermione: "I release you from murder (1761) and I approve her marriage bed, whenever her father gives her." At the moment of his speaking, however, Orestes has Hermione by the throat and is ready to kill her. This quick switch from threatened murder to marriage seems almost laughable to the modern reader.

Conclusion?

At this point, I wish I had an Apollo or the Dioskouroi to come and set it all right. I have tried to show what can happen when you look at Electra's several incarnations from the perspective of work in queer theory. First, it reveals the gender ambiguity of Electra—leading us to look at her as an example of a girl who is pressed to develop manliness through mourning for her father but who is then like a woman all dressed up with nowhere to go. She is on the margins, not quite a woman, but not a girl. Then, we have seen that her gender is bound up with her mourning, which is sometimes viewed as self-indulgent and excessive, thus appearing to be a form of melancholy. As in activism around grief in our own times, her mourning has political effects (especially in Sophocles and Euripides). Her resistance to the powers that be and her political fight against the tyrants are reminiscent of the emergence of queer activism out of death and loss. Finally, this perspective has led me to look at Electra's rejection of her mother and her overblown or incestuous love of her father and brother as somehow connected and constructing a queer subtext. All of these, her gender ambiguity, her melancholy, her aggressive disavowal of femininity (both mother and sister in Sophocles), and her excessive attachment to her father and brother make her a potentially disruptive figure.

In antiquity some versions of the myth give Electra short shrift (Aeschylus); some condemn her to life on the outside of the house (Sophocles), and some, like Euripides, re-inscribe her in the norms of femininity through the enforcement of a marriage to her brother's best friend. It will take a modern version of the play to develop the active resistance of this non-normative heroine.

Notes

Special thanks to my co-editors and Barbara Gold and Walter Penrose Jr for their careful reading of this essay, to my students who found Electra so unpleasant that I decided I had to work on her, and to research assistant Caroline Grunewald and the librarians at Hamilton College. Translations from the Greek are my own, except where otherwise noted, and are to the Oxford Classical Texts.

1 Jan Bremmer calls mourning "her trademark" (Bremer 1994: 113; see also Kitzinger 1991).
2 On women's homoeroticism in Classics, see, for instance, Brooten 1996; Rabinowitz and Auanger 2002; Boehringer 2007. There is an extensive literature, mostly from the 1990s, on the difference between the terms "gay and lesbian" and "queer." For example, Teresa de Lauretis's introduction to a special issue of the journal *differences* uses both: "Queer Theory: Lesbian and Gay Sexualities," defining her use of the word "queer" to refer to the resistance offered by gay and lesbian sexualities (de Lauretis 1991: iii), as well as to "mark a certain critical distance from the latter [lesbian and gay], by now established and often convenient, formula" (iv). Judith Butler (1997a) moves back and forth between the terms. See Crimp 2002: esp. 192–3 on queer theory's "break with earlier lesbian and gay studies." By offering a more capacious umbrella, "queer" has political advantages for the formation of a coalition

of individuals oppressed in different ways through their sexuality or gender expression (for a more detailed working out of this discourse, see Rabinowitz 2002b).

3 I am especially indebted to the work of Judith Butler on Antigone, whom she calls "not quite a queer heroine" (2000: 72). She argues that "Antigone does emblematize a certain heterosexual fatality that remains to be read" (2000: 72). In addition to Butler on Antigone and melancholy, see Taxidou 2004: 20–1.

4 For general considerations of the three (sometimes four) Electras, see the introductions of Kamerbeek 1974, Jebb 1894, March 2001, Kells 1973, Denniston 1939, and to a lesser extent West 1987 and Cropp 1988; Aelion 1983: 11–61. For Sophocles as antithesis to Euripides, see Michelini: 1987: 185. For the reception of three Electras, see Bakogianni 2011. On the revenge motif, see Burnett 1998; McHardy 2008: 103–12.

5 Historically after Solon, women's lament was limited because their voices raised in public were dangerous since they might lead to vendettas (Alexiou 1974; Foley 2001: 21–55, with further bibliography). On lamentation and women's role especially in tragedy, see Seremetakis 1991; Holst-Warhaft 1992, 2000; Seaford 1994; Blok 2001: 104–9; Foley 2001: 21–55; McClure 2001; Taxidou 2004: 8–9, 88–9; Dué 2006; for a recent summary see Dué 2012.

6 Freud 1957: 244; on pleasure and mourning in Electra, see Honig 2010: 9; on melancholy and trauma, see Griffiths 2011.

7 See Halberstadt-Freud 1998: 41–3 for the importance of the desire for the mother for feminist psychoanalytic critics. See also Irigaray 1985: 66–73.

8 The resistance she offers may account for her unpopularity. See Goldhill 2012: 201, noting that "At some juncture, as the Victorian nineteenth century turned into the twentieth century of modernism, the figure of Sophocles' Electra changed from a sympathetic, tender, loving, constant heroine into an over-emotional, murderous, disturbed woman, violently perverted by her own hatred." On the unattractive Euripidean Electra, see Ormand 2009: 253, and n. 28 below. Cf. Michelini 1987: esp. 3–19, on the way that the classical ideal affected the judgment of Euripides.

9 Her role as mourner has been discussed, for instance by Foley 2001: 145–71; on the importance of her female gender, see Woodard 1964 [1965], 1966; on the dialectic of word and deed see Gellie 1972; Kitzinger 1991; Wheeler 2003.

10 Electra is always a *parthenos*, even in Euripides where she is married (Ormand 1999; March 2001: 151 on lines 164–5, Jebb 1894: xix–xx on her name from *alektros* [citing Ael. *Var. Hist.* 4.26]; Kamerbeek 1974: 2). On prolonged maidenhood and disease, Pl. *Tim* 91c, Hippocr. *Nature of the Child* 4; *On Women* 3–4; King 1983: 111–17, 2005: 157–8, as ideology 159; Demand 1994: 95–8. See Wheeler 2003, also Penrose 2006. Marriage and motherhood was prescribed as a cure for the "erotic fascination with death" (King 1998: 78); when Electra is married she only plays at being a mother in Euripides.

11 We might take that plot element as the kind of routing of male desire through a woman analysed by Sedgwick 1985.

12 I will treat Sophocles and Euripides as branches from the Aeschylean trunk without debating the priority of one or the other.

13 On the tyrannicide motif, see Juffras 1991.

14 For an early treatment of this motif, see Winnington-Ingram 1948; Zeitlin 1978 [1996].

15 Young Iphigeneia is a goat, Aesch. *Ag.* 232; other animals, Ar. *Lys.* 1308; Soph. *Ant.* 477–8; on coming of age, see King 1983: 111–12, 1998: 76–7; Sourvinou-Inwood 1988; Dowden 1989: 9–48, esp. 26–32; Demand 1994: 102–20, esp. 112, contra Faraone 2003.

16 On marriage as constraint in the Persephone myth, see Parca and Tzanetou 2007: 3–4.

17 Jebb 1894: xxxii–xlii emphasizes the epic conception of the play, and its Homeric "colouring" (xli)— concluding that the vengeance is unproblematic; he does question whether "Athenians, familiar with the lyric and the dramatic *Oresteia*, … [would] feel that the story, as told by Sophocles, reached a true conclusion." Denniston 1939: xxiv asserts that the audience of the Sophoclean *Electra* would find "no suggestion that the matricide raises any moral problem at all"; Whitman 1951: 159–63; Gellie 1972: 130 thinks the audience reacts "to both the good spirits and the matricide"; Kells 1973, 1986 disagrees with the cheerful reading; Winnington-Ingram 1980: 246 calls it "a grim play"; Segal 1981: 249 points out that after the *Oresteia*, one could not forget about the punishment; March 2001: 15–20 is on the side of a brighter interpretation; Wright 2005 on the debate and for a dark reading.

18 Foley 2001: ch. 3.2 on the differences in the ways they handle revenge and vendetta.

19 Woodard 1964; cf. Kitzinger 1991: 302–5 who sees the prologue as revealing two kinds of speech, 302, n. 13; Gellie 1972: esp. 108–9; 116–17; Segal 1981: esp. 250, 249–91 offers a structuralist reading

based on opposites; Burnett 1998: 121–32; McCoskey 2009: 224; Dué 2012: 241–6 on lament and women's speech.

20 Whitman 1951: 156 marvels that critics have found Chrysothemis "fundamentally right" "though weak."

21 In the scholarship her excessive mourning is held against her; as a character in Sophocles and Euripides she is often seen as "too extreme, too unpleasant" (Conacher 1967: 201, citing Kitto; Michelini 1987: 187, n. 23 with further references; Goldhill 2012: 201–30). This fits with one of the major discussion points about the Sophocles: what is its position on the matricide (see above, n. 17)? Perhaps critics do not like the disruption of norms any more than did the ancients (cf. Michelini 1987: 188 who sees the negative view of Euripides' *Electra* resulting from "generic" problems).

22 See Gardiner (1987: 141–2, 142 n. 10 for other sources) on chorus. Gardiner thinks that there is a conspiracy of men matched by one of women (1987: 146), which is dissolved when Chrysothemis exits after the sisters' second confrontation (1987: 153). Cf. Burton 1980: 186–8. On the question of citizenry in both Electra plays, see Ormand 2009.

23 Gardiner points out that this is a question, and she argues that it does not "imply rebuke" (1987: 143). I would say that it indicates her excess and self-willed suffering.

24 On her character and the quality of reason, see Burton 1980: 186; on reason as an element in the portrayal of a tragic hero, see Knox 1964: 13–15, 19–26. It is on this point of excess that I find students are often entirely unsympathetic to Electra.

25 Speaking outside is typically forbidden to women in Athens (the classic statement is Pericles' in Thuc. 2.45.2), though not in other Greek cities, e.g. Sparta (Pomeroy 2002: 9).

26 March 2001: 174 on lines 516–18 on the relationship between mother and daughter implied here and the gender norms underlying her criticism.

27 Burton 1980: 186 takes the chorus as possibly married to citizen men who are in opposition.

28 They are also the norms for anyone who is the weaker, thus they have conservative political import: do not stand up for what you believe in unless you are guaranteed a victory. While the play does not make Electra an entirely sympathetic character—the chorus and Chrysothemis seem saner—in the end, the chorus comes around and praises her (1089, 1095). Like Antigone, Electra is most decidedly not a woman-identified woman, not filled with love or desire for her sister (*pace* Strauss' *Elektra* where she almost seems to make love to her); she has energetically turned away from both women in her life.

29 On masculine toughness and feminine capacity to love, see Gellie 1972: 120.

30 Lyons 2012: 105–9; Gellie 1972: 116 refers to her "tormented feminine introversions" replaced by a "spacious and shadowless world of colour and movement" when Orestes enters.

31 Cf. Gardiner 1987: 156 sees this as reasonable, not cold.

32 Cf. Gellie 1972: 125 who sees her as "the woman you can't shut up"; McCoskey 2009: 233 on the masculinity of revenge and subordination of Electra; Burnett 1998: 120.

33 Kells 1986: 153–5 discusses staging and concludes by saying " … if you try to *stage* the play on either of the conventional assumptions, *you have no ending*." That is what I am arguing happens to Electra (Goldhill 2012: 20). Cf. Jebb 1894 and Gellie 1972, e.g., who take the ending as the text saying "The End" (Gellie 1972: 129); Jebb 1894: 203 on line 1510, sees "no presage of trouble to come," though in the introduction he allows for ambiguity in the audience response (xlii).

34 Some find the ending a simple vindication of the children (March 2001: 15–20 with bibliography); Gardiner does not find the ending exulting (1987: 159–60); Gellie 1972: 130 believes that "Electra [is] living with her own brand of Furies." Dunn 2012: 109 argues that the ending suggests that "the drama of Electra's personality is complete." McCoskey 2009: 242, n. 38 hypothesizes that the audience might think of the mythic marriage to Pylades, remarking that it would be a "personification of the banality that awaits her." Goldhill 2012: 17–21 argues that it must at least pose questions for the audience.

35 On the dominance of the Strauss-Hofmannsthal version of Electra in later performances, see Goldhill 2012: 201.

36 Zeitlin 1970: 650, nn. 21, 22 on references to marriage to death; on the effects of sexual inactivity, see Hipp. *Mul.* 1.2. Cf. Cropp 1988: 102 on line 44. Grube 1941: 303 calls her "a woman whose desire for revenge has through continuous brooding become a completely self-centred obsession!"; he further (313) sees her in the end as "hysterical and half-crazed."

37 On the importance of the ritual, see Zeitlin 1970; Ormand 2009: 253–4, 268.

38 This is a point that is debated in the scholarship and relevant to her gender performance. See O'Brien 1964: 28; Zeitlin 1970. Conacher 1967: 205 on self-martyrdom; Michelini 1987: 189–93 defends Electra from these charges because she has been denied her status; she sees her as "hopelessly alienated from the heroic world by the wrong she has suffered" (1987: 227).

39 Conacher 1967: 207 makes much of her bitterness and concern for "her own outcast situation" as compared to the "nobler motives which animate Sophocles' Electra." She is refused the possibility of making a "sympathetic impression" (208).

40 In the end, Mossman 2001: 384 argues that perhaps the polarity of male/female was not as distinct as we often claim it to have been. It might be challenged as well as maintained here. I would agree.

41 O'Brien 1964: 17–18 makes the connection to the gorgon; Cropp 1988: 180 on line 1221 points out that the image might refer not only to Perseus (citing Headlam, *Classical Review* 15, 1901: 99).

42 Cf. Sophocles where there is no doubt expressed, and like Aeschylus where he is also pursued by Erinyes.

43 On male friendship, see Chapter 29, Boyarin, this volume; Halperin 1990: 75–87, on the relationship of such friendships to kinship structure, in particular siblings, on homoeroticism as a later lens, 86–87.

44 Kamerbeek 1974: 22 on lines 15, 16 also calls him that in Sophocles.

Bibliography

Aelion, R. (1983) *Euripide: Héritier d'Eschyle*, vol. 1. Paris: Belles Lettres.

Alexiou, M. (1974) *Ritual Lament in Greek Tradition*. Cambridge: Cambridge University Press.

Bakogianni, A. (2011) *Electra Ancient and Modern: Aspects of the Tragic Heroine's Reception*. London: Institute of Classical Studies.

Blok, J. (2001) "Virtual voices: Toward a choreography of women's speech in classical Athens", in A. Lardinois and L. McClure (eds) *Making Silence Speak: Women's Voices in Greek Literature and Society*. Princeton, NJ: Princeton University Press, pp. 95–116.

Boehringer, S. (2007) *L'homosexualité dans l'antiquité grecque et romaine*. Paris: Belles lettres.

Bremer, J.M. (1994) "A daughter fatally blocked: Von Hofmannsthal's *Elektra*", in H. Hillenaar and W. Schonau (eds) *Fathers and Mothers in Literature*. Amsterdam: Rodopi, pp. 113–21.

Brooten, B. (1996) *Love between Women: Early Christian Responses to Female Homoeroticism*, Chicago Series on Sexuality, History, and Society. Chicago, IL: University of Chicago Press.

Burnett, A. (1998) *Revenge in Attic and Later Tragedy*. Berkeley, CA: University of California Press.

Burton, R. (1980) *The Chorus in Sophocles' Tragedies*. Oxford: Clarendon Press.

Butler, J. (1990) *Gender Trouble: Feminism and the Subversion of Identity*. New York: Routledge.

——(1997a) "Against proper objects", in E. Weed and N. Schor (eds) *Feminism Meets Queer Theory*. Bloomington, IN: Indiana University Press, pp. 1–30.

——(1997b) *The Psychic Life of Power: Theories in Subjection*. Stanford, CA: Stanford University Press.

——(2000) *Antigone's Claim: Kinship between Life and Death*. New York: Columbia University Press.

Conacher, D.M. (1967) *Euripidean Drama: Myth, Theme and Structure*. Toronto, ON: University of Toronto Press.

Crimp, D. (2002) *Melancholia and Moralism: Essays on AIDS and Queer Politics*. Cambridge, MA: MIT Press.

Cropp, M. (1988) *Euripides: Electra*, with trans. and commentary. Warminster: Aris & Phillips.

de Lauretis, T. (1991) "Queer theory: Lesbian and gay sexualities", *Differences: A Journal of Feminist Cultural Studies* 3: iii–xviii.

Demand, N. (1994) *Birth, Death, and Motherhood in Classical Greece*. Baltimore, MD: Johns Hopkins University Press.

Denniston, J.D. (ed.) (1939) *Euripides: Electra*. Oxford: Oxford University Press.

Dodds, D.B. (2003) "Adolescent initiation in myth and tragedy: Rethinking the black hunter", in D. Dodd and C. Faraone (eds) *Initiation in Ancient Greek Rituals and Narratives: New Critical Perspectives*. London and New York: Routledge, pp. 71–84.

Dowden, K. (1989) *Death and the Maiden*. New York: Routledge.

Dué, C. (2006) *The Captive Woman's Lament in Greek Tragedy*. Austin, TX: University of Texas Press.

——(2012) "Lament as speech act in Sophocles", in K. Ormand (ed.) *Companion to Sophocles*. Malden, MA: Wiley-Blackwell, pp. 236–50.

Dunn, F. (2012) "Electra", in K. Ormand (ed.) *Companion to Sophocles*. Malden, MA: Wiley-Blackwell, pp. 98–110.

Faraone, C. (2003) "Playing the bear and the fawn for Artemis: Female initiation or substitute sacrifice?", in D. Dodd and C. Faraone (eds) *Initiation in Ancient Greek Rituals and Narratives: New Critical Perspectives*. London and New York: Routledge, pp. 43–68.

Foley, H. (2001) *Female Acts in Greek Tragedy*. Princeton, NJ: Princeton University Press.

Freud, S. (1957 [1917, 1915]) "Mourning and melancholia", in J. Strachey and A. Freud (eds) *The Standard Edition of the Complete Psychological Works of Sigmund Freud*, vol. 14. London: Hogarth Press.

Gardiner, C. (1987) *The Sophoclean Chorus: A Study of Character and Function.* Iowa City, IA: University of Iowa Press.

Gellie, G.H. (1972) *Sophocles: A Reading.* Melbourne, VIC: Melbourne University Press.

Goldhill, S. (2012) *Sophocles and the Language of Tragedy.* New York: Oxford University Press.

Griffiths, J. (2011) "The abject *eidos*: Trauma and the body in Sophocles' *Electra*", in J. Parker and T. Parker (eds) *Tradition, Translation, Trauma: The Classic and the Modern.* Oxford: Oxford University Press, pp. 229–43.

Grube, G.M.A. (1941) *The Drama of Euripides.* London: Methuen.

Halberstadt-Freud, H.C. (1998) "Electra versus Freud: Femininity reconsidered", *International Journal of Psychoanalysis* 79: 41–56.

Halperin, D.M. (1990) *One Hundred Years of Homosexuality: And Other Essays on Greek Love.* New York: Routledge.

Holst-Warhaft, G. (1992) *Dangerous Voices: Women's Lament in Greek Literature.* London and New York: Routledge.

——(2000) *The Cue for Passion: Grief and its Political Uses.* Cambridge: Harvard University Press.

Honig, B. (2010) "Antigone's two laws: Greek tragedy and the politics of humanism", *New Literary History* 41: 1–33.

——(2011) "Ismene's forced choice: Sacrifice and sorority in Sophocles' *Antigone*", *Arethusa* 44(1): 29–68.

Irigaray, L. (1985) *Speculum of the Other Woman*, trans. G.G. Gill. Ithaca, NY: Cornell University Press.

Jebb, R.C. (1894) *Sophocles: The Plays and Fragments. Part VI. The Electra.* Cambridge: Cambridge University Press.

Juffras, D. (1991) "Sophocles' *Electra* 973–85 and tyrannicide", *Transactions of the American Philological Association* 121: 99–108.

Kamerbeek, J.C. (1974) *The Plays of Sophocles. Commentaries. Part V: Electra.* Leiden: Brill.

Kells, J.H. (ed.) (1973) *Sophocles: Electra.* Cambridge: Cambridge University Press.

Kells, J.H. (1986) "Sophocles' *Electra* revisited", in J.H. Betts, J.T. Hooder, and J.R. Green (eds) *Studies in Honour of T.B.L. Webster.* Bristol: Bristol Classical Press, pp. 153–60.

King, H. (1983) "Bound to bleed: Artemis and Greek women", in A. Cameron and A. Kuhrt (eds) *Images of Women in Antiquity.* Detroit, MI: Wayne State University Press, pp. 109–27.

——(1998) *Hippocrates' Woman: Reading the Female Body in Ancient Greece.* London and New York: Routledge.

——(2005) "Women's health and recovery in the Hippocratic Corpus", in H. King (ed.) *Health in Antiquity.* London: Routledge, pp. 150–61.

Kitzinger, R. (1991) "Why mourning becomes Elektra", *Classical Antiquity* 10: 298–327.

Knox, B. (1964) *The Heroic Temper: Studies in Sophoclean Drama.* Berkeley, CA: University of California Press.

Lardinois, A. and McClure, L. (eds) (2001) *Making Silence Speak: Women's Voices in Greek Literature and Society.* Princeton, NJ: Princeton University Press.

Lyons, D. (2012) *Dangerous Gifts: Gender and Exchange in Ancient Greece.* Austin, TX: University of Texas Press.

McClure, L. (2001) "Introduction", in A. Lardinois and L. McClure (eds) *Making Silence Speak: Women's Voices in Greek Literature and Society.* Princeton, NJ: Princeton University Press, pp. 3–16.

McCoskey, D. (2009) "The loss of abandonment in Sophocles' *Electra*", in D. McCoskey and E. Zakin (eds) *Bound by the City: Greek Tragedy, Sexual Difference, and the Formation of the* Polis. Albany, NY: SUNY Press, pp. 221–45.

McHardy, F. (2008) *Revenge in Athenian Culture.* London: Duckworth.

March, J. (2001) *Sophocles: Electra.* Warminster: Aris & Phillips.

Michelini, A. (1987) *Euripides and the Tragic Tradition.* Madison, WI: University of Wisconsin Press.

Mossman, J. (2001) "Women's speech in Greek tragedy: The case of Electra and Clytemnestra in Euripides' *Electra*", *Classical Quarterly* 51: 374–84.

O'Brien, M. (1964) "Orestes and the Gorgon: Euripides' *Electra*", *American Journal of Philology* 85: 13–39.

Ormand, K. (1999) *Exchange and the Maiden: Marriage in Sophoclean Tragedy.* Austin, TX: University of Texas Press.

——(2009) "Electra in exile", in D. McCoskey and E. Zakin (eds) *Bound by the City: Greek Tragedy, Sexual Difference, and the Formation of the Polis.* Albany, NY: SUNY Press, pp. 247–73.

Parca, M. and Tzanetou, A. (2007) *Finding Persephone: Women's Rituals in the Ancient Mediterranean*. Bloomington, IN: Indiana University Press.

Penrose, W. (2006) "Bold with the bow and arrow: Amazons and the ethnic gendering of martial prowess in ancient Greek and Asian cultures", unpublished PhD thesis, City University of New York.

Pomeroy, S. (2002) *Spartan Women*. Oxford: Oxford University Press.

Rabinowitz, N.S. (2002a) "Excavating women's homoeroticism in ancient Greece: The evidence from vase painting", in N.S. Rabinowitz and L. Auanger (eds) *Among Women: From the Homosocial to the Homoerotic in the Ancient World*. Austin, TX: University of Texas Press, pp. 106–66.

——(2002b) "Queer theory and feminist pedagogy", in S.S. Casal and A. Macdonald (eds) *21st Century Feminist Classrooms: Pedagogies of Identity and Difference*. New York: St Martin's Press, pp. 175–202.

Rabinowitz, N.S. and Auanger, L. (eds) (2002) *Among Women: From the Homosocial to the Homoerotic in the Ancient World*. Austin, TX: University of Texas Press.

Scott, J. (2005) *Electra after Freud: Myth and Culture*. Ithaca, NY: Cornell University Press.

Seaford, R. (1994) *Reciprocity and Ritual: Homer and Tragedy in the Developing City-State*. Oxford: Oxford University Press.

Sedgwick, E.K. (1985) *Between Men: English Literature and Male Homosocial Desire*. Ithaca, NY: Cornell University Press.

Segal, C. (1981) *Tragedy and Civilization: An Interpretation of Sophocles*. Cambridge, MA: Harvard University Press.

Seremetakis, C.N. (1991) *The Last Word: Women, Death and Divination in Inner Mani*. Chicago, IL: University of Chicago Press.

Sorum, C. (1982) "The family in Sophocles' 'Antigone' and 'Electra'", *Classical World* 75: 201–11.

Sourvinou-Inwood, C. (1988) *Studies in Girls' Transitions: Aspects of the Arkteia and Age Representation in Attic Iconography*. Athens: Kardamitsa.

Taxidou, O. (2004) *Tragedy, Modernity and Mourning*. Edinburgh: Edinburgh University Press.

Vidal-Naquet, P. (1986) *The Black Hunter: Forms of Thought and Forms of Society in the Greek World*, trans. A. Szegedy. Baltimore, MD: Johns Hopkins University Press.

West, M.L. (ed. and trans.) (1987) *Euripides: Orestes*. Warminster: Aris and Phillips.

Wheeler, G. (2003) "Gender and transgression in Sophocles' *Electra*", *Classical Quarterly* 53: 377–88.

Whitman, C. (1951) *Sophocles: A Study of Heroic Humanism*. Cambridge, MA: Harvard University Press.

Willink, C. (1986) *Euripides: Orestes*. Oxford: Clarendon Press.

Winnington-Ingram, R.P. (1948) "Clytemnestra and the vote of Athena", *Journal of Hellenic Studies* 68: 130–47.

——(1980) *Sophocles: An Interpretation*. Cambridge: Cambridge University Press.

Woodard, T. (1964 [1965]) "*Electra* by Sophocles: The dialectical design", *Harvard Studies in Classical Philology* 68: 163–205; 70: 195–233.

——(1966) "The *Electra* of Sophocles", in T. Woodard (ed.) *Sophocles: A Collection of Critical Essays*. Englewood Cliffs, NJ: Prentice Hall, pp. 125–46.

Wright, M. (2005) "The joy of Sophocles' Electra", *Greece & Rome* 52: 172–94.

Zeitlin, F. (1970) "The Argive festival of Hera and Euripides' *Electra*", *Transactions of the American Philological Association* 101: 645–69.

——(1978 [1996]) "The dynamics of misogyny: Myth and mythmaking in the *Oresteia* of Aeschylus", *Arethusa* 11: 149–84; repr. in F.I. Zeitlin (ed.) *Playing the Other: Gender and Society in Classical Greek Literature*. Chicago, IL: University of Chicago Press, pp. 87–122.

——(1996) *Playing the Other: Gender and Society in Classical Greek Literature*. Chicago, IL: University of Chicago Press.

13

OF LOVE AND BONDAGE IN EURIPIDES' *HIPPOLYTUS*

Monica S. Cyrino

Such an *eros* for love, knotted beneath my heart,
poured a thick mist upon my eyes,
stealing the tender wits out of my chest.
(Archilochos, fragment 112)

Eros once again limb-loosener rattles me,
sweet-bitter inexorable creature.
(Sappho, fragment 130)

Eros, *eros*, dripping desire upon the eyes,
bringing sweet soul's grace to those he attacks,
may he never show himself with evil against me,
may he not come against me all out of rhythm.
(Euripides, *Hippolytus* 525–9)[1]

Introduction: *Eros*

In his ferocious tragedy of passion gone awry, *Hippolytus*, Euripides portrays the destructive power and violent rippling effects of antagonistic *eros*, giving dramatic expression to a traditional image he inherited from earlier Greek writers and artists.[2] When the ancient Greek poets articulated the universal feeling of erotic desire, whether expressed by a male or female poet or character in a poem or play, it was almost never described as a pleasant experience. *Eros* in Greek poetry is characterized as having both hostile intentions and deleterious consequences.[3] The poets depict the experience of erotic desire using metaphors of war, athletic contests, natural disasters, disease, madness, with all of these attacks leading inexorably to total physical and mental devastation. *Eros* can be depicted as a harmful outside entity, aggressively pursuing victims, a supernatural force that attacks and invades the body and mind of the lover in order to assume control and ultimately to demolish the individual into tiny indistinct fragments.

These Greek literary images of the power of *eros* suggest a dynamic where offense and defense both take the field at once, in a struggle between the integrity of the self and a dangerous coming-into-contact with the other: the onset of desire becomes something of a tangible personal threat, where the substance and coherence of the lover's body are made vulnerable to violation. From the Greek poets we get the impression of an acute sensibility about personal boundaries, an intense concern for preserving the definition of the self, the very unity of which is at risk under the onslaught of *eros*.[4] Anne Carson describes the aftereffect of this collision: "The self forms at the edge of desire."[5] The lover, in an effort to resist erotic disintegration, is compelled to acknowledge and appreciate the enclosure of his or her own bounded identity at the very moment those edges are perceived as being loosened, unfastened, blurred, melted, torn apart, and utterly plundered by desire. What the lover experiences, then, is the loss of personal integrity, and an unraveling of one's sense of self.

These Greek literary descriptions of the effects of the erotic experience suggest that a sudden perception of the breach inside the lover's vital connective tissue may be what *eros* is all about: the verb *erao, eramai* in Greek denotes "to love, want, long for, lust after, desire eagerly."[6] An individual in love longs for what he or she does not have, and wants to satisfy that hunger for remembered connection, and to fill the hollow in the belly that desire has gnawed open.[7] As Carson argues: "The presence of want awakens in him the nostalgia for wholeness."[8] The lover is immediately, painfully, alerted to the nature of that glowing vacancy-sign in the Eros Motel: it is the space between the self and the desired other, and the only way to negotiate this immense distance is through the extremely hazardous gesture of reaching outside the self across the boundary of flesh in an attempt at physical fusion. Joy Harjo portrays the intrusive reach of *eros* in her poem "Motion": "I tremble and grasp at the edges of myself; I let go into you."[9] In Greek literature, sexual activity is often described by the verb *mignumi*, as well as by the noun *mixis*, which connotes a kind of "mingling": you "blend" yourself with the beloved, blur your distinctions, and "mix it up" in the act of lovemaking.[10]

But to reach out and touch the other, to let *eros* "loosen the limbs" in the erotic experience (as Sappho describes the physical effect of *eros lusimeles*, the "limb loosener," in fragment 130, quoted above), necessarily means a disturbing loss of one's own bodily integrity. Every *liaison* is rendered *dangereuse*, as it were. The Greek poets recognized the considerable personal peril involved in venturing out into the space, as Carson expresses it, "between reach and grasp, between glance and counterglance, between 'I love you' and 'I love you, too'";[11] the verses of the Greek poets record the excruciating sensation of dangling in that spacious verbal interval as pursuit turns to capture, prey enters net, shoot becomes score. So here is the inescapable problem posed by *eros*: the lover learns to value the existence of her own borders at the very moment she finds herself desperately wanting to dissolve them in erotic *mixis* with another.

How does the lover seek to resolve this dilemma? *Eros* in Greek poetry teaches the lover the boldness necessary to cross the space of desire, and encourages the requisite daring to face dissolution of the self in acknowledgment, however temporary or fleeting, of the beloved other. This lesson of alterity, as Euripides boldly demonstrates in the *Hippolytus*, is utterly irresistible: you refuse it at your own risk. In Greek mythology, the extreme nature of the personified god of desire supports this universal concept of love's coercive force and audacity.[12] The Greek god Eros is portrayed not as an innocent baby playing at darts, but a handsome adolescent athlete, a gambler, dark-haired and dangerous, greedy for gifts and endorsement deals, with a muscular body and a competitive urge: the ballistic equipment he uses is divine, and his shot placement is deadly.[13] The wings of Eros represent the swiftness with which the god closes the distance between the lover and the beloved other;[14] his titanium-shaft arrows strike with perfect accuracy the tender back of the victim's neck, initiating the lover into the knowledge of bounded limits and heightened vulnerability. Game over, sudden death, Eros wins again.

Eros is often portrayed as the child of Aphrodite, goddess of sexual love and beauty, from her adulterous affair with Ares, the buff and brutal god of war (Aphrodite has no legitimate children with her husband, Hephaestus, god of the forge).[15] As I have argued elsewhere, Aphrodite is both the most popular – in terms of the ubiquity of her cult worship – and the most potent Greek deity, and the scope of her power is manifested in her liminality, her capacity for "in-betweenness," and her ability to be literally in two places at once.[16] Aphrodite's world is one of blending and mingling, of tangling together people and ideas, of mediation between categories that are usually kept opposed. "She makes hungry where most she satisfies," as Shakespeare wrote of Cleopatra.[17] As the goddess who graces those most intimate moments shared by humans, Aphrodite crosses easily between mortal and divine spheres; in her straightforward promiscuity, she confuses traditional male and female roles; and she joins the physical, sexual instincts of the natural world with the sophisticated "arts of love" – such as cosmetic orna-mentation, erotic persuasion, and sexual seduction – considered an indispensable part of civi-lized culture by the ancient Greeks. Aphrodite both binds and unravels: she loosens the lover's limbs in desire, then induces the lover to merge with the other in the fusion of sexual activity, what the modern poet Anne Sexton would much later call "the bedded-down knot."[18]

Aphrodite's daughter Harmonia – "she who binds together" – personifies this act of cou-pling. The Greek verb *harmozo* means "to fit together, join, unite," and is the *mot juste* to describe the ligature formed by betrothal and marriage: as we might say in English, couples who wed "tie the knot" or "get hitched." In Greek literature, the standard conjugal metaphor is "the yoke of marriage," that is, the image of two horses hitched together drawing one chariot in smooth cooperation.[19] Thus, the erotic knot is a pervasive symbol in Greek literature in the representation of two individuals joining together into one whole, but the merger is not always smooth and trouble-free: this image of binding also suggests the parallel yet opposite actions of stricture and freedom, of pressure and release, of tying tight and loosening.[20] And it is the goddess Aphrodite who inhabits this liminal space between lover and beloved where erotic bonds can be both tightly fastened and released.

In representing the ambivalent nature of *eros*, its tensely integrated duality, the mirror of Aphrodite is more than just an accessory of vanity: through her association with and deploy-ment of the mirror, the goddess exposes the lover to the doubling mechanism of desire.[21] In ancient Greek vase paintings, the goddess is sometimes depicted holding a mirror, and real mirrors were often dedicated to Aphrodite in her sanctuaries and shrines.[22] The bronze bedside case-mirrors that survive from Greek antiquity, mostly from the late classical and early Hellenistic periods, are frequently decorated with images of Aphrodite, or scenes of erotic encounters, and some even show avid eye contact between lovers;[23] this is in contrast to the ubiquitous erotic red-figure symposium cups depicting orgies or raucous sexual acts in which the participants assume positions (usually *a tergo*) where they necessarily look away from each other.[24] Using her mirror as a pedagogical tool, the ultimate visual aid, Aphrodite can compel the lover not only to recognize oneself through the other's desiring eyes, but also to see and desire the reflection that is seen: one mirror holds two faces. In the act of erotic reaching and desired *mixis*, the mirror projects the self both onto and beside the other, blended yet separate, coupled yet isolated.

The test of double vision is tough, however, and not everyone passes: Narcissus, in one possible interpretation of a notorious mythological example, failed to perceive the depths of himself in the surface image of the beautiful other, and his loss of personal substance was complete and irrevocable. For the lover willing and able to see, the mirror offers insight into the ambiguity of *eros*, and even the chance to contemplate the possibility of self-knowledge. What Aphrodite teaches the lover, then, is a lesson in perspective in which desire and identity merge together; the tools of her husband, the metal-working god, Hephaestus, stand ready to fuse lover and beloved together in a bonded whole.[25] It is this Aphrodite that Euripides stages at the opening of his play, *Hippolytus*, the goddess who will emphasize as the drama unfolds the universal significance of the binding and release of *eros* for both men and women alike, and who will ruthlessly illustrate the brutal consequences for those to refuse who allow the erotic experience to bind them to another.

Eros and Hippolytus

In the prologue speech of Euripides' play *Hippolytus*, Aphrodite reveals her distress over a certain mortal who rejects the lesson of her overwhelming divine power, and decides to put him through some special tutoring.[26] In the city of Troezen lives the young Hippolytus, who is clearly failing the erotic curriculum in "Plays Well with Others."[27] Hippolytus is the illegitimate son of Theseus, king of Athens and second most important hero in the Greek tradition (after Herakles); the boy's mother was an Amazon warrior, either abducted or seduced by Theseus during one of his many heroic exploits.[28] Aphrodite is angry to discover that Hippolytus refuses to honor her, and instead chooses to worship only her half-sister, Artemis, the virgin goddess of the hunt and the untouched natural world. "He says that I am the worst of the gods," Aphrodite complains at the start of the play, "and considers *her* to be the greatest of the gods" (*Hippolytus* 13, 16). To ignore one god in favor of another is unspeakably dangerous, playing into the sibling rivalries and venomous jealousies of the famously dysfunctional Olympian family.[29] And the Greeks would certainly call such neglect of a god an act of *hubris*: that is, a crime of human arrogance that throws the world off balance, and so upsets the cosmic order that it draws a compensatory movement of *nemesis*, or retribution, from the gods to put everything right again. The pendulum swings back into place, and some poor human or family of humans gets punished in the process: this tragic structure recalls that of Euripides' *Bacchae*, where Dionysus occupies a similarly untenable position of neglect and exacts an equally brutal revenge as Aphrodite does in the *Hippolytus*.[30]

Thus, Euripides sets up this dramatic plot as a basic punishment myth, with Aphrodite as the injured deity seeking redress.[31] As noted above, Aphrodite, goddess of erotic *mixis* and sexual binding and release, joins Dionysus, god of intoxication, out of body experience, and ecstatic release, as the deity most often denied by mortals in the Greek mythological and literary tradition.[32] This is perhaps because both gods demand a certain kind of "looseness" from their worshippers: but when uptight humans refuse to "let go" – as they so often do – they are punished with an enforced disintegration, which is much more painful and very messy. Consider poor Pentheus in Euripides' *Bacchae*, torn up by his mother and the other maenads for denying the divinity and power of Dionysus. Likewise, whenever someone insults the goddess of love, refusing to dissolve the self and bond with another in blended *eros*, Aphrodite punishes the offender directly with an immoderate desire for an inappropriate target: we know how Smyrna (or Myrrha) refused to worship Aphrodite, and was subjected by the goddess to an incestuous desire to sleep with her own father.[33]

But here in our story, the mythological pattern of Aphrodite's vengeful intervention takes something of a detour. At the beginning of the play, Aphrodite announces her plan to use a tool, to inspire an "innocent other" with illicit passion in order to accomplish her revenge against Hippolytus: she chooses as her cat's paw Phaedra, the most recent young trophy wife of Theseus.[34] So technically, Phaedra is the stepmother of Hippolytus, perhaps even close to him in age and sexual attractiveness, yet as her stepson he is a totally unsuitable object whom Aphrodite now compels her to love.[35] As Aphrodite boasts in the prologue, "Phaedra's heart is in the grip of terrible *eros* by my design" (*Hippolytus* 27–8). The Greeks would have seen Phaedra's desire for her stepson as a scandal, improper and even incestuous.[36] In this case, then, Aphrodite proposes a toxic erotic mix, an outrageous recipe. She will use the unsuspecting queen as a double for herself, since they are both scorned by Hippolytus, with the result that Phaedra will become a text to teach the youth a lesson about the power of Aphrodite and the experience of *eros* over which she holds sway, and a prescription to cure him of his *hubris*.[37] Phaedra will be held up like a mirror to make Hippolytus face his own rejection of the desiring other, and force him to learn the dynamics of the sexual ties he refuses to experience. As Sophie Mills explains: "Aphrodite's honour has been wounded and her punishment will be viciously precise – what worse punishment could there be for someone who hates sexuality than a forced encounter with incestuous adultery?"[38] The goddess weaves together a binding *logos*, a strategy of deception and false charges, of emotional repression and linguistic constraints, employing Phaedra as the instrument of her cruel plot.[39]

As we shall see, Aphrodite's vengeance will result in the staging of scenes where knots are fastened at vulnerable pressure points, and where amorous bondage is simulated and even perverted: using the boy's own father to effect the fatal binding, Aphrodite directs the dramatic intrigue to entangle Hippolytus in the constricting bonds of punishment.[40] When Aphrodite finally compels Theseus to loosen the tangle of reins and embrace his son, at that crucial point the boy will be forcibly dissolved, released from the ropes of *eros* only by his death.

But, by denying love's power, isn't Hippolytus just asking for it? In the logic of divine retribution, the answer is yes. His appearance onstage after the speech of the goddess confirms that here we have a clearly negative paradigm of the perils of ideological extremism.[41] This is the fanatically chaste youth who refuses to grow up, who rejects the biologically expected and politically necessary transition from boyhood to adult male sexuality, whether for homosexual pleasure or heterosexual procreation – he is a kind of *puer aeternus* meets Peter Pan. In outline, the story of Hippolytus also follows the mythic pattern of a failed adolescent initiation: one example is that of Phaethon, who cannot do his father's job flying the sun-chariot and crashes to the ground; or again Actaeon, who is not prepared for his encounter with the revealed nudity of the goddess Artemis and is shredded to bits.[42] Like Hippolytus, both suffer total disintegration: the boy most emphatically does not become a man.[43]

But in the case of Hippolytus, he is obstinate in his double bind: he refuses even to imagine the power of sexuality, and vehemently declines to fulfill his father's role of sleeping with the mother (even Oedipus did that). Hippolytus' name means "loosener of horses," and indeed he devotes himself to hunting in the wild pure meadows away from the cosmopolitan lures of the palace. He wears his ostentatious virginity like a badge of his opposition to the process of erotic fusion of self and other, suggesting his exaggerated anxiety about keeping his own personal boundaries intact. As we say nowadays, he is wound pretty tight. His refusal to bond, blend, or connect to another in *eros* is what Froma Zeitlin calls "an asyndeton … in the grammar of life."[44] To the ancient Greeks, virginity in mortals, and especially sexual celibacy in males, is an unnatural state, appropriate only at certain early stages of life, and then only temporarily: the fruit is better picked green than left to wither on the tree.[45] So the poet may have wanted us to see Hippolytus' abstinence from *eros* as an extreme stance, unhealthy in someone of his age and gender, as well as a direct affront to the goddess of love. "I like no god who is adored at night," he sniffs demurely (*Hippolytus* 106).

Although he renounces both Aphrodite and her mortal agent Phaedra, Hippolytus is not just gynophobic, but he is allo-phobic as well, terrified of coming into contact with the edge of another.[46] It is not merely ironic that the only other being he acknowledges is Artemis, whose own most defining characteristic in Greek mythology, as I have argued elsewhere, is her aggressive and often violent distancing of herself from others.[47] Thus, this drama is not just about Hippolytus' one-time denial of his stepmother's invitation to an adulterous, ostensibly incestuous sexual rendezvous, a sordid plot device Euripides has the vengeful Aphrodite stage, no doubt, for its extreme dramatic value as a sexual and political scandal. Rather, this drama is ultimately about the implications of Hippolytus' persistent rejection of Aphrodite and his unremitting refusal to allow *eros* to blend his single self with another in the bond of love.

The very essence of the other in this play is represented by Phaedra, "the shining one," who now by Aphrodite's plan incurs the most urgent desire for this inaccessible wild-child. Phaedra is a princess of Crete, from that notoriously taurophilic family: Europa was seduced by the god Zeus in the form of a bull, and their son was Minos, king of Crete, Phaedra's father; her mother was Pasiphae, "the all-shining," daughter of Helios the Sun, who so lusted after her husband's beautiful bull that she cross-species-dressed as a cow to make love to him, thus giving birth to the hybrid Minotaur. Phaedra's family history is important here, since the Greeks would have believed that a proclivity towards sexual extravagance was genetically encoded in her bloodline, an inheritance like eye or hair color, and utterly inevitable: the poets speak of "Cretan women" as a byword for erotic excess.[48] This hereditary Cretan sensuality, "the pull backward" as one critic identifies it,[49] makes it easier for the audience to accept that Phaedra is unwittingly cast in the role of victim and tool of Aphrodite, and that she is doomed to be a civilian casualty during the attack against Hippolytus.

At first Phaedra will try to repress her desire, in a stubborn effort to preserve her own personal bodily integrity, which she reveals in an excessive concern for her honor as the wife of Theseus and mother of his two legitimate male heirs.[50] The dilemma within Phaedra models the struggle between Aphrodite and Artemis, the eternally divided female image, between the two sides of sexuality/sensuousness (Aphrodite's sphere of influence) and chastity/motherhood (Artemis, although a virgin, is the goddess of childbirth and the female procreative cycle). In the classical Greek conception, the idea of the feminine is an enigmatic "double sign," a constant and not always successful attempt at reconciling these split categories:[51] the female image is often used by the ancient Greek authors to represent the world of ambiguity and conflict, "an evil you want to embrace," as Pandora is described in the famous Hesiodic paradox (*Works and Days* 57–8). Playing a crucial role in Euripides' depiction of Phaedra is the figure of the sexually transgressive adulterous wife, who to the Greeks represents a confusion of roles, in that she embodies the contaminating mixture between the two opposing sides of the feminine coin – both wife and lover, chastity and passion – or what Zeitlin might describe as "a cultural oxymoron."[52]

The figure of the adulteress thereby suggests an alluring but risky attempt to reconstruct the substance of the self by allowing the intimate juxtaposition, even blending of these two apparent opposite sides. Thus, in her impulse towards extramarital *eros*, Phaedra confounds the categories of virtuous wife and desiring lover, purity and pollution, secrecy and revelation. Her divine counterpart in infidelity is, of course, the mastermind of this illicit erotic binding, the promiscuous Aphrodite, married to hard-working Hephaestus but ever unfaithful to him. This is a goddess who regularly encourages mortal women to commit adultery: remember that she blithely gives Helen, wife of Menelaus, to the Trojan Paris as a gift. In our story, Aphrodite defines the conflict within the ambivalent self, using the female double meaning of Phaedra, and through her achieves the desired revenge: Hippolytus will learn the complexity of his own self when he is forced to confront his eroticized reflection in the mirror of Phaedra, whose name means "the Shining One."

Euripides complicates the dramatic tension by conflating the theme of divine punishment with the old "Potiphar's wife" motif, familiar from Near Eastern and other Greek sources.[53] In this pattern, a married woman falls in love with another man: when she is rebuffed by the object of her desire, she exacts vengeance by falsely accusing him of rape or attempted sexual assault and reports it to her husband, a man of power, who then punishes the alleged offender. But here the playwright adds a plot twist: Aphrodite as a character is dramatically necessary not only to reveal her own wrathful agency, but also to disclose what Phaedra is keeping bound up inside of her – her overwhelming passion for Hippolytus. The queen resolves to repress the *eros* she considers a shameful violation of her duty to her husband; but that blocked desire, an impediment both to the plot and to the goddess of love's design, ties her mortal body up in knots, binding her face under her obscuring veil, and causes Phaedra to suffer a debilitating lovesickness.[54]

The women of the chorus tell us, "She lies afflicted upon a bed of sickness, keeping herself inside the house, and fine cloths shadow her golden head" (*Hippolytus* 131–4). While Phaedra's intentions are honorable, her failure to accept the *eros* she feels starts the downhill slide to cat-astrophe in this play: her disease will prove both very contagious and very deadly. Erotic illness drives Phaedra outside of the house and away from that interior domestic space symbolic of her married life with Theseus, since "the secret of adulterous desire is incompatible with the house and the social values it objectifies, so that the woman is no longer 'at home' with herself."[55] Phaedra's exit through the door of the house, that gesture of tentative reach outside herself in the direction of the beloved other, brings her closer to Aphrodite's planned loosening of the bonds of secret desire: as soon as she appears onstage, an arrival mid-wived by her concerned Nurse,[56] Phaedra's struggle for containment will begin to fail. The queen's unbinding, divinely coerced, will lead to the various thwarted and fatal bindings in the play. She tears off her veil, once a symbol of her chastity and her silence, which she used to cover her repressed *eros* as securely as the house itself did, and cries out her desire to run to the woods and join in the hunt.[57] Thus is Phaedra liberated from the house, released from her head wrapping, unbound.

Phaedra's Nurse, not surprisingly, thinks the queen has gone mad from her illness. And although she does not yet know what disease ails her mistress, the Nurse is determined to bring her back to health in any way she can.[58] Phaedra stubbornly clings to the fast-dissolving threads of her secret, but little by little the Nurse succeeds in releasing the truth: that Phaedra is dying of love for Hippolytus. Devoted to the suffering woman she loves as her own daughter, and out of a practical concern to save Phaedra's life, the Nurse adopts the active role of physician to end the patient's lovesickness. Now if Phaedra had consulted a doctor for treatment, it is likely that his prescribed therapy would be intercourse, or at least the simulation of it, since her husband Theseus has been away from home for some time: current Hippocratic medical theory supported social mores by linking female health to conjugal sexual activity and reproduction.[59] So, well aware that allopathic measures will fail, the Nurse suggests to Phaedra a remedy that follows the medical trend towards homeopathy, since her prescription promises to arouse rather than calm Phaedra's desire. "It's not fine words you need," the Nurse cajoles, "you need the man" (*Hippolytus* 490–1). She makes Phaedra a seductive offer, proposing a solution that the weakened, lovesick queen is in no condition to resist: the Nurse suggests – with an ambiguity that will later allow Phaedra to claim she misunderstood the plan – that she will persuade Hippolytus to reciprocate Phaedra's passion.

But the Nurse's *pharmakon*, her remedy, proves to be a dose of bad medicine, which instead of curing the patient, in fact poisons her:[60] this will cause Phaedra to counter with a course of self-medication leading to her own death. For when the Nurse confronts Hippolytus with the queen's secret, the youth fiercely rejects Phaedra and her love, unknowingly complying with Aphrodite's scheme of revenge. The Nurse commits an act of malpractice of the gravest kind, and pays for it by the violent severing of her bond with Phaedra. As the queen laments, angrily repudiating the Nurse's loving but misguided attempt to help: "She destroys me by telling him my pains: she loves me but did not heal this illness" (*Hippolytus* 596–7). Now the secret of adulterous desire, that double sign, as it alienates Phaedra from her would-be protectress, is transmitted from Phaedra through the Nurse to Hippolytus; the secret penetrates the once inviolable limits of his body, making him conscious of the boundary between the outside and the inside of the self. Hippolytus pledges to keep Phaedra's secret concealed in that interior physical space, the existence of which he must simultaneously acknowledge. "My tongue swore, but my heart is unsworn," he complains, now painfully aware of his split self (*Hippolytus* 612).[61] Like his virginity, Hippolytus' oath of secrecy is an effort at containment, but it actually threatens the integrity of the self, as the secret divides him in two, and forces him to participate in Phaedra's experience of duality, her oscillation between repression and revelation, silence and speech. "He will share in this disease of mine," the queen promises with her last breath on stage (*Hippolytus* 730–1).[62] When *eros* is denied, Aphrodite reacts swiftly "to confound the identity of one with an other by replacing radical disjunction with hidden identification."[63] Thus, the oath becomes the figurative knot – which will later be manifest in the real leather knots of the horses' reins – that fatally binds Hippolytus to Phaedra.

Phaedra now retreats in silence back into the house, back to her state of erotic incarceration, desperate to redraw the boundaries of her body and her reputation that were loosened to such disastrous results. She fastens a twisted noose – a *brochos*, or "slip knot" in Greek – to the rafters of her marriage chamber and hangs herself, closing off one of the open ends of her woman's body, that porous physical nature too dangerously receptive to blending with the other in the bonds of love.[64] Note how the rope tied to the ceiling above her conjugal bed calls attention to the symbolic framework of the house and her place within it, as she reconnects herself to the domestic space in her role as wife of Theseus and mother of his legitimate sons. "From the roofbeams of her bridal chamber, she yokes a hanging noose-knot to her white throat," cries the chorus (*Hippolytus* 768–72), adopting the matrimonial metaphor of the yoke to portray Phaedra's act of self-destructive binding. As Barrett succinctly describes this scene, "Hanging oneself involves two fastenings: of the rope to the beam and of the rope to one's neck."[65] With her throat caught in the snare, effectively choking off her ability to speak, and with her body hidden in the bedroom, behind closed doors, Phaedra is locked into a double prison, an impermeable obstacle between herself and others. Sealed in death, Phaedra is re-contained within a position of muteness and secrecy, as she restores herself to the interior of the house, the private place of woman's traditional glory. Moreover, Phaedra also redeems her cherished image as a "virtuous wife" by staging her suicide in the noble tragic manner. But even the "honorable" Phaedra proves the Greek rule that women are deceitful, since her death is an act of *metis* or "cunning":[66] the knot she ties around her throat sets a fatal trap for Hippolytus. The dead woman, silenced forever, can still speak.

Theseus storms onstage and commands that the bolts of the palace doors be released, and that his wife's corpse be untied from its knotted noose and revealed to his sight: Phaedra, enveloped in her bridal-chamber-tomb, is once again forcibly detached from the chaste confines of the house and made to expose herself to spectators. There is an astonishing interplay here, as Nicole Loraux points out, between the hidden and the seen, between concealment and revelation, in which "we do not see a woman's death, but do see the dead woman."[67] And as mournful and shocking as this scene is, the dramatic action continues in earnest, as scripted by Phaedra herself: her conspicuous corpse becomes an important stage element, invoking the absent woman's silent presence, and bearing manifest proof against Hippolytus, the fictitious evidence for his crime. An uncanny evocation of such a moment can be found in Sylvia Plath's poem *Edge:* "Her dead / Body wears the smile of accomplishment."[68] For fastened with a knot and hanging from Phaedra's hand is a writing tablet, the *deltos,* containing the false accusation of rape against Hippolytus: as Theseus sees it, he cries, "What is this tablet attached to/hanging from her hand?" (*Hippolytus* 856–7).[69] The mute witness of her corpse together with the lying letter serves as a dual envoy carrying a "message of erotic violence."[70] "It shouts, the tablet shouts aloud of cruel hurt!" exclaims Theseus as he reads (*Hippolytus* 877). Taking on the dead woman's speaking role, the *deltos* becomes an actor in the drama, the queen's verbal stunt-double, and Phaedra manipulates it like a ventriloquist.

Using the *deltos* to cover up her shame, wrapped on itself and imprinted with her seal, Phaedra also presents an image of the inviolate wife: when Theseus unfolds and reads the tablet, he replays the husband's first "loosening" of his virgin bride's belt and his "knowing" of her sexually. The word *deltos* often appears in Greek literature to describe the visible female genitalia, where the pubic hair has been cropped into the popular inverted triangle shape, perhaps based on the shape of the capital letter *delta*:[71] indeed, Euripides seems to be well aware of the deeper analogies implicit here. Like a woman's body, the wax inner surface of the *deltos* receives impressions, and like her mouth and genitals, the leaves of the *deltos* open and close to deliver an ambiguous, sometimes even duplicitous, message of female sexuality. Phaedra's *deltos*, her speaking yet silent sex, bound to her lifeless body, is a text to teach Hippolytus a lesson about *eros*, a new *logos* to bind him in punishment.[72] And through the deception of the *deltos*, its false charge of criminal desire, Aphrodite can fulfill her favored mode of vengeance in terms of erotic reciprocity: Hippolytus is now forced to take on the role he rejected, to become the *erastes*, the unlawful lover of his father's wife, in word if not in actual deed.[73] Because of his refusal to blend in *eros*, and by failing to worship Aphrodite, Hippolytus is transformed into the unwilling double of what he sought to avoid. The reflection is totally unexpected, as he sees a dual image: the goddess' mirror has become the instrument of his own destruction, his blurring of self and identification with the other.

For his alleged crime, Hippolytus is condemned and banished from the land by his father, the hero Theseus.[74] With this act, the boy learns another level of alterity, as he is even further removed from society: to his marginal status as a bastard son is added the stigma of pollution belonging to the exile.[75] Hippolytus chafes under the constraints of his oath of silence, founders with the useless double-talk in which he is forced to engage to defend himself, and strains against the recognition of his own duality that Phaedra's secret *eros* has compelled him to experience, now longing vehemently for another one to share his suffering.[76] "I wish there were another me to look me in the face and weep for the pains we are suffering," he cries (*Hippolytus* 1078–9), now at last understanding his own personal complexity, his physical permeability, and the depths beneath the surface. Hippolytus has been penetrated, and his loss of innocence is irrevocable, just as very soon his loss of self, with Poseidon's help, will be permanent.[77]

As he leaves Troezen, Hippolytus is driving his chariot along the seashore when from the waves comes a monstrous bull, sent by the god Poseidon upon the curse of his son, Theseus. The divine bull bellows and charges the team, panicking the horses and overturning the chariot, entangling Hippolytus in the reins and dashing him against the rocks. "He is dragged, bound in an inextricable knot," comes the servant's report (*Hippolytus* 1236–7). The scene of Hippolytus' fatal breakdown is openly evocative of the sexuality he refused in life.[78] His death has parallels in other punishment myths where the one who refuses to accept the yoke of *eros* is destroyed by the yoke of horses and chariot, in the typical Greek narrative balance of crime and penalty.[79] In Greek myth and literature, horses that break from the reins and run wild are associated with rampant, often violent, sexuality; the erotic appeal of bulls has already been mentioned in connection with the women of Crete. The seashore itself is also a liminal location redolent of sex, the site of erotic kidnappings, and the foamy birthplace of Aphrodite floating on the half-shell. In punishing him, the goddess relocates Hippolytus from the meadow of chastity he chose to the beach of sexuality he tried to escape. By her power he is first bound up in his horses' reins, a simulated erotic knot, then utterly dissolved in death: Hippolytus is transformed into the one "loosened by horses,"[80] a passive victim of *eros*, the "loosener of limbs."

In the final scene of the drama, the goddess Artemis appears as *dea ex machina* and reveals to Theseus how, in a dispute between Olympian sisters, the entire network of tragic events has been orchestrated by Aphrodite: Phaedra's secret desire, the Nurse's ill-conceived remedy, Hippolytus' oath of silence, and the lie of the *deltos*. Artemis forgives Theseus for his ignorant curse against Hippolytus, "for it was Aphrodite who wanted this to happen, to satisfy her passion" (*Hippolytus* 1327–8). When a barely-alive Hippolytus is carried onstage, his body battered and broken, Artemis urges him to reunite with his father, to reintegrate his scattered self into the adult male principle represented by Theseus, to repair their ruptured relationship through the mutual witness of each other's suffering.[81] Hippolytus recognizes that it is the compulsion of *eros* triggering this change in him: through his experience of standing in Phaedra's place, "sharing in her disease" (as she warned he would do at lines 730–1), and the painful perception of his own duality, Hippolytus has learned the lesson of reciprocity that allows him now to blend with his father in the bond of filial love. As Zeitlin affirms: "We recognize here the power of Aphrodite that, when refused, converts rapture to pain and *eros* to death."[82] Aphrodite's divine instruction also binds Hippolytus to an erotic destiny, joining him to Phaedra for eternity in the cult of brides who will sing their story of love: Hippolytus will be forced to repeat the duplicitous message of the *deltos* forever.[83] The poor boy, newly aware of his sensory needs, even reaches for his beloved Artemis, to connect with her in a final act of devoted affection. "Goodbye, blessed virgin," he whispers as she turns away, "how lightly you leave a long companionship" (*Hippolytus* 1440–1). But the goddess recoils from his touch and refuses to meet his gaze as she departs from the scene, her very remoteness an ironic comment on the ideal of chastity for which he is dying.

In the end, Hippolytus veils his head as he dies, replaying the woman's binding gesture in her vain attempt to preserve an interior space and contain her desire, which he now reiterates as he shares in her experience of erotically induced illness: this visible moment of physical affinity reveals that he has learned not only to play well with others, but to "play the other" well.[84] Compelled by the vengeful Aphrodite to look into the reflection of the "shining one," Hippolytus can see, wrapped as he is in the veil, that he is now Phaedra: and it is Aphrodite, goddess of *mixis*, who forced the two to meld into a single burnished bond. Thus, in staging this drama, Euripides vividly demonstrates Aphrodite's ruthless power in wielding the universal force of *eros* to bind and release both men and women alike, as he unravels before the audience's eyes the immense and implacable wrath of divinity denied.

Notes

1 The Greek text and numbering of the lyric fragments are from Campbell 1967. The text of Euripides is from Barrett 1964. All translations of Greek verses are my own.

2 See now the outstanding new volume edited by Sanders et al. 2013, especially chapters on the image of violent *eros* in Sappho (D'Angour, 59–72); Greek drama (Thumiger, 27–40; Sanders, 41–59; Robson, 251–66); and Athenian art and cult (Stafford, 175–208).

3 For the negative portrayal of the effects of *eros*, see Thornton 1997. On the Greek poets' use of metaphors of disease and madness for erotic experience, see Cyrino 1995. The literary features of *eros* are discussed by Calame 1999. On the representation of the divinity and personification of Eros, see Breitenberger 2007.

4 My introductory discussion is indebted to Carson 1986: esp. 3–11; 26–45.

5 Carson 1986: 39.

6 See *LSJ s.v. eramai* II.

7 On the difference between *eros* and *pothos*, see Robson 2013: 252–4, with numerous references, where *eros* is explained as a more aggressive desire, with a greater possibility of being fulfilled, while *pothos* is a more passive feeling of longing that rarely achieves its object.

8 Carson 1986: 31.

9 Harjo, "Motion," 1983.

10 On erotic *mixis*, see Cyrino 2010: 32–5, with references.

11 Carson 1986: 30.

12 For the depiction of the cosmic violence of the boy-god Eros, see Cyrino 2010: 44–9.

13 For Eros as a rough ball-player, see Anacreon fr. 358; Eros as a greedy gambler, see Apollonius of Rhodes *Argonautica* 3.112–55. On the depiction of Eros as an aggressive, athletic pursuer, see Stafford 2013: 179–89.

14 Note the forceful velocity of Eros in Ibycus fr. 286. On the wings of Eros, see Carson 1986: 49; Breitenberger 2007: 159–63.

15 On Eros as the most prominent and individualized attendant of Aphrodite, see Breitenberger 2007.

16 On Aphrodite's cultic, mythological, and literary persona, see Cyrino 2010. On the liminality of the goddess, see Friedrich 1978: 132–48.

17 *Antony and Cleopatra*, Act II Scene 2.

18 Sexton, "The Interrogation of the Man of Many Hearts," 1969.

19 On the yoke in conjugal erotic imagery, see Rosenzweig 2004. Euripides' Medea refers to the "yoke of marriage" at *Medea* 242. The other common use of this yoking/binding metaphor in Greek is for "the yoke of slavery," suggesting a rather more negative connotation of bondage: again there is a modern echo where the two ideas of marriage and servitude are combined in the colorful phrase "my ball and chain," used affectionately to refer to one's spouse.

20 The earliest references to erotic knots and binding in Greek poetry portray the negative aspects of the experience: Eros is coiled in a tense knot beneath the lover's heart in Archilochos, fr. 112; and Eros binds the lover in the nets of Kypris in Ibycus, fr. 287. See Cyrino 1995: 77–9, 107–9.

21 On the mirror as a symbol of erotic doubling, see Carson 1986: 72–4. For the mirror as a tool of knowledge, see Luschnig 1988.

22 See Cyrino 2010: 65–6 on the association of Aphrodite and mirrors in Greek art and cult.

23 For a discussion of the sexual imagery represented on ancient Greek case-mirrors, see Stewart in Kampen 1996: 136–54.

24 On the argument that such positions intentionally preclude eye-contact, see Sutton Jr in Richlin 1992: 11; see also Frontisi-Ducroux in Kampen 1996: 81–100; Cairns 2005: 123–55.

25 Plato, *Symposium* 192d–e.

26 My discussion of the *Hippolytus* is indebted to the critical arguments and explorations presented in Zeitlin 1996: 219–84, especially on the imagery of knots (225–32) and mirrors (269–73). Rabinowitz 1993: 155–69 approaches the play with a feminist reading of its conservative ideological assertions in the representation of female sexuality. Mills 2002 offers an insightful overview of the major dramatic themes as well as an excellent survey of various critical interpretations of the play.

27 The phrase comes from primary school report cards, and is used here as a playful variation on the title of Zeitlin's *Playing the Other* (1996).

28 On Hippolytus' maternal heritage, see Barrett 1964: 8–9; Mills 2002: 92–3.

29 See Mills 2002: 91 for the punishment of Hippolytus as the direct result of his arrogance towards Aphrodite.

30 For the comparison, see Zeitlin 1996: 228.

31 On the mythological theme of punishment as a dramatic motif in the play, see Cyrino 2010: 99–102.

32 Dionysus' divinity is denied by the Thracian Lycurgus (Homer, *Iliad* 6.130–40; Apollodorus 3.5.7; Hyginus, *Fabulae* 132); by the Thracian Boutes (Diodorus 5.50); by the daughters of Minyas at Orchomenos (Plutarch, *Q. Gr.* 38); and of course by his Theban cousin, Pentheus (Euripides, *Bacchae*); for more examples, see Dodds 1960: xxv–xxxvi. Aphrodite's divinity is denied by Smyrna, also known as Myrrha (Apollodorus 3.14.3–4); by the women of Lemnos (Apollonius, *Argonautica* 1.609–39, Apollodorus 1.9.17); and of course by Hippolytus (Euripides, *Hippolytus*); see Cyrino 2010: 95–102.

33 Cyrino 2010: 95.

34 For Phaedra as "innocent other," see Zeitlin 1996: 224; as Aphrodite's tool, 219–24; as the goddess' substitute/agent, 273. Mills 2002: 107 notes that even the "honorable" Phaedra is subject to the dictates of the mythological tradition.

35 See Rabinowitz 1993: 155 for the threat posed by Phaedra's sexuality to her husband's son.

36 On stepmothers in the Greco-Roman world, see Watson 1995. For the figure of the amorous stepmother in Greek tragedy, see McHardy 2005: 129–50.

37 The motif of the education of Hippolytus is analyzed by Zeitlin 1996: 222–4.

38 Mills 2002: 78.

39 On Phaedra's agency in the plot, see Rabinowitz 1993: 155–69. On the power of Phaedra's speech to propel the plot forward, see McClure 1999: 112–57.

40 Rabinowitz 1993: 173–88 unpacks the "Oedipal narrative" in the relationship between Theseus and Hippolytus, emphasizing the intensity of the father–son bond in Greek tragedy.

41 For the nature of Hippolytus' behavior as a kind of extreme form of elitism, see Mills 2002: 65–8.

42 On Actaeon, see Zeitlin 1996: 282–3; on Phaethon, see Reckford 1974: 414–21; Zeitlin 1996: 236.

43 See Mitchell-Boyask 1999: 42–66 on the motif of failed adolescent initiation in the play.

44 Zeitlin 1996: 229.

45 See Sissa 1990 on the concept of virginity as understood by the ancient Greeks. On the depiction of male virginity in the *Hippolytus*, see Zeitlin 1996: 231–6; Mills 2002: 64–5.

46 On the suggestion of homosexuality in the figure of Hippolytus, see Rabinowitz 1993: 174. Poole 1990: 134–5 reads homosexual overtones in the relationship of Theseus and Pirithous.

47 On Hippolytus' woefully flawed perception of his companionship with Artemis, see Mills 2002: 77. For the fiercely aloof character of Artemis in Greek mythology, see Cyrino 2010: 99–100.

48 See, for example, Aristophanes' *Frogs* 849–50, for the excessive erotic passions of women from Crete. Mills 2002: 103 notes that Crete, to the Athenian audience, had a reputation as a land of "sexual irregularity."

49 Reckford 1974.

50 On Phaedra's excessive concern for and near obsession with her honor, see Goff 1990: 35; Zeitlin 1996: 220–2; Mills 2002: 54, 59–60.

51 For the female as an ambiguous or dual sign, see Zeitlin 1996: 236–9.

52 Zeitlin 1996: 238 notes the "cultural oxymoron" evident in Greek ideas about female chastity/sexuality.

53 The story of Joseph and the wife of Potiphar is told in Genesis 39:1–20. On the use of the "Potiphar's wife" motif in the play, see Barrett 1964: 6; Zeitlin 1996: 224, 280–1.

54 Cyrino 1995 surveys the various symptoms of erotic *nosos* as portrayed in Greek poetry.

55 Zeitlin 1996: 243. On the dramatic implications of Phaedra's oscillating movement between internal and external spaces, see 243–4.

56 On the role of the Nurse in encouraging Phaedra, see Rabinowitz 1993: 159–65.

57 Head coverings and their removal are always crucially significant in Greek literature: compare the scene in Homer, *Iliad* 22.466–72, where Andromache faints upon seeing Hector's corpse being dragged outside the walls of Troy, and her multipart headgear, a gift from Aphrodite on her wedding day, tumbles from her head as she falls. On Phaedra's veil, see Zeitlin 1996: 244–5.

58 On the Nurse's role in the crisis, and especially her no-nonsense philosophy of relativism, see Mills 2002: 62–3.

59 The secondary literature on Hippocratic gynecology has in recent years become vast. See, for example, Hanson 1990 and King 1998, who discuss the implication of prescribing regular sexual activity and reproduction for female sexual health in ancient times.

60 For the dangerous ambiguities of the *pharmakon*, see Goff 1990: 48–9; Mills 2002: 63–4.

61 Perhaps the most famous line in the play: Zeitlin 1996: 251 pinpoints it as the moment Hippolytus first recognizes his own duality.

62 Critical views vary regarding Phaedra's motivation in uttering this line: see Zeitlin 1996: 222, 233–4, 247; Mills 2002: 61.

63 Zeitlin 1996: 252.

64 On the hanging of Phaedra as a feminine suicide, see Loraux 1987: 17. See Goff 1990: 38 on how the act of hanging serves to diminish Phaedra's sexuality.

65 Barrett 1964: 311.

66 Zeitlin 1996: 220 notes: "In the end, the honorable Phaedra only seems to corroborate the supposition of woman's essentially duplicitous nature." See also Rabinowitz 1993: 1165–9 on the destructive consequences of deceitful female speech.

67 Loraux 1987: 22.

68 Plath's poem "Edge" (in *The Collected Poems* 1992) is often considered the final poem she wrote before she committed suicide in February 1963.

69 See *LSJ s.v. artao*: the verb refers to both the act of fastening and the state of hanging after being attached.

70 On the pivotal function of the *deltos* and its symbolism, see Zeitlin 1996: 245–7.

71 Zeitlin 1996: 245–6 n. 58 collects all the relevant evidence.

72 For the suicide note as a kind of love letter, see Goff 1990: 38.

73 The *deltos* facilitates the fulfillment of Aphrodite's usual mode of erotic intervention: see Zeitlin 1996: 282.

74 For an insightful discussion of the tensions between father and son in this final scene, see Rabinowitz 1993: 173–88.

75 On the various critical interpretations of Hippolytus' illegitimacy, see Mills 2002: 93–4. On bastardy in ancient Greece, see Ogden 1996.

76 See Goff 1990: 17; Zeitlin 1996: 251; Mills 2002: 90 on how the oath of Hippolytus binds him utterly and thus acts to suppress the truth of Phaedra's accusations.

77 On the loneliness expressed by Hippolytus in his rather tone-deaf exchange with the enraged Theseus, see Mills 2002: 70–2.

78 Commentators note both bull and waves are obvious symbols of sexuality: see Mills 2002: 135 n. 19.

79 For example, the myth of Glaucus of Corinth, son of Poseidon, who in some traditions had also offended Aphrodite; see Zeitlin 1996: 279 n. 113.

80 On the reversal of the name's meaning, see Zeitlin 1996: 225–6.

81 On the reconciliation of Hippolytus and Theseus and their shared suffering, see Zeitlin 1996: 248–9; Mills 2002: 70–2.

82 Zeitlin 1996: 248.

83 Barrett 1964: 3–6 summarizes the ancient cults of Hippolytus; see also Reckford 1974: 431; Zeitlin 1996: 233–4, 267. Mills 2002: 70–1 notes that the cult set up in Hippolytus' memory emphasizes by an extreme negative paradigm the necessity of making a successful transition from childhood to adult marriage – even though he could not have married Phaedra, he arrogantly rejected marriage altogether.

84 Zeitlin 1996: 244–5 discusses the repetition of the gesture as a sign that at the end of the play Hippolytus has assumed Phaedra's place and repeats her earlier experience of lovesickness.

Bibliography

Barrett, W.S. (ed.) (1964) *Euripides: Hippolytos*. Oxford and New York: Oxford University Press.

Breitenberger, B. (2007) *Aphrodite and Eros: The Development of Erotic Mythology in Early Greek Epic and Cult*. London and New York: Routledge.

Cairns, F.L. (ed.) (2005) *Body Language in the Greek and Roman World*. Swansea: Classical Press of Wales.

Calame, C. (1999) *The Poetics of Eros in Ancient Greece*, trans. J. Lloyd. Princeton, NJ: Princeton University Press.

Campbell, D.A. (ed.) (1967) *Greek Lyric Poetry: A Selection of Early Greek Lyric, Elegiac and Iambic Poetry*. London: Bristol Classical Press.

Carson, A. (1986) *Eros the Bittersweet: An Essay*. Princeton, NJ: Princeton University Press.

Cyrino, M.S. (1995) *In Pandora's Jar: Lovesickness in Early Greek Poetry*. Lanham, MD: University Press of America.

——(2010) *Aphrodite*. London and New York: Routledge.

D'Angour, A. (2013) "Love's battlefield: Rethinking Sappho fragment 31", in E. Sanders, C. Thumiger, C. Carey, and N.J. Lowe (eds) *Erôs in Ancient Greece*. Oxford: Oxford University Press, pp. 59–72.

Dodds, E.R. (ed.) (1960) *Euripides Bacchae*. Oxford: Oxford University Press.

Friedrich, P. (1978) *The Meaning of Aphrodite*. Chicago, IL: University of Chicago Press.

Frontisi-Ducroux, F. (1996) "Eros, desire, and the gaze", in N.B. Kampen (ed.) *Sexuality in Ancient Art*. Cambridge: Cambridge University Press, pp. 81–100.

Goff, B.E. (1990) *The Noose of Words: Readings of Desire, Violence and Language in Euripides' Hippolytos*. Cambridge and New York: Cambridge University Press.

Hanson, A.E. (1990) "The medical writers' woman", in D.M. Halperin, J.J. Winkler, and F.I. Zeitlin (eds) *Before Sexuality: The Construction of Erotic Experience in the Ancient Greek World*. Princeton, NJ: Princeton University Press, pp. 309–38.

Harjo, J. (1983) *She Had Some Horses*. New York: Thunder's Mouth Press.

King, H. (1998) *Hippocrates' Woman: Reading the Female Body in Ancient Greece*. London and New York: Routledge.

Loraux, N. (1987) *Tragic Ways of Killing a Woman*. Cambridge, MA: Harvard University Press.

Luschnig, C.A. (1988) *Time Holds the Mirror: A Study of Knowledge in Euripides' Hippolytus*. Leiden: Brill.

McClure, L. (1999) *Spoken Like a Woman: Speech and Gender in Athenian Drama*. Princeton, NJ: Princeton University Press.

McHardy, F. (2005) "From treacherous wives to murderous mothers: Filicide in tragic fragments", in F. McHardy, J. Robson, and F.D. Harvey (eds) *Lost Dramas of Classical Athens: Greek Tragic Fragments*. Exeter: University of Exeter Press, pp. 129–50.

Mills, S. (2002) *Euripides: Hippolytus*. London: Duckworth.

Mitchell-Boyask, R. (1999) "Euripides' *Hippolytus* and the trials of manhood (the ephebia?)", in M.W. Padilla (ed.) *Rites of Passage in Ancient Greece: Literature, Religion, Society*. Lewisburg, PA: Bucknell University Press, pp. 42–66.

Ogden, D. (1996) *Greek Bastardy in the Classical and Hellenistic Periods*. Oxford: Oxford University Press.

Plath, S. (1992) *The Collected Poems*. New York: Harper Perennial.

Poole, W. (1990) "Male homosexuality in Euripides", in A. Powell (ed.) *Euripides, Women and Sexuality*. London and New York: Routledge, pp. 108–50.

Rabinowitz, N.S. (1993) *Anxiety Veiled: Euripides and the Traffic in Women*. Ithaca, NY and London: Cornell University Press.

Reckford, K.J. (1974) "Phaedra and Pasiphae: The pull backward", *Transactions of the American Philological Association* 104: 307–28.

Robson, J. (2013) "The language(s) of love in Aristophanes", in E. Sanders, C. Thumiger, C. Carey, and N.J. Lowe (eds) *Erôs in Ancient Greece*. Oxford: Oxford University Press, pp. 251–66.

Rosenzweig, R. (2004) *Worshipping Aphrodite: Art and Cult in Classical Athens*. Ann Arbor, MI: University of Michigan Press.

Sanders, E. (2013) "Sexual jealousy and *Eros* in Euripides' *Medea*", in E. Sanders, C. Thumiger, C. Carey, and N.J. Lowe (eds) *Erôs in Ancient Greece*. Oxford: Oxford University Press, pp. 41–59.

Sanders, E., Thumiger, C., Carey, C., and Lowe, N.J. (eds) (2013) *Erôs in Ancient Greece*. Oxford: Oxford University Press.

Sexton, A. (1969) *Love Poems*. Boston, MA: Houghton Mifflin.

Sissa, G. (1990) *Greek Virginity*, trans. A. Goldhammer. Cambridge, MA: Harvard University Press.

Stafford, E.J. (2013) "From the gymnasium to the wedding: *Eros* in Athenian art and cult", in E. Sanders, C. Thumiger, C. Carey, and N.J. Lowe (eds) *Erôs in Ancient Greece*. Oxford: Oxford University Press, pp. 175–208.

Stewart, A. (1996) "Reflections", in N.B. Kampen (ed.) *Sexuality in Ancient Art*. Cambridge: Cambridge University Press, pp. 136–54.

Sutton, R.F. Jr (1992) "Pornography and persuasion on Attic pottery", in A. Richlin (ed.) *Pornography and Representation in Greece and Rome*. Oxford and New York: Oxford University Press, pp. 3–35.

Thornton, B.S. (1997) *Eros: The Myth of Ancient Greek Sexuality*. Boulder, CO: Westview Press.

Thumiger, C. (2013) "Mad *erôs* and eroticized madness in tragedy", in E. Sanders, C. Thumiger, C. Carey, and N.J. Lowe (eds) *Erôs in Ancient Greece*. Oxford: Oxford University Press, pp. 27–40.

Watson, P.A. (1995) *Ancient Stepmothers: Myth, Misogyny and Reality*. Leiden: Brill.

Zeitlin, F.I. (1996) *Playing the Other: Gender and Society in Classical Greek Literature*. Chicago, IL and London: University of Chicago Press.

14

DOG-LOVE-DOG

Kynogamia and Cynic sexual ethics

Dorota Dutsch

The problem with *kynogamia*

The 2009 film *Dogging: A Love Story*, directed by Simon Ellis, provoked visceral reactions from critics and audiences. "Dogging" refers in British English to sex in public places, and the critics' moral disgust for the "sleazy" and "sordid" practices blended with their comments on the film's aesthetic shortcomings.[1] Public sex has its considerable capacity to shock because it violates a deep-rooted desire to separate private from public, human from animal, clean from dirty, rational from mindless. And yet, as I argue in this chapter, one ancient ethical system presented public sex as rational and ethical behavior. The Greek term for public sex, *kynogamia* (dog marriage), is reminiscent of "dogging." *Kynogamia* is linked in ancient testimonies with the Cynics, or "Dogs," especially with a philosophical couple active in the fourth century BCE, Crates of Thebes and Hipparchia of Maroneia.[2] Sextus Empiricus, Tatian, Clemens, and Theodoretus speak of Crates and Hipparchia practicing *kynogamia* in the middle of the busy Stoa Poikile.[3] Lactantius and Isidore further assert that other Cynic couples followed their example, and that the Cynic school was in fact named after this dog-like behavior by its adherents.[4] While "public sex" is the prevalent contextual meaning of *kynogamia*, the tenth-century Byzantine encyclopedia *Suda* claims that Crates coined the term to describe his marriage (*gamos*) with the fellow Cynic—not any specific sexual practice.[5] In fact the only meaning of the word listed in the *LSJ* is "*Dog wedding*, used by Crates of his own marriage."[6] Should we, then, dismiss the notion of Cynics having sex in public as an invention of generally hostile later biographers? While it is, of course, impossible to verify whether the tales about Crates and Hipparchia correspond to historical practices, I will argue that the concept of *kynogamia* resonates deeply with the thought of early Cynics and can serve as a useful focal point for reconstructing their sexual ethics.

The term *kynogamia* has a double meaning. The first element, *kyno*, denotes "dog" and connotes "Dog," that is, a Cynic philosopher. The second element, *gamia*, appears in several compound nouns denoting diverse marriage practices, including *mono-* and *poly-gamia*.[7] In its primary meaning, "dog marriage," *kynogamia* is an oxymoron deriding the institution of marriage: dogs obviously do not wed; they mate as they please. The secondary meaning of *kynogamia*, "Cynic philosophers' marriage," hints at a program for a Cynic anti-marriage, suggesting that the philosophers' sexual practice should be modeled on that of the eponymous animal.[8] Scholars tend to dismiss *kynogamia* as a marginal topic, a colorful detail of the Cynic lore, or to assume that such reports are meaningful only as a token of the Cynic rejection of traditional marriage, which is thus assumed to have conveyed a critique of contemporary sexual mores but no positive program.[9]

My contention in the present essay is that reports of Cynic *kynogamia* are, on the contrary, closely linked to a positive proposal of sexual ethics. There are good reasons to expect that tales about *kynogamia* would have been part of a program linked to and illustrative of Cynic philosophy. Lack of inhibition is the Cynic trademark: biographical sources often portray Cynics as fond of drawing public attention to their bodies and bodily functions. Since such portrayals consistently represent the Cynics' bodily acts as witty efforts to draw attention to specific teachings, it is reasonable to expect that the stories about public sex are programmatic.[10] Given the nature of the Cynic teachings, their program must be gleaned from the famous sayings (*chreiai*), anecdotes, and literary allusions handed down in philosophical biography.[11] In order to identify this positive proposal of a sexual ethics, I will draw mostly on Diogenes Laertius' (D.L.) *Lives of Philosophers* from the third century CE.[12] I will begin by situating *kynogamia* firmly within the general aesthetics of the early Cynics' public performance as presented by D.L. To that end, I discuss several notorious acts of the arch-Cynic, Diogenes of Sinope, highlighting both the ways in which the early Cynics reportedly used bodies to produce meaning and the core values conveyed by such performances. My next move will be to analyze the comments on sexuality among the prolific testimonies to Diogenes of Sinope's thought, and show that they form a coherent ethical program. I will then compare Diogenes' sexual ethics to the comedic testimonies to Crates' life. Finally, I turn to Hipparchia's biography to ask how the Cynics' practice of correct sexual relations—including public sex—was imagined to have affected the most famous female adherent of the sect.

Lack of inhibition and the aesthetics of the Cynic performance

The Cynics offered practical advice on living a happy life and demonstrated the efficacy of their beliefs through public actions.[13] To Diogenes of Sinope, choosing to read about philosophy, rather than interacting directly with a philosopher, was like choosing a painting of figs over fresh fruit (D.L. 6.49). Since public performance was a privileged means of conveying Cynic ideas, and since the famous sayings (*chreiai*) of the Cynics share certain linguistic features, scholars often assume that many of the *chreiai* were ultimately derived from street performances.[14] In the absence of direct evidence, it is hard to assess the testimonial value of the anecdotes about the Cynics' public behavior (as opposed to their words); but such vignettes are at least a viable record of how the Cynics' street performances were remembered.[15] In those recollections of Cynic acts, the performer is equipped with certain telltale props, whose "invention" is attributed to either Antisthenes or Diogenes of Sinope: the double folded cloak (*tribon*), the wallet (*pera*), and the staff (*bakteria*).[16] Thus costumed, the Cynic exercises his or her right to free speech (*parrhesia*).[17] Verbal artistry and succinct wit are typical of the Cynic performance as portrayed in the biography. The puns attributed to Diogenes are, as Bracht Branham (1996) has argued, of a very specific character: all require that the audience take a creative leap from one discursive matrix to another.[18] Diogenes claimed, for example, that people who do not own the Cynic's wallet (*pera*) should be called *ana-peroi,* which means "physically disabled," or "stunted in development." By forcing his listener/reader to leap from absence of a Cynic prop to bodily disability, Diogenes makes a powerful statement about Cynicism as being the only path toward becoming a fully functioning human being (6.33). The coinage *kynogamia,* which invites the mind to move from mating dogs to philosophical marriage and back, uses a similar linguistic tour de force. Furthermore, public sex would also have found parallels in Diogenes of Sinope's use of the body for rhetorical purposes. Consider, for example, this concise anecdote about Diogenes at a party (D.L. 6.46):

ἐν δείπνῳ προσερρίπτουν αὐτῷ τινες ὀστάρια ὡς κυνί· καὶ ὃς ἀπαλλαττόμενος προσεούρησεν αὐτοῖς ὡς κύων.

At a feast some men tossed bones at him, as though he were a dog;
And he in response urinated at them, as though he were a dog.

The dinner guests in this anecdote appropriate the Cynic's humorous self-designation; they imply that the "Dog" is not entitled to his portion of meat at a feast, but should have bones tossed at him, as if he were indeed a canine. This gesture, which reduces the Cynic to the status of scavenger, also seems to imply that Diogenes' rejection of civilized manners is disingenuous: for all his posturing, the Cynic depends for his livelihood on the very society whose silly conventions he criticizes. Diogenes' rebuttal draws attention to his freedom to do as he pleases, which results from his rejection of social conventions. By urinating at the other guests, Diogenes also asserts his credentials as a radical ready to put his words into action. The verb *prosoureo* denotes Diogenes' action literally and metaphorically, as it means "to urinate in somebody's direction" as well as "to show disrespect to someone."[19] The epiphora "as though he were a dog" further establishes a tit-for-tat poetics, underscoring the justice of Diogenes' revenge and warning the audience/reader to take Diogenes at his word: when the Cynic says "I piss," he indeed urinates.[20]

Several anecdotes about Diogenes of Sinope's views on sex also show the philosopher using his body to demonstrate his teachings. D.L. reports that Diogenes of Sionope used to "do the works of Demeter and Aphrodite alike in public." Once, while practicing manual self-stimulation (*cheirourgon*) in the middle of a street, the Cynic apparently compared the two, saying: "If only I could fill my stomach by rubbing it!" (D.L. 6.69). This saying, which Laertius also recounts elsewhere (6.46), implies that the sage can deal with *eros* freely and with great ease and will not shy away from demonstrating this achievement in public.[21] Diogenes' lack of inhibition also shows that the Cynic sage is able to turn sex (and references to sex) into an effective rhetorical device.

The ease with which Diogenes uses his body as a teaching prop is not, however, to be taken for granted. The anecdote briefly mentioned above, about Crates, the inventor of the term *kynogamia*, and Zeno, the future founder of Stoicism, presents immunity to embarrassment as an art that requires both talent and practice (D.L. 7.3). As apprentice to Crates, Zeno was apparently making excellent progress in most aspects of his training except *anaischyntia*, "unabashedness."[22] In order to free his disciple from his bashfulness, Crates made Zeno carry a clay pot full of lentil porridge across the Kerameikos. Embarrassed, Zeno tried to cover the pot, but Crates surprised him: he hit the pot and broke it with his staff, causing the brown substance to flow down his apprentice's legs. As Zeno turned to flee, mortified that the passers-by might think that he had just had a very public bowel movement, Crates responded with a line from an unknown drama: "Why flee, little Phoenician? Nothing terrible has happened to you." Crates is obviously mocking Zeno's concern for appearances; after all, his pot contained only lentil soup. The ability not to be embarrassed by one's actual bodily functions would, according to this logic, require a higher degree of self-mastery, and public intercourse would indeed have to be considered an impressive demonstration of *anaischyntia*.

The term *anaischyntia* deserves a few words of explanation. According to Aristotle, shame was a consequence of behavior that revealed vice in one's character.[23] The Cynics thought that no vice was revealed either by apparent incontinence or by public sex. There was, therefore, no need to feel shame. Hence, Diogenes' consistent use of the term *anaischyntia*, rather than *anaideia* (which modern scholars tend to adopt to speak of the Cynic attitude), is understandable;

anaideia would denote lack for respect of others and oneself, which is not a quality that the Cynics would have claimed for themselves.[24] *Anaischyntia* does not imply a wholesale denial of shame, but rather a rejection of the usual judgments about what are and are not *aischra*. Sayings of Diogenes of Sinope, in *DL* (6.65), offer examples of a constructive program of Cynic morality, based on a new kind of shame. They are conveyed in a series of questions Diogenes asked of various interlocutors, introduced by the formula "Are you not ashamed of … ?" (οὐκ αἰσχύνῃ;). Acts that Diogenes would have considered transgressions against the proper sense of shame include lack of care for one's soul, lack of attention to one's body, and lack of respect for one's father. As Anthony Long concisely put it, the Cynics rejected "manners not morals" (1996: 35).

The new morals were to be based directly on the authority of nature, *physis*, which Diogenes of Sinope ranked above *nomos*, law or custom (D.L. 6.71). The above-cited anecdotes about Diogenes imply that to the Cynics, the most important manifestation of nature was the flesh and blood person and his or her freedom from unnecessary constraints. A full bladder or sexual urges would, as functions of *physis*, have priority over social conventions.[25] The philosopher's body thus works, in the Cynic discourse, as the stage upon which the laws of physical necessity are seen to act. The philosopher is expected to not only cater to them freely but also to make a performance of his (or her) disregard for empty conventions.[26] The simplest implication of public lovemaking would, then, be that sex, a natural function of the human body, should not be perceived as shameful and that people should be free to satisfy their urges anywhere and at any time. But Cynic sexual morals entail a more complex notion of "sex according to nature" than an apology for sex as a bodily function that one ought to be free to perform in public. In order to grasp this notion, we will now take a look at the comments on sex attributed to Diogenes of Sinope, and at the philosophical and literary background to his definition of correct sexuality.

Diogenes' Cynic *gamos* and Plato's *Republic*

The Cynic validation of nature over custom was not a call for self-indulgence. On the contrary, the ideal Cynic strives for a life based on reason (6.24) and restraint; Diogenes advocates simple food, water, and indifference to discomfort (6.34, 6.44). Sex should also be simple. Diogenes' program of sexual ethics consists of both a critique of current mores and a proposal for a Cynic solution. The critique addresses the diverse sexual relationships in which a Greek man would typically engage. Marriage should be avoided. There is never a right time to marry: a young man is too young, an old one, too old (6.54). A mistress will rule over her lover even if he happens to be a king (6.63; cf. 6.61 and 6.66). A prostitute is poison dipped in honey (6.60; cf. 6.61, 6.66). Seducing someone else's wife is not worth the risk (6.68). In brief, none of the conventional licit or illicit relationships in which a woman is the beloved obtains Diogenes' approval. Relationships in which the beloved is male receive no better press. Diogenes repeatedly chastises young men for exposing themselves to unwanted advances: one dines with Persian officials (6.46), another plays *kottabos* in the baths (6.46), others wear flashy clothes (6.46, 6.47); yet others adopt provocative postures (6.53, 6.65). Lest we conclude that this is a crusade against male attractiveness, a woman exposing her charms while praying is likewise rebuffed (6.38). These short *chreiai* depict situations in which the potential beloveds might forsake mastery over their bodies for a material reward that is not worth such a sacrifice, or that is no reward at all. In fact, freedom might be lost in the process and freedom is, indisputably, one of the central values of Cynicism.[27]

Freedom is at stake in both the warnings Diogenes addresses to potential objects of desire, and in the warnings to lovers who risk becoming enslaved to their objects of desire. Taken together, Diogenes' warnings imply that the sexual practices of his contemporaries are inherently harmful to both the lover and the beloved, precisely because they jeopardize the freedom of both.[28] This view is most clearly articulated in the comment that Diogenes is said to have addressed to a young man putting on fancy clothes: "if this is for a man, you are unlucky (*atycheis*); if for a woman, you are unjust (*adikeis*)" (6.54). In other words, in order to want to sell oneself, one has to be short on luck, while, in order to try to seduce a woman, one must lack moral principles. Thus, to be the loved one (*eromenos*) is a misfortune; to be the lover (*erastes*) is an injustice.

Diogenes, however, also offers instructions on how to have morally correct sex. If sexual relations that constitute a danger to a person's freedom are objectionable because of this danger, then relations that do not pose such a danger should be unobjectionable. We can now see the anecdote in which Diogenes praises self-stimulation (6.46 and 6.69) in a new light. If the most important criterion of sexual ethics were avoiding imposition of any kind on the lover or beloved, then Cynic philosophy would indeed have placed *cheirourgia* (self-stimulation) as the most ethical form of human sexuality. But so radical a sexual *autarkeia* (self-sufficiency) was not the only practice that the Cynics deemed moral. Rather, Diogenes' anecdote about masturbation purposely sets the stakes too high.[29] A second-best option would be a sexual relationship that infringes as little as possible on the freedom of both the lover and the beloved.

Traces of a positive attitude toward sex and procreation can be found in D.L.'s summary of the views of Antisthenes, whose ideas, he claims, were the inspiration for both Diogenes of Sinope and, most relevant to the current discussion, Crates (6.15). Antisthenes apparently taught that enlightened men should form unions (*gamesein*) with women of the noblest disposition (as opposed to the best looks) and have children with them (6.11); he also insisted that women had the same predisposition toward virtue as men (6.12). No comparably enthusiastic statements about marriage are attributed to Diogenes of Sinope, but he apparently did formulate a definition of the correct relationship between a man and a woman, stating that women should be *koinai* and that man should persuade his partner to live with him (rather than negotiate with her male relatives). The adjective *koinos* means "common" or "shared," but I will avoid translating it for the moment (6.72):

ἔλεγε δὲ καὶ κοινὰς εἶναι δεῖν τὰς γυναῖκας, γάμον μηδένα νομίζων, ἀλλὰ τὸν πείσαντα τῇ πεισθείσῃ συνεῖναι· κοινοὺς δὲ διὰ τοῦτο καὶ τοὺς υἱέας.

And he [Diogenes] said that women should be *koinai*, not recognizing any union (*gamos*) besides one in which a man, who has persuaded a woman (to live with him), cohabits with a woman who has been persuaded (by him); and for this reason, sons should be also *koinoi*.

Diogenes' proposal for a correct union consists of three elements: (1) women should be *koinai*; (2) marriage entails free choice on the part of the woman as well as on the part of the man; (3) children should be *koinoi*. The second point, conveying the importance of freedom from imposition, appears logical in light of the above analysis of Diogenes' *chreiai*. The first point however, suggesting at first glance that women be objects shared by all men, seems to contradict the idea that women have the choice to accept or reject attempts at persuasion. In order to understand the meaning of *koinos* in this context, I propose to compare Diogenes' use of this adjective with the famous proposal for philosophers' sharing (*koinonia*) of women and children, namely, Socrates' arrangements for the guardians in the fifth book of Plato's *Republic*.[30]

At 451c of the *Republic*, Socrates defines *koinonia* as tantamount to the abolition of two aspects of marriage: the acquisition (*ktesis*) of wives and the possession (*chreia*) of women and children. "Sharing" in this philosophical context connotes abolition of private entitlement to and responsibility for women (and children), which is not the same as joint access to women.[31] Because of the chronological and contextual proximity, it is reasonable to expect that Diogenes is using *koinos* similarly. If *koinos* refers to the elimination of marriage and family, the women who are *koinai* are not "shared" by all men but "exempt from control" of one man, each woman being potentially available to any man who can persuade her to live with him.[32] While in Plato's imaginary republic, wise rulers arrange mating festivals and decide *de facto* which woman is available to which man, the Cynic *gamos* calls for women to make their own decisions: "that he who has persuaded live with her who has been persuaded."[33] This free union that respects the wishes of both partners constitutes the innovative core of Diogenes' proposal for the Cynic *gamos*. But how does this proposal relate to *kynogamia*?

Let us keep Plato and his guardians in mind for another moment, for there is one more useful hint about Diogenes' idea of marriage in the subtext of Plato's *Republic*. And this hint has to do with the intellectual abilities of dogs, and of philosophers of both sexes. The starting point for Socrates' discussion of the aptitudes of male and female guardians is a comparison between dogs and human beings (451d4–e5). Guard dogs, he points out, share the same duties, regardless of their sex, even after they mate, although the females are considered weaker (cf. 455c6–e1). Dogs provide Socrates with a model for natural behavior that justifies the claim that male and female guardians must mate, receive the same training, and do the same work—regardless of their sex.

The same conceit—that dogs are a paradigm of natural relations between sexes—informs the term *kynogamia*. The concept of Cynic union thus resonates both with the series of jokes about Cynics as "Dogs" (see above) and with a fourth-century BCE debate on whether or not women can practice philosophy and attain the same virtues as men. Several of Socrates' disciples offered answers to this question: the answer given by Antisthenes was, as we have seen, emphatically positive; Plato's was a cautious "yes, but not to the same degree"; Diogenes of Sinope's definition of *gamos* implies that women have at the least the same competence to make decisions about their own bodies as do men.[34] Crates' and Hipparchia's *kynogamia* appears in this context as an embodied answer to the question of the relative abilities of men and women. If *anaischyntia* is a virtue, then the public practice of heterosexual intercourse demonstrates that women are men's equals with respect to their ability to disregard empty conventions.

Before we turn to testimonies regarding the couple's shared life, it will be useful to summarize what we have found out so far about Cynic recommendations for a healthy sexuality. First and foremost, sex is natural, so there is nothing shameful in it, on the condition—and this is the greatest challenge—that it does not violate anyone's freedom. Self-stimulation, a staple of biographical accounts of the life of Diogenes of Sinope, is presented as the simplest solution to this challenge. But a union between heterosexual partners who have come to a mutual agreement is another viable option. This option comes with an important proviso: in order for a woman's consent to be valid, she must be free to give it, and, therefore, *koine*, exempt from male tutelage and available to whomever *she* chooses.

This proposal for *gamos* still leaves an important lacuna in our knowledge about Cynic sexuality: the relationships between men. Or perhaps it does not. From a Greek man's point of view, a relationship arranged by mutual consent and involving no financial obligations (unlike relationships with either a *hetaira* or a wife), a relationship in which one's partner is one's intellectual equal, would be usually possible only between men. It is worth noting that the language of persuasion and consent is part of the vocabulary and culture of male courtship, as represented in Plato's *Symposium*.[35] Diogenes of Sinope's focus on (male) persuasion and (female) consent (τὸν πείσαντα τῇ πεισθείσῃ συνεῖναι) in his definition of the Cynic *gamos* would thus imply that a relationship between a lover (*erastes*) and his beloved (*eromenos*) should be the model for the ideal heterosexual union. The Cynic "sex according to nature" would therefore entail far more than a license to make love on the street: in order to be "natural," sexual relations must be ethical. The Cynics' rejection of manners but not morals means that individuals engaging in correct relationships must be capable of making choices dictated by their *physis*.

Crates of Thebes and the literary echoes of *kynogamia*

The epistolographic tradition of the Second Sophistic fashioned Crates into an ardent proponent of gender equality.[36] In one fictitious letter to Hipparchia (28) he is presented as correcting Plato's famous statement that women have the same kinds of abilities as men, but are always weaker (455e1): Crates insists that women's nature is in fact no weaker than men's.[37] Nothing so radical is to be found in D.L.'s life of Crates, in which Crates comes across as a comic caricature of a philosopher. Physically deformed (6.91–2), he makes a spectacle of his resistance to hardships in ways verging on masochism: immune to cold and heat, he wears a thick cloak in the summer and rags in winter (6.87); impervious to insults, he deliberately exposes himself to public humiliation (6.86, 6.87, 6.90–2). But there are two testimonies that, by virtue of the dating of their sources, strongly suggest that Crates and Hipparchia were known in the fourth century BCE for their application of radical ideas about gender and sexuality to their own life and the education of their children. The most direct witness to this reputation is a fragment of *Didymai* by Menander (Kock fr. 117, 118; cf. D.L. 6.93), Crates' younger contemporary. The speaker of the lines in question is a man who addresses a woman, inviting her to imagine a fate very much like that of Hipparchia:

συμπεριπατήσεις γὰρ τρίβων᾽ ἔχουσ᾽ ἐμοί,
ὥσπερ Κράτητι τῷ κυνικῷ ποθ᾽ ἡ γυνή,
καὶ θυγατέρ᾽ ἐξέδωκ᾽ ἐκεῖνος, ὡς ἔφη
αὐτός, ἐπὶ πείρᾳ δοὺς τριάκονθ᾽ ἡμέρας.

You will walk around wearing the double-cloak with me,
Just as once with Crates the Cynic his wife did,
And that man married off his daughter, as he said,
"Giving her away for trial, for thirty days."

Menander's speaker draws attention to two unorthodox behaviors of the Cynics. First, he presents Crates and Hipparchia as walking together, both dressed in the standard Cynic outfit. Identical clothing underscores their equality and shared lifestyle, and their life-long performance of the creed that men and women can strive to achieve the same virtues. Whether or not the addressee of this comic utterance embraced the prospect of the Cynic life with enthusiasm, this fragment is a crucial reminder that contemporaries envisioned Crates and Hipparchia's shared life as a proposal that others were invited to adopt.

In the next two lines, the speaker mocks Crates (but not Hipparchia) for giving his (their?) daughter away for an unconventional "trial marriage." By fourth-century Greek standards, this month-long relationship is suspiciously reminiscent of a contract with a *hetaira*.[38] So Crates is in fact accused of acting as a pimp for his own daughter. No matter whether this reference to Crates' daughter's short-lived sexual relationship and his tolerance of it has any historical value, the fragment bears witness to Crates' staunchly liberal attitude toward sexual unions, including that of his own daughter. "Crates the anti-father" is also the protagonist of another anecdote in which Cynic sexual morals are deliberately conflated with the mores surrounding prostitution

(D.L. 6.88). Drawn from Eratosthenes of Cyrene's (276–195 BCE) work *On Comedy*, this account presents Crates taking his and Hipparchia's son Pasicles to a brothel and instructing him that this was "how his father was married."[39] Here, again, Crates features as a father instilling lax sexual morals in his child. These two anecdotes about children suggest that the Cynic redefinition of family both undermined the traditional role of the Greek father and put him in charge of a program of Cynic sexual education. The satire of the sexual ethics of free love as equivalent to prostitution would have been especially biting if Crates was indeed the passionate critic of prostitution evinced by his *chreiai*.[40] These testimonies demonstrate that as public figures, Crates and Hipparchia passed for radical advocates of equality (fr. 117) and sexual of freedom (fr. 118 and D.L. 6.88), who practiced what they preached.

In order to find a less hostile take on Crates' sexual ethics, we must turn to a later source, a *chreia* that Augustine apparently found in Cornelius Nepos' *De viris illustribus* (first century BCE).[41] This *chreia* contains the earliest allusion to Crates and Hipparchia having sex in public; it is humorous but nevertheless sympathetic to the Cynic couple's resolve to live by their principles:

> amplexare factum illud Cratae Thebani, hominis locupletis et nobilis, cui adeo fuit cordi secta cynicorum ut relinquens paternas opes Athenas cum uxore migraverit Hipparchide, pari animo istius philosophiae sectatrice cum qua cum concumbere in publico vellet, ut refert Cornelius Nepos et illa occultandi gratia palli velamen obduceret, verberata est a marito "tuis sensibus nimirum," inquit, "parum adhuc docta es, quae, quod te recte facere noveris, id aliis praesentibus facere non audeas."

> Consider this famous deed of Crates of Thebes, a wealthy and noble man, who was so passionate about Cynic ideas that, leaving behind the wealth of his father, he moved to Athens with his wife Hipparchia, who was an equally zealous follower of this doctrine. And when he wanted to lie down with her in public, and she, as Cornelius Nepos reports, pulled over her cloak as a cover, she was scolded by her husband: "obviously you are not yet wise," he said, "since you don't dare to do in the presence of others what you know well to be the right thing to do."

This *chreia* represents a rather self-righteous and patronizing Crates: he rebukes Hipparchia in public, telling her that she still has a lot to learn. Even so, the story casts her as Crates' partner and fellow practitioner of Cynicism. First, Augustine writes (possibly already echoing Nepos) that Hipparchia admired the Cynics with an enthusiasm equal to that of Crates (*pari animo*). Then, Crates speaks of her hesitation as a result of insufficient training (*parum adhuc docta*) rather than some inherent weakness. He expects Hipparchia to accept his argument and consent because she knows that his request is reasonable, not because she simply must obey him. Most important, Nepos' source seems to have presented the ability and willingness to have intercourse in public as a virtue, a proof of strength and moral competence, rather than a moral weakness. This perception not only coincides with our analysis above of the Cynic unabashedness, but also informs D.L.'s account of Hipparchia's life.

Hipparchia's story in Diogenes Laertius

Although we have so far mostly turned to D.L. as source of anecdotes about the life of ancient Cynics, it is important to keep in mind that he was also a writer whose choices reflect a system of beliefs about generation and transmission of philosophical knowledge. Sexual relationships, as Warren has observed (2007: 144–5), play an important role in Diogenes' construction of the history of philosophy: Diogenes systematically presents homoerotic relationships between masters and disciples as underlying the patterns of transmission of knowledge.[42] Knowledge and intimacy are even more closely intertwined in the rare cases of female philosophers: it is as a beloved, either a philosopher's sexual partner or his child, that the female disciple receives training from her master and lover or father.[43] Most women never outgrow the role of loyal recipients of male knowledge to become independent thinkers, and are mentioned only in passing. The life of Hipparchia of Maroneia is exceptional: not only is it much longer than that of any other female philosopher, but she is also said to have advocated her own ideas (on women's education) in public. Given Diogenes' underlying assumptions about intimacy and transmission of knowledge, Hipparchia's unorthodox position as a thinker can be expected to reflect the ideology of the Cynic union. I propose to show that in Diogenes' account, Hipparchia's unorthodox sexual conduct is positively linked to her intellectual and philosophical capabilities.

The tale begins with a humorous episode in which Crates demonstrates the validity of the Cynic approach to bodily functions. Hipparchia's brother, Metrocles, a student of Theophrastus, disgraces himself by breaking wind in public. When the distressed youth contemplates suicide, Crates intervenes, persuading him that bodily functions are not shameful and thus saving his life (6.94–5). Impressed by this demonstration, Hipparchia becomes enamored of Crates' teachings. The account of the circumstances under which they became partners illustrates an array of virtues that are preconditions for the Cynic partnership, and is worth citing *in extensor* (6.96–7).

καὶ ἤρα τοῦ Κράτητος καὶ τῶν λόγων καὶ τοῦ βίου, οὐδενὸς τῶν μνηστευομένων ἐπιστρεφομένη, οὐ πλούτου, οὐκ εὐγενείας, οὐ κάλλους· ἀλλὰ πάντ' ἦν Κράτης αὐτῇ καὶ δὴ καὶ ἠπείλει τοῖς γονεῦσιν ἀναιρήσειν αὑτήν, εἰ μὴ τούτῳ δοθείη. Κράτης μὲν οὖν παρακαλούμενος ὑπὸ τῶν γονέων αὐτῆς ἀποτρέψαι τὴν παῖδα, πάντ' ἐποίει, καὶ τέλος μὴ πείθων, ἀναστὰς καὶ ἀποθέμενος τὴν ἑαυτοῦ σκευὴν ἀντικρὺ αὐτῆς ἔφη, "ὁ μὲν νυμφίος οὗτος, ἡ δὲ κτῆσις αὕτη, πρὸς ταῦτα βουλεύου· οὐδὲ γὰρ ἔσεσθαι κοινωνός, εἰ μὴ καὶ τῶν αὐτῶν ἐπιτηδευμάτων γενηθείης." εἵλετο ἡ παῖς καὶ ταὐτὸν ἀναλαβοῦσα σχῆμα συμπεριῄει τἀνδρὶ καὶ ἐν τῷ φανερῷ συνεγίνετο καὶ ἐπὶ τὰ δεῖπνα ἀπῄει.

She fell in love with Crates' words and lifestyle, and was not attracted to the wealth, high birth, or good looks of any of her suitors. Crates was everything for her. She even threatened her parents that she would do away with herself, unless she was given to him in marriage. When her parents asked him to dissuade her, Crates did everything he could. Finally, unable to convince her, he rose, took off his garments, and spoke facing her: "Such is the bridegroom; this is all his property; think about it. For you will not be my partner unless you come to share my ways of living." And the girl chose. Putting on the same clothing, she went about with her man, lived with him in public, and even attended dinner parties.

It is noteworthy that the anecdote opens with Hipparchia pursuing Crates, and that she is therefore styled as the lover, not the beloved. The motif of love is somewhat problematic in the light of Diogenes of Sinope's views that passion jeopardizes the lovers' freedom, although Antisthenes recommended that the sage should fall in love. It may be that Crates and Hipparchia could be considered the followers of Antisthenes rather than Diogenes in this respect, although Crates himself is said to have authored a couplet claiming that love had to be cured with hunger, time, or, failing both, suicide.[44] At any rate, Diogenes Laertius is careful to say that while Crates was the focus of Hipparchia's attention, she was, in fact, in love with his teachings. Her lack of interest in suitors who represent the conventional values of good looks, wealth, and youth indicates her aptitude to become a Cynic. Likewise, Crates' lack of interest in the attractive prospect of marrying a young girl from a well-to-do family demonstrates his exemplary Cynic indifference toward the usual *desiderata*. Finally, attempting to dissuade Hipparchia, Crates resorts to frontal nudity, in a masterful show of *anaischyntia*. But Hipparchia is unfazed. Her reaction proves that, unlike another famous disciple of Crates, Zeno (he of the lentil soup), she has the makings of a true Cynic. Naked, Crates states his conditions: only if she is sure of making a conscious decision, knowing that he owns nothing but his body, can Hipparchia be his partner.

The emphasis on consent is strongly reminiscent of the phrase "he who has persuaded would live with her who has been persuaded" from Diogenes of Sinope's definition of a Cynic union. The absence of the term "wife" from this mock-wedding scene is also remarkable: Hipparchia becomes Crates' partner, *koinonos*, not his wife, *gyne*. Without embarrassment or hesitation, the girl adopts the demeanor (*schema*) of the Cynic, attends dinner parties, and lives with Crates in public.[45] Hipparchia from now on mirrors Crates, leading a Cynic's life. When D.L. states that Hipparchia "used to live with [Crates] in the open" (ἐν τῷ φανερῷ συνεγίνετο) he might be alluding to the tales about public sex, since the Greek verb συγγίνομαι can have, just like the English "to live with," sexual overtones (*LSJ* s.v.3).[46] More importantly, the arrangement is presented as Hipparchia's choice; in fact, she is styled, at least at the beginning, as the one who persuades while Crates is being persuaded. Their union is thus based on a verbal contract between consenting partners, who share clothing, lifestyle, food, and sex. The ideal to which Crates' and Hipparchia's union aspires is strikingly similar to the union between two male lovers.

As a love story, the beginning of Hipparchia's passion recalls the classic account of the disciple's love for his master, Plato's representation of Alcibiades' passion for Socrates in the *Symposium* (215a–217). Just like Socrates, Crates was apparently physically repulsive (6.91).[47] And just like Alcibiades, Hipparchia has suitors who surpass the philosopher in beauty and wealth. Yet, like Socrates' disciple, she is able to see beyond the conventional values, and falls in love with philosophy. By the standards famously formulated by Diotima in the *Symposium* (210a–212a), this kind of desire for something beyond the body makes Hipparchia into a philosopher.

In the final section of Diogenes' description of her life, Diogenes presents Hipparchia as a philosopher in her own right, showing off her wit and moral stamina. She attends a dinner party; Crates seems to be absent (or at least is not mentioned), but another philosopher, Theodore the Atheist, is present, and he and Hipparchia engage in a public debate. Theodore apparently argues that a given action is always inherently just or unjust, no matter who performs it. Hipparchia responds that, if this were true, then—given that it is not unfair for Theodore to hit himself—it would not be unfair for Hipparchia to hit him as well (6.97–8). Unable to find a counterargument, her adversary pulls down her cloak:

ὁ δὲ πρὸς μὲν τὸ λεχθὲν οὐδὲν ἀπήντησεν, ἀνέσυρε δ' αὐτῆς θοἰμάτιον· ἀλλ' οὔτε κατεπλάγη Ἱππαρχία οὔτε διεταράχθη ὡς γυνή. ἀλλὰ καὶ εἰπόντος αὐτῇ "αὕτη ἐστὶν ἡ τὰς παρ' ἱστοῖς ἐκλιποῦσα κερκίδας;" "ἐγώ," φησίν, "εἰμί, Θεόδωρε· ἀλλὰ μὴ κακῶς σοι δοκῶ βεβουλεῦσθαι περὶ αὐτῆς, εἰ, τὸν χρόνον ὃν ἔμελλον ἱστοῖς προσαναλώσειν, τοῦτον εἰς παιδείαν κατεχρησάμην;" καὶ ταῦτα μὲν καὶ ἄλλα μυρία τῆς φιλοσόφου.

He did not answer anything to what she said, but pulled down her cloak. Hipparchia, however, did not panic and was not confused despite being a woman. But when he said to her [citing Euripides' *Bacchae* 1236]: "Is this the woman who has abandoned her shuttle by her loom?" She answered, "Yes, Theodore, I am this woman. You cannot possibly be thinking that I have not made the right decision for myself if I have devoted to education the time that I would have otherwise wasted at the loom?" This story and many others circulate about this female philosopher.

Theodore attempts to dismiss Hipparchia's achievement by reminding everyone present that she is a woman. He does so in two symbolic gestures. First, he pulls down her *himation*, a garment that can be used metonymically for citizenship and authority.[48] She does not react, and D.L. remarks that her composure is surprising in a woman. Second, Theodore cites from Euripides' *Bacchae* a line (1236) that implies that unspeakable things happen when women abandon their looms. The speaker of the line in the play, Agave, the mother of Pentheus, comes down from the mountains and boasts to her father that she has left her loom in order to accomplish greater deeds. In her arms she carries the remains of her own son Pentheus, whom she has murdered in her frenzy. So Theodore's attack is a vicious attempt to present Hipparchia's refusal to stay at home and spin her wool as monstrous: the female intellectual is styled as a madwoman proud to have murdered her own child. Hipparchia's response is, conversely, perfectly rational. She speaks of her enlightened choice based on her assessment of the value of weaving versus acquiring an education. The loom stands for conventional female duties, the *nomos*, and Hipparchia's rejection of this duty is a Cynic gesture par excellence. Nothing, however, underscores her Cynic credentials as clearly as her indifference to being partially disrobed. This image mirrors Crates' nakedness in the mock-wedding scene and offers the most poignant testimony to Hipparchia's moral and intellectual status as his equal and a superior of some male philosophers, including the defeated Theodore. If living in public with her husband was a part of Hipparchia's training in *anaischyntia*, this triumphant ending implies that it has served her very well indeed.

Conclusion

Our study of *testimonia* to Cynic sexual ethics has revealed an intellectual background against which *kynogamia* acquires a profound ethical meaning. The philosophers whom the tradition represents as prone to making love on the street represent a school whose sexual ethics held personal freedom as an essential value. A correct union between man and woman was one in which "he who has persuaded would live with her who has been persuaded." Such relations are possible between men and women only if one assumes that both partners are equals capable of making informed decisions and free to dispose of their bodies as they see fit—even to make love in the Stoa, should this be their wish. Stories about Crates and Hipparchia wearing the same clothes, sharing the same lifestyle, and having sex on the street publicize a sexual ethics based on equality of aptitudes between men and women.

This equality has its inherent limits: the *testimonia* present Hipparchia as the junior partner in the relationship, whose highest achievement is to become a mirror image of her partner, as Epictetus put it, "another Crates" (3.22.76.2). But despite these limitations, the Cynic partnership's connection to ethics of equality makes *kynogamia* an important episode in the history of ancient sexualities. After all, love between male philosophers, which, as I argue, is the likely model for the Cynic *gamos*, also entails (an at least initial) asymmetry, one that has to do with age and experience. In the end, the account of Crates and Hipparchia's public intercourse is a provocative rhetorical device that draws readers' attention to the radical personal freedom advocated by the Cynics, including its most outrageous aspect: a woman's freedom to dispose of her body as she saw fit.

Notes

1 The adjective "sleazy" was used by Catherine Shoard in the *Guardian* (2009); "sordid," by Eduard Porter in the *Sunday Times* (2009). Bell (2006) discusses the mass media's coverage of and role in the publicizing of "dogging": he terms the media's attitude toward dogging "moral panic." See also Johnson 2007: 543 n. 73 and his observation on the legal response to "dogging" as a measure of public attitudes.

2 On the origin of the name from the gymnasium of Cynosargos, where Antisthenes used to lecture, see D.L. 6.13; cf. D.L. 6.60–1.

3 Sextus Empiricus (*Pyrrhoniae Hypotheses* 1.153.3), Tatian (*Oratio ad Graecos* 3.3.4), Clemens (*Strommata* 4.19.122), and Theodoretus (*Graecarum Affectionum Curatio* 12.49.8).

4 See Lact. *Divin. Inst.* 3.15.21 and Isid. *Ethym* 8.6.14.

5 A *TLG* search yields five instances of the word; four (note 4 above) clearly refer to public sex; only Suda (under kappa; 2341.5) refers to marriage: γήμας δὲ Ἱππαρχίαν τὴν Μαρωνεῖτιν κυνογαμίαν τὸν γάμον ἐκάλεσε. ("Having married Hipparchia of Maroneia, he [i.e. Crates] called their union *kynogamia*.")

6 Branham and Goulet-Cazé 1996: 10 in the introduction to the co-edited collection mention *kynogamia* only briefly, defining it as "marriage."

7 E.g., *agamia, epigamia, monogamia,* and *polygamia, LSJ* ad voc. Lonsdale 1979: 149–50 has conveniently collected references to Athenian attitudes toward dogs; see especially Thuc. 2.50.

8 Taylor 2003: 173–226 compares the roles women, including wives of philosophers, played in diverse schools of Greek philosophy and offers a convenient list of female stereotypes (2003: 213–23). Taylor considers only the Pythagoreans as examples of wifely virtue and dismisses Hipparchia because she was not an independent thinker but was "presented as important only in her relationship with Crates" (Taylor 2003: 201).

9 Desmond states that on account of "her *kynogamia*," Hipparchia was "the most colorful" of the handful of female philosophers (2008: 27). Moles 1995: 139 notes briefly that her attitude toward marriage was part and parcel of the Cynics' qualified rejection of the institutions of the *polis*. Trapp 2007: 165 calls *kynogamia* an "anti-marriage" meant to reveal the mistakes embodied by conventional marriage.

10 On the Cynics' use of the body for rhetorical purposes, cf. Branham 1996: 100–1.

11 The genre of *chreiai* was particularly popular in the fourth and third centuries BCE: Gow 1965: 12–13; for their role in rhetorical education, see Hock and O'Neil 2002; on their use to convey gendered discourse, see McClure 2003.

12 See Long and his references (1996: 30–1) for the rationale for distinguishing between Diogenes Laertius's portrayal of early Cynics and their representation in writers who alter their portrayal to reflect later philosophical developments, such as Epictetus, Lucian, Dio Chrysostom, and Julian. Sources of D.L. often go back to the fourth century BCE: For Crates, see also the discussion on Menander and Eratosthenes in the section, on Crates of Thebes; the life of Diogenes of Sinope contains references to the fourth-century BCE comic playwright Eubulus (6.30), fourth-century BCE scholar Zoilus of Perga, as well as Theophrastus.

13 On Cynic performance, see Branham's insightful analysis of the Cynic rhetoric (1996: 81–104); cf. Bosman's comments on the Cynics' behavior in public as performance meant to advertise Cynicism (2006: passim).

14 On the authenticity of the *chreiai*, see Long 1996: 30–1; cf. Fischel 1968: 372–411, who argues that the *chreiai* cited by D.L. are Hellenistic.

15 This interest in praxis ensued from a rejection of the traditional philosophical education in subjects other than ethics; e.g., music, astronomy, geometry (D.L. 6.73). On the Cynics' rejection of culture, see Branham and Goulet-Cazé 1996: 23.

16 See D.L. 6.13 and 6.22.

17 On Cynic attitude toward frank speech, see Hultin 2008: 81–7 and his references.

18 See Branham 1996: 99–100.

19 For Aristophanic usage, see *LSJ* ad loc.

20 In a similar story in which bodily fluids are used to make a point (*DL* 6.32), Diogenes visits a stately house; as he enters it, someone warns him not to spit on anything in these noble surroundings. Diogenes immediately spits—directly into the face of the man who has warned him—explaining that this is the least noble receptacle he could find. By stipulating that costly objects take precedence over the physical needs of Diogenes, the man has given up his own precedence over costly objects. Diogenes' spitting is more than a random misbehavior: just like his urination, it conveys a message about the Cynic's personal dignity and his freedom to act as he wishes.

21 So Trapp 2007: 156. According to Dio Chrysostom, Diogenes maintained that it was absurd that men, who in general are unwilling to pay anything for having their hand or foot rubbed, spend fortunes on one particular body part (8.17–20).

22 Cf. also 7.112, where Diogenes reports that Zeno thought that shame (*aischyne*) was one of the emotions caused by fear.

23 *Rhet.* B 84b2; cf. Konstan 2006: 103 and 301 n. 42.

24 D.L. uses the term *anaideia* only once discussing Zeno, who apparently vied with a certain nameless Cynic as to who was more shameless (7.17). Kruger 1996: 225–6 argues that Diogenes' *anaideia*, as presented by Dio Chrysostom and Lucian, consisted of a programmatic violation of commonsense notions. (I am grateful to David Konstan for his helpful comments on an earlier version of this section.)

25 See Branham 1996: 98–9 on the human body as an example of nature in the Cynic discourse; Kruger 1996: 233–4 on the body as symbol of social order in Julian's representation of Diogenes.

26 Subject to the dictates of the body and changing circumstances, the enactment of the Cynic *sophia* was, ideally, spontaneous; Long 1996: 30.

27 On freedom as one of the central values of Cynicism, see e.g., Moles 1995: 112; Branham and Goulet-Cazé 1996: 24, 26–7; Long 1996: 29, 34, 37.

28 These anecdotes can be seen as critical of some kinds of Greek masculinity and as misogynistic; see especially the famous anecdote praising an olive tree which women used for hanging themselves (6.52).

29 Diogenes once described his strategy as modeled on the trainers of a chorus, who set the note a little high to ensure that most of the singers would hit the right note (6.35).

30 D.L. clearly connects Diogenes' and Plato's proposal in 7.131. Desmond 2008: 95 draws attention to this similarity of contexts, but contrary to the arguments presented here, he understands *koinonia* as referring to a community of wives, and, following Epictetus *Diss.* 3.22.7, presents the Cynic's attitude toward sexual relationships and procreation as strongly negative.

31 On abolition of the nuclear family as the most important implication of *koinonia*, see Gardner 2000: 227–31 and her critique of the early feminist readings of the passage by Pomeroy 1974, Annas 1976, and Okin 1977; cf. also Halliwell 1993 ad loc.

32 Children of such unions are also *koinoi*. It is hard to say how Diogenes, if he ever developed the idea, imagined the care for these free children, but anecdotes about Crates suggest that the father was expected to play some role in their education; see p. 251–2.

33 As Aristotle had already recognized (*Politics* Book 2 = 1261a 1–19), this is motivated by a desire to strengthen the unity of the state.

34 For an argument that Socrates might have assumed that virtue was independent of gender, see Scaltsas 1992.

35 See 182b 5: πείθειν τοὺς νέους; (to persuade young men [to become the beloved]) or 217d 1: ὅμως δ' οὖν χρόνῳ ἐπείσθη (that [Socrates] would nevertheless yield in time).

36 On the dating of the letters, see Malherbe 1977: 27–9.

37 Admittedly, Crates uses this argument to persuade his partner to join him.

38 See Cohen 2006: 109–14 for a discussion of testimonies for contracts for erotic work undertaken by Athenian citizens both male and female.

39 Crates, in the anecdote, then proceeds to explain to his son that while intrigues and unhappy marriage are fit for tragedy, affairs with prostitutes are good for comedy, the kind of material very likely to have been drawn from Eratosthenes.

40 D.L. (6.88) gives as his source the work of the third-century BCE polymath Eratosthenes of Cyrene, who was the author of a work on comedy; cf. Geus 2002.

41 Aug. Contra *Iulian. Respons.* 4.43 = 8.17–20 = *De vir. illustr.* Malcovati fr. 14.

42 Warren 2007: 144–5.

43 The only truly independent figure is Axiothea of Philius, who wore men's clothing (3.46). Another Platonist, Lasthenia of Mantinea (3.46), is usually presented as a lover of Speusippus. The children of philosophers include Cleoboulus' daughter Cleoboulina (1.91), Aristippus' daughter Arete (2.72, 2. 86), and the nameless daughter of Stilpo of Megara (2.120). Pythagoras' philosophically inclined daughter Damo and wife Theano fit neatly into this pattern of family practicing wisdom under the watchful eye of a father figure (8.42). The philosophical liaisons include Lais and Aristippus (2.85) and Theodete and Phila and Arcesilaus (4.40); several *hetaerae* are mentioned in connection with Epicurus: Leontion (10.4, 10.5, 10.7) and Hedia, Erotion, and Nikidion (10.7); Epicurus is also said to have had an affair with a female disciple named Themista, who was married (10.5).

44 "Love should be cured with hunger, if this does not help, with time, if this does not work, with a rope" (D.L. 6.86 = *Anth. Pal.* 9.497).

45 In doing so, she acted like a courtesan; cf. Isaeus, *On the Estate of Pyrrhus* 3.13–14.

46 For a parallel, see: [Demosthenes], *Against Neaera* 59.33.

47 The authority cited just above, Zeno of Citium, seems to be Diogenes' (alleged) source of the information on Crates' appearance; see also the epigram Crates allegedly composed on his own death (6.92), in which he apparently calls himself a hunchback.

48 It is the *himatia* that the Athenian women take from their husbands in Aristophanes' *Ecclesiazousae* in order to pose as men. In Ar. *Ec.* 333 Blepyros' neighbor complains that because he could not find his *himation* he is now wearing his wife's dainty *crocotidion*; cf. Plut. *Brut.* 17, *Cor.* 14, *Cam.* 10, where *himation* is the equivalent of the Roman toga. Notably, the reference to *himation* in this passage is surprising, because, as a Cynic, Hipparchia should be wearing the famous double cloak, the *tribon*.

Bibliography

Annas, J. (1976) "Plato's *Republic* and feminism", *Philosophy* 51: 307–21.

Bell, D. (2006) "Bodies, technologies and spaces: On 'dogging'", *Sexualities* 9: 387–407.

Bosman, P. (2006) "Selling cynicism: The pragmatics of Diogenes' comic performances", *Classical Quarterly* 56(1): 93–104.

Branham, R.B. (1996) "Defacing the currency: Diogenes' rhetoric and the invention of cynicism", in R.B. Branham and M.O.G. Goulet-Cazé (eds) *The Cynics: The Cynic Movement in Antiquity and its Legacy*. Berkeley, CA: University of California Press, pp. 81–104.

Branham, R.B. and Goulet-Cazé, M.O.G. (1996) *The Cynics: The Cynic Movement in Antiquity and its Legacy*. Berkeley, CA: University of California Press.

Cohen, Edward E. (2006) "Free and unfree sexual work", in C.L. Faraone and L.K. McClure (eds) *Prostitutes and Courtesans in the Ancient World*. Madison, WI: University of Wisconsin Press, pp. 95–124.

Desmond, W.D. (2008) *Cynics*. Stocksfield, UK: Acumen.

Fischel, H.A. (1968) "Studies in Cynicism and the ancient Near East: The transformation of a *chria*", in J. Neusner (ed.) *Religions in Antiquity: Essays in Memory of Erwin Ramsdell Goodenough*. Leiden: Brill, pp. 372–411.

Gardner, C. (2000) "The remnants of the family: The role of women and eugenics in Republic V", *History of Philosophy Quarterly* 17(3): 217–35.

Geus, K. (2002) *Eratosthenes von Kyrene. Studien zur hellenistischen Kultur-und Wissenschaftsgeschichte, Münchener Beiträge zur Papyrusforschung und antiken Rechtsgeschichte*, 92. Munich: C.H. Beck.

Gow, A.S.F. (1965) *Machon: The Fragments*. Cambridge: Cambridge University Press.

Halliwell, S. (1993) *Republic 5*. Warminster: Aris & Phillips.

Hock, R.F. and O'Neil, E.N. (2002) *The Chreia and Ancient Rhetoric Classroom Exercises*. Atlanta, GA: Society of Biblical Literature.

Hultin, J.F. (2008) *The Ethics of Obscene Speech in Early Christianity*. Leiden: Brill.

Johnson, P. (2007) "Ordinary folk and cottaging: Law, morality, and public sex", *Journal of Law and Society* 34(4): 520–43.

Long, A.A. (1996) "Diogenes, Crates, and Hellenistic ethics", in R.B. Branham and M.O.G. Goulet-Cazé (eds) *The Cynics: The Cynic Movement in Antiquity and its Legacy*. Berkeley, CA: University of California Press, pp. 28–46.

Lonsdale, S.H. (1979) "Attitudes towards animals in ancient Greece", *Greece & Rome* 2(26.2): 146–59.

Konstan, D. (2006) *The Emotions of the Ancient Greeks: Studies in Aristotle and Classical Literature*. Toronto, ON: University of Toronto Press.

Kruger, D. (1996) "The bawdy and society: The shamelessness of Diogenes in Roman imperial culture", in R.B. Branham and M.O.G. Goulet-Cazé (eds) *The Cynics: The Cynic Movement in Antiquity and its Legacy*. Berkeley, CA: University of California Press, pp. 222–39.

McClure, L. (2003) "Subversive laughter: The sayings of courtesans in Book 13 of Athenaeus' Deipnosophistae", *American Journal of Philology* 124(2): 259–94.

Malherbe, A.J. (1977) *The Cynic Epistles: A Study Edition*, Sources for Biblical Literature. Missoula, MT: Scholars Press.

Moles, J.L. (1995) "The cynics and politics", in A. Laks and M. Schofield (eds) *Justice and Generosity, Proceedings of the 6th Symposium Hellenisticum*. Cambridge: Cambridge University Press, pp. 129–60.

Okin, S.M. (1977) "Philosopher queens and private wives: Plato on women and the family", *Philosophy and Public Affairs* 6: 345–69.

Pomeroy, S. (1974) "Feminism in Book V of Plato's *Republic*", *Apeiron* 8: 33–5.

Porter, E. (2009) Review of *Dogging: A Love Story*, *Sunday Times*, 23 December 2009. Available online at www.thesundaytimes.co.uk/sto/culture/film_and_tv/film/article193607.ece (accessed 30 October 2012).

Scaltsas, P.W. (1992) "Virtue without gender in Socrates", *Hypatia* 7(3): 126–37.

Shoard, C. (2009) Review of *Dogging: A Love Story*, *The Guardian*, 17 December 2009. Available online at www.guardian.co.uk/film/2009/dec/17/dogging-a-love-story (accessed 30 October 2012).

Taylor, J.E. (2003) *Jewish Women Philosophers of First Century Alexandria: Philo's* Therapeutae *Reconsidered.* Oxford: Oxford University Press.

Trapp, M.B. (2007) *Philosophy in the Roman Empire: Ethics, Politics, and Society.* Aldershot, UK: Ashgate.

Warren, J. (2007) "Diogenes Laertius, biographer of philosophy", in J. König and T. Witmarsh (eds) *Ordering Knowledge in the Roman Empire*. Cambridge: Cambridge University Press, pp. 133–49.

15

NAMING NAMES, TELLING TALES

Sexual secrets and Greek narrative[1]

Sheila Murnaghan

ὦ ψυχά, πῶς σιγάσω;
πῶς δὲ σκοτίας ἀναφήνω
εὐνάς, αἰδοῦς δ᾽ ἀπολειφθῶ;

My soul, how can I stay silent?
But how can I cast off shame
and reveal a hidden union?
(Euripides, *Ion* 859–61)

As Creusa finds the courage to reveal her long-concealed union with Apollo, Euripides aligns the powerful narrative at the heart of his *Ion* with the disclosure of a sexual secret. Such disclosures make good stories, interesting in part for their sexual content, but even more, I suggest, for the circumstances that lead to their telling. As Peter Brooks argues in *Reading for the Plot*, narratives engage us in the desires of their characters, which we follow through a trajectory of frustration and fulfillment, propelled by a corresponding passion for knowledge. Among the strongest of those desires, more powerful even than erotic longing or material ambition, is the wish to tell one's own story, "the more nearly absolute desire to be heard, recognized, listened to" (Brooks 1984: 53), so that narratives often include an account of their own origin in a character's quest for recognition. But a story like Creusa's can only be told after a difficult struggle with fear and shame, which have to be overcome before one party in a sexual encounter breaks the bond of silence to reveal what had been a shared and exclusive secret.

This discussion concerns accounts of heterosexual encounters across a range of genres in archaic and classical Greek literature, from hymn, to tragedy, to historiography, in which the exposure of a sexual secret underlies and enables the narrative, explaining its genesis and defining its motivation. These accounts bring out the tricky power dynamics of heterosexual relationships, in which gendered differences are subsumed in a delicate equilibrium. As scholars of ancient Greek sexuality have stressed, such relationships were always by definition asymmetrical, with the male as the dominant partner.[2] But the fact that they were also private – as much so when sanctioned and open as when illicit and clandestine – itself indicates an element of mutuality: an equal investment in silence that betokens tacit acquiescence in the balance of power between male and female.

This equilibrium can be seen in the *Odyssey*'s early and definitive account of an ideal marriage. Odysseus and Penelope are not equal in power or opportunity, nor are they held to the same standard of sexual fidelity, but they are set apart and united by an equal investment in their marriage and in the exclusive possession of their household. Their inequality is softened by *homophrosynê* or likeness of mind, of which the proof is a shared secret.[3] Odysseus and Penelope's secret concerns their marriage bed, but it signifies, not what they do together there (briefly recounted through the sober metaphor of a law or ritual: λέκτροιο παλαιοῦ θεσμόν, "the ritual of their longstanding bed" [*Od.* 23.296]), but the stability of their relationship, symbolized by the immovable bedpost and secured by Penelope's willing assent to the terms of her marriage.[4] Their shared attachment to the bed effects what Foucault has termed "the stylization of an actual dissymmetry."[5] Narratives engendered by the breaking of a sexual secret point to less settled, more contested relations between male and female; incorporating the voices of characters who overcome shame in order to be heard, they draw their impetus from, in some cases the assertion of power, in others its exposure and resistance.

My first examples involve those matings of gods and mortals that are a basic element of Greek mythology and especially of heroic genealogy, events so frequent and indispensable that individual occurrences can be lumped together in extended catalogue poems. Only when such matings disrupt expected patterns do they generate more elaborated accounts, as in the *Homeric Hymn to Aphrodite*.

The *Hymn to Aphrodite* beautifully illustrates the connection between sexual desire and the progress of a narrative. The starting point of the action is the abrupt imposition of desire, recounted in several crisp formulations: Zeus casts sweet desire (ἵμερον ἔμβαλε, 45, 53) into Aphrodite's heart; she falls in love (ἠράσατ', 57); desire seizes her (ἵμερος εἷλεν, 57). The result is rapid forward motion over a broad expanse of space: she rushes (σεύατ', 66) to Troy, making her way swiftly (ῥίμφα, 67) through the clouds; when she arrives on Ida, she goes straight (ἰθύς, 69) to Anchises' hut. Her appearance there inspires a complementary trajectory as *eros* seizes Anchises (ἔρος εἷλεν, 91) and reimposes itself (144) after she has deflected the doubts that make him initially reluctant to act; at that point, he wants to have sex with her "right now" (αὐτίκα νῦν, 151). These two arcs of desire converge as the pair then go to bed together.

But we are only in a position to be caught up in this forward progress because a confidence has been broken: the secret of Aphrodite's true identity has been revealed by both participants, for each of whom the differential between Aphrodite's status as a goddess and Anchises' as a mortal is too provocative to keep under wraps. Before they have sex, Aphrodite, in order to overcome Anchises' well-founded caution, recasts their relationship as one between well-matched humans; she spins a false tale about being a Phrygian princess, with her sights set on a properly conducted marriage, anticipating the setting in which, according to human conventions, female desire appropriately arises. Under these fabricated conditions of ordinary human intercourse, the expected gender differential (already introduced through her feigned concern with marriage) comes into play, and the male seizes the initiative. Anchises takes Aphrodite's hand (λάβε χεῖρα, 155) and she follows him to the bed, where he undresses her. This process is described in appreciative detail, crowned by an assertion of Anchises' innocence: as far as he knew, the relationship between them was what his actions implied (161–7).

> οἳ δ' ἐπεὶ οὖν λεχέων εὐποιήτων ἐπέβησαν,
> κόσμον μέν οἱ πρῶτον ἀπὸ χροὸς εἷλε φαεινόν,
> πόρπας τε γναμπτάς θ' ἕλικας κάλυκάς τε καὶ ὅρμους.
> λῦσε δέ οἱ ζώνην ἰδὲ εἵματα σιγαλόεντα

261

ἔκδυε καὶ κατέθηκεν ἐπὶ θρόνου ἀργυροήλου
Ἀγχίσης· ὃ δ' ἔπειτα θεῶν ἰότητι καὶ αἴσῃ
ἀθανάτῃ παρέλεκτο θεᾷ βροτός, οὐ σάφα εἰδώς.

When they had climbed into the well-made bed,
he removed the shining ornaments from her body,
the pins and twisting bracelets, the earrings and necklaces,
he untied her sash and took off her brilliant clothes
and placed them on a chair that was studded with silver nails.
Anchises then, by the will of the gods and immortal fate,
went to bed with a goddess, himself a mortal, not knowing the truth.

And yet, once their desires have been satisfied, Aphrodite herself is unwilling to keep Anchises in the dark and maintain their seeming parity; she wakes him up to assert her divine status and finally, obliquely, her identity, which she slips in, in the form of an epithet, as part of an injunction against ever mentioning it (μηδ' ὀνόμαινε, 290); she promises punishment from Zeus, εἰ δέ κεν ἐξείπῃς καὶ ἐπεύξεαι ἄφρονι θυμῷ / ἐν φιλότητι μιγῆναι ἐυστεφάνῳ Κυθερείῃ, "if you speak of it and thoughtlessly boast / that you mingled in love with beautiful-garlanded Cytherea" (286–7). Like other gods who name themselves with more fanfare during epiphanies, and like Odysseus with the Cyclops, Aphrodite cannot let her exercise of power remain anonymous. In her case, this assertion of power entails a further twist involving gender: as a female goddess with a merely mortal lover, Aphrodite is concerned to disown the traditional subordination of the female to the male.

At the same time, however, Aphrodite insists that Anchises must himself conceal what she reveals. She threatens harsh punishment at the hands of Zeus if he publicizes their mating and supplies him a cover story to use instead, since the existence of his son will inescapably point back to some sexual act; once again, she generates a false tale in which the sharp power differential between them is occluded. She instructs him to explain that the mother of his son was an ordinary, anonymous wood nymph like the ones who will fill in for her in the task of raising Aeneas.[6] Nothing is said here of Anchises' disobedience, but later myths suggest that he did incur the threatened punishment, and it seems likely that this poet was aware of that feature of the story even if he chose not to mention it (Richardson 2010: 243; Schein 2013: n. 4).

The poet–narrator of the *Hymn* implies that his information comes from the omniscient Muse rather than from human gossip, but by ending his narrative with Aphrodite's injunction he puts himself in a position of bad faith that parallels Anchises' implied betrayal, telling a story that, on his own account, Aphrodite would prefer to have suppressed. The result is a double-edged hymn, which at once glorifies and embarrasses its subject and so exemplifies the close intertwining of praise and blame in archaic Greek poetry. That intertwining is illuminated by the mixture of motives underlying both the revelations of Aphrodite and Anchises and Aphrodite's resistance to further disclosure. The formulation of Aphrodite's prohibition (εἰ… ἐπεύξεαι, "if you boast," 286) makes it clear that Anchises' revelation is a glorifying boast – a claim to recognition of status, like her own self-identification, that will also extend to his son Aeneas. But the news of their equally sought mating is also for Aphrodite the basis of a humiliating taunt: on the one hand, Anchises' desire for Aphrodite is a sign of her power over him, an effect of the supreme beauty and charm that the hymn evokes and celebrates; on the other hand, Aphrodite's desire for Anchises is a sign that she is also herself subject to that same power, which has been appropriated by Zeus and imposed on her. Erotic desire has a disturbing capacity to overturn established hierarchies, because it places one being, of whatever status, under the power of another, as this story of a goddess helplessly in love with a mortal illustrates. Under such circumstances, the outcome is a zero-sum game – Anchises' conquest is his glory but Aphrodite's shame (which is why she is in such a hurry to reassert the upper hand) – and a story that simultaneously conveys praise for one and blame for another – Anchises' potential boast is for Aphrodite a humiliating taunt.[7]

The hymn's status as a taunt is made clear by Aphrodite, both through her insistence that its events should stay secret and through the tone she has set when telling similar stories about her fellow divinities, reveling in her successful commingling of gods with mortal women and goddesses with mortal men. By the end of the narrative, Aphrodite's ability to tell such tales has been foreclosed, as she herself explains (252–6).

νῦν δὲ δὴ οὐκέτι μοι στόμα χείσεται ἐξονομῆναι
τοῦτο μετ' ἀθανάτοισιν, ἐπεὶ μάλα πολλὸν ἀάσθην,
σχέτλιον, οὐκ ὀνομαστόν, ἀπεπλάγχθην δὲ νόοιο,
παῖδα δ' ὑπὸ ζώνῃ ἐθέμην βροτῷ εὐνηθεῖσα.

Now I can no longer open my mouth to name
this deed among the immortal gods, since I was duped,
wretchedly, unspeakably. I went out of my mind
and put a child under my sash, going to bed with a mortal.

As a result, Aphrodite is subject to constant taunting among the gods: she complains to Anchises that because of him she will now every day be the recipient of ὄνειδος (247), a term which stands for blame poetry within epic and epinician poetry (Nagy 1999: 226). And now the poet can call on the Muse for subject matter that includes what Aphrodite herself finds unspeakable (οὐκ ὀνομαστόν, 251): Μοῦσά μοι ἔννεπε ἔργα πολυχρύσου Ἀφροδίτης, "Tell me Muse about the doings of golden Aphrodite" (1).

The *Hymn to Aphrodite* finds the impetus for several poetic genres, both negative and positive, including its own, in the publicized "doings of Aphrodite." The connection drawn here is echoed in other programmatic episodes in early Greek poetry. The sexual revelation is a mainstay of invective, associated with several definitive practitioners of the form. Achilles' unspoken desire for Penthesileia is among the provocative topics aired by Thersites, the prototypical blame poet of the Trojan legend.[8] Sexual disclosure as a powerful form of discourse appears both in the biographical traditions surrounding Archilochus and in his works. Reports of sexual escapades, such as orgies in sanctuaries, figured in the invectives through which Archilochus supposedly drove Lycambes and his daughters to suicide (West 1974: 25–8). In the surviving "Cologne epode" (196a West), sexual slurs concerning Neobule, one of those daughters, are deployed by the speaker in his own reported seduction of another woman, whose own privacy is violated by the poem, to the speaker's advantage.

In the *Homeric Hymn to Hermes*, sexual disclosure is the subject of a foundational poetic performance that also blurs the boundary between hymn and invective. As soon as Hermes invents the lyre, he sings a song that is at once reminiscent of theogonic poetry and explicitly compared to taunting (54–9; described with a verb, κερτομέω, that can designate blame poetry [Nagy 1999: 261, 263]):

θεὸς δ' ὑπὸ καλὸν ἄειδεν
ἐξ αὐτοσχεδίης πειρώμενος, ἠΰτε κοῦροι
ἡβηταὶ θαλίῃσι παραιβόλα κερτομέουσιν,

ἀμφὶ Δία Κρονίδην καὶ Μαιάδα καλλιπέδιλον,
ὡς πάρος ὡρίζεσκον ἑταιρείῃ φιλότητι,
ἥν τ' αὐτοῦ γενεὴν ὀνομακλυτὸν ἐξονομάζων·

And to [the lyre] the god sang beautifully,
improvising, trying things out, just the way
young men at feasts throw out taunting gibes;
he sang about Zeus son of Cronus and Maia with beautiful shoes,
telling how they shared lovers' words in companionable closeness,
and naming his own famous-named lineage.

Hermes, like the poet of the *Hymn to Aphrodite*, and like the poet of his own hymn, makes a song out of a sexual encounter that has been a secret. At the beginning of the poem, we are told that Zeus and Maia mate in her remote cave, in the dead of night (νυκτὸς ἀμολγῷ, 7), when Hera is asleep, escaping the notice of both gods and men (λήθων ἀθανάτους τε θεοὺς θνητούς τ' ἀνθρώπους, 9). But unlike those anonymous singers, Hermes has a personal stake in the contents of his song, which establishes his own status by identifying his parents and especially his divine father. The amorous conversation of Zeus and Maia generates a more pointed form of discourse that elevates its speaker at the cost of their privacy.[9]

Hermes' ambitions clarify one of the main pressures driving the exposure of such secrets: the resulting child's wish to claim a glorious lineage. That motive is one impetus behind the revelations of the *Hymn to Aphrodite*, as Aphrodite herself indicates when she frames the false tale she dictates to Anchises as the answer to a future question about Aeneas' mother.[10] The child is a further interested party, with his own need to be recognized and his own objections to having the power differential between the two lovers cloaked in secrecy. In the *Hymn to Hermes*, Zeus willingly descends to the level of the insignificant nymph Maia (much as Aphrodite descends to the level of Anchises); to hide his affair from Hera, Zeus joins Maia in her obscure circumstances, which are symbolized by the humble cave that conveniently conceals their lovemaking.[11] But those obscure circumstances are intolerable to Hermes; as he explains to Maia, he is determined that they will leave that cave behind to share in the pleasures and privileges of Olympus (166–72), and so he must expose what the cave has concealed and claim his birthright as the son of Zeus.

Hermes' self-asserting song comes in a context in which the establishment of his paternity is a pressing and provocative matter, since it bears on the distribution of divine power (itself the principal subject of the Homeric hymns [Clay 1989: 3–16]): his status as Zeus' son means that room must be found for one more Olympian, mostly at the expense of Apollo. In the different poetic context of the Hesiodic *Catalogue of Women*, the focus of the narrative is on the establishment of multiple heroic genealogies among humans (West 1985: 2), and the recurrent divine–human couplings that structure the work can be presented as routine preludes to the stories of those heroic offspring. Thus the opening lines of the catalogue forecast many similar tales of illustrious women who slept with gods, beginning with ὅσσαις δὴ παρέλεκτο πατὴρ ἀνδρῶν τε θεῶν τε, "however many as the father of men and gods [i.e. Zeus] slept with" (fr. 1.15). The verb used here, παραλέχομαι, is specifically associated with secret sex (Irwin 2005: 42–3); this is in keeping with the way such liaisons are at once openly acknowledged, so that the crucial genealogical point can be made, and yet protected by an element of concealment, such as the mountain-like wave that rises up to hide the lovemaking of Poseidon and Tyro in the episode narrated in the catalogue of heroines in *Odyssey* 11 (235–52).[12]

This discreet combination of brief mention and concealment recurs in other poetic contexts in which the superior status of human heroes is traced to their mixed divine–human parentage.

In the mythical narrative of Bacchylides 17, Theseus meets an act of aggression by Minos with matching conception stories:

> If the noble daughter of Phoenix, the girl whose name spells love [Europa], bore you, peerless among mortals, after mingling with Zeus under the crags of Mt. Ida, well the daughter of rich Pittheus bore me, after drawing close to the sea god Poseidon, when the azure-haired Nereids gave her a golden veil.
>
> (*Bacchylides 17.29–38*)

The woman's inferiority to her divine lover is softened by reference to her father's wealth and high status, and the act itself is hidden, in the recesses of a rocky mountain or through the gift of a veil (κάλυμμα, 38). Allusions to stories of this type are, not surprisingly, a staple of the epinician odes that celebrate those heroes' remoter descendants (Kearns 2013: 57–8).

In tragedy, by contrast, with its focus on trauma and conflict, the difficult revelation and confrontation of hidden knowledge, including sexual secrets, is a frequent driver of the plot.[13] In Euripides' *Bacchae*, the most overtly metatheatrical of our surviving tragedies, this feature of the genre is rooted in the mythology of Dionysus himself. Dionysus' situation is like that of Hermes, except that his human mother Semele is even humbler than Maia. For Dionysus' divinity to be properly recognized, it is essential that Semele's union with Zeus be affirmed. The plot of the *Bacchae* springs from Dionysus' frustration and rage when the story of his conception is distorted. In the prologue, Dionysus identifies himself immediately as "the son of Zeus ... whom Cadmus' daughter Semele bore" (1–2) and then explains why he has come to Thebes and stirred up its women (26–31):

> ἐπεί μ' ἀδελφαὶ μητρός, ἃς ἥκιστα χρῆν,
> Διόνυσον οὐκ ἔφασκον ἐκφῦναι Διός,
> Σεμέλην δὲ νυμφευθεῖσαν ἐκ θνητοῦ τινος
> ἐς Ζῆν' ἀναφέρειν τὴν ἁμαρτίαν λέχους,
> Κάδμου σοφίσμαθ', ὧν νιν οὕνεκα κτανεῖν
> Ζῆν' ἐξεκαυχῶνθ', ὅτι γάμους ἐψεύσατο.

> For my mother's sisters – the last ones who should –
> deny that Dionysus was begotten by Zeus.
> Semele, they say, was seduced by some mortal,
> and passed the blame to Zeus for her illicit passion –
> a clever gambit that Cadmus thought up. That's why Zeus killed her,
> they proclaim: because she made up their union.

Dionysus' begetting, like Aeneas' in the *Hymn to Aphrodite*, becomes the subject of a war of words in several genres, with prose forms now mixed in with poetry. Semele's own account, implicit but unrecorded, has been hijacked by her sisters, who have labeled it a lie and a sophistic stratagem. Asserting their superiority, they have allied themselves with invective over encomium to substitute their own moralizing tattle for the truth; in doing so, they project a banal but demeaning equality on the encounter, linking Semele with just "some mortal." The events of the play, through which Dionysus disproves their version by displaying his own power, are equated by him with another speech form, the legal defense: δεῖ...Σεμέλης τε μητρὸς ἀπολογήσασθαί μ' ὕπερ / φανέντα θνητοῖς δαίμον' ὃν τίκτει Διί, "and I must speak in defense of my mother Semele, revealing myself to mortals as a god whom she bore to Zeus" (39–42). This formulation casts in civic terms a claim that is central to another Dionysian genre, the dithyramb. The dithyramb frequently stresses the honor due to Semele as the consort of Zeus and mother of Dionysus (cf. Pindar, *Dithyrambs* fr. 70b.30–1, fr. 75.11, 19); this theme is reinforced by mythical narratives in which Dionysus rescues Semele from Hades and makes her a goddess (Hesiod, *Th.* 940ff., Pi., *O.* 2.25, Apollod. 3.5.3).

The *Bacchae*'s chorus of maenads makes a passing reference to rites in Semele's honor (997), but the play itself, as defined by its dramaturgical protagonist, replaces such myths of rescue and apotheosis with the vindication of a mortal woman's truthfulness. This comes at great cost to her entire family, as her own insistence on knowing the truth has come at great cost to her, and her own voice is never heard. In the *Ion*, however, Euripides draws on the resources of tragedy to give a voice to Semele's counterpart, Creusa, whose account of her own sexual encounter with Apollo is the centerpiece of the play.[14] As has already been noted, Creusa's testimony is strongly marked as the outcome of a struggle with powerful feelings of shame, which have kept her experience a long-held secret. As in the *Bacchae*, the truth is elicited as the corrective answer to a false tale of a more ordinary mortal coupling: Creusa's old retainer explains Xuthus' discovery of Ion as his son by imagining that he slept with a slave and sent the resulting child to be raised at Apollo's temple, planning if necessary to shift the blame to the god (815–31).

Creusa tells her story in two forms, specific to tragedy, that Euripides develops as vehicles for the voicing of normally unspeakable truths, the lyric monologue and the stichomythic exchange. In her monologue, she apostrophizes Apollo with an unprecedented description of what it feels like to be a human girl overpowered by an Olympian god (887–96).

ἦλθές μοι χρυσῷ χαίταν
μαρμαίρων, εὖτ' ἐς κόλπους
κρόκεα πέταλα φάρεσιν ἔδρεπον,
ἀνθίζειν χρυσανταυγῆ·
λευκοῖς δ' ἐμφὺς καρποῖσιν
χειρῶν εἰς ἄντρου κοίτας
κραυγὰν Ὦ μᾶτέρ μ' αὐδῶσαν
θεὸς ὁμευνέτας
ἆγες ἀναιδείᾳ
Κύπριδι χάριν πράσσων.

You came at me, and dazzled me
with your golden hair.
I was piling up petals,
gleaming yellow in my lap.
Gripping my pale wrists,
you made me lie down in a cave,
while I screamed "Mother!" –
a god and a lover
without shame,
answering to Aphrodite.

In the dialogue that follows, the sympathetic questions of the old man lead her to reiterate the horror of a forced encounter (939–41).

Κρέουσα: ἐνταῦθ᾽ ἀγῶνα δεινὸν ἠγωνίσμεθα.
Πρεσβύτης: τίν᾽; ὡς ἀπαντᾷ δάκρυά μοι τοῖς σοῖς λόγοις.
Κρέουσα: Φοίβῳ ξυνῆψ᾽ ἄκουσα δύστηνον γάμον.

Creusa: There I fought a bitter fight.
Old Man: How so? Your words are bringing me to the point of tears.
Creusa: I mated with Phoebus against my will in a miserable union.

The plot of the *Ion* is organized in such a way that what Creusa here discloses still remains a secret within the larger world of the play.[15] This allows for an outcome in which Creusa is protected from the shame that applies even to victims of rape (Cairns 1993: 308–9), and normative social relations are upheld, including the fiction of relatively parity between Creusa and her husband Xuthus, even as Ion's divine paternity is affirmed. At the same time, the play's external audience, as well as a select internal audience of the Old Man and the sympathetic chorus, have been granted a rarely heard perspective on the power differential that is cloaked by sexual secrecy. Apollo's mating with Creusa is experienced by her as an abuse of power in the form of a rape, and this is all the more shocking because the story follows the familiar contours of those conventional genealogical reports which are generally left unnarrated.[16] Creusa's shame is different from Aphrodite's embarrassment at her own desire: it stems from an experience that Creusa has not sought but that, because it does not comply with human conventions, dishonors her nonetheless. Her long-maintained commitment to silence about their union may echo Apollo's, but that does not mean that she shares his motives for keeping quiet; her revelation disproves the ostensible connection between silence and acquiescence. With his notable attunement to the inner lives of women, Euripides has used the broken sexual secret as a medium for opening up painful questions about sex and power that more discreet accounts paper over.

Already in his own day, Euripides was famous for bringing out the affinities between mythical heroines and ordinary Athenian women (cf. Ar. *Frogs* 1043–56), and Creusa's helplessness before Apollo echoes the vulnerability of all women to rape (Rabinowitz 1993: 201), much as Medea's problems as a foreigner in Corinth echo the experiences of all women who marry and enter the unfamiliar terrain of their husband's house (cf. Eur. *Medea* 238–40). Turning to the fifth-century context that informs Euripidean tragedy, we find more explicit descriptions of the well-balanced (if not strictly equal or symmetrical) sexual relationship that defines an ideal union, which we have already met in the *Odyssey*, and narratives concerning historical as well as mythological figures generated by disturbances of that balance.

In the conceptual universe of classical Greece, sex between men and women occurs ideally within the institution of the *oikos*, a realm of private activity in general that surrounds the particular privacy of sexual relations. The *oikos* is a constituent of the public sphere of the *polis* yet differentiated from it, both because it is private and because it encompasses a wider range of personnel, including women, slaves, and children, as well as free male citizens. In the context of the *polis*, those male citizens are theoretically not only similar but equal, but in the *oikos* they intersect with those who are dissimilar and unequal. The *oikos* harbors, and keeps out of sight, two forms of potentially disruptive difference that are played down in public life: differences in wealth between citizens, and differences in legal and social status between citizen men and others, among them women.

The concealment of women within the household is in theory (no matter what may have happened in practice) essential to the well-being of the *polis*, because the visibility of women is understood as a sign of dysfunction. In a widespread classical conception of social order, for women to be silent and out of view is a sign that all is well. Men are properly exercising their superior authority, so that women are cared for and their interests are protected; women are happily cooperating with the social structures in which they find themselves, and the irrationality and wayward sexuality to which women are subject are under control. Under such conditions, women have no reason to emerge from their hidden quarters to speak or act, as they regularly do in tragedy, the genre in which dysfunction is dramatized. There is an ethic of secrecy about women, symbolized in the essential role of veiling in the wedding ceremony (Cairns 1996: 80; Llewellyn-Jones 2003: 215–58), which is linked, paradoxically, to the idea that there should be no secrets to tell. Instead of the more familiar paradox of the "open secret," we have a closed non-secret, at once inaccessible and incapable of generating an interesting story.

This paradox is reflected in texts from the classical period that, in contrast to tragedy, give us idealized pictures of a well-functioning society. Of these, by far the most famous is Pericles' advice at the end of the Funeral Oration: "If I must say something about female virtue, for those of you who are now widows, I will put it all in a brief admonition. There is great glory in not being worse than your existing nature and great glory for her who has the least reputation among men whether for praise or for blame" (Thucydides 2.45.2). Pericles describes a situation in which women fulfill their nature at its best by doing nothing that men would want to talk about, a category that applies to good actions that would generate praise just as much as to bad actions that would generate blame (so here too, in this negative formulation, those seemingly antithetical types of speech are closely linked).

The lack of anything to say prescribed by Pericles is complemented by the full-scale discussion of an ideal classical *oikos*, the house of Ischomachus, including an extensive portrayal of Ischomachus' wife, found in Xenophon's *Oeconomicus*, which actively demonstrates that there is nothing remarkable happening behind the closed doors of the house. As readers of the dialogue, we never go inside the house, which remains off-limits to us, but rather hear about it indirectly from Socrates, who reports the description given to him on another occasion by Ischomachus. But Ischomachus' detailed account assures us that the house has no secrets, a point that is reinforced by his eager willingness to answer any question Socrates puts to him.

In constructing this reassuring picture, Xenophon plays down the element of difference that characterizes the *oikos* in relation to the *polis* and is itself an internal feature of the *oikos*. He portrays a husband and wife who are markedly disparate in age, experience, and authority; the marriage is in fact described through Ischomachus' anodyne account of how he instructed his wife in her proper role. But in his teaching, Ischomachus characterizes their relationship as a κοινωνία, "partnership," a concept that extends to their sexual relationship in which they are said to be καὶ τῶν σωμάτων κοινωνήσοντες ἀλλήλοις, "also sharing their bodies with one another" (10.4), with the explicit and equally sought goal of producing children (7.11). As with the marriage of Odysseus and Penelope, there is a stress on the equal investment of both in the success of the household, however disparate their material contributions, which effects a "necessary equalization of initial differences between the husband and the wife" (Foucault 1985: 156). Ischomachus depicts their daily activities as complementary, differing primarily in the very matter of visibility, since the wife's proper sphere of activity is indoors and the husband's is outdoors (7.20–5). The wife's commensurate enthusiasm for their joint enterprise is displayed in her happy assent to Ischomachus' teaching, which is glossed by Socrates as "manly understanding" (10.1). The well-ordered household is compared to a *polis* and the wife, as she assumes her proper role, is compared to a magistrate, a *nomophulax* (Murnaghan 1988).

In the first book of the *Politics*, Aristotle similarly politicizes and equalizes the relationship of husband and wife. The wife, he says, is ruled by the husband, but in a manner that he calls "political" (πολιτικῶς), as opposed to the way in which a father rules his children, which is "monarchical" (βασιλικῶς).

> In most political offices, it is true, there is an alternation of ruler and ruled, since they tend by their nature to be on an equal footing and to differ in nothing; all the same, when one rules and the other is ruled, [the ruler] seeks to establish differences in external appearances, forms of address, and prerogatives … The male always stands thus in relation to the female.
>
> (Aristotle, *Politics* 1, 1259b)

In a conceit that is illogical but evidently useful, the relation of husband and wife is compared to rotating offices in a *polis*, in which the difference between ruler and ruled is insignificant because it is understood to be both arbitrary and transitory. For the married couple, however, the difference is not temporary and reversible but intrinsic and permanent.

In these formulations, marriage is defined as an equilibrium supported by contradictions: the wife must be hidden, but there is nothing to hide; she is subordinated to her husband, but she is also his equal partner. Less idealizing genres, including – as we have seen – tragedy, expose these contradictions, showing their instability under the pressure of challenging but predictable circumstances. A final set of examples is supplied by Herodotus' *Histories*, a prose narrative with many affinities to tragedy,[17] in a series of episodes in which the narrative is propelled by the revelation of sexual secrets. These episodes occur at important junctures in the narrative, when power changes hands in illegitimate or unexpected ways,[18] and so contribute significantly to the implicit analysis of power, especially tyrannical power, and the causes and effects of its volatility, that runs through the *Histories*.

The first and most prominent of these is the opening story of Gyges and the wife of Candaules, which is brought in as background to what Herodotus presents as the first real event of his narrative, Croesus' subjection of Greek peoples, but serves to introduce key themes of tyrannical power and historical change.[19] Like the *Hymn to Aphrodite*, the narrative begins with the sudden onset of desire, as the Lydian king Candaules falls in love with his own wife (ἠράσθη ἑωυτοῦ γυναικός, 1.8.1). If Candaules had reacted to this simply by having sex with her, there would be no story to tell, only conventional marital relations, protected at once by polite discretion and by their inherent banality. But he feels the need to convince another man, his spear-bearer Gyges, of his wife's exceptional beauty, and so decides that Gyges must hide in their bedroom and watch the queen undress for bed.[20] Recognizing Candaules' proposal as a serious violation of proper norms, Gyges tries to refuse. But Candaules insists, assuring Gyges that the queen will never know what has happened. In this he is wrong; she detects Gyges' presence and the result is Candaules' undoing.

In his attempt to dissuade Candaules, Gyges invokes an aphorism, ἅμα δὲ κιθῶνι ἐκδυομένῳ συνεκδύεται καὶ τὴν αἰδῶ γυνή, "when a woman takes off her dress she also takes off her shame" (1.8.3), which clarifies one of the most important, but also generally unspoken, motives for privacy in marriage. Alone with her husband, a woman expresses a sensuality that she should display only to him. This point is made in a less punchy but more explicit way in a recommendation attributed by Diogenes Laertius to Theano, the wife of Pythagoras: τῇ δὲ πρὸς τὸν ἴδιον ἄνδρα μελλούσῃ πορεύεσθαι παρῄνει ἅμα τοῖς ἐνδύμασι καὶ τὴν αἰσχύνην ἀποτίθεσθαι, ἀνισταμένην τε πάλιν ἅμ' αὐτοῖσι ἀναλαμβάνειν, "And she advised a woman going in to her own husband to put off her shame with her clothes, and on leaving him to put it on again along with them."[21] The wife's active sexuality, which is acknowledged here, is only hinted at in most treatments of marriage. One reason for that can be seen in the *Odyssey*, where the possibility of Penelope as a desiring subject is connected to the fear, which is raised by her dream and by her appearance to the Suitors in Book 18, that she might be interested in someone other than her husband. In the *Oeconomicus*, Ischomachus does, in the course of demonstrating to his wife that she would be more alluring without makeup, cause her to say that she would rather touch his skin in its natural state than covered with lead or other cosmetics (10.6). The occlusion of women's sexuality within marriage is effectively dramatized in the *Hymn to Aphrodite*: as Aphrodite's blatant desire is satisfied within a relationship figured proleptically as a marriage, the demonstrative gesture of taking off the woman's clothes is assigned to the man.

Once her αἰδώς has been violated through the conversion of her proper act of self-display to her husband into an inappropriate show for an outsider, Candaules' wife also puts off her shame in a metaphorical sense as well: like Creusa, she emerges from silence and invisibility to speak of what has been done to her. Not only does the queen's willingness to speak recall Euripides' character, but her testimony is represented in the surviving tragic fragment that (whether it is earlier or later) closely parallels Herodotus' narrative. In the one extant speech of the "Gyges tragedy,"[22] the queen reveals to a group of loyal supporters, presumably represented by the chorus, what she experienced during the preceding night. In Herodotus' version, in which the events that transpire in the bedroom can be told by the narrator, we hear her speaking in ways that actively shape the course of Lydian history. She confronts Gyges and presents him with a choice: "Either the one who planned these things must die, or you, the one who saw me naked and did what is not right" (1.11.3). Her words both name what has been done to her and point to the public consequences of her private violation. As she moves to restore the lost exclusivity of her marriage, she brings about what her tragic counterpart also recognizes as the logical implication of a third person in the bedroom. In the tragic version, the queen says that when she first saw Gyges she feared he was an assassin with designs on Candaules. Herodotus' queen assures that he plays out that role: she forces him to murder the king and replace him as her husband, bringing about dynastic change and setting the stage for the defeat of Croesus five generations later (explicitly defined by the Delphic oracle as punishment for a δόλος γυναικηίος, "a woman's treacherous act" 1.91.9).

Candaules' wife not only discloses what has been done to her, but she stages a re-enactment of Candaules' scheme that brings to light its implications, revealing aspects of tyrannical power that Candaules himself does not fully grasp. While Candaules has placed Gyges in their bedroom with the idea that Gyges can simply see the queen and then disappear as if nothing had happened, the queen herself places him there once again ("the attack will come from the same place where he exposed me naked," she explains, again naming Candaules' transgression [1.11.5]) and insists that he act out the logical consequences of being there. Through her determination that what Gyges has seen he must also take possession of, and that when he takes possession of her he must also take possession of the throne, the queen conveys an understanding of political power as rooted in the exclusive control of hidden resources, which is further elaborated throughout the work.

The many stories that make up the *Histories* reflect a vision of political power as inherently unstable and endlessly productive of change, in part because the successful exercise of power depends on maintaining a precarious balance between secrecy and display. The possible connection between revealing a source of power and losing that power is illustrated in the story of Gyges' descendant Croesus, who insists on showing the Athenian wise man Solon his money, much as Candaules insists on showing Gyges his wife. Unlike Gyges, Solon is able to witness Croesus' wealth without being drawn into the historical process of rise and fall; standing outside that process, he articulates both its inevitability and the unreliability of wealth as a source of happiness. But it is nonetheless clear that Croesus' foolish need to show off contributes to the complex of factors that make his fall at the hands of the Persian Cyrus inevitable.[23]

The most successful wielder of power in the *Histories* is Cyrus' ancestor Deioces, the founder of the Medean dynasty, who not only occupies the role of ruler but actually invents it. A gifted man in love with absolute rule (ἐρασθεὶς τυραννίδος, 1.96.2), living at a time when the Medes have no central government, Deioces manipulates the people by making himself indispensable as an arbiter of disputes so that they decide that they must have a king and choose him for that role. He then forces them to build a capital city with a heavily fortified palace at its center and hides himself within it, instituting a series of royal protocols by which his subjects are kept out of his presence and all business is conducted through messengers. In this way, he fends off the jealous rivalry of other men who knew him before as one of them: "if they didn't see him, he would appear to be a person of a different order (ἑτεροῖος)" (1.99.2). Like a harmonious husband and wife, Deioces makes a secret out of what is entirely ordinary. As a result, he reigns for fifty-three years, unites all of the Medes under his rule, and passes his kingdom on to his son.

Deioces' strategy is a definitive recipe for unchallenged political power and a tour de force. It works through the manufacture of difference out of secrecy itself, through concealing the fact that there is nothing to hide. Because Deioces' purchase on power resides in himself (in the cleverness in which he *is* different from other men), he has a rare self-sufficiency that is key to his success. More typically, for rulers like Candaules and Croesus, their power is vested in possessions of high value, whether a supremely beautiful woman or a large amount of gold. And they feel the need to affirm their power by showing off their valuable possessions and soliciting the validation of other men (Travis 2000: 339–40). This inevitably exposes them to rivalry, as Deioces shrewdly recognizes, and as the wife of Candaules makes clear by requiring Gyges, despite his passivity and reluctance, to become Candaules' rival and usurper. And while Candaules and Croesus may be excessive and deluded in their longing for confirmation, they are faced with a difficult challenge, since power is hard to exercise if it is wholly concealed. What must be hidden must also be known to exist, and it is hard to pull off Deioces' feat of maintaining power by showing nothing.

The similarities between the Gyges and the Croesus stories suggest an affinity between wealth and a desirable woman as comparable sources of monarchical power; both need to be kept hidden in the inner bedroom or treasure rooms of the Lydian royal palace as both are also kept hidden in the private houses of democratic Athens. As assets, women resemble wealth, and their value is enhanced when accompanied by wealth.[24] The wealth a woman brings to a marriage can help to equalize her relations with her husband, compensating for her inferior status. Thus Aphrodite, in her false tale, stresses the rich gifts of gold and clothing that her prominent Phrygian parents will supply (139–40), and Theseus when asserting his genealogy in Bacchylides 17 specifies that his mother is the daughter of "rich Pittheus." As the basis of a story about power's loss or limitation, the exposure of a woman is, however, especially interesting because her value is sexual (and so the removal of her clothes is required for Gyges' appraisal just as it is required for Anchises' mating with Aphrodite) and because she is capable of communicating the secrets of the bedroom, herself supplying the material for an intriguing exposé.

Candaules' misstep reveals the instability of tyrannical power, which is hard to display without inspiring rivals (so that even a spectator without ambitions, like Gyges, becomes the king's rival); as a character later in the *Histories* puts it, tyranny is "precarious" (σφαλερόν) because it has "many lovers" (πολλοὶ…ἐρασταί, 3.53.4). But it also suggests that such power is inherently abusive, as it leads him to violate norms of sexual privacy and to treat his wife as a possession to be shown off. The abusiveness of tyrannical power is further elaborated in a series of related stories set in the tyrant's bedroom, in which the tyrant's mistreatment of his wife involves not just exposing her but misusing her in some further way. These stories substantiate the general claim of Otanes, in his speech against monarchy during the Persian debate on government in Book 3, in which he links the tyrant's disregard for law and convention with his sexual mistreatment of women: "he disrupts traditional customs; he forces women; and he kills men without trial" (3.80.5).[25]

The tyrant's excessive power compared to everyone else is expressed through an abuse of the inherent power differential between husband and wife that is usually masked by the privacy of the bedroom, where it ought to be counterbalanced by mutual respect: the sign of that excess is the wife's defection from the pact of secrecy that defines her marriage. Whether Greek or Eastern, these tyrannical figures are measured against an essentially Greek norm of monogamous marriage (Rosselini and Saïd 1978: 1003), in keeping with a Greek tendency to make the properly functioning *oikos* the basis and precondition of a successful political order (Blok 2002: 241–2).

The first of these stories involves the Athenian tyrant Peisistratus. In the second of the three tries that it takes before he can establish himself in Athens, Peisistratus seizes power through a clever trick and then consolidates that power by marrying the daughter of his powerful former opponent Megacles. But because he has heard that Megacles' family is under a curse, and because he already has grown sons, he wants to avoid having children with his new wife and so he has intercourse with her οὐ κατὰ νόμον, "not in the customary way" (1.61.2; that is, penetrating her anally). This is insulting to her, not because of the act itself, but because Peisistratus is using his legitimate wife solely for pleasure and not for procreation, forestalling the shared goal of marital sex and depriving his wife of her honorable role as a mother (Holt 1998: 234).[26] At first the wife keeps this hidden (ἔκρυπτε) but then (perhaps in response to a question, Herodotus speculates) she tells her mother. Her mother tells her father, who is outraged at the dishonor to himself, breaks off his alliance with Peisistratus, and reunites with Peisistratus' enemies; as a result, Peisistratus is obliged to leave Athens and start all over again. Here the news of the wife's mistreatment is elicited by her interested parents and passed from daughter to mother to father until it results in political change.

Another story, which also involves the flow of information from wronged wife to outraged father, concerns a time of troubled succession in the Persian royal family, when Cambyses' throne is usurped by a Magus named Smerdis, who pretends that he is actually Cambyses' brother, also named Smerdis, who has been secretly murdered by Cambyses. The false Smerdis is exposed by the prominent Persian Otanes (the same man who shortly afterwards proclaims the sexual deviance of tyrants), whose daughter is one of the several wives of the real Smerdis taken over by the false Smerdis. Breaking through the seclusion of the royal household, Otanes manages to communicate with his daughter by sending her secret messages. In response to his first inquiry, she is unable to say whether her current husband is the real or the false Smerdis, so he entrusts her with the mission of finding out.

> If he is not really the son of Cyrus, but instead the man I think he is, he cannot get away with sleeping with you and holding power over Persia, but must be punished. This is what you must do. The next time he shares your bed, once you are sure he's asleep, feel for his ears. If he turns out to have ears, know that you are married to Smerdis, the son of Cyrus; if not, then Smerdis the Magus.
>
> *(3.69.2–3)*

Although Smerdis is not guilty of a sexual offense in the way that Peisistratus is, his usurpation is formulated as a sexual crime: sleeping with Otanes' daughter as an imposter is as worthy of punishment as seizing political power, and Smerdis' transgression can only be detected through physical contact between husband and wife in bed. Smerdis' illegitimacy is reflected in a physical deficit, which is the result of an earlier punishment, and which is only uncovered in the most private circumstances. Here too there is a faint hint of the wife's sexuality, in the form taken by her brave act of discovery – reaching in the dark for a hidden body part (Purves 2013: 34–5). Otanes' daughter undertakes the experiment, does discover that her husband lacks ears, and communicates this to her father, who initiates a successful conspiracy against him. In this episode, the power imbalance that destabilizes the marital relation is twofold: like any tyrant, Smerdis takes too much power by seizing the throne; as a lowly criminal lacking royal lineage, he is inferior in status to Otanes' daughter, the rightful ruler's concubine and the daughter of a prominent Persian.

Finally, a story involving the most egregious of the Greek tyrants, Periander of Corinth, which is told to the Spartans by the Corinthian Socles in an attempt to dissuade them from reinstating tyranny in Athens by restoring Peisistratus' son Hippias (5.92η.1–4).[27] Periander loses an item that has been entrusted to him by a friend and sends to an oracle of the dead to find out where it is. The ghost of his dead wife Melissa appears to his messengers and says she cannot answer his question because she is cold and naked, since the clothes that were buried with her were never properly burned. As a token of her truthfulness – so that Periander will know this message really comes from her – she adds that Periander has baked his loaves in a cold oven. Periander knows at once what she is talking about: as Socles explains, she is alluding to the fact that he had intercourse with her after she was dead. Periander immediately calls all the women of Corinth to the temple of Hera, where he has them stripped by his guards; their clothes are collected in a pit and burned while he prays to the spirit of Melissa. Then he sends to the oracle again, and Melissa's ghost tells him where he has put his friend's possession.

Once again, the tyrant's excess is expressed in an act of sexual outrage against his wife, which might have remained secret except that she reveals it. Here the power of the outraged wife to make known what she has suffered transcends even her death and takes on an oracular force. The form taken by the wife's revelation is in this case particularly complex. On the one hand, it is a cryptic message, a puzzling metaphor that might reinforce and safeguard Periander's secrecy if it were not that Herodotus' internal narrator Socles intervenes to translate it for his internal audience and thus for us. On the other hand, she, like the wife of Candaules, sets in motion a clarifying restaging of her husband's original crime. She causes him to re-enact his assault on her through a violation of the entire female population of Corinth, which takes the form of removing their clothes. Like Candaules' wife, she does not allow tyrannical high-handedness to remain a secret of the bedroom, but insists that the public, political implications of excessive power must be brought to light as the tyrant's private violation of female honor is translated into a public one. In this case, the particular tyrant in question is not overthrown, but that outcome is transferred to the occasion of the story's retelling, since Socles succeeds in persuading the Spartans not to reinstall Hippias in Athens.

In these stories, Herodotus makes a broad point about the evil and instability of excessive power through the compelling scenario of a woman driven to reveal the secrets of the bedroom. Like Euripides, he draws attention to the vulnerability of women, who are inhibited by shame from disclosing what is done to them. The daughters of Megacles and Otanes communicate only through private channels within the family (and only when asked) and leave it to their fathers to reveal and act upon the abuses to which they testify; the bolder wives of Candaules and Periander are heard in the context of public speech forms available to women, the dramatic dialogue and the oracular utterance, and they themselves dictate the further actions that will publicize the conditions of their mistreatment.

The case of Melissa shows how the voice of the wronged wife serves as a vital building block of the historian's narrative, because it appears in a history within the *Histories*. Socles traces the history of the Corinthian tyrants from generation to generation, stressing their cruel misdeeds, including in his account several oracles and prophecies; and like Herodotus, he claims for himself the authority of personal knowledge, asserting that the Spartans would never have made their proposal if they had experienced tyranny first hand, as the Corinthians have (5.92α.2).[28] Herodotus grounds his narrative in revelations like Melissa's, as the authors of the Homeric hymns ground theirs in the revelations of Aphrodite, Anchises, and Hermes, and Euripides grounds his in the revelations of Creusa. Across multiple periods and genres, such revelations generate narratives that draw attention to the precarious balance between male and female, which secrecy typically protects. Drawn in by our curiosity about the sexual and the hidden, we are led to appreciate the diverse consequences – from the elevated status brought by a distinguished lineage to the bitter humiliation of rape and abuse – when the unspoken disparity built into relations of sexual difference becomes too great to be kept quiet.

Notes

1 My thanks to Mark Masterson and Nancy Rabinowitz for helpful comments on an earlier draft, and to Alex Purves for showing me her forthcoming work on enclosed spaces in Herodotus and for many conversations on topics addressed in this essay.

2 For a strong and influential statement of this view, see Halperin 1990: 30. In classical literature, the first extensive portrayals of sexual symmetry between men and women are found in the Greek novels of the imperial period (Konstan 1994).

3 Odysseus appears to include exclusive shared knowledge in his description of a happy marriage to Nausicaa, which ends μάλιστα δέ τ' ἔκλυον αὐτοί, "they know it best themselves" (*Od.* 6.185). The meaning of this phrase is, however, uncertain. See Hainsworth in Heubeck et al. 1988 ad loc.

4 For a far-reaching discussion of Odysseus and Penelope's bed, including its significance as an emblem of their "relative symmetry," see Zeitlin 1996: 19–52.

5 Foucault 1985: 151. Foucault applies this description to an ethic of fidelity for husbands as well as wives that emerged in philosophical discussions from the fourth century BCE on; as he points out, the fidelity of men differed from that of women because it depended on a self-mastery that men alone were believed to possess.

6 On these nymphs as occupying an intermediate status between mortality and immortality, see Clay 1989: 193–6.

7 On the *Hymn*'s blurring of the distinction between praise and blame, see Bergren 1989: 1–2. On the relationship of praise and blame in the Greek poetic tradition more generally, see Nagy 1999: 222 ff. Recent overviews of the powers of Aphrodite, with further bibliography, include Cyrino 2010 and Blondell 2013: 1–26.

8 *Aithiopis* p.67, 25–6 B = 47, 7–12 D. On Thersites as a blame poet or satirist in this episode, see Rosen 2007: 91–8 and Fantuzzi 2012: 267–79. A later example is Cerambus, whose story is told by Antoninus Liberalis, a mythographer of the first to third centuries CE. Inventor of the syrinx and first human player of the lyre, Cerambus is turned by the nymphs into a beetle, an animal closely identified with invective, because of his taunting discourse, in which he claims that one of them had sex with Poseidon (*Metamorphoses* 22), see Svenbro 1999; Steiner 2009: 110–15. Demodocus' song at *Odyssey* 8.266–366 recounts the literal exposure of a secret affair: Hephaestus traps Aphrodite and Ares in bed together and makes a spectacle of them. On this episode as a paradigmatic account of Homeric laughter, see Halliwell 2008: 77–86.

9 Talk between lovers and talk about love are equally the province of Aphrodite. In the *Theogony*, she receives παρθενίους ὀάρους, "maidens' conversations" (205) as part of her sphere of power; in the *Homeric Hymn to Aphrodite*, she herself claims to use ὀάρους καὶ μήτιας, "conversations and tricks," to bring couples together (249). Cf. *Il.* 6.156, 14.216, and 22.127. In Pindar and later authors, ὄαρος itself comes to refer to song (cf. Pi. *P.* 1.98; *N.* 3.11; *N.* 7.69).

10 As Bergren notes, this motive mirrors Aphrodite's own compulsion to name herself (1989: 37): "[t]o keep Aphrodite from boasting of the workings of her ὀάρους … would be tantamount to forbidding a

mortal to utter his own genealogy." The need to assert Aeneas' genealogy will keep the memory of Aphrodite's union with Anchises alive, despite her injunction and even if, as has been argued (Clay 1989: 166–70), this is the last instance in cosmic history of this type of unequal mating.

11 This is, in effect, an intensification of the concealment proper even to sanctioned lovemaking, which is reflected in the cloud with which Zeus covers himself and Hera during their encounter in *Iliad* 14, at her insistence (*Il.* 14.330–45).

12 On secrecy in love affairs among the gods in general, see Richardson 2010: 254.

13 As feminist scholarship on tragedy has stressed, the genre is particularly compelling as a medium for the normally occluded voices of women, although these are always mediated through the interests and conventions of a male-authored and male-directed genre. See especially Rabinowitz 1993; Zeitlin 1996: 341–74; Wohl 1998; McClure 1999; Foley 2001.

14 On the affinities between Semele and Creusa, see Murnaghan 2006: 107–9.

15 In the prologue, Hermes announces that one of the goals of the plot is keeping Apollo's sex with Creusa a secret (72–3). On the play's intertwining of revelation and concealment, see Lee 1997: 30–1.

16 For an analysis that stresses Euripides' exceptional rendition of the raped women's perspective, especially in comparison to other versions of similar tales, see Scafuro 1990. Kearns (2013) contrasts Euripides' treatment of Creusa's rape with Pindar's account of Apollo and Cyrene in *Pythian* 9 (to which Euripides may be alluding): Pindar minimizes the differential between the two by giving Cyrene extraordinary powers and describes their union in language that evokes a formal marriage. As Rabinowitz points out (1993: 195–201, 2011: 10–11), Creusa's report is qualified in ways that prevent her identification as simply a victim. Earlier in the play, the chorus has voiced the conviction that such stories never turn out well for the resulting children (507–8).

17 For a nuanced account of Herodotus' relationship to tragedy, see Chiasson 2003.

18 See Brooks 1984: 26 on usurpation as "preeminently what it takes to incite narrative into existence."

19 On the importance of this episode and other related stories involving powerful women for the structure of the *Histories*, see Wolff 1964; Tourraix 1976.

20 On the significance of Candaules' bedroom and other enclosed spaces in the *Histories*, see Purves 2014.

21 Diog. Laert. 8.43. For both the meaning of Gyges' aphorism and the comparison, see Cairns 1996: 80–1, 2012: 185–6.

22 The "Gyges Tragedy" can be found in Page 1951.

23 For an analysis that stresses the far-reaching implications of seeing in the Gyges episode, see Travis 2000, esp. 355, for discussion of the consequential differences between Gyges and Solon as spectators.

24 The similar roles of Candaules' wife and Croesus' gold in these two prominent narratives is one of several ways in which Herodotus acknowledges the status of women as objects of exchange within marriage, as delineated by Lévi-Strauss (1969); the sequence of repeated violations of this norm through bride thefts that opens the narrative (*Histories* 1.1–4) is another. On marriage and the exchange of women in the Homeric epics, see Von Reden 2003: 49–55; in tragedy, see Rabinowitz 1993; Wohl 1998.

25 For an account of how Herodotus' narrative bears out Otanes' analysis of tyranny, see Lateiner 1989: 167–85. On tyrants' general association with *eros* in Herodotus, see Hartog 1988: 330. On Herodotus' treatment of this theme in relation to a widespread association between tyranny and sexual excess and abuse throughout Greek culture, see Holt 1998: 225–37.

26 As Dewald argues (1993: 61–2), Candaules similarly insults his wife by viewing her only as object of desire (perhaps what is meant by the information that ἠράσθη, "he fell in love" with her); when she exchanges him for Gyges, she fulfills her proper dynastic role and becomes the ancestress of Croesus. Aphrodite's loss of status through her liaison with Anchises is reflected in the way that she, by contrast with mortal women, experiences motherhood as humiliation.

27 On this speech and the interpretive issues it has raised, with bibliography, see Moles 2007.

28 On the metahistorical character of this speech, see Moles 2007: 255–6.

Bibliography

Bergren, A. (1989) "The *Homeric Hymn to Aphrodite*: Tradition and rhetoric, praise and blame", *Classical Antiquity* 8: 1–41.

Blok, J. (2002) "Women in Herodotus' *Histories*", in E.J. Bakker, I.J.F. de Jong, and H. van Wees (eds) *Brill's Companion to Herodotus*. Leiden: Brill, pp. 225–42.

Blondell, R. (2013) *Helen of Troy: Beauty, Myth, Devastation*. New York: Oxford University Press.

Brooks, P. (1984) *Reading for the Plot: Design and Intention in Narrative*. New York: Alfred A. Knopf.

Cairns, D.L. (1993) *Aidôs: The Psychology and Ethics of Honour and Shame in Ancient Greek Literature*. Oxford: Clarendon Press.

——(1996) "'Off with her ΑΙΔΩΣ': Herodotus 1.8.3–4", *Classical Quarterly* 46: 78–83.

——(2012) "Vêtu d'impudeur et enveloppé de chagrin: Le rôle des métaphores de 'l'habillement' dans les concepts d'émotion en Grèce ancienne", in F. Gherchanoc and V. Huet (eds) *Les vêtements antiques: S'habiller, se déshabiller dans les mondes anciens*. Paris: Éditions Errance, pp. 149–62.

Chiasson, C. (2003) "Herodotus' use of Attic tragedy in the Lydian *logos*", *Classical Antiquity* 22: 5–36.

Clay, J.S. (1989) *The Politics of Olympus: Form and Meaning in the Major Homeric Hymns*. Princeton, NJ: Princeton University Press.

Cyrino, M. (2010) *Aphrodite*. New York: Routledge.

Dewald, C. (1993) "Reading the world: The interpretation of objects in Herodotus' *Histories*", in R.M. Rosen and J. Farell (eds) *Nomodeiktes: Greek Studies in Honor of Martin Ostwald*. Ann Arbor, MI: University of Michigan Press, pp. 55–70.

Fantuzzi, M. (2012) *Achilles in Love: Intertextual Studies*. Oxford: Oxford University Press.

Foley, H.P. (2001) *Female Acts in Greek Tragedy*. Princeton, NJ: Princeton University Press.

Foucault, M. (1985) *The Use of Pleasure*. New York: Random House.

Halliwell, S. (2008) *Greek Laughter: A Study of Cultural Psychology from Homer to Early Christianity*. Cambridge: Cambridge University Press.

Halperin, D.M. (1990) *One Hundred Years of Homosexuality: And Other Essays on Greek Love*. New York: Routledge.

Hartog, F. (1988) *The Mirror of Herodotus: The Representation of the Other in the Writing of History*. Berkeley, CA: University of California Press.

Heubeck, A., West, S., and Hainsworth, J.B. (1988) *A Commentary on Homer's Odyssey*, Vol. 1. Oxford: Clarendon Press.

Holt, P. (1998) "Sex, tyranny, and Hippias' incest dream (Herodotos 6.107)", *Greek, Roman and Byzantine Studies* 39: 221–41.

Irwin, E. (2005) "Gods among men? The social and political dynamics of the Hesiodic *Catalogue of Women*", in R. Hunter (ed.) *The Hesiodic Catalogue of Women: Constructions and Reconstructions*. Cambridge: Cambridge University Press, pp. 35–84.

Kearns, E. (2013) "Pindar and Euripides on sex with Apollo", *Classical Quarterly* 63: 57–67.

Konstan, D. (1994) *Sexual Symmetry: Love in the Ancient Novel and Related Genres*. Princeton, NJ: Princeton University Press.

Lateiner, D. (1989) *The Historical Method of Herodotus*. Toronto, ON: University of Toronto Press.

Lee, K.H. (1997) *Euripides Ion*, with introduction, translation, and commentary. Warminster: Aris and Phillips.

Lévi-Strauss, C. (1969) *The Elementary Structures of Kinship*. Boston, MA: Beacon Press.

Llewellyn-Jones, L. (2003) *Aphrodite's Tortoise: The Veiled Woman of Ancient Greece*. Swansea: Classical Press of Wales.

McClure, L. (1999) *Spoken Like a Woman: Speech and Gender in Athenian Drama*. Princeton, NJ: Princeton University Press.

Moles, J. (2007) "'Saving' Greece from the 'ignominy' of tyranny? The 'famous' and 'wonderful' speech of Socles (5.92)", in E. Irwin and E. Greenwood (eds) *Reading Herodotus: A Study of the Logoi in Book 5 of Herodotus' Histories*. Cambridge/New York: Cambridge University Press, pp. 245–68.

Murnaghan, S. (1988) "How a woman can be more like a man: The dialogue between Ischomachus and his wife in Xenophon's *Oeconomicus*", *Helios* 15: 9–22.

——(2006) "The daughters of Cadmus: Chorus and characters in Euripides' *Bacchae* and *Ion*", in J. Davidson, F. Muecke, and P. Wilson (eds) *Greek Drama III: Essays in Honour of Kevin Lee*, BICS Supplement 87. London: Institute of Classical Studies, pp. 99–112.

Nagy, G. (1999) *The Best of the Achaeans*, rev. edn. Baltimore, MD: Johns Hopkins University Press.

Page, D. (1951) *A New Chapter in the History of Greek Tragedy*. Cambridge: Cambridge University Press.

Purves, A. (2013) "Haptic Herodotus", in S. Butler and A. Purves (eds) *Synaesthesia and the Ancient Senses*. Durham, NC: Acumen, pp. 27–41.

——(2014) "In the bedroom: Interior space in Herodotus' *Histories*", in K. Gilhuly and N. Worman (eds) *Space, Place, and Landscape in Ancient Greek Literature and Culture*. Cambridge: Cambridge University Press, pp. 94–129.

Rabinowitz, N.S. (1993) *Anxiety Veiled: Euripides and the Traffic in Women*. Ithaca, NY: Cornell University Press.

——(2011) "Greek tragedy: A rape culture?", *Eugesta* 1: 1–21.

Richardson, N. (2010) *Three Homeric Hymns: To Apollo, Hermes, and Aphrodite*. Cambridge: Cambridge University Press.

Rosen, R.M. (2007) *Making Mockery: The Poetics of Ancient Satire*. New York: Oxford University Press.

Rosselini, M. and Saïd, S. (1978) "Usages des femmes et autres *nomoi* chez les 'sauvages' d'Hérodote", *Annali della Scuola Normale di Pisa* 8: 949–1005.

Scafuro, A. (1990) "Discourses of sexual violation in mythic accounts and dramatic versions of the 'the girl's tragedy'", *differences* 2: 126–59.

Schein, S.L. (2013) "Divine and human in the *Homeric Hymn to Aphrodite*", in R. Bouchon, P. Brillet-Dubois, and N. Le Meur Weissman (eds) *Hymnes de la Grèce antique: Approches littéraires et historiques*. Lyon: Publications de la Maison de l'Orient et de la Méditerranée, pp. 295–312.

Steiner, D. (2009) "Beetle tracks: Entomology, scatology, and the discourse of abuse", in I. Sluiter and R. M. Rosen (eds) *Kakos: Badness and Anti-Value in Classical Antiquity*. Leiden: Brill, pp. 83–117.

Svenbro, J. (1999) "Der Kopf des Hirschkäfers Kerambos und der Mythos des 'Lyrischen'", *Archiv für Religionsgeschichte* 1: 133–47.

Tourraix, A. (1976) "La femme et la pouvoir chex Hérodote: Essai d'histoire des mentalités antiques", *Dialogues d'histoire ancienne* 2: 369–86.

Travis, R. (2000) "The spectation of Gyges in P. Oxy. 2382 and Herodotus Book 1", *Classical Antiquity* 19: 330–59.

Von Reden, S. (2003) *Exchange in Ancient Greece*. London: Duckworth.

West, M.L. (1974) *Studies in Greek Elegy and Iambus*. Berlin: De Gruyter.

——(1985) *The Hesiodic Catalogue of Women*. Oxford: Clarendon Press.

Wohl, V. (1998) *Intimate Commerce: Exchange, Gender, and Subjectivity in Greek Tragedy*. Austin, TX: University of Texas Press.

Wolff, E. (1964) "Das Weib des Masistes", *Hermes* 92: 51–8.

Zeitlin, F.I. (1996) *Playing the Other: Gender and Society in Classical Greek Literature*. Chicago, IL: University of Chicago Press.

16

ANCIENT WARFARE AND THE RAVAGING MARTIAL RAPE OF GIRLS AND WOMEN

Evidence from Homeric epic and Greek drama

Kathy L. Gaca

The first feminist scholarly wave of studying women in antiquity, and the sexual mores regulating their lives, began to take shape in the 1970s, around the same time as the revival of military historical interest in ancient warfare. Since then, studies of ancient warfare and of women and sexual mores in antiquity have generally proceeded as though the research findings in each field have little reason to be engaged with one another.[1]

Ancient military historians have been at work in their field, with greater intensity and a higher profile of academic and public interest since Keegan 1976, 1987 (e.g., Pritchett 1971–91), many of them partly stimulated by Keegan's engaging style and insights about battles in Western warfare over time and the roles of commanders and their men therein.[2] With rare exceptions, these studies of ancient warfare retain a virtually exclusive focus on fighting-age adult males in their organized hierarchies under command, often reaching a high degree of technicality about weaponry, bodily armor, and armament overall, and also about the logistics, strategies, and tactics of commanders maneuvering their adult male forces. As a result the subject can seem a specialized male-oriented topic for military history buffs. To be a woman working with these studies can feel rather like ending up in the wrong locker room and hiding out in one of the stalls.

As for women and sexual mores in antiquity, scholars exemplified by, but not limited to, contributors to this *Sex in Antiquity* collection have likewise been productively at work in this still developing field, as indicated by the field's evolving name. First known as "women in classical antiquity" or "women in antiquity" in the time of Pomeroy 1975 and Keuls 1985,[3] this field is now more generally ancient cultural studies with a focus on women, gender, and sexuality in the Ancient Near East and Mediterranean. Unlike "military historians," we as scholars have no self-evident, shared, and concise name for this research field and our collective identity in it. Yet most and probably all of us share the sociopolitical identity of being feminist, or at least have strong enough feminist or womanist sympathies to have been drawn to the field of women, gender, and sexuality. This field is committed to paying attention to gender or socially constructed sex difference in antiquity, as well as to other layers of identity and labeling, whether imposed, voluntary, or semi-voluntary, that helped shape separate classes and groups with different social outlooks. These layers include, for instance, ethnicity, religiosity, age progression and its social markings from early girlhood and boyhood, and the status of being slave or free or in between freedom and slavery—the in-between status including recently manumitted slaves.[4] The resultant complexity of the gender and other research interests in this evolving field in ancient cultural studies resists any one succinct name.

The broad-based exploratory engagement that characterizes women, gender, and sexuality studies is part of a continuing effort to press toward inclusivity in our research, in particular by recognizing the diversity in our subject matter; thus we attempt to bring the hitherto marginalized of antiquity into view and to keep them there. From this perspective, it is outdated to perpetuate the longstanding focus on freeborn adult males, with at best a token recognition of the rest. Androcentrism, especially in its unquestioned focus on those with freeborn status, is the old narrow habit we are still working to go beyond. Nonetheless it is very much a part of the project of women, gender, and sexuality studies to examine currents in masculinity and manliness, not least because these inquiries can help us to understand how social orders that presume androcentrism and various patterns of gender separatism historically came about.

Given the different research approaches and orientations in the two fields, ancient warfare has until recently been scarcely in evidence in studies of women, sex, and gender in antiquity.[5] Conversely, women are accorded some conventional kinds of recognition in scholarship on ancient military history, such as being seen as active supporters of their menfolk in war and as grieving widows and mothers of fallen fighters (Schaps 1982; Loman 2004). Yet in these studies it is rare to investigate the treatment meted out to women and girls seized as war captives and the norms of gender and sexuality that inform and develop from this martial aggression in antiquity.[6]

However, in ancient populace-ravaging warfare,[7] the focused martial use of aggravated sexual assault and other bodily and psychological torments against war-captive girls and women make it imperative to bring the two fields together to develop an integrated exploration of rape warfare against girls and women and its social repercussions in the ancient world, as I have argued thus far in dispatches from my beachhead of studying ancient warfare with commitments rooted in ethics, political philosophy, and women, gender, and sexuality studies. This article is another contribution toward this end.

As I have argued elsewhere (Gaca 2010, 2011a, 2011b, 2012, 2014), practices of aggravated rape and keeping alive, and of aggravated rape and killing, or leaving to die, were inflicted on women and girls among peoples targeted and hit with the martial aggression known as populace-ravaging warfare. In these articles I have further argued the following related claims, which can only be summarized and not reproduced here: (1) The subjugation and enslavement of non-combatant captives were fundamental to populace-ravaging warfare. That is what this warfare was substantively for. (2) Sexual aggression was integral both to what it meant to subjugate or enslave war-captive girls and women and to how they were treated thereafter as unfree persons. (3) Populace ravaging, given its sex- and age-based methods of deciding who was to be killed (or left with little chance to survive) and who was to be kept alive, was designed exclusively or primarily to seize young females as live captives. (4) As sexually ravaged subjugates, these girls and young women were available for ongoing sexual and other exploitative maltreatment, as decided by their captors or new owners.

In the next section, "Seeing ancient warfare inclusively," I present substantive new evidence for my third claim about the acquisitive martial fixation on young females and I note the sexual tenor of this fixation. Then, in much of the rest of this article I further bear out my second claim that the aggression was sexual against war-captive girls and young women wanted alive (Gaca 2011a, 2012, 2014), and I do so by exploring additional important evidence from Homeric epic and Greek drama that in this article is elucidated for the first time. Hence, aggravated heterosexual rape was not merely a regular practice but an important purpose in these man-to-man armed conflicts.[8]

Community-minded men trained in methods of defense against ravaging warfare provided the first line of defense. This included forming local defense coalitions committed to rushing to the aid of fellow communities under this kind of attack (e.g., Hom. *Od.* 9.39–61). Ravaging aggressors generally aimed to slaughter, or to torture and slaughter, the males among the people targeted for attack, be it all the males including boys or the adult males of fighting age, as further discussed in the next section, "Seeing ancient warfare inclusively." Getting them out of the way, especially males of fighting age, was the premeditated lead-in to the likewise premeditated finale of seizing girls and young women alive in order to rape them and thereby turn them into subjugates who were isolated and bereft of their kin groups. The young women and girls could then be used for sexual and other exploitative labors as their captors or new owners saw fit. This is one basic way in which heterosexual rape became a socially normative rape culture in antiquity,[9] for while raping freeborn girls and women was an outrage contrary to ancient civil norms, such as the rape of Dinah (Gen 34:1–31) and of Lucretia, raping young female war captives kept alive was a customary practice within ravaging martial hierarchies and the social orders they came to constitute and develop.[10]

It is no coincidence that the ancient freeborn civil norm against heterosexual rape was trampled on in the process, for to conduct organized martial sexual violence with impunity against previously freeborn women and girls of targeted peoples was key to the populace-ravaging enterprise of taking away their day of freedom (ἐλεύθερον ἦμαρ) and the civil social protections and privileges of that freedom, as Homer first pointed out long ago.[11] Once they were forced into the demoted status of slaves and other kinds of social subjugates (e.g., war-captive concubines), they and their deracinated female offspring in principle remained sexually usable with impunity by their male keepers and by any men to whom their keepers granted or rented sexual access.

This is not to suggest that girls and women in this position had no means to get out from under this use of power, for resourceful they were, even if that meant exploiting others. For example, they might acquire girls for sexually exploitative purposes, like the brothel madame Nicarete in Athens, herself a disadvantaged freedwoman (ἀπελευθέρα, ps.-Demosth. 59.18–19) who gained her advantage at the expense of the seven young slave girls she acquired and prostituted, the young Neaera included. Consequently, to seize young women and girls to put through their paces of customary rape was one basic objective and function of populace-ravaging warfare over antiquity, from small village hits and minor rural sweeps to major city conquests and the overrunning of large regions. Of those kept alive, some female captives were used in the forces and largely compelled to help populate them,[12] and others were traded to other owners. Each ravaging attack on hitherto freeborn girls and women struck yet another blow against the ancient civil norm that to rape daughters and mothers of other men was a crime deserving of serious penalty. And as for already enslaved or freed women and girls seized along with freeborn girls and women, ravaging demolished any strategies they devised hitherto to help cope with their lot.

As an integral part of isolating and disempowering the girls and young women wanted alive as sexual subjugates, many other members of their communities were killed in addition to the core group of fighting-age adult males. Fully grown females and older non-fighting-age males alike were also killed, whether by quick dispatch, or being tortured and killed slowly, or being seriously injured and left to die. A number in this group, for whom no counts or percentages are on record, were women judged not worth keeping alive on some grounds, such as those who seemed too mature. This is not to say that these women merely seemed too old, although some of them presumably were elderly and killed as part of the mocking torment (*ludibrium*) to which elderly women and men were subjected in ravaging aggression, partly because they were deemed not worth being kept as human plunder.[13] Rather, women liable to being gang-raped and killed or left for dead were too fully formed as adults to be co-opted en masse into an ongoing pliability and docility as subjugates, be they in the possession of their martial captors or of other owners, for those with possession would want the captives to compliantly do their bidding. Some of the fully mature women are on record being gang-raped and killed outright or left behind in a condition of having been repeatedly raped (e.g., en masse or in turn, ὑπὸ πλήθεος or ἐκ διαδοχῆς) and injured and maltreated in other respects (e.g., subjected to starvation and sleep deprivation, ἥ τε ἀσιτία καὶ ἡ ἀυπνία), and thus likely to die from being denied the necessities of life (περιφθειρομένας δι' ἔνδειαν τῶν ἀναγκαίων).[14] It is hard to imagine a harsher way to turn the girls and young women kept alive into dazed submissives of their conquerors and other buyers than to experience their mothers, grandmothers, and other female role models and caregivers being treated this way, as well as being raped and dominated themselves.

Here I extend my arguments farther by looking closely at Homeric, classical Greek, and select post-classical Greek and later evidence about the young women and girls wanted alive. In addition to further showing the sexual tenor of this aggression, my aim is to demonstrate that the sexual aggression against them was not the unlimited-access and likely lethal gang rape but a controlled-access rape in which the likelihood of survival was greater. I also show early Homeric evidence that this practice was a matter of top-down orders and thus of martial policy. My culminating emphasis is on the girls long overlooked in the history of this warfare,[15] the underage or barely pubescent girls. The "underage" standard used here is one familiar from Old World antiquity: Girls still too young to become legitimate wives with parental approval in classical Athens. It is important to use this ancient civil age standard so as to appreciate that the martial standard in antiquity is even younger than the customary minimum bridal age of fourteen or fifteen years old in Athens.

Seeing ancient warfare inclusively

To comprehend ancient populace-ravaging warfare and to fit the martial sexual subjugation of war-captive women and girls into the picture, we need to transform the predominant modern understanding of ancient warfare as organized armed violence of men killing and men being killed, exclusively or foremost in battles. The latter approach to ancient warfare explores how battle worked in antiquity, partly in response to Keegan's influential *The Face of Battle*.[16] Yet battle is often only the first part of ancient warfare and its far-reaching social consequences, as argued in my recent studies mentioned above (see bibliography). Insofar as the lethal force in this aggression has the significant purpose to seize and subjugate alive the young and youthful sectors among the attacked people—females exclusively or mainly depending on the range of lethal force methods employed—it is time to start looking at what populace-ravaging warfare does to those kept alive, once the martial signal is given to turn from inflicting carnage to ravaging captives alive (Polyb. 10.15.8). It is shortsighted to concentrate on the killing in such warfare, adult male armed conflict foremost, without considering the en masse round-up, by one method, of girls and young women alive or, by another method, of girls and young women along with preadolescent boys. By analogy, we would not conceptualize bank robbery in terms of the hold-up strategies, weapons, and casualties, while paying little or no attention to the heist.[17] The two methods are as follows.

Depending on the incident, the orders given, and peer pressure at work, ravaging martial aggressors typically use one of two main methods of populace ravaging. By one method, they seek to take alive no one but girls and women, and mainly young women. This means trying to eliminate captured boys and the rest of the members of the captured populace, including women not wanted alive and liable to being gang-raped to death. By another method, the aggressor forces try to take alive girls and mainly young women but also preadolescent boys. This means eliminating many of the rest in the captured populace, especially fighting-age males adolescent and older.

The policy of taking only girls and young unmarried women alive is well attested in the Old Testament. For example, in Moses' directive in Numbers 31—a directive presented as authorized by the Lord God (31:2)—only virgin girls are to be kept alive by Israelite forces after their conquest of the Midianite people. Everyone else is to be killed, boys included, and here married women are expressly to be killed as well, though not a word is said about whether any of the married women are raped to death.[18] This method, which includes pandemic male slaughter, has a broad but sporadically attested cross-ethnic martial representation from Homeric epic through late antiquity.[19] The policy of commandeering women and girls and also some preadolescent boys alive is especially well known as a Greek, Macedonian, and Roman martial practice that in Greek is called "andrapodizing" (Gaca 2010: 117–61), such as the Athenian martial conquest of Melos according to Thucydides (Thuc. 4.115.1–4). The top-down nature of this policy is especially clear where accounts are given of the prior deliberations, such as Thucydides' account of the famous Athenian decision to andrapodize Mytilene and then reversing this decision the next day (Thuc. 3.28.2, 35.1–36.6, 49.1–50.3). In both ravaging methods, therefore, the proverbial "women and children" seized alive are not women of all ages but mainly young women. The children vary between being only female or female and male, depending on whether preadolescent boys are wanted alive or dead in any particular ravaging incident.

In late antiquity, for instance, Synesius of Cyrene makes it clear that Moorish Ausurian forces ravaging near Cyrene in North Africa for a time were seizing boys alive along with young female captives, but then reverted to killing boys and keeping only the young female captives alive (*Epist.* 125). Thus, girls are generally wanted alive in both methods, and boys in some number are wanted alive in the second method. The women wanted alive are mainly young. Further, the children wanted alive, girls always, and boys too by the andrapodizing method, are generally old enough to be mobile and to feed themselves, able to function without needing the daily nurture and care that maternal figures give to infants and very young children.[20] The aggression of populace-ravaging warfare in antiquity was extremely violent in its entirety and degrading for everone involved, including the perpetrating armed forces, a number of them press-ganged, that is, forcibly recruited and then coerced, enticed, and corrupted into this behavior by being threatened with serious penalty for failing to comply.[21]

I refer to the aggressive male armed forces who are coerced and enticed into ravaging as "martial," not "military," because ideologically and historically military forces take up arms to fight in defense against the aggressive doings of ravaging martial forces.[22] This is not to deny that military defensive aggression can take on martial qualities, such as making a preemptive strike to liquidate peoples deemed to be intransigent ravagers.[23] But the difference is clear incident by incident, for in each incident we need only ask which forces are trying to haul off women and children of other men and which forces are trying to stop this from being done or to retrieve and restore abducted children and women to their remaining menfolk. The former are martial forces and the latter military.

Thus, as noted previously, the sectors of the ravaged populace to be seized alive are, historically, either exclusively or predominantly made up of female captives; the overwhelming majority of them young. They are exclusively female when the orders and aims are to kill all the males, boys of all ages and grown men alike. They are predominantly female when the orders and aims are to kill fighting-age males.[24] A number of the young female captives are put to auxiliary uses by martial forces, such as having to be breadmakers and cooks (Josep. *AJ* 41), be it on campaign or in settlements that the armed forces called home, at least for those martial groups that had such settlements, as opposed to martially roving forces "without roofs" and no place to call home.[25] The sector of females in the populace wanted alive are generally the same age as girls in the present day who are on the threshold between preschool and kindergarten, girls throughout grade school, and girls turning into women in high school and college in societies that grant this sort of education to their female members. Female educational level is worth mentioning because one of the first social repercussions of populace ravaging is to terminate the civil education that the captured and attacked girls and women receive in any era, be it at home with their mothers or in schools. In the modern day, this is unforgettably shown in the reuse of school buildings and their classrooms, among other locations, for the purpose of detaining and subjecting the girls and young women to organized rape, rape, and more rape.[26] The substituted martial "education" of the girls and women proceeds along radically different lines in its lessons, such as this blunt but practical advisory threat in how to survive given by a paramilitary soldier from Montenegro to young Bosnian Muslim female captives. The girls should submit to being raped and never talk about it, for "listen, it's better to be fucked than to be beaten and fucked."[27]

By contrast, war-captive boys who were seized and kept alive from their andrapodized people were not subjected to public martial demonstrations of rape. To suppose that ancient Greek norms of male pederasty made them regular targets in this performance of social degradation may initially seem plausible but is not the case. Greek male pederasty was a power-imbued sexual protocol between freeborn men and and freeborn blossoming boy-youths. This sexual conduct was in principle not an outright sexual mauling of the boys against their will. Instead it was conducted with characteristic adult male enticements, pressures, and attempts to lure and seduce.[28] As Hieron states in Xenophon's biography of this Syracusan Greek tyrant, sexual mauling is characteristic of ravaging warfare (λεηλασία), and this is repugnant in Greek freeborn male pederasty, where the protocol called for submissive ἀφροδίσια on the boys' part. Plato and the early Stoic Zeno strongly concur.[29]

War-captive boys were egregiously maltreated too when andrapodized and kept alive, but generally by means of boy-specific norms of organized martial violence, such as being beaten or castrated at the decision of their captors.[30] These norms did not carry over to the armed forces sexually degrading captured boys too in an organized public way. The forces did not tear off boys' garments and adornments with such force that even the stripping caused injuries.[31] The forces also did not throw boys down to sexually penetrate them anally and orally, as they did to their sisters and mothers, mainly but by no means in a strictly vaginal way (Gaca 2012: 105, and see too 97). This was the treatment meted out to captured girls and women, and the treatment was especially violent against female captives not wanted alive. Further, when preadolescent boys were killed off, there is no evidence to indicate that they were first raped or gang-raped and then killed. They are instead portrayed being conspicuously slaughtered, such as being run through with a sword and having their heads bashed on the ground.[32] Upon conquest, forcible pederasty could of course also be practiced against andrapodized war-captive boys.[33] But these male–male relations of sustained post-conquest sexual abuse are beyond my present focus, which is on the sexual violence employed in the heterosexual martial aggression of populace-ravaging warfare itself and on the ensuing normative rape culture that then circumscribes the lives of war-captive girls, young women, and their female descendants.

Regardless of whether or not preadolescent boys are included as captive subjugates wanted alive, populace ravaging retains a female-specific trajectory with characteristic sexual assault strategies against girls and women, and these have been persistently downplayed or overlooked in the history of this warfare since antiquity. As indicated above, in a ravaged populace, women of all ages are subjected to martial sexual aggression. The girls and young women wanted alive are generally subjected to more regulated forms of rape that are conducive to having them survive, as opposed to the uncontrolled and often lethal gang rapes carried out against women who for various reasons are not wanted alive.[34]

In the rest of this article I give additional evidence for the specifics of targeting girls and young women wanted as live captives (beyond that elucidated in Gaca 2012), and I further demonstrate its sexual tenor, starting with Homeric epic.

Taking the day of freedom away from women and girls

In the *Iliad* and *Odyssey*, the overriding emphasis of populace-ravaging warfare is on the forcible seizing of "women" alive, that is, "womenfolk" in the traditional sense of female persons as their own quasi-race or human species (the γένος γυναικῶν or the φῦλον or φῦλα γυναικῶν), which includes preadolescent girls.[35] As Achilles states in the *Iliad*, when he along with his fellow marauders set out on their war raids (διαπορθήσας, see *Il.* 2.691), they killed adult males in town after town by the sea and inland (9.325–9), 23 towns in total, not yet counting Troy, in order to take the "day of freedom away (ἐλεύθερον ἦμαρ)" from "women taken as plunder (ληΐάδας γυναῖκας)" by hauling them into captivity.[36] The Trojan and allied men trying to defend their communities and settlements from ravaging aggression likewise grasp that the driving motive of the Achaean aggression is to abduct and dominate the womenfolk from the communities once their menfolk are overthrown. Hector, for instance, declares to Diomedes, "You will never take away our women (γυναῖκας) in your ships."[37]

In the *Iliad*, in the walled camp of the Achaeans and their allies, the ravaged and abducted womenfolk include two pubescent κοῦραι roughly about the age of Nausicaa. The first is Chryseis, who is likely still virginal when Agamemnon first rapes her and tries to keep her for himself, for virgins are a choice prize for the main overlord or for his elite male beneficiaries (e.g., Polyb. 10.19.3–7, Joseph. *Vit.* 414). Another likely indicator of Chryseis' young age is that her father Chryses is the one determined to get her back, and no mention is made of any husband of Chryseis who has been killed. To kill a husband and turn a young wife into an enslaved widow are martial aggressor points to brag about, as noted, for instance, in the future in store for the widowed and enslaved Andromache, who will be taunted and caused fresh pain (νέον ἄλγος) in captivity by being called Hector's (former) wife, Ἕκτορος ἦδε γυνή (*Il.* 6.460–3). Nothing of this sort is said about Chryseis. The second κούρη is the hitherto young wife, Briseis, who is turned into a brotherless, fatherless, and husbandless widow by Achilles and his forces before Achilles wins her sexually as his war prize (*Il.* 19.291–300) and tries to keep her for himself.[38] On the historical record, Scipio Africanus supposedly refused his beautiful virgin war prize and gave her back to her father (Polyb. 10.19.3–7), or to her Celtiberian fiancé Allucius (Livy 26.50.1–14); yet Valerius Antias disbelieves the account about Scipio's refusal, seeing it as a case of historical revisionism.[39] He instead maintains that the virgin was kept and used by Scipio "for his pleasures and passions" (*in deliciis amoribusque*, Aul. Gell. 7.8.6), just as is done in the *Iliad*.

There are additional ravaged and abducted womenfolk (γυναῖκες) in the *Iliad* who are likewise allocated as the property of a single warrior, such as the γυνή Diomede, daughter of Phorbas, whom Achilles uses as his bedmate after Agamemnon takes Briseis away from him, and the unnamed women whom Achilles hands away as prizes to victorious warriors in Patroclus' funeral games, along with objects including tripods, kettles, horses, mules, cattle, and a hefty lump of iron.[40] As "womenfolk" are anonymous and given no descriptors indicative of their age, it is not clear whether these prizes are girls, women, or some of both. It is also not clear whether the three other named female captives in the *Iliad* are women or girls who are each allocated as belonging to one man, Hecamede, whom the Achaean warriors picked out for Nestor because of his skill as military adviser (*Il.* 11.624–7, 14.6–7), Iphis given to Patroclus by Achilles, and Diomede used by Achilles (*Il.* 9.664–8) after Agamemnon takes Briseis away.

Agamemnon likewise promises Teucer a prospective woman prize for his prowess once Troy is ravaged, just as Patroclus has already been given Iphis by Achilles. Agamemnon does not divulge to Teucer whether this promised woman is a girl or a more developed woman. And stingy as Agamemnon notoriously is with his war-captive womenfolk (*Il.* 2.226–8), he also indicates that he might just give Teucer a tripod or two horses with a chariot instead (*Il.* 8.281–91). Seeing that the individually named female captives are high-status gains as daughters and former wives of once prominent men (van Wees 1992: 252), the men now killed off, these female captives are generally to be understood as having shapeliness, a high-quality mind, and a capable skill set in women's work, all of which Agamemnon brags that Chryseis has no less than does his wife Clytemnestra (*Il.* 1.113–15). They may not all be as gorgeous as Briseis and "look like golden Aphrodite," as Homer puts it (*Il.* 19.282). Nonetheless, the dream captive for ravaging warriors to take by sexual force is an ancient analogue to the sexy schoolgirl centerfold, although in antiquity the women clustered around that young age actually were raped. They were not consenting adult female partners engaging in sex play and pretending to be budding schoolgirls, and they were not images of sexual fantasy.[41]

The presence of relatively few named pubescent girls and women in the *Iliad* should not leave the impression that female war captives in the Achaean and allied camp amount only to a token presence overall—this or that captive regional princess in the occasional tent. Other war-captive girls and women are to be understood as interned there, and periodically the camp would be restocked with young and youthful female ἀνδράποδα in considerable numbers.[42] As indicated above, an integral and important part of why the Achaean and allied forces go to war is because they seek to seize womenfolk so as to "take their day of freedom away" (20.193–4, cf. 6.455), that is, so as to subjugate and exploit them in considerable numbers, both directly and by trafficking them to be slaves and other kinds of social subjugates for other owners (see *Il.* 7.470–7). Their presence as imprisoned captives in number in the walled camp is better disclosed when Achilles and Agamemnon have and use unnamed γυναῖκες as discretionary prize items, and also when Achilles and the uppity Thersites point out that Agamemnon is keeping many of them for himself (*Il.* 2.226–8, 9.323–33).

Further, in Homeric epic, Achilles and Odysseus are both given the epithet πτολίπορθος to convey their proficiency as ravagers of womenfolk from attacked cities and towns.[43] Why Achilles has the epithet is already clear. Odysseus likewise earns the epithet given the many female war captives that he puts on board his ships before departing from Troy (*Od.* 3.153–4). Evidently they are not enough, for after leaving, he and his comrade forces on their way back from Troy kill male Cicones in order to seize their wives (ἄλοχοι, *Od.* 9.39–42). Also, an audacious Homeric simile indirectly shows Odysseus' familiarity with this practice by likening his tears about his return travel woes to that of a captive woman convulsed with grief and throwing herself upon her slaughtered husband (πόσις), only to be spear-whipped into submission and taken off for toil and hardship (*Od.* 8.523–30).

Despite the euphemistic descriptor of calling abducted and ravaged females "wives" (ἄλοχοι) in Homeric epic (e.g., *Il.* 2.355, *Od.* 9.41), which implies that the captive females are of a marriageable age and already married wives, armed forces engaged in populace ravaging primarily want emerging adolescent young women and girls verging on adolescence. As Aeschylus puts it, war-captive girls are seized before the time of legitimate marriage (*Sept.* 334), which for him meant girls younger than fourteen or fifteen, the conventionally minimum Athenian female marital age.[44] The aim of ravaging forces to seize female captives in girlhood as well as in pubescence is further shown in the *Iliad* and *Odyssey* alike, where the ravaging warriors regularly seize alive women (γυναῖκας), children (τέκνα), and young children (νήπια τέκνα) from the settlements they torch and from the rural areas they devastate (*Il.* 9.590–4, *Od.* 14.263–5 = *Od.* 17.432–4). It is important to see that τέκνα here includes girl children and may mean girls primarily, for this sense is consonant with the rest of the Homeric evidence about the Achaean martial focus on seizing womenfolk, preadolescent and in their sexual prime, as war captives. Old Testament evidence indirectly confirms this focus by showing Israelite forces ravaging the Midianites with a view to taking only the virgin-aged and virginal Midianite womenfolk alive, that is, only the girls (e.g., Num. 31:1–47).[45]

The Achaean martial fixation on girls is conveyed powerfully in the Homeric simile about the little girl and her mother in *Il.* 16.7–11. Though long regarded as an endearing cameo scene of domesticity during peacetime between a mother and her very young daughter (κούρη νηπίη, *Il.* 16.7–8), I have argued that this simile reveals the martial destruction of normal domestic life for a young daughter and her mother who are being chased down and are about to be captured by ravaging Achaean warriors (Gaca 2008: 145–71). Euripides likewise points out this martial determination to seize young girls in what I argue is his adaptation of this mother–daughter simile in his *Trojan Women* (Gaca 2008: 165, n. 57, cf Eur. *Tr.* 1089–93). It is not until the Hellenistic era, when Aristarchus carries out his extensively revisionist assessment of Homeric epic, that *Il.* 16.7–11 is altered and in effect airbrushed into the heart-warming domestic scene that it has since been taken to be. Thus, Homeric epic provides exemplary insight into the main lineaments of the martial practices by which the girls and women are seized and socially demoted and degraded through populace ravaging. Beyond epic, the sustained determination to seize women and (girl and boy) children or strictly girls and women alive is further borne out in the multiethnic mores of populace-ravaging ancient warfare, as I have argued elsewhere (Gaca 2010, 2012: 93–8, 93 nn. 28–9, 96 n. 37, 2014).

The sexual ravaging of war-captive women and girls

Let us now turn to salient Greek evidence that further discloses the sexual tenor of the ravaging aggression against captured freeborn daughters and women,[46] beyond that which I have discussed elsewhere (Gaca 2012: 93–106, 2014). Here I begin once again with Homeric epic and proceed from there to Greek drama.

The *Iliad* does not take long to indicate that martial mass rape is a top-down part of the aggressors' command structure, not a "boys will be boys" accompaniment of war. Nestor in the *Iliad* first highlights the sexual assault in store for the young women of Troy once the city is conquered. As Agamemnon's most senior military adviser, he issues the command that the soldiers on the Achaean side unconditionally must fulfill, under pain of death, before any of them can leave Troy and go home: "Let no one be eager to return home until he has slept with a wife (ἀλόχῳ κατακοιμηθῆναι) among the Trojans" in revenge for Helen's sufferings (*Il.* 2.354–6). As stated by Kirk (1985: 153), the "mass rape (which is what it amounts to) is phrased in a typically epic—that is, bowdlerized—way, almost as if one were simply to take one's place in the marital bed for a long night's rest" (Gaca 2008: 149). Homeric epic likewise uses this sort of euphemism for post-conquest sexual coercion back in the Achaean camp: Diomede "laid down next to (παρκατέλεκτο)" Achilles, as did Iphis next to Patroclus (ἐλέξατο) when he laid down (*Il.* 9.663–8), and Agamemnon envisions Teucer's prospective captive woman clambering up into bed with Teucer (εἰσαναβαίνοι, *Il.* 8.291) once Troy is conquered.

In Euripides, by contrast, the post-conquest norm of warriors owning and continuing to sleep with their female captives back in camp is explicitly recognized as habitual rape. Euripides states that Agamemnon will "forcibly copulate (γαμεῖ βιαίως)" with war-captive Cassandra, getting her into his bed through "shady nuptials (σκότια νυμφευτήρια)" (*Tr.* 44, 252). Similarly, the later Homeric scholia recognize that it is habitual rape for warriors to own and continue to "lie next to (παριαύειν)" their female captives back in camp. All this "lying" and so-called "sleeping with" is done with force (τὸ βίαιον), just as Penelope's suitors forcefully bed with the female slaves in Odysseus' house (*Od.* 22.37), for the female captives are unwilling objects of coercion (schol. on *Il.* 9.336d, Erbse vol. 2 p. 468). They are not willing agents making love together in bed out of mutually shared desire and then snuggling together for sweet sleep (γλυκὺς ὕπνος) afterwards.

The martial norm of institutionalized rape is also described as "the copulation of an unwilling female person with a willing male person (γάμος ἀκούσης καὶ ἑκόντος)."[47] This apt phrase appears in the scholia on the epic *Halieutica* (*Lore of the Sea*) by Oppian of the second century CE. In relation to *Hal.* 1.529–32, the scholiast is explaining Oppian's adventurous presentation of supposed tortoise sexuality to convey the intense pain involved when a spear-conquered female captive is raped as a war prize. To appreciate the power of his simile, one needs to get beyond the incongruity of his ideas about tortoise copulation and pay attention to the simile. In tortoise sexuality, according to Oppian, the females find it utterly excruciating for male tortoises to mount them. They abhor and greatly fear copulating, because the male's penis is an inflexible and extremely painful bony prong that becomes even sharper when he is ready for sex. So unbearable is this prong for the female tortoises that they struggle with great intensity against mating. They bite at the males and are bitten back, and this spurs the males to become willingly desirous of copulating with their resistant female targets, "until the male, conquering," couples with her in coerced love-making, "just as with female human booty, a prize of war (ἠΰτε ληϊδίην, πολέμου γέρας)" (see Oppian, *Hal.* 1.529–35, esp. 530–2, and schol. on Opp. *Hal.* 1.529, Bussemaker 1849). Surviving girls and women subjected to such rape in recent and still living memory confirm that the penetrative experience is excruciating.[48] Bony prongs are not on record in contemporary ravaging martial rape, but similar kinds of hard foreign objects are used for this purpose, such as beer bottles and gun barrels (e.g., Vranic 1996: 43).

Even though much of Homeric epic communicates the martial rape of a coerced spear-conquest bedmate as though it were sexual copulation in legitimate marriage, Priam cuts through this Homeric euphemism about sleeping and bedding with Trojan wives to acknowledge the impending mass rape on site once Troy is conquered. Unless the doomed Hector survives to continue defending the city, Priam will see "his daughters and daughters-in-law mauled (ἑλκηθείσας θύγατρας, ἑλκομένας νυούς) by the destructive hands of the Achaeans" (*Il.* 22.62–5). The mauling is sexual, for ἕλκειν (or ἑλκεῖν) here signifies aggravated rape, just as it does when Tityus "raped (ἕλκησε)" Zeus' consort Leto (*Od.* 11.580).

The sense of ἕλκειν specific to heterosexual rape is synonymous with the Homeric ῥυστάζειν, which is a frequentative of ἐρύειν, "drag along," and, like ἕλκειν, stresses the dragging or mauling involved in attacking and subjecting female persons to aggravated rape. The *Odyssey* uses ῥυστάζειν to convey what Penelope's suitors are doing to the female slaves in Odysseus' house (*Od.* 16.108–9 = 20.318–19). A definition of ῥυστάζειν presented in the *Etymologicum magnum* (Gaisford) thus further illuminates the sexual nature of the impending violence against Priam's daughters and daughters-in-law by Achaean and allied fighters, for ῥυστάζειν means "to sexually maul (ἕλκειν) and to copulate with a woman through force and compulsion (τὸ μετὰ βίας καὶ ἀνάγκης ἕλκειν καὶ μίγνυσθαι γυναικί)."[49] This is a concise and apt definition of aggravated heterosexual rape. As Porphyry puts it more succinctly, ἕλκειν meaning "sexually maul" is ἕλκειν εἰς ὕβριν in the sexually specific legal sense of ὕβρις as rape.[50] This succinct definition likewise indicates the salient aspects of aggravated rape—sexually penetrative mauling through sheer force. This is what Nestor and the Homeric narrator call "sleeping or bedding down with" and what Priam refuses to hide under these covers.

Hector is blunt and honest like his father when he tells Andromache that she faces the sure prospect of a sexual mauling (ἑλκηθμοῖο) on site when Troy is conquered. He hopes to be dead and gone before hearing her outcry for help (βοή) when she is taken and subjected to aggravated rape (*Il.* 6.464–5). The scholia strongly empathize with Hector's perspective here: "Of all the horrors [of war], the rape of women is the worst."[51]

Even though Hector's dread focuses on the victimizing of Andromache, she will hardly be screaming alone, for, as Priam makes clear, the sexual attack on her is part of a bigger Achaean martial plan of aggravated sexual assault to be carried out against all of his daughters and daughters-in-law, Andromache included. But Priam too is overly selective, for the Achaean plan of retribution is not limited to raping only the female members of a king's extended family as punitive payback against him and his male relatives, as it is on later occasions to punish several Greek tyrants (Diod. Sic. 13.112.3–4, 14.44.4–5, Aelian, *Var. Hist.* 9.8, Strabo 6.1.8, Plut., *Timol.* 13.8–10). The Achaean and allied aim is to turn all the surviving female inhabitants of Troy into their raped inmates. And, as noted previously, it is not as though the men in the lower echelon of the Achaean forces have much choice in this martial rape project. Even though many of them would rather just go home (*Il.* 2.142–210), any fighters in league with Agamemnon who would act on this impulse would be killed on the spot, as Nestor makes clear, for abandoning this required mandate of mass rape and Trojan mission accomplished (*Il.* 2.354–9).

Yet Homeric epic nowhere indicates that underage girls are subjected to martial rape as a routine part of populace-ravaging warfare. For example, as noted above, Nestor's phrase about each Achaean warrior having to rape a Trojan "wife" (ἄλοχοι, *Il.* 2.355) leaves the impression that preadolescent girls and as yet unmarried virgins still in emergent adolescence are not raped at this time, even though captive virgins were historically premier among the prizes. To understand why this impression is wrong, and why Aeschylus and his scholia are correct about underage girls being seized and raped, we have to proceed beyond Homeric epic to Herodotus and then to a further consideration of Aeschylus on the seizing of war-captive girls before their time of legitimate marriage.

The martial rape of underage girls

The norm of martial rape against captive girls in populace-ravaging ancient warfare can be hard to discern in Greek given the collective Greek use of "womenfolk" (γυναῖκες), that is, "women" in the traditional cultural sense that subsumes girls as little women among the γένος γυναικῶν, rather as though preadolescent girls were like Russian *matryoshka* or nesting dolls in which even the littlest *matryoshka* is already a diminutive woman in her shape. To this usage is to be added a related twist of semantic irony: In ancient civil traditions, to commence sexual relations in legitimate marriage, that is, in parentally approved and community celebrated unions (e.g., *Il.* 18.491–5), is traditionally what turns virgins into women in the other traditional sense of womanhood: being an adult female who is sexually and procreatively active with her husband. By analogy with this norm, once preadolescent girls and pre-nubile virgins are martially raped and dominated as war captives, they too are often simply called "women (γυναῖκες)" even though they are still underage—a usage facilitated by girls already being seen as little women among womenfolk.

Here is one striking example to show the problem of taking underage girls as women: Herodotus refers to Athenian girls at Brauron as "women" (γυναῖκες) in the legendary or semi-legendary incident of Pelasgian raiders ambushing, subjugating, abducting, and eventually impregnating these so-called women.[52] This abduction need not have happened as narrated for what is important here: Herodotus describing raped girls as women. The age of girls who worshipped Artemis of Brauron clustered around ten but they could have been as young as seven or even five.[53] This means that even older girls at Brauron would still be several years away from being conventionally marriageable παρθένοι of fourteen or fifteen years old in Athenian civil society (Gaca 2012: 102 n. 55). And at the youngest, the girls were more than double their lifespan away from being able to bear children and enter a legitimate marriage. Iconographic evidence further confirms that the female celebrants at Brauron were girls no older than, for instance, American Girl Scout Brownies (five to nine years old) or Juniors (nine to eleven years old) or their international Girl Guide age-group equivalents. This is the case because Greek red-figure vase fragments depict sexually undeveloped girls in a race during this festival for Artemis.[54] Hence, Herodotus' so-called Athenian "women" at Brauron would have been flat-chested and still pretending that they were bears at the time of their legendary abduction. They accelerate into being γυναῖκες in Herodotean discourse because sexual initiation traditionally marks the entry of marriageable virgins into adult womanhood through the norms of legitimate civil marriage, and also because virgin girls are womenfolk in the "nesting dolls" sense, no matter how young they are.

Further, Aeschylus, an experienced military man trained in defense skills, clearly indicates in *Seven against Thebes* that girls close to or in emergent adolescence are premier targets for sexual mauling and forcible removal when a community or settlement is subjected to martial ravaging. The chorus of female Thebans in Aeschylus' play is a composite of girls in preadolescent and early adolescent years: παῖδες and παρθένοι (*Sept.* 792, 110, and so too the *dramatis personae* list). What is more, all of these girls and virgins are still living at home in the nurturing care of their mothers (παῖδες μητέρων τεθραμμέναι). A city's collective "slave yoke" (δούλιον ζυγόν) devastates the sexual bodies of the girls, virgins, and women living there in two ways (792–3). At the time of conquest, they are raped along with women, which the chorus depicts as the time when "the overthrown female captives, young and mature, are hauled around by their hair horse-style while their garments are ripped off" (326–8).

Next, the chorus of girls and virgins stresses the ravaged community's grief and lamentation over the young females in particular being plucked raw and forced from their homes on an "abhorrent journey" and coerced into "a bed of spear-conquest" (333–5).[55] This is the martial action that the historian Appian likewise calls "the hauling off of virgins (παρθένων ἀπαγωγαί)" by Hasdrubal's forces near the end of the Second Punic War (218–201 BCE). Hannibal expressly delegated Hasdrubal to oversee this hauling off and to have their forces carry it out so as to "enrich (πλουτίσας)" the forces with virginal girls in big lots by the city load. The virgins were taken en masse from the cities that Hannibal's forces had taken over in southern Italy and were then stripped of their wealth, virgins foremost, upon evacuating (App. *Hann.* 243–6). Diodorus confirms that in populace-ravaging warfare, virgins are raped at a time "not suitable for their age group (οὐκ οἰκεία τῆς ἡλικίας)" (Diod. Sic. 13.58.1–2; Gaca 2012: 93–4). As Aeschylus further explains, each girl ends up with "the man who lucks out and gets to keep her as his own spear-captive bed inmate (εὐνὰν αἰχμάλωτον / ἀνδρὸς εὐτυχοῦντος, 364–5)," even when the girls are "before the age of legitimate marriage (νομίμων προπάροιθεν, 333)."[56]

The *Septem* scholia vividly explicate and clinch my case that the ravaging martial norm involves sexually assaulting and commandeering underage girls from the attacked people: "Warfare (πόλεμος) does not wait for them [virgins, παρθένους] to become ripe (πέπονας),[57] but plucks everything at one time." It is a norm "worthy of outcries in lament (κλαυθμοῦ ἄξιον)" for the unripe girls "to have their virginity taken away at the wrong time (ταῖς παρὰ τὴν ἀκμὴν διακορευομέναις)" and to be compelled "to change houses by the law of war (ταῖς παρθένοις ἀλλάξαι τοὺς οἴκους νόμῳ πολέμου)."[58]

Further, Aristophanes in one of the fragments, all of them sparse,[59] from his comedy *Old Age* (Γῆρας) makes it clear that not all of the underage captive girls become spear-conquered girl wives in enemy houses. Some of them are turned into underage or "pre-virginal hetaeras" (ὑποπαρθένους ἑταίρας, fr. 141 Edmonds). These sexually undeveloped or underdeveloped girls are prostituted as one type of hetaera known as being like "hard salty olives (τὰς ὑποπαρθένους, ἁλμάδας ὡς ἐλάας, / στιφράς)" that are picked green and have to be soaked in brine to be edible, as opposed to those prostituted as another type known as "tree-ripened olive hetaeras (τὰς δρυπετεῖς ἑταίρας)." The latter are sexually developed, unlike girls seized unripe from their so-called trees, that is, from their devastated families and communities, through ravaging warfare. Further, a number of mature Athenian men (ὦ πρεσβῦτα) had the reputation of becoming rather like olive connoisseurs and of developing a distinct taste for one or the other, as Aristophanes likewise notes in the same fragment. The same is likely the assumed norm for avuncular old Nestor with Hecamede, although Homer only suggests this delicately by highlighting the sex appeal of her lovely hair (ἐϋπλόκαμος Ἑκαμήδη, *Il.* 14.6), just as he does the beautiful hair of Briseis (κούρης ... Βρισηΐδος ἠϋκόμοιο, *Il.* 2.689).

Even though Greek sources divulge that underage girls in general are sexually ravaged, they do not clearly reveal whether sexually attacked "pre-virgin" girls are on average, say, closer to ten than five years old, and if so, whether this indicates that girls abducted alive were ever considered too young and thus off limits for ravaging soldiers to rape. It would appear, however, that no statutory rape age limit applied, not even one calibrated to our kindergarten. A pragmatic restraint might have been at work to facilitate keeping young captive girls uninjured and alive. But if there is, it is not in evidence, and any pragmatism about waiting to rape them in several years would remain morally problematic and differ from the principled civil legal concept of statutory rape and its unconditional hands-off age limit.

Suffice it to say, then, that captive girls were subjected to ravaging rape at an age younger than the generally minimum Greek bridal age of fourteen or fifteen, younger still than the ten-year-old Athenian captive brides, and even half that age. This means that not even the generally youngest biological age for procreative child brides in any civil society, eleven or twelve years old, provides a reliable minimum age limit for the sexual ravaging of captive girls. To the extent that they were sexually attacked at this young age, especially in a serial way, their casualty rate would have been high, as is confirmed by the thirteenth-century Byzantine historian Pachymeres (see Gaca 2012: 96 n. 37) and by modern testimonials.[60]

It nonetheless appears that soldiers in their assault on female captives generally preferred to sexually attack and dominate those with at least some pubescent shapeliness. They were not by and large driven by a passion for little girls, unlike committed "green-olive" pedophiles who want their girls small and who lose interest once the girls start to mature and sexually develop. The primary desired age group for conquering armies to sexually assault en masse and abduct into a social condition of being spear-conquered and sexually subjugated are generally girls closer to middle school than preschool in their age, as well as adolescent females and women in their sexual prime. In Homeric epic, they are κοῦραι and γυναῖκες; in Aeschylus, they are παρθένοι and παῖδες; and in Diodorus the daughters raped in the Carthaginian martial conquest of Selinus in 409 BCE are too young for marriage, but close to being marriageable (ἐπίγαμοι, Diod. Sic. 13.58.1).

However, the problem of supply and demand would have been conducive to the sexual assault on preadolescent girls by ravaging forces, both during the en masse sexual assault and thereafter in the shift toward post-conquest sexual exploitation of female captives. The premier young adolescent and attractive female captives tended to be kept in the upper echelons of a martial hierarchy. This would mean that the demand for the especially desired young female bodies was likely to exceed the available supply in the ranks. Soldiers in the lower echelons thus had an incentive to rape underage girls rather than remain empty-handed themselves. As one result of this distribution system, a taste for underage girls who survived this treatment did develop back in the cities, as Aristophanes indicates for the city of Athens, where some men learned to crave pre-virginal hetaeras as though they were salty finger food (Aristoph. fr. 141 Edmonds).

Conclusion

As argued here, to see ancient warfare as it has long been constructed, with its focus on fighting-age men engaged in battle with lethal aims, is to overlook or downplay the important historical trajectory of populace-ravaging warfare. Further, to see populace-ravaging warfare as terminating with men killing and men being killed, and with massacre more generally, is to confuse the heavily lethal means of this warfare, including the gang rape and killing of mature women, with its purposeful end of seizing live young captives, be the captives (1) preadolescent boys and girls and women, mainly young women, through andrapodizing; or (2) strictly girls and young women, mainly young women, through the pandemic slaughter of males of all ages, including preadolescent boys, as well as raping and killing mature women. The consequence of this way of thinking is to ignore or give scant attention to the longstanding and major "what for" of populace-ravaging warfare—to seize, dominate, and exploit girls and women alive from the attacked peoples, with or without preadolescent boys seized too as live captives. It is important to appreciate the prevalence of such warfare in antiquity and its ulterior motive of raping and reducing young and youthful women and girls to a miserable life after killing or raping and killing a number of their mature and close female and male caregivers, role models, and siblings. This transforms our understanding of what much of ancient warfare was substantially for, what much of the adult male fighting and killing were about in antiquity. As Justin puts it in his epitome of Pompeius Trogus' Hellenistic history, children and mothers (*liberi, matres*) are the ones "for whom wars are customarily taken up (*pro quibus bella suscipi solent*)" by armed defenders, so as to protect their women and children from the acquisitive rapacity and exploitative abuses of ravaging martial aggressors (26.2.3, cf. Aen. Tact. *prol.* 2). When the defenders and the rest of their community were overwhelmed, heterosexual rape played an important role in the subjugating conquest and ensuing treatment of young war-captive girls and women kept alive, and in killing or leaving for dead the women not wanted alive. This, then, is why ancient warfare should be of strong interest on the agenda of researching women, gender, and sexuality in antiquity.[61]

No small part of this research agenda will be to investigate the social conditioning that informs martially aggressive masculinity in populace-ravaging warfare. This sort of inquiry is needed to better account for the potent brew of coercion and enticement organized from the top down and through peer pressure in the ranks that drives men in ravaging armed forces to conduct these practices. Some ravaging fighters in the modern day see it as the mark of real men as "fiery boys" and "fiery steeds" to rape and commandeer mainly the girls and young women of their enemy,[62] once the fighters have carried out their killing assignment. What is at work martially socializing them into this weird bravado, to see themselves as flaming wonder boys and blazing stallions in this sexual violence, and not as despicable thugs and bullies?

This inquiry would in turn allow another notion of manly heroism to come into better view and deeper appreciation from antiquity onwards—that of lesser sung but more authentic men in collective defense coalitions. These would include Hector, Sarpedon, and Eteocles and his fellow Theban defenders in legend; and, historically, the philologist and bishop Eustathius who stayed put in his conquered city of Thessalonica, at great danger to himself, in order to help "the remaining children of his city (τὰ λοιπὰ τέκνα τῆς πόλεως)" during the ravaging of his city in 1185 CE. By τέκνα he, like Oedipus in Thebes (Soph., *Oed. Tyr.* 1), refers to all the city's inhabitants, but especially the young generation. Eustathius was held in awe by many for his selfless bravery, and especially by the Byzantine historian Nicetas Choniates (Eustath. *Capt. Thess.*, Nicetas Choniates *c.*1155–1217, *Hist.* 307–8). Men of this sort did all they could to stop or subdue populace-ravaging aggressors who were trying to gain hold primarily of the girls and young women in their own and allied communities so as to rape them into submission and to subject them to lives of toil and hardship from then on (cf. *Od.* 8.523–30). This masculinity merits κλέος, not that of the goons.

Notes

1 "Ancient" and "antiquity" here are geographically and culturally specific to the Old World west of the Caucasus range and centered on the Mediterranean. Translations from Greek and Latin are my own. For biblical Hebrew I utilize the New English Bible (NEB), with the relevant Hebrew checked in the original. Critical editions of primary Greek sources not listed in the bibliography are generally cited in Berkowitz and Squitier 1990³. Critical editions of primary Latin sources are OCT or Teubner. My deep thanks to the editors, especially Nancy S. Rabinowitz and Mark Masterson, and to readers for their many helpful insights and comments.

2 e.g., Hanson 1989, 1991. For recent summations of this productivity, see Sabin et al. 2007; Campbell and Tritle 2013 and the extensive bibliographies therein.

3 This convention appears in book titles through the mid-1990s, such as the edited collections of Foley 1981; Cameron and Kuhrt 1983; Skinner 1987; Hawley and Levick 1995; McAuslan and Walcot 1996; McHardy and Marshall 2004.

4 One way in which this in-between status worked was that manumitted female slaves could be required to stay and continue working for their former owners. The παραμονή clause in the Delphic manumission inscriptions regularly requires manumitted girls and women and the children they produce to stay and keep working for their former owners, Tucker 1982: 225–36.

5 Scodel 1998 is an important exception; and see too Chapter 3, Solvang, this volume.

6 Exceptions include van Wees 1992; Kern 1999; Gaca 2008, 2010, 2011a, 2011b, 2012, 2014; Burstein 2012.

7 The verbs used to communicate this type of warfare include, for example, διαρπάζειν in Greek and *diripere* and *depopulari* in Latin, πορθεῖν in Homeric epic and Greek histories, and "andrapodizing (ἀνδραποδίζεσθαι, ἐξανδραποδίζεσθαι)" targeted peoples in Greek historical and other narratives. See further Gaca 2010, 2012.

8 Space constraints permit only this summary of my claims argued in Gaca 2010, 2011a, 2011b, 2012, 2014.

9 For a thoughtful and balanced theorizing of rape as normative in modernity and Greek tragedy, see Rabinowitz 2011.

10 Polyb. 10.38.1, Dion. Hal. *Ant. Rom.* 4.82.2, and see Gaca 2012: 94.

11 *Il.* 20.193–4, see too 6.454–5, 9.138–9 = 9.280–1, 9.325–7, 16.830–3.

12 Nicolaus of Damascus, fr. 53 and Eur. *Tr.* 562–7.

13 For example, Roman martial forces and their paramilitary grooms and camp attendants (*calones, lixae*) "kept dragging elderly men and women of advanced age into mocking torment" (*grandaevos senes, exacta aetate feminas, vilis ad praedam, in ludibrium trahebant*), Tac. *Hist.* 3.33, regarding the factional Roman martial ravaging of Cremona in 69 CE.

14 ὑπὸ πλήθεος, Hdt. 8.33; περιφθειρομένας δι᾽ ἔνδειαν τῶν ἀναγκαίων, Isoc. *Epist. Archid.* 9.10, ἐκ διαδοχῆς and ἥ τε ἀσιτία καὶ ἡ ἀυπνία, Paus. 10.22.4. For further explication of this and other evidence, see Gaca 2012, esp. 93–106.

15 The striking lack of scholarly attention given to sexually attacked girls in populace-ravaging warfare is thoughtfully considered by Nordstrom 1997 in relation to the protracted martial ravaging of Mozambique; this armed conflict started in 1977.

16 Keegan 1976, which studies battles at Agincourt in 1415, Waterloo in 1815, and along the Somme in 1916.

17 The illustrative validity of this analogy presupposes my arguments about populace-ravaging warfare sketched above and argued at length in Gaca 2010, 2011a, 2011b, 2012, 2014.

18 Deut. 20:13–14: "Putting all the males to the sword" is not the Greek, Macedonian, and to a lesser degree Roman martial norm of ἡβηδόν male massacre, that is, killing captured males who are fighting-age adolescents and older, Gaca 2010: 117–61. For example, when David and his forces subjugate the land of Edom, he and his armies spend half a year working to exterminate all the males therein, only for the young boy Hadad, the Edomites' future avenger, to escape this pandemic male killing by taking refuge in Egypt (1 Kgs 11:14–25). If this were ἡβηδόν male massacre, Hadad would not have had to flee to survive. So too in Gen. 34, Simeon and Levi are said to have "killed every male" (Gen. 34:25) among the Hivites. See also Num. 31:1–47 and Judg. 21:8–15.

19 *Il.* 6.55–60, Herod. 1.146.2, Paus. 7.2.5–6, 10.22.3–4, Strabo 4.6.8, Synesius *Epist.* 125.

20 Infants and very young children of both sexes are too dependent and unlikely to survive, and some of them are said to have been killed off and even conspicuously slaughtered. For some of the biblical evidence, see Kern 1999: 85 and for some of the Greek evidence, see Gaca 2010: 139–40.

21 For example, Julius Caesar wanted the Gallic Eburones ravaged and exterminated because their fighting men, under Ambiorix, destroyed one of his Roman legions in 54 BCE. For this purpose, Caesar called out (*evocare*) his recently subjugated and now Roman-affiliated local ancillary forces, Germanic and Gallic alike. Notable among them were the remaining Germanic Sugambri, whose people were already worsted once as targets of Caesar's martial vengeance (*ulcisci, Gal.* 4.19.4). Caesar presents the Sugambri forces as though they were naturally plunder-driven (*in bello latrociniisque natos*) and thus eager to ravage the Eburones. Yet they had no readily viable choice but to respond to Caesar's martial call-out to ravage the Eburones or suffer yet again themselves. Caesar also makes it clear that he issued this call-out expressly to prevent his own more valued Roman legionary forces from being subjected to the dangers and lures of ravaging, *Gal.* 4.18.1–19.4, 6.34.1–35.10.

22 One of the best representations of the difference is in Aesch. *Septem,* the restrained yet determined resolve of Eteocles and his forces defending Thebes and the furiously crazed and boasting Argive warriors such as Capaneus and Parthenopaeus with their terrifying shields.

23 The attack on the Germanic Aduatuci by Julius Caesar's Roman legions is a good example of this sort of preemptive strike. The Aduatuci were a group settled in Gaul as captives and camp followers under the armed guard of 6,000 men. They were left behind there by the main martial forces of the populace-ravaging Cimbri and Teutones, who were later defeated and heavily reduced in number by Marius and his Roman forces in 102–101 BCE. According to Caesar, the Aduatuci persisted in ravaging ways locally. Upon Caesar's demand, they adopted the stance of surrendering to him, but were afraid of what neighboring hostile peoples would do to them once they handed over their weapons to him. Nonetheless they complied outwardly in their disarmament by throwing many of their weapons down from the city wall into a ditch. Then, as Caesar puts it, the Aduatuci "experienced peace that day with their city gates opened" (*portis patefactis eo die pace sunt usi*), *Gal.* 2.32.1–2. But then the Aduatuci tried to escape in the night. To stop (as Caesar saw them) these inveterate populace-ravagers from getting away, Caesar unleashed his Roman forces against them. The people among the Aduatuci who were not killed Caesar sold in one big wholesale lot into slavery, numbering 53,000 according to the wholesale buyers, Caesar, *Gal.* 2.29.1–33.7. From Caesar's perspective, this Roman martial liquidation of the Aduatuci was justifiable defense to stop their populace-ravaging ways in the region.

24 Gaca 2010: 117–61, 2011a: 73–88.

25 For examples of the latter, see Paus. 10.22.3–4 (a Celtic detachment of forces under Brennus) and Caes. *Gal.* 1.36.6 (Ariovistus and his Germanic forces).

26 In Bosnia, for example: Doboj Central High School, UN Annex IX.II.A.18, pp. 19–20; a high school in Foca, Annex IX.II.A.20, p. 23, under the direction of M. Cherif Bassiouni (printout online at www.ess.uwe.ac.uk/comexpert/anx/IX-A.htm [accessed July 2014 from the same archive as http://archive.today/Bb7s]); and the unnamed juvenile File 373, Vranic 1996: 166–7.

27 UN Annex IX, "Rape and Sexual Assault [in Bosnia]," II.A.20, p. 24.

28 One of the best sustained descriptions of these customs is that of the youthful Alcibiades when he unsuccessfully tries to turn the tables and use them on the older Socrates, Pl. *Symp.* 217a2–19d2.

29 Xen., *Hiero* 1.36, and so too Pl. *Symp.* 181c2–4: the eroticism of the heavenly Aphrodite sort, which is felt strictly by men for boys, is "without sexual violence (ὕβρεως ἀμοίρου)." So too the early Stoic Zeno, SVF 1.251 = Sextus *Math.* 11.190.

30 Captive boys subjected to conspicuous slaughter: early archaic Mykonos pithos, metopes 8, 14, 17, 19; Ervin (1963) pls. 23b, 26, 27, 28b; Hdt. 3.147.1. Castration: Hdt. 6.32; App. *BCiv.* 2.13.91; Joseph.

Ap. 2.270; Lib. *Decl.* 1.80. Aggravated battery: Dem. *In Arist.* 23.141; App. *Mith.* 186; Dio Cass. 30–5.102.9, and see further further Gaca 2012: 104–5.

31 For instance, ripping and disfiguring women's earlobes by yanking off their pierced earrings, Soz. 8.23.3–4. On the martial stripping off of women's and girls' garments and the fierce intensity used, see further Gaca 2012: 99–101 and Diod. Sic. 17.35.7.

32 Ervin 1963: pls. 23b, 26, 27, 28b.

33 Xen. *An.* 4.6.1–3; 7.4.7–11. Tacitus suggests likewise about a captive youth (outstanding in his figure (*quis forma conspicuus*), the masculine counterpart of a fully developed *adulta virgo* or virgin-aged girl captive also mentioned by Tacitus, *Hist.* 3.33.

34 Young women and girls who resist are also likely to be killed, although the first express evidence known to me for this is relatively recent, e.g., Carnegie Endowment 1993 [1913]: 307.

35 γένος γυναικῶν (Hes. *Theog.* 590, Pin. *Pyth.* 4.49–52, Eur. *Med.* 1085–9, *Hipp.* 616–24, 1249–54, *Cycl.* 186–7), φῦλον γυναικῶν (Hes. *Scut.* 4–6, *Cat.* fr. 1.1–2), or φῦλα γυναικῶν, Hom. *Il.* 9.130, 9.272.

36 *Il.* 20.193–4, see too 6.454–5, 9.138–9 = 9.280–1, 9.325–7, 16.830–3.

37 *Il.* 8.164–6, see too 6.450–5, 19.291–4, *Od.* 9.39–42.

38 Chryseis as κούρη: *Il.* 1.98, 1.111; Briseis as κούρη: *Il.* 1.275, 1.298, 1.336–7, 1.392, 2.377, 2.689, 9.106, 9.637–8, 18.444–5, 19.55–8, 19.261. Briseis a young bride at the time of her conquest, *Il.* 19.290–9; Briseis belonging to Achilles once the Achaean warriors "picked her out (ἔξελον)" as his prize (γέρας), *Il.* 16.56–7.

39 See Sutton 1982 on the extensive artistic tradition about Scipio as narrated in Polybius' and Livy's versions of this incident.

40 *Il.* 23.259–61. The γυναῖκες set forth as contest prizes to victors in Patroclus' funeral games, *Il.* 23. 263, 512–13, 704–5.

41 Here is a reasonably well-documented modern instance of this problem, from Bosnian Muslim testimonies dating from 1992: A woman, Fatima, from the Bosnian town of Miljevina, relates that Serbian forces stopped the transport bus of Muslim refugees fleeing Miljevina that she was on, before the bus could cross into territory safer for Muslims. At that time, she states, "a girl was carried off" from the bus by the forces, a girl also from Miljevina and known to Fatima. "Her name is Alma B. She was twelve years old and gorgeous. While we were between Ustikolina and Osanica they stopped the bus and took her out. Later in Gorazde I met Edi, a man I knew from Miljevina. ... I asked him if he knew anything about Alma, and he told me she had been in the brothel in Miljevina and slit her wrists there," Stiglmayer 1994: 108. Why Alma resorted to suicide is indirectly indicated by another Bosnian Muslim woman, the twenty-year-old Hasiba, based on her own experience of being taken to the Vilina Vlas Hotel as a forced brothel: "The whole hotel was filled with our girls and women, each one prettier than the next ... The Chetniks were there with the girls" in the rooms. "There was nothing they didn't do with them, you only had to stop and look. In every room there were women, men, screams, noise, songs, everything," Stiglmayer 1994: 130. In these testimonials, the use strictly of first names, generally pseudonyms, is to protect the witnesses against reprisals.

42 Gaca 2011b: 115–16 and 116 n. 12; see too Burstein 2012: 101–3 on non-Greek captive women as coerced birth-givers and mothers of Greeks (and/or Macedonians) among Alexander's forces in Bactria.

43 Achilles: *Il.* 8.372, 15.77, 21.550, 24.108, Odysseus: *Il.* 2.278, *Od.* 8.3, 9.504, 9.530, 14.447, 16.442, 18.356, 22.283, 24.119.

44 See Gaca 2012: 102–3 and n. 55 with bibliography ad loc. Note also Sourvinou-Inwood 1988: 78 n. 87.

45 This practice, of keeping only young female captives alive, is also known in the *Iliad*. In retaliation against Trojan treachery during the duel of Paris and Menelaus, Agamemnon expressly states that once Troy is sacked, all the captured boys will be slaughtered, such that even pregnant women will be cut down as prospective bearers of male infants (*Il.* 6.55–60). For one striking historical counterpart to the latter practice, see Strabo 4.6.8.

46 Historically, female slaves among ravaged people are also captured and, presumably, also subjected to martial sexual aggression. Yet their experience is not described in Homeric epic, where it is assumed that ravaging means taking the freedom away from (freeborn) girls and women. Further, the ravaged female slave experience is not described as such in Greek drama. However, female slaves are in Homer's Troy (e.g., *Il.* 6.323, 374–81, 399–400, 22.449), so one would imagine their presence is presupposed by Euripides in his portrayal of the screaming female captives of Troy being distributed to the Greek contingents, *Tr.* 28–31. Greek historians do convey that slaves as δουλικὰ σώματα (as opposed to ἐλεύθερα σώματα) can be ravaged and andrapodized, e.g., Polyb. 2.6.6–8, but they do not disclose any gender difference in how female and male slave bodies are respectively assaulted.

47 As exemplified in Opp. *Hal.* 1.529 and here in the Oppian scholia, γάμος and its verbal counterpart as of the early Roman empire often means "copulate" without any necessarily marital connotations. So too, for instance, Tatian, *Orat. ad Graecos* 8.2: "Aphrodite takes pleasure in the embraces of sexual copulation (Ἀφροδίτη δὲ γάμου πλοκαῖς ἥδεται)"; see also Gaca 2003: 235–9.

48 "I had never realised that suffering could be this intense," Jan Ruff-O'Herne in her memoir as a very young Australian woman of Dutch descent who was also used as a so-called comfort woman by Japanese forces, along with mainly Korean women, cited in Askin 1997: 77. The testimony of the Bosnian Muslim Selma: "I couldn't speak because of the pain"; the testimony of anonymous case File 373: "Every time I was raped I was also beaten by the Serbs. … They kicked me with their boots and with a wooden stick," Vranic 1996: 116–18, 166. The Bosnian Muslim Azra: "It was no normal rape. When it was over the blood kept flowing out of me," Stiglmayer 1994: 108.

49 *Etym. Magn.* s.v. ῥυστάζειν. As Eustathius further explains (*Comm. in Od.*, vol. 2, p. 116 (Stallbaum)), "It is to be understood that ῥυστάζειν generally signifies the forceful rape of women (βίαιον ἑλκυσμὸν γυναικῶν), just as τὸ ἑλκῆσαι does, as previously shown." Hence ἕλκειν and Homeric ἑλκεῖν convey not simply "a suggestion of ravishment," as stated by Cunliffe 1924, s.v. ἕλκω and ἑλκέω. It means aggravated rape.

50 *Zetemata codicis Vaticani* 334 Schrader.

51 Literally, "the rape of women is worse than all the horrors [of war]," hence the worst of them all: δεινῶν γὰρ πάντων χείρων ἡ τῶν γυναικῶν ὕβρις, bk. 6.454a2, p. 208 Erbse vol. 2. See too Lib., *Orat.* 59.157: "If anyone were to ask anyone, what is the most grievous of the customary pains to suffer for people (ἀνθρώποις) whose lot is armed capture, right away and without having to look it over at all, one would say it is the shame of the womenfolk (τὴν τῶν γυναικῶν αἰσχύνην)." Further, "For every instance of beheading at the [Tokyo war crimes] trial, there were countless accounts of gang rape. Is gang rape worse than beheading? Given the evidence I listened to at the International Military Tribunal of the Far East, the answer would appear to be *yes*," Arnold C. Brackman, a United Press correspondent, as cited in Askin 1997: 164.

52 On raiders evading, and attempting to evade, the risk of having to kill menfolk in considerable numbers by attacking girls and women at a womenfolk-only festival, see Gaca 2011a: 82–3.

53 As stated in the Suda, s.v. Ἄρκτος ἢ Βραυρωνίοις entry 3958: "Women acting as bears would carry out the festival for Artemis, dressed in saffron-colored robes, being neither older than ten nor younger than five years old." The scholion on Aristoph. *Lys.* 645 ed. Dübner 1877 specifies the same general age range of the young female celebrants and refers to them as παρθένοι and κόραι. Aristophanes indicates that the age of ten was probably more the norm, or at least older than seven years old as a lower age limit, *Lys.* 641–7, Sourvinou-Inwood 1988: 59–66.

54 Herod. 4.145.2, 6.138.1–4 and esp. 1–2. On the potsherds (Sourvinou-Inwood 1988: Plate 1), the girls have adult women standing with them, but the girls are the womenfolk, as confirmed by the Suda naming the Brauronian female celebrants γυναῖκες who are "neither older than ten nor younger than five years old" (see also note 53).

55 For a fuller discussion of this summation about Aeschylus' *Seven against Thebes*, see Gaca 2012: 102. In l. 335 I diverge from Page's OCT edition of Aeschylus (1972) and follow the manuscript reading στυγερὰν ὁδόν.

56 As another of the *Septem* scholia similarly notes, "It is worthy of great lament for girls (ταῖς κόραις), the ones just starting to pluck virginal adolescence (ταῖς ἄρτι δρεπομέναις τὴν παρθενίαν), to be taken captive (αἰχμαλωτισθῆναι) before reaching the time of marriage (πρὸ τοῦ ἐλθεῖν εἰς ὥραν γάμου) and to go away as slaves (δούλαις) into a strange land (ξένην χώραν)," 333–5d Smith.

57 The body of a young "ripe" woman is likewise said to be "full of juice (*suci plenum*)," Terence, *Eun.* 318.

58 Schol. in Aesch. *Septem* 333–5b, and see too 333–5c, d, and f (Smith). 333–5e is also relevant but lacunose. Schol. 333–5b reasonably treats the manuscript reading ὠμοδρόπων as though it modified νομίμων in name, but in function as though it were the adverb ὠμοδρόπως. The adverbial ὠμοδρόπως is Lowinski's emendation accepted by Page.

59 There are 23 fragments in total: three of three lines, including fr. 141; four of two lines; 12 of one line; and four of one word—little to go by in discerning the plot line. However, in conjunction with fr. 141, fr. 139 suggests, as one would expect from Aristophanes, that this play concerns horny old men. In fr. 139 perhaps one old man in a pederastic mode is following boys around (παιδάρια), a ball and strigil in hand, and an unknown speaker is apparently wondering whether this is appropriate behavior for a man of his age: εἰ παιδαρίοις ἀκολουθεῖν δεῖ σφαῖραν καὶ στλεγγίδ' ἔχοντα. Fr. 141 reads in full:

ὦ πρεσβῦτα, πότερα φιλεῖς τὰς δρυπετεῖς ἑταίρας / ἢ σὺ τὰς ὑποπαρθένους, ἁλμάδας ὡς ἐλάας, / στιφράς;

60 This testimony from the seventeen-year old Bosnian Muslim Mirsada: "Stojan, the camp guard ... was the most ruthless among them. He even raped ten-year-old girls, as a 'delicacy.' Most of those girls didn't survive," Searles and Berger 1995: 174–5.

61 This is also why women, gender, and sexuality should be of strong interest in ancient warfare studies.

62 Helsinki Watch 1993: 180; Stiglmayer 1994: 140.

Bibliography

Askin, K.D. (1997) *War Crimes against Women: Prosecution in International War Crimes Tribunals*. The Hague: Nijhoff.

Berkowitz, L. and Squitier, K.A. (1990) *Thesaurus Linguae Graecae: Canon of Greek Authors and Works*, 3rd edn. New York: Oxford University Press.

Burstein, S. (2012) "Whence the women?: The origin of the Bactrian Greeks", *Ancient West and East* 11: 97–104.

Cameron, A. and Kuhrt, A. (eds) (1983) *Images of Women in Antiquity*. New York: Routledge.

Campbell, B. and Tritle, L.A. (2013) *The Oxford Handbook of Warfare in the Classical World*. New York: Oxford University Press.

Carnegie Endowment (1993 [1913]) *The Other Balkan Wars: A 1913 Carnegie Endowment Inquiry in Retrospect, with a New Introduction by George F. Kennan*. Washington, DC: Carnegie Endowment for International Peace.

Cunliffe, R.J. (1924) *A Lexicon of the Homeric Dialect*. Norman, OK: University of Oklahoma Press.

Ervin, M. (1963) "A relief pithos from Mykonos", *Archaiologikon Deltion* 18: 37–75.

Foley, H. (ed.) (1981) *Reflections of Women in Antiquity*. New York: Gordon and Breach Science.

Gaca, K.L. (2003) *The Making of Fornication: Eros, Ethics, and Political Reform in Greek Philosophy and Early Christianity*. Berkeley, CA: University of California Press.

——(2008) "Reinterpreting the Homeric simile of *Iliad* 16.7–11: The girl and her mother in ancient Greek warfare", *American Journal of Philology* 129: 145–71.

——(2010) "The andrapodizing of war captives in Greek historical memory", *Transactions of the American Philological Association* 140: 117–61.

——(2011a) "Girls, women, and the significance of sexual violence in ancient warfare", in E.D. Heineman (ed.) *Sexual Violence in Conflict Zones*. Philadelpia, PA: University of Pennsylvania Press, pp. 73–88.

——(2011b) "Manhandled and 'kicked around': Reinterpreting the etymology and symbolism of *Andrapoda*", *Indogermanische Forschungen* 115: 110–46.

——(2012) "Telling the girls from the boys and children: Interpreting παῖδες in the sexual violence of populace-ravaging ancient warfare", *Illinois Classical Studies* 35–6: 85–109.

——(2014) "Martial rape, pulsating fear, and the overt sexualizing of girls (παῖδες), virgins (παρθένοι), and women (γυναῖκες) in antiquity", *American Journal of Philology* 135: 303–57.

Hanson, V.D. (1989) *The Western Way of War: Infantry Battle in Classical Greece*. New York: Knopf.

——(1991) *Hoplites: The Classical Greek Battle Experience*. New York: Routledge.

Hawley, R. and Levick, B. (eds) (1995) *Women in Antiquity: New Assessments*. New York: Routledge.

Helsinki Watch (1993) *War Crimes in Bosnia-Hercegovina*, vol. 2. New York: Human Rights Watch.

Keegan, J. (1976) *The Face of Battle*. New York: Penguin.

——(1987) *The Mask of Command*. New York: Viking.

Kern, P.B. (1999) *Ancient Siege Warfare*. Bloomington, IN: Indiana University Press.

Keuls, E.C. (1985) *The Reign of the Phallus: Sexual Politics in Ancient Athens*. New York: Harper & Row.

Kirk, G.S. (1985) *The Iliad: A Commentary*, vol. 1, Books 1–4. Cambridge: Cambridge University Press.

Loman, P. (2004) "No women no war: Women's participation in ancient Greek warfare", *Greece & Rome* 51: 34–54.

McAuslan, I. and Walcot, P. (1996) *Women in Antiquity*, Greece and Rome Studies. New York: Oxford University Press.

McHardy, F. and Marshall, E. (2004) *Women's Influence on Classical Civilization*. Routledge: New York.

Nordstrom, C. (1997) *Girls and Warzones: Troubling Questions*. Uppsala: Life and Peace Institute.

Pomeroy, S.B. (1975) *Goddesses, Whores, Wives, and Slaves: Women in Classical Antiquity*. New York: Schocken Books.

Pritchett, W.K. (1971–91) *The Greek State at War*, vols 1–5. Berkeley, CA: University of California Press.

Rabinowitz, N.S. (2011) "Greek tragedy: A rape culture?", *Eugesta* 1:1–21. Available online at http:// eugesta.recherche.univ-lille3.fr/revue/pdf/2011/Rabinowitz.pdf (accessed 15 July 2013).

Sabin, P.A.G., van Wees, H., and Whitby, M. (eds) (2007) *The Cambridge History of Greek and Roman Warfare*. New York: Cambridge University Press.

Schaps, D. (1982) "Women of Greece in wartime", *Classical Philology* 77: 203–4.

Scodel, R. (1998) "The captive's dilemma: Sexual acquiescence in Euripides' *Hecuba* and *Troades*", *Harvard Studies in Classical Philology* 98: 137–54.

Searles, P. and Berger, R.J. (1995) *Rape and Society: Readings in the Problem of Sexual Assault*. Boulder, CO: Westview Press.

Skinner, M.S. (ed.) (1987) "Rescuing Creusa: New methodological approaches to women in antiquity", *Helios* 13(2): Special Issue.

Sourvinou-Inwood, C. (1988) *Studies in Girls' Transitions: Aspects of the Arkteia and Age Representation in Attic Iconography*. Athens: A. Kardamitsa.

Stiglmayer, A. (1994) *Mass Rape: The War against Women in Bosnia-Herzegovina*, trans. M. Faber. Lincoln, NE: University of Nebraska Press.

Sutton, P.C. (1982) "The continence of Scipio by Gerbrandt van den Eeckhout (1621–74)", *Philadelphia Museum of Art Bulletin* 78: 2–15.

Tucker, C.W. (1982) "Women in the manumission inscriptions at Delphi", *Transactions of the American Philological Association* 112: 225–36.

van Wees, H. (1992) *Status Warriors: War, Violence, and Society in Homer and History*. Amsterdam: J.C. Gieben.

Vranic, S. (1996) *Breaking the Wall of Silence: The Voices of Raped Bosnia*. Zagreb: Biblioteka Antibarbarus.

17

"YES" AND "NO" IN WOMEN'S DESIRE

Edward M. Harris

If one were to select a few pieces of evidence from the sources for life in ancient Greece, one might get the impression that a woman's consent did not count for much. Take, for instance, Greek marriage practices. From New Comedy we learn that the standard formula in a contract of marriage was "I give you this woman for the purpose (or the ploughing) of legitimate children" (Men. *Pk.* 1013–14; *Sam.* 897–901; *Dys.* 842–4). The amount of the dowry given by the father might also be settled at this time.[1] The agreement was between two men, the father or other male relative and the future husband. The woman was not one of the contracting parties; she was passed from the household of one man to that of another. Her consent was not required. In the best study of ancient Greek marriage, Vérilhac and Vial observe that

> Greek marriage was never an act by which two spouses were joined one to the other on an equal footing. Marriage necessarily involved three people – the husband, the wife and the person who gave her away. Not only was the presence of the third person indispensable; it was he who had the principal role and took the initiative in the legal act. The active role lay in the hands of the two men, the husband and the father of the wife. The last of these three, except in very rare exceptions, had a passive role.[2]

The father had the right to terminate the marriage without his daughter's consent.[3] A husband might indicate in his will whom his wife should marry after his death (Dem. 36.28–9). If the wife inherited her father's estate and had no brothers, she would become an *epikleros* in Athenian law. The nearest male relative in this case had the right to claim her in marriage and take her into his home without obtaining her consent.[4] In the eyes of the law women's consent appears to have had no place.

One of the laws about just homicide might give one the same impression. There were three main categories of homicide in Athenian law: deliberate homicide, homicide against one's will, and just homicide or homicide according to the law. The last category covered cases in which the killer had the right to use deadly force and could not be punished for causing death. One of the cases was that in which a man caught someone on top of his wife, sister, mother, daughter or concubine kept for the purpose of free children (Dem. 23.53–4). In a passage from Lysias' speech *Against Eratosthenes* (1.30–5) the speaker Euphiletus claims that this law applied only to seducers (*moichoi*) caught in this position, but this makes little sense.[5] If one were to accept this interpretation of the law, a man who caught someone having sex with his wife would first have to ask him whether she had been willing or not. If she had not consented, he would have to wait until the assailant had finished and bring him to court because the law did not allow him to kill the man who had not seduced but employed force. As the passage from Demosthenes' speech *Against Aristocrates* makes clear, the law applied both to men who used force and those who used persuasion. The woman's consent made no difference as far as the law was concerned. Whether the woman was willing or not, her husband or male relative had the right to kill the man having sex with her.

These two isolated pieces of information about women in ancient Greece might lead one to think that men paid no attention to women's consent in sexual matters and regarded women merely as passive objects, bodies without a will. Passman has gone so far as to claim that:[6]

> In the patriarchal world, erotic desire and marriage are too dangerous to be joined. The implication is that the only proper marriage will be rape, because it must be against the desire of the woman; the only proper bride is the intact virgin; the only proper motherhood is that which comes about as a result of rape. Desire (on the part of the woman) and reproduction are incompatible.

Osborne believes that:[7]

> in limiting scenes of female pursuit to the case of the winged Eos, pot painters were able both to suggest that women did desire men and to suggest that female desire could not be active in the real world. [So] ... by playing with the contexts in which they showed Eos' pursuit, painters presented the sexual desire of Eos as socially threatening, like the excess of the Satyr, and as potentially overpowering for men (like Helen).

Goldhill asserts that "in the classical period, it is hard to find a narrative of female desire that does not end in disaster".[8] According to Halperin, sex in classical Greece "was not a private quest for mutual pleasure that absorbed, if only temporarily, the social identities of its participants" and "was not conceived as a collective enterprise in which two or more persons jointly engaged, but as an action performed by one person upon another".[9] Finally, Konstan thinks that Greek authors paid little or no attention to women's desire before the second century BCE. For Konstan, "sexual symmetry", mutual desire between men and women, was a new development reflected in the Greek novel and in Plutarch's *Erotikos* written long after the classical period.[10]

These views assume that men in the ancient Greek world always viewed women's desire as dangerous and that men were unconcerned whether they did or did not arouse desire in a woman before or during the sexual act. Thus it made little difference whether a woman said yes or no to sexual relations; her consent did not count, and men did not wish that their desire were reciprocated.[11] The aim of my own contribution is to present evidence showing that men in ancient Greece did notice whether women said yes or no in sexual matters and therefore recognized that women had a will of their own and could make decisions about their bodies. Greek males may have evaluated these decisions according to different criteria from the ones we are encouraged to employ today in the European Union and the United States, but they knew that a woman could decide for herself. In some cases, they also treated women who said yes very differently from a woman who said no in the same circumstances. Male authors also depicted the victims of sexual violence in such a way as to invite the sympathy of their audience. Finally, several texts indicate that men might find a woman's desire not a threat to their power or potentially disruptive but very desirable in a wife or a lover.

Several passages reveal that men did make a distinction between women who said yes and those who said no and treated the former in a different way from the latter. In Xenophon's *Hiero* (3.3) the tyrant stresses the importance of friendship and affection in daily life.

> States too are well aware of the importance of the part friendship plays in helping people to live well and pleasantly. At any rate, it is not uncommon for the laws of communities to allow people to kill seducers, and only seducers, with impunity, and the thinking behind this law is obviously that seduction impairs the affection a wife feels for her husband. After all, if sex takes place without the woman's consent, this does not make the slightest difference to the regard her husband feels for her, as long as the affection she feels for him remains inviolate.

One must not ignore the rhetorical context of the passage; Hiero is stressing the serious nature of seduction as a crime and therefore exaggerates when he claims the laws of the Greek *poleis* allowed men to use deadly force only against seducers. If the laws of Athens provide any guidance, this is not true: one was allowed to kill several other categories of offenders with impunity.[12] What is relevant for our topic is that Hiero discusses two different situations – the first in which the wife is seduced and implicitly has sex willingly with another man and the second in which the woman does not give her consent. The effects of each situation are quite different: in the first the woman's emotional bond with her husband is damaged; in the second the emotional bond may remain intact. The comparison of seduction and sexual violence is approached from the male perspective, not that of the woman. Hiero evaluates each according to the impact it has on a man's relationship with his wife, not on her feelings. Yet if we can take Hiero's attitude as typical, it is obvious that a husband placed much value on the quality of his emotional relationship with his wife. In this analysis, seduction was not so much a violation of his rights over his wife (though it was that too) as a disruption of the feelings shared by the two spouses. If a man did not care about how his wife felt about him, there would be no point in making this comparison.

There is a similar comparison in Lysias' speech *Against Eratosthenes* (1.32–6). The speaker Euphiletus, whose wife has been seduced, draws a similar distinction between cases in which the woman is persuaded to have sex and those in which she is compelled by force. Like Hiero, Euphiletus compares the impact of each offence against him in terms of its effect on his relationship with his wife. Seduction leads to alienation of affection and gives the seducer emotional control over the wife; the victim of sexual violence hates the aggressor. Once more we observe that it is very important for the husband whether his wife consents to sex with another man or not.[13]

The laws of Athens also treated the woman who had allowed herself to be seduced differently from one who resisted a man's sexual advances. There was no disability imposed on a woman who was the victim of sexual violence.[14] Men like Herodotus (1.4.2) may have suspected that the woman who claimed to have been forced to have sex was really lying. As we will see, however, when it was clear that the woman was the victim of abuse, men might react with pity and sympathy. On the other hand, according both to Aeschines in his *Against Timarchus* (1.183) and Apollodorus in his *Against Neaira* ([Dem.] 59.86) the woman who was caught with a *moichos*, that is a seducer, was banned from public sacrifices and could not adorn herself in public.[15] If a woman did attend, anyone who wished had the right to do anything he wished as long as he did not kill her. The wording of the law and the meaning of the word *moichos*, which should be translated seducer, not adulterer, indicate that the penalties applied both to married women and to unmarried women. The law therefore treated women who consented to having sex with a man to whom she was not married and those who were forced to do so very differently.

In a valuable essay Alan Sommerstein has shown that "tragedy gives no countenance to the fashionable view that for classical Athenian men, a (free) woman's consent was a matter of little or no importance".[16] He starts by examining the Potiphar's wife scenario. This kind of plot occurs seven times in tragedies which have survived either intact or in fragments (Euripides' *Hippolytus Stephanephoros*, *Hippolytus Kalyptomenos*, *Stheneboia*, *Phoenix*, *Peleus*, and *Tennes*, which has also been attributed to Critias, and Sophocles' *Phaedra*). In each play a woman is worried that she may be accused of adultery and attempts to throw suspicion onto a man by accusing him of sexual violence. As Sommerstein remarks,

> If consent or non-consent in such matters had been thought to have been of little significance, no sane person would have done such a thing, particularly when safer and equally effective alternatives were readily available. (…) A society in which this story-pattern was popular, or even comprehensible, must have been a society in which, while a woman who willingly committed adultery was abhorred, a woman raped was seen as an innocent victim.

For instance, in Euripides' *Hippolytus* Phaedra thinks it makes all the difference in the world whether or not people think Hippolytus used force against her. In her suicide note, she explicitly states "Hippolytus dared to touch my bed by force" (885–6). Similar charges appear to have been levelled by Phthia in Euripides' *Phoenix* and by Stheneboia against Bellerophontes in the play named after her.

Next Sommerstein turns to plays in which an unmarried girl is forced to have sex against her will and becomes pregnant, then is threatened with punishment by her father. There are two varieties: in the first and more frequent version the aggressor is a god or hero like Heracles; in the second the girl is the victim of violence from her brother or father. For some of the plays the evidence is too fragmentary to determine whether the girl was willing or not, but in some it is obvious that she was not. Sommerstein draws attention to a fragment attributed by Wilamowitz-Moellendorff to Euripides' *Auge* (*trag. adesp.* 402), in which a character asks, "Did you take your pleasure by force or did you persuade the girl?" If Wilamowitz-Moellendorff is correct, the question may have been posed by Aleos, the father of Auge, who was raped by Heracles.[17] As Sommerstein observes, the line reveals that this character "thought it important to know whether she was raped or seduced, presumably because it would affect how he dealt" with his daughter.[18]

What Sommerstein does not examine is how the victims of sexual violence are portrayed and how other characters react to their suffering. Is the audience encouraged to view the victims sympathetically or with indifference? What do other characters say, both men and women, when they hear what has happened to these victims? In the *Prometheus Bound* of Aeschylus Io recounts her dreams in which she has seen visions telling her about Zeus' desire for her and instructing her to go to Lerna's meadow so that the god may satisfy his passion for her. She informs her father, who is alarmed and consults the oracle at Delphi. The oracle commands him to cast his daughter out of his house. Both part with much sorrow, and Io is transformed into a cow and wanders for many years (Aeschylus *Prometheus Bound* 640–86). The chorus does not blame her for refusing to submit to the god. Instead they cry out (Aeschylus *Prometheus Bound* 687–95):

> Never did I think that such dreadful words would reach my ears; never did I think such unbearable sufferings, painful to the eye, shameful and full of terror, so would chill my souls with a double-edged goad. Alas, alas for your fate. I shudder when I look on Io's fortune.

Prometheus predicts more suffering but he does not condone Zeus' actions (Aeschylus *Prometheus Bound* 736–41):

> Do you now think the tyrant of the gods is hard in all things without difference? He was a god and tried to lie in love with this girl who was mortal, and on her he brought this curse of wandering; bitter indeed you found your marriage with this suitor, young woman.

One also finds sympathy for the victim of sexual violence in Euripides' *Ion*.[19] In the prologue Hermes relates how Creusa was compelled by Apollo to have sex and bore a child, whom she abandons. Hermes rescues the child and brings him to the temple of Apollo at Delphi where he serves as a slave of the shrine. Creusa marries Xuthus but when they cannot have children, they go to the oracle of Apollo to find a solution. Creusa arrives before her husband and talks to the temple slave who she does not realize is actually her son. She tells the story of a woman who was the victim of sexual violence at the hands of Apollo and bore a child whom she exposed. When he hears the story, Ion exclaims "the god does wrong and the mother suffers". After Creusa leaves he protests against Apollo's injustice (Euripides *Ion* 436–47):

> But I must take Apollo to task. What's got into him? Using violence then abandoning virgins? Secretly fathering children and then nonchalantly letting them die? You should be the last to do this. Phoebus, you have the power, so you should make virtue your goal. Human wickedness is punished by the gods, so how can it be right for you gods to make laws for us and then to be guilty of breaking those same laws yourselves? If – not that it will happen, but just for the sake of argument – if you and Poseidon and Zeus, the lord of the heavens, are going to be brought to book by humans for all the sexual violence you've committed, the penalties will empty your temples.

Aeschylus' play *The Suppliant Women* is a drama about women who have fled from Egypt to Argos to avoid being forced into marriage against their will. In the opening lines of the play, the Danaids say they have arrived in Argos fleeing the impious marriage of the sons of Egypt. They call the men who pursue them *hybristes* and ask the Argives to prevent them from entering their beds against their will (*akontôn*) (37–9). When they appeal to the gods for justice, they call on them to hate *hybris* (81) and to observe the destructive results of *hybris* (104; cf. 528). If the Argives do not protect them, they threaten to hang themselves (160; cf. 461–5). Their father takes their side and asks how could a man who marries (i.e. has sex with) an unwilling woman taken from an unwilling man be righteous (227–8). Like Sisyphus, the Egyptians will not avoid punishment for their crimes in Hades (230–2). The king of Argos sees the justice of their request, but cannot offer them protection unless the people agree (365–9). He obviously sympathizes with these women: as he departs to consult the Argives, he prays that they too will hate the *hybris* of the men who pursue the Danaids (487). After the Argives grant their request for protection, an Egyptian herald arrives and demands that the Danaids leave with him (821–31). They denounce his *hybris* (845), but he ignores their protest and orders them to come with him whether willing or not (860–1). The king makes good on his promise to protect the Danaids from violence and drives the Egyptians away (911–49). In this play the king and the assembly of male citizens condemn the threatened rape of the Danaids and are willing to risk war to defend them.

We have now seen that men viewed women who said yes and those who said no very differently and that they might be sympathetic to the victims (actual or potential) of sexual violence. But did Greek husbands consider it important whether their own wives consented to sexual relations with them? Was women's desire ever considered desirable by men? Men certainly noticed whether a woman had desire and consented to sexual relations and when she did not. But did they prefer women who were willing and felt desire? Or were they all sadists who could not enjoy sex unless the woman felt suffering and humiliation? I am not going to deny that there were men in ancient Greece who took pleasure in inflicting pain – but this does not get us very far; sadistic attitudes and behaviour are a lamentable but widespread phenomenon. My question is different – are there passages which suggest that a man might prefer a willing partner to an unwilling one?

Let us begin with Aristophanes' *Lysistrata*. The lead character wishes to stop the war between Athens and Sparta and convinces the women of Athens to stop having sex with their husbands until they make peace. She makes her co-conspirators take an oath (Aristophanes *Lysistrata* 217–32; trans. Henderson 2000):

Lysistrata: At home in celibacy shall I pass my life –
Calonice: At home in celibacy shall I pass my life –
Lysistrata: wearing a saffron dress and all dolled up –
Calonice: wearing a saffron dress and all dolled up –
Lysistrata: so that my husband will get as hot as a volcano for me –
Calonice: so that my husband will get as hot as a volcano for me –
Lysistrata: but never willing shall I surrender to my husband.
Calonice: but never willing shall I surrender to my husband.
Lysistrata: If he should use force to force me against my will –
Calonice: If he should use force to force me against my will –
Lysistrata: I will submit coldly and not move my hips.
Calonice: I will submit coldly and not move my hips.
Lysistrata: I will not raise my Persian slippers toward the ceiling.
Calonice: I will not raise my Persian slippers toward the ceiling.
Lysistrata: I won't crouch down like the lioness on a cheesegrater.
Calonice: I won't crouch down like the lioness on a cheesegrater.

This passage strongly suggests that a husband might have sex with his wife against her will – but would he have preferred a willing partner? If men did not care whether their wives enjoyed sex, the threat to "submit coldly and not move my hips" would not have any effect on Athenian husbands. This threat only makes sense if men enjoyed sex more when their wives enjoyed it too.[20] If the ideal were to make love to a woman who was frigid, passive and unfeeling, Lysistrata's ruse would not be very practical. In fact, Lysistrata explicitly says, "men get no pleasure in sex when they have to force you (*pros bian*)" (Aristophanes *Lysistrata* 163).[21]

A husband's preference for a willing partner is also found in Xenophon's *Oeconomicus*. This treatise encompasses all aspects of life at home and dispenses some advice about the right kind of marriage. Socrates has received this advice from a wealthy farmer named Ischomachus. Ischomachus reports a discussion he has with his wife about cosmetics (X. *Oec.* 10). She wishes to put on make-up to make herself more desirable to her husband. He tells her this is not necessary – a natural complexion and a healthy body is all that he desires. He compares making love to his wife to sex with a slave girl.

As for what my wife looks like, when there's a decision to be made between her and a slave girl, then when she is less made up and more tastefully dressed, she becomes an object of desire, and especially because she is granting her favours willingly, whereas the slave has no choice but to yield.

Ischomachus not only notices whether his partner is willing or not; he actually prefers a willing partner over an unwilling partner. The former is more desirable. His wife says that man and wife "are partners in each other's bodies" and Ischomachus agrees. We noted above that the woman is passive in the marriage agreement. Once in the household, she becomes a willing partner and shares in the pleasure of the bed. Her husband does not see this as menacing but welcomes this attitude because it makes lovemaking more stimulating for him.[22]

The role of mutual desire in marriage is also described in the pantomime at the end of Xenophon's *Symposion* (9.2–7).[23] The entire passage deserves careful study:

(2) After that, first a chair was set down in the room, and then the Syracusan came in. "Gentlemen," he said, "Ariadne will enter the bedroom which she shares with Dionysus. Then Dionysus will arrive, having become a little tipsy with the gods, and will go to join her; then they will have some fun with each other."

(3) So, in came first Ariadne, decked as a bride, and she sat down on the chair. Without Dionysus appearing yet, the bacchic rhythm was played on the *aulos*. Then they really did admire the dancing-master, for as soon as Ariadne heard the music she reacted in such a way that anybody would have known she was delighted with what she heard. She didn't go to meet him, and she didn't get up either, but she plainly only just kept still.

(4) When Dionysus caught sight of her, he danced up to her as lovingly as one possibly could, knelt down, embraced her and kissed her. Despite looking bashful, she embraced him with affection in return, and seeing it, the drinkers clapped their hands and shouted encore, all at the same time.

(5) When Dionysus got to his feet and raised Ariadne with him, then there really were gestures of embracing and kissing to behold! People could see that Dionysus was really good-looking, and that Ariadne was beautiful, and that they weren't just in fun, but were kissing truly mouth to mouth, and everyone watched in eager expectation.

(6) They could hear Dionysus asking her if she loved him and her giving him such an assurance back that not only Dionysus < ... > but everyone there could have sworn an oath together that the boy and girl were really in love with each other; they didn't look like people who had been taught the moves, but like people at last allowed to do what they had long been wanting to do.

(7) Eventually, when the party saw them wrapped around each other and apparently going to bed, the bachelors swore to get married, and the married men mounted their horses and road away to have the company of their wives.

Several features of this description are noteworthy. Xenophon is no doubt inverting the traditions of the symposion, which was more likely to end in sex with the *hetairai* or musicians who often attended or in a brawl (cf. Pl. *Symp.* 223b). As a philosopher, he is trying to domesticate the practices of the symposion, which was potentially disruptive, and turn them to socially useful ends. Although this is only a pantomime in which the actors play roles and feign real emotions, Xenophon stresses the realism (*alêthinôs*) of the acting: the actors were so natural that all the spectators were ready to swear that the two really loved each other. Throughout the passage

Xenophon evokes the mutual desire of Dionysus and Ariadne. Dionysus does not make love to an inert body; they are playing with each other (*paizountai pros allêlous*). She is aroused by the Bacchic rhythm of the music. She then attempts to restrain herself like a respectable wife, but it is obvious she finds it difficult. After the god kisses her, she willingly returns his affection. Because she is a respectable woman, she blushes (*aidoumenê*), but her modesty does not prevent her from reciprocating.[24] Dionysus wants to know if Ariadne loves him, a sign that he prefers a willing partner.[25] He obviously wants to hear Ariadne say "yes!" What is most striking is the stimulating effect which the pantomime has on the men at the symposion. In this state of arousal they do not rush out to find a *hetaira*, but either run home to their wives or swear to get married. The thought of sexual pleasure with a willing partner inspires them to think of connubial bliss.[26]

This evidence about the role of women's desire in marriage shows that Apollodorus' statement that "we keep *hetairai* for the sake of pleasure, concubines to look after or daily physical needs and wives for the purpose of bearing legitimate children and serving as a trustworthy guardian of our households" is potentially misleading. It gives the impression that the only role of the wife was to provide legitimate offspring and to keep house and that only a *hetaira* could provide physical pleasure.[27] The passage from Xenophon's *Symposion* reveals that sexual pleasure was an important part of the bond between husband and wife.

A woman's desire might also be seen as socially beneficial. In his *Constitution of the Spartans* (1.5) Xenophon discusses Lycurgus' laws about marriage.

> He noticed too that during the time immediately succeeding marriage, it was usual elsewhere for the husband to have unlimited intercourse with his wife. The rule that he adopted was the opposite of this: for he laid it down that the husband should be ashamed to be seen entering his wife's room or leaving it. With this restriction on intercourse the desire of the one for the other must necessarily be increased, and their offspring was bound to be more vigorous than if they were surfeited with one another.

Here woman's desire is not just sexually attractive – it brings social benefits. Xenophon does not say that only the intensity of the father's desire, but that of both partners determine the health of the child. The greater the libido of the parents, the mightier the child. And one might add, the mightier the army of the state. One should not attempt to transform Xenophon into a proto-feminist. If he places a positive value on woman's desire, he does so not because he believes that she has a right to enjoy sex and choose her partners. Xenophon views women's desire "functionally – as a means of producing children for men – rather than as an autonomous domain of desire, a subjectivity of one's own".[28] In other parts of the treatise Xenophon (*Lac. Pol.* 1.7–9) commends the practice of husbands lending their wives to other men for the purpose of having children, hardly an enlightened habit by our standards. He wishes to maximize women's desire only because it serves the interests of the state. He does not view the satisfaction of desire as a worthy end in itself. In fact, he disapproves of normal marriages in which the husband has sex with his wife frequently in the first few months. That said, he still believes that a woman's desire can play a positive role in strengthening the family and the state.

The idea that reproduction results from the mutual desires of man and wife is also found in Plato's *Timaeus* 91b–d (trans. Bury 1952):

> And the marrow, inasmuch as it is animate and has been granted an outlet, has endowed the part where its outlet lies with a love for generating by implanting therein a lively desire for emission. Wherefore in men the nature of the genital organs is disobedient and self-willed, like a creature that is deaf to reason, and it attempts to dominate all

because of its frenzied lusts. And in women again, owing to the same causes, whenever the matrix or womb, as it is called – which is an indwelling creature desirous of child-bearing – remains without fruit long beyond the due season, it is vexed and takes it ill; and by straying all ways through the body and blocking up the passages of breath and preventing respiration it casts the body into the uttermost distress, and causes, moreover, all kinds of maladies; until the desire and love of the two sexes unite them.

For reproduction to take place both partners must feel desire. For Plato, as for the Hippocratic writers, sexual pleasure is linked to reproduction. But the desire for sexual pleasure is present in both partners and leads them to make love. There is no suggestion in this passage that the ideal wife would be frigid or that female desire was something that could not exist in the real world. Here desire is seen almost as a disease that can only be cured by sexual pleasure. Or as Halperin says, "in the absence of men, women's sexual functioning is aimless and unproductive, merely a form of rottenness and decay, but by the application of male pharmacy it becomes at once orderly and fruitful".[29] What is potentially deleterious is not desire *per se*, but unfulfilled desire.[30]

A woman's thwarted desire as the cause of trouble is also a powerful theme in tragedy. Some critics believe that women's desire in tragedy is inherently disruptive, a threat to family and community.[31] Certainly Phaedra's desire for her stepson in Euripides' *Hippolytus Kalyptomenos* has terrible consequences, but not all tragedies about female desire conform to this pattern. In Aeschylus' *Oresteia* the trouble stems from Agamemnon's ambition, which causes him to sacrifice his daughter and to stay away from home for ten years. On his return home, his desire for Cassandra leads him to introduce the slave into his house, which was a breach of Greek custom. It was socially acceptable for a man to go to a brothel or keep a mistress provided he did not bring her home. In a speech attributed to Andocides (4.14) the speaker criticizes Alcibiades for bringing both slave and free *hetairas* into his house after receiving the largest dowry in Greece for his wife. This forced his wife to leave him and go to the archon to register for a divorce. The speaker clearly regards Alcibiades' behaviour as outrageous and insulting (ὑβριστής). In a marriage contract from Ptolemaic Egypt between a woman from Cos and a Greek from Alexandria, which must reflect general Greek attitudes, the husband agrees not to bring other women into the house (ἐπεισάγεσθαι) and thereby insult his wife.[32] If he did so, he would have been in breach of their agreement. The Greek audience who viewed the *Oresteia* would have seen Agamemnon's attempt to introduce Cassandra into his house as deeply shocking. Clytemnestra takes a lover in part because her husband has left her alone and unsatisfied, then takes revenge on her husband in part for killing her daughter and for insulting her by introducing Cassandra into their home (Aesch. *Ag.* 1440–2, 1444–7). Clytemnestra goes too far in seeking revenge; the proper recourse would have been for her to leave the household and return to her father's family. Yet had Agamemnon not left in the first place, there is no reason to think that there would have been a tragedy. By neglecting his wife's desire, Agamemnon brings tragedy on himself.[33] And his own desire for Cassandra only makes the situation worse.

Heracles offends Deianeira in the same way in Sophocles' *Trachiniai*. Here again it is a man's desire for a woman which threatens his household. Heracles falls in love with Iole, and when her father Eurytus, the king of Oechalia, refuses to let him have an affair with her, he invades his country, kills him and sacks the city (351–68; cf. 472–83). While he is away for a long time, Deianeira remains loyal and worries about her husband (36–48, 141–52). She is too modest to admit that she desires her absent husband, but the chorus express for her what decorum prevents her from saying: she cannot put "to rest without tears the longing (πόθον) in her eyes" (107).[34] Her love and concern for him prompt her to send her son Hyllus to find him (61–93), and at first she rejoices at the news of his imminent return (293–4).

Her joy turns to sorrow when she learns that one of the women captured by Heracles and brought to Trachis by Lichas is Iole (351–8). As a good wife, Deianeira has tolerated Heracles' affairs with women in other places (457–60), but living with another woman under the same roof is more than she can endure (536–51; trans. Lloyd-Jones 1994–6):

> For I have taken in the maiden – but I think she is no maiden, but taken by him – as a captain takes on a cargo, a merchandize that does outrage to my feelings. And now the two of us remain beneath one blanket for him to embrace; such is the reward that Heracles, who is called true and noble, has sent me for having kept the house so long. I do not know how to be angry with my husband now that he is suffering severely from this malady; yet what woman could live together with this girl, sharing a marriage with the same man? For I see her youth advancing, and mine perishing; and the desiring eye turns away from those whose bloom it snatches. That is why I am afraid that Heracles may be called my husband, but the younger woman's man.

Deianeira desires her husband and is worried that he will pay more attention to the younger woman. Although she tries not to be angry with Heracles, Deianeira is clearly hurt that her reward for looking after the house for so long is to receive a rival in her own home. She distinguishes between Heracles falling in love, which she does not reproach, and bringing another woman into the house, which is intolerable.[35] Her desire for her husband leads her to make a fatal mistake: she anoints his tunic with a potion given to her by the centaur Nessus, which she thinks will restore his love to her. But she discovers Nessus has tricked her and that the potion is a poison that brings about Heracles' death. Hyllus at first curses his mother when he learns what she has done, but later recognizes that she is not to blame (1136, 1138–9). After all, her intent was good (χρηστὰ μωμένη) because all she wanted was to be close to her husband. Heracles too understands that Nessus, not she, is responsible for his death (1157–63). It is not Deianeira's passion which brings about the tragedy; as Hyllus says near the end of the play, it is Heracles' passion for Iole which is responsible (1233–7). Her only fault is her naivety in trusting Nessus, an error she quickly realizes (706–11, 714–18).[36]

For the final part of this chapter, I would like to turn to some tales about women's desire found in the *Erotika Pathemata* ("Sufferings in Love") by Parthenius of Nicaea.[37] Parthenius was a poet and grammarian who was captured in the Third Mithridatic War (74–63 BCE) and taken to Rome. He wrote thirty-six prose tales in this work for the Roman poet Cornelius Gallus.[38] The stories are summaries of earlier works, some dating to the fourth century BCE, most of which are now lost.[39] We now have a valuable new edition with translation and commentary by Jane Lightfoot (whose translations I use in this chapter). To my knowledge, these stories have not been studied for the light they cast on attitudes towards women's desire. Many of the stories are tragic; but in most cases it is men's passion that causes the misfortune. Men fall in love with other men's wives,[40] men attempt to rape women[41] and fathers have sex with their daughters.[42] Some of the stories portray a woman's adulterous love,[43] a mother's incestuous passion for her son[44] or a young woman falling in love with the enemy and committing treason.[45] Yet other stories about women's desire have happy endings. Let us begin at the beginning with the first story in the collection, *Lyrcus*.

> When Io of Argos was stolen by pirates, her father Inachus dispatched various searchers to track her down, among them Lyrcus, son of Phoroneus. He traversed vast areas of land, crossed huge tracts of sea, but finally, when he could not find her, gave up out of weariness. To Argos he would not return, for fear of Inachus; so he went

instead to Caunus and called upon Aegialus, whose daughter Heilebia he married; they say that on seeing Lyrcus the girl fell into love (*eis erôta elthein*) and pleaded with her father to have him. He portioned off not the smallest share of his kingdom and other possession and made Lyrcus his son-in-law. A long time elapsed, but Lyrcus had no issue; so he went off to Didyma to consult the oracle about begetting children. The god told him that he would father children on the first woman he had intercourse with when he left the temple. In great delight he began to hurry back to his wife, convinced that the oracle would turn out as he wished. But when his voyage brought him to Bybastus, he was most cordially entertained there by Staphylus, Dionysus' son, who encouraged him in some heavy drinking; and once the quantities of alcohol had softened him up, Staphylus put him to bed with his daughter Hemithea. He did this because he had advance knowledge of the oracle, and he wanted Lyrcus to father children on his daughter. There had been some contention as to which of them should sleep with the stranger, so overcome were they both with desire. On the next day Lyrcus realized what he had done when he saw Hemithea lying next to him. He took it badly and blamed Staphylus bitterly for deceiving him; but afterwards, since there was nothing he could do, he took off his belt and gave it to the girl, telling her to save it for their son when he grew up: it would be a token when the boy should come looking for his father in Caunus. And so he sailed away. When Aegialus learnt about the oracle and Hemithea, he tried to banish Lyrcus from his country, and from then on there was constant fighting between the supporters of Lyrcus and those on Aegialus' side. But Heilebia was Lyrcus' staunchest ally, for she would not repudiate her husband. Afterwards, when the son of Hemithea and Lyrcus had grown up (he was called Basilus), he arrived in Caunus, where he was recognized by the now aging Lyrcus, who made him leader of his own people.

In this tale it is the woman who falls in love with the man and takes the initiative in asking her father to allow her to marry him. Her desire is not a threat to the social order. In fact, her request enables her father to gain a good son-in-law. There is no reason to connect the desire of the wife with the failure to have children. According to the narrator it is Lyrcus "who has no issue", which appears to imply that he is the one who is infertile and has to consult the oracle to find out how to become fertile. If he had not been deceived by Staphylus, he would have returned home, slept with Heilebia and had children with her. What is disruptive in this tale is not female desire, but the plots of one man, Staphylus, and the weakness of another, Lyrcus. Both of the daughters of Staphylus desire Lyrcus, but it is their father who enables one to consummate her desire and cause the conflict between Aegialus and Lyrcus. Their desire is not *per se* disruptive – it is their father's meddling that creates the problem. On the other hand, Hemithea's desire is not incompatible with deep loyalty to her husband. Despite his weakness and Staphylus' deceit, she remains loyal to Lyrcus in the conflict between father and son-in-law. Woman's desire can play a positive or a harmful role in human relations. It is not something inherently evil, which needs to be suppressed at all costs.[46]

In another tale it is the failure of a husband to reciprocate his wife's desire that leads to tragedy (*Leucone*). Had the husband done his duty to his wife, she would not have suffered, and he would not have felt remorse. It is the man's inability to control his own love of hunting, which is responsible for the suffering of both.

> In Thessaly Cyannippus, son of Pharax, fell in love with a very beautiful girl, Leucone. He asked permission from her parents and married her. Now, he was very fond of hunting and used to spend the day in pursuit of lions and boars, coming home at night

to the girl in such a state of exhaustion that he sometimes did not even speak to her and simply fell into a deep sleep. She was annoyed and distressed and did not know what to do, and made it her special concern to spy on Cyanippus and find out what it was that he was doing to make him find so much pleasure in his sojourns in the mountains. So she hitched her dress up as far as her knees and, in secret from her maids, entered the woods where Cyanippus' bitches were chasing a stag. But they were pretty wild, maddened after a long day's hunting and tore her quite to pieces. No one else was present. And in this way, out of desire for her husband (διὰ πόθον ἀνδρός), the girl met her end. When Cyanippus came up and found the mangled body of Leucone, he was full of grief. He summoned his attendants, heaped up a pyre and placed her on it. He then threw the bitches on top of the pyre, and finally, bewailing the girl deeply, he killed himself.

The neglected wife Leucone is treated sympathetically in the narrative, and her husband implicitly admits his own guilt by committing suicide. Erotic love holds the marriage together, and when the husband pays no attention to his wife's desire, the result is tragic.

The final story (*Pallene*) provides a happy ending for this chapter. This story comes from Theagenes and from Hegesippus' *Palleniaca*. The former is otherwise unknown, but the latter poet has been dated to the fourth century BCE.[47]

It is also said that Sithon, king of the Odomanti, had a lovely and charming daughter Pallene, whose fame spread far and wide, and for whose sake suitors came not only from Thrace itself but also from further afield, from Illyria and from among the people settled on the banks of the Tanais. (2) First Sithon had the incoming suitors fight (him) < >, taking the girl, while the one who showed himself the weaker was to die; and in this way he killed off a great many. (3) Later, when the greater part of his strength had left him and he resolved to get the girl married, he ordered two new arrivals, Dryas and Cleitus, to fight with each other with the girl as a prize. One was to die, the survivor to have the girl and the kingdom. (4) When the appointed day dawned, Pallene (who, so it turned out, had fallen in love with Cleitus) was very much afraid for him. She had not the heart to confess this to any of those around her; but her cheeks so ran with tears that eventually her old tutor realized and diagnosed her condition. He told her to keep her spirits up, that things would go just as she wanted. Secretly he approached Dryas' charioteer, promising him a great deal of money if he would not insert the linch-pins of the chariot wheels. (5) So when they went out to battle and Dryas charged at Cleitus, the wheels fell away from under the car, and Cleitus rushed up to him as he lay there and dispatched him. (6) But Sithon realized his love-struck daughter's strategem. He heaped up an enormous pyre and set Dryas on top. He was going to slay Pallene on it, too, only a divine visitation stopped him; the heavens opened and a huge shower of rain burst forth, and Sithon relented. He treated the assembled Thracian crowd to wedding-feast, and let Cleitus have the girl.

The narrative introduces Pallene in positive terms. Her father by contrast comes across as violent and cruel, killing all her suitors. Pallene feels passion for Cleitus but is too modest to express her feelings. It is left to her tutor, a slave, to notice her distress and to look for a solution, which threatens to overturn her father's plans and defies his authority. The tutor plays a role similar to that of Phaedra's nurse in Euripides' *Hippolytus*; each character tries to help a woman suffering from love to fulfil her desire but ends up creating more trouble for them. In the case of Pallene, however, the gods come to the rescue and unite her with the object of her desire. Marriage brings together two willing partners in mutual bliss.

This study has been perforce selective in its analysis of the evidence. One could also have examined stories in which a woman's desire led to tragedy and suffering. But the aim of this essay was not to be comprehensive, but rather to question some views held by modern scholars. First, we have found that women's desire was not always seen as threatening or transgressive. Second, Greek men did not consider the ideal wife to be frigid and passive. As the wife of Ischomachus says (without him disagreeing), man and wife were partners in each other's bodies. Third, the possibility of "sexual symmetry" in marriage was already present in the classical period. Finally, it would be both inaccurate and unfair to call ancient Greece a "rape culture". Greek men did condone some forms of sexual violence which are now outlawed, but other forms were condemned and subject to harsh penalties.[48] Men in ancient Greece often held misogynistic views and placed restrictions on women's conduct. But they did pay attention to when a woman said no and preferred it when she said yes.[49] And their own sexual pleasure might be enhanced when they knew it was mutual.

Notes

1 On the practice of dowry see Vérilhac and Vial 1998: 125–208.
2 Vérilhac and Vial 1998: 265 (my translation).
3 For the practice of *aphaeresis* see Dem. 41.6 with Cohn-Haft 1995.
4 On the *epikleros* see Karabélias 2002; Cudjoe 2010: 191–202, 247–52.
5 Cole 1984, followed by Goldhill 1995: 166, attempts to defend Lysias' interpretation of the law, but see Harris 1990 (= Harris 2006: 283–93). The conclusions of this essay have been widely accepted; see Harris 2006: 94. For discussion of Athenian attitudes towards acts of sexual violence see Harris 2006: 297–332, which has now been endorsed by Kaffarnik 2013 and Bathrellou 2012, 151 n. 1.
6 Passman 1993: 58.
7 Osborne 1996: 76–7; cf. Rabinowitz 1993: 19: "any form of female desire could be perceived as a threat to the family and the Athenian polis". Osborne's analysis of the portrayal of the myth of Eos on Greek vases is well criticized by Lefkowitz 2002 and Lewis 2002: 203.
8 Goldhill 1995: 149.
9 Halperin 1990: 266. Halperin's statements cover both heterosexual and homosexual relationships. Halperin believes that sex in classical Athens "was rather a declaration of one's social identity, an expression of one's public status". Yet how could an act performed in the privacy of a closed bedroom convey a social message when no one was watching?
10 See Konstan 1994: 57 n. 58: "In the Classical period, *erôs* was not normally perceived as the basis of a permanent conjugal bond." On Plutarch's *Erotikos* see Brenk 1988.
11 See, for example, Omitowoju 1997, 2002. For a critique, see Harris 1997; Sommerstein 2006.
12 For the categories of just homicide see *Ath. Pol.* 57.3 and Dem. 23.53–61 with MacDowell 1963: 70–81. There is also evidence that it was permitted to kill tyrants or those aiming at tyranny in Ilion (Dareste et al. 1898: no. XXII, lines 19–36).
13 For a similar distinction between a case of seduction and one of sexual violence see Men. *Dys.* 289–98 with Brown 1991 and Harris 2006: 313–14.
14 Harrison 1968, 35–6 with n. 1, observed that an inserted document at [Dem.] 59.87 contains a law stating that the the husband who caught his wife in adultery was not permitted to remain married under pain of *atimia*. He then argues by analogy that "it would seem that the victim of rape was liable to just the same treatment as she who had been a willing co-operator in the adultery". There are three objections to this argument. First, the document found at [Dem.] 59.87 is a forgery inserted into the text at a later date and contains no reliable information; see Canevaro 2013: 190–6. Second, even if the document were genuine, there is no reason to believe that the same treatment must have applied to women who had allowed themselves to be seduced and those who had been forced to have sexual relations against their will. Athenian law recognized that those acting under compulsion were not responsible for their actions. See Harris 2013: 286–9, 290–1, 298–300. Third, X. *Hier.* 3.3 gives the

impression that men whose wives had been the victims of sexual violence would keep them, provided that their affection for them was undiminished.

15 On these passages see respectively Kapparis 1999: 354–7; Fisher 2001: 336–7.

16 Sommerstein 2006: 244. Sommerstein 2006: 245 is incorrect however to deny that the Greeks did not have a word which has the same semantic field as the modern English word "rape" when he claims that the term *biasmos* was equivalent in meaning. *Pace* Sommerstein, this word refers generally to acts of violence – see Aeneas Tacticus 24.15. One should also note that the word *biasmos* is almost never used to describe sexual violence. Rabinowitz 2011, 13–16 rightly notes that rape is a key theme in Euripides' *Trojan Women* and *Andromache*.

17 Wilamowitz-Moellendorff 1935: 201.

18 Sommerstein 2006: 238.

19 For discussion of the sexual violence in this play see Harris 2006: 320–3 with references to earlier discussions.

20 Dover 1973: 71 rightly observes that "the central idea of the play, that a sex-strike by citizens' wives against their husbands can be imagined as having so devastating an effect, implies that the marital relationship was much more important in people's lives than we would have inferred simply from our knowledge of the law and our acquaintance with litigation about property and inheritance"; but does not comment on the men's attitudes towards women's desire.

21 Stroup 2004: 41 argues that "For a wife to be represented trading in her sexuality meant for the fifth-century audience of comedy that she is no longer, for all intents and purposes, a wife." In this scene Stroup claims that drinking from a *kylix* transforms these women into *hetairai* because this kind of cup was only used at symposia, which married women did not attend. But what made a woman a *hetaira* was not drinking from a *kylix* but attending a symposion where she drank in the presence of men who were not their relatives (Isaeus 3.14; [Dem.] 59.24, 33). The use of the *kylix* in this scene is better understood in the thematic context of female appropriation of traditional male customs and pre-rogatives. Stroup 2004: 59 also claims that "Myrrhine is itself an Attic *hetaira* name" and that this is part of Lysistrata's "hetairization of the wives". But the name Myrrhine was used for respectable women – see *IG* i³ 1330 (Myrrhine the priestess of Athena Nike).

22 For another comparison between making love to free women and making love to slaves see Timocles fr. 24A (Kassel-Austin): "What a big difference it makes between spending the night with a young girl (*koriskê*) and with a whore (*chamaitypê*). Wow, her firmness, her complexion, her breath – ye gods! The fact that everything isn't there on a plate – you have to struggle a bit and get slapped in the face and beaten by soft hands: it's sweet, almighty Zeus." I would like to thank the editors for drawing my attention to this passage.

23 I would like to thank my colleague Dr Ivana Petrovic for drawing my attention to this passage.

24 Cf. Ormand 1999: 34 who notes that vase paintings and texts suggest the possibility "of female sexual subjectivity within the legitimate sphere of matrimony" but "similarly bury it under competing images of female decorum and reluctance".

25 A willing Ariadne is also depicted in vase paintings. See, for example, the Apulian calyx crater dated to *c*.340 BC by the Hippolyte Painter (Antikenmuseum Basel inv. 468). Note also the frequent appearance of Eros in wedding scenes. As Sutton (1992) 27 rightly notes, "Eros operates in both an active and passive sense, expressing both the emotion felt by the bride and the feeling she engenders in the groom."

26 Konstan (1994: 57 n. 58) realizes that this passage poses difficulties for his view that there was no sexual symmetry in Greek marriage during the classical period. See Kaimio 2002, who shows that "eros in tragedy is not only a destructive force leading to adultery, but also a powerful force inside the marriage".

27 Cf. Lacey 1968: 113, with n. 24.

28 Halperin 1990: 283.

29 Halperin 1990: 283. Halperin rightly notes that in this passage, and several from the Hippocratic writers, women's sexual and reproductive functions are combined.

30 The Hippocratic writers have relatively little to say about women's desire – see Dean-Jones 1992: 89 n. 36. The reason for this may be that these writers were mainly interested in physiology rather than emotions.

31 For a study of the destructive aspects of female desire in the tragedies of Sophocles see Ormand 1999.

32 *P. Eleph.* 1, lines 1–18 (= Hunt and Edgar [1932] no. 1) with Yiftach-Firanko 2003: 189–90, 312–14; cf. *P. Giss.* 2, lines 19–20.

33 As Kaimio 2002: 99 points out, Medea's rage is provoked by her thwarted desire for sex (Eur. *Med.* 265ff., 568ff., 1336ff.). For the idea that men are responsible for their wives' adultery by leaving them alone, see Ar. *Lys.* 403–13.

34 Cf. Kaimio 2002: 104–6 for a perceptive analysis of the play's imagery evoking Deianeira's desire. As Robson (2013) shows, the word *pothos* usually "expresses longing for someone or something that is missed or has been missing". This can apply to places or things, but also extends to objects of sexual desire.

35 In their lemmata on this passage neither Easterling 1982: 140–2 nor Davies 1991: 151–5 comment on Heracles' insult to his wife or compare her outrage with the reaction of Alcibiades' wife when he brought *hetairai* into their house.

36 Note also that Deianeira's desire for her husband is not connected with desire for children. She misses his love and companionship.

37 Goldhill 1995 appears to be unaware of these stories. Konstan 1994: 124 n. 51 mentions them only *en passant*.

38 For biographical details see Lightfoot 1999: 9–16.

39 Even though some of these stories date to the Hellenistic period, there is no need to believe that the position of women changed during this period, leading to a quasi-emancipation (e.g. Pomeroy 1984). See the important study from van Bremen 1996.

40 XXV: *Phayllus*.

41 XX: *Leiro*. Orion tries to rape Leiro and is killed by her father Oenopion.

42 XXVIII: *Cleite*. In XXXII: *Assaon*, he tries to marry his daughter Niobe, but she refuses.

43 XIV: *Antheus*; XVIII: *Neaira*; XXIII: *Chilonis*; XXVII: *Alcinoe*; XXXI: *Thymoetes* (Euopis, the wife of Thymoetes, has an incestuous affair with her brother).

44 XVII: *Periander's Mother*.

45 XXI: *Peisidice*; XXII: *Nanis*.

46 Cf. XXXVI: *Arganthone*, in which Rhesus courts Arganthone by going hunting with her. She falls in love with him, and they marry. After he is killed in the Trojan War, she dies from grief. Stories like this one show that literary works portrayed "sexual symmetry" before the Greek novels written during the Roman Empire (*pace* Konstan 1994).

47 Lightfoot 1999: 403.

48 On Athenian attitudes towards sexual violence see Harris 2006: 297–332.

49 I would like to thank Susan Deacy for inviting me to speak at a conference about Women's Desire held at Roehampton University in February 2009. I would also like to thank Mary Bachvarova and Kirk Ormand for reading over a draft of this essay, making suggestions for improvements (which I have tried my best to follow), and for drawing my attention to several items of bibliography I had overlooked. I would also like to thank Alan Shapiro for reading over the essay and discussing representations of women's desire in vase painting. Finally, I would like to thank the editors of this volume for many helpful suggestions and constructive criticisms.

Bibliography

Bathrellou, E. (2012) "Menander's *Epitrepontes* and the festival of the Tauropolia", *Classical Antiquity* 31(2): 151–92.

Brenk, F.E. (1988) "Plutarch's *Erotikos*: The drag down pulled up", *Illinois Classical Studies* 13: 457–71.

Brown, P.G.McC. (1991) "Athenian attitudes to rape and seduction: The evidence of Menander's *Dyskolos*", *Classical Quarterly* 41: 533–4.

Bury, R.G. (1952) *Timaeus, Critias, Cleitophon, Menexenus, Epistles.* Cambridge, MA: Harvard University Press.

Cairns, D. and Liapis, V. (eds) (2006) *Dionysalexandros: Essays on Aeschylus and His Fellow Tragedians in Honour of Alexander Garvie.* Swansea: Classical Press of Wales.

Canevaro, M. (2013) *The Documents in the Attic Orators: The Laws and Decrees in the Public Speeches of the Demosthenic Corpus.* Oxford: Oxford University Press.

Cohn-Haft, L. (1995) "Divorce in Classical Athens", *Journal of Hellenic Studies* 115: 1–15.

Cole, S.G. (1984) "Greek sanctions against sexual assault", *Classical Philology* 79: 97–113.

Cudjoe, R.V. (2010) *The Social and Legal Position of Widows and Orphans in Classical Athens*, Symboles, 3. Athens: Centre for Ancient Greek and Hellenistic Law, Panteion University of Social and Political Sciences.

Dareste, R, Haussoullier, B. and Reinach, T. (1898) *Recueil des inscriptions juridiques grecques*, vol. 2. Paris: Ernest Leroux.

Davies, M. (1991) *Sophocles' Trachiniai.* Oxford: Oxford University Press.

Deacy, S. and Pierce, K.F. (eds) (1997) *Rape in Antiquity: Sexual Violence in the Greek and Roman Worlds*. London and Swansea: Duckworth and Classical Press of Wales.

Dean-Jones, L. (1992) "The politics of pleasure: Female sexual appetite in the Hippocratic Corpus", *Helios* 19: 72–91.

DeForest, M. (ed.) (1993) *Women's Power, Men's Game: Essays on Classical Antiquity in Honor of Joy K. King*. Wauconda, IL: Bolchazy-Carducci.

Dover, K.J. (1973) "Classical Greek attitudes to sexual behaviour", *Arethusa* 6(1): 59–73.

Easterling, P. (ed.) (1982) *Sophocles' Trachiniai*. Cambridge: Cambridge University Press.

Fisher, N.R.E. (2001) *Aeschines: Against Timarchos*. Oxford: Oxford University Press.

Goldhill, S. (1995) *Foucault's Virginity: Ancient Erotic Fiction and the History of Sexuality*. Cambridge: Cambridge University Press.

Halperin, D.M. (1990) "Why is Diotima a woman? Platonic *erôs* and the figuration of gender", in D.M. Halperin, J.J. Winkler and F.I. Zeitlin (eds) *Before Sexuality: The Construction of Erotic Experience in the Ancient Greek World*. Princeton, NJ: Princeton University Press, pp. 257–308.

Halperin, D.M., Winkler, J.J. and Zeitlin, F.I. (eds) (1990) *Before Sexuality: The Construction of Erotic Experience in the Ancient Greek World*. Princeton, NJ: Princeton University Press.

Harris, E.M. (1990) "Did the Athenians regard seduction as a worse crime than rape?", *Classical Quarterly* 40: 370–7 (= Harris 2006: 283–95).

——(1997) "Review of Deacy and Pierce 1997", *Echos du monde classique/Classical Views* 40: 483–97.

——(2006) *Democracy and the Rule of Law in Classical Athens: Essays on Law, Society, and Politics*. New York: Cambridge University Press.

——(2013) *The Rule of Law in Action in Democratic Athens*. Oxford: Oxford University Press.

Harrison, A.R.W. (1968) *The Law of Athens I: Family and Property*. Oxford: Oxford University Press.

Henderson, J.J. (2000) *Aristophanes III: Birds, Lysistrata, Women at the Thesmophoria*. Cambridge, MA: Harvard University Press.

Hunt, A.S. and Edgar, C.C. (eds) (1932) *Select Papyri*. Cambridge, MA: Harvard University Press.

Kaffarnik, J. (2013) *Sexuelle Gewalt gegen Frauen in antiken Athen*. Hamburg: Kovac.

Kaimio, M. (2002) "Erotic experience in the conjugal bed: Good wives in Greek tragedy", in M.C. Nussbaum and J. Sihvola (eds) *The Sleep of Reason: Erotic Experience and Sexual Ethics in Ancient Greece and Rome*. Chicago, IL: Chicago University Press, pp. 95–119.

Kampen, N.B. (ed.) (1996) *Sexuality in Ancient Art: Near East, Egypt, Greece, and Italy*. Cambridge: Cambridge University Press.

Kapparis, K.A. (1999) *Apollodorus: Against Neaira [D. 59]*. Berlin: Walter de Gruyter.

Karabélias, E. (2002) *L'épiclérat attique*. Athens: Académie d'Athènes.

Konstan, D. (1994) *Sexual Symmetry: Love in the Ancient Novel and Related Genres*. Princeton, NJ: Princeton University Press.

Lacey, W.K.C. (1968) *The Family in Classical Greece*. Ithaca, NY: Cornell University Press.

Leſkowitz, M.R. (2002) "'Predatory' goddesses", *Hesperia* 71: 325–44.

Lewis, S. (2002) *The Athenian Woman: An Iconographic Handbook*. London and New York: Routledge.

Lightfoot, J. (1999) *Parthenius of Nicaea: The Poetical Fragments and the Ἐρωτικὰ παθήματα*. Oxford: Oxford University Press.

Lloyd-Jones, H. (ed. and trans.) (1994–6) *Sophocles*, 3 vols. Cambridge, MA: Harvard University Press.

MacDowell, D.M. (1963) *Athenian Homicide Law in the Age of the Orators*. Manchester: Manchester University Press.

Nussbaum, M.C. and Sihvola, J. (eds) (2002) *The Sleep of Reason: Erotic Experience and Sexual Ethics in Ancient Greece and Rome*. Chicago, IL: Chicago University Press.

Omitowoju, R. (1997) "Regulating rape: Soap operas and self-interest in the Athenian courts", in S. Deacy and K.F. Pierce (eds) *Rape in Antiquity: Sexual Violence in the Greek and Roman Worlds*. London and Swansea: Duckworth and Classical Press of Wales, pp. 1–24.

——(2002) *Rape and the Politics of Consent in Classical Athens*. New York: Cambridge University Press.

Ormand, K. (1999) *Exchange and the Maiden: Marriage in Sophoclean Tragedy*. Austin, TX: University of Texas Press.

Osborne, R. (1996) "Desiring women on Athenian pottery", in N.B. Kampen (ed.) *Sexuality in Ancient Art: Near East, Egypt, Greece, and Italy*. Cambridge: Cambridge University Press, pp. 65–80.

Passman, T. (1993) "Re(de)fining women: Language and power in the Homeric hymn to Demeter", in M. DeForest (ed.) *Women's Power, Men's Game: Essays on Classical Antiquity in Honor of Joy K. King*. Wauconda, IL: Bolchazy-Carducci, pp. 54–77.

Pomeroy, S.P. (1984) *Women in Hellenistic Egypt from Alexander to Cleopatra*. New York: Wayne State University Press.

Rabinowitz, N.S. (1993) *Anxiety Veiled: Euripides and the Traffic in Women*. Ithaca, NY and London: Cornell University Press.

——(2011) "Greek tragedy: A rape culture?" *Eugesta* 1: 1–21.

Richlin, A. (ed.) (1992) *Pornography and Representation in Greece and Rome*. New York and Oxford: Oxford University Press.

Robson, J. (2013) "The language(s) of love in Aristophanes", in E. Sanders, C. Thumiger, C. Carey and N.J. Lowe (eds) *Erôs in Ancient Greece*. Oxford: Oxford University Press, pp. 251–66.

Sanders, E., Thumiger, C., Carey, C. and Lowe, N.J. (eds) (2013) *Erôs in Ancient Greece*. Oxford: Oxford University Press.

Sommerstein, A. (2006) "Rape and consent in Athenian tragedy", in D. Cairns and V. Liapis (eds) *Dionysalexandros: Essays on Aeschylus and His Fellow Tragedians in Honour of Alexander Garvie*. Swansea: Classical Press of Wales, pp. 233–51.

Stroup, S.C. (2004) "Designing women: Aristophanes' *Lysistrata* and the 'hetairization' of the Greek wife", *Arethusa* 37(1): 37–74.

Sutton, R.F. (1992) "Pornography and representation on Attic pottery", in A. Richlin (ed.) *Pornography and Representation in Greece and Rome*. New York and Oxford: Oxford University Press, pp. 3–35.

van Bremen, R. (1996) *The Limits of Participation: Women and Civic Life in the Greek East in the Hellenistic and Roman Periods*. Amsterdam: J.C. Gieben.

Vérihac, A.M. and Vial, C. (1998) *Le mariage grec du vie siècle av. J.-C. à l'époque d'Auguste*. Paris: École française d'Athènes.

von Willamowitz-Moellendorff, U. (1935) *Kleine Schriften I: Klassische Poesie*. Berlin: Weidman.

Yiftach-Firanko, U. (2003) *Marriage and Marital Arrangements: A History of the Greek Marriage Document in Egypt, 4th Century BCE–4th Century CE*. Munich: C.H. Beck.

18

FANTASTIC SEX

Fantasies of sexual assault in Aristophanes[1]

James Robson

The rape, sexual assault and sexual objectification of women are recurrent motifs in Old Comedy and – along with the rape theme so common in New Comedy – have attracted their fair share of attention from scholars. Work on the topic includes that of Alan Sommerstein (1998) whose study "Rape and young manhood in Athenian comedy" aims to establish a taxonomy of sexual assault in Old and New Comedy and compares and contrasts its presentation and characteristics in the two genres. Stephen Halliwell (2002) has also articulated his thoughts on what he calls "shamelessness": the element which, he suggests, underpins sex and sexuality in Aristophanes' work. This interest in rape in comedy is mirrored for other genres, too. Nancy Rabinowitz (2011) has recently written on rape in tragedy, for example, in an article that looks at non-consensual sex through the lens of modern feminist scholarship and explores ways in which tragedies containing rape can be productively read and taught in the light of contemporary ethical concerns. Scholars such as Harris (2004; Chapter 17, this volume) also continue to explore the way in which the crime we call "rape" and issues of female consent were understood in ancient Greece, building on a rich seam of classical scholarship in this area.[2]

The aim of this chapter is to provide a fresh examination of fantasies of sexual assault as an Aristophanic *topos*. "Shamelessness", the term favoured by Halliwell to describe Aristophanic sexuality, would seem to fit these remarkable passages particularly well. The fantasies are brazen, public articulations of male desire: in addition to the audience, there are always on-stage listeners privy to the fantasy, often including the would-be victim herself. Halliwell (among others) is right, of course, to stress the special circumstances of comedy and the dramatic festival that allow such extreme articulations of sexuality to be part of the public discourse of Athens: the poet is afforded special licence.[3] But given this context of *parrhesia*, it is interesting to note that the assaults are nevertheless rule-bound: the victims are typically of lowly status, typically voiceless and, crucially, the fantasy is always projected, never accomplished. In Aristophanic comedy, no man actually commits a rape; no woman is ever raped.[4]

The contrast between the portrayal of rape in Aristophanes and in Menander is worth exploring briefly. The fact that male-on-female rape in Old Comedy only ever exists as a fantasy (or occasionally a threat)[5] removes the need so familiar from New Comedy to deal with the practical consequences of rape: there is no resulting pregnancy, for example, and no need for the dramatist to ensure that the woman is married off (rapes in New Comedy routinely lead to marriage and always result in the birth of a child, it seems; none of this is true of Old

Comedy). The rape of free, unmarried, citizen girls in New Comedy evidently raised important issues for contemporary Athenians such as the loss of honour both for the girl and her family and the need for redress, whereas in Aristophanes the status of the would-be victims and/or their relationship to the men who fantasize about assaulting them allow many of the key concerns that surface in New Comedy to be sidestepped.[6]

What we characteristically find in Aristophanes, then, is something very different from rape in New Comedy: not rape in the *past*, but fantasies or threats about rape in the *future*; not the rape of another citizen's unmarried daughter, but rather – as we shall see – fantasies of forced sex with a pilfering slave (*Acharnians*), a pliant prostitute (*Peace*) and the fantasist's own wife (*Lysistrata*).[7] Crucially, then, unlike the molested girls of New Comedy, the extent to which the victims in Old Comedy would have been able to seek any redress in classical Athens if they were actually raped in the way envisaged is questionable, to say the least.[8] And so in one sense, Aristophanic Comedy might be thought of as explicitly exploring the possibilities that citizen men's privileged social position opens up for them in the (hetero)sexual realm. While in New Comedy a rapist has to face the consequences of his actions (notwithstanding the fact that these "consequences" might involve nothing more than marrying the girl he has raped),[9] there are no such repercussions for rape fantasists in Aristophanes. Indeed, the kinds of women who feature in Aristophanic rape fantasies are those from whom citizen men in Athens could potentially demand sex in real life. In short, the imagined rapes of Old Comedy both reflect and reinforce the realities of power dynamics inherent in gender and social roles in the city.[10]

But a close reading of these sexual assault fantasies is capable of revealing more than this about male sexual attitudes towards women, and in the discussion that follows I intend to look at four key passages in detail, exploring what they have to say about male desire and male attitudes towards rape. I shall first concentrate on the two most substantial fantasies in Aristophanes' plays, namely *Acharnians* 263–79 and *Peace* 894–904, examining above all the language and emotional direction of each and considering the qualities they share. Having established the fundamental characteristics of the fantasies, I go on to examine two passages which, I believe, provide an instructive contrast with the *topos* as a whole: these are *Lysistrata* 973–80, where the fantasy involves sex with a citizen woman, and *Birds* 1253–6, which – unusually – contains a direct sexual threat against a goddess, Iris. These two passages represent, I suggest, first a subversion, then an inversion of the *topos*.

A key part of my analysis of these depictions of rape in this chapter will consist in exploring them in their literary and poetic context – not just *what* is said, but *how* it is said – with a view to establishing the centrality of these passages to the Aristophanic project as a whole. Aesthetic considerations are relevant, of course, for assessing how the descriptions of sexual assault are conceived by their author and how they might have been received by the nominally (though not exclusively) male audience:[11] hence why I take time to analyse each passage as a piece of literature. Of particular note is the upbeat way in which sexual assault can be presented by Aristophanes – a pleasurable act for the would-be rapist with the trauma for the would-be victims very much downplayed. But I shall also show that Aristophanes' descriptions of the assaults display an awareness that male sexual aggression can be experienced by a woman as an expression of power: rape can be envisaged as a punishment, for example, or as an act of tyrannical aggression.

A note on terminology. I use the word "rape" in this chapter despite the difficulties in applying the term to the world of the ancient Greeks, who had no single, comparable term. Typically in classical Greek texts, the act that we would call "rape" is described *not* as a sexual act which lacked the consent of one of the parties (the absence of consent being key to the definition of rape in modern, western legal codes),[12] but one which involved force and/or humiliation. Thus, Greek authors commonly use words cognate with *bia*, "force", "violence", or *hybris*, "insolence", "outrage", with words such as *damazesthai*, "subdue", *aischunein*, "shame", and *adikēma*, "wrongdoing", also featuring in descriptions of forced sex.[13] As we shall see, these elements of force, outrage, humiliation, subjugation and wrongdoing feature in an assortment of ways in Aristophanic rape fantasies, too.

Acharnians 263–79: The Phallic Song

Let us turn first to *Acharnians* 263–79, the so-called Phallic Song, *phallikon*.[14] This song is delivered by Dicaeopolis as he celebrates his own, personal Country Dionysia while his family looks on, his return to his rural deme having been made possible by the private peace treaty he has made with Sparta. This lyric has been the subject of much discussion, most notably by Michael Silk (2000) in *Aristophanes and the Definition of Comedy*, some of whose comments I shall examine presently. Significant for our purpose is that it contains a sexual assault fantasy concerning a slave-girl, Thratta, at lines 271–5. Since this fantasy forms an organic whole with the rest of the lyric, it will be important to consider the song in full.

> Φαλῆς, ἑταῖρε Βακχίου
> ξύγκωμε, νυκτοπεριπλάνη-
> τε, μοιχέ, παιδεραστά,
> ἕκτῳ σ' ἔτει προσεῖπον εἰς
> τὸν δῆμον ἐλθὼν ἄσμενος,
> σπονδὰς ποιησάμενος ἐμαυ-
> τῷ πραγάτων τε καὶ μαχῶν
> καὶ Λαμάχων ἀπαλλαγείς.
> πολλῷ γάρ ἐσθ' ἥδιον, ὦ Φαλῆς Φαλῆς
> κλέπτουσαν εὑρόνθ' ὡρικὴν ὑληφόρον,
> τὴν Στρυμοδώρου Θρᾷτταν ἐκ τοῦ φελλέως,
> μέσην λαβόντ', ἄραντα, κατα-
> βαλόντα καταγιγαρτίσαι.
> Φαλῆς, Φαλῆς,
> ἐὰν μεθ' ἡμῶν ξυμπίῃς, ἐκ κραιπάλης
> ἕωθεν εἰρήνης ῥοφήσει τρύβλιον·
> ἡ δ' ἀσπὶς ἐν τῷ φεψάλῳ κρεμήσεται.

Sommerstein's translation of the passage is as follows:[15]

> Phales, companion of Bacchus,
> fellow-reveller, night-rover,
> adulterer and pederast,
> after six years I address you,
> returning gladly to my deme,
> having made a peace for myself,
> released from broils and battles
> and Lamachus.
> For it's far more pleasant, Phales, Phales,
> to find a blooming young girl carrying stolen wood,
> Strymodorus' Thratta from the Rocklands,

and to take her by the waist, and lift her up,
and throw her down, and stone her fruit!
Phales, Phales,
if you drink with us, for your hangover
in the morning you shall slop down a bowl of peace;
and my shield shall be hung up in the sparks.

For Silk, this ode is Aristophanes at his lyric best – it is an example of "hybrid" lyric, "low lyric *plus*"[16] – an innovative combination of high and low lyric genres which, Silk suggests, is Aristophanes' "real accomplishment" in this area.[17] Certainly this song is remarkable for its pace, its conciseness and its linguistic and emotional exuberance. In his various discussions of the song, Silk brings out these features and others – the rapid changes in stylistic pitch, the specifics detailed by Dicaeopolis that "issue in a universal acclamation of life".[18] "Formally and rhythmically … ", Silk comments, "the lyric as a whole is a joy, with the iambics conforming perfectly to the exuberant mood and the rapidity of thought … and the ode powerfully organized".[19] Halliwell suggests that along with Dicaeopolis' "earthy sex drive" a thinking spectator might also have "a sense of … [Dicaeopolis'] ludicrous grossness", but his is a lone voice.[20] Given the subject matter, what is surprising is the innocuous spell that the song seems to weave on modern scholars. To Reckford the ode is "only slightly indecent", for Henderson it is "playful sexual aggressiveness" and even "wholesome sex".[21]

Before looking closely at the sexual assault fantasy itself, let us, then, consider some of the features which contribute to this ode's mood. There are, to be sure, risqué elements from the very beginning. The addressee is Phales, the personified Hard-On, who, we note, is immediately linked to theatre's patron deity, Dionysus. Each of the epithets that follow is ever more scurrilous and remarkable than the last: *xunkōme*, "fellow-reveller", is hardly exceptional for a follower of Bacchus, whereas in the epithet *nuktoperiplanēte*, "night-rover", there is already a suggestion of irrespectability, though nothing to merit opprobrium *per se*.[22] Only then do we encounter the racy climax of the series, *moiche* and *paiderasta*,[23] "adulterer" and "pederast", words for which we are, I think, all the more prepared – and all the less shocked by – since we have already entertained the notion of obscenity. The image conjured up of "a wild revelling-band wandering the streets at night in search of sexual opportunity"[24] stands in striking contrast to Dicaeopolis' current rural isolation – just as the sexual imagery of this passage is striking given the presence of his wife and daughter on stage.

No sooner are these scurrilous elements mentioned than the tone changes, and Dicaeopolis talks of his happy return to his deme with the highly alliterative phrase *hektōi s' etei proseipon eis …* (266). Lines 266–70 contain an arresting combination of concrete specifics and elements of fantasy: the general Lamachus and the sixth year of the war are realities for the audience,[25] whereas the private peace treaty, the return to the countryside and the release from troubles are fantasies that Aristophanes has created for his play.

At 271–5 we have the rape scene itself. Phales is now appealed to once more (and by implication his associations of wine and sexual wrongdoing evoked), and it is suggested that there is something is even *more* sweet than the images of peace and freedom we have encountered – illicit sex in the form of the rape of a slave-girl. The girl has a name, Thratta, belongs to Strymodorus, and the sex act is given a location, *phelleus* (Sommerstein translates "the Rocklands")[26] – the real and fictional names reflect the intertwining of fantasy and concrete reality present earlier in the ode (and this is further complemented by the grammatical intermingling of items discernible in line 271: *kleptousan heuronth' hōrikēn*).[27] The description of the assault, which Silk suggests is "intensely physical in its effect",[28] includes an arresting series of participles following the law of increasing members and displays heavy assonance. All this is finally topped with the much-discussed coinage *katagigartisai*.[29]

μέσην λαβόντ᾽, ἄραντα, κατα-
βαλόντα καταγιγαρτίσαι.

… to take her by the waist, and lift her up,
and throw her down, and stone her fruit!

katagigartisai – which Sommerstein translates "stone her fruit", Silk "press her grape" – combines elements from throughout the ode: it is suggestive of wine, which is in turn suggestive of peace (the word *spondai*, "peace treaty"/ "libations", links the two). In addition *katagigartisai* here is made suggestive of sex, of Phales and, of course, the god who unites all these elements, Dionysus. The dense, suggestive imagery, with its concreteness and physicality, is continued in the last lines of the ode, and themes and images important to the play are returned to once more – the sparks of the fire remind us of the wood-burning Acharnians, dawn reminds us of Dicaeopolis' lonely wait on the Pnyx and the overarching theme is again that of peace.

An interesting proposition put forward by Silk is that this ode shares characteristics with many songs from musicals in that it can stand alone, being neither dramatically probable nor necessary where it occurs in the play – he adds, though, that "its dramatic relevance on a broad thematic level is … apparent",[30] and there is a sense in which this is true for the song in relation to the Aristophanic corpus as a whole.[31] Its subjects of wine, sex, freedom and peace, its wordplay, pace and variety would appear central to the world as seen through Aristophanes' eyes.

I have taken some time to establish the effectiveness and mood of this ode for a number of reasons. One, quite simply, is to demonstrate that a fantasy of sexual assault can lie at the heart of the most Aristophanic of passages. From a modern perspective, of course, Aristophanes may legitimately be considered morally problematic for celebrating a rape in this way and, what is more, doing so in the midst of what a scholar like Silk would suggest is one of his most brilliant pieces of writing. It is instructive, too, that Dicaeopolis' fantasy assault of Thratta occurs in the most uplifting of celebratory contexts – a celebration that Dicaeopolis shares with his family – and is associated with Aristophanic virtues such as peace and wine. All these elements are bound together, as we have seen, by the coinage *katagigartisai*, "stone her fruit", "press her grape".[32] This ode is densely written, its expression exuberant and exciting – and these are elements we see repeated in the next sexual assault fantasy we shall consider.

Before we leave this ode, we should note one final detail of the assault, namely that Thratta is caught in the act of stealing wood (*kleptousan … hulēphoron*, 272). Thratta's name already implies that she is a slave and the setting of the assault, "the Rocklands", sounds remote.[33] Dicaeopolis' fantasy could hardly be more guilt free. A female slave is caught stealing – she surely deserves punishment and will neither have any means of complaining about her treatment nor, even if she did, any witnesses to the act. Indeed, the way in which the fantasy is set up neatly skirts around many of the issues that make forced sex problematic for classical Athenians. A citizen's punishment of a slave is difficult to cast as an act of *hybris*,[34] for example, and a slave's wrongdoing arguably justifies the use of force, *bia*. Not that the element of force is dwelt upon in this description: Thratta's manhandling amounts to being lifted by the waist and thrown down – an image taken from wrestling – with the sex act itself described by the oblique coinage *katagigartisai*. The presence of Dicaeopolis' wife and daughter lends an odd dynamic here, to be sure, but among other things they serve as instructive examples of citizen women whose assault by a stranger would be seen in a very different light.

Peace 894–904

Let us move on now to another Aristophanic passage featuring a fantasy of sexual assault, *Peace* 894ff. This is another remarkable piece of writing, albeit for a new set of reasons, as we shall see. It comes not long after the *parabasis* when Trygaeus brings back to earth two women whom Hermes has entrusted to him during his trip to Olympus, Opora ("Harvest") and Theoria ("Showtime" in Sommerstein's translation). Trygaeus has made preparations to marry Opora, who has gone inside, and he plans to give Theoria to the Prytaneis as Hermes has instructed. When Trygaeus, his slave and Theoria are on the stage alone, the two men begin to discuss Theoria in sexual terms. For example, when he hears the name Theoria, the slave exclaims (872–4):

Οι.   τίς αὑτηί; τί φής;
      αὕτη Θεωρία 'στιν, ἣν ἡμεῖς ποτε
      ἐπαίομεν Βραυρωνάδ' ὑποπεπωκότες;

Slave: Who's this girl here? What did you say? Is this the Showtime we used to have when we'd screw our way to Brauron after a few drinks?

   The sexual comments continue. For instance, the slave later remarks on Theoria's *prōktopente-tērida*, "quadrennial bum" (876), and even touches her saying, when challenged by Trygaeus, that he is "staking a claim to camping space for my prick (*peos*) for the Isthmian games" (879–80). Then, after a series of sexual innuendoes concerning cunnilingus (885), Theoria's availability for sex (889–90) and her genitalia (891–3) – during which she removes her clothes (887–8) – Trygaeus delivers the following lines before finally presenting her to the Prytaneis (894–904).[35]

Τρ.   ἔπειτ' ἀγῶνά γ' εὐθὺς ἐξέσται ποεῖν
      ταύτην ἔχουσιν αὔριον καλὸν πάνυ,
      ἐπὶ γῆς παλαίειν, τετραποδηδὸν ἑστάναι   896a
      καὶ παγκράτιόν γ' ὑπαλειψαμένοις νεανικῶς
      παίειν, ὀρύττειν, πὺξ ὁμοῦ καὶ τῷ πέει·
      τρίτῃ δὲ μετὰ ταῦθ' ἱπποδρομίαν ἄξετε,
      ἵνα δὴ κέλης κέλητα παρακελητιεῖ,
      ἅρματα δ' ἐπ' ἀλλήλοισιν ἀνατετραμμένα
      φυσῶντα καὶ πνέοντα προκινήσεται,
      ἕτεροι δὲ κείσονταί γ' ἀπεψωλημένοι
      περὶ ταῖσι καμπαῖς ἡνίοχοι πεπτωκότες.

Tr.   And *then*, now you've got her, first thing tomorrow you'll be able to hold a splendid athletic meeting – to wrestle on the ground, to stand her on all fours, to anoint yourselves and fight lustily in the free-style, knocking and gouging with fist and prick at once. After that, the day after tomorrow, you'll hold the equestrian events, in which rider will outride rider, while chariots will crash on top of one another and thrust themselves together puffing and panting, and other charioteers will be lying with their cocks skinned, having come unstuck in the bends and twists.

Behind this passage it is no doubt possible to discern the relish and delight the poet has taken in creating what Henderson describes as a "wild mélange of metaphors".[36] Particularly note-worthy is the way in which Aristophanes plays with the metre and combines sound effects and imagery in a striking marriage of form and content. The lines in which the sexual assault is described – while Theoria is present on stage – are 896–8, but as with the Phallic Song of the *Acharnians*, I shall aim to place this assault in the context of the passage as a whole.

Let us begin by briefly looking at some of the passage's more prominent features. In the first two lines, Aristophanes establishes a subtly heightened register. Lines 894–5 are cast in strictly tragic-compatible metre[37]– there are no comic resolutions here – and while none of the diction is high-flown, the non-standard hyperbaton between noun and adjective in the phrase *agōna … kalon* also makes a nod towards the poetic rather than the everyday. Any elevation in tone is soon undermined, though, both metrically and lexically, with the introduction of *double entendres*.

The most remarkable instance of Aristophanes' metrical playfulness in this passage comes at 897–8. Line 897 contains first and second "foot" anapaests plus a resolution of the fourth princeps, not exceptional in itself for a piece of comic verse, but this anapaestic rhythm is picked up in 898, a line whose scansion is of particular interest. The resolutions and word-division contained in 898 are such that the first two iambic metra could alternatively be scanned as four "feet" of a marching anapaest: *kai pankration g' upaleipsamenois* (— — UU—| UU—UU—).[38] This metre no doubt serves to underline the agonistic imagery of these lines and of the sex act itself.

The vocabulary and imagery employed by Aristophanes in these lines are similarly noteworthy. The athletic images follow neatly from the slave's mention of the Isthmian games we noted earlier at 879–80 and, indeed, the order of events – wrestling, pancration, horse-racing – seems to follow that of the games themselves.[39] The vocabulary becomes more and more suggestive – from *palaiein*, "to wrestle", to *tetrapodēdon*, "on all fours" (896a), to *hupaleipsamenois*, "anointed" – anointing also has erotic overtones – to *neanikōs*, "lustily" (897). And the progression continues at 898: *paiein*, "to strike", can be used in a sexual sense – as we have seen in the slave's question at 874 – and *oruttein*, "to gouge", also has sexual associations elsewhere in Aristophanes (*Birds* 442–3). The climax of the series is *tōi peei*, "with the cock" (instead of the expected *tō skelei*, "with the legs").[40] Thus the imaginative ascent of *double entendres* culminates in an unambiguous obscenity.[41]

Following these lines, the fantasy takes flight – even the chariots are personified with sexual overtones (901–2). There are a number of heavy assonantal series and the piling on of sounds and of bodies is added to by the *figura etymologica* of 900, *kelēs kelēta parakelētiei*, "rider will outride rider" (*kelēs* also being the name of a sexual position).[42] As a whole the passage is an exuberant, seductive *tour de force* of sound and image, form and content – a "wild mélange" indeed.

But at the heart of this energetic passage lies a sexual assault fantasy of a young woman. The first point to observe here being how Theoria is characterized. Just as in the *Acharnians* passage it is made clear that Thratta is no "respectable" citizen's daughter – she is a slave and is caught stealing – in the *Peace* we learn that Theoria has a sexual past.[43] The slave's question "Is this the Showtime we used to have when we'd screw our way to Brauron after a few drinks?" (873–4) invites us to think of her as a prostitute – in short, Theoria is hardly a respectable woman either (an element which would no doubt have been underlined in the scene's staging).[44]

In real life, a prostitute might have struggled to establish that her sexual assault qualified as *hybris* (there seems to be no question of Neaera receiving satisfaction in law for the *hybris* she claims to have suffered when she was gang raped, for example: [Dem.] 59.33 and 37).[45] Second, we should note that while Theoria is envisaged as being subject to a physical assault, there is no mention in the fantasy of her suffering or being injured: the assault certainly contains elements of violence, *bia*, but the violence and subjugation is presented as sport. A further important detail about the *Peace* passage (and here it stands in contrast to that of the *Acharnians*) is that Trygaeus' fantasy is not simply vicarious but also democratic in its conception. Theoria's assault is envisaged as being at the hands of the Prytaneis, and so by implication, by Athens' citizen body as a whole (which in turn creates an interesting dynamic between stage and audience). Indeed, Theoria's prospective availability for all citizen men contrasts sharply with the assault undergone by Thratta in the *Acharnians* at the hands of just one man and in a remote location. Sexual assault and peace would seem to go hand in hand: Theoria's assault, like Trygaeus' peace, is for all citizen men; Thratta's assault, like Dicaeopolis' peace, is for the enjoyment of one citizen alone.[46]

One final point to be made about the *Peace* scene is that both girls – Opora and Theoria – belong to a group of figures which Bella Zweig (1992) describes as "mute nude female characters". Certainly, not all such characters are the subject of *explicit* sexual assault fantasy – although that they are viewed in a sexual light is hardly a matter for dispute[47] – but, nevertheless, they *do* seem to share the associations with peace, a return to normality and youthfulness which we have observed in the cases of Theoria and Thratta (the latter may perhaps be regarded as a mute nude female character *in absentia*).[48] Indeed, Opora, whom Trygaeus marries, could be said to represent the personal benefits of peace just as Theoria does the public ones. Diallage, "Reconciliation", the mute nude female character in the *Lysistrata*, has her body used as a map by the Athenians and Spartans as they settle their territorial disputes under Lysistrata's watchful eye (1112–88). What unites the two sides in their desire for *peace* is their desire for *sex* – and for sex with Diallage in particular. Here we have another sexually available, compliant female, then, serving as a symbol of peace. Spondae, "Peace Treaties", in the *Knights* (1389) doubtless fulfil a similar function.[49]

Lysistrata 973–80

By examining these two sexual assault fantasies and locating them within the wider context of scenes where abstract figures become objects of sexual desire, we have seen how a man's sexual dominance of a compliant female is a common Aristophanic image representative of peace. These women are typically of lower social status and, in some cases, the sexual objectification of their bodies is tacitly witnessed or actively overseen by citizen women (tacitly in the case of Dicaeopolis' wife and daughter; actively in the case of Lysistrata). Since the social status of women is an important dynamic in these fantasies, it will be instructive now to examine a further short passage from the *Lysistrata* which constitutes an anomalous case of sexual assault – both in terms of the description of the incident and the relationship between the assailant and victim. The passage in question is *Lysistrata* 973ff., a short lyric sung by Cinesias who is in a state of sexual frustration, as are all the young men in this play, because of the sex strike. His song comes at the end of a long scene in which his wife, Myrrhine, has teased him by promising sex only to disappear with the rejoinder "make sure, darling, you vote for making peace" (950–1). Cinesias bemoans his fate in a short lyric (954–8) to which the men's chorus replies in sympathy (959–66). Shortly afterwards, Cinesias sings the following ode in which he envisages his wife being made to have sex with him unwittingly through divine intervention (973–80).

μιαρὰ μιαρὰ δῆτ'· ὦ Ζεῦ Ζεῦ
εἶθ' αὐτὴν ὥσπερ τοὺς θωμοὺς
μεγάλῳ τυφῷ καὶ πρηστῆρι
ξυστρέψας καὶ ξυγγογγύλας
οἴχοιο φέρων, εἶτα μεθείης,
ἡ δὲ φέροιτ' αὖ πάλιν εἰς τὴν γῆν,
κᾆτ' ἐξαίφνης
περὶ τὴν ψωλὴν περιβαίη.

She's a villain, a villain! Oh, Zeus, Zeus,
I wish you would strike her, as if she were a heap of corn,
with a great whirlwind and hurricane,
sweep her aloft, roll her up,
carry her off, and then let go of her,
so she would fall back to earth
and then all of a sudden
land a-straddle of my peeled prick!

The anomalies of the situation are obvious at once. Myrrhine is radically different from other would-be victims of sexual assault in that she is a citizen woman with a speaking part in the play and is portrayed as wilful and able to defy her husband's advances. What is more, the song represents neither a celebration of peace nor the success of an old man's scheme (which in the *Achamians* and *Peace* amount to much the same thing). Rather the ode articulates a young man's exasperation in the face of his continued sexual frustration, a state of affairs to which, as Myrrhine reminds us, he and the other men could put a stop to simply by voting to end the war. Noteworthy, too, is the fact that, unlike other sexual fantasies, Cinesias' song is sung when there are no women on stage – a fact which further serves to underline his inability to find a female partner for sex.

To be sure, some of the features of this passage are familiar to us from the other sexual assault fantasies we have looked at. There is an element of violence, *bia*, for example, with the woman imagined as being swept up and cast down, and the climax is accompanied by an obscenity at 980 in the form of *psōlē*, "pealed prick" (cf. *Peace* 903, *apepsōlēmenoi*). What we lack, however, is the fullness and the palpable enjoyment of the sexual act by the man that we found in *Achamians* and *Peace*. There is no lingering on the sexual act itself, none of the wrestling imagery found in both Thratta's rape and that of Theoria – indeed, the description is altogether more stark. The passage is given some life by occasional bursts of alliteration (the taus and thetas of 974, the pis and psis of 977–8, the jingle of *eita metheiēs*, 977), and repetition serves (perhaps a little crudely) to highlight some of the paired items of which there is such an abundance. This repetition comes in the form of whole words (*miara miara*, 973), prefixes (*xustrepsas kai xungongulas*, 976) and, in the final three lines, semantic elements (*viz.* the semi-chiastic arrangement of verb/adverb(s)/prepositional phrase) and both pairing and repetition serve linguistically to underline Cinesias' obsession with the sexual coupling currently occupying his speech and actions.[50]

Yet while the ode does possess vigour, it fails to engender any vicarious pleasure in Cinesias' fantasy, lacking as it does both the inventiveness of language and imagery, the metrical diversity and, crucially, the provocative detail of the passages from the *Achamians* or *Peace*. The simpler expression of this ode may, however, fruitfully be seen as indicative of Cinesias' sexual frustration. In short, this is a wartime image which contrasts sharply with the sheer male joy of peacetime sex – in wartime a husband must fantasize even about sex with his own wife, whereas in peacetime his imagination may run far more freely. The overall effect is that we look on as observers of Cinesias' frustration, confident that the resolution of his difficulties will come not in the form of a Zeus-sent whirlwind but rather a vote for peace. The Aristophanic association of peace and sex is surely nowhere as apparent as in the *Lysistrata*.

Birds 1253–6

In the *Lysistrata* passage we encountered a subversion of the *topos* of sexual assault fantasy, in that we are presented with an unengaging sexual act whose very starkness derives from its rootedness in war rather than peace. As a further demonstration of how the motif of sexual assault is conceived and utilized by Aristophanes, and how the status of the would-be victim is all important, let us briefly look at another passage, *Birds* 1253–6, which also neatly highlights the link between brutal sex and war. At the stage of the play where we find the projected sexual assault, the goddess Iris is on her way to visit mankind to tell them to sacrifice to the gods, unaware that Peisetaerus and the birds have imposed themselves between earth and heaven and so are now the ones receiving the benefits of sacrifices. Peisetaerus declares that the birds are now mankind's gods (*ornithes anthrōpoisi nun eisin theoi*: 1236) and threatens Iris with violence, death and finally with rape.

σὺ δ᾽ εἴ με λυπήσεις τι, τῆς διακόνου
πρώτης ἀνατείνας τὼ σκέλει διαμηριῶ
τὴν Ἶριν αὐτήν, ὥστε θαυμάζειν ὅπως
οὕτω γέρων ὢν στύομαι τριέμβολον.

And if *you* annoy me at all, then I'll take on the servant first – raise up her legs and screw her, yes, Iris herself, so as to amaze her how at my age I'm still hard enough to stand three rammings!

To make an important distinction, what we have here is a *threat* of rape rather than a rape fantasy *per se*.[51] This astonishing, hybristic insult to a god demonstrates well Peisetaerus' growing arrogance and the bellicose position he has adopted. What is interesting to observe once more is the way that the scene plays on the conventions of sexual assault fantasy that we observed in the previous passages. The threat to Iris is a declaration of war rather than peace – an inversion of the *topos* – a further inversion being that Iris is neither compliant and passive like Thratta and Theoria nor absent like Myrrhine. Indeed, exceptionally in the context of sexual assault, Iris is both nominally of higher status than her would-be assailant and is able to voice a protest (1257):[52]

διαππαγείης, ὦ μέλ᾽, αὐτοῖς ῥήμασιν.

Blast you to pieces, Mister, you and your language.

Sexual assault here is directly linked to concepts of power. Were it to take place, Peisetaerus' rape of Iris would help to establish a new world order and symbolize his dominance over the gods (indeed the threat itself is a symptom of the fact that Peisetaerus is challenging the status quo: this is a threat to use force, *bia*, too, and symbolically to subjugate, *damazesthai*, the gods). In the other examples we have seen, sexual assault merely confirms an existing power relation between the sexes (and does so, we should note, implicitly rather than explicitly).[53]

While the *topos* of sexual assault is in part inverted in this passage, certain elements common to sexual fantasies are nevertheless present – inventive language such as *diamēriō*, "spread her thighs" (1254) – a word Aristophanes uses only in this play[54] – and *stuomai triembolon*, "I have a hard-on ready for three rammings" (1256).[55] Furthermore, the boast of 1256, *gerōn ōn*, "still at my age … ", echoes numerous claims by old men in Aristophanes to be rejuvenated, both sexually and in other ways, following the success of their particular scheme.[56] Despite the refocusing of the sexual assault motif, *Birds* 1253–6 can still be said to form a continuum with other envisaged acts of sexual assault in Aristophanes' plays. To be sure, Peisetaerus' high-spirited tone sits uncomfortably with the violence of the threat he is making, but this duality is obviously a feature of Aristophanes' artistic vision for this play, since Peisetaerus and his new city are consistently presented in a morally ambivalent light.[57]

Conclusion

To conclude, let me suggest that sexual assault in Aristophanes is typically (though by no means exclusively) presented in a celebratory light and its expression by the poet tends to display particular energy and exuberance. We have seen, too, how sexual assault fantasies form a continuum with other scenes describing sex, and how men's potential to enjoy uninhibited sex may be viewed as a metaphor for peace. In this regard it is interesting that our examples of sexual assault fantasy are almost exclusively drawn from Aristophanes' so-called "peace plays" (*Acharnians*, *Peace* and *Lysistrata*),[58] the one exception being the anomalous example from the *Birds* (a "war" play?).

Many of the features we find in sexual assault fantasy seem central to the Aristophanic project – exuberance, humour, freedom from cares, *parrhesia*, sexuality – and it is these qualities combined with the energy of the writing which, I suggest, have led even modern readers to overlook the morally questionable nature of the fantasies we find at *Acharnians* 263–79 and *Peace* 894–904.[59] We should also note other details which help make these fantasies guilt free – for an ancient male audience, at least. Thratta is a slave-girl (already of lowly status) who is caught in the act of stealing; Theoria is most likely a prostitute (certainly she has a sexual past) and the fantasy allotment of Diallage's body parts – a sexual fantasy if not quite an assault – is overseen by another woman.[60] What is more, the celebratory mood predominates in both the *Acharnians* and *Peace* passages, with the issue of force, *bia*, sidelined (though not wholly ignored) and the voiceless victims portrayed as broadly compliant and not *envisaged* as being harmed (indeed the fact that the fantasy is projected rather than accomplished means, on one level, that the issue of harm simply does not arise).[61]

Furthermore, the fact that the would-be victims do not speak robs them of any personality and makes it hard for an audience to engage with their plight: rather, the emotional focus of each assault is the exuberant pleasure of the sexual acts as described by their would-be perpetrators. Of note, too, is that at the point of the sexual assault itself in these fantasies, the emphasis is firmly on the sex act itself – and not, say, on the beauty of the "victim". The woman's physical appearance may be mentioned before the assault (Thratta is "blooming", for example, and Myrrhine tantalizes Cinesias with her beauty) but at the moment of sex – which is marked by an inventive coinage (*katgigartisai* in *Acharnians*; *diamēriō* in *Birds*) or a primary obscenity (*peos* and *apepsōlēmenoi* in *Peace*; *psōlē* in *Lysistrata*) – the focus is very much on the physicality of the encounter and the genital act.

The passages from the *Lysistrata* and above all from the *Birds* form useful points of contrast and comparison to the celebratory sexual assault fantasies of *Acharnians* and *Peace*. One point which the *Birds* passage helps to confirm, for instance, is the potential for rape to be used aggressively to degrade the victim – here, *hybris* and the issue of control come to the fore, with Peisetaerus' sexual threat to Iris representing a challenge to the power of the gods. Likewise, the *Lysistrata* passage serves to demonstrate the lack of pleasure which sexual assault fantasy can be thought to offer in times of war and women's dominance over men.

If we consider these passages as a whole, we note that the fantasies in which spectators are invited to take the most vicarious pleasure are those where the dominance of the assailant over his victim is at its clearest and in which, arguably, the exuberance of the language and the set-up of the scenes serve to downplay issues such as violence, *bia*, and *hybris*. At one end of the spectrum are the goddess Iris and the citizen woman Myrrhine, who at the time of Cinesias' fantasy holds a good deal of power over her husband. At the other end are the slave-girl thief, Thratta, and the obliging prostitute-figure, Theoria, both of whose assaults are described in uplifting terms. In short, the status of the victim and the level of coercion required are both crucial to the level of enjoyment the protagonist can hope to gain from the assault. On the one hand, the rape of the goddess Iris is portrayed as an act of arrogant aggression, on the other the repercussion-free assault of a non-citizen woman is one of the key pleasures a man can hope to enjoy on making peace.[62]

Importantly, though, the example of Iris should persuade us that Aristophanes *does* understand the potential of rape to degrade and harm (and, indeed, to take this one step further, one could also argue that an awareness that sexual assault can harm the victim goes part of the way to explaining the use of agonistic imagery found in the *Acharnians* and most notably the *Peace* passage – after all, wrestling and the pankration are zero-sum competitions in which physical injuries *are* incurred).[63] To repeat what was said above, though, the focus is never the victim's suffering and the strongest condemnation we find in Aristophanes' plays is Iris' exasperated "Blast you to pieces, Mister, you and your language" (*Birds* 1257).

Distress and suffering is thus an element which Aristophanes, understandably enough perhaps, chooses to omit from his peacetime sexual assault fantasies and this, in turn, raises an interesting set of questions about how the male members of the audience might have regarded both sexual assault in general and these Aristophanic fantasies in particular. After all, these scenes display an intriguing mixture of, on the one hand, delight in unbounded and uncomplicated sex with a compliant and voiceless partner and, on the other, a recognition of the ability of rape to harm and degrade (especially if the victim is a woman of status). This suggests a sensitivity towards the plight of victims of sexual assault with which Athenian men are rarely credited by modern scholars – albeit one which belongs to a carefully crafted fantasy world where issues of blame and consent are neatly avoided. In Aristophanes' Old Comic vision of the world sexual assault belongs to an off-stage imaginary world where men can fulfil their urges without causing hurt to anyone. Or in other words, Aristophanes' vision of sexual assault is fantastic sex indeed.

Notes

1 Special thanks are due to Felix Budelmann, Ed Sanders and my fellow editors for their comments on earlier drafts of this chapter.

2 Important contributions to the study of rape in classical Athens include Cole 1984, Keuls 1985, chs 6–8, Carey 1995, Harris 1990, 2004, Lefkowitz 1993, Stewart 1995, Omitowoju 2002 and the essays in Deacy *et al.* 1997.

3 Halliwell 2002: 122.

4 Sommerstein 1998: 105.

5 As Sommerstein 1998: 105 notes, "[i]t is not always easy to draw a line distinguishing rape from non-rape in Old Comedy", and the ten examples he lists include not just instances "where, if the victim had been of citizen status, a charge of *hybris* might well seem appropriate", and where "physical force" is applied, but also examples where "the woman/boy is blatantly treated as a mere thing". In this chapter I have chosen to examine what I see as the four most clear-cut instances of rape. It should be noted, too, that two of Sommerstein's examples concern same-sex relations: the objectification of a non-speaking boy at *Eq.* 1384–6 and the Inlaw's stated preparedness to bugger the cross-dressing tragic poet Agathon at *Th.* 59–62.

6 On the rapes of New Comedy, see esp. Pierce 1997; Sommerstein 1998: 105, 110; Omitowoju 2002: 137–233. There is an important continuum between the conceptualization of sex in lyric (and especially sympotic) poetry and Old Comedy – as the presence of sexual assault fantasies in primarily *lyric* passages reflects. An important point of comparison, for instance, is the tendency of sex to be imagined rather than realized, the exceptions being mostly iambic (most famously the Cologne Archilochus, fr. 196a West-Merkelbach).

7 A further way of articulating the difference between Old and New Comic rapes is that rapes in New Comedy all qualify as acts of *moicheia* ("seduction") – which is never the case in Aristophanes. For an overview of scholarship on the crime of *moicheia*, see Robson 2013: 19–102; on *moicheia* as "seduction" (rather than "adultery"), see esp. Harris 1990.

8 For an overview of the legal possibilities for prosecuting rape in Athens, see Robson 2013: 110–13. There is, however, no unequivocal example of rape being prosecuted in an Athenian courtroom.

9 See e.g. Brown 1993; Pierce 1997; Scafuro 1997: 239–40, 246–59; Sommerstein 1998; Harris 2004: 43–4, 50–1.

10 Sommerstein 1998: 109 comes to a similar conclusion: "[r]ape in Old Comedy is, unashamedly, precisely what present-day feminists often declare it to be: it is an *aggressive* assertion of *superiority* – superiority of gender, superiority of social status, or (most often) both at once". An interesting point to consider when assessing the role of rape fantasy in any culture are the competing ways which Sutton outlines of understanding pornography. The *"peitho"* model essentially sees viewers persuaded to emulate what they see, while the *"catharsis"* model sees pornography as providing a release for potentially dangerous fantasies and passions (Sutton 1992: 6–7). Sutton leaves it to his readers to judge what kind of audience ancient Athenian men might have been.

11 Modern discussion of the vexed question as to whether women attended the dramatic festivals in significant numbers include Henderson 1991a; Goldhill 1997; Carter 2011: 49–50; Roselli 2011. Sommerstein 1997: 65 makes the point that "whether or not their audience actually was male or even nearly so, dramatists seem to regard it as such … On the whole it is true that dramatists, tragic and comic alike, wrote as male Athenian citizens for male Athenian citizens". The tension between actual and notional audience is explored by Henderson 1991a: 134 and Carter 2011: 52.

12 For an overview of scholarship on female consent, see Robson 2013: 102–5.

13 On the vocabulary of rape, see Cole 1984: 98: *adikēma* is not a word listed by Cole, but is used of forced sex at Hdt. 1.2 and Eur. fr. 272b (*Auge*); cf. Lys. 1.2. Rabinowitz 2011: 1–8 provides a thoughtful account of modern scholarship on rape and the issues of dealing with Greek sources (see also Robson 2013: 102–15). Harris's important study of rape in classical Athens (2004) demonstrates the key role that the perceived presence or absence of *hybris* played for the Greeks when it came to condemning or condoning rape. See also Harris, this volume.

14 As commentators on this passage are wont to point out, it is Phallic Songs, *ta phallika*, which are said by Aristotle (*Poet.* 4.1449a10–15) to be a precursor of comedy.

15 The translations in this chapter are based on those of Sommerstein 1980 (*Acharnians*), 1985 (*Peace*), 1987 (*Birds*) and 1990 (*Lysistrata*).

16 Silk 1980: 133, which he also calls "hybrid": see Silk 2000: 166–7, where he also discusses the reception of his earlier article.

17 Silk 2000: 180.

18 Silk 2000: 185.

19 Ibid. For a detailed analysis of the metre, see Parker 1997: 126–9.

20 Halliwell 2002: 122. For criticism of Silk's (and others') view of the ode, see Halliwell 2002: 120–2 and 136 n. 1.

21 Reckford 1987: 457; Henderson 1991b: 59–60; Bowie 1993: 26 – all quoted and commented on by Halliwell 2002: 121–2; cf. Reckford 1987: 48.

22 Halliwell (2002: 121) and Olson (2002: 263 n.) concur that the image here is of an urban *kōmos* in search of sexual opportunity. Halliwell notes the contrast between this and 271–5 where a solitary man is to be found in the most rural of settings (2002: 123): "adultery for Phales' urban phallus, rural rape for his own".

23 On the significance of *moichos*, see Todd 1993: 276–9; Olson 2002: ad loc.; Robson 2013: 91–8 (with references).

24 Olson 2002: 263 n.

25 Olson (2002: ad loc.) reasons that the last such Rural Dionysia would have been celebrated in late 432 and thus ἕκτῳ, "sixth", here "must be evidence either of a somewhat casual attitude towards chronology … or of the Greeks' occasional readiness to count exclusively".

26 For bibliography see Bowie 1993: 105 n. 12; Silk 2000: 186 n. 60.

27 This use of a remote, wild location is arguably present in lyric representations of sexual fantasy, too, such as Anacreon 417 (the Thracian filly).

28 Silk 2000: 123. Much of the imagery is drawn from wrestling: García Romero 1995: 59; Olson 2002: ll. 274–5 ad loc.

29 On *katagigartisai* see Starkie 1909: ad loc.; Taillardat 1965: 100; Henderson 1991b: 166; Halliwell 2002; and Olson 2002: ad loc., who adds to the discussion of this word the possibility that it evokes the act of penetration (as opposed to the squeezing out of a stone or pip): thus "stick my grape stone/penis into her".

30 M.S. Silk, "Putting on a Dionysus Show", *Times Literary Supplement* 28 August 1998.

31 Halliwell (2002: 122) – albeit on different grounds – talks of "the song's status as a microcosm of its genre".

32 Silk 2000: 187 " … we may suggest that such heartfelt exuberance is persuasive counsel for its own guilt-free standpoint; particularly so, when we note that the song is in no sense an individual's self-glorification: for Dicaeopolis' wife and daughter are both present and, indeed, given supporting roles in the celebratory ritual".

33 Indeed, this wilderness setting stands in stark contrast to the city in which Dicaeopolis is forced to reside prior to his private peace treaty; like the slave girl, this location is a fantasy which he alone can enjoy.

34 *Pace* Cohen who argues that slaves and foreigners – prostitutes included – were meaningfully protected by Athenian legislation concerning *hybris* (including from sexual exploitation: Cohen 2000: 116–23, 2005: 213–19).

35 Line 896b – πλαγίαν καταβάλλειν, εἰς γόνατα κύβδ' ἰστάναι – is omitted here: on which see Sommerstein 1985: ad loc.; Olson 1998: ad loc.

36 Henderson 1991b: 169. As Sommerstein 1998: 113 n. 17, notes – probably rightly – the chorus' stated intention to have sex with Opora at *Peace* 1337–40 (τρυγήσομεν αὐτήν, "we shall gather her vintage") "should be regarded as a jocular pretence".

37 There is, of course, no strict line to be drawn between tragic and comic versification as far as the iambic trimeter is concerned – rather, certain features such as resolution and the abuse of Porson's law occur with greater frequency in comedy. Nevertheless, as I have argued elsewhere, Aristophanes seems to be sensitive to the possibilities offered by versification for undermining or establishing a given register (what I have termed "clashes" and "coincidences"): Robson 2006, ch. 5, esp. 176–83.

38 On this metre, see West 1982: 53–4. The first "foot" of an anapaestic sequence is frequently spondaic. Tonally, the rhythm may serve to pull the listener in two directions. On the one hand, the rhythm is hardly "tragic compatible"; on the other, as Dover 1997: 161 comments: "dactylic and anapaestic rhythms have a double association with moralizing dicta and proverbs, and with heroic narrative".

39 See García Romero 1995: 67 and Olson 2002: ad loc. García Romero also comments at length on the agonistic(-cum-sexual) imagery in this passage (67–76). We may note, too, that the description of Theoria's assault not only shares imagery with that of Thratta in the Phallic Song but also its tendency to concreteness. Thus he says of *Peace* 894ff., 67: "[i]l ne s'agit pas de la description systématique d'une rencontre amoureuse, mais plutôt d'une succession de 'flashes', de moments isolés et concrets … ".

40 See scholia on this line: RVΓ, RV^bisΓ.

41 On this "build up" to the introduction of obscenities, see Robson 2014: 40–9, esp. 46–8.

42 A position for which a prostitute could command a large fee, too: see Davidson 1997: 118.

43 "Respectable" in this chapter is simply used to mean non-prostitute (on the problems inherent in the term see, e.g., Rabinowitz 2002: 134).

44 On another level, Theoria's allegorical nature (she is "Showtime" personified) already locates her in the realm of fantasy.

45 Relevant, too, is that the sex with respectable women was also punishable as *moicheia*, whereas sex with prostitutes was not: [Dem.] 59.66.

46 Once more, parallels with lyric are apposite here. As Kurke and others have argued (e.g. Kurke 1997) sympotic poetry tends to flatter female symposiasts, avoiding any mention of financial transaction (and indeed of words like "hetaira") and instead dwelling on the benefits of sexual union to the woman. This *Peace* passage could be said to "democratize" this *topos*: here the prostitute is available to all.

47 Zweig (1992: 77) lists only two examples of mute female characters not subject to exposure: the abstraction of Peace herself in *Peace* and the Queen of Heaven in *Birds*.

48 As Zweig, ibid., comments, "Peace is notably a time for men's unfettered enjoyment of women's sexuality", of which she list examples at 77–8. See also Sommerstein 1998: 109.

49 Sommerstein lists this passage as an example of a projected rape. Spondae certainly qualify as mute nude female characters and they are discussed sexually in language reminiscent of the *Peace* scene (cf., for instance, the use of καλός at *Eq.* 1390 and *Pax* 891, λαμβάνω at *Eq.* 1392 and *Pax* 847 and 875, and παραδίδωμι at *Eq.* 1394 and *Pax* 888). It must be said, however, that no *explicit* assault is envisaged. This also holds true for a number of other scenes which Sommerstein describes as rape, such as *Eq.* 1384–6, *V.* 768–9 and *Lys.* 160–6. Numerous other scenes where male characters make lustful comments about girls, women and boys, but where no assault is envisaged, have also been excluded from the present discussion. Worse Argument's statement at *Nu.* 1070 *is* of interest, however: γυνὴ δὲ σιναμωρουμένη χαίρει, "a woman enjoys being mauled".

50 Henderson 1987: 971–2 n. suggests that repetition is a "Euripidean mannerism" and views this ode, 973–9 n., as essentially a prayer with a surprise ending – a wish for Myrrhine to suffer forced copulation rather than death. Such tragic elements that there are doubtless provide an effective contrast to the ode's low features.

51 On this scene, see Dunbar 1995: 612–14 and 1253–6 n., who notes (613–14) that the assault of divine females was most likely a *topos* in satyr plays.

52 Iris would no doubt have appeared on the *ekkyklēma* and so have towered over Peisetaerus physically – a piece of staging that also illustrates the fact that she has arrived in Cloudcuckooland from the gods above.

53 It could be argued that another victim of assault, Theoria, is a "goddess", but her status and presentation is clearly different from that of Iris as is the way in which their assaults are envisaged.

54 On *diamēriō* see Dunbar 1995: 669 n.

55 Cf. the coinage used in respect of the mute Spondae at *Eq.* 1391, which, as Sommerstein comments (1998: 106) "ostensibly means something like 'thirty-yearise up them' but which can also, with only a little comic licence, be etymologised as 'pierce them three times'".

56 See Halliwell 2002: 125. For other instances of the jingle *gerōn ōn* see Dunbar 1995: ad loc.

57 See, for example, the readings of the play by Konstan 1997; von Möllendorff 2002: 108–13. *Pace* Henderson 1997, who argues for a mainly positive view of Peisetaerus' rule.

58 Leaving aside Sommerstein's more problematic examples: see n. 36 above.

59 A tension neatly summed up by Sharrock 1998: 184.

60 On the question of the importance of the woman's status to the way sexual assault is regarded, see Harrison 1997: 195.

61 Although Zweig 1992: 87 maintains that there is "no mutuality".

62 It is also important to note who articulates these fantasies. Characteristically, it is the male protagonist of the play (or in Cinesias' case, the male character with the largest role in the play). In other words, these fantasies routinely originate with the dominant male.

63 It is interesting that the idea of rape as punishment comes into more than one passage: Thratta is caught stealing (*Ach.* 272), Iris is threatened with rape *if she annoys* Peisetaerus (*Av.* 1253) and even Myrrhine is cast as wicked: she is called *miara*, "a villain" (*Lys.* 973). Perhaps there is more to say about Aristophanes legitimizing – or feeling he *has* to legitimize – acts of sexual aggression.

Bibiography

Bowie, A. (1993) *Aristophanes: Myth, Ritual and Comedy.* Cambridge: Cambridge University Press.

Brown, P. (1993) "Love and marriage in Greek New Comedy", *Classical Quarterly* n.s. 43: 189–205.

Carey, C. (1995) "Rape and adultery in Athenian law", *Classical Quarterly* n.s. 45: 407–17.

Carter, D.M. (2011) "Plato, drama and rhetoric", in D.M. Carter (ed.) *Why Athens?* Oxford: Oxford University Press, pp. 45–67.

Cohen, E. (2000) "'Whoring under contract': The legal context of prostitution in fourth-century Athens", in V. Hunter and J. Edmondson (eds) *Law and Social Status in Classical Athens.* Oxford: Oxford University Press, pp. 113–47.

——(2005) "Laws affecting prostitution at Athens", *Symposion: Vorträge zur griechischen und hellenistischen Rechtsgeschichte* 19: 201–24.

Cole S.G. (1984) "Greek sanctions against sexual assault", *Classical Philology* 79: 97–113.

Davidson, J. (1997) *Courtesans and Fishcakes: The Consuming Passions of Classical Athens.* London: HarperCollins.

Dover, K.J. (1997) *The Evolution of Greek Prose Style.* Oxford: Clarendon Press.

Dunbar, N. (1995) *Aristophanes: Birds.* Oxford: Clarendon Press.

García Romero, F. (1995) "Ἔρως Ἀθλητής: Les métaphores érotico-sportives dans les comédies d'Aristophane", *Nikophoros* 8: 57–76.

Goldhill, S. (1997) "The audience of Athenian tragedy", in P.E. Easterling (ed.) *The Cambridge Companion to Greek Tragedy.* Cambridge, Cambridge University Press, pp. 54–68.

Halliwell, S. (2002) "Aristophanic sex: The erotics of shamelessness", in M.C. Nussbaum and J. Sihvola (eds) *The Sleep of Reason: Erotic Experience and Social Ethics in Ancient Greece and Rome.* Chicago, IL and London: University of Chicago Press, pp. 120–42.

Harris, E.M. (1990) "Did the Athenians regard seduction as a worse crime than rape?", *Classical Quarterly* 40: 370–7.

——(1997) "Review article: Susan Deacy and Karen Pierce, eds., *Rape in Antiquity: Sexual violence in the Greek and Roman worlds*", *Échoes du monde classique/Classical Views* 41, n.s. 16: 483–96.

——(2004) "Did rape exist in classical Athens? Further reflections on the laws about sexual violence", *Dike* 7: 41–83 (repr. in E.M. Harris (2006) *Democracy and the Rule of Law in Classical Athens: Essays on Law, Society, and Politics*. Cambridge: Cambridge University Press, pp. 297–32).

Harrison, T. (1997) "Herodotus and the ancient Greek idea of rape", in S. Deacy and K.F. Pierce (eds) *Rape in Antiquity: Sexual Violence in the Greek and Roman Worlds*. London: Duckworth/Classical Press of Wales, pp. 185–208.

Henderson, J. (1987) *Aristophanes: Lysistrata*. Oxford: Oxford University Press.

——(1991a) "Women and the Athenian dramatic festivals", *Transactions of the American Philological Association* 121: 133–47.

——(1991b) *The Maculate Muse: Obscene Language in Attic Comedy*, 2nd edn. New York and Oxford: Oxford University Press.

——(1997) "Mass versus elite and the comic heroism of Peisetairos", in G.W. Dobrov (ed.) *The City as Comedy: Society and Representation in Athenian Drama*. Chapel Hill, NC and London: University of North Carolina Press, pp. 135–48.

Keuls, E. (1985) *The Reign of the Phallus: Sexual Politics in Ancient Athens*. Berkeley and Los Angeles, CA and London: University of California Press.

Konstan, D. (1997) "The Greek polis and its negations: Versions of utopia in Aristophanes' *Birds*", in G.W. Dobrov (ed.) *The City as Comedy: Society and Representation in Athenian Drama*. Chapel Hill, NI and London: University of North Carolina Press, pp. 3–22.

Kurke, L. (1997) "Inventing the *hetaira*: Sex, politics, and discursive conflict in archaic Greece", *Classical Antiquity* 16: 106–50.

Lefkowitz, M. 1993. "Seduction and rape in Greek myth", in A.E. Laiou (ed.) *Consent and Coercion to Sex and Marriage in Ancient and Medieval Societies*. Washington, DC: Dumbarton Oaks Research Library and Collection, pp. 17–37.

Olson, S.D. (1998) *Aristophanes: Peace*. Oxford: Oxford University Press.

——(2002) *Aristophanes: Acharnians*. Oxford: Oxford University Press.

Omitowoju, R. (2002) *Rape and the Politics of Consent in Classical Athens*. Cambridge: Cambridge University Press.

Parker, L.P.E. (1997) *The Songs of Aristophanes*. Oxford: Oxford University Press.

Pierce, K.F. (1997) "The portrayal of rape in New Comedy", in S. Deacy and K.F. Pierce (eds) *Rape in Antiquity: Sexual Violence in the Greek and Roman Worlds*. London: Duckworth/Classical Press of Wales, pp. 163–84.

Rabinowitz, N.S. (2002). "Excavating women's homoeroticism in ancient Greece: The evidence from Attic vase painting", in N.S. Rabinowitz and L. Auanger (eds) *Among Women: From the Homosocial to the Homoerotic in the Ancient World*. Austin, TX: University of Texas Press, pp. 106–66.

——(2011). "Greek tragedy: A rape culture?", *EuGeStA (Journal on Gender Studies in Antiquity)* 1: 1–21.

Reckford, K.J. (1987) *Aristophanes' Old-and-New Comedy*. Chapel Hill, NC and London: University of North Carolina Press.

Robson, J. (2006) *Humour, Obscenity and Aristophanes*. Tübingen: Narr.

——(2013) *Sex and Sexuality in Classical Athens*. Edinburgh: Edinburgh University Press.

——(2014) "Slipping one in: The introduction of obscene lexical items in Aristophanes", in S.D. Olson (ed.) *Ancient Reception and Comedy: Essays in Honour of Jeffrey Henderson*. Berlin and Boston, MA: De Gruyter, pp. 29–50.

Roselli, K.D. (2011) *Theater of the People: Spectators and Society in Ancient Athens*. Austin, TX: University of Texas Press.

Scafuro, A. (1997) *The Forensic Stage: Settling Disputes in Greco-Roman Comedy*. Cambridge: Cambridge University Press.

Sharrock, A. (1998) "Re(ge)ndering gender(ed) studies", in M. Wyke (ed.) *Gender and the Body in the Ancient Mediterranean*. Oxford: Blackwell, pp. 179–90.

Silk, M.S. (1980) "Aristophanes as a lyric poet", *Yale Classical Studies* 26: 100–51.

——(2000) *Aristophanes and the Definition of Comedy*. Oxford: Oxford University Press.

Sommerstein, A.H. (1980) *The Comedies of Aristophanes*, vol. 1: *Acharnians*. Warminster: Aris & Phillips.

——(1985) *The Comedies of Aristophanes*, vol. 5: *Peace*, 2nd edn. Warminster: Aris & Phillips.

——(1987) *The Comedies of Aristophanes*, vol. 6: *Birds*. Warminster: Aris & Phillips.

——(1990) *The Comedies of Aristophanes*, vol. 7: *Lysistrata*, 2nd edn. Warminster: Aris & Phillips.

——(1997) "The theatre audience, the *dēmos* and the *Suppliants* of Aeschylus", in C. Pelling (ed.) *Greek Tragedy and the Historian*. Oxford: Claredon Press, pp. 63–79.

——(1998) "Rape and young manhood in Athenian comedy", in L. Foxhall and J. Salmon (eds) *Thinking Men*, Leicester-Nottingham Studies in Ancient Society, vol. 7. London and New York: Routledge, pp. 100–14.

Starkie, W.J.M. (1909) *The Acharnians of Aristophanes*. London: Macmillan.

Stewart, A. (1995). "Rape?" in E.D. Reeder (ed.) *Pandora: Women in Classical Greece*. Princeton, NJ: Princeton University Press, pp. 74–90.

Sutton, R.F. Jr (1992) "Pornography and persuasion on Attic poetry", in A. Richlin (ed.) *Pornography and Representation in Greece and Rome*. New York and Oxford: Oxford University Press, pp. 3–35.

Taillardat, J. (1965) *Les images d'Aristophane: Études de langue et de style*. Paris: Belles Lettres.

Todd, S.C. (1993) *The Shape of Athenian Law*. Oxford: Clarendon Press.

von Möllendorff, P. (2002) *Aristophanes*. Hildesheim: Olms

West, D.L. (1982) *Greek Metre*. New York and Oxford: Clarendon.

Zweig, B. (1992) "The mute nude female characters in Aristophanes' plays", in A. Richlin (ed.) *Pornography and Representation in Greece and Rome*. New York and Oxford: Oxford University Press, pp. 73–89.

PART III

Republican, imperial and late-ancient Rome

19

THE BISEXUALITY OF ORPHEUS[1]

Matthew Fox

These phenomena of the play area have infinite variability, contrasting with the relative stereotypy of phenomena that relate either to personal body functioning or to environmental actuality.

(Winnicott 1971: 91)

Introduction

My aim in this contribution is not to offer new information about sex in antiquity, but rather to provide a different perspective on the question of sexuality and interiority, focused through Ovid's depiction of the bisexual Orpheus. Ovid tells Orpheus' story in the ninth to the eleventh books of the *Metamorphoses*, where his response to the double death of Eurydice is first a change of sexual partner (from Eurydice to boys), and then a series of narratives, in which Orpheus takes the role of the poet to tell myths dominated by problematic sexual unions (Pygmalion, Myrrha, Venus and Adonis). Orpheus has been a figure of particular interest in twentieth-century reception, acting as a kind of ur-artist for Rilke and Cocteau, and for the latter, an embodiment of his own preoccupations with art and homosexuality. Ovid's treatment of the mythical poet casts an interesting light on current conceptions of male homosexuality in Rome, and offers the opportunity to examine how ideas about ancient sexuality relate to the tactics we adopt in reading the sources that reveal them. My approach is explicitly literary in its orientation, but one purpose of this contribution is to demonstrate that literary dynamics and the history of sexuality cannot be neatly demarcated. This particular part of Ovid's epic demands a reading that takes questions of sexuality and questions of poetic creativity together. In what follows, some readers may feel that I sacrifice clear historical understanding for the purposes of unlocking poetic dynamics. I would argue that such a polarity itself is only one way of understanding the nature of historical investigation. If our historical categories do not serve to allow ancient texts to speak more eloquently, then they are failing in their main function.

Much current work on ancient sexuality presents itself as carrying out a kind of historical sociology. Evidence, taken mostly from fictional texts (poetry, novels, plays and dialogues), is treated as though it is recording values and opinions in a historical reality that is readily accessible.[2] The nature of the object of study in this work is seldom in doubt: even if ancient categories are taken to be fundamentally different from our own, we still want to know about ancient homosexuals. It is our interest in homosexuality in our own world that stimulates our interest in ancient sexuality. The causes for reflecting on the differences between our own handling of sexual behaviour and those represented in ancient literature are complex.[3] But it is difficult to know how far it is possible to think past so dominant a category as "homosexuality", especially since it (like its forerunners) has played so important a role in defining the difference between ancient and modern sexual values. Nevertheless, since Foucault, and even for those who dislike his work, it has been a core principle of gender research that differences in categorization will enable the distinctness of ancient practices and identities to be grasped in their historical specificity. Most scholarship on the history of sexuality proceeds as though the main obstacle to be overcome is difficulty in categorization, rather than the problem of evidence, as if ancient sexual practices and desires were in fact properly documented in the literature in which they are represented.

My difficulty with this approach comes in part from personal inclination towards historical scepticism. Concerning the far better recorded details of the political structures of the Roman Republic, P.A. Brunt wrote: "The historian of Rome can be likened to a man standing at the entrance of a cavern of vast and unmeasured dimensions, much of it impenetrably dark, but here and there illuminated by a few flickering candles" (Brunt 1988: 92). It seems to me those who are confident of the sexual dynamics of the Romans do not often exercise such caution.[4] In terms of the complex picture of love and relationships present in Roman poetry (whether in epic, elegy or satire), it is more convenient to present a clearly delineated set of dynamics that frame the evidence presented by individual poetic moments, than to attempt to contain a rich body of material within an analytical structure that is sufficiently flexible to allow for its complexity. The ideas of "performativity", and "self-fashioning", particularly as they have been explored in the Roman rhetorical context as a method for understanding how masculinity was "constructed", are good examples both of the virtues, but also of the shortcomings, of our existing paradigms.[5] The rigidity of a "construct", or the finite nature of "performance" are comfortably concrete metaphors for considering the expression of emotions. They provide an emblematic way of discussing behaviour, one that focuses on the outcome or product rather than the process. Such metaphors are particularly effective when discussing a goal-driven genre such as rhetoric or declamation. But a different perspective is opened up with the challenge laid down by the sentence from Winnicott that I have chosen as an epigraph. Put briefly, current models of ancient sexuality, concerned as they largely are with bodily function and with "environmental actuality" (the social arrangements which regulate the use of body, and its public presentation), do not pay sufficient attention to what is probably of far greater concern to the ancient authors who provide us with evidence. Like Winnicott, they too, I would argue, are concerned with "the play area": the workings of the imagination, of creativity and of dynamics in the inner world of the individual. They were also, like him, interested in how that world intersected with its more public expression, in the worlds of art, politics and religion.

We accept without question that sex is of vital importance to these realms in our own world. This essay argues that evidence does exist that it was of similar importance to the Romans, and that sex and sexuality need to be understood, at least in part, as the manifestation of emotional processes as much as social or political ones, and as opportunities for imaginative exploration. Roman sexual subjectivity is not just about the outside, about the public anxiety about the correct use of the body and social status of sexual partners. And even if being Roman was to a large extent thought of in those terms, we are not thereby obliged to pass over evidence of an interest in the inner life, and in the relationship between individual sexual expression and identity. In Rome too, homosexuality could be good to think with;[6] even to play with.

The metamorphosis of Orpheus' sexuality

Ovid's treatment of the story of Orpheus is a rare thing: a text that discusses directly an individual's change from one kind of sexual desire and behaviour to another. If Orpheus were alive today, we would not hesitate to call this a change of sexuality; our current models for Roman values, which focus on hierarchies rather than the gender of those who act as partners to a man, do not favour the idea that it is historically appropriate to talk of sexuality in that manner at all. But the juxtaposition of this episode with the one that immediately precedes it, telling of the love of Iphis for Ianthe that results in a change of actual sex, makes clear how important the ideas of sex and transformation are to the Orpheus episode.[7] Like the vast majority of metamorphoses in the poem, Iphis' depends on a corporeal alteration, from female to male. Orpheus' change is entirely internal, and the obvious thematic similarity with the Iphis/Ianthe episode raises the possibility that it is Orpheus' sexual behaviour, his choice of sexual partners, that is under scrutiny. In what follows, I shall explore the internal alternation in the poet that causes a change in the objects of his desires. It does, I think, give us reason to think about the relationship between inner life and sexual behaviour in a manner at odds with current critical trends.

We are used to thinking of (or aspiring to render accurately) a value-free equivalence in antiquity between boys and women as the targets or origins of desire. As Lucretius puts it:[8]

> sic igitur Veneris qui telis accipit ictus,
> sive puer membris muliebribus hunc iaculatur
> seu mulier toto iactans e corpore amorem,
> unde feritur, eo tendit gestitque coire
> et iacere umorem in corpus de corpore ductum.

> So the one who receives the blows of Venus' darts
> Whether a boy with girlish limbs has thrown it
> Or a woman, casting forth love from her whole body,
> He leans to the place he was struck from, desires to unite,
> And cast the fluid drawn from his body into the body.

> *(Lucr. 5.1052–6)*

Lucretius' deliberate repudiation of a distinction between desiring women and desiring boys is corroborated by much Latin poetry, and, indeed, much Greek. That situation would seem to reflect historical reality, so the scholarly neglect of the theme of sexuality in this part of *Metamporphoses* is itself expressive of the hermeneutic situation just discussed. However, Ovid seems to have a different sense of the matter, telling us, succinctly, in another poem, that he personally draws a distinction between love with women and love with boys. The reason is the fact that in his view, the sexual climax is not mutual:[9]

> odi concubitus, qui non utrumque resolvunt
> hoc est, cur pueri tangar amore minus.

> I hate acts of intercourse where both parties do not achieve release. That is the reason
> why I am less touched by the desire for a boy.

> *(Ars Am. 2.683–4)*

That is suggestive, and in expressing it as he does, Ovid makes clear that there is more at stake than simply sexual enjoyment. The idea of *tangar* (I am touched) encompasses the idea of emotional as well as physical fulfilment, and although it could be interpreted in a non-meta-phorical way, with *amor* as a physical force, I think it would be more accurate to see in the idea of "touched by *amor*" a deliberately broad range of meanings. The interaction of the poet with women is clearly richer than his interaction with boys; a state of affairs corroborated, of course, by the marginal role played by male partners in his *oeuvre*.

I bring in these two introductory texts in order to support a particular reading of the story of Orpheus. In different ways, they both suggest that his change of sexual partner is worth detailed scrutiny, and the passage from *Ars Amatoria* invites us to think about the emotional differences between love for women or boys as a possible topic for poetic treatment. In his elaboration of the story of Orpheus, Ovid allows us to see in more depth how Orpheus' rejection of women, and preference for boys, resonates with his psychic state. As the main point of the narrative is to explore Orpheus as a figure crushed by grief, we need not shy away from looking into his psyche. Orpheus' situation may not be typical, and most of our evidence for Roman sexual practice does not invite so close an interest in the interior drivers of sexual behaviour. But even admitting how unusual it is, Ovid's account of Orpheus' mentality does provide food for thought not just about the sudden preference for boys over women, but beyond that, through the disturbing subjects of the myths he himself narrates, about the darker side of sexuality more generally – the occasions where sexual behaviour expresses particularly problematic psychological states.

Following Hellenistic models (principally, it seems, the fourth-century BCE poet Phanocles) and Vergil, *Georgic* 4, Ovid depicts Orpheus as shattered by the death of his beloved Eurydice.[10] She had trodden on a poisonous snake in the dances following their marriage, and been carried off to the underworld. Orpheus' unique capacities as a poet enable him to enter that world, charm it into submission and strike a bargain with its rulers: to return to life with Eurydice on condition that he not look at her during the ascent. In lines of remarkable power, Ovid shows that the desire to look is stronger than reason, and as Eurydice slips back underground, she does not complain: for what should she complain of except that she was loved?[11] One point of the story is to introduce the idea that passion, desire and possession constitute a dangerous combi-nation, one that thwarts self-control, and places individuals in insufferable situations, an idea that is given ample airing in the rest of Book 10. More immediately, the manifestations of Orpheus' grief are his withdrawal to a mountainous wilderness, and the transferral of his erotic interests to young boys:[12]

> tertius aequoreis inclusum Piscibus annum
> finierat Titan, omnemque refugerat Orpheus
> femineam Venerem, seu quod male cesserat illi,
> sive fidem dederat; multas tamen ardor habebat
> iungere se vati: multae doluere repulsae.
> ille etiam Tracum populis fuit auctor amorem
> in teneros transferre mares citraque iuventam
> *aetatis breve ver et primos carpere flores.*

The third Sun had finished its year, closed by fishy Pisces, and Orpheus had shrunk from all womanly love; either because it had gone badly for him, or because he had given a pledge of fidelity. However a passion gripped many women to join themselves to the poet, and many grieved at rejection. For he was the instigator for the people of Thrace to transfer their love to tender males, and this side of youth, to snatch the brief spring of their age and the first flowers.

(Met. 10.79–86)

There are many interesting details here: the poet has two explanations for Orpheus' lack of interest in *venus feminea*: either some kind of pledge given to Eurydice, or because the turmoil produced by the loss of his wife acted as a deterrent. In other words, either his previous experience of love, with Eurydice, was so catastrophic that the idea of union with another woman became somehow impossible, or his fidelity to Eurydice left boys as the only option open to him. Another woman would have been a betrayal. The *tamen* (82) and *etiam* (84) suggest that the sequel was in some sense a consequence of his celibacy. Many women found him attractive, but, to their grief, he showed no interest in them: he had instead become the pioneer of paederastic love in Thrace. The causal chain is a clue to the end of Orpheus' story, and his life: the women, as maenads, take revenge in the grotesque Bacchanal with which the following book opens, and which culminates in the image of Orpheus' still-singing head floating down the river Hebrus, and the reuniting of Orpheus with Eurydice in the afterlife.[13] Perhaps in contrast to the brutality meted out by the women, the poet here chooses images of spring and flowers to depict the sexual pleasure to be had from young men of a certain age. It is impossible to say, I think, how aberrant Orpheus' tastes would seem to Ovid's readers. Thrace is not Rome, so perhaps there is a degree of distancing. Our conventional view of Roman erotics makes even the idea of *multae doluere repulsae* ("many women grieved at their rejection") more likely to be a description of an imaginary world than any form of female behaviour recognizable from the discussion of sexual roles in historical Rome.

Perhaps, along similar lines, Orpheus' taste for particularly young boys conjures up a strange fictional world in the mythic past, in which real paedophilia took place, even if it was unpopular with women; and where, until Orpheus' arrival, such love was unknown. *Citra iuventam* allows for the possibility that *iuventa* was a more usual stage at which young men could be found attractive: the age, presumably, at which adolescents were thought of as sexually appealing.[14] On the other hand, the intensity of the imagery suggests that Ovid is playing on his readers' own erotic sensibilities, drawing them in to sympathize with the poet's desires. That interpretation would be supported by the paederastic myths that occur in the remainder of the book, mostly given as embedded narratives from Orpheus himself, which certainly employ the familiar dynamic of evoking the allure of the beloved as a way of involving the reader in the unfolding plot. My aim in picking apart these lines is in part to show how difficult a matter it is to locate a clear idea of sexual behaviour that corresponds to anything we can realistically surmise about how such matters were handled in Ovid's own world. The text produces its own world, and (as so often) it is unclear how that world connects with historical reality.[15]

The question of the relation of this story to the nature of Roman sexuality is not limited to the evaluation of the particular kinds of activity either that Orpheus enjoyed, or that Ovid's readers would have regarded as outside the range of acceptable behaviour. In the story of Orpheus' bisexuality, there is a larger challenge to our paradigms. The move from devoted husband to paederast is presented as having complex psychological ramifications, and there is something perverse and dangerous about the transition. In both Vergil and Ovid, Orpheus' tragic death is the direct result of his repudiation of the local women, and in Ovid (as in Phanocles), that rejection of intercourse with women is compounded by his turning towards young men. Such a scenario is a far cry from the prevailing orthodoxies concerning Roman masculinity. The idea that choice of sexual object is determined by an internal emotional state is one that is absent from constructivist, identity-based or performance-centred notions of sexuality. Such approaches do not generally allow for an examination of the relationship between subjectivity and sex, since sexual behaviour is a marker of an external attribute: identity based upon social and economic position and gender, and carefully preserved against violation of conventional categories.[16]

It may be true in a historical sense that ancient societies were closely regulated and con-formist. But this "fact" has lulled scholars into accepting the idea that behavioural patterns and social expectations were static and clearly defined, and material (such as the Orpheus story) that demands a different model for examining images of action and behaviour can be passed over. There is nothing in the prevalent models of ancient masculinity that can account for Orpheus' choice of boys over women. His position as penetrating adult male remains unaltered, and this places him, even in fiction, in the role of a normal man. Nor does the idea of woman's revenge against paederasty find any echo in current conceptions of norms of Roman sexuality. But this is precisely the value of this episode. Ovid's treatment makes it clear that something unusual is going on in Orpheus' psyche, and the narrative which Orpheus delivers over the course of *Metamorphoses* 10 is noteworthy for its interest in the perverse. It may be, therefore, that our sense of Roman normality can thereby be left untouched: if an ancient Greek poet comported himself in this way, then that need not trouble conceptions of Roman sexual orthodoxy. But to pursue that interpretation would be to squander the much richer opportunities which Ovid's texts offer: to see what it is that interests Ovid in his exploration of Orpheus' inner world. In the end, that in itself may motivate us to rethink categorizations that are too eagerly historicist.

Orpheus' imagination

Orpheus announces the theme of his narrative in the following manner:

"ab Iove, Musa parens, (cedunt Iovis omnia regno)
carmina nostra move! Iovis est mihi saepe potestas
dicta prius: cecini plectro graviore Gigantas
sparsaque Phlegraeis victricia fulmina campis.
nunc opus est leviore lyra, puerosque canamus
dilectos superis inconcessisque puellas
ignibus attonitas meruisse libidine poenam."

"Mother Muse, make Jove the start of our poetry (everything is subject to the rule of Jove). Often before I've spoken of the power of Jove: I have sung with a heavier plectrum of the Giants, and the thunderbolts of victory scattered over the Phlegraean fields. Now a lighter lyre is needed, and let us sing of boys desired by the gods and girls surprised by illicit fires to deserve, through passion, their punishment."

(Met. 10.148–54)

There are clearly multiple layers of meaning in these lines.[17] But it is the combination of two distinct elements that give the poetic programme its most salient characteristics. We find first the narrowing of the poetic range more familiar from elegy, and most clearly elaborated by Propertius (*leviore lyra*). Then there is the choice of theme: boys beloved by the gods, and girls who succumbed to illicit desire and who end up paying the penalty. By combining these two ideas, Orpheus borrows the confessional *persona* of the elegist, but standing in for themes taken from the life of the poet are these two particular types of *eros*. The interesting question, of course, is how far these themes do in fact re-enact the personalizing rhetoric of elegy, even though they are not ostensibly autobiographical. The poetic aspirations of the elegist, associated with the slighter poetics, bring with them subjects more personal than those of the epic tales to which he is more accustomed.

These girls and boys do not seem to correspond immediately to that agenda, beyond the fact the love stories are more suited to a lighter genre than to epic. But clearly enough, the boys desired by gods can be aligned to Orpheus' own sexual metamorphosis. The illicit, and punished, desires of girls are less obvious in their relevance, but it is not a big leap to connect the dismal vision of doomed passion to the negative experience of Orpheus with Eurydice. There thus emerges the possibility that the stories of misalliance that follow are a displacement of the internal disturbance that characterizes Orpheus' situation. The key to reading Orpheus as a poetic emblem, and as a character, is to understand these bad love stories as expressions of his own troubled perspective on love.

Fitting to the character of the poem, the stories all involve some kind of metamorphosis. In those transformations we find further confirmation that the loss of Eurydice has brought Orpheus not only to a change of love object, but to a particularly negative view of what love itself consists of. This should not surprise us. After all, the second death of Eurydice has put Orpheus in a unique relationship to love and attachment. Rather than, as an ordinary mortal, having to accept the death of his wife, he has had the power to use his skill as a poet and musician to resurrect her, only to have her die again. Ovid's elaboration of that situation presents Orpheus as a figure in an extreme process of mourning, but also as one who has an exaggerated view of the nature of emotional attachment and separation. Ordinary humans can resurrect a dead person only in the imagination.[18] Orpheus has done it in actuality, and by virtue of his potent poetic power. It is therefore appropriate that in his proem he promises the loves of the Gods, those embodiments of omnipotence, as subject matter; and when he starts the sequence with Jupiter's love for Ganymede we would be right to sense that he is not just taking Jupiter as a starting point, but that he is also identifying with him. Jupiter is the king of the gods, Orpheus the incorporation of the ultimate in poetic power. They are brought together here as lovers of young men.

In part, the myths do fulfil this opening programme, while also sustaining Ovid's own interest in metamorphosis.[19] Orpheus' tales respond well both to the demands of his explicit programme, and to the pressure for a metamorphosis to round off each episode – the exact nature of the metamorphosis responding to Orpheus' obsession with erotic impossibilities (an obsession, of course, that is shared by many of the narrators in the poem). Jupiter's love for Ganymede finds him transformed into an eagle. Phoebus' for Hyacinthus involves the death and transfiguration of the beloved.[20] That of Pygmalion for his sculpture mirrors the transition from inanimate to animate that characterizes Orpheus' grief (see pp. 342–3). By turning ivory to flesh, it also reverses the petrifaction that is the punishment of the Propoetides, the compatriots of Pygmalion, who raise such disgust in him that he prefers his manufactured mistress to any living woman.[21] The lineage of Pygmalion links the remaining stories in the book; his grand-daughter Myrrha's incestuous passion for her father forming the dramatic centrepiece of the book, and Myrrha's son/brother, Adonis, inspiring his mistress, the goddess Venus herself, in her own aetiology of her hatred of hunting and wild beasts as she tells the long story of Atalanta. Adonis is woven more closely into the thematic coherence of the book, in that his ability to attract Venus is revenge for Myrrha's passion.[22] By the death of Adonis, Venus is punished for inspiring the worst form of incestuous passion in Myrrha.

That Orpheus' contemplation of the perverse aspects of love should produce a long mono-logue where he dramatizes a failed passion of Venus herself reminds us that Orpheus' inspiration is drawn not from some abstract interest in perversity, but from a desire to explore a topic that we can perhaps best encapsulate in a question: "Why, even when we are capable of exercising a high degree of control over the natural world, are we unable to remain in charge of the one thing upon which our own happiness depends?" Orpheus' stories all share this preoccupation, and they gain coherence if we interpret the tales as explorations of the powerlessness of the individual to control the outcome of his passions. His unprecedented power to charm trees, stones, even the underworld, did not enable him to control his desiring gaze long enough to see Eurydice return to the world of the living. That sense of the ability of desire, and sexual obsession, to cause the individual to fail (even if that individual is a god), and to find that their desire overcomes both their will and their sense of self-preservation, is a recurrent theme in the stories Orpheus tells.

So what picture of love does Orpheus provide? There are a number of coherent threads. Most obvious among them is that in all these episodes, love occurs in conjunction with separation: in some episodes enormous obstacles are overcome in order for the union to take place at all (Myrrha, Pygmalion, Atalanta); in others, metamorphosis results as compensation for the loss of, or final severing from, the beloved (Hyacinthus, Adonis – and Cyparissus, though he lies outside Orpheus' narration). All these obstacles point to one inevitable lesson: the encounter with the other, in Orpheus' discourse, is an intensely problematic arena. In every episode, there is an incompatibility between the partners, whether because of their divine or human status, or because of social taboo. In the case of Pygmalion, the gulf is between animate and inanimate. The poet's inspiration comes from fantasizing ways through what, in this universe, is the impossible nature of the loving relationship. Given the intensity of Orpheus' grief, it makes sense to regard this series of stories as a form of mourning: Orpheus is trying to work out his own grief, and the stories that he narrates show him reordering ideas of desire and loss in an attempt to find some kind of inner peace. The prelude (narrated by Ovid in the description of the grove that gathers round to hear Orpheus' song, 10.86–147) makes the central topic of mourning clear enough: it is the story of Cyparissus, beloved of Apollo, who kills himself in grief over his beloved pet stag, and whose final plea to the god is to be able to mourn for all time, *ut tempore lugeat omni* (10.135). He thus becomes the cypress tree, symbol of mourning.[23]

Some of the stories have a recuperative, wish-fulfilment quality, suggesting that Orpheus is approaching a satisfactory sense of closure. Others are more ambiguous in their resolution, and suggest not just that love is doomed and desire at best futile, but also that it is dangerous to the integrity of the self, as Orpheus knows from his own experience. Outside his song, he has found paederasty the appropriate response to his own catastrophe, and there is some reflection of that solution within the song: Jupiter's love for Ganymede involves his changing himself into an eagle. That could be read as a redemptive trajectory. The transformation into an eagle is ennobling and appropriate to the grandeur of Jupiter, as well as effective in enabling the conquest to succeed. But although it is one of the few "happy endings" in Orpheus' book, it is still one in which even the supreme being feels required to find a new corporeal form.[24] As in the story of Iphis, love cannot be fulfilled by remaining within the standard human form (though in this case, divine). Similar is Phoebus' love for Hyacinthus, which results in the transformation of the beloved into the flower. It is a parable of aesthetic sublimation, of desire moving beyond the body to a beautiful eternal reminder. But in both cases, the outcome of passion for a boy could hardly be described as an affirmation of identity, for either partner.

We have the sense that Orpheus' paederastic relationships may not be very satisfying, an idea present in Phanocles' account.[25] Do his imaginings of heterosexual love provide a happier ending, even though this is a form of erotic gratification he has now rejected? Pygmalion's desire for his sculpture mirrors the transition from inanimate to animate that marked Orpheus' grief earlier: at the point of Eurydice's death, Ovid provides two *exempla* featuring petrification (10.64–71: a nameless man, Olenos and Lethaea). So the metamorphosis of Pygmalion's sculpture suggests overcoming the rigidity of that grief, the thawing of the stoniness which is Orpheus' response to loss. If stone is death, the strength of Orpheus' love for Eurydice produces the fantasy of

Pygmalion's statue brought to life, and as Sharrock showed, the idea of the manufactured female beloved is a metaphor for the poetic process itself.[26] So at first sight Orpheus is taking comfort in an idealization of heterosexuality, and an optimistic vision of the power of the creative artist. By imagining an artist who can bring life even out of ivory, Orpheus/Ovid is replaying the vision of poetic mastery; except, of course, it is only through Venus' intervention that he avoided the rather alarming life, so vividly depicted at 10.252–69, of adoring an ivory mannequin. Pygmalion's story is a close reversal of the punishment of the Propoetides, those compatriots whose shamelessness spurs him (Pygmalion) to prefer an inanimate manufactured mistress. As well as the optimistic vision, therefore, there is also, in this section of the narrative, a sense of futility and, in the sequel (Myrrha's passion for her father), that futility becomes more negative, leading to catastrophe. It is not difficult to detect a disturbing misogyny in this entire section, one that mirrors Orpheus' own rejection of *venus feminea*:[27]

> sunt tamen obscenae Venerem Propoetides ausae
> esse negare deam; pro quo sua numinis ira
> corpora cum fama primae vulgasse feruntur,
> utque pudor cessit, sanguisque induruit oris,
> in rigidum parvo silicem discrimine versae.

> But the obscene Propoetides dared to deny that Venus is a goddess: for this, by the anger of her divinity, they are said to have been the first who spread both their bodies and their reputation among the people. And as their shame failed, and the blood of the face congealed, with little difference they were turned into rigid flint.
>
> *(Met. 10.238–42)*

The Propoetides are petrified because they are incapable of proper expressions of shame when they cross the boundary into prostitution.[28] As the product of Orpheus' imagination, they represent a grim response to heterosexuality, against which Pygmalion's idealized lifeless woman makes sense. Blushing and shame are the appropriate response to transgression, while vulgarizing their bodies and reputation is the corollary of failing to recognize that Venus as a goddess. It is worth noting that although his grief makes him reject *venus* in its female version, in most of Orpheus' narrative, Venus the goddess is strongly idealized, manifesting some of the characteristics of power she has in Lucretius. The idealization results in a splitting of his narrative material into the idealizing and the abjected. The dichotomy between, on the one hand, desire and life, and, on the other, death and desire's end, comes to be expressed as a dialectic between flesh and not-flesh, and in the Pygmalion episode in particular, it is the power of Venus that enables that transition to occur.

Theodorakopoulos has pointed out, adopting concepts from Melanie Klein, that Ovid is concerned throughout *Metamorphoses* with a cycle of grief and reparation. She argues that the dynamic of metamorphosis itself reflects an ongoing process whereby anxiety is expressed in terms of disintegration, and that the way in which that anxiety is allayed is through a fantasy of reintegration, of bodily wholeness which constitutes a form of reparation.[29] The advantage of this approach is that it provides a basis for looking at the poem as the charting of a continuous process of emotional variation, rather than pinning down the individual metamorphoses as parables. Klein's work was taken further by Winnicott, both of them sharing an interest in thinking about fundamental emotional attachments as "internal objects".[30] That approach is useful for analysing a text like this, in which a set of stories are themselves the expression of an internal mental state, and where the fantastic context, both of the poem as a whole, and of Orpheus' narrative in particular, provides an opportunity for unfettered imaginative elaboration.[31] The optimistic notion of reparation does not by itself do justice to the pessimistic and often grotesque quality of much of Ovid's narration, although in psychological terms, imaginative responses to trauma can, as well as heal, also continue to reinforce the trauma. From that perspective, the idea that Orpheus' narrative is a space in which "internal objects" can be repeatedly rearranged, and given a variety of narrative resolutions, in a response to unresolved grief, gives a useful coherence to the entire episode.

The reference to Orpheus' love for boys is, in this context, tantalizingly brief, and Ovid does not give enough information to enable it to be interpreted as either a healing, or a traumatic, behaviour. Nor, as I suggested above, do the dynamics of the particular myths produce a neat idea of Orpheus resolving his grief through the production of satisfactorily compensatory paederastic poetry. Thus it is difficult to form a view about how that choice relates to the disturbing vision of relationships that his stories express. Perhaps it is just a refuge from more complex amatory dynamics. The fact that Ovid does not elaborate on his explanation for Orpheus' change, nor allow space in the poem for his experience outside the secluded grove, nor, indeed, give us any information about the lives of his sexual partners, would reinforce such an interpretation. Equally, the withdrawal from the world, and the immersion in morbid contemplation of the erotics of failure, could suggest that paederasty represents some kind of minimal compensation, the only kind of union in which the poet could find pleasure, given his evident difficulty with women.

That image emerges more clearly in Phanocles' version, and is hinted at by Ovid's minimal explanation, that he bestowed his love on boys because things had gone badly for him hitherto (*male cessserat illi*). Beyond these rather minimal fragments, the only source for a deeper understanding is Orpheus' narration itself. Within that, two aspects seem to me to be particularly revealing, even if the core of Ovid's view of Orpheus' change remains mysterious: the impossibility of a satisfactory process of mourning for Eurydice, and the related interest in the interface between the body, desire and the environment. In Orpheus' grief-laden universe, the boundaries between these elements become unusually unstable even by the poem's own extreme standards; and Ovid is not slow to mark the moral and emotional transgressions which are then matched by the chaotic reordering of the internal and external worlds.

What does Orpheus want?

To my mind, the obvious answer to this question is Eurydice.[32] But where is she in his narrative? In the processes of pathological mourning described by Klein (1948) and Bowlby (1980), grief-stricken individuals fixate upon the person they have lost. Ovid takes a different tack. Rather than giving us repeated references to Eurydice, he removes her entirely from the text, except when Orpheus returns to her in death, when he is able to gaze at her safely once more, thus overcoming the trauma of the fatal backward gaze that triggered the catastrophe:

> hic modo coniunctis spatiantur passibus ambo,
> nunc praecedentem sequitur, nunc praevius anteit
> Eurydicenque suam iam tutus respicit Orpheus.

> Now with their paces joined they walk together, now he follows her as she leads, now in front he goes before her, and now Orpheus looks back safe at his Eurydice.

(Met. *11.64–6*)

Taking a lead from those theories, there is a certain logic that can help diagnose Orpheus' dysfunctional mourning. As his poetry avoids those ideas of positive and successful love which the memory of Eurydice might provide, so his fantasies revolve around perversion, and his stories repeatedly demonstrate the failures of desire. The displacement of Eurydice in his imagination matches the fact that Orpheus has achieved in life what most mourning can only dream of, the return of the lost beloved. Having lost her again, he has also lost all interest in the conventional mourning process. What he is left with is the love of boys, and a barely restrained interest in illicit sexual unions. The most disastrous of all these forms the centrepiece of Book 10: the story of Myrrha's passion for her father. It is singled out by a dramatic second prologue, a clear sign of the pivotal role of this episode:

> dira canam; procul hinc natae, procul este parentes;
> aut, mea si vestras mulcebunt carmina mentes,
> desit in hac mihi parte fides, nec credite factum;
> vel, si credetis, facti quoque credite poenam.

> I will sing dire matters: go far from here, daughters, be far from here, parents. Or, if my songs will charm your minds, may trust in me here be lacking, and don't believe what was done. Or, if you believe it, also believe in the punishment.

> *(Met. 10.300–3)*

The word *poena* here, repeated from Orpheus' first prologue (10.154), reinforces the idea of punishment for perverse desire, a punishment that is in this case the transformation of Myrrha, after a long and novelistic account of her scheme to get her own father into bed, into the endlessly weeping myrrh tree. At a stretch, Atalanta too can be thought to be among those girls who paid a penalty for their desire, but effectively, Orpheus' first prologue refers to Myrrha, and the reiteration here of the word *poena* grants prominence to the sense of sexual transgression and punishment. An extended discussion of the Myrrha would lengthen this chapter inordinately.[33] The crucial feature is what Nagle terms the "prurience" of the narrative: in the face of the exhortation to disbelieve, Ovid produces (predictably) a luridly vivid narrative, drawing on a range of familiar tropes of unrequited love which give the taboo-breaking quality of Myrrha's passion a hyper-real quality, and which heighten reader involvement. The effect is disorientating: a further demonstration of the power of Ovid–Orpheus' verse, able to conjure even the most unthinkable act in elegant language which will, as he predicted, charm (*mulcebunt*) the readers into following this "romance" even into the parental bed.

It is a different way of dramatizing Orpheus' interest in the furthest extremes of desire, which are depicted with a repulsive kind of appeal.[34] As Orpheus' prologue predicts, we read this, but would rather not be doing so. The rescue, if there is one from this abyss, comes gradually, first in the small details of the metamorphosis itself, then in the continuation of the narrative sequence into more optimistic territory. Myrrh is, after all, a useful commodity: *est honor et lacrimis* (10.501), says Ovid, describing the permanent reminder of Myrrha's story in the reputation for myrrh as a product:

> quae quamquam amisit veteres cum corpore sensus,
> flet tamen et tepidae manant ex arbore guttae.
> est honor et lacrimis, stillataque robore myrrha
> nomen erile tenet nulloque tacebitur aevo.

Although she has lost her old senses with her body, she still weeps and warm tears exude from the tree. Those tears are honoured too, and the myrrh lifted from the bark has a high name, and in no age will it fail to be spoken of.

(Met. 10.499–502)

A minimal benefit can emerge even from this story of perverse desire, and tears themselves can be a boon.[35] But immortality is double edged. The metamorphosed tears are a sign of the perpetuation of Myrrha's grief, while their eternal reputation is an allegory for Ovid's own aspirations to fame.[36]

It is not difficult to see the resonance of these ideas to Orpheus. The preoccupation with survival, reputation, death and grief is also manifest in the account of his death (Met. 11.1–84), lending greater coherence to isolated motifs in Orpheus' narration. The central idea is expressed in the dialectic of flesh and non-flesh to which I have already referred: stone, wood, ivory; and in the idea of posthumous perpetuation, itself a kind of concretization of subjectivity beyond the individual human life. We find examples of the permanent and renewable immortalization of grief (Cyparissus, Hyacinthus, Myrrha), and of continuing to grieve even after the loss of the body (Myrrha, Orpheus). Myrrha's grief has a more useful material outcome than the other plant metamorphoses, and the motif of productive tears, even in the face of such dire subject matter, provides some possibility of progress, albeit only by producing a continual reminder of mourning. Or perhaps it is in this idea of mourning as a permanent state that Orpheus tries to find redemption, since it is the nature of poets' work to aim at perpetuation. Notions of compensation and reparation only provide a partial explanation, but other aspects of Orpheus' tales, in particular the sexual symbolism of some of the details of the narrative, do suggest a more active dynamic of libido and gratification that opens a further perspective.

After Orpheus has finished singing of the Propoetides, and of Pygmalion and his descendants, Ovid comes to describe the missiles of the maenads that destroy the poet. His song is powerful enough initially to deflect them harmlessly from the sky, but as they drown out his music, its magical effect is lost, and the stones fulfil their trajectory. The forces of creativity and destruction are in tension, and that tension has a libidinous quality, as if poetic creation were itself some kind of sexual process. Much of Metamorphoses, as, indeed, much of Ovid's other poetry, expresses that idea.[37] We are dealing with a dynamic of desire, expressed in terms of hardening and softening, tension and slackening, a corporeal preoccupation that is familiar in a poet whose major concern is desire.[38] There is not a simple equation that supports the idea of phallic symbolism in the details of these stories, whereby desire is consistently connected to moments of rigidity, and the change to flesh to the softening after gratification. But there is a different type of pattern. The drive to destroy Orpheus becomes a firm line of fire once the maenads' voices have cancelled out that of the poet: the stones themselves then inflict their damage. They are propelled by revenge, revenge that comes from a thwarted desire for intercourse with Orpheus: en hic est nostri contemptor, "behold our despiser", exclaims the leading Bacchant.[39] So there is a phallic, goal-orientated quality to the flight of the stones, properly realized once the effect of the poet's voice has been eliminated and becoming an orgy of destruction. This is an inexact reversal of the potency that enables Pygmalion, as the gratification of his desire, to bring his sculpture into flesh. The softening of the ivory is the resolution of his story, and the culmination of his creative effort. While the sculpture remains inanimate, his desire remains heightened, its gratification deferred. As it becomes human, his desire can be fulfilled, but that also marks the end of Pygmalion's narrative thread. The maenads' missiles mirror this dynamic: their aim is thwarted, and the rigidity of their trajectory continually slackened, as long as the poet can sing. But as soon as they cannot hear him, they fly to their target, putting an end to his life, and to his narrative presence – excepting the pathetic epilogue of the singing severed head, and the only – inevitable – conclusion: that Orpheus can only find peace and silence in being reunited with Eurydice in death. Ovid kills Orpheus off, but this act of poetic suicide is, following a suggestion of Klein's, a way of reuniting the poetic self with its loved object, rather than allowing the revenge of the maenads to triumph.[40] The maenads, conversely, continue in the story, until Bacchus punishes them by transforming them into a grove. Desire here is productive and destructive in turns, and creativity is sometimes working with desire to produce gratification, and sometimes against it, to thwart and silence it, often in the most sadistic terms. Ovid uses Orpheus to explore his interest both in the stasis that immortalization entails, and in the sexualized tensions that allow the love poet to work. It is a dynamic that, as this *carmen perpetuum* itself demonstrates, can never be satisfactorily resolved.

The behaviour of external objects cannot properly be seen as different from the behaviour of human bodies: they are both, after all, the products of poetic imagination. The stories told here underline that point, making the alteration of the body a marker of the limits of human agency, and of the moral independence of the universe from human wishes. The Propoetides' narrative moment is brief: their flesh changes not through the action of their own desire, but as a manifestation of the bodily functions themselves. The act of blushing in shame, understood as a normal bodily response, is extrapolated to the flow of blood, and life in general, in the body, so that once it is suspended, animation comes to an end, and bodies are petrified.

Although only one short anecdote, it is crucial for Orpheus' discourse, since it suggests an autonomous physical truth, a corporeal reality that limits the idea of the individual having control over their physical, and indeed sexual, fate. The thought is entirely appropriate to the man who has been able to exert the power to bring the underworld to a halt, but who has not been able to quell his desire to gaze upon his beloved; it is useful to remember Lacan's definition of the gaze as almost like a bodily organ.[41] Although the notion of *poena*, punishment, entails the idea that the individual could have behaved differently, in all of Orpheus' tales, the protagonists, gods included, are driven by forces beyond themselves, and suffer the physical consequences. The Propoetides' own bodies, as, indeed, Myrrha's, decide their fate, restoring moral balance.[42] There is a sad inevitability too in Orpheus' fate: the revenge of the maenads intertwined with his sexual alteration, which, in the light of the surrounding context, we can more confidently interpret as dictated by his own body: an unreflecting expression of a physical desire, rather than any deliberate choice. Ovid's own equivocation on the causes of Orpheus' turn to paederasty discourages the view that it was driven by any kind of reason or consciousness. The manner in which Orpheus describes the dynamics of desire, in the stories that he tells, also evokes its involuntary nature. Only the maenads see it as reprehensible, and there is no trace, I think, of Ovid showing their retribution as justified.[43] Indeed, their brutal punishment, turned (like Myrrha) to trees, and the outpouring of grief from the whole of nature on the poet's death, present it as a tragedy.[44] But it is clearly the rejection of women that has led to Orpheus' death, and that rejection is an expression of the same dark vision of love which runs through his song.

Orpheus' excessive mourning provides Ovid with plenty of material: stories that revolve around the tightening and slackening of desire, and which measure the erotic stakes against basic bodily function. So many of them end with the extinction of the body that it is best to understand Orpheus' own narrative as a final poetic act: a speculative shuffling of the objects of desire by one for whom ultimate gratification lies in death. That shuffling, however, is still carried out with an eye to eternity, and to the productive value of song. In these terms there is little to distinguish Orpheus' narrative from much of the rest of *Metamorphoses*. That in itself, however, strengthens the argument that Ovid is using the archetypal poet to explore a wider preoccupation with the dynamics of desire and loss in imaginative production.

Conclusions

Metamorphoses is a rich and chaotic piece of writing, a fantastic elaboration upon change that cannot easily be pressed into service to provide information about historical reality. Fantasy, however, will always reveal something about reality, and fantasy will always need it to provide the component elements which it can reorder and distort. I am still tempted to draw some relatively simple conclusions regarding the light shed by the Orpheus episode on Roman sexual values. Orpheus' sexuality is conditioned by his emotional state, and the dynamics of sexuality are linked directly by Ovid to that state. The condition of the lover of boys, in this case, appears to be one predicated on psychic self-sufficiency, a physical manifestation of the flight from the lost beloved which has its fantastic counterpart in the troubling stories of thwarted love that Orpheus tells.

All the subjects in Orpheus' narrative have insurmountable difficulties with the objects of their desire, and in parallel, Ovid spends no words on describing the poet's boy-partners. That fact in itself does to some degree reinforce the current orthodoxies of masculinity: passive partners in homosexual pairs only enter the textual record when their age and status make such a role inappropriate, and they thus become the target of satire, polemic or forensic attack.[45] Recalling the comment in *Ars Amatoria* on the absence of pleasure for *pueri* as Ovid's sexual partners, it seems that by casting Orpheus as a paederast, he is designating him as someone who is unconcerned about their sexual pleasure. Calling him the *auctor* of paederasty in Thrace, he may be suggesting a political gesture to disseminate this mode of subjectivity; although perhaps the word just suggests that he is the first (as well as reminding readers to be aware of the overlap between Orpheus and Ovid). At all events, Orpheus' removal from humankind is mirrored in what he imagines human love consists of, and a correspondence between that, his inordinate creativity, and his sexual preference, lies at the centre of this text.

I hope I have succeeded in establishing that questions of literary interpretation cannot be sidestepped when using ancient texts in the discussion of sex and sexuality. We cannot understand Orpheus' paederasty without also coming to a view about how far Ovid's technique encourages us to regard it as a perversion, or as a guilty pleasure, shared with his readers. Nor can we get a full sense of what paederasty means, as an alternative to marital fidelity, without considering the reflections on love, relationships and sexuality with which Orpheus' narrative is invested. The text itself, to my eyes, does not offer simple conclusions, nor a coherent picture of how sexuality and creativity intersect. But if the picture is less clear in historical terms, I hope that these reflections on the erotic dynamics of the narrative, and on the relationship between the workings of poetic imagination and sexuality, will nevertheless appear pertinent. There is in this text a preoccupation with the connection between grief, mourning, subjectivity and poetry, which will continue to demand our attention, even as it defeats a linear analysis. It is also a text that makes clear that sex cannot be separated from broader conceptions about the dynamics of narrative, about the image of the body and about the emotional world of readers, both ancient and modern.[46]

Notes

1 I use the terms "sexuality", "bisexuality" and "homosexuality" for the sake of convenience, and in an attempt to keep what is at times a dense paper at least stylistically uncluttered. Readers should not thereby forget that these are modern terms, which have more unwanted anachronistic associations than circumlocutions such as "same-sex desire/sexual behaviour" or "lack of discrimination between the gender of sexual partners". See Gunderson 2003: 153 for a stronger version of this polemic.

2 E.g. Ormand 2009; Williams 2010, both of which handle an impressive array of literary texts with considerable sensitivity, within a framework determined by historical aspirations. Note, too, the scepticism of Skinner 2005: 252. On Ovid, Ormand 2005: 80–4 finds it natural to preface his reading with

a detailed summary of the state of our understanding of the historical facts of Roman views of homosexuality. Similarly Volk 2010: 87–8, and Williams 2010: 275, read Orpheus' change to paederasty as confirmation of the prevailing model of Roman sexuality.

3 See Orrells 2011 for an account of the role of homosexuality in the evolution of classical scholarship.

4 See Langlands 2006: 15–17.

5 So the excellent, and rightly influential studies, Gleason 1995; Gunderson 2003; Dugan 2005.

6 The phrase originates in the English translation of Lévi-Strauss (see Leach 1970: 34). In spite of Leach's reservations its reuse had overcome the distortions of its origin.

7 Ormand 2005.

8 Translation a slightly modified, more literal version of Melville 1997.

9 See Makowski 1996: 30.

10 On Phanocles' version see Stern 1979; Hopkinson 1988, which includes the text (45–6) and commentary, and Barchiesi 2006: 286–8, which explores the paederastic tradition on Orpheus.

11 *quid enim nisi se quereretur amatam?* (*Met.* 10.61).

12 Published translations into English tend to shy away from Ovid's precision here. But the Budé version is accurate (italics added): "Ce fut même lui qui apprit aux peuples de la Thrace à reporter leur amour sur des *enfants* mâles et à cueillir les premières fleurs de ce court printemps de la vie qui précède la jeunesse" (Lafaye 1955: ad loc.).

13 *Met.* 11.1–66. In Vergil's version, Orpheus simply remains celibate, and roams the icy landscape alone, lamenting what has happened: *Georgics* 4.516–22.

14 Langlands 2006: 11–12 gives a possible example of a sensationalist response to paedophilia, pointing out the difficulty of correctly interpreting the word *pueri* (which Ovid does not use of Orpheus' partners).

15 Ormand 2005 and Makowski 1996 approach this in different ways. Makowski reads the Orpheus tale as evidence of Ovidian homophobia; Ormand 2005: 90 rejects that idea. I think both neglect narrative dynamics in their discussion of Orpheus' sexuality. On Ovid's "realism", see Feldherr 2010: 3–5; on illusions of reality, Rosati 1983; Hardie 2002b; on visualization (crucial to Ovid's fictional world) Fondermann 2007.

16 Halperin 2007 explains the scepticism in gay discourse towards psychological or psychoanalytic explanations of identity.

17 See Böhmer 1980: 62–3; Makowski 1996: 35–6; Barchiesi 2006: 285–6. Most obvious is the echo of Aratus; on the tradition of Aratean imitation, see Fantuzzi 1980. The image is of a poet rather in the mould of the one imagined by Vergil in *Eclogue* 6, which, given its interest in metamorphic myths (including Atalanta), must have haunted Ovid.

18 Cf. Winnicott 1971: 22.

19 On the intersection and distinction between the two narrators, see Barchiesi 2006; Liveley 1999: 201.

20 On Hyacinthus, and his double, Cyparissus, see Fulkerson 2006.

21 See Salzman-Mitchell 2008: 303 4 on hardening/softening in *Metamorphoses*.

22 Describing the adolescence and growth in beauty of Adonis: *iam placet et Veneri matrisque ulciscitur ignes* – "Now he pleases even Venus and avenges his mother's passions" (10.524).

23 The metamorphosis itself is effected by means of bodily fluids: Cyparissus loses his blood through his weeping, *per immensos egesto sanguine fletus* (10.136), and so his limbs turn vegetal. Later, the Propoetides and Myrrha both undergo changes based on either blood or tears: extreme physical expressions (one a little more metaphorical than the other) of the emotional impact of grief: weeping/bleeding so much you are turned into a tree/stone. For a recent summary of the role of grief in *Met.* see Gentilcore 2010.

24 *inventum est aliquid quod Iuppiter esse, / quam quod erat, mallet*; "something was discovered that Jupiter would rather be than what he was" (10.156–7).

25 See Stern 1979: 139–40.

26 Sharrock 1991; Fondermann 2007; Feldherr 2010: 259–71. Salzman-Mitchell 2008 urges necessary caution about the exact significance of ivory in this episode.

27 As Makowski 1996: 27–8 points out, there was a tradition, present in Plato and other sources, of Orpheus as a misogynist, even without the accompanying turn to boys.

28 Liveley 1999.

29 Theodorakopoulos 1999.

30 Rudnytsy 1993 provides an introduction to object relations theory in literary criticism.

31 Winnicott's interest in the places of the imagination is particularly relevant here. See Winnicott 1971: 95–110.

32 I recognize that many would disagree. Makowski 1996: 28–9 sees Ovid deliberately minimizing the idea of mourning as presented in Vergil, and making the paederastic phase a demonstration that he has entirely forgotten his devotion to his wife.
33 See Nagle 1983; Lowrie 1993; Fantham 2004: 78–80.
34 As Barchiesi 2006: 291–3 points out, Ovid is also concerned with the question of Myrrha's geographical location, and a contrast between Pangaia and Italy.
35 Cf. Klein 1948: 327–8 on the positive possibilities for overcoming mourning via positive internal preservation of the loved object.
36 *Met.* 15.870–9.
37 Hardie 2002a 10–15; Sharrock 2002a: 99 ("Writing poetry, for Ovid, is not just *about* 'sexuality'; it is itself an erotic experience"); Sharrock 2002b.
38 Liveley 1999.
39 *Met.* 11.7. In an interesting variation from Phanocles, Ovid keeps the women out of earshot for the entirety of Orpheus' narration. In Phanocles it is hearing Orpheus' homoerotic outpourings that provokes revenge. The difference strengthens the interpretation I put forward here.
40 Klein 1948: 296.
41 See e.g. Quinet 1995.
42 Cf. Liveley 1999: 202 "the second metamorphosis of the Propoetides may be seen not as a punishment, but as a kind of self-transformation", with discussion of the scholarship.
43 *pace* Makowski 1996: 29–36. I therefore see little evidence here of Ovidian homophobia.
44 *Met.* 11.44–50.
45 Skinner 2005: 214–16; Ormand 2009: 136–7; Williams 2010: *passim*.
46 This paper has had a long gestation, and I would like to thank audiences at seminars in Cambridge and London, and at *Feminism and Classics VI*. I have been fortunate to work alongside inspiring Latinists who have been generous with advice: in Glasgow, Luke Houghton and Costas Panayotakis; in Birmingham, Elena Theodorakopoulos, to whose friendship, and insights into Latin poetry, I owe an enormous amount. The bibliography on *Metamorphoses* is now formidably large, and I apologisze to the many scholars whose work I have not been able to take into account.

Bibliography

Barchiesi, A. (2006) "Voices and narrative 'instances' in the *Metamorphoses*", in P. Knox (ed.) *Oxford Readings in Ovid*. Oxford: Oxford University Press, pp. 274–319.
Böhmer, F. (1980) *P. Ovidius Naso: Metamorphosen: Kommentar, Buch X–XI*. Heidelberg: Carl Winter.
Bowlby, J. (1980) *Attachment and Loss*, vol. 3: *Loss: Sadness and Depression*. London: Hogarth Press.
Brunt, P.A. (1988) *The Fall of the Roman Republic*. Oxford: Clarendon Press.
Dugan, J.R. (2005) *Making a New Man: Ciceronian Self-fashioning in the Rhetorical Works*. Oxford: Oxford University Press.
Fantham, E. (2004) *Ovid's Metamorphoses*. Oxford: Oxford University Press.
Fantuzzi, M. (1980) "Ἐκ Διὸς ἀρχώμεσθα: Arat. Phaen. 1 e Theocr. XVII 1", *Materiali e Discussioni per l'Analisi dei Testi Classici* 5: 163–72.
Feldherr, A. (2010) *Playing God: Ovid's Metamorphoses and the Politics of Fiction*. Princeton, NJ: Princeton University Press.
Fondermann, P. (2007) *Kino im Kopf: Zur Visualisierung des Mythos in den "Metamorphosen" Ovids*. Göttingen: Vandenhoek & Ruprecht.
Fulkerson, L. (2006) "Apollo, Paenitentia, and Ovid's 'Metamorphoses'", *Mnemosyne* 59(3): 388–402.
Gentilcore, R.M. (2010) "The transformation of grief in Ovid's *Metamorphoses*", *Syllecta Classica* 21: 93–118.
Gleason, M. (1995) *Making Men*. Princeton, NJ: Princeton University Press.
Gunderson, E. (2003) *Declamation, Paternity, and Roman Identity*. Cambridge: Cambridge University Press.
Halperin, D.M. (2007) *What DO Gay Men Want?* Ann Arbor, MI: University of Michigan Press.
Hardie, P. (ed.) (2002a) *The Cambridge Companion to Ovid*. Cambridge: Cambridge University Press.
Hardie, P. (2002b) *Ovid's Poetics of Illusion*. Cambridge: Cambridge University Press.
Hardie, P., Barchiesi, A. and Hinds, S. (eds) (1999) *Ovidian Transformations: Essays on Ovid's Metamorphoses and its Reception*, Cambridge Philological Society Supplementary Vol. 23. Cambridge: Cambridge Philological Society.
Hopkinson, N. (1988) *A Hellenistic Anthology*. Cambridge: Cambridge University Press.
Klein, M. (1948) *Contributions to Psychoanalysis 1921–1945*. London: Hogarth Press.

Lafaye, G. (1955) *Ovide: Les Métamorphoses*. Paris: Les Belles Lettres.

Langlands, R. (2006) *Sexual Morality in Ancient Rome*. Cambridge: Cambridge University Press.

Leach, E. (1970) *Lévi-Strauss*. London: Fontana.

Liveley, G. (1999) "Reading resistance in Ovid's *Metamorphoses*", in P. Hardie, A. Barchiesi and S. Hinds (eds) *Ovidian Transformations: Essays on Ovid's Metamorphoses and its Reception*. Cambridge: Cambridge Philological Society, pp. 197–213.

Lowrie, M. (1993) "Myrrha's second taboo, Ovid *Metamorphoses* 10.467–68", *Classical Philology* 88(1): 50–2.

Makowski, J.F. (1996) "Bisexual Orpheus: Pederasty and parody in Ovid", *The Classical Journal* 92: 25–38.

Melville, R. (1997) *Lucretius: On the Nature of the Universe*. Oxford: Oxford University Press.

Nagle, B.R. (1983) "Byblis and Myrrha: Two incest narratives in the *Metamorphoses*", *The Classical Journal* 78(4): 301–15.

Ormand, K. (2005) "Impossible lesbians in Ovid's *Metamorphoses*", in R. Ancona and E. Greene (eds) *Gendered Dynamics in Latin Love Poetry*. Baltimore, MD: Johns Hopkins University Press, pp. 79–110.

——(2009) *Controlling Desires*. Westport, CT: Praeger.

Orrells, D. (2011) *Classical Culture and Modern Masculinities*. Oxford: Oxford University Press.

Quinet, A. (1995) "The gaze as object", in R. Feldstein, B. Fink and M. Jaanus (eds) *Reading Seminar XI: Lacan's Four Fundamental Concepts of Psychoanalysis*. Albany, NY: SUNY Press, pp. 139–48.

Rosati, G. (1983) *Narciso e Pigmalione: Illusione e spettacolo nelle Metamorfosi di Ovidio*. Florence: Sansoni.

Rudnytsy, P.L. (ed.) (1993) *Transitional Objects and Potential Spaces: Literary Uses of D.W. Winnicott*. New York: Columbia University Press.

Salzman-Mitchell, P. (2008) "A whole out of pieces: Pygmalion's ivory statue in Ovid's *Metamorphoses*", *Arethusa* 41(2): 291–311.

Sharrock, A.R. (1991) "Womanufacture", *Journal of Roman Studies* 81: 36–49.

——(2002a) "Gender and sexuality", in P. Hardie (ed.) *The Cambridge Companion to Ovid*. Cambridge: Cambridge University Press, pp. 95–107.

——(2002b) "Ovid and the discourses of love: The amatory works", in P. Hardie (ed.) *The Cambridge Companion to Ovid*. Cambridge, Cambridge University Press, pp. 150–62.

Skinner, M. (2005) *Sexuality in Greek and Roman Culture*. Malden, MA: Blackwell.

Stern, J. (1979) "Phanocles' fragment 1", *Quaderni Urbinati di Cultura Classica* 3: 135–43.

Theodorakopoulos, E. (1999) "Closure and transformation in Ovid's *Metamorphoses*", in P. Hardie, A. Barchiesi and S. Hinds (eds) *Ovidian Transformations: Essays on Ovid's Metamorphoses and its Receptions*. Cambridge: Cambridge Philological Society, pp. 142–61.

Volk, K. (2010) *Ovid*. Chichester: Wiley-Blackwell.

Williams, C. (2010) *Roman Homosexuality*, 2nd edn. New York: Oxford University Press.

Winnicott, D.W. (1971) *Playing and Reality*. London: Routledge.

20

READING BOY-LOVE AND CHILD-LOVE IN THE GRECO-ROMAN WORLD

Amy Richlin

In memory of John J. Winkler (1943–90)

Meaning is made at the point of reception.[1] Ten years after Stonewall, in 1978, K.J. Dover, Professor of Greek at St Andrews, published *Greek Homosexuality*, the first study of the subject by a prominent academic. The book's publication was made possible by the open discussion of sexuality that followed the sexual revolution. Dover's book coincided with Michel Foucault's last project, the *History of Sexuality* (vol. 1, first French edition, 1976; English translation, 1978; vols. 2–3, 1984); subsequent work on the ancient sex/gender system focused on its differences from modern Euro-American systems in its practice of male same-sex erotics, making a "useable past" for the political activism of the 1990s. Athens and Plato held a central place.[2] In the process, some aspects of the ancient system were played down. Writers of the late nineteenth century, however, found this past usable in somewhat different ways; their perspective points up the historicity of our own. Scholarly perspectives may well shift once again.

Mine have, and more than once. My research on Roman slavery led me to rewrite the entry on "Sexuality" for the *Oxford Classical Dictionary* (2012) to locate the key difference between ancient and modern sex/gender systems in the institution of slavery and in the normative understanding that persons became sexual subjects at puberty. This second claim was based in longstanding discussions of the age of Roman girls at marriage and of the desirable ages for boys expressed in pederastic literature. Now I think that I was wrong, and that slavery enabled sexual use at any age: there is, in fact, substantial evidence to suggest that enslaved persons were used for sex before they reached puberty, and that free children were also sometimes objects of desire. This raises the fraught question of whether the lexical blurring in the words for "child/slave/beloved boy" in Greek and Latin represents a blurring, in practice, of categories that today most people would wish to keep separate – "child" and "sex object." An unpleasant question to ask about the founding states of Western civilization, for the sake of whose charms we habitually overlook their use of slaves. For scholars, the *erastês* and *erômenos* have become familiar figures; it would be harder to get used to thinking of owner and *puerulus* as sex partners, or to see Ganymede as a child, as Lucian does. Indeed, it would be impolitic.

Boy–love and the recent history of the study of ancient sexuality

The words *puer* in Latin, *pais* in Greek, have a threefold lexical range:

(1) "child" (unisex, but often male)
(2) "male slave" (of any age)
(3) "(beautiful) boy, object of sexual desire"

This third sense goes along with a sex/gender system richly attested from Anacreon to Philostratus, but only sporadically after Nemesianus (late 200s CE). The textual form that parades the system in operation is love poetry, in which details are given about boys' appearance, age, and civil status; at the same time, these poems are fictional and conventional (as is argued by Apuleius in his *Apologia*), but then so is autobiography (for example, Libanius' insistence on his boyhood chastity).[3] Love poetry nonetheless shows what an educated readership found appealing. The image of the beautiful boy – coy, teasing, a torment to his lovers, who only sometimes mention paying a fee for the use of his body – is complicated by the fact that a world without slavery was unknown to these writers; where war, poverty, and piracy flourished, children were always at risk of being sold into slavery, wherein the sexual vulnerability of prostitutes differed only in its business model from the sexual vulnerability of any slave. The consent of slave boys is unreal, their very agency obscured within the Schwarzschild radius of slavery, while the sexual agency of free boys, with whom sex was in any case off-limits by Roman custom, was obscured by the always-felt analogy with the sexual use of those enslaved.[4]

Here I disagree with arguments put forward by Thomas Hubbard, Beert Verstraete, and Riccardo Vattuone, among others. I would never doubt that the ardent poets felt love, any more than I would doubt that some boys loved in return – Marcus Aurelius did, although at eighteen he was a bit old to be an *erômenos* and indeed calls himself the *erastês* of the much older Fronto (*Addit.* 7.1; see Richlin 2006). We might place the future emperor at the extreme upper end of the range of power available to free boys. Nor would I deny the agency of enslaved persons, their capacity to desire; but I agree with C.W. Marshall, who compares the desires expressed by slave prostitutes, as represented in New Comedy, with the desires expressed by the children in Thai brothels (Marshall 2013: 192–6, with photographs of graffiti).

Persons labeled "boys" today, of course, are not felt to have sexual agency at all. Scholarly discussion of ancient pederasty since Dover has held the practice to involve boys from puberty to their late teens, with variations: Roman texts cite the exchange of the purple-bordered *toga praetexta* for the all-white *toga virilis* at puberty as also the time when a citizen boy might become the target of lust, and be willing to succumb (Cicero *Cael.* 9–10), and the age at which this happens is usually specified as around fifteen; the Greek epigrammatist Strato, in several poems, sets out the age range for pederasty as twelve to eighteen; invective attacks on the Stoics accused them of desiring young men into their late twenties; and this tallies with actual recommendations by the early Stoics of sex between teachers and students.[5] However, the normative picture of this upper limit has been challenged by Mark Masterson (2014) for late antiquity (but with clear ramifications for earlier centuries), and I am belatedly beginning to doubt the lower limit as well.

Consideration of this issue has perhaps been delayed by the political motivations that have characterized the arguments about pederasty since Dover, from a range of perspectives. John Boswell (1980) wanted to take invective (against *cinaedi*) along with expressions of desire (for boys) as evidence for a socially approved "homosexuality"; Ramsay MacMullen (1982) wanted to prove Boswell wrong; more recently James Davidson, arguing against Dover and Foucault, has wished to deny the existence of most sexual activity for males *under* eighteen (Davidson 2007); Thomas Hubbard has argued not only that Davidson is wrong but that ancient texts demonstrate boys' own agency and desire (2009, 2010). Among less well-known apologists for pederasty as boy-love, Beert Verstraete (2012) emphasizes the love displayed by Catullus in the Juventius poems, by Tibullus in the Marathus poems, and especially by Horace in the Ligurinus poems; he argues that all these boys are imagined as free, hence (by implication) autonomous.[6]

The political agenda of the 1970s made it urgent for there to have been a time in the history of the West when male–male sex was normal, and there was a tendency to argue that pederasty, despite the sound of the word, had nothing to do with what is now reviled as pedophilia. I have said so myself to numerous undergraduate classes since the early 1980s, taking the man/boy-yes, man/man-no structure as an opportunity to practice cultural relativism. The argument goes that *pueri* were not considered "children"; that although for us (in the US) the age of consent (sexual personhood) is eighteen, in antiquity the age of sexual personhood was puberty, so what appears to be an overlap with pedophilia is not, even though *pueri* were, ideally, under eighteen; and that, while pedophilia is a pathology, pederasty was socially acceptable, for, at least in the urban locations we know best, writers like Catullus addressed, with no change in tone, both boys and women.[7] After all, girls were considered, in Roman law, to be eligible for marriage at the age of twelve, and no one in antiquity saw any problem with that, except for medical writers concerned about childbearing. The citizen boys in Plato's dialogues took center stage, helped by the fact that Plato's boys run through the lines of later Greek and Latin literature.

The problem of slavery, the lack of a real correspondence between ancient pederasty and any modern civil rights agenda, and the harsh Greco-Roman strictures against sex between adult males, or against gender-bending affect – these were generally not discussed, or glossed over, for understandable political reasons. Nor, ironically, was it easy to see the inconcinnity between ancient practice and modern programs before all the research was done, by which time queer studies had moved on to modernity. Pederasty only made sense as a model for gay liberation in the 1970s because, in late antiquity, the church condemned all male–male sex indifferently, often confusedly, and this attitude has continued, taking in lesbians along the way. So, then, to those combating this condemnation, a time when *some* same-sex love was all right could be viewed as good news for *all* same-sex love (see Hexter 2006 for Boswell's motivations). Or for all the same-sex love a writer might wish to champion; the effeminate male and the lover of boys have not been the public face of the civil rights agenda, and this has affected the directions taken by scholarship on ancient sexuality.[8] For lesbians, Sappho poses a relatively unproblematic role model, especially since so little is known of the social conditions under which she lived (see Rabinowitz 2002). The main point was the historical contingency of sexual systems, but the eloquence of Plato and Sappho exudes a glamour still palpable in many histories, as if their texts offered normative models for all ancient sex/gender systems.

No matter what might be argued about adolescents, however, few now want to argue for the sexual personhood of those below puberty, although such a claim is perhaps implicit in Vattuone's defense of intergenerational love (this term is preferred to "child abuse" by its proponents, who wish to differentiate pedophilia from what Laes, summarizing Vattuone on Plato (Laes 2010a: 40), calls "mutual consent and gratifying friendship"). Freud talked about children's sexuality; Kinsey researched it; Marge Piercy's feminist utopian novel *Woman on the Edge of Time* included children among the sexual persons in its future world.[9] Christian Laes titled an article "When classicists need to speak up" (2010a), positing that attention to "ancient sexuality" could help to historicize current ideas about childhood; he contends (Laes 2011: 276) that "what today seems like a self-evident division into sexless or sexually isolated children and sexual adults was not made in Antiquity," and that "it is not up to the historian to pass judgment" (2011: 290). But all reading entails judgment, including the choice of what to discuss. Indeed we should discuss the eroticized children in Greco-Roman sources. They are not sexual subjects; in the 2010s, it does not seem possible to view the system these texts betoken in a positive light, but it was not always so.

The sexual use of children: Some Roman stories and their readers

Historical and moralizing texts show a concern to protect free children from sexual abuse, not only in the extreme case of war but in everyday life. Ancient writers of history ventriloquize the fear that a battle will result in the rape of a people's women and children (see Gaca 2010–11); this fear is echoed in a titillating way by the images of captive children on Roman monuments, which, Jeannine Uzzi (forthcoming) argues, are just as specularized as the images of their mothers. Inhabitants of the city of Rome could look at them as they walked past the columns of Trajan and Marcus Aurelius, just as they could have looked at their live correlatives on the platforms of the slave market (in some cases, as fellow objects for sale). In fourth-century Gaul, Ausonius wrote a poem-cycle about his *alumna*, Bissula, in which the physical features that mark her as a German war captive (*Bissula* 3) are praised as beautiful in the vocabulary of the *sermo amatorius*; he calls her *Sueba virguncula*, "a little Suebian girl," with blue eyes and blonde hair, *delicium, blanditiae, ludus, amor, voluptas* (*Bissula* 1.2, 3.10, 4.1).[10] How or why he came to introduce this cycle with two lines evoking the *Priapea* (2.1–2, ~ *Pr.* 1.1–2) is a matter of dispute, but these lines do mark the poems as erotic in intent. Kathy Gaca (2010–11) argues that the *paides* in Greek accounts of sexual atrocities after battle are meant to be girls, but sometimes the threat to young boys is also made explicit, as in Livy's version of the legend of Cloelia for an Augustan audience.

This captive *virgo*, given the opportunity by the enemy general to return home with her choice from the remaining (male) hostages, after consulting the whole group chose the *impubes* (those under puberty), because it made most sense "for that age to be freed from the enemy which was most likely to attract injury" (2.13.10).[11] R.M. Ogilvie takes "injury" here to mean "*muliebria pati*," on which more below; Livy's readers, according to Suetonius, also experienced Augustus' separation of theater seating so that boys wearing the *toga praetexta*, among other classes, should have their own section, near to their *paedagogi* (*Aug.* 44.2): a public mark of perceived risk. Ogilvie points out that Servius, retelling the story of Cloelia in the 400s CE, changes the *impubes* to *virgines* (1965: 267): times had changed, along with readers' expectations – also their sense of decorum, of what could be mentioned.

The *toga praetexta* should have been enough of a distinguishing mark, but Plutarch, in the 100s CE, wonders whether the Roman *bulla*, an amulet worn by free boys, was meant to distinguish them from slave boys, so no one will make a mistake and "love" them (*erân*, QR 288A); the Neronian satirist Persius describes himself dedicating his *bulla* to the household gods when he put aside his *toga praetexta* and began his life as a sexual subject (*S.* 5.30–3). Plutarch, who calls the *bulla* the *paidikon … parasêmon*, the "sign of childhood" (288B), believes that Romans going back to early times felt it not wrong to "love" slave boys of the same age as these free boys wearing the *bulla*, and says "to this day, their comedies bear witness to this." The age at which the ceremony was carried out was not fixed; the physical signs of puberty may or may not have been a prerequisite; what is clear is that the change from *toga praetexta* to *toga virilis* marked a change in status in Roman terms, from protected youthful category to sexual autonomy.[12]

That there was reason to worry about free boys even before they took off the *bulla* is suggested by a story in Valerius Maximus (early first century CE) about a man who lost a court case because he bragged about his sexual use of a girl and a *puer praetextatus* (8.1.*absol*.8). The wording is significant: *carmen quo puerum praetextatum et ingenuam virginem a se corruptam poetico ioco significaverat*, "a poem in which he had indicated, in a poetic quip, that a *puer praetextatus* and a freeborn virgin girl had been corrupted by him." To the poet, a joke; to the moralizing orator, a sexual transgression (*corruptam*). We can see what an extreme version of such a joke might have looked like in Petronius' novel (*Sat.* 25), where a seven-year-old girl has sex with the sixteen-year-old Giton while other characters watch in amusement. Encolpius, unwilling to let go of Giton, objects that the girl is too young to bear "the law of taking it like a woman (*muliebris patientiae*)"; Quartilla answers, "Is she younger than I was, when I was taken by (*passa sum*) my first man?" Within the system of the novel, these characters are certainly depraved; the episode is still meant to be funny.

Catullus 56 is explicitly presented as a funny joke about raping a boy. This seven-line poem has not been much discussed by historians of Roman sexuality, perhaps because both text and sense are uncertain and its attitude is so far from that of Catullus' Juventius poems.[13] This poem is much more like the *Priapea*, in which the ithyphallic god threatens to rape those who would steal from him; the boy is identified only by the term *pupulus*, which probably indicates a young age; his status is not clearly indicated as slave or free – readers are left to infer this. Four of the poem's seven lines are taken up by an address to someone named Cato; the rape is accomplished in only three cryptic lines:

> Oh what a ridiculous thing, Cato, what a funny thing,
> worthy of your ears and your guffaw (*cachinno*)!
> Laugh, as much as you love me, Cato, at Catullus:
> the thing is ridiculous and too funny.
> I just caught (*deprendi*) the little boy (*pupulum*) [of my girl (*puellae*)]/ [at a girl]
> thrusting (*trusantem*); him I, so please Dione [Venus' mother, a stand-in for Venus],
> struck (*cecidi*) with my stiff (*rigida*) [prick] like an ox-team pull (*protelo*).

Problems: how old is a *pupulus*? Is *puellae* genitive, so "of (my) girl," that is, "belonging to Lesbia"? Or is it dative after *trusantem*, so, "[doing something] *at* or *to* a girl"? (In this case, the unmodified *pupulum* would make him Catullus' property.) Since the verb *truso* is found nowhere else in Latin, is the manuscript tradition here corrupt? If not, what does *trusantem* mean? It would be derived from *trudo*, "thrust."

Among commentators, I will turn to Robinson Ellis; best known today as a character in Tom Stoppard's play *The Invention of Love*, he belongs to homophile Oxford in the time of Victoria.[14] The 1889 edition of his Catullus commentary spends most of a two-page introduction to c. 56 on the identity of the poem's Cato. The action attracted less of his attention, but, unlike many commentators (this is what makes him so useful), he does comment substantially (Ellis 1889: 198–9):

> The incident itself, if my view of it is right, is a piece of childish precocity, such as might have pleased Sterne, and which has its counterpart in the mock marriage of two children, one a girl of seven, in Petron. S. 25, as well as in the more modern narrative of Casanova (Mémoires, tom. i. p. 41, ed. Brux. 1871). Bährens, reading in 6 *Crusantem*, another form of *Crisantem* (L. Müller Lucil. p. 229) imagines the situation as follows [I here translate Bährens' Latin]: "Those two little ones (*parvoli*) had been playing husband and wife, but because they were not yet perfectly acquainted with conjugal matters, the boy like a woman had the girl placed above himself like a man, and he shimmied (*crisavit*) at her (that is, he wiggled his buttocks during intercourse). Our poet, therefore, laughs at the roles of male and female turned upside down by

half-aware little ones, and punishes them in this way: he causes the little boy (*puer-ulum*) who was conducting himself like a woman, to suffer womanish things (*muliebria pati*) like a woman." This has the merit of explaining the dat. *puellae*: cf. Priap. xix.4 *Crisabit tibi fluctuante lumbo* [She (a dancing girl) will shimmy for you, with swaying hips].

Several things must strike the current reader: the unruffled, indulgent tone of "a piece of childish precocity," echoing Bährens' "little ones" and "our poet"; the parallels from the world of *curiosa* (Sterne, Petronius, Casanova, the *Priapea*); Bährens' own interpretation of the poet's action as a punishment; and Ellis' concluding concern to explain the case of *puellae*. Ellis' use of "two children" indifferently of a seven-year-old and a sixteen-year-old (*Sat.* 97.2) marks a blurring now significant. Both Ellis and Bährens read *pupulus* as "little boy." Instead of the unparalleled *trusantem*, Bährens imagined *crusantem* to make *puellae* dative and then invented an elaborate scenario to match it, for the verb *criso* is used only of women in Latin. Evidently the speaker has found the *pupulus* doing something that prompts the speaker to rape him.[15]

Ellis bolsters Bährens' reading by his explanation of *deprendi* (56.5), which he notes is used "of persons taken in adultery or the like." He briskly dispenses with line 8: *protelo* is "properly applied to a team of oxen drawing in even successive pulls," with a double entendre on *pro telo*, "in place of a weapon"; *rigida* is compared to another adjective used substantively for *mentula*, "prick" (Catull. 80.6); several parallels are given for the verb *caedo* ("beat," "strike") to refer to sexual penetration. Perhaps reading his own schoolboy days at Rugby onto this poem via the common experience of Roman schoolboys, he adds, "The word [*cecidi*] is probably chosen as suiting *pupulum* in the sense of flogging *ferula scuticaque cecidit* [with the stick and the whip he struck them] Suet. Gramm. 9" (citing Suetonius on Roman schoolmasters).[16]

What is really interesting is Ellis' explanation of *pupulum*: "seems here to be [equivalent to] *pupum*, a word of endearment used by the common people = *pusionem* or *puerulum*. Suet. Calig. 13 *laetissimo obviorum agmine incessit super fausta omina sidus et pullum et pupum et alumnum appellantium* [As he went along, the line of people became most joyful as he passed, and called him, amongst names of good omen, 'star' and 'chick' and 'boy doll' and 'fosterling']. Cali-gula was twenty-five at the time. Ellis' equivalents include one used elsewhere of boys who were the object of pederastic affection (*pusio*, cf. Juvenal 6.34, where sex with a *pusio* is recommended in lieu of marriage) and one that means "little boy" (*puerulus*); similarly, Sue-tonius' list of endearments mixes the term *pullus* ("chick," "young creature," but also "beloved boy") with *pupus* ("boy doll") and *alumnus* ("slave foster son").[17] Age lines blur, while this group of words beginning with *pŭ*, all of which are associated with childhood, conveys feelings ambiguously parental or erotic: like "baby." What became of the term *pullus* in Lombard Italy in the late 700s CE can be seen in comparing the second-century dictionary of Pompeius Festus ("The ancients used to call a boy whom someone loved his *pullus*," 284L) with its epitome by Paul the Deacon ("A boy who was loved obscenely by someone was called the *pullus* of the man by whom he had been loved," 285L).[18] The main point: Catullus thought what happened was funny, and expects his reader to think so, too; some have done so. The age of the *pupulus* is unspecified but young; his status is unspecified, but surely servile.

A last illustration of the sense of *pusio*: the lost third-century poet Septimius Serenus used it in a context that associates the boy with the idea that the age of seven was marked by the falling out of teeth (*pusioni meo / septuennis cadens*, "my boy's seven-year-[teeth] falling out"). Edward Courtney, explicating this fragment (1993: 410), adduces a story of the younger Seneca, who retails in his *Moral Epistles* (12.3) his own cruel joke about an aged slave. At his country estate one day, where everything seemed to be falling apart, he was expostulating with the present farm manager (himself a slave):

> Turning to the door, I said, "Who's that guy? That decrepit guy? It's a good thing you moved him over to guard the entry, because he's certainly looking out the door [i.e., towards the grave]. Where did you find that guy? What possessed you to pick up some other family's corpse for burial?" But the guy said, "Don't you recognize me? I'm Lucky (*Felicio*) – you used to bring me winter-festival presents (*sigillaria*). I'm the son of the farm-manager Philositus, I'm your little darling (*deliciolum*)." I said, "That guy is completely crazy. Has he become a *pupulus*, even my darling (*delicium*)? Could be: his teeth are falling out as fast as they can."

Here both *pupulus* and *delicium* are associated with the loss of baby teeth; the riddling joke-type is familiar from Plautus (Fraenkel 2007: 28–37). The slave-name *Felicio* provokes the question, lucky for whom? It is matched in texts and inscriptions by names like *Paegnium* ("Plaything"), *Ganymedes*, *Eros* (very common).[19] Felicio's luck, manifested in his early life by gifts and pet names, has long since run out; his status as son of the old *vilicus* has ended with his placement now as door-guard, a low position within the household (cf. Suet. *Gram.* 27.1). The callousness here displayed toward slaves, not only their bodily integrity but their personal worth, can be paralleled in texts starting from Plautus around 200 BCE on through Apuleius in the 100s CE. (In Plautus, at least, the slave's point of view is acted out onstage alongside the owner's: *eheu, quam illae rei ego etiam nunc sum parvolus* – "Alas, how little I am as yet for doing that thing," *Pseud.* 783, a boy prostitute.) Valerius Maximus, evoking indignant pity, refers to the *puer praetextatus* and the *virgo ingenua* as *corruptus/a*, but, in another case, recounts how a defendant used a putative assignation with a *puer servus* as an excuse for being caught in a married man's bedroom (8.1.*absol*.12): "no self-control" (*intemperantia*), chides Valerius. Status matters to him, not age. The restatements and changes in Servius and Paul the Deacon indicate a new attitude (all pederasty is wrong and, when possible, we will not discuss it) but not a new understanding of what was at stake.[20] Nor are parallels hard to find in Greek (see subsection, The sexual use of small children, below).

To a reader today, one of the most shocking instances of the callousness of the ancient sex trade comes up in a pair of poems by the epigrammatist Martial, thanking the emperor Domitian for restricting the castration and prostitution of children (9.6, 9.8):

> No boy (*puer*) cut by the skill of the greedy dealer
> mourns the loss of his ripped-away manhood,
> nor does the wretched mother give her prostituted boy-baby (*prostituto … infanti*)
> the wages counted out by the arrogant pimp.
>
> (Martial 9.6.4–7)

> As if small were the injury to our sex
>   that males were prostituted to be made foul by the public,
> now cradles belonged to the pimp, so that, snatched from the teat,
>   a boy (*puer*) asked for the dirty money with his wailing:
> bodies too young (*inmatura*) were paying unspeakable penalties.
>
> (Martial 9.8.1–5)

Hyperbolic as they are, these poems assume a readership that accepts as factual the sale of young children into prostitution by impoverished families; Domitian's ban is accepted by legal historians as part of his moral agenda (Grelle 1980). It seems not to have ended the practice.

The sexual use of small children: What were **deliciae?**

The stories above link the *pupulus* that Catullus rapes with Seneca's *delicium, deliciolum, pupulus.* The nature and function of the children called by some form of the term *deliciae* in Latin is something of a mystery, because numerous texts mention them without reference to any use as sex objects. *Deliciae* just means "darling," "delight," but it also has a technical sense: a slave child kept as a special pet. There are epitaphs to *deliciae*, some of whom are girls; their age is often specified, and it is often pre-puberty. Some are actual epitaphs, gravestones; others are fictional, epigrams – a surprisingly popular subject.[21] *Ipsimi nostri delicatus decessit, mehercule margaritum, catamitus*, says Trimalchio (*Sat.* 63.3): "Our owner's *delicatus* died, a pearl, by God, a Ganymede."[22] Were *deliciae*, at times, eroticized? This question has elicited conflicting answers from scholars since the 1990s; the ambiguous evidence has set up a clear illustration of the workings of reception. Here I will go back a century to Theodor Birt's 42-page 1892 Latin treatise, "A second short commentary on Catullus, concerning images of *Amores* in ancient art and concerning the tiny children [or 'boys'] kept as pets [or 'darlings'] by the ancients": *de pueris minutis in deliciis habitis*.[23] This very obscure work is buried in the University of Marburg's listing of faculty and the lectures they would be offering in the summer semester of 1892, and I myself would never have seen it if not for the erudition of Jack Winkler.[24] Birt's arguments, although strange, open up issues seldom discussed today.

In his treatise, Birt (1892) reviews a substantial amount of textual and visual evidence; he includes ten illustrations, for example Figure 20.1 (his fig. VI). It is hard to know what he thought he was doing. 1892, in Germany as well as in England, was the height of the aesthetic

Figure 20.1 Pusio in slave chains; figure VI from Birt 1892, after F. de Clarac, *Musée de Sculpture Antique et Moderne* (Paris: Victor Texier, 1826-52). Drawing by Amy Richlin.

movement; Birt's coeval Baron von Gloeden (1856–1931), the German expatriate who produced artistic photographs of Sicilian boys dressed (lightly) as Eros or Theocritean shepherds, was in full swing. Von Gloeden did not, however, work as a university professor, which Birt did; the University of Marburg was old, respected, conservative. Birt's work cannot have been scandalous.

The treatise is ostensibly a commentary on a single poem by Catullus, 55, in which the poet searches for someone named Camerius, who (Birt argues) was the poet's *deliciae*; discussion of *deliciae* then completely overshadows analysis of the poem. In order to make his case, Birt reiterates the following points (the pages use Roman numbering):

- Men and women kept little boys as toys (*deliciae*); they were no older than six years old; they were kept "not without sex" (*non sine venere*, x); cf. xviii, xxi, xxvi.

- Art reflects life, and life comes first; all the representations we see in art of *Amores* and *Erôtes* are drawn from what the artists saw around them: xvii, xx (twice), xxi (on his fig. IX, see below), xxv (twice), xxvi (*non cessabo*, he says, truly), xxvii, xxix–xxx, xxxi, xxxiii (twice).

- Artists saw *deliciae* especially in the houses of the rich, who were also the ones who paid for the works of art we see (xx, xxiii, xxv).

- QED: boys with wings, boys without wings, boys depicted as *Amores* – all are interchangeable in art (xxv).

- Furthermore: the whole idea came from Alexandria, where there was a special market for these children, who thus were imported to Rome (xxxi ff.); it catered to the wealthy (xxxii).

To build up his picture of *deliciae*, Birt looks at many texts, following no historical sequence. Those he repeatedly cites include a group of stories about emperors, most of them wicked – but not all. Most notorious is the story in Suetonius about Tiberius and his goings-on on the island of Capri (*Tib.* 44.1):

> He was branded with a still greater and more disgusting disgrace, so that it is hardly right for it to be recounted or heard, much less believed: people said that he trained boys in their earliest youth (*pueros primae teneritudinis*), whom he called "fishies" (*pisciculi*), to busy themselves between his thighs as he was swimming, and to play, going for him gently with their tongues and nibbling; and it was even said that he took babies (*infantes*), well developed while not yet weaned, and held them to his groin as if to the nipple, being, after all, more inclined to this kind of lust due to his nature and age.

The emphasis on suckling here recalls the images in Martial's poems on the control of the sex trade. Birt refers to the Suetonius passage but quotes only the words *pueros primae teneritudinis*, to reinforce his point about age. Of Tiberius, he says severely, "What misdeeds it is said the emperor committed with these [boys], I will not repeat; it can be seen in the author" (Birt 1892: xii). The *praeteritio* so effected is similar to Suetonius' own declaration that he should not tell the story, nor should we believe it.

Birt argues for the presence of very young children as toys in the houses of the mighty on the basis of several tendentious stories from historians writing, like Suetonius, long after the events recorded – Plutarch, Cassius Dio, Herodian. All might be said, like Plutarch, to be fond of anecdotes, in the case of Cassius Dio the more scurrilous the better; all wrote in Greek, and exhibit some degree of ethnographic voyeurism. Dio, writing about the wedding of Octavian and Livia in 38 BCE, says (48.44), "[at the wedding,] a *paidion* from the whispering ones (*psithurôn*), usually naked, that women keep to amuse themselves, … said to [Livia], 'What are you doing there, Ma'am?'" Birt is interested in this passage partly because the keeping of such children is here associated with women; such children, he notes, are often described as talkative, and many of them are naked (xii, xviff., xxxv–vi).[25] He comments on the nudity of infants in Christian art: "of course, in a child before puberty, nakedness has a simple charm without offense, a sort of sanctity" (xvii); as will be seen, he writes in a Christian context (see Stevenson 1998 on the meaning of Hellenic nudity within late-Victorian Christianity). We might add that, for Dio, this is specifically a "child" (*paidion*); that, because *paidion* is neuter, we cannot be sure this is a boy; that it is not just talkative but, oddly, whispering; and that, unlike Martial's wailing babies, it is at least old enough to talk. In another story from Dio (67.15), the *deliciae* of the emperor Domitian contribute to his downfall when they find the list he has made of his enemies and give it to Domitian's wife, who was on the list: "he (Domitian) put [the list] under the pillow on the bed on which he used to take a rest, and a *paidion*, one of the naked whispering ones (*psithurôn*) who slept with him in the daytime, found it and took it." Birt also quotes in full a story about the wicked emperor Commodus from Herodian, who wrote fifty years after Commodus' death and evidently copied the story directly from Dio on Domitian (1.17.3):

> There was a *paidion*, really a baby (*panu nêpion*), one of the ones who go naked or dressed in gold and precious stones, the kind Roman voluptuaries always like. Commodus liked him so much that he often lay down with him; he was called "Philo-commodus."

This child does the same thing that Domitian's *paidion* did: he finds the list, does not know what it is, and gives it to Commodus' mistress. What interests Birt here: the very young age; the attested popularity of such children with wealthy Romans; the nudity; the ornament. What we might note: again, bedmates; the sleight of hand which translates "Commodus likes child" into "child likes Commodus," a renaming typical of owners' representations of slave sex objects.

Plutarch injects gossip about *delicia* into Cleopatra's court (*Ant.* 59.4): "[The historian Dellius had complained that] at Rome Sarmentus was drinking Falernian wine. This Sarmentus was a *paidarion* among the *paignia* of Caesar [Octavian], those whom the Romans call *dêlikia*." Here Plutarch translates *delicium* directly into Greek as *paignion*, and places among the *paignia* this *paidarion*, "small child"; in Plautus' *Persa*, "Paegnium" is the name of a boy slave whose sexual use is the subject of joking throughout the play (192, 229–32, 284–5, 804–5). This view through Plutarch's ethnographic eye is complicated by the fact that Sarmentus was a grown-up, attested elsewhere as Maecenas' freedman, a *scriba* and a *scurra* (sources at Gowers 2012: 200): here a probable trace of Antonian propaganda.[26] Birt is interested in this story because many child-figures in literature and art are shown drinking, or associated with drinking imagery; on this passage, he exercises his imagination, as he likes to do, and says, "I will not argue if you imagine Sarmentus as often drunk" (xxvii). He adduces as corroborating evidence his figure IX, a drawing of a relief from the Villa Pamphili that shows babies crawling around among banqueters and being given wine to drink. This illustration typifies Birt's use of art at several removes from any original context: he mixes drawings and photographs; the drawing comes from Eduard Gerhard's *Antike Bildwerke* (1827–44), a standard reference work by the founder of the DAI but, in 1892, ageing; the relief itself came from a seventeenth-century villa in Rome, where the piece was detached from its original setting. Birt's use of drawings makes clearer how deracinated our knowledge has been: the "Berlin Painter" epitomizes the physical remove of Attic vases northward, and Dover's "List of Vases" (1978: 205–25) provides a gazetteer. The story to date is borrowed, layer upon layer.

Amid these stories of profligacy, Birt includes a down-to-earth anecdote in Suetonius about Augustus (1892: xi; *Aug.* 83):

> To relax, he either used to go fishing with a hook and line, or play with knucklebones and dice and nuts with little boys (*pueris minutis*), whom he used to collect from everywhere, ones attractive for their looks and chatter, especially Moors and Syrians.

Innocuous, for readers not put off by the idea of shopping for children. Not just any children, either, but exotic children, like von Gloeden's Sicilians; this kind of shopping is discussed for more modern periods by Robert Aldrich (2002), in the context of sex tourism (see esp. 2002: 280–1); cf. now Boone 2014: 51–107, 270–86.[27] A double exoticism, not apparent to the modern reader, inheres in the ethnicities named here: boys praised as attractive by Suetonius' coevals are Greek or Greek-Egyptian, while Moors and Syrians are associated with ugliness, coarseness, and suitability for slavery.[28] Ausonius' Bissula shows up on the same page in Birt. Yet the next page presents Augustus' grandsons Gaius and Lucius, and a young son of Germanicus: after his death, Livia dedicated an image of him dressed as Cupid in the temple of Venus, and Augustus had it placed in his bedroom and used to kiss it. Or so Suetonius says (*Calig.* 7).

Birt's examples emphasize how art and life were interwoven, as decorative real-life *deliciae* imitated images of children and *erôtes* (thus, children with wings). Underlying Birt's eccentric insistence stands the thought-provoking point that, in the Greco-Roman iconosphere, Eros looks like a small child. Birt is concerned to show that sculpture and painting were only copying scenes from daily life, but gaze theory since John Berger has traced the feedback loop whereby art and libido are co-implicated. This is borne out by Birt's stories about children dressed up to look like *erôtes*, as in Plutarch's description (*Ant.* 26.2) of Cleopatra, on her golden barge, dressed up like Aphrodite, with "boys/children (*paides*) made to look like *Erôtes* in paintings, [who] stood on each side of her and fanned her."

Art forms life here, while life forms art: the spectacle, if it happened, makes meaning out of real bodies; then Plutarch comes along a century later, and makes a written spectacle; and so this image ricochets down the centuries, acted out again here and there, in a Shakespeare play, in an opera, until at last it reaches the movies, and the *paides* (if they are still there) lose most of their original meaning; for most people. Again, however, since the word *paides* is gender-neutral, we are left with the now uncomfortable possibility that the children's gender was immaterial – age was enough. The age of Cleopatra's *paides* has to be extrapolated from extant images of *erôtes*, which certainly appear to be childish. Thus Birt speculates on two boys described by Martial (1892: xii) – for once, a current event, the death of two young slaves in the arena (2.75.5–7): "Two boyish (*puerilia*) bodies from the tender (*tenera*) crowd / that was freshening the bloody dirt with rakes: / that savage and accursed [lion] killed them with maddened teeth." Birt is interested in their age – the word *tener* is used by Suetonius to describe Tiberius' trained boys – but he also guesses that the *pueri* might have worn costumes, since "*Amores* often play with lions." Martial seems to take for granted the placement of these children as a sort of ornamental janitor service in the bloodstained arena.

Birt also likes the *Imagines* of Philostratus, a group of little-read Severan texts only recently the subject of scholarly discussion. They were, however, collected relatively early on in the buildup of the Loeb Classical Library; erotic texts loom large in the early series titles, even though explicit language was bowdlerized. Philostratus' *Imagines* are word-paintings of works of art, some real, some imaginary; the Loeb volume, unusually, includes illustrations – again, a combination of drawings and photographs. The translator, Arthur Fairbanks, lists his affiliation as "Professor of Fine Arts in Dartmouth College," and his translation suggests a strong familiarity with the works of Walter Pater, who caused such a sensation with his erotic definition of friendship in the "Conclusion" to his essays on the Renaissance (1873; *Marius the Epicurean* came out in 1885, *Plato and Platonism* 1893, *Greek Studies* posthumously in 1895). It comes as no surprise to find that Fairbanks earned a PhD in Germany in 1890; his 1931 translation, a retirement project, illustrates the persistence of the nineteenth century into the twentieth.[29]

Fairbanks emphasizes in his "Introduction" that Philostratus addresses his *Imagines* to an unnamed boy (1931: xxiii). Here is his version of a small section of Philostratus' *Imagines* 1.6, which describes a painting of Cupids (Fairbanks 1931: 23, 25):

> For here are four of them, the most beautiful of all, withdrawn from the rest; two of them are throwing an apple back and forth, and the second pair are engaged in archery, one shooting at his companion and the latter shooting back. Nor is there any trace of hostility in their faces; rather they offer their breasts to each other, in order that the missiles may pierce them there, no doubt. It is a beautiful riddle; come, let us see if perchance I can guess the painter's meaning. This is friendship, my boy, and yearning of one for the other. … In a word, the first pair in their play are intent on falling in love, while the second pair are shooting arrows that they may not cease from desire.

Fairbanks illustrates this passage with a drawing of a sarcophagus showing "Erotes boxing and wrestling"; Birt cites *Imagines* 1.6 to argue that mythic small boys are shown in art playing boyish games (xxvii). This and other works of Philostratus are intensely homoerotic, and would have been read as markedly so in the 1890s–1930s, when poems about boys, and art depicting athletes, were very much part of a thinly disguised vogue (Stevenson 1998).[30]

The literal eroticization of young children – turning them into *erôtes* – forms part of Birt's argument about a supposed child market at Alexandria, which he takes to be supported by the many images of Cupid, or just of babies, in chains or in cages (see Figure 20.1). A popular theme, "Wer kauft Liebesgötter," had inspired a poem by Goethe later set to music by Schubert; Birt fears he may be accused of "indolence" if he omits it (xxxii). He outlines the analogies drawn in antiquity between young children and young birds in order to justify his idea that a baby shown with wings is really just a baby, not a Cupid (xxxii–xxxv). Here, among other lexical items, he quotes the fragment from Pompeius Festus discussed in the section, The sexual use of children, above: "The ancients used to call a boy (*puer*) whom someone loved his chick (*pullus*)." The babies in the market, then, are being sold like little birds. In order to argue that poets were describing something they had actually seen, he adduces an epigram by the poet Meleager (first century BCE), which he takes to be about such a market. "I cannot help quoting the most brilliant part," he says, printing lines 1–3, 7–10 (xxxii). Here is the poem in full (*AP* 5.178, trans. Paton 1916):

> Sell it! though it is still sleeping on its mother's breast. Sell it! why should I bring up such a little devil? For it is snub-nosed, and has little wings, and scratches lightly with its nails, and while it is crying often begins to laugh. Besides, it is impossible to suckle

it; it is always chattering and has the keenest of eyes, and it is savage and even its dear mother can't tame it. It is a monster all round; so it shall be sold. If any trader (*emporos*) who is just leaving wants to buy a baby (*paida*), let him come hither. But look! it is supplicating, all in tears. Well! I will not sell thee then. Be not afraid; thou shalt stay here to keep Zenophila company.

Zenophila is addressed in other poems as the poet's mistress; the little creature described here is Eros, recognizable by his conventional attributes. The scratching, in particular, is often mentioned in epigram as a sexy thing to do. Yet the creature is also a baby slave whose owner has decided to sell him. Birt was interested in its young age, and its chatter, and in the fact that it was for sale in the market (viz. the presence of the trader). Meleager came from Gadara in Syria; Birt insists that this is something he might have seen himself, and he comments approvingly on the poem, "See how carefully Meleager has observed the likeness of little tiny children (*puerulorum … minutorum*)" (xxxiii). As in Martial's poems about the sale of unweaned children by their mothers, the young slave is defined as saleable in relation to its mother's breast; the baby's tears are treated with kindly indulgence: "Well! I will not sell thee." (The "Well!" is another Walter Pater mannerism, natural in Paton, whose translation of the *Greek Anthology* for the Loeb series spanned the years 1916–18; cf. Nisbet 2013.)[31]

Birt supports his arguments for the Alexandrian child market (xxxi, xxxvii) with brief reference to two poems in Statius' *Silvae* in which the poet eulogizes dead slave boys by differentiating them from children sold among Egyptian goods. The first boy belonged to the wealthy Atedius Melior, the second to Statius himself. Two passages in these poems bear marked similarities:

> The whirl of a barbarian *catasta* did not turn you about,
> nor, a child (*infans*) for sale mixed up with Egyptian wares
> and speaking specially composed witticisms and well-rehearsed words,
> did you, flirtatious (*lascivus*), seek an owner, and get one belatedly.
> Your home is here, your origin from here …
>
> *(Silvae 2.1.72–6)*

> I did not love a child (*infantem*) I shopped for from an Egyptian ship,
> a talkative *deliciae*, trained in the abusive language (*convicia*) of his native Nile,
> too impudent with his tongue and witticisms:
> he was mine, mine …
>
> *(Silvae 5.5.66–9)*

What interested Birt, and must interest us, is that, as part of the grooming of these children for sale, they are taught to say "impudent" phrases (cf. Bernstein 2005: 267). Birt might have pointed out that this is another way in which they resemble birds; Statius also has a poem lamenting Melior's dead parrot (*Silvae* 2.4). The transgressive speech of *deliciae* is remarked on by Roman moralizers, notably Quintilian (*Inst.* 1.2.7–8), who places the children amid scenes from a decadent household – like *scurrae*, or *kinaidoi*, who served similar functions in wealthy houses in this period (cf. Richlin forthcoming).

Birt's Statius passage comes from a string of poems on boys threaded through the *Silvae*: three laments for dead freed-slave boys (2.1, on "Glaucias, the *delicatus* of Atedius Melior"; 2.6, a "Consolation to Flavius Ursus on the loss of his *puer delicatus*"; 5.5, fragments of a "Dirge for my *puer*"); 3.4, on the locks of hair dedicated by Domitian's boy eunuch Earinos; 5.2, "Praises of Crispinus, son of Vettius Bolanus." It is doubted that the titles, although ancient, are original

(Newlands 2011: 7); if not, they show how an ancient editor read the boys addressed in 2.1 and 2.6: as *delicati* – erotic objects.[32] The five poems interlock in ways that conflate the virtues of the noble boy with those of beloved slaves – directly so, in the consolation to Flavius Ursus; the lost children are lamented as the mourner's flesh and blood, their chastity is insisted upon, their parents rate a nod; then again, their beauty is praised as in pederastic poetry; Melior's boy is decked in purple and jewels (2.1.132–5) like the children in Herodian, and Statius ends 2.6 by telling Flavius Ursus that fate will send him "another Philetos" to console him (2.6.103–5). The laments for Atedius Melior's boy and Statius' own boy present detailed descriptions of their babyhood and childhood; what remains of 5.5 specifies only that the boy is an *infans* (9), while Melior's died at the age of twelve (Statius says the boy's status precluded Melior's dressing him in the *praetexta*, 2.1.136).

Martial, who courted the same patrons as Statius (Newlands 2011: 22–3), produced two epigrams also commemorating Melior's Glaucias (6.28, 6.29): *cari deliciae breves patroni*, Martial calls him (6.28.3) – "brief pet of his dear former owner." Yet for Martial, too, the boy is chaste (6.28.6, 6.29.2) as well as beautiful (6.28.7, 6.29.5–6). Over two hundred years later, Ausonius, who loved to imitate Martial, turned out a lament for Glaucias (*Epig.* 53) that raises his age to sixteen, stresses his transition into manhood out of his former epicene beauty, and imagines him transformed into the favorite either of the queen or the king of the underworld, for whom he will be Adonis or *Catamitus* (53.8). So Ausonius rewrote Martial for his readers; so Martial and Statius wrote Melior's desire in order to please him.

The oddity of Statius' very odd poems has produced a range of readings among different groups of readers: Roman family historians (most recently Bernstein 2005; Laes 2010b, 2011: 223–30); literary critics writing on Statius (Newlands 2011); historians of sexuality (Asso 2010, who points out that Hubbard included *Silvae* 2.6 in his 2003 sourcebook on ancient homosexuality). In general, the family historians and some readers of Statius have interpreted *Silvae* 2.1, with 5.5, as laments for a foster child; Neil Bernstein (2005) singles out "status inconsistency" as the reason for the poem's odd air of overkill (why show such grief for a former slave?); all then must explain the poem's markedly erotic elements. Other readers of Statius, and historians of sexuality, have read the boys in 2.1 and 2.6 as *delicati*, hence eroticized; Paolo Asso (2010) lays out the many erotic intertexts for *Silvae* 2.1, including the related poems in the *Silvae* plus Statius' *Achilleid*, but then must explain the poem's markedly non-erotic elements. The Roman reality adumbrated by these texts is best summed up by Beryl Rawson on *deliciae* (2003: 261): "The line between indulgent affection and sexual exploitation must have been blurred."[33]

How the line is blurred is shown by two groups of poems in Martial: three famous epigrams lamenting a dead six-year-old slave girl named Erotion (5.34, 5.37, 10.61), and three less famous ones to a boy named Diadumenus (3.65, 5.46, 6.34).[34] The two groups are linked by the format of 5.37 and 3.65: both poems list physically attractive features, with elaborate comparisons to luxury goods. Erotion is *dulcior, mollior, delicatior,* the poet's *amores, gaudium, lusus;* Diadumenus exhales delicious scents. Erotion is dead (5.37.14), so her poem is a lament; Diadumenus is cruel, and gives *basia* (3.65.9), so his poem is a love poem; until late in each poem, however, it would be hard to tell the difference. The difference is brought home in Martial 5.46:

> Since I don't want kisses (*basia*) except those I've taken despite your struggles (*luctantia*),
> and your anger pleases me more than your face,
> so that I may want you more, Diadumenus, I often strike you (*caedo*):
> here's what I get: you neither fear me nor love me.

Martial's *caedo* here brings us back to Catullus' *cecidi* in c. 56, and indeed Martial often has Catullus in mind; 6.34, another kiss-poem, is modeled on Catullus 5 and 7, and 5.46 also recalls c. 99 on *basia* stolen from Juventius. The epigram form, with its typical intertextuality, lets Martial hold a costume party, teasing the historian: life or literature? Bernstein (2005: 271–3) analyzes both Melior's boy and Statius' poem on the boy as commodities. I would add that, as high-art laments are a form of entertainment, so readers of Statius and Martial must have taken pleasure in grief for dead slave children. This grief was "sentimental," as in the songs of Stephen Foster, only insofar as neither art form advocated social change. Whatever was the real physical relationship between Melior and Glaucias, whose age is solidly located before puberty, the poem's insistence on chastity must be arguing against readers' expectations of what an owner might do with such a huggy-kissy child – whose cuddly behavior is lovingly detailed (2.1.51, 60–6).

The insistence on chastity in praise poems likewise provoked a contemporary skepticism, seen in a running gag in the *Cena Trimalchionis* (68.6–69.5, 74.8–75.5): compare Trimalchio on a *puer* he kissed, *non propter formam, sed quia frugi est* ("not because of his beauty, but because he's honest," 75.4) with Niceros on his (married) girlfriend, whom he loved *non corporaliter ... aut propter res venerias ... sed magis quod benemoria fuit* ("not for her body, or for sex, but more for her good character," 61.7). Trimalchio's autobiography incorporates his sexual use, as *deliciae*, by both his master and mistress, and scholars have often noted his defensive line "What the master orders is no disgrace" (*nec turpe est quod dominus iubet*, 75.11); he also, however, says (75.10) how small he was when he came from Asia, how he longed for his beard to appear (cf. Statius *Silvae* 2.1.53–4), but, despite this, how his sexual service lasted fourteen years. Statius through a jaundiced eye.

A teasing pleasure informs another text Birt likes (xxvii, xxxvi–vii): Lucian *Dialogues of the Gods* 10, on Zeus and Ganymede. Although Birt barely quotes from it, he insists on its importance, and a look at the text explains why (trans. Macleod 1961):

Zeus: Come now, Ganymede. We've got there, so you can give me a kiss right away ...
Ganymede: You're just a kidnapper (*andrapodistês*), if you ask me. ... Won't you be taking me back to Ida today?
Zeus: Of course not. ...
Ganymede: Then my daddy will be looking everywhere for me ... I miss him already.
Zeus: [The italicized section is what Birt quotes] *How simple the child is, how innocent he is! Still just a child* (*pais*), *that's what he is.* Look here, Ganymede, you can say good-bye to all those things, and forget all about them ...
Ganymede: But what if I want to play? Who will play with me? There were a lot of us who were of my age on Ida.
Zeus: You have someone to play with here too – there's Eros over there – and lots and lots of knucklebones as well. ...
Ganymede: But how could I possibly be any use to you? ... Where shall I sleep at night? With Eros, my playmate?
Zeus: No, that's why I carried you off up here; I wanted us to sleep together.
Ganymede: Can't you sleep alone? Will you prefer sleeping with me?
Zeus: Yes, when it's with a beautiful boy like you (*houtô kalos*).
Ganymede: ... I'll be an awful nuisance to you, tossing and turning all night long.
Zeus: That's just what I'll like best – staying awake with you, kissing and hugging you again and again. [The word for "hugging" here, *periptussôn*, is used by Agathon of Eros himself in Plato's *Symposium* (196a), with the sense "permeate."]

The joke here is that the boy is too young and innocent to know what is about to happen to him: the knucklebones, the emphasis on play, the ignorance of pederasty, all mark him as childish, and Zeus comments on his childish innocence. Ganymede was the paradigm of the *erômenos*, and figures as such in a thousand epigrams ("Zeus came as an eagle to godlike Ganymede," *AP* 5.65.1). He appears on the cover of Craig Williams' book *Roman Homosexuality*, in the version painted by Rubens, where he looks about sixteen, requiring quite a large eagle (an instance of Counter-Reformation ambivalence about Ganymede's age). There is no doubt in Lucian's dialogue that the boy is about to be raped, although Lucian does not say so, nor is "rape" part of his formulation; he emphasizes the boy's ignorance in order to titillate the reader, especially through the omission of any detailed answer to the question "What do you want me for?" Compare the end of *Dialogues of the Courtesans* 5, which leaves the reader hanging on the question of what *tribades* do in bed. The boy calls Zeus an *andrapodistês* – a slave-trader (Macleod's translation somewhat obscures the full sense); the girl Amymone says the same of Poseidon as he carries her off ("You're an *andrapodistês*," *Dialogues of the Sea-Gods* 8.3); and Lucian here and elsewhere shows an interest in the sexual initiation of young girls (*Dial. Court.* 6; *Dialogues of the Sea-Gods* 15). He must be anticipating a readership that shares these tastes.

Birt's comment on Lucian's "Zeus and Ganymede" is startling (xxxvi–xxxvii):

> Indeed there is nothing of this kind in works of comedy either sweeter (*dulcius*) or which could do more to soothe the soul than the dialogue I recall reading of the baby (*infantis*) Ganymede with great Jupiter, done by Lucian in *Dialogues of the Gods* [10]: for Lucian achieved there a painterly expression of both the charming ignorance of life and the love of chatter and that continuous and simple impulse to ask questions that is natural to small children (*puerulorum*). And Jupiter himself points this out: "*How simple the child is, how innocent he is! Still just a child (*pais*), that's what he is.*" And so Ganymede here, as Lucian describes him, is the same to Jupiter as Sarmentus was to Augustus and Camerius was to Catullus.

Birt knew what Zeus wanted Ganymede for; does he think that Lucian de-sexes Ganymede, just as the supposed Sarmentus, and Birt's imagined Camerius, were non-erotic for Octavian and Catullus? Or does he imagine all as both erotic and childish? Until the explicit critique of sex/gender systems that began in the 1970s, it was common for those few scholars who wrote about ancient sexuality to adopt the point of view of their sources. Birt invites his reader along with him to fantasize that Catullus used to dress Camerius up to look like Cupid (xlii). Bizarrely, he imagines that a teeny-tiny Cupid has flown onto his little page to make an objection, like Tinkerbell (*rursus ecce in chartulam Cupido minusculus nobis involat*, xxxvii). At the end, he figures the making of his argument as the catching of this "well-hidden runaway" – placing himself in Catullus' place, looking for Camerius.

It would be easy to believe, at this point, that Birt was in sympathy with Catullus. It is not just the eruption of Tinkerbell onto the page; at several points he does show that he understood what Ganymede did. After all, he started out with the statement that *deliciae* were kept *non sine venere*. As well as the dictionary entry from Festus, he quotes from a late ancient Greek/Latin dictionary that glossed *pullarius* as *paiderastês* (Goetz 392; Birt xxxiv); on *pullarius*, he cites a poem by Ausonius (*Epig.* 65 = 73 Green) that includes graphic lines on anal sex, although he does not quote that part. He drags in a late Latin poem about Cupid "pissing into a philosopher's asshole" (xxxviii). At the very end he presents Catullus c. 56 in full – in order to show that Catullus' Lesbia also had a *deliciae*. "The thing is funny, hilarious," as he puts it; his Latin again merges with the quoted text itself. Birt takes the poem to mean that an *infans* is serving as a slave to lust (*lasciviae inservire*), and compares the "unworthy tales" about Tiberius – and Lucian's *Dialogue* about Jupiter and Ganymede.

So you would think that Birt believed that small children were used for sex. At times he seems to like the idea, or at least find it "charming." But in the conclusion to his treatise, he leaves the reader less certain (xxxix):

> I strongly urge this one point, that we not believe that only lustful pleasure or improper luxuriousness was the single or principal source of the custom [of keeping *deliciae*]. For we are dealing with that age, in general, in which also our Lord Jesus both ordered the children (*infantes*) to come to him and embraced them.

Reading boy-love and child-love

Times change, and reading changes with them. Birt in 1892 seems to be participating in the sort of aestheticized pederasty well described by Jane Stevenson, in which the love of boys is simultaneously Christian and sexy (Stevenson 1998). For an historically minded bystander in 2014, it is hard to find in Greek and Roman texts any clear distinctions between the categories "pet slave child" and "sex object slave boy," while free children and fantasy children were also sometimes the target of lust; in art, babyish *amores* were ubiquitous, and children looked like Ganymedes or Erotes, not angels. It would seem that there was no strongly felt lower age limit in pederasty. Readers have interpreted this material to suit their own ideas, at every level from textual criticism (Shackleton Bailey's "her" for "him") to oil painting. Ancient pederasty, from a late nineteenth-century perspective, was literally the love of boys, not distinguished as a category from children, and the Uranian poets, for example, did not see this as a problem, even if better known writers like John Addington Symonds and Edward Carpenter preferred to stress the love between manly companions like the Sacred Band of Thebes.[35] In Theodor Birt's world, in the world of Robinson Ellis, of the first Loeb translators, the Uranian writers were an underground river that deeply watered contemporary aesthetics. In turn, nineteenth-century scholarship formed twentieth-century scholarship, feeding from Gerhard to Beazley to Dover.[36] The year 1968 both opened things up and closed things off. From a twenty-first-century perspective, pederasty did overlap with what we now call pedophilia; in discussing it as a social practice we can now no more view it through the lens of cultural relativism than we can slavery. We need to think more about how pederasty and slavery were interrelated. Nor was a boy's freedom, despite Verstraete's heartfelt arguments, any guarantor of his independent action, even if it made a lover show respect; even if Catullus imagined Juventius as free, he still thought raping the *pupulus* was funny.

Yet we cannot read our own experiential categories onto a group of cultures that had sexually objectified young males for a millennium. In John Berger's famous dictum about the male gaze, "Men look at women. Women watch themselves being looked at. This determines not only most relations between men and women but also the relation of women to themselves" (Berger 1972: 47). For "women" read "boys." Or "children" – this shows how terms matter. Amid the wave of theory touched off by Berger, one point was vociferously repeated: women who are acculturated in this way not only internalize such objectification, but also, in some cases, enjoy it (discussion in Richlin 1992b: xiv–xviii) – another way in which meaning is made at the point of reception. This defense of the gaze, however, was never extended to children, and never tested by slavery.

Notes

1 For this axiom of reception theory, see Martindale 1993 and ensuing work. Many thanks to the editors for their patience. Portions of this essay were presented at the 2013 Paul Rehak Symposium on Greek and Roman Art and Gender at the University of Kansas; thanks to John Younger for the invitation, and, for discussion, to my co-presenters Eve D'Ambra and Jeannine Diddle Uzzi, to Stanley Lombardo at Kansas, and to the poet Trish Reeves in Kansas City. Christian Laes kindly sent me a copy of his essay on pedophilia/pederasty (2010a).

2 A surprising amount of work came out of Yale: Jeffrey Henderson published his study of Aristophanic sexual language, *The Maculate Muse* (1975), while teaching there (it had been his Harvard dissertation, and he was in close communication with Dover due to their shared interest in Aristophanes); John J. Winkler was teaching there at the same time, and both were on my dissertation committee (1978); my director, Gordon Williams, coincidentally Dover's former colleague at St Andrews, went on to direct Craig Williams' 1992 dissertation; Thomas K. Hubbard completed his dissertation there in 1980. Meanwhile, John Boswell, then a young professor in the History Department, was at work on his own studies in ancient and medieval sexuality, the first major book appearing in 1980; Ralph Hexter, then a graduate student in Comparative Literature, was his research assistant. Across the country, David Halperin was finishing his PhD at Stanford (1980), where Winkler had been hired in 1979.

3 Apuleius *Apologia* 9–13; Libanius *Autobiography* 7, 12.

4 On the overlap between subordinate groups in classical Greece, see esp. Golden 1984: 316–20, and, on age demarcations, 321–2, with Golden 1985. For the legal status of male/male sex in Greece and Rome, see Cohen 1991; Dover 1978: 19–38; Fantham 1991; Masterson 2014; Richlin 1992a: 224, 1993; Williams 2010: 103–36, 214–16.

5 For statements of these norms, see Dover 1978: 84–7; on the Stoics, Gaca 2003: 75–81 (adolescents both male and female); Hubbard 2003: 5–6 and *passim*; Richlin 1992a: 36–7; Williams 2010: 19; most recently, Laes 2010a, 2011: 262–8, 281 (he rightly comments that age is very rarely mentioned, but ends, following Williams, with a range of twelve to twenty).

6 See also Laes 2010a, a general overview largely agreeing with Verstraete's approach; both accord attention to Vattuone 2004, who blames feminism and the nanny state for the image of the monstrous pedophile and the lack of respect for intergenerational love (a stock argument; cf. Hubbard 2009; Laes 2010a: 32 n. 56, 2011: 276; esp. Mader 2005: 411–12, for a serious historical treatment). Parts of Laes 2010a reappear in Laes 2011: 222–77, which covers many of the texts dealt with below. Cf. Hubbard 2000, published by a small press and bearing the endorsement of the North American Man-Boy Love Association. Verstraete and Provencal's 2005 publication was held back by Haworth Press until an article by Bruce Rind was removed by the editors; this controversy continues on the internet.

7 For the lack of a concept of an age of consent in antiquity, see Laes 2010a: 47–8; 2011: 275. Consent did matter, however, although differently in different places: free boys in classical Athens are said to have exercised consent (Dover 1978: 81–4); by Roman custom, sex with a free boy was *stuprum*, an assertion that the boy had consented being no defense (Fantham 1991, see esp. Valerius Maximus 6.1.10); slaves had no right to refuse. Consent was, then, a matter of civil status.

8 On "sissyphobia" see Bergling 2001; Kendall and Martino 2006. Critiques of "homonormativity," going back at least to Lisa Duggan (2003: 50, 65), advocate a range of queer sexualities outside the model of binary heterosexuality, but do not address child-love; see Stryker 2008 for the earlier use of "homonormativity" among transgender persons. On the particular problems of homonormativity for adolescents, see Cover 2012.

9 Kinsey *et al.* 1948: 157–81; Piercy 1976: 129–31.

10 For discussion, see also Laes 2011: 258–9.

11 Note that the Etruscan king promises to send Cloelia home < *intactam* > *inviolatamque* (2.13.8), on the model of Scaevola, identified at 2.12.2 as *adulescens nobilis*, who is sent home *intactum inviolatumque* (2.12.14): cautionary tales for Augustan youth.

12 See Dolansky 2008: 50, 62–3 nn. 15–17 on the dedication of the *bulla* and *toga praetexta*; 49 and 61 n. 11 on evidence for the connection between this ritual and physical puberty. On girls' amulets, see D'Ambra 2007: 124–5; Olson 2008: 144.

13 The poem is briefly discussed by Lateiner 1977; briefly discussed in Richlin 1992a: 152, 249–50 n. 23; not discussed by Fitzgerald 1995; included by David Wray in a list of 69 poems that "feature Catullus performing or threatening aggression" (2001: 113); mentioned among the essays in Skinner's *Companion to Catullus* only as "the description of a sexual encounter" in a discussion of "Cato" in the poem (Lorenz 2007); not discussed by Williams 2010.

Amy Richlin

14 *ODNB*: Robinson Ellis (1834–1913), educated at Rugby and Balliol; taught at Trinity College, Oxford, and University College, London, ending as Professor of Latin and fellow of Corpus Christi College, Oxford. On homophile Oxford, see Dowling 1994.

15 For more recent discussion of the vocabulary in this passage, see Adams 1982: 145–6, who calls Bährens' *crusantem* "bizarre"; he follows Kroll and A.E. Housman in keeping *trusantem* and understanding it to mean "masturbating." He cites, following Bährens, the textual critic D.R. Shackleton Bailey, who also indulged his own imagination and changed "him" (line 6) to "her," arguing that "'logic ... suggests that the object of Catullus' intervention ... should be not the boy, but his playmate.'" Adams gives no opinion on the meaning of *puellae* except to say that it cannot be dative; he is certain at least that *caedo* here signifies a punishment. The now-standard commentator is succinct: "Take *pupulum puellae* together: 'my girl's little boy-servant'" (Thomson 1997 ad loc., with further bibliography). Note Thomson's understanding of *pupulus* to imply slave status (presumably he, like others, here uses "servant" to mean "slave").

16 See most recently Laes 2011: 132–47 on *grammatici* and corporal punishment.

17 These terms are not discussed in Adams 1982. Other uses of *pusio* also blur age and status: Cicero *Cael.* 36, *Tusc.* 1.57, Apuleius *M.* 9.7.

18 For a brief discussion, see Richlin 1992a: 288–9; Williams 2010: 25.

19 For *Eros* and compounds (*Hermeros, Niceros, Phileros*), 1,027 examples in Clauss-Slaby for Rome alone; for *Ganymedes*, only six in Rome, but cf. *CIL* 6.35769, to a dead freed child whose freed parents are inscribed in verse comparing their son to Cupid and Ganymede, and also (if he had lived) to Phoebus, Bromius, and Narcissus. See the subsection, The sexual use of small children, below on Statius' poem to Melior's boy.

20 Here I disagree with John Martens' argument (2009) that early Christian writers used *paidophthorein* to mean "sexually abuse children." This term is the moral equivalent of *corrumpere* in Valerius Maximus (see John Cassian *Conl.* 13.5.3–4 for a direct translation of *paiderastês* as *corruptor puerorum*), but indicates no special sense of childhood as a protected state. Similarly Laes 2011: 268–75.

21 On the epigraphic evidence, most recently Laes 2003: 305–16; cf. n. 19. For full discussion of relevant Roman art, and conclusions close to my own, see George 2013, which appeared while this essay was in press.

22 Reading Jacobs' emendation *catamitus* for mss. *caccitus*.

23 Available online at de.wikipedia.org/wiki/Theodor_Birt (fullest information) (accessed 29 June 2014): Theodor Birt (1852–1933), classicist and fiction writer (under the pen-name Beatus Rhenanus); studied at Leipzig and Bonn; taught at Marburg from 1878 to 1921, as Ordinarius from 1886 on; served as Rector 1902–3. Not in *ADB*. Birt is briefly credited at Laes 2003: 299.

24 He sent it to me to read in the fall of 1977; Stanley Lombardo remembers the day Winkler discovered it in the University of Texas library when they were graduate students together. See Richlin 1992a: 258 n. 9 for a 1727 source Winkler found in the library of the Kinsey Institute.

25 On this point, I would tentatively propose that the word *infantaria* at Martial 4.87.3 means, not "a woman who looks after babies" (*OLD*), but "a woman enamored of babies," on the model of *glabraria*, "a woman enamored of beardless young men" (Mart. 4.28.7, cf. Williams 2010: 83 with note), or *pullarius*, "a man enamored of boys" (Petr. *Sat.* 43.8, but this is an emendation; Ausonius *Epig.* 73.5, where Green adduces Plautus *Per.* 751 *virginaria*; see the section, The sexual use of children, above on *pullus*).

26 Dellius, who was a house historian for Antony, retained a reputation as a joker; he changed sides repeatedly during the Civil Wars, and wrote some *epistulae lascivae* addressed to Cleopatra, evidently after siding at last with Octavian (Sen. *Suas.* 1.7).

27 Exoticism in this story is also addressed by Asso 2010: 679 n. 53.

28 Greeks and Greek-Egyptians: Martial 4.42, 4.66.9, cf. 2.43; Asiatic Greek boys contrasted with Moors, Juvenal 5.52–60. Syrians: litter-bearers in Martial (7.53.10, 9.2.11, 9.22.9) and Juvenal (6.351); cf. Plautus *Mer.* 413–16; Starks 2010.

29 See Sorenson n.d. for Fairbanks' ties to the world of homophile art collectors in the early 1900s.

30 Homoerotics in Philostratus *Imagines*: 1.20, *Satyrs*, with 1.21, *Olympus* (both on Olympus, beloved of Marsyas); 1.23, *Narcissus*; 1.24, *Hyacinthus*; 2.32, *Palaestra* (cross-gender); cf. 1.5, *Pêcheis*, a description of the famous statue showing tiny children climbing over the body of a naked man. (The children represent the "cubits" of inundation, the man represents the Nile; the Vatican has a copy, which appears as Fairbanks 1931 fig. 1 = Birt 1892 plate III, with discussion at xxi and xxxvii.) In Fairbanks' Loeb, see also the *Imagines* of the younger Philostratus: 1, *Achilles on Scyros*; 8, on Eros playing

370

knucklebones with Ganymede (illustrated by fig. 29, a drawing from a "Pompeian wall-painting" in which each looks to be about four years old; this word-painting of an imaginary painting is in turn based on Ap. Rhod. 3.117ff.); 14, *Hyacinthus*; also, in Fairbanks, the *Descriptions* of Callistratus: 3, *Statue of Eros*; 5, *Statue of Narcissus*; 11, *Statue of a Youth* (the "Diadoumenos" of Praxiteles). On the Philostrati, see now Bowie and Elsner 2009; on Philostratus' *Love Letters,* Goldhill 2009. Goethe wrote on the *Imagines*, and they strongly evoke Alma-Tadema and his kin; the Uranian journal *Artist and Journal of Home Culture* ran a double series on "Subjects for Pictures" in 1889. See Mader 2005: 384–6 on Uranian translations of Philostratus and similar projects; see further the section, Reading boy-love and child-love below.

31 *ODNB* William Roger Paton (1857–1921); in Oscar Browning's house at Eton (1871–3); friend of Oscar Wilde; active as an epigrapher in the Greek islands from 1884, in which year he met the 14-year-old Irene Olympitis, marrying her the following year; an adventurous life in the eastern Mediterranean, and many publications, including a selection of erotic poems from Book 5 of the *Greek Anthology.*

32 Similarly Asso 2010: 676 n. 42.

33 Also quoted in Asso 2010: 665 n. 6; compare Laes 2011: 284 on the "double meaning" of *delicium.*

34 For Erotion and bibliography, see Bernstein 2005: 257 n. 2, 267 n. 49; Laes 2011: 256–8; for Diadumenus in Martial 3.65, Richlin 1992a: 39–40.

35 On the Uranians, see D'Arch Smith 1970; Mader 2005. On von Gloeden and related art in this period, see Aldrich 1993: 87–111, 144–52; Boone 2014: 271–5; Reed 2011: 97–109; Stevenson 1998. On nineteenth-century German scholarship and pederasty, see Dynes 2005. Also see Matzner 2010 on the reception of Greek ideas in the early gay rights movement in Germany. Symonds' 1873 *A Problem in Greek Ethics* can be found on Rictor Norton's website, with publication history, available online at http://rictornorton.co.uk/symonds/greek.htm (accessed 29 June 2014). On Carpenter, see Rowbotham 2008: 186–91.

36 On the relationship between Sir John Beazley, the great authority on Greek vases, and the poet James Elroy Flecker, in their Oxford days, see Sherwood 1973.

Bibliography

Adams, J.N. (1982) *The Latin Sexual Vocabulary*. London: Duckworth.

Aldrich, R. (1993) *The Seduction of the Mediterranean: Writing, Art and Homosexual Fantasy*. London: Routledge.

——(2002) *Colonialism and Homosexuality*. London: Routledge.

Asso, P. (2010) "Queer consolation: Melior's dead boy in Statius' *Silvae* 2.1", *American Journal of Philology* 131: 663–97.

Berger, J. (1972) *Ways of Seeing*. London and Harmondsworth: BBC and Penguin.

Bergling, T. (2001) *Sissyphobia: Gay Men and Effeminate Behavior*. New York: Southern Tier Editions.

Bernstein, N.W. (2005) "Mourning the *puer delicatus*: Status inconsistency and the ethical value of fostering in Statius, *Silvae* 2.1", *American Journal of Philology* 126: 257–80.

Birt, T. (1892) *De Amorum in arte antiqua simulacris et de pueris minutis apud antiquos in deliciis habitis commentariolus Catullianus alter,* incorporated in *Indices lectionum … quae in Academia Marpurgensi per semestre aestivum … habendae proponuntur*. Marburg: Robert Friedrich.

Boone, J.A. (2014) *The Homoerotics of Orientalism*. New York: Columbia University Press.

Boswell, J. (1980) *Christianity, Social Tolerance, and Homosexuality: Gay People in Western Europe from the Beginning of the Christian Era to the Fourteenth Century*. Chicago, IL: University of Chicago Press.

Bowie, E. and Elsner, J. (eds) (2009) *Philostratus*. Cambridge: Cambridge University Press.

Cohen, D. (1991) *Law, Sexuality and Society: The Enforcement of Morals in Classical Athens*. Cambridge: Cambridge University Press.

Courtney, E. (ed.) (1993) *The Fragmentary Latin Poets*. Oxford: Clarendon Press.

Cover, R. (2012) *Queer Youth Suicide, Culture and Identity: Unliveable Lives?* Burlington, VT: Ashgate.

D'Ambra, E. (2007) *Roman Women*. Cambridge: Cambridge University Press.

D'Arch Smith, T. (1970) *Love in Earnest: Some Notes on the Lives and Writings of English "Uranian" Poets from 1889 to 1930*. London: Routledge and Kegan Paul.

Davidson, J.N. (2007) *The Greeks and Greek Love: A Radical Reappraisal of Homosexuality in Ancient Greece*. London: Weidenfeld & Nicolson.

Dolansky, F. (2008) "*Togam virilem sumere*: Coming of age in the Roman world", in J. Edmondson and A. Keith (eds) *Roman Dress and the Fabrics of Roman Culture*. Toronto, ON: University of Toronto Press, pp. 47–70.

Dover, K.J. (1978) *Greek Homosexuality*. London: Duckworth.

Dowling, L. (1994) *Hellenism and Homosexuality in Victorian Oxford*. Ithaca, NY: Cornell University Press.

Duggan, L. (2003) *The Twilight of Equality? Neoliberalism, Cultural Politics, and the Attack on Democracy*. Boston, MA: Beacon Press.

Dynes, W.R. (2005) "Light in Hellas: How German classical philology engendered gay scholarship", in B.C. Verstraete and V. Provencal (eds) *Same-Sex Desire and Love in Greco-Roman Antiquity and in the Classical Tradition of the West*. Binghamton, NY: Haworth Press, pp. 341–56.

Ellis, R. (ed.) (1889) *A Commentary on Catullus*, 2nd edn. Oxford: Clarendon Press.

Fairbanks, A. (trans.) (1931) *Philostratus: Imagines; Callistratus: Descriptions*. London: Heinemann.

Fantham, E. (1991) "*Stuprum*: Public attitudes and penalties for sexual offences in Republican Rome", *Echos du Monde Classique/Classical Views* 35: 267–91.

Fitzgerald, W. (1995) *Catullan Provocations: Lyric Poetry and the Drama of Position*. Berkeley, CA: University of California Press.

Foucault, M. (1978) *The History of Sexuality, Volume I: An Introduction*, trans. R. Hurley. New York: Vintage Books.

Fraenkel, E. (2007) *Plautine Elements in Plautus*, trans. T. Drevikovsky and F. Muecke. Oxford: Oxford University Press.

Gaca, K.L. (2003) *The Making of Fornication: Eros, Ethics, and Political Reform in Greek Philosophy and Early Christianity*. Berkeley, CA: University of California Press.

——(2010–11) "Telling the girls from the boys and children: Interpreting *paides* in the sexual violence of populace-ravaging ancient warfare", *Illinois Classical Studies* 35–6: 85–109 [published 2012].

George, M. (2013) "Cupid punished: Reflections on a Roman genre scene", in M. George (ed.) *Roman Slavery and Roman Material Culture*. Toronto, ON: University of Toronto Press, pp. 158–79.

Golden, M. (1984) "Slavery and homosexuality at Athens", *Phoenix* 38: 308–24.

——(1985) "*Pais*, 'child' and 'slave'", *L'Antiquité Classique* 54: 91–104.

Goldhill, S. (2009) "Constructing identity in Philostratus' *Love Letters*", in E. Bowie and J. Elsner (eds) *Philostratus*. Cambridge: Cambridge University Press, pp. 287–305.

Gowers, E. (ed.) (2012) *Horace: Satires Book I*. Cambridge: Cambridge University Press.

Grelle, F. (1980) "La 'correctio morum' nella legislazione flavia", *Aufstieg und Niedergang der römischen Welt* 2(13): 340–65.

Henderson, J. (1975) *The Maculate Muse: Obscene Language in Attic Comedy*. New Haven, CT: Yale University Press.

Hexter, R. (2006) "John Boswell's gay science: Prolegomenon to a re-reading", in M. Kuefler (ed.) *The Boswell Thesis: Essays on Christianity, Social Tolerance, and Homosexuality*. Chicago, IL: University of Chicago Press, pp. 35–56.

Hubbard, T.K. (ed.) (2000) *Greek Love Reconsidered*. New York: W. Hamilton.

——(2003) *Homosexuality in Greece and Rome: A Sourcebook of Basic Documents*. Berkeley, CA: University of California Press.

——(2009) Review of James Davidson, *The Greeks and Greek Love*. H-Histsex in *H-Net Online*. Available online at http://h-net.msu.edu/cgi-bin/logbrowse.pl?trx=vx& list = H-Histsex& month = 0902& week = b& msg = Ug%2BYuljwHAbsmjyw%2BhMXhQ> (accessed 10 February 2009).

——(2010) "Sexual consent and the adolescent male, or what can we learn from the Greeks?", in T.K. Hubbard (ed.) *Boys' Sexuality and Age of Consent* (= special issue of *Thymos: Journal of Boyhood Studies*, 4.2). Harriman, TN: Men's Studies Press, pp. 126–48.

Kendall, C. and Martino, W. (eds) (2006) *Gendered Outcasts and Sexual Outlaws: Sexual Oppression and Gender Hierarchies in Queer Men's Lives*. New York: Harrington Park Press.

Kinsey, A.C., Pomeroy, W.B., and Martin, C.E. (1948) *Sexual Behavior in the Human Male*. Philadelphia, PA: W.B. Saunders.

Laes, C. (2003) "Desperately different? *Delicia* children in the Roman household", in D.L. Balch and C. Osiek (eds) *Early Christian Families in Context: An Interdisciplinary Dialogue*. Grand Rapids, MI: Eerdmans, pp. 298–324.

——(2010a) "When classicists need to speak up: Antiquity and present day pedophilia", in V. Sofronievski (ed.) *Aeternitas Antiquitatis*. Skopje, Macedonia: Association of Classical Philologists, pp. 30–59.

——(2010b) "*Delicia*-children revisited: The evidence of Statius' *Silvae*", in V. Dasen and T. Späth (eds) *Children, Memory, and Family Identity in Roman Culture*. Oxford: Oxford University Press, pp. 245–72.

——(2011) *Children in the Roman Empire: Outsiders Within*. Cambridge: Cambridge University Press.

Lateiner, D. (1977) "Obscenity in Catullus", *Ramus* 6: 15–32.

Lorenz, S. (2007) "Catullus and Martial", in M.B. Skinner (ed.) *A Companion to Catullus*. Oxford: Wiley-Blackwell, pp. 418–38.

Macleod, M.D. (trans.) (1961) *Lucian*, vol. VII. Cambridge, MA: Harvard University Press.

MacMullen, R. (1982) "Roman attitudes to Greek love", *Historia* 31: 484–502.

Mader, D.H. (2005) "The Greek mirror: The Uranians and their use of Greece", in B.C. Verstraete and V. Provencal (eds) *Same-Sex Desire and Love in Greco-Roman Antiquity and in the Classical Tradition of the West*. Binghamton, NY: Haworth Press, pp. 377–420.

Marshall, C.W. (2013) "Sex slaves in New Comedy", in B. Akrigg and R. Tordoff (eds) *Slaves and Slavery in Ancient Greek Comic Drama*. Cambridge: Cambridge University Press, pp. 173–96.

Martens, J.W. (2009) "'Do not sexually abuse children': The language of early Christian sexual ethics", in C. B. Horn and R.R. Phenix (eds) *Children in Late Ancient Christianity*. Tübingen: Mohr Siebeck, pp. 227–54.

Martindale, C. (1993) *Redeeming the Text: Latin Poetry and the Hermeneutics of Reception*. Cambridge: Cambridge University Press.

Masterson, M. (2014) *Man to Man: Desire, Homosociality, and Authority in Late-Roman Manhood*. Columbus, OH: Ohio State University Press.

Matzner, S. (2010) "From Uranians to homosexuals: Philhellenism, Greek homoeroticism and gay emancipation in Germany 1835–1915", *Classical Receptions Journal* 2: 60–91.

Newlands, C.E. (ed.) (2011) *Statius: Silvae Book II*. Cambridge: Cambridge University Press.

Nisbet, G. (2013) *Greek Epigram in Reception: J.A. Symonds, Oscar Wilde, and the Invention of Desire, 1805–1929*. Oxford: Oxford University Press.

Ogilvie, R.M. (ed.) (1965) *A Commentary on Livy Books 1–5*. Oxford: Oxford University Press.

Olson, K. (2008) "The appearance of the young Roman girl", in J. Edmondson and A. Keith (eds) *Roman Dress and the Fabrics of Roman Culture*. Toronto, ON: University of Toronto Press, pp. 139–57.

Paton, W.R. (trans.) (1916) *The Greek Anthology*, vol. 1. London: Heinemann.

Piercy, M. (1976) *Woman on the Edge of Time*. New York: Knopf.

Rabinowitz, N.S. (2002) "Introduction", in N.S. Rabinowitz and L. Auanger (eds) *Among Women: From the Homosocial to the Homoerotic in the Ancient World*. Austin, TX: University of Texas Press, pp. 1–33.

Rawson, B. (2003) *Children and Childhood in Roman Italy*. Oxford: Oxford University Press.

Reed, C. (2011) *Art and Homosexuality: A History of Ideas*. Oxford: Oxford University Press.

Richlin, A. (1992a) *The Garden of Priapus: Sexuality and Aggression in Roman Humor*, rev. edn. Oxford: Oxford University Press.

——(1992b) "Introduction", in A. Richlin (ed.) *Pornography and Representation in Greece and Rome*. Oxford: Oxford University Press, pp. xi–xxiii.

——(1993) "Not before homosexuality: The materiality of the *cinaedus* and the Roman law against love between men", *Journal of the History of Sexuality* 3(4): 523–73.

——(trans.) (2006) *Marcus Aurelius in Love*. Chicago, IL: University of Chicago Press.

——(forthcoming) "Retrosexuality: Sex in the Second Sophistic", in W. Johnson and D. Richter (eds) *A Companion to the Second Sophistic*. Oxford: Wiley-Blackwell.

Rowbotham, S. (2008) *Edward Carpenter: A Life of Liberty and Love*. London: Verso.

Sherwood, J. (1973) *No Golden Journey: A Biography of James Elroy Flecker*. London: Heinemann.

Starks, J.H. Jr (2010) "*Servitus, sudor, sitis*: Syra and Syrian slave stereotyping in Plautus' *Mercator*", *New England Classical Journal* 37.1: 51–64.

Stevenson, J. (1998) "Nacktleben", in D. Montserrat (ed.) *Changing Bodies, Changing Meanings: Studies in the Human Body in Antiquity*. Ann Arbor, MI: University of Michigan Press, pp. 198–212.

Stryker, S. (2008) "Transgender history, homonormativity, and disciplinarity", *Radical History Review* 100: 145–57.

Thomson, D.F.S. (ed.) (1997) *Catullus*. Toronto, ON: University of Toronto Press.

Uzzi, J.D. (forthcoming) "Ethnicity and sexuality in Roman imperial relief: Reconstructing the pederastic gaze", in P.F. Biehl and G. Coşkunsu (eds) *Children as Archaeological Enigma*. Albany: SUNY Press.

Vattuone, R. (2004) *Il mostro e il sapiente: Studi sull'erotica greca*. Bologna: Patron Editore.

Verstraete, B.C. (2012) "Reassessing Roman pederasty in relation to Roman slavery: The portrayal of *pueri delicati* in the love-poetry of Catullus, Tibullus, and Horace", *Journal of International Social Research* 5: 157–67.

Verstraete, B.C. and Provencal, V. (eds) (2005) *Same-Sex Desire and Love in Greco-Roman Antiquity and in the Classical Tradition of the West*. Binghamton, NY: Haworth Press (= *Journal of Homosexuality* 49).

Williams, C.A. (2010) *Roman Homosexuality*, 2nd edn. Oxford: Oxford University Press.

Wray, D. (2001) *Catullus and the Poetics of Roman Manhood*. Cambridge: Cambridge University Press.

21

WHAT IS NAMED BY THE NAME "PHILAENIS"?

Gender, function, and authority of an antonomastic figure[1]

Sandra Boehringer[2]

Antiquity has left us few works by women. Even if recent research by specialists in the Greek and Roman worlds sometimes enables us to discover unpublished fragments, learn new names, and bring to light aspects of women's participation in the cultural, scientific, and artistic life of political communities, it is undeniable that they play only a minor part in the record that has come down to us. The reasons for this are numerous and vary greatly according to period and geographical area in the ancient world, but one can say with justice that, in general, the vast majority of those to whom the ancients attribute authorship of a work – "the author function"[3] (in choral works, epic, drama, epigram, and historiography) – are men.

Yet there is an exception, one field where women's names are more numerous and visible than men's, and that is in the field of treatises and manuals of an erotic or pornographic character (in the modern sense of the term).[4] Holt Parker, in a 1992 study devoted to ancient erotic manuals, noticed that, aside from a few masculine names – such as Botrys of Messana,[5] the inventor of *paignia*, or Paxamos,[6] the author of a *Dodekatechnon* – it is essentially women's names that appear. We can infer from the elliptical manner in which these authors are mentioned that their names would have been well known to literate audiences. Thus, Astyanassa,[7] according to the Souda, was a servant of Helen who discovered sexual positions and produced a book about them, and Elephantis was one of her followers. Tiberius owned a work by Elephantis. Suetonius writes of the work as having the form of a didactic treatise.[8] The *Carmina Priapea* and Martial also refer to her "obscene" and "lascivious" work.[9] Other women authors appear in our texts, such as Salpē, Pamphilē, Nikō of Samos, and Kallistratē of Lesbos.[10] But one name stands out: that of Philaenis.

Philaenis[11] is the most often mentioned of the female authors to whom the authorship of an erotic treatise or manual is attributed, and she is the only one whose works we know directly. A dozen sources refer to her, and the publication, in 1972, of a few papyrological fragments of what seems to be her manual (P. Oxy. 2891) allows us to infer that Philaenis' work probably dates from the middle of the fourth century BCE and that it was particularly well known during the following centuries up until imperial times.[12] Thus, there existed, during antiquity, a field of discourse attributed for the most part to women, in which, furthermore, the most famous name is a woman's. This fact deserves to be emphasized.

Philaenis has particular status for another reason. Three times, in Greek and Latin works, her name is found in feminine homoerotic contexts. Yet, while orators' speeches overflow with accusations or praise for famous men who loved boys, while historians mention names of women who lost their honour in adulterous relationships with men, in the case of documents evoking sexual or loving relationships between women, the names of either fictional characters or real persons are rare:[13] those figures or names that do appear generally refer to the world evoked in the text's fiction and only exceedingly rarely to an extradiegetic context. In this regard, Philaenis appears doubly exceptional. Yet, even though her status as author of an erotic manual was the subject of more than twenty articles towards the end of the twentieth century, the connection with the field of female homoeroticism has scarcely been mentioned and studied even less.

When female figures do appear, be it as poets or authors of medical treatises, contemporary researchers, historians, and philologists often suspect the use of a pseudonym by a male author.[14] Was Philaenis a woman? What kind of works are the *poïēmata* of Philaenis?[15] The very question of the author's gender raises questions, broad and complex, about authority/authorship in antiquity. The question also brings up the issue of sexuality, in societies "before sexuality",[16] and contemporary prejudices which tend to assimilate debauchery and prostitution to female homosexuality. In the end, this is not about determining if Philaenis really existed and if she was a woman, but rather trying to define what is named by the name "Philaenis".

The name of an author

The various references to Philaenis' work lead us to believe that it was a manual describing a long list of sexual positions. The discovery of three papyrus fragments and the publication of the text in 1972 have brought to light the work's wider characteristics: not merely an annotated list of sexual positions, it was probably an *ars amatoria* (περὶ ἀφροδισίων). But before going any further, a clarification must be made. The modern term "pornography" is a "false friend": a πορνογράφος does not write texts with content that is erotic and/or considered obscene, but writes about prostitution and courtesans. The ancient equivalent of our "pornographic author" was rather, even if the term was rarely used, an ἀναισχυντογράφος, somebody who writes about shameless things.[17] What characterizes, in antiquity, the works that we moderns consider pornographic is not so much the content (sex and eroticism are not sufficient to define the pornographic genre) as its similarity to other technical genres and its didactic dimension: an *ars amatoria* (or a περὶ ἀφροδισίων) contains advice and presents itself as addressed to a public that wants to be instructed on erotic matters by an expert.[18]

The three fragments attributed to Philaenis found in Oxyrhynchos (P. Oxy. 2891, fr. 1–3) originate from the second century CE. They are short and very lacunose, and some passages are hardly decipherable. E. Lobel published the first edition of these fragments; several articles completing, re-editing, and correcting that first transcription followed this edition.[19] Since the text is lacunose,[20] and the *testimonia* are sometimes contradictory (if only in the matter of the author's geographical origin), reconstitutions remain very hypothetical. One point is certain, though: the text is in prose. Philaenis is therefore not a poet, contrary to what some philologists have stated – even though the sources themselves are silent on this point.[21]

The text, whose incipit is composed of a *sphragis* traditional in form, i.e., in the third person, is explicitly attributed to Philaenis: τάδε συνέγραψε Φιλαινὶς Ὠκυμένους. What follows is a transcription (Table 21.1) and a translation.[22]

> Fr. 1 (col. i): Philaenis the Samian, daughter of Okymenes, wrote this work for those who want to know the true things in life and not just in passing ... having worked at

Table 21.1 The three fragments attributed to Philaenis (P. Oxy. 2891, fr. 1–3, ed. Lobel)

Fr. 1		Fr. 3
col. i	col. ii	col. ii
τάδε συνέγραψε Φιλαι-	περὶ πειρασῶν	..]υφ[]. [
νὶς Ὠκυμένους Σαμ[ία (?)	δεῖ τοίνυν τὸν πειρῶ[ν-	..]ν τῇ διανοία[ι
τοῖς βουλομέμοις με-	τα ἀκαλλώπιστον ..[	μεν, τὴν μὲν [
θ. [ ] ς τὸν βίον. ε-	καὶ ἀκτένιστον, ὅπ[ως	ὡς ἰσόθεον [
ξα[κ]αὶ μὴ παρέρ-	ἂν τῇ γυναικ‹ί› μὴ [δοκῇ	οὖσαν, τὴν δὲ αἰσχρὰ[ν
γω[ς κτλ.	ἔπεργος εἶναι,κτλ.	ὡς ἐπαφρόδιτον, τ[ὴν
		δὲ πρεσβυτέραν ὡς [
		αν φάο[ ]ων εἶναι, (?)[
		> ----
		περὶ φιλημάτ[ων

it myself ... (col. ii): About seductions: it is necessary that the seducer be unbeautified and uncombed so that the woman has no realisation of what he is doing ... Fr. 3 (col. ii) ... in thoughts ... by saying that a woman ... is like a goddess, that an ugly woman is full of charm, and that an old woman is like a young maid. How to kiss ...

The work, as can be deduced from these short excerpts, was composed of various sections. The second fragment introduces a section on various ways to seduce (περὶ πειρασμῶν), and the end of the third fragment a section on kisses (περὶ φιλημάτων). Some indirect sources mention further analysis of erotic positions (a subject that was sometimes used to designate the work through metonymy: περὶ σχημάτων[23]), but nothing of that kind appears here.

This papyrus is the only trace of an erotic manual that has come down to us. But if these fragments demonstrate the existence of this type of work – for which until now we have only had indirect sources – they do not confirm with certainty the existence of a specific work (that of Philaenis) or of Philaenis herself. It is possible that the celebrity of the work attributed to Philaenis in classical times conferred a generic value upon the expression "Philaenis' work": this term in ordinary language could be used to refer to several works of the same kind.[24] The fragments themselves could be excerpts from a manual whose real author, adopting the name of the famous author, used Philaenis' by-line and produced an imitation of the original manual (if this "original" manual ever existed).

Moreover, even if these fragments prove that, in antiquity, saying "Philaenis' work" signified *something*, they in no way prove that it was Philaenis herself (if she ever existed) who wrote the manual (the issue of the work's attribution recurs often in the *testimonia*, as we will see). Here, Philaenis is the name of an author expressing herself in the *sphragis*: it is a fictional name. It may or may not match reality. Having these fragments in our possession does not prove that Philaenis ever wrote or existed; on the other hand, it does prove that this type of work existed – the indirect *testimonia* thus are confirmed – and it proves that the (feminine) *persona* of Philaenis, as well as the attribution of this type of work to this *persona*, were part of the cultural representations current in Greek and Roman times.

The name of a debauched woman and/or an expert in *aphrodisia*

These observations may seem particularly cautious, especially considering that the writing of erotic manuals, as we said in the introduction, is for the most part attributed to women. Why such reservations in the attribution of these fragments' "paternity" to Philaenis, an author who is a woman? I have done this in order to avoid taking for granted ancient *testimonia* when they deal with women and eroticism. I am following the advice of John Winkler who, in his work *Constraints of Desire*, produced this useful warning:[25]

> Most of our surviving documents simply cannot be taken at face value when they speak of women. As long as the discussion is centered on *gunaikes*, citizen-wives, there is a large interference in the data from male speakers' sense of social propriety … it seems that most of men's observations and moral judgments about women and sex and so forth have minimal descriptive validity.

It is therefore without postulating *a priori* any sexual identity, any identifying characteristic (profession, place of origin), or any author function, that I shall analyse the main contexts where Philaenis or a Philaenis is mentioned – contexts which can seem difficult to comprehend, as an approach to the evidence is sometimes made difficult by editions and commentaries that mix, without distinction, ancient and contemporary categories of sexuality (the latter with its ideological layers, from the 1950s until the end of the twentieth century).[26]

The first two significant occurrences[27] of our author's name appear in two epigrams from the third century BCE in the *Greek Anthology*; the authorship of these epigrams suggests that Philaenis lived a little while before the writing of the poems, towards the end of the fourth century or at the beginning of the third century BCE.[28] This piece of information, vague as it is, is already more precise than what we know about the other authors of such manuals.

Aeschrion of Samos, in a funerary epigram written in the first person, makes Philaenis speak. He has her say that it was Polycrates,[29] and not herself, who wrote the erotic work, and that she is neither a debauched woman nor a prostitute. Aeschrion probably lived in the time of Aristotle. We know nothing more about this poet. Only this one epigram has come down to us:[30]

> I, Philaenis, renowned amongst men, rest here, after living long into old age. Frivolous sailor, you who round the cape, do not mock me, do not laugh, do not despise me. No, by Zeus, in the name of the young people resting underground, I was not a debauched woman (μάχλος) with men, offered to anyone (δημώδης). It is Polycrates of Athenian birth, a sort of subtlety of words (λόγων τι παιπάλημα) and a perfidious tongue (κακὴ γλῶσσα), who wrote what he wrote. As for me, I know nothing about it.

The same pattern (the attribution of Philaenis' work to someone else) appears in the writings of Dioscorides. An imitator of Asclepiades and Callimachus, Dioscorides wrote towards the middle of the third century in Alexandria. It is highly probable that he was inspired by Aeschrion (not vice versa). In his epigram, he makes Philaenis, the fictional and fictive enunciator, refuse authorship of writings slanderous to women and shameful, without giving any further details. Dioscorides introduces her as a Samian:[31]

> Here is the tomb of Philaenis, the Samian. You, sir, dare to address me and come close to my stele. I am not the one who wrote slanderous things against women, and who did not consider Shame a goddess: I am a respectable woman (φιλαιδήμων), I swear by my tomb. And if someone, shaming me, made up that monstrous story (λαμυρὴν … ἱστορίην), may time reveal their name and, once this miserable reputation is pushed away, may my bones rest in peace.

Aeschrion and Dioscorides, in these twin epigrams, apparently take up defence of Philaenis in order to remove all blame from her – this at least is how A. Cameron interprets these epigrams.[32] A. Gow and D. Page consider another interpretation: maybe Aeschrion is aiming not to save Philaenis from disgrace but to attack Polycrates.[33] K. Tsantsanoglou, meanwhile, takes the position on these two epigrams that Polycrates, as a sophist, wrote the erotic manual under the name of Philaenis in an overtly parodic manner and that it constitutes important evidence about this Athenian writer.[34] Yet it seems, as B. Baldwin briefly states, that some scholars have taken these two epigrams too seriously: they probably are humorous.[35] How indeed can one better perpetuate (or launch) a rumour than by refuting it, after having at some length brought it to light? We know nothing about Aeschrion, but, on the other hand, we do know that humour and clever winks of the eye are important aspects of Dioscorides' work (of which forty epigrams have come down to us). In his erotic epigrams for example, he reuses the *topoi* of love epigrams and subverts them with figures and terms that are susceptible to *double-entendre*.

The construction of these two epigrams, that is to say the elaborate presentation of denials by Philaenis' *persona*, shows their humorous aim: instead of making her say who she "really" is in the affirmative (an honest and modest woman), both Aeschrion and Dioscorides choose to make her say, in the negative form, what she is not. The contrast between the form of the epigram (a funerary epigram) and the vocabulary employed – coarse (μαχλός), suggestive (λαμυρή), and rare but expressive (δημώδης) – as well as Dioscorides' pun on the poet's name – corroborates this interpretation.[36] Far from restoring Philaenis' honour, Aeschrion and Dioscorides, in parodic fashion, propagate a rumour that establishes a particularly derogatory reputation. Furthermore, these two epigrams testify that she, or at least her *persona*, was well known at the time. Dioscorides is indeed interested in the great figures of his time and he may have written fictive epitaphs for famous poets.[37] The humour of these two authors' epigrams implies that the reader would have the necessary knowledge of the *persona* in question and of her life and/or reputation.

Indirect *testimonia* from the same general period (fourth–third centuries BCE) mention the name of Philaenis and give some indications of the nature of her work – without providing anything further about the author herself. These *testimonia* come from Aristotle, Timaeus (fragments in Polybius), Chrysippus of Soli, and Clearchus of Soli (both in Athenaeus).[38] Philaenis is classified in the same category as authors of erotic treatises or as an author of a gastronomy treatise. In the passages from Athenaeus, her work is used to illustrate the philosophical *topos* of harmful effects of excess of all kinds.

A few centuries later, in Rome, the author of an epigram in the *Carmina Priapea*, a collection of inscriptions associated with statues of Priapus and compiled in the first century CE, refers, comically, to Philaenis' work in order to suggest the numerous and various erotic postures that were described there:[39]

> There comes in addition to these things the sign of shamelessness, this obelisque erected by my lecherous limb. Right up to it, the *puella* – I nearly said her name! – is accustomed to come with the one who shags her (*cum suo fututore*), and if she has not completed all the positions described by Philaenis (*tot figuris, quas Philaenis enarrat*), she leaves, still itching for it (*pruriosa*).

Priapus has just listed all his misfortunes, but the worst remains his "member" uselessly erected, which does not even have a beneficial influence on the erotic powers of the *fututor*.[40] The *puella* is unsatisfied and unappeased, and her sexual frustration arises from the fact that she has not experimented with all the positions (*figurae*) transmitted by Philaenis. The mentioning of Philaenis' name is not a reference to some prostitute or madam: it refers to an organized discourse (note *enarrat*) that circulated and had consequences for knowledge among *puellae* of erotic games and practices.[41]

The figure of a sexually insatiable *puella* provides a threatening image of women and one can see in this *carmen* an expression of anxiety – which is completely in harmony with the *Carmina Priapea* as whole – anxiety over the ineffectual powers of Priapus in sexual matters (the poem describes at length the difficult situations that the god faces), and anxiety about a possible reversal of power between the sexes, once the *puellae* have read Philaenis' discourse and come to understand the frustration in which they might be left. Of course, this suggested reversal cannot be taken literally, and it is described to make passers-by laugh (but laugh about what?).[42] However, parody or not, it is certain that the allusion to Philaenis is richer than an allusion to a famous prostitute would be, and that there is, in the connotations and implications of this word, "Philaenis", an idea of excessiveness, of a certain knowledge about sex (and not only of a practice), of a knowledge that can be feminine in its mode of transmission. Again, the reference to Philaenis is scarcely developed, her name alone is sufficient to evoke in public awareness both her work and the reputation attached to it.

The name of a didactico–erotic work

Philaenis' work is also mentioned in texts that originated later. In the second century CE, Lucian mentions, in the same elliptical way as the *Carmina Priapea*, the "tablets" of Philaenis as a striking example of a text containing coarse and vulgar terms. This is in a passage from *Pseudologista*, which contains a lengthy *psogos* against Timarchus. The narrator has just enumerated a list of terms which he (Timarchus) uses regularly and asks:[43]

> Indeed in what books do you find these words? Probably buried in the corner of a funeral oration from one of the poets, full of mould and cobwebs, or from somewhere out of the tablets of Philaenis (ἐκ τῶν Φιλαινίδος δέλτων), which you hold in your hand. In any case, they are worthy of you and your mouth!

A *prosopopoeia* by the tongue follows, complaining about the numerous affronts to which its owner subjects it, as well as a list of Timarchus' nicknames connected to his oral sex practices. Again, the mere expression αἱ Φιλαινίδος δέλτοι functions as a paradigm for works containing indecent and obscene language.

Likewise, when Lucian, in one of his *Dialogues of the Courtesans*, has a prostitute mention a woman named Philaenis, no details are given. The context suggests, to be sure, that this woman practises the same profession.[44] But can this really be only the name of a courtesan?

Krobyle: So, Korinna, it was not as bad as you thought, not to be a virgin anymore and become a woman. You realise it now after you have been with a handsome young lad, and you have received a *mina* as your first salary! With it I will straightaway buy you a necklace!

Korinna: Yes, my dear mummy, but with stones that shine like Philaenis' necklace (οἷος ὁ Φιλαινίδος ἐστίν).

Krobyle: Certainly. But also listen to what I am going to tell you, about what one should do with men and how to behave with them.

One could see here just the name of a flamboyant courtesan, but it is highly probable that it is also an implicit reference, for an informed audience, to the famous author of the erotic and didactic work; we know, thanks to the passage from the *Pseudologista*, that Philaenis' work was known by Lucian and his audience. One can therefore read this attribution not as a name thrown out as a reference to the supposedly debauched life of Philaenis (which, in this context, would not bring anything new to the dialogue), but rather as a nod in the direction of her didactic know-how: this dialogue not only describes the daily life of prostitutes, but provides an exchange between a daughter, a courtesan to be, and her mother, who explains how to seduce men so that she may earn as much money as possible. In a recent and particularly convincing study,[45] Kate Gilhuly has underlined the metadiscursive issues of this dialogue and the importance of transmitting knowledge and *savoir faire* from the teacher to her student – "the Sophist as *hetaira*", as she analyses it.[46] In my opinion, Lucian underlines this theme by mentioning the name of Philaenis. It functions as an allusion that will speak to a particular audience.

At around the same time, this name gradually became a *topos* in a different context: the Patristic discourse of blame and disapproval. In the second century CE, Justin mentions Philaenis' work as exemplary of works that provide a shameful education,[47] and Tatian speaks of horrible creations and refers to the works of Philaenis and Elephantis together.[48] The two Christian apologists mention this work in the context of general condemnation of the art, thought, and customs of the Greeks, and the example of Philaenis appears as a most representative work to denounce. As for Clement of Alexandria, he condemns those who exhibit paintings inspired by Philaenis as if they were representations of Heracles' physical exploits.[49] The reputation of Philaenis' work continues to be well attested among the Church Fathers.

Thus, this Greek work, known since the third century BCE in Greece, becomes famous in Rome, and it seems that no comparable writer working in Latin arose. This manual becomes a "classic": *the* pornographic manual to refer to, and an ideal illustration of the decline of morals – little by little acquiring generic value. The expression "Philaenis' treatise", the name of a work written by a woman with a Greek name, no longer strictly designates the writings of this author, but becomes, in certain contexts, a metonymy referring to all didacto-pornographic writings.

Philaenis is NOT a "courtesan's name"

Before continuing our enquiry, a clarification is in order. As Holt Parker has shown in his study on pornography, there is often, in the case of pornographic writings, a confusion in the ancient audience between the author and the content of the work: one is convinced that, in order to write on such a subject, one needs personal experience and therefore must be particularly debauched (which does not necessarily imply being a prostitute of either sex). This is the case with Aeschrion and Dioscorides who, in these two humorous epigrams, pretend to defend the morality of Philaenis while echoing (or creating?) a derogatory rumour. Yet nothing in the information that has come down to us enables us to say that the ancients asserted that Philaenis "really" was a courtesan or a prostitute: the most "informed" sources (one thinks of Athenaeus, who was particularly fond of this kind of anecdote) mention her work, and sometimes its reprehensible characteristics, but they do not speak of the life that Philaenis led. On the other hand, even if Philaenis was not introduced as a courtesan, it appears that ancient discourse constructed a certain image of her *persona* by sometimes, but not always, presenting her as a debauched woman.

Yet it is necessary to distinguish what is being said of her, when she is the subject of a precise and extended discourse, from what she connotes when her name simply appears without explanation or development. Contemporary researchers have indeed sometimes asserted that Philaenis *was* a courtesan, or that she connoted prostitution (this observation appears in a number of commentaries and translations).[50] The first argument for this interpretation is that, as a female author of *pornographia*, her name, in antiquity, would connote prostitution. Yet just because ancient authors who mention Philaenis' work specify how debauched the author was, it does not follow that, in a text or an epigram, a short allusion to Philaenis is simply an allusion to debauchery or prostitution. Surely there were sufficient women and courtesans in antiquity with a confirmed reputation – Thais or Lais – who could fulfil this function without ambiguity.

The second argument is that the name Philaenis was a "typical name" for a female prostitute, since other characters bearing the same name are very frequently prostitutes.[51] This point, which often resurfaces when dealing with women's names, is based on a fallacy. With the exception of famous characters of mythology (evoked in tragedy) or the rare great women figures (evoked in historiography), simple female citizens are rarely named in the non-epigraphic texts (if one compares them with the sheer number of masculine names); those of whom we speak are those who appear on the public scene, and are therefore often courtesans or prostitutes: the female characters in middle comedy or Roman comedy constitute good examples.[52] Since *hetairai* are more often mentioned than simple citizens or metics (whose names it was improper to give if they were "respectable" women), it is not surprising that this or that name is often that of a prostitute. But it does not follow that the name itself connotes prostitution. Louis Robert brilliantly asserted, as regards women characters in Hellenistic poetry and in particular Dorkion, in the *Greek Anthology*,[53]

> We must keep ourselves from thinking that a name such as Dorkion is a "courtesan name" … for a long time in the past, women's names were made known from authors who spoke of courtesans: Athenaeus, Latin comedy, Lucian, Aristaenetus, etc. Little by little, inscriptions have made known women's names as a whole … The "names of the courtesans" appeared in the most normally constituted families.[54]

Thus, as long as one subscribes to the argument that the name of Philaenis designates a courtesan, the texts where the name appears are interpreted as describing prostitutes; the philologist is then easily influenced by the scholiast of the Byzantine times who writes "Poem addressed to Philainis the Prostitute" of a poem where nothing indicates that the young girl in tears is in fact a prostitute.[55] So, once the corpus is compiled with such criteria in mind, it is difficult for contemporary researchers to escape this fallacy.[56]

In order to extract oneself from this vicious circle, one can simply bring up the fact that, repeatedly in the *Greek Anthology*, the name does not designate a prostitute, but a woman about whom nothing is specified, a young girl who died at an early age, a widow mourning, or a woman tenderly loved.[57] The name also appears in Greek epigraphic sources, where, among nearly thirty examples, it frequently accompanies the mention of the father or sometimes of a *kurios*; one can also find epitaphs by the husband for his deceased wife.[58]

Thus, in contexts where brief allusions appear, the name of Philaenis cannot be read as an allusion to a debauched way of living in general: the *Carmina Priapea*, the *Pseudologista*, and the *Dialogues of the Courtesans* refer, rather, to a specific Philaenis, and more particularly to the knowledge that she produced and transmitted.

The name of an anti-erotic character

In the discursive context of Martial's epigrammatic satire, the name of Philaenis appears without referring *a priori* to the author of manuals, and without its being characterized as the name of a prostitute. Over the course of the *Epigrams*, a character-type is constructed: the references to this name appear each time in a sexual context, which is the object of a derogatory caricature by the poet, and it is particularly repulsive.[59] Does it have anything to do with Philaenis, the author of a manual?

P. Laurens, a specialist in ancient epigram, has shown that one of Martial's techniques is characterized by "the use of pseudonyms more or less systematically associated with determined characters": the conception of the satirical epigram by Martial is not one "directed against individuals but against types".[60] The same name does not designate a specific person, who existed and whom Martial had met, but it very often refers, as various commentators have noticed, to a larger group of individuals afflicted with the same faults or behaving in the same manner.[61] He does not concern himself with chronological or narrative verisimilitude: in book 9, Philaenis is dead, but she is found again very much alive in book 12. For the satirist, it is a matter of constituting types of individuals with characteristics which appear as facets, each of which is sufficient but not necessary. Let us consider, in the first place, to what kind of individual the name Philaenis refers.

The first occurrence of the name Philaenis in the collection appears in a playful epigram, in the form of a riddle, about her physical appearance. The answer to the riddle comes out crudely at the end of the epigram: Philaenis looks like a penis.

> Why do I not kiss you (*basio*), Philaenis? You are bald (*calva*).
> Why do I not kiss you, Philaenis? You are red *(rufa)*.
> Why do I not kiss you, Philaenis? You are one-eyed (*lusca*).
> Whoever kisses those things, Philaenis, sucks dick (*fellat*).

Three times in the *Epigrams* she is described as one-eyed: at 2.33, these elements deprive Philaenis of feminine characteristics, as ugly as a *mentula*; at 4.65, the fact that she is one-eyed (*lusca*) is associated with a constant leaking from her other eye (with a strong sexual connotation); at 12.22, this infirmity makes an indecent being of her: "blind (*caeca*), she would be prettier (*decentior*)".[62]

The character is not any more attractive in smell: at 9.62, one learns that she hides her body odour with that of purple dye. Let us quote the humorous *paronomasia*: "it is the smell (*odore*) that she likes, not the colour (*colore*)!" She is a repulsive character: at 10.22, the speaker finds a stratagem to protect himself from her kisses, clearly meaning that her breath is foul because of her indulgence in oral sex. One learns further, at 9.40, that she is ready to practise fellatio, an act associated with oral defilement and bad smell. The epigram 9.29, where the poet creates a parody of a funeral epigram, definitively finishes the portrait:

> Philaenis, having traversed aeons of Nestorean old age, are you now carried away so quickly to the hellish waters of Dis? Yet you had not reached the great age of the Sibyl of Cumae: she was three months older than you! Ah, what a tongue falls silent! A thousand cages at the slavemarket did not prevail over her, not the crowd who loves Serapis, nor the curly-haired gang belonging to the morning's school master, nor the bank with its din from Strymon's flock of cranes. Who will now know how to call down the moon with Thessalian *rhombus*? What madam (*lena*) will know how to sell these and those beds? May the earth be light for you and may you be covered with soft sand, so that the dogs cannot dig up your bones!

The tone of this last poem recalls that of the fictive epitaphs by Aeschrion and Dioscorides (Hellenistic epigrams were generally a source of inspiration for the Latin poets). Here, Philaenis is not compared to a prostitute, but to a madam (*lena*). The evocation of a ready and noisy tongue, well known by everyone, and with an important reputation, could be an allusion to the *persona* of the manual's famous author.

What appears to be common to the epigrams where this name appears is a particularly repulsive physical and moral portrait (something that is not, let us remember, specific to this character – portraits of ugly men and women, weak and deformed because of repeated sexual practices, are legion in Martial's work). Among the *topoi* which Paul Veyne has enumerated in his study on love elegy, the hair, light complexion, appearance, and subtle and sweet smell of a healthy body are the erotic traits of a desired and beloved being.[63] Philaenis is nothing like that. On the contrary, in order to create the sort of person embodied in Philaenis, Martial reworks and subverts these clichés. Each characteristic is drawn from this general typology, which works like a construction kit where one may add or substract components at will. The body is in general the target of these attacks, and they confer upon her an identity, a type. In these seven epigrams, the author successively makes this character into the very portrait of an anti-erotic woman.

The name of a tribad

The last argument that allows us to argue that Philaenis does not simply connote prostitution is that the two other important contexts where a Philaenis appears present her not as a prostitute but as a *tribas*.[64] We will see, a little later, that this characteristic enables us to make a connection back to the woman-author.

The rare Latin word *tribas* appears three times in Martial's work, and of these three occurrences, two concern Philaenis.[65] Difficult to translate on account of the few occurrences that have come down to us, the word refers to a form of sexual practice.[66] Yet, this practice is far from the character's only one, as illustrated by epigram 7.67.[67]

> The tribad Philaenis buggers (*pedicat*) boys,
> And more savage than a hard-on of a husband,
> She bangs (*dolat*) eleven girls in a day.
> And she plays ball, wearing gym shorts
> And she gets dirty with the sand of the playing field,
> And lifts weights, even studs[68] would find heavy, with an easy arm,
> And muddy from the dirty *palaestra*,
> She takes a beating from an oiled instructor.
> Nor does she dine or recline before
> She has puked up seven pints of undiluted wine;
> To which she thinks she should return
> When she has eaten sixteen meat pies.
> After all this, when she's feeling sexy,
> She doesn't give blowjobs (she thinks this isn't macho enough),
> But she just eats the middles of girls (*sed plane medias vorat puellas*).
> May the gods give you back your brain, Philaenis,
> If you think it's macho to lick cunt.

Contrary to what one might think, this portrait does not consist of a description of the physical traits of the character, even less of a virile lesbian (the "butch" type[69]). It is, rather, an enumeration of a succession of activities: one does not know anything about Philaenis' physical traits nor anything about her life (age, social status, occupation).[70] Her body is deprived of all distinguishing features, ready to be modelled by social practices (including sexual practices). In fact, Martial puts on display the complexity of moral evaluation concerning sexual practices in Rome.[71] One cannot be *virilis* just by wanting to: it is not enough to have a body that is firm and not softened, and to perform this or that practice; one must above all understand, according to the person one is, the nuances and subtleties of what is, and what is not, worthy of a Roman citizen. If Philaenis makes Martial's audience laugh, it is not because she "masculinizes" herself (there is nothing virile in this practice for a Roman), it is because she does not know the rules of *pudicitia*, and becomes, by her own will, a character with a repulsive body.

Therefore, this is not about the visible appearance of a type illustrating a specific sexual category ("the lesbian"): the physical traits of Philaenis are not (as has sometimes been said) the signs of "homosexuality". Rather, Martial gives us a view of the impact that diverse practices (athletic, alimentary, sexual) have on the body of his character in extreme situations. This aspect of the character is underlined in another epigram:[72]

> Philaenis, tribad of the tribads themselves,
> you rightly call the woman you fuck (*futuis*) your "girlfriend" (*amicam*).

If one considers the portrait of Philaenis produced by Martial, one notices that the recurring trait is that she is a person whose characteristics are pushed to the extreme. Her homoerotic practices are an element that contributes to making her, in a more general way, the paradigm of an obscene and anti-erotic woman.[73]

At this point, one might be tempted to suppose that there is no connection between the author-Philaenis and the repulsive and anti-erotic Philaenis of the *Epigrams*, and that reading Martial has led us far from the manual under discussion. Yet the echoes between the fictive epitaphs by Aeschrion and Dioscorides and epigram 9.29 and another passage from a work by Lucian enable us not only to establish a connection between these two characters, but also to go further in our enquiry into what is named by the name "Philaenis".

An antonomastic character

It is in the *Erotes*, a dialogue for a long time attributed to an imitator of Lucian, but whose authenticity is now generally accepted, that one finds Philaenis mentioned and a link established with the theme of sexual relationships between women.[74] The passage to be discussed presently is all the more interesting because it is our only evocation of female homoeroticism in the context of an erotic *sunkrisis*.[75]

This dialogue has been the object of numerous works in the study of ancient sexuality, and Michel Foucault devotes a whole chapter to it in *The Care of the Self*.[76] As David Halperin shows,[77] the object of this dialogue is not to oppose homosexuality and heterosexuality:[78] the defender of love with boys does not, *at any point*, present himself as the champion of homosexuality in general terms, and if there is indeed one point on which Charicles and Callicratidas agree, it is in rejecting love between two adult men. The one who prefers women presents sexual relationships between adult men with disgust. As for Callicratidas, he makes no argument to counter this idea and focuses his points on paederasty. It appears that what the characters of this dialogue, Charicles and Callicratidas, but also Theomnestus and Lycinus, ultimately have in common, and what distinguishes them from citizens in general, is their extremism: the first two not only have definitively fixed choices but, most importantly, consider that theirs is the only acceptable one; the other two have either extreme sexual practices (Theomnestus) or non-existent ones (Lycinus).

It is possible to read this dialogue, by an author famous for his humour, his sophisticated erudition, and his eminently metadiscursive works,[79] as a sort of "case-study", playful and wise, on what is normal as regards kinds of sexual practice (boys or women) and quantity (intense versus non-existent) – from the point of view of the (male) lover.

It is in the epilogue of the speech of Charicles, the defender of men's love of men for women, that the name Philaenis appears. The arguments which are deployed may seem familiar to us, but we must detach ourselves from this sensation, built up by centuries of discourse on sex, and keep in mind the fact that this is our sole reference to relationships between women in the context of a *sunkrisis* (a rarity which, as we will see, is underlined in a meta-discursive way by the author himself):[80]

> "Whoever makes love with a woman or with a boy, well, Callicratidas, for him it is possible to feel pleasure and to come in two ways, whereas men can in no way offer the pleasure that women give. This is why, if this type of pleasure suits you, let us clearly keep a distance between us men: yet, if unions between men suit men, well, in the future, women should also love each other (ἐράτωσαν ἀλλήλων καὶ γυναῖκες)! Come on, new era, legislator of alien pleasures, after imagining new ways for men's pleasure, grant the same freedom to women also, and may they make love with each other, like men (καὶ ἀλλήλαις ὁμιλησάτωσαν ὡς ἄνδρες). Harnessed to this object built in the shape of licentious parts, monstrous indicator of their sterility, may woman, like a man, bed down with woman. May this word, that we hardly ever hear and that I even feel shame pronouncing, I mean *tribadistic lust* (τριβακῆς ἀσελγείας), openly parade (πομπευέτω)! May the bedrooms of our women be each a Philaenis dishonouring her androgynous loves (Φιλαινὶς ἀνδρογύνους ἔρωτας ἀσχημονοῦσα)! Should it not be better – and how much better! – that a woman be driven to manly pleasure rather than that the nobility of men be made effeminate?" All tensed up and emotional on account of these matters, Charicles ceased speaking, having a terrible and fierce glare in his eyes. It seems to me that this was a purificatory act offered against the love of boys.

After having developed an argument that is rather conventional and sprinkled with expected clichés about paederastic relationships, Charicles resorts to an unexpected point, whose connection with reciprocity does not appear to follow logically. The place of this argument at the very end of his speech is not insignificant. According to the rules of rhetoric, the last point of a discourse aiming to persuade should be a strong one. It is important to find the right ending, an image sufficiently dense and expressive to support by itself the thesis, which has already been developed at length. Our orator ignores all rational reasoning, however, and proceeds by means of syllogism and short cuts. If relations between men are recognized, he says in substance, then one must also recognize relations between women. The implicit element that enables this assertion is the following: relations between men and relations between women belong to a common set, that of relations between persons of the same sex. This is a shocking argument. The *topoi* of monstrosity and sterility, already used to blame love between men, are reused, as well as the hackneyed *topos* of the inexorable degradation of the human race: we will enter upon a new age, even more terrible than the iron one.

The logic is as follows: the more horrifying is the picture, the stronger will be the rejection of this kind of sexual relations, and the more convincing his discourse. But Charicles loses his bet. No one in his audience could possibly accept his first implication, postulating a common category of relations between men and relations between women, and even less are they going to consider paederastic relations equivalent to the monstrous picture of women instructed by Philaenis and discovering reciprocal love. What Lucian shows by making Charicles produce such an extreme discourse, full of clichés and tasteless descriptions, indicates the strategic place occupied in this debate by the brief allusion to sexual relationships between women. To speak of such a thing, however noble the reasons one has for doing so, is disastrous: Callicratidas was right to abstain when Charicles chose a very bad card to play.

Here, then, it emerges clearly that, if Charicles uses the name of Philaenis, it is not to evoke some courtesan who might influence chaste spouses, but rather to evoke an image of abnormal love, frightening and repulsive. The metaphor "may the bedrooms of our women be each a Philaenis" is rather crude, and rhetoricians of the time would probably have found it unsophisticated. Be that as it may, it is there to shock the imagination: Charicles presents the danger of relationships between women as an important threat; the danger is not related to the world of prostitution, but could penetrate into the γυναικωνῖτις of each οἶκος. Processions (πομπαί, vid. πομπευέτω) no longer have their primary religious and solemn meaning; Philaenis deforms and mangles the usual erotic practices. It is difficult to translate the expression ἀνδρογύνους ἔρωτας ἀσχημονοῦσα, which indicates an infraction of the norms of decency, through the deformation of love into androgynous love, and which very probably echoes, as a pun, the legendary erotic "figures" (σχήματα) from the manual said to be "of Philaenis": Philaenis "disfigures" (ἀσχημονοῦσα) the figures of love, according to Lucian's character.

This pun and the reference to Philaenis let us know that Lucian's audience was familiar with her. The name of this transtextual and transhistorical personage refers to a character exterior to the *Erotes*, where it is not mentioned in any other place; the author resorts to the audience's indirect or direct knowledge of Philaenis, of the pornographic manual, and especially of the connotations attached to this name. The point is not that the *gynaekeia* are going to "become" this woman, but that they are going to be filled with what is named by the name "Philaenis". This name acquires here an antonomastic value.

A famous name

In Greek and Latin discourses mentioning sexual relationships between women, rare are the authors who provide the names of persons (real or fictive). Occurrences of the term *tribas*/τριβάς are also few (little more than a dozen), and the contexts in which the term appears are explicit. It is appropriate to add to this list the unique use of the adjective τριβακή. Table 21.2 shows a summary of their appearances. I have also included occurrences of the late term *frictrix*/*fricatrix* (the meaning of which is difficult to deduce in Tertullian, but which has the meaning of τριβάς in Hermes Trismegistus).[81]

Studies of Philaenis, the author of an erotic manual from the fourth or second century before the common era, do not generally integrate her with the character in Martial's *Epigrams* who

Table 21.2 Summary of Greek and Latin discourses mentioning same-sex relationships between women

1st century CE	Phaedrus and Seneca the Elder	*tribas*
	Martial	*tribas*
2nd century CE	Ptolemy	τριβάς
	Vettius Valens	τριβάς
	Lucian	τριβακή
3rd century CE	(Tertullian)	(*frictrix*)
	Pomponius Porphyrio	*tribas*
	Manetho	τριβάς
4th century CE	Hermes Trismegistus	*fricatrix*
5th century CE	Caelius Aurelianus	*tribas*
	Hephaistion	τριβάς

appears at the end of the first century of our era. G. Burzacchini is one of the rare commentators who has explicitly established a link, but without analysing it any further.[82] Yet if one studies carefully the history of the rare word τριβάς/*tribas*, one notices that the only non-astrological context where the Greek word τριβάς appears (in the form of its derived adjective τριβακή) is in the text of Lucian's *Amores*, and this a few decades after the use of the Latin word in Martial's epigrams. *In both cases* the name Philaenis appears. It seems highly likely, therefore, that Martial and Lucian allude to the "same" Philaenis, or, to be precise, to the same "thing" that is named by the name "Philaenis".

Lucian's antonomastic use of the name, Martial's use of it in his creation of a character of a woman, and its probable use by the ancients generally to designate any erotic work, enable us to deduce that Philaenis was a famous figure in Greek and Roman culture, a celebrity.

Sex, knowledge, power

At the end of this journey, it no longer seems relevant to wonder whether Philaenis really was a woman, whether she truly wrote an erotic manual, and whether the fragment of P. Oxy. 2891 is indeed an excerpt of it, for it is not to her, *stricto sensu*, that the texts refer. Different images of Philaenis succeed each other and, in each context, they are built up and staged to provoke disgust, laughter, or fear. This figure is threatening because of her skills in erotic matters. Practical skills, connected to personal experience? No, not necessarily, even if the ancients sometimes mention that possibility. Practical skills connected to the profession of a prostitute? I have shown that prostitution is not a characteristic of this personage. In reality, this word evokes the figure of one who knows about sex with men *and* women (which, from the perspective of an author with a female name, deserves to be underlined), who writes about and systematizes this knowledge, who transmits it: her knowledge of eroticism, of its forms, and of its persuasive strategies confer upon her authority and reputation. Famous for this knowledge and for her skills as an author transmitting it, the figure of Philaenis comes to be credited with a menacing force and power. Her name has acquired a particular function: it has become a content word, the signifier of a complex of ideas which goes beyond gender identity and includes the "author function" as an important element.

Notes

1 This chapter was translated from the French by Luc Arnault and Mark Masterson.
2 I would like to thank Mark Masterson warmly for his thoughtful advice, patience, and work on the English translation of this text; Ruby Blondell for her help and valuable remarks as we were in a Platonic context (Pisa, 2013); and Nancy Rabinowitz for her support and the discussion we had in 2008 in Cork, Ireland. Any mistakes are, of course, my sole responsibility.
3 For a definition of Foucault's notion of "author function" adapted to antiquity, see Calame 2004, 2013.
4 We will come back later to the definition of this discursive genre described here in modern terms and therefore anachronistic.
5 Polybius 12.13.1; Athenaeus 7.321f–322a. He lived in the fifth century according to Jacoby (*FGrH* 566), but towards 340 BCE according to Parker (1992: 94).
6 Souda, *s.v.* Parker 1992 suggests the first century CE.
7 Souda, *s.v.*
8 Suetonius, *Tiberius* 43.
9 The sources date for the most part from the second century CE and it is difficult to determine just when she lived. See Souda, *s.v.*; Suetonius, *Tiberius* 43; Martial, *Epigrams* 12.43.4; *Priapea* 4.2; Tatian, *Discourse to the Greeks* 34.3. Parker (1992) suggests the first century CE, Baldwin (1990) the first or second century CE.

10 For Salpē, see Athenaeus 7.321f–322a after Alcimos and Nymphodoros; for Pamphilē, see Souda *s.v.*; for Nikō of Samos, Kallistratē of Lesbos, and Phytonicos of Athens, see Antisthēne quoted by Athenaeus 5.220.

11 The transcription of the Greek term Φιλαινίς is Philainis, and the transcription of the Latin term is Philaenis.

12 Baldwin 1990; Herrero Ingelmo and Montero Cartelle 1990; De Martino 1996.

13 See my study on feminine homosexuality in antiquity (Boehringer 2007a, 2013).

14 The attribution of erotic manuals to women is, according to H. Parker (1992: 92), a timeless characteristic of the pornographic genre, a feminine name being the pseudonym of a man who writes for a masculine audience, but attributes to women a disproportionate interest in sex.

15 Aristotle, *De Divinatione per Somnum* 464b.

16 See Halperin *et al.* 1990.

17 Polybius 12.13.2.

18 On the definition of ancient pornography, see De Martino 1996. For a more general treatment of sexual knowledge in antiquity see King 1994.

19 The text is edited in vol. 39 of *P. Oxy.* (Lobel 1972). See also the studies following this edition: Merkelbach 1972; Tsantsanoglou 1973; Luppe 1974, 1998; Marcovich 1975.

20 Cataudella 1973; Marcovich 1975; Parker 1989.

21 P. Waltz, in his edition of the *Greek Anthology* (Waltz 1938: 201), as well as Macleod, in his edition of *Erotes* (Macleod 1967: 194) speak of Philaenis as a poet. Here a first modern prejudice is already betrayed, maybe connected to the idea that poetry is more feminine than prose.

22 I use here the edition of Lobel. For the translation I have used the following supplements: Fr 1 col i: l. 4-5: διεξάγειν τὸν βίον (Lobel 1972); l. 4: μεθ' ἱστορίης (Tsantsanoglou 1973: 185, followed by Parker 1992); l. 6: αὐτὴ πονέσασα (Tsantsanoglou 1973: 187, followed by Parker 1992). Fr 3 col ii: l. 7-8: ὡς νέαν φάσκων εἶναι (Parker 1989).

23 Clement of Alexandria, *Protrepticus* 4.61.2 (τὰ Φιλαινίδος σχήματα). See the section, The name of a didactico-erotic work, and n. 63.

24 Various pieces must have been passed around under this name (Thomson Vessey 1976). One can go further and say that, much later, it was used to designate some pieces that were explicitly not by Philaenis, merely because of these erotic or pornographic characteristics.

25 Winkler 1990: 5–6.

26 Tsantsanoglou 1973: 192; Thomson Vessey 1976: 81, according to whom, in ancient popular belief, prostitutes were often assimilated to lesbians (see *contra* Boehringer 2007a: 285; Boehringer 2007c).

27 The name Philaenis appears in a fragment of the historian Timeus (fourth to third century BCE) transmitted to us by Polybius (12.13.1; *FGrH* 566F35), but the excerpt is short.

28 Gow and Page think rather the beginning of the fourth century BCE (Gow and Page 1965, vol. II: 3); Maas 1938 suggests the third century.

29 In a scholion to Pseudo-Lucian (*Erotes* 28), Arethas speaks not of Polycrates but of Philocrates as an author of comedies. For the error of this scholiast, see Cameron 1998. See also Cataudella 1973 and Tsantsanoglou 1973, *contra* Baldwin 1990.

30 *Greek Anthology* 7.345 = Aeschrion 1 GP. The attribution to Aeschrion is thanks to Athenaeus (8.335b).

31 *Greek Anthology* 7.450 = Dioscorides 26 GP.

32 Cameron 1981/1995: 513, n. 68.

33 Gow and Page 1965, vol. 2: 3–4.

34 Tsantsanoglou 1973: 194. See *contra* Whitehorne 1990.

35 Baldwin 1990: 4.

36 Notice the paronomasia and etymological play between φιλαιδήμων ("one who loves decency", l. 5) and Φιλαινίδος (l. 1).

37 Gow and Page 1965, vol. 2: 235–6.

38 Aristotle, *De Divinatione per Somnum* 464b; Timaeus in Polybius 12.13.1–2; Chrysippus of Soli (third century BCE) in Athenaeus 8.335b–e; Clearchus of Soli (fourth–third century BCE) in Athenaeus 10.457e.

39 *Carmina Priapea* 63.13–18.

40 On Priapus' sad sexuality, see the analysis by F. Dupont and T. Éloi (1994), which introduces their French translation of *Carmina Priapea*.

41 Cazzaniga (1959) reads *narrat*, while Parker (1988) suggests the more compelling *enarrat*: an *enarratio* is an explanation more detailed and precise than a simple *narratio*.

42 On laughter driving away anxiety caused by the swollen member of Priapus (who neither gives nor experiences sexual pleasure), see Dupont and Éloi 1994: 13–17.

43 Lucian, *Pseudologista* 24.

44 Lucian, *Dialogues of the Courtesans* 6.1.

45 "This scene belongs to a tradition of didactic literature in its representation of advice given by an adult to a youth who is on the cusp of coming of age" (Gilhuly 2007: 68).

46 Gilhuly 2007: 83.

47 Justin, *Apology* 2.15 (διδάγματα αἰσχρά).

48 Tatian, *Discourse to the Greeks* 34.3 (ἄρρητοι ἐπίνοιαι).

49 Clement of Alexandria, *Protrepticus* 4.61.2 (τὰ Φιλαινίδος σχήματα ὡς τὰ Ἡρακλέους ἀθλήματα).

50 For example, Chambry 1933–4, vol. 3: 514, n. 177; Plant 2004: 45–6.

51 Tsantsanoglou 1973: 192, among others.

52 The name of Philaenis appears in Mytilene on a mosaic originating in the middle of the fourth century CE (Webster and Green 1978: XZ37) that represents a scene taken from a comedy by Menander.

53 *Greek Anthology* 12.161.

54 Robert 1968: 340–1.

55 *Greek Anthology* 5.186 (lemma c, for the commentary: εἰς φιλαινίδα πόρνην).

56 The mention of Samos as the geographical origin of Philaenis has sometimes led to false conclusions among modern commentors who connect her with Samian women who are represented as debauched or "homosexual" (another chronic misconception) in particular in the case of an epigram by Asclepiades (*Greek Anthology* 5.207). To "save the Samians" from accusations of debauchery and prostitution, see Boehringer 2007c.

57 It is to such a "refreshed" reading, without *a priori* assumptions, that A. Cameron invites us, in a study entitled "Asclepiades' girlfriends" (Cameron 1981/1995: 494–519).

58 See for example ED 14, IG 12.1.764; ED 178. I would like to thank Marie Augier for her valuable remarks regarding the cultural contexts of a number of the epigraphic texts in which the name Philaenis appears.

59 For a more comprehensive study, see Boehringer 2011.

60 Laurens 1965: 315.

61 See C. Williams on Postumus (2004).

62 12.22.3.

63 Veyne 1983.

64 D. Thomson Vessey and K. Tsantsanoglou – according to whom, in ancient popular belief, prostitutes were assimilated to lesbians – claim misleadingly that the name of Philaenis is connected to the idea of prostitution, when they argue that she is … accused of being a tribad (Tsantsanoglou 1973: 192; Thomson Vessey 1976: 81).

65 For the occurrences and dates of origin of this term, see Boehringer 2007a: 272 ff.

66 It can obviously not be translated by "lesbian", a term which implies the existence of categories of heterosexuality and homosexuality (see Halperin 1997; Boehringer 2007a, 2014). Let us add that in antiquity, the geographic designation of Lesbos does not work as a marker of feminine homosexuality (the island of Lesbos is only connected to feminine homoeroticism in Lucian, *Dialogues of the Courtesans* 5); and let us also remember that the verb *lesbiazein* often designates fellatio (see, among others, Dover 1978: 223; Jocelyn 1980: 30–3; Adams 1982: 202; Lardinois 1989: 15–35). For a summary of these issues and their significance for the study of sexual relationships between women in antiquity, see Boehringer 2007a: 61–3 and Boehringer forthcoming.

67 Martial 7.67, trans. from Hubbard 2003, adapted.

68 On the rare term *draucus*, see Housman 1930: 114–16; Williams 1999: 88, n. 126.

69 Several commentators refer to this epigram to justify their interpretation of the *tribas* as a homosexual and virile woman. Yet at 1.90, the term *tribas* designates Bassa, whom the narrator thought a "Lucretia" for a long time, and whose physical appearance did not imply any erotic practices at all.

70 I summarize here analysis conducted from another perspective in my book (Boehringer 2007a: 288–95).

71 On the perception of oral sex, see Williams 1999: 197–203; Dupont and Éloi 2001: 197–203.

72 Martial 7.70, trans. from Hubbard 2003, adapted.

73 See Boehringer 2007a: 143ff. and 311ff.

74 See Jope 2011 on the authenticity of *Erotes* and their attribution to Lucian.

75 For a study of these erotic comparisons, see Boehringer 2007b.

76 Foucault 1984: 243–61; see also Goldhill 1995: 102–9.

77 Halperin 1992.
78 Contrary to what the editor of Lucian, Matthew D. Macleod, writes, among others, in his first edition of the text in 1967 (vol. 8: 147).
79 On the generic hybridity of Lucian, see Briand 2007.
80 *Erotes* 27–8.
81 See Boehringer 2007a: 272–5; see B. Brooten ("Predetermined erotic orientations: Astrological texts" in Brooten 1996: 115–41) for bibliography and list of references. Yet, the interpretation she makes of this corpus is subject to debate: David Halperin criticizes her use of modern categories of "homosexuality" and "orientation" to which she resorts in her analysis of these passages (see Halperin 1997: 64–8). See also her reply (Brooten 1998).
82 Burzacchini 1977: 240. Brick, in an article on Martial (1851: 383), also points out that the poet translated the Greek name of Philaenis in these two epigrams, but without developing the connection further. G. Burzacchini (1977) is not interested in the fact that Philaenis is, twice, called a *tribas*, but links this characteristic to the more general *topos* of prostitution.

Bibliography

Adams, J.N. (1982) *The Latin Sexual Vocabulary*. London: Duckworth.
Baldwin, B. (1990) "Philaenis, the doyenne of ancient sexology", *Corolla Londiniensis* 6: 1–7.
Boehringer, S. (2007a) *L'homosexualité féminine dans l'antiquité grecque et romaine*. Paris: Les Belles Lettres.
——(2007b) "Comparer l'incomparable: La *sunkrisis* érotique et les catégories sexuelles dans le monde gréco-romain", in B. Perreau (ed.) *Le choix de l'homosexualité: Recherches inédites sur la question gay et lesbienne*. Paris: Epel, pp. 39–56.
——(2007c) "*All'Hagêsichora me teirei* (Alcman fr. 3): Ce que les travaux sur la sexualité apportent aux recherches sur le genre", in N. Ernout and V. Sebillotte Cuchet (eds) *Problèmes du genre en Grèce ancienne*. Paris: Publication de la Sorbonne, pp. 125–45.
——(2011) "Le corps de Philaenis ou les ravages du sexe dans les *Épigrammes* de Martial", in L. Bodiou and M. Soria-Audebert (eds) *Corps outragés, corps ravagés: Regards croisés de l'antiquité au moyen age*. Turnhout: Brepols, pp. 231–48.
——(2013) "Female homoeroticism", in T.K. Hubbard (ed.) *A Companion to Greek and Roman Sexualities*. Malden, MA: Blackwell, pp. 150–64.
——(forthcoming) "The illusion of sexual identity in Lucian's *Dialogues of the Courtesans* 5", in R. Blondell and K. Ormand (eds) *Ancient Sex, New Essays*. Columbus, OH: Ohio State University Press.
Briand, M. (2007) "Les dialogues des morts de Lucien, entre dialectique et satire: Une hybridité générique fondatrice", in A. Eissen (ed.) "*Dialogue des morts*", *Otrante* 22: 61–72.
Brick (Ten), B. (1851) "De duobus in Philaenidem epigrammatis", *Philologus* 6: 382–4.
Brooten, B.J. (1996) *Love between Women: Early Christian Responses to Female Homoeroticism*. Chicago, IL and London: University of Chicago Press.
——(1998) "Lesbian historiography before the name? Response", *GLQ: A Journal of Lesbian and Gay Studies* 4(4): 606–30.
Burzacchini, G. (1977) "Filenide in Marzial", *Sileno* 3: 239–43.
Calame, C. (2004) "Identités d'auteur à l'exemple de la Grèce classique: Signatures, énonciations, citations", in C. Calame and R. Chartier (eds) *Identités d'auteur dans l'antiquité et la tradition européenne*. Grenoble: J. Millon, pp. 11–40.
——(2013) "Soi-même par les autres: Pour une poétique des identités auctoriales, rythmées et genrées (Pindare, *Parthénée* 2)", *Métis* hors série 1: 2–38.
Cameron, A. (1981) "Asclepiades's girlfriends", in H.P. Foley (ed.) *Reflections of Women in Antiquity*. London: Gordon & Breach, pp. 275–302; rev. and expanded in A. Cameron (1995) *Callimachus and His Critics*. Princeton, NJ: Princeton University Press, pp. 494–519.
——(1998) "Love (and marriage) between women", *Greek, Roman and Byzantine Studies* 39: 137–56.
Cataudella, Q. (1973) "Recupero di un'antica scrittrice greca", *Giornale Italiano di Filologia* 25: 253–63.
Cazzaniga, I. (ed.) (1959) *Carmina Ludicra Romanorum: Pervigilia Veneris Priapea*. Turin: G.B. Paravia.
Chambry, E. (ed. and trans.) (1933–4) *Lucien de Samosate: Œuvres complètes*. Paris: Garnier.
De Martino, F. (1996) "Per una storia del 'genere' pornografico", in O. Peccere and A. Stramaglia (eds) *La letteratura di consumo nel mondo greco-latino*. Cassino: Universita degli studi di Cassino, pp. 295–341.
Dover, K.J. (1978) *Greek Homosexuality*. London: Duckworth.
Dupont, F. and Éloi, T. (1994) *Les jeux de Priape: Anthologie d'épigrammes érotiques*. Paris: Gallimard.

——(2001) *L'Érotisme masculin dans la Rome antique*. Paris: Belin.

Foucault, M. (1984) *Le souci de soi: Histoire de la sexualité*, vol. 3. Paris: Gallimard.

Gilhuly, K. (2007) "Bronze for gold: Subjectivity in Lucian's *Dialogues of the Courtesans*", *American Journal of Philology* 128: 59–94.

Goldhill S. (1995) *Foucault's Virginity: Ancient Erotic Fiction and the History of Sexuality*. Cambridge: Cambridge University Press.

Gow, A.S.F. and Page, D.L. (eds) (1965) *The Greek Anthology: Hellenistic Epigrams*. Cambridge: Cambridge University Press.

Halperin, D.M. (1992) "Historicizing the subject of desire: Sexual preferences and erotic identities in the pseudo-Lucianic *Erotes*", in D.C. Stanton (ed.) *Discourses of Sexuality: From Aristotle to AIDS*. Ann Arbor, MI: University of Michigan Press, pp. 236–61; repr. in J. Goldstein (ed.) (1994) *Foucault and the Writing of History*. Oxford: Wiley-Blackwell, pp. 19–34.

——(1997) "Response: Halperin on Brennan on Brooten", *BMCR* 97.12.03. Available online at http://bmcr.brynmawr.edu/1997/97.12.03.html> (accessed 15 March 2013); repr. as "The first homosexuality?", in M.C. Nussbaum and J. Sihvola (eds) (2002) *The Sleep of Reason: Erotic Experience and Sexual Ethics in Ancient Greece and Rome*. Chicago, IL and London: University of Chicago Press, pp. 29–68.

Halperin, D.M., Winkler, J.J., and Zeitlin, F.I. (eds) (1990) *Before Sexuality: The Construction of Erotic Experience in the Ancient World*. Princeton, NJ: Princeton University Press.

Herrero Ingelmo, M.C. and Montero Cartelle, E. (1990) "Filenide en la literatura grecolatina", *Euphrosyne* 18: 265–74.

Housman, A.E. (1930) "*Draucus* and Martial 1 1.8.1", *Classical Review* 44: 114–16.

Hubbard, T.K. (2003) *Homosexuality in Greece and Rome: A Sourcebook of Basic Documents*. Berkeley, CA: University of California Press.

Jocelyn, H.D. (1980) "A Greek indecency and its students: ΛΑΙΚΑΖΕΙΝ", *Proceedings of the Cambridge Philological Society* 206: 12–66.

Jope, J. (2011) "Interpretation and authenticity of the Lucianic *Erotes*", *Helios* 38(1): 103–20.

King, H. (1994) "Sowing the field: Greek and Roman sexology", in R. Porter and M. Teich (eds) *Sexual Knowledge, Sexual Science: The History of Attitudes to Sexuality*. Cambridge: Cambridge University Press, pp. 29–46.

Lardinois, A. (1989) "Lesbian Sappho and Sappho of Lesbos", in J.N. Bremmer (ed.) *From Sappho to De Sade: Moments in the History of Sexuality*. London and New York: Routledge, pp. 15–35.

Laurens, P. (1965) "Martial et l'épigramme grecque du Ie᷑ siècle ap. J.-C.", *Revue des études latines* 43: 315–41.

Lobel, E. (1972) "P. Oxy. n 2891", in E. Lobel (ed.) *The Oxyrhynchus Papyri*, vol. 39. London: Egypt Exploration Society, pp. 51–4.

Luppe, W. (1974) "Nochmals zu Philainis, Pap. Oxy. 2891", *Zeitschrift für Papyrologie und Epigraphik* 13: 281–2.

——(1998) "Zum Philainis Papyrus (P. Oxy. 2891)", *Zeitschrift für Papyrologie und Epigraphik* 123: 87–8.

Maas, P. (1938) "'Philainis', in Pauly-Wissowa", *Realencyclopädie des klassischen Altertumswissenschaft* 19(2): 2133.

Macleod, M.D. (ed. and trans.) (1967) *Lucian*, Vol. 8. Cambridge, MA: Harvard University Press.

Marcovich, M. (1975) "How to flatter women: P. Oxy. 2891", *Classical Philology* 70: 123–4.

Merkelbach, R. (1972) "Φαυσώ", *Zeitschrift für Papyrologie und Epigraphik* 9: 284.

Parker, H.N. (1989) "Another go at the text of Philaenis", *Zeitschrift für Papyrologie und Epigraphik* 79: 49–50.

——(1992) "Love's body anatomized: The ancient erotic handbooks and the rhetoric of sexuality", in A. Richlin (ed.) *Pornography and Representation in Greece and Rome*. New York and Oxford: Oxford University Press, pp. 91–111.

Parker, W.H. (ed.) (1988) *Priapea: Poems for a Phallic God*. London and Sydney, NSW: Croon Helm.

Plant, I.M. (ed.) (2004) *Women Writers of Ancient Greece and Rome: An Anthology*. Norman, OK: University of Oklahoma Press.

Robert, L. (1968) "Discussion in: W. Ludwig, 'Die Kunst des Variation im Hellenistischen Liebesepigramm'", in *L'Épigramme grecque, Fondation Hardt, entretiens sur l'antiquité classique* 14. Genève: Droz, pp. 340–1.

Thomson Vessey, D.W. (1976) "Philaenis", *Revue belge de philologie et d'histoire* 54: 78–83.

Tsantsanoglou, K. (1973) "The memoir of lady of Samos", *Zeitschrift für Papyrologie und Epigraphik* 12: 183–95.

Veyne, P. (1983) *L'Élégie érotique romaine: L'Amour, la poésie et l'occident*. Paris: Seuil.

Waltz, P. (ed.) (1938) *Anthologie grecque*, vol. 4. Paris: Les Belles Lettres.

Webster, T.B.L. and Green, J.R. (1978) *Monuments Illustrating Old and Middle Comedy*, 3rd edn, rev. and enlarged by J.R. Green, *Bulletin of the Institute of Classical Studies* Supplement 39, London: Institute of Classical Studies.

Whitehorne, J.E.G. (1990) "Filthy Philainis (P. Oxy. XXXIX 2891): A real lady?", in M. Capasso, G. Messeri Savorelli and R. Pintaudi (eds) *Miscellanea philologica in occasione del bicentenario dell'edizione della Charta Borgiana*, vol. 2. Florence: Gonnelli, pp. 529–42.

Williams, C.A. (1999) *Roman Homosexuality*. New York and Oxford: Oxford University Press.

——(2004) *Martial Epigrams: Book Two*. New York: Oxford University Press.

Winkler, J.J. (1990) *The Constraints of Desire: The Anthropology of Sex and Gender in Ancient Greece*. New York and London: Routledge.

22

CURIOSITAS, HORROR, AND THE MONSTROUS-FEMININE IN APULEIUS' METAMORPHOSES

Hunter H. Gardner

Pleasure pursues beautiful objects—what is agreeable to look at, to hear, to smell, to taste, to touch. But curiosity (*curiositas*) pursues the contraries of these delights with the motive of seeing what the experiences are like, not with a wish to undergo discomfort, but out of a lust for experimenting and knowing. What pleasure is to be found in looking at a mangled corpse, an experience which evokes revulsion (*quod exhorreas*)? Yet wherever one is lying, people crowd around to be made sad and turn pale. … To satisfy this diseased craving, outrageous sights are staged in public shows.

(Augustine, *Confessions*, 10.35.55; trans. Chadwick 1991)

The monstrous–feminine: A peculiar type of horror

The horrific, that which might make one shudder (*exhorreas*), was long recognized in antiquity as a source of *curiositas*, if not pleasure, as Augustine attempts to distinguish by recalling a famous passage from Plato's *Republic* (439e). As ancient arena culture has been replaced by increasingly synthetic spectacles of the cinema, the psychic and social functions of a bloody good show continue to offer seemingly endless cause for speculation. In an influential treatment of Roman performances of "Fatal Charades" (1990), Kathleen Coleman has drawn attention to the way that violent punishment of prisoners in the highly public context of the arena strengthens ideologies of dominance and submission and offers audiences psychic reassurances: aside from the penal functions performed by the public execution of prisoners (retribution, humiliation, correction, and deterrence), Coleman speculates on the psychological factors—identification with agents of punishment, fascination with the moment of death, and interest in the horrific (that *curiositas* maligned by Augustine)—that helped produce an audience eager to view death scenes inspired by the shared cultural currency of Greco-Roman myth (Coleman 1990: 57–60).

In this essay, I consider the social and psychic function of a particular kind of punitive spectacle, that of a condemned murderess, in Apuleius' second-century "novel"[1] the *Metamorphoses*. This work of prose fiction chronicles the adventures of its narrator and protagonist, Lucius, whose story begins with an account of his journey to Hypata in Thessaly. Along the way he is charmed by the tale of Aristomenes, who recounts how vengeful witches murdered his friend and traveling companion Socrates. After he arrives in Hypata, Lucius is a guest at the house of a local notary, Milo, and embarks on a series of erotic adventures with Milo's servant Photis, adventures that put him in disastrous proximity to the transformative witchcraft practiced by Photis' mistress Pamphile (Books 1–3): magic attracts Lucius' (proleptically asinine) *curiositas*, and, after applying the wrong ointment to his body, he is metamorphosed into an ass. Our narrator thereupon is abducted, sold, discarded, and beaten, while frequently overhearing bawdy or horrific tales and observing atrocities among the human race (Books 4–9). Finally, in Corinth, Lucius is pampered, indulged, and procured to satisfy the sexual appetite of a well-born *matrona*, described as an "asinine Pasiphae" (10.19), and performs his services to such satisfaction that his owner, Thiasus, is prompted to make a public spectacle of him (Book 10). This *spectaculum*, the proposed fatal charade of the novel's penultimate book, presents the threat of death and dismemberment with a *vilis aliqua*, a "certain contemptible woman" (10.23), whose crimes and punishment intersect spectacularly with her gender. Avoiding the threatened fate, Lucius at last finds his path to redemption through the goddess Isis and service to her cult (Book 11).

This paper attempts to determine the relationship between Lucius' near-death experience as a spectacle bound for the arena and the novel *in toto*, and offers two basic propositions: first, that the proposed coupling between Lucius and the murderess re-enacts certain dynamics of Aristomenes' unfortunate voyeurism of women behaving badly in the novel's opening tale, and, second, that the threat of contact (*contagium*) between Lucius and the condemned woman plays a critical role in his climactic restoration to human form. Lucius' own curiosity about the horrors enacted by the novel's female characters allows him to identify woman's threatening properties—increasingly "on display" (*incoram*, 10.23) for public consumption—and ultimately distinguish them from the maternal and nurturing properties that he identifies in his restorative vision of the goddess Isis.[2] The proposed copulation between ass (Lucius) and condemned woman, the culmination and inversion of his asinine *curiositas*,[3] functions as a necessary prospect he must face before resuming his human identity and reclaiming a place in the social order. My aim here is to demonstrate how the narrator's spectacular confrontation with aspects of feminine sexuality that he identifies as threatening is a primary mechanism allowing him to experience redemption.

The initial crime of the nameless condemned woman, the *vilis aliqua*, is motivated by sexual jealousy over a presumed rival; her subsequent transgressions, involving a complete rejection of motherhood through the murder of her daughter, also foreground her gender. Her punishment, moreover, forced copulation with an ass while being thrown to the beasts (*damnata ad bestias*; cf. 10.23, 28), highlights both her feminine sexuality and her transgression of the norms appropriate to it.[4] Here we can look to the larger realm of Roman discourse to find the logic behind Apuleius' representation of penal processes. Coleman's review of the literary evidence for staged executions suggests that Thiasus' spectacular coupling of Lucius the ass with the woman in the arena was inspired by a familiar mode of punishment (Coleman 1990: 63; cf. Mart. *Lib. Spect.* 5). She also notes that representations were occasionally crafted to forge a link between the instrument of execution and some symbol of the criminal's former power (1990: 54), the source of which, in the case of a woman forced to copulate with an animal, would implicitly lie in her sexual appetite construed as subhuman. Might the audience at Corinth—might we too as attentive *lectores*?—derive a particular satisfaction from viewing the unnamed woman's formerly threatening sexual capacities undone in the arena?

This unnamed murderess, as the final portrait of savage womanhood in the novel, serves as a provocative and summary reflection of the *femmes fatales* who have plagued male protagonists since Aristomenes' opening tale of the witch Meroe. Aristomenes' account of the witch foregrounds his role as spectator (albeit an unwilling one) of feminine transgressions and establishes a model for viewing subsequent horrors in the text; as we shall observe, Aristomenes' inability to maintain his relatively remote status anticipates Lucius' troubling involvement in the punishment of Book 10's murderess. Together these episodes serve a bracketing function that prompts readers of the novel to reconsider their own voyeurism and the nature of the *curiositas* that propels their interest in this particular text: the threat posed by these women, mounted specifically with regard to their sexually appetitive and emasculating functions, proves to be a critical catalyst to Lucius' salvation through another version of feminine subjectivity, the benign Isis, whose generative properties counter the threatening aspects of woman demonstrated throughout Lucius' experiences as an ass.

The horrific aspects of the *Metamorphoses*, especially in the tales that Lucius is privileged to hear in his asinine form, have been noted in passing by readers throughout the last century.[5] I would like to identify more precisely the nature of that horror and demonstrate its conceptual link with the female body. In the novel, threatening women are associated with blood and bodily waste; they jeopardize the integrity of the human form and are frequently linked with pollution; and they transgress the boundaries between life and death. Similar properties of woman as a symbolic category have been theorized as "abject" by the psychoanalyst and cultural theorist Julia Kristeva (1982) and applied to the pleasures of horror films by Barbara Creed, who uses the abject to account for the psychic satisfaction associated with viewing the "monstrous-feminine" (Creed 1993). According to Kristeva, the abject status of woman as a construct emerges from the maternal functions frequently assigned to her: as mother she participates in mapping the child's body, leading the infant through the processes by which sites of bodily waste, primarily feces and urine, but also blood, saliva, vomit, pus, and bile are identified and regulated through social taboos (Kristeva 1982: 71–5; Creed 1993: 13). According to such a model of infantile development, the subject needs confrontation with the abject, allowing "filth and prohibition to brush lightly against each other" (Kristeva 1982: 71), in order to separate from the mother–child dyad, and thereby enter the symbolic order.

Kristeva views this process of confrontation with the abject and ensuing separation from the maternal bond as an integral component of psychic development, the completion of which various psychoanalytic models mark by the child's recognition of the phallus and the threat of castration that such recognition entails. The source of the threat of castration is traditionally identified with the father figure; Freud noted the possibility of the castrating mother only to dismiss it and assign this role to the father,[6] who stands as the "third term," severing the asocial dyad of mother and child and giving birth to a social order of patriarchy in the process. Woman in turn becomes threatening either because she appears castrated (and thus serves to remind the masculine subject of the possibility of castration), or because she is symbolically endowed with a phallus and thus aligned with processes of masculine aggression. Creed argues against the premise that woman's sexual threat is recognized and tamed in horror films exclusively through being associated with phallicism, as occurs in horror films that leave a single (often masculinized) female survivor, the knife-wielding "Final Girl," to eradicate the sexually deviant male killer (Clover 1989; cf. Creed 1993: 125–7). Instead she explains woman's frequent depiction as castrating according to a revision of Freud's model of infantile development, which would assign significantly more power, if also greater potential for harm, to the female genitalia.

In arguing for a revision of the "way in which genitals might horrify," Creed observes that the penis, frequently representative of the phallus, is marked as an instrument of violence not because it castrates, but because it threatens "to penetrate and split open, explode, tear apart." The vagina likewise can be dangerous, particularly in its representation as the "mythical *vagina dentata* which threatens to devour, to castrate via incorporation" (157). This is the very conflict—between Lucius' enlarged, bestial *membrum* and Pasiphae's dangerously infinite womb—staged in Book 10 of the *Metamorphoses*. The terms of this conflict suggest that the horror readers identify in the novel is born not only from woman's link with the abject (her association with the body's remainders, those elements of decay cast off as a human subject departs from the material conditions of birth), but also from the dangerous capacity of her womb, and its consequences for the male genitalia, that accompany her abject status.

Horror films frequently dramatize a conflict with the monstrous-feminine by representing the *femme castratrice* and *vagina dentata* as threats whose containment restores both the male protagonist and the social order he is defending.[7] This recovery allows a unique kind of satisfaction, explained better through a psychosexual model that assumes woman castrates through the power of her genitals to devour, rather than one that renders her threatening only by allowing her to wield a lost phallus. Such satisfaction is also applicable to the discursive realm of Apuleius' novel, where the language of watching frequently constructs readers as viewers who paradoxically delight—and satisfy their *curiositas*—in woman as a symbol of the abject.[8] By examining Apuleius' wicked women as a variety of this monstrous-feminine we not only have a better grasp on the psychological reassurances that readers get from experiencing a unique type of "horror"—from the Latin verb *horreo*, the shuddering that follows on the heels of the portentous and the *unheimlich*; we can also offer one answer to the question of why Lucius must get full view of such gendered monstrosities before he can become human again.

Meroe: A model for viewing the monstrous-feminine

Women and the erotic desires they express prove disastrous in the novel's opening tale of Aristomenes and become increasingly so for the narrator as he makes his way to the novel's climax in Book 10. It has been nearly twenty years since Konstan (1994) argued for a kind of sexual symmetry—based on mutual desire and expressed by social equals—that governed representations of male and female protagonists in the Greek novel. Since that time scholars have responded to his thesis with caveats against overestimating the equality of the sexes in the Greek novel and argued that its empowered and virtuous women underwrite ideologies that are not necessarily egalitarian.[9] Still, Konstan's assertion that women in the few surviving Roman novels, in contrast to their Greek counterparts, are frequently presented as sexually threatening has found little disagreement. The desires of women that bracket Lucius' journey, introducing him as a human and concluding in his asinine experiences, are represented as both dangerous and horrific, and may be considered among the innovations by which Apuleius transforms his source, epitomized in the surviving *Lucius, or the Ass* (= *Onos*), into a story of salvation and conversion. As Konstan notes (1994: 126–7; cf. Tatum 1979: 23), destructive passions of women emerge in particular from the embedded tales that Apuleius apparently added to the Greek original:[10]

> Meroe and Pamphile are in a class apart from amorous women like Manto in *An Ephesian Tale* or Heliodorus' Arsace, who are motivated by a species of *eros* recognizably akin to that which drives the hero and heroine themselves. Apuleius' witches, on the contrary, incarnate a will to total domination.

To understand better what these creatures with a "will to total domination" are doing in Apuleius' novel, we now turn to our initial encounter with Meroe, whose transgressions are presented not only as a horrific spectacle, but as one that has a covertly restorative function. As noted above, Meroe's vengeance against her erstwhile lover Socrates is narrated by Aristomenes, whom Lucius encounters on his journey to Hypata. While Lucius stresses the aural pleasure gleaned from this first Milesian tale in the novel (1.2), he also uses a revealing anecdote to defend its veracity. Having witnessed an Athenian acrobat swallow a sword (1.4), our narrator not only confirms the reality of the marvelous, but also anticipates its healing function. Lucius describes a young boy who shimmies up the sword like a snake writhing around the staff of Asclepius, the healing god. Winkler observes that an implied structural parallel lurks in this introductory anecdote, so that the recollection of popular entertainment transformed into "therapeutic vision" might shape our interpretation of the novel as a whole (Winkler 1985: 30).[11]

All the same, it is not a stretch to claim "horrific" status for the story of Meroe and the vengeance she enacts on Socrates: even scholars who define fictional horror as a modern phenomenon look to Apuleius' tale of Aristomenes as a significant forerunner (e.g., Carroll 1990: 13). Meroe is supernatural, impure, threatening and thus demonstrates the most basic properties of the monster in the horror genre.[12] But her narrative also implies that the horrific can be gendered, insofar as it horrifies partly *because* of its representation as feminine. Such horror, moreover, is both tempting and "affecting" to observe—that is, Meroe's actions provoke a certain response in the novel's readership, one guided by the internal response of the characters in the narrative (Carroll 1990: 17–18). While Apuleius' female monstrosities are indebted to portraits of women in Latin satire and epigram, as well as in Petronius' *Satyricon*,[13] our narrator's incredulous attitude toward the miraculous and threatening (*mira nec minus saeva*, 1.11) and his probing *curiositas* prompt his readers to view such images of transgressive femininity from a radically different perspective. In other words, Apuleius' innovation lies not so much in the abject properties that he assigns to women as in the way that he positions his characters as spectators of such properties. While the witch and her transgressions were popular in ancient literature, Apuleius has shaped his account of her actions in a way that foregrounds not only her associations with the abject, but also, through the responses of Lucius and Aristomenes, the perils and satisfactions of watching it.

Apuleius constructs the relationship between Meroe as spectacle and Aristomenes as curious onlooker at the expense of the ironically named Socrates,[14] initially referred to as a "wretched spectacle of suffering" (*miserum aerumnae spectaculum*, 1.6). And yet Socrates is also represented as a potential spectator, since he posits a direct correlation between his sufferings (*aerumnae*) on account of Meroe and his pursuit of a famous gladiatorial show (*qui dum voluptatem gladiatorii spectaculi famigerabilis consector, in has aerumnas incidi*, 1.7). For Socrates the pleasure (*voluptas*) of a good show will be replaced initially by Meroe and *voluptas Veneria* (1.8), and finally by suffering the kind of violence he might have observed more happily from a distance.

Telling of his reaction to Socrates' account of his experience, Aristomenes constantly directs his audience of fellow travelers to view that experience as a staged performance. He begs Socrates to tone down the dramatics, which (ironically) underscores the dimensions of spectacular dramatization: *oro te inquam aulaeum tragicum dimoveto et siparium scaenicum complicato et cedo verbis communibus* ("please, remove the tragic curtain and fold back the stage drapes, and tell it to me in plain language!" 1.8). Though Aristomenes resists Socrates' hyperbole, we have been directed to interpret Socrates first and then Meroe, who is linked explicitly with Euripides' stage heroine Medea (1.10), in spectacular terms. Meroe's specific atrocities are both highly visible (according to Socrates, performed before the sight of many, *in conspectum plurium*, 1.8) and are sparked by a sexual jealousy that results in a torturous inversion of sexual pleasures: one unfaithful lover is transformed into a beaver prone to self-castration; the wife of another is burdened with perpetual pregnancy (1.9). This is not to say that all of Meroe's transgressions are sexually motivated and manifested, but rather that these are among the most salient and most relevant to the increasingly anxious Socrates.

Up to this point in the tale Aristomenes has only had his anxiety aroused to a rueful blend of dread and curiosity (1.11). On the same night, after Socrates concludes his account and collapses with exhaustion, Aristomenes will become transformed from an attentive listener into an eyewitness through his metaphorical metamorphosis into a tortoise. The forceful entrance of the witches, Meroe and Panthia, into the room shared by the two men causes Aristomenes' cot to collapse and land on top of him (1.12):

> *tunc ego sensi naturalitus quosdam affectus in contrarium provenire. nam ut lacrimae saepicule de gaudio prodeunt, ita et in illo nimio pavore risum nequivi continere, de Aristomene testudo factus.*

> Then I experienced the natural occurrence that certain reactions are expressed through their opposites. For just as tears often spring from joy, thus even in that excessive fright I was not able to restrain my laughter, made (as I was) from Aristomenes into a tortoise.

As an affective response to the sight of Meroe and Panthia, Aristomenes' fear yields to uncontrollable laughter, and we are led to anticipate the shifting moods that will govern Lucius' own story of transformation. Aristomenes' metamorphosis into a "tortoise," peering out from beneath his mattress, anticipates Lucius' own transformation in the novel as well as the covert perspective on marvelous events that such transformation enables. The human intellect housed in animal form affords a unique mode of viewing and satisfaction of curiosities, a satisfaction not without its liabilities—and not without the prospect of becoming involved in a spectacle one would prefer to view from a distance, as Aristomenes' (and Lucius' own) fate will show. The implicit warning embedded in the tale of Aristomenes and Lucius' inability to heed its relevance for his own *curiositas* have been often acknowledged, but in need of further consideration is the gendered nature of the visions that so often become the object of that *curiositas*, and the specific warnings about monstrous women that those visions offer.

Before Meroe and Panthia exact vengeance on the sleeping Socrates, they discover the voyeur under the mattress, condemn Aristomenes explicitly for his *curiositas* (1.12), and consider the punishment appropriate to it. Panthia devises a singularly spectacular castigation, one that again evokes the horrors of Euripidean tragedy: *quin igitur inquit soror hunc primum bacchatim discerpimus vel membris eius destinatis virilia desecamus* ("but, sister," she said, "why don't we tear this one limb from limb first, in a bacchant frenzy, or cut off his genitals after we've bound his limbs," 1.13). Aristomenes, still partially concealed in tortoise form, is threatened with either dismemberment or castration, the first of which relies on a "colorful neologism" (*bacchatim*, Scobie 1975: 107) to frame the women as Bacchants, eager to tear apart Pentheus, who, while also playing the voyeur, is mistaken for a beast in Euripides' play. The second threatened punishment aligns Meroe and Panthia with the *femme castratrice*, a role Meroe has already played with a former lover.[15] Aristomenes is spared, as recommended by Meroe, to perform burial rites for his friend, though Meroe's utter lack of concern for Socrates' well-being in all other respects suggests that a more pressing concern—the need for an eyewitness?—ensures Aristomenes' survival. The most spectacular deed committed by Meroe involves pilfering Socrates' heart after slitting his throat, so that she violates the integrity of his body in a manner recalling bacchant dismemberment, but with remarkably tidy results, as a sponge quickly staunches the flow of blood (1.13). The text thus horrifically recalls woman's role as mother mapping the body and regulating its abject fluids: Meroe asserts uncanny power over the blood that ought to pulse from the veins in Socrates' neck.

Aristomenes meanwhile crosses even further the boundary between passive viewer and active participant in the havoc wreaked by Panthia and Meroe. The remarkable absence of blood that marks Socrates' demise is compensated for by the flood of urine that the two women release over Aristomenes: *varicus super faciem meam residentes vesicam exonerant, quoad me urinae spurcissimae madore perluerent* ("squatting astride over my face they empty their bladders to the point that their most foul urine drenched me with moisture").[16] We are not offered an explanation for the flooding experienced by Aristomenes, but it is one that marks him indelibly. The scent of urine lingers with him upon his reunion with the undead Socrates (1.17), where the superlative *spurcissimus umor* returns us to the original *spurcissima urina* (1.13). By describing the urine as *spurcus* ("foul, filthy") Aristomenes links the fluid with a range of polluting substances in Latin literature as well as with sexual acts like fellatio (*OLD* s.v. 1b–c, 2 b).[17] He initially describes himself as lifeless (*inanimis*; cf. *semimortuus*) and "covered with urine, as if I had just come out of my mother's womb" (*lotio perlitus, quasi recens utero matris editus*, 1.14). The likeness between urine and the fluids of childbirth proposed by Aristomenes genders the horror he details for our amusement as feminine, raising the possibility of Meroe's reproductive function, only to subvert it by confirming her roles as murderess and necromancer. As survivors of these "bogeywomen" (*lamiae*, 1.17) Aristomenes on a literal level, but Lucius also in metaphorical kinship with him, will exist on the precarious border between life and death—the former as an outcast from his *patria* (1.19) and the latter as an outcast from the human race.

Summing up his nocturnal experience for Socrates, and using language that points to the spectacular nature of his encounter with the monstrous-feminine, Aristomenes refers to these women as representations of reality, or more specifically, as "cruel and savage dreams" (*diras et truces imagines*, 1.18). Throughout the novel, the temptations of visual spectacle—here manifested as captivating horror, elsewhere as compelling physical perfection[18]—function as a complementary antithesis to the blindness (*caecitas*, 11.15) of *fortuna* that governs Lucius' wayward journey. Constant fascination with the visual only draws him further into the impenetrable darkness of "fortune that does not see" (*caeca fortuna*, 7.2). Meroe, as one *dira et trux imago* (a mistaken dream that becomes dangerously real for Aristomenes), creates a template for other images of threatening women in the *Metamorphoses*—from Lucius' first encounters in Hypata with Photis and Pamphile to the stories of cunning, adulterous wives (9.5–7, 9.14–22) and Phaedra-like stepmothers (10.2–12) that he overhears in asinine form.[19] By the end of the novel, however, Meroe will assume an additional function as foil for Isis and the restorative *imagines* sent by the goddess in her foresight (*nocturnis imaginibus*, 11.13; *hanc ... imaginem*, 11.20; *nocturnae imagini*, 11.27; cf. *imaginabor*, 11.25). Such dreams in Book 11 ostensibly offer a path to salvation, and are realized for Lucius in a way that reverses (rather than confirms—as in the case of Aristomenes) his relegation from the symbolic order.

Exposing atrocities: A punishment that fits the crime

Before his encounter with the visions sent by Isis, however, Lucius must submit to the horrifying prospect of a union with the *vilis aliqua* in Book 10. The criminal murderess is, like Meroe, overdetermined as the object of a spectacle, both in her proposed punishment in the arena and in Lucius' theatrically inspired narrative of her crimes. Moreover, the part assigned to the narrator in her fatal charade places him in the very role of voyeur-turned-participant formerly played by Aristomenes. While, as Tatum observes (1969: 514–16), Lucius himself remains at a sanguine distance from the horrific tales of adultery and vengeance to which he is privy for much of the novel, the narrative developments of Book 10 jostle our narrator into significantly greater proximity to the horrors he describes, and a number of verbal cues in the text prompt us to consider Lucius as the object of a spectacle rather than as a curious bystander.

As an ardent promoter of *munera*, Lucius' final owner, "Thiasus," evokes both the frenzy of a bacchic procession and the joys of watching one;[20] the Dionysian connotations of his name, however, also signal the ease with which such joys are converted into peril and, in so doing, recall the bacchant antics of Meroe and Panthia. Thiasus in Book 10 assumes the role of *sititor novitatis* ("one who thirsts for novelty") that Lucius, in his eagerness to hear Aristomenes' "absurd and monstrous" lies (*absurda … immania*, 1.2), had at the start of the novel assigned to himself.[21] After learning of his ass' unusual appetite for human delicacies, Thiasus enhances both his reputation and his fortune by adorning Lucius in sumptuous clothes and showing off his "variety of tricks" (*multiformibus ludicris*, 10.19). Such exposure leads our narrator into a transgressive dalliance with an attractive but voracious *matrona* of Corinth, a dalliance eagerly overseen by his trainer, as if "rehearsing for a new show" (*novum spectaculum praeparando*, 10.23).

As various scholars have commented, the final segment of Lucius' asinine experiences relies heavily on the language of the stage.[22] In his initial sexual performances, Lucius cannot predict the horror that awaits him, failing to observe the monster behind the lovely Corinthian *matrona*, though his allusion to the desires of Pasiphae marks her as deviant (10.22). The *matrona*'s sexual capacity, while at first confirming Lucius' single virtue in asinine form (his *vastum genitale*), also threatens to deny him that asset, as she "clasped me very tightly and took in absolutely all of me" (*artissime namque complexa totum me prorsus, sed totum recepit*, 10.22), leaving Lucius to wonder whether his considerable virility could satisfy her. This aspect of the sexual dynamic between ass and *matrona* hints at the same castration fear that defined Aristomenes' encounter with the witches Meroe and Panthia, though Lucius' experience is inflected as a distinct fear of being devoured within the *matrona*'s monstrous womb. Such fear is played out to sobering (if also humorous) conclusion in the *Onos*, where Loukios patently fails to please his former mistress after he has resumed his more modestly proportioned human form (56 [= 141–5 in Macleod 1967]).

Apuleius' Lucius, by contrast, will have no desire to revisit his sexual escapades or the voracious women associated with them after the threat of death as a *spectaculum* in the arena. His resumption of human form is forestalled by an expanded vision of the woman condemned to the beasts, leaving us to speculate further on both the horror about to take place and the titillating and repulsive spectacle of the *matrona* who secured this further engagement for him. While some scholars have gleaned in the episode of the Corinthian *matrona* a reciprocal affection between ass and lady, and interpreted it as marking Lucius' progress toward reclaiming his humanity, such affections are callously limited by a survival instinct:[23] the narrator's fear of rupturing her delicate form is prompted by his own wariness of being thrown to the beasts (*bestiis obiectus*) as punishment for so doing (*dirrupta nobili femina*, 10.22). The anxieties that surround his sexual encounter with the *matrona*, rather than marking progress toward enlightenment, anticipate the very encounter with the monstrous-feminine that Lucius will just barely avoid with the condemned murderess.

The tale of the *vilis aliqua* is, unlike most in the novel, introduced with particular relevance to Lucius: the two figures are bound by the nature of their fates, both of which hinge on a display of sexual violation—the murderess' ceremonial loss of *pudicitia*—made available for eager public consumption (*quae mecum incoram publicans pudicitiam populi caveam frequentaret*, 10.23). Zimmerman remarks on the terse introduction to the tale of the condemned woman, which conspicuously fails to promise the reader any aesthetic pleasure (2000: 295), and may reflect our narrator's sobering realization of how his fate is interwoven with hers. We might also ask, however, in light of the absence of aural pleasure and charming distraction, what affect we should experience by hearing it. Generically, the tale begins by offering the New Comic scenario of the abandoned citizen daughter whose real identity will be confirmed onstage, and then rapidly gestures toward tragedy—except that there is nothing tragic about our leading lady, who bears a greater resemblance to popular conceptions of the modern sociopath in her systematic eradication of anyone who interrupts her designs.[24]

Lucius' introduction to the tale posits an "inborn affection/reverence" expected of mothers (*insita matribus pietate*, 10.23), drawing on the comic type who secretly gives up her infant daughter in order to save the child from exposure. The detail not only underlines the condemned woman's flippant rejection of her maternal role later in the story (Schlam 1978: 103; cf. Zimmerman 2000: 298), but also redraws a polarization of feminine virtue and vice that will eventually lead, on the one hand, back to the coerced and horrifically farcical *matrimonium* Lucius is supposed to suffer in the arena and, on the other hand, to a spiritual wedlock with Isis that he achieves in its stead. We do not have to travel far for this fork in the road, as the *vilis aliqua* (also referred to as an *uxor*) enters the tale as a virtual extension of *caeca Fortuna* and *saeva Rivalitas*. This *uxor* mistakenly suspects the daughter, brought up by neighbors and now a recently married *puella*, of having an affair with her husband, who is actually the *puella's* brother. The *uxor's* first *facinus* is to lure her assumed rival into seclusion and then torture her to death (10.24). From there the *uxor*, under the guise of healing her grief-stricken, ailing husband, acts swiftly to hire an unscrupulous doctor to poison him; in so doing she catches the doctor off guard and forces him to drink his own poison in front of concerned onlookers in order to prove its salutary effects (10.25–7). The doctor lives long enough to report the *vilis aliqua's* crime to his wife, who in turn seeks payment from the murderess, but is duped into deferring her demands until she has handed over the rest of the poison. With this additional dosage, the *uxor* is able to kill off her own daughter, now an impediment to the inheritance of her dead husband's estate, and the wife of the doctor, who manages to disclose the tale to authorities just moments before her death (10.27–8).

With five murders to her credit, three of them committed on family members, the *vilis aliqua* outdoes the crimes of her predecessors in the novel in number and kind. The vengeance Meroe was able to enact on unfaithful lovers and sexual rivals through witchcraft is reduced in the case of the *vilis aliqua's* first victim, her wrongly presumed rival, to an act of physical torture—but, as with Meroe's vengeance, it is an act that directs us to view it as a product of feminine monstrosity. Despite the *puella's* protestations of innocence, the *uxor* "savagely killed [her] by thrusting a hot firebrand between her thighs" (*titione candenti inter media femina detruso crudelissime necavit*, 10.24). By drawing attention to the pain inflicted on the area between the young woman's thighs, and making this the mechanism of her death, the tale recalls the *femme castratrice* who haunted the novel earlier. While the *puella*, of course, cannot suffer literal castration, her particular fate also involves Lucius more closely in the horror that he narrates. Earlier in the novel, Lucius in asinine form nearly experiences castration—an assault involving his own thighs (*femina*[25])—at the hands of a sadistic boy (7.23, *dissitis femoribus emasculare*); he is saved from such a fate when the boy is attacked by a vicious she-bear, but soon finds his genitalia again under threat when the boy's mother seeks vengeance for her son's death (7.28; Zimmerman 2000: 313): as the mother approaches Lucius' genitals with a firebrand, the ass uses a stream of liquid dung in a literal explosion of scatological humor to blind his assailant (*liquida fimo strictim egesta*).

Indeed, humor and horror remain constant bedfellows in the novel, and in the tale of the *vilis aliqua* in particular. Zimmerman (2000: 313–14) describes the ensuing litany of the murderess' crimes as evoking either sympathy (for the *puella*, husband and daughter) or humor (the spectacularly drawn out death scenes of the doctor and his wife). And yet, in so brief an account of nameless victims, even the most innocent cannot elicit sympathy so much as a shudder at the cruelty of their deaths. The murders following the death of the *puella* are articulated as a sequence of horrors determined largely by the feminine construction of their maker. "That excellent wife" (*illa uxor egregia*, 10.24, as Lucius ironically refers to her) turns from implied genital mutilation to poison (a stereotypically "feminine" murder weapon in antiquity), and spreads her bloody hands far and wide in the process (*lateque cruentas suas manus porrigit*, 10.27).

Of the adjectives used to describe her, *truculenta* (used twice; from *trux*, "fierce, savage, cruel," 10.26) evokes the novel's template for wicked women, the witches Meroe and Panthia, whose images were *truces et dirae* (1.18). This *uxor*'s deeds and their telling by the moribund spouse of the doctor are marked as particularly horrific, *cunctis atrocitatibus expositis* (10.28), but also informed by legal language that anticipates the attempt to define her crimes and thus devise an appropriate punishment (Zimmerman 2000: 346).

As the *vilis aliqua*'s story is transformed from narrative inset to exposition of her punishment that will directly impact Lucius, we are allowed the prospect of viewing her monstrous nature in the spectacular light of the arena. Lucius offers an initial evaluation of her condemnation, summoning both the possibility of *talio* (so that "the punishment suits the crime"[26]) and its failure to cohere in this particular case, as the *praeses* "sentenced her to be thrown to the beasts, indeed less than she deserved, but because no other worthy punishment could be devised" (10.28; *illam, minus quidem quam merebatur, sed quod dignus cruciatus alius excogitari non poterat, certe bestiis obiciendam pronuntiavit*). The punishment cannot address the full extent of this woman's *atrocitates*, but (so it is implied) it is somehow worthy (*dignus*) of them. As such we should ask ourselves in what way the murderess' ritual wedding to Lucius in the arena enacts justice for the internal audience of Corinthian viewers as well as a kind of poetic justice for the *lectores* who know her story.

By framing their forced public copulation as a kind of marriage ceremony (10.29), Lucius reflects on his relatively pleasurable union with the *matrona* earlier in Book 10, though, as noted above, the resulting elision between the two women also shades the *matrona* with colors of the murderess' monstrosity. The *vilis aliqua*, however, is patently not an adulteress—her disavowal of all familial *fides* sprang from excessive desire for her husband. Why then renew the famously horrific mating of Minos' wife with a bull? This kind of *talio*, I would argue, works not simply to address the horrific wife of the embedded tale, but to exorcise the demons of desirous, threatening, and castrating women who have disrupted the social order with increasing severity throughout Lucius' journey. By somewhat inappropriately parading the *vilis aliqua* as an unfaithful wife of mythological proportions, the narrative concentrates on what makes woman, as constructed throughout the *Metamorphoses*, threatening: her castrating power and her abject nature together make her less than fully human and leave her relegated outside the symbolic order. At the end of Lucius the ass' narrative we are offered a kind of defilement ritual, a brushing up against the abject in order to distinguish and expel it from the social order, and allow the ass' return to his own "clean and proper body" (Kristeva 1982: 102) and his proper place in the human and, indeed, symbolic order.

The internal audience cannot sense our not-quite-human narrator's concerns about such mingling, but we *lectores* are made doubly aware of it. By confusing the ritual of a wedding with the threat of *contagium*—from *contingo* and literally "touching, contact with" (*OLD* s.v. 1)—Lucius represents this spectacle as a kind of publicly sanctioned ceremony of pollution (*priusquam scelerosae mulieris contagio macularer vel infamia publici spectaculi depudescerem*, 10.29). After describing the visually splendid pantomime of the judgment of Paris that serves as a prelude and stark contrast to the impending and no doubt fatal charade, Lucius defines his performance again as *contagium scelestae pollutaeque feminae* ("contact with the wicked and polluted woman") and connects it intimately with his experience of fear (*metu etiam mortis maxime cruciabar*, 10.34). We never quite glimpse the horror that threatens our frantic narrator—most of all because he makes his escape prior to having to go through with it— but in light of the elaborate narrative background now constructed for its display, we should ask ourselves: what ideological work is Lucius' near brush, or almost "touching," with the monstrous-feminine doing?

Conclusion: healing horrors

His eyes were riveted. He imbibed madness. Without any awareness of what was happening to him, he found delight in the murderous contest and was inebriated by bloodthirsty pleasure … But even now this experience was stored away in his memory as a kind of remedy for the future (*ad medicinam futuram*).

(Augustine, *Confessions*, 6.8.13–19.14, trans. Chadwick 1991)

If, as our narrator muses over the stunning vision of Paris' fateful choice in the pantomime sequence, beauty corrupts good judgment, can horror somehow heal, or confirm our sense of self? In summing up his friend Alypius' transformative addiction to the cruelties of the amphitheater, Augustine notes that the very memory of such transformation—as Alypius is defeated by *curiositas* (*victus curiositate*, 6.8.13) under the power of "most frightful pleasures" (*immanissimis voluptatibus*, 6.8.13)—was enough to provide Alypius with a remedy against future lapses. Similarly, while it is a critical commonplace that *curiositas* is one of Lucius' flaws, it is also evident that his abiding curiosity in the horrific is what catapults him to the peculiar form of salvation he finds at the end of the novel.

It has been argued that horror films exist largely to explore the problem of woman's sexuality, a force both desirable and threatening to the male psyche (Neale 1980: 61; cf. Clover 1989; Creed 1993; Greven 2011). Cinema's focus on the female form as vulnerable reinstates woman as castrated victim; as Creed reminds us, however, she is also frequently depicted as castrating, allowing her defeat to sooth male anxieties. Both representations within the medium of film rely on cinematographic methods, rather different from those in Apuleius' novel, to construct and explore the gendered aspects of human identity. Still, Apuleius' text finds a kinship with cinematic successors not only in the way that it privileges Lucius' direct representation of the visual (Elsom 1989; cf. Slater 1998: 39), but also insofar as it creates monsters driven by sexual desires to commit atrocities that raise a shuddering in the audience. Apuleius evokes a particular brand of horror by gendering his monstrosities and exploiting what is most threatening about woman's sexuality, a threat tamed provisionally by the spectacle of a "certain contemptible woman's" demise in the arena, and finally by substituting the threat of woman for the *salus* (11.1) she might offer in the image of Isis.

The initially unnamed goddess of Book 11 is not herself devoid of abject properties: instead, her threatening aspects—links with Hecate and the underworld (11.2, 5) that recall Meroe's opening antics—are sublimated, organized, and unified under the more salutary and beneficent symbol and name of Isis. As the wealth of visual details about Isis' manifestation suggest (*miranda species*, 11.3), woman in this form remains the object of a spectacle, and one that (again) inspires fear, this time coupled with joy rather than *curiositas* (*pavore et gaudio*, 11.7). Lucius can reenter the social contract because he has confronted the abject in visions of remarkably wicked women and finally seen it properly subordinated in the figure of the Egyptian goddess.

To be sure, visual marvels will continue to hold Lucius rapt, but new objects of his gaze displace the old entertaining, but horrifying ones: so our narrator expounds at length on the ironically ineffable image of the goddess he spies in the religious procession honoring her (11.11); after entering Isis' sanctuary in newly restored human form, Lucius remarks on the marvelous *simulacra* of the goddess, and one *specimen* of her in particular holds his gaze as he recalls former misfortunes (11.17). As Lucius proceeds down the path toward initiation, directives from the goddess are, as noted earlier (see p. 399), frequently articulated as visions or *imagines*, this time restorative ones that effectively supplant the threatening *imago* of Meroe described by Aristomenes. The language of visions to describe a process of revelation and conversion may be conventional, but in light of the novel's sustained interest in images of the monstrous-feminine, the construction of Isis and her entourage as a new kind of spectacle prompts readers to revisit the images of women they have seen through the eyes of the hapless narrator of Books 1–10. From there, as attentive *lectores*, we might measure not only the disparity between representations of Isis and those of her wicked predecessors, but perhaps gain a new awareness of the rigidly systematic organization of female vices and virtues that makes such images meaningful.

Kristeva argues that, historically, it has been the function of religion to purify the abject, but with the disintegration of these "historical forms" of religion, the processes of purification now depend on "that catharsis *par excellence* called art" (Kristeva 1982: 17). For Creed, the horror film in particular performs this function, in its capacity to "bring about a confrontation with the abject … in order finally to eject the abject and redraw the boundaries between human and non-human" (Creed 1993: 14). I have argued here that we can observe similar workings in Apuleius' artistry, as our protagonist is increasingly touched by the abject, only to expel it in a final gesture that literally discards his animal form, thus erasing his debt to nature and (re-) achieving symbolic status. This reading does not deny the author's awareness of significant, and potentially ironic, slippage in the polarized constructions of women on which he relies to mark his narrator's progress. Whether or not we read Lucius' conversion as sincere, the confrontation with the abject and the reclamation of the boundaries between human and animal performed by the text—as well as the role assigned to frightening women in that process—is indisputable. As woman is visibly and publically reduced to the status of beast (whether willingly or punitively), the novel re-inscribes a link with the material and natural world that makes her a symbol of the abject, of all that Lucius must eject to make himself human again.[27]

Notes

1 On the genre of the *Metamorphoses* and its relationship to other ancient prose fiction, see, e.g., Walsh 1970; Hägg 1983; Schlam 1992: 18–28; Tatum 1994.

2 Isis' life-giving qualities are especially apparent in Lucius' prayer in Book 11 and in Isis' response to it. The first manifestation of the goddess he invokes is "nourishing Ceres" (*Ceres alma*, 11.2) and, as Isis, she promises to extend his life beyond its fated years, if he remains suitably devout (11.6). Cf. also her role as "holy and eternal savior of humankind, who forever bountifully nurtures mortals" (*sancta et humani generis sospitatrix perpetua, semper fovendis mortalibus munifica*, 11.25).

3 By many accounts, *curiositas* is Lucius' most definitive and problematic characteristic; see Schlam 1992: 48 and 139 n. 1 for a brief overview of the scholarship. *Curiositas* is attested only once before Apuleius, in Cicero's letters (*Att.* 2.12.2), but used frequently after him in Tertullian, Augustine, and other early Christian writers, and often with reference to visual spectacles (*TLL* 4.1489.69–71; 4.1490.24–31). Walsh 1988: 76 views *curiositas* as a "key to the novel," presented with an ambiguity that Augustine will revise to condemnation in his *Confessions*. For Apuleius' influence on Augustine's articulation of *curiositas* as a kind of "misguided desire," see Shumate 1996: 243–6.

4 I do not mean to imply that sexuality and gender are coterminous in the novel, though they clearly overlap; cf. Morales 2008: 46. The *vilis aliqua* transgresses gender norms in her lack of the obedience and fidelity expected of a *matrona*, and in rejecting maternity; she commits no sexual transgression, but can be viewed as violating sexual norms in her vindictive jealousy of a presumed rival.

5 Tatum (1969: 524) cites from Auerbach's well-known reading of the novel's horrific aspects in *Mimesis*; see Auerbach 2003: 60–1; see also Puccini-Delbey (2003: 78) who, drawing on the work of Bataille (1956 [1979]), finds the novel's horrors heightened by its frequent antitheses of extreme pleasure and grief.

6 As he observes in "From the history of an infantile neurosis," 86, cited in Creed 1993: 155–6.

7 Examples of the *femme castratrice* are found in *Psycho* (Hitchcock 1960), *Deep Red* (= *Profondo Rosso*, Argento 1975), *Carrie* (De Palma 1976), and *Fatal Attraction* (Lyne 1987). For the devouring and dangerous properties of the female womb, see also *The Brood* (Cronenberg 1979) and the *Alien* films

(1979–97). Most recently, Ridley Scott's *Prometheus* (2012), a prequel to the *Alien* series, stages a similarly gendered conflict as its denouement, in which the hyper-masculine Prometheus figure is devoured by a very feminized and vaginal alien proto-life force. While Creed's thesis offers a persuasive account of the dynamics of gender in the horror genre, its limitations have also been recognized, e.g., by Greven (2011), whose reading of modern horror (*c*.1960–90) demonstrates that the genre explores the tensions surrounding a subject's desire to return to the womb as often as it expresses dread over the archaic mother figure; esp. 13–15.

8   Cf. Elsom 1989 on the cinematic qualities of the *Metamorphoses*; she is primarily interested in the similar narrative strategies of filmmakers and Apuleius—in particular, the gulf created between what Lucius the protagonist can see, but not affect, resembles the camera/viewer's ability to capture but not affect onscreen reality. Her comparison between cinematographic technique and the novel's narrative strategies anticipates Slater, who also posits a comparison between Lucius as narrator and the camera as director of our gaze: "up until [Book 11], Lucius has been a camera, recording what he sees and making us see it too" (Slater 1998: 39).

9   For important modifications to the sexual symmetry observed by Konstan, see esp. Montague (1992); Egger (1994); Haynes (2003); and Morales (2008).

10 For the story as Apuleius' innovation, but one modeled on motifs from folklore, see Scobie 1975: 87–8.

11 This is not to say that Winkler privileges the therapeutic vision (on the contrary, he stresses the need for readers to suspend prejudgments), but only that it is one interpretive key which with which we are teased from the very start.

12 On basic properties of the monster, see Carroll 1990: 27–35. Cf. also Amsa 2009: 5–13 for "unintelligibility" as a property of the monster, though his study extends beyond the monster of the horror genre to examine its composition across a range of literatures and media, both ancient and contemporary. As Carroll (1990) points out, the horror genre (unlike mythology, folklore, and other fantastical genres) constructs the monster as a creature that cannot be "accommodated by the metaphysics of the cosmology that produced them" (16), a status intimately connected with its capacity to evoke fear.

13 Cf. Ash 2012: 442 on two factors that influence literary portraits of men and women: "preconceived rules of a given literary genre" and the "practice of creative allusion, which involves filtering one character or situation through another pre-existing text." Puccini-Delbey argues (2003; cf. 2007: 205) that Apuleius' diction of female sexuality is more restrained than his Latin forerunners in satire and lyric ("essentiellement euphémique," 69). While Apuleius may describe female genitalia using less graphic terminology, the invective tone he uses to characterize certain women, especially those in the latter books of the novel, is fairly severe; e.g., the wife of the poor workman in Book 9, "notorious for her exceptional lasciviousness" (*postrema lascivia famigerabilis*, 9.5); the Phaedra-like character of Book 10 is described as "that dreadful woman, a unique example of stepmotherly maliciousness" (*dira illa femina et malitiae novercalis exemplum unicum*, 10.5).

14 For the significance of names and the storytellers who name (or fail to name) characters in the *Metamorphoses*, see Hijmans 1978.

15 For the prominence of castration in the novel, see Scobie 1975: 108, who cites van Thiel 1971–2: 68, 50.

16 Images of urinating women are relatively rare in Latin, but see Juvenal's upper crust *matronae* urinating near the temple of *Pudicitia* (6.308–13). Scobie (1975: 109) compares the act with Petr. *Satyr.* 62 and comments on possible ritualistic significance.

17 Cf. esp. *Met.* 7.10 and 8.29, for the adjective's associations with sexual conduct.

18 For this antithesis in the novel, see Puccini-Delbey 2007: 202–8.

19 Cf. Tatum 1969: 494 n. 29 on parallels between Meroe and other wicked wives in the later books.

20 From the Greek θίασος; see *OLD* s.v. 1.

21 For Thiasus as one who thirsts for novelty, see esp. 10.16 (*novitate spectaculi laetus*). The phrasing used to describe him is not identical to that used to describe Lucius, but the parallel is rightly asserted by Zimmerman 2000: 27.

22 See Zimmerman 2000: 15, 20 and Fick 1990 on Book 10's designation as "Liber de Spectaculis."

23 Shumate, who offers an otherwise astute reading of Lucius' epistemological and moral progress in the novel, remarks on the "spirit of mutual caring" that defines the episode (Shumate 1996: 125).

24 Zimmerman 2000: 444 describes the movement from "expected happy dénouement to horror story."

25 *Femur*, "thigh," forms its oblique cases from two different stems (*femin-* and *femor-*); Apuleius uses both.

26 Or, according to the *OLD*, "exact compensation in kind."

27 I would like to thank Steven Smith, Casey Moore, and James Tatum for their insightful comments on an earlier draft of this paper. Suggestions from Mark Masterson and the volume editors have significantly improved the final version. Any errors or oversights that remain are entirely my own.

Bibliography

Amsa, S.T. (2009) *On Monsters: An Unnatural History of our Worst Fears*. Oxford: Oxford University Press.

Ash, R. (2012) "Women in imperial Roman literature", in S.L. James and S. Dillon (eds) *A Companion to Women in the Ancient World*. Malden, MA: Wiley-Blackwell, pp. 442–52.

Auerbach, E. (2003) *Mimesis: The Representation of Reality in Western Literature*, trans. W. Trask. Princeton, NJ: Princeton University Press.

Bataille, G. (1956 [1979]) *Madame Edwarda*. Paris: Pauvert.

Carroll, N. (1990) *The Philosophy of Horror, or Paradoxes of the Heart*. New York and London: Routledge.

Chadwick, H. (trans.) (1991) *Saint Augustine: Confessions*. Oxford and New York: Oxford University Press.

Clover, C.J. (1989) "Her body, himself: Gender in the Slasher film", in J. Donald (ed.) *Fantasy and the Cinema*. London: BFI Publishing, pp. 91–133.

Coleman, K.M. (1990) "Fatal charades: Roman executions staged as mythological enactments", *Journal of Roman Studies* 80: 44–73.

Creed, B. (1993) *The Monstrous-Feminine: Film, Feminism, and Psychoanalysis*. London and New York: Routledge.

Egger, B. (1994) "Women and marriage in the Greek novels: The boundaries of romance", in J. Tatum (ed.) *The Search for the Ancient Novel*. Baltimore, MD: Johns Hopkins University Press, pp. 260–82.

Elsom, H. (1989) "Apuleius and the movies", in H. Hoffman (ed.) *Groningen Colloquia on the Novel: Volume II*. Groningen: E. Forsten, pp. 141–50.

Fick, N. (1990) "Die Pantomime des Apuleius (*Met.* X, 30–34, 3)", in J. Bländsdorf (ed.) *Theater und Gesellschaft im Imperium Romanum*. Tübingen: Francke, pp. 223–32.

Greven, D. (2011) *Representations of Femininity in American Genre Cinema: The Woman's Film, Film Noir, and Modern Horror*. New York: Palgrave Macmillan.

Hägg, T. (1983) *The Novel in Antiquity*. Oxford: Oxford University Press.

Haynes, K. (2003) *Fashioning the Feminine in the Greek Novel*. London: Routledge.

Hijmans, B.L. (1978) "Significant names and their function in Apuleius' *Metamorphoses*", in B.L. Hijmans Jr and R. Th. van der Paardt (eds) *Aspects of Apuleius' Golden Ass*. Groningen: Bouma, pp. 107–22.

Konstan, D. (1994) *Sexual Symmetry: Love in the Ancient Novel and Related Genres*. Princeton, NJ: Princeton University Press.

Kristeva, J. (1982) *Powers of Horror: An Essay in Abjection*, trans. L. Roudiez. New York: Columbia University Press.

Macleod, M.D. (trans.) (1967) *Lucian* (in 8 vols), vol. 8. Cambridge, MA: Harvard University Press.

Montague, H. (1992) "Sweet and pleasant passion: Female and male fantasy in ancient romance novels", in A. Richlin (ed.) *Pornography and Representation in Ancient Greece and Rome*. New York and Oxford: Oxford University Press, pp. 231–49.

Morales, H. (2008) "The history of sexuality", in T. Whitmarsh (ed.) *The Cambridge Companion to the Greek and Roman Novel*. Cambridge: Cambridge University Press, pp. 39–55.

Neale, S. (1980) *Genre*. London: BFI Publishing.

Puccini-Delbey, G. (2003) *Amour et désir dans les Métamorphoses d'Apulée*. Brussels: Éditions Latomus.

——(2007) *La Vie sexuelle à Rome*. Paris: Tallandier.

Schlam, C.C. (1978) "Sex and sanctity: The relationship of male and female in the *Metamorphoses*", in B.L. Hijmans Jr. and R. Th. van der Paardt (eds) *Aspects of Apuleius' Golden Ass*. Groningen: Bouma, pp. 95–106.

——(1992) *The Metamorphoses of Apuleius: On Making an Ass of Oneself*. Chapel Hill, NC: University of North Carolina Press.

Scobie, A. (1975) *Apuleius Metamorphoses (Asinus Aureus) I: A Commentary*. Herstellung: Verlag Anton Hain.

Shumate, N. (1996) *Crisis and Conversion in Apuleius' Metamorphoses*. Ann Arbor, MI: University of Michigan Press.

Slater, N.W. (1998) "Passion and petrification: The gaze in Apuleius", *Classical Philology* 93: 18–48.

Tatum, J. (1969) "The tales in Apuleius' *Metamorphoses*", *Transactions of the American Philological Association* 100: 487–527.

——(1979) *Apuleius and the Golden Ass*. Ithaca, NY: Cornell University Press.

——(1994) "Introduction:The search for the ancient novel", in J. Tatum (ed.) *The Search for the Ancient Novel*. Baltimore, MD: Johns Hopkins University Press, pp. 1–19.

Van Thiel, H. (1971–2) *Der Eselsroman*, vols 1–2. Munich: Beck.

Walsh, P.G. (1970) (repr. 1995) *The Roman Novel: The Satyricon of Petronius and the Metamorphoses of Apuleius*. Cambridge: Cambridge University Press.

——(1988) "The rights and wrongs of curiosity (Plutarch to Augustine)", *Greece & Rome* 35: 73–85.

Winkler, J.J. (1985) *Auctor & Actor: A Narratological Reading of Apuleius' The Golden Ass*. Berkeley, CA: University of California Press.

Zimmerman, M. (2000) *Apuleius Madaurensis: Metamorphoses, Book X: Text, Introduction, and Commentary*. Groningen: E. Forsten.

23

MAKING MANHOOD HARD

Tiberius and Latin literary representations of erectile dysfunction

Judith P. Hallett

(43) *secessu vero Caprensi etiam sellaria excogitavit, sedem arcanarum libidinum, in quam undique conquisiti puellarum et exoletorum greges monstrosique concubitus repertores, quos spintrias appellabat, triplici serie conexi, in vicem incestarent coram ipso, ut aspectu deficientis libidines excitaret. cubicula plurifariam disposita tabellis ac sigillis lascivissimarum picturarum et figurarum adornavit librisque. Elephantidis instruxit, ne cui in opera edenda exemplar imperatae schemae deesset. in silvis quoque ac nemoribus passim Venerios locos commentus est prostantisque per antra et cavas rupes ex utriusque sexus pube Paniscorum et Nympharum habitu quae palam iam et vulgo nomine insulae abutentes "Caprineum" dictitabant.*

(44) *maiore adhuc ac turpiore infamia flagravit, vix ut referri audirive, nedum credi fas sit quasi pueros primae teneritudinis, quos pisciculos vocabat, institueret, ut natanti sibi inter femina versarentur ac luderent lingua morsuque sensim adpetentes; atque etiam quasi infantes firmiores, necdum tamen lacte depulsos, inguini ceu papillae admoveret, pronior sane ad id genus libidinis et natura et aetate. quare Parrasi quodque tabulam, in qua Meleagro Atalanta ore morigeratur, legatam sibi sub condicione, ut si argumento offenderetur decies pro ea sestertium acciperet, non modo praetulit, sed in cubiculo dedicavit. fertur etiam in sacrificando quodam captus facie ministri acerram praeferentis nequisse abstinere, quin paene vixdum re divina peracta ibidem statim seductum constupraret simulque fratrem eius tibicinem; atque utrique mox, quod mutuo flagitium exprobrarant, crura fregisse.*

(45) *feminarum quoque, et quidem illustrium, capitibus quanto opere solitus sit inludere, evidentissime apparuit Malloniae cuiusdam exitu, qua perductam nec quicquam amplius pati constantissime recusantem delatoribus obiecit ac ne ream quidem interpellare desiit, "ecquid paeniteret"; donec ea relicto iudicio domum se abripuit ferroque transegit, obscaenitate oris hirsuto atqui olido seni clare exprobrata. unde nota in Atellanico exhodio proximis ludis adsensu maximo excepta percrebuit, "hircum vetulum capreis naturam ligurire."*

(43) But at his retreat on the island of Capri, Tiberius also devised "the rear-endings," a site suited for his secret sexual passions, where throngs of girls and males-for-hire, who were long past their sexual prime, gathered together there from everywhere, inventors of freakish sexual activity, whom he called

"fundamentalists"; having connected to one another in "three-way couplings," they would, one trio after another, perform sexually shameful acts before him so that he might stir his failing sexual passions by watching. He decorated the sleeping places, situated all over, with paintings and statues of the most sexually explicit scenes and bodies, and furnished these locales with sex manuals by the Greek woman Elephantis, so that there might be no illustration of an erotic position commanded for performance lacking to anyone in engaging in a sexual act. In the forests and glades, moreover, he set up "Sex Spots," and young people of either sex soliciting for partners through the caves and the hollow rocks, in the costumes of Pans and nymphs, a place which those at that time openly called "the Caprineum," "Old-Goat's Park," with a punning misuse of the island's name, Capri.

(44) He became notorious because of a still greater and more shameful reputation for disgraceful conduct, behavior that may not be appropriate to be discussed or heard, much less believed: for instance, that he got little boys of a tender toddler age, whom he called his little fishies, into a routine that involved moving back and forth between his thighs as he swam and acting playfully by seeking him slowly with tongue and biting, and that he also guided babies, fairly sturdy specimens, although not yet weaned, to his penis as if it were a breast, since by both temperament and age he was particularly inclined to this type of sexual passion. For this reason he not only chose to keep, but even prominently exhibited in his bedroom, a painting by Parrhasius, on which Atalanta gave pleasure to Meleager orally, though the work had been bequeathed to him on the condition that if he were made uncomfortable by the subject matter he would instead receive a million sesterces. It is also said that during a sacrifice, overpowered by the physical appeal of the attendant bearing incense, he was unable to keep himself under control, to the point that when the ceremony was barely over he immediately pulled him aside and raped him and his brother, the flute-player, and soon thereafter, because they together complained of his shameless conduct, had their legs broken.

(45) To what extent Tiberius was in the habit of obtaining pleasure from the heads of women, even those of noble background, was most clearly revealed by the death of a certain Mallonia. He handed her over to informers after she had been brought to him and was refusing most emphatically to endure anything more, and he did not stop interrupting even when she was under interrogation, asking "whether she was regretting anything," until, after she had departed from the courtroom, she hurried home and stabbed herself, audibly castigating the hairy and malodorous old man for the vileness of his mouth. From this incident an insult in an Atellan farce at the next dramatic performances, welcomed with the greatest enthusiasm, made the rounds, "the old goat was licking the birthing parts of the roe-deer."

(Suetonius, Tiberius *43–5)[1]*

My discussion seeks to situate this tripartite passage from Suetonius' life of the Julio-Claudian emperor Tiberius in its larger Roman literary, historical, and cultural context. Written in the early second century CE, it purports to provide a detailed account of sexual proclivities exhibited by the aged Tiberius, who was born and won a string of military victories during the late first century BCE and held political sway during the early first century CE.[2] I will argue that various verbal and thematic similarities between this passage—which focuses chiefly on what we would today call Tiberius' problems with erectile dysfunction—and several other Latin poetic and prose texts help illuminate what Suetonius himself is implying, and what Suetonius' Roman readers would have inferred, about the difficulties faced by this military and political leader in physically proving himself a true Roman man.[3]

The prose passages come from Suetonius' own biographies of Tiberius' two immediate predecessors, Julius and Augustus Caesar. Suetonius also represents them as failing to perform sexually as true Roman men, especially Roman military and political leaders, were expected to do: by successfully penetrating their female and male partners with hard, erect male organs. But I will accord initial and greater attention to poetic texts, by Catullus and Horace respectively, that represent men seeking remedies for erectile difficulties.[4] These texts long predate Suetonius' lives of the Caesars, and share key vocabulary and themes with his description of Tiberius here. As I will argue below, they also may allude to a woman belonging to Tiberius' own, noble Claudian family. These texts are, therefore, likely to have influenced Suetonius' biographies of Tiberius and other Julio-Claudian emperors. While none of them are ordinarily read in conjunction with this Suetonian passage, all of them intertextually illuminate and are illuminated by it.[5] The affinities between this passage and the poems by Catullus and Horace, moreover, suggest that Suetonius assumes a learned readership whose familiarity with these Catullan and Horatian texts will add depth and point to his own. His emphasis on Tiberius' own literary learning may further account for his decision to call these poems to mind.[6]

Suetonius' apparent evocations of these earlier poems not only help to document, as do his assertions about Tiberius' militarily accomplished political predecessors, that he, like my discussion itself, seeks to situate Tiberius' efforts to overcome erectile dysfunction in a larger Roman literary and cultural context. They also testify to a concept of Roman masculinity more complex and nuanced than that articulated by earlier studies: inasmuch as it recognizes and tries to account for the challenges posed by the vicissitudes of male erectile functioning. Such challenges, of course, remind us that the cultural performance of Roman manhood in its fully realized state was indubitably hard, just like the optimal, if not everlasting, condition of the physical organ that served as its symbol.

Suetonius on Tiberius' manly malfunctions

Most scholarly discussions of this Suetonian passage obscure or even overlook an important detail that it foregrounds about Tiberius' sexual conduct; namely, his frequent failure to attain and sustain an erection, from the time he became emperor in 14 CE, when he was fifty-five, until his death in 37 CE, when he was seventy-eight.[7] Perhaps scholars are distracted by the spotlight Suetonius throws on the outlandish efforts and huge expenditures that Tiberius, utilizing the vast human and financial resources at his disposal as Rome's ruler, was able to invest in making and keeping his male organ hard.[8]

Chapter 43, as we have seen, describes Tiberius' costly visual sexual aids, beginning with the males and females he hired to perform acrobatic group sexual acts, at a site called the *sellaria*, which I have translated, "rear endings," on his island retreat at Capri. I have translated Suetonius' words that euphemistically describe Tiberius' motivation for arranging these entertainments, *ut aspectu deficientis libidines excitaret*, literally, as "so that he might stir his failing passions by watching." They acknowledge, however, the emperor's need for visual stimulation to make and keep his organ hard. Suetonius emphasizes other visual modes of sexual stimulation also on display at Capri: the sexually explicit poses of the painted and sculptural figures decorating its sleeping places as well as the erotic manuals filling them. In addition, the passage mentions the solicitation of partners by young people, costumed as lustful figures from Greek mythology, in locales not only known as *Venerios locos*, "Sex Spots," but also referred to, in a pun on the name of Capri itself, as the *Caprineum*, "Old Goat's Park." This word alludes in turn to Tiberius' own "goatishness," mentioned again—to create a "ring composition" effect—at the end of chapter 45.[9]

In chapter 44 Suetonius euphemistically describes, and at the same time expresses strong disapproval of, the physical, mostly oral activities in which Tiberius engaged to remedy his erectile problems. First, training young boys, whom he called "little fishies" (*pisciculos*), to move back and forth through his thighs, and arouse his genital area with their tongues and teeth, as he swam. Second, obtaining another form of oral stimulation from unweaned babies by guiding them to his penis as if it were a breast, to be pulled at vigorously. Third, exhibiting in his bedroom a sexually stimulating painting by the fourth-century BCE Greek artist Parrhasius. Suetonius states that it depicted the mythic female figure Atalanta orally pleasuring her successful suitor Meleager; his language suggests that it portrayed Atalanta as also being orally pleasured herself.[10]

Finally, in chapter 45, Suetonius relates that Tiberius sought oral sexual gratification from women, and even, when forcing his unwanted attentions on them, tried to arouse them with his mouth. Such are the implications of Suetonius' euphemistically phrased claims that Tiberius obtained pleasure "from the heads of women" (*feminarum ... capitibus*); that a woman named Mallonia castigated him in a courtroom for the "vileness of his mouth" (*obscaenitate oris*); and that a popular play insulted him with the phrase "the old goat was licking the birthing parts of roe-deer" (*hircum vetulum capreis naturam ligurire*). Suetonius evidently contrasts the grown women that Tiberius forced to stimulate him orally with the boys and babies described in his previous chapter, by emphasizing that they received oral sexual gratification of their own in return for fellating him.[11]

By merely enumerating Tiberius' expensive, imaginative efforts to become and stay tumescent, and representing them as efforts involving and viewed by others, Suetonius attests that Tiberius was forced to acknowledge his sexual inadequacies to the Roman public. He testifies, too, that such acknowledgments caused Tiberius to undergo considerable public humiliation, in the halls of justice and on the Roman stage. Yet, somewhat paradoxically, Suetonius accords Tiberius' sexual inadequacies a measure of sympathy at the same time that he criticizes Tiberius' attempts to overcome them: by using language and themes featured in earlier Latin erotic poetry about male impotence and its oral remedies. The intertextual dynamic constructed by Suetonius thereby draws on a Latin literary tradition in which male poets, writing in the first person, admit, both directly and indirectly, to their own, albeit temporary, sexual failures. What is more, these poet-speakers—Catullus and Horace—voice this admission for literary as well as erotic reasons.

Manly malfunctioning in Catullus and Horace

By writing in the first person about their sexual failures, Catullus and Horace seek to claim authority, albeit of a different kind from that wielded by a Roman ruler and commander-in-chief: authority on both love and poetry. They describe these bouts of impotence to emphasize that erotic activity itself can involve physical and emotional disappointments as well as successes. What is more, through attesting to their own episodes of erectile dysfunction, in a realistic, though fictionalized, effort to prove their expertise on amatory matters, these love poets seek to elicit sympathy from their audiences.[12]

Suetonius is, of course, writing in the third person about the activities of Tiberius, a dead historical figure, and not his own love life. He aims to elicit moral disapproval of Tiberius' conduct, especially shameful in a Roman head of state. Still, by merely evoking these earlier erotic poems, he situates Tiberius' sufferings from and endeavors to cure erectile dysfunction in a pedigreed Latin literary tradition. Through these intertextual strategies, Suetonius is representing Tiberius himself as more human, and hence more comprehensible to his readers. Even this rich, powerful, military and political leader, Suetonius implies, encountered physical difficulties faced by other, ordinary, Roman males, and struggled to prove himself a true Roman man. While Suetonius may openly disapprove of Tiberius, he nonetheless stresses the commonalities among emperor, erotic poets, and his male readers; his own prose also gains authority and power from this web of literary associations.

The contribution to this literary tradition by the earlier of these poets, the mid-first-century BCE Catullus, merits our special scrutiny. Several recent studies have furnished both linguistic and literary evidence to substantiate a claim that Catullan readers have been making for centuries. Namely, that in his second and third poems, literally about the *passer*, pet sparrow, of his female beloved, Catullus also uses the noun *passer* metaphorically, to describe his own male member. By using this figure of speech, then, Catullus invites readers to interpret both poems as an extended sexual double entendre.

Such studies, however, do not regard these Catullan poems, both of which Suetonius recalls in describing Tiberius' sexual proclivities, as about either erectile dysfunction or oral sexual stimulation.[13] Yet the similarities between these two poems and Suetonius' text strongly suggest that all three treat these very topics. These textual affinities also allow us to use Suetonius' later, more sexually explicit passage about Tiberius' impotence and its remedies to illuminate the earlier, more euphemistically phrased Catullan poems.

Let us now turn to the text of these two poems—which here includes that of the three lines, also in the hendecasyllabic meter, directly following Poem 2 (frequently labeled "2a")—so as to consider in detail their affinities with Suetonius, *Tib.* 43–5, and what these affinities imply.[14] I have provided literal translations of both.

> passer, deliciae meae puellae,
> quicum ludere, quem in sinu tenere,
> cui primum digitum dare appetenti
> et acris solet incitare morsus,
> *cum desiderio meo nitenti*   5
> carum nescioquid lubet iocari,
> et solaciolum sui doloris,
> credo, ut tum gravis acquiescat ardor:
> tecum ludere sicut ipsa possem
> *et tristis animi levare curas!*   10
>
> tam gratum est mihi quam ferunt puellae
> pernici aureolum fuisse malum,
> quod zonam solvit diu ligatam.

Sparrow, erotic delight of my girl, with whom she is accustomed to play, whom she is accustomed to hold in her embrace, whom she is accustomed to touch with her fingertip as he seeks her, and from whom she is accustomed to stir up sharp bites, when it pleases my shining desire to act playfully with something cherished and a little relief for her emotional pain, I believe, and so that her vehement passion may subside: if only I were able to play with you as she herself is, and to relieve the sad cares of my mind.

This [playing with the sparrow] is as pleasing to me as they say the golden apple was to the swift girl, which loosened her maiden zone tied for so long a time.

(Catullus, Poem 2 and "2a")

Lugete, o Veneres Cupidinesque,
et quantum est hominum venustiorum:
passer mortuus est meae puellae,
passer, deliciae meae puellae,
quam plus illa oculius suis amabat—   5
nam mellitus erat suamque norat
ipsam tam bene quam puella matrem,
nec sese a gremio illius movebat,
sed circumsiliens modo huc modo illuc
ut solum dominam usque pipiabat: 10
qui nunc it per iter tenebricosum
illud, unde negant redire quemquam.
at vobis male sit, malae tenebrae
Orci, quae omnia bella devoratis:
tam bellum mihi passerem abstulistis.   15
o factum male! o miselle passer!
Tua nunc opera meae puellae
Flendo turgiduli rubent ocelli.

Mourn, o Venuses and Cupids, and however great the quantity of people with a special affinity for the goddess Venus: the sparrow of my girl is dead, the sparrow, erotic delight of my girl, whom she loved more than her own eyes. For he was honey-sweet and knew my girl herself as well as a girl child knows her mother. Nor did he move himself from her lap, but jumping around, now here, now there, constantly chirped for her, his mistress alone. And now he journeys through that shadowy passage, from which they say no one journeys back. But may you suffer evil, evil shadows of the underworld, you who devour all beautiful things: you have taken such a beautiful sparrow from me. O action causing pain! O poor little sparrow. Because of your work now the little eyes of my girl, slightly swollen, are red from crying.

(Catullus, Poem 3)

Catullus 2 portrays the pet bird of his female beloved as a plaything that brings pleasure to her. Catullus 3 depicts the bird as having died and brought her sorrow. Suetonius' passage about Tiberius immediately calls both poems to mind by associating human sexual performance with animals. Even when we read both Catullan poems literally, they describe the pet bird as involved in erotic play with Catullus' beloved. Suetonius, as we have seen, notes that Tiberius' partners were called "little fishies" (*pisciculos*) and roe deer (*capreis*), that Tiberius himself was disparaged on stage as a "he-goat" (*hircum*) and that Tiberius' sexual playgrounds on Capri were referred to as "the Old-Goat's Park" (*Caprineum*).[15]

Suetonius makes prominent use of Catullus' vocabulary and themes in these two poems, especially 2, as well. For example, Suetonius employs the verb *ludere*, "to play, perform," in both its simple form and the compounded *inludere*, to describe Tiberius' erotic activities. The verb *ludere* appears twice in Catullus 2: at line 2 and line 9, in the first instance as a complementary present active infinitive with *solet*, a form of the verb *solere*, "to become accustomed."[16] Suetonius similarly uses *inludere* as a complementary present active infinitive with a form of the same verb (*solitus sit inludere*), in chapter 45. Poem 2 shares with Suetonius' account of Tiberius' sexual conduct the noun *morsus*, "biting," and the verb *appetere*, "to seek avidly."[17] On the thematic level, the three lines of 2a, as we shall observe, refer to the sexual activity of the mythic maiden Atalanta. At *Tiberius* 44, as we have observed, Suetonius claims that an erotically explicit painting that Tiberius displayed in his bedroom depicted her as engaging in oral sexual activity.

If we understand the noun *passer* as referring to the male organ of the poet-speaker as well as a pet bird, many details in Poem 3—which laments the death of the *passer*—allow us to read it as portraying the poet-speaker in a state of impotence, and indeed ruefully recalling that his male organ was orally ministered to by his beloved in the past. These details include the reference to the dead bird as "honey-sweet" (6), implying that it received oral attention from his beloved. They also include the charge, leveled at the "evil shadows of the underworld" that "you who eat up (*devoratis*) all beautiful things have taken so beautiful a sparrow from me" (13–15)—which characterizes the realm of the dead as, like the beloved herself, receiving the *passer* orally.

Yet Suetonius' echoes of Catullus 3 offer additional corroboration for interpreting the *passer* in that poem as the male organ of its poet-speaker. Suetonius (*Tib.* 43) clearly uses the word *opera*, "work, effort," in a sexual sense by employing the gerundive phrase *in opera edenda* to describe those who followed the instructions of the illustrated sex manuals on Capri, and hence to signify "in engaging in a sexual act." This usage allows us to assign Catullus' phrase *tua opera* an erotic meaning as well, with the statement "owing to your work now the eyes of my girl are red" as a reference to the organ's erectile failure, and to the sadness this failure causes his beloved.[18] So, too, Suetonius appears to recall, and invite his readers to recall, Catullus' address to Venuses and Cupids, as well as to people with a special affinity to the erotic goddess Venus (*venustiorum*), by referring to the places that Tiberius established for erotic encounters as *locos Venerios*, "locales of Venus" or "Sex Spots."

Nevertheless, if Catullus is employing the word *passer* to refer to the poet-speaker's male organ as well as his female lover's pet bird in Poem 2, it is more difficult to imagine the sexual scenario operating in that poem. After all, in lines 3–4 Catullus literally portrays the *passer* as seeking the poet's beloved when she touches him with her fingertip, and as bestowing sharp bites, evidently on her fingertips as well, in response. Such biting actions would be impossible for a male organ to perform.[19] Yet the grammatical complexities of Catullus' Latin also allow another translation, one that describes the beloved as engaged in caressing and biting: that is, orally stimulating and arousing the male organ of the poet-speaker. The ambiguity of the dative form *cui*, a relative pronoun which represents the *passer* in subordinate clauses containing the two present active infinitives *dare* and *incitare* here, allows a second translation: "[the *passer*] whom she is accustomed to touch with her fingertip as he seeks her, and on whom she is accustomed to intensify her own sharp bites."[20] An erotic scenario centered on mutual oral stimulation—the *puella* fellating Catullus, Catullus performing cunnilingus on the *puella*—would help account for Catullus' statements in this poem that "playing with the pet bird" provides his beloved with "a little relief from her emotional pain," and that she engages in this playful activity "so that her vehement passion may then subside." Such statements may suggest that oral stimulation of her genitalia by him, and of his genitalia by her, in and of themselves afford his *puella* pleasure. Yet they may also imply that her oral exertions make his organ hard enough to penetrate her vaginally, and bring her further sexual satisfaction.

Catullus' use, in Poem 2, of words—such *as ludere*, *appetere*, and *morsus*—later employed by Suetonius to describe the oral stimulation of both male and female genitalia renders an erotic scenario of this sort even more plausible. The poet-speaker's subsequent wish that he "would be able to play with the bird as his female lover does," "to relieve the sad cares of his own mind" fits this scenario, too. It serves as an indirect way of expressing desire for oral self-stimulation and self-gratification, a physically difficult if not impossible act.[21]

The affinities between Catullus' Poem 2 and Suetonius' passage about Tiberius' sexual proclivities also allow us to connect the three lines of 2a with the rest of Poem 2. In these three lines, the poet-speaker asserts that some unnamed thing is "as pleasing" to him as "the golden apple, which loosened her maiden zone, was to the swift girl." Commentators agree that here Catullus refers obliquely to the pleasures experienced by the mythic maiden Atalanta, after she wed, and yielded her virginity to, the swiftest of her suitors.[22] This man is said to have thrown a golden apple in Atalanta's path, causing him to defeat her in a footrace, and thereby win her hand.

Commentators have not associated the unnamed "pleasing thing" in 2a with the wish of the poet-speaker at the end of Poem 2 to "relieve the sad cares of his own mind" by playing with the pet bird of his beloved. But Catullus depicts Atalanta's pleasure as occasioned by a sexual act that ends her virginity, which requires a hard male member. Furthermore, Suetonius' description of the painting in Tiberius' bedroom that represented Atalanta and Meleager as engaged in oral sexual gratification offers further evidence for identifying "the pleasing thing" as the poet's wish for sexual fulfillment when away from his beloved, fulfillment necessitating oral stimulation, which can facilitate penetrative sexual activity.[23]

In this second, sexual, reading of Poems 2 and 3, then, Catullus portrays himself, the poet-speaker, as suffering from erectile dysfunction, and confessing his need for oral stimulation from his female partner to gratify her sexually. His description of Atalanta as experiencing sexual pleasure herself renders it likely that he here depicts himself as pleasuring his female partner orally; what is more, he seems to voice a desire to perform the physically difficult if not impossible act of fellating himself. Two poems by Horace, *Epodes* 8 and 12, composed in the decades immediately after Catullus wrote, recall these and other Catullan poems. They further develop the Latin literary tradition on which Suetonius' portrayal of Tiberius' sexual difficulties draws.[24] Significantly, by evoking Catullus as they portray their poet-speaker as suffering from impotence, and needing remedial oral gratification, Horace's two poems also strengthen an interpretation of Catullus 2 and 3 as treating these two topics.

In the first of these poems, *Epode* 8, the male poet-speaker vividly acknowledges the limpness of his penis: first asking an older, erotically demanding female partner "That you, disgusting female of advanced age, have the nerve to ask what is weakening my male muscles" (1–2 *rogare longo putidam te saeculo / vires quod enervet meas*); later inquiring "You don't imagine, do you, that my male muscles grow less stiff because they are uneducated, or that my manly part lies less limp?" (17–18 *illiterati num minus nervi rigent, / minusve languet fascinum?*). He then demands oral sexual stimulation from her as a condition for his successful sexual performance, "So that you may call my organ up from its proud groin, it is necessary that you keep working on it with your mouth" (19–20 *quod ut superbo provoces ab inguine / ore allaborandum est tibi*). In line 7, Horace calls Catullus' *passer*-poems to mind with the verb *incitare*, "to arouse," which Catullus employs in line 4 of Poem 2.[25]

Yet Horace also characterizes the aging woman unable to arouse the poet-speaker as a wealthy aristocratic matron. He claims that triumphal funeral masks of her ancestors are slated to grace her funeral (11–12 *funus atque imagines / ducant triumphales tuum*), and that especially round and hence costly pearls (13–14 *rotundioribus / onusta bacis*) weigh her down. With such details he calls to mind Clodia Metelli, the wealthy, aristocratic woman whom scholars assume Catullus portrays as his beloved in his poetry, under the metrically equivalent, literarily flavored pseudonym of Lesbia.[26] While Catullus does not refer to his beloved by this name in Poems 2 and 3, at 7.14.3–4 the later poet Martial employs the name Lesbia for Catullus' beloved when describing her grief over the loss of her pet bird.

In *Epode* 12, Horace again echoes Catullus' poetry in addressing another woman whom he cannot satisfy sexually. He characterizes her as a more violent version of Catullus' beloved in Poem 2. Whereas in Catullus 2 the beloved of the poet-speaker plays with her pet bird, "so that her vehement passion may subside" (8 *ut tum gravis acquiescat ardor*), this woman "hurries to calm down her untamed sexual rage" (9 *indomitam properat rabiem sedare*). Horace represents this woman as finding fault with him because he is "always soft for one performance with her," but managed "three times a night" with another woman named Inachia (14–16 *"Inachia langues minus ac me,/Inachiam ter nocte potes, mihi semper ad unum/mollis opus"*). So, too, he portrays her as comparing him unfavorably with another male "in whose untamed groin a male muscle, firmer than a new tree on the hillsides holds fast" (18–20 *"cum mihi Cous adesset Amyntas/cuius in indomito constantior inguine nervus/quam nova collibus arbor inhaeret?"*). He also assigns this woman a speech in which she likens him, the poet-speaker, and herself as sexual performers to animals: referring to him as resembling a female lamb and roe deer in his fearful flight, and to herself as similar to wolves and lions in her pursuit (*"o ego non felix, quam tu fugis, ut pavet acris/agna lupos capreaeque leones"?*).

Yet this woman first curses one Lesbia for "having pointed out you, a lifeless bull, to me" when she was seeking a man to satisfy her sexually: 16–17 *pereat male, quae te/Lesbia quaerenti taurum monstravit inertem*. By using the name that Catullus employs for his beloved, and by representing this Lesbia as responsible for bringing him, the sexually inadequate poet-speaker, to the bed of this sexually dissatisfied woman, Horace both evokes and criticizes Catullus' poems featuring his beloved, particularly but not only those referring to her as Lesbia. Like Catullus' two poems about his *puella* and her pet *passer*, Catullus' poems about his beloved that refer to her specifically as Lesbia ordinarily portray her with respect and affection, even when registering unhappiness with her conduct toward him.[27] Horace, though, merely represents this Lesbia as procuring a young male lover for an older married woman, and a male lover incapable of pleasing her at that. At the same time he depicts himself as resembling Catullus' poet-speaker in 2 and 3, albeit by admitting openly rather than obliquely to erectile dysfunction and need for oral stimulation.

The mere admission of impotence by Horace's poet-speaker in both of these poems, along with his demand for an oral remedy, would seem to have influenced Suetonius' portrait of Tiberius. Significant, too, are Horace's depiction of his female partner in *Epode* 8 as resembling the wealthy aristocratic matron—Clodia Metelli—whom Catullus is alleged to have called Lesbia in his poems, and Horace's use of the name Lesbia itself for the female procuress in *Epode* 12. For Clodia Metelli, Catullus' Lesbia, was in fact a member of the same noble family, the Claudii, as Tiberius himself. Indeed, Suetonius begins his life of Tiberius by discussing some of Tiberius' more memorable male and female ancestors. Among them is the brother of Clodia Metelli, the demagogue Publius Clodius Pulcher. Suetonius describes him at *Tiberius* 2.4 as having himself adopted out of the patricians into the plebeians for the sake of expelling Cicero from the city. Catullus refers to this same man at 79.1 as "Lesbius" and puns on his cognomen Pulcher.[28] Catullus' actual connections with and depictions of Tiberius' ancestors may have played a role in Suetonius' decision to recall Catullus' words when describing the sexual inadequacies of Tiberius. Horace's evocations of Catullus' beloved in these two *Epodes* may have influenced Suetonius too.

Various details in Suetonius' description of Tiberius also suggest Horace's influence. Suetonius not only likens sexually performing humans to animals, but also utilizes Horace's vocabulary: *turpis*, "disgusting" at *Tiberius* 44 (so Horace, *Epodes* 8.5); *hirsutus*, "hairy" at 45 (so *Epodes* 12.5); *inguen*, "groin" at 44 (so *Epodes* 8.19 and 12.19); *caprea*, "roe deer" and *hircus*, "he-goat" at 45 (so *Epodes* 12.5 and 26). To be sure, at *Tiberius* 45 Suetonius quotes the words of a popular stage farce in describing Tiberius' performance of cunnilingus with the phrase *hircum vetulum capreis naturam ligurire*. But this phrase itself, with its reference to roe deer and a he-goat, may have sought to evoke Horace *Epode* 12. The punning associations between another Latin word for he-goat, *caper*, with the name of *Capri* itself, and the nickname for Tiberius' "Sex Spots"—*Caprineum*, "Old-Goat's Park"—mentioned in *Tiberius* 43 are relevant in this connection as well.[29]

Suetonius and the manly malfunctioning of Julius and Augustus Caesar

Suetonius' biographies of Tiberius' immediate predecessors, the military and political leaders Julius and Augustus Caesar, merit examination as well, since they also help contextualize Suetonius' portrayal of Tiberius' sexual inadequacies. While at *Divus Augustus* 62.1 Suetonius suggests that Augustus may have been unable to consummate his first marriage, he does not portray either man as suffering from chronic erectile dysfunction. Rather, he merely reports accusations that they allowed themselves to be penetrated anally and orally by other adult men, thereby failing to perform sexually as true, "penetrating" Roman men should. Notwithstanding this important difference, Suetonius represents both men as resembling Tiberius in that both acknowledged these sexual failures of their own. Furthermore, he seems to imply that their admission of these inadequacies helped provide them with authority and credibility in their chosen pursuits. In this way Suetonius also represents these successful military and political figures as similar to the love poets of their own day.

At *Divus Julius* 22.2, Suetonius relates that Julius Caesar was overjoyed when, in 59 BCE, the Roman Senate assigned him, in the face of major opposition, the command of three key provinces. Suetonius reports that Caesar then claimed *insultaturum omnium capitibus*, "he would jump on the heads of all his opponents." Yet, Suetonius continues, when told, dismissively, that such conduct "would not be easy for any woman" (*facile hoc ulli feminae fore*), Caesar replied, playfully, that Queen Semiramis had ruled Syria and a group of women, the Amazons, and had held a great part of Asia.

A recent commentator explains the phrase *insultaturum omnium capitibus*, here translated "jump on the heads of all opponents," merely as an "obscenity."[30] She refers readers to Suetonius' use of the same phrase at *Tiberius* 45, when describing the emperor's "obtaining pleasure from the heads of women" (*feminarum capitibus … inludere*). But there, as we have seen, the phrase describes Tiberius' forcing women to stimulate him orally because he could not become hard otherwise. Admittedly, in indicating that Caesar claimed, albeit metaphorically, to have sought oral stimulation from his opponents, Suetonius may be attributing him with a figurative act of *irrumatio*, forcing his foes to fellate him, and implying that he possessed a hard male organ.[31]

Nevertheless, Suetonius may intimate that Caesar was not necessarily claiming, at least figuratively, to be hard. For Suetonius also states that when these opponents then called Caesar a woman, Caesar did not object to this insult. At 49.4, moreover, Suetonius reports that Caesar did not protest when his own men, in his own military triumph, recalled his sexual submission, as a young man, to King Nicomedes of Bithynia. Such statements, then, allow us to infer that Julius Caesar was comfortable with publicly acknowledging his sexual inadequacies, in his case adopting the passive, penetrated role rather than failing to achieve erection, including them in his qualifications to serve as a military and political leader. While we can only speculate as to why he admitted to these sexual failings, it seems most likely that Caesar wished to communicate that he shared concerns and experiences with the ordinary men he led in battle.

Suetonius' life of Augustus, too, cites various charges impugning Augustus' masculinity, and implying that he suffered from sexual difficulties. At *Augustus* 68, he not only reports accusations that Augustus was unable to consummate his first marriage, but also charges that he had been rendered womanly (*effeminatum*) and anally penetrated by his great uncle and adoptive father Julius Caesar, indeed adopted because of his shameful submission (*stupro meritum*). So, too, he reports that Augustus was subjected to public abuse on the Roman stage, where he was likened to a castrated priest of the goddess Cybele.[32] Suetonius is not, incidentally, our only ancient source testifying that Augustus was insulted in this way. Lead sling bullets, actual military weapons, surviving from the battle of Perusia in 41 BCE address him as Octavia, employing the feminine form of his family name Octavius, and announce their intention of penetrating him anally.[33] Suetonius' testimony, however, is significant for depicting Augustus as tolerating insults of this kind. Here, too, we can only speculate about Augustus' motives. But Augustus, too, may have sought military and political credibility, and gained public support, from owning up to his, albeit temporary, problems with sexually functioning as Roman males should.

Suetonius' description of how the aged and hopelessly impotent Roman emperor Tiberius and his two illustrious predecessors Julius and Augustus Caesar dealt with and acknowledged their unmanly behavior—whether it took the form of erectile dysfunction, as it did in the case of Tiberius, or submitting to penetration by other men, as it did in the instances of Julius and Augustus Caesar—merits attention for several reasons. First, that Suetonius draws on a tradition of learned literary representation developed by the Latin erotic poets Catullus and Horace to describe Tiberius' erectile dysfunction. Suetonius' portrayal of Tiberius' sexual proclivities in fact helps illuminate these earlier Latin poetic texts, and proves itself richer and more complex when read in conjunction with them. Tiberius' own associations with literary learning, as well as the identity of the historical woman to whom Catullus and Horace allude, a member of Tiberius' own Claudian family, may also account for Suetonius' choice of literary models.

But Suetonius also testifies that politically powerful and militarily successful Romans such as Tiberius and his two predecessors resemble erotic poets such as Catullus and Horace: in admitting that they did not always function sexually, with hard, penetrating male organs, in accordance with Roman cultural expectations of normative manhood. Such willingness to acknowledge these sexual inadequacies recognizes that the male organ cannot always be hard and penetrative. It also complicates the definition of what Roman manhood entailed, in both poetic representation and historical reality.

Notes

1 All translations from the Latin are my own. For the meanings of *sellaria,* which I have translated as "rear endings," and *spintrias,* which I have translated as "fundamentalists," see Champlin 2011. On the basis of Tacitus, *Annales* 6.1—which claims that the designations of *sellaria* and *spintriae* originated with Tiberius' sexually degenerate practices on Capri—as well as other literary and linguistic evidence, he argues that the former signifies "The Brothel" and the latter "bracelet worker." He thus takes strong issue with the *OLD,* 1728 and 1805, as well as with earlier translations: e.g. Hurley's revision of Rolfe (1998), which renders these words as "holey places" and "analists" respectively.
For *exoletorum,* which I translate as "males-for-hire, long past their sexual prime," I follow Williams 1999: 84, who argues that "the term *exoletus* denoted a male prostitute past the age of adolescence who might … play the insertive role in penetrative acts with his male clients, but who might just as well also play the receptive role." Curiously, although ch. 44 describes Tiberius as hiring, and watching, acts that involve anal penetration, Suetonius only mentions one act of anal penetration that Tiberius actually performed: in the final sentence of 44, where he relates that the emperor forcibly and disgracefully sodomized (*constupraret*) a sacrificial attendant and his brother. While he acknowledges that Tiberius in this instance was capable of sustaining an erection and penetrating two partners in short order, in 44–5 he otherwise focuses exclusively on Tiberius' oral sexual activities, especially those aimed at making Tiberius hard.
2 For Tiberius' life and career, see Levick 1976, who does not discuss either this passage or Tiberius' life on Capri.

3 For Roman physical constructions of manhood, see, for example, Williams 1999: 125–49, whose discussion of its sexual dimensions focuses on insertive behavior without considering erectile function.

4 Various textual details suggest that Suetonius was also familiar with, and alludes to, two later literary representations of male erectile dysfunction: Ovid, *Amores* 3.7 and Petronius' account of Encolpius' impotence at *Satyricon* 126ff. Both Ovid and Petronius evoke the Catullan and Horatian texts discussed in this paper, contributing to as they modify the Latin literary tradition upon which Suetonius draws. Considerations of space in this study do not permit discussion of these texts, and how Petronius parodies Ovid's poet-speaker in his characterization of Encolpius; for discussion of the complex intertextual relationship between *Amores* 3.7 and *Satyricon* 126ff., see McMahon 1998; Courtney 2001: 193–4; Hallett 2012b.

5 My choice of the term "intertextuality" to describe the verbal and thematic affinities shared by Suetonius' biography of Tiberius and four poems by Catullus and Horace draws on the discussion of Hallett (2009), based on Heath (2002). I regard these texts as "immediately produced by the author as well as by the language, society and ideology that have themselves produced the author," the result of active authorial agency and intention.

6 For Tiberius' own literary learning, see Suetonius, *Tiberius* 70: his imitation of "neoteric" poets associated with Catullus—Euphorion and Parthenius—may in part prompt Suetonius' apparent evocations of Catullus 2 and 3, discussed in the following section, Suetonius on Tiberius.

7 An exception is McMahon 1998: 48. He briefly states that "the account by Suetonius of the emperor Tiberius' impotence and his efforts to remedy it (*Tiberius* 42–5), while descriptively graphic and subject to the usual consideration of authorial bias, affords no real difficulty of interpretation for the purposes of this study"; he lists voyeurism and pedophilia, but not oral stimulation, as Tiberius' remedial activities. Champlin, for example, does not acknowledge Tiberius' erectile dysfunction as part of the "sexual dynamic" on Capri. Skinner 2005: 276–7 limits her discussion of male impotence to Petronius, *Satyricon* 126ff.

8 See, for example, Champlin 2011: 329–31, who foregrounds the details describing the expense, complexity, and scale of the sexual set-up on Capri, viewing them as evidence that "real prostitution is not involved but rather an extreme form of traditional, elaborate private theatricals."

9 See *OLD* 1983: 269 and 798 s.v. *caper* and *hircus*, the Latin words for male goat. It does not attribute sexual connotations to the former, and merely claims that the latter is "applied to persons as a term of abuse, implying lack of refinement, etc." Yet the very first example this entry cites as evidence for *hircus* in this sense is Plautus, *Casina* 550 (*illius hirci inprobi edentuli*, "of that disgraceful toothless goat"), which dates to the early second century BCE. These words specifically criticize the *senex* Lysidamus, a lecherous old man lusting after the title character, a young female slave-girl, who also forces his sexual attentions, by oral exertions *inter alia*, on an adult male slave.

10 See Hallett 1977a for the "middle voice" phrase *ore morigeratur* as describing the mutual oral gratification of Atalanta and Meleager; the statement in 45 that Tiberius himself performed cunnilingus on women adds to the plausibility of this interpretation. For Catullus 2 and 2a as evidence for Atalanta's association with mutual oral gratification, see later in this section.

11 Williams 1999: 81, 162, 199, 301 discusses Tiberius' sexual stimulation by *fellatio*, "fondness for cunnilinctus" and abuse of boys, but does not consider the role played by his erectile dysfunction in his sexual conduct, nor why Tiberius orally stimulated the females but not the boys who fellated him.

12 See Hallett 2012a, writing about Catullus, Tibullus, and Ovid. The discussion of Horace, *Epodes* 8 and 12 by McMahon 1998: 31–4 rightly emphasizes that Horace is writing invective, not "love poetry" of the kind immortalized by Catullus and the Latin love elegists. Even so, Horace seeks to create sympathy for his poet-speaker and affirm his own erotic authority in such misogynistic poems.

13 See, for example, Hooper 1985; Thomas 1993. While Adams 1982: 31–3 is not convinced that *passer* in Catullus 2 and 3, and in Martial 11.6.16 "were intended in a double meaning," he nonetheless provides further evidence in support of such an interpretation, quoting the statement by the grammarian Festus (p. 410) that "in mimes in particular they call the male organ *strutheum*, indeed because of the lasciviousness of the sparrow (*salacitate passeris*), which in Greek is called *struthos*." See also the discussion of Dyson 2007: 257.

14 For the three lines following Catullus 2, and their textual history, see Quinn 1970: 94–6; by separating them from Catullus 2 merely by a series of "dots," he differs from, e.g. Wiseman 1985: 121, who refers to them as 2b, and regards them as three surviving lines of a separate poem.

15 For animals and in particular birds as sexual metaphors, frequently representing the penis ("often treated as having a personality and life of its own"), see Adams 1982: 29–34.

16 On the sexual connotations of *ludere*, and of the related nouns *ludus* and *lusus* elsewhere in Latin, see Adams 1982: 162, 223, 225.

17 Compare Suetonius *Tib.* 44 (*luderent lingua morsuque sensim adpetentes*) to Catullus 2.4 (*morsus*) and 2.3 (*appententi*). *Adpetere* and *appetere* are merely alternative spellings of the same word.

18 In noting the use of both *opera* and *opus* as sexual metaphors, Adams 1982: 157 connects them with "the male part in the [sexual] act"; while he does not cite Suetonius, *Tiberius* 43 as his evidence, he does mention Horace *Epode* 12.16, discussed later in this section.

19 Mark Masterson has suggested that the bites may be a veiled reference to playful thrusting or a metaphorization of penetration as a kind of thrusting. However, while the act of applying dental pressure to the male organ may strike contemporary readers as painful rather than playful, an ancient audience may have reacted differently—as Suetonius himself suggests by his statement that Tiberius' "fishies" sought his organ with "tongue and biting."

20 For the transitive verb *incitare*, "to speed up," see Glare 1982: 868. It often describes the arousal of the male organ. At 16.9, in fact, Catullus may employ this verb in precisely this sense (*et quod pruriat incitare possunt*), although—as Mark Masterson observes—the phrase *quod pruriat* here may refer to sexually stimulating thoughts. The direct object of *incitare* at 2. 4 would be the *morsus*, bitings, by the *puella*.

21 Strikingly, Catullus portrays such a physical endeavor, and terms it extremely shameful, when talking about the disgraceful Gellius at 88.7–8: *nam mihil est quicquam sceleris, quo prodeat ultra/non si demisso se ipse voret capite*, "for there is no evil deed beyond which he might transgress, not if he should eat himself up with his head lowered."

22 See, for example, Quinn 1970: 95, for the identification of the "swift girl" as the mythic Atalanta; while Suetonius refers to her male "suitor" as Meleager, he is also known as Milanion and Hippomenes.

23 Wiseman 1985: 257 cites a quote from the later grammarian Nonius Marcellinus 195L, *Catullus … de meo ligurire libido est*, "Catullus [writes] it is my sexual passion to lick, on my own account." If these words were expressed by Catullus in the first person as poet-speaker, they may well testify to his "fondness for cunnilinctus." And as Suetonius uses both *libido* and *ligur[r]ire* for Tiberius' sexual activities, the latter in connection with the performance of cunnilingus, he may be recalling this Catullan passage as well.

24 On the representation of the poet-speaker's impotence in Horace, *Epodes* 8 and 12, see McMahon 1998: 31–3, who—citing studies by Fitzgerald and Mankin—interprets "the coarse description of sexual matters and especially of impotence … as [presenting] a truly Archilochean picture of Late Republican Rome." Yet he does not consider the relationships between these poems and Catullus' poetry, or note that Horace's language is more refined than that of Catullus, since he refrains from the primary obscenities that Catullus favors, such as *fellare, irrumare,* and *mentula.* See Richlin 1983: 1–31 for levels of Latin erotic diction.

25 Strikingly, *saeculum*, employed in line 1, is also the last word in Catullus' poem 1, immediately before the *passer*-poems 2 and 3.

26 For Clodia Metelli, see, for example, Wiseman 1985: 15–53 and Skinner 2011.

27 Two major exceptions are poem 58 and 72. The first crudely accuses Lesbia of "manually stimulating the grandsons of great-spirited Remus (5 *glubit magnanimi Remi nepotes*) in alleys and crossroads"; the second, addressed to Lesbia herself, claims to desire her more even as he values her less.

28 For Publius Clodius Pulcher in Catullus 79, see Wiseman 1985: 131, 172 as well as Skinner 2011: 133–5. Skinner also cites Suetonius, *Tiberius* 1–2 on 23–4, when discussing Clodia's "family mythology."

29 It is certainly possible that these two passages draw on a more extensive, common tradition of Latin sexual description, and Suetonius is not necessarily evoking this particular Horatian text. But the multiple affinities between the two texts render a close relationship more likely.

30 So Hurley in Rolfe 1998: 62 n. 37

31 *Insultare* is not a synonym of *inludere.* According to Glare 1982: 933, the verb, like its English derivative "insult," implies mockery of its object. In this figurative display of bravado, Caesar may have implied that he did not need oral stimulation to achieve an erection when compelling his opponents to fellate him. But whereas a hard organ is required for anal (and vaginal) penetration, it is not necessary for insertion into the mouth.

32 See Suetonius, *Divus Augustus* 62.1–2 and 68.

33 See Hallett 1977b.

Bibliography

Adams, J.N. (1982) *The Latin Sexual Vocabulary*. London: Duckworth.

Champlin, E. (2011) "Sex on Capri", *Transactions of the American Philological Association* 141(2): 315–32.

Courtney, E. (2001) *A Companion to Petronius*. Oxford: Oxford University Press.

Dyson, J. (2007) "The Lesbia poems", in M.B. Skinner (ed.) *A Companion to Catullus*. Malden, MA, Oxford and Carlton, VIC: Wiley-Blackwell, pp. 254–75.

Glare, P.W. (1982) *Oxford Latin Dictionary*. Oxford: Oxford University Press.

Hallett, J.P. (1977a) "*Morigerari*: Suetonius, Tiberius 44", *L'Antiquité Classique* 47: 96–200.

——(1977b) "*Perusinae glandes* and the changing image of Augustus", *American Journal of Ancient History* 2: 151–71.

——(2009) "Sulpicia and her resistant intertextuality", in D. van Mal-Maeder, A. Burnier, and L. Nunuz (eds) *Jeux de voix: Énonciation, intertextualité et intentionalité dans la literature antique*. Bern and Berlin, pp. 141–53.

——(2012a) "Authorial identity in Latin love elegy: Literary fiction and erotic failings", in B.K. Gold (ed.) *A Companion to Roman Love Elegy*. Malden, MA, Oxford, and Chichester: Wiley-Blackwell, pp. 269–84.

——(2012b) "Anxiety and influence: Ovid's *Amores* 3.7 and Encolpius' impotence in *Satyricon* 126 ff.", in M.P. Futre Pinheiro, M.B. Skinner, and F.I. Zeitlin (eds) *Narrating Desire: Eros, Sex and Gender in the Ancient Novel*. Berlin and Boston, MA: DeGruyter, pp. 211–22.

Heath, M. (2002) *Interpreting Classical Texts*. London: Duckworth.

Hooper, R.W. (1985) "In defence of Catullus' dirty sparrow", *Greece & Rome* 32(2): 162–78.

Levick, B. (1976) *Tiberius the Politician*. London and New York: Routledge.

McMahon, J.M. (1998) *Paralysin Cave: Impotence, Perception, and Text in the Satyrica of Petronius*. London, New York and Köln: Brill.

Quinn, K. (ed.) (1970) *Catullus: The Poems*. London and Basingstoke: Macmillan.

Richlin, A. (1983) *The Garden of Priapus: Sexuality and Aggression in Roman Humor*. New Haven, CT and London: Yale University Press.

Rolfe, J.C. (1998 [1913]) *Suetonius*, Vol. 1, rev. edn by D.W. Hurley. Cambridge, MA: Harvard University Press.

Skinner, M.B. (2005) *Sexuality in Greek and Roman Culture*. Malden, MA, Oxford and Carlton, VIC: Wiley-Blackwell.

——(2011) *Clodia Metelli: The Tribune's Sister*. Oxford: Oxford University Press.

Thomas, R. (1993) "Sparrow, hares, and doves: A Catullan metaphor and its tradition", *Helios* 20: 131–42.

Williams, C.A. (1999) *Roman Homosexuality*. Oxford: Oxford University Press.

Wiseman, T.P. (1985) *Catullus and his World: A Reappraisal*. Cambridge: Cambridge University Press.

24

TOGA AND *PALLIUM*

Status, sexuality, identity

Kelly Olson

This study examines the ancient material and literary evidence for Roman men in Greek dress, considering the toga and the *pallium*, two important items of outerwear for the Romans. Despite the strong social resonances of each, sometimes the garments themselves, paradoxically and somewhat unexpectedly, cannot be distinguished in Roman material representations. This paper will challenge some long-held assumptions about the identification of toga and *pallium*, and also examine the bearing the occasional adoption of Greek costume had not only on the formation of cultural identity but also on the construction of gender and sexual personality. A man's clothing communicated not only rank and status, ethnicity and identity, but also reflected and strengthened a man's sense of his masculine self.

The history of fashion is just as complex as any other branch of history, and Roman fashion has not lacked for treatments. Lillian Wilson published *The Roman Toga* and *The Clothing of the Ancient Romans* in 1924 and 1938 respectively. Meyer Reinhold published two seminal studies on clothing, one on the history of purple (1970) and another on the usurpation of status symbols (1971). Bonfante-Warren began her invaluable work on the clothing of the Etruscans in 1973 (and her *Etruscan Dress* has recently been reissued in an updated edition). But even so, "the study of dress in the ancient world has been shamefully undervalued" (Llewellyn-Jones 2002: vii). Scholarship in English on ancient costume has until recently lagged sadly behind fashion studies in other fields, and the clothed body has suffered from a lack of critical analysis. Many previous studies of ancient dress often dealt only with matters of interest to the antiquarian: the precise shape and size of the toga, for instance, or the possible shades of clothing dyes (e.g., Wilson 1924, 1938). But dress studies have evolved greatly in the last twenty years or so, beginning with the publication of Sebesta and Bonfante's *The World of Roman Costume* in 1994:[1] scholars have moved away from the "rather sterile 'costume history' that for so long dominated the field" to sophisticated analyses of dress and its communicative properties.[2] Dress is now a fast-growing topic within the field of classical studies, and works have appeared in English on such diverse topics as how dress was utilized in the speeches of Cicero, the social meaning of the bordered toga, the cultural resonances of female dress, and how male identity was reflected in clothing choices in late antiquity.[3]

These achievements are all the more noteworthy because talking about ancient dress is complicated in a way that it is not for clothing scholars of more modern societies. "Historians of dress in the ancient world do not, for the most part, have the luxury of artifact-based research … we rely heavily on visual representations in a range of media, and literary texts from a range of genres" (Harlow 2005: 143). In addition, many of the clothing terms found in ancient literature have unexplainable meanings, in part because we have probably lost many nuanced and colloquial words for items of clothing which varied according to time and place. Thus the historian of ancient clothing must face "the difficulty of coping with an incomplete vocabulary of changing technical and colloquial terms" (Llewellyn-Jones 2003: 25).

Despite the limits of the evidence, clothing, that intimate record of human experience, provides valuable insight into ancient culture. Clothing in Roman society was a sign system, a code, with its own language and purpose; an arrangement of symbols that could reflect and even help construct the social order. Clothing was important in ancient visual symbolism because it articulated rank, which had to do with one's juridically defined place in the social hierarchy, and with social status, the prestige accorded one by society. Ideally, "the form, fabric, and color of a garment announced a person's condition, quality, and estate. It did so juridically, clearly, unabashedly, and without justifications" (Perrot 1994: 15). Thus, in the contest for social distinction, clothing played a significant role,[4] and dressing was, in principle, an act of political and social signification. Social role and status were preferably read instantly via one's clothing in Roman antiquity: "a quick look would take in the full meaning of dress" (Perrot 1994: 81, of ancien régime France).

But clothing could also lie. Although clothing was at once the sign and the generator of rank, such symbols in a highly mobile society like that of Rome (within particular boundaries) did not render the social structure fixed, as there was both omission of and usurpation of sartorial status symbols by those who had and had not the right to wear them.[5] Because it was hard to enforce legislation concerning status symbols; because many of them were a function of wealth; and because sometimes they were omitted, vestimentary signs served to visualize the social hierarchy but not necessarily to reinforce it. It was not in fact always easy to tell a person's rank or status from his or her clothing alone, which could convey a multitude of fictions to the viewer instead of facts; the disturbing truth was that clothing could insinuate things about the wearer that were half-truths or outright falsehoods. "For sight does not seem to embrace accurate results, but the mind in its judgment is rather often deceived by it," wrote Vitruvius.[6] Thus clothing and status did not always necessarily correspond, and garments at Rome could produce confusion, rather than clarification, of social boundaries.

In addition, certain garments were prescribed or proscribed because of the values, ideas, and constraints of Roman society. Clothing had the power to articulate rank, communicate status, wealth, and power, but also to express the relation between the sexes, reflect values, and embody anxieties. It could announce tradition, prerogative, gender, age, social class, marital status, sexuality, and ethics.[7] It was part of the cultural language, a visual code that ideally guided the viewer through a complex network of social and sexual relations. Thus, Roman clothing articulated concerns of gender and sexuality: through the toga and *pallium* for example, a man made it known to those around him what kind of man he actually was; which of the many ways of being a man he had chosen.

Such details were essential because the visual was fundamental to the way Romans constructed social meaning. One scholar believes the ancients were "accustomed to and highly attuned to visual modes of communication so that visual literacy reigned supreme over verbal literacy; pictures and visual clues often took priority over words" (Elsner 1998: 11; Petersen 2009: 182). Symbols and images were signs in the system of visual communication. The Romans recognized that visual imagery could often be more effective than the spoken word in conveying ideas: "less vividly is the mind stirred by what finds entrance through the ears than by what is brought before the trusty eyes, and what the spectator can see for himself," wrote Horace.[8] Seeing "was the privileged source of knowledge" (Barton 2001: 58). Plautus wrote: "look and then you'll know" (*Bacc.* 1023: *em specta, tum scies*); "those who see know distinctly" (*Truc.* 490: *qui vident plane sciunt*); and "they believe because they see" (*Asin.* 202: *credunt quod vident*). Social structure was created and generated by viewing: symbols of power or rank made the social structure and hierarchy of power visible, and in turn these images helped produce the hierarchy.

Self-presentation was so important because Roman ethicists saw aesthetics and morality as being inextricably linked. Cicero wrote that the eyes judge beauty, color, and shape, "and even other more important things, for they also recognize virtues and vices" (*ND* 2.145: *atque etiam alia maiora, nam et virtutes et vitia cognoscunt*). Literally, one was what one wore. Deviation from the male vestimentary code at Rome could thus bring social censure, ridicule, slander, and accusations of unsuitability for politics.[9] The primary modern theorist of the link between affect and behavior is Judith Butler, who holds that gender is not something that one *is* but something that one *does*; in other words, the appearance of the "subject" is an effect of performance (Butler 1990, 1993: 315; Cornwall and Lindisfarne 1994: 38). But for the Romans, effeminacy and masculinity were not things that could be put on and off at will, or created by wearing a certain type of clothing. For them, outward show was *always* a manifestation of the inner self—a sure reflection of one's morals and character.

With all this at stake, the study of Romans in Greek dress—why certain men chose to wear Greek dress and what bearing it had on Roman cultural identity—raises complicated questions, and the meaning of the practice is by no means easy to decipher. After an outline of ancient literary opinion on the toga and the Greek *himation* (called the *pallium* by the Romans), I will examine the two garments in material evidence from the late Republican to the Julio-Claudian era. I argue for an interpretation of Romans in Greek dress which focuses not only on cultural definition and erudition, but also on sexuality, gender, class, and wealth, asserting that a Roman dressed in Greek clothing was a polyvalent figure. My argument is that although toga and *pallium* are always distinguished in Roman literary evidence, and scholars often try to identify the two garments in material representations, they are not always recognizable. Our failure to distinguish the two of them in the visual sources has to do in part with the ways in which clothing was significant in Roman social ideology, in terms of class, masculinity, and Roman identity itself.

The spatial and temporal parameters of this study are restricted to Italy, mainly to what has been termed "the central period" in Roman history; that is, roughly 200 BCE to 200 CE, although I use evidence occasionally which falls outside these boundaries. Interdisciplinarity is vital to the field, and here I make use of a variety of written evidence as well as the wealth of available material sources. I have outlined the drawbacks and advantages to such a method elsewhere.[10]

Toga

Arguably the most important item of dress in Roman antiquity for citizen males was the toga, a garment which enjoyed a long lifespan and numerous changes in size and draping.[11] A large semicircle or an ellipse of cloth, the toga was woven to shape on a loom, with measurements that would depend on the size of the wearer, his financial means, and perhaps the draping popular during a particular chronological period. The short or thin toga of the Republican era (scholars estimate its dimensions at 16 × 5 feet) may have been called the *toga exigua*, although this is a modern term.[12] The garment is perhaps depicted on the Arringatore statue (Figure 24.1),[13] and seems occasionally to have been worn in the empire by individuals as a deliberate evocation of earlier Republican days. The term *toga exigua* is taken from a remark of Horace on Cato's dress: "what, if a man were to ape Cato with grim and savage look, with bare feet and the cut of a

Figure 24.1 The Arringatore: Aulus Melus, before 100 BCE. National Archaeological Museum, Florence. D-DAI-ROM 63.601.

scanty gown (*toga exigua*), would he thus set before us Cato's virtue and morals?"[14] This might also be the toga to which Quintilian refers when he remarks (specifying no date), "in olden times there were no overfolds (*sinus*); after that the overfolds were very short."[15]

Soon after or even contemporaneous with the Arringatore statue, togas seem to become larger and longer, with softer and looser folds. In the late Republic, the toga became more voluminous, and scholars estimate that by the late first century CE the garment measured about 19½ by 10 feet.[16] It differed in manner of draping as well. Seen in the *Ara Pacis* procession (Figure 24.2), this is the type of toga in which the *sinus*[17] appears, and the *umbo*, a largely decorative clump of drapery pulled up from the folds of the toga which ran up the left side of the wearer but helped hold the drapery together.[18] One additional characteristic of this toga was an excess of material which, in a religious sacrifice, could be drawn over the head.[19] But there seem to have been several different toga drapes in use at any one time, and varying sizes of togas during all periods.[20] The *Vicomagistri* relief (early 20s BCE; Figure 24.3), for example, shows that togas of more than one size and style were worn by different men in the same ceremony.[21] Augustus, in his policy of moderation in dress, is reported to have worn togas neither scanty nor full (Suet. *Aug.* 73: *togis neque restrictis neque fusis*). Horace did not like over-wide togas, and wrote that "a narrow toga befits a client of sense."[22] Perhaps wide togas which used an excess of fabric (exceedingly expensive in antiquity) were seen as symptomatic of luxury and decadence:[23] such huge lengths of cloth were expensive.

In material representation, the imperial toga is conventionally distinguished by its lower curved edge, the *sinus*, the *umbo*, and the long end hanging or dragging between the feet (the *lacinia*; Bieber 1959: 415; Figure 24.2).[24] Republican togas were somewhat different in draping and voluminousness, but the curved edge is also present. Due both to the ceremonial nature of Roman material representation, and to the fact that it was the immediately recognizable and unmistakable mark of a citizen, the toga is often thought to be the garment represented in Roman statuary and on gravestones.

The toga as a visual text could denote several things. First, of course, the toga was an immediate and conspicuous marker of the Roman citizen: non-citizens were forbidden to wear it.[25] The word *togatus* was often used by itself to designate such men,[26] and Virgil described the Romans as the *gens togata*.[27] According to Seneca, the emperor Claudius wished to see the whole world in a toga.[28] That the toga remained the quintessential Roman garment for centuries is due to the fact that the toga was one of the means by which Roman men divided themselves off from men of other races. The quality of *Romanitas*, of being Roman, was made known and in part generated by the garment.

The toga had a high symbolic content as well. Cicero explained that the toga is the symbol of harmony and repose, and weapons of unrest and war.[29] The orator employing metonymy might elegantly substitute "Ceres" for corn, "Liber" for wine, and "toga" for peace.[30] The term could also mean urbanity, sophistication, and city life.[31] Cicero praised Caesar as one who was *clarus in toga*, distinguished in civil life (*Fam.* 6.6.5; cf. Liv. 22.26.2; Luc. 5.382). To be forgetful of Rome and city life was *oblitus togae* (Hor. *Carm.* 3.5.10). An urbane manner of speaking was *verba togae* (Pers. 5.14). Martial termed sophisticated epigrams *urbanae togae*, in contrast to scurrilous verses (11.16.2). Valerius Maximus described civil strife as *violentiae togatae* (9.7.1), while ready courage in peace was *togata praesentia* (3.7.5, and see 3.2.17). During the empire, the term *togatus* also became synonymous with client status, since clients greeted and accompanied their patrons in the toga.[32]

Despite the importance of the toga as a symbol of urbanity and citizenship, we find numerous instances in literature of the omission of the toga, and that is because it was never a convenient garment. The mark of the male citizen was supposedly the toga, but poorer men (free

Figure 24.2 Ara Pacis: procession, south side, 12 BCE. Museo dell' Ara Pacis. Art Resource orz054071.

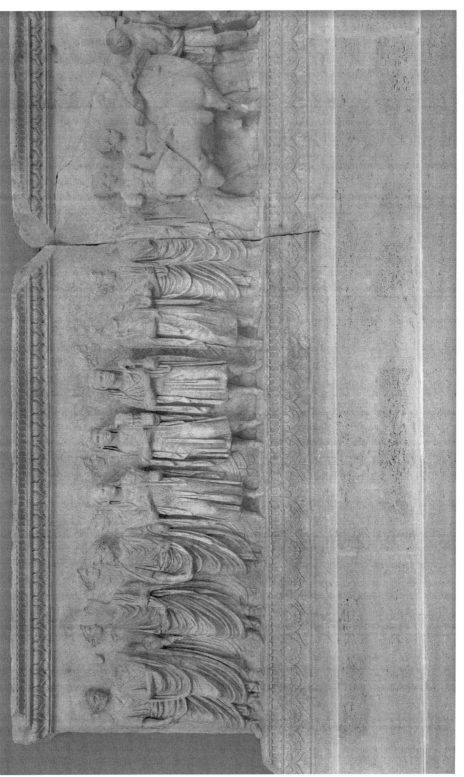

Figure 24.3 Vicomagistri relief, early 20s BCE. Rome: Vatican Museums, Museo Gregoriano Profano, inv. 1156/7. Bestand-Microfiche-D-DAI-ROM 57.1004.

and freed) would not necessarily have owned or worn one, since it was expensive (Hor. *Epod.* 4.8; Mart. 2.44.1–4); hard to care for (Tert. *Pall.* 5.1–2; Bradley 2002; Granger-Taylor 1982); hot (Mart. 12.18.5); and cumbersome (Tert. *Pall.* 5.1–2). Or possibly a poor man would own just one toga: Martial (4.66) tells us of a provincial man who lived a frugal life with one toga; Juvenal (3.171–9) related that men in rustic parts of Italy wore tunics regularly, and only donned a toga at their own funeral. Many passages in ancient literature attest to the joys of not donning the toga.[33]

The toga is a "classic example of 'emblemic style,' an artifact marked with a distinctive form that transmits a clear message to a defined target about conscious affiliation or identity."[34] But intriguingly the toga is never overtly characterized in ancient literature as masculine or manly clothing. It only really reveals itself as a masculine garment when its *absence* is spoken of: on foreigners, slaves, and women. The toga then was quintessential Roman male attire because it was the garb of the citizen, who was also ideally an active and dominant male. If ancient sexuality was also about domination, then the toga-less person was voteless, powerless, and penetrated. Persons who did not wear the toga were located outside traditional power structures.[35]

Philhellenism[36]

It is a well-known fact that things Greek were much sought and genuinely admired at Rome in the first and second centuries BCE, after Greece came under Roman control. Familiarity with Greek literature, culture, and language signaled that one was powerful, educated, and tasteful, and, most of all, wealthy: great sums of money were paid out for Greek slaves, actors, and art. But there were some Romans who felt this affectation of Greek culture was taken to extremes. Alongside the elevation of Greek culture grew a perception of Greeks as effeminate and Greek culture as morally enervating. A Greek life of pleasure, according to some writers, included the elements of feasting, sexual pleasure, wine, indolence, and literature (versus an idealized "Roman" life of frugality and military virtue), and Roman authors often attributed decline in Rome to contact with the soft Greek east.[37] Similarly, wearing Greek clothing could also mark one as anti-Roman (see below, p. 430).[38]

But for many men, especially those of the elite, familiarity with Greek literature, customs, and art, as well as the purchase and consumption of Greek goods, was a source of prestige. Upper-class Romans therefore had to perform a balancing act: to be cultured was to be familiar with Greek customs, yet to be overly familiar or enthusiastic about such customs invited charges of softness. Thus Cicero in his oration against Verres (the corrupt governor of Sicily; *Verr.* 2.4.94), is at pains to convince his audience that he himself knows nothing about Greek art—yet we possess his letters asking his friend Atticus to send him suitable Greek sculptures for his library and villa (e.g., *Ad Att.* 1.8.2. 1.9.2). This is the typical ambivalence of the cultured Roman.[39] Ambiguity appears as the principal characteristic of Rome's attitude towards Hellas: "the strains surface repeatedly in our texts. Many public figures at Rome expressed familiarity, admiration, and close involvement with Greek culture … yet one can as readily multiply example of ostensible hostility, repugnance, and alienation" (Gruen 1992: 223–4).

It could be that certain Romans went so far as to view the assumption of the *pallium* therefore as an abrogation of manhood: "an effeminate appearance and excessive preoccupation with one's looks could be presented as typical of a Greek" (Edwards 1993: 93).[40] Greek sandals, often seen as womanish (Gell. *NA* 13.22), the special dinner costume called the *synthesis*, or a long tunic, or one that was long-sleeved, might all be suspect (Dalby 2000: 122–3).[41] Thus, Greek clothing on a Roman man could have indicated several simultaneously valued and unvalued resonances: erudition and culture, effeminacy, wealth, even rejection (for some) of the basic qualities of *Romanitas* and/or Roman masculinity—conflicting concepts which often would have been encapsulated in the *pallium*.

Pallium[42]

The *pallium*, a Latin word without a Greek derivation,[43] was the wide Greek cloak or mantle, square-shaped, with four corners and many folds (Bieber 1959: 398; Figure 24.4). The word the Greeks used for the *pallium* is *himation*, but as Wallace-Hadrill has noted, "so little loading does the word carry in Greek that authors like Plutarch are happy to use it to refer to the Roman toga."[44] First mentioned in Plautus and Terence,[45] the Greek mantle continued to be popular throughout Roman antiquity: the *pallium* had the longest history of any of the cloaks worn by the Romans. Greeks are referred to as *palliati* (e.g., Suet. *Aug.* 98), but the *pallium* was often associated with the literati: Gellius names it as the cloak of the philosopher (13.8.5, 9.2.4). Tertullian states that the *pallium* is the dress of grammarians, rhetors, sophists, doctors, and poets. But the garment was worn by others as well.[46]

Wilson claims Romans always wore a tunic underneath the *pallium* (1938: 81), but Tertullian states that Cato, "by baring his shoulder at the time of his praetorship, favoured the Greeks no less by his palliate attire" (*Pall.* 3.7.3: *idem Cato iuridicinae suae in tempore humerum exertus, haud minus palliato habitu Graecis favit*). Like the Greeks, Cato at least wore his *pallium* with no tunic underneath, although this may be a reference to his habit of wearing the toga in a similar fashion.[47]

Of course, the *pallium* could be a poor garment or a rich one (Wallace-Hadrill 2008: 51) and *pallia* could differ greatly in appearance. Some *pallia* were luxurious: Verres (Cic. *Verr.* 2.5.31, 2.5.86) and Caligula sported purple *pallia* (Suet. *Calig.* 35); Trimalchio had an expensive scarlet one (*Satyr.* 32.2: *coccineo pallio*).[48] The mantle could also be short: the *palliolum*.[49] Thus Cicero quoting Caecilius Statius (d. 186 BCE) speaks of wisdom hidden under a shabby *palliolum* (*Tusc. Disp.* 3.56: *sub palliolo sordido*); actors wear these in comedy (Pl. *Cas.* 246 [an old man], 934 [a slave]; Pl. *Miles* 1179–80 [a sailor]). Giton wears one at Petr. *Satyr.* 98.7. Ovid recommends that the pale and sickly lover go about with his head covered by a *palliolum* (*Ars* 1.734); in Seneca (*Nat.* 4.13.10) and Quintilian (*Inst.* 11.3.144) the *palliolum* is worn by those who are unwell.

Although Bieber (1959: 415) has claimed that the *pallium* remained unchanged in size and draping throughout the central period, there surely must have been different sizes, types of drapes, and fabrics for different persons according to status, situation, and financial means.[50] Whether long and full or short and convenient, for some Romans there might have been no difference: the *pallium* was not the toga, and perhaps represented the debased fashion of a conquered territory.

The habit of wearing Greek clothing was one for which men could be exonerated or excoriated. Cicero (*Post. Rab.* 28) gives us examples of famous Romans who assumed outlandish Greek-style clothing, none of whom were blamed or censured: Sulla wore a *chlamys* and *crepidae* (a short Greek cloak and sandals); in Cicero's time the statue of Lucius Scipio on the capitol bore a *chlamys* and *crepidae*; P. Rutilius Rufus stopped wearing the toga when he fell into the hands of Mithridates at Mytilene and donned a *pallium* and *socci* (slippers).[51] Rabirius also had to assume Greek dress upon arriving at Alexandria to take up his position as *dioecetes*, treasurer of the king's revenues (Cic. *Rab. Post.* 28; his trial was in 54 BCE). Rabirius was criticized for wearing the *pallium* and "other ornaments not commonly worn by a Roman man,"[52] but Cicero lists other men who wore Greek clothes: "they were unassailed even by popular talk, let alone by judicial proceedings" (*Rab. Post.* 27: *quorum impunitas fuit non modo a iudicio, sed etiam a sermone*). Decades later, Augustus distributed Greek *pallia* to his companions (Suet. *Aug.*

Figure 24.4 The Greek *pallium:* statue of Aeschines, 340–330 BCE. National Archaological Museum, Naples, inv. 6018. D-DAI-ROM 31.751.

98; Wallace-Hadrill 2008: 38), and his political advisor, the notoriously dandified Maecenas, wore a *pallium* (Sen. *Epp.* 114.6).[53]

On the other hand, in Plautus a *malacum pallium* (*Bacch.* 71: an effeminate *pallium*) is contrasted to a solder's cuirass (*lorica*). In 205 BCE, complaints were made about Scipio Africanus for wearing the *pallium* with sandals at a gymnasium in Sicily;[54] at Cic. *Verr.* 2.5.137 the corrupt Verres was criticized for wearing a tunic and a purple *pallium* while a governor; at 2.5.31 for a long tunic and a purple mantle (*cum pallio purpureo talarique tunica*); at 2.5.86 also in slippers (*soleatus*).[55] Some thought the (future) emperor Tiberius wrong to wear a *pallium* and *crepidae* on Rhodes while in exile 6 BCE–2 CE (Suet. *Tib.* 13.1).[56] Hadrian only wore the *pallium* to banquets outside Italy (*HA* Hadrian 22). When Severus appeared before Marcus Aurelius in a *pallium*, he was given a toga from the emperor's own wardrobe (*HA* Sev. 1.7). In third-century Carthage a Roman citizen could still be criticized for wearing the garment, as Tertullian makes clear.[57] There was no actual law against wearing the *pallium* in place of the toga. But elite men were disparaged for wearing the *pallium* when it was assumed permanently, or when the official or social position of the wearer made it inappropriate, as it seemed to indicate effeminacy or a rejection of Roman values. An elite Roman could assume the *pallium* occasionally as an outer cloak, but if he entirely discarded the toga for the *pallium*, he was censured no matter where he was living; perhaps this pertained in the middling classes as well. There was a dangerous amount of rejection of both *Romanitas* and manliness in the wearing of such a garment.

While philhellenism was held by some to be suspicious generally, there may have been more specific factors at work in Roman criticism of the *pallium*: namely, a class assumption. The *pallium* was associated with erudition and effeminacy, but it was also the ordinary rectangular cloak of the regular person; the garment of the non-political and thus of the lower classes.[58] Thus the garment could be associated with poverty or non-elite status; Christians[59] likely adopted the *pallium* because they originally came from the lower middle classes or had been slaves. The Christian author Tertullian gives us the aphorism *a toga ad pallium*; that is, sinking from a higher position to a lower one (*Pall.* 5.1). Isidore of Seville and the fragment of Plautus he quotes, underline this:[60]

> A *pallium* is that with which the shoulders of attendants are covered so that, while they are providing service, they may hurry about unencumbered. Plautus says (*fr.* 177): "if you are to amount to anything, hang a *pallium* on your shoulders, and let your feet go as fast as they can."

To take another example, Tertullian criticizes his fellow Carthaginians saying that once the *pallium* was worn "by everyone" but that now it is ignored and even derided (i.e., in favor of the toga: *Pall.* 1.3.1: *pallium tamen generaliter uestrum immemores etiam denotatis*). Thus in addition to its associations with the *literati*, the *pallium* was identified as the garment of the derided slave and the ordinary man.

The *pallium* was easy to put on: "there is nothing so convenient as the *pallium*," Tertullian states, "even if it is double (*duplex*), as that of Crates. On no occasion is there a waste of time in dressing, for all the effort it takes is loosely covering oneself" (*Pall.* 5.3.1–3).[61] Interestingly, however, the difficulty of donning the toga and the hindrance to movement it presented was a sign of status for Roman citizens: the hallmark of the upper classes was not freedom of movement but encumbrance—the encumbrance of the voluminous and demanding toga. Slaves and the lower classes hurried, and needed clothing which would facilitate this (whether it was a *pallium* or a *palliolum*) while the upper classes had no such need. Even if it was long and full, the *pallium* was likely much more convenient than the toga, whose folds had to be arranged in a prescribed manner, and were not supposed to be changed by movement (Bieber 1959: 415).

The Roman upper classes attached great importance to distinctions in dress. In one case, two advocates appeared before the emperor Claudius, squabbling over whether the man accused of fraudulently assuming Roman citizenship should appear in court in a toga or in a *pallium*. Interestingly, Claudius ruled that the man must change back and forth, depending on whether he was being defended or accused. Suetonius presents this anecdote to show the emperor's eccentricities, but Bablitz has correctly noted that

> [W]e can instead see in Claudius' solution his real understanding of how clothing could affect perceptions within the courtroom. At least one of the advocates believed that the litigant's adoption of clothing that could either support or refute his case was a real threat.[62]

As Petersen has noted, one's role in Roman society was marked by external appearances and by the legibility of those appearances (2009: 182–6).

Thus the *pallium* was the ordinary rectangular cloak of the regular person, the garment of the non-political, but also associated with Greeks, philosophers, *literati*, and (later) Christians. Greek clothing could thus indicate effeminacy, financial, cultural, or intellectual status, or even a willful rejection of *Romanitas*. This is a good example of the ability of clothing to allow for multiple interpretations, depending on the viewpoint of the observer.[63]

Palliati *in Roman material sources*

The toga was the immediately recognizable and unmistakable mark of a Roman citizen and by extension of Roman masculinity, and men anxious to show their rank and status were often depicted in it on tombstones, for example. What has puzzled scholars is the apparent presence of numerous citizen men in Roman material representations who appear to have had themselves commemorated wearing not the toga, the badge of the Roman citizen, but the *pallium*.[64]

Identifying and interpreting clothing in Roman visual sources carries with it several problems. As Natalie Kampen noted (1981: 98–9), clothing in reliefs and statues may often have functioned as ideogram (i.e., a written character or picture symbolizing the idea of a thing), rather than as an indication of what men actually wore. Thus, togate men who appear in commercial scenes (such as in Figure 24.5) are described by modern scholars, probably correctly, as customers, or as the manager or owner of the shop. But the fact that such men are togate may simply be due to artistic convention. The man in question may not be in the habit of always wearing the toga: the workers, who are pictured in tunics, may in fact be free or freed workers and may have the right to wear the toga themselves. But it is probably to show status distinctions that differentiating clothing is deployed in these representations, and not sociological description. In other words, the owner/manager/customer is above the others in employment status, though possibly not in juridical status, and the toga is quite likely the convention chosen to represent that fact. This shows the toga's strength as an ideological symbol, and is in addition an example of clothing employed as visual shorthand for legal or moral status.[65]

It must also be said in addition that the classification and identification of the different types of Roman male clothing by modern scholars in visual sources can be vague, and even confusing. It seems to me it is much more difficult to tell whether or not it is the toga or the *pallium* depicted in reliefs and statuary than scholars have previously thought (especially true of "window" reliefs). For instance, the detailed microfiche collection of the Deutsches Archäologisches Institut gives several categories of men and their clothing in Roman art, but why a certain statue or relief has been set under one heading rather than under another is not always

Figure 24.5 Commercial scene of knife-sellers. Rome: Vatican Museums, Galleria Lapidaria 147, inv. 9277. Bestand-Microfiche D-DAI-ROM 1020.

clear. For instance, in the Roman male statuary collection there are categories entitled "Nackt mit Schultermantel" ("naked with shoulder-mantle"; usually military statues, but not always); "Mantelstatuen: himation mit rechter armschlinge" ("Statues with mantles: right arm wrapped in a *himation*"; no tunic); and "Mantelstatuen: Oberkörper ganz oder teilweise nackt" ("Statues with mantles: upper body completely or partially naked"). Categories of *togati* include "Toga unter dem rechten Arm durchzegogen" ("right arm wrapped in a toga," often called the "pallium-wrap"); and "Toga auf beiden Schultern aufliegend" ("toga resting on both shoulders"). What follows is an attempt to question some of these categories.

1. Several statues are classed in the DAI microfiche under the heading of "Mantelstatuen": men in *himation/pallium* with no tunic (such as Figure 24.6) but I would argue that several of these statues might instead show a Roman man in a toga with no tunic. As we have seen, the toga and tunic were supposed to be worn together, but Romans in the regal period allegedly wore the toga with no inner tunic. Aulus Gellius mentions this practice (6.12.3), and Pliny (*Nat.* 34.23) states that statues of Romulus and Tatius erected in the time of Tarquinius Priscus were depicted without the tunic.[66] Cato the Younger reportedly went out in public in warm weather with a *campestre* under his toga instead of an under tunic, citing the habits of regal Romans as an illustrious precedent.[67] By way of comparison, the figure of Aeneas sacrificing to the Penates on the west panel on the Ara Pacis shows him in a toga with no tunic (Figure 24.7).[68]

2. There are photographs in the DAI database variously labeled as "Mantelstatuen" or men in *himatia* (with tunic, arm tightly wrapped, such as DAI 71.1540, 81.3365) or Roman men in togas but a *"pallium"* wrap (with tunic, arm tightly wrapped). As mentioned, the toga is conventionally distinguished from the *pallium* by its curved edge, *sinus*, and *umbo* (Bieber 1959: 415)—but these identifications are complicated by the fact that in the early first century BCE and into the early empire the toga was often draped and the arm held as though the man were in a *pallium*. The *palliatus* pose had a long history in Greece (from the fourth century BCE onward), and also found its way into Etruscan statuary.[69] The toga in the *pallium* drape is marked by the tight *sinus* in which the arm is held high and close to the chest, and the length of the garment almost reaching the shoes (both characteristics are mentioned by Quintilian).[70] Of course, the paint which was on statues has now disappeared: if the man was a magistrate, presumably he would be in the *toga praetexta* of the office holder, with a purple border along the *sinus* (Figures 24.8, 24.9 and 24.10).[71]

3. The clothing of men in "window" reliefs, previously identified by many as togate (e.g., George 2006: 20; Kleiner 1987: 171, no. 49; Figure 24.11), I maintain cannot be identified with any certainty. The figures are often accompanied by inscriptions which name the men as citizens; and thus it is often assumed that the voluminous wrap covering the man's upper body is the toga. But in the absence of *sinus*, *umbo*, or curved lower edge (and/or an inscription naming the man as a citizen male), I argue that it could just as well be the *pallium* that is depicted, for reasons mentioned below.

It seems likely that many of the portraits previously identified by scholars as *"palliati"* could be *togati* instead. Many of the men that Bieber claims are *palliati* look to me and to other scholars like *togati* (1959: 376–7, n. 31; as well as her figs 10, 11, 12, 24–7, 35; her evidence dates 80 BCE–360 CE). It can even be argued of one late Republican funerary relief (the married couple from the Via Statilia, Figures 24.8–9) that the man is in a *pallium* (Bieber 1959: 385) or a toga (Goette 1990: 108: A b 16; Kleiner 1977: 145–6; Stone 1994: 16). Nonetheless, if they are *palliati*, their presence on Roman citizen tombstones at all, when the toga was supposedly an all-important marker of

Figure 24.6 Man in a *himation* or toga? Early first century CE. National Archaeological Museum, Naples, inv. 6210. D-DAI-ROM 83.2141.

Figure 24.7 Ara Pacis Augustae, west relief panel: Aeneas, 13–9 BCE. Rome: Ara Pacis Museum. Art Resource ART66821.

Figure 24.8 Pallium-drape toga: grave relief of a married couple from the Via Statilia, 75–60 BCE. Musei Capitolini: Centrale Montremartini, Rome: inv. 2142. D-DAI-ROM 2001.2051.

Figure 24.9 Pallium-drape toga: grave relief of a married couple from the Via Statilia; man's toga, 75–60 BCE. Musei Capitolini: Centrale Montremartini, Rome: inv. 2142 (photo: author).

Figure 24.10 Pallium-drape toga: Eurysaces, late first half of first century BCE. Rome: Porta Maggiore. D-DAI-ROM 33.749.

Figure 24.11 Window relief, two men and a woman. Ascoli Piceno. Bestand-D-DAI-ROM 37.412.

citizenship and status, is puzzling, although it accords nicely with literary sources (e.g., Pliny *Epp.* 5.6.45; Juv. 11.203–4; Tert. *Pall.* 5) which mention the omission of the toga.

Scholars differ as to the reasons for the presence of *palliati* in Roman material representations. Bieber goes so far as to claim that most of the men on tombstones have been misidentified as togate rather than palliate, and that unless one was a member of the imperial court or a high-ranking official, the *pallium* was the garment assumed, rather than the toga (Bieber 1959: 413). She states that the *pallium* was portrayed in portrait statues with good reason, "for it represented the people as they actually were" (1959: 415).[72] Bieber admits many of her artistic examples of men wearing the "*pallium*" are from Greece itself or Greek colonies, but still believes that most *palliati* in material representations are from the Roman upper middle class who affected Greek learning and culture. It might be assumed that such men were orators or philosophers, but some are self-proclaimed magistrates or doctors (Bieber 1959: 412). Stone (1994: 16) on the other hand believes many men labeled by Bieber as *palliati* are in fact togate, partially due to direct imitation by the artists, but also to direct Greek influence on how the toga was actually worn.[73] Stone further contends that perhaps the popularity of the toga is questionable and may in fact be overemphasized as the "typical" dress of the Roman male (Stone 1994: 17, 21–4).

In his sophisticated 2008 study, Wallace-Hadrill states that the *palliatus* pose was due to direct Greek influence on how Roman clothing was worn, and that intense imitation by Roman orators of Attic rhetorical models in the first century BCE produced a sort of sartorial copying, up to a certain point. "At precisely the period at which Augustus not merely encourages the use of the toga, but backs it with the force of law in the Forum, the toga makes a sharp movement away from its immediate preceding phase of 'hellenisation.'"[74] Thus perhaps Roman identity was "threatened or undermined by the abandonment of so charged a marker as the *toga.*"[75] Colivicchi (2000) complicates the matter even further. Tombstone reliefs from the Greek island of Ancona in the Hellenistic age (a very small number, from the last decades of the second century BCE and the first decade of the first century BCE) show men on reliefs who seem to wear *himatia* but which Colivicchi argues wear Roman *togae exiguae*, due to the distinctive curved lower edge. Thus, there is a possibility that garments labeled as "*pallia*" on Roman statuary by modern scholars could be *togae exiguae*.

Conclusions

This article has briefly challenged a long-held assumption about male clothing in Roman material representations (that toga and *pallium* are garments distinguishable from one another), and has sketched out a problem which demands much more detailed work. My own conviction regarding *pallium* and toga on tombstones is that the two are not always distinguishable. One reason for this is because visual evidence is rarely concerned with giving its viewers an exact replication of the toga, or indeed any piece of clothing, at any one time. In addition, the fact that there are several reliefs on which we cannot tell if the man is wearing a toga or *pallium* is surely not due entirely to our own ignorance (as Wallace-Hadrill points out: 2008: 45). Perhaps it was important that the toga and *pallium* be distinguished, but the fact that in the material evidence they are not, at least for a certain time period, is interesting: possibly the men shown in vague *pallium*-togas do not have the right to wear the toga and are thus being deliberately ambiguous about their status. Perhaps the *pallium* drape in toga-wearing developed as a way of showing one's erudition yet not leaving off the badge of Roman citizenship—the perfect blend of *Romanitas* and Greek learning. Perhaps we are looking not at the *pallium* but at the *toga exigua*. Or perhaps the important thing for the wearer was neither toga nor *pallium* per se, but merely some sort of voluminous draped outer garment which indicated education, freedom from manual labor, and pretensions to status in a general way.

Of course, the textual evidence tells us that for some Romans the *pallium* continued to carry the stigma of its problematic origins: depending on who viewed it and who wore it, it could represent Greek erudition or the low character of the conquered person or base citizen; perhaps even the effeminacy and untrustworthiness associated with the Greeks. Both the *pallium* and toga had their own ideological and emotional force, and as clothing both remained integrally connected to the social and sexual order.

Notes

1 Male dress for instance is explored by Blonski 2008; Croom 2002; Davies 2005; Delmaire 2004; Deniaux 2003; Dolansky 2008; Goette 1990; Harlow 2004; Heskel 1994; Huet 2008; Palmer 1998; Sebesta 2005; Stone 1994.

2 Edmondson and Keith 2008b: 1.

3 Harlow 2004; Heskel 1994; Olson 2008; Sebesta 2005.

4 See Owen-Hughes 1983; Reinhold 1971; Roche 1994.

5 On usurpation of symbols of male rank (which carried criminal implications: Paul. *Sent.* 5.25.12), see Olson 2002: 389–90; Reinhold 1971.

6 Vitruvius *De Arch.* 6.2.2.

7 See Olson 2008: 1, with references; Olson forthcoming; Perrot 1994: 6–8 (of ancien régime France).

8 Hor. *Ars* 180–2: *segnius irritant animos demissa per aurem / quam quae sunt oculis subiecta fidelibus et quae/ ipse sibi tradit spectator.* See also Cic. *de Orat.* 2.357.

9 In Republican Rome, the reading of morality became an aesthetic practice (Corbeill 1996: 151, 156, 169); see also Bourdieu 1984: 44–50.

10 Olson 2008: 2–4.

11 Several authors state the toga was of Etruscan origin: Dio. Hal. 3.60–1; Livy 1.83; Serv. *Aen.* 2.781. Hafner (1969); Stone (1994: 13 and 38 n. 3) believe the toga was worn by the Etruscans although they called it the *tebenna*. On the *tebenna,* see Bonfante 2003: 15, 39, 45, 48–55, 102; Bonfante-Warren 1973: 612; Polybius 10.4.8, 26.10.6. On Etruscan togate sculpture, see Hafner 1969. On changes in toga size and draping, see Goette 1990; Wilson 1924. On the toga generally, see see Bieber 1959; Christ 1997; Croom 2002: 41–9; Dyck 2001; Goette 1990; Stone 1994; Wilson 1924, 1938: 36–54.

12 Stone thinks this was probably a witticism and would not usually have been used to designate the early Republican toga (1994: 16). On Republican togas, see Goette 1990: 20–8; Pausch 2008: 26; Stone 1994: 15–17; Wilson 1924: 17–44.

13 On this statue, see Dohrn 1968; Fittschen 1970; Goette 1990: 21, A a 2; Granger-Taylor 1982. The Arringatore can be dated to sometime before 100 BCE (Granger-Taylor 1982).

14 *quid? siquis voltu toruo ferus et pede nudo / exiguaeque togae simulet textore Catonem, / uirtutemne repraesentet moresque Catonis?* (*Epp.* 1.19.12–14; and see Cic. *de Orat.* 2.91). Mayer (1994: 261) states it is unclear which Cato is meant, but that the younger seems more likely, "given his moral authority."

15 *Inst.* 11.3.137: *nam veteribus nulli sinus, perquam breves post illos fuerunt.* Quintilian gives no specific dates. On the dress of the Roman orator, see Bablitz 2007: 191–2; Gunderson 2000: 59–86. On the *sinus,* see below.

16 On the toga in this period, see Goette 1990: 20–31; Stone 1994: 17–21; Wallace-Hadrill 2008; Wilson 1924: 43–60.

17 On the development of the *sinus,* see Goette 1990: 3–6, 20–101; Stone 1994: 17–38; Wallace-Hadrill 2008: 49; Wilson 1924: 40–9, 61–116. Stone believes that while the evolution of the *sinus* is unknown, "it may represent observation of a similar use of an overfold over the torso on the *himatia* on some Greek statues" (see Stone 1994: 17, and Bieber 1961: figs 132–5, 138–9, 163–6, 176, 249, 779–81).

18 Stone 1994: 17. On the evolution of the *umbo,* see Goette 1990: 29–97; Stone 1994: 17–38; Wilson 1924: 49, 67.

19 Stone (1994: 20) writes that the *capite velato* look was achieved by loosening the *umbo* and pulling the excess material up over the head, as in the figure behind Livia on the Ara Pacis (Stone 1994: fig. 1.6). He further notes that Augustus is able to be *capite velato* without loosening the *umbo,* another sign of the increasing size of the toga during the Augustan era, as seen in the statue of Augustus in the Terme

Museum, Rome (inv. 56230; Zanker 1988: 127–9 and fig. 104; Stone 1994: n. 45). On the *capite velato* gesture, see Linderski 2002: 348, with references.

20 See Kampen 1981: 98–9.

21 On this relief, see Stone 1994: n. 47, with references; Pollini 2012: 309–53.

22 *arta decet sanum comitem toga; Epp.* 1.18.30.

23 Clothing was so valuable that it was often the target of thieves (Mart. 8.48, 8.59; Petr. *Satyr.* 12, 30; Cat. 25), or could be pawned or sold outright for ready cash (Petr. *Satyr.* 12). Clothing is taken as surety in the *P. Oxy.* (see Liu 2009: 72 n. 68 for examples)—for small as well as large amounts of money, showing that customers came from all kinds of socio-economic backgrounds. This is because in antiquity cloth and clothing were expensive in a way unknown today: Wild calculates that the cost of materials and labour for a late-antique tunic were around 2,296 denarii: by comparison, a day's wage for a stonemason was fifty denarii, and pork was twelve denarii per Roman pound by the fourth century CE (Wild 1994: 30–1).

24 *Lacinia*: see *TLL* 7.2.834–5.

25 *Dig.* 49.14.32. See also Sen. *Apol.* 3; Tac. *Agr.* 21; Pliny *Epp.* 4.11.3 (a man who had been banished); Suet. *Claud.* 15.2.

26 Cic. *Phil.* 5.5.14, *Sul.* 85, *de Orat.* 1.24.111, *Rosc.* 135, *Rab. Post.* 27; Sall. *Jug.* 21.2; Livy 3.52.7.

27 Virg. *Aen.* 1.282. In Athen. *Deip.* 5.213 togate Romans are easily picked out by assassins.

28 *constituerat enim omnes Graecos Gallos Hispanos Britannos togatos videre; Apol.* 3.

29 *Pis.* 73: *sed quia pacis est insigne et otii toga, contra autem arma tumultus atque belli.*

30 Cic. *de Orat.* 3.167; see also Vell. 1.12.3, Cassius Dio 41.17.

31 Harlow 2004: 51: the toga marked a man as a civic being, who embodied *gravitas* and *pietas*.

32 Mart. 1.108, 2.74, 3.46, 6.48, 9.100, 10.18.4, 10.47, 10.74.3, 10.82, 11.24.11, 14.125; Juv. 1.96, 7.142.

33 Livy 3.26.7–10; Mart. 10.47.5, 12.18.5; Pliny *Epp.* 5.6.45; Juv. 11.203–4; Tert. *Pall.* 5; George 2008; Turcan 2007: 208–12.

34 Wallace-Hadrill 2008: 41–2; see Shennan 1989: 18; Wiessner 1983: 257.

35 Richlin (1993: 532) has noted that "the highly class-stratified nature of Roman society is an essential component in the construction of Roman sexuality—the two systems can hardly be understood independently."

36 On philhellenism, see Gruen 1992, especially 52–83, 223–71; Mellor 2008; Petrochilos 1974; Spawforth 2012; Wallace-Hadrill 2008. Scholars today have sought to move away from the, as it were, boundary-marking terms of "Romanization," and "Hellenization," (Mattingly 2002, 2004; Wallace-Hadrill 2008) in favor of examining mutual influence and cultural dialogue between Greece and Rome, both of which make "philhellenism" a logical term.

37 See Gruen 1992; Mellor 2008.

38 Women, too, adopted Greek hairstyles, footwear, and jewelry, but rather than indicating pretensions to erudition (as it could do for men), this may have marked a woman out as sexually available. Such Greek articles for women indicated sexual appeal and were fashionable—it is noteworthy that they are never spoken of in literary sources as enhancing or revealing a woman's intellect or taste. And indeed, some did not like even this trend: Juvenal counts nothing "more offensive" (*rancidius*) than the fact that women do not consider themselves beautiful unless they are adorned in Greek fashion (6.184–200). At Mart. 10.68, a married woman is chided for using sexy Greek terms of endearment. Women wore Greek slippers (Fortunata's Greek slippers are embroidered in gold at Petr. *Satyr.* 67; see also Pl. *Aul.* 510; Sen. *Ben.* 7.21.1); Greek turbans (Prop. 2.29A.15; Pliny *Nat.* 35.58; Juv. 3.66); or *mitellae*, Greek woven headbands (Virg. *Copa* 1; Apul. *Met.* 7.8, 8.27). Greek names for poetic women "probably suggested" romance or sex (Dalby 2000: 127).

39 See also Cic. *ad Quint. Frat.* 1.1.6, in which the Greeks are called the most civilized of all people (*humanissimum*), but later, "false, untrustworthy, and schooled in over-complaisance by long servitude" (1.1.16: *sic vero fallaces sunt permulti et leves et diuturna servitute ad nimiam adsentationem eruditi*). See also 1.1.27–8, 1.2.4.

40 On Greeks and effeminacy see Polyb. 31.25.2–5; Cic. *de Rep.* 2.4.7–8, 4.4.4; Nepos *pr.* 4, *Alcibiades* 7.2.2–3; Mart. 10.65; Dalby 2000: 122–3; Edwards 1993: 33–4.

41 Cic. *Cat.* 2.22; Verg. *Aen.* 9.614–20; Gel. 6.12.1–2, 13.22. See Pausch (2008: 41–3) on the character and position of Greek clothing in Roman society.

42 On the *pallium* see Pausch 2008: *pallium*: 26–8, *TLL* 10.1.133–7.

43 On the ancients' etymological derivation of *pallium*, see Varr. *LL* 5.133; Schol. Pers. 5.14; Isid. *Orig.* 19.24.1. The term was also used of couch-coverings and bedclothes: Ov. *Am.* 1.2.2; Mart. 1.109.11; Juv. 6.236; Apul. *Met.* 3.9.7.

44 e.g., Plut. *Brutus* 17, *Coriolanus* 14; Wallace-Hadrill 2008: 51. See also Wilson 1938: 80.

45 e.g., Plaut. *Men.* 658; Ter. *Phorm.* 844.

46 *Pall.* 6.2.1–2, with Turcan 2007: 214–16.

47 On this passage, see Turcan 2007: 139. On the toga with no tunic, see below, nn. 75–6.

48 A purple *pallia* woven with gold is mentioned at *HA* Carin. 20.5.

49 See *TLL* 10.1.132–3.

50 See Wilson 1938: 81–3.

51 Cos. 105 BCE. *RE* 'Rutilius' 34.

52 *Rab. Post.* 25: *aliqua habuisse non Romani hominis insignia.* The insignia are unspecified.

53 Apparently he wore it wrapped around his head with his ears sticking out, like a mime actor.

54 Livy 29.29.12; Val. Max. 3.6.1; Plut. *Cato* 3.7. Gruen (1992: 223) notes that it was likely that critics "directed their reproaches not at Hellenism as such but at the unseemliness of a Roman commander and representative of the *res publica* behaving in an undignified and inappropriate fashion."

55 The *pallium* is worn with an unbelted tunic at Tert. *Pall.* 5.3. On the resonances of the ungirded tunic, see Corbeill 1996: 160 n. 82; Edwards 1993: 90; Graver 1998: 620; Olson forthcoming; Richlin 1992: 92.

56 Tiberius doubtless reassumed the correct *toga praetexta* in place of the *pallium* when he returned to Rome (Suet. *Tib.* 17).

57 Thus Tertullian's *de Pallio*; see Daniel-Hughes 2011: 48–53; Wallace-Hadrill 2008: 56.

58 See for instance Tert. *Pall.* 5.4, in which the *pallium* is made to say: "I owe nothing to the forum … nothing to the Campus Martius, nothing to the Senate-house. I do not watch for a magistrate's function, do not occupy any platform for speakers, do not attend to the governor's office. I do not smell the gutters, nor adore the bar in court, nor wear out benches, nor disturb proceedings, nor bark pleas. I do not act as a judge, a soldier, or a king: I have withdrawn from public life" (*ego … nihil foro, nihil campo, nihil curiae debeo; nihil officio aduigilo, nulla rostra praeoccupo, nulla praetoria obseruo; canales non odoro, cancellos non adoro, subsellia non contundo, iura non conturbo, causas non elatro; non iudico, non milito, non regno: secessi de populo*). See also Turcan 2007: 208–12.

59 "The power struggle between Christians and Romans used dress as a signifier" (Harlow 2004: 63). Tertullian himself naturally associates the toga with Roman luxury and decadence (*Pall.* 5.5; see Turcan 2007: 208–12), and the *pallium*, in contrast, suggested piety and modesty. On the Christian *pallium*, see Daniel-Hughes 2011: 45–61; Turcan 2007.

60 *Orig.* 19.24.1: *Pallium est quo ministrantium scapulae conteguntur ut, dum ministrant, expediti discurrant. Plautus (frag. 177): si quid facturus es, adpende in humeris pallium, / et pergat quantum valet tuorum pedum pernicitas.* For running slaves in comedy who wear the *pallium* wrapped around their necks or shoulders, see Pl. *Capt.* 778–9; Ter. *Phorm.* 844.

61 See Turcan 2007: 86–7, 199–201. On the meaning of *duplex*, see Casson 1983: 194–9.

62 Bablitz 2007: 84; Suet. *Claud.* 15.2. See also Sen. *Contr.* 9.3.13.

63 See Bartsch 2000; Elsner 1995, 2000; Nelson 2000a, 2000b.

64 See Bieber 1959; Stone 1994: 16–17, 40 n. 30; Vessberg 1941: pls. 25–31; Wallace-Hadrill 2008. The comparison of the juridical status of men (determined from inscription) with the clothing in which the men are depicted is something that has been seldom done and which could benefit from in-depth scholarly investigation.

65 Certainly the Romans had plenty of literary examples of this: see Cic. *Phil.* 13.13.28; Juv. 13.33; Livy 6.41; Suet. *Aug.* 38.2.

66 On these statues, see Palmer 1998: 60–1; Stone 1994: 38–9.

67 Asc. *ad Cic. In Scaurianam: Cato praetor iudicium, quia aestate agebatur, sine tunica exercuit campestri sub toga cinctus. In forum quoque sic descendebat iusque dicebat, idque repetierat ex vetere consuetudine secundum quam et Romuli et Tati statuae in Capitolio et in rostris Camilli fuerunt togatae sine tunicis* (Clark 1907); see Wilson 1924: 26. Plut. *Coriol.* 14. Plutarch (*Cat. Min.* 6) repeats this story.

68 On this panel see now Rehak 2001, with references.

69 Bieber 1959: 377–85; Hafner 1969.

70 "There are some features of dress which have themselves changed somewhat with the changing times. The ancients had no *sinus*, and their successors very short ones (*perquam breves post illos fuerunt*). Accordingly, as their arms (according to Greek custom) were kept within their clothes, they must have used different gestures from ours in the *prooemium*" (*Inst.* 11.3.137–8). And further: "the ancients used to let the toga fall right down to the heels, like a Greek *pallium* (*togam veteres ad calceos usque demittebant, ut Graeci pallium*) and this is recommended by Plotius and Nigridius, who wrote on gesture in that period [first half of the first century BCE] … [Plinius Secundus] … says that Cicero used to wear his

toga like this to conceal his varicose veins, although this fashion is to be seen also in statues of persons who lived after Cicero's time" (*Inst.* 11.3.143).

71 Scholars often mislocate the *praetexta* border along the lower edge of the toga: e.g., Linderski 2002: 359; Wilson 1924: 52–3. For the location of the purple border along the *sinus* on the *toga praetexta*, see now Goldman 1994: 229; Granger-Taylor 1982: 10–13.

72 She also writes that the reason the *pallium* was worn was because Augustan decrees prescribing use of the toga were not always followed (399). We should note however that there is no extant law which states Augustus made omission of the toga illegal, although Suetonius (*Aug.* 40, 44) does make mention of the aediles policing the area of the Forum and its neighborhood to be certain everyone was in a toga and not in a grey tunic or *lacerna*.

73 Stone 1994: 16; see refs here n. 30.

74 Wallace-Hadrill 2008: 50.

75 Wallace-Hadrill 2008: 50; Suet. *Aug.* 40 and 44.

Bibliography

Bablitz, L. (2007) *Actors and Audience in the Roman Courtroom.* London and New York: Routledge.

Barton, C. (2001) *Roman Honor: The Fire in the Bones.* Berkeley, CA: University of California Press.

Bartsch, S. (2000) "The philosopher as Narcissus: Vision, sexuality, and self-knowledge in Classical antiquity", in R. Nelson (ed.) *Visuality before and beyond the Renaissance: Seeing as Others Saw.* Cambridge: Cambridge University Press, pp. 70–97.

Bieber, M. (1959) "Roman men in Greek himation (*Romani pallati*): A contribution to the history of copying", *Proceedings of the American Philosophical Society* 103: 347–417.

——(1961) *The Sculpture of the Hellenistic Age*, 2nd edn. New York: Columbia University Press.

Blonski, M. (2008) "Les sordes dans la vie politique romaine: La saleté comme tenue de travail?", in F. Gherchanoc and V. Huet (eds) *S'habiller, se déshabiller dans les mondes ancien, Mètis* 6: 41–56.

Bonfante, L. (2003) *Etruscan Dress*, 2nd edn. Baltimore, MD: Johns Hopkins University Press.

Bonfante-Warren, L. (1973) "Roman costumes: A glossary and some Etruscan derivations", *Aufstieg und Niedergang der römischen Welt* 1(4): 584–614.

Bourdieu, P. (1984) *Distinction: A Social Critique of the Judgement of Taste*, trans. R. Nice. Cambridge, MA: Harvard University Press.

Bradley, M. (2002) "'It all comes out in the wash': Looking harder at the Roman *fullonica*", *Journal of Roman Archaeology* 15: 20–44.

Butler, J. (1990) *Gender Trouble: Feminism and the Subversion of Identity.* London and New York: Routledge.

——(1993) "Imitation and gender insubordination", in H. Abelove, M.A. Barale, and D.M. Halperin (eds) *The Lesbian and Gay Studies Reader.* London and New York: Routledge, pp. 307–20.

Casson, L. (1983) "Greek and Roman clothing: Some technical terms", *Glotta* 61(4): 193–207.

Christ, A. (1997) "The masculine ideal of 'the race that wears the toga'", *Art Journal* 56(2): 24–30.

Clark, A. (ed.) (1907) *Asc. ad Cic. In Scaurianam; Orationum Ciceronis quinque enarratio.* Oxford: Oxford University Press.

Cleland, L., Harlow, M., and Llewellyn-Jones, L. (eds) (2005) *The Clothed Body in the Ancient World.* Oxford: Oxbow Books.

Colivicchi, F. (2000) "Dal *pallium* alla toga: Ancona fra ellenismo e romanizzazione", *Ostraka* 9(1): 135–42.

Corbeill, A. (1996) *Controlling Laughter: Political Humor in the Late Roman Republic.* Princeton, NJ: Princeton University Press.

Cornwall, A. and Lindisfarne, N. (1994) "Dislocating masculinity: Gender, power, and anthropology", in A. Cornwall and N. Lindisfarne (eds) *Dislocating Masculinity: Comparative Ethnographies.* London and New York: Routledge, pp. 11–47.

Croom, A.T. (2002) *Roman Clothing and Fashion.* Stroud, Gloucs. and Charleston, SC: Tempus (paperback edn).

Dalby, A. (2000) *Empire of Pleasures: Luxury and Indulgence in the Roman World.* London and New York: Routledge.

Daniel-Hughes, D. (2011) *The Salvation of the Flesh in Tertullian of Carthage: Dressing for the Resurrection.* New York: Palgrave MacMillan.

Davies, G. (2005) "What made the Roman toga *virilis*?" in L. Cleland, M. Harlow, and L. Llewellyn-Jones (eds) *The Clothed Body in the Ancient World.* Oxford: Oxbow Books, pp. 121–30.

Delmaire, R. (2004) "Le vêtement dans les sources juridiques du bas-empire", *Antiquité Tardive* 12: *Tissus et vêtements dans l'antiquité tardive*: 195–202.

Deniaux, E. (2003) "La *toga candida* et les élections à Rome sous la République", in F. Chausson and H. Inglebert (eds) *Costume et société dans l'Antiquité et le haut Moyen Âge*. Paris: Picard, pp. 49–55.

Dohrn, T. (1968) *Der Arringatore*. Berlin: Gebr. Mann.

Dolansky, F. (2008) "*Togam virilem sumere:* Coming of age in the Roman world", in J. Edmondson and A. Keith (eds) *Roman Dress and the Fabrics of Roman Culture*. Toronto, ON: University of Toronto Press, pp. 47–70.

Dyck, A.R. (2001) "Dressing to kill: Attire as a proof and means of characterization in Cicero's speeches", *Arethusa* 34: 119–30.

Edmondson, J. and Keith, A. (eds) (2008a) *Roman Dress and the Fabrics of Roman Culture*. Toronto, ON: University of Toronto Press.

——(2008b) "Introduction", in J. Edmondson and A. Keith (eds) *Roman Dress and the Fabrics of Roman Culture*. Toronto, ON: University of Toronto Press, pp. 1–20.

Edwards, C. (1993) *The Politics of Immorality in Ancient Rome*. Cambridge: Cambridge University Press.

Elsner, J. (1995) *Art and the Roman Viewer: The Transformation of Art from the Pagan World to Christianity*. Cambridge: Cambridge University Press.

——(1998) *Imperial Rome and Christian Triumph*. Oxford: Oxford University Press.

——(2000) "Between mimesis and divine power: Visuality in the Greco-Roman world", in R. Nelson (ed.) *Visuality before and beyond the Renaissance: Seeing as Others Saw*. Cambridge: Cambridge University Press, pp. 45–69.

Fittschen, K. (1970) "Der Arringatore: Ein römischer Bürger?", *Römische Mitteilungen* 77: 177–84.

George, M. (2006) "Social identity and the dignity of work in freedmen's reliefs", in E. D'Ambra and G.P. R. Métraux (eds) *The Art of Citizens, Soldiers and Freedmen in the Roman World, BAR* International Series 1526, pp. 19–29.

——(2008) "The 'dark side' of the toga", in J. Edmondson and A. Keith (eds) *Roman Dress and the Fabrics of Roman Culture*. Toronto, ON: University of Toronto Press, pp. 94–112.

Goette, H.R. (1990) *Studien zu römischen Togadarstellungen*. Mainz: von Zabern.

Goldman, N. (1994) "Reconstructing Roman clothing", in J.L. Sebesta and L. Bonfante (eds) *The World of Roman Costume*. Madison, WI: University of Wisconsin Press, pp. 101–32.

Granger-Taylor, H. (1982) "Weaving clothes to shape in the ancient world: The tunic and toga of the Arringatore", *Textile History* 13(1): 3–25.

Graver, M. (1998) "The manhandling of Maecenas: Senecan abstractions of masculinity", *American Journal of Philology* 119: 607–32.

Gruen, E.S. (1992) *Culture and National Identity in Republican Rome*. Ithaca, NY: Cornell University Press.

Gunderson, E. (2000) *Staging Masculinity: The Rhetoric of Performance in the Roman World*. Ann Arbor, MI: University of Michigan Press.

Hafner, G. (1969) "Etruskische Togati", *Antike Plastik* 9: 23–45.

Harlow, M. (2004) "Clothes maketh the man: Power dressing and elite masculinity in the later Roman world", in L. Brubaker and J.M.H. Smith (eds) *Gender in the Early Medieval World: East and West, 300–900*. Cambridge: Cambridge University Press, pp. 44–69.

——(2005) "Dress in the *Historia Augusta:* The role of dress in historical narrative", in L. Cleland, M. Harlow, and L. Llewellyn-Jones (eds) *The Clothed Body in the Ancient World*. Oxford: Oxbow Books, pp. 143–53.

Heskel, J. (1994) "Cicero as evidence for attitudes to dress in the late Republic", in J.L. Sebesta and L. Bonfante (eds) *The World of Roman Costume*. Madison, WI: University of Wisconsin Press, pp. 133–45.

Huet, V. (2008) "Jeux de vêtements chez Suétone dans les vies des Julio-Claudiens", in F. Gherchanoc and V. Huet (eds) *S'habiller, se déshabiller dans les mondes anciens, Mètis* 6: 127–58.

Kampen, N. (1981) *Image and Status: Roman Working Women in Ostia*. Berlin: Mann.

Kleiner, D.E.E. (1977) *Roman Group Portraiture: The Funerary Reliefs of the Late Republic and Early Empire*. New York: Garland.

——(1987) *Roman Imperial Funerary Altars with Portraits*. Rome: Bretschneider.

Linderski, J. (2002) "The pontiff and the tribune: The death of Tiberius Gracchus", *Athenaeum* 90(2): 339–66.

Liu, J. (2009) *Collegia Centonariorum: The Guilds of Textile Dealers in the Roman West*. Leiden: Brill.

Llewellyn-Jones, L. (2002) "Introduction", in L. Llewellyn-Jones (ed.) *Women's Dress in the Ancient Greek World*. Swansea: Classical Press of Wales, pp. vii–xv.

——(2003) *Aphrodite's Tortoise: The Veiled Woman of Ancient Greece*. Swansea: Classical Press of Wales.

Mattingly, D. (2002) "Vulgar and weak 'Romanization', or time for a paradigm shift?" [review of S. Keay and N. Terrenato (eds) (2001) *Italy and the West: Comparative Issues in Romanization*. Oxford: Oxford University Press], *Journal of Roman Archaeology* 15: 536–40.

——(2004) "Being Roman: Expressing identity in a provincial setting", *Journal of Roman Archaeology* 17: 5–26.

Mayer, R. (ed.) (1994) *Horace: Epistles Book 1*. Cambridge: Cambridge University Press.

Mellor, R. (2008) "*Graecia capta*: The confrontation between Greek and Roman identity", in K. Zacharia (ed.) *Hellenisms: Culture, Identity, and Ethnicity from Antiquity to Modernity*. Aldershot: Ashgate Publishing, pp. 79–126.

Nelson, R. (2000a) "Descartes' cow and other domestications of the visual", in R. Nelson (ed.) *Visuality before and beyond the Renaissance: Seeing as Others Saw*. Cambridge: Cambridge University Press, pp. 1–21.

——(ed.) (2000b) *Visuality before and beyond the Renaissance: Seeing as Others Saw*. Cambridge: Cambridge University Press.

Olson, K. (2002) "*Matrona* and whore: The clothing of women in Roman antiquity", *Fashion Theory* 6(4): 387–420.

——(2008) *Dress and the Roman Woman: Self-Presentation and Society*. London and New York: Routledge.

——(2014) "Masculinity, appearance, and sexuality: Dandies in Roman antiquity", *The Journal of the History of Sexuality* 23: 182–205.

Owen-Hughes, D. (1983) "Sumptuary law and social relations in Renaissance Italy", in J. Bossy (ed.) *Disputes and Settlements: Law and Human Relations in the West*. Cambridge and New York: Cambridge University Press, pp. 69–100.

Palmer, R.E.A. (1998) "Bullae insignia ingenuitatis", *American Journal of Ancient History* 14: 1–69.

Pausch, M. (2008) *Die römische Tunika*. Augsberg: Wißner.

Perrot, P. (1994) *Fashioning the Bourgeoisie: A History of Clothing in the Nineteenth Century*, trans. R. Bienvenu. Princeton, NJ: Princeton University Press.

Petersen, L.H. (2009) "'Clothes make the man': Dressing the Roman freedman body", in T. Fögen and M. Lee (eds) *Bodies and Boundaries in Greco-Roman Antiquity*. Berlin: Walter de Gruyter, pp. 181–214.

Petrochilos, N. (1974) *Roman Attitudes to the Greeks*. Athens: National and Capodistrian University of Athens, Faculty of Arts.

Pollini, J. (2012) *From Republic to Empire: Rhetoric, Religion, and Power in the Visual Culture of Ancient Rome*. Norman, OK: University of Oklahoma Press.

Rehak, P. (2001). "Aeneas or Numa? Rethinking the meaning of the Ara Pacis Augustae", *The Art Bulletin* 83(2): 190–208.

Reinhold, M. (1970) *History of Purple as a Status Symbol in Antiquity*. Brussels: Coll. Latomus.

——(1971) "The usurpation of status and status symbols in the Roman empire", *Historia* 20: 275–302.

Richlin, A. (1992) *The Garden of Priapus*, 2nd edn. Oxford: Oxford University Press.

——(1993) "Not before homosexuality", *Journal of the History of Sexuality* 3: 523–73.

Roche, D. (1994) *The Culture of Clothing: Dress and Fashion in the Ancien Régime*, trans. J. Birrell. Cambridge and New York: Cambridge University Press.

Sebesta, J.L. (2005) "The *toga praetexta* of Roman children and praetextate garments", in L. Cleland, M. Harlow, and L. Llewellyn-Jones (eds) *The Clothed Body in the Ancient World*. Oxford: Oxbow Books, pp. 113–20.

Sebesta, J.L. and Bonfante, L. (eds) (1994) *The World of Roman Costume*. Madison, WI: University of Wisconsin Press.

Shennan, S.J. (1989) "Introduction: Archaeological approaches to cultural identity", in S. J. Shennan (ed.) *Archaeological Approaches to Cultural Identity*. London: Unwin Hyman, pp. 1–30.

Spawforth, A. (2012) *Greece and the Augustan Cultural Revolution*. Cambridge: Cambridge University Press.

Stone, S. (1994) "The toga: From national to ceremonial costume", in J.L. Sebesta and L. Bonfante (eds) *The World of Roman Costume*. Madison, WI: University of Wisconsin Press, pp. 13–45.

Turcan, M. (ed.) (2007) *Tertullian: Le manteau (de Pallio)*. Paris: Les Éditions du Cerf.

Vessberg, O. (1941) *Studien zur Kunstgeschichte der römischen Republik*. Lund: C.W.K. Gleerup.

Wallace-Hadrill, A. (2008) *Rome's Cultural Revolution*. Cambridge: Cambridge University Press.

Wiessner, P. (1983) "Style and social information in Kalahari San projectile points", *American Antiquity* 48: 253–76.

Wild, J.P. (1994) "Tunic no. 4219: An archaeological and historical perspective", *Riggisberger Berichte* 2: 9–36.

Wilson, L.M. (1924) *The Roman Toga*. Baltimore, MD: Johns Hopkins University Press.

——(1938) *The Clothing of the Ancient Romans*. Baltimore, MD: Johns Hopkins University Press.

Zanker, P. (1988) *The Power of Images in the Age of Augustus*, trans. A. Shapiro. Ann Arbor, MI: University of Michigan Press.

25

REVISITING ROMAN SEXUALITY

Agency and the conceptualization of penetrated males

Deborah Kamen and Sarah Levin-Richardson

"Does ['passive'] suggest a man who fails to enact his desires … ? One who sits at home waiting for the phone to ring?"

(Williams 2010 [1999]: 230)

In the realm of sexual matters, the Romans were particularly concerned with the issue of who penetrated whom. Penetrating was associated with freeborn status, masculinity, and social dominance, whereas being penetrated was associated with servility, femininity, and social inferiority. This conceptual model, sometimes called the "penetration paradigm," has found widespread (though not univocal) acceptance among scholars, since it accounts for the majority of ancient evidence regarding Roman sexual ideology.[1]

Recent scholarship has proposed nuances for this model, pointing out that some types of sexual behaviors cannot be understood, or understood alone, through the framework of penetration.[2] Building on this scholarship, we re-explore depictions of penetrated men in literature and graffiti, finding a distinction between men who sought their own penetration and those who were not thought of as agents in their own penetration. Ultimately, we argue that in addition to the primary conceptual axis of penetration (penetrating versus penetrated), the Romans further envisioned a secondary axis of agency (activity versus passivity) in the sexual act.

Agency and the penetration model

Scholars have been slow to explore the issue of agency in ancient sexuality, partly due to the dominance of the penetration model, and partly due to a terminological issue: namely, the convention of using the terms "active" and "passive" to refer, respectively, to the penetrating and the penetrated partner. This vocabulary, we argue, conflates penetration with agency, and while the two terms often coincide, they are in fact distinct concepts.

We are not the first to voice dissatisfaction with this terminology, especially with the labeling of all penetrated individuals as "passive." Amy Richlin, for example, notes, "'Passive' misleadingly connotes inaction; this is not a phenomenon we have named well" (1993: 531); and James Davidson has expressed similar concerns about the use of this vocabulary to describe Greek sexuality, asserting that the penetrated partner "was certainly not inactive" (Davidson 1998:

177).[3] Therefore, we propose a new use of the words "active" and "passive" based on the model of Latin grammar. As Charisius, a fourth-century CE grammarian, explains:[4]

> activum est quod facere quid significabit, ut "lego," < vel > corporis motum significans, ut "salio," vel animi, < ut > "provideo" ... passivum est activo contrarium, quod pati quid significat, ut "uror."
>
> *(Char. 211.27, 29; text Schad 2007: 12, 292)*

> Active is that which will indicate doing something, like "I say," indicating a motion either of the body, like "I mount," or of the mind, like "I foresee" ... Passive is the opposite of active, [and is] that which indicates enduring something, like "I am burned."

If we apply these definitions to the sexual realm, "activity" should refer to more than just penetration; it should encompass, for example, performing a sex act, moving one's body during sex, or moving one's soul (i.e., desiring).

In this chapter, we explore male sexuality, looking specifically at the representation of penetrated males as "active" or "passive" based on the definitions above.[5] We focus primarily on the literary and epigraphic use of the nouns *cinaedus* (which is hard to define; see below) and *pathicus* ("sexually penetrated male"), as well as the following verbs and their associated participles: *irrumare* and *irrumari* ("to face-fuck" and "to be face-fucked"), *fellare* ("to suck cock"), *pedicare* and *pedicari* ("to ass-fuck" and "to be ass-fucked"), *futui* ("to be fucked"), and *cevere* ("to waggle the buttocks"). We pay attention to grammar (e.g., active versus passive voice, subjects versus objects), as well as descriptions of agency, movement, and desire. Through these close readings, we argue that some penetrated males (the *irrumatus* and the *pedicatus/fututus*) were conceptualized as passive, while others (the *fellator* and the *cinaedus/pathicus*) were characterized as active.[6] We use these Latin terms (*irrumatus, pedicatus/fututus, fellator, cinaedus/pathicus*) as heuristic labels for individuals performing particular behaviors, though as seen below, other terminology is sometimes used. Moreover, we do not suggest that these terms are fixed identities.[7]

Passive penetrated males

The *irrumatus*

Because *irrumatio*, "face-fucking," was a violent act—namely, oral rape—its victim was conceptualized as an unwilling or inactive participant, in contrast to those who were said to perform fellatio (*fellare*; see below).[8] A male whose mouth was forcibly penetrated could be described either with passive forms of the verb *irrumare*, or as the direct object of the same verb. In either case, his passivity was stressed.

In both literature and graffiti, *irrumatio* often appears in implicit or explicit threats. For example, one graffito from Pompeii reads, *L(ucius) Habonius sauciat / irrumat Caesum / Felic(e)m*, "Lucius Habonius wounds, face-fucks Caesus Felix" (*CIL* IV 10232a). The use of the verb *saucio*, paired with *irrumo*, amplifies the violence directed towards the victim.[9] A set of graffiti from Rome takes a more laconic approach, twice recording in close proximity: *ir(r)umo te Sexte*, "I face-fuk you, Sextus" (*AE* 1949 3). The Latin poet Catullus often threatens to "face-fuck" his enemies, as when he tells the frugal Aurelius to keep away from Catullus' favorite boy, whom Aurelius has been anally penetrating (*pedicare*, 21.4).[10] If he doesn't, Catullus will turn the tables and attack him with "face-fucking" (*irrumatione*, 21.8). Catullus reinforces Aurelius' passivity with the very last word of the poem, saying that Aurelius will be *irrumatus*, "face-fucked" (21.13).[11] *Irrumatio* is used as a threat in the epigrams of the poet Martial, too, as when a certain Gallus is warned that his female lover's husband is quite likely to "face-fuck" (*irrumat*) him if the husband catches him (2.47.4; cf. 2.83.5).

Other examples of threats come from the Priapic Corpus.[12] These poems are written from the perspective of the woodland deity Priapus, guardian of gardens, who threatens thieves with rape by his oversized phallus. In one poem, he warns a thief: "you will be ass-fucked" (*pedicabere*) for a first offense, "I will face-fuck" (*irrumabo*) you for a second, and for a third violation, Priapus warns the thief, *pedicaberis irrumaberisque*, "you will be ass-fucked and face-fucked" (*Priap.* 35). The thief must *poenam patiare*, "endure the punishment" (35.4), with a play on *pati*'s associations both with passivity (as in the grammarians above) and with being subject to sexual penetration (e.g., Adams 1982: 189–90). In none of these cases does the threatened individual *want* to engage in oral sex; rather, the implication is that he is an unwilling, passive party in his penetration.

The *pedicatus/fututus*

Anally penetrated males who did not seek their penetration could be described with passive forms of the verb *pedicare*, "to ass-fuck" (and less often *futuere*, "to fuck"), or as objects of *pedicare*.[13] The passive participles *pedicatus* and *fututus*, while not used in literary texts, do appear in graffiti. Most often, the terms are paired with just a name, as in *Ditio Betu(s) / pedicatus*, "Ditio Betus the ass-fucked" (*AE* 1992 1151) from the Alps and *Deeicatu(s) / pedicatus*, "Deeicatus [= Delicatus] the ass-fucked" (*CIL* XI 6690.6) from Northern Italy.[14] Another graffito, from Pompeii, lists three "fucked" individuals in a kind of matrix: *Ny(m)phe fututa*, "Nymphe the fucked [female]" frames one column reading *fututa Perenni(s)*, "Perennis the fucked [female]," and another stating *Amomus fututus*, "Amomus the fucked [male]" (*CIL* IV 8897). The passivity of the *fututus / pedicatus* is perhaps best illustrated by the following graffito from Northern Italy, which focuses on the actions and agency of the penetrator, as opposed to the penetrated: *Antioc(h)us pedicatus / ego qui feci non / nego*, "Antiochus [has been] ass-fucked. I, the one who did it, don't deny it" (*AE* 2002 550).

As with *irrumare*, *pedicare* was often used in threats. One Priapic poem promises a would-be thief *tu … pedicabere*, "you will be ass-fucked," with Priapus' *fascino pedali*, "foot-long phallus" (*Priap.* 28.3). In another (discussed above), the deity threatens anal rape for first- and third-time offenders (*pedicabere*, 1; *pedicaberis*, 5). These Priapic threats may help to explain a graffito from Pannonia, which reads *pidico qui ta(n)cunt*, "I ass-fock those who touch [= steal?]" (*AE* 2008 1083), and part of a mathematical compass from Germany, which warns *ponis aut pidico te*, "put [me?] down or I [will] ass-fock you" (Thüry 2008: 299).

In addition to being used against thieves, *pedicatio* ("ass-fucking") also features in threats against nosy and envious individuals. When a busybody asks Martial why he keeps well-endowed slave-boys, Martial replies, *pedicant … curiosos*, "they ass-fuck nosy people" (Mart. 11.63.5). Two graffiti from Numidia similarly warn, *pedico / invide*, "I ass-fuck, jealous one" (*ILAlg* 2.3.8277) and *curiosos pedico / invide cacas*, "I ass-fuck nosy people, jealous one; you [will] shit" (*AE* 1976 709). The implication of the latter seems to be that defecation will follow from the *invidus* or *curiosus* individual being anally penetrated.

Forms of *pedicare* were also used in humorous threats against readers. At its simplest, we find *ego qui lego pedicor*, "I who read am ass-fucked" (*AE* 1959 63) in a graffito from Gaul, while another incarnation, also from Gaul, is more detailed: *III vices pidico qui legeret / [l]ege vade qu(a)ere quis vae [tibi dicat?]*, "Three times I ass-fock he who would read this; read, go away, seek who [says] woe [unto you]" (*AE* 1983 684). Two elaborate variations from Pompeii state, *amat qui scribit pedicatur qui legit / qui obscultat prurit pathicus est qui praeterit*, "he who writes, loves; he who reads, is ass-fucked; he who listens, itches; he who passes by, is a *pathicus*" (*CIL* IV 2360 Add. 219, 465, 704; and *CIL* IV 4008).[15] Once again, the reader of the graffito is being threatened with anal rape.

In sum, *irrumati, pedicati,* and *fututi* routinely show a lack of sexual agency, movement, and desire for being penetrated.

Active penetrated males

The *fellator*

Common to both literature and graffiti are statements (or accusations) that a male has performed fellatio. Unlike the passive victims of *irrumatio*, who lack volition and agency, the subjects of the active verb *fellare*, "to suck cock," are conceptualized as agents in their oral penetration. In graffiti, for example, we often find simple statements connecting a male name with a second- or third-person form of *fellare*, as in *Felix fel(l)at*, "Felix suks cock" (*CIL* IV 1869 Add. 213) and *Valentine fel(l)as*, "Valentinus, you suck cock" (*CIL* IV 8413) from Pompeii.[16] These graffiti highlight the agency of the male performing fellatio not only by using an active verb, but also by leaving out mention of any object of fellatio.[17]

Literature often portrays fellatio as willingly performed. For example, in one epigram, Martial calls attention to a particular man's behavioral faults (*vitium* is the word used), which include drinking too much wine, writing bad poetry, vomiting, being extravagant, and, as the punch line, practicing fellatio (*fellas*) (2.89). Another poem targets a man who, as a youth, *lambebat medios improba lingua viros*, "licked men's middles with his lusty tongue" (2.61.2), that is, acted as a desiring agent. Now that the man has become a base gossiper (Williams 2004 ad loc.), Martial says, *haereat inguinibus potius tam noxia lingua: / nam cum fellaret, purior illa fuit*, "it would be better that his impure tongue stick to men's loins, for when he sucked cock it was cleaner" (2.61.7–8). Martial plays on the common trope that oral sex pollutes the mouth, but what is particularly relevant here is the stress on the man's agency through the active verbs *lambebat, haereat,* and *fellaret*.[18] The lust of a male for performing fellatio is described in still another epigram: *aspicit nihil sursum, / sed spectat oculis devorantibus draucos / nec otiosis mentulas videt labris*, "He doesn't ever glance up, but gazes at athletes with voracious eyes, nor does he look at their cocks with lips idle" (Mart. 1.96.11–13). His active desire for this act is expressed, in this case, by his lusty eyes and mouth.

That performers of fellatio were considered agents is additionally suggested by the word *fellator*, "cock sucker," an agent noun composed of the root *fell-* and the agentive suffix *-tor*. This word is particularly common in graffiti, and in at least eight examples, *fellator* appears alone with a male name, as in *[E]pafroditus / fella[t]or*, "Epafroditus the cock sucker" (*CIL* IV 10073c) from Pompeii.[19] Other Pompeian graffiti add further details: Narcissus is called *fellator maximus*, "greatest cock sucker" (*CIL* IV 1825a Add. 212), and Secundus is said to be a *fel(l)ator rarus*, "cock suker of rare talent" (*CIL* IV 9027; trans. Varone 2002: 140). One graffito proclaims, *Cosmus Equitiaes / magnus cinae/dus et fellator / est suris apertis* …, "Cosmus, slave of Equitia, There is a grand *cinaedus* and cock sucker, with his legs open" (*CIL* IV 1825 Add. 212, 464; see also Varone 2002: 140 n. 238), suggesting that Cosmus desires both oral and anal (*magnus cinaedus … suris apertis*) penetration.

Fellatores, moreover, were characterized by their habitual behavior. For example, a certain Vacerra is said by Martial to be an informer, a slanderer, a swindler, a dealer, a gladiator-trainer, and a cock sucker (*fellator*) (11.66.1–3). In another epigram, a man returning to Rome after fifteen years is greeted with kisses by a number of unappealing characters, including (among others) a weaver, a fuller, a cobbler, and a cock sucker (*fellator*) (12.59).[20] Just as a slanderer or a cobbler performs his defining actions repeatedly, so too does the *fellator* habitually perform fellatio.

Finally, the distinction between the agency of the *fellator* and the passivity of the *irrumatus* is made particularly clear in Martial's attack on Zoilus, who dines luxuriously while his guests go hungry. Martial implies that the guests might want to get back at Zoilus by performing *irrumatio* on him, but as the surprise ending reveals, *nec vindicari ... possumus: fellat*, "We are not able to get our revenge—he sucks cock" (3.82.33). Because Zoilus *wants* to perform fellatio and is the agent of his actions (*fellat*), the enforced passivity of *irrumatio* is no longer an option.[21]

The *cinaedus/pathicus*

The Latin word *cinaedus* comes from the Greek word κίναιδος, which is of uncertain origin.[22] The ancient lexicographers proposed various etymologies for κίναιδος, including derivation from κενὸς αἰδοῦς, "empty of shame," and κινεῖν τὰ αἰδοῖα, "to move one's shameful parts" (*Etym. Magn.* s.v. κίναιδος). The association of κίναιδος with both shameful behavior and movement is seen in the use of *cinaedus* as well. Although in early Latin (and occasionally also in later texts) *cinaedus* was used primarily to designate dancers, with an emphasis on their bodily movements,[23] in time it came to have a broader semantic range: most often it referred to a male who desired to be penetrated anally or was effeminate,[24] but it could also designate a male who was lustful in general. Thus, a *cinaedus* might also perform oral sex on males and females and even penetrate females and (albeit rarely) males.[25] This constellation of characteristics has led scholars to disagree about the defining attribute of the *cinaedus*: for some, he is primarily a gender deviant; for others, a male penetrated by other men.[26]

For the purposes of this chapter, we will focus on a particular aspect of the *cinaedus*: his active role in his own penetration. Since there is no verb "to act like a *cinaedus*," the Romans expressed the agency of the *cinaedus* by speaking of his desire to be anally penetrated and his bodily movement during this act.

First, *cinaedi* and males of a similar ilk are depicted as wanting to be penetrated. So, for example, while the thieves in the Priapic Corpus are most often passive, extra humor is added by presenting some as stealing *in order to* be penetrated. In one poem, Priapus insinuates that this is the case with thieves who continue to steal from his garden, even though much better crops, in much greater supply, can be found nearby (51). In another poem, he mentions a thief who *furatum venit huc amore poenae*, "comes here to steal, with love for the punishment" (64.1–2). The conceptual importance of desire and agency is made explicit in this poem's conclusion: Priapus refuses to punish the thief since he would not be an unwilling victim (64.3; cf. Mart. 3.82, discussed above).

In other instances, one of Martial's *cinaedi* is said to *prurit*, "to itch," that is, "to yearn sexually" (6.37.4), and the Latin author Gellius' *cinaedus* has *oculos ludibundos atque inlecebrae voluptatisque plenos*, "eyes that are wanton and full of enticement and desire" (3.5.2). The Latin satirist Lucilius' cinaedus is a *sectator*, a "pursuer" (1140–1), and Virro, the *cinaedus* of Juvenal's ninth satire, not only pursues with flattering love-notes (*blandae adsidue densaeque tabellae sollicitent*; 9.36–7) but also pays to be penetrated (9.39, 41). We see another man who pays to be penetrated in a graffito from Pompeii: *ratio mi cum ponis / Batacare te pidicaro*, "When you hand over the money, Batacarus, I will ass-fock you" (*CIL* IV 2254 Add. 216).[27] Catullus describes two *cinaedi* as *vorax*, "voracious" (29.10, 57.8), and once gives agency to the *culo ... voraciore*, "rather voracious anus," of a *cinaedus* (33.4).

Martial combines two common traits of the *cinaedus* when he claims that Hyllus pays to be penetrated and that his anus *vorat*, "devours" (2.51.6).[28] In another epigram, he repeatedly stresses the desire of a penetrated man (2.48):

> percidi gaudes, percisus, Papyle, ploras.
> cur, quae vis fieri, Papyle, facta doles?
> paenitet obscenae pruriginis? an magis illud
> fles, quod percidi, Papyle, desieris?

> You rejoice in being plowed, Papylus, but after you've been plowed, you cry. Why, Papylus, do you lament the deeds you wish to be done? Do you regret your impure itch? Or do you weep rather because you've stopped being plowed?

Likewise, the desire of (some) penetrated males is highlighted by a character in a farce of Pomponius: *ut nullum civem pedicavi per dolum, / nisi ipsus orans ultro qui occuiniceret*, "I have ass-fucked no citizen by deceit, unless he himself, begging for it, is the type who bends over of his own accord" (148–9).

As with the man who "bends over of his own accord," sometimes the agency of *cinaedi* is made manifest through their enthusiastic bodily movements, whether in attracting men or in the act of sex. For example, a certain *cinaedus* is warned not to "move his loins" (*movere lumbos*) beneath his stola while summoning (*vocare*) men arriving at the ports (Verg. *Catal.* 13.21, 24). In the *Priapea*, a man addresses his flaccid penis thus: *nec tibi tener puer / patebit ullus, imminente qui toro / iuvante verset arte mobilem natem*, "no tender boy will open up for you, who, when the bed beckons, shakes his supple buttocks with pleasing skill" (*Priap.* 83.21–3). The boy, like a *cinaedus*, is both penetrable and described with words indicating agency and movement (*patebit, verset, mobilem*).[29]

The *cinaedus'* movement in sex is perhaps best seen in an episode of Petronius' novel, the *Satyricon*, in which the narrator Encolpius is attacked by a *cinaedus* at a party. Encolpius relates: … *immundissimo me basio conspuit. mox et super lectum venit atque omni vi detexit recusantem. super inguina mea diu multumque frustra moluit*, "[the *cinaedus*] slobbered on me with the filthiest kiss. Next, he clambered on the bed and undressed me by force, though I was unwilling. He vehemently ground [his buttocks] on my groin for a long time, in vain" (23.4–5). The *cinaedus* then moved on to the narrator's friend Ascyltus and *clunibus eum basiisque distrivit*, "bruised him with his buttocks and kisses" (24.4). The *cinaedus* is the subject of multiple verbs of action (*conspuit, venit, detexit, moluit, distrivit*), of which *moluit* has an overtly sexual connotation.[30] His actions and desire are set in stark contrast to Encolpius, who is not the subject of any finite verbs in this passage and moreover is made into the passive victim in this attempted sex act (*omni vi … recusantem*).[31]

In other instances, verbs such as *ceveo*, "to waggle the buttocks," are used to describe the sexual movement of *cinaedi* and those with similar characteristics.[32] In Juvenal's ninth satire, the interlocutor Naevolus complains to Juvenal that his stingy patron is a *cinaedus* who *computat et cevet*, "calculates [the cost] and waggles his buttocks" (9.40); that is, the patron pays to have Naevolus penetrate him.[33] Another Naevolus, this one a presumed *cinaedus*, is said to *pulchre … ceves*, "waggle his buttocks beautifully" when anally penetrated (*pedicaris*) (Mart. 3.95.13). In Satire 2, Juvenal attacks hypocritical men who speak of virtue but *clunem agitant*, "shake their buttocks." In one instance, he has someone pose a rhetorical question to one of these hypocrites: *ego te ceventem, Sexte, verebor?*, "Am I to respect you, Sextus, who waggle your bottom?" (2.21). An adverbial form of *ceveo* appears in Pompeian graffiti, as in *Trebonius Eycini ceventinabilite[r] / arrurabe[l]iter*, "Trebonius of Eycinius, buttocks-wagglingly, boorishly(?)" (*CIL* IV 4126), and *inclinabiliter /*

ceventinabiliter, "bowingly; buttocks-wagglingly" (*CIL* IV 5406).[34] The pairing of *ceventinabiliter* with *inclinabiliter* in the latter example may suggest being penetrated in anal sex, in addition to movement.[35]

The term *pathicus* shows up considerably less frequently than *cinaedus* in Latin literature and graffiti, making it difficult to determine how *pathici* were conceptualized. Derived from the Greek παθικός, the word is related to the verb *pati*, "to endure"; in the case of males, it indicates enduring anal penetration (Williams 2010 [1999]: 193). Despite this etymology suggesting passivity, the near-interchangeability of the terms *pathicus* and *cinaedus* hints that at least some *pathici* were thought to be agents.[36] Particularly illuminating are a set of inscribed lead bullets attacking Octavian (the future Augustus): one addresses him as *pat(h)ice* (*CIL* XI 6721.39), and others more explicitly depict him as a desiring agent in his own penetration, including one reading *esureis et me celas*, "you hunger for and hide me" (*CIL* XI 6721.34). The situation evoked may be one of anal or oral sex, both of which are suggested by other bullets in this cache.[37]

Thus, while all of the males discussed in the previous sections were penetrated (either orally or anally), an important distinction was made by the Romans between males who were conceptualized as agents in their own penetration (*fellatores, cinaedi*, and *pathici*), and those who were not (*irrumati, pedicati*, and *fututi*).[38] Literature and graffiti convey this agency by representing the former group of individuals (and those who engage in similar practices) as performing, moving their body in, or desiring a sexual act.

Further repercussions

This distinction between active and passive penetrated males has further repercussions for our conceptual map of Roman sexuality, providing nuances to models set forth by Craig Williams and Holt Parker. Parker's teratogenic ("monster-producing") grid (1997: 49) provides a visualization of the penetration paradigm, organizing sexual acts and persons around the role in penetration (which he calls "active" and "passive") as well as bodily orifice (vagina, anus, mouth) (see Table 25.1).

As the most comprehensive illustration of Roman sexuality, this model has been widely influential. However, in grouping together all penetrated individuals under the label "passive," this model obscures the potential agency of some of these individuals. Williams's chart of sexual verbs (2010 [1999]: 178) (see Table 25.2), on the other hand, allows for precisely this agency, as well as eschewing the terms "active" and "passive" as glosses for one's role in penetration.

Table 25.1 Teratogenic grid (adapted from Parker 1997: 49)

	Vagina	Anus	Mouth
Active			
Activity	*futuere*	*pedicare*	*irrumare*
Person	*fututor*	*pedicator/pedico*	*irrumator*
Passive			
Activity	*futui*	*pedicari*	*irrumari/fellari*
Person			
Male	*cunnilinctor*	*cinaedus/pathicus*	*fellator*
Female	*femina/puella*	*pathica*	*fellatrix*

Table 25.2 Chart of sexual verbs (based on Williams 2010 [1999]: 178)

	Insertive	Receptive
Vaginal	*futuere*	*crisare*
Anal	*pedicare*	*cevere*
Oral	*irrumare*	*fellare*

Neither model, however, encompasses *both* active *and* passive penetrated individuals, or fully represents the complex relationship between penetration and agency.

Thus, we propose a revised model for Roman sexuality that adds an axis of agency (active versus passive) subordinate to the main axis of penetration (penetrating versus penetrated). Building from Parker's model, we have changed his terms "active" and "passive" to "penetrating" and "penetrated," and have clarified his category "activity" by renaming it "verb."[39] We then divide penetrated men into active and passive, supplementing Parker's model with the bold entries below in Table 25.3.[40]

The distinction between active agents and passive non-agents, seen in Table 25.3, was not insignificant. While all penetrated men were non-normative objects of scorn (some of the "monsters" of Parker's grid; see 1997: 54), the Romans at the same time drew distinctions between *pedicati/fututi* and *cinaedi/pathici*, and between *irrumati* and *fellatores*. In oratory and satire, for example, accusations or insinuations that someone was not only penetrated but also an *agent* in his own penetration were particularly defamatory.[41] At times, this difference could have legal consequences, too. While a sexually penetrated male could suffer legal disadvantages—namely, in the form of not being able to bring a suit on another's behalf—there were exceptions for those who had been raped by pirates or enemies during war (*Dig.* 3.1.1.6).[42] Thus, one's sexual agency had the potential to affect one's legal rights: being willingly penetrated could result in civic restrictions, whereas being an unwilling party did not.

In sum, we have shown that Romans considered agency an important component in the conceptualization of penetrated males. More broadly, through the expansion of the penetration paradigm to include agency, we hope to have more fully and accurately represented the ideology of Roman sexuality.

Table 25.3 Penetration-agency model for male sexuality (modified from Parker 1997: 49)

	Orifice		
	Vagina	Anus	Mouth
Penetrating			
Verb	*futuere*	*pedicare*	*irrumare*
Person	*fututor*	*pedicator/pedico*	*irrumator*
Penetrated			
Verb	*futui*	*pedicari*	*irrumari/fellare*
Person			
Male **(passive)**	—	***pedicatus/fututus***	***irrumatus***
Male **(active)**	—	***cinaedus/pathicus(?)***	***fellator***
Female	*femina/puella*	*pathica*	*fellatrix*

Notes

1 For the penetration model of Roman sexuality, see, e.g., Richlin 1992 [1983]; Parker 1997; Walters 1997; Ormand 2008; Williams 2010 [1999], with further bibliography on 412 n. 16. For the penetration model of Greek sexuality, see, e.g., Dover 1978; Foucault 1985; Halperin 1990; Winkler 1990; Ormand 2008. For a critique of the penetration model, see, e.g., Davidson 1998; Davidson 2001; Davidson 2007.

2 See, e.g., Langlands 2006; Ormand 2008 (especially pp. 128–45); Kamen 2012; Levin-Richardson 2013; Kamen and Levin-Richardson forthcoming.

3 For a discussion of the terms "active" and "passive," see also Edwards 1993: 72–3 with 72 n. 36; Younger 2005, e.g. xiv–xv; Williams 2010 [1999]: 230–1, 258, 261, 309 n. 16. As an alternative, Williams offers the terms "insertive" and "receptive."

4 Grammarians on the meaning of *activus*: Plin. ap. Pomp. 5.227.25; Macr. *exc.* 5.652.21; Diom. 1.336.26; Sacerd. 6.430.18; Char. 211.27; Cled. 5.18.35; Prisc. 2.373.15 (cited in Schad 2007: 12). On the meaning of *passivus*: Plin. ap. Pomp. 5.227.26; Macr. *exc.* 5.652.22; Diom. 1.336.32; Char. 211.29; Cled. 5.18.36; Prisc. 2.374.1 (cited in Schad 2007: 292). We thank Curtis Dozier for his insights on the Latin grammarians.

5 In a future article (Kamen and Levin-Richardson forthcoming), we explore the relationship between agency and penetration with respect to female sexuality. We demonstrate that some women in Roman culture were conceptualized as sexual agents despite being penetrated (*fututrices* and *fellatrices*), while others were conceptualized as agents *and* penetrators (*tribades*).

6 Since the term *pathicus* is related to *pati*, "to endure" (see p. 455), we expected the *pathicus* to be a passive penetrated male. However, despite the etymology, the evidence (discussed on p. 455) seems to suggest at least some *pathici* were agents.

7 For the *cinaedus* as a sexual identity, however, see Richlin 1993; Taylor 1997; cf. Parker 1997 and Williams 2010 [1999]: 239–45.

8 On *irrumare*, see Krenkel 1980; Richlin 1981; Adams 1982: 125–30; Richlin 1992 [1983]: 26, 69, and *passim*; Williams 2010 [1999]: 178, 218, and *passim*.

9 On "wounding" as a sexual metaphor in Latin, see, e.g., Adams 1982: 152; on this graffito, see Adams 1982: 127, 152.

10 For threats involving *irrumatio* in Catullus, see also 16.1, 16.14, 37.8. For other examples of males as objects of *irrumatio*, see Catull. 28.10, 74.5; Mart. 3.96; *Priap.* 13.2, 22.2, 74.2; *CIL* IV 1473, 10030.

11 The adjective *irrumatus* can also be used in a transferred sense: Martial describes bath waters as being "irrumated" (*undis … irrumatis*) because penises have been inserted in them (Mart. 2.70.3). Rarely, the victims of the threat of *irrumare* are non-human: e.g., guard-dogs (*custodes … irrumatos*, *Priap.* 70.13).

12 For threats of *irrumatio* in the Priapic Corpus, see *Priap.* 35.2, 35.5 (discussed on p. 451), 44.4, 56.6. Many other Priapic poems use different vocabulary to threaten thieves with rape.

13 In addition to the examples discussed on p. 451–2, see also Pompon. 148; Laber. 34; Catull. 21.4, 16.1, 16.14; *Priap.* 3.9, 38.3; Mart. 1.92.14, 3.98.2, 6.56.6, 7.10.1, 7.67.1 (the penetrator is the *tribas* Philaenis), 9.69.2, 10.64.6, 11.45.8, 11.94.6, 12.16.3; *AE* 1992 1150; *AE* 1994 1394 and 1876; *CIL* IV 1691 Add. 211, 1882 Add. 465, 2048 Add. 215, 2375 Add. 220, 8805, 10090; *CIL* XIII 10017.41; *CLE* 1899; *Suppl. Ital.* 670. It is important to note that passive forms of the verb *pedicare* can also be used to describe the sexual acts of individuals who might more properly fall under the category of the actively desiring *cinaedus* than the passive *pedicatus* (e.g. Mart. 3.95.13, 7.62.5–6, and perhaps also 7.10.1). See further p. 453–5.

14 Another possible translation for *x pedicatus* is "x has been ass-fucked."

15 In this case, we have provided a corrected version of the text based on the two exemplars. The former graffito continues with *ursi me comedant et ego verpa(m) qui lego*, "may bears devour me, and I who read am a dick [or: may I who read eat dick]"; the latter continues with *scribit [p]edicator / Septu[m]ius*, "the ass-fucker Septumius writes [this]." See also Williams 2010 [1999]: 294 and 428 n. 23. For another graffito of this type, see *CIL* IV 1798.

16 See also *AE* 1951 158a (which may be preceded by a greeting); *CIL* IV 1284, 1631, 1850, 1851 Add. 213, 1852a Add. 213, 1869 Add. 213, 2004 Add. 214, 3144 (the name, however, is unclear), 3200, 4652 (note that the case here seems to be genitive), 8413, 8461, 10628; Stylow and Ventura Villanueva 2009; Cf. Mart. 7.10.1: *fellat Linus*. For more elaborate graffiti with a male subject of *fellare*, see *CIL* IV 1623 Add. 209, 7243, 8230, and possibly 2402 Add. 222.

17 Only one graffito includes the recipient of the act: *Martialis fellas Proculum*, "Martialis, you suck Proculus" (*CIL* IV 8841).

18 For fellatio as polluting, see, e.g., Richlin 1992 [1983]: 26–9; Williams 2010 [1999]: 218–24.

19 See also *AE* 2000 304, *CIL* IV 1708, 1784 (there was more to the graffito originally, but the meaning of its few legible letters is unknown), 2169 Add. 215, 2170 Add. 215, 4580, 4997, 10073c, 10222. Two graffiti have just the word *fellator* (*CIL* IV 4209, 4548), perhaps addressing the reader as such. For other *fellatores*, see *CIL* IV 2400, 3494 (on which see especially Clarke 2003: 161–70; Clarke 2005: 273–82), 5408, 8400.

20 See also Mart. 11.30 and 95, both of which focus on the unsavoriness of *fellatores'* mouths; cf. Mart. 14.74, in which a crow is said not to be a *fellator*, since it is so noisy.

21 For a similar situation with anal sex, see *Priap.* 64.

22 On the meaning and etymology of κίναιδος/*cinaedus*, see Kroll *RE* s.v. Kinaidos; Williams 2010 [1999]: 193–7; Younger 2005: 31–2. On the *cinaedus*, see, e.g., Richlin 1992 [1983] *passim*; Richlin 1993; Gleason 1995: 64–7; Parker 1997 *passim*; Taylor 1997; Ormand 2008: 19 and *passim*; Williams 2010 [1999] *passim*. On the κίναιδος, see, e.g., Winkler 1990: 45–70; Davidson 1998: 167–82; Davidson 2007: 52–64; Ormand 2008: 19 and *passim*.

23 On *cinaedi* as dancers: Colin 1952–3: 329–35; Corbeill 1997. See, e.g., Plaut. *Mil.* 668 and *Stich.* 769, 772; Scip. min. *Orat.* fr. 30; Lucil. fr. 1.32; Petron. *Sat.* 23.2; Plin. *Ep.* 9.17.1; Non. 5M; *CGL* v.65.7.

24 Being anally penetrated: Plaut. *Asin.* 628 and *Aul.* 422; Catull. 16.1–2, 57.1; Petron. *Sat.* 23.5 (see further p. 454), 24.2, 24.4 (see further below); Mart. 2.43.14, 3.73, 6.16, 6.37, 6.39.12–13, 9.63 (according to Adams 1982: 141), 12.16.2–3; Juv. 2.10; Suet. *Aug.* 68.1; Gell. *NA* 3.5.2; *CIL* IV 2319b (see Varone 2002 [1994]: 137 and Williams 2010 [1999]: 427 n. 19); 2332. Being effeminate: Plaut. *Men.* 513, *Poen.* 1318; Verg. *Catal.* 13.17, 21; *Priap.* 45.2–3, 6; Phaedr. 5.1, Appendix 10.2, 20; Petron. *Sat.* 21.2, 23.2; Mart. 6.16.1, 6.39.12, 7.58.2, 10.40, 10.98.3–4, 11.21.7; Juv. 2 *passim*; Suet. *Aug.* 68.1; Apul. *Met.* 8.24, 26; Gell. *NA* 3.5.2, 6.12.5.

25 Performing oral sex on males: *Priap.* 25.5; Petron. *Sat.* 21.2 and 23.2 (on which see Schmeling with Setaioli 2011, ad loc.); Juv. 9.35 (possibly also Catull. 16.1–2; Mart. 2.43.14, 9.63; *CIL* IV 1825 Add. 212, 464). Performing oral sex on females: Verg. *Catal.* 13.32; *LSO* 2. Penetrating females: Lucil. 30.1058; Catull. 57.8, 9; Mart. 6.39.12–13; Gell. *NA* 3.5.2; *AE* 2000 303. Penetrating males: Petron. *Sat.* 21.2 (that this scenario is unusual, see Schmeling with Setaioli 2011, ad loc.); cf. *CIL* VI 248 Add. 3004 and 3756.

26 For the *cinaedus* as a gender deviant, see, e.g., Ormand 2008: 19; Williams 2010 [1999]: 177–8, 193–4, 232–43; see also Edwards 1993: 63–97. For the *cinaedus* as a male penetrated by men, see, e.g., Richlin 1993.

27 For *cinaedi* in graffiti: *AE* 1994 1061, *AE* 2000 303 (if the name is male); *CIL* II 11 Add. 781; *CIL* IV 1485a, 1772, 1802, 1825 Add. 212 and 464, 2312, 2334, 2338 Add. 218, 2409 Add. 222, 3079, 3114, 3336, 4082, 4201 Add. 704, 4206, 4602, 4703, 4917, 5095, 5156, 5268, 8146, 8531, 10043, 10078a, 10086b, 10098c, 10143, 10654c, 10671; *CIL* XI 6728.21; *RIB* 2.4.2447.28a.

28 For other examples of males wanting to be anally penetrated, see, e.g., Mart. 2.47, 54, 62; 3.71; 11.88.

29 However, for the distinction between *pueri* and *cinaedi*, see Williams 2010 [1999]: 203–8, 237.

30 See Adams 1982: 152–3 on the sexual connotations of *molo*; in this passage, however, he suggests that the *cinaedus* may be masturbating.

31 For *vis* as rape, see *OLD* s.v. *vis*, 2a.

32 Williams 2010 [1999]: 178, 202 takes *ceveo* to be the reciprocal action of *pedico* (see p. 456). Sometimes the verb is used more metaphorically: see, e.g., Pers. 1.87. On the meaning of *ceveo*, see also Mussehl 1919; Fraenkel 1964 [1920].

33 That Naevolus is the penetrating party is made clear at 9.43–5; that his patron is a *cinaedus* is indicated by αὐτὸς γὰρ ἀφέλκεται ἄνδρα κίναιδος, "the *kinaidos* himself entices a man" (37).

34 For *arrurabiliter* as "à la manière d'un rustre," see Bader 1962: 281.

35 For the sexual use of *inclino*, see Adams 1982: 192. A form of *ceveo* (*ceventes*) is also found in graffiti to describe anally penetrated males (*CIL* IV 4977).

36 Conflation of *pathicus* and *cinaedus*: Catull. 16.2, 57.1–2. Other similarities include: being anally penetrated (Catull. 16.2, 57.1; Juv. 9.130; *CIL* XI 6721.7, 10, 11, 34); effeminacy (Juv. 2.93–101); performing oral sex on men (Catull. 16.2; Juv. 2.95; *CIL* XI 6721.9, 34 (possibly)); and penetrating females (Catull. 57.8–9).

37 For anal sex, see, e.g., *CIL* XI 6721.7, 10, 11; for oral sex: *CIL* XI 6721.9. For other *pathici*, see Catull. 112; Juv. 9.133; *CIL* IV 2360 Add. 219, 465, and 704, 4008; *CIL* IX 6089.5. For *pathicus* as an adjective, see Mart. 12.95.1, 3.

38 See also Williams 2010 [1999]: 263 and *passim*, who argues that penetrated men were conceptualized differently based on their desire or lack thereof.

39 We have also corrected the verb *fellari* to *fellare* in the category of oral penetration. In Kamen and Levin-Richardson forthcoming we add a category for active penetrating women, and distinguish between active and passive penetrated women.

40 We remove Parker's entry *cunnilinctor* [sic] in the "penetrated male—vagina" category, since this spot logically ought to demarcate the (impossible) category of a man penetrated in his vagina (!) (cf. Parker 1997: 51, 57), as the other categories denote individuals penetrated in their anus or mouth. In a future article, we hope to return to where the *cunnilingus* fits into this model.

41 A good entry point for scholarship on sexual invective is Richlin 1992 [1982].

42 *removet autem a postulando pro aliis et eum, qui corpore suo muliebria passus est. si quis tamen vi praedonum vel hostium stupratus est, non debet notari,* "however, [the edict] prevented anyone who endured womanly things with his body from bringing a suit on another's behalf. But if someone was raped by pirates or enemies, he shouldn't be so marked." For discussion of this passage, see, e.g., Richlin 1993: 558–61; Ormand, 2008: 178–81; Williams 2010 [1999]: 214–16. Whether penetrated males suffered other legal disadvantages (including *infamia* or prosecution under the *Lex Scantinia*) is debated: see, e.g., Richlin 1993; Ormand 2008: 176–81; Williams 2010 [1999]: 130–6, 214–16, and further bibliography at 362 n. 95.

Bibliography

Adams, J.N. (1982) *The Latin Sexual Vocabulary*. Baltimore, MD: Johns Hopkins University Press.

Bader, F. (1962) *La formation des composés nominaux du latin*. Besançon: Les Belles Lettres.

Clarke, J. (2003) *Art in the Lives of Ordinary Romans: Visual Representation and Non-elite Romans in Italy, 100 BC–AD 315*. Berkeley, CA: University of California Press.

——(2005) "Representations of the *cinaedus* in Roman art", *Journal of Homosexuality* 49: 271–98.

Colin, J. (1952–3) "Juvénal, les baladins et les rétiaires d'après le MS. d'Oxford", *Atti della Accademia delle Scienze di Torino* 87–8: 315–86.

Corbeill, A. (1997) "Dining deviants in Roman political invective", in J.P. Hallett and M.B. Skinner (eds) *Roman Sexualities*. Princeton, NJ: Princeton University Press, pp. 99–128.

Davidson, J. (1998) *Courtesans and Fishcakes: The Consuming Passions of Classical Athens*. New York: St Martin's Press.

——(2001) "Dover, Foucault and Greek homosexuality: Penetration and the truth of sex", *Past & Present* 170: 3–51.

——(2007) *The Greeks and Greek Love: A Radical Reappraisal of Homosexuality in Ancient Greece*. London: Weidenfeld & Nicolson.

Dover, K.J. (1978) *Greek Homosexuality*. Cambridge, MA: Harvard University Press.

Edwards, C. (1993) *The Politics of Immorality in Ancient Rome*. Cambridge: Cambridge University Press.

Foucault, M. (1985) *The History of Sexuality*, Volume 2: *The Use of Pleasure*, trans. R. Hurley. New York: Random House.

Fraenkel, E. (1964 [1920]) "*Cevere* im Plautustext", in *Kleine Beiträge zur klassischen Philologie*. Rome: Edizioni di storia e letteratura, pp. 45–52.

Gleason, M. (1995) *Making Men: Sophists and Self-Presentation in Ancient Rome*. Princeton, NJ: Princeton University Press.

Halperin, D.M. (1990) "One hundred years of homosexuality", in *One Hundred Years of Homosexuality: And Other Essays on Greek Love*. New York: Routledge, pp. 15–40.

Kamen, D. (2012) "Naturalized desires and the metamorphosis of Iphis", *Helios* 39: 21–36.

Kamen, D. and Levin-Richardson, S. (forthcoming) "Lusty ladies in the Roman imaginary", in R. Blondell and K. Ormand (eds) *New Essays in Ancient Sexuality*. Columbus, OH: Ohio State University Press.

Krenkel, W. (1980) "Fellatio and irrumatio", *Wissenschaftliche Zeitschrift der Wilhelm-Pieck-Universität Rostock* 29: 77–88.

Langlands, R. (2006) *Sexual Morality in Ancient Rome*. Cambridge: Cambridge University Press.

Levin-Richardson, S. (2013) "*fututa sum hic*: Female subjectivity and agency in Pompeian sexual graffiti", *Classical Journal* 108: 319–45.

Mussehl, J. (1919) "Bedeutung und geschichte des Verbums *cēvēre*", *Hermes* 54: 387–408.

Ormand, K. (2008) *Controlling Desires: Sexuality in Ancient Greece and Rome*. Westport, CT: Praeger.

Parker, H.N. (1997) "The teratogenic grid", in J.P. Hallett and M.B. Skinner (eds) *Roman Sexualities*. Princeton, NJ: Princeton University Press, pp. 47–65.

Richlin, A. (1981) "The meaning of *irrumare* in Catullus and Martial", *Classical Philology* 76: 40–6.

——(1992 [1983]) *The Garden of Priapus: Sexuality and Aggression in Roman Humor*, rev. edn. New York: Oxford University Press.

——(1993) "Not before homosexuality: The materiality of the *cinaedus* and the Roman law against love between men", *Journal of the History of Sexuality* 3: 523–73.

Schad, S. (2007) *A Lexicon of Latin Grammatical Terminology*. Pisa: F. Serra.

Schmeling, G. with Setaioli, A. (2011) *A Commentary on the Satyrica of Petronius*. Oxford: Oxford University Press.

Stylow, A.U. and Ventura Villanueva, Á. (2009) "Los hallazgos epigráficos", in R. Ayerbe Vélez, T. Barrientos Vera, and F. Palma García (eds) *El foro de Augusta Emerita*. Mérida: Instituto de Arqueología de Mérida, pp. 453–523.

Taylor, R. (1997) "Two pathic subcultures in ancient Rome", *Journal of the History of Sexuality* 7: 319–71.

Thüry, G.E. (2008) "Die erotischen Inschriften des instrumentum domesticum: Ein Überblick", in M. Hainzmann and R. Wedenig (eds) *Instrumenta inscripta latina 2*. Klagenfurt: Verlag des Geschichtsvereines für Kärnten, pp. 295–304.

Varone, A. (2002 [1994]) *Erotica Pompeiana: Love Inscriptions on the Walls of Pompeii*, trans. R.P. Berg. Rome: "L'Erma" di Bretschneider.

Walters, J. (1997) "Invading the Roman body: Manliness and impenetrability in Roman thought", in J.P. Hallett and M.B. Skinner (eds) *Roman Sexualities*. Princeton, NJ: Princeton University Press, pp. 29–43.

Williams, C.A. (2004) *Martial: Epigrams: Book Two*. Oxford: Oxford University Press.

——(2010 [1999]) *Roman Homosexuality*, rev. edn. New York: Oxford University Press.

Winkler, J.J. (1990) *The Constraints of Desire: The Anthropology of Sex and Gender in Ancient Greece*. New York: Routledge.

Younger, J.G. (2005) *Sex in the Ancient World from A to Z*. London: Routledge.

26

THE LANGUAGE OF GENDER

Lexical semantics and the Latin vocabulary of unmanly men

Craig Williams

Interpretations of the sex–gender systems of ancient Greece and Rome cannot, in the nature of things, be based on the "thick descriptions" familiar from cultural anthropology, derived as they are from observations of living individuals and groups and the complex interplay of their behaviors and utterances. We have but a thin network of material surviving from Greek and Roman antiquity on the basis of which to construct our interpretive models: physical remains on the one hand, texts on the other. We are arguably *readers* of both kinds of material, and those of us who were trained as readers of Greek and Latin texts certainly should and do pay a great deal of attention to words, singly and in combination.

It would thus seem a natural thing to use the tools developed by linguists working in the field of lexical semantics when we make assertions about what certain Greek or Latin words "mean"; but surprisingly few classicists have done so (and my own previous work is no exception). In this paper I aim to show, in an introductory and heuristic way, how some of the conceptual and terminological tools developed by linguists can add further precision, accuracy, and nuance in our interpretations of ancient Greek and Roman sex–gender systems as they are expressed in and through language. I focus here on some items from the Latin vocabulary of masculinity, but of course the methods and tools of lexical semantics can just as fruitfully be applied to the vocabulary of femininity, and to Greek or indeed to any other language. As a way into the Latin language of masculinity, I have chosen to concentrate on the vocabulary of unmanliness, on the conviction that exploration of deviations from a cultural or linguistic norm, of the marked as opposed to the unmarked, can give us especially clear insights into how systems of meaning work.

Further precision and accuracy regarding this vocabulary is clearly still needed. Glosses of *mollis*, *impudicus*, *pathicus*, and *cinaedus* in scholarly writings and translations continue to range, widely but seemingly interchangeably, from "effeminate" to "queer" and "queen," from "fairy" to "faggot," from "pansy" to "bugger," from the quasi-clinical "passive homosexual" to the exotic "pathic."[1] Yet the tools used by generations of classical philologists point to some significant distinctions among those Latin words. Attention to etymology shows us, for example, that *mollitia* ("softness," built on the same Indo-European root as *mulier*, "woman") fundamentally has to do with womanliness, femininity, and effeminacy broadly conceived, and not with any one sexual practice in particular; that *impudicus* signals the negation of ideals of sexual

461

decency or *pudicitia* (and if we supplement etymology with a survey of usage, we see that there is a gendered distinction between the feminine *impudica*, which typically suggests that a woman has had sex with someone other than her husband, and the masculine *impudicus*, which typically suggests that a man has been sexually penetrated); that *pathicus* evokes the receptive role in penetrative sexual acts (Greek *paskhein*, Latin *patior*); that *cinaedus* (a Greek loan word, probably in turn borrowed from a non-Indo-European language of Asia Minor but in some ancient etymologies connected with the Greek phrases *kinein to sōma* or *kineisthai ta aidoia*, "to move the body" or "to stimulate the genitals") evokes the suggestively gyrating movements of male dancers, thus anchoring effeminacy in the body and in particular the hips and buttocks.[2]

So far, so good; but there is clearly more to be said, and lexical semantics can help us say more. In what follows I do not attempt to offer a comprehensive or systematic overview of so complex and debatable a field, but instead offer a representative sampling of concepts and terminology which seem particularly relevant to the Latin vocabulary of masculinity, suggesting how they can help us reformulate or refine some of the questions we have been asking for the past few decades. I organize my discussion around three basic questions which semanticists explore: (1) how to describe the meanings of words using other words (*semantic representation in metalanguage*); (2) how to describe the semantic relations between different words (*sense relations*); (3) how to describe relationships among various senses of a single word (*polysemy*) in ways that complement traditional lexicography.

General issues

Lexical semantics can be defined as the study of meaning of individual words (as opposed to meaning at the level of sentence or utterance, social meaning, and so on) in natural languages (as opposed to artificial or computer languages).[3] The big questions – such as those concerning the relationships between words and concepts, language and experience, words and culture – have been debated for centuries, in some cases millennia, and continue to be debated to this day. On nearly every point having to do with semantics, both major and minor, linguists have disagreed; and nearly every example cited in studies of semantics is up for debate among native speakers. Indeed, linguists are the first to emphasize that discussion of semantics will always be ongoing, not only because disagreement is possible on nearly any example or any model proposed, but also because of the larger and deeper point that word meanings and distinctions between them are marked by a high degree of indeterminacy or "fuzziness."[4]

At the outset we must also acknowledge the qualifications on what we can know about the lexical semantics of ancient languages such as Greek and Latin. Many assertions about semantics (for example, which usages are normal, acceptable, questionable, or simply impossible) are based on native speakers' intuitions as tested in surveys, or on linguists' own reflections on their native language. In the cases of languages which have no more native speakers, we must rely on a tiny and hardly random sampling of material in the form of those literary texts which have survived, along with inscriptions and – an especially small sample – graffiti. In other words, we have no unmediated access to the primary speech genres of direct, interpersonal, verbal communication and only partial access to the secondary or written speech genres in these languages.[5] Still, Greek and Latin were natural languages and we have every reason to expect that their semantics, like their morphology and phonology, will follow the basic patterns found in most or all other natural languages. So the experiment is worth trying, as long as we remain conscious of the limitations confronting us, and cautious about making assertions regarding the "normal" or "acceptable" or "standard" senses of a given word, or about what might be "questionable" or "impossible" Latin.

Although linguists have adopted no single comprehensive system of terminology, they have widely adopted the distinction between *word* and *lexeme*. The former may seem a commonsense notion, but in fact there have been long and inconclusive debates about how precisely to define what constitutes a word and what does not. (We cannot, for example, rely on the conventions of writing, since the majority of natural languages in human history never adopted a writing system, and even among those which have done so, there is a great deal of variety on the point of how, or whether, to visually mark boundaries between units in an utterance.) And so the term *lexeme* is commonly used to refer to "a unit of the lexicon" or a "vocabulary-unit of a language"; lexemes are "abstractions of actual words that occur in real language use" or "groupings of one or more word-forms that are individuated by their roots and/or derivational affixes."[6] *Love, loved, loving* are three different word-forms but one and the same lexeme; *bat* ("flying animal") and *bat* ("instrument for hitting a ball") are the same word-form but two different lexemes. For some linguists, moreover, an idiomatic phrase with unpredictable meaning (such as *to give up*) consists of two or more words but constitutes a single lexeme; and while probably no one would identify bound morphemes such as *un-* or *-ism* as words, for some linguists they count as lexemes.

If there is one thing that all semanticists agree on, it is a lively skepticism regarding any simple statements about what a given word "means." Introductory books on semantics written in English regularly begin with a demonstration of the multiple meanings of the verb *to mean* and the noun *meaning*, culminating with the implicit or explicit recommendation to carefully circumscribe their use in any systematic analysis. Beyond this, however, there is no universally accepted system for describing the different ways in which a lexeme can be said to have "meaning." But a tripartite scheme is common. *Denotation* is the class of entities of which a proposition using a given lexeme is or is not true, and thus has to do with the lexeme's relationship to extralinguistic categories (e.g., *dog* as an animal possessing various characteristics which distinguish it from cats, pigs, or birds). A lexeme's *sense* is one specific way in which it is used, as opposed to other ways, and is thus fundamentally a matter of the relationship between and among lexemes (e.g., *dog* as opposed to *hound*). And a lexeme's *reference* is the specific entity at stake in a particular utterance (e.g. *this* dog as opposed to the class of dogs in general).

The fact that I am writing about one language in another brings me to an issue of particular importance. As John Lyons writes, "words cannot be defined independently of other words that are (semantically) related to them and delimit their sense" and "looked at from a semantic point of view, the lexical structure of a language – the structure of its vocabulary – can be regarded as a network of sense relations."[7] The lexical structure of a given natural language thus consists of a network of sense relations which by definition *cannot be the same* as that in any other natural language. Exploration of the range of theoretical and practical issues which flow from this insight lies at the heart of the thriving field of translation studies. Along with lexical semantics and linguistics in general, classicists have much to learn from translation studies, but also – since we are not native speakers of the languages we study and thus have the benefit of an analytic distance – not a little to offer.[8]

Semantic representations in metalanguage

A major preoccupation of lexical semantics has been the question of how to represent the senses of a given lexeme of a given natural language by using other lexemes of the same or another natural language. While some have argued that senses have no constituent parts, more influential over the past decades have been approaches such as *lexical decomposition* or *componential analysis*, which assume that senses can indeed be broken down into building blocks or units, sometimes called "universal sense-components" and generally represented in upper case. Linguists taking such approaches not infrequently speak the language of logic, for example seeking to identify those components which are "necessary and sufficient conditions" for a given sense.[9]

A system of analysis using binary components with the logical operators (+) or (-) is usually introduced early in textbooks on semantics. Latin *vir* could be represented as [+HUMAN] [+ADULT] [+MALE] and *femina* as [+HUMAN] [+ADULT] [-MALE], while *pathicus* might be [+HUMAN] [+MALE] [-SEXUALLY PENETRATING]. Clearly, however, so simple a scheme will work only for a small number of lexemes, and it quickly runs up against difficult, perhaps intractable, questions. How, for example, should we identify the components? Should they really be binary, and if so, which option should be the default, and why? The question of which option should be the default takes on particular urgency in the case of lexemes having to do with sex and gender. As one linguist puts it:

> The question is of considerable theoretical interest if we are seriously concerned with establishing an inventory of universal sense-components. It is in principle conceivable that there is no universally valid answer. What is fairly clear, however, is that, as far as the vocabulary of English is concerned, it is normally MALE that one wants to treat as being more general and thus, in one sense, more basic. Feminists might argue, and perhaps rightly, that this fact is culturally explicable.[10]

With all its qualifications ("in principle conceivable"; "fairly clear"; "as far as"; "normally"; "one wants"; "in one sense"; "might argue"; "perhaps rightly") this formulation is a semanticist's version of a complex set of questions which lie at the very heart of gender studies. As it happens, another linguist has argued that if binary notation is to be used, it is actually FEMALE that should be the default − but precisely because it is the "marked" term, whereas MALE is "unmarked." His arguments are carefully limited to the linguistic: "In a great many cases, the word from a related pair referring to a female is formed from the word referring to the corresponding male by the addition of a morphological mark in the form of an affix" (e.g. *prince/princess, lion/lioness*), whereas "cases where the word referring to a male is derived from the word referring to a female are extremely rare in English" (e.g. *widow/widower*); and "in general only the term referring to males can also have a generic use" (e.g. *actors, dogs, mankind*; cases such as *ducks* and *cows* are in the minority).[11] Of course there is much more at stake here, but even if we keep our focus on strictly linguistic issues, some pressing questions suggest themselves. *Why* is this linguistic pattern so common in English? What about other languages? And what about those exceptions within English?

I have dwelt on these examples not because componential analysis using binary features is still accepted among semanticists as a universally valid tool − it is not − but rather to illustrate how posing questions of lexical semantics can help us sharpen or reformulate the questions about gender that we classicists have been posing of the Greek and Latin textual tradition for decades. In fact, binary componential analyses of this type are generally introduced in textbooks on semantics only as a heuristic first step in the direction of other systems for semantic representation in metalanguage. One of these relies on hierarchically ordered sets of *meaning postulates*. These are representations in metalanguage of what a lexeme necessarily implies or "entails," a relationship represented by the symbol $\rightarrow$ (thus $p \rightarrow q$ signifies that p entails q, which is to say that "the truth of q necessarily follows from the truth of p, and the falsity of q necessarily follows from the falsity of p").[12] Such postulates are listed in a hierarchical order, beginning with those which seem indispensable to the sense of the lexeme in all "possible worlds," and sequentially proceeding to those which might more and more probably be dispensed with in some possible worlds. John Lyons gives the following example of hierarchically ranked meaning postulates for the lexeme *bachelor*:

bachelor → "unmarried"
bachelor → "adult"

"and," he adds, "perhaps also" this third:

bachelor → "man"

To call a person a *bachelor* logically entails, first, that he is unmarried; second, that he is an adult; third, that he is male. In no possible world could a person who is married be called a *bachelor* "without some other associated change in the sense of either *bachelor* or *unmarried*"; but in one possible world, Lyons suggests, children could get married and thus the lexeme *bachelor* would not entail "adult."[13] Precisely this example illustrates how open so much of this is to debate, for it could just as well be argued that maleness is more fundamental to the lexeme *bachelor* than is adulthood – or not.[14]

In all their debatability, some hierarchically ordered meaning postulates for some relevant Latin lexemes might look like this:

mollis → "soft, tender"
mollis → "womanish, effeminate"
mollis → "like a woman in character: weak, uncontrolled, self-indulgent, luxurious"
mollis → "like a woman sexually: self-indulgent, uncontrolled, addicted to pleasures"
mollis → "like a woman sexually: enjoys being penetrated"

impudicus → "male"
impudicus → "indecent"
impudicus → "sexually indecent"
impudicus → "sexually penetrated"

pathicus → "male"
pathicus → "sexually penetrated"
pathicus → "enjoys being sexually penetrated"

The experiment of creating and arranging such postulates sharpens our focus on some key questions. In the case of *impudicus*, for example, this experiment highlights the priority of the sense "sexually indecent" over the sense "sexually penetrated," and draws attention to the absence of a postulate "enjoys being penetrated," in a noticeable and probably significant contrast with *pathicus*. For it is worth considering the possibility that, while to call a man *impudicus* typically implies that he has been penetrated, to call him *pathicus* is to underscore the pleasure he takes in that sexual role.[15]

The exercise of formulating meaning postulates also raises a issue fundamental to languages which, like Latin, inflect adjectives for gender: how does grammatical gender relate to biological sex on the one hand and semantics on the other, and how should these relationships be represented in metalanguage?[16] One might argue, for example, that since Latin morphologically distinguishes masculine from feminine gender in first- and second-declension adjectives, the first meaning postulate listed above for *impudicus* and *pathicus* ("male") should be omitted, and that we should instead create a semantic representation for the ungendered stem forms *impudic-* and *pathic-*. On the other hand, I have argued elsewhere that feminine *impudica* and *pathica* are different from masculine *impudicus* and *pathicus* not merely on the point of male or female sex. Women's *impudicitia* generally consists in having sexual relations with someone other than one's husband, and the adjective *impudica* particularly suggests adulteresses on the one hand, prostitutes on the other, while men's *impudicitia* generally consists in being sexually penetrated.[17] And whereas masculine *pathicus* suggests male pleasure in being anally penetrated, feminine *pathica* is not limited to that specific mode of penetration, but suggests an exuberant desire on the part of a receptive partner which is potentially stimulating to his or her penetrative partners.[18] In short, it seems preferable to set up separate hierarchical meaning postulates for the feminine adjectives, such as these:

> *impudica* → "female"
> *impudica* → "sexually indecent"
> *impudica* → "has sex with partners other than her husband"
> *impudica* → "adulteress"
> *impudica* → "prostitute"
>
> *pathica* → "female"
> *pathica* → "sexually penetrated"
> *pathica* → "enjoys being sexually penetrated"
> *pathica* → "stimulating to partners"

Another recent approach to semantic representation abandons the search for "necessary and sufficient conditions" in favor of "typical and atypical features" of a given lexeme, and identifies *preferential features (P-features)* which in any particular instance may be overridden.[19] The lexeme *bird* comes with the P-feature *can fly*, and this is automatically true of all lexemes referring to all kinds of birds. But the lexeme *ostrich* overrides this P-feature, having *cannot fly* as its own P-feature without thereby altering the semantics of the lexeme *bird* (and if one specific ostrich were able to fly, this "token" would override the P-feature of its "type" *ostrich* without contradicting or changing the semantics of the type). With regard to the Latin vocabulary of masculinity, I might reformulate what I have argued elsewhere as follows: a P-feature of *vir* is *sexually penetrates others* and a P-feature of *cinaedus* is *enjoys being sexually penetrated*, but neither *impudicus* nor *mollis* has either of these as a P-feature: the former because it has no preferential feature which concerns the issue of enjoyment, the latter because it has no preferential feature which concerns the issue of penetrative role.

Sense relations

Another major question posed by lexical semantics is how to describe with precision and accuracy the relationships *between* lexemes, or more specifically between certain senses of different lexemes: for example between *hot* in the sense "having a high temperature" (and not the sense "heavily spiced") and *cold* in the sense "having a low temperature." Here, too, there is much debate and no universally adopted set of terminology, but one distinction is common. If the lexemes in question belong to different classes or parts of speech and thus can form syntactic units, many linguists speak of *syntagmatic* sense relations (such as those between the relevant senses of the adjective *hot* and of nouns like *day*, *sauce*, or *head*). If the lexemes belong to the same word-class or part of speech and can, without violating syntactic rules, be substituted for each other within an utterance, linguists speak of *paradigmatic* sense relations (such as those among the relevant senses of the adjectives *hot, warm, cold, sunny, cloudy*, all of which may modify the noun *day*).

In the sphere of syntagmatic semantic relations, if two or more lexemes belonging to different classes or parts of speech attract each other, they can be called *philonyms* (*merry* and *Christmas*), whereas if the combination results in a semantic clash, they can be called *xenonyms* (*merry* and *Easter*).[20] Using this terminology, we might say that *femina, mulier*, and *puer* are all philonyms of *mollis*, and that *vir* is a xenonym of *mollis*. Adding the terminology of antonymy and synonymy (to which we will turn in the next paragraph), we might say that *mollis* is an antonym not only of the obvious *durus* but also of the somewhat less obvious *fortis*, which is itself a philonym of *vir*.[21] This is to reformulate in terms of lexical semantics one of the basic features of the sex–gender system informing the Latin textual tradition: that it is *women and boys* (rather than women and men, or females and males) who are normative objects of male desire, and that women and boys are contrasted with fully masculine men – and perhaps therefore desirable – because of their qualities of "softness" and "weakness," which themselves stand in strong contrast with Roman masculinity. The experiment of describing the semantics in this way makes the binarisms underlying the system, in all their rigidity, that much clearer, just as it reminds us that not all of the scenarios of desire which we find in the surviving textual tradition (not to mention the endless variety and messiness which must have characterized lived experience then as now) always fit these or other binary schemes.[22]

As for paradigmatic semantic relations: if we are dealing with closeness, nearness, or similarity, we are in the realm of *synonymy*, while opposition, contrast, or exclusion take us to the realm of *antonymy*.[23] These are widely familiar terms in their non-technical senses, but the work done by linguists allows us to reformulate or refine what we might say about larger questions of gender in the Latin textual tradition as they are played out in language. In the area of antonym relations, some linguists distinguish between *complementary* or *contrastive antonyms*, which seem to leave no room for middle ground (*even* and *odd, dead* and *alive, to stay* and *to go*), and *contrary antonyms* (such as *short* and *tall, old* and *young, to love* and *to hate*) where there is clearly a middle ground and the lexemes have a scalar or gradable quality. Yet it has been observed that even such seemingly clearcut cases of complementarity as *dead* and *alive* can take on gradable qualities ("He's more dead than alive"). The argument that all complementary antonym pairs are potentially gradable obviously has ramifications that go far beyond the narrowly linguistic. In Latin, literary and cultural study of the representation of eunuchs, hermaphrodites, and intersexed persons invites being supplemented by, for example, semantic inquiry into the lexemes *semivir* and *semimas* and their implications for the workings of the antonymy *vir/mas* vs *femina/mulier*.[24]

As for synonym relations, semanticists are in general agreement that very few words in natural languages are *absolute synonyms*, i.e. totally substitutable in denotation, connotation, and social meaning as well as in their syntagmatic relations; much more common are *near-synonyms*.[25] Lexical semantics teaches us, then, to be skeptical of translations or scholarly arguments which imply or explicitly claim that *impudicus, mollis, pathicus*, and *cinaedus* are synonymous with each other and leave it at that. Yet how we might more precisely describe the relations between these lexemes and their various senses remains an open question. Such lexemes do not, for example, seem amenable to representation as branching hierarchies of taxonomic or meronymic types (taxonomy: *cutlery* is categorized into *fork, knife, spoon*, and *spoon* in turn is divided into *teaspoon, tablespoon, soup spoon*; meronymy: *arm* is divided into its parts *shoulder, elbow, wrist, hand*, and this last into *palm, fingers, knuckles*, etc.). Another possibility considered by David Cruse is the concept of *lexical cluster*, informal groupings of near-synonyms in which the structuring is not as clearly articulated as in taxonomic or meronymic hierarchies. Cruse distinguishes between "centered clusters," which have a "more or less clear core" of one or two lexemes (the cluster *walk, amble, stroll, stride, saunter* has *walk* as its core; the cluster *brave, courageous, intrepid, gallant, fearless, valorous, heroic, plucky*, etc. could be said to have a two-member core consisting of *brave* and *courageous*) and "non-centered clusters" in which the lexemes are "spread over a spectrum of sense, but there is no superordinate item."[26] The concept of lexical cluster suggests itself in the case of the lexemes *impudicus, mollis, pathicus*, and *cinaedus*, as well as the colorful compounds *scultimidonus* and *intercutitus*, and no doubt other lexemes now lost to us.[27] But it is not immediately clear whether this is a non-centered cluster or one with a center, and if the latter, which lexemes are at the core. On Cruse's criteria, the most likely candidate for core element seems to be *mollis* in the sense "enjoys being penetrated" (sense 9 below), yet in the absence of native speakers, such questions must remain unanswered.

Various techniques for graphically representing paradigmatic sense relations have been developed. Especially common are box diagrams of a given semantic field carved into distinct semantic spaces, each of which is occupied by various lexemes (e.g. the field COOK and the lexemes *bake, boil, roast, simmer*, and so on).[28] Such diagrams will hardly work for all lexemes and all semantic fields, but when they are appropriate their advantages are clear. They concisely illustrate the range of lexical possibilities within a given semantic field; they distinguish between and show the hierarchical relationship between more general and more restricted sense of the same lexeme (e.g. *drink* "take in liquids by the mouth" and *drink* "take in alcoholic liquids by the mouth"); and they make clear any gaps in the semantic field, i.e. spaces which are not occupied by any single lexeme or set of lexemes. See Figure 26.1 for a first attempt at a box diagram of Latin lexemes of varying registers (some but not all of them obscene) occupying a semantic field we might identify as MALE SEXUAL AGENT.[29]

A few important points emerge from this attempt. First there are the gaps, visual reminders that a given language's lexemes very rarely, perhaps never, occupy all possible spaces within a given semantic field. In the case at hand, one gap reminds us that not all possible spaces within the subfield "man who penetrates" are occupied by lexemes: there is, for example, no Latin lexeme with a sense "man who sexually penetrates effeminate males." As far as we can tell,

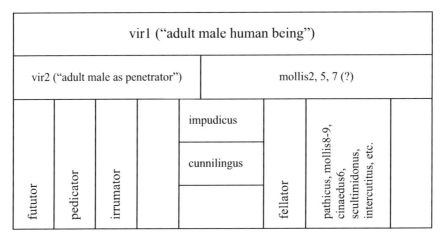

Figure 26.1 The semantic field male sexual agent.

Latin obscenities casting men in the penetrating role all have to do with the mode of penetration – vaginal, anal, or oral – and not with the sex of their partners; there are no attested Latin obscenities denoting "woman-fucker" or "*cinaedus*-fucker." Then there is the important point that some senses of the lexemes *impudicus, mollis, cunnilingus* straddle the divide between "penetrating" and "being penetrated." *Impudicus* can refer to a pimp, for example, without entailing that he has been sexually penetrated, and a man may be called *mollis* without any entailment with regard to penetrative role. The case of *cunnilingus* is particularly interesting. On the one hand a man who orally pleasures women can be represented as less than fully manly, worse even than a *fellator*. On the other hand there is an obscene epigram of Martial's, as so often joking but precisely in its jokiness revealing certain habits of thought. Pondering the case of a castrated priest of Cybele who enjoys performing cunnilinctus, the epigram culminates with the remark that by undergoing castration, this man has sacrificed his manhood, and yet: "You are a man with your mouth." The poem's point lies precisely in paradox, and the paradox rests on an assumption that a man who performs cunnilinctus can at least potentially be represented as playing the "man's" sexual role of vaginal penetration.[30]

Polysemy

In some cases, various senses of a single word-form are so different from each other that speakers of the language generally perceive them to be distinct words, sometimes in line with etymological origins, sometimes not: examples in English include *bat* ("flying animal") and *bat* ("instrument for hitting a ball"), *sole* ("bottom of foot or shoe"), *sole* ("type of fish"), and *sole* ("alone, only"). This phenomenon is called *homonymy*, and a common convention is to distinguish among lexemes by means of subscript numerals: bat_1 and bat_2 or $sole_1$, $sole_2$, $sole_3$. In other cases, however, speakers generally perceive the existence of a single lexeme with different senses, and this is what most linguists identify as *polysemy*: examples in English are the different senses of *drink* in the sentences "Dogs drink frequently" and "He only drinks at parties" or of *book* in the sentences "Hand me that book" and "That book is controversial." The different senses of a lexeme are sometimes marked with letters – *drink* (a) and *drink* (b) – and sometimes, especially in box diagrams, with subscript numerals. In what follows, I indicate different senses of a single lexeme with in-line numerals – *moll*-(1) and *moll*-(2) – in order to underscore the distinction from homonymous lexemes.[31] Polysemy is rarely experienced as an obstacle in everyday communication, especially between native speakers of a language, who continuously perceive and send out cues for the selection or exclusion of specific senses, or else engage in puns and other kinds of word-play.[32] But the theoretical issues continue to draw attention in the field of lexical semantics, and for those of us who seek to interpret the sex–gender systems of an ancient culture through its words, a review of the work that linguists have done in this field can only help.[33]

A crucial point on which there is widespread agreement is that identification of the different senses of a polysemous lexeme and the criteria for delimiting them are inescapably subjective processes, always open to debate: a point which urges all the more caution on us as we attempt to describe the semantics of a language which has no native speakers.[34] Some of the terms used to describe the semantic processes which result in polysemy are familiar enough to classicists, for example *metaphor, metonymy, synecdoche, narrowing,* and *broadening*.[35] Perhaps less familiar to classicists but potentially helpful is the distinction between *vagueness* (the lack of specificity of a given sense with regard to one or more criteria) and *ambiguity* (multiple senses, i.e. polysemy proper). Various tests have been developed for establishing whether vagueness or ambiguity exists in the case of a given lexeme, and while there have been challenges to the validity of some or all of these tests, many continue to find value in the usefulness of the distinction. An important point, moreover, is that "since vagueness, polysemy and homonymy apply at different levels of consideration (single sense, single lexeme, different lexemes), it is sometimes the case that a single word-form can illustrate all of these phenomena."[36] Thus we could say that the lexeme *moll-* is ambiguous, its senses ranging from "soft" to "cowardly" to "enjoying being penetrated," and that some of these senses in turn are vague. For example: is a man who is called *mollis* in the sense "enjoys being penetrated" necessarily associated with exclusively male sexual partners? Elsewhere I have argued that such a man might be imagined as enjoying being penetrated by female partners; to rephrase my argument as a matter of semantics, the relevant sense of the polysemous lexeme *moll-* is vague on the point of the sex of the man's partner.[37]

How might we represent on a page or computer screen the senses of a polysemous lexeme and the relationships among them? Classicists are fortunate to be able to draw on a rich lexicographical tradition which has produced detailed lists of senses, structured with varying degrees of complexity and illustrated by relevant quotations from ancient texts. The articles of the *TLL* catalogue usage in dazzling, sometimes dizzying detail, and their meticulously articulated structure allows readers with sufficient Latin to perceive some important distinctions: when, for example, the adjective *mollis* refers to human beings as opposed to animals, things, qualities, or actions; whether it is being used in its "proper" or "transferred" sense (*proprie* or *translate*); whether the sense has a positive or negative value (*in bonam partem* or *in malam* [sometimes *deteriorem*] *partem*). And there are frequent indications of other Latin adjectives with which *mollis* has a relation of similarity or synonymy (*i.q.*) or contrast (*opp.*). See Figure 26.2 for the structure of the *TLL* article on the adjective *mollis*.

But precisely because of their mass of detail, intricate outline structure, and exclusive use of a spare Latin, *TLL* articles – particularly such long and complex articles as that for *mollis* – do not make it easy for their readers to perceive recurring themes or internal connections among the senses of a given word, or between a given word and others, whether forms of the same lexeme (*mollio, mollis, mollitia, mollitudo*) or of others (*mollis, puer, cinaedus*). Even on its own terms, the terminological apparatus of the *TLL* raises without answering some basic questions of semantics. Are we to take *i.q.* literally, "the same as"? Surely not; but more precise distinctions of synonymy or near-synonymy are left unmade. Where is the line drawn between *i.q.* and *fere i.q.* and why? And while the distinction between *in bonam* and *in malam partem* is of obvious utility, its either/or quality necessarily flattens out cases of ambiguity or questions of degree, and raises without being able to answer the question of *why*, and with reference to which cultural norms, certain senses are "good" or "bad."

The more compact and user-friendly articles of the *OLD*, for their part, allow readers quickly to perceive basic features of a word's semantics. See Figure 26.3 for the structure of the *OLD* article on the adjective *mollis*. But *OLD* articles share with those of *TLL* a tendency to make such a large number of distinctions (in this case, on the basis of the kinds of things, qualities, or persons of whom the given word is predicated) that one finds a small number of English glosses (e.g. "soft" or "gentle") scattered throughout the article, raising the question of whether the various subentries indeed correspond to what semanticists would describe as different *senses* of the lexeme. Indeed, by their very nature, dictionary entries may too easily give a false impression of straightforwardly linear and chronological processes (*from* sense 1 *to* sense 2 *to* sense 3, etc.) and they certainly obscure the relationships *between* senses.

As a complement to dictionary entries, linguists have thus experimented with drawing *polysemy networks* as a means of visually representing the relationships among a lexeme's

I.   **proprie** pertinet ad corpora non dura neque rigida

    A. strictius, i.q. tactui cedens, non durus
        1. generatim
            a. de rebus naturalibus
                i. de rebus aeriis
                ii. de terra, solo, agro sim.
                iii. de herbis, plantis, arboribus, lignis sim.
                      1. de ipsis plantis
                      2. de partibus plantarum (fere i.q. offensionibus obnoxius)
                          a. de fructibus
                          b. de aliis partibus
                iv. de materia corporum
                v. de cera, metallis, lapidibus sim. (interdum agitur de rebus, quae e duris tractando molliuntur)
                vi. de umoribus tangenti, natanti cedentibus
                vii. de harena, pulvere sim.
                viii. de materiis accuratius non definitis
            b. de rebus ad usum animantium paratis sive natura mollibus sive mollioribus tractando factis
                i. de cibis
                ii. de vestimentis, vittis sim.
                iii. de lectis, feretris sim., quae impositis culcitis al. molliora fiunt
                iv. de aliis rebus
            c. de animantibus
                i. de ipsis corporibus, i.q. ossibus minus duris praeditus, tener
                      1. hominum (fere mulierum vel puerorum)
                      2. animalium
                ii. de carnosis partibus
                iii. de osseis partibus
                iv. de lana, capillis sim.
                v. de excrementis

        2. i.q. languidus
            a. de corporibus animantium (in re veneria i.q. impotens coeundi)
            b. de partibus corporum
            c. de armis

    B. latius, i.q. flexibilis, mobilis

        1. de membris
        2. de motibus corporis
        3. de plantis (opp. lentus)
        4. de rebus arte tractatis (in imag. de verbis tamquam rebus corporeis; audacius de operibus arte fingendis – opp. rigidus)

II.   **translate** pertinet ad ingenia, mores, actiones animantium ac statum rerum

    A. de animantibus rebusque ad homines pertinentibus
        1. in bonam partem i.q. mitis, placidus, lenis, obsequens, gratus, tolerabilis, mediocris, blandus
            a. de rebus ad homines (deos, bestias) pertinentibus
                1. de actionibus hominum (deorum)

2. de eventis, condicionibus vitae sim., i.q. iucundus, amoenus, facilis
   a. generaliter
   b. de eventis iniquis, i.q. tolerabilis, minus durus
3. de animis, vultibus, affectibus
4. de dictis, sententiis, mandatis sim.
   a. generatim
   b. potius i.q. blandus, tener
5. de carminibus
   a. generatim
   b. de poesi elegiaca
6. de genere dicendi vel compositionis, pertinet at stilum remissum, tenuem, nihil duri asperique habentem; transfertur ad ipsum hominem; in carminibus
7. de numeris, rhythmis, sonis sim.
   a. generatim
   b. speciatim pertinet ad harmoniae doctrinam

b. de ipsis hominibus (de umbris mortuorum; de deis; adde de rebus quasi affectibus humanis praeditis, fere i.q. propitius)
c. de animalibus
   1. natura mitibus, pacificis
   2. domitis, mansuetis

2. in deteriorem vel etiam contemnendam partem, i.q. parum obduratus, effeminatus, dissolutus, iners (fere i.q. lascivus, i.q. nimis misericors)
   a. de hominibus
      1. de animis, mentibus, moribus sim.
      2. de actionibus rebusque humanis (animalium)
      3. de ipsis hominibus (dea)
         a. generatim; per enallagen; de re pro persona; de civitatibus, quarum incolae effeminatae sunt; de parte corporis, i.q. lascivus
         b. speciatim de pathicis, cinaedis sim.
            A. adi.
            B. subst.
   b. de animalibus
      1. i.q. iners, ignavus, timidus, imbellis
      2. i.q. delicatus, offensionum non patiens

B. de statu rerum naturalium
   1. pertinet ad temperiem
      a. de tempestate, umbra, caelo; de spatiis temporum; inde de ipsis regionibus miti caelo fruentibus
      b. de ventis placidis
   2. pertinet ad vim attenuatam, gradum delenitum
      a. de fluviis, undis sim.; sim. de pulsu
      b. de regionibus paulum declivibus rebusque leniter curvatis
      c. de medicamentis vi leni praeditis
      d. de igne leni
      e. de variis rebus i.q. modicus
   3. pertinet ad saporem sive odorem

Figure 26.2 Structure of the *TLL* article *mollis*.

1 Yielding to the touch; soft
       b soft (with cushions or sim. covering; also with grass)
       c (applied to food, usu. as a term of commendation)
       d (applied as a comparative term to things normally considered as hard)
       e (used to describe the class *cephalopoda*; cf. Gk μαλάκια)

2 (of the body or its parts) Lacking firmness, soft, flabby, flaccid

3 Soft, tender
       a (as typical of women; also of emasculated males)
       b (as typical of youth)
       c (of statues, as giving the illusion of real flesh)

4 Supple, flexible, loose, pliant
       a (of the body or its parts)
       b (of other things)

5 (of persons) Physically weak, feeble

6 (of terrain, roads, etc.) Providing easy going
       b (of slopes) gentle (also, of curves)

7 Easily borne, tolerable, mild
       b (of climate, weather) mild, soft, relaxing (also of places, regions)
       c (of tasks, journeys, etc.) easy to accomplish

8. Agreeably soft to the senses (other than touch), mild
       b (of speech, verse, rhet. style, etc.) free from harshness, smooth

9 (of actions) Gentle, soft
       b (of things) gently moving or acting

10 (of conditions, activities, etc.) Of a calm or peaceful nature, unwarlike
       b (of sleep, etc.)

11 Gentle, conciliatory, complaisant, kindly
       b (of words, actions, etc.)

12 Easily influenced, impressionable, susceptible, sensitive

13 Effeminate in character, weak, cowardly
       b (of actions, opinions, etc.) lacking firmness, weak

14 (of animals) Mild in nature, gentle

15 Effeminate in appearance or behaviour, womanish; (esp.) denoting a passive partner in male homosexual intercourse
       b (of things or actions) unmanly, womanish

16 (of movement) Languid, voluptuous
       b (of writings) amorous

Figure 26.3 Structure of *OLD²* article *mollis.*

senses – which, it is important to note, are not conceived in exactly the same way, or in the same quantity, as the subheadings of dictionary entries.[38] In one type of network, the senses are placed in boxes connected by lines and radiating out from a core sense; the thickness of the lines around each box signifies how logically close it is to the core sense; each box is given a mnemonic phrase inspired by an attested usage; and the processes leading from one box to another are sometimes described with such terms as "radial categories" and "experiential bases." In another type of network, a tree is drawn; the senses are numbered; and the lines connecting one sense with another are sometimes labeled with the type of semantic relationship at stake (for example *metonymic*, a relationship of conceptual association, as opposed to *taxonomic*, a relationship of part for whole or similar categorization).[39] See Figure 26.4 for tentative lists of the relevant senses of two polysemous lexemes which are key elements in the language of masculinity informing the Latin textual tradition (*cinaed-* and *moll-*, the latter restricted to senses referring to human beings), and Figures 26.5 and 26.6 for equally tentative partial polysemy networks for these two lexemes, constructed respectively as a network of linked boxes and as a tree.

As partial and tentative as they are, such networks can reveal important points and inspire constructive debate. Figure 26.5, for example, graphically demonstrates the semantic distance between senses 3 (type of fish and bird) and 6 (an effeminate man who enjoys being anally penetrated) of the lexeme *cinaed-*. Its use of broken lines to connect certain senses reminds us, moreover, that senses of a lexeme are not hermetically sealed off from each other and that sometimes there is an especially close association between certain senses. In the case of *cinaedus*, the core sense "dancer" is closely linked both with the image of suggestive movements of hips and buttocks and with origins in Asia Minor, and both of these senses in turn facilitate what I have elsewhere described as a "conceptual continuum" between the figure of the *cinaedus* in the sense "effeminate man who enjoys being anally penetrated" and the figure of the *gallus*, a eunuch priest of the goddess Cybele.[40]

The exercise of drawing such a network raises some interesting and difficult questions: where, for example, to locate the box representing the sense illustrated by Catullus' use of the *cinaed-* lexeme to refer to a woman called a "whore" (*scortillum*, Catull. 10.3), who shamelessly asks him for the loan of his eight-man litter (*illa, ut decuit cinaediorem, / 'quaeso' inquit …* , Catull. 10.24–5)? Is this sense (apparently "shameless, outrageous") closer to, or logically derived from, the sense "effeminate male who enjoys being anally penetrated" or the sense "effeminate dancer who suggestively wiggles his hips"? I have tentatively opted for the former, but have drawn a dotted line to suggest a relationship with the latter as well.

For its part, Figure 26.6 highlights the key metonymic process at the head of this part of the polysemy network for the lexeme *moll-*: that which leads from sense 1 "physically soft" to sense 2 "womanish" and thence to all other senses, a structural feature which highlights the point that all other senses in this partial network are implicitly coded as feminine. Some linguists might describe the metonymic movement from sense 1 to sense 2 as having an "experiential basis," but its prominent position in the polysemy network is no less revealing of cultural habits of thought: why is *this* physical feature associable with female bodies more prominent in the semantics of *moll-* rather than others? Next, the network allows us to observe that sense 3 "inactive, lazy" is fairly distant from the others, and we also see in the contiguity of the complementary senses 8 and 9 the key role of sexual penetration in the Latin semantics of gender: the feminine is here associated not, say, with the unique capacity to give birth, but with the sexual role of being penetrated. Finally, the exercise of drawing a polysemy network for *mollis* draws attention to a question with important implications: where to locate senses 6 and 7 ("sexually attractive to women" and "sexually attractive to men"), and indeed whether to separate the two out or else collapse them *cinaed-* **(1)** 'male dancer': Plaut. Mil. 668 (*ad saltandum non cinaedus malacus aequest atque ego*); Lucil. 32 Marx (*stulte saltatum te inter venisse cinaedos*); Plin. Epist. 9.17 (*scurrae, cinaedi, moriones mensis inerrabant*)

cinaed- **(2)** 'dancer who makes suggestive and stimulating movements': Stich. 760 (*celeriter / lepidem et suavem cantionem aliquam occipito cinaedicam / ubi perpruriscamus usque ex unguiculis*)

cinaed- **(3)** 'type of fish': Plin. NH 32.146, 37.153 [cf. the bird called *kinaidion* in Greek (Hesych. s.v.) also known as *seisopugis* 'butt-shaker' (Schol. to Theocr. 2.17)]

cinaed- **(4)** 'dancer from Asia Minor': Plaut. Stich. 769 (*qui Ionicus aut cinaedicust, qui hoc tale facere possiet?*)

cinaed- **(5)** 'a *gallus,* castrated priest of Mother Goddess': Suet. Aug. 68 (*versum in scaena pronuntiatum de gallo Matris Deum tympanizante: videsne ut cinaedus orbem digito temperat?*); Apul. Met. 8.26 (*chorus cinaedorum*)

cinaed- **(6)** 'effeminate man' [imagined playing various sexual roles or none in particular]: Plaut. Poen. 1318 (*te cinaedum esse arbitror magis quam virum*); Catull. 57 (*pulchre convenit improbis cinaedis / . . . non hic quam ille magis vorax adulter*); Phaedr. Fab. 5.1.15-16 (*"quisnam cinaedus ille in conspectum meum / audet venire?*); Gell. NA 3.5.2 (*nihil interest quibus membris cinaedi sitis, posterioribus an prioribus*)

cinaed- **(7)** 'man who enjoys being anally penetrated': Catull. 33 (*cinaede fili, culo voraciore, nates pilosas*); Mart. 6.37 (*culum non habet, est tamen cinaedus*)

cinaed- **(8)** 'shameless, outrageous' [of a woman called a "whore"]: Catull. 10.3, 24–5 *scortillum. . . / hic illa, ut decuit cinaediorem, / 'quaeso' inquit . . .*

moll- (1) 'physically soft': Cels. De medic. 2.1.13 *maximeque in mollioribus corporibus, ideoque praecipue in muliebribus*

moll- (2) 'womanish': Plin. N.H. 25.61.1 *vetant dari senibus, pueris, item mollis ac feminei corporis animive*

moll- (3) 'inactive, lazy': Hor. Epod. 14.1 *mollis inertia;* Ov. Met. 11.648 *molli languore*

moll- (4) 'self-indulgent, luxurious': Cic. Off. 1.106 *quam sit turpe diffluere luxuria et delicate et molliter vivere;* Cic. Fin. 1.37 *voluptaria, delicata, mollis . . . disciplina;* Sen. Epist. 84.1 [*voluptates*] *molliunt et enervant*

moll- (5) 'sexually self-indulgent, sensual': Hor. C. 2.9.17–19 (*desine mollium / tandem querellarum et potius nova / cantemus Augusti tropaea*); 4.1.4–7 (*desine, dulcium / mater saeva Cupidinum, / circa lustra decem flectere mollibus / iam durum imperiis*); Prop. 2.1.1–2 (*quaeritis unde mihi totiens scribantur amores, / unde meus veniat mollis in ora liber*)

moll- (6) 'sexually attractive to women': Sen. Contr. 2.1.6 *incedentem ut feminis placeat femina mollius;* Ov. Ars 1.595–6 *si vox est, canta; si mollia bracchia, salta, / et quacumque potes dote placere, place;* Juv. 6.63–4 *chironomon Ledan molli saltante Bathyllo / Tuccia vesicae non imperat, Apula gannit*

moll- (7) 'sexually attractive to men': Hor. Epod. 11.4 *mollibus in pueris aut in puellis urere*

moll- (8) 'unable to penetrate others; castrated; impotent': Hor. Epod. 12.15–16 (*Inachiam ter nocte potes, mihi semper ad unum / mollis opus*), Petr. Sat. 134.2 (*mollis, debilis, lassus tamquam caballus in clivo*), Lucan 10.133–4 (*infelix ferro mollita iuventus / atque exsecta virum*), Mart. 7.58.5 (*deseris imbelles thalamos mollemque maritum*)

moll- (9) 'enjoying being penetrated': Phaed. 4.16.1: *tribadas et molles mares* (cf. 14 *ita nunc libido pravo fruitur gaudio*); Juv. 9.38: *mollis avarus* (cf. 9.40 *computat et cevet,* 130 *numquam pathicus tibi derit amicus*)

Figure 26.4 Some senses of the polysemous lexemes *cinaed-* and *moll-*.

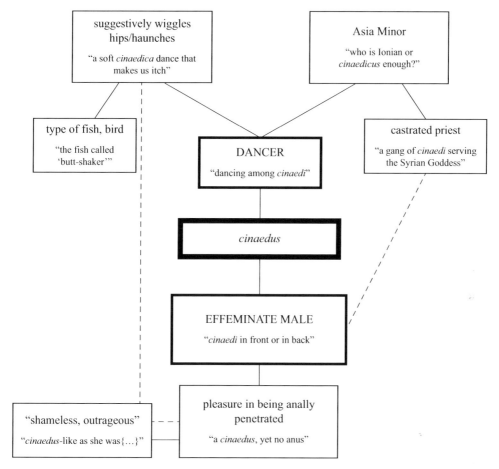

Figure 26.5 Polysemy network of *cinaedus*.

into a single sense "sexually attractive." In Figure 26.6 I have tentatively distinguished between the two and placed them underneath sense 5 ("sexually self-indulgent, sensual"), thereby highlighting the features of sense 5 as the source of attraction.

But one conceivable alternative would be to place them underneath sense 2, parallel to senses 3, 4, 8, and 9, thereby highlighting the feature of "womanish softness" as source of attraction – to both men and women. The positioning of sense 2 in this network reminds us that the language of softness as embodied in the lexeme *moll-* when applied to human beings is always already gendered as feminine. But this alternative configuration would more prominently highlight the homoerotic configuration of one kind of feminine desire we find in the Latin textual tradition: women are represented as potentially finding effeminate men attractive. The degree to which we foreground this point in our attempt to create a polysemy network for the *moll-* lexeme has obvious implications for our broader understanding of the sex–gender system informing the Latin textual tradition. And the very exercise of drawing, questioning, and redrawing polysemy networks like these concretely illustrates how the tools of lexical semantics can sharpen our focus as we seek to interpret the Greek and Latin languages of gender.

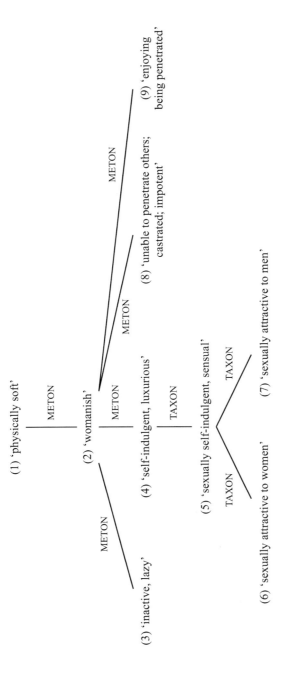

Figure 26.6 Partial polysemy network of the *moll-* lexeme.

(1) 'physically soft'

METON

(2) 'womanish'

METON

(3) 'inactive, lazy'

METON

(4) 'self-indulgent, luxurious'

TAXON

(5) 'sexually self-indulgent, sensual'

TAXON

(6) 'sexually attractive to women'

TAXON

(7) 'sexually attractive to men'

METON

METON

(8) 'unable to penetrate others; castrated; impotent'

METON

(9) 'enjoying being penetrated'

Notes

1 See Williams 2010: 230–1, 261, for arguments in favor of banning both the "pathic" and the "passive homosexual" from the pages of scholarship. Half technical term and half opaque euphemism, as far as I can tell the "pathic" is a creature who exists today only in the pages of English-language classical scholarship and translations. As James Robson suggests to me, use of this pseudo-Latin word in English may well be an instance of what is known in translation studies as "foreignization" (see Venuti 2008).

2 See Williams 2010: 139–44, 191–7.

3 In what follows, I limit myself to English-language studies of lexical semantics, making particular use of Lyons 1995, Cruse 2000, 2011, Murphy 2010. Introductions to the subject in other languages include Blank 2001 and Polguère 2003.

4 Lyons 1995: 126: "It is, after all, a matter of dispute whether it is possible, even in principle, to give a complete analysis of the sense of all lexemes in the vocabularies of natural languages. As I have emphasized on several occasions, it is, to say the least, arguable that the sense of some natural-language lexemes is to a greater or less degree fuzzy and indeterminate."

5 See Bakhtin 1986 for the concept of speech genres, defined as "relatively stable types of utterance," both oral and written, which are marked by thematic content, linguistic style (lexicon, phrasing, grammar), and compositional structure. Bakhtin distinguishes between *primary* speech genres of "unmediated speech communion" and *secondary* genres of writing of all kinds, including the entire range of traditionally identified literary genres.

6 Quotations respectively from Lyons 1995: 47, 51; Cruse 2000: 87; Cruse 2011: 76.

7 Lyons 1995: 102; he returns to the issue briefly at 40–2, 89–90.

8 English-language introductions to translation studies include Venuti 2012 and Bassnett 2014.

9 In addition to those which I discuss in this section, approaches to semantic representation which have been explored over the past decades include the construction of attribute-value matrices; the identification of core features and peripheral features; the search for family resemblances (associated with Wittgenstein's influential analysis of the semantics of *game*); generative lexicon; natural semantic metalanguage.

10 Lyons 1995: 109–10.

11 Cruse 2000: 258, 2011: 225.

12 Lyons 1995: 117.

13 Lyons 1995: 127.

14 To be sure, a woman might conceivably be called a *bachelor* just as a man might be called an *old maid* – with irony, for example, or in a queer adoption of the straightlaced vocabulary of heterosexuality. But it could be argued that such a usage, precisely because ad hoc or strategic, would not affect the core sense of the lexeme, whereas a putative lexicalization of *bachelor* to refer to a *married* person would be tantamount to fundamentally changing the semantics of the lexeme.

15 For the possibility that masculine *impudicus* suggests only the fact of being penetrated without suggesting a man's pleasure in the role, consider Haterius' remark, quoted at Sen. Contr. 4.pr.10, about *impudicitia* as a slave's lot in life (*necessitas*) and a freedman's duty (*officium*), along with the poetic Priapus' penetrative threat (Priap. 59.2: *si fur veneris, impudicus exis*, "If you have come here as a thief, you will leave *impudicus*") and the word-form *impudicatus*, glossed by Festus as *stupratus, impudicus factus* (Paul. Fest. 109M). To be sure, *impudicus* could be insulting (Cic. Cael. 30: *"adulter, impudicus, sequester" convicium est*), but it may not only be an accident of survival that in the published Latin graffiti *cinaedus* has 31 occurrences, *pathicus* 9, and *impudicus* none.

16 See Cruse 2000: 272–4, 2011: 277–8 for a brief overview.

17 See Williams 2010: 103–6. Langlands 2006 de-emphasizes the gendered distinction.

18 *Priap.* 40.4 (*hoc pathicae summi numinis instar habent*); cf. 25.3 (*sceptrum quod pathicae petunt puellae*), 48.3–5 (*cum mens est pathicae memor puellae*), 73.1–2 (*obliquis quid me, pathicae, spectatis ocellis? / non stat in inguinibus mentula tenta meis*). As I suggest at Williams 2010: 388, in these texts *pathica* seems partly synonymous with *proterva* (*Priap.* 58.3–4), *pruriens* (*Priap.* 26.4), and *cupida* (*Priap.* 80.3). Similar questions have been posed of the Greek feminine *katapugaina* and the occasional feminine use of the form *katapugōn* itself (cf. Dover 1989: 113–14, 142–3); the key difference from *pathica* is that the etymology of the Greek term directly refers to anal intercourse (*pugē*, "buttocks").

19 See Murphy 2010, sec. 4.2, inspired by the work of Ray Jackendoff.

20 Cruse 2000: 193–4, 224, 2011: 179–91 abandons this terminology, speaking instead of "co-occurrence preferences" (whereby one lexeme is the "selector" of others, which are "selectees") as opposed to "semantic clash" (subdivided into "inappropriateness," "paradox," and "incongruity").

21 *Femina, mulier, puer* as philonyms of *mollis*: Cic. D.N.D. 2.66 *effeminarunt autem eum Iunonique tribuerunt, quod nihil est eo mollius*; Plaut. Pseud. 172–3 *auditin? vobis, mulieres, hanc habeo edictionem. / vos, quae in munditiis, mollitiis deliciisque aetatulam agitis*; Hor. Epod. 11.3–4: *amore qui me praeter omnis expetit / mollibus in pueris aut in puellis urere. Mollis* as xenonym of *vir*: Cic. Epist. ad Brutum 17.1.8 *cum enim mollius tibi ferre viderer quam deceret virum*; Quint. I.O. 5.9.14 *fortasse corpus vulsum, fractum incessum, vestem muliebrem dixerit mollis et parum viri signa. Mollis* as antonym of *fortis*: Lucan 10.133–5 *nec non infelix ferro mollita iuventus / atque exsecta virum; stat contra fortior aetas / vix ulla fuscante tamen lanugine malas. Fortis* as philonym of *vir*: Cato, Agr. pr.4.2 *ex agricolis et viri fortissimi et milites strenuissimi gignuntur.*

22 Consider, for example, the advice given by the hypermasculine god Priapus in a poem of Tibullus, in the course of which the kinds of young men who are imagined as arousing a man's desire have qualities which are lexically marked as both masculine and feminine (Tibull. 1.4.13–14: *hic, quia fortis adest audacia, cepit; at illi / virgineus teneras stat pudor ante genas*).

23 I rely on Murphy 2010 for what follows.

24 For general discussion see Brisson 2002.

25 A commonly cited example of seemingly absolute synonyms which actually differ in one or more of these ways is the pair *big* and *large*, which are not in fact entirely substitutable. Some have argued that pairs like *sofa* and *couch*, *groundhog* and *woodchuck*, are indeed absolute synonyms; but others have countered that in these cases, too, differences in tone and register preclude absolute synonymy. See Murphy 2003 for full discussion.

26 Cruse 2000: 193–4. Cruse's criteria for determining the core elements of centered clusters are: "(1) They are expressively neutral. (2) They are stylistically unmarked, that is, they occur in a wider range of registers than any of the other items. (3) They are propositionally superordinate." Cruse 2011 omits the term "lexical clusters" entirely.

27 Fragments of ancient lexicography give us tantalizing glimpses at some exuberantly coarse word-formation for words describing men who have been sexually penetrated. *Intercutitus* is explained as deriving from *intercus* ("guts, intestines") and *scultimidonus* as deriving from *scultima*, in turn said to be a contraction of *scortorum intima*. See Festus 100.24 (*intercutitus: vehementer cutitus, hoc est valde stupratus*) and CGL 4.xviii (*scultimidoni qui scultimam suam quod est podicis orificium gratis largiantur; dicta scultima quasi scortorum intima*). We know nothing about how commonly used these words were or what their register and tone were; but we can be confident that there were others like them.

28 See Lehrer 1974 for detailed discussion of semantic fields with examples from various languages.

29 Box diagrams for English lexemes typically restrict themselves to a single word-class (e.g. nouns, adjectives, verbs). The lexemes included in Figure 26.1, some of them most readily identifiable as nouns and others as adjectives, reflect a basic morphosyntactic feature of Latin: the porous boundary between adjectives and substantives. Adjectives like *impudicus* and *mollis* are regularly substantivized, and along with the noun *cinaedus* we find the comparative adjective *cinaedior* (Catull. 10.24).

30 Mart 3.81 (with the punchline in v. 6: *sacra tamen Cybeles decipis: ore vir es*). Another epigram graphically represents cunnilinctus as penetration with the tongue (Mart. 11.61: *lingua maritus, moechus ore Nanneius*). For discussion of *cunnilingi* as more objectionable and perhaps even less manly than *fellatores* see Williams 2010: 218–24.

31 This non-trivial typographical issue brings us to the heart of a theoretical problem. How do we distinguish between cases of polysemy and homonymy, and on what basis? Native speakers' intuitions about when we are dealing with two or more different words on the one hand, or different senses of the same word on the other, are a good place to begin but cannot be the only criterion, since not all native speakers always agree; and what about languages which have no more native speakers? In fact, some linguists (possibly the majority in recent years) argue that rather than seeking to establish a clearcut distinction between the two phenomena, we might do better to perceive a continuum. See for example Nerlich and Clarke 2003.

32 See Williams 2013 for a reading of Catullus 16 with attention to the poem's cues for various senses of the *moll-* lexeme.

33 See Duranti 1997 for a general introduction to linguistic anthropology. Ravin and Leacock 2000 and Nerlich and Clarke 2003 are both inspired by the role of cognitive linguistics in opening up what had sometimes been conducted as a rather narrowly linguistic inquiry to broader questions of psychology, anthropology, and culture. Lakoff and Johnson 1980 has been especially influential in discussions of the cultural implications of metaphor.

34 Cf. Fillmore and Atkins 2000: 101: "Even for lexicographers there are no objective criteria for the analysis of a word into senses or for systematically extracting from corpus data the kinds of information useful to dictionary users."

35 For an overview see Blank 2003, esp. Table 1 (with a distinction between diachronic and synchronic perspectives).
36 Murphy 2010, sect. 5.2.4.
37 Williams 2010: 233–9, on the basis of a reading of Phaedrus, *Fables* 4.16, and Seneca, *Epistulae morales* 95.20–1.
38 For example, the study of English *to crawl* in Fillmore and Atkins 2000 cites 52 sentences using the verb, and on the basis of this material identifies 20 senses (representing them as a visual network of linked boxes), and quotes published dictionary entries which divide *crawl* into only 5 or 6 sub-entries.
39 For an example of first type see Fillmore and Atkins 2000 (English *to crawl* and French *ramper*), and of the second type Blank 2003 (English *man* and French *parler*).
40 Williams 2010: 195–6, 229–30.

Bibliography

Bakhtin, M. (1986) *Speech Genres and Other Late Essays*, trans. V.W. McGee. Austin, TX: University of Texas Press.
Bassnett, S. (2014) *Translation Studies*, 4th edn. London: Routledge.
Blank, A. (2001) *Einführung in die lexikalische Semantik für Romanisten*. Tübingen: Niemeyer.
——(2003) "Polysemy in the lexicon and in discourse", in B. Nerlich, Z. Todd, V. Herman, and D.D. Clarke (eds) *Polysemy: Flexible Patterns of Meaning in Mind and Language*. Berlin and New York: Mouton de Gruyter, pp. 267–93.
Brisson, L. (2002) *Sexual Ambivalence: Androgyny and Hermaphroditism in Greco-Roman Antiquity*, trans. J. Lloyd. Berkeley, CA: University of California Press.
Cruse, A. (2000) *Meaning in Language: An Introduction to Semantics and Pragmatics*, 2nd edn. Oxford: Oxford University Press.
——(2011) *Meaning in Language: An Introduction to Semantics and Pragmatics*, 3rd edn. Oxford: Oxford University Press.
Dover, K.J. (1989) *Greek Homosexuality*, updated edition with a new postscript. Cambridge, MA: Harvard University Press.
Duranti, A. (1997) *Linguistic Anthropology*. Cambridge: Cambridge University Press.
Fillmore, C.J. and Atkins, B.T.S. (2000) "Describing polysemy: The case of 'crawl'", in Y. Ravin and C. Leacock (eds) *Polysemy: Theoretical and Computational Approaches*. Oxford: Oxford University Press, pp. 91–110.
Lakoff, G. and Johnson, M. (1980) *Metaphors We Live By*. Chicago, IL and London: University of Chicago Press.
Langlands, R. (2006) *Sexual Morality in Ancient Rome*. Cambridge: Cambridge University Press.
Lehrer, A. (1974) *Semantic Fields and Lexical Structure*. Amsterdam: North-Holland.
Lyons, J. (1995) *Linguistic Semantics: An Introduction*. Cambridge: Cambridge University Press.
Murphy, M.L. (2003) *Semantic Relations and the Lexicon: Antonymy, Synonymy, and Other Paradigms*. Cambridge: Cambridge University Press.
——(2010) *Lexical Meaning*. Cambridge: Cambridge University Press.
Nerlich, B. and Clarke, D.D. (2003) "Polysemy and flexibility: Introduction and overview", in B. Nerlich, Z. Todd, V. Herman, and D.D. Clarke (eds) *Polysemy: Flexible Patterns of Meaning in Mind and Language*. Berlin and New York: Mouton de Gruyter, pp. 3–30.
Nerlich, B., Todd, Z., Herman, V., and Clarke, D.D. (eds) (2003) *Polysemy: Flexible Patterns of Meaning in Mind and Language*. Berlin and New York: Mouton de Gruyter.
Polguère, A. (2003) *Lexicologie et sémantique lexicale: Notions fondamentales*. Montréal, QC: Presses de l'Université de Montréal.
Ravin, Y. and Leacock, C. (eds) (2000) *Polysemy: Theoretical and Computational Approaches*. Oxford: Oxford University Press.
Venuti, L. (2008) *The Translator's Invisibility: A History of Translation*, 2nd edn. London: Routledge.
——(2012) *Translation Studies Reader*, 3rd edn. London: Routledge.
Williams, C. (2010) *Roman Homosexuality*, 2nd edn. Oxford and New York: Oxford University Press.
——(2013) "The meanings of softness: Some remarks on the semantics of *mollitia*", *Eugesta: Journal on Gender Studies in Antiquity*, 3: 240–63.

27

REMAKING PERPETUA

A female martyr reconstructed

Barbara K. Gold

I begin with the following question: when we read an ancient text written by a woman (or purportedly written by a woman), is the feminist project to rescue this woman from the scrapheap of history and attempt to recover a fleshed-out, fully historicized figure? Or should we attempt rather to examine the cultural and social contexts, the social relationships, and the (re) construction of this woman by later, mostly male, authors, in hopes of finding the excluded or oppositional traces, the remnants of the female voice?

This question is especially vexing in a case such as the Christian martyr Perpetua. Here we may have a text written by an early Christian woman, but our entrance into the text and our process of discovering Perpetua is consistently blocked and stymied by the men who shaped, read, and produced her: her editor/confessor/redactor, the Christian fathers, in particular Augustine, who sermonized about her, and even those contemporary male writers who have appropriated her. She has been portrayed as both a virgin and a whore by her narrator and later by Augustine.[1] Elizabeth Clark, in her article "The Lady Vanishes," asks how feminist historians, and in particular church historians, can approach, analyze, and understand early Christian ascetic women (known mainly through texts written about them by men). "Has then," she asks, "the lady vanished?" She responds by saying that "we cannot recover her pure and simple from texts," but we can try to know her through the traces she leaves, "embedded in a larger social-linguistic framework" (Clark 1998: 31).

Constructing women from late antiquity

Constructing any ancient subject is a difficult proposition; trying to construct an ancient woman subject is that much more difficult because we have so few texts from the hands of women. Even when we do have a female-authored text, it could be argued that the author is reflecting a society or time period founded on male values, but at least here we will hear a woman's voice, which we can situate in a particular time, place, and cultural environment. Those of us who work in the classical, late antique, or early Christian periods are often constrained by sources such as the church fathers, who used deeply embedded ideologies to represent women as they wanted them to be seen. Clark discusses "a long tradition of Christian males whose selective reading of biblical texts, buttressed by a misogynistic inheritance from antiquity, was designed to create," according to Althusser's formulation, "'good [female] subjects' who work 'all by themselves', freely submitting to their inferior status."[2] In other words, such subjects are unwittingly a part of the practices of their culture or society; they "'recognize'," according to Althusser, "the existing state of affairs, ... that 'it really is true that it is so and not otherwise', and that they must be obedient ... " (Althusser 1971: 181). Various strategies of containment were used to carry out this project; these included naturalizing, universalizing, and using norms from past myth or history to define female subjects.[3] In any one of these processes, the plurality and individuality of individual "women" becomes the rhetorical or ideological construct "woman," and thus the subjectivity of women is erased.

By characterizing women as weak, cowardly, passive, overly passionate, permeable, deceptive, corporeal, and irrational, a writer could position this female subject as part of a long line of women with similar negative character traits and behaviors, and thus as someone who was acting in character and just as we would imagine. And any women who try to break out of this mold and to appropriate or emulate male traits are usually seen as, at best, hybrid and puzzling creatures, or, at worst, creatures who have transgressed their bounds unsuccessfully without being able to become the other.[4] Women are thus stuck between two impossible situations: to be stereotyped as a "woman" is to be denigrated as having a set of negative characteristics; however, to be cast as a woman trying to be a man is to leave the world of woman (in which she could operate successfully within the bounds of her limitations) but to fail always to make a successful transition to manhood since she could not ever truly become a man.

Women's traditional traits are similarly underscored and made to seem real by the system of naturalizing and normalizing employed in masculine and aristocratic narratives. Here, instead of overtly ascribing female traits to an entire sex or tribe (so we might say, "these are the vices typical of the female sex"), such conventionally ascribed female traits are seen as part of the natural order of things and accepted without challenge by both those who set the rules (normally men) and those who are governed by them (normally women). It is the observer or person with power whose ideology determines what is deemed "natural" (although traces of oppositional voices may be heard in many texts, and in particular in a text like Perpetua's; cf. Gold 1993: 84). One example of a "natural" condition in late antiquity is virginity; this is the "natural" condition to which women should aspire. Any deviation is unnatural. Another "natural" condition is women's subjection to, or inferior position to, men. Should they try to be in a dominant role, they risk being portrayed as creatures who have transgressed set boundaries.

Another mechanism employed to mark women's behavior as natural or unnatural is the use of historical or mythological precedent to put a woman into a historical continuum and to set proper boundaries and models of behavior. Both biblical women (Mary, Eve) and classical figures (Polyxena, Iphigenia, Lucretia) serve this purpose and help to define female traits that have a venerable pagan past and are then put to use in Christian ideology.

Such ways of constructing woman have a long history in classical/pagan works and had been developed long before Christian writers appropriated them for their own uses.[5] We might point specifically to Roman satire (Juvenal, Martial) for constructions of gender and gender-deviant behaviors, but such delineations are also found in many other genres, notably philosophy (Aristotle, Seneca, Cicero), history or biography (Tacitus, Suetonius), epic, oratory, and elegy (Catullus, Propertius, Ovid). There were thus many models that the Christian fathers could use to contain women. One can question the motivations for using these strategies (as we will below), but we can also ask the question posed by Spivak: can we ask a male writer who is embedded in such a hegemonic discourse and who is in total control of the subjects (objects) to provide us with concepts and strategies that do not "appropriate or displace the figure of woman"? (Spivak 1983: 170).

Given the embeddedness of male writers and commentators in their discourse and culture, one further question must be asked before we turn to our specific subject, Perpetua. When a male writer praised a woman as a "good woman," did he mean a woman who acted like a woman, or a woman who acted like a man (since men provided the desired ideal, but an ideal that women could never truly reach)? Could a woman who displayed *virilitas* or *andreia* ("manliness") be a proper woman? Or did this transgression of boundaries mean that she was neither a good and proper woman nor a good "man"? This is a question we will need to ask of Perpetua.

What do we know about Perpetua?

I turn now to one particularly fascinating woman of the imperial Roman period, Perpetua, an early Christian martyr. Here are the few facts available from the third-century CE text that contains her prison narrative.[6] The *Passio Sanctarum Perpetuae et Felicitatis* tells us the story of the martyrdom of Perpetua, a young Roman woman living in or near Carthage and a catechumen or Christian in training. She and four of her fellow Christians were arrested in or near Carthage in the year 203 CE and, after a brief trial, they were martyred in the reign of the emperor Septimius Severus. Part of the text of the martyrdom is purported to have been written in Perpetua's own hand (*manu sua et suo sensu*, "in her own hand and reflecting her own feelings," 2.3) while she was in prison awaiting her martyrdom. This text has taken on an importance larger than its slim size would lead us to expect. It is the earliest extended prose piece in Latin that we have by a Christian woman, and it will be an important model for later martyr texts. It gives insight into an early period of Christianity and into the context surrounding the life of a provincial Roman family in the third century CE. And it focuses on a figure who is (though the mother of a young child and so not in fact a virgin) a precursor to the later ascetic figures such as the two Macrinas, Olympias and Melania in the third to fifth centuries, who, having renounced their marriages and children, led celibate lives devoted to God.[7]

Every detail we know about Perpetua is found in the *Passio*, a text that is purportedly written by three authors: sections 1–2, 11.1, and 14–21 by an anonymous narrator, sections 3–10 by Perpetua, and sections 11.2–13 by Saturus, a fellow martyr. We know only that she was in her early 20s, a nursing mother of a baby son, and an unbaptized Christian when she was arrested. Arrested along with Perpetua were Felicitas (another woman, perhaps a slave), Revocatus (probably also a slave), Secundulus and Saturninus; the aforementioned Saturus turned himself in at a later time.

Vibia Perpetua was probably from a Roman family of good standing living in or near Carthage. Her family must have been thoroughly Romanized, having probably received citizenship under the emperor Tiberius.[8] She is described as being *honeste nata, liberaliter instituta, matronaliter nupta* ("well-born, brought up in a manner befitting a free person, and married in the fashion of a respectable Roman woman," *Passio* 2.1). Her family consisted of her father (with whom she has a difficult relationship), mother, maternal aunt, two brothers (one of whom is also a Christian), and an infant son. She had another brother who had died young of facial cancer. There is no mention of her husband; many reasons have been offered for his absence. He could have been dead, on an extended trip, or estranged from Perpetua and her family (if, for example, he was not a Christian; cf. Bremmer 2002: 87–8). Or, it is entirely possible that Perpetua followed the path of many women after her, who divested themselves of their prior familial relationships, including husbands and children, when they themselves became Christians so that they might dedicate themselves to God.[9] Cooper has even suggested that Perpetua could have been a concubine, whose child was born out of wedlock. This would explain why her son was cared for during her imprisonment and after her death by her own family and not by her husband and his family (Cooper 2011: 688–90).

Most of these biographical details, however, are given not by Perpetua but by the editor in the frame of the narrative. Perpetua's text presents an account of several meetings with her father after her arrest, a few details of her trial and her stay in prison, and four visions that she had in prison. Perpetua's account of the interactions with her father indicates a strong connection with him. She describes four difficult visits from him when he comes to dissuade her from what he feels is a foolish and inexplicable march toward martyrdom and death, an act that will, he feels, have dire consequences not only for her but also for her family (we hear his side of the story only through her words).

The men in Perpetua's text

The text of Perpetua's *Passio* is divided into four sections by three different authors:

Sections 1–2: a theological introduction attesting to the power and efficacy of reading and hearing the deeds of martyrs, followed by a brief description of the events surrounding the arrest of five catechumenal Christians. These sections and sections 11.1 and 14–21 are by the narrator or editor, whose identity remains unknown.
Sections 3–10: a first-person narrative (or diary or journal, Heffernan 1995: 320–5; Formisano 2012: 330), purported to have been written by Perpetua and containing four visions. There is no independent evidence about the authorship of this section (or any of the sections), only the statement of the anonymous narrator that sections 3–10 were written in Perpetua's own hand. Sections 11.2–13: the vision of Saturus, one of Perpetua's fellow martyrs, purportedly written by Saturus.
Sections 14–21: a concluding narrative, probably by the same narrator as sections 1–2, detailing the fates and deaths of the martyrs, with some detail about the birth of the baby of Felicitas just before the martyrdom and death of Perpetua herself; a concluding section returns to the theme of section 1, glorifying the martyrs and commending their deeds to be read and emulated by all later Christians (see Shaw 2004: 301 for a schematic representation).

There are, then, at least three voices heard in this text: one female (if Perpetua is the author of sections 3–10), and at least two males, Saturus and the unnamed editor. Even, however, sections 3–10 could hardly have been directly recorded by her, given her dire and restricted conditions in the prison. In regard to this, Heffernan says,

> If we are to believe the author's claim that these remarks were written in prison, it surely is pertinent to ask where Perpetua got the necessary materials, time, and space, both psychic and physical, to write these lines? … It is difficult to imagine how an individual could write such elaborately constructed sentences … under such impossible circumstances.
>
> *(Heffernan 1995: 322–3)*

Heffernan argues that our extant account of the *Passio* likely came from a reconstruction of a verbal report, possibly given by Perpetua herself, and that any original record, "whether written or dictated," had to have undergone extensive editing (Heffernan 1995: 324).[10]

So to what extent is this the text of Perpetua, a female martyr? At best, we must imagine that Perpetua dictated her visions and thoughts to one of her visitors in prison, perhaps the editor, who then edited what she had conveyed to him and subsequently added the framing narrative. This editor thus had the opportunity to shape Perpetua as he wanted; it is he who has the final word on her martyrdom and death. The narrative also contains a number of male figures, who control Perpetua's actions in various ways, and frequent masculinizing language as well. Even the gender identity of Perpetua herself is called into question by her actions and by the roles she plays in the *Passio*.

Let us look at how the figure of Perpetua develops over the course of the *Passio*. Perpetua's account of her imprisonment is largely comprised of four visions that came to her before her execution: the first, in which she steps on the head of a serpent, climbs a ladder, and sees a godlike figure; two visions centering on her dead brother, Dinocrates; and a final vision the day before her execution. It is the fourth vision (*Passio* 10) that has aroused the greatest interest.

In this vision, Perpetua's transgressive behavior is foregrounded in a startling way. Here, Pomponius, a Christian who had visited her in prison, comes for Perpetua.[11] He leads her to the amphitheater and then departs. Perpetua sees a large and boisterous crowd in the arena (10.5) and is surprised not to find any wild beasts attacking her. Instead she sees an Egyptian "hideous to look at" (10.6: *Aegyptius foedus specie*). Then she claims, "I was disrobed, and I became male" (10.7: *expoliata sum et facta sum masculus*), using an adjective *masculus* rather than a noun for "man" (*vir, mas*). Standing opposite her is her opponent rolling in the sand of the arena (10.7); this Egyptian must stand for the Devil, who would, she claimed, be her true opponent in her actual contest on the following day.[12] Another man appears, a paternal figure as in her first vision; he was clothed in purple robes and carried a rod (*virga*) like the owner and trainer of gladiators (*lanista*, *Passio* 10.8). This man is a Christ figure, there to present Perpetua for a martyr's death in the amphitheater just as an *agônothete* or director of the games might present gladiators in the pagan games.

There follows a brutally physical battle between Perpetua and the Egyptian, a pankration which consists of wrestling, punching, and kicking. Perpetua knocks the Egyptian down, trampling on his head and winning the promised reward. The *lanista* says then to Perpetua, "Peace be with you, daughter" (*Passio* 10.13), while the crowd cheers and her supporters sing psalms.

In this vision, we can see the logical development of the theme of the fearless woman who refuses to be subordinated to her familial roles. As Castelli says, Perpetua's victory "is described *as* and *by* the stripping off of feminine gender" (Castelli 1991: 42; emphasis in the original). Perpetua's sudden, brief transformation in 10.7 into a *masculus* is necessary in order to explain her victory over the large Egyptian man but also a sign of confidence in her ability to win. She *must* prevail because she is fighting for God.[13] Her victory is marked by her signifying male body; as Tilley says, the transformation might be seen as a "culturally conditioned affirmation of Perpetua's ultimate victory" (1994: 844). In antiquity, the male body was considered the cultural and physical norm. Biblical metaphors contained many masculine images that "reinforced prejudice for male superiority" (Tilley 1994: 844; Eph. 4:13, 6:11–17; Rom. 13:12). "Male" and "female" became metaphors for particular moral categories, with male standing for strong, superior, and female standing for weak, inferior. A person had to be "male" or "virile" in order to be strong, to fight against beasts or demons, or to bear up bravely under difficult circumstances. The designations "male" and "female" became interchangeable terms that could indicate either sex. Thus sex was transcended and gender identity became fluid and temporary, referring to a common human nature. The terms came to describe less a static state or a particular sexual category than a moral category: to "become female" indicated moral weakness or degeneracy; to "become male" indicated the attainment of "a higher state of moral and spiritual perfection" (Vogt 1985: 72–80).[14] By this reading, we would understand that, when Perpetua becomes male, she has been strengthened and turned into an athlete who can prevail over her Egyptian opponent, and that she has reached a higher spiritual state.

Women were considered to be engaging in transgressive behavior when they exhibited courage or made conscious choices about their lives (Miles 1989: 55). Both mothers and fathers were puzzled and terrified by this behavior. According to the *Passio*, Perpetua's father was angered by her stubbornness and independence of thought (*Passio* 3.3), and Thecla's mother exclaimed "Burn the lawless woman" when Thecla rejected marriage (*Acts of Paul and Thecla* 20). The criticism in such cases was not leveled at the male behaviors but rather at women who were trying to act like men and against their female nature. Philo, the first-century CE Jewish philosopher, tries to make sense of this contradiction when he says: "Progress is nothing else than the giving up of the female gender by changing into the male, since the female gender is material, passive, corporeal, and sense-perceptible; while the male is active, rational, incorporeal and more akin to mind and thought" (Philo, *Questiones et solutiones in Genesim* 1.8, quoted in MacDonald 1987: 99).[15]

One way that women could "become male" was to follow the path of asceticism, discarding their former world of husband, children, and goods (as Perpetua did), becoming celibate, and taking on "a new status that elevated them beyond the deficiencies of the female condition" (Clark 1986: 43; cf. Clark 1979: 54–8). Jerome makes a clear pronouncement on this when he claims that at the point at which a woman prefers Jesus Christ to her husband and babies, "she will cease to be a woman and will be called a man" (Jerome, *Comment. on Ep. to the Ephesians* III [Eph. 5:28]). At this point, she is considered man's equal, not his inferior; Jerome famously quotes Paul, who had earlier said that "in Christ Jesus there is no male and female" (Jerome, *Ep.* 71.2.2; 75.2.2). With their female gender identity and family relations effaced, says Jerome, all that remains is for women to "transcend their femaleness."

Perpetua is transformed into what Aspegren has called "the male woman" through various narrative techniques (Aspegren 1990: 133–43). She is clearly a leader among her group of fellow martyrs; she controls, in one way or another, all the men in her story: her father (3.1–3, 5, 6.1–5, 9); the procurator Hilarianus (6.3–4); an arguing pair of bishop and presbyter (13.1–4); the tribune in the prison (18.5–6); the gladiator who is assigned to kill her (21.9–10). It is she who powerfully holds and deflects the gaze of the onlookers in the amphitheater by her *vigor oculorum* ("power of her gaze," 18.2). And the imagery used in her fourth vision, where she fights the Egyptian athlete, is full of masculinizing words and actions: not only the obvious *facta sum masculus* (10.7), but phallic words and symbols like the *virga* and *ramus* that the *lanista* carries (and which Perpetua will then receive, 10.8, 10.12), and the sword which the Egyptian will wield against her (10.9).[16]

Such a transformation into a male body later became a common trope for holy women in particular; so Castelli says, "the mark of true holiness is that the women become men" (1991: 42–7; quote, p. 42). This transformation took many different forms (cutting one's hair, acting in a masculine way, transvestism), but it was not often a physical metamorphosis (even if in a dream or for a brief time) into a male body.[17]

Perpetua's actions in her section of the narrative cast her in a dominant and controlling role. She is independent and brave, and, as noted above, she is a leader of her group. She takes a dominant position over her father, who is cast into an increasingly feminized position as her narrative progresses.[18] She hands over her baby to her family with some anxiety, giving up her maternal role (6.7–8). When Roman prison guards try to force her to dress for the "games" in the pagan robes of Ceres (and the men in the robes of Saturn), she refuses their demand and they back down (*Passio* 18.4–6). She is portrayed as a fierce combatant in her fourth vision when she fights against her Egyptian opponent. And, when she says that her father wanted to attack her "as if he was going to pluck my eyes out" (*Passio* 3.5), Bal has argued that this is evidence for "Perpetua's tendency to self-identification as male," with a Freudian glance at the relationship between blinding and castration anxiety (Bal 1991: 232 n. 14).

The masculinizing of Perpetua becomes even more complex if we compare her own recounting of the story to the framing narrative in which Perpetua becomes a character in the drama. The external narrator, who introduces Perpetua in section 2 and tells the story of her martyrdom and death in sections 14–21, takes care to highlight her feminine side. In section 20, where Perpetua and Felicitas prepare to meet the beasts, we discover that the animal chosen to dispatch the two women martyrs (not their male companions) was a fierce heifer ("in order to mimic [*aemulatus*] their sex even as regards the beast," 20.1).[19] The authorities (or the Devil, *diabolus*) chose the heifer to make a cruel joke, as a rebuke to women who had the boldness to renounce their conventional roles and a reminder that women should stay within their appropriate bounds. Perpetua and Felicitas could no longer be regarded as real women.[20]

In this same section, after her battle with the heifer, Perpetua is cast by the editor/narrator in a demure, feminine role. After she is thrown by the heifer, she

> fell onto the small of her back. And when she sat up, she rearranged the tunic that had been torn away from her body to cover her thigh, being more concerned with her modesty than her pain. Then she asked for a hairpin and pinned up her disheveled hair; for it was not fitting to suffer martyrdom with her hair loose since she might seem to be mourning in her hour of glory.
>
> *(Passio 20.3–5)*

This Perpetua, so concerned with the typical feminine preoccupations of modesty and keeping a proper demeanor, hardly seems to accord with the more aggressive, confident Perpetua we see in her sections of the narrative (3–10).

After Perpetua's fourth and final vision, she says,

> Then I woke up. And I understood that I was going to fight not against animals but against the Devil. But I also knew that victory was to be mine. This is what I did up to the day before the games.
>
> *(Passio 10.13–15)*

In her final lines, she gives control of the ending, and of her own end, to the narrator: "As for what happened during the games themselves: anyone who wants to write about that may do so" (10.15). At this point Perpetua is appropriated by the male (or so we assume) narrator, who closely controls her story, presenting the complex figure of a martyr who takes charge of her own death and yet also a woman who displays a typical female preoccupation with modesty and correct comportment. The gender fluidity and ambiguity revealed throughout the *Passio*, but in particular in the antiphonal structure of the first-person Perpetuan narrative and the framing third-person account by the narrator, shows us a Perpetua who has an ambiguous identity: a feminized male subjectivity, and a resubjugated female subjectivity (Burrus 2008: 71). Castelli says of this gender ambiguity,

> Just as her narrative remains open-ended and therefore ambiguous, it also narrates an ambiguity toward gendered imagery and gendered identity on the part of its main character; whereas Perpetua's own story calls narrative closure and fixed gender identity into question, the framing narrative finishes the story and puts Perpetua back into the conventions of gender, as a woman (*femina*).
>
> *(21.10; Castelli 1991: 35)*

It is difficult to say where exactly such an ambiguous gender portrait found its impetus: perhaps in the developing Christian theology in early writers such as Paul where one finds statements like "there is no male and female"; perhaps in the destabilization of subjectivity and the new idea of the self in the early empire and the Second Sophistic; or perhaps in the reaction of early Christians to Roman social hierarchies.[21]

Augustine and the church fathers on female subjectivity and behavior

The church fathers and Christian writers in the early Roman empire and in the two to three centuries after Perpetua's death in 203 CE often took as their topic of conversation the ascetic women of the church, who were "more like men than nature would seem to allow."[22] The kind of gender ambiguity and complexity displayed by a Christian woman like Perpetua set in motion a series of debates among the church fathers about the appropriate roles for women to play. Such women of great courage and fortitude were both admired for displaying masculine qualities but also held suspect and feared because they did not stay within the expected gender boundaries and act according to code. So John Chrysostom purportedly claimed about the abbess Olympias, "Don't say 'woman' but 'what a man!' because this is a man, despite her physical appearance."[23] Likewise Gregory of Nyssa says about Macrina, "A woman is the starting-point of the narrative; if indeed a woman; for I do not know if it is proper to name her who is above nature out of [the term] nature" (Gregory of Nyssa, *Vita Macrinae* 1). And in a non-Christian writing of the same period, Porphyry addresses Marcella, telling her, "Do not preoccupy yourself with the body, do not see yourself as a woman since I no longer hold you as such. Flee in the spirit everything feminine (θηλυνομένων) as if you had a male body that enveloped you."[24] Even the very terms for manly feminine virtue are problematic: Olympias and Melania are called ἡ ἄνθρωπος (using the generic word for man with a feminine article); and the words ἀνδρεία in Greek and *virilis* in Latin are used for manliness or manly courage, each containing the word for man (ἀνήρ and *vir*).[25]

The holy women after Perpetua's time (and after the time of martyrdom) in the third–fourth centuries thus were in a peculiarly liminal position, somewhere between male and female, and it was this that gave them their special status and prepared them for the spiritual perfection or holiness that they strove to achieve (Castelli 1991: 45–6). While Paul had said earlier (in the first century) that "in Christ Jesus there is no male and female" (Gal. 3:28, quoted by Jerome *Ep.* 71.2.2; 75.2.2), this ideal of the effacement of gender difference, with its utopian and transgressive possibilities, seems to have been overwhelmed by the long-standing hierarchy of male over female. The belief in two genders with two distinct sets of inherent strengths and weaknesses stubbornly persists alongside the developing Christian idea of virginal holy women who transcended gender differences. It is not that gender characteristics do not exist for fourth-century writers like Chrysostom, but rather that such women as Olympias successfully struggle to overcome them (see Burrus 2008: 70–1; Castelli 2008: 84).

What does this mean for Perpetua, who substantially predates the ascetic women of the later third–fourth centuries? Although Perpetua was herself not strictly speaking a virgin or an ascetic (this type seems to have evolved from the earlier female martyrs after the age of martyrdom[26]), she certainly is a prototype, who has no husband in the *Passio* and severs ties with her family, including her baby son. Her transformation into a male in *Passio* 10.7 has precedent in an even earlier martyrdom found in the Letter of the Churches of Lyon and Vienne (dated from 177 CE), in which a woman named Biblis, who had denied Christianity, was put under torture and was transformed from a weak and unmanly (ἄνανδρος) woman into a Christian (Cobb 2008: 89–90). There is then an equivalence drawn between being manly and being Christian. The gender instability and porousness we see in the *Passio* does not start with Perpetua; it is present already in the martyr literature and in the New Testament. But Perpetua famously enacts this transformation and provides both inspiration for later holy women and a source of anxiety for writers such as Gregory of Nyssa, Chrysostom, Jerome, and Augustine.

Augustine's containment of Perpetua

By the time of Augustine (354–430), the cult of Saints Perpetua and Felicitas had become very popular, and the *Passio* had become a standard part of the liturgy. When Augustine gave his sermons on their annual feast day, he was confronted with a problem. How does Augustine come to terms with this brave, courageous, almost virile martyr, whose acts he could not ignore since she had become a much read part of church liturgy? His only choice was to accept the *Passio* as an authentic text, but he chose to reinterpret this text for his audiences so that it would be palatable both to them and to himself, and to remake Perpetua into a figure that his church could admire.[27]

Augustine wrote at least three sermons in honor of Perpetua, 280–2, and he mentioned her again in sermon 159A. Another sermon mentioning Perpetua has been found that is of dubious attribution and is probably not by Augustine.[28] Perpetua is also present in his philosophical work *De Natura et Origine Animae*. Perhaps this last work is the most interesting of his disquisitions on the martyrdom of Perpetua because it was not written for a specific occasion as were the sermons; rather, here he introduces one of Perpetua's visions somewhat gratuitously to make a theological point against his adversary, Vincentius Victor.

Let us look first at the sermons written for the anniversary of the martyrdom of Perpetua, Felicitas, and their companions. These were sustained reflections written on the occasion of their feast day, March 7.[29] Augustine, who was constrained at least to acknowledge the martyrdom of Perpetua and Felicitas on the day that was named for this event, dwells at some length in Sermons 280–2 on their heroic exploits (puzzled though he was by the fact that the day was named only for the two female martyrs and not for their male companions). It is not unusual that Augustine acknowledges the martyr acts of Perpetua and Felicitas since he often celebrated the feast days of martyrs. But it is surprising that he devotes at least three entire homilies to this pair as this was not his common practice.[30]

It is also notable that at least one of Augustine's sermons on Perpetua, 280, was given immediately following the reading of the text of Perpetua's martyrdom:

> we heard when they were read to us (*cum legerentur, audivimus*) the encouragement they received in their divine visions and the triumphs in their martyrdoms; and all these things, laid out and illuminated by the light of words, we heard with our ears, we saw with our minds, we honored with our religious devotion, and we praised with love.
>
> *(280.1)[31]*

We can surmise then that her text was read as part of the liturgy each year on her feast day, and this was followed by a homily, which was sometimes centered on her.

Augustine had to account for the fact that a woman, marked by womanly weakness (*fragilitas feminea*, 281.1), was able to perform such courageous acts, to outperform the men in her group (so that the feast day was named only for the women, *Serm.* 282), to become male in her fourth vision, and to resist and repudiate all the men who tried to control her (her husband perhaps, her father, Hilarianus, the jailer who sentenced her, and even the gladiator sent to dispatch her at the end). How was this possible? The female martyrs prevailed, according to Augustine, because where the sex is weaker, the crown is more glorious (*Serm.* 281.1). They are the more admired because they are women, who are weaker by nature and so not expected to perform brave and heroic physical deeds. This then sufficiently explains why the feast day is named only for the two women.

Augustine is still left, however, with the uncomfortable figure of the female hero or the virile woman. He is anxious to take apart this hybrid character and fit her into a more comfortable mold for his contemporary audience.[32] One strategy is to appeal to the Pauline idea that there will be no male and female (*Serm.* 280.1; cf. Gal. 3:28); the sexes will be as one, so that even in the body of a woman, the manliness (*virtus*) of mind will conceal the sex of the flesh. But Augustine uses another strategy to foreground Perpetua's feminine nature. He admits that she stood up against her father (who was the Devil's tool); but he preserves her role as a loving daughter, saying that she responded to him in a temperate fashion, neither dishonoring him nor yielding to his deceits (*Serm.* 281.2). She fights bravely, but she and Felicitas are both mothers, inhabiting the ultimate female role.[33] Of course the true female forebear for women is Eve, the source of womanly weakness and inferiority.[34] Augustine connects to Eve Perpetua's stepping on the head of the serpent in her first vision: "the head of the ancient serpent, the ruin of the woman as she fell, became a step for this woman as she ascended" (*Serm.* 280.1). This is not a connection made explicit in the *Passio*, but Augustine draws it out in order to connect Perpetua not only with womanhood in general or womanly weakness as a trait but with the original sin brought to women by Eve.[35] It was this she overcame by her chastity, her masculine courage, and her devotion to Christ, a devotion so great that it took her out of herself (*quo amore alienata*) and enabled her to endure the torments of the arena in an altered state (cf. *Passio* 20.8–9; Augustine, *Serm.* 280.4).

Augustine then is concerned to wrest Perpetua away from the masculinized roles that she inhabits in at least her own section of the *Passio*[36] and to focus on her feminine roles and feminized behavior. She was a good daughter and a mother (interestingly, Augustine says that only one of the women was a mother, Perpetua [*Serm.* 282.2]; this is presumably because Felicitas gave birth only just before the martyrdom). In *Serm.* 282, Augustine says that Perpetua and Felicitas were *non solum feminae, verum etiam mulieres fuerunt* ("were not only of womankind but were also *mulieres*"). Shewring (1931: 56) translates *mulieres* as "very women" while Hill (1994: 81) translates it as "wives"; I might translate it as "grown women."[37] Clearly Augustine must mean that Perpetua and Felicitas were not only biological women but also performed normative femininity in their relations of woman to man or wife to husband.[38] He thus manages to highlight their most womanly aspects (motherhood, lactation, sexuality), their masculine courage, and their sainthood. To achieve sainthood, they had to cast aside their previous familial roles; this rejection of early ties to family is strongly urged by Augustine in his *Sermo de honorandis vel contemnendis parentibus* (*Serm.* 159A = Dolbeau 1996b, *Serm.* 3, especially Chapter 11, where he addresses the *infirmum sexum*). It then becomes possible for women to have it all: fecundity and family, and then (once they have renounced sexuality and family ties) chastity or virginity and virile courage, and finally martyrdom and sainthood.[39] Augustine says that, because they were women and mothers, strong emotional attachments added to the innate weakness of their sex (*Serm.* 282.2); this ultimately worked to their advantage because their enemies assumed weakness and inability to withstand torture. These attachments produced an inner masculine strength (*interioris hominis cautissimo et fortissimo robore*) that broke the enemy's attacks.

Augustine celebrates Perpetua and Felicitas together in his sermons, and he puns endlessly on their names, frequently inserting the phrase 'perpetual felicity' (*Serm.* 281.3, 282.1 [twice], 282.3). This is a source of annoyance for anyone trying to read his sermons with any degree of seriousness. What exactly is the point? He seems obsessed in these sermons with the fact that the feast day is named only for the two female martyrs and not their male companions. He deals with this fact (a fact he was bound to accept) by so closely entwining Perpetua and Felicity that they become one; they are Woman. The repetition of their names (*perpetua felicitas*) serves as almost a chant to mark and embody their roles with a memorable, rhetorical, ritualized mnemonic device. Was this, as some think, a way to mock them? I suggest, rather, that Augustine was trying to find a means, using a masculinizing rhetoric, of memorializing them as a pair of women linked in their everlasting sanctity.[40] By appropriating their very names into his own discourse, Augustine is able to take control of the very substance of the *Passio*.

One other work of Augustine outside of the sermons, *De Natura et Origine Animae*, contains a particularly interesting mention of Perpetua. The use of Perpetua here (without Felicitas) is to some extent gratuitous; Augustine did not have to bring her into the text (as he did in his sermons on her feast day). In *De Nat*. 1.10.12, Augustine, while refuting the views of Vincentius Victor on baptism, adduces evidence from Perpetua's second and third visions about her brother Dinocrates. Vincentius Victor had apparently argued that Perpetua had the power to intercede for the child Dinocrates when he died and to save his soul, although he had not yet been baptized. Augustine denies this and claims there is no evidence that Dinocrates was not baptized (arguing *ex silentio*), thus undercutting Perpetua's power and authority. He makes two further comments, which undermine the importance and authority of the *Passio*. First, he says that the work was not part of canonical scripture (*nec scriptura ipsa canonica est*) and thus deserved less reverence than many people were giving it. He then adds, "Nor did she write – or whoever wrote it (*vel quicumque illud scripsit*) – that this little boy had died without being baptized," and consequently questions the authorship and authenticity of the *Passio* (while at the same time feeling the need to cite her).[41]

Augustine's treatment both of Perpetua and of her text in this work shows him caught in a dilemma, as he is in his sermons. He cannot dismiss her since she is a figure of importance who holds a firm place in the liturgy and church tradition. Therefore he chooses to foreground her text while at the same time undercutting its authority with the three-pronged attack detailed above: Perpetua might not have had the power to intercede for her dead brother; the *Passio* was not part of canonical scripture; Perpetua might not be the author of any part of the *Passio*. It is worth taking into account as we examine Augustine's frequent attempts at balancing the many different aspects of these complex issues that this balancing is a reflection not only of his own probably conflicted attitudes but also of his need to address a pluralistic audience of Christians with many different identities that he was trying to pull together.[42]

Augustine and Lucretia

Augustine's attitude toward Perpetua and his containment of women can also be illuminated by his treatment of another Roman woman, Lucretia, made famous by Livy. In Book 1 of the *City of God* (Chap. 19), Augustine re-examines the story of Lucretia, the chaste wife of Collatinus, who was raped by Sextus Tarquinius and subsequently killed herself. Before her suicide, she takes revenge by making her husband, father, and their trusted friends promise to avenge her rape. According to Livy, this event was the pretext for the overthrow of the Etruscan kings by L. Junius Brutus and the beginning of the Roman republic (Livy 1.58). In Augustine's treatment of the story in the *City of God*, he takes quite a different approach to the normally revered figure of Lucretia than we find elsewhere.[43] Lucretia was for Augustine "an ambivalent model of heroism," as Trout says, embodying features both of womanly *pudicitia* and also of masculine fortitude and heroism (Trout 1994: 57). Thus she inhabits uncomfortably (for Augustine, at any rate) two different worlds, just as Perpetua did. Augustine faults Lucretia on several counts: she committed suicide (a practice which Augustine rejects as immoral) even though she was not guilty, thus adding her crime to the crime of Tarquinius; she used sexual purity as an excuse for heroic action (*non est pudicitiae caritas, sed pudoris infirmitas*); she cared too much for her own honor and shame in the public eye (*laudis avida nimium, City of God* 1.19). Further, Lucretia's act of volitional death was carried out by stabbing herself with a knife, a traditionally male way to die (this detail is not mentioned by Augustine, but is a part of Livy's account).[44]

Lucretia was a powerful symbol, taken from Roman history, for the Romans, an exemplum to be followed by Roman women. She is also, I suggest, a possible model for a strong female figure like Perpetua, who guided the knife in the gladiator's hand to her own throat when he was unable to complete the task (*Passio* 21.9) and could thus be accused of having committed volitional death, using a male method of dying.[45] And Perpetua, like Lucretia, was an ambivalent figure, embodying at once female chastity (or nearly so) and modesty, yet a masculine fortitude and demeanor (no lowered eyes for Perpetua, *Passio* 18.2), sacrificing herself (perhaps needlessly or too publicly) for a higher principle and perhaps too conscious of her own honor and shame.[46] And like Lucretia, Perpetua's own story has been transformed by the many men who wrote it.

Conclusion

So male authors from Perpetua's own time onward have shaped her tale and her subjectivity. "What chance was there," Brent Shaw asks, "for any Perpetua to tell her story?" (Shaw 2004: 322). Perpetua would hardly recognize herself in any of the later representations and refigurings of herself and her tale.[47] Even in the *Passio*, which was likely written a short time after her martyrdom, Perpetua has been revised by her editor/narrator. Farrell, commenting on Augustine's "canonization of Perpetua," says that the *Passio* invites the kind of insinuations that Augustine makes about its purported authorship (i.e., that it might not be by Perpetua), "surrounded as it is by an interpretive frame that may be as tendentious in its interpretation as Augustine is in his" (Farrell 2012: 311). And Shaw pines for the "small and fragile thing" that was the original *Passio* of Perpetua, which however, "from the start … was buried under an avalanche of male interpretations, rereadings, and distortions" (Shaw 2004: 322).

For a long while, Perpetua (the woman and the text) was the product of male commentators, editors, and sermonizers. This subversive woman and her text were absorbed into a masculine, dominant discourse and changed beyond recognition. The narrator of the *Passio* makes her into the *matrona Christi, Dei delicata* ("the wife of Christ, the *delicata* of God," *Passio* 18.2) and later a *puellam delicatam* (20.2). Some people translate *delicata* as "darling," "favorite," "beautiful," but *delicata* usually has an erotic sense, as with its predecessor in earlier Latin, *deliciae*, used often of pet slaves kept for sexual purposes.[48] At the opposite pole, Augustine transforms her into a *virgo casta* (*Serm.* 281.1), a woman shorn of womanly weakness. So, as Sigismund-Nielsen says,

> both the narrator of the *Passio* and Augustine had to change her in order to make this extraordinary Roman woman fit into their Christian framework. One made Perpetua a whore, the other a virgin. Both reflect the perfervid contempt in which the early Church held women.
>
> *(Sigismund-Nielsen 2012: 117)*

More recently, feminist scholars of early Christianity have tried to find new ways of uncovering "the voice of the victim" (Cooper 1998).[49] Cooper finds an access in the *Passio* to the "vivid, bold, and unapologetic voice of the martyr herself," a woman who understands well that her own voice will be out of her control after her death (Cooper 1998: 157; cf. *Passio* 10.15). It is not the case that all women scholars speak with the same voice (any more than all male scholars do), but rather that they are far more reluctant to appropriate Perpetua as male scholars and church fathers in the past have done. Scholars like Bal, Burrus, Cameron, Castelli, Clark, Cooper, Kraemer, Perkins, and Tilley have given us a whole new Perpetua to consider. As Cameron says,

> the rhetoric of the early church was a male rhetoric, and it is only recently that readings of it have also not been male readings. Thus the entire debate about the "position of women in the early church" has taken place, and still must take place, within a framework of male textuality … there was no simple way in which the Fathers of the fourth century could write about women.
>
> *(Cameron 1989: 184, 200)*[50]

Virginia Burrus gives us one of the more interesting accounts of the "torturable female body" (Burrus 2008). For Burrus, Perpetua is evidence of a "new" Christian subjectivity, an identity in which gender had become more malleable and much less easy to define (Burrus 2008: 59), although still necessary as a category of definition. Perpetua can be – and has been – seen as a figure of feminized virility or virilized femininity, a figure who can provide a "site of ambivalent identification for female readers," or an object of male voyeurism (Burrus 2008: 70–1). She is a site of continual contestation. As Marina Warner has said, "meanings of all kinds flow through the figures of women, and they often do not include who she herself is" (Warner 1985: 331).

Coda

Maureen Tilley ends her study of the *Passio Sanctarum Perpetuae et Felicitatis* with a section entitled "Twisting the Tradition" (1994: 851–2). There she points out that Perpetua and Felicitas were "liturgically rendered virgins" by the thirteenth century. Much later their feast day was moved from March 7 to March 6 to make way for a male saint. Finally, under Vatican II, they reclaimed March 7 as their own, and their status was no longer said to be "virgins," "a gesture to the historical bodiliness of these mothers" (852). The voice of Perpetua continues to be strong and clear despite the processes of reinterpretation, misinterpretation, resubjugation, and victimization that she has undergone.

Notes

1 See on this Sigismund-Nielsen 2012: 117, and the conclusion to my essay.
2 Clark 2008: 101; cf. Althusser 1971: 181–2.
3 See Clark 2008 on these strategies used by the Church Fathers. The phrase "strategies of containment" is taken from Jameson 1981: 52–4. It is through such a strategy that authors are "able to project the illusion that their readings are somehow complete and self-sufficient" (Jameson 1981: 10).
4 See on similar stereotyping in the early empire, Gold 1998, esp. 375–6.
5 Carson 1990; Gold 1993, 1998; Vidén 1993; Gleason 1995: 82–102; Shaw 1996, esp. 279, n. 26 and bibliography cited there.
6 See Gold 2013.
7 See on this Cooper 2011, esp. 688–90.
8 See Bremmer 2002: 87 for discussion of the name Vibius and its probable provenance.
9 See Castelli 1991: 44–7. See too Heffernan 1988: 233–4, who gives as one possible reason for Perpetua's missing husband "the idea that following baptism the renunciation of the marriage debt was an achievement of the highest good."
10 See, with Heffernan, the remarks by F. Dolbeau (1996a: 313), who thinks it entirely possible that Perpetua could have written sections 3–10 in the days leading up her execution when she was imprisoned under better conditions. See also now Heffernan 2012: 3–8: "we cannot claim with apodictic certainty that either she [Perpetua] or Saturus 'authored' their respective narratives, but the weight of

the cumulative historical evidence in the text persuades me that they did, and that this is a text authored in the early third century and edited by a close contemporary" (5). There is certainly disagreement over the authority of sections 3–10 of the narrative and Perpetua's role in it. See Bremmer and Formisano 2012: 5–6; also Chapters 2, 10, and 15 in the Bremmer and Formisano (2012) book.

11 Pomponius is often compared to the pagan dignitary who brings the participants to the contest, but, as Bremmer points out, his dress, especially the absence of a belt, marks him as a Christian, not a pagan (2002: 114–15).

12 The Egyptian may also be used to signify the paradigm of a strong athlete. Bremmer (2002: 116) cites L. Robert (1982) here for Robert's influential interpretation of the athletic contest in the fourth vision. Bremmer points out that the Egyptians were the "athletes par excellence of the Roman Empire," and therefore it is not surprising that an Egyptian would be Perpetua's opponent here. But also the Devil was often represented as black, and this may have affected the choice of the Egyptian for Perpetua's contest.

13 Lateiner, in writing of sexual and gender transformations in Ovid, says that "Ovid's treatment of transsexualities and transvestisms … dwells on the instrumental and social consequences of their transits" (Lateiner 2009: 151); the same might be said of Perpetua's transformation into a male in her contest with the Egyptian.

14 Metaphors of woman turning into man and woman becoming male were commonly used in Gnosticism. See Clement of Alexandria, who says "the woman … when she has freed herself of the cravings of the flesh, achieves perfection in this life as the man does … for souls are … neither masculine nor feminine, when they no longer marry nor are married. Perhaps she is thus turned into a man, the woman who is no more feminine than he, the perfect, manly, woman" (cf. Vogt 1985: 73; see Clement, *Stromateis* VI.100.6).

15 Cf. Castelli 1991: 44–5, who points out that there are many encomia to women who "become male" and yet also condemnation and mistrust. For example, cutting one's hair, as Thecla did, to try to disguise oneself as a man or as a rejection of self-beautification, was seen as negative since "women's hair stands for their subjugation" (Castelli 1991: 44).

16 Cooper (1998: 154–6) points out that such a masculinized representation of women and the violence inherent in it can be viewed as pornographic; the audience is invited to view a woman who is courageous but inherently vulnerable, and is titillated by this image.

17 We have many examples of such women, most of them after Perpetua's time but a few before her, for example, Thecla. There are certainly parallels between the stories of Perpetua and Thecla, and it is tempting to think that Perpetua must have read her story. See on this Bremmer 1998: 176ff., 2002: 107ff.; he asks whether Perpetua had read the *Acts of Paul* and knew enough Greek to do so.

18 On the increasing feminizing of Perpetua's father, see Castelli 1991: 37ff.

19 See here Burrus (2008), esp. 69, where she discusses the "exaggerated strategies of feminization" that are almost "parodic" in the final version of the *Passio*. She says, "The self-dreamed Perpetua is made male in order to meet an intensely masculinized adversary, but in the realm of the intensely 'literal', the doubled female figures of Perpetua and Felicitas face a 'mad heifer', an adversary that the narrator assures 'was an unusual animal', 'chosen that their sex might be matched with that of the beast' (*PPF* 20.1)".

20 See on this Shaw 2004: 289–91.

21 See on this Burrus 2008, esp. 59, for references (with full bibliography) to discussions of the new subjectivity by Barton, Gleason, Perkins, and Shaw, and Burrus 2008: 70–1. Perkins, Burrus says, suggests that "by the second century, the ancient 'self' was slipping from its moorings in a mind-over-matter subjectivity grounded in conventional patriarchal familial roles, precisely by becoming more fluid, able to encompass and turn to strategic advantage stances marked as 'feminine', such as embodiment, passability and even penetrability" (Burrus 2008: 59, n. 16; Perkins 1995).

22 Palladius, *Lausiac History*, Prol. 5, trans. W.K. Lowther Clarke (London 1918), 37. Such women received accolades for their manly piety but were also condemned and feared for their gender ambiguity and their casting off of traditional roles. See Castelli 1991: 44–5.

23 Palladius, *Dialogus de vita S. Ioannis Chrysostomi* in Migne, *PG* 47.56, cited by Castelli 1991: 45 and n. 22.

24 Porphyry *Ad Marcellam*, cited by Castelli 2008: 83–4 and note 61.

25 See on this Castelli 2008: passim, esp. 83–6. She (citing Cora Lutz) notes that Musonius Rufus defends using the word ἀνδρεία ("manliness") for women, but that Plutarch, in his *On the Bravery of Women*, uses the term ἀρετή, which does not have the same male denotation (Castelli 2008: 86). See also Clark 1986: 45, who says that the phrase "manly courage" in Greek is almost a tautology "since the word for courage, *andreia*, indicates its masculine association."

26 See Castelli 2008: 76–7, citing Brock; Clark 1986: 45, who says that "the church fathers frequently asserted that asceticism was a new form of martyrdom, one in which we could be martyred daily." Cf. Jerome, *Ep.* 130 to Demetrias, where Jerome compares the courage of the virginal young maiden, who renounced marriage, to the courage shown by martyrs like Agnes (130.5).

27 Cobb 2008: 109 calls the process "creative exegesis."

28 Sermons 280–2 of Augustine are widely regarded as genuine (Migne, *PL* 38, col. 1280–6; van Beek 1936: 149★–156★). Another manuscript, containing more parts of Sermon 282 (282 auct.) was discovered in 2007 in the Erfurt University Library and is regarded as genuine; see Schiller et al. 2008: 251–60 for a discussion and pages 260–4 for the *editio princeps* of the text. Two other sermons, 394 and 394A, are not regarded as genuine but rather were composed by someone writing in the style of Augustine, perhaps Quodvultdeus, Bishop of Carthage in the early fifth century and a younger contemporary of Augustine. These are classified as *sermones dubii*; see Dolbeau 1995, 2005: 337–54 for a complete discussion of 394A; he rejects them as genuine mainly on stylistic grounds. See also on Sermons 280–2, Shaw 2004: 314–19; Elm von der Osten 2008: 275–98. Perpetua is mentioned in, though not central to, another sermon (labeled 159A by Farrell 2012: 309, n. 28); in Dolbeau 1996b, this is Sermon 3, *De Honorandis vel Contemnendis Parentibus*.

29 The augmented version of Sermon 282 discovered in Erfurt is important because it has phrases in it used also in the *Acta*, and therefore Augustine must have known the *Acta* (which are then earlier than was previously thought).

30 Another woman, Guddene, was martyred at almost the same time as Perpetua and Felicitas (on June 27, 203) in Carthage. We have a sermon written by Augustine for Guddene's feast day (Sermon 294), but in this sermon, which is on the topic of the baptism of infants, Augustine makes no mention of Guddene. For the text of Guddene's martyrdom, see Quentin 1908: 174. See on her martyrdom Shaw 2004: 325 (see also his comment in 2004: 315 and n. 79 on the fact that Augustine often used the occasion of a saint's birthday to deliver a sermon on another subject entirely, as in the case of Crispina). Shaw makes the case that the difference between Perpetua and Guddene was one of class: Perpetua provoked multiple responses from Augustine because she was of a higher social status and thus had to be reckoned with (of course Felicitas was probably a slave, but one might argue that she was privileged by Augustine because of her relationship with Perpetua). Shaw says, "In this social setting … the fact of gender was strongly, if not decisively, modulated by that of class" (325). Cf. also Cobb 2008: 178–9, n. 77; she comments on the fact that, while Augustine often acknowledges saints' days, he "rarely incorporates the saint into his homily." Perpetua also attracted more attention and refutation because we have a document purported to be written in her own words.

31 For the Latin text of Sermons 280–2, see van Beek 1936: 149★–154★.

32 Shaw says, "he is interested in making her experiences concordant not with traditional practices, but also with present and future thinking" (2004: 319).

33 See Heffernan 2012: 365, who says that Augustine was anxious to divert attention away from her "feminine heroism"; Shaw 2004: 316–19; Cobb 2008: 107–11.

34 See on representations of Eve in antiquity Flood 2011, especially 7–48.

35 See Burrus 2008: 67.

36 See Shaw 2004; Gold 2013. There is, however, disagreement about whether Perpetua is presented as a masculine or feminine figure; cf. Perkins 2009, who stresses that, apart from Perpetua's fourth vision, it is a mother's body and not a man's that is central in the *Passio* (165; cf. also 166–7). See also Cobb 2008: 176, n. 53. On gender in the *Passio*, see Williams 2012.

37 *Mulier* is often used in opposition to *virgo* (and often in parallel to *femina*) to designate a woman who is married or has had sexual experience; see *TLL* VIII 1571, 3–1575, 20, esp. 1574, 5–34. But cf. Augustine *Serm.* 282.3, where Augustine discusses the men in the group along with Perpetua and Felicitas. It was not the case that the day was named after the women, he says, because "women (*feminae*) were preferred before men (*viris*) for the worthiness of their conduct, but because the weakness of women (*muliebris infirmitas*) more marvelously did vanquish the ancient Enemy and also the strength of men (*virilis virtus*) contended to win a perpetual felicity" (see Shewring 1931: 56).

38 Quodvultdeus, Bishop of Carthage in the early fifth century, is much more explicit. He says that both Perpetua and Felicitas are mothers, one pregnant and in labor, and one nursing ("una earum erat praegnans, alia lactans. Felicitas parturiebat, Perpetua lactabat," *Sermo de tempore barbarico* 5 in van Beek 1936: 156★).

39 On the link between virginity/chastity and fecundity, see Weitbrecht 2012: 150–66, esp. 159; see also Cameron 1989 on virginity used as a metaphor and on the relationship of virginity to misogyny; Tilley

1994: 851: "what even God could not do, according to the medievalists, the church did: Perpetua and Felicitas were liturgically rendered virgins."
40 See on this Heffernan 1995: 316, n. 6. Heffernan refers to Aug. *Serm.* 282.2, and says that Augustine "finds the *Passio* of interest for its use of rhetoric, citing the *paronomasia* in the names of Perpetua and Felicitas with the virtues his Christian congregation should cultivate."
41 See on this passage van Beek 1936: 154⋆; Steinhauser 1997: 244–9, esp. 247; Farrell 2012: 308–11.
42 See Rebillard 2012: 61–91, esp. 74–9. Rebillard addresses here the multiple identities of Christians and the bishop's duty to bring his congregation together.
43 See Trout 1994 for a good discussion of Augustine's treatment of Lucretia in the *City of God*. Trout says that by re-textualizing Lucretia, "Augustine intended to confront contemporaries with the culturally subversive implications of a Christian understanding which discounted the values that symbol had so long denoted" (55).
44 Trout 1994: 57 and n. 19. Cf. also Tertullian *Ad Mart.* 4.4, who similarly says that Lucretia "stabbed herself in the presence of her kinsfolk to gain glory for her chastity." See also Loraux 1987.
45 Tertullian had already offered Lucretia among others as an example of people who in the pagan past had showed strong resistance by committing suicide (*Ad Mart.* 4.3–6). His exempla are mainly men, but Lucretia stands at the head of the list. See Weigel 2012: 189, who suggests that Perpetua's martyrdom can thus be seen not only as an *imitatio Christi* but also as an *imitatio Lucretiae*.
46 See Trout 1994: 62–5 for these themes in Augustine's treatment of Lucretia in *City of God* (*De Civ. Dei*) 1.19. On the figure of Lucretia as a pre-Perpetuan example of male fortitude in a female body, see Weigel 2012: 189–93; Williams 2012: 71–2. The Roman author Valerius Maximus says about Lucretia, a paragon of chastity, that "her manly spirit (*virilis animus*) was allotted a woman's body (*muliebre corpus*) by a malicious error of fate" (6.1.1).
47 See Sigismund-Nielsen 2012: 103 on this point.
48 See Amat 1996: 250.
49 These scholars are often, but not always, female. Brent Shaw, for example, has written an interesting critique of the *Passio* employing what I would call feminist techniques (Shaw 2004).
50 See also Cameron's note on the "valiant efforts to rehabilitate early Christian writing as women's writing" (1989: 184, n. 1).

Bibliography

Althusser, L. (1971) "Ideology and ideological state apparatuses (notes towards an investigation)", in L. Althusser (ed.), *Lenin and Philosophy and Other Essays*, trans. B. Brewster. New York: Monthly Review Press, pp. 127–86.
Amat, J. (ed., comm.) (1996) *Passion de Perpétue et de Félicité suivi des Actes*. Paris: Les Éditions du Cerf.
Aspegren, K. (1990) *The Male Woman: A Feminine Ideal in the Early Church*, ed. R. Kieffer, Uppsala Women's Studies (Acta Universitatis Upsaliensis). Stockholm: Almqvist & Wiksell International.
Bal, M. (1991) "Perpetual contest", in M. Bal (ed.) *On Story-Telling: Essays in Narratology*, ed. D. Jobling. Sonoma, CA: Polebridge Press, pp. 227–41.
Beek, C.I.M.I. van (1936) *Passio Sanctarum Perpetuae et Felicitatis*, vol. 1. Nijmegen: Dekker and Van de Vegt.
Bremmer, J.N. (1998) "The novel and the apocryphal acts: Place, time and readership", in H. Hofmann and M. Zimmerman (eds) *Groningen Colloquia on the Novel*, vol. 9. Groningen: Egbert Forsten, pp. 157–80.
——(2002) "Perpetua and her diary: Authenticity, family and visions", in W. Ameling (ed.) *Märtyrer und Märtyrerakten*. Wiesbaden: Franz Steiner Verlag, pp. 77–120.
Bremmer, J.N. and Formisano, M. (eds) (2012) *Perpetua's Passions: Multidisciplinary Approaches to the Passio Perpetuae et Felicitatis*. Oxford: Oxford University Press.
Burrus, V. (2008) "Torture and travail: Producing the Christian martyr", in A.-J. Levine and M.M. Robbins (eds) *A Feminist Companion to Patristic Literature*. London: T & T Clark International, pp. 56–71.
Cameron, A. (1989) "Virginity as metaphor: Women and the rhetoric of early Christianity", in A. Cameron (ed.) *History as Text: The Writing of Ancient History*. Chapel Hill, NC: University of North Carolina Press, pp. 181–205.
Carson, A. (1990) "Putting her in her place: Woman, dirt, and desire", in D.M. Halperin, J.J. Winkler, and F.I. Zeitlin (eds) *Before Sexuality: The Construction of Erotic Experience in the Ancient Greek World*. Princeton, NJ: Princeton University Press, pp. 135–69.

Castelli, E.A. (1991) "'I will make Mary male': Pieties of the body and gender transformation of Christian women in late antiquity", in J. Epstein and K. Straub (eds) *Body Guards: The Cultural Politics of Gender Ambiguity*. New York: Routledge, pp. 29–49.

——(2008) "Virginity and its meaning for women's sexuality in early Christianity", in A.-J. Levine and M. M. Robbins (eds) *A Feminist Companion to Patristic Literature*. London: T & T Clark International, pp. 72–100.

Clark, E.A. (1979) *Jerome, Chrysostom and Friends: Essays and Translations*, Studies in Women and Religion 2. Lewiston, NY: Edwin Mellen.

——(1986) "Devil's gateway and bride of Christ: Women in the early Christian world", in E. Clark (ed.) *Ascetic Piety and Women's Faith: Essays on Late Ancient Christianity*, Studies in Women and Religion 20. Lewiston, NY: Edwin Mellen, pp. 23–60.

——(1998) "The lady vanishes: Dilemmas of a feminist historian after the 'Linguistic Turn'", *Church History* 67(1): 1–31.

——(2008) "Ideology, history and the construction of 'woman' in late ancient Christianity", in A.-J. Levine and M.M. Robbins (eds) *A Feminist Companion to Patristic Literature*. London: T & T Clark International, pp. 101–24 (originally published in *Journal of Early Christian Studies* 2(2 [1994]): 155–84).

Cobb, L.S. (2008) *Dying to be Men: Gender and Language in Early Christian Martyr Texts*. New York: Columbia University Press.

Cooper, K. (1998) "The voice of the victim: Gender, representation and early Christian martyrdom", in G.M. Jantzen (ed.) *Bulletin of the John Rylands University Library of Manchester*, 80: *Representation, Gender and Experience*, pp. 147–57.

——(2011) "A father, a daughter, and a procurator: Authority and resistance in the prison memoir of Perpetua of Carthage", *Gender and History* 23(3): 685–702.

Dolbeau, F. (1995) "Un sermon inédit d'origine Africaine pour la fête des Saintes Perpétue et Félicité", *Analecta Bollandiana* 113: 89–106.

——(1996a) "Chronica Tertullianea et Cyprianea, 1995: Actes des Martyrs", rev. of T.J. Heffernan, "Philology and authorship in the *Passio Sanctarum Perpetuae et Felicitatis*", (*Traditio* 50 [1995]: 315–25), *Revue des Études Augustiniennes* 42: 312–13.

——(ed., comm.) (1996b) *Vingt-six sermons au peuple d'Afrique*, Paris: Institut d'Études Augustiniennes.

——(2005) *Augustin et la prédication en Afrique: Recherches sur divers sermons authentiques, apocryphes ou anonymes*. Paris: Institut d'Études Augustiniennes.

Elm von der Osten, D. (2008) "'*Perpetua Felicitas*': Die Predigten des Augustinus zur *Passio Perpetuae et Felicitatis* (S. 280–2)", in Th. Fuhrer (ed.) *Die christlich-philosophischen Diskurse der Spätantike: Texte, Personen, Institutionen*. Stuttgart: Franz Steiner Verlag, pp. 275–98.

Farrell, J. (2012) "The canonization of Perpetua", in J.N Bremmer and M. Formisano (eds) *Perpetua's Passions: Multidisciplinary Approaches to the Passio Perpetuae et Felicitatis*. Oxford: Oxford University Press, pp. 300–20.

Flood, J. (2011) *Representations of Eve in Antiquity and the English Middle Ages*. New York: Routledge.

Formisano, M. (2012) "Perpetua's prisons: Notes on the margins of literature", in J.N Bremmer and M. Formisano (eds) *Perpetua's Passions: Multidisciplinary Approaches to the Passio Perpetuae et Felicitatis*. Oxford: Oxford University Press, pp. 329–47.

Gleason, M.W. (1995) *Making Men: Sophists and Self-Presentation in Ancient Rome*. Princeton, NJ: Princeton University Press.

Gold, B.K. (1993) "'But Ariadne was never there in the first place': Finding the female in Roman poetry", in N.S. Rabinowitz and A. Richlin (eds) *Feminist Theory and the Classics*. New York: Routledge, pp. 75–101.

——(1998) "'The house I live in is not my own': Women's bodies in Juvenal's satires", *Arethusa* 31: 369–86.

——(2013) "'And I became a man': Gender fluidity and closure in Perpetua's prison narrative", in D.G. Lateiner, B.K. Gold, and J. Perkins (eds) *Roman Literature, Gender, and Reception: Domina Illustris*. New York: Routledge, pp. 153–65.

Heffernan, T.J. (1988) *Sacred Biography: Saints and their Biographers in the Middle Ages*. New York and Oxford: Oxford University Press.

——(1995) "Philology and authorship in the *Passio Sanctarum Perpetuae et Felicitatis*", *Traditio* 50: 315–25.

——(2012) *The Passion of Perpetua and Felicity*. Oxford: Oxford University Press.

Hill, E. (1994) *The Works of Saint Augustine: A Translation for the 21st Century*, Sermons III.8. Hyde Park, NY: New City Press.

Jameson, F. (1981) *The Political Unconscious: Narrative as a Socially Symbolic Act*. Ithaca, NY: Cornell University Press.

Kraemer, R. (2008) "When is a text about a woman a text about a 'woman'?: The cases of Aseneth and Perpetua", in A.-J. Levine and M.M. Robbins (eds) *A Feminist Companion to Patristic Literature*. London: T & T Clark International, pp. 156–72.

Lateiner, D. (2009) "Transsexuals and transvestites in Ovid's *Metamorphoses*", in T. Fögen and M. Lee (eds) *Bodies and Boundaries in Graeco-Roman Antiquity*. Berlin and New York: Walter de Gruyter, pp. 125–54.

Loraux, N. (1987) *Tragic Ways of Killing a Woman*, trans. A. Forster. Cambridge, MA: Harvard University Press.

MacDonald, D.R. (1987) *There is No Male and Female*. Philadelphia, PA: Fortress Press.

Miles, M.R. (1989) *Carnal Knowing: Female Nakedness and Religious Meaning in the Christian West*. Boston, MA: Beacon Press.

Perkins, J. (1995) *The Suffering Self: Pain and Narrative Representation in the Early Christian Era*. London: Routledge.

——(2009) "The rhetoric of the maternal body", in J. Perkins (ed.) *Roman Imperial Identities in the Early Christian Era*. New York: Routledge, pp. 159–71.

Quentin, H. (1908) *Les martyrologes historiques du moyen age: Étude sur la formation du martyrologe romain études d'histoire des dogines et d'ancienne litterature ecclésiastique*. Paris: Lecoffre.

Rebillard, É. (2012) *Christians and Their Many Identities in Late Antiquity, North Africa, 200–450 CE*. Ithaca, NY: Cornell University Press.

Robert, L. (1982) "Une vision de Perpétue martyre à Carthage en 203", *Comptes rendus de l'Académie des inscriptions et belles lettres* 228–76 (reprinted in his *Opera minora selecta* V (Amsterdam 1989): 791–839).

Schiller, I., Weber, D., and Weidmann, C. (2008) "Sechs neue Augustinuspredigten, Teil I (mit Edition dreier Sermones)", *Wiener Studien* 121: 227–84.

Shaw, B.D. (1996) "Body/power/identity: Passions of the martyrs", *Journal of Early Christian Studies* 4(3): 269–312.

——(2004) "The passion of Perpetua", in R. Osborne (ed.) *Studies in Ancient Greek and Roman Society*. Cambridge: Cambridge University Press, pp. 286–325 (originally published in *Past and Present* 139 [1993]: 3–45).

Shewring, W.H. (1931) *The Passion of Saints Perpetua and Felicity: A New Edition and Translation of the Latin Text Together with the Sermons of S. Augustine*. London: Sheed and Ward.

Sigismund-Nielsen, H. (2012) "Vibia Perpetua – an indecent woman", in J.N Bremmer and M. Formisano (eds) *Perpetua's Passions: Multidisciplinary Approaches to the Passio Perpetuae et Felicitatis*. Oxford: Oxford University Press, pp. 103–17.

Spivak, G.C. (1983) "Displacement and the discourse of woman", in M. Krupnick (ed.) *Displacement: Derrida and After*. Bloomington, IN: Indiana University Press, pp. 169–95.

Steinhauser, K.B. (1997) "Augustine's reading of the *Passio Sanctarum Perpetuae et Felicitatis*", *Studia Patristica* 33: 244–9.

Tilley, M.A. (1994) "The passion of Perpetua and Felicity", in E. Schüssler Fiorenza (ed.) *Searching the Scriptures*, vol. 2. New York: Crossroad, pp. 829–58.

Trout, D. (1994) "Re-textualizing Lucretia: Cultural subversion in the *City of God*", *Journal of Early Christian Studies* 2(1): 53–70.

Vidén, G. (1993) *Women in Roman Literature: Attitudes of Authors under the Early Empire*. Göteburg: Acta Universitatis Gothoburgensis.

Vogt, K. (1985) "'Becoming male': One aspect of an early Christian anthropology", in E. Schüssler Fiorenza and M. Collins (eds) *Women: Invisible in Theology and Church*. Edinburgh: T & T Clark, pp. 72–83.

Warner, M. (1985) *Monuments and Maidens: The Allegory of the Female Form*. New York: Athenaeum.

Weigel, S. (2012) "Exemplum and sacrifice, blood testimony and written testimony: Lucretia and Perpetua as transitional figures in the cultural history of martyrdom", trans. J. Golb, in J.N Bremmer and M. Formisano (eds) *Perpetua's Passions: Multidisciplinary Approaches to the Passio Perpetuae et Felicitatis*. Oxford: Oxford University Press, pp. 180–200.

Weitbrecht, J. (2012) "Maternity and sainthood in the medieval Perpetua legend", in J.N Bremmer and M. Formisano (eds) *Perpetua's Passions: Multidisciplinary Approaches to the Passio Perpetuae et Felicitatis*. Oxford: Oxford University Press, pp. 150–66.

Williams, C. (2012) "Perpetua's gender. A Latinist reads the *Passio Perpetuae et Felicitatis*", in J.N Bremmer and M. Formisano (eds) *Perpetua's Passions: Multidisciplinary Approaches to the Passio Perpetuae et Felicitatis*. Oxford: Oxford University Press, pp. 54–77.

28

AGATHIAS AND PAUL THE SILENTIARY

Erotic epigram and the sublimation of same-sex desire in the age of Justinian

Steven D. Smith

Around the middle of the sixth century CE in Constantinople, the poet and lawyer Agathias of Myrina composed the following verses denouncing male same-sex desire:[1]

αὐτή μοι Κυθέρεια καὶ ἱμερόεντες Ἔρωτες
τήξουσιν κενεὴν ἐχθόμενοι κραδίην.
ἄρσενας εἰ σπεύσω φιλέειν ποτέ, μήτε τυχήσω
μήτ' ἐπολισθήσω μείζοσιν ἀμπλακίαις.
ἄρκια θηλυτέρων ἁλιτήματα· κεῖνα κομίσσω,
καλλείψω δὲ νέους ἄφρονι Πιτταλάκῳ.

Cythereia herself and the Loves that excite desire, in their hatred of me, will melt my empty heart. If I am ever eager to love males, let me not succeed and let me not slip in these greater sins. Sinning with the opposite sex is enough: that I'll take, but I'll leave youths behind for foolish Pittalacus.

(AP 5.278 Agathias)

This poem was part of an anthology of epigrams by contemporary poets that was collected and arranged by Agathias himself in Constantinople around 567 and came to be known as the *Cycle*, much of which survives transmitted in sequences scattered throughout the *Greek Anthology*, a tenth-century collection. Though Agathias' *Cycle* appeared shortly after the accession of Justin II (565), most of the poems date from the final decades of Justinian's reign.[2] In the verse preface, Agathias describes himself and his contemporaries as the "parents of new song" (νέης γενετῆρες ἀοιδῆς, *AP* 4.4.68), reviving classical epigram for a new age. Agathias divided the collection thematically into seven books, but this essay is concerned primarily with the erotic epigrams of Book 6 (preserved in Book 5 of the *Greek Anthology*), in which Aphrodite intervenes, "stealing the song" (μέλος κλέπτουσα, *AP* 4.4.83).

A reasonable reaction after reading the epigram quoted above is to wonder why Agathias felt the need to announce in verse form his apparent distaste for the love of males. Even if we grant that this epigram offers literary evidence of the poet's erotic disposition (a conclusion I think unwarranted), the question remains: why does the repudiation of male same-sex desire appear in this poetry? One explanation is that this poem was composed at a time when the emperor Justinian (r. 527–65) aggressively persecuted men who engaged in or were thought to have engaged in sexual relations with other males. It is the goal of this essay, then, to propose what effect, beyond that of fear, Justinian's persecutions had on writers of the period for whom same-sex desire might not otherwise have posed a problem or might even have been an attractive subject. The increasingly Christian world of late antiquity did not altogether eradicate representations of same-sex desire; in the fifth century, for example, Nonnus' *Dionysiaka* lavishly depicted a sensuous homoerotic relationship between Dionysus and the satyr Ampelus, and from that love grew the vine, the source of Dionysus' divine gift to mortals.[3] But turning to the poetry of the sixth century to look for such expressions of same-sex desire, one finds either silence or loud protestations of disavowal.[4] This silence and explicit disavowal cannot, however, be the end of the discussion; same-sex desire found poetic expression during the age of Justinian, albeit in a sublimated and ambiguous manner.

Persecution

By the sixth century, legislation against male same-sex sexual activity was not new in the Roman world,[5] but the legal persecution of such activity intensified during the reign of Justinian. In only the second year of his reign (528), Justinian began a purge of bishops and other men accused of engaging in sexual activity with other males and we have graphic evidence of this purge from several authors: the perpetrators were arrested, castrated, paraded in public, and killed; the castration may have been the cause of their deaths.[6] Justinian also expanded the *Lex Iulia de Adulteriis Coercendis* to punish with death also those men "who dare to exercise their unspeakable lust with males" (*qui cum masculis infandam libidinem exercere audent, Institutes* 4.18.4).

Following his revision of the *Lex Iulia*, Justinian issued two new imperial regulations (*novellae constitutiones*) on the same topic, *Novellae* 77 (538) and 141 (559), which sought to prevent God's wrath against whole cities and populations tolerating male same-sex sexual activity. The intensity of Justinian's anxiety about the earthquakes and plague that occurred during his reign – signs, he thought, of God's anger – is reflected in the laws' scathing rhetoric. The first law targets primarily "those possessed by the power of the devil" (ὑπὸ τῆς διαβολικῆς ἐνεργείας συνεχόμενοι, Schöll and Kroll 1895: 382) who "have both plunged themselves into grievous licentiousness and do what is the opposite of nature itself" (καὶ ταῖς βαρυτέραις ἀσελγείαις ἑαυτοὺς ἐνέβαλον καὶ αὐτῆς τῆς φύσεως τἀναντία πράττουσι). The second law demands repentance – and failing that, punishment – of "those growing putrid together with the loathsome and unholy deed justly hateful to God; indeed we mean the corruption of males, which in an ungodly manner some dare, males with males, by committing obscenity" (τοὺς τῇ μυσαρᾷ καὶ θεῷ μεμισημένῃ δικαίως ἀνοσίᾳ πράξει συνσαπέντας· λέγομεν δὴ τὴν τῶν ἀρρένων φθοράν, ἣν ἀθέως τολμῶσί τινες ἄρρενες ἐν ἄρρεσι τὴν ἀσχημοσύνην κατεργαζόμενοι, Schöll and Kroll 1895: 704).[7] The emperor's intolerance has Biblical justification: the last phrase from this passage is a virtual quotation of Paul's Epistle to the Romans (ἄρσενες ἐν ἄρσεσιν τὴν ἀσχημοσύνην κατεργαζόμενοι, 1:27).

In order to convey the impact of Justinian's persecutions and at the same time to clarify what I mean throughout this essay by male same-sex sexual activity (as opposed to classical Greek *paiderastia*), it is worth considering briefly the summary of these events by one of Agathias' contemporaries, the Syrian chronicler John Malalas:

And at this time some of the bishops from various provinces were slandered in the belief that they were living wickedly concerning the things of the body and were sleeping with males [*arsenokoitountes*]. Among whom was Ēsaias of Rhodes, one of the chief officers of the night watch of Constantinople, and likewise also one from Thracian Diopolis named Alexandros. They, in accordance with the divine ordinance, were brought to Constantinople, and having been examined were condemned by Victor, the city prefect, who punished them: Ēsaias after merciless torture he exiled, and Alexandros after castration he paraded in a hearse; and straightaway the same emperor commanded those being discovered in erotic relationships with boys [*paiderastiai*] to be castrated. And at this time were arrested many men who sleep with men [*androkoitai*], and after castration they died. And thereafter fear descended upon those plagued by a desire for males [*tēn tōn arrhenōn epithumian*].

(Malalas 18.18 Thurn 2000)

In this paragraph Malalas is concerned in a general sense with the persecution of adult men engaging in sexual activity with members of their own sex. The terms or phrases that Malalas uses are: *arsenokoitein* ("to sleep with males"), *paiderastia* ("desire for boys"), *androkoitēs* ("a man who sleeps with adult men"), and *hē tōn arrhenōn epithumia* ("the desire for males"). The first three are compound words, the initial stems of which (*arseno-*, *paid-*, and *andro-*) all deserve closer inspection: I take *arsenes* to refer to persons of the male sex generally, regardless of age, while *paides* refers to boys and *andres* refers to adult men. The first of Malalas' terms, the verb *arsenokoitein*, is a scriptural allusion to the First Epistle to the Corinthians, in which Paul includes men who sleep with males (*arsenokoitai*, 6:9) in a catalogue of those who will fail to inherit the kingdom of God. Malalas' use of the verb *arsenokoitein* also echoes Justinian's imperial prohibition in the *Novellae* of sexual activity between males, regardless of age or sexual role. Within this general conception of male same-sex desire and activity there are variants: the terms *paiderastia* ("[a man's] desire for boys") and *androkoitēs* ("a man who sleeps with men") imply respectively the concepts *to paiderastein* ("[a man's] having sexual desire for boys") and *to androkoitein* ("[a man's] sleeping with adult men"). The former had an ancient and famous pedigree within Greek culture; the latter, though, appears for the first time in Malalas.[8] Both, however, were prohibited under Justinian, because both fall under the more general Christianizing prohibition against sexual activity between males.

Following the model implied by Malalas' passage, therefore, in this essay I maintain the distinction between *paiderastia* (sexual desire for boys) and *androkoitein* (a man's sexual activity with other adult men), if only to signal the continued awareness in the sixth century of the long cultural heritage of *paiderastia*. The point remains, though, that even the ancient pedigree of *paiderastia* does not save it from Christian condemnation. During the reign of Justinian, for a man to be caught in bed with a boy is just as bad as being caught in bed with a grown man. Both are thought to be grave perversions requiring stern correction. Consequently, though contemporary classicizing poets may refer to *paiderastia*, it is with the acute awareness that this is but one expression of a larger repertoire of prohibited same-sex desires and activities.

The fraught atmosphere created by Justinian's persecutions shaped the erotic poetry of the period, but Agathias and his peers should not be thought of as merely cowering in fear of castration and death, though those were certainly legitimate fears. It says much, for example, that they chose to write sensuous erotic epigram at all in the face of that fear. Moreover, the poetry of Agathias' circle was a highly developed discourse of artifice, whose very claim of artificiality belies a subversive power to question and challenge Justinian's cultural program. Indeed, the *Cycle* contains enough questionable material that it would have stood out as frankly provocative within Justinian's pious Christian society. And although some of Agathias' erotic epigrams express a disavowal of same-sex desire, the erotic poetry of Agathias and Paul is nevertheless an early illustration of how same-sex desire could be artfully, surreptitiously articulated within a morally conservative Christian context that was intolerant of such desires.[9] In what follows, I offer a brief survey to show that much work remains to be done to uncover the levels of dissimulation – and particularly sexual dissimulation – in literature from the age of Justinian.[10]

This dissimulation and sublimation should not be surprising, for, as Eve Sedgwick reminds us, "in the vicinity of the closet, even what *counts* as a speech act is problematized on a perfectly routine basis."[11] Likewise, according to Foucault,

> there is no binary division to be made between what one says and what one does not say; we must try to determine the different ways of not saying such things ... There is not one but many silences, and they are an integral part of the strategies that underlie and permeate discourses.[12]

It may already be clear to some readers that many of my interpretations in this essay are informed by queer theory, especially as represented by the work of Judith Butler and Eve Sedgwick. Butler has developed ways of thinking about gender as socially constructed and about the phantasmatic quality of the supposedly natural heterosexual opposition between male and female, while Sedgwick has offered a model for thinking about male same-sex desire as but one phenomenon within a broader homosocial continuum.[13] Bringing these theoretical insights to a reading of Agathias' *Cycle* is justified on the grounds that Justinian's legislation against male same-sex sexual activity (a) sought to reinforce as divine law the illusion that the only natural expression of erotic desire was sex between male and female; and (b) was consequently instrumental in the formation of the closet in late antiquity. By positing the existence of a "closet" in late antiquity, I do not mean to imply also the existence in late antiquity of a homosexual identity, which is of course a modern phenomenon. This emergent closet did, however, impact the expression of desire in contemporary erotic poetry. I contend that the epigrams of Paul and Agathias sublimate same-sex desire by affecting denial of that very desire, by adopting female personae, and by representing that desire as emergent within an erotic triangle containing one woman and two men.

One last note before turning to the poems themselves. Agathias included the epigrams of at least 23 poets in his collection,[14] but I restrict my analysis to the poems of Agathias and Paul, and do so for two reasons. First, Agathias and Paul wrote most of the erotic epigrams included in the *Cycle*. Of the 86 poems from the *Cycle* in Book 5 of the *Greek Anthology*, 63 (nearly 75 percent) are by Agathias and Paul, and Paul, with 40 poems, is the most prolific contributor by far. Second, there is evidence in both the *Cycle* and the *Histories* that Agathias and Paul were close friends.[15] I venture therefore to identify the sublimation of same-sex desire in epigrams by two poets who are known to have shared a deep homosocial bond. I do not foreclose the possibility that the bond between Agathias and Paul may even have been erotic, but I also do not insist on this point. The intimate homosocial bond, I suggest, would be a sufficient basis for an increased sensitivity to homoeroticism and its attendant anxieties in the age of Justinian. At the very least, the intense homosocial bond facilitates a poetic flirtation with the homoerotic.

Affected denial

In two epigrams by Agathias, the speaker distances himself from homoerotic desire, a gesture that I identify as affected denial. There was a tradition for such poems extending back to the

Hellenistic and Imperial periods, though similar poems by Rufinus, Marcus Argentarius, and Meleager are more graphically sexual in nature.[16] It is noteworthy that the first of these poems by Agathias immediately follows a similar epigram by his contemporary Eratosthenes Scholasticus, himself a poet of the *Cycle*.[17] It is possible that Agathias wrote his poem in imitation of the poem by Eratosthenes and that their juxtaposition in the collection was meant to show off the way Agathias varied and adapted the motifs in the earlier epigram.[18] The artificial context therefore immediately poses a serious challenge to the sincerity of Agathias' claims in the poem. There is more to be said, though, about this playful expression of disavowal, and so it is worth quoting the first of these poems again in its entirety:

> αὐτή μοι Κυθέρεια καὶ ἱμερόεντες Ἔρωτες
> τήξουσιν κενεὴν ἐχθόμενοι κραδίην.
> ἄρσενας εἰ σπεύσω φιλέειν ποτέ, μήτε τυχήσω
> μήτ' ἐπολισθήσω μείζοσιν ἀμπλακίαις.
> ἄρκια θηλυτέρων ἀλιτήματα· κεῖνα κομίσσω,
> καλλείψω δὲ νέους ἄφρονι Πιτταλάκῳ.

> Cythereia herself and the Loves that excite desire, in their hatred of me, will melt my empty heart. If I am ever eager to love males, let me not succeed and let me not slip in these greater sins. Sinning with the opposite sex is enough: that I'll take, but I'll leave youths behind for foolish Pittalacus.

> *(AP 5.278 Agathias)*

Despite the reference to Aphrodite and the Erotes, as several scholars have noted, the message would have appealed to ascetic Christian morality.[19] Agathias lived in a world where, in public discourse at least, all sex was sinful, though heterosexual sex was less so than sex between males. And although the speaker of the poem loudly refuses sex with males, the more grievous sin, it is clear that he is not repulsed by the idea. The two negative subjunctive verbs in verses 3 and 4 suggest in fact that the speaker not only has sexual desires for males but that he also has the drive to act on those sinful desires. "Let me not succeed," the poet declares, implying that against his supposedly better judgment he may actually persist in his erotic pursuit of males. The additional prayer, "let me not slip in these greater sins," shows that his claim/wish for only heterosexual desire is defined in contradistinction to and by his disavowal of same-sex desire. The speaker's exclusively heterosexual desires, in other words, are not a natural disposition, but a practice that must be continually reinforced.[20]

This interpretation is borne out by the learned allusion with which the epigram concludes: "but I'll leave youths behind for foolish Pittalacus" (καλλείψω δὲ νέους ἄφρονι Πιτταλάκῳ, *AP* 5.278.6). Agathias expects his readers to be familiar with a famous scandal from antiquity. Pittalacus was a public slave in Athens who was addicted to gambling and whose homoerotic besottedness and dramatic jealousy Aeschines famously reported in his speech *Against Timarchus* (55–66). Viansino suggests that Agathias' reference to Pittalacus might be a function of Agathias' involvement with law, a lawyer's classical *exemplum*.[21] But consideration of Pittalacus' story as told by Aeschines reveals a problematic relationship between *erōs* and ethics that is relevant to the deeper theme of self-control in Agathias' poem. Aeschines was outraged that Timarchus, a free citizen and a *meirakion* old enough to know better, should have prostituted himself to a mere public slave of the city (δημόσιος οἰκέτης τῆς πόλεως, 54). "And I myself have heard," he declared, "that such acts and such outrages were committed by this man against the body of

Timarchus that I – by Olympian Zeus! – would not dare to mention them to you" (καὶ τοιαῦτα πράγματα καὶ τοιαύτας ὕβρεις ἐγὼ ἀκήκοα γεγονέναι ὑπὸ τοῦ ἀνθρώπου τούτου εἰς τὸ σῶμα τοῦ Τιμάρχου οἵας ἐγὼ μὰ τὸν Δία τὸν Ὀλύμπιον οὐκ ἂν τολμήσαιμι πρὸς ὑμᾶς εἰπεῖν, 55).

But Pittalacus, it turns out, was a loser in love: he could not keep the young man for long, for his beloved Timarchus was quickly seduced by a certain Hegesander, arousing Pittalacus' jealousy and causing Pittalacus to become a nuisance to the new couple. One night in a drunken folly, Timarchus and Hegesander broke into Pittalacus' house, destroyed his belongings, and killed his pet birds; they then tied Pittalacus to a column and whipped him violently. The next morning Pittalacus made a public spectacle of himself, sitting naked as a suppliant at the altar of the mother of the gods. Timarchus and Hegesander feared that Pittalacus' melodramatic display would bring to light their scandalous behavior, and so Timarchus, by promising sexual favors, managed to persuade Pittalacus to relent. But Pittalacus was duped, for Timarchus never made good on his promises. Pittalacus attempted to bring lawsuits against Timarchus and Hegesander, but eventually, realizing how influential Hegesander was, he gave up trying to get his revenge on the pair.

Pittalacus' story is one of powerlessness, both over himself and over his circumstances. His slavish nature is reflected in his inability not only to demonstrate self-control in his private life (witness his addiction to gambling and his erotic obsession with Timarchus) but also to claim any kind of authority in his public life: Pittalacus was deluded in thinking that he, as a mere public slave, could have any hope of prevailing in litigation against a free citizen as wealthy and as popular as Hegesander. But what fascinated later generations was Pittalacus' erotic mania, which was perceived as an ethical failure to exercise control over his desires. The fourth-century sophist Libanius in one of his *progymnasmata* conjures an elaborate anecdote in which the philosopher Theophrastus defines *erōs* as "something experienced by an idle soul" (πάθος ψυχῆς σχολαζούσης, 3.4). Within the imaginary context of Libanius' rhetorical exercise, Pittalacus serves as a classical example of just such a soul: he and others like him "were slaves to such loves" (τοιούτοις ἐδούλευον ἔρωσιν, 3.4.12) because of the laziness of their lives and because they failed to foster the intellect.

Returning to the final verse of Agathias' poem ("but I'll leave youths behind for foolish Pittalacus"), we will ask why Pittalacus is "foolish" (*aphrōn*). He is not a fool simply because he is obsessed with *paiderastia*, habitually pursuing youths as objects of desire. The word *aphrōn* (ἄφρων) indicates an important lack: Pittalacus is without *phrēn* (φρήν), the critical psychic capacity associated with the intellect.[22] His foolishness, in other words, derives from the fact that he has not the ethical will or purpose to suppress his erotic desires for males. Consequently, by contrasting himself with the notorious Pittalacus, the speaker in Agathias' poem implicitly characterizes himself as the opposite of one who is *aphrōn*, that is, he is *sōphrōn*, literally one whose *phrēn* (φρήν) is *sōs* (σῶς), safe and intact, and therefore a man "having control over the sensuous desires."[23] The allusion to Pittalacus, then, reinforces the idea in the preceding verses that the heterosexual *sōphrosynē* required of Christian scripture and imperial law is an ongoing process of self-formation based on the denial of very real and pressing desires. A man's not having a desire for other males is not, then, a natural disposition; on the contrary, the man remains so haunted by those desires that he must pray in a state of fear: "let me not succeed and let me not slip in these greater sins."

Though it treats an erotic theme, Agathias' other poem of affected denial is technically an exhortation and is therefore found not in Book 5 with the other erotic poems of the *Greek Anthology*, but in the protreptic epigrams of Book 10:

καλὸν μὲν στυγόδεμνον ἔχειν νόον· εἰ δ' ἄρ' ἀνάγκη,
ἀρσενικὴ φιλότης μή ποτέ σε κλονέοι.
Θηλυτέρας φιλέειν ὀλίγον κακόν, οὕνεκα κείναις
κυπριδίους ὀάρους πότνα δέδωκε φύσις.
δέρκεο τῶν ἀλόγων ζῴων γένος· ἦ γὰρ ἐκείνων
οὐδὲν ἀτιμάζει θέσμια συζυγίης·
ἄρσενι γὰρ θήλεια συνάπτεται· οἱ δ' ἀλεγεινοὶ
ἄνδρες ἐς ἀλλήλους ξεῖνον ἄγουσι γάμον.

It is a fine thing to have a mind that hates marriage. But if you must, may the love of males not harass you. To love the opposite sex is a small evil, because revered nature gave them Aphrodite's songs. Look at the race of senseless beasts: none of them dishonors the laws of coupling, for the female joins with the male. But men, full of trouble, make marriages to each other that are strange.

(AP 10.68 Agathias)

McCail has noted the allusion to Paul's First Epistle to the Corinthians (λέγω δὲ τοῖς ἀγάμοις καὶ ταῖς χήραις, καλὸν αὐτοῖς ἐὰν μείνωσιν ὡς κἀγώ, 7:8) with which the poem begins as well as the allusion to the argument from nature in Paul's Epistle to the Romans (1:27). There are also important parallels to Justinian's *Novella* 141. Like Justinian (Schöll and Kroll 1895: 704), Agathias too cites Paul's argument from nature as the basis for his moral authority. Furthermore Agathias' phrase ἄνδρες ἐς ἀλλήλους echoes Justinian's paraphrase of Paul on the subject of sex between men (ἄρρενες ἐν ἄρρεσι, *Nov.* 141, Schöll and Kroll 1895: 704; cf. Paul's Epistle to the Romans 1:27).[24] Mattsson reads the poem as an expression of heartfelt sincerity and Averil Cameron sees it as an unproblematic "vehicle for moralizing," while McCail goes even further, not just reading the epigram as a sincere product of Agathias' Christian morality, but suggesting that the poet was a collaborator in the emperor's campaign to purge Constantinople of male same-sex sexual activity.[25]

The first rationale provided by the poet for disavowing sex between males occurs in the second couplet: making love to the opposite sex is a small evil, and for this reason nature (φύσις) gave women "the songs of Aphrodite" (κυπριδίους ὀάρους). The poet must mean, of course, that nature has endowed women with the powers of seduction, but it is noteworthy that that power is described here as *song*: the erotic attraction of women derives not from some innate physical presence, but from their skill in crafting verse. The accusative plural form ὀάρους occurs only once more in the *Cycle*: in the preface Agathias describes Aphrodite's intervention in the collection, conceding that she "may divert our path into elegiac poetry (lit. "songs of elegiac poetry") also into sweet erotic passions" (εἰς ὀάρους ἐλέγοιο παρατρέψειε πορείην / καὶ γλυκερούς ἐς ἔρωτας, *AP* 4.4.84–5). Within the verse world of the *Cycle*, then, erotically inspired poets like Agathias share the power of erotic song with women. Even in a mode ostensibly expressive of conservative morality, Agathias' language evokes the erotic mode of Book 5 of the *Cycle*, disruptively assimilating his own moralizing poetry with songs of feminine seduction.

The poet then challenges the reader to "consider the race of irrational beasts" (δέρκεο τῶν ἀλόγων ζῴων γένος).[26] The argument that same-sex desire is unnatural extends back to Plato (*Lg.* 836c).[26] The argument from nature was, in fact, so hackneyed even by the first century CE as to prompt Plutarch's criticism that philosophers invoked it "as though there were no proof of nature within ourselves" (*De amore prolis* 493c2). The argument from nature is treated with irony in the Greek novels, which illustrates that a privileged heterosexual desire based on the example of nature could be unveiled as the product of a sophistic art.[27] Within the epigrammatic tradition, moreover, one finds the following remarkable verses by Strato:

πᾶν ἄλογον ζῷον βινεῖ μόνον· οἱ λογικοὶ δὲ
τῶν ἄλλων ζῴων τοῦτ᾽ ἔχομεν τὸ πλέον
πυγίζειν εὑρόντες. ὅσοι δὲ γυναιξὶ κρατοῦνται,
τῶν ἀλόγων ζῴων οὐδὲν ἔχουσι πλέον.

Every irrational creature merely fucks. But we, possessed of reason, have this over the other creatures: we discovered butt-fucking. And whoever are dominated by women, they are nothing more than the irrational beasts.[28]

(*AP 12.245* Strato)

Strato humorously reverses the discourse to argue that male same-sex sexual activity is not an unnatural perversion, but actually a cultural advance that distinguishes humans from irrational animals. This is just the sort of epigram that Agathias was careful not to include in the *Cycle*. He knew Strato's poetry, though, and by crafting his own epigram in opposition to *paiderastia* on the basis of an argument from nature, Agathias slyly appeals to the sophisticated reader's knowledge of this poem by Strato in particular. In the entirety of the *Greek Anthology*, the phrase ἀλόγων ζῴων occurs *only* in these two poems. Viansino too notes the connection with Strato's epigram, but he leaves no room for irony: the allusion merely serves "per la dimostrazione contraria."[29] Agathias dresses the whole of the epigram in pious rhetoric from the New Testament, but the allusion to Strato's humorously "progressive, evolutionary view"[30] of male same-sex desire undermines the genuineness of the Christian moralizing. Agathias may have purged the *Cycle* of epigrams sympathetic to same-sex desire and included some seemingly earnest poems against such desire, thereby toeing the official line as laid out most recently in the edict of 559. But in this hortatory epigram he also arguably deploys a studied literary allusion to subversive effect.

The poet's final statement in the closing verses of the epigram are also tantalizing for their latent potential to disrupt the poem's ostensible message: "But men, full of trouble (ἀλεγεινοί), make marriages to each other that are strange (ξεῖνον)" (7–8). The adjective ἀλεγεινοί ("full of trouble") recalls the horses of Achilles, "troublesome to tame" (ἀλεγεινοὶ … δαμήμεναι, *Il.* 10.402–3), or even the "troublesome waves" (ἀλεγεινὰ … κύματα, *Od.* 8.183; 13.91, 264) that Odysseus could not conquer. The word evokes a force of nature impossible to subdue, and its application here to men who "make marriages to each other" suggests that no amount of Christian scripture or imperial law will completely eradicate male same-sex desire. Even the poet's claim that such marriages are ξεῖνον is suffused with ambiguity. As an adjective, the word often connotes that which is "foreign," "strange," or "unusual." But as is well known, the same word when used as a noun has a double meaning, for ὁ ξεῖνος (ὁ ξένος in Attic) is the stranger who can become the guest-friend, forever connected to his host by the bond of hospitality. So prevalent was the positive meaning of this word that by the classical period, it was frequently combined with the word for "friend" in the formulaic expression ξένος καὶ φίλος.[31] Even the negative adjectival use of the word in Agathias' poem could have triggered this cloud of positive associations. Therefore, despite the poet's apparent intention to impugn sexual desire between males, his description of their coupling as a ξεῖνον γάμον ("strange marriage") nevertheless extends to their union the potential for an all but sacred intimacy.[32]

Feminine personae

A salient feature of Roman love elegy is the apparent reversal of gender roles, and Barbara Gold, Maria Wyke, and others have addressed the subversive power of that reversal.[33] Whether direct or indirect, the influence of Latin love elegy on Agathias and Paul is worth exploring.[34]

Moreover, the theoretical insights of feminist scholarship on Latin love elegy are helpful in considering the *explicit* gender reversal of the poet's voice and the subversive potential of this reversal in two poems by Paul and Agathias in which it facilitates (a) the possibility for a male poet to articulate same-sex desire while safely concealed behind the persona of a woman; and (b) an alternative vision of the homosocial world of sixth-century Constantinople.

First, Paul's poem:

Ἱππομένην φιλέουσα νόον προσέρεισα Λεάνδρῳ
ἐν δὲ Λεανδρείοις χείλεσι πηγνυμένη
εἰκόνα τὴν Ξάνθοιο φέρω φρεσί· πλεξαμένη δὲ
Ξάνθον ἐς Ἱππομένην νόστιμον ἦτορ ἄγω.
πάντα τὸν ἐν παλάμῃσιν ἀναίνομαι· ἄλλοτε δ' ἄλλον
αἰὲν ἀμοιβαίοις πήχεσι δεχνυμένη
ἀφνειὴν Κυθέρειαν ὑπέρχομαι. εἰ δέ τις ἡμῖν
μέμφεται, ἐν πενίῃ μιμνέτω οἰογάμῳ.

Kissing Hippomenes, I set my mind on Leander. And while planted on the lips of Leander, I bear in my heart an image of Xanthus. And while embracing Xanthus, I lead my heart back to Hippomenes. I spurn each one that's in my grasp, and sometimes receiving one man and sometimes another in my promiscuous arms, I seek to procure for myself a rich Cytherea. And if someone finds fault with me, let him be content with the poverty of monogamy.

(AP 5.232 Paul)

There are precedents in the *Greek Anthology* for a lover's expression of being torn between multiple loves, but these are to be found among the epigrams celebrating *paiderastia* in Book 12.[35] The novelty of Paul's approach is that he articulates similar desires, but in the voice of a woman. Just as Agathias' seemingly anti-pederastic poem subverted its own message by alluding to Strato's praise of *paiderastia*, so Paul's manipulation of the theme of multiple loves likewise draws the reader's attention back to the homoerotic desire of the *Musa Puerilis*, another name for the predominantly pederastic twelfth book of the *Anthology*. The choice of persona cannot be explained away merely as Paul's wish to describe, as Viansino calls it, "la capricciosità del cuore femminile";[36] the female persona is, rather, another way in which male same-sex desire has been sublimated to conform with the compulsory heterosexuality of Justinian's Constantinople. Let me explain.

Even though the epigram speaks in a heterosexual idiom, a provocative, transgressive sexuality remains.[37] The freedom with which Paul articulates a promiscuous sexual desire for men – even disguised behind a female persona – is surprising. The speaker's desire for multiple partners is not treated on its own terms, but in stark contrast to what is termed "the poverty of monogamy" (πενίῃ οἰογάμῳ), a long-established Christian ideal by the time Paul was writing.[38] As in Agathias' poem above, the default alternative to monogamous heterosexual marriage is "the love of males" (ἀρσενικὴ φιλότης, *AP* 10.68.2), and Paul's speaker revels in her countercultural desire. Moreover, whereas the love elegies of Propertius, Tibullus, and Ovid subvert traditional Roman conceptions of gender by casting a male narrator in the disempowered, effeminate role of *servus amoris*, Paul here jettisons the figure of the male narrator altogether in what amounts to a queer disavowal of masculine authority: in fact Paul becomes the woman himself and embraces an overt sexuality to accompany so transgressive an act. If he cannot write explicitly homoerotic epigrams, he will perform a kind of literary "drag."

It is profitable to consider the sexually subversive quality of Paul's epigram in terms of Judith Butler's theory that normative notions of gender and desire are merely illusions that are reified by means of repeated performance and imitation.[39] Paul's epigram may be read as an exaggerated inversion of one normative standard for gender performance, an inversion that finds expression in the celebration of a woman's thoroughly transgressive desire. Masculine asceticism, heterosexual monogamy, and subservient femininity all find their opposites on wonderful, lurid display in this poem. Furthermore, Paul transforms traditional epigrammatic material – an adult male lover's besottedness for multiple boy loves – into something new: a woman's erotic desire for multiple adult men. Paul thus appears to heterosexualize a traditionally homoerotic poetic mode, but the heterosexual desire to which the poem gives voice, flagrantly resisting monogamy in favor of a "rich Cythereia," represents a voracious sexuality that is just as disruptive as the ἀρσενικὴ φιλότης outlawed by both Christian scripture and Justinian's laws. Paul's epigram therefore opens up a theoretical space where sympathetic readers may deconstruct (or at least take pleasure in the sensuous flouting of) the normative heterosexual paradigm authorized by the Church and Justinian. I concede that *mimēsis* ("imitation") was the traditional, dominant practice in the literary cultures of Greece and Rome and rhetorical role-playing was to be expected. But in the right hands and with the right motivation, *mimēsis* could be something more than the mere imitation of classical models.[40] A case in point is when *mimēsis* irreverently thematizes gender and transgressive sexual desire, as Paul's epigram does, demonstrating that the play of masks in literary *mimēsis* can give a voice to abject subjects and desires and at the same time provide a necessary camouflage.

The adoption of a female persona in Agathias' epigram has a very different effect:

ἠϊθέοις οὐκ ἔστι τόσος πόνος ὁππόσος ἡμῖν
ταῖς ἀταλοψύχοις ἔχραε θηλυτέραις.
τοῖς μὲν γὰρ παρέασιν ὁμήλικες, οἷς τὰ μερίμνης
ἄλγεα μυθεῦνται φθέγματι θαρσαλέῳ,
παίγνιά τ᾽ ἀμφιέπουσι παρήγορα καὶ κατ᾽ ἀγυιὰς
πλάζονται γραφίδων χρώμασι ῥεμβόμενοι·
ἡμῖν δ᾽ οὐδὲ φάος λεύσσειν θέμις, ἀλλὰ μελάθροις
κρυπτόμεθα ζοφεραῖς φροντίσι τηκόμεναι.

For bachelors there is not so much suffering as is the experience for us soft-hearted females. Their peers are there for them and they tell them in a confident voice what troubles their mind, and they attend the games to console themselves and they wander the streets surrounded by the colors of paintings. We on the other hand are not allowed even to see the light, but are hidden in our chambers, consumed with gloomy thoughts.

(AP 5.297 Agathias)

Whereas Paul adopts a female persona to give voice to transgressive sexual desires, Agathias' female persona is more pensive; it is that of a sheltered woman who looks out with envy at the world of men and their rich urban life. The world described by the woman in the poem is the very world inhabited by Agathias and Paul, but it is striking how Agathias strives to look at that world through another's eyes. The transference of perspective inflects the homosocial bonds between peers and friends with a newfound intimacy: the woman sees men together, pouring their hearts out to each other and unburdening themselves in a way that is inaccessible to women. And that they are able to forge these bonds so publicly intensifies the speaker's feeling of solitude: men speak to each other with confidence, they go to the hippodrome together, they become as much an object of the public gaze as the city's artistic splendors. This poem may also reflect Agathias' own partial distance from the world to which he ostensibly belongs, if he has same-sex desire with which he struggles. If so, sympathetic readers might sense a double tragedy implied in the poem's emphatic final words. The gloomy thoughts that consume the heart are felt equally by the woman concealed in her dusky chamber and by the poet, who, already putting up a front, must speak from behind a mask of the other gender to describe the (ironically) public lives that men lead together in Constantinople.

Erotic triangles

The term "erotic triangle" refers to a male–female erotic relationship that is complicated by the involvement of a second male, either an intimate friend of the male lover or a rival for the affections of the female beloved. In developing a queer approach to the erotic triangle in late Greek epigram, I have in mind the theorization of male homosocial desire proposed by Eve Sedgwick, whose identification in modernity of a radical disruption in the continuum between male homosocial relationships and same-sex sexual activity[41] holds true also for sixth-century Byzantium as a result of Justinian's legislation. Although an ostensibly heterosexual erotic triangle, focusing male desire on the female member of the triangle, might seem to redirect or dilute homoerotic desire, the relationship between men only ends up becoming intensified. Two paired epigrams from the *Cycle* in particular reveal a complex social and sexual entanglement between Agathias and Paul via an erotic triangle.

In the first of the two poems that follow, Agathias, who is busy with his legal studies, writes to Paul wishing that he could be present with him and an anonymous young woman in the idyllic country setting that they are enjoying.[42] In his response, Paul encourages his companion to give more heed to *erōs* and less to law. Here are both epigrams:

> ἐνθάδε μὲν χλοάουσα τεθηλότι βῶλος ὀράμνῳ
> φυλλάδος εὐκάρπου πᾶσαν ἔδειξε χάριν·
> ἐνθάδε δὲ κλάζουσιν ὑπὸ σκιεραῖς κυπαρίσσοις
> ὄρνιθες δροσερῶν μητέρες ὀρταλίχων,
> καὶ λιγυρὸν βομβεῦσιν ἀκανθίδες· ἡ δ' ὀλολυγὼν
> τρύζει, τρηχαλέαις ἐνδιάουσα βάτοις.
> ἀλλὰ τί μοι τῶν ἦδος, ἐπεὶ σέο μῦθον ἀκούειν
> ἤθελον ἢ κιθάρης κρούσματα Δηλιάδος;
> καί μοι δισσὸς ἔρως περικίδναται· εἰσοράαν γὰρ
> καὶ σέ, μάκαρ, ποθέω καὶ γλυκερὴν δάμαλιν,
> ἧς με περισμύχουσι μεληδόνες. ἀλλά με θεσμοὶ
> εἴργουσιν ῥαδινῆς τηλόθι δορκαλίδος.

There the land, verdant with blooming branch, displays all the favor of fruitful foliage. And there birds, the mothers of tender chicks, chirp beneath the shady cypresses, and goldfinches buzz clearly, and the singing bird makes its low murmuring sound, haunting the jagged brambles. But what delight in those things is there for me, since I was wishing to hear your conversation more than the notes of the Delian lyre? And a double desire spreads round about me, for I long to look upon you, blessed friend, and the sweet calf – my care for her makes me smoulder. But the law keeps me far away from that tender deer.

(AP *5.292 Agathias*)

θεσμὸν Ἔρως οὐκ οἶδε βιημάχος, οὐδέ τις ἄλλη
ἀνέρα νοσφίζει πρῆξις ἐρωμανίης.
εἰ δέ σε θεσμοπόλοιο μεληδόνος ἔργον ἐρύκει,
οὐκ ἄρα σοῖς στέρνοις λάβρος ἔνεστιν ἔρως.
ποῖος ἔρως, ὅτε βαιὸς ἁλὸς πόρος οἶδε μερίζειν
σὸν χρόα παρθενικῆς τηλόθεν ὑμετέρης;
νηχόμενος Λείανδρος ὅσον κράτος ἐστὶν ἐρώτων
δείκνυεν, ἐννυχίου κύματος οὐκ ἀλέγων·
σοὶ δέ, φίλος, παρέασι καὶ ὁλκάδες· ἀλλὰ θαμίζεις
μᾶλλον Ἀθηναίη, Κύπριν ἀπωσάμενος.
θεσμοὺς Παλλὰς ἔχει, Παφίη πόθον. εἰπέ, τίς ἀνὴρ
εἰν ἑνὶ θητεύσει Παλλάδι καὶ Παφίη;

Eros, fighting violently, does not know law, nor does any other deed separate a man
from the madness of love. But if the work of legal administration keeps you, then
furious Eros does not reside in your breast. What sort of Eros is that, when a short
passage over the sea can separate your body far from your maiden? Leander, when he
swam, showed how great the power of the Erotes is, since he had no fear of the swell
of the sea at night. But for you, my friend, there are boats nearby. But you pay more
attention to Athena, rejecting Cypris. Pallas possesses laws, the Paphian passion. Tell
me: what man serves Pallas and the Paphian together?

(AP 5.293 Paul)

Agathias' description of the *locus amoenus* turns out to be a priamel, since he reveals in the seventh
verse that the true source of his enjoyment would be to hear Paul's conversation (σέο μῦθον
ἀκούειν). The phrase is borrowed from Nonnus, who uses a variant of μῦθον ἀκούειν 19 times.[43]
Only once however does Nonnus use the phrase σέο μῦθον ἀκούειν: during Dionysus' lament
for his beloved satyr, Ampelus (11.336). Furthermore, Nonnus' scene is set in a grove (ἐνὶ λόχμῃ,
11.333), similar to the *locus amoenus* described by Agathias. Apparently Agathias has in mind this
paradigmatic scene of same-sex romance from late Greek poetry. In the same passage from
Nonnus the reference to Apollo's loss of his beloved Hyacinthus (11.328–30) parallels Agathias'
desire to hear Paul's conversation even more than the strains of Apollo's lyre (ἢ κιθάρης
κρούσματα Δηλιάδος, *AP* 5.292.8).

The implicit homoeroticism of Agathias' verse becomes all the more apparent when one
considers a similar expression in an epigram by Meleager, in which the poet wishes to hear the
voice of his beloved Heliodora "rather than the son of Leto's cithara" (ἢ τᾶς Λατοΐδεω
κιθάρας, *AP* 5.141.2).[44] Agathias claims that a "double desire spreads round about me" (μοι
δισσὸς ἔρως περικίδναται, *AP* 5.292.9), but the use of this particular verb ends up highlighting
the exclusivity of his relationship with Paul: περικίδνασθαι ("to spread round about") occurs
only once before the sixth century (Quintus of Smyrna, *Posthomerica* 7.1), and then again *only* in
two epigrams by Paul (*AP* 9.651, 765) and in this epigram by Agathias. It is as if the two poets
are speaking their own special language.[45] Beyond these philological subtleties, though, Agathias treats his relationship with Paul with remarkably explicit eroticism: not only is Agathias
possessed by *erōs*, but he longs to "look upon" his dear friend – even Viansino senses in the
verb, εἰσοράαν, "un implicito valore erotico."[46]

Of course Agathias allows himself to get away with such homoerotic swooning because his
erōs is divided between Paul and the anonymous young woman, whose presence as a heterosexual object of desire is meant to desexualize the *erōs* that is directed at Paul. But the presence

of the young woman in this poem, it should be noted, is phantasmatic. Not only does the girl not possess a name, she has no human form. Twice she is animalized, but even in animal form her identity is unstable, as she shifts from being first a calf (δάμαλις) and then a deer (δορκαλίς). The girl, it can safely be said, is more of an idea than a real person. What really matters to Agathias is his relationship with Paul.

Paul reciprocates, responding to the sentiments, imagery, and language of his friend's poem in the identical number of verses. Where Agathias pleaded at the end of his poem that law (θεσμοί, AP 5.292.11) kept him from his love, Paul's poem deftly picks up where Agathias' leaves off: Erōs doesn't know law. Paul's point, that Erōs is dominant and invincible, is neatly formulated by the first two words of the poem: the phrase θεσμὸν ῎Ερως (AP 5.293.1) demotes Agathias' nominative plural θεσμοί into a mere accusative singular and promotes Erōs into the nominative subject of the sentence. Indeed Erōs dominates the entire poem, as Paul playfully upbraids his friend for his continued absence: why should a narrow strait separate lovers? Whereas Agathias longed for the voice and vision of his friend, Paul focuses on the physicality of Agathias' *body* (σὸν χρόα, AP 5.293.6). In the same line, the girl receives her only mention in the poem (παρθενικῆς τηλόθεν ὑμετέρης), though she remains anonymous, just as in the mythological allusion that occupies the middle of the poem the poet focuses solely on the male lover Leander, who bravely swam across the Hellespont because of love. Paul makes no mention of Hero at all. Unlike Leander, however, Agathias could merely hop on a boat. Instead, he is more committed to law than love, which prompts Paul's concluding remark about the impossibility of serving both Athena and Aphrodite at the same time.

Contrasting love and law by means of their mythological analogues was a commonplace in late antiquity,[47] but the alliterative coupling of the names Pallas and Paphiē is a sixth-century innovation, occurring twice more in Agathias' *Cycle* and again in an Anacreontic couplet by the contemporary poet Georgius Grammaticus.[48] Paul's playful nomenclature at the end of the epigram is thus another reminder that despite the alleged heterosexual content, these erotically charged poetic inventions were the product of an intensely homosocial milieu: they were composed for and circulating among elite male peers who were laboring together to create and refine their own stylized poetic language. The pair of poems by Agathias and Paul is a perfect example of what Sedgwick describes as "male homosocial desire within the structural context of triangular, heterosexual desire."[49] The licit object of Agathias' sexual desire might be the anonymous calf/deer/maiden, but the intellectual and creative energy that was spent on these refined literary products binds the poets together: they speak their own language that excludes almost entirely the female member of the triangle.

The tension between Pallas and Paphiē with which the poem concludes deserves further consideration. Given the reciprocity of form and content between the two poems, one might have expected Paul to respond to Agathias' "double desire" with a δισσὸς ἔρως in kind. Instead, he mentions only "your maiden" (AP 5.293.6), remaining silent about his own status as an object of his friend's desire. Despite their intense bond, illustrated by their reciprocal exchange of verses in a shared, artificial language, Paul's response reinforces the absence which Agathias' initial epigram was meant to remedy. What kind of love is it, he asks, that separates you from your beloved? Agathias, he asserts, for all his protestations, has demonstrated himself the acolyte of a legal authority that has nothing to do with real desire. Combined with Agathias' voluntary absence from the *locus amoenus*, the associative link between Pallas Athena and the unnamed παρθενική even suggests an attenuation of Agathias' erotic attraction to the maiden: in a move that one could describe as ascetic, Agathias has chosen a divine virgin at the expense of an earthly virgin.

Throughout his poem, Paul contrasts Erōs with θεσμός,[50] which I have translated as "law," but whose etymology from the verb τιθέναι ("to put or place") suggests "that which has been laid down" by human dictates and by human practice, as opposed to that which is inherent in nature. Paul thus conceives of law as an artificial constraint on the forces of nature, and to Agathias' seemingly harmonious διϲϲὸϲ ἔρωϲ that finds expression only in a self-imposed absence and denial Paul responds by asserting that it is impossible to be true to desire while at the same time submitting to convention. Paul's epigram therefore speaks to the very dilemma with which the whole of this essay has been concerned: the problem of expressing male same-sex desire in an atmosphere hostile to such desire. Paul's flirtatious response to Agathias that he serves Pallas more than Paphiē may on the surface neutralize the potentially dangerous homo-erotic desire to which Agathias' poem gives voice. But Paul also insists that Erōs has a will of his own; the god puts up a violent fight (βιημάχοϲ, *AP* 5.293.1) and in this respect he is like the stubborn men in Agathias' other poem, "full of trouble" (ἀλεγεινοί, *AP* 10.68.7), who make marriages with each other. In conjunction with Erōs and in resistance to a virgin Athena, a "rich Cythereia" (ἀφνειὴ Κυθέρεια, *AP* 5.232.7) abides, and one way or another, in spite of Christian scripture, imperial law, or even a poet's protestations to the contrary, the "love of males" (ἀρϲενικὴ φιλότηϲ, *AP* 10.86.2) will find expression.

Conclusion

One will look in vain for explicitly sympathetic representations of same-sex desire in the literature of the sixth century, but that hardly means that same-sex desire itself was exterminated as a result of Justinian's aggressive legislation and persecution. I have attempted to trace the contours of same-sex desire within a collection of epigrams whose composition is known to have been the product of an intimate homosocial bond between two poets. Scholars of late Greek poetry are quick to announce the level of education and sophistication required to compose epigrams like those in Agathias' *Cycle*; it is consequently necessary to approach the poems themselves with appropriately sophisticated interpretive strategies. Thus, when Agathias loudly disavows male same-sex desire in sixth-century Constantinople, amid an atmosphere hostile to such desires, it must at least be considered that Agathias is writing with irony. Similarly, the adoption of feminine personae offered opportunities for male poets safely to voice sexual desire for other males as well as to articulate a feeling of difference from the heteronormative life of the city. In all of these poems, finally, it is apparent that heterosexual *sōphrosynē* can only be sustained by means of men's ongoing suppression within themselves of their own abiding desire for other males. Reading with sensitivity and attuned to the possibility that same-sex desire has not been altogether eradicated in sixth-century Constantinople, we see a little more clearly what may be described as the early queer sensibilities of Agathias and his circle.

Notes

1 I wish to thank Derek Krueger, Ilaria Marchesi, Mark Masterson, and James Robson for their comments on earlier drafts of this essay. For the text of the *Greek Anthology*, I have used the Budé editions of Waltz 1929 (Books 1–4); Waltz and Guillon 1929 (Book 5); Irigoin et al. 2011 (Book 10); and Aubreton et al. 1994 (Book 12). Abbreviations of names and titles in this essay are the same as those found in Liddell and Scott's *Greek–English Lexicon*. All translations are my own. All dates are Common Era (CE) unless otherwise indicated. Names of Greek authors and texts have been Latinized or retain their conventional English spelling. I do not posit that a homosexual identity existed in late antiquity; throughout this essay, therefore, I rigorously avoid the term "homosexual" in favor of the phrase "same-sex."

2 Averil Cameron 1970: 13. The *Souda* provides the title *Kyklos*, but it should be noted that Agathias himself does not use this term. See Baldwin 1996: 99.

3 *D.* 10.175–338, 11.117–291.

4 It is worth noting that there is no entry for "homosexuality" *vel sim.* in the index of the *Cambridge Companion to the Age of Justinian.* See Maas 2005.

5 See *CTh.* 9.7.3 (342), *Coll.* 5.3 (390), and *CTh.* 9.7.6 (439).

6 Procopius *Arc.* 11.34–6; Malalas pp. 364–5 Thurn; Theophanes p. 177 de Boor; Kedrenos 1:645–6 Bekker. Bailey 1955: 79 attempts to minimize Justinian's zeal in eliminating same-sex sexual activity. See also Boswell 1994: 146–61, 219, 245.

7 Bailey 1955: 76–7 dates *Novella* 141 to 544. See also Dalla 1987: 203–4; Crompton 2003: 147.

8 The verb *androkoitein* appears also in a first-century BCE document from Egypt (*Berliner griechische Urkunden* 1058.30) and in the sixth-century medical writer Aëtius of Amida (1.139.7, 16.17.14, 16.34.58); in all these instances, though, the subject of the verb is female, not male.

9 For the religious appropriation of homoerotic admiration for the masculine body beyond the age of Justinian, see Krueger 2006.

10 Kaldellis 1997, 1999, 2003, focusing on religion and philosophy, do not address sexual dissimulation, but identify corollary structures of dissidence in Agathias' *Histories.*

11 Sedgwick 1990: 3.

12 Foucault 1990: 27.

13 See Sedgwick 1985; 1990 [2008]; Butler 1990, 2004.

14 See Cameron and Cameron 1966: 8; Schulte 2006.

15 *AP* 5.292–3 and Agathias, *Histories* 5.9. Cameron and Cameron 1966: 17–19 argue that Agathias and Paul were nearly the same age, Paul perhaps slightly younger, and both were in their early thirties around the time that Agathias published the *Cycle.* But this would mean that Paul would have been less than 30 years old at the time he was commissioned by Justinian to compose the verse *ekphrasis* of Hagia Sophia, which, while certainly possible, is unlikely (cf. Veniero 1916; McCail 1969; Madden 1995; De Stefani 2011). Madden 1995 argues that Paul was the older of the two by a generation, which would by no means preclude an intimate relationship. It has been suggested that Agathias married Paul's daughter. For refutation of this notion, with bibliography, see Cameron 1970: 6. For a reading of Agathias' *Histories* as the work of a dissident intellectual, see Kaldellis 1997, 1999, 2003.

16 *AP* 5.19, 116, 208, and 12.41. See also Ovid *AA* 2.683 Lucian *Am.* 25f., and Ach. Tat. 2.35.

17 See Schulte 2006: 40–1.

18 See Cameron 1993: 48.

19 Mattsson 1942: 57–8, 63–4; Viansino 1967: 97; McCail 1971: 212–13.

20 Thus Butler 2004: 129: "That heterosexuality is always in the act of elaborating itself is evidence that it is perpetually at risk, that is, that it 'knows' its own possibility of becoming undone: hence, its compulsion to repeat which is at once a foreclosure of that which threatens its coherence. That it can never eradicate that risk attests to its profound dependency upon the homosexuality that it seeks fully to eradicate and never can or that it seeks to make second, but which is always already there as a prior possibility."

21 Viansino 1967: 97.

22 *LSJ* φρήν I.3, 4.

23 *LSJ* σώφρων II.1.

24 McCail 1971: 214–15.

25 Mattsson 1942: 60–1; Cameron 1970: 21; McCail 1971: 259.

26 Goldhill 1995: 46–111.

27 Ach. Tat. 2.35–8; Longus 4.12.

28 Obscene language is warranted: on the verbs βινεῖν and πυγίζειν, see Henderson 1975: 35, 202.

29 Viansino 1967: 97.

30 Goldhill 1995: 63.

31 D. 18.46, 21.110; X. *An.* 2.1.5; Lys. 19.19.

32 *AP* 5.302 is another example of affected denial (cf. Theognis 425–8, *AP* 9.359, 360, 446, and 10.56). McCail 1971: 216 and Viansino 1967: 100, both read the poem as sincere. But the poem cannot be taken seriously, as the coarse humor of the final verses undermines the moralizing tone that precedes them.

33 Gold 1993; Wyke 1994.

34 See Cameron 1966: 211; Viansino 1967: ix *et passim*; Yardley 1980: 239–43; Martlew 1996: 108–10.

35 *AP* 12.5, 88–91, 93–5, 244.

36 Viansino 1963: 151.

37 This transgressive quality is noted by Waltz and Guillon, who argue, somewhat improbably because so ambitiously, that the speaker in the poem cannot be an *hetaira*, but a "grande dame corrompue de la cour de Justinien" (1929: 103 n. 1).

38 Athenagoras *Supplicatio pro Christianis* 33.4; Theophilus *Apologia ad Autolycum* 3.15; Tertullian *De exhortatione castitatis* 9; Minucius Felix *Octavian* 24.11, 31.5. See Viansino 1963: 151.

39 See Butler 1999: 174–80; 2004: 127–8.

40 Cf. Whitmarsh 2001: 26–38.

41 Sedgwick 1985: 27.

42 Cameron 1970: 1 n. 5.

43 *D.* 3.342, 11.82, 11.336, 29.361, 33.283, 35.48, 40.35, 40.145, 42.431; *Paraphrasis* 1.206, 5.151, 5.177, 8.122, 9.175, 10.72, 11.14, 13.118, 18.179, 19.60.

44 Waltz and Guillon 1929: 128 n. 2.

45 The verb would not be seen again in Greek literature until the fourteenth century, when it appears in a poem by Manuel Philes (5.26.85).

46 Viansino 1967: 46.

47 Lib. *Progymnasmata* 11.18; Nonnus *D.* 20.245, 24.297; *AP* 5.272 (Paul), 6.48.5 (anon.), 6.283.4 (anon.), 7.59.93 (Julianus); and Musaeus 153; cf. Propertius 1.2.30. See Viansino 1963: 150.

48 *AP* 6.59.1 (Agathias) and 9.633.1 (Damocharis Grammatikos). See Kaster 1988: 286–7.

49 Sedgwick 1985: 16.

50 Θεσμόν, verse 1; θεσμοπόλοιο, verse 3; and θεσμούς, verse 11.

Bibliography

Aubreton, R., Irigoin, J., and Buffière, F. (eds) (1994) *Anthologie Grecque, Tome XI, Anthologie Palatine, Livre XII*. Paris: Les Belles Lettres.

Bailey, D.S. (1955) *Homosexuality and the Western Christian Tradition*. London: Longman's, Green and Co.

Baldwin, B. (1996) "Notes on Christian epigrams in Book One of the *Greek Anthology*", in P. Allen and E. Jeffreys (eds) *The Sixth Century: End or Beginning?* Brisbane, QLD: Australian Association for Byzantine Studies, pp. 92–104.

Boswell, J. (1994) *Same-Sex Unions in Pre-modern Europe*. New York: Villard Books.

Butler, J. (1990; 2nd edn 1999) *Gender Trouble: Feminism and the Subversion of Identity*. New York and London: Routledge.

——(2004) "Imitation and gender insubordination", in S. Salih and J. Butler (eds) *The Judith Butler Reader*. Malden, MA: Blackwell Publishing, pp. 119–37.

Cameron, Alan (1993) *The Greek Anthology from Meleager to Planudes*. Oxford: Clarendon Press.

Cameron, Alan and Cameron, Averil (1966) "The Cycle of Agathias", *Journal of Hellenic Studies* 86: 6–25.

Cameron, Averil (1966) "Review of *Paolo Silenziario: Epigrammi*, ed. Giovanni Viansino", *Journal of Hellenic Studies* 86: 210–11.

——(1970) *Agathias*. Oxford: Clarendon Press.

Crompton, L. (2003) *Homosexuality and Civilization*. Cambridge, MA: Belknap Press of Harvard University Press.

Dalla, D. (1987) *"Ubi Venus mutatur": Omosessualità e diritto nel mondo romano*. Milan: A. Guiffrè.

De Stefani, C. (ed.) (2011) *Paulus Silentiarius: Descriptio Sanctae Sophiae; Descriptio Ambonis. Bibliotheca Scriptorum Graecorum et Romanorum Teubneriana*. Berlin and New York: De Gruyter.

Foucault, M. (1990) *The History of Sexuality, Volume 1: An Introduction*. New York: Vintage Books.

Gold, B. (1993) "'But Ariadne was never there in the first place': Finding the female in Roman poetry", in N.S. Rabinowitz and A. Richlin (eds) *Feminist Theory and the Classics*. New York: Routledge, pp. 75–101.

Goldhill, S. (1995) *Foucault's Virginity*. Cambridge and New York: Cambridge University Press.

Henderson, J. (1975; 2nd edn 1991) *The Maculate Muse*. Oxford and New York: Oxford University Press.

Irigoin, J., Maltomini, F., and Laurens, P. (eds) (2011) *Anthologie Grecque, Tome IX. Anthologie Palatine, Livre X*. Paris: Les Belles Lettres.

Kaldellis, A. (1997) "Agathias on history and poetry", *Greek, Roman and Byzantine Studies* 38(3): 295–305.

——(1999) "The historical and religious views of Agathias: A reinterpretation", *Byzantion* 69: 206–52.

——(2003) "Things are not what they are: Agathias Mythistoricus and the last laugh of Classical culture", *Classical Quarterly* 53(1): 295–300.

Kaster, R.A. (1988) *Guardians of Language: The Grammarian and Society in Late Antiquity*. Berkeley, CA: University of California Press.

Krueger, D. (2006) "Homoerotic spectacle and the monastic body in Symeon the New Theologian", in V. Burrus and C. Keller (eds) *Toward a Theology of Eros: Transfiguring Passion at the Limits of Discipline*. New York: Fordham University Press, pp. 99–118.

Maas, M. (ed.) (2005) *The Cambridge Companion to the Age of Justinian*. Cambridge and New York: Cambridge University Press.

McCail, R.C. (1969) "The cycle of Agathias: New identifications scrutinised", *Journal of Hellenic Studies* 89: 87–96.

——(1971) "The erotic and ascetic poetry of Agathias", *Byzantion* 41: 205–67.

Madden, J.A. (1995) *Macedonius Consul: The Epigrams*. Hildesheim, Zurich, and New York: Georg Olms.

Martlew, I. (1996) "The reading of Paul the Silentiary", in P. Allen and E. Jeffreys (eds) *The Sixth Century: End or Beginning?* Brisbane, QLD: Australian Association for Byzantine Studies, pp. 105–11.

Mattsson, A. (1942) *Untersuchungen zur Epigrammsammlung des Agathias*. Lund: H. Ohlssons Boktryckeri.

Schöll, R. and Kroll, W. (eds) (1895) *Corpus iuris civilis*, vol. 3. Berlin: Weidmann.

Schulte, H. (2006) *Paralipomena Cycli: Epigramme aus der Sammlung des Agathias*. Trier: WVT Wissenschaftlicher Verlag Trier.

Sedgwick, E.K. (1985) *Between Men: English Literature and Male Homosocial Desire*. New York: Columbia University Press.

——(1990 [2008]) *Epistemology of the Closet*. Berkeley, CA, Los Angeles, CA, and London: University of California Press.

Thurn, I. (ed.) (2000) *Ioannis Malalae Chronographia*. Berlin and New York: Walter de Gruyter.

Veniero, A. (1916) *Paolo Silenziario: Studio sulla letteratura bizantina del VI secolo*. Catania: F. Battiato.

Viansino, G. (1963) *Paolo Silenziario: Epigrammi*. Turin: Loescher.

——(1967) *Agazia Scolastico: Epigrammi*. Milan: Casa Editrice Luigi Trevisini.

Waltz, P. (ed.) (1929) *Anthologie Grecque, Tome I. Anthologie Palatine, Livres I–IV*. Paris: Les Belles Lettres.

Waltz, P. and Guillon, J. (eds) (1929) *Anthologie Grecque, Tome II. Anthologie Palatine, Livre V*. Paris: Les Belles Lettres.

Whitmarsh, T. (2001) *Greek Literature and the Roman Empire: The Politics of Imitation*. Oxford and New York: Oxford University Press.

Wyke, M. (1994) "Taking the woman's part: Engendering Roman love elegy", *Ramus* 23: 110–28.

Yardley, J.C. (1980) "Paulus Silentiarius, Ovid, and Propertius", *Classical Quarterly* 30(1): 239–43.

29

FRIENDS WITHOUT BENEFITS

Or, academic love

Daniel Boyarin

For Virginia Burrus, who taught me the meaning of queer friendship

It is, perhaps, not too extravagant to suggest that in the history of western thought there are three great explorations of the philosophy of love, Plato's, Augustine's, and Freud's. If, for the former two, sex is either the gateway or the obstacle to love (which remains to be seen), for the latter, love is the mystification of sex (or one possible one). In this essay I hope to explore the proposition that all love in the west from Plato into the Christianity and Judaism of late antiquity is platonic love. The goal, as in so much of my work, is to thoroughly displace the notion of the natural in human behavior, insisting on its absolute, fundamental queerness.

Academic love; or Plato as an early neoplatonist

The question of the meaning of "platonic love" is not a simple one. The question might most summarily be raised by asking (as I did in a previous article): "What do we talk about when we talk about (platonic) love"?[1] In order to proceed further I shall summarize the argument of that article regarding one of the key texts for this investigation, the *Symposium* of Plato.[2] The *Symposium* has been read in various ways in the thousands of years since it was produced. Throughout the late-ancient and medieval periods, it was understood that platonic love was a love that did not involve, that "transcended," physical sex. It is this understanding, of course, that has led as well to the "vulgar" usage: "Their relationship was platonic," meaning, of course, only that they did not have sex with each other. In the Reformation, in the hands of figures such as John Milton, this interpretation shifted, according to Thomas Luxon, in the direction of an understanding of platonic love that was not predicated on a dualism between body and spirit and consequently did not at all reject physical sexuality entirely. The older interpretation was retained during this same period by such commentators as the Italian humanist neoplatonists, the de Mirandolas and Ficinos and their like, and Montaigne as well (Luxon 2005).

   To this day these two interpretations are in play among scholars, as we shall see, with Foucault, for example, taking on Milton's reading, while Kenneth Dover on the other hand reads Plato as the Platonists do.[3] This difference in interpretation turns on several cruces in Plato's text itself. One crux has to do with the ratio of Pausanias' account of "heavenly love" to

Diotima's account of ideal Eros. The *Symposium*, it will be remembered, consists of a series of encomia to eros delivered by various "real" (and perhaps some made-up) characters from Socrates' world, followed by an elaborate reported dialogue between Socrates himself and the Peloponnesian prophetess Diotima, who teaches Socrates the proper theory of erotics. The character Pausanias, for his contribution, presents a highly idealized (some might say apologetic) picture of Athenian pederasty, in which an older man takes under his wing a younger (beard-less) man, and in exchange for sexual gratification, teaches the younger man what he needs to know to be an upstanding Athenian. This form of pederastic relation is dubbed by him as heavenly love, while Pausanias also identifies another form of love as "vulgar," because it is primarily or exclusively concerned with sexual pleasure.

Diotima provides an even more exalted version of pederastic love in which sex is transcended entirely in favor of a partnership of minds and souls in contemplation of the Truth. In most interpretations of the *Symposium*, Diotima's philosophy of love is taken to represent platonic love, Plato's own ideology of eros. Some earlier interpretative traditions simply conflated Pausanian heavenly love and Diotima's philosophical eros, referring to both as "platonic love" and assuming that in neither was sex actually practiced.[4] Other, better readers, seeing that in heavenly love à la Pausanias there *is* sex involved, assume that such is the case for Diotiman/platonic love, as well, thus again nearly conflating the two.[5] Luxon, who refers to Diotima/Socrates' presentation as an "even more glorified version of homoerotic relations," adopts a form of the latter position. This formulation gets, to be sure, the point that there is a difference between Pausanian heaven and Platonic heaven but does not emphasize enough to my taste the oppositional character of Diotima/Socrates (and thus platonic love) to that of Pausanias' "elaborate apologetic for Athenian pederasty," as Luxon so pithily describes it. I would maintain that the neoplatonist reading of the *Symposium* is at least as tenable as Milton's, if not much more so.

Kenneth Dover, in contrast to Foucault and those of his persuasion, makes clear distinctions between Plato's Pausanias (as the representative of the "best" of Athenian eros) and Diotima, writing, for instance, that in Plato "*heterosexual eros is treated on the same basis as homosexual copu-lation*, a pursuit of bodily pleasure which leads no further …, and in *Symposium* it is sub-rational, an expression of the eros that works in animals."[6] Dover thus discriminates plainly between the sexual practices of Athenians in general—even in their most high-minded, heavenly form—and Plato's disdain for all physical sex. Plato, in this view, promotes an erotics that is almost in binary opposition to the erotics of Athens as best represented in Pausanias' speech, and this is consistent with, indeed part and parcel of, Plato's whole antagonistic stance vis-à-vis the life of the polis itself.

According to Foucault, "[Plato] does not trace a clear, definitive, and uncrossable dividing line between the bad love of the body and the glorious love of the soul," and, for Foucault, "both the *Phaedrus* and the *Symposium* are quite clear on this point."[7] My own reading of the *Symposium*, on the other hand, points up the radical difference between Platonic and Pausanian (demotic Athenian) love, disrupting the Foucauldian inclination to place Plato's theory of eros on more of a continuum with (rather than in opposition to) classical Athenian pederastic prac-tice.[8] As we will see, this will have enormous consequences for our reading of patristic and Talmudic love, as well.[9]

The break that Plato makes with customary Athenian erotic mores is as sharp as the most pious Victorian scholar could imagine, indeed sharper, because many of them did not have clearly in their minds the physicality of that non-platonic Athenian love. Greek love and pla-tonic love thus need to be clearly distinguished.[10] Platonic love, while eros it is, has nothing to do with physical touch, but such love is intended only for a particular elite. For those blessed few, it is understood that from the very beginning their desire will be for the refined corporeal pleasure of seeing the beautiful person and thence it will develop finally into contemplation of the form of Beauty itself. Thus, contrary to at least some generally held contemporary readings of Plato, I believe that ideal platonic love is, indeed, a matter of complete elite celibacy, and as such had a more profound effect on Christian mores than is currently imagined (Boyarin 2006). This analysis should help us keep clearly separate the two different Christian ideals, procreationism for the many, celibacy for the elite. Whether or not this has anything to do with "the mysticism of the East," as Jowett would have it, it does, I think, have everything to do with the conceptions of the relations of the political body to the spiritual one in late-ancient Judeo-Christianity. Christian celibate eros—the eros, for instance, of a Jerome and a Paula (Burrus 2003: 60–9)—is neither the antithesis nor yet the product of heavenly Greek love but finds its genealogy rather in the total break with sex and the city initiated by "platonic love."

Platonic love itself, however, has its own very ancient genealogy. Before there was platonic love, there was heroic friendship.[11] Halperin uncovers this institution, or rather that which he refers to as a "social label," by discussing the instance of Achilles and Patroclus in the context of the portrayals of the friendships of Gilgamesh and Enkidu in the ancient Mesopotamian epic and David and Jonathan in the Bible ("Heroes and their pals"; Halperin 1990: 75–87). In showing that in both of these cases the role of friendship came to greater prominence, took on the "meaning, the values attached to it" only in its later revisions, in approximately the Homeric age, Halperin argues that there is a

> possibility, then, that we may regard the friendship between Achilles and Patroclus depicted in our text of the *Iliad* not as some fixed, unchanging, and immovable feature of the epic but as a historical artifact, the product of a particular turn of thought at a particular juncture in the artistic elaboration of the traditional material.
>
> *(Halperin 1990: 76–7)*

For my present purposes what is even more to the point is to regard this very specific historical cultural development as one that was common around the Mediterranean, east and west, at a certain particular juncture in cultural history, such that the tributaries that flow into late-ancient Judeo-Christianity from both Hellas and Israel share ancient common sources (Halperin 1990: 84).

Halperin has well described the characteristics of heroic friendship, arguing that

> The male couple constitutes a world apart from society at large, and yet it does not merely embody a "private" relation, of the sort that might be transacted appropriately in a "home". On the contrary, friendship helps to structure—and, possibly, to privatize—the social space; it takes shape in the world that lies beyond the horizon of the domestic sphere, and it requires for its expression a military or political staging-ground.
>
> *(Halperin 1990: 77)*

This formulation points to, and Halperin more than hints at, the tension between the realm of heroic male friendship and the spaces of relations with women and especially the *oikos*, the home. Working out this tension seems, then, to be a major theme of all varieties of ancient Mediterranean culture, whatever their "religious" self-identifications. Absolutely compellingly, Halperin makes the point that when David cries over the death of Jonathan, "Your love to me was wonderful, passing the love of women," it is not to imply that he had a sexual relationship with Jonathan, but rather that the power of the friendship of male "souls" for each other (the term "soul" is an anachronism) is greater than the love of bodies enacted in conjugal relations. "Jonathan's love for David was astonishing because—even *without* a sexual component—it was stronger and more militant than sexual love" (Halperin 1990: 83). It would not be unfair to conclude, then, that at least for a moment the biblical narrative provides friendship, bonds of affective intimacy between men, as a more fundamental relation in the ordering of human society than relations of conjugality.[12] Insofar as that fundamental relation imagines itself as based on and produced by equality between the partners, I will coin the term homonormative for it. Over a millennium later, Jewish culture, in its rabbinic and Christian versions, was still exploring this structural conflict between the ties that bind a "man" to his family and those that tie him intimately to another man or men.

For Plato, as for platonists, Christian, Jewish, and "others," celibate relations were clearly sharply superior to any physical, sexual relations, homosexual or heterosexual. That is the whole point of the move from Pausanias to Diotima, as I read the text. In Plato himself, in the relationship of Socrates to Diotima, and in early Christian celibate male–female friendship, women had already been introduced as partners into the homonormative economy of "friendship," such that the very reason that Diotima is a woman is to make clear that since there is to be no physical sex anyway, women are as good as men.[13] This point has been made fairly explicitly by at least one prominent Christian platonist, Clement of Alexandria:

> As then there is sameness [with men and women] with respect to the soul, she will attain to the same virtue; but as there is difference with respect to the peculiar construction of the body, she is destined for child-bearing and house-keeping.
>
> *(Clement of Alexandria 1989: 20)*

Without the flesh, the gender translation is so much less problematic.[14] It makes a great deal of sense, then, that, as Carolinne White has discussed, "the growth of interest in the possibilities of friendship on a personal, ecclesiastical, and theological level may also be connected with the growth of the ascetic movement" (White 1992: 9).

Monks and their gals: Platonic love and the place of Christian women

Based on my reading of the *Symposium* I would like at this juncture to offer three propositions. The first is that the relationship between Socrates and Diotima is being presented to us not only as being about platonic love but also as being an instance of platonic erotic love.[15] (Of course, I am not hinting at anything so vulgar as "Socratean heterosexuality," but perhaps at a platonic protest against the notion that philosophical eros—of the sort without touching—need necessarily be confined only to men.) As such, it is the positive foil for which Pausanias' demotic love is the negative. In platonic love the love between a man and a woman is as good as the love of men for men. Second, it is absolutely conditioned on the renunciation of physical sex. Third, this contempt for sex is not, thereby, inscribed as contempt for the female body but for the sexual body per se. I suggest that these three propositions together will enable us to move toward a more complex understanding of the Christian eros of asceticism and the relations between the sexes that it implies.

The question of the origins of Christian permanent sexual renunciation is central to the study of early Christianity, and Peter Brown has been one of the major voices in offering answers. On the one hand, he rejects totally the notion that this peculiarly radical sexual practice is to be straightforwardly explained as a reaction against an alleged "pagan" (or late-Roman) dissoluteness (Brown 1988: 22–3):

> The evidence that we have considered so far gives little support to the widespread romantic notion that the pre-Christian Roman world was a sunny "Eden of the

unrepressed." Still less is it possible to explain, and by implication to excuse, the austerity of Christian sexual ethics, and the novelty of the Christian emphasis on total sexual renunciation, as if it were no more than an understandable, if excessive, reaction to the debauchery that prevailed among the cultivated classes of the Empire.

On the other hand, neither will Brown allow that this innovation is simply a continuation of earlier practice:

> To be frank: I have frequently observed that the sharp and dangerous flavor of many Christian notions of sexual renunciation, both in their personal and their social consequences, have been rendered tame and insipid, through being explained away as no more than inert borrowings from a supposed pagan or Jewish "background."
>
> *(Brown 1988 : xvi)*

I shall certainly not think, then, of inert borrowings, still less of backgrounds, but I do want to suggest in the light of my reading of the *Symposium* that the connection between at least certain Christian notions of sexual renunciation and those of Plato is closer than we might have thought. My thesis is rather that much (or, more modestly put, some) of the most important versions of Christian sexual renunciation represent a profoundly Christian recasting of the erotics of Diotima.[16] Robert Markus has already made an observation similar to the one underlying this notion (1970: 132):

> But may it not be true, also, that the feeling we have on reading Plato's *Symposium* that the love there finally shown us is, at bottom, really so "very Christian," is not wholly due to our being duped by the pervasive and corrupting influence of Platonic moulds in the tradition of Christian thought? This is the approach I want to explore here; to try to discern in the Platonic "dialectic of love" the features which have recommended it to Christian thinkers like St. Augustine and the pseudo-Dionysius and, through them, to St. Thomas Aquinas; to find, within it rather than in our gullibility, the source of its perennial fascination to Christian minds.

The reading of the *Symposium* offered here is intended to take Markus' feeling in quite a different direction than he does, into the consideration of eros in the history of sexuality itself and, I hope, to lead us deeper into an understanding of Christian platonism and its role in the formation of Christian eros.[17] Brown writes:

> It is not sufficient to talk of the rise of Christianity in the Roman world simply in terms of a shift from a less to a more repressive society. What was at stake was a subtle change in the perception of the body itself. The men and women of later centuries were not only hedged around with a different and more exacting set of prohibitions. They had also come to see their own bodies in a different light.
>
> *(Brown 1988: 30)*

A different light, precisely from what? Brown, of course, is the last to lose sight of the complexity of that very Roman world that he invokes. In emphasizing, after all, the profoundness of the shift from the non-Christian to the Christian, however, he underestimates this point. I think we ought not underestimate the (delayed) impact of Plato's revolutionary—as I have claimed— understanding of eros and its role in the lives of philosophers, and that if we do not do so, we shall understand better the platonic love of the late-antique Christian life, as well.

Brown has exposed much of this in writing of the so-called gnostic sect Valentinianism (second to fourth centuries).[18] Brown remarks that the Valentinian study-circles in which spiritual men and women gathered together with their teacher remind one of the ancient philosopher's study-circle. He does not go beyond this bare formal comparison, however, writing that "by claiming that the redeemed had overcome sexual desire, Gnostics were able to accept women as equal partners in the intense group-life of a Christian intelligentsia" (Brown 1988: 119). Brown fails to note here that the deepest ground for such "overcoming" of sexual desire—or rather its transformation into a spiritual eros—was also a product of the philosopher's (rather a specific philosopher's) theory and, presumably, practice. Brown's own descriptions bring us close to the ambiance of the *Symposium* (1988: 119):

> Love "for ever warm and still to be enjoyed," the happy merging of two beings, an exuberant fertility: these were not disowned by the believer. They were sought, instead, at the undivided core of the universe, in the Place of Fulness. They were not to be found through the body, nor along the shattered images of the physical world. This strongly symbolic mentality made the physical world transparent to mighty spiritual events. Because of this, the Valentinians contributed directly to the spinning of one fine strand in the sensibility of continent Christians of all shades of opinion. Along with the Christians of the Great Church, they presented the intimate passing on of an irreplaceable, saving wisdom as the truest form of procreation.

I think this strand reveals itself spun of platonic filaments, that undivided core and passing on of saving wisdom, that particular merging of beings.

Brown seeks to render clear a sharp difference between figures like Clement, Plotinus, and Porphyry, on the one hand, and figures such as Origen and Methodius, on the other—platonists all, as he does not fail to note—with respect to their sensibilities and ideologies regarding sexuality. For Brown, Clement and, like him, Plotinus and Porphyry, while themselves (at any rate some of them) celibate, do not exclude married sex from the realm of value in the spiritual life. For Clement, in particular, sex for the young is an accepted and necessary step on the spiritual ladder that will lead to full Christian gnosis and salvation:

> more like Clement in his attitude to sexuality than Origen, Plotinus looked at the body from a huge height. His own ascetic regimen included total chastity, yet he moved with ease among patrons and disciples whose married state he took for granted. A fine-tuned body, as vibrant as a well-used lyre, was his ideal.[19]

Brown emphasizes that for Porphyry, it seems, the greatest spiritual danger was in the eating of meat: "The ingestion of animal meat summed up for Porphyry far more appropriately than did the hot passions of the bed the vulnerability of the human spirit to the cloying materiality that weighed in upon it on every side" (Brown 1988: 182).

Origen, according to Brown, is an entirely different matter indeed. For him, it seems, there is nothing redeemable about actual human sexuality. Brown makes clear that for this alleged disciple of the very same Clement, there is no way to see actual physical sex as a step on a ladder of salvation. All that such experience can do is to dull the human spirit. Brown does, of course, recognize the powerful contribution that Plato has made to the formation of Origen's sexuality: "Origen's attitude to marriage was so much sharper than that of Clement mainly because of the streak of 'wild' Platonism that ran through his thought" (Brown 1988: 173). Given this, however, it becomes harder and harder to follow Brown and see the difference between Origen, on the one hand, and Porphyry, on the other, as "the divergence between pagan and Christian notions of renunciation" (Brown 1988: 180).

What I would like to suggest, given my reading of the *Symposium*, is that the difference between these two groups of platonists with respect to sexuality lies precisely at the fault line between the two types of approved (but not equally so) eros in Plato.[20] At any rate, with respect to Clement, I would offer his stance as a close analogy to the story of heavenly love expressed by Pausanias, while Origen's "wild Platonism," at least in this matter, seems best understood as the product of a deep understanding, perhaps then not so wild after all, of platonic love. For Clement, it would seem (following Brown's own description), the grace and pleasure of the marriage bed provide precisely that first step on the ladder of saving gnosis that the physical love of the pederastic couple provide in Pausanias' account of heavenly love. For Plotinus too, although not engaging in sex himself, sexual intercourse can provide that first intimation and teacher of spiritual ecstasy. Both of these platonists and Plutarch too[21] are, paradoxically, in at least this one area, not entirely platonic insofar as they reflect the views of Socrates' interlocutors and not Socrates or Plato (*ex hypothesi*), as we can see once we delineate clearly the difference within Plato himself.[22] Origen, however, with his absolute theoretical commitment to perpetual physical virginity and the "wild Platonism" of the erotic energy of his spiritual quest, seems closest to Diotima, very close indeed, I would hazard, in his understanding of the possibilities for human eros.

In her pioneering and by now near-classic studies of the place of women in patristic social thought, Elizabeth Clark notes that for John Chrysostom (fourth to fifth century), Christian ideas about sex were directly contrary (and contradictory) to those of Plato. Chrysostom refers to virginity (perpetual virginity for women) as a *politeia*, thus directly implicating it as the counterpart and exact opposite of Plato's notions of women-in-sexual-common, as described in Book 5 of the *Republic*: "The claim he wished to press was that the true republic which would change women's status was not to be found in Plato's commonwealth but in Christian asceticism" (Clark 1979: 16). Somewhat ironically, I would claim, precisely in advancing the claims of a virginal *philosophia* over against marriage as the basis for women's freedom, Chrysostom (and even more ironically perhaps Tertullian too) are manifesting precisely the view that I have taken to be platonic. Echoing Clement, and ultimately as I have argued Plato himself, "Chrysostom accorded virgins a remarkably elevated status. In the worldly order, he believed, a woman could not equal a man or assume functions traditionally considered masculine, but in the spiritual order she can and does" (Clark 1979: 19).

At the same time, in another essay, Clark wonders how it is that on the basis of an ancient philosophical ideal that "by definition excluded friendship between the sexes" we are "to interpret the phenomenon of intersexual friendship which developed in early Christianity, in particular the friendships with women which the fourth-century church fathers Jerome and John Chrysostom developed" (Clark 1979: 35). Clark's query is founded on the assumption that for all ancient philosophy, including Plato, the possibility of friendship between a man and a woman was denied in theory and in practice. It is my suggestion here that one answer to Clark's puzzlement is that it was precisely Plato who provided the model for such intersexual friendship in the depiction of the relationship between Diotima and Socrates, as contrasted with the relation of Pericles and Aspasia on the one hand, and Agathon and Pausanias on the other.[23] (It is, of course, of great interest that Agathon and Pausanias are not even representatives of the ideal couple of man and boy described by Pausanias himself as the Athenian ideal, but are two men.) In this triangulation of possibilities, notwithstanding this anomaly, Plato is, I suggest, arguing that the friendship of celibate philosophers with each other, regardless of gender, is superior to the love that includes sex, whether the love of a man for a boy (or another man) or the love of a man for a woman. It is this, at least theoretical, possibility that, I suggest, provided the blueprint for ascetic cross-gender friendship in the Christian world.[24] This has consequences, moreover, for our evaluation of patristic friendships. Diotimas of God are not only honorary men (without denying for a minute the dominance of the "male" androgyne), but also people who have left sex (and thus gender) behind, *as have the celibate men, frequently representing themselves as women.*[25] Virginia Burrus has captured this nuance perfectly when she wrote of Gregory of Nyssa (2000: 96–7):

> If Christ can be all things to all people, any gendering of the object of desire will also do: the beloved is equally divine whether figured as the queenly Sophia or the incorruptible Bridegroom, concludes Gregory (*De Virg.* 20). Indeed, most of the time Gregory's "inner man" seems happy to play the woman in relation to the "Good Husband" for whom he bears deathless children, protects his chastity (20), and even keeps house (18).[26]

Or as she put it most strikingly,

> Mobilizing androgyny's fluidity on behalf of a different love, Gregory's vertically oriented "philosophic logos" does not flow in channels of gendered plurality but begets a singular—and singularly graceful—masculine subjectivity that derives its position of transcendent dominance "from its power to *eradicate the difference between the sexes.*"[27]

To be sure, that very transcendence itself is most often figured as masculine (Boyarin 1998: 117–35), but the dichotomy of gender is nevertheless seriously disrupted and not only in one direction. Female men of God can be constru(ct)ed in two ways it seems—both anatomically female (spiritual) men of God and anatomically male (spiritual) *female* men of God—and these transsexuals can be (at least in principle) friends, and not *just* friends, much as Socrates and Diotima. Eros abides.[28] I think that I have at least the suggestion of a partial answer to Clark's query of thirty-five years ago; there is at least something in the classical philosophical tradition that empowers our Fathers and their Friends.

In a beautiful essay, Mark Jordan has directly explored the profound nexus between the *Symposium* and Augustine.[29] Studying the close encounter of Socrates and Alcibiades at the end of the text, Jordan shows how deeply erotic Plato's imagination of that encounter is, and, moreover, how it then sets the stage for an Augustinian theory of erotically charged relations with God, as well as (and this is, as Jordan emphasizes, highly important) erotically charged and passionate relations with other celibate men. Referring to an anecdote of Augustine's about two imperial officials who devote themselves to Christian celibacy on reading Antony's Life, Jordan writes,

> Each man, it turns out, was already engaged, but their fiancées, hearing the news, conveniently agreed to dedicate their virginity to God. The shackle is woman (*femina*), and the support is one's comrade, partner (*socius*). Abandoning the flesh does not mean abandoning same-sex friendship.
>
> *(Jordan 2006: 34–5)*

Jordan brilliantly sums up: "What we call Augustine's 'conversion' is not a change of belief. It is an amorous refusal of the prevailing economy of male-female sex in favor of (male-male?) celibacy with God" (Jordan 2006: 35). Not disagreeing with Jordan, but perhaps adding something, I would suggest that one distinct innovation of the platonic love that moves into Christian celibacy with God, in precisely the way that Jordan has evoked it, is a kind of imagined transcending of the binary of gender itself (although not, as we have seen in the case of Augustine himself) one that imagines at least a *socius* who is female (Diotima), a *femina*, who is male (Agathon).[30] In either case, the opposition is made between the shackles of the sexual relation with all the entanglement in the polis that that entails and the celibate philosophical friendship with its (imagined) space of autonomy and freedom.

The tension between a thus sublimated—but again, no less erotic—sex and the city is framed for Plato himself as the resistance of philosophy to rhetoric; for early Christians as the resistance of the ascetic to the everyday, and for the (Babylonian) rabbis of late antiquity, as we are about to see, in an intricate and tense and ultimately impossible staging of the conflict of the values of marriage and procreation (the values of the ancient city) with the values of the spiritual *Män-nerbund* (Sacred Band) of the study of Torah.

Rabbis and their pals: Platonic love in rabbinic Babylonia

Thomas Luxon argues (2005: 79):

> Aristotle, Cicero, Plutarch and Montaigne regarded friendship as the quintessentially human, if not originary, relation. Though it was not difficult to find biblical examples of homosocial friendships, the Bible, beginning with Genesis, advanced marriage as the original and most fundamental form of human society. When God saw that it was not good for Adam to be alone (Gen. 2:18), he made a woman to remedy his solitude.

The rabbis who told the familiar story we are about to reread (and in other texts as well) seem to be engaged in the same problematic of weighing the gravity of marriage versus homosocial friendship. The rabbis seem well aware of the structural faults in their own attempts at this reconciliation of their contradictory values. One term in the binary seems always fated to undermine the other and yet a clear dominance cannot be established. The Talmud simply will not settle down on one view or another with respect to the ratio between physical and spiritual eros (with women and men respectively). This may, in fact, be one explanation for the famed rabbinic tacit refusal to write systematically at all and their vaunted penchant to express all values in the form of narrative. One might imagine that this is the very condition of the world and the human situation in the eyes of the rabbis, to be unable to find adequate solutions to the most profound of human dilemmas and to remain in ambiguity and tension forever.

The Babylonian Talmud tells a tale of homoerotically charged friendship between two rabbis that has been oft interpreted by now in the scholarly literature (not least oft by me). In the current reading, I would see this narrative as engaged in a confrontation of the same kinds of dilemmas with which both early Platonism and its Christian variants are occupied as well. In this story, heteronormativity is confronted with homonormative friendship (or perhaps the homonormative friendship is confronted with heteronormativity in the very diegesis itself, thus making it a powerful site for the thematization of an ideological aporia). To summarize the plot: Resh Lakish is a well-known Jewish brigand and pursuer of female flesh. On a certain occasion he observes from afar the paragon of male beauty and radiance, Rabbi Yoḥanan, bathing in the Jordan and swoops down upon this figure of sexual allure by vaulting on his lance. The manuscripts explicitly thematize the question of heteronormativity by indicating that there was some ambiguity about the gender of that alluring figure in the eyes of his/her suitor. After some byplay involving the parallelism and competition of the sexual life with the life of Torah-study,

Rabbi Yoḥanan offers Resh Lakish the possibility of both: me for your friend (*socius*), my sister for your wife (*femina*). Rabbi Yoḥanan's slightly indecent proposal reminds me of none so much as one made by Queen Elizabeth I to Mary, Queen of Scots, that the latter marry Elizabeth's own favorite, Robert Dudley, "and come to England, 'to be conversant with her, Elizabeth, in this realm, and live with her.'" As Luxon remarks of this queer idea, citing contemporaneous comment (2005: 24–5):

> "Seeing they two [Elizabeth and Mary] cannot be joined in marriage, the second degree to make them and their realms happy is that Mary marry him whom Elizabeth favours and loves as her brother." All of the unresolved tensions and implicit contradictions involved regarding marriage as a friendship were thrown into sharp relief as these two queens managed and mismanaged their marriages and nonmarriages and pseudomarriages …

Likewise, *mutatis mutandis*, for *our* heroes. Their own inability to marry, as it were, is mediated by their shared erotic connection with a "female" object of desire, on the one hand, the Torah that they study together as "friends," *havruta*, and on the other, by the shared human female object, sister of one, wife of the other. The classic structures of Eve Sedgwick's "between men" or Irigaray's *hommo-sexualité* (precisely not, of course, *homo*sexuality) are thus perfectly reproduced and doubled in the story on the sexless plane of friendship and the sexualized plane of marriage.

But meanwhile back at the Yeshiva, at first things seem to be going quite well. Resh Lakish studies well and vigorously and becomes a great Talmudic scholar and, while it is not named as such, he and Rabbi Yoḥanan clearly enter into the highly privileged rabbinic version of platonic friendship, the *havruta*. However, as love-relations frequently do, this one too, turns sour. That souring and its bitter sequel are where, to my mind, the tension between friendship and marriage is most richly thematized in rabbinic literature (Baba Metsia 84a):

> Once they were disputing in the Study House: "the sword and the lance and the dagger, from whence can they become impure?"[31] Rabbi Yoḥanan said, "from the time they are forged in the fire." Resh Lakish said, "from the time they are polished in the water." Rabbi Yoḥanan said, "a brigand is an expert in brigandry" [i.e. sarcastically: You should know of what you speak; after all, weapons are your metier]. He [R.L.] said to him [R.Y.], "What have you profited me. There they called me Rabbi and here they call me Rabbi!" He (R. Yoḥanan) said, "I have indeed profited you, for I have brought you near under the wings of the *Shekhina*".[32] He [R.Y.] became angry, and Resh Lakish became ill [owing to a curse put on him by R.Y.]

It is here that we remark most clearly on the ambivalence built into this text. On the one hand, just as Rabbi Yoḥanan is to be apprehended as one of the great culture-heroes of the rabbis, one would expect that his inscription of the superiority of the love of Torah between men over the love of women would be the "winner" in any ideological contest within the text. But, on the other hand, it hardly seems reading anything into this text to see that that is hardly the case. Resh Lakish's outburst: "What have you profited me? There they called me Rabbi and here they call me Rabbi!" remains a very powerful indictment of the "pretensions" of the rabbinic sacred band. Resh Lakish is protesting that the male–male eros of the study house is precisely supposed to be non-hierarchical and non-violent in its nature, but Rabbi Yoḥanan has just proven that it is neither. In fact, hardly conforming to the expressed ideal of dialogue in *havruta*, this male–male friendship reproduces rather precisely the very ancient pattern described by Halperin, of

> structural asymmetry, consisting in an unequal distribution of precedence among the
> members of the relationship and a differential treatment of them in the narrative: one
> of the friends has greater importance than the other; the latter is subordinated—
> personally, socially, and narratologically—to the former.
>
> *(Halperin 1990: 78)*

Resh Lakish's outburst is culturally precise, then: You offered me something entirely new, so you claimed, a set of relations that you call "Torah," or "under the wings of the Shekhina," but what I got was simply the same-old, same-old of hierarchical heroic friendship.

The rivenness, the incoherence, of their own ideology of friendship and family seems thematized in the continuation of the Talmudic narrative itself. Although the "true" meaning of Rabbi Yoḥanan's invitation to Resh Lakish was that he join the homoerotic brotherhood of those who "learn" Torah together, there is a human woman involved, Rabbi Yoḥanan's sister according to the flesh, who has, moreover, become a mother in the meantime. Her place in the economy is elegantly delineated in the narrative:

> His sister [Rabbi Yoḥanan's sister; Resh Lakish's wife] came to him [Rabbi Yoḥanan]
> and cried before him. She said, "Look at me!" He did not pay attention to her. "Look
> at the orphans!" He said to her "Leave your orphans, I will give life" (Jeremiah 49:11).
> "For the sake of my widowhood!" He said, "Place your widow's trust in me."

It is hard for us to imagine a more devastatingly clear statement of Rabbi Yoḥanan's position here than the "'Look at me!' He did not pay attention to her," nor a more devastatingly clear inculpation of that position.

The Talmud thus seems to be asserting the supreme value of textual intercourse at one and the same time as it is undermining the pretensions of such value. In the Talmud, at any rate, *contra* the claims made for platonic love by some critics, there is no doubt that such insistences on male–male equality in the intellectual world are as false-appearing as they are in the world of heterosexual "love" or, for that matter, as far from mutuality and equality of desire or power as Pausanian pederasty.

For Halperin, the great departure of Plato is from the hierarchical model of sex to one of mutual desire and pleasuring ("Why is Diotima a woman?"; Halperin 1990: 113–51). Halperin goes on to indicate that this reciprocity of active desire, "Plato's remodeling of the homoerotic ethos of classical Athens ... has direct consequences for his program of philosophical inquiry." It results in an ethos of true conversation in which "mutual desire makes possible the ungrudging exchange of questions and answers which constitutes the soul of philosophic practice" (Halperin 1990: 133). This seems to be what my alleged platonist Rabbi Yoḥanan is suggesting as well, but, counters the bitter Resh Lakish: Your promises of mutuality and reciprocity were entirely false. In truth, all you expected of me, brother Yoḥanan, was to be passive and receive your logos into my corpus. In his verbally violent and highly dismissive response to the disagreement on the part of his "friend" Rabbi Yoḥanan indicates that nothing indeed has changed at all. Paradoxically by saying that Resh Lakish is still a brigand, he is indicting his own practice with colleagues as no different from the practices of a band of brigands, precisely the charge that Resh Lakish brings against him. You are still a brigand means, in effect, I am still a brigand. The *bet hamidrash*, the space of the allegedly non-acquisitive true and mutual eros of men with men, is being set up as superior to the sexualized space of the family and that very set-up is being deconstructed as violent and hierarchical at one and the same time. Plato's dialectic is, I have argued, much closer in ethos to the absolute hierarchical, domination patterns of heroic friendship than Plato (or "Rabbi Yoḥanan") would have us believe.

This incoherency or rupture in the narrative is the product of social and theoretical tension. At the same time that the eros of men with men is presented as superior to the eros of the family, rabbinic Judaism insists on the absolute necessity and virtue of marriage and procreation for everyone, thus setting up an irresolvable tension between almost contradictory ideas of what is the fundamental and basic, the quintessential human relation, friends or family. It is almost as if Rabbi Yoḥanan himself represents Platonism, and his sister and her family the claims of the polis. For the rabbis, from tannaitic times, the notion of an elite separating off physically from the main body of the Jewish people is anathema, and with that, anathema as well, the thought that 'as for procreation, we will leave that for the ignoramuses.'[33] Rather than separating the population into two groups as some Jewish platonists (notably Philo) and some Christians would do, the rabbis seem rather to separate the spheres of a valorized homoerotic intellectual passion and a subordinated functional heterosexual world of getting and spending within the same male lives. Rabbi Yoḥanan would put it memorably: A millstone round his neck and he will learn Torah?!—but, nevertheless, the rabbi marries.

The analogy with the Protestant *institution* of marriage as friendship, only partial to be sure, but, nevertheless, a genuine analogy, may be revealing, for both its similarities and differences from the dilemma dramatized in our Talmudic tragicomedy. These Reformers, also, as Luxon remarks, "promoted [marriage] energetically for everyone, even (or especially) clergymen" (Luxon 2005: 28), producing as Luxon shows only too well a set of irresolvable dilemmas that plague us until now. The rabbinic attempt to conjoin celibacy and marriage in the same human life would seem to be, for obvious reasons, just as shot with contradiction.

It is simply no longer adequate, as perhaps I once imagined, to draw distinctions between Hellenistic Judaisms and that of the rabbis, or even platonized Judaisms and that of the rabbis. Sometimes, in certain texts, the rabbis indeed assert marriage and even the love of husband and wife as friendship. It was this moment that I documented in my *Carnal Israel*, a moment in which, for instance, a bride and groom can be referred to liturgically as loving friends. But so much else had to be papered over (I hope unintentionally) to render this distinction, including overlooking some very important differences between Palestinian and Babylonian rabbinisms. The Babylonian rabbis who retold our story, at any rate, seem caught between platonic and other Hellenistic understandings of marriage and society. They do not seem to subscribe to the common Hellenistic notion (expressed in the *Symposium* by Aristophanes, by Zeno, by the Hellenistic novels) that "Eros is a god who contributes to the city's security"[34]—our story perceives a passion much more corrosive to civic life than that—but neither will the narrative accept and revel in that corrosiveness (as Plato would have perhaps and surely some of the wilder of the "wild Platonists" of the Christian world, as well).

Michael Satlow (2001) has argued for a fundamental difference between Palestinian and Babylonian Jewish marriage ideologies. Noting that Babylonian sources almost never, if ever, speak of the *oikos* as a value in itself while Palestinian texts do so ubiquitously, he argues compellingly that the whole issue of marriage was quite differently configured for the Palestinians than for the Babylonians. According to Satlow the difference is to be explained by analogy with a difference between Hellenistic philosophies, with the Palestinians representing "Stoic" positionings of marriage as necessary for the good ordering of society,[35] and the greater Babylonian ambivalence about marriage, particularly in its relation to Torah-study, as closer to other Hellenistic philosophical positions, such as those of the Cynics (Satlow 2001: 33). Accepting his distinction, I would rather propose that the Palestinian view of the heterosexual marriage and *oikos* as the very foundation of ordered society represents more generally held views both popular and learned, while the Babylonian rabbinic virtual hostility to the *oikos* is closer to elite philosophical views heavily impacted by platonism.

The analysis of the Talmudic text presented here (and not considered by Satlow in this context at all) would bear out the suggestion that Babylonian rabbinism, more exclusively the product of a scholastic social formation, is closer to the position of Plato himself, as articulated in the *Symposium* and the *Phaedrus*.[36] As Alan Bloom has put it so sharply:

> This movement [from family to polis] is recapitulated in the *Republic*, with its noble lie, myths, and bizarre sexual regulations, where first the family is annihilated in the name of the city, and then the philosophers, who are to be its rulers, do not want to turn away from their contemplations to descend to the city's cavelike darkness.
>
> *(Bloom 2001: 66)*

However, Babylonian rabbinism must be riven by this antipathy as well, for whatever the attractions that celibacy might hold for any group of rabbis, their commitment to marriage and the foundation of families seems at least equally as strong. Hence the vacillations and oscillations of our story.

Strikingly, it is not entirely clear from the Talmudic text that it adopts the same position that we do instinctively, for when Rabbi Yoḥanan repents, it is of the failure of his love for Torah and the consequent failure of his love for Resh Lakish that he repents and not of the callous treatment of his sister:

> Resh Lakish died, and Rabbi Yoḥanan was greatly mournful over him. The Rabbis said, "What can we do to comfort him? Let us bring Rabbi El'azar the son of Padat whose traditions are brilliant, and put him before him [Rabbi Yoḥanan]." They brought Rabbi El'azar the son of Padat and put him before him. Every point that he would make, he said, "there is a tradition which supports you." He [R.Y.] said, "Do I need this one?! The son of Lakish used to raise twenty-four objections to every point that I made, and I used to supply twenty-four refutations, until the matter became completely clear, and all you can say is that there is a tradition which supports me?! Don't I already know that I say good things?" He used to go and cry out at the gates, "Son of Lakish, where are you?" until he became mad. The Rabbis prayed for him and he died.

As we see from this quotation, not only is it Rabbi Yoḥanan who seemingly has no care—even in penitential retrospect—for his sister, the wife of Resh Lakish, nor for his own nephews and nieces; the text shows no such concern either. It does not even bother to narrate their undoubtedly sad fate, let alone waste any energy on lamenting it. On the one hand, the text has raised that family to our consciousness; they cannot be simply ignored on the rabbinic reading of human life, but on the other hand, that raising to consciousness is almost immediately suppressed—but not, of course, never, of course, totally, the net result being a dialectic or an oscillation between two positions of critique of Rabbi Yoḥanan and seeming approbation of his denigration of sexual and kinship ties.

I can even pursue this reading a little further. Rabbi Yoḥanan's turning away from his sister surely manifests simple callousness and a critique of his ethics. But it also can be read as a representation of a highly critical perspective on human kinship, one not inconsistent with Rabbi Yoḥanan's near-platonism throughout the narrative. As Luxon has pointed out, kinship was itself considered an inferior, fleshly claim on human loyalty (Luxon 2005: 37, 46–7). Rabbi Yoḥanan's own indifference to his sister's plight, followed by an insistence that she ignore the plight of her own "one flesh"—what care I for your widowhood; what for your loss of sexual companionship?—as well as of her and his flesh and blood, the children, can be seen also as a chilling cultural response to all such claims and not just a moment of pique and arrogance. He, having divorced Resh Lakish, simply cannot stand the clangor of such inferior claims, just as for David the ties of conjugality were suddenly irrelevant, for Achilles the love of Patroclus was superior to the love one bears to brother or son (Halperin 1990: 84). If the love he bore for Resh Lakish, his soul-mate, has failed him, then what use are such inferior connections produced by the matings of bodies? This places our story somewhere between David's "Dearer was thy love to me than the love of women" and the "Jesus'" (and Paul's *mutatis mutandis*) insistence that only by abandoning family is it possible to be saved.[37] How different in ethos, after all, is this picture from the depiction of Paula leaving behind her little son, "pleading with his mother at the dock not to desert him"?[38] This dock itself represents the very liminality that Clark has pointed out of the monastic, man or woman, halfway between this world and another one (Clark 1979: 49). This liminality is not, then, I would suggest (or not only or even primarily), a limen between genders but rather one between the world of fleshly relations, of kinship and sex, and the world of friendship.

Friendship itself is liminal. Classicists have made this point clearer for us. Thus Halperin's remark that, "Friendship is the *anomalous* relation: it exists outside the more thoroughly codified social networks formed by kinship and sexual ties; it is 'interstitial in the social structure' of most western cultures" (Halperin 1990: 75). While in Halperin's first clause, one might think him to be saying that friendship is less natural than physical ties that bind, his final phrase shows clearly that he understands this ascription of naturalness, this depiction of interstitiality of friendship, to be a social construct as well. David Konstan has made this point in slightly different terms (1996: 1):

> … while the idea of friendship is not uniform over various cultures or even within a single culture at any given moment, the core of the relationship … may be characterized as a mutually intimate, loyal, and loving bond between two or a few persons that is understood not to derive primarily from membership in a group normally marked by native solidarity, such as family, tribe, or other such ties. Friendship is thus what anthropologists call an achieved rather than an ascribed relationship, the latter being based on status whereas the former is in principle independent of a prior formal connection such as kinship or ethnicity.

This helps us to go a bit further in answering some historical questions. If friendship represents indeed the triumph of achieved ties (that is ties that are described as achieved) within a given cultural or social formation over ties that are deemed to be natural within that culture, such as ties of sex and kinship, then it is not surprising that in an early Christian culture, entirely based—at least initially—on the superiority of achieved to ascribed ties, celibate friendship, the very symbolic antithesis of ascribed ties, becomes so central (Drake 1996: 3–36). This ties Christian renunciation with the very core of Christianity in a way that is not dependent on hatred of the body, sex, or women at all but rather intimately imbricated in fundamental theological commitments of the renunciation of the claims of kinship (the Pauline flesh) in the name of a universalism. This provides, as well, further explanation for the incredible pressure and stress that unsettles our rabbinic narrative. While the rabbis (and earlier biblical culture as well) feel the strong pull toward the achieved relation of friendship and its superiority over the ascribed relations of kinship, rabbinic Jewish society with its absolute commitment to the value of ethnicity, the flesh, cannot possibly settle down there.

The attraction of asceticism and even celibacy for the ancient rabbis (and not only other ancient Jews, as had been pointed out in a breakthrough essay by Steven Fraade in 1986), has been overlooked until very recently. Recent scholars, however, have gone beyond Fraade in realizing how fraught the issue of celibacy was *within* the rabbinic community itself,[39] thus showing us, once again, how unstable are the differences we ascribe to Christianity from Judaism. This leads one away, ever further away, from absolute (or near-absolute) binary oppositions between platonistic and rabbinic cosmologies and anthropologies; I see much more contiguity now at least in some rabbinic texts. My thinking until recently had comprehended the apparent inner tensions of rabbinic literature as being the product of a contention between the rabbis and earlier/other Jewish groups on this issue (Boyarin 1993: 61–76). At most, I allowed that an earlier and more Palestinian version of rabbinism had been closest to the ascetic ideals but that this shifted dramatically in Babylonian rabbinism (Boyarin 1993: 46–57). Most recently, however, stimulated by the excellent scholarship of a new generation, I have concluded that the tensions and ambivalence over corporeality and sexuality were right at the heart of the rabbinic movement itself. What was once easier to see as a heterogloss between the rabbis and the fathers now seems to be a complicated set of heteroglosses within the rabbinic community, as well.

I have tried to expose the deeply unsettled (and unsettling) ambiguity of the rabbinic text on the question of homoerotic desexualized love and its relations to bodies, sex, and procreation, an exposure in part rendered possible by reading it in the light of two cognate reflections on these ratios, that of Plato and that of early Christianity. In the past, and especially in *Carnal Israel*, I tended to lift up only the positions that seemed most antithetical to "Christian" or "Hellenistic" ones. I now would see those very positions as always mixed and conditioned by the presence within the Talmud itself of positions much closer to those of contemporary Others in the Mediterranean world. On my current reading, the Talmudic narrative constructs and reveals an ideology of sexuality that is not nearly as different from that of the *Symposium* as I would have previously imagined, nor as clearly oppositional to that of patristic Christianity as I would have previously inscribed. The same dual(istic) structure of corporeal vs non-corporeal passion (the same "instinct"[40]) is being advanced with the intensely homoerotic (but desexualized) male–male spiritual bonding over the seeking of wisdom (Sophia, Philosophia, Torah) clearly placed into a hierarchical circumstance in which it is read as far superior to the mere physical eros of sex with women and procreating children.[41]

Robert Markus famously remarked that "there just is not a different culture to distinguish Christians from their pagan peers, only their religion" (Markus 1990: 12). One comes to wonder more and more if the same statement might be made, *mutatis mutandis* and perhaps somewhat hyperbolically, about Jews as well.

Notes

1 Boyarin 2006: 3–22, 375–84.
2 A much fuller version of the argument only summarized here has also been made by me in Boyarin 2009: 290–308. The version presented here supersedes in some sense both this version and the one from 2006.
3 Not entirely surprising, then, that Foucault sees more of a break between Greek and Christian asceticisms, as noted by Elizabeth A. Clark 1988: 622, esp. 625, n. 13.
4 Nygren 1969: 303. See too for this position Cohen 1991: 175.
5 "One should keep in mind that [Platonic] 'asceticism' was not a means of disqualifying the love of boys; on the contrary, it was a means of stylizing it and hence, by giving it shape and form, of valorizing it," Foucault 1986: 245.

6 Dover 1989: 163 (emphasis added).

7 Foucault 1986. 238.

8 See also Vlastos 1981: 39–40 whose view of the matter is very like Foucault's.

9 For the argument upon which this conclusion is based, see Boyarin 2006.

10 Konstan, seemingly, would locate this very split before Plato, arguing that it "is the constitutive role played in the construction of Greek *erōs* by pederastic relations between men and boys which produced a rather sharp distinction between amatory and amicable ties," Konstan 1996: 6. This is a point of some importance as it goes to the question of the very ancient roots of classical and late antiquity.

11 Halperin 1990: 75–87. Lest anyone worry that I am conflating *philia* and *eros* here, it is clear from the *Lysis* that Plato sees them as not at all in opposition to each other, for in that dialogue (221d) *epithumia* (desire) is understood as the basis for friendship. See Robinson 1986: 75–6 and discussion in Konstan 1996: 73. Fascinating is the logical trap that Plato gets himself into, precisely by identifying the basis for friendship as desire, such that good men (those who have what they desire, the Good) cannot be friends, a hardly intelligible conclusion, hence the aporia of Robinson 1986: 83. On the other hand, for clear distinctions between *epithumia* and *eros*, see Halperin 1985: 172; for less clear ones, see Halperin 1985: 190, n. 8, by which I only mean that these are closer to each other than some might imagine.

12 "Those representations, moreover, all seem to exhibit a similar paradox: although their textual strategies make kinship and conjugality into privileged loci of signification for representing friendship, they also make friendship into a paradigm case of human sociality. They invoke kinship and conjugality, in other words, only to displace them, to reduce them to *mere* images of friendship," Halperin 1990: 85.

13 Although I will not treat them here, the connections of both Gregory of Nyssa's *Life of Macrina* and *On the Soul and Resurrection* with platonic texts, especially the *Symposium* and Methodius' all virgin-girl *Symposium*, also help to make this point. See Virginia Burrus 2000: 112–22 on Gregory.

14 It is certainly apposite to note here that Plotinus also had women among his close friends. Although White herself does not connect them, this is surely to be juxtaposed to Plotinus' own insistence that "Some [friendships belong] to the joint entity [consisting of body and soul], some to the inner man [soul alone]," cited in White 1992: 42. It seems intuitively right that Plotinus would ascribe his cross-gendered friendships to the latter category, although his text is, as White points out, cryptic. In this context, it is also worth noting that Synesius' explicit platonizing theory of friendships of different orders subtends his special relationship with Hypatia in apparently similar fashion.

15 In this respect my position is quite opposite to that of Mark Jordan (2006), for which see brief discussion in the section, Monks and their gals.

16 Nygren's rather obsessive insistence on how thoroughly everyone in early Christianity (and especially Origen) were enamored of eros is actually, for all the distaste with which he presents it, a partial recognition of this point. Unfortunately, as I have argued, Nygren seems to have had very little idea about what the *Symposium* actually means. A *locus classicus* for the writing of a Christian woman as Diotima is, of course, Gregory of Nyssa's life of his sister Macrina, which I hope to treat at some length in the longer version of this essay. See Burrus 2003: 58 and literature cited there.

17 I wish to emphasize that Markus (1970), like Jowett 1875, and in absolute contradistinction to Nygren and many others, does not see in the deep platonism of Christian thinking something that discredits (or contaminates) the latter. See too Vlastos 1981: 11–12, n. 28, who allows something much more like Christian agape into his Plato than some others (especially Nygren) do.

18 On which see Markschies: 1992.

19 Brown 1988: 179, citing Dodds 1965: 24–6.

20 In adducing Clement, then, as an argument that "Platonism restrained, and often helped to overcome, the tendency to a sometimes positively frenzied dislike of this world and of the body, which seems to have curiously deep roots in the religion of the Incarnation," Armstrong 1972: 38, I humbly suggest that Armstrong is not paying sufficient attention to the rivenness of Platonism itself.

21 Veyne 1987: 43.

22 Veyne himself would rather identify these attitudes as products of Roman culture, Veyne 1987: 43, which is hardly "wrong" too, of course.

23 Clark 1979: 39. *Contra* Clark, however, it does need mentioning that there are at least some persistent ancient reports of women among the academicians (Gaiser 1988: 154, cited in Hadot 2002: 61), supporting my suggestion that platonic theory allowed for, even articulated, such friendship (in the friendship of Socrates and Diotima) as well (see Boyarin 2006). Given my view on this matter, that is, if it makes any sense, one would not need to assume that Chrysostom had read the *Lysis* in order to

form an idea of male–female friendship, or of friendship at all. Gregory of Nyssa, had, however, read the *Symposium* in modeling his relationship with his sister Macrina on that of Socrates and Diotima in the *Dialogue on Resurrection and the Soul*, for which see Burrus 2000: 112–22.

24 For a Jerome perhaps but not, e.g., for Augustine, who writes that "Eve could not have been created primarily to be Adam's companion for 'how much better would two male friends live together, alike for company and conversation, than a man and a woman,'" White 1992: 10.

25 Partially disagreeing with Clark 1979: 48. Of course I am not denying the ample evidence that such women were represented as virtual men frequently enough, for which see Clark 1979: 56–7; but I am suggesting that it is less necessary and central than one might have thought. Let us not forget, of course, that *andreia* is a quality for which both women and men have to struggle. One of the arguments against any simplex assumption that ascetic women are rendered men is that ascetic men can also be represented as women, as argued by Burrus 2003: 20, 59, 91, and in Burrus 2000 throughout but esp. Burrus 2000: 111, 131–3. This does not constitute a claim of feminism for these men (Burrus 2000: 84, citing Loraux, "the man gains in complexity while the woman loses substance," Loraux 1995: 14–15).

26 Citing Loraux 1995: 13–14. Gregory himself, it should be mentioned, was married and had an intricate relation to the celibate movement, for discussion of which see Burrus 2000: 84–97. Especially relevant is Burrus' comment, "However, if Gregory defines virginity as 'the practical method' by which the soul maintains its upward gaze and resists being dragged down, swinelike, 'to the emotions belonging to flesh and blood' (*De virg.* 5), he may also intend that 'marriage' be interpreted more metaphorically, as a problem of erotic orientation resulting not from domestic and procreative coupling *per se* but rather from a failure to remain detached from the painful and distracting trivialities of the 'common life,'" Burrus 2000: 90. If so, then we can infer how he "read" his own marriage as a sort of virginity.

27 Burrus 2000: 97. The last citation is from Irigaray 1985: 74.

28 For a both moving and brilliant analysis of the conceptual distinction and relation between sexual desire and eros, see Halperin 1985: 182–5.

29 Jordan 2006: 23–37. This is the best place to remark that Jordan's essay was of immeasurable help to me in reforming my reading of the *Symposium*, as that reading appeared finally in my *Socrates and the Fat Rabbis* (Boyarin 2009).

30 Jordan's piece, a response to my earlier writing Boyarin 2006, curiously mistakes me at one point. In my assertion of the justness of Jowett's 1875 reading, I hardly meant to endorse his notion that Plato has some unique (and universally Christian) disdain for homoerotic passion. *Pace* Jordan, Boyarin's (platonic) Socrates does *not* condemn male–male copulation; he, rather, expresses disdain for all copulation without distinction between male–male and male–female. This is a distinction that makes an enormous difference. My regard, to be sure, for Diotima is quite a bit higher than Jordan's, but this is precisely because I read her as lover of Socrates and not the one who would repress love.

31 Raw materials are not subject to ritual impurity, but finished implements or vessels are. The question that this text asks is, then, what constitutes the completion of production for these various weapons?

32 This sentence is not in the ms. and is clearly an addition in the text, but I cite it from the print as it is very revealing of the meaning of the narrative, as a whole, and indeed supportive of my reading (it would seem to be an ancient gloss). R. Y. is not made to say that he profited R. L. by providing him with a wife but only by having provided him with the spiritual female object of desire, the *Shekhina*.

33 That is, there is the class of the ignoranti (the *'ammei h'araṣot*) but the Sages are enjoined not to separate themselves from this crowd. Much more can and will need to be said on this point, but it approximates my thinking at present.

34 Long and Sedley 1987: 430.

35 For brilliant and trenchant comments on the role of Stoicism in the development and propagation of this morality, see Veyne 1987: 44–5. On Antipater and Musonius, cited by Satlow, see Veyne 1987: 46–7.

36 Satlow himself reads this position as "cynic," which it well might be, but if so, I would argue it is such as a legacy of cynicism's own platonic lineage.

37 The clear Gospel preference for Martha over Mary inscribes this hierarchy in another way, Clark 1979: 7.

38 Clark 1979: 51.

39 Naeh 1997: 73–89; Koltun-Fromm 2001: 205–18; Satlow 2003: 204–25; Diamond 2004.

40 As already pointed out in Boyarin 1993: 65 but with much greater clarity and power in Rosen-Zvi 1999: 55–84.

41 Let us not forget, then, that Socrates himself was married with children (perhaps his children were very naughty). Plato, most assuredly, was not.

Bibliography

Armstrong, A.H. (1972) "Neoplatonic valuations of nature, body and intellect", *Augustinian Studies* 3: 35–59.

Bloom, A.D. (2001) "The ladder of love", in A.D. Bloom and S. Bernadete (eds/trans.) *Plato's Symposium*. Chicago, IL: University of Chicago Press, pp. 57–177.

Boyarin, D. (1993) *Carnal Israel: Reading Sex in Talmudic Culture*, The New Historicism: Studies in Cultural Poetics, vol. 25. Berkeley, CA: University of California Press.

——(1998) "Gender", in M.C. Taylor (ed.) *Critical Terms for the Study of Religion*. Chicago, IL: University of Chicago Press, pp. 117–35.

——(2006) "What do we talk about when we talk about Platonic love: Towards a genealogy of Christian sex", in V. Burrus and C. Keller (eds) *Toward a Theology of Eros: Transfiguring Passion at the Limits of Discipline*. New York: Fordham University Press, pp. 3–22, 375–84.

——(2009) *Socrates and the Fat Rabbis*. Chicago, IL: University of Chicago Press.

Brown, P. (1988) *The Body and Society: Men, Women, and Sexual Renunciation in Early Christianity. Lectures on the History of Religions*, n.s. 13. New York: Columbia University Press.

Burrus, V. (2000) *"Begotten, Not Made": Conceiving Manhood in Late Antiquity*. Figurae: Reading Medieval Culture. Stanford, CA: Stanford University Press.

——(2003) *The Sex Lives of Saints: An Erotics of Ancient Hagiography*. Divinations: Reading Late Ancient Religion. Philadelphia, PA: University of Pennsylvania Press.

Clark, E.A. (1979) *Jerome, Chrysostom, and Friends: Essays and Translations*. Studies in Women and Religion, vol. 2. New York and Toronto, ON: Edwin Mellen Press.

——(1988) "Foucault, the Fathers, and sex", *Journal of the American Academy of Religion* 56(4 Winter): 619–41.

Clement of Alexandria (1989) "The instructor", in A. Roberts and J. Donaldson (eds) *The Fathers of the Second Century, The Anti-Nicene Fathers*, vol. 2. Grand Rapids, MI: Wm. B. Eerdmans, pp. 207–98.

Cohen, D. (1991) *Law, Sexuality, and Society: The Enforcement of Morals in Classical Athens*. Cambridge: Cambridge University Press.

Diamond, E. (2004) *Holy Men and Hunger Artists: Fasting and Asceticism in Rabbinic Culture*. Oxford: Oxford University Press.

Dodds, E.R. (1965) *Pagan and Christian in an Age of Anxiety: Some Aspects of Religious Experience from Marcus Aurelius to Constantine*. Cambridge: Cambridge University Press.

Dover, K.J. (1989) *Greek Homosexuality*, updated and with a new postscript. Cambridge, MA: Harvard University Press.

Drake, H.A. (1996) "Lambs into lions: Explaining early Christian intolerance", *Past and Present* 153: 3–36.

Foucault, M. (1986) *The History of Sexuality*, Volume 2: *The Use of Pleasure*, trans. R. Hurley. New York: Random House.

Fraade, S.D. (1986) "Ascetical aspects of ancient Judaism", in A. Green (ed.) *Jewish Spirituality from the Bible through the Middle Ages*. New York: Crossroad pp. 253–88.

Gaiser, K. (1988) *Philodems Academica: Die Berichte über Platon und die Alte Akademie in zwei herkulanensischen Papyri*. Stuttgart-Bad Canstatt: Frommann-Holzboog.

Hadot, P. (2002) *What is Ancient Philosophy?* Cambridge, MA: Harvard University Press.

Halperin, D.M. (1985) "Platonic *erōs* and what men call love", *Ancient Philosophy* 5: 161–204.

——(1990) *One Hundred Years of Homosexuality: And Other Essays on Greek Love*. New York: Routledge.

Irigaray, L. (1985) *This Sex Which is Not One*, trans. C. Porter and C. Burke. Ithaca: Cornell University Press.

Jordan, M. (2006) "Flesh in confession: Alcibiades beside Augustine", in V. Burrus and C. Keller (eds) *Toward a Theology of Eros: Transfiguring Passion at the Limits of Discipline*. New York: Fordham University Press, pp. 23–37.

Jowett, B. (1875) *The Dialogues of Plato*, 2nd edn, trans. B. Jowett. Oxford: Clarendon Press.

Koltun-Fromm, N. (2001) "Yoke of the holy-ones: The embodiment of a Christian vocation", *Harvard Theological Review* 94.2: 205–18.

Konstan, D. (1996) *Friendship in the Classical World*. Key Themes in Ancient History. Cambridge and New York: Cambridge University Press.

Long, A.A. and Sedley, D.N. (1987) *The Hellenistic Philosophers*. Cambridge/New York: Cambridge University Press.

Loraux, N. (1995) *The Experiences of Tiresias: The Feminine and the Greek Man*. Princeton, NJ: Princeton University Press.

Luxon, T.H. (2005) *Single Imperfection: Milton, Marriage, and Friendship*. Pittsburgh, PA: Duquesne University Press.

Markschies, C. (1992) *Valentinus Gnosticus? Untersuchungen zur valentinianischen Gnosis mit einem Kommentar zu den Fragmenten Valentins*. Wissenschaftliche Untersuchungen zum Neuen Testament. Tübingen: J.C. B. Mohr.

Markus, R.A. (1970) "The dialectic of eros in Plato's *Symposium*", in G. Vlastos (ed.) *Plato: A Collection of Critical Essays*. Modern Studies in Philosophy. Garden City, NY: Anchor Books, pp. 132–43.

——(1990) *The End of Ancient Christianity*. Cambridge: Cambridge University Press.

Naeh, S. (1997) "Freedom and celibacy: A Talmudic variation on tales of temptation and fall in Genesis and its Syrian background", in J. Frishman and L. Van Rompay (eds) *The Book of Genesis in Jewish and Oriental Christian Interpretation: A Collection of Essays*. Traditio Exegetica Graeca 5. Louvain: Peeters, pp. 73–89.

Nygren, A. (1969) *Agape and Eros*, trans. P.S. Watson. New York: Harper and Row.

Robinson, D.B. (1986) "Plato's *Lysis*: The structural problem", *Illinois Classical Studies* 11: 63–83.

Rosen-Zvi, I. (1999) "The evil instinct, sexuality, and forbidden cohabitations: A chapter in Talmudic anthropology", *Theory and Criticism: An Israeli Journal* 14 (Summer): 55–84.

Satlow, M.L. (2001) *Jewish Marriage in Antiquity*. Princeton: Princeton University Press.

——(2003) "And on the earth you shall sleep: Talmud Torah and rabbinic asceticism", *Journal of Religion* 83: 204–25.

Veyne, P. (1987) "The Roman Empire", in P. Ariès and G. Duby (eds) *A History of Private Life I: From Pagan Rome to Byzantium*. Cambridge, MA: Belknap Press of Harvard University Press, pp. 6–50.

Vlastos, G. (1981) "The individual as object of love in Plato", in Gregory Vlastos (ed.) *Platonic Studies*. Princeton, NJ: Princeton University Press, pp. 3–42.

White, C. (1992) *Christian Friendship in the Fourth Century*. Cambridge: Cambridge University Press.

30

TOWARD A LATE-ANCIENT PHYSIOGNOMY

Mark Masterson

In the *Codex Theodosianus*, the massive legal code from 439 CE preserving edited laws going back to 313, the emperors frequently address their elite subordinates (individuals and the senate itself) with lavish complimentary language that attributes qualities of lofty abstraction and light to them. At 1.15.8, for example, the emperors Valens, Gratian, and Valentinian II address Hesperius, a praetorian prefect, as "Your Shining Judgment" (*Illustris Censura Tua*). Elsewhere in the code, "Your Sublimity" (*Sublimitas Tua*) appears over 75 times[1] and "Your Loftiness" (employing the word *culmen*) a number of times as well.[2] These salutations, exemplary (for there are others similar to them), can be associated with designations of precedence in the senatorial order. By the year 400, every man of senatorial rank would have held one of the following three ranks (lowest to highest): *clarissimus*/λαμπρότατος[3] ("most bright"), *spectabilis*/σπεκταβίλιος[4] (or περίβλεπτος[5]) ("well-worth looking at"), and *illustris*/ἰλλούστριος[6] ("utterly illuminated").[7] Only the lowest, *clarissimus*, was hereditary, while the other two higher ranks were bestowed in recognition of service.[8] It is important to note two things about these titles. First, they are significant as the number of senators will increase ten-fold over the course of the fourth century,[9] and the imperial bureaucracy, which will create ever more senators, grows well into the sixth.[10] Second, this glamorous elite manhood is a thing of paradox; though presented in the late-ancient sources as abstract and shining, late-Roman elite manhood has an essential connection to heredity and service, both of which are material and have no necessarily gleaming evanescence about them.

Like the elite men serving the emperor, philosophers and holy men, illumined, seem to belong to the next world, while at the same time remaining involved with things of this earth. The late fourth- to early fifth-century writer Eunapius tells how the body and clothing of Iamblichus (the late third- to early fourth-century philosopher) used to acquire a golden hue when he was at his devotions.[11] Theurgists, late-ancient practitioners of pagan religious rites such as sacrifice, were often figured as bathed in light.[12] But even as Iamblichus and the theurgists gleamed, they also engaged in physical acts of blood sacrifice and other pagan practices. Recalling the situation with senators and pagan holy men, light and transcendence marked out Christian ascetics[13] and saints' relics[14]—even as materiality was never far away. Christian holy men often became grand through physical acts of self-deprivation in service to God, and inscrutable relics, even as they were deemed wholly sufficient to bring about the divine presence of the saint, were all the same insistently material and fragmentary.

Elite male subjectivity (or its remnants in relic form) considered in this way presents aspects that would have appeared old in late antiquity. The appeals to light and spectacle meant to underscore grandeur can be seen as the continuation of prior practice. For the Latin speaker in the prior centuries of empire, glory (*gloria*) was a shining thing (Lendon 1997: 274). Among the Greek speakers, honor (e.g., *timē*/τιμή or *doxa*/δόξα) was often illuminated (Lendon 1997: 278–9). Nonetheless, the numbers of men designated in this way, the exaggerations of abstraction, and the zealous creation of classifications (e.g., *clarissimus*, *spectabilis*, *illustris*) are all novel to late antiquity. In similar fashion, the evanescent thing of all value finding its opposite in less valuable materiality recalls Plato and is therefore old. But the interaction of these Platonizing concepts in late antiquity proves to be new because it repositions an old structure's hierarchized terms. For example, late-Platonic philosophy will question the separation of matter from the transcendent, and the philosopher Iamblichus will even propose that the soul is embodied. The similarity between these developments in philosophy and the mixture of transcendence and materiality in late-Roman manhood is manifest: in both the immaterial and material meet and interact in ways that surpass and/or complicate a prior hierarchy.

At this point of convergence between old and new, and between immaterial and material, lies the business of this paper, which is consideration of a work, likewise old and new, that is concerned with gender: the anonymous Latin physiognomy from the fourth century CE. As a specimen of a genre of technical writing old by the time of late antiquity and a work that describes and polices gender, this relatively unsophisticated treatise at the same time offers a topology of subjectivity—a proposed arrangement of an unseen psychic interior, i.e., mind and soul, and the relation of this interior to the body—that is late ancient and has discernible connections to late-Platonic philosophy. Furthermore, when reflecting on his method, Anonymous proposes that bodies of men and women—which he grants share qualities, i.e., men have feminine qualities, and women masculine ones—can be analyzed to produce the categories by which they may be understood. At first seeming unconvincing and circular, as physiognomy on this understanding will need a miracle to be effective, Anonymous' technical commentary then features a metaphorization of physiognomy as the reading of text. This is the miracle required, as a "miraculous" similarity between the reading of bodies and that of texts covers over the scandalous circularity of pure categories being produced from hybrid bodies: letters, syllables, and the rest signify in a manner correlative to the way body parts do in physiognomy. Although letters themselves raise questions, successful reading of text disables the concerns of logic, and this glamorous success renders the body legible to the physiognomist after all. This metaphorization of physiognomy as reading also recalls the paradox of subjectivity in late antiquity. As mere graphic evidence and hybrid bodies against expectation point to wholeness not able to be accounted for logically, so late-Roman elite manhood or Christian ascetic sanctity is in this world and the next, mixing up the material with the transcendent. Before discussion of Anonymous' topology of subjectivity and his reflections on his working methods, however, a few words on the science of physiognomy are in order.

Physiognomy in late antiquity and before

Physiognomy, or the science of reading the body for signs of inner character and future destiny, was old by late antiquity. It first shows up some 800 years earlier and maintains a constant presence in Greek and Roman imaginations down to the late empire and beyond.[15] There are two treatises extant from the fourth century CE, an anonymous one in Latin (the focus of this paper) and one in Greek by Adamantius.[16] Both treatises consist in large part of copied/translated material. Adamantius admits (at *Physiognomonica* 1.1), for example, that he presents the words of the famous rhetor and physiognomist Polemon (*c.*88–144 CE), and Anonymous mentions Loxus (whose dates are uncertain[17]) and Aristotle, in addition to Polemon (*Anon. Lat.* 1).

Not surprisingly, both of these late-ancient physiognomies have been hunting grounds for scholars looking for the words of earlier thinkers, and both, fragmented, have played starring roles in narratives of the use of physiognomy in earlier centuries (e.g., Gleason 1995). This paper, as its title indicates, has an interest in what makes one of these works, the anonymous Latin one, late ancient, for its mere existence and references to physiognomy in other late-ancient texts attest to the continuing relevance of this science for understanding subjectivity. The historiographer, Ammianus Marcellinus, for example, includes in his necrologies of deceased emperors and *caesar* Gallus descriptions of their bodies that clearly owe much to physiognomy.[18] Both Iamblichus and the philosopher Porphyry assert that Pythagoras practiced physiognomy.[19] Frank (2000: 134–70) persuasively connects physiognomy to descriptions of Christian ascetics. It is therefore worth asking what can be learned about late-ancient ideas of gender from this work.

The object of physiognomic analysis was usually a man, although women on occasion were objects of study.[20] Women appear to have been used mostly to identify characteristics that, detected in a man, would mark him as effeminate. Indeed, the occasional appearance of two sexes is overwhelmed by the insistent and ironic marking of the unmarked category of man who, through the excess of authorial attention to the male sex and masculine gender, comes to stand for the human. But the physiognomists did not expend all this energy only to describe men; these works were meant to police them too. In an important study of elite manhood in the Roman empire of the first and second centuries CE, Gleason notes that physiognomy, while seemingly a science of observation and classification, is better conceived as "belong[ing] to a large-scale coercive social process"[21] of enculturation of elite men to their roles as leaders of society, enculturation that separated the worthy from the unworthy.[22] This function for physiognomy continued in late antiquity. Speaking of the embeddedness of physiognomy in late-ancient power relations, Kuefler notes that there was a "social utility"[23] to the identification of effeminacy in men in late antiquity; physiognomy designated those who deserved to wield authority (the free, the Roman, the masculine) and stigmatized those who did not (the servile, the non-Roman, the effeminate), even as it masqueraded as disinterested.[24] Since physiognomy still acted as a means of social control in late antiquity, close reading of Anonymous' reflections on the practice of physiognomy for what it has to say about late-ancient men is warranted. The coming close reading brings into view a topology of subjectivity that has discernible connections to sophisticated notions about personhood in late-ancient philosophy and to the paradoxical configurations of elite masculinity, secular and sacred; a modest document with "social utility" has commonalities with ambitious and rarified personages and systems of thought.

Animus and *anima*

Anonymous begins by proclaiming that the worth of physiognomy is that it enables an understanding of the mind (*animus*) from the observed characteristics of the body:[25]

> In the first place it should be established what good physiognomy does. It does good because it examines and discerns the quality of the mind from the quality of the body.
>
> (*Anon. Lat. 2*)

Anonymous here suggests a proportionality of some kind between mind and body. This suggestion made, Anonymous then turns to the soul (*anima*). He presents Loxus' notion[26] that the blood is the home of the soul and that bodies give signs based on the quality of the interaction between soul/blood and body:[27]

> A certain Loxus established that blood was the abode of the soul. Moreover, each body and the parts of the body, which give signs, give signs divergent in proportion to the liveliness and sluggishness of the blood, in proportion to whether the blood is thin or thick, and in proportion to whether it has free and direct passages or twisted and narrow ones.
>
> (Anon. Lat. *2*)

Having posited blood as the dwelling place of the soul/*anima*, Anonymous does not explain what the *anima* is (which he did not do, either, for the *animus*) or what it means for it to have a physical abode. From here, blood substitutes for the soul and the production of signs (*signa*) for the physiognomist to read depends on the interplay of blood and body, as the two of them shape each other. Character is, to this extent, an epiphenomenon of physicality. Also, it seems that the *animus* is more transcendent than the *anima* because of the latter's association, if not coincidence, with physical blood. The soul's physicalization and, at the same time and with some paradox, its nature as both physical and abstract also have a perceptible pedigree in other late-ancient discourses.[28]

Anonymous' association of the soul with blood recalls the role blood plays in the depiction of martyrs and their relics. Writing in the mid-390s in his sermon "On the Praise of Saints," Victricius sees blood as tantamount to the soul of the martyr: "blood, upon the reward of divinity, bursts into flame after martyrdom" (Victric. 8.10–11: *sanguis … post martyrium praemio divinitatis ignescit*). The "reward of divinity," which is to be understood as eternal life, comes about through the fiery dematerialization of blood after the martyr's sacrifice. Making a similar point a little later, Victricius states that blood exists in both terrestrial form and transcendent transformation:[29]

> We declare that the flesh is held together by the glue of blood, and we assert that the spirit [*spiritus*], dripping with blood's dew, has drawn to itself the word's fiery ardor.
>
> (*Victric. 9.32–4*)

Similarly, Emperor Julian (writing in the early 360s in his ninth oration, "To the Uneducated Cynics") offers up a duplex soul that recalls Anonymous' pairing of *animus* and *anima* (note especially that one half of the soul is passionate and diffused):[30]

> Since one part of the soul (*psyche*/ψυχή) is more god-like, which we call mind [*nous*/νοῦς] and intelligence [*phronēsis*/φρόνησις] and silent reason [*logos*/λόγος], whose herald is voiced speech made up of words and phrases; and since there is yoked to it another part (of the soul) which is intricate and multiform, a beast promiscuous in passion and desire and many-headed—isn't it necessary to look steadily and unswervingly at the opinions of the many before we master this beast and persuade it to obey the god within us, or, rather, the divine part of the soul?
>
> (*Jul. Or. 9.15 [197a–b]*)

Julian's topology of subjectivity presents a bisected soul. One part, "the god within us," is uniform and unchangeable (by implication) and therefore can be regarded as equivalent to the *animus*—and, characteristically prolix, Julian provides three names for this part: "mind," "intelligence," and "reason." The changeable and multiform part of the soul, in contrast, involves itself with things of the world and is affected by them. The "god within us" must govern this counterpart to Anonymous' *anima* carefully because of its tendency to become overly involved in the world of emotions and possessions ("a beast promiscuous in passion and desire"). Julian also remarks that this part of the soul is "many-headed." In saying this, Julian simplifies a passage from Plato's *Republic*, a work well known in late antiquity,[31] in which Socrates and Glaukon "fashion an image of the soul in words,"[32] an image which has three parts to it. The first part is in the "form of a changeful and many-headed beast,"[33] and its heads are both tame and feral. Socrates compares this beast to the Chimaera, Cerberus, or Scylla as it, like them, is an example of "many forms grown into one."[34] The other two parts of the soul in Plato's text are in the forms of a lion and a human. The ideal situation is that the human will control the monster and persuade the lion to side with him (*R.* 9.589a-b). This reference to the *Republic* illustrates Julian's notion of a multiform and beastly part of the soul needing the governance of the more rational part. Reading Julian and Plato with Anonymous suggests what might have occurred to an educated reader of the physiognomy in late antiquity: making *anima* both blood and not blood, and therefore putting the soul in a tense, inconsistent relationship with physicality, Anonymous' topology recalls Julian's conception, which he surely developed from Plato,[35] and so, to some audiences at least, this relatively unsophisticated physiognomy, embedded in power relations, has a perceptible philosophical sheen.

There are similar ideas in other late-Platonic thinkers which can be connected to Anonymous' topology of subjectivity. Going back to the second (Mind/*nous*/νοῦς) and third (Soul/*psychē*/ψυχή) of Plotinus' hypostases ("The One" being the first, of course[36]) and which Porphyry subsequently used (with some modifications),[37] Iamblichus proposes a distinction between Mind (*nous*/νοῦς) and Soul (*psychē*/ψυχή) that resembles Anonymous' one between *animus* and *anima*. He speaks of classes of being that govern the world at *De Mysteriis* 1.7,[38] and contrasts the highest governing force in the universe to the lowest. The greatest and most rarified (identified as Mind/*Nous* at 1.7/21.14), while authoring the world, is unaffected by mortal things. In contrast, the lower and least rarified (called Soul/*Psyche* at *Myst.* 1.7/22.3) is affected by that which it rules and has a close association with the created world:[39]

> The one (*sc.* Mind/νοῦς) is highest, transcendent, complete in itself, while the other (*sc.* Soul/ψυχή) is last, left behind, and rather incomplete; the one can do all things unitarily all at once in the present moment, while the other can do whole things neither all at once, nor all of a sudden, nor without division. The one, without perturbation, produces and manages all things, and the other has the nature to incline downward and to be turned towards the things that come into existence and which are subject to governance.
>
> (*Myst. 1.7 [21.1–6]*)

A little further on in the *De Mysteriis*, Iamblichus notes that lofty Mind comprehends all things existent all at once, while Soul needs time and space. While the former is unconditioned or absolute, the latter is affected by things around it:[40]

> The one (*sc.* Mind/*Nous*), in accordance with its singular penetrating strength, embraces the fulfilments of whole actualizations and essences. The other (*sc.* Soul/*Psychē*) metamorphoses from one thing to another and makes its way from the imperfect to the perfect. The former possesses utter height and incomprehensibility. It is greater than any measure and it is formless in that it cannot be limited by any form. The latter is mastered by downward momentum, passing states, and physical inclinations. It is held fast by the attractions of the worse and appropriation by secondary

powers. In sum, the latter takes its appearance from entities of all kinds and from their specifications.

(Myst. 1.7 [21.7–14])

The sublime governor of the universe, Mind is the perfect thing unaffected by what it governs. Soul, on the other hand, takes charge of matter and changes according to what it has to deal with; Soul mediates between the intellectual and material realms.[41] Steel (1978: 65) writes of Soul in Iamblichus' conception of it:

> As a *whole* it remains in itself and is identical to itself and as a *whole* it proceeds outside of itself and changes. Further, it does not do this alternatively—now remaining and then proceeding—but this occurs simultaneously: ἅμα ὅλη μένει καὶ πρόεισι [*At one and the same time it remains whole and proceeds outward*[42]]. This is the central idea of Iamblichus' vision of the soul.

The distinction Anonymous draws between *animus* and *anima*, so that one is more transcendent than the other, therefore, has correlates in late-ancient philosophic innovations, the ultimate basis of which was in Plato. (Anonymous' distinction also has an analogue in Victricius' theorization of the martyr's transcendent soul manifesting as flaming blood.) Although the names vary (Julian speaks in the first place of the soul, while Iamblichus speaks of Mind), in both of these thinkers, and similarly in Anonymous, there is a transcendent part to the unseen in subjectivity and a part that mediates between the transcendent and the body, just as, for example, the emperor's elite man, who sports the title of *Illustris Censura Tua*, has both his physicality and an abstract dimension.

Sympathy and the nature of the soul

The next words of Anonymous look quite Iamblichan through their emphasis on the soul's power over the body and its liability, at the same time, to feeling effects from its close relationship to materiality:[43]

> Moreover, others think that just as the soul is the shaper [*figuratrix*] of the body through *sympathy* (*per συμπάθειαν*[44]), so the soul takes its appearance from the quality of the body (also through *sympathy*).

(Anon. Lat. 2)

The appearance of *sympathy* to account for the effect of physiognomy ties Anonymous' treatise even more closely to the philosophical discourses that have just been discussed.[45] Omnipresent in the ancient philosophical systems,[46] *sympathy* is a name for the idea that all things in the universe are interconnected. *Sympathy* accordingly validates conclusions drawn from surface manifestations about hidden depths and is useful in physiognomy. Furthermore, through its origin in philosophy long ago, it was attractively authoritative. Historically it had been most of all associated with the Stoics and had for them designated "the presence of the divine logos through all things, that is, the material basis of the connection of every part of the existing cosmos" (Struck 2004: 189).

Sympathy appears in philosophical and para-philosophical works throughout late antiquity. For example, Emperor Julian, writing in his prose hymn "To the Mother of the Gods," sees *sympathy* at work in the coordination between the demigod Attis' bestowal of form on matter and the movement of the sun at the equinox (*Or.* 8.11 [171b–c]). In Adamantius' *De Ventis* (47.20–4), the planets and stars affect earthly affairs through *sympathy*. *Sympathy* appears a number of times in the works of Iamblichus and names a force coursing through and connecting a structured universe. According to Pythagoras, Iamblichus says, mallow should not be eaten because it is "the first herald and seal of the *sympathy* of heavenly things toward things earthly" (*VP* 24 [109]).[47] At *Myst.* 5.7 (207.8–13), as part of his explanation of the effectiveness of sacrifice,[48] Iamblichus describes the underlying connection between all things as *sympathy*.

To demonstrate the power of *sympathy* he sees connecting soul and body, Anonymous then provides two illustrations. In the first, the soul is compared to liquid in a bottle. The bottle governs the liquid's form in the way the body governs the soul's. In the second comparison, which is a representation of the same point, Anonymous notes that breath will make a different sound depending on whether it is sent through a pipe, flute, or trumpet. The soul is:[49]

> just like liquid contained in a bottle—it takes its shape from the bottle; just like breath blown into a pipe, flute, or trumpet—for although the breath is the same, the trumpet, pipe, and flute nevertheless make different sounds.
>
> *(Anon. Lat. 2)*

These similes illustrate only one half of the dynamic which Anonymous sets out prior to their deployment; they show twice that the soul is affected by its embodiment and not the other half, how the soul is the shaper (*figuratrix*) of the body. Perhaps the point about the power the unseen has over the body, which can be connected ultimately to the famous Platonic forms, is one Anonymous feels hardly needs an illustration after a simple statement of it. It is easy to document instances of the transcendent figuring material things in late-ancient philosophical literature.[50] In any case, and allowing the presence of Anonymous' examples to govern the form of the present argument, it is time to contextualize Anonymous' idea that "the soul takes its appearance from the quality of the body."

The inclination of the soul toward the body, affected while remaining itself, recalls Iamblichus' observation that the soul, even as it remains a recognizable entity, "is mastered by downward momentum, passing states, and physical inclinations" (*Myst.* 1.7 [21.12]: ῥοπῇ καὶ σχέσει καὶ νεύσει κρατεῖται). Providing a quotation from Priscianus that also presents Iamblichus' views,[51] Shaw points out that Iamblichus thought that the human soul was the lowest of the ethereal deities and that a signal characteristic of its lower status was its lack of uniformity and abundance of otherness (in comparison to, say, Mind). Shaw remarks (1995: 101–2 [emphasis in original]):

> Among the hierarchy of immortal entities, the human soul possessed the greatest degree of otherness (*heterotēs*/ἑτερότης). This caused it to identify with what was other to itself, and the corporeal body became the context of its self-alienation. Priscianus says: "Our soul [being one] remains one and is multiplied at the same time in its inclination to the body; it neither remains purely nor is changed entirely, but somehow it both remains and proceeds from itself, and when *it is made other to itself* the sameness with itself is made faint."[52]

Otherness in the soul keeps it from having the self-identity that other ethereal entities have. Indeed, this otherness makes the soul better able to deal with the otherness of the body; in performing its duty of enlivening the body, the soul naturally goes out from itself and experiences change while doing so. Indeed, Iamblichus saw the soul as completely descended into the body,[53] as a number of scholars have shown.[54] In asserting that the soul completely descended into a body and this world, Iamblichus rejected what he presented as a sort of Gnostic or Manichaean error in

Plotinus and Porphyry, for these philosophers insisted on the soul's transcendence of the world.[55] In asserting this reciprocal relationship between the soul and the body, Iamblichus thought himself a better Platonist than his two illustrious predecessors and, to the point in the present instance, there is demonstrable commonality once again between philosophy and the physiognomy of Anonymous. The physiognomy, as it polices gender in late antiquity, makes use of a concept, *sympathy*, that connects it to philosophy, and this connection proposes that at the level of the body and soul is a relation similar to that which connects elite men to heaven and which, as an ineffable force, pervades and gives structure to the universe.

Types and text

Anonymous next distinguishes between the types (*genera*)[56] of masculine and feminine. He finds focusing on differences between the types the incorrect way to proceed; it is better to keep in mind that men and women often share qualities:[57]

> The first division and distinction of this study are that one type (*genus*) is masculine and the other is feminine. And this is not to be understood on the terms that sexes and types (*sexus et genera*) are naturally distinct but [on the terms] that the masculine type is frequently to be detected in the feminine and the feminine [frequently] in the masculine.
>
> *(Anon. Lat. 3)*

A distinction between types needs to be made but bodies give conflicting signals. Male and female bodies share features, and this fact can be correlated to substantial similarities between the male and female types. This passage perhaps provides evidence of at least a little independence in the ancient world of anatomical sex from what we now call gender.[58] But what is to the point is the difficult pass to which Anonymous has come. While he notes that the two types need to be distinguished, the types and sexes share qualities with one another. Determining the nature of masculinity and femininity will not be a simple matter of looking at a(ny) man in his totality and a(ny) woman in hers and through comparison inferring the nature of masculinity and femininity. According to Anonymous, nothing is naturally all masculine or all feminine and notions of masculine and feminine are drawn from composite sources in a circular process whereby the likely (or actual) subjects for analysis are productive of the various categories through which they are analyzed. It therefore is not clear whether a reliable mode of measurement can be devised.

After a technical comment on the relationship between the Greek and Latin terms he uses[59] and seeming sensitive to the arbitrariness of his procedures, Anonymous lays down axioms about men's and women's minds and bodies:[60]

> In the first place, therefore, the mind (*animus*) of the masculine type and, in contrast, that of the feminine have to be posited (*constituendus*). Next the signs of each body have to be indicated (if not all of them, at least those which are able to open the way for this examination).
>
> *(Anon. Lat. 3)*

In attributing gendered qualities to the mind, Anonymous possibly contradicts the present reading of his physiognomy, which will prefer to assign such qualities to the soul instead. But perhaps the contradiction is only seeming. In remarks made in his discussion of *sympathy*, Iamblichus says that Mind's power and sway are the enabling condition for Soul's ability to act upon material reality:[61]

Accordingly, Mind (*nous*/νοῦς), on the one hand, as leader and emperor of those things which are and as a method demiurgic of everything, is always present in a manner similar to the gods, i.e., perfectly, self-sufficiently, and faultlessly according to a singular potentiality situated purely in itself; while Soul (*psychē*/ψυχή), on the other hand, partakes of a partial and multiform Mind (*nous*/νοῦς), which looks directly at the management of the whole, and (Soul) itself, arising in different forms at different times, has a concern also for the soulless realm [*lit.* "soulless things"/*ta apsycha*/τὰ ἄψυχα].

(*Myst. 1.7 [21.14–22.5]*)

Mind manifests as "a partial and multiform Mind" in places where Soul is doing its work, even down to the level of Soul's management of the ironically named "soulless realm," by which Iamblichus means rocks, plants, bodies of water, and the like. Going even further afield (and into the fifth century), Anonymous' altering the definition of the mind is a visible precursor to the fifth-century philosopher Proclus' formulation of a pervasive Mind (*nous*/νοῦς) whose extent runs higher *and* lower than that of Soul.[62] In any case, and moving past this possible contradiction, which can be finessed by recourse to the late-Platonic thinkers' ever ready propensity to make ever more precise abstract distinctions about the nature of things, what of the bodies Anonymous is surveying?

As discussed above (p. 543), Anonymous offers no stable basis either for generating evaluative criteria or for determining which parts of the body will be expressive or in what way they will be expressive. The process is circular and the hybridity of bodies makes the operation even more uncertain. Perhaps to bridge this abyss that has opened up due to the circularity of his reasoning, Anonymous compares the acquisition of skill in reading bodies physiognomically to the process of becoming a masterful reader of literature (in the hope that the image, magical and miraculous, will do the work that straight-on description clearly cannot[63]):[64]

For just as in the study of literature (*litterae*), since there are twenty-four letters (*elementa*)—according to the Greeks—through which each word (*vox*) and the language as a whole (*omnis sermo*) is understood, so also in physiognomy, through the "letters" set before us (*propositis elementis*), the most wide-ranging avenue for this investigation is revealed. For if we have learned all the syllables (*syllabae*) in boyhood, and when the power of the syllables has been realized (according to which each language [*sermo*] comes forth), shortly we see in detail a marshaling of the literature (*litterae*) that the language possesses.

(*Anon. Lat. 3*)

It is hardly surprising that Anonymous should have recourse to this metaphorization of physiognomy's action. Polemon compared physiognomy to reading, as can be discovered in one of the Arabic translations of his physiognomy.[65] But more importantly, the identification of similarity between the signs (*indicia*) of the body and the twenty-four letters (*elementa*) of written and spoken language is powerful. A reader is compelled by his or her success in making meaning from the written words to entertain the notion that physiognomy experiences similar success as it interprets its own set of communicative signs. Furthermore, in this physiognomy and that of Adamantius, observation of bodily signs elicits actual speech in much the same way that letters will, for in the ancient world silent reading was exceptional. To take some examples, in Anonymous' work, the physiognomists will "say" or even "declaim" (*Anon. Lat. 1.9*: *dicerent, pronuntiabant*) what they have seen, while, in the physiognomy of Adamantius, the observation of the body leads the physiognomist to "say" (λέγε [Adam. 1.3.19]; ἐρεῖς [Adam. 1.3.24]) what has been discovered.

By late antiquity, letters had a long history of representing physical realities. Lucretius proposed that letters (*elementa*) on a page should suggest to a reader the play of atoms that is the universe's reality (Lucr. 1.823–9). Rhetorical theory mapped the orator's body in text, and boys learned to become men by interacting with handbooks (Gunderson 2000: 4; 14[66]). Lamberton (1986: 76–7) discusses a similar metaphorization of the physical universe through language in the fragments of Numenius, where this middle-Platonic philosopher (second century CE) posed the question as to whether the universe was best thought of as composed of elements individually or as combinations of these same elements. The word Numenius used for element was *stoicheion* (στοιχεῖον). This Greek word, similar to the Latin *elementum*, can refer either to one of the four elements (earth, water, air, and fire) or to a letter of the alphabet. Furthermore, the word for composites of these elements is *syllabai* (συλλαβαί). *Stoicheion* and an adverb derived from *syllabai* (*syllēbdēn*/συλλήβδην) allowed Numenius to offer a visualization of the universe employing a metaphor of reading:[67]

> But what is being? Is it these four elements (*stoicheia*), earth, fire, and the two natural elements in between? Are these, then, the things that really are, either collectively (*syllēbdēn*) or according to each one of them?
>
> *(On the Good fr. 3.1–4)*

Language here is a metaphor for the ultimate reality of the physical world, just as the canonic four elements and their combinations that comprise the universe are a metaphor for language.

While speaking of the body as a text to be read *in a text being read* out loud or silently is a powerful move for reasons situated in the moment of reading or in the history of letters being associated with the physical world, questions about both physiognomy and language emerge when Anonymous' comparison is analyzed even more closely. As already noted, circularity is present in Anonymous' text: there is a need to categorize persons (whose bodies are hybrid concatenations of masculine and feminine elements) as predominantly one or the other, even as it is stipulated that these bodies are productive of the evaluative criteria. It is not clear how a would-be physiognomist is supposed to proceed with security. Furthermore, the crucial point about the gender of masculine and feminine minds is likewise merely asserted and then enters into the general circularity of Anonymous' procedure. The explanatory model of language Anonymous offers raises similar questions. Just as the *constituendum* has to be defined beforehand in the case of physiognomy, which makes the physiognomist dependent on unpresented criteria, so the would-be interpreter of literary language has need of convention and a storehouse of concepts to make his or her progress from the *elementa* through the *syllabae*, *vox*, and *sermo* to *litterae*. The significatory power of lofty literature is a site of contest as the indeterminacies of reference starting with the *elementa* are passed up through the syllables and speech because the need for extraneous convention and concepts has not lessened. The only hope for elucidation is a resort to more language which intensifies the problem and brings to mind the similarly problematic determination of masculine and feminine via observation of hybrid bodies.

Anonymous' comparison between learning to read the body and learning to read a text therefore is an apt one: each of these modes of reading fails in similar ways. In both cases a syntax of parts is supposed to yield a language that will encompass the whole either of the person or of *litterae*. The circularity of the description of the bases of physiognomy is patent; that of language is less apparent perhaps, but, in any case, rendered obvious by the context of the comparison. The claim, however, in both cases is that failure is only apparent and that success occurs. The visible and logically insufficient *elementa* (bodily or graphic) point to a wholeness miraculously achieved through connection to things outside of the terms provided: success in making meaning from reading words contests and ultimately overwhelms the claims of logic to discover problems with the legibility of both letters and bodies.

When Anonymous offers visions of wholeness that succeed in spite of demonstrable illogicalities, the glorious men of imperial address, called by such titles as "Your Shining Judgment," should come to mind:[68] the unstable suite of qualities of these elites—light-filled grandeur, its head amid the stars, has feet, defined by lineage and busy in service, on the ground—recalls the visible elements, letters, or body parts, that gesture to a wholeness guaranteed by reference to things beyond what is directly to hand. Anonymous' late-ancient physiognomy accordingly reflects the tensed and aspiring liveliness of elite subjectivity, as it also is of a piece with innovative understandings of the relation between soul and body being developed in late-ancient philosophy. Anonymous' little work on the reading of bodies for clues into character and gender plays a tune perceptibly shaped by late-ancient discourses concerned with status and philosophy.

Finally, it should be noted again that the attention paid to women, as is typical of the genre of physiognomy, is but glancing. Indeed, and this is an old and continuing story, Anonymous conceives of subjectivity in unitary terms and the general presumption underlying his text is that speaking of the human ultimately means speech about the man; the hybridity of bodies that poses such a challenge to logic is a superficial aspect of this sex that is functionally but one.[69] Perhaps this sex, capacious and transcendent of the binary, is a dynamo whose workings in late antiquity would benefit from closer consideration.[70]

Notes

1 E.g. Emperor Julian [sends the following words] to Mammertinus, the Praetorian Prefect: "May *Your Sublimity* call together the *rectores* of the Provinces …" (*CTh*.1.15.4 [362]) (*Imp. Iulianus a. ad Mamertinum praefectum praetorio. Rectores provinciarum Sublimitas Tua conveniat …*). See Gradenwitz 1925 [1970]: 240 for a list of occurences of *sublimitas* in the Codex. This translation and all others in this paper are my own. Here is a list of primary texts and editions referred to in this paper: Adamantius, *Physiognomonica* (*TLG*) and *De Ventis* (*TLG*); Ammianus Marcellinus, *Res Gestae* (Seyfarth 1978); *Codex Theodosianus* (Mommsen and Meyer 1905); Eunapius, *Lives of the Philosophers* (Civiletti 2007); *Gesta Senatus* (Mommsen and Meyer 1905); Iamblichus, *De Mysteriis* (Des Places 1966) and *De Vita Pythagorica* (Dillon and Hershbell 1991 = Deubner/Klein 1975); Emperor Julian, *Or.* 8 (Rochefort 2003), *Or.* 9 (Rochefort 2003), and *Or.* 11 (Lacombrade 2003); Lucian, *Rhetorum Praeceptor* (*TLG*); Lucretius, *De Rerum Natura* (J. Martin 1969); Marinus, *Vita Procli* (Saffrey and Segonds 2002); Numenius, *On the Good* (*TLG*); Plato, *Republic* (*TLG*); Paulinus of Nola (Hartel and Kamptner 1999); *De Physiognomonia Liber* (André 1981); Porphyry, *Vita Pythagorae* (*TLG*); Saloustios, *De Deis et Mundo* (Rochefort 2003); Simplicius (Pseudo)/Priscianus (*TLG*); Victricius, *De Laude Sanctorum* (Demeulenaere 1985).
2 *Culmen* occurs in the *Gesta Senatus* and in the following places in the *Codex*: 1.29.1 [364 CE], 1.29.3 [late 360s or early 370s], 1.29.4 [368], 6.24.4 [387], 6.30.23 [422], 7.4.32 [412], 7.4.35 [423], 8.4.18 [394], 8.7.10 [369], 11.20.5 [424], 12.1.175 [412], 13.11.7 [396], 14.16.1 [409], 15.5.4 [424], 16.2.37 [404]. See Corcoran's presentation (1996: 324–34) of the wide variety of abstract terms that the emperors give to those they address.
3 See Jones 1964: 1228; Mason 1974: 65, 179; Millar 1983: 91.
4 *LSJ* Supplement 1996.
5 *LSJ* Supplement 1996.
6 Jones 1964: 1229; Lampe 1961.
7 Of the three terms, *clarissimus* and *illustris* are well attested in the fourth century, and *spectabilis*, less seen, is establishing itself by 400. For more, see Chastagnol 1992: 293–324; Gizewski 2012; Groß-Albenhausen 2012a, 2012b; Hirschfeld 1901; Jones 1964: 528–30; Löhken 1982: 112–34; Salzman 2002: 37–8.
8 Jones 1964: 529, 1221; *CTh.* 6.4.10 (356 CE).

9 Heather 1998: 190.

10 See Kelly 2004; Kelly 1998 for more.

11 Eunapius, *Lives of the Philosophers* 5.1.8 (Wright [1921] 458/364); see Civiletti 2007: 326–34 (esp. 333–4) for discussion of many instances of a light-filled and/or golden appearance attributed to notable men in late antiquity. See, too, Struck 2004: 227–9 and Goulet 2001: 47 on the gloriously illumined impression the fifth-century philosopher Proclus makes in the biography Marinus wrote of him (*Vita Procli* 3). For more on the frequent appearance of light at the point of connection between a theurgist/philosopher and the divine, see Cremer 1969: 104–6; Lewy and Tardieu 1978 [1956]): 467–1; Sodano 1984: 255–7; cf. Lamberton's remarks on Plotinus' resort to light to describe the One (1986: 90).

12 Iamblichus, *Myst.* 1.12 (41.3–8).

13 This is a frequent refrain in the literature (see, e.g., Frank 2000 or Miller 1994).

14 See, e.g., Miller 2005: 47, 2000b: 226–7, 234. On a related note, Brown 1981: 73 draws attention to Paulinus' characterization of the martyred saint Felix as a star; Paulinus says of Felix that "the martyr is at once a star at his shrine and a remedy for those who worship [him]" (*Carmina* 19.15: *martyr stella loci simul et medicina colentum est*).

15 See Förster's invaluable 1893 collection of ancient physiognomic *loci*. Swain 2007, Gleason 1995, Barton 1994: 95–131, and Evans 1969 feature panoramic discussions of this science.

16 Swain 2007: 2–3, Gleason 1995: 30–2, Barton 1994: 102, and Evans 1969 all agree that the treatises by Anonymous and Adamantius date from the fourth century (although Gleason is slightly hesitant in the case of Anonymous).

17 His dates are probably Hellenistic, but there has been debate about this. See Boys-Stones 2007: 58–9 for discussion.

18 Gallus: 14.11.28; Constantius II: 21.16.19; Julian: 25.4.22; Jovian: 25.10.14; Valentinian I: 30.9.6; Valens: 31.14.7. See Sabbah 1978: 421–8 for discussion of Ammianus Marcellinus' use of physiognomy.

19 Iamblichus *Vit. Pyth.* 17.71 and 17.74; Porphyry *Vit. Pyth.* 13.2, 13.7, and 54.14–15.

20 See, e.g., *Anon. Lat.* 6; Adam. 2.2.23–43.

21 Gleason 1995: 76 (cf. Barton 1994: 113 noting the coincidence of topics in physiognomy with the *topoi* of invective).

22 Gleason 1995: 164, cf. xxvii, 80, 161; Barton 1994: 115–18.

23 Kuefler 2001: 30.

24 Cf. Barton 1994: 119–24.

25 *primo igitur constituendum est quid physiognomonia profiteatur.* < *profitetur* > *itaque ex qualitate corporis qualitatem se animi considerare atque perspicere.*

26 For more on Loxus, see Boys-Stones 2007: 58–64.

27 *et Loxus quidem sanguinem animae habitaculum esse constituit, corpus autem omne et partes eius quae signa dant, pro vivicitate vel inertia sanguinis et prout tenuis seu crassus magis fuerit vel cum liberos habuerit ac directos meatus vel cum perversos et angustos, dare signa diversa.*

28 Boys-Stones understands Anonymous to be using *anima* and *animus* as synonyms for one another (2007: 60). I see Anonymous making a distinction between them most of the time, a distinction based in the physicalization Anonymous accords the *anima*. All the same, Anonymous revisits the notion of blood housing the soul (*anima*) in Section 12 of the physiognomy where he notes again, and using similar language, that Loxus has established that the blood is "the seat of the soul" (*sedem … animae*). Anonymous further states in this section that thin blood: "fosters the intellect's [*mens*] talent and excites the mind's [*animus*] keenness and does not suppress its mobility and motion" (*Anon. Lat.* 12) (*mentis … ingenium confovet et acumen animi excitat nec intercludit mobilitatem eius ac motum*). So while it later seems that the more transcendent entity, the *animus*, is affected by physical things, it nonetheless appears that Anonymous does not physicalize it to the same degree.

29 *carnem dicimus glutino sanguinis contineri, spiritum quoque madentem sanguinis rore flammeum Verbi adfirmamus duxisse ardorem.* For more on Victricius' treatment of blood, see Clark 1999: 370; Hunter 1999: 428.

30 οὐκοῦν ἐπειδὴ τὸ μέν ἐστι τῆς ψυχῆς ἡμῶν θειότερον, ὃ δὴ νοῦν καὶ φρόνησίν φαμεν καὶ λόγον τὸν σιγώμενον, οὗ κῆρυξ ἐστὶν ὁ διὰ τῆς φωνῆς οὑτοσὶ λόγος προϊὼν ἐξ ὀνομάτων καὶ ῥημάτων, ἕτερον δέ τι τούτῳ συνέζευκται ποικίλον καὶ παντοδαπόν, ὀργῇ καὶ ἐπιθυμίᾳ ξυμμιγές τι καὶ πολυκέφαλον θηρίον, πότερον χρὴ πρὸς τὰς δόξας τῶν πολλῶν ἀτενῶς ὁρᾶν καὶ ἀδιατρέπτως, πρὶν ἂν τοῦτο δαμάσωμεν τὸ θηρίον καὶ πείσωμεν ὑπακοῦσαι τῷ παρ᾽ ἡμῖν θεῷ, μᾶλλον δὲ θείῳ.

31 Plato's works arguably had achieved scriptural status by late antiquity (Miller 2000a: 212; Shaw 1995: 8).

32 Pl. *R.* 9.588b: εἰκόνα πλάσαντες τῆς ψυχῆς λόγῳ.

33 Pl. *R.* 9.588c: ἰδέαν θηρίου ποικίλου καὶ πολυκεφάλου.

34 Pl. *R.* 9.588c: συμπεφυκυῖαι ἰδέαι πολλαὶ εἰς ἓν γενέσθαι.

35 Cf. to that which Socrates says at Pl. *R.* 4.431a (soul has a better and worse part) and at 4.442a–b (in a triplex soul, the logical and passionate parts of the soul are to rule over the part susceptible to bodily pleasures).

36 See, e.g., Plot. 5.2.1.1–28.

37 See Lilla 1992: 587b–589a; Lloyd 1967: 287–93; Struck 2004: 207–9; Wallis 1995 [1972]: 110–18.

38 In his *De Mysteriis*, a lengthy treatise in ten books, Iamblichus re-theorized pagan religious practice (prayer and physical ritual actions such as blood sacrifice) as theurgy ("God-Work"; *theourgia*/θεουργία).

39 τὸ μέν ἐστιν ἄκρον καὶ ὑπερέχον καὶ ὁλοτελές, τὸ δὲ τελευταῖον καὶ ἀπολειπόμενον καὶ ἀτελέστερον· καὶ τὸ μὲν πάντα δύναται ἅμα ἐν τῷ νῦν μονοειδῶς, τὸ δὲ οὔτε ὅλα οὔτε ἀθρόως οὔτε ἐξαίφνης οὔτε ἀμερίστως. καὶ τὸ μὲν ἀκλινῶς ἀπογεννᾷ πάντα καὶ ἐπιτροπεύει, τὸ δ᾽ ἔχει φύσιν ἐπινεύειν καὶ ἐπιστρέφεσθαι πρὸς τὰ γιγνόμενά τε καὶ διοικούμενα.

40 καὶ τὸ μὲν κατὰ μίαν ὀξεῖαν ἀκμὴν τὰ τέλη τῶν ἐνεργειῶν ὅλων καὶ οὐσιῶν συνείληφε, τὸ δ᾽ ἀπ᾽ ἄλλων εἰς ἄλλα μεταβαίνει, καὶ ἀπὸ τοῦ ἀτελοῦς προχωρεῖ εἰς τὸ τέλειον. ἔτι τῷ μὲν ὑπάρχει τὸ ἀκρότατον καὶ ἀπερίληπτον, κρεῖττόν τε παντὸς μέτρου, καὶ ἀνείδεον οὕτως ὡς ὑπ᾽ οὐδενὸς εἴδους περιωρισμένον, τὸ δὲ καὶ ῥοπῇ καὶ σχέσει καὶ νεύσει κρατεῖται, ὀρέξεσί τε τοῦ χείρονος καὶ οἰκειώσει τῶν δευτέρων κατέχεται, λοιπόν τε παντοδαποῖς καὶ τοῖς ἀπ᾽ αὐτῶν μέτροις εἰδοποιεῖται.

41 See Steel 1978: 52–69 for discussion of Soul's position in Iamblichus' thought as mediator between the intellectual realm and matter. See, too, Shaw 1995: 98–106; Sodano 1984: 248–9; Struck 2004: 208.

42 Steel's own Greek, I believe. This language is close to that in the *In De Anima* of Pseudo-Simplicius (which Steel attributes to Priscianus, who, Steel argues, replicates Iamblichus' views): see 11.6.14–15, 11.90.20–1, 11.229.18–19, or 11.242.25–6.

43 *ceteri autem tam figuratricem corporis animam esse arbitrantur < per συμπάθειαν > quam ex qualitate corporis animam speciem mutuari ...*

44 In the *apparatus criticus* of his 1981 edition, André notes that the phrase *per συμπάθειαν* (which André includes in his text) may in fact be a later addition. Förster approves this addition in his 1893 edition on the authority of both Du Moulin's 1549 edition and notations appearing in the margins of manuscript E, which dates from some time in the thirteenth or fourteenth centuries. It is therefore a reading that is not the oldest (the earliest manuscripts are from the twelfth century), but it is not without plausible authority both on the basis of its going back as far as it does and on the basis of its consonance with the philosophic tradition in general (which Anonymous cites at the beginning of the work). Repath (Swain 2007: 556) excises the phrase and Boys-Stones, while accepting the excision, nonetheless believes that Anonymous has *sympatheia* in mind (Boys-Stones 2007: 63).

45 For another view of this part of Anonymous' argument, see Boys-Stones 2007: 62.

46 Fowden 1986: 75–8; Struck 2004: 189–92; Van Liefferinge 1999: 62–5.

47 πρώτη ἄγγελος καὶ σημάντρια συμπαθείας οὐρανίων πρὸς ἐπίγεια.

48 See Clarke 2001: 39–57; Shaw 1995: 153–4, 158; Van Liefferinge 1999: 87–8 for more on sacrifice according to Iamblichus.

49 *sicuti humor constitutus in vasculo qui speciem ex vasculo mutuatur et sicut spiritus infusus in fistulam vel in tibiam vel in tubam; nam cum uniformis sit spiritus, diversum tamen sonat tuba, fistula, tibia.*

50 In late-ancient sources, see Aristides Quintilianus (fl. circa 300 CE), as discussed in Boys-Stones 2007: 114–16; Iamblichus, *Myst.* 1.8 (28.11–29.3), 1.17 (50.11–51.8), 3.17 (139.10–13), or 5.3 (201.1–9); Emperor Julian's Helios hymn (*Or.* 11.9 [135C]); Saloustios (mid-fourth century), *De Deis et Mundo* 9.2, 9.4, and 17.2.

51 Iamblichus' *De Anima* is lost and has had to be reconstructed from various places. One place has been the *In De Anima* of Pseudo-Simplicius, which most scholars believe was written by Priscianus.

52 Pseudo-Simplicius (*sc.* Priscianus), *In De An.* 11.223.28–32: μία γὰρ οὖσα ἡ ψυχὴ ἡ ἡμετέρα ... ἅμα τε μένει μία καὶ πληθύνεται ἐν τῇ πρὸς σῶμα ῥοπῇ, οὔτε μένουσα καθαρῶς οὔτε ἐξισταμένη παντελῶς, ἀλλὰ καὶ μένουσά πῃ καὶ προϊοῦσα ἀφ᾽ ἑαυτῆς καὶ τῷ ἑτεροιοῦσθαι πρὸς ἑαυτὴν ἀμυδροῦσα τὴν πρὸς ἑαυτὴν ταὐτότητα. See also Finamore and Dillon 2002: 14–15 and 30–1, 91–3 (passage 7).

53 E.g., fragment 28 in Finamore and Dillon 2002: 56–7, 156–9.

54 For more on Iamblichus' contention that the soul completely descended, see Shaw 1995: 59–126; Smith 1995: 104–13; Steel 1978: 38–45. (Steel and Shaw likewise emphasize the connection between Iamblichus and Plato on this score.)

55 Iamblichus somewhat misrepresented Plotinus' views of the soul as being completely transcendent for, in fact, there was tension, if not contradiction, in Plotinus' position (Steel 1978: 44–5).

56 I was tempted to translate *genus* here as "gender." But study of *TLL* 6.2.1895.35–72—the section ("*de sexu*") that canvasses the use of *genus* in and around things now translated by the words "(biological) sex" or "gender"—suggested that the distinction between bodily substrate (sex) and performance (gender) is not consistently captured by a contrast between *sexus* and *genus*. Indeed, *sexus* and *genus* are often (though not always) synonymous. "Type" is Repath's (Swain 2007: 557) helpful and suitably vague translation (cf. Gleason 1995: 59).

57 *prima igitur divisio observationis huius atque discretio ea est ut alterum masculinum genus sit, alterum femininum. quod non ea ratione accipiendum est qua naturaliter sexus et genera discreta sunt, sed ut plerumque etiam in feminino masculinum genus et in masculino femininum deprehendatur.*

58 Gleason 1995: 58–60.

59 *denique quod masculinum nos dicimus,* < ἀρσενικόν >, *quod femininum,* < θηλυκὸν > *physiognomones dicunt* (*Anon. Lat.* 3).

60 *primo igitur constituendus est animus masculini et econtra femini, deinde corporis utriusque designanda indicia sunt et, si non omnia, ea tamen quae viam dare considerationis huiusce possint.*

61 νοῦς τοίνυν ἡγεμὼν καὶ βασιλεὺς τῶν ὄντων τέχνη τε δημιουργικὴ τοῦ παντὸς τοῖς μὲν θεοῖς ὡσαύτως ἀεὶ πάρεστι τελέως καὶ αὐταρκῶς καὶ ἀνενδεῶς, κατὰ μίαν ἐνέργειαν ἑστῶσαν ἐν ἑαυτῇ καθαρῶς, ἡ δὲ ψυχὴ νοῦ τε μετέχει μεριστοῦ καὶ πολυειδοῦς εἰς τὴν τοῦ ὅλου τε προστασίαν ἀναποβλέποντος, καὶ αὐτὴ τῶν ἀψύχων ἐπιμελεῖται ἄλλοτε ἐν ἄλλοις εἴδεσιν ἐγγιγνομένη.

62 Struck 2004: 229–32.

63 Anonymous does not hope in vain. Plato himself will depart from staged dialectic and opt for an illustrative *mythos* (μῦθος), the myth of Er in the *Republic* (10.614b–621d) being a famous example. Then too, imagery is often used to finesse a difficulty in an argument, such as the one Anonymous is having; although Anonymous is not a philosopher, a comment by Penelope Deutscher, who is relaying the opinion of Michèle Le Dœuff, is applicable here: "Among the textual work which imagery can … do is … 'conceal,' or substitute for, problems in a philosopher's argument" (1997: 62).

64 *nam sicut in studio litterarum, cum sint viginti quattuor elementa secundum Graecos quibus omnis vox et omnis sermo comprehenditur, ita et in physiognomonia propositis elementis latissima observationis huius via panditur. nam et si syllabas omnes in prima aetate didicimus, concepta vi syllabarum, prout quisque sermo provenerit, mox litterarum ex quibus constat ordinem pervidemus.*

65 Förster 1893: Vol. 1, 120.9–12 (note Swain's salutary words of caution [2007: 5] about the reliability of the Arabic text).

66 Gunderson 2000: 165 also points out a metaphor in Lucian (*Rh. Pr.* 9). There, rhetorical excellence is a muscular body and the well-defined features of this hard body are called *grammai*, which are also the lines that form letters of the alphabet.

67 ἀλλὰ τί δή ἐστι τὸ ὄν; ἆρα ταυτὶ τὰ στοιχεῖα τὰ τέσσαρα, ἡ γῆ καὶ τὸ πῦρ καὶ αἱ ἄλλαι δύο μεταξὺ φύσεις; ἆρα οὖν δὴ τὰ ὄντα ταῦτά ἐστιν, ἤτοι συλλήβδην ἢ καθ᾽ ἕν γέ τι αὐτῶν,

68 Holy men or saints' relics could just as easily come to mind too.

69 Irigaray 1985 [1977].

70 See Burrus' discussion (2000) of Gregory of Nyssa for a more than good start down this road.

Bibliography

Barton, T. (1994) *Power and Knowledge: Astrology, Physiognomics, and Medicine under the Roman Empire*. Ann Arbor, MI: University of Michigan Press.

Boys-Stones, G. (2007) "Physiognomy and ancient psychological theory", in S. Swain (ed.) *Seeing the Face, Seeing the Soul: Polemon's Physiognomy from Classical Antiquity to Medieval Islam*. Oxford: Oxford University Press, pp. 19–124.

Brown, P. (1981) *The Cult of the Saints: Its Rise and Function in Latin Christianity*. Chicago, IL: University of Chicago Press.

Burrus, V. (2000) *"Begotten, not Made": Conceiving Manhood in Late Antiquity*. Stanford, CA: Stanford University Press.

Chastagnol, A. (1992) *Le Sénat romain à l'époque impériale: Recherches sur la composition de l'Assembleé et le statut de ses membres*. Paris: Les Belles Lettres.

Civiletti, M. (trans. and comm.) (2007) *Eunapio di Sardi: Vite di filosofi e sofisti*. Milan: Bompiani.

Clark, G. (1999) "Victricius of Rouen: Praising the saints", *Journal of Early Christian Studies* 7(3): 365–99.

Clarke, E. (2001) *Iamblichus' De Mysteriis: A Manifesto of the Miraculous*. Aldershot: Ashgate.

Corcoran, S. (1996) *The Empire of the Tetrarchs: Imperial Pronouncements and Government, AD 284–324*. Oxford: Clarendon Press.

Cremer, F. (1969) *Die chaldäischen Orakel und Jamblichs de Mysteriis*. Meisenheim am Glan: A. Hain.

Deutscher, P. (1997) *Yielding Gender: Feminism, Deconstruction and the History of Philosophy*. New York: Routledge.

Evans, E. (1969) "Physiognomics in the ancient world", *Transactions of the American Philosophical Society* 59(5).

Finamore, J. and Dillon, J. (2002) *Iamblichus: De Anima*. Leiden: Brill.

Förster, R. (1893) *Scriptores Physiognomonici Graeci et Latini*. Leipzig: Teubner.

Fowden, G. (1986) *The Egyptian Hermes: A Historical Approach to the Late-Pagan Mind*. Cambridge: Cambridge University Press.

Frank, G. (2000) *The Memory of the Eyes: Pilgrims to Living Saints in Christian Late Antiquity*. Berkeley, CA: University of California Press.

Gizewski, C. (2012). "Illustris vir", in H. Cancik and H. Schneider (eds) *Brill's New Pauly*. Available online at www.brillonline.nl/subscriber/entry?entry=bnp_e523310 (accessed 2 March 2012).

Gleason, M. (1995) *Making Men: Sophists and Self-Presentation in Ancient Rome*. Princeton, NJ: Princeton University Press.

Goulet, R. (2001) *Études sur les vies de philosophes dans l'antiquité tardive: Diogène Laërce, Porphyre de Tyr, Eunape de Sardes*. Paris: Vrin.

Gradenwitz, O. (1925 [1970]) *Heidelberger Index zum Theodosianus*. Berlin: Weidmann.

Groß–Albenhausen, K. (2012a) "Spectabilis", in H. Cancik and H. Schneider (eds) *Brill's New Pauly*. Available online at www.brillonline.nl/subscriber/entry?entry=bnp_e523310 (accessed 2 March 2012).

——(2012b) "Vir clarissimus", in H. Cancik and H. Schneider (eds) *Brill's New Pauly*. Available online at www.brillonline.nl/subscriber/entry?entry=bnp_e523310 (accessed 2 March 2012).

Gunderson, E. (2000) *Staging Masculinity: The Rhetoric of Performance in the Roman World*. Ann Arbor, MI: University of Michigan Press.

Heather, P. J. (1998) "Senators and Senates", in A. Cameron and P. Garnsey (eds) *The Cambridge Ancient History 13: The Late Empire, AD 337–425*. Cambridge: Cambridge University Press, pp. 184–210.

Hirschfeld, O. (1901) *Die Rangtitel der römischen Kaiserzeit*. Berlin: K. Akademie der Wissenschaften.

Hunter, D. (1999) "Vigilantius of Calagurris and Victricius of Rouen: Ascetics, relics, and clerics in late Roman Gaul", *Journal of Early Christian Studies* 7(3): 401–30.

Irigaray, L. (1985 [1977]) *This Sex Which Is Not One*, trans. C. Porter. Ithaca, NY: Cornell University Press.

Jones, A. (1964) *The Later Roman Empire, 284–602: A Social Economic and Administrative Survey*. Baltimore, MD: Johns Hopkins University Press.

Kelly, C. (2004) *Ruling the Later Roman Empire*. Cambridge, MA: Belknap Press of Harvard University Press.

——(1998) "Emperors as gods, angels as bureaucrats: The representation of imperial power in late antiquity", *Antigüedad: Religiones y Sociedades* 1: 301–26.

Kuefler, M. (2001) *The Manly Eunuch: Masculinity, Gender Ambiguity, and Christian Ideology in Late Antiquity*. Chicago, IL: University of Chicago Press.

Lamberton, R. (1986) *Homer the Theologian: Neoplatonist Allegorical Reading and the Growth of the Epic Tradition*. Berkeley, CA: University of California Press.

Lendon, J. (1997) *Empire of Honour: The Art of Government in the Roman World*. Oxford: Oxford University Press.

Lewy, Y. and Tardieu, M. (1978 [1956]) *Chaldaean Oracles and Theurgy: Mysticism, Magic, and Platonism and the Later Roman Empire*. Paris: Institut d'Études Augustiniennes.

Liefferinge, C. van (1999) *La Théurgie des Oracles Chaldaïques à Proclus*. Liège: Centre international d'étude de la religion grecque antique.

Lilla, S. (1992) "Neoplatonism", in A. Berardino (ed.) *Encyclopedia of the Early Church*. New York: Oxford University Press, pp. 585B–593A.

Lloyd, A. (1967) "The later Neoplatonists", in A. Armstrong (ed.) *The Cambridge History of Later Greek and Early Medieval Philosophy*. London: Cambridge University Press, pp. 269–325.

Löhken, H. (1982) *Ordines dignitatum: Untersuchungen zur formalen Konstituierung der spätantiken Führungsschicht*. Köln: Böhlau.

Mason, H. (1974) *Greek Terms for Roman Institutions: A Lexicon and Analysis*. Toronto, ON: Hakkert.

Millar, F. (1983) "Empire and city, Augustus to Julian: Obligations, excuses and status", *Journal of Roman Studies* 73: 76–96.

Miller, P. (1994) "Desert asceticism and 'the body from nowhere'", *Journal of Early Christian Studies* 2: 137–53.

——(2000a) "Strategies of representation in collective biography: Constructing the subject as holy", in T. Hägg and P. Rousseau (eds) *Greek Biography and Panegyric in Late Antiquity*. Berkeley, CA: University of California Press, pp. 209–54.

——(2000b) "'The little blue flower is red': Relics and the poetizing of the body", *Journal of Early Christian Studies* 8(2): 213–36.

——(2005) "Relics, rhetoric, and mental spectacles", in G. de Nie, K. Morrison, and M. Mostert (eds) *Seeing the Invisible in Late Antiquity and the Early Middle Ages*. Turnhout: Brepols Publishers, pp. 25–52.

Sabbah, G. (1978) *La Méthode d'Ammien Marcellin-Recherches sur la Construction du Discours Historique dans les Res Gestae*. Paris: Les Belles Lettres.

Salzman, M. (2002) *The Making of a Christian Aristocracy: Social and Religious Change in the Western Roman Empire*. Cambridge, MA: Harvard University Press.

Shaw, G. (1995) *Theurgy and the Soul: The Neoplatonism of Iamblichus*. University Park, PA: Pennsylvania State University Press.

Smith, R. (1995) *Julian's Gods: Religion and Philosophy in the Thought and Action of Julian the Apostate*. New York: Routledge.

Sodano, A. (trans., intro., comm.) (1984) *Giamblico: I Misteri Egiziani: Abammone, Lettera a Porfirio*. Milan: Rusconi.

Steel, C. (1978) *The Changing Self: A Study on the Soul in Later Neoplatonism: Iamblichus, Damascius, and Priscianus*. Brussels: Paleis der Academiën.

Struck, P. (2004) *Birth of the Symbol: Ancient Readers at the Limits of Their Texts*. Princeton, NJ: Princeton University Press.

Swain, S. (ed) (2007) *Seeing the Face, Seeing the Soul: Polemon's Physiognomy from Classical Antiquity to Medieval Islam*. Oxford: Oxford University Press.

Wallis, R. (1995 [1972]) *Neoplatonism*. Indianapolis, IN: Hackett.

Wright, W. (1921) *Philostratus and Eunapius*. Cambridge, MA: Harvard University Press.

INDEX

Entries in *italics* denote figures; entries in **bold** denote tables.